SOUTHERN AFRICAN POLITICAL HISTORY

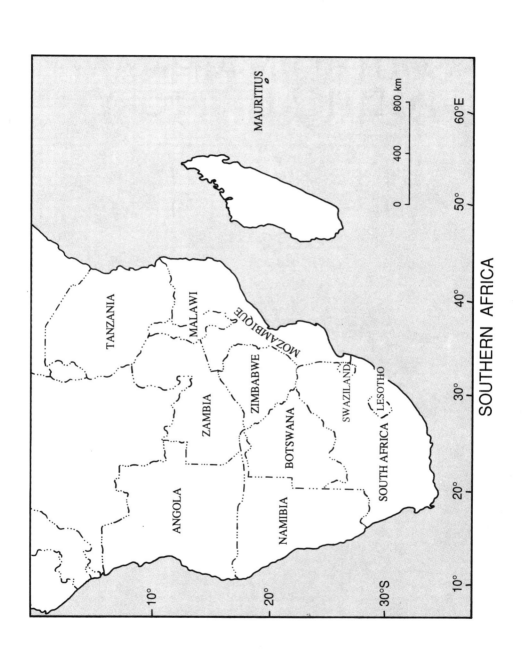

SOUTHERN AFRICA

SOUTHERN AFRICAN POLITICAL HISTORY

A Chronology of Key Political Events from Independence to Mid-1997

Compiled by
Jacqueline A. Kalley,
Elna Schoeman, and L. E. Andor

Assisted by Abdul Samed Bemath,
Claire Kruger, and Beth Strachan

Foreword by Peter Vale

GREENWOOD PRESS
Westport, Connecticut • London

Library of Congress Cataloging-in-Publication Data

Kalley, Jacqueline A. (Jacqueline Audrey)
Southern African political history : a chronology of key political
events from independence to mid-1997 / compiled by Jacqueline A.
Kalley, Elna Schoeman, and L. E. Andor ; assisted by Abdul Samed
Bemath, Claire Kruger, and Beth Strachan ; foreword by Peter Vale.
p. cm.
Includes bibliographical references and index.
ISBN 0-313-30247-2 (alk. paper)
1. Africa, Southern—Politics and government—Chronology.
I. Schoeman, Elna. II. Andor, L. E. (Lydia Eve) III. Title.
DT1147.K35 1999
968'.0009'045—dc21 98-44996

British Library Cataloguing in Publication Data is available.

Library of Congress Catalog Card Number: 98-44996
ISBN: 0-313-30247-2

First published in 1999

Greenwood Press, 88 Post Road West, Westport, CT 06881
An imprint of Greenwood Publishing Group, Inc.

Printed in the United States of America

The paper used in this book complies with the
Permanent Paper Standard issued by the National
Information Standards Organization (Z39.48-1984).

10 9 8 7 6 5 4 3 2 1

Dedicated to our wonderful JSH support staff, Cathy Viljoen, Helena Mitchell, Hedda Newman and Anne Katz—in appreciation

Contents

Foreword

This book marks beginning and end. It sets out a chronology of the region with the `states' of Southern Africa as the primary focus. As elsewhere in the world, this is an accepted way of organizing political knowledge: and for half a century it has been the established way of explaining Southern African affairs. But state-based understandings record only a moment in the history of a region which is in the midst of deep change. Southern Africa has been acutely affected by the ending of apartheid: scarcely a day passes in which the countries of the region are not drawn together in one kind of an exchange or another.

In the sheer exuberance of these, it seems scarcely credible to believe that a short decade ago the region was at war, its politics were framed by discourses which were set in simple binaries - white versus black, colonialism versus decolonialization; majority-rule versus minority rights; order versus anarchy. These interpretations of reality undoubtedly helped to shape the course of regional relations which were marked by chasm, clash and conflict. The result was as tragic as it was predictable. Pinned against the ropes `by the force of history', South Africa's ruling minority seemed determined to go down fighting and, regardless of world opinion, to drag the peoples of the region with them.

But the seeming inevitability of this pattern of politics gave way, in the early-1990s, to new political discourses. There are no simple ways to capture the momentum and the magnitude of the shift from war-talk to peace-talk. Today the mood is of merge, mingle and mix: of interdependencies - in water, in electrical power, in health, in environmental affairs. The premier regional institution, the Southern African Development Community (SADC), has been encouraged to promote the signing of protocols of understanding in a wide variety of functional areas and there is talk of a regional parliament.

This does not mean, as any crude analysis of the wealth of data in this book will suggest, that the nation-state (or the system it promoted) is dead in Southern Africa. The emergence of the new South Africa suggests, in sharp contrast, that states may have been accorded a new lease on life. We know however that the region can never be the same: the same careful analysis of this book tells us why by pointing to the new region which is being built in Southern Africa.

As they have done so often, Jacqueline Kalley and Elna Schoeman have brought the highest professional standards to this work. Their record shows how, quite selflessly, they have worked together producing or editing thirty-one books in the highly acclaimed SAIIA Bibliographical Series and ten volumes of Southern Africa Update - A Bibliographical Survey. Additionally they have produced several independently published bibliographical contributions, a considerable number of articles in academic journals and conceived and published SARDIUS - the Southern African Research, Documentation, Information User Service - a CD ROM compilation which is now published by National Inquiry Services Centre (NISC) in the United States. Together this constitutes, probably, the single most dedicated body of work in international relations in Southern Africa's history.

The institutional base which they have used to produce this work, the Jan Smuts House Library, has been closed. It is simply outrageous that budgetary priorities should have shifted at the very moment when the prospects for peace look the strongest and the opportunity for tackling the longer-term problems of poverty and disease in the region seem so promising. The next phase of Southern African studies will look beyond the political discourses which have been exclusively framed by states; with its open-ended perspective, this book and its companion volume, which provides in-depth data on the region, represent a useful bridge to academic work that will help to shape Southern Africa in the new millennium. The question is to whom will scholars and the public turn to for bibliographical guidance.

Peter Vale
Professor of Southern African Studies
University of the Western Cape

Introduction

AIM

This work seeks to bring together information on the political development of the South African Development Community (SADC) member countries since their independence from colonial rule. In the case of South Africa, the republican status attained in 1961 was selected as the starting point. Ease of information retrieval is the prime focus of this chronology. The main component is a detailed chronology of political events as they unfolded in the post independence period. The twelve members of SADC form the regional parameters of this study, each with its unique history. Subsequent to the compilation of this work, two further states have joined SADC, namely the Seychelles and the Democratic Republic of the Congo.

The index provides quick access to key developments and the role played by both political parties; individual personalities and treaty information where available. Additional data on the Southern African region, including an in-depth list of acronyms, statistics, biographical and political party information may be found in the companion volume to this work entitled: Southern African Political Handbook. Two indexes provide ease of access to the text - a comprehensive subject index and a name index. The subject index focuses on keywords appropriate to swift information retrieval. This follows a subject rather than country orientation, given the arrangement of the work. However, these keywords are thereafter limited to specific countries. The name index comprises personal names only.

ACKNOWLEDGEMENTS

Typing assistance was cheerfully rendered by Cathy Viljoen, Hedda Newman, Anne Katz, Lynette Sackstein, and Adam Tikly. We thank them for their meticulous work.

Without the facilities and extensive resources of Jan Smuts House Library, Johannesburg, this work would not have been easily feasible. We acknowledge its seminal role in this regard and its wider role in promoting research in Southern Africa and mourn its demise.

J.A. Kalley, E. Schoeman and L.E. Andor
Jan Smuts House Library, October 1998

Acronyms

ACDP (South Africa)	African Christian Democratic Party
ACP	Africa the Caribbean and the Pacific (Lomè Convention)
AD (Angola)	Democratic Alliance
ADM (Mozambique)	Mozambique Democratic Alliance
ANC (South Africa)	African National Congress
ANCWL (South Africa)	African National Congress Women's League
ANCYL (South Africa)	African National Congress Youth League
APLA (South Africa)	Azanian People's Liberation Army
AWB (South Africa)	Afrikaner Weerstandsbeweging
AZAPO (South Africa)	Azanian People's Organisation
BCP (Lesotho)	Basotho Congress Party
BDP (Botswana)	Botswana Democratic Party
BIP (Botswana)	Botswana Independence Party
BLS States	Botswana, Lesotho and Swaziland
BNP (Lesotho)	Basotho National Party
BPP (Botswana)	Botswana People's Party

BPU (Botswana)	Botswana Progressive Union
CAF	Central African Federation
CCFADM (Mozambique)	Joint Commission for the Formation of the Mozambican Defence Force (Commissâo Conjunta dos Forças Armadas da Defensa do Moçambique)
CMVF (Angola)	Joint Verification and Monitoring Commission
COMESA (Southern Africa)	Common Market for Eastern and Southern Africa
COMIRA (Angola)	Military Council of Angolan Resistance (Conselhe Militar de Resistencia Angolana)
CONSAS (Southern Africa)	Constellation of Southern African States
COSAS (South Africa)	Congress of South African Students
COSATU (South Africa)	Congress of South African Trade Unions
CP (South Africa)	Conservative Party of South Africa
CSR (Malawi)	Congress for the Second Republic
CWUSA (South Africa)	Communication Workers' Union of South Africa
DP (South Africa)	Democratic Party
DTA (Namibia)	Democratic Turnhalle Alliance
ECC (South Africa)	End Conscription Campaign
FAA (Angola)	Angolan Armed Forces (Forças Armada Angolanas)
FADM (Mozambique)	Armed Forces for the Defense of Mozambique (Forças Armadas de Defensa de Moçambique)
FALA (Angola)	Armed Forces for the Liberation of Angola (Forcas Armadas de Libertaçâo de Angola)
FAPLA (Angola)	Popular Armed Forces for the Liberation of Angola (Forcas Armaddas Populares de Libertaçao de Angola)
FF (South Africa)	Freedom Front
FLEC (Angola)	Front for the Liberation of the Enclave of Cabinda (Frente de Libertaçâo de Enclave de Cabinda)
FLS (Southern Africa)	Front Line States
FOSATU (South Africa)	Federation of South African Trade Unions
FNLA (Angola)	National Front for the Liberation of Angola (Frente Nacional de Libertaçâo de Angola)

FPLM (Mozambique)	Popular Forces for the Liberation of Mozambique
FRELIMO (Mozambique)	Front for the Liberation of Mozambique (Frente de Libertaçâo de Moçambique)
FUMO-PCD (Mozambique)	Mozambique United Front-Democratic Convergence Party
FUS (Mozambique)	United Salvation Front
GAT (Angola)	Monitoring Task Group
GRAE (Angola)	Revolutionary Government of Angola in Exile (Governo Revolucionario da Angola no Exilio)
HRC (South Africa)	Human Rights Commission
IBA (South Africa)	Independent Broadcasting Authority
KZN (South Africa)	KwaZulu Natal
LESOMA (Malawi)	Socialist League of Malawi
LMY (Malawi)	League of Malawi Youth
MAFREMO (Malawi)	Malawi Freedom Movement
MCP (Malawi)	Malawi Congress Party
MDU (Malawi)	Malawian Democratic Union
MK (South Africa)	Umkhonto we Sizwe
MMM (Mauritius)	Movement Militant Mauricien (Mauritian Militant Movement)
MNR (Mozambique)	Mozambique National Resistance Movement (Movimento Nacional do Resistencia da Mocambique) later RENAMO
MPLA-PT (Angola)	Popular Movement for the Liberation of Angola-Workers Party (Movimento Popular para a Libertaçao de Angola-Partido de Trabalho) (People's Movement for the Liberation of Angola)
MSM (Mauritius)	Movement Socialist Mauricien (Mauritian Socialist Movement)
NACTU (South Africa)	National Council of Trade Unions
NCOP (South Africa)	National Council of Provinces
NEDLAC (South Africa)	National Economic, Development and Labour Council
NFZ (Zimbabwe)	National Front Zimbabwe

NGK (South Africa)	Nederduitse Gereformeerde Kerk
NOCSA (South Africa)	National Olympic Committee of South Africa
NUM (South Africa)	National Union of Mineworkers
NUMSA (South Africa)	National Union of Metalworkers of South Africa
NUSAS (South Africa)	National Union of South African Students
OMA (Angola)	Organization of Angolan Women (Organizaçao da Mulher Angolana)
OTM (Mozambique)	Mozambican Workers' Organisation
PF (Rhodesia)	Patriotic Front
PIDE (Mozambique)	International Police for the Defence of the State (Polisia Internacional a de Defensa do Estado)
PLAN (Namibia)	People's Liberation Army of Namibia
RDP (South Africa)	Reconstruction and Development Programme
RENAMO (Mozambique)	Mozambican National Resistance (Resistência Nacional Moçambicana)
RF (Zimbabwe)	Rhodesian Front
SABC (South Africa)	South African Broadcasting Corporation
SACC (South Africa)	South African Council of Churches
SACP (South Africa)	South African Communist Party
SACU (Southern Africa)	Southern African Customs Union
SADC (Southern Africa)	Southern African Development Community
SADCC (Southern Africa)	Southern African Development Coordination Conference
SANDF (South Africa)	South African National Defence Force
SATCC (Southern Africa)	Southern African Transport and Communication Commission
SDP (Botswana)	Social Democratic Party
SDP (Malawi)	Social Democratic Party
SEF (Mozambique)	Programme of Economic and Financial Restructuring (Programa de Saneamento Econômico and Financeiro)
SNASP (Mozambique)	National Service of Popular Security (Service Nacional de Segurança Popular)
SWANU (Namibia)	South West African National Union

SWAPO (Namibia)	South West Africa People's Organization of Namibia
TANU (Tanzania)	Tanzania Africa National Union
TAZARA (Tanzania)	Tanzania-Zambia Railway Route
TMC (South Africa)	Transitional Metropolitan Council
UDF (Malawi)	United Democratic Front
UDF (South Africa)	United Democratic Front
UDI (Zimbabwe)	Unilateral Declaration of Independence (Southern Rhodesia-Zimbabwe)
UDP (Lesotho)	United Democratic Party
UFMD (Malawi)	United Front for Multi-Party Democracy
UNAVEM (Angola)	United Nations Angola Verification Mission
UNIP (Zambia)	United National Independence Party
UNITA (Angola)	National Union for the Total Independence of Angola (Uniao Naçional para a Independência Total de Angola)
UNOMOZ (Mozambique)	United Nations Operations in Mozambique (also referred to as ONUMOZ)
UNTAG (Namibia)	United Nations Transition Assistance Group for Namibia
ZANU-PF (Zimbabwe)	Zimbabwe African National Union - Patriotic Front
ZDP (Zimbabwe)	Zimbabwe Democratic Party
ZIPRA (Zimbabwe)	Zimbabwe People's Revolutionary Army

Sources Consulted

Africa Contemporary Record (London, Great Britain: Africa Research Ltd, 1968/9-1997)

Africa Institute Bulletin (Pretoria, South Africa: Africa Institute of South Africa, 1961-1997)

Africa Research Bulletin: Economic Series (Exeter: Great Britain: Africa Research Ltd, 1964-1997)

Africa Research Bulletin: Political Series (Exeter:Great Britain: Africa Research Ltd, 1964-1997)

Africa Review (Exeter: Great Britain: World of Information, 1985-1997)

Africa South of the Sahara (London: Great Britain: Europa Publications, 1971-1997)

Annual Register of World Events (London: Great Britain: Longman, 1954-1997)

Europa World Yearbook (London: Great Britain: Europa Publications, 1971-1997)

International Who's Who (London: Great Britain: Europa Publications, 1972/3-1997)

Keesing's Record of World Events (London: Great Britain: Keesings Publications), 1967/8-1997)

South Africa by Treaty: A Chronological and Subject Index by J. Kalley (Johannesburg: South Africa: South African Institute of Affairs, 1987)

South African Institute of International Affairs Press Cuttings

United Nations Treaty Series (New York: United States: United Nations, 1946/7-1997)

Who's Who of Southern Africa (Johannesburg: South Africa: Ken Donaldson, 1959-1997)

SOUTHERN AFRICAN POLITICAL HISTORY

CHRONOLOGY OF KEY POLITICAL EVENTS

ANGOLA

10 Nov. 1975   Last of Portuguese troops leave Angola. The High Commissioner proclaims Angolan independence from midnight, without an official transfer of authority to a new government.

11 Nov. 1975   Dr. Agostinho Neto is invested as President of The People's Republic of Angola. Holden Roberto simultaneously declares 'The Popular and Democratic Republic of Angola' with Huambo as the temporary seat of a joint FNLA-UNITA government.

14 Nov. 1975   The new government of the People's Republic of Angola is sworn in by Dr. Neto.

16-19 Nov. 1975   A Central African 'emergency diplomatic conference' is by President Bongo of Gabon, in Libreville, to seek ways of enabling Angola to form a government of national union. Countries attending are: Cameroon, Chad, Zaire, Gabon, Central African Republic, Sao Tomé and Principe and the Congo People's Republic.

18 Nov. 1975   South African Foreign Minister Dr. Hilgard Muller denies reports that South African men and equipment are supporting the joint FNLA and UNITA forces in Angola.

23 Nov. 1975   FNLA and UNITA establish a coalition government, based, temporarily, at Huambo, to begin functioning 1 December 1975. Its composition, announced in Carmona, is as follows: Prime Ministers: Johnny Pinnock Eduardo and José Ndelé.
Ministers: Interior: M. Katalayé; Foreign Affairs: H.V. Neto; Information: W.F. Santos; Education & Culture: J. Wanga; Agriculture & Fisheries: D. Fernandes; Planning & Finance: G. Tavares; Economy & Trade: J.P. Mouzinho; Natural Resources: I. Jacob; Transport & Communication: A. Dembo; Industry & Energy: N. Kabangu; Public Works: J. Vahekeni; Justice: O.M. dos Santos. Secretaries of State: Foreign Affairs: M. Kakumba; Information: M. Sebastino; Planning & Finance: L.M. Alfonso. The two Prime Ministers will have alternating mandates of one month. The Health and Social Affairs portfolios, and the post of Secretary of State for the Interior, have not yet been allocated. According to the constitutional agreements signed between UNITA and the FNLA in Kinshasa, just prior

	to independence, a 24-member Revolutionary Council will also be set up, together with a Joint Defence High Command.
25 Nov. 1975	MPLA's counter-offensive, backed by Soviet airlift and Cuban 'advisers', halts UNITA advance.
27 Nov. 1975	The South African Minister of Defence, P.W. Botha appeals to the West to play a more direct role in preventing the Soviet Union establishing a permanent foothold in Angola.
3 Dec. 1975	An influx of refugees into Zambia from Moxico province is reported.
18 Dec. 1975	Radio Lisbon announces that UNITA and the MPLA have reached agreement, after talks between their leaders, Dr. Jonas Savimbi and Dr. Agostinho Neto, in Lusaka, (Zambia) and Luso, (Angola). The talks are also attended by the Portuguese High Commissioner in Angola, vice-Admiral Rosa Coutinho.
19 Dec. 1975	The United States senate votes to halt all further arms supplies to anti-MPLA forces in Angola.
Jan. 1976	The MPLA gains decisive military victories on all fronts.
10-13 Jan. 1976	An emergency meeting of the forty six member states of the OAU ends in deadlock over the Angola question.
27 Jan. 1976	The United States House of Representatives votes to endorse the Senate's ban on further military aid to the anti-Marxist factions.
11 Feb. 1976	Angola is officially admitted to the OAU. Great Britain recognizes the MPLA government.
22 Feb. 1976	Portugal recognizes the MPLA government.
10 Mar. 1976	Diplomatic relations are established with Portugal.
15 Mar. 1976	The leaders of Cuba, Guinea and Guinea-Bissau announce that they will give the People's Republic of Angola all aid needed to expel remaining South African troops from Angolan territory. A Summit Meeting of the three countries and Angola close with a warning to South Africa in a communiqué from Conakry (Guinea) where the four nation summit is held.
16-18 Mar. 1976	Two days of talks between an Angolan delegation and the Zambian government are held in Lusaka in an attempt to normalize strained relations. More than 12,000 Angolan refugees settled in camps on the Zambian border with Angola are thought to be UNITA supporters and their repatriation to Angola is suggested.
27 Mar. 1976	Last South African troops withdraw from guarding the Cunene River Hydroelectric Project and leave Angola.
31 Mar. 1976	A United Nations Security Council resolution condemns SA aggression against Angola.
Apr. 1976	Heavy fighting in Cabinda enclave.

1 Apr. 1976	The South African Air Force Commande Lieut.-General Rodgers admits that twenty eight South African soldiers have been killed and 100 wounded during the involvement in Angola.
5 Apr. 1976	Jannie de Wet, Commissioner-General for the Indigenous People of South West Africa meets with MPLA representatives in Angola. First direct diplomatic contact between Luanda and Pretoria since independence.
6 Apr. 1976	An agreement is concluded between Angolan and South West African officials allowing work to resume on the Cunene River Hydro-electric Irrigation Project. Angola will guarantee the security of the project and its workers; the border will be respected; two check points will be set up. Portuguese and Angolan workers are resuming work. An agreement on the Cunene River Hydro-electric Irrigation Project is reached at a secret meeting attended by senior personnel. It effectively constitutes recognition by South Africa of the MPLA government.
7-10 May 1976	The UNITA party congress, held at Cuanza, draws up a manifesto calling for an intensification of the armed struggle, against the regime imposed by the Cubans and Russians.
15 May 1976	Signs acceptance agreement to the constitution of the World Health Organization.
19 May 1976	Diplomatic relations with Portugal are broken off.
21 May 1976	Signs a treaty with the World Health Organisation for technical advisory assistance (provision II).
26 May 1976	Establishment of a Soviet Union trade delegation in Angola.
26 May 1976	Establishment of an Angolan trade delegation in the Soviet Union.
26 May 1976	Signs trade treaty with the Soviet Union.
4 June 1976	Ratifies with declarations, the ILO convention on the minimum age for admission for children and employment at sea (no. 7); weekly rest in commerce and offices (no. 106); crew accommodations on board ship (no. 92); food and catering for crews on board ship (no. 68); discrimination in employment and occupation (no. 111); organization in employment service (no. 88); abolition of forced labour (no. 105); forced or compulsory labour (no. 29); marking of weight of heavy packages transported by vessels (no. 27); protection and integration of indigenous and other tribal or semi-tribal populations in independent countries (no. 107); abolition of penal sanctions for breaches of contract of employment for indigenous workers (no. 104); industrial undertakings (no. 14 and no. 1) pertaining to weekly rest and hours of work; labour inspection in industry and commerce (no. 81); creation of minimum wage-fixing machinery (no. 26); right to organize aid bargain effectively (no. 98); seafarers (no. 73, 108, 91); certification of able seamen (no. 74); certification of ships' cooks (no. 69); women - light work employment in industry (no. 89); employment during the night (no. 6), employment on underground work in mines (no. 45); equal remuneration for work of equal value for men and women workers (no. 100); workmen's compensation for accidents (no. 17), equality of treatment for national and

foreign workers involved in accidents (no. 19), in agriculture (no. 12), occupational diseases (no. 18); night work of young persons employed in industry (no. 6).

7 June 1976

First session of the fifty member International Commission of Inquiry on Mercenaries established by the Angolan government, comprising representatives of twenty seven countries.

11 June 1976

The trial of thirteen British and American mercenaries opens in Luanda. The accused mercenaries are named as:
British: Costas Georgiu, known as 'Col. Callan' (25) born in Cyprus, but now a British citizen; Andrew Mackenzie (25); John Barker (35); Malcolm McIntyre (27); Cecil Fortuin (31); Kevin Mar chant (25); Michael Woseman (27); John Lawlor (26) and Colin Evans (28)
Americans: Daniel Gearheart (34); Gary Acker (21); Gustavo Grillo (27) born in Buenos Aires, but listed as an American citizen.
Irish: John Nammock (2)

11 June 1976

In a communiqué, released in Nairobi, UNITA pledges to intensify its guerrilla campaign against the MPLA government to force it into negotiations on the formation of a government of national unity. Tactics and strategy, agreed upon at a party conference on the Cuanza River, include continued attacks, sabotage, the formation of food producing units and the creation of an armed people's militia to protect food-producing units. UNITA's elected Political Bureau, led by Dr. Savimbi is sharply critical of the continuing Soviet and Cuban presence and demands the withdrawal of all foreign troops.

23 June 1976

American veto in the Security Council is used to block Angola's admission to the United Nations.

28 June 1976

Sentences on the mercenaries are pronounced by the People's Tribunal. Four of the accused are sentenced to death. The remaining nine receive prison sentences of from sixteen to thirty years.

11 July 1976

Radio Luanda announces that the four white mercenaries sentenced to death by a Revolutionary Court have been executed. The four were Costa Georgiou (Colonel Callan), John Derek Barker, Andrew Gordon Mackenzie and David Francis Gearhart.

26 July 1976

President Castro promises Cuban troops will remain in Angola for as long as they are required.

29 July 1976

Adherence to the multilateral convention pertaining to the conservation of Atlantic tunas.

15 Aug. 1976

Additions to the International Health Regulations signed.

27 Aug. 1976

Cuban-led Angolan government troops are striking at various points in the extreme south of Angola. Following their occupation of the town of Dirico more than 1,000 Angolan refugees have crossed the border into Namibia.

3 Sept. 1976

The foreign ministers of Portugal and Angola meet in Cape Verde and agree to a renewal of relations and to the setting up of two commissions to resolve outstanding issues.

30 Sept. 1976	Protocol for the continuation in force as an extension to the International Coffee Agreement.
Oct-Nov-Dec. 1976	Heavy fighting in Southern Angola between the MPLA supported by Cuban troops and by SWAPO guerrillas and UNITA.
1 Oct. 1976	The South African Commissioner-General for South West Africa, Jannie de Wet, calls for help from the International Red Cross and the United Nations to care for and assist a new wave of some 5,000 refugees crossing from Angola into Namibia, fleeing a `reign of terror' in southern Angola.
4 Oct. 1976	Adherence to the multilateral convention pertaining to the conservation of living resources in the Southeast Atlantic.
8 Oct. 1976	Heads of State Neto and Brezhnev sign a twenty year treaty of friendship and cooperation in Moscow.
21 Oct. 1976	Holden Roberto, leader of FNLA claims in Brussels that the FNLA and UNITA now control two-thirds of Angola. He alleges that there are more than 30,000 Cuban troops already in the country, with more arriving daily.
1 Nov. 1976	The admission of Angola to UNESCO membership is approved.
9 Nov. 1976	Acceptance of UNESCO constitution.
19 Nov. 1976	A new influx of Angolan refugees has reached Botswana where they will join the 2,000 already housed at Etosha.
19 Nov. 1976	According to the Zambian Home Affairs Minister, Aaron Milner, there are now over 14,000 Angolan refugees in Maheba refugee camp in north-west Zambia. Several hundred more have recently crossed into Zambia from southern Angola.
22 Nov. 1976	Angola is admitted to the United Nations. The United States abstains.
26 Nov. 1976	Changes in the constitution are published. The President, Dr. A. Neto, replaces the Prime Minister as executive head of government.
10 Dec. 1976	South Africa's Prime Minister gives an assurance that South Africa has no territorial ambitions in Angola; but expresses deep concern at Soviet and Cuban involvement.
10 Dec. 1976	The United Nations Commissioner for Namibia, Sean MacBride, alleges that South Africa is preparing an invasion of Angola for January 1977. The South African Minister of Defence, P.W. Botha, denies this.
15 Dec. 1976	A co-operation agreement between Angola and the Cape Verde Islands is signed.
27 Dec. 1976	The Zambian government bans UNITA from operating in Zambia and orders all UNITA officials to leave the country.
31 Dec. 1976	A UNITA military situation report by Commander-in-Chief Colonel S. Chiwale claims that UNITA controls five provinces (Cuando-Cubango, Cunene, Bie, Huambo and Moxico) and operates in three

others (Benguela, Mossamedes and Huita).

12 Jan. 1977	The Chief Minister of Ovambo, Pastor Ndjoba estimates that more than 10,000 Angolan refugees have been assimilated into Ovamboland. About 5,000 are also living in refugee camps and approximately the same number have returned to Angola. The Ovambo government has now requested the closure of the border.
3 Feb. 1977	A statement by South Africa's Defence Department gives reasons for South Africa's initial involvement and the extent of its activities in Angola.
18 Feb. 1977	Signs assistance treaty with the UNDP.
3 March 1977	Accession to the Universal Postal Union including Additional Protocols, General Regulations, insured letters, postal parcels and the Universl Postal Convention.
10 Mar. 1977	Angolan forces invade Zaire's Shaba Province.
25 Mar. 1977	The withdrawal of South African troops in completed.
13 Apr. 1977	In Windhoek the Commissioner General for the Indigenous Peoples of South West Africa, Jannie de Wet, reports that fierce fighting between the combined forces of the MPLA, SWAPO and Cuba and those of UNITA continues unabated in southern Angola. Refugees continue to cross the border into Ovamboland.
15 Apr. 1977	Radio Angola reports that the MPLA have launched a 'search and destroy' operation against UNITA in central Angola.
17-18 Apr. 1977	The Presidents of Angola, Botswana, Mozambique, Tanzania and Zambia hold a Frontline Summit in Luanda to discuss Southern African problems in general and Rhodesia in particular.
22-25 Apr. 1977	Official visit by President Neto to Yugoslavia.
26-28 Apr. 1977	President Neto visits Poland. A joint declaration on friendship and cooperation is signed.
27 May 1977	President Neto announces that an attempted uprising led by Commander Nito Alves, former Minister of Internal Administration and José van Dunem, Political Commissioner of the Armed Forces, has been crushed.
28 May 1977	The bodies of six leading members of the MPLA, who were kidnapped and killed by the insurgents, are found in a Luanda suburb. They are Major S.V.D. Mingas (Minister of Finance), Commander P. da Silva and Commander E. da Costa (all three members of the MPLA Central Committee and Council of the Revolution); Commander J. Daiva and Commander M. Goncalves (both members of the Council of the Revolution); and Commander E. Neto of the political police force. A.G. Neto, Director of Economic Affairs at the Foreign Ministry is also, later confirmed, to have died.
28 May 1977	President Neto says in a broadcast that there will be no pardon for the insurgents, and little time will be wasted on trials.

31 May 1977	A massive purge is underway in the wake of the unsuccessful coup attempt by the 'Poder Popular'. Among those detained is the Deputy Chief of Staff of the Army, Commander P.J. Caetano (Commander Monstro Imortal).
2 June 1977	Several Portuguese nationals are arrested for complicity in the attempted coup d'etat, including Colonel J.V. Gomes.
6 June 1977	Acceptance of membership to Inter-Governmental Maritime Consultative Organization.
10 June 1977	Major J.I. da C. Mar tins, formerly Minister of Labour in Portugal, is detained as implicated in the uprising.
11 June 1977	The Minister of Internal Trade, D.A. Machado, is dismissed from his post and subsequently arrested, following disclosures by a ringleader in the attempted overthrow of the government, P. Fortunato (Provincial Commission of Luanda) concerning the aims of the insurrection.
18 June 1977	Cuba announces that it has stopped withdrawing its troops from Angola.
17 Aug. 1977	The Central Committee of the MPLA has amended the Constitution to grant President Neto increased powers to appoint and dismiss the government.
31 Aug. 1977	Cabinet changes. The Prime Minister, L. do Nascimento takes over Internal Trade as an additional portfolio. I. G. Mar.tins (Governor of the Bank of Angola) is appointed Minister of Finance.
12 Sept. 1977	The Minister of Health, Major M.A. de Almeida resigns. No immediate replacement is announced.
27-29 Sept. 1977	President Neto visits Moscow for talks with President Brezhnev, and other Soviet leaders, covering the situation in Africa.
16 Oct. 1977	The Cabinda Enclave Liberation Front (FLEC) proclaims the 'Independent State of Liberated Areas of Cabinda' in a communique from Loavo. The Cabindan Armed Forces (FAC) have meanwhile set up a new organization claiming to replace FLEC.
4-11 Dec. 1977	The First Congress of the MPLA is held in Luanda, attended by over 450 delegates. A resolution is passed restructuring the MPLA into a Marxist-Leninist political party. MPLA - Party of Labour (MPLA-PT) to be guided by the principles of scientific socialism. Its constitution, statutes and programme are drawn up.
7 Jan. 1978	President Neto announces Cabinet reshuffle involving nine portfolios. New appointments: M.P. Pacavira (Agriculture); F.F. Muteka (Transport); Major A. do C.B. Ribeiro (Industry and Power); A. da C. L. da Camara (Fisheries); R.A.V.F. de Almeida (External Trade); P.P. Joao (Internal Trade); C. Vahekenny (Secretary of State for Social Affairs); I.T.A. Machado (Secretary of State for Communications); A.V. de Carvalho (Governor of National Bank).
25 Jan. 1978	The Angolan government dissolves the Roman Catholic radio station 'Radio Ecclesia' and nationalizes its assets by a decree stating that the MPLA government would henceforth hold monopoly control over the information

	media.
8 Feb. 1978	A report by the British Christian Aid Association gives the country with the largest number of refugees as Zaire, with 470,000 fleeing Angolans. Second is Angola with 470,000 fleeing Angolans. 220,000 from Zaire's Shaba Province and 5,000 from Namibia.
Mar. 1978	MPLA launches a two pronged onslaught against UNITA in Cuando Cubando province, including air attacks.
4 Apr. 1978	At a news conference in London, UNITA's Information Secretary, Jeremiah Chitunda, confirms a major offensive around Serpo Pinto in Cuando Cubando province. Forces against UNITA include 5,000 Cubans, 1000 MPLA government troops and about 1,000 SWAPO guerrillas. Nigerians, Guineans, Congolese and East Europeans are also present.
5 Apr. 1978	More than 700 civilian refugees have crossed the border and are being taken in charge by South African forces in north-eastern Kavango.
4 May 1978	South Africa raids SWAPO bases in Angola.
5 May 1978	The South African Chief of Staff Operations Lt.-Gen. Jack Dutton says in Pretoria that South African forces have attacked and destroyed a guerrilla base manned by SWAPO within Angola, near the mining town of Cassinga. A communiqué signed by Angolan Defence Mininster Iko Carreira, states that the attack was upon 'the Namibian refugee camp in the town of Cassinga'. The number of SWAPO guerrillas operating from Southern Africa is estimated to be between 3000 and 5000. There has been a renewed exodus of refugees from Ovamboland to Angola, now said to number about 30,000.
6 May 1978	The incursion by South Africa is condemned by the United Nations Security Council in a resolution demanding the withdrawal of all South African forces from Angola.
7 June 1978	A UNITA spokesman in London reports that the offensive by some 6000 Cubans with air support, begun on 4 June in Bié, Huambo and Cuando-Cubango provinces, has been routed.
20 June 1978	In a major policy speech the United States Secretary of State, Cyrus Vance, indicates that the United States should seek to improve ties with President Neto's government.
21-24 June 1978	Don McHenry, the United States Deputy Permanent Representative at the United Nations, visits Luanda for informal talks on matters of mutual interest.
26 June 1978	A three year treaty of friendship and cooperation is concluded between Angola and Portugal, following a summit meeting in Guinea Bissau between President Ramatho Eanes of Portugal, and President Neto.
26 June 1978	A joint communiqué is signed by Presidents Neto and Eanes undertaking to promote the rapprochement between Angola and Portugal on a basis of respect for national independence, sovereignty, territorial integrity, equality- and non-interference.

2 July 1978	Dr Neto indicates at a press conference that his government has 'no reservations' about establishing diplomatic relations with the United States and that the decision depends on Washington.
15 July 1978	Angola's Foreign Minister, Paolo Jore, indicates that the government plans to diversify its relations with all other countries in accordance with its policy of non-alignment.
15-17 July 1978	Angolan and Zairean delegations hold talks in Brazzaville aimed at normalizing their relations.
21-22 July 1978	A second round of talks follow. Agreements concerning the reopening of the Benguela Railway and the repatriation of refugees are reached.
22 July 1978	The United States Department of State replies that it is pleased with Dr. Neto's offer; but that the Cuban presence in Angola is a matter of concern.
10 Aug. 1978	According to the United Nations High Commissioner for Refugees (UNHCR) 2,347 Angolans have applied for repatriation to Angola. Most are expected to return by the end of 1978. An airlift is being organized by Portuguese and Angolan officials with government approval.
19-21 Aug. 1978	An official visit by President Neto to Kinshasa seals the reconciliation between Angola and Zaire.
19 Sept. 1978	A treaty of friendship and cooperation between Mozambique and Angola is signed in Maputo.
15-17 Oct. 1978	An agreement for close cooperation between Zaire and Angola is signed in Luanda at the close of President Mobutu's State visit.
17 Oct. 1978	A joint communiqué from Presidents Neto and Mobutu asks the UNHCR to provide increased aid to speed the voluntary repatriation of refugees from both Angola and Zaire. Zaireans crossing into Angola are meantime being disarmed and sent to refugee camps. The camps themselves have been moved further away from the border.
7 Nov. 1978	General mobilization is ordered by Major Iko Carreira, the Defence Minister, in anticipation of a major airborne attack from South Africa.
10 Nov. 1978	A UNITA communiqué released in Paris gives details of UNITA's attacks on the Benguela Railway.
11 Nov. 1978	In a speech marking the third anniversary of independence, President Neto accuses South Africa of waging an undeclared war against Angola.
11 Nov. 1978	Angola closes its airspace to flights between South Africa and Europe.
13 Nov. 1978	A UNITA special communiqué from Paris reports a major Angolan government offensive against UNITA in central and southern Angola, involving 20,000 troops - Angolan, Cuban, East German, Katangan and Portuguese.
14 Nov. 1978	The United Nations Special Committee on Apartheid appeals to all governments to help Angola repel South African aggression.

21 Nov. 1978   The United States Deputy Secretary of State for African Affairs, Richard Moose, arrives in Luanda, with a strong American delegation.

6 Dec. 1978   The Angolan and Zairean envoys in Lusaka disclose that about 4,000 Angolan and Zairean refugees who fled into Zambia have been repatriated during the past two months.

6-9 Dec. 1978   Following the meeting of the MPLA-PT's Central Committee it is announced that Lopo do Nascimento has been dismissed as Prime Minister and as secretary of the Politburo, that Cdr. C.R. Dilolua has resigned as Second Deputy Prime Minister and as a member of the Politburo and that the directors of national television and of Jornal de Angola have been removed from office.

10 Dec. 1978   In a speech marking the twenty second anniversary of the founding of the MPLA, President Neto states the government's intentions of eradicating devisive influences and acquiring greater direct control of Ministries.

11 Dec. 1978   A Presidential decree announces the removal of the two remaining Deputy Prime Ministers, J.E. dos Santos and Commander P. de C. dos S. van Dunem and three ministers.

13 Dec. 1978   Visit to Angola by Senator George McGovern of the United States Democratic Party.

22 Dec. 1978   A series of new appointments to the government are announced by ANGOP.

11 Jan. 1979   In an interview published in Lisbon, Dr. Jonas Savimbi claims that UNITA is present throughout most of Angola and is tightening its grip on the country. Only the presence of 28,000 Cuban troops gives the MPLA the upper hand.

17 Jan. 1979   Four ministerial appointments are made in decrees issued from the Presidency: F.F. Muteka (Transport and Communications); P. de C. van Dunem (Provincial Co-ordination); E.T.A. Machado (Communications, Deputy Minister); H. do C.A. Machado (Agriculture and Forestry Resources, Deputy Minister).

17 Jan. 1979   In a fifth decree E.T.A. Machado is dismissed from his post as State Secretary for Communications.

17 Jan. 1979   The government reorganization includes the following new appointments: J.E. dos Santos - Planning and Chairman of National Planning Commission; H.P.B. da Silva - Housing and Construction; M.A. dos P. Mangueira - Deputy Minister for Housing and Construction; C.A. van Dunem - Internal Trade; F.G.G. Martins - Deputy Minister for Internal Trade; P.P. Joao - Deputy Minister for External Trade; A.J.F. Neto - Deputy Minister for Health; P. de C. dos S. van Dunem - Provincial Co-ordination; F.F. Muteka - Transport and Communications; E.T.A. Machado - Deputy Minister for Communications; H. do C.A. Machado - Deputy Minister for Agriculture and Forestry; J.V.D. Mingas - Secretary of State for Physical Education and Sport; A. Nsikalangu - Secretary of State for Co-operation. Mr. Muteka took on the additional responsibility for Communication. A. Machado was promoted from Secretary of State to Deputy Minister for Communications. The Ministry of Health, left vacant in September 1977, had been assumed

at the end of that year by D. da Cruz.

18 Jan. 1979   A statement by UNITA spokesman Mr. Chitunda in London indicates that UNITA is ready to talk to President Neto's forces, but only when all Cuban forces have been withdrawn from Angola.

22 Jan. 1979   A trade agreement is signed in Luanda between Portugal and Angola, at the conclusion of a visit by a Portuguese delegation led by the Minister of Trade and Tourism A.R. Carreira.

6 Feb. 1979   The National Front for the Liberation of Angola (FNLA) is reported to have renewed guerrilla warfare in Northern Angola, and to be gaining local support.

17-19 Feb. 1979   An official friendship visit is undertaken by Erich Honecker, Chairman of the East German Council of State and General Secretary of the Socialist Unity Party (SED) Central Committee, at the invitation of President Neto. A twenty year treaty of friendship and cooperation is signed and a joint communiqué issued by the two leaders.

26 Feb. 1979   Rhodesia's Air-Force launches an air strike against a guerrilla base near the eastern Angolan town of Luso, said to contain 1500 Zimbabwe People's Revolutionary Army (ZIPRA) trainees, loyal to the Patriotic Front.

6 Mar. 1979   South African troops and planes attack SWAPO guerrilla bases in Angola. Facts are disclosed by the South African Prime Minister in the House of Assembly.

14 Mar. 1979   Maj.-Gen. Geldenhuys (General Officer Commanding South West Africa Command) announces that a second air strike against SWAPO bases has been undertaken.

20 Mar. 1979   United Nations Security Council meets to consider a complaint by Angola against South Africa's 'intensified' air and ground attacks on Angolan territory.

28 Mar. 1979   United Nations Security Council adopts a resolution strongly condemning South Africa by twelve votes to none (Britain, France and the United States abstaining).

12-14 Apr. 1979   President Ceausesu of Romania visits Angola. A twenty year treaty of friendship and co-operation is signed as well as a protocol on economic, industrial and technical cooperation and an agreement between the two countries political parties.

25 Apr. 1979   A decree issued by Zambia's Western Province member of the Central Committee, Felix Luputa, orders Zambian police and immigration officials to 'round up' the 2,410 Angolan refugees living illegally in villages in Sikongo.

19 May 1979   UNITA forces capture the town of Calai after a two hour battle during which UNITA drives the MPLA from their main base about 5 km outside the town.

19 May 1979   A member of the National Front for the Liberation of Angola (FNLA)

Political Bureau, Hendrik Vaal Neto, claims in Lisbon that the FNLA is holding talks with UNITA, aimed at forming a common front against the MPLA government, that the FNLA has attacked and destroyed several oil storage depots and that it controls six provinces and large areas of the north and north east.

24 May 1979
ANGOP reports that Vaal Neto has been expelled from Portugal.

5 July 1979
ANGOP reports that President Neto has promulgated a law making military service for three years obligatory for all Angolans on reaching the age of eighteen.

21 July 1979
A four-day session of the Portuguese-Angolan Joint Cooperation Commission ends with the signing in Lisbon of a cultural agreement and a cooperation agreement in the socio-cultural, technical and scientific spheres.

25 July 1979
President Neto has made several ministerial and party changes, including ten Provincial Commissars, under decrees dated 25 July. Appointments include: K. Paiama (Interior Minister); A.C. do A. Martins (Secretary of State for Culture); R.A.V.D. Mingas (Secretary of State for Physical Education and Sports).

3 Aug. 1979
In a report released at the United Nations in New York, Angola estimates damage caused by South African air and ground attacks in its territory since 1976 at $293 million, and demands compensation.

11 Aug. 1979
A recently formed guerrilla movement, the Popular Movement for the Liberation of Cabinda, (PMLC) claims in Kinshasa that it has made a successful attack on a Cuban base near Tshiowa.

10 Sept. 1979
President Agostinho Neto's death in Moscow, from inoperable cancer is announced in a medical bulletin, quoted by the official Soviet news agency, Tass. An Angolan delegation, including Lucio Lara and Pascual Luvualo fly to Moscow. The MPLA Bureau decree forty-five days of mourning.

17 Sept. 1979
The funeral ceremonies for President Neto take place in Luanda at the Palace of the People. The first funeral oration is read by the President of the Organization of African Unity (OAU), President Tolbert of Liberia.

21 Sept. 1979
José Eduardo dos Santos is sworn in as Angola's second President, following a unanimous decision by the Central Committee of the MPLA-PT.

21 Sept. 1979
In his inauguration speech President dos Santos reaffirms the objectives of non-alignment and friendly relations and cooperation with all countries, but stresses Angola's continuing support for liberation movements in Southern Africa.

13 Oct. 1979
Angolan government troops cross the border into Kavango, northern Namibia, for the first time.

14 Oct. 1979
Zambia, Zaire and Angola sign a mutual non-agression pact, and a series of economic cooperation agreements, following a summit meeting of their three Presidents at Ndola on the Zambian copper belt.

27 Oct. 1979
The decision to ban Angolan opposition leaders, taken by the People's

Revolutionary Movement (MPR)'s Political Bureau is announced in Kinshasa.

31 Oct. 1979   In a communiqué from the MPLA Politbureau South Africa is accused of raiding into Southern Angola, 120 miles north of the border, and attacking the towns of Mocamedes and Lubango.

31 Oct. 1979   Angola requests an urgent meeting of the United Nations Security Council and accuses South Africa of launching a two-pronged attack deep into Angola.

2 Nov. 1979   The Security Council adopts a resolution calling on South Africa to respect Angolan sovereignty and requesting urgent assistance for Angola, to strengthen her defence capacity.

7 Nov. 1979   President dos Santos reshuffles his Cabinet in areas connected with the national economy. Appointed by decree: L.P.F. do Nascimento (Foreign Trade Minister); R.A.V.F. de Almeida (Planning Minister); A.J.G. de Carvalho (Fisheries Minister).

12-15 Nov. 1979 Proposals based on an Angolan suggestion for a demilitarized zone (DMZ) extending fifty kilometres either side of the Angolan and Zambian border with Namibia are the subject of a United Nations working paper discussed at meetings in Geneva.

14 Nov. 1979   The leader of the FNLA, Holden Roberto, is expelled from Senegal.

17 Nov. 1979   The Zaire government announces that Angolan refugees living in Zaire will not be allowed to settle along the borders with Angola, or in the Cabinda enclave. An estimated 700,000 Angolans now live in Zaire.

9 Dec. 1979   A thirty five member Soviet military mission arrives in Luanda, to assess the needs of Angola's army in the face of 'constant enemy attacks'.

28 Jan. 1980   The Angolan News Agency ANGOP reports that Ministers from Angola, Mozambique, Guinea Bissau, Cape Verde and Sao Tomé and Principe have agreed at their four day meeting in Luanda, 24-27 January, to increase support to national liberation movements, including SWAPO in Namibia and the ANC in South Africa.

12 Feb. 1980   The Defence Minister, Cdr. I. Carreira has been relieved of his post. By an official decree the President José Dos Santos will share control over defence matters with the Chief of Staff of the Angolan armed forces.

16 Feb. 1980   A national commmmission to study the implementation of people's power holds its first session.

22 Mar. 1980   A joint communiqué issued in Havana, after an official visit by President dos Santos, expresses Angola's and Cuba's full solidarity with the Afgan people and declares Cuba's firm and unshakeable support for Angola and its revolution. Cuban military and civil aid is to continue at all levels.

28 Mar. 1980   Acting on a request from Angola the United Nations Security Council passed a resolution condemning South Africa for its premediated, persistent and sustained invasions of Angola.

12 May 1980	The Angolan Ministry of Defence reports a South African incursion into Cunene Province and the killing and wounding of civilians.
21 May 1980	A Radio Luanda announcement reports a South African attack in Cuando-Cubango Province, 60 km from the border. Reprisal raids are threatened.
7 June 1980	South African military forces enter Angola and begin large scale operations in the southern provinces of Cunene and Cuando-Cubango.
13 June 1980	South Africa's P.W. Botha discloses a major preemptive strike into Angola, in which SWAPO's operational command headquarters has been destroyed in a 'shock attack'.
24 June 1980	At a press conference in Luanda the Angolan Interior Ministry announce that 120 Angolans have been arrested for alleged involvement in 'bomb squads' planting explosives in public places in Luanda. This attempted destabilization is blamed on South Africa.
26 June 1980	E. de Figuerido, the Angolan Permanent Representative at the United Nations calls for an urgent meeting of the Security Council.
27 June 1980	Security Council resolution condemns South Africa's persistent armed invasions, demands the immediate withdrawal of all its forces and the payment of compensation.
28 June 1980	Angola claims that South African troops are still occupying parts of Southern Angola, including the commune of Ovale and have installed a command post at Mulemba.
3 July 1980	In a joint communiqué covering a visit to Angola by President Mobutu of Zaire, South African attacks on Angola are repudiated and solidarity is expressed with the Angolan people, with their government and with the MPLA Workers' Party. Diplomatic relations are to continue from now on at an ambassadorial level.
9 July 1980	The Angolan News Agency announced a sweeping government reshuffle. New appointments include Armed Forces Chief of Staff P.M. Tonha (Defence); Lieut-Colonel A. Rodrigues (Interior Ministry); K. Paiama (State Security); B. Ribeiro (Industry); P. van Dunem (Energy); M.A. Managueira (Housing) and J. Ferreira (Secretary of State for Housing).
12 July 1980	Further ministerial changes are announced. The membership of the Council of Ministers incorporating the latest changes was as follows: M.A.E.R. Quito (Interior); K. Paiama (State Security); P.M.T. Pedale (Defence); P.T. Jorge (Foreign Affairs); R.A.V.F. Almeida (Planning); C.A. van Dunem (Internal Trade); L.F.F. do Nascimento (External Trade); Dr. D.A. Boavida. (Justice); Cdr. P. de C. dos S. van Dunem Loi (Energy); J.A. do C.B. Ribeiro (Industry); D.E. Quimba (Provincial Co-ordination); A.A.M. de Carvallo (Health); H.P.B. da Silva (Labour and Social Security); M.A. dos P.B. Mangueira (Construction); A.J.G. de Carvalho (Fisheries); M.P. Pacavira (Agriculture); F.F. Mutsla (Transport and Communication); A. Lucoque (Education); I.G. Martins (Finance); J. Morais (Petroleum). L.J.F. Diandengue appointed Secretary of State for Housing, other Secretaries of State in the Council being A.J. do A. Martins (Culture);R.A.V.D.Mingas

(Physical Education and Sport) and M. da A. Vahekenny (Social Affairs).

31 July 1980	ANGOP reports 529 violations of Angolan territory by South Africa during the period January to June 1980.
5 Aug. 1980	Anami Akakpo, Togo's Foreign Minister and head of the OAU committee of inquiry into damage caused in Cunene and Cuando-Cubango provinces by South African raids reports in Luanda on committee findings.
7 Aug. 1980	It is officially announced that sixteen UNITA guerrillas, convicted of making a series of bomb attacks in Luanda and sentenced to death on 29 July, were executed on 5 August.
11 Aug. 1980	Angolan authorities confirm a UNITA attack on oil installations at Lobito port.
11 Aug. 1980	UNITA announces a general offensive throughout the country to `avenge the memory' of its sixteen activists executed in Luanda on 5 August.
12 Aug. 1980	The military staff of FNLA set up a new organization COMIRA (Comité Militar da Resistencia Angolana) under the leadership of P. Tuba and H.V. Nato.
19 Aug. 1980	The official news agency ANGOP announces that a 206 member National People's Assembly is to be installed in November 1980 to replace the existing Council of the Revolution as the supreme organ of state. Provincial people's assembles will also be elected.
20 Aug. 1980	Z. Estevas, Director of the Department for the Institution of People's Power indicates that meetings are already being held throughout the provinces to enable voters to choose an electoral college.
21 Aug. 1980	An Angolan revolutionary tribunal, sitting in Huambo, sentenced nine members of UNITA to death for 'counter-revolutionary activities and crimes against the people'; sentences later carried out by firing squad.
23 Aug. 1980	In reprisal a UNITA tribunal pronounces death sentences against fifteen MPLA soldiers and the sentences are carried out immediately.
23 Aug. 1980	Voting for electoral colleges which will choose the members of the National Assembly and the provincial assemblies begins, in the southern province of Cunene.
15 Sept. 1980	It is reported in Paris that Holden Roberto, leader of the National Front for the Liberation of Angola (FNLA) has been overthrown by his military leaders, and that the FNLA has itself been replaced by the Military Council for Angolan Resistance (COMIRA).
26 Sept. 1980	Sweeping amendments are made to the Constitution, calling for elections to the provincial and national assemblies. The National Assembly will become the supreme organ of state power in place of the Revolutionary Council. The elective process is to be completed before 4 December.
11 Nov. 1980	The National Assembly is installed, and eighteen provincial legislatures created.

19 Nov. 1980	A United States House-Senate conference on the 1980-81 Foreign Aids Authorization Bill blocks an attempt to repeal the Clark Amendment. Instead it adopts a modified version of the ban maintaining the requirement that any proposal by the President to provide support for military or paramilitary operations in Angola should be submitted to Congress, which could only approve such assistance by a joint resolution of both houses.
1 Dec. 1980	A people's revolutionary court at Cuito (Bie province) sentences four UNITA members to death as 'counter-revolutionaries'.
17-23 Dec. 1980	An extraordinary congress of the MPLA-PT is held in Luanda to assess Angola's economic progress and to approve economic plans for 1981-85. President dos Santos' position as head of state and party leader is confirmed by the congress. Membership of the Central Committee is to be increased from fifty five to seventy five.
2-3 Jan. 1981	Cuban and Angolan forces are attacked by South African troops and aircraft 310 km north of Namibia, in the vicinity of Uia and Mujombe.
14 Jan. 1981	South African forces begin a new offensive in Cunene province, and attack Cuamato.
16 Jan. 1981	AIM reports that eleven basic commodities are seen to be rationed.
28 Jan. 1981	Le Monde reports that 'protected villages' are being imposed on the population of the Central Plateau to defend them against UNITA guerrilla attacks.
7 Feb. 1981	A memorandum is drafted, principally by Dr. Chester Crocker, Assistant Secretary of State-designate for African Affairs, arguing that American recognition of Angola should not be considered until Cuban troops have left the country and that no settlement should be made at Dr. Savimbi's expense.
17 Feb. 1981	The Front-line States summit meeting at Lusaka warns South Africa to stop training dissidents hostile to Angola's government.
21 Feb. 1981	A Defence Ministry communiqué released in Luanda reports an increase in South African air attacks and incursions.
Mar. 1981	The Secretariat of the Central Committee of the MPLA-PT: Cadres - J.E. dos Santos Organization - L. Lara Ideology, Information & Culture - A. Lukoki Defence and Security - J. Paulo (Dino Matross) Justice - H. de C. Santos 'Onambwe' Economic and Social Policy - R. de Almeida Productive Sector - M. P. Pacavira Foreign Relations - A. Van-Dunem 'Mbinda' Administration and Finance - I.T.A. Machado
7 Mar. 1981	The South African Air Force strikes the SWAPO orientation camp near Lubango, about 200 kms north of the Namibian border.
8 Mar. 1981	An Angolan court sentencees eighteen UNITA members to death for participating in bomb attacks.

19 Mar. 1981	The United States government asks Congress to repeal the Clark Amendment banning all aid to anti-government forces in Angola.
20 Mar. 1981	President José dos Santos announces ministerial changes. Political appointments: L. do Nascimento (Planning); A.L. Teixeira (Education); A.V. Gomes (Agriculture) F.G.G. Martins (Internal Trade). Secretaries of State: P.P. Joao (Cooperation); R.T.M. Gil (Social Affairs); Capt. J.D.F. Tuta (War Veterans); B. da S. Cardoso (Culture).
16 Apr. 1981	Presidents of the Frontline States, meeting in Angola, criticize the Reagan Administration's policies and denounce actions to destabilize the MPLA government.
3 May 1981	United States Senate, Foreign Relations Committee, approves a measure to lift the Clark Amendment, provided that the future aid (i.e. to UNITA) is tied to substantial progress in resolving the Namibian conflict.
12 May 1981	United States House of Representatives Foreign Affairs Committee approves measures involving the retention of the Clark Amendment, by nineteen votes to five.
30 July 1981	A communiqué from the Angolan Defence Ministry in Luanda accuses South Africa of invading Cunene Province, seizing seven towns and encircling the provincial capital, Ondjiva. South Africa denies this.
Aug.- Sept.1981	During 'Operation Protea' up to 5,000 South African troops occupy most of Cunene Province.
23 Aug. 1981	Operation Protea launched.
26 Aug. 1981	Angola claims it has been invaded by two South African armoured columns and that combat areas in Southern Angola are under heavy air bombardment. President dos Santos appeals to the United Nations for help.
26 Aug. 1981	The South African Prime Minister P.W. Botha confirms that South African troops have been fighting inside Angola. He explains the South African incursion as part of continuing follow-up operations against terrorists.
28 Aug. 1981	General Constand Viljoen, the Chief of Staff of the South African Army claims South African troops have completed their 'limited task' inside Angola and are returning to their bases in Namibia.
30 Aug. 1981	Luanda announces South African forces have occupied Ngiva, and nine other towns in Cunene Province.
31 Aug. 1981	The United States uses its veto to block a United Nations Security Council resolution condemning the South African raid into southern Angola. The vote, 13-1 with Great Britain abstaining.
4 Sept. 1981	Operation Protea ends, according to South African army chief, Johannes Geldenhuys.
12-13 Sept. 1981	A special OAU meeting in Nigeria appeals to African States to provide military support to Angola.

21 Sept. 1981	OAU chairman, President Moi of Kenya, appeals for military aid for Angola.
1 Oct. 1981	President dos Santos visits Col. Gaddafy in Tripoli, following an offer of military aid by Libya.
12 Oct. 1981	A friendship and cooperation treaty is signed by President José dos Santos and the Czechoslovak President Gustav Husak in Prague.
19 Oct. 1981	A treaty of friendship and cooperation between North Korea and Angola is signed in Pyongyang by President Kim and President dos Santos.
1-20 Nov. 1981	South African armed forces launch another major offensive'Operation Daisy', allegedly a search-and-destroy operation against the SWAPO base at Chitequeta, near Cassinga.
2 Nov. 1981	President dos Santos dismisses his Minister for Petroleum and appoints Lt.-Col. P. de C. dos S. van Dunem Loi, the Minister for Energy to take temporary charge, until a new appointment is made.
24 Nov. 1981	President dos Santos meets President Diouf of Senegal in Cape Verde, leading to the later establishment of diplomatic relations at ambassadorial level.
27 Nov. 1981	The British Royal Navy headquarters at Northwood have confirmed that the Soviet Union is setting up a new South Atlantic fleet to be based at Luanda.
30 Nov. 1981	UNITA claims responsibility for the major fire at Luanda's state-run oil refinery.
3 Dec. 1981	Luanda radio reports the dismissal of Lieutenant-Colonel F. da C. Gato, Commander of the Air Force and of Lieutenant-Colonel D.M. Ndozi, Deputy Chief of General Staff.
7 Dec. 1981	Through the military incursion 'Operation Protea' South African forces have destroyed SWAPO bases inside Angola and dismantled SWAPO's military command structure.
11 Dec. 1981	Yugoslav news agency TANJUA reports from Luanda that President dos Santos has appealed for direct contacts and the normalization of relations between the United States and Angola.
12 Dec. 1981	K. Paihama has been dismissed as Minister of State Security and replaced by Colonel J.M.P.D. Matroce.
14 Dec. 1981	United States House-Senate conference approves the 1981-82 Foreign Aid Authorization Bill which retains the Clark Amendment.
22 Dec. 1981	The Angolan ambassador to France, Luis de Almeida, reaffirms that the government will never negotiate with UNITA, nor with its leader Savimbi.
24 Dec. 1981	ANGOP claims a force of over 2000 COMIRA insurgents is being trained in Zaire, with the object of invading northern Angola.
27 Dec. 1981	South African aircraft bomb targets in Moxico Province.

29 Dec. 1981	Luanda claims a South African force, backed by airpower, has attacked Evale, 68 kms north of Ngiva.
15-16 Jan. 1982	Talks are held in Paris between Dr. Chester Crocker and P.T.1982 Jorge, Angolan Minister of Foreign Affairs, as part of a continuing dialogue between the two countries.
24 Jan. 1982	In an interview published in The Observer, Dr. Savimbi maintains his interest in the idea of a government of national reconciliation and claims UNITA has established unofficial contacts with the MPLA-PT.
24 Jan. 1982	Soviet news agency TASS reports that during a visit by an Angolan delegation, led by Lucio Lara (MPLA Secretary-General) and Col. P.M.T. Pedale (Minister of Defence), to the Soviet Union, the two countries have signed a programme of economic and technological cooperation for the period 1981-85.
5 Feb. 1982	A joint Angolan-Cuban communiqué issued at the end of a visit by Cuban Foreign Minister, I.M. Peoli, states that the presence of Cuban troops is a sovereign and legitimate act by both countries and has nothing to do with the problems of Namibia.
16 Feb. 1982	Senegal is to establish diplomatic relations with Angola at ambassadorial level with immediate effect.
2 Mar. 1982	Luanda's oil refinery resumes production. The re-opening is formally inaugurated by P.M. Touha (Defence Minister) representing the President and P.C. Van-Dunem (Energy and Oil Minister).
15-19 Mar. 1982	President Eanes of Portugal pays a state visit to Angola. Agreements are signed on financial relations, industrial cooperation, transport, energy and tourism.
23 Mar. 1982	Zambia intends to repatriate 9,000 refugees from Maheba camp near Solwezi, in the northwest, following acceptance of Angolan government conditions by the office of the United Nations High Commissioner for Refugees.
25 Mar. 1982	UNITA communique, issued in Lisbon, claims all the refugees are UNITA members, many well known militants, and their repatriation will endanger their lives.
5 Apr. 1982	Angolan Defence Minister Colonel P.M.T. Pedale announces South African attacks in Huila Province, southern Angola, including air strikes.
16-19 Apr.1982	Portuguese President Eanes visits Angola to discuss the1982 Namibian issue. As a gesture of goodwill President dos Santos has promised to release three Portuguese political prisoners held in Luanda for the last six years. Several economic agreements are reached.
22 Apr. 1982	South African Defence Minister General Magnus Malan threatens raids deep into Angola in retaliation for SWAPO attacks in Namibia.
23 Apr. 1982	ANGOP reports five people sentenced to death for collaborating with UNITA against the government.

4 May 1982	The Internal Trade Minister F.G.G. Martins is dismissed by presidential decree.
9 May 1982	President dos Santos supports President Kaunda's decision to hold direct talks with South Africa's Prime Minister, P.W. Botha, on 30 April, over Namibian independence.
13 May 1982	Three Cabindan separatists are sentenced to death and eighteen others are jailed.
16 May 1982	South African planes bomb the Kassinga district.
3 June 1982	UNITA claims their forces are operating within 125 miles of Luanda.
16-22 June 1982	At its tenth Ordinary Session the MPLA Central Committee launches a recruitment drive to raise membership to 60,000.
8 July 1982	The Angolan Foreign Minister sets out the terms on which Cuban forces would be withdrawn from Angola, and stresses that the presence of the estimated 20,000 Cubans in Angola is a bilateral question between Angola and Cuba.
Mid-July 1982	Radio Nacional de Angola announces the dismissal of M.P. Pacavira, MPLA Party Secretary for the Sector of Production, part of a purge demotions and transfer of respected civilian party leaders and officials.
26 July 1982	An Economic, Social and Scientific Agreement is signed in Luanda by the French Aid Minister, J.P.C.G. Penne.
26 July 1982	Signs general agreement with France on cooperation.
26-31 July 1982	UNITA Party Congress is held at Mavinga, attended by over 1,500 delegates and by Western reporters. Savimbi's Presidency is confirmed, M. Nzau Puna is re-elected Secretary-General, D.A. Chilingutila remains Chief of Staff of FALA.
12 Aug. 1982	South Africa admits it is involved in a 'follow-up' operation against SWAPO guerrillas in Angola.
15 Aug. 1982	In government changes involving major economic portfolios the following appointments are made: L.F. do Nascimento (Planning); I.G. Mar.tins (External Trade); A.P. dos Santos (Internal Trade); A.T. de Matos (Finance).
21-22 Sept.1982	The heads of state of Portugal's five former African colonies, Angola, Mozambique, Cape Verde, Guinea Bissau and Sao Tomé and Principe, attend a summit meeting in Praia, Cape Verde.
27 Sept. 1982	An agreement on economic, scientific and technical co-operation is signed with Cuba.
28 Sept. 1982	China recognises the government of Angola.
4 Oct. 1982	In the United Nations General Assembly Angola's Foreign Minister, Paulo Jorge, accuses South Africa of making ninety-six landings of

helicopter-borne troops during the first nine months of 1982, as well as staging eighteen air raids and 580 reconnaissance flights.

25 Oct. 1982	UNITA communiqué claims the capture of Candono government barracks on 19 October, 167 miles east of Luanda.
25 Oct. 1982	A general agreement in the military field is signed with the Hungarian Defence Minister.
25 Oct. 1982	UNITA say they captured the Roman Catholic Archibishop of Lubango, Alexandre do Nascimento, by mistake, and promise his early release.
Nov. 1982	UNITA capture Lumbala in Moxico Province.
5 Nov. 1982	UNITA, raiding at Calulo, come to within 130 miles of Luanda.
8 Nov. 1982	South African marines make a seaborne raid north of Namibe and destroy bridges on the Ghiane River.
9 Nov. 1982	E. Honecker, Chairman of the East German Council of State, promises that military cooperation between Angola and East Germany will be intensified.
16 Nov. 1982	A prisoner exchange, involving three United States citizens, three Soviet military men, a Cuban, about ninety Angolan soldiers held by South Africa, and the return of the bodies of three South African soldiers from Angola, takes place in Luanda.
Dec. 1982	The Angolan army's 16th Brigade conducts a major counter-insurgency sweep through Cuando-Cubango.
7 Dec. 1982	A MPLA-PT Central Committee grants President dos Santos special powers to carry out certain aspects of Angola's overall emergency plan.
8 Dec. 1982	Top level delegations from the Angolan and South African governments meet on the island of Sal in Cape Verde for secret talks over the future of Namibia and the possible cessation of hostilities between South Africa and Angolan forces in southern Angola.
10 Dec. 1982	A unanimous decision by the MPLA Central Committee gives President dos Santos sweeping emergency powers to implement an emergency plan affecting defence and security, the economy and the state apparatus.
10 Dec. 1982	UNITA communiqué calls on the MPLA government to form a 'government of national union'.
23-25 Dec. 1982	UNITA attack targets within Huambo city.
27 Dec. 1982	A.T. de Matos is appointed Governor of the Angolan National Bank.
29 Dec. 1982	UNITA reports that its four-day Christmas offensive has extended its operations into Uige Province on the Zairean border.
29 Dec. 1982	The acting officer commanding the South West Africa Territory Force, Brigadier W. Meyer, indicates in Windhoek that South African forces are involved in a seek and destroy mission in southern Angola against SWAPO

bases and forces.

5 Jan. 1983	UNITA communiqué declares its wish to start talks with the MPLA-PT to restore peace in Angola, secure national reconciliation and form a government of national unity.
7 Jan. 1983	MPLA Party purge confirmed. C. Andrade and V. Lara imprisoned, some thirty other activists, including Ruth Lara, suspended.
15 Jan. 1983	The Angolan ambassador to Lisbon discusses with President Eanes the possibility of Portugal providing training assistance to the Angolan armed forces.
18 Jan. 1983	UNITA launch a devastating attack on Angola's second largest dam and hydroelectric power station at Lomaum in Benguela Province.
9 Feb. 1983	A protocol of cooperation in the field of culture is signed with Benin.
9 Feb. 1983	The MPLA has re-admitted eighteen of the thirty party militants suspended. Ruth Lara is still suspended and C. Andrade still held in detention.
10-13 Feb.1983	Official visit to Great Britain by the Angolan Foreign Minister, P. Jorge.
11 Feb. 1983	Foreign Minister P. Jorge, declares in London that there is no question of any conciliation or reconciliation between the Angolan government and UNITA.
22-24 Feb.1983	The People's Assembly votes to extend its term of office until 1986 and resolves that a new electoral law be drafted.
23 Feb. 1983	Talks are held on Sal, Cape Verde between delegations from South Africa and Angola. No agreement is reached.
25 Feb. 1983	Luanda announces that the People's Assembly has ratified legislation providing for death sentences for convicted spies.
12 Mar. 1983	UNITA captures sixty-four Czech and twenty Portuguese technicians during a three hour battle at the Alto Catumbela hydro-electric complex in Benguela Province.
15-16 Mar.1983	Interior Minister, Lt.-Col. A. Rodrigues holds talks in Paris with Frank Wisner of the United States State Department's Bureau of African Affairs.
21 Mar. 1983	Cuba airlifts another 7,000 troops to Angola.
21 Mar. 1983	A force of 2,000 Cubans, backed by a strike force of Mig combat aircraft moves south to Menongue.
21 Mar. 1983	UNITA's Deputy Secretary for Foreign Affairs, Tito Chingunji confirms that the twenty one Czech children captured by UNITA will be unconditionally released.
12-14 Apr.1983	The Interior Minister, Lt-Col. A. Rodrigues visits Washington for talks with the Secretary of State, George Schultz and Vice President George Bush.

19 Apr. 1983	UNITA offers to release Dr. Marea Hudeckova, a Czech hostage, in exchange for Philippe Augoyard a French national, serving an eight year sentence in Afghanistan convicted on spying charges.
20 Apr. 1983	J.H.V. de Melo Dias is appointed Minister of Construction.
20 Apr. 1983	UNITA captures the Benguela railway junction, Munhango.
24 Apr. 1983	President dos Santos dismisses several ministers.
16 May 1983	TASS reports that Soviet President Andropov has promised to increase Soviet arms supplies to Angola.
20 May 1983	An agreement on cooperation between the CPSU and the MPLA-PT, a plan for party links between the two parties and a protocol on cultural and scientific cooperation between the USSR and Angola for 1983-84 are signed. A joint Soviet-Angolan communiqué is published. President dos Santos leaves the Soviet Union after a five day working visit marking the seventh anniversary of the Soviet-Angolan Treaty of Friendship and Cooperation.
20 June 1983	The Minister of Health, M. de Carvalho is relieved of his post by Presidential decree, and is replaced by A.J.F. Neto.
27 June 1983	A tripartite Angolan-Zambian-Zairian summit is held in Lubumbashi. President dos Santos holds a five hour meeting with Presidents Mobutu and Kaunda to discuss border security problems, refugee questions and the fate of the Benguela railway.
29 June 1983	A new law approved by the People's Assembly and the President restricts the movements of foreigners in the country.
30 June 1983	Forty five Czechoslovak hostages released by UNITA arrive in Johannesburg en route to Czechoslovakia.
July 1983	UNITA holds the town of Mussende, 300 km south east of Luanda, with a UNITA brigade of 2000 men.
2 July 1983	By Presidential decree, dismissals: P.P. Joao (Secretary of State for Cooperation); B.S. van Dunem (Secretary of the Council of Ministers). Appointments: C.A. Fernandes (Secretary of State for Cooperation); P.P. Joao re-appointed, with the position of Secretary of State.
18 July 1983	Angola declares an amnesty for all UNITA and FNLA rebels, both within and outside the country.
18 July 1983	UNITA rejects amnesty offers.
25-26 July 1983	Belgian Foreign Minister, L. Tindemans visits Luanda and signs agreements on economic cooperation, food and the repair of Benguela railway rolling stock.
30 July 1983	UNITA estimates the number of Cuban troops and civilian advisers at 30,000 - 40,000; Western sources at 19,000 - 25,000.
31 July 1983	Angola introduces a new internal defence law, putting power and

	responsibility for security into the hands of military councils appointed by the President.
31 July 1983	Front Line States, including Angola, at the end of a two-day meeting at Kadoma, Zimbabwe, announce restrictions on South African based foreign correspondents who will not, in principle, be allowed to work in Front Line States.
1 Aug. 1983	UNITA attacks Cangamba.
4 Aug. 1983	UNITA launches a major offensive involving 10,000 guerrillas throughout central and eastern Angola.
14 Aug. 1983	FAPLA garrison withdraws from Cangamba.
22 Aug. 1983	Angola admits that the south-eastern town of Cangamba has fallen to UNITA, after a two-week battle.
26 Aug. 1983	President dos Santos states his conditions for a Cuban withdrawal at a mass rally in Luanda.
4 Sept. 1983	UNITA forces capture the town of Calulo, 200 km from Luanda, taking twenty-seven Spanish, Brazilian and Portuguese hostages.
30 Sept. 1983	President dos Santos introduces conscription to the armed forces.
Oct. 1983	FAPLA launches a concerted counter-offensive against UNITA, to continue into 1984.
6 Oct. 1983	Ambassador Luis de Almeida, Angola's senior official in Europe, releases the government's White Paper detailing South African attacks on Angola since 1975 at a press conference in London.
2 Nov. 1983	UNITA begins a new offensive expected to last six months.
7 Nov. 1983	UNITA ambushes a military train near the city of Malange.
8 Nov. 1983	UNITA shoots down an Angolan Boeing 737 at Lubango.
16 Nov. 1983	UNITA takes seventeen foreign hostages, five Britons and twelve Portuguese citizens during raids in Moxico Province.
6 Dec. 1983	The South African Defence Force begins a new offensive by moving into position in the Cunene buffer zone.
15 Dec. 1983	In a letter to the United Nations Secretary General, South Africa offers to begin, from 31 January 1984, disengaging troops stationed in Angola, provided that Luanda takes reciprocal steps to see that its own troops, as well as those of Cuba and SWAPO do not exploit the resultant situation.
16 Dec. 1983	The United Nations Security Council begins a debate on South Africa's military intervention in Angola.
18-19 Dec. 1983	President dos Santos attends the fourth summit of the Heads of State of the five Portuguese speaking African countries in Bissau.

20 Dec. 1983	United Nations Security Council resolution demands that South Africa unconditionally withdraws forthwith all its occupation forces from the territory of Angola.
22 Dec. 1983	South African forces occupy Cassinga in Huila Province.
23 Dec. 1983	General C. Viljoen acknowledges that South African forces are engaged in a limited campaign against SWAPO bases.
29 Dec. 1983	South African jets attack the SWAPO base near Lubango in southern Angola.
30 Dec. 1983	President dos Santos accepts the South African proposal, on conditions implying South Africa's abandoning of the 'linkage' issue.
3 Jan. 1984	Angola accepts the principle of a thirty day truce with South Africa, in a letter to the United Nations, on certain conditions, including the withdrawal of all South African troops from Angolan territory.
6 Jan. 1984	The United Nations Security Council condemns South Africa for its military attacks on Angola and demands the immmediate withdrawal of South African forces now in Angola, and hints at future consideration of sanctions.
7-16 Jan.1984	Fighting between FAPLA and UNITA is reported in the Samba-Lucala district of Kwanza Norte.
8 Jan. 1984	South African security forces begin to withdraw from southern Angola.
12 Jan. 1984	Tass reports that joint Soviet-Cuban-Angolan consultations have been held in Moscow, and agreement has been reached on assistance to Angola.
19 Jan. 1984	South Africa rejects Angolan conditions for a thirty day ceasefire.
31 Jan. 1984	South African Prime Minister, P.W. Botha announces that South Africa is to begin to disengage its forces from Angola with immediate effects.
16 Feb. 1984	Trilateral conference between South Africa, Angola and United States, acting as mediator, results in the Lusaka Accord, and the setting up of a Joint Ceasefire Commission.
24 Feb. 1984	UNITA seizes seventy seven foreign technicians, including sixteen Britons and forty-six Portuguese, in an attack on a diamond mine at Cafunfu, which causes a substantial drop in diamond earnings.
20 Mar. 1984	In a joint statement issued in Havana, at the end of two days of talks between Presidents dos Santos and Castro, Cuba undertakes to withdraw its troops from Angola provided South Africa ends its aggression and its support for UNITA.
25 Mar. 1984	UNITA attacks Sumbe, 160 miles south-east of Luanda, on the Atlantic coast.
26 Apr. 1984	Ninety released UNITA hostages arrive in Johannesburg.
27-28 Apr.1984	Angola attends the conference of Portuguese-speaking African countries in

Maputo, Mozambique.

27 Apr. 1984	Dr. Savimbi offers talks with the MPLA government aimed at forming a government of national unity.
4 May 1984	Mass trial begins before the Luanda People's Revolutionary Court of 124 defendents accused of diamond smuggling, foreign exchange offences, and in a few cases, spying for the United States. State officials and army officers are involved, together with sixty foreigners. The trial ends on 30 October 1984.
12 May 1984	Sixteen British hostages are released to Sir John Leahy, special British Foreign Office envoy, at the guerrilla headquarters in Jamba.
4 June 1984	UNITA has taken several American prisoners in a raid on Quibala, 170 miles south-east of Luanda.
12 June 1984	UNITA attacks Quibala, strategic crossroads town in Kwanza Sul and takes eleven foreign hostages.
7 July 1984	H. de C. Santos is appointed Minister of Industry by Presidential Decree.
12 July 1984	The oil pipeline in Cabinda is sabotaged.
29 July 1984	Sabotage incident in Luanda harbour affecting the Angolan freighter Lundoge and the East German Arensee.
3-4 Sept. 1984	Angola attends the two day conference of Front Line States and the Socialist International in Arusha, Tanzania. The linkage of Cuban troop withdrawal from Angola with independence for Namibia is condemned.
10 Sept. 1984	A further twenty-five hostages are freed by UNITA and flown to Johannesburg.
10-15 Sept. 1984	President dos Santos visits France, Italy and Spain for talks with political and industrial leaders.
13 Sept. 1984	Diplomatic relations are established with Malta.
Oct. 1984	US Representative Frank Wisner visits Luanda. Angola concedes the principle of linkage between the issue of Cuban troops and the implementation of UN Resolution 435.
8 Oct. 1984	More than 1,500 FNLA members surrender to the government's Defence and Security forces and pledge support for the MPLA.
9 Oct. 1984	UNITA sabotages Luanda's power supply.
15 Oct. 1984	President dos Santos calls on the Reagan Administration to establish diplomatic relations with Luanda.
22 Oct. 1984	P.T. Jorge, Foreign Minister since 1976, is dismissed. President dos Santos assumes his duties until a new appointment is made.
1-9 Nov. 1984	UNITA hold an Extraordinary Congress in Jamba. Major Vakulukuta is

removed from his post as Commander of the central southern front, Brigadier A. Chendorara is appointed Chief-of-Staff of UNITA's FALA.

11 Nov. 1984   President dos Santos reveals his plan for a phased withdrawal of some 20,000 Cuban troops stationed south of the 13th parallel.

11 Nov. 1984   A trilateral Angolan-Brazilian-Soviet agreement is signed on the construction of a $900m. hydroelectric dam at Kapanda on the Rio Kwanza.

21 Nov. 1984   UNITA release fourteen more hostages, including three Bulgarians captured on 25 March 1984.

5-6 Dec. 1984   President dos Santos visits Kinshasa. Regional security talks are held with Presidents Mobutu and Kaunda.

8 Dec. 1984   UNITA attacks the municipality of Longonjo.

20 Dec. 1984   UNITA attacks the city of Huambo, but is repulsed.

20-21 Dec. 1984   President dos Santos visits Mozambique. A joint communiqué declares Angola's solidarity with the efforts of Mozambique to ensure the full implementation of the Nkomati Accord.

29 Dec. 1984   UNITA again attacks Cafunfo, mining equipment is destroyed and twenty-five foreigners abducted.

1 Jan. 1985   President dos Santos rules out any possibility of a coalition government with UNITA in his New Year message.

2 Jan. 1985   Pitched battle at Carfunfo, in northern Angola. UNITA captures Cafunfo and takes hostages.

14-19 Jan.1985   President dos Santos addresses the first National Congress of the MPLA-PT in Luanda. In his opening address he speaks of the Cuban sacrifices made for the Angolan revolution and affirms the Soviet Union as the main supplier of military equipment.

16-17 Jan.1985   The Central Committee of the MPLA-PT appoints new members of the Party Secretariat.

18 Jan. 1985   A South African battle force completes a two-day conventional warfare exercise, code-name `Iron Fist' in the operational area of Namibia near the Angolan border.

29 Jan.-1 Feb.   Angolan-Zairean joint commission meets in Kinshasa. Agreements are
1985   reached on border trade and customs, the conservation of common natural resources, medical cooperation and the implementation of the 1981 cultural and scientific accord.

3 Feb. 1985   An extensive reshuffle of the Council of Ministers includes the creation of three super-ministries, headed by Ministers of State, K. Paiama (Inspection and Control), P. van Dúnem (Productive Sphere) and M.M. Café (Economic and Social Sphere).

6 Feb. 1985   L. do Nascimento leaves the Planning Ministry to become Provincial

	Commissioner in Huila and Chairman of the Military Council in the 5th Military Region, in the south-west.
6-9 Feb. 1985	President dos Santos visits Kinshasa. An agreement is signed on 9 February on defence, security and the circulation of persons and goods. A Joint Commission to oversee security along the 2,600 km common border is set up.
27 Feb. 1985.	UNITA claims to have shot down a Boeing 737 aircraft near Lubango.
8 Mar. 1985	A. Van Dúnem `Mbinda' is named as Foreign Minister.
14 Mar. 1985	UNITA releases twenty-two hostages captured on 29 December at Cafunfo, after a forced march of about 375 miles to Jamba.
16 Mar. 1985	A bomb explodes outside the Hotel Almirante in Huambo city, injuring 50 people. UNITA later claims responsibility.
18 Mar. 1985	The United State Assistant Secretary of State for African Affairs, Chester Crocker, holds talks in Cape Verde with Angola's Interior Minister, Colonel A. Rodrigues, `Kito'.
21 Mar. 1985	Crocker meets `Pik' Botha in South Africa and presents a compromise package on Cuban troop withdrawal from Angola.
22 Mar. 1985	Saboteurs cut the main power lines from Cambambe Dam to Luanda, disrupting power supplies to the capital for five days.
23 Mar. 1985	President dos Santos states that the Cape Verde meeting did not achieve any positive results.
4 Apr. 1985	Power lines from Cambambe to N'dalatando are sabotaged, depriving much of Kwanza Norte and Malanje provinces of electricity for ten days.
15 Apr. 1985	South African Foreign Minister `Pik' Botha announces that the disengagement of the South African Defence Force from Angola will be completed in a matter of days.
17 Apr. 1985	The last of South African forces leave the border post of Santa Clara and are received by General Constand Viljoen at Oshikango in Namibia.
30 Apr. 1985	Angola signs the Lomé Convention.
10 May 1985	UNITA raids the diamond mine at Luo soon after President dos Santos had addressed MPLA officials in the same area in Lunda Norte Province.
13 May 1985	South African Minister of Defence General Magnus Malan states that the South African Defence Force will send units into Angola again, if FAPLA fails to curb SWAPO activities.
16 May 1985	The Joint Monitoring Commission, established to oversee the implementation of the Lusaka Accord, is dissolved.
21 May 1985	A South African commando unit attempts sabotage to oil industry installations in Cabinda.

24 May 1985	A United States State Department spokesman expresses `deep displeasure' over the Cabinda incident and a formal protest is lodged in Pretoria by the U.S. Ambassador to South Africa, Mr. Herman Nickel.
28 May 1985	Leader of the sabotage team, Captain W.P. du Toit, gives a detailed account of the mission at a news conference in Luanda.
June 1985	Political Bureau of the MPLA-PT J.E. dos Santos; A. Van-Dúnem `Mbinda'; A.d.S. França; F.M.P. Nvunda; J.M.P.D. Matross; K. Payama; M.A.D. Rodrigues; P. Luvualu; P.deC. dos S. Van Dúnem; P.M. Tonha; R.A.F.V. de Almeida. Alternate members - A.J. do A. Martins; M.M. Café.
1-2 June 1985	Savimbi hosts a conference in Jamba of anti-government guerrilla groups from Afghanistan, Laos and Nicaragua and UNITA, at which an alliance called the `Democratic International' is formed.
11 June 1985	The United States Senate votes by 65 to 34, to repeal. the `Clark Amendment' which prohibits US military and financial support for UNITA.
18-19 June	President dos Santos visits Gabon and Ivory Coast. A general co-operation agreement is signed with President Houphouet-Boigny of Ivory Coast.
20 June 1985	The United Nations Security Council unanimously adopts Resolution 567 (1985) condemning South Africa for this most recent act of aggression.
10 July 1985	The United States House of Representatives votes, by 236 to 185, to repeal the `Clark Amendment'.
13 July 1985	The Angolan government breaks off all contacts with the United States in protest at the Congressional votes on the Clark Amendment repeal.
Mid-July 1985	FAPLA begins an offensive along the Benguela railway to Cazombo in Moxico Province and towards Mavinga.
Aug. 1985	The office of the United Nations Commissioner for Refugees (UNHCR) estimates 70,000 Angolan refugees now in the Shaba region of Zaire, in a serious situation, as a consequence of UNITA activities near the Zairean border.
2 Aug. 1985	FAPLA offensive against UNITA controlled regions in the south-east begins and lasts until October 1985.
8 Aug. 1985	President Reagan signs the Foreign Aid Authorization Bill, incorporating the repeal of the Clark Amendment opening the way for United States aid to UNITA.
14 Aug. 1985	A Roman Catholic priest, a nun and five medical orderlies die in an ambush as they drive to a hospital in Cunene Province.
20 Aug. 1985	Another bomb blast occurs in Huambo city.
2-8 Sept. 1985	The non-aligned Foreign Minister's Conference is held in Luanda, attended by high level delegations from more than 100 countries.

9 Sept. 1985	The Luanda Declaration on Southern Africa, issued by the Non-Aligned Movement, includes a clause demanding a complete and unconditional withdrawal of South African troops from Angola.
16 Sept. 1985	General C. Viljoen announces a South African Defence Force follow-up operation into Cunene Province.
20 Sept. 1985	General Magnus Malan admits publicly in Pretoria that South Africa has provided material, moral and humanitarian help to UNITA.
20 Sept. 1985	Resolution 571 (1985) is adopted unanimously by the United Nations Security Council, in the context of a complaint by Angola over a South African incursion in mid-September.
21 Sept. 1985	TASS reports a Soviet government statement condemning South Africa for a barbarous act of aggresion against Angola and demands the immediate and complete termination of its hostilities.
29 Sept. 1985	FAPLA forces capture the town of Cazombo, after fifty-two days of fighting, but fail to take Mavinga.
1 Oct. 1985	A Bill (HR 3472) is introduced in the United States House of Representatives to authorize $27 m. worth of humanitarian assistance to UNITA.
7 Oct. 1985	South Africa is unanimously condemned in the Security Council for aggression against Angola in Resolution 574 (1985).
22 Oct. 1985	A 'Promotion of Democracy in Angola' Bill (HR 3598) is introduced in the United States House of Representatives which would ban almost all loans to Angola, as well as new investment and trade.
22-25 Oct.1985	President dos Santos visits New York to attend the 40th anniversary celebrations of the United Nations and renew diplomatic contacts with the United States.
23 Oct. 1985	A second UNITA Aid Bill (HR 3609) is introduced to authorize the provision of $27m. worth of military aid to Savimbi's forces.
23 Oct. 1985	A United Nations Commission of Inquiry, set up under Resolution 571, concludes a ten-day fact-finding visit to the provinces of Cunene, Huila and Cuando Cubango.
25 Oct. 1985	President dos Santos flies to Havana, together with FAPLA's Chief of Staff Colonel A. França for talks with Castro.
6 Nov. 1985	A New York Democrat, T. Weiss, and sixteen other members of the United States House of Representatives introduce a Bill (HR 3690) to reinpose a ban on sending aid to Angolan organizations.
11 Nov. 1985	The tenth anniversary of independence from Portugal is celebrated.
11 Nov. 1985	At a press conference in Jamba, Savimbi appeals for United States military aid for UNITA, and sees no prospects for a negotiated peace.

27-28 Nov.1985	Talks take place in Lusaka between Chester Crocker and Colonel A. Rodrigues.
2 Dec. 1985	The FAPLA garrison at Calueque is attacked by the South African Defence Force.
2-10 Dec.1985	The second Ordinary Congress of the MPLA-PT is held in Luanda. President dos Santos is re-elected unanimously as President of the Party and Head of State.
9 Dec. 1985	The composition of a new ninety member Central Committee is announced. Changes to membership results in a majority for the supporters of President dos Santos.
12 Dec. 1985	Full members of the Political Bureau, elected by the Central Committee are named: President dos Santos; A. van Dúnem 'Mbinda'; A. dos S. Franca 'Ndalu'; F.M. Paulo 'Dino Matross', K. Paihama, M.A.D. Rodrigues 'Kito'; P. Luvualu; P. de C. dos S. van Dúnem 'Loi', P.M. Tonha 'Pedale'; R.A. de Almeida.
15 Dec. 1985	ANGOP confirm that two South African reinforced battalions have entered Angolan territory in Cunene Province, followed two days later by three more battalions.
16 Dec. 1985	A South African incursion is reported to have taken place over the previous four days in the direction of Ngiva, Cunene Province. A major invasion is expected.
30 Dec. 1985	Five missionaries are killed in an ambush on a convoy in Huila Province. UNITA seizes two Brazilian nuns.
31 Dec. 1985	The United States Conservative Caucus announces that it plans to buy equity in Chevron, the parent of Cabinda Gulf Oil Company, in an effort to 'change the corporation's pro-Soviet activities in Angola'.
8 Jan. 1986	United States Assistant Secretary of State for African Affairs, Chester Crocker, arrives in Luanda for talks.
8-9 Jan. 1986	Talks between Colonel A. Rodriques and Chester Crocker take place again in Lusaka.
13 Jan. 1986	The South African Defence Force attack Mupa, in Cunene Province, c. 135 km north of the Namibian border.
18 Jan. 1986	The Secretariat of the MPLA-PT Central Committee is named: President dos Santos - Cadres and Organization; Mr. de Almeida - Ideology; A. van Dunen - External Relations; Mrs. Café - Economic and Social Affairs & Production; S.A. Petra 'Petroff' - Agrarian Policy; P. 'Dino Matross' - State and Judicial Bodies; P.M. Júnior - Youth and Social Organizations; J.V. Sempora - Administration and Finance.
27 Jan. 1986	In a communiqué, issued in the course of a tripartite meeting in Moscow, the government of Cuba and the Soviet Union reaffirm their commitment to the Angolan government, including the maintenance in Angola of Cuban troops.

29 Jan. 1986	Chester Crocker admits the Reagan Administration has advised Chevron, and other United States companies operating in Angola,that they should consider U.S. national interests, as well as their own corporate interests.
29 Jan.-6 Feb. 1986	Savimbi arrives in Washington for a nine day visit. He is received at the White House and holds separate meetings with the Secretary of State and the Defence Secretary.
30 Jan. 1986	High level talks are held in Moscow by the USSR, Cuba and Angola to examine possible developments in Angola in the light of the U.S. Administration's idea of providing assistance for UNITA.
Late Jan. 1986	The United States White House informs the Congressional Intelligence Committee of plans to provide covert military aid to UNITA financed from the CIA's contingency fund.
3 Feb. 1986	Changes to the Council of Ministers are announced on this date, on 6 February and 22 February.
4 Feb. 1986	President Reagan, in his 'Agenda for the Future' message to Congress indicates support for UNITA's struggle against Soviet-Cuban imperialism.
7 Feb. 1986	Fidel Castro, in an address to the Third Congress of the Cuban Communist Party, rules out the possibility of withdrawing Cuban troops from Angola before the implementation of Resolution 435, and the abolition of apartheid, and warns the United States that 'we are prepared to stay in Angola, ten, twenty or thirty more years, if need be'.
12 Feb. 1986	Chevron sends its president, John Silcon, to Luanda to assure President dos Santos that it will stay and continue its development programme.
18 Feb. 1986	The United States government confirms that it has decided to provide military aid to UNITA and that 'the process is in motion'.
19 Feb. 1986	Angola denounces the American decision to provide covert aid to UNITA, and maintains the move amounts to 'a declaration of war'.
26 Feb. 1986	President dos Santos attends the 27th Congress of the Communist Party of the Soviet Union in Moscow and meets with President Castro, as well as Soviet leaders.
4 Mar. 1986	UNITA claims a successful attack on Andrada's diamond mine and the capture of 180 foreign workers, together with a large quantity of diamonds.
4 Mar. 1986	South African President P.W. Botha sets 1 August as the deadline for the start of the implementation of Resolution 435, but demands a firm and satisfactory agreement before that date on the withdrawal of the Cubans.
8 Mar. 1986	Angolan government rejects the South African proposal.
17 Mar. 1986	UNITA releases the 180 foreign hostages into Red Cross care in Zaire.
18 Mar. 1986	In a letter to the UN Secretary-General J. Pérez de Cuellar, President dos Santos indicates Angola's deep outrage at the United States Administration's military support for UNITA, asks him to assume the role of mediator in

Southern Africa since the U.S. action has jeopardized its credibility as a mediator. He reveals a secret document The Mindelo Act of January 1984, whose terms the United States have not kept.

30 Mar. 1986	Washington Post reports that the military hardware being supplied to UNITA includes United States 'Stinger' surface-to-air missiles, indicating a policy change by the Administration.
5 Apr. 1986	President dos Santos appoints seven new government officials Provincial Commissioners of Benguela, Moxico, Bie, Huambo and Kwanzo Norte, respectively: J.M. Lourenco, J.B. Ndonge, M.J.C. Maco, M. Monakapui 'Bassovava', P.T. Jorge. Also appointed A.J. dos Santos, Vice-Minister of Foreign Trade and M. Bento, Secretary of State for War Veterans.
8 Apr. 1986	Communiqué issued after a one day meeting of six Frontline States in Luanda states that by welcoming Savimbi to Washington the United States has lost credibility as a mediator in Southern Africa.
28-29 Apr.1986	A summit meeting of the five Portuguese-speaking African countries in Luanda accuses the United States of 'supporting organized terrorism'.
May 1986	The Defence and Security Council: President J.E. dos Santos Ministers: Defence - P.M. Tonha 'Pedale'; Interior - M.A. Rodrigues 'Kito'; State Security - vacant Ministers of State Productive Sphere - P. de C. van Dúnem 'Loy'; Edonomic and Social Sphere - M. Mambo Café; Inspector and Control - K. Paihama; Chief of Staff of FAPLA - A. dos S. França 'Ndalu'; MPLA-PT Central Committee - R. de Almeida - Secretary for Ideology.
2 May 1986	President Mobutu insists that relations with Angola are 'correct' and that Zaire will never be used as a base for destabilization.
6 May 1986	During a visit to Moscow by President dos Santos, the Soviet leader Gorbachev pledges continued support for the commitments made to Angola in its treaty of friendship and co-operation.
8 May 1986	Zairean ambassadors around the world formally deny charges that Zaire is being used as a conduit for United States aid to UNITA.
12 May 1986	Savimbi warns Zambia that he will retaliate if UNITA forces are attacked from Zambian territory.
17 May 1986	Indian Prime Minister Rajiv Gandhi visits Luanda. A permanent Indian embassy is established and an agreement for technical and economic cooperation is signed.
19-25 May 1986	South African troops launch attacks deep inside Angola.
26 May 1986	A South African force is moving through Cunene Province near Calueque.
June 1986	Government forces begin an offensive against UNITA bases in Southern Angola.

5 June 1986	Ships and oil storage tanks in Namibe harbour are attacked by South African frogmen from a missile carrying launch. One ship is sunk and two damaged.
10 June 1986	The South African Defence Force deny responsibility for the raid on Namibe port.
11 June 1986	UNITA attacks economic and social infrastructures in Cabinda.
18 June 1986	A draft resolution, proposed by five non-aligned countries in the United Nations Security Council, to condemn the recent attack on the port of Namibe is vetoed by Great Britain and the United States.
10 July 1986	President Mobuto of Zaire visits Angola, a communiqué is issued in Luanda reaffirming cooperation along the common border, the accord for security and control, and stressing the 'Zairean peoples solidarity with Angola's fair struggle'.
6 Aug. 1986	Ministry of Defence communiqué notes an increase in South African forces in Cunene Province and in air flights over Angolan territory.
10-11 Aug.1986	Attacks by South African armoured units begin on Cuito Cuanavale, and are repelled.
18 Aug. 1986	President dos Santos declares he would welcome a meeting with President Reagan and invites him to visit Angola.
22 Aug. 1986	The head of UNITA's intelligence service, Brigadier I. Chindondo, claims chemical weapons have been used against UNITA troops on at least three occasions, including during the battle for Cuito Canavale.
26 Aug. 1986	J.T.P. Teixeira is appointed Director of Defence and Security Department of the Central Committee.
26-31 Aug.1986	UNITA holds its sixth congress at Jamba. Jeremias Chitunda is elected as Vice-President. M. N'Zau Puna remains Secretary- General. Tito Chingunji becomes Secretary for Foreign Affairs.
2 Sept. 1986	In a speech to the Non-Aligned Summit in Harare, President Castro indicates that Cuba is prepared to keep its troops in Angola 'for as long as apartheid remains in South Africa'.
16 Sept. 1986	An Angola-delegation pays a five-day visit to the Kassai region in Zaire. The Kissama frontier post is to be opened on an experimental basis, and a regional commission is to be formed to help maintain stability along the border.
17 Sept. 1986	The United States Administration's policy on covert aid is endorsed by a vote in the House of Representatives.
18 Sept. 1986	UNITA warns that 'if UNITA is attacked from Zambia, then Zambia itself will be regarded as a war zone'.
10 Oct. 1986	UNITA's Chief of Staff Brigadier A. J. Chendorara is killed in a road accident. He will be replaced by UNITA's operational military head Brigadier D.A. Chilingutila.

16-17 Oct.1986	Z.E. Juliano, Commissioner of Uige province, visits Kwitu-Ngongo in Zaire. Security arrangements are discussed. The two countries agree to set up a working group to study common border problems.
23 Oct. 1986	Dr. Savimbi presents his case to conservative members of the European Parliament in Strasbourg, appeals for peace talks and indicates his willingness to negotiate with the MPLA government.
27 Oct. 1986	Angola's Ambassador to France, L. de Almeida, formally protests over Savimbi's visit, threatens undisclosed measures against France, and relocates his residence to Bonn.
11 Nov. 1986	In a speech to mark the eleventh anniversary of independence, President dos Santos unequivocally rejects the idea of negotiations with UNITA.
13-15 Nov.1986	Angolan plans to participate in the Franco-African summit in Lomé are rescinded.
14 Nov. 1986	The South African Defence Force launches a 'pre-emptive raid into Angola against SWAPO bases in Cunene Provinces.
17 Nov. 1986	UNITA guerrillas open a new military front in the north in Uige Province, said by Angolan sources to be supplied through Zaire. Angola reinforces its defences in Cabinda and in Soyo town.
19 Nov. 1986	President dos Santos makes Ministerial changes: Minister of Construction - J.G. Cabelo Branco; Minister of State for Town Planning, Housing and Water - F.J. Fragata; Governor of the Central Bank - A. Inacio.
9 Dec. 1986	Angola establishes diplomatic relations with Venezuela.
10 Dec. 1986	New ranks are established for the army and the navy. The President J.E. dos Santos becomes the first full General. Other appointments: Colonel-General P.M. Tonha 'Pedale'. Lieutenant-Generals - A. Franca, F.M. Paira, A. Rodrigues; Major-Generals - J.M. Paulo, P.B. Lima, J.L. Neto, Z. Pinto, A.C. de Carvalho.
15-19 Dec.1986	Egyptian Minister of State for Foreign Affairs, Dr. Boutros Boutros-Ghali, visits Angola.
18 Dec. 1986	A South African Defence Force raid into Cunene Province is repulsed by FAPLA between Mongua and Xangongo.
6 Jan. 1987	Influx of refugees from Angola into Zambia brings their estimated number to more than 75,000.
7 Jan. 1987	General George Meiring, commander of the South West Africa Territorial Force (SWATF) complains that Angola is attempting to challenge South Africa's air superiority in the region and warns of a possible conventional clash.
24 Jan. 1987	A South African-led military offensive begins, Angolan forces suffer considerable losses, South African troops occupy five municpalities around Mongua.

30 Jan. 1987	President dos Santos opens the first session of the new National People's Assembly.
Feb. 1987	Zaire denies reports that the CIA is making use of Kamina airfields to fly military supplies to UNITA.
1 Feb. 1987	A New York Times investigative report confirming the airlift of arms to UNITA through Zaire, holds it 'inconceivable' that this supply operation could be taking place without President Mobuto's knowledge.
8 Feb. 1987	UNITA attacks Camabatela in Kwanza Norte Province.
13 Feb. 1987	St. Lucia officials confirm that aircraft of the privately owned St. Lucia Airways are apparently being used by the CIA to transport arms for UNITA from the United States to Zaire.
26 Feb. 1987	UNITA massacres civilians at Damba, Uige Province, according to ANGOP.
5 Mar. 1987	President Chissano of Mozambique visits Angola. A joint communiqué blames the apartheid regime for tension and war in Southern Africa.
10-11 Mar.1987	A tripartite Angolan-Soviet-Cuban strategy meeting takes place in Moscow.
22 Mar. 1987	C.A. Fernandes is appointed as Minister of Transport and Communications.
24 Mar. 1987	C.D.F. da Cunha is sworn in as Provincial Commissar for Luanda Province.
26 Mar. 1987	Savimbi offers to hold a truce along the Benguela Railway and to guarantee safe travel through UNITA-controlled territory on condition that an 'international inspection group' is set up to ensure the railway is not used for military purposes. The MPLA government refuses to respond.
28-30 Mar.1987	President Ceausescu of Romania leads a high-level delegation of officials to Angola.
1-4 Apr. 1987	President dos Santos visits India for talks with the Indian Prime Minister Rajiv Gandhi, President Zait Singh and other senior officials.
4-5 Apr. 1987	President dos Santos visits Vietnam.
6 Apr. 1987	At an informal meeting in Brazzaville, arranged by the chairman of the Organization of African Unity, the governments of Angola and the United States agree to resume official talks on Southern African issues.
16 Apr. 1987	Tripartite Angolan-Zairean-Zambian talks on the reopening of the Benguela Railway to international freight traffic are held in Luanda.
30 Apr. 1987	Presidents dos Santos, Mobutu and Kaunda meet in Lusaka and make a joint commitment to reopen the Benguela railway and to carry out the required rehabilitation work, estimated to cost $280 m.
12 May 1987	President dos Santos, in a speech at Maquela do Zombo, twenty miles south of the Zairean border, says that Angola does not want war with Zaire, but would continue to use diplomatic channels to counter the border instability.

13 May 1987	UNITA forces attack Maquela do Zombo, possibly crossing over from Zaire.
18 May 1987	ANGOP reports President dos Santos has dismissed I.G. Martins, Minister of Foreign Trade and A.P. dos Santos Junior, Minister of Internal Trade, from their posts.
21-22 May 1987	Angola attends the Lusophone countries 'Group of Five' summit meeting in Maputo.
5 June 1987	South African forces attack the FAPLA base at Arnhanca, 50 km into Angolan territory.
10 June 1987	The United States Administration proceeds with a second annual installment of covert aid to UNITA, amounting to $15,000,000.
18 June 1987	An unscheduled encounter takes place between members of the Angolan delegation in Washington and UNITA supporters, including its Washington representative, Marcos Samondo.
29 June 1987	Angola reports an air attack by South Africa on army positions in Ongiva, capital of Cunene Province.
12 July 1987	In a statement, issued in Lisbon, and signed by UNITA Chief of Staff General D.A. Chilingutila, UNITA claim a successful attack on airport installations at Menongue in south-eastern Cuando-Cubango Province, on 28 June.
14-15 July 1987	A formal round of negotiations take place in Luanda between the United States represented by Chester Crocker and Angola's Minister of State, Lieutenant-Colonel P. de C. Van-Dúnem 'Loy'.
22 July 1987	Angola reports that government troops have forced two battalions of South African troops to withdraw from Ongiva after seven weeks of sporadic fighting.
25 July 1987	Angola reports to the Organisation of African Unity ad hoc Commission in Lusaka that nearly 7,000 South African troops are currently in Southern Angola.
27 July 1987	United States Congressional Democrats accuse the Reagan Administration of circumventing the will of Congress by conducting a covert supply operation to UNITA. The operation and Zaire's role in it will be increasingly scrutinized.
30 July-2 Aug. 1987	President Castro of Cuba and President dos Santos meet in Havana, agree to make their common position on Cuban troop withdrawal 'more flexible', and willing to hold talks with the United States in order to pursue a negotiated settlement.
24 Aug. 1987	Angola proposes to the United States government a four-point formula for possible agreement, calling for the withdrawal of South African troops from Southern Angola, the cessation of South African aggression, respect for Angola's sovereignty and territorial integrity and the implementation of United Nations Security Council Resolution 435 (1978) on Namibian

independence.

26 Aug. 1987   A road-bridge on the outskirts of Cuito Cuanavale, vital to FAPLA's supply lines, is sabotaged, allegedly by South African frogmen using limpet mines.

Sept.-Nov. 1987   Fighting takes place near the Lomba River, midway between Cuito Cuanavale and Mavinga.

4 Sept. 1987   Lieutenant-Colonel A.C. Neto is presented as Commander of the Air Force.

7 Sept. 1987   South African Army Officer Captain Wynand du Toit, captured in 1985, is freed in Maputo as part of a major prisoner exchange involving two European anti-apartheid activists freed by South Africa and 122 Angolan prisoners held by UNITA.

8-9 Sept.1987   Dr. Crocker discusses the Angolan-Cuban position with President dos Santos.

9 Sept. 1987   UNITA abduct three Swedes in Bengo Province, about fifty km from Luanda.

13 Sept. 1987   Fierce fighting is reported in the Lomba River region, twenty-five km north of Mavinga.

16 Sept. 1987   J.G. Dias is appointed Minister of Internal Trade.

21 Sept.-1 Oct.   President dos Santos tours Western Europe, successively visiting France,
1987   Belgium, Italy and Portugal.

21-23 Sept.1987   President dos Santos visits France and meets President Mitterand and Prime Minister Chirac. A military agreement is obtained, including the provision of military equipment. The French government promises support for Angola's membership of the IMF and World Bank.

25 Sept. 1987   Dr. Chester Crocker holds further talks with Angolan officials in Brussels.

27 Sept. 1987   President dos Santos visits Portugal for talks with President M. Soares and The Portuguese Prime Minister, Prof. A.C. Silva, culminating in the signing of an economic and technical agreement.

2-23 Oct.1987   UNITA forces, with South African ground and air support, repulse a government offensive after a major confrontation centring on Mavinga.

3 Oct. 1987   South African Minister of Defence, General Magnus Malan confirms that South African troops are actively deployed in Southern Angola, as a limited military presence to curb the movements of SWAPO guerrillas.

14 Oct. 1987   UNITA is believed responsible for the crash of a Red Cross cargo plane about forty km from Cuito, resulting in the suspension of a feeding programme for 100,000 people in the central plateau.

15 Oct. 1987   UNITA troops, led by Dr. Savimbi, have beaten off military offensives by Cuban and Soviet-backed Angolan government forces along the line of the Lomba River, some 50 kms north of Mavinga.

16 Oct. 1987	Angola applied for membership of the International Monetary Fund. The United States indicates it will oppose the application.
28 Oct. 1987	President dos Santos appoints two new ministers, F.J.R. da Cruz as Minister of Fishing and D. das C.S. Rangel Minister of Foreign Trade.
29-30 Oct.1987	West German Foreign Minister, Hans-Dietrich Genscher, visits Angola.
2 Nov. 1987	A preemptive attack is launched by the South African Defence Force and the South West Africa Territory Force on a SWAPO base in Angola.
7 Nov. 1987	President dos Santos and Castro meet in Moscow, attending celebrations marking the 70th anniversary of the Bolshevik Revolution and agree to send in seasoned Cuban troops to bolster FAPLA's defences in the south of Angola.
11 Nov. 1987	Chief of the South African Defence Force, General Johan Geldenhuys, admits for the first time that his forces are fighting alongside UNITA and claims Angolan government forces are directly assisted by Soviet and Cuban troops using tanks, ground-to-air missiles, MiG-23 fighter aircraft and attack helicopters.
13 Nov. 1987	Savimbi acknowledges the crucial role United States supplied anti-aircraft missiles are playing in repulsing the government offensive. He presents evidence at an international press ceremony at Jamba that Cubans are directly involved in the fighting.
14 Nov. 1987	President P.W. Botha of South Africa pays an unannounced visit to South African troops in Southern Angola.
16 Nov. 1987	After a one-day meeting in Luanda, the Front Line States demand international military aid for Angola to defeat South Africa's invasion.
17 Nov. 1987	The Organization of African Unity states that Britain and the United States can no longer dissociate themselves from the ongoing situation, and pretend not to be involved, when the territory and sovereignty of Angola are violated. It calls on the international community to impose mandatory and comprehensive sanctions on South Africa.
20 Nov. 1987	South African Minister of Foreign Affairs, 'Pik' Botha indicates South Africa will keep its troops on the present battlefield in Angola until Cuban troops and Russian troops and advisors are withdrawn and invites the United Nations Secretary-General J.P. de Cuellar to visit south-eastern Angola to familiarize himself with the extent of Russian and Cuban involvement.
25 Nov. 1987	A United Nations Security Council resolution unanimously condemns South Africa's 'continued and intensified acts of aggression' against Angola and calls upon South Africa to remove its forces immediately and unconditionally.
5 Dec. 1987	The South African military announce that a gradual withdrawal of its troops is underway. This is not confirmed by a United Nations delegation visiting Angola.
10 Dec. 1987	President dos Santos declares that experienced Cuban troops - the 50th

Division under the command of General Arnaldo Ochoa Santos - are to take up positions near the Namibian border, and are to engage directly with South African troops.

23 Dec. 1987 A further United Nations Security Council resolution is approved condemning South Africa for its delay in implementing its November resolution.

28-29 Jan.1988 A further round of talks is held in Luanda at which J.R. Valdés-Saldana, a senior member of the Cuban politburo, is present and the United States is represented by Chester Crocker. For the first time it is accepted that all Cuban troops could be withdrawn under a regional security arrangement.

20 Feb. 1988 The South African Air Force attacks two SWAPO bases in Southern Angola in retaliation for a bomb blast at a bank in Oshakati.

29 Feb. 1988 Colonel P. van Dunem `Loy' on an official visit to Great Britain, claims that 9,000 are involved in the invasion of southern Angola, and that immense damage is being done.

6 Mar. 1988 General Magnus Malan proposes direct discussions with the Soviet Union regarding the cessation of Soviet involvement in Angola and the establishment of a neutral and non-aligned Angolan government. The proposal is rejected by a Soviet government spokesman.

9-11 Mar.1988 United States, Angolan and Cuban delegations meet, and continue discussions on 17-18 March.

13 Mar. 1988 Dr. Savimbi reveals a complex web of negotiations involving South Africa, the Soviet Union, the United States and Angola to reporters at his bush headquarters. He comments on improved communications and that when real negotiations start, he will have to be present.

14 Mar. 1988 The South African Foreign Minister R.F. `Pik' Botha and Dr. Chester Crocker meet in Geneva to discuss a new peace proposal by Angola concerning a timetable for Cuban troop withdrawal.

15 Mar. 1988 South Africa releases twelve Angolan soldiers at Luanda airport, in exchange for the bodies of two South Africans killed during a sabotage operation in 1985.

18 Mar. 1988 Lieutenant-Colonel Ngueto, commander of Angola's sixth military region, reports that FAPLA still controls the town of Cuito Cuanavale, despite regular artillery attacks on the Cuito River bridge and Cuito Cuanavale bridge.

4 Apr. 1988 President dos Santos disbands the Commission for the Reorganisation of the State Security Ministry set up in 1986.

14 Apr. 1988 An OAU team fail to persuade the United States administration to end its support for UNITA.

19 Apr. 1988 General J. Geldenhuys, Chief of the South African General Staff releases a South African version of the war, admits that thirty one South Africans have been killed and around ninety injured since May 1987, in the two operations

codenamed Modular and Hooper. The number of South African troops involved is given as a maximum of 3,000 as against an estimated 25,000 FAPLA forces.

19 Apr. 1988	South African Defence Force General Jan van Loggerenberg claims it has never been the SADF's intention to capture Cuito Cuanavale because of the difficulties of defending it. However bombardment has largely destroyed its strategic value.
3-4 May 1988	First quadripartite meeting between Angola, Cuba and South Africa, under the mediation of the United States, is held in London. Constructive progress made on the question of the total withdrawal of Cuban troops. Leading the respective delegations: A. Van Dúnem 'Mbinda', the Angolan Minister of External relations, Mr. Risquet, Neil van Heerden, Director-General of the South African Department of Foreign Affairs and Dr. Chester Crocker.
12 May 1988	Senior Angolan and South African government representatives meet in Brazzaville and agree to hold further bilateral sessions.
17 May 1988	A donors conference, held in Geneva under the auspices of the United Nations Disaster Relief Organization, is attended by forty countries and thirty five non-governmental agencies pledge $75,000,000 worth of aid to Angola.
30 May 1988	South Africa warns that it will be forced to act if the Cuban advance into southern Angola, to within forty miles of the Namibian border, threatens its interests as a regional power. The Cuban forces are said to include six infantry regiments totalling 15,500 men.
6-8 June 1988	The Angolan-Zairean Joint Commission on Defence and Security meets in Luanda, and agrees to reinforce security along the 2,600 km boundary.
24-25 June 1988	Second quadripartite meeting is held in Cairo, with Foreign Ministers participating. Discussion centres on independence for Namibia, on the withdrawal of South African troops and of Cuban troops, with the United States pressuring for a compromise. Also present, in Cairo, is Vladillen Vaslev, head of the Southern Africa department of the Soviet Foreign Ministry.
27 June 1988	Angola starts withdrawing its troops from Sao Tomé.
27 June 1988	South Africa reports a Cuban bombing raid on the dam at Calueque, and direct ground clashes with heavy casualties.
29 June 1988	Air attacks by Cuban MiG-23s on Calueque dams are condemned by South Africa as a possible set back to the peace process, and as confirmation of the suspicions that the Cuban command in Angola ignores the Angolan government in Luanda.
30 June 1988	Dr. Savimbi meets President Reagan during a visit to the United States and urges the U.S. Congress to renew aid to UNITA.
30 June 1988	Repeated reports indicate UNITA is preparing to move its southern base, Jamba, to Quimbele, near the northern border with Zaire. United States military supplies would reach it through the Zairean port, Matadi.

11 July 1988   The Ministry of Foreign Trade and the Ministry of Internal Trade are to merge into one, by Presidential decree, for administrative reasons.

11-13 July 1988   Third quadripartite meeting is held in New York. The fourteen `Principles for a Peaceful Settlement in Southwestern Africa' are accepted.

22-23 July 1988   A secret two-day top-level military meeting between Angola, South Africa and Cuba is held on the Cape Verdean island of Sol. The delegations are led by the Chiefs of Staff of their armed forces, respectively Colonel A. Franca `Ndalu', General J. Geldenhuys, and General U.R. Deltoro.

25 July 1988   A fresh contingent of 22,000 Cubans, combined with FAPLA troops and SWAPO guerrillas, under the command of General Polos Frias, former head of the Cuban military mission, are moving along a 280-mile front, in some instances merely twelve miles from the Namibian border.

26 July 1988   President Castro, speaking in Havana, commits himself for the first time to the `gradual and total' withdrawal of his troops from Angola, subject to the satisfactory conclusion of a peace agreement.

2-5 Aug.1988   Fourth quadripartite meeting is held in Geneva. In the `Protocol of Geneva', signed 5 August, agreement is reached on an immediate ceasefire.

3 Aug. 1988   The initial withdrawal of South African troops is completed.

8 Aug. 1988   The ceasefire is publicly announced in the Joint Statement on a Ceasefire Agreement for Namibia and Angola South African troops are to withdraw from Angolan territory by 1 September 1988 and the implementation of United Nations Resolution 435 is to begin on 1 November 1988.

9 Aug. 1988   UNITA rejects the ceasefire.

10 Aug. 1988   South African troops withdrawal begins, and is to be completed by 1 September 1988.

11 Aug. 1988   UNITA claims to have occupied Chamutete in Huila Province as part of a new military offensive.

22 Aug. 1988   A ceasefire agreement is formally signed by Angola and South Africa, at Ruacana. It provides for the formation of a Joint Military Monitoring Committee (JMMC) to determine rules for the application of the agreement and to monitor violations. Signatories: for Angola A.J. Maria, Presidential Secretary for Defence and Security for Cuba L.C. Frias; W. Meyer, officer Commanding the SWA Territory Force.

24-26 Aug.1988   Fifth quadripartite meeting in Brazzaville, focuses on a timetable for the withdrawal of Cuban troops.

27-28 Aug. 1988   A Cuban delegation meets UNITA representatives in Abidjan.

30 Aug. 1988   The last South African troops cross over into Namibia, before the agreed deadline of 1 September 1988, and the Cubans pull back to an agreed position.

7-9 Sept.1988   Sixth quadripartite meeting is held in Brazzaville. Various conflicting proposals are submitted, but no accord is concluded.

13 Sept. 1988   Munhango, Savimbi's birthplace falls to government forces.

17 Sept. 1988   ANGOP reports that the government forces have captured five towns from UNITA-Cangumbe, Munhango, Cangongo, Sautar and Luando - key points on UNITA's route to the north.

26-29 Sept.1988   Seventh quadripartite meeting is held in Brazzaville. Further discussions ensue.

6-9 Oct. 1988   Eighth quadripartite meeting is held in New York. No accord is concluded. Major obstacles still remaining include the exact schedule for the withdrawal of Cuban troops and the status of Jonas Savimbi.

Nov. 1988   At the UNITA conference J. Chitunda becomes UNITA's representative in Washington, P.M. Alicences Secretary for Foreign Relations, T. da C. Fernandes President of the Foreign Relations Commission, J. Valentine Head of the Information Department and Tito Chingunji is persuaded to return from Washington to Jamba - where he is placed under house arrest.

11-15 Nov.1988   Ninth quadripartite meeting is held in Geneva and draws up the Second Protocol of Geneva, to be submitted for approval.

18 Nov. 1988   The Second Protocol of Geneva is approved by Angola and Cuba. It includes agreement on the timing of the withdrawal of Cuban troops.

19 Nov. 1988   New appointments are made: F.J. Fernandes becomes Minister of Health and J.L. da Costa e Silva the new Cabinet Secretary.

22 Nov. 1988   South Africa approves the Second Protocol of Geneva.

30 Nov.-3 Dec. 1988   Tenth quadripartite meeting in Brazzaville discusses the question of control of the withdrawal of Cuban troops.

13 Dec. 1988   Eleventh quadripartite meeting is held in Brazzaville. A four-point accord is signed in the Palace of the People by Angola, Cuba and South Africa.

14 Dec. 1988   The President denounces the creation of special forces of a commando nature secretly set up within the Ministry of the Interior, headed by A. Rodrigues `Kito'.

14 Dec. 1988   Mrs. M. Mambo Café is transferred from her position as Minister of State for Economic and Social Affairs to that of Secretary for Youth and Social Organization in the MPLA.

22 Dec. 1988   The Foreign Ministers of Angola, Cuba and South Africa formally sign the Brazzaville Agreements at the United Nations headquarters in New York. The main agreement covers independence for Namibia, the withdrawal of all South African troops by 1 April 1989 and giving effect from the same date to the UN Security Council's Resolution 435 of 1978.

24 Dec. 1988   South African Foreign Minister `Pik' Botha tells a press conference at the United Nations that while South Africa remained sympathetic and friendly to UNITA aid to UNITA will cease `as from today'.

26 Dec. 1988	The Angolan People's Assembly approves a one-year amnesty for UNITA members, to begin on 4 February 1989.
27 Dec. 1988	Heads of state of Angola, Botswana, Tanzania, Mozambique and Zimbabwe meeting in Lusaka urge the United States President- elect, George Bush, to end support for UNITA.
28 Dec. 1988	A formal request to the United Nations for aid in meeting the estimated US$800,000,000 cost of the Cuban withdrawal is made by President dos Santos in a letter to the UN Secretary- General.
(1st week) Jan. 1989	Angolan government announces a peace plan, including the offer of general amnesty to UNITA defectors and calls for the exile of Savimbi.
5 Jan. 1989	The ANC agrees to close its military training bases in Angola, according to President dos Santos.
6 Jan. 1989	Savimbi is given an electoral promise by the Bush Administration that the United States would continue 'all appropriate and effective assistance' to UNITA until there is national reconciliation.
8 Jan. 1989	The ANC announces it will close down its bases in Angola.
10 Jan. 1989	The withdrawal of Cuban troops begins.
11 Jan. 1989	President dos Santos appeals to the United States to accord diplomatic recognition to the MPLA government.
12 Jan. 1989	UNITA rejects President dos Santos' call to lay down arms. Peace is possible only if the MPLA government agrees to negotiate with UNITA.
16 Jan. 1989	A ninety member United Nations verification team monitor the departure of the Cuban troops and report 3,000 have already left.
27 Jan. 1989	United States officials state that talks are taking place between the United States and Angola, with a view to agreeing to some degree of diplomatic representation.
29 Jan. 1989	President dos Santos insists that there will never be any negotiations with the 'terrorist organization' (UNITA).
4 Feb. 1989	The government offers amnesty to anybody prepared to renounce violence and accept the authority of the MPLA-PT regime comes into force.
6 Feb. 1989	Electricity supply to Luanda from the Cambamba dam.
8 Feb. 1989	UNITA launches a military offensive.
14 Feb. 1989	The peace initiative by President Houphouet-Boigny is supported by UNITA, who are postponing their annual rainy-season offensive to facilitate efforts at reconciliation. Savimbi explains his own peace terms as a power-sharing arrangement for two years, leading to democratic elections.
24-25 Feb.1989	First ordinary session in Luanda of the Joint Commission for Verification and Implementation of the Peace Agreements of 22 December.

13 Mar. 1989   Savimbi propopses an eight-point peace plan, including a unilateral four-month moratorium on offensive military operations.

16 Mar. 1989   The Presidents of Zaire, Congo, Gabon, Zimbabwe, Mozambique, Zambia and Sao Tomé and Príncipe attend a regional summit in Luanda, to address the problem of the ongoing civil war with dos Santos.

27-28 Apr.1989   Senior representatives of Angola, Cuba and South Africa meet in Cape Town to review their peace plan. Members of the Joint Commission are joined for the two-day conference by an American envoy and Vyacheslav Ustinov, a veteran Soviet diplomat.

16 May 1989   The Presidents of Zaire, Congo, Gabon, Zimbabwe, Mozambique, Zambia, Sao Tomé and Príncipe and Angola meet in Luanda and endorse the MPLA governments peace plan. The joint summit statement says the eight African nations will co-ordinate efforts to end foreign involvement in Angola and guarantee security and stability. The peace plan includes a proposal for a peace zone along the Benguela Railway.

Late May -   A government delegation tours Spain, France, Great Britain West Germany,
Early June 1989   Italy and Belgium to discuss arreas in interest payments owing on Angola's national debt.

22 June 1989   President Mobutu of Zaire convenes in Gbadolite a summit meeting involving twenty African countries, at which a ceasefire was formally agreed, to begin midnight 23 June. A declaration proclaims national reconciliation and sets up a commission to prepare the implementation of a reconcilition plan, on the basis of a seven-point Angolan government plan. A meeting and a handshake between President dos Santos and Savimbi is widely reported as symbolizing a breakthrough. The agreement however is differently construed by the government and by UNITA.

23 June 1989   President Kaunda of Zambia expresses support for the Gbadolite Declaration.

23 June 1989   South Africa's Foreign Minister `Pik' Botha notes the progress made at the Gbadolite summit, trusts that the use of violence will come to an end, but notes that there is much uncertainty and disinformation surrounding the Declaration.

24 June 1989   The ceasefire is to start at midnight.

27 June 1989   Savimbi is quoted as saying he is happy with the ceasefire but denies he ever agreed to go into exile.

29 June 1989   Portuguese news agency, Lusa, reports that the Angolan government is to offer UNITA three senior posts and the governships of four key provinces.

29 June 1989   UNITA successfully sabotages Luanda's power supply facilities.

23 July 1989   An Angolan airliner carrying local government officials is shot down by a heat-seeking missile in UNITA-held territory. Forty-two people die in the crash, the ceasefire is violated and the peace process jeopardized.

22 Aug. 1989   Dos Santos meets with eight African heads of state at the Committee for

Reconciliation Conference convened by President Kaunda of Zambia. The Committee endorses the version of the Gbadolite Agreement accepted by the Angolan government.

23 Aug. 1989   President dos Santos claims the ceasefire is in jeopardy because the United States and South Africa continue to arm UNITA.

24 Aug. 1989   Savimbi announces that his 50,000 strong army is resuming hostilities in protest at remarks by President Kaunda of Zambia. Kaunda had said that Savimbi agreed to go into temporary exile and that his forces would be absorbed into existing government institutions.

24 Aug. 1989   United States State Department officials confirm UNITA report that government troops are moving eastward from Cuito Cuanavale towards Mavinga in UNITA territory and maintain that the ceasefire 'never really took hold' and that military activity by both sides is gradually increasing. The United States rejects dos Santos' suggestion that Washington is responsible but confirms that the United States plans to continue arming UNITA.

25 Aug. 1989   South African Acting President F.W. de Klerk flies into Zaire for urgent talks with President Mobutu over renewed guerrilla warfare in Angola, and the consequent 'delicate situation'.

28 Aug. 1989   Acting President F.W. de Klerk meets with President Kaunda in Livingstone to discuss the 'very serious' situation.

18 Sept. 1989   Assistant United States Secretary of State for African Affairs Herman J. Cohen urges Savimbi to attend a second round of negotiations in Kinshasa, Zaire. Savimbi rebuffs the offer. Eight African heads of state meet at the invitation of President Mobutu, but the effort to revive the Angolan peace process fails. The leaders of Zambia, Angola, Congo, Gabon, Mozambique, Sao Tomé and Príncipe and Egypt do little more than reiterate their version of the Gbadolite Agreement.

20 Sept. 1989   President Mobutu temporarily terminates United States access to Zairean airstrips, thereby denying UNITA access to its covert military assistance.

25-28 Sept. 1989   UNITA holds an Extraordinary Congress at Jamba to show support for Savimbi. It calls for direct negotiations with the MPLA, a cease-fire, the release of prisoners of war, the formation of a transitional government and the scheduling of multi-party elections. Savimbi himself categorically rejects the call for his exile, and for UNITA's integration.

Mid-Oct. 1989   A series of indirect meetings between MPLA and UNITA representatives take place at a Mobutu estate in the south of France, but no communiqué is issued. Present are Jonas Savimbi, President Mobutu, P. de C. van Dunem for Angola, 'Pik' Botha for South Africa and Herman Cohen for the United States.

17 Oct. 1989   Savimbi leaves France for Africa. Herman Cohen claims the United States has encouraged Savimbi to continue to work with President Mobutu towards a peaceful settlement, but is ready to continue to support UNITA until national reconciliation is achieved.

31 Oct. 1989   The heads of state of Gabon, President Bongo, Sao Tomé and Príncipe, P. da Costa, Zambia, Kenneth Kaunda and Cote d'Ivoire, President Houphouet-Boigny, met in Yamoussoukro in the Cote d'Ivoire to discuss the Angolan conflict. The meeting reaffirms that the Zairean President Mobutu will continue to play a mediating role and President Houphouet-Boigny that of adviser.

8 Nov. 1989   Angola and Swaziland establish diplomatic relations in a ceremony held in the United Nations headquarters.

24 Nov. 1989   President dos Santos decrees a minor government reshuffle.

19-22 Dec.1989 The first meeting of the China-Angola Joint Commission convenes to analyze economic, trade and technical cooperation opportunities for the two countries.

23 Dec. 1989   The government launches a major military offensive against Mavinga, involving 20,000 MPLA men, 400 armoured vehicles and a core airpower force of MiG-23s, MiG-25s and Mi-35 helicopters. An estimated $1bn worth of advanced Soviet military hardware fuels the MPLA's effort to win the Mavinga engagement and destroy UNITA in its Jamba headquarters.

30 Dec. 1989   President dos Santos broadcasts the government's latest proposals for a settlement, reiterating that a ceasefire could only follow recognition of the legitimacy of the government, envisaging elections within five years, and offering new guarantees of freedom of association.

Jan. 1990   Fighting intensifies, particularly near Mavinga.

8 Jan. 1990   UNITA dismisses the government's settlement proposals, as containing nothing new and reiterates its demand for an interim coalition administration and multiparty elections.

15 Jan. 1990   The government calls off its massive three-week military offensive against UNITA, reportedly under pressure from the Soviet Union.

15-18 Jan. 1990 The Central Committee of the MPLA-PT recommends certain democratic reforms for consideration but reaffirms that the single-party system remains the most appropriate.

21 Jan. 1990   UNITA attacks a village 22 km north of Lobito with missile launchers, mortars and machine guns. Among those killed are four Cuban soldiers.

25 Jan. 1990   The Angolan and Cuban governments announce a temporary suspension of the Cuban troop withdrawal.

27-30 Jan. 1990 Jonas Savimbi visits Portugal and holds discussions with President Soares and with Prime Minister A.C. Silva.

28-29 Jan. 1990 President José Sarney of Brazil signs a joint communique with President dos Santos confirming their commitment to cooperation in areas of trade, culture, education, technology transfer and development.

30 Jan.-   Talks take place between Israeli and Angolan officials to
5 Feb. 1990   strengthen friendship and understanding.

31 Jan. 1990	Dr. Savimbi breaks off a European tour as UNITA strongholds come under a heavy air offensive around Mavinga and government troops advance to about 12 km from the town.
Feb.-Mar.1990	Fierce fighting takes place for control of the south-eastern town of Mavinga, a UNITA advance base.
2 Feb. 1990	MPLA government claim its FAPLA forces have captured Mavinga. UNITA deny this.
5 Feb. 1990	A joint Angola-USSR energy subcommission convenes for a week-long meeting in Luanda to discuss bilateral cooperation on energy.
6 Feb. 1990	The Portugese News Agency LUSA reports that Angola has presented new peace proposals to Zairean mediators.
6 Feb. 1990	Angolan military sources report the military situation in the Mavinga region is still fluid and fighting continuing.
7 Feb. 1990	President Mobutu welcomes the heads of state of Gabon, Congo and Cameroon to a mini summit at N'Sele, on the Angolan peace problems. President dos Santos does not attend.
21 Feb. 1990	UNITA claims that chemical weapons have been used against it, have received confirmation from Western experts in a statement saying that 'chemical bombs have gassed the population in this region recently and for many years'.
23 Feb. 1990	The MPLA government denies UNITA claims that it has used chemical weapons in the Mavinga area.
24 Feb. 1990	Dr. Savimbi is reported to have been wounded in the bombing of Jamba. This is denied by UNITA.
25 Feb. 1990	Cuban troop withdrawals resume after a one-month suspension.
27 Feb. 1990	President dos Santos decrees a minor cabinet reshuffle.
Mar. 1990	UNITA Chief of Staff Gen. D.A. Chilingutila is replaced by Gen. A. Pena 'Ben Ben'.
1 Mar. 1990	South African Foreign Affairs Minister 'Pik' Botha pays the first official visit by a South African Minister since 1975, and meets President dos Santos and Lt.-Col. P. de C. Van Dúnem 'Loy', to discuss the abandonment of the single-party system in Africa and of apartheid in South Africa.
2 Mar. 1990	The government claims to have twice bombed UNITA's headquarters at Jamba. President dos Santos is optimistic that peace talks will restart, but is keen to find an alternative group of mediators to the group of eight led by Mobutu.
5 Mar. 1990	Savimbi states that he is ready to accept an immediate ceasefire, provided the government abandon its military gains of the last two months. A transitional government should be formed.

18 Mar. 1990	Soviet Foreign Minister Eduard Shevardnadze visits Luanda during his tour through Southern Africa and meets with President dos Santos. They discuss peace issues in the context of the USSR's new role as observer in the Angolan peace process.
20 Mar. 1990	President dos Santos and United States Secretary of State, James Baker, meet in Windhoek and agree that a ceasefire is necessary as a first step to a political settlement.
Late Mar.1990	The war reaches a stalemate at a point north of Mavinga, near the Lomba River.
Late Mar. - 6 Apr. 1990	Limited air strikes are launched over Jamba. Following a mini-summit on Angola, in Sao Tomé and Príncipe, attended by the Presidents of Congo and Gabon and Sao Tomé and Príncipe: President dos Santos confirms that diplomatic moves are encouraging talks between the government and UNITA.
9 Apr. 1990	UNITA offers an immediate ceasefire and direct talks, both without conditions.
24-25 Apr.1990	Preliminary talks between MPLA and UNITA are held in Evora, Portugal, chaired by the Portuguese Secretary of State for Foreign Affairs, J.D. Barroso. The talks coincide with a three-day conference in Lisbon, attended by about 1,400 Angolan professionals of all political persuations to discuss terms under which Angolan exiles could return to replace Cuban and Eastern Bloc personnel.
27 Apr. 1990	FLEC attacks a petroleum installation on the Congolese border and seizes hostages.
29 Apr. 1990	UNITA communiqué describes the talks as extremely positive and decides to stop all hostile propaganda against the Luanda government.
30 Apr. 1990	The second stage of the withdrawal of Cuban forces is completed by the end of April.
May-June 1990	UNITA stages a counter-offensive and FAPLA forces withdraw from the Mavinga region.
1 May 1990	Savimbi repeats his wish for peace talks with dos Santos, recognises him as head of state, but refuses to accept the MPLA-PT as the legitimate government.
7 May 1990	Chief of Staff, Lieutenant-General A. dos S. França 'Ndalu' is tranferred from the Mavinga front to command the new Cuanza-Bengo front, between Luanda and Uige province to counter a UNITA offensive there.
9 May 1990	UNITA communiqué claims a victory in the battle for Mavinga on 6 and 7 May, the withdrawal of FAPLA forces from the area, and a decisive ending to the government offensive launched in December 1989.
17 May 1990	Talks are held in Zaire between UNITA's Jonas Savimbi and United States Secretary of State for African Affairs Herman Cohen.

19-20 May	An agreement is concluded by Angola and Namibia to form a Joint Commission to maintain security along their 1,000 km border. An agreement on the movement of people and goods across the two borders is also signed.
25 May 1990	Agence France Presse (AFP) reports that the United States has decided to grant $10m in emergency aid to UNITA, in addition to its annual aid of $50m. The military aid will, for the first time, include anti aircraft missiles of greater range than Stinger missiles.
7 June 1990	A UNITA communiqué proposes a three-month truce starting 22 June.
11 June 1990	President dos Santos signs a law creating a Ministry of Information to meet the current demands of the country's socio-economic and political developments.
16 June 1990	B. da S. Cardoso is appointed Information Minister, J.D. Van Dúnem, Planning Minister and A. Jaime Finance Minister.
18 June 1990	UNITA withdraws its delegation after two days of talks on 16-17 June between MPLA-PT and UNITA representatives held near Lisbon.
18 June 1990	It is reported that the United States Bush Administration is seeking congressional approval for an additional US$1015,000,000 in covert aid to UNITA, to supplement a $50,000,000 CIA assistance programme.
18 June 1990	P. da C. Neto is appointed Governor of the Central Bank.
20 June 1990	The government's Information Ministry warns UNITA leadership of the consequences of its interruption of the talks in Portugal.
3 July 1990	The Central Committee of the MPLA announces that the People's Republic of Angola will evolve towards a multi-party system.
3 July 1990	An inter-ministerial Co-operation Accord is signed by the Bulgarian Foreign Minister, Enyo Savov, to strengthen bilateral friendship and cooperation in various areas.
20 Aug. 1990	The government claims FAPLA has repulsed an attack on Andulo city (Bie province) and denies UNITA has overrun the Caculuma barracks (Malange province).
24 Aug. 1990	L.M. Dias is appointed Minister of Justice.
27-31 Aug.1990	Session of talks between the MPLA government and UNITA hosted by Portuguese mediators in Lisbon end without agreement on a truce, but with consensus that the Soviet Union, the United States and Portugal shall monitor an eventual ceasefire.
12 Sept. 1990	Savimbi and President Mobutu hold lengthy talks in Goma (eastern Zaire) on the contents of a message from the OAU ad hoc Committee on Southern Africa, delivered to President Mobutu by visiting ANC Deputy President, Nelson Mandela.
24-28 Sept.1990	Delegations representing the MPLA government and UNITA meet near

Lisbon for a fourth session of direct negotiations on a peace agreement. Two joint sub-commissions are formed, one to examine further 'political principles' and the other to examine military issues and aspects of the ceasefire.

2 Oct. 1990

Jonas Savimbi meets President Bush in the course of a visit to the United States to lobby for the continuation of CIA aid.

10 Oct. 1990

President dos Santos cancels a visit to the USA in protest against 'hostile United States policy'.

Mid-Oct. 1990

The United States House of Representatives, after a public debate on Central Intelligence Agency funds, rejects a proposal to cease 'covert' CIA support for UNITA, amounting to some U.S.$60,000,000 annually.

25-26 Oct 1990

The Central Committee of the MPLA-PT endorses a reform programme, including a proposed transition to multiparty politics, for presentation to a Party Congress scheduled for December 1990.

7 Nov. 1990

The army posts of Defence Minister and General Chief of Staff, previously held by P.M.T. Pedale and A. Franca Ndalu respectively, are taken over by President J.E. dos Santos himself in his capacity as Commander-in-Chief of the Angolan Armed Forces.

12 Nov. 1990

By decree L.F.F. do Nascimento becomes a special assistant to the President, A. de O. Silvestre has taken over the portfolio of Trade and Industry and F.A. da G. Teixeira becomes the new central bank Governor.

16-20 Nov.1990

Five days of negotiations at Estoril, Portugal between the MPLA government and UNITA end with an eighty per cent agreement on a ceasefire document drawn up by the Portuguese mediating team.

29 Nov. 1990

UNITA attacks Luanda's oil refinery.

4-9 Dec. 1990

At the third Congress of the MPLA-PT, in Luanda, delegates agreed on a reform package and endorse wide-ranging changes including the replacement of the party's Marxist ideology by a commitment to 'democratic socialism'. Discuss plans for the President and legislature to be elected by universal secret ballot, for a revised constitution which would guarantee freedom of expression, permit the formation of political parties and end the MPLA-PT's control over the armed forces.

7 Dec. 1990

Savimbi undertakes to accept a ceasefire on condition that the Angolan government legalizes opposition parties.

12 Dec. 1990

The United States and Soviet Union arrange a meeting in Washington between Jonas Savimbi and the Soviet Foreign Minister Eduard Shevardnadze.

13 Dec. 1990

After a meeting with United States President George Bush, Savimbi says that peace prospects have improved, that his goal was a truce early in 1991 and free and fair elections by the end of the year. After the White House talks a five party discussion between United States, Soviet and Portuguese officials and MPLA and UNITA representatives work on the parameters of a peace settlement.

21 Dec. 1990   The government decides to suspend the United Nations Special Aid Programme for Angola.

28 Dec. 1990-
2 Jan. 1991   A UNITA conference on the negotiating process is held in Jamba, in the presence of Political Bureau and Central Committee members and personnel of the Armed Forces' Supreme Command, as well as UNITA's representatives abroad and other delegates.

9 Jan. 1991   President dos Santos announces changes to the Angolan Council of Ministers.

10 Jan. 1991   Cuba's Ambassador to Zimbabwe Enmelio Caballero, indicates that, while Cuba is ahead of schedule in withdrawing its troops from Angola, it reserves the right to respond to unprovoked UNITA attacks.

23 Jan. 1991   The MPLA government accepts 'with only slight amendments' a peace plan to end the civil war.

6-8 Feb. 1991   The sixth round of peace talks, postponed from 28 January, fail to take place, despite ensuing rounds of consultations among the Portuguese mediating team, the Soviet and United States observers and the MPLA and UNITA delegations.

7 Feb. 1991   UNITA claims that government military aircraft are dropping chemical bombs on several villages in Luanda province. Specifically mentioned are deaths and devastation at Sasanji village, near the provincial capital Saurimo.

10 Feb. 1991   UNITA attacks and takes the north-western port of Ambriz. Foreign employees of the oil companies flee the scene.

12 Feb. 1991   The Council of the Republic will in future play a definitive role in the revision of the constitution and the creation of the main legal instruments and other requirements relating to the establishment of a multi-party system. The Council will consist of five members of the People's Assembly, nominated by its standing commission, the Chief Justice of the People's Supreme Court, an official from each of the recognised churches, and grass roots organizations together with people nominated by the President and traditional authorities.

13 Feb. 1991   Angolan MiG-23 aircraft bomb Bagani in northern Namibia. An urgent meeting of the Angolan-Namibian Joint Commission on Security is called. The Angolan embassy expresses its regret and promises to pay compensation.

14 Feb. 1991   The United Nations Development Programme (UNDP) asks the Angolan government to permit the immediate resumption of humanitarian aid distribution to war and drought affected areas.

19 Feb. 1991   In a communiqué issued by the People's Assembly in Luanda, the following Ministries and Secretariats of State are established:
Ministry for Territorial Administration; Ministry of Public Works and Urbanisation; Ministry of Commerce; Ministry of Petroleum; Secretariat of State for the Promotion and Development of Women; Energy and Water Affairs; Secretariat of State for Construction Materials; Secretariat of State for Energy and Water Affairs; Secretariat of State for Geology and Mines

and Secretariat of State for Housing.
The Ministry of Agriculture will from now on be called the Ministry of Agriculture and Rural Development and the Ministry of Labour and Social Security will from now on be called the Ministry of Labour, Public Administration and Social Security.
The following ministries and secretariats of state were abolished:
Ministry of State Security; Ministry of Construction; Ministry of Labour and Social Security; Ministry of Foreign Trade; Ministry of Domestic Trade; Ministry of Energy and Petroleum; Secretariat of State for Urbanisation, Housing and Water Affairs and Secretariat of State for Co-operation.

21 Feb. 1991   Presidents dos Santos of Angola, Sassou-Nguesso of Congo and Pinto da Costa of Sao Tomé and Príncipe arrive in Libreville for a quadripartite summit on developments in the Angolan peace process with President Bongo of Gabon.

4-5 Mar. 1991   Talks take place in Lisbon involving Soviet, United States and Portuguese mediators, and new proposals are made.

5 Mar. 1991   Changes in government are carried out. New appointments are made:
Ministers: L.F.F. do Nascimento - Territorial Administration; J.L. Lamboite - Oil; D.J. de Jesus - Labour, Public Administration and Social Security; J.E.G. Cabelo Branco - Public Works and Urbanization; V.P. Nicolao - State Secretary for Housing
State Secretaries:
A.L. de J. Neto - Construction materials; J.Q.M. Mota - Energy and Water; J.D.A. Dias - Geology and Mining; K. Paihama - Commission for Luanda Province.

12 Mar. 1991   The government agrees to the resumption of UN food and medical relief convoys, subject to United States guarantees of non-interference by UNITA.

17 Mar. 1991   UNITA concluded its seventh Congress at Nkramati and states it will sign a ceasefire agreement as soon as a date is set for multiparty elections. Jonas Savimbi is re-elected President of UNITA.

3-29 Apr.1991   The sixth round of peace talks brokered by Portugal, United States and the Soviet Union are held at Bicesse, near Estoril, Portugal. Key issues are the establishment of a single army, modalities of a ceasefire and elections.

5 Apr. 1991   President dos Santos visits Spain and holds talks with Prime Minister F. Gonzalez on co-operation projects.

7 Apr. 1991   The government accuses UNITA of launching an offensive involving ten battalions against the eastern city of Luena.

8 Apr. 1991   During talks with French ministers on his visit to France, President dos Santos asks for French participation in training his army and police force and for support in rescheduling Angola's foreign debt.

9 Apr. 1991   UNITA Vice-President Jeremias Chitunda says that the resolution of the conflict is contingent on the signing of a ceasefire and the holding of free, fair and internationally monitored elections.

23 Apr. 1991   United States Assistant Secretary of State for African Affairs, Herman J.

	Cohen and Soviet Deputy Foreign Minister Vladmir Kasimirov arrive at the peace talks. A workable settlement appears possible.

29 Apr. 1991 Savimbi announces in London that a peace agreement will be initialled on 30 April and formally signed on 30 May 1991.

29 Apr. 1991 Reuter reports that UNITA has ordered its forces to drive government troops out of the area centred on Luena in the Eastern Province, Moxico.

1 May 1991 A ceasefire is agreed to and a peace agreement initialled. Hostilities are to end by 15 May, peace documents to be formally signed at the end of May 1991. Angola's first multi-party elections are to be held between September and November 1992.

11 May 1991 A multi-party system comes into effect.

14 May 1991 The ceasefire comes into effect at midnight.

16 May 1991 UNITA attack and capture the village of Monte Belo in Benguela Province.

19 May 1991 All Angolan refugees in Zambia are to be repatriated. Some of the more than 8,000 are already returning.

27 May 1991 The last 119 Cuban troops arrive home in Havana, five weeks ahead of schedule.

31 May 1991 The formal signing of the peace agreement takes place in Lisbon, in the presence of United States Secretary of State James Baker, Soviet Foreign Minister Aleksander Bessmertnykh, United Nations Secretary-General Javier Pérez de Cuéllar, and President Museveni of Uganda, Chairman of the Organization of African Unity.

2 June 1991 President dos Santos joins an estimated 40,000 people in an ecumenical thanksgiving Mass in Luanda, to mark the end of sixteen years of civil war.

3 June 1991 The Soviet government welcomes the signing of the Estoril Agreement, and intends 'to fulfil vigorously the accords reached in connection with the settlement in Angola, including in the sphere of ending arms deliveries to that country, on the understanding that all whom this concerns will do likewise'.

13 June 1991 Zimbabwe pledges multi-faceted assistance to Angola to minimise eventual difficulties following the end of the war.

17 June 1991 The first meeting of the Joint Political and Military Commission together with Soviet, United States and Portuguese representatives begins in Luanda.

3 July 1991 The government states it proposes to meet with FLEC in a bid to secure peace in Cabinda.

4 July 1991 The British Minister for Overseas Development, L. Chalker, is received by President dos Santos and meets the UNITA delegation to the Joint Political and Military Commission. British investment projects are discussed and British assistance promised.

9 July 1991	The Kinshasa, Zaire, based FLEC claims that a joint MPLA-UNITA force of 6,000 men are mounting an offensive against FLEC guerrillas, before United Nations observers arrive to monitor the peace accord.
10 July 1991	It is announced that Senegal has been approached by the United Nations to prepare to send military observers to Angola to help monitor the ceasefire.
19 July 1991	Fernando José França Van-Dúnem is appointed as Angola's first Prime Minister since 1977. R. Caseiro becomes Planning Minister.
26 July 1991	The release of hundreds of Angolan prisoners of war is suspended, one day after 107 UNITA prisoners are freed in Luanda. Significant discrepancies emerge over the number of prisoners held by UNITA.
1 Aug. 1991	The Joint Political and Military Commission (CCPM), overseeing the peace process reports delays in the implementation of the accord. Only 10-20 per cent of prisoners have been exchanged and not all monitoring mechanisms are in place.
10 Aug. 1991	The liberation of prisoners resumes.
13 Aug. 1991	Assembly points are ready to accept troops from both sides.
31 Aug. 1991	The leader of the Angola National Liberation Front (FNLA) returns to Angola after sixteen years of exile, and intends standing in the forthcoming presidential elections.
2 Sept. 1991	The Democratic Renewal Party (PRD) becomes the first political party to receive sanction from Angola's Supreme People's Court to begin political activities throughout the country.
3 Sept. 1991	The Portuguese Prime Minister Cavaco Silva arrives in Luanda on a three-day official visit.
10-17 Sept.1991	UNITA suspends its participation in the Joint Political and Military Commission (CCPM), and lists seven conditions for its return.
14 Sept. 1991	Alberto Correia Neto is sworn in as Chief of General Staff of FAPLA. Major-General Joao de Matos is appointed Ground Forces Commander.
15-16 Sept.1991	President dos Santos visits the United States to begin establishing diplomatic relations and meets President George Bush.
20 Sept. 1991	The Joint Political and Military Commission proceedings resume.
22 Sept. 1991	President dos Santos holds discussions in London with British Prime Minister John Major, focusing on Britain's possible contribution to the creation of a single national army.
27 Sept. 1991	Jonas Savimbi returns to Luanda for the first time since the start of the sixteen year civil war.
10 Oct. 1991	The United States and United Nations airlift of food and other essential items begins to avert crises among the estimated 200,000 demobilized soldiers.

20 Oct. 1991	Savimbi announces that UNITA's general headquarters are being transferred from Jamba to Luanda, to create a greater UNITA presence in Luanda.
21 Oct. 1991	In a minor government reshuffle S.A. Pittra 'Petrof' is appointed Deputy Minister of the Interior in charge of public order and Commander General of the Police, O.S. Van-Dúnem is appointed Minister of Youth and Sports and M. Moco Secretary-General of the MPLA.
10 Nov. 1991	President dos Santos announces that a general election will take place on a date provisionally set for the second half of September 1992.
12 Nov. 1991	A curfew is imposed in Cabinda after clashes between government forces and FLEC supporters.
14 Nov. 1991	General J. de Matos, chief of the government's ground forces, and General A.C. Numa, commander of UNITA's northern front are sworn in as the Supreme Command of Angola's armed forces.
21 Nov. 1991	The governments of Angola, Cuba, Namibia and South Africa, members of the Joint Commission created by the Brazzaville Protocol of 13 December 1988 have, by consensus, concluded that the Commission has complied fully and honourably with its objectives and it holds its final meeting and issues its final declaration.
22 Nov. 1991	President dos Santos, by decree, delegates some of his duties to the Prime Minister, F.F. van Dunem, who will now chair the sessions of the Council of Ministers, manage and coordinate government activity and issue orders and instructions to members of government and other officials.
5 Dec. 1991	While opening a meeting of the UNITA political commission in Luanda, Savimbi calls on the United Nations to send experts to Angola immediately to help prepare for the September 1992 elections.
13 Dec. 1991	Jonas Savimbi, President of UNITA and President J.E. dos Santos meet at Futungo de Belas Palace in a cordial atmosphere. Issues addressed include the situation in Cabinda, the activities of the Joint Political and Military Commission (CCPM) and the possible holding of a multiparty conference.
3 Jan. 1992	Four British tourists are killed and two others injured in an ambush near Quilengues in southern Angola. The government launches an official inquiry.
10 Jan. 1992	The senior high command of the proposed unified army takes up its duties.
11 Jan. 1992	A new Monitoring Task Group (GAT) is created to strengthen the implementation of the peace accord. It includes members of the government, of UNITA and of the United Nations Angola Verification Mission.
14-26 Jan.1992	Representatives of the government and of twenty six political parties meet in Luanda to discuss the transition to democracy. UNITA declines its invitation.
17 Jan. 1992	UNITA troops are reported to have re-occupied three district capitals in Bengo Province in northern Angola. UNITA is reported to be withdrawing its confined troops from containment camps. Government forces are also

filtering back to towns and cities.

22 Jan. 1992	Italy is providing aid estimated at US$142,000,000.
23 Jan. 1992	South Africa and Angola agree to establish formal diplomatic ties. Initially 'interest offices' will be established in Luanda and Pretoria.
30 Jan. 1992	M. de A. Monteiro is appointed Finance Minister and S.B. Lavrado Governor of the National Bank.
1 Feb. 1992	The government and UNITA begin talks on the recommendation of the multi-party conference. A new political party, The National Union for the Beacon of Democracy and Development of Angola (UNLDDA) is launched.
5 Feb. 1992	Signs an agreement with Hungary on the abolition of visa requirements for holders of diplomatic passports.
10 Feb. 1992	UNITA and the Angolan Democratic Forum (FDA) apply to the Supreme Court for registration as political parties.
28 Feb. 1992	The European Community (EC) Vice-President Manuel Marin, announces that the EC is making available a sum of $10m for support towards the Angolan electoral process. Also recommended is a total sum of ECU 200m to resolve the problem of the rehabilitation of Angola and simultaneously to help the social reintegration of ex-fighters from both armies, FAPLA and FALA.
2 Mar. 1992	Demobilization of the government army and UNITA troops begins.
6 Mar. 1992	UNITA confirms that two of its most senior officials, General M. N'Zau Puna and General T. da Costa Fernandes, have left the organization. They arrive in Paris, where they accuse Dr. Savimbi of various crimes, including the execution of Wilson dos Santos and Tito Chingundji.
22 Mar. 1992	Dr. Savimbi warns the country that the MPLA is planning to launch an attack on UNITA. His soldiers at assembly points are ordered to stay on alert.
24 Mar. 1992	Angolan Defence Minister Pedro Maria Tonha meets his South African counterpart, Roelf Meyer, in Pretoria. Cooperation between the two countries is to be strengthened 'on certain issues', including the location of land mines.
24 Mar. 1992	In a statement issued in Paris, Generals N'Zau Puna and Fernandes accuse UNITA of human rights abuses and political killings.
24 Mar. 1992	Two tripartite accords are signed in Luanda concerning the creation of a Commission responsible for promoting the voluntary repatriation of Angolan refugees from Zambia and Zaire. They are signed by Angolan Social Affairs State Secretary, R. dos Santos, the Zairean Ambassador and the Zambian Chargé d'Affairs, as well as by the regional chief for the UNHCR.
31 Mar. 1992	The United States Secretary of State James Baker demands from Savimbi a full explanation of the changes made by the defecting UNITA Generals.

31 Mar. 1992	More than 3,000 MPLA (government) and FALA (UNITA) soldiers are demobilized.
2 Apr. 1992	In the opening session of the National People's Assembly, President dos Santos announces that multiparty presidential and legislative elections will be held on 29 and 30 September 1992. He accuses UNITA of violating the May 1991 peace accord, and of preventing free political activity in its controlled areas.
3 Apr. 1992	Angola's Parliament adopts a package of laws to govern the country's first multiparty elections in September. These define the terms for voter registration, set time limits for the election campaign and create a National Electoral Council (CNE) to manage the poll and establish the new Parliament. Voting is to take place on 29 and 30 September.
5 Apr. 1992	UNITA accepts the government's timetable for the elections.
7 Apr. 1992	UNITA defector General M. N'Zau Puna claims that 20,000 UNITA soldiers, hidden near Licua, will be mobilized should UNITA lose the elections.
9 Apr. 1992	President dos Santos reshuffles his government following the resignation of L.F.F. do Nascimento. Col. A.P. Kassomo becomes Minister of Territorial Administration, A.L. Brandao Minister of Transport and Communications, M. de F. Jardim Minister of Fisheries, F.R. da Cruz, Governor of Cuanzo Sul Province, and N.F. dos Santos State Secretary for Social Affairs.
9 Apr. 1992	The Peoples Assembly ratifies amendments to the Law on Political Parties allowing political groups applying for registration to submit only 1,500 signatories instead of 3,000, provided that 100 signatures come from each of the registered fourteen provinces.
18 Apr. 1992	Savimbi denies allegations that he is keeping a clandestine army of 20,000 men in the south of Angola and claims 94% of some 40,000 of his guerrillas are in containment areas under United Nations supervision.
23 Apr. 1992	The People's Supreme Court registers the Social Renewal Party (PRS).
27 Apr. 1992	Resignations from the Democratic Renewal Party (PRD) destroy its chances in the multiparty elections in September.
7-12 May 1992	The MPLA-PT holds its third Special Congress. Significant changes are made in the party structure. Membership of the Central Committee is increased from 180 to 193 and includes businessmen, intellectuals and some former dissidents, including Daniel Chipenda.
9 May 1992	The National Electoral Council (CNE) is inaugurated. Chaired by O.M. dos Santos, it will monitor the elections.
20 May 1992	Voter registration opens in five of the eighteen provinces.
4-9 June 1992	Pope John Paul visits Angola and urges Angolans to unite for peace.
7 June 1992	Two former senior UNITA cadres, T. do C. Fernandes and M. N'zau Puna, have formed a Democratic Reflection Tendency (DRT), and call for an

	Extraordinary Congress of the entire UNITA party to be held in Luanda at the end of July.
10 June 1992	UNITA radio denounces the MPLA government for hypocrisy over the Pope's visit claiming that during their term of office they have 'transformed churches into barracks and holy places into carnage grounds'.
July 1992	All factions of the Front for the Liberation of the Cabinda Enclave (FLEC) agree to boycott the elections.
8 July 1992	The United Nations Security Council, in a non-binding statement, urges the government and UNITA to exercise restraint, halt violent incidents and permit open voter registration, and, swiftly to implement the peace accords. It appeals to member states to provide electoral assistance and equipment.
13 July 1992	MPLA supporters fire on UNITA supporters at a political rally at Malanga, northern Angola. Two are killed, many wounded.
17 July 1992	By decree President dos Santos calls for Presidential and Legislative elections to be held simultaneously on 29 and 30 September.
Mid-July 1992	Daniel Chipenda resigns as organizer of the MPLA's election campaign and from the MPLA Central Committee, indicating that he may stand for President as an independent. He claims support within UNITA and seeks support from other opposition parties.
23 July 1992	UNITA leader, Dr. Jonas Savimbi's candidacy for the Presidency is officially announced.
27 July 1992	At its Fourth Ordinary Session the MPLA Central Committee approves the list of MPLA candidates for legislative elections and unanimously nominates President dos Santos as the sole candidate for the Presidential elections.
30 July 1992	Twelve candidates have registered for the presidential elections to be held 29-30 September 1992. They include the incumbent president J.E. dos Santos, for the MPLA-PT, Jonas Savimbi, leader of UNITA, Holden Roberto, FNLA leader and Daniel Chipenda, proposed by the Angolan National Democratic Party (PNDA).
31 July 1992	A total of 4,300,000 Angolans have been registered to vote. The United Nations team extend this deadline by another ten days.
3 Aug. 1992	Fighting continues in the city of Malanje, 350 km inland from Luanda.
17 Aug. 1992	The People's Supreme Court publish the final list of presidential candidates. The following is a list in the order they will appear on the voting papers: L. dos Passos (Democratic Renewal Party); H. Roberto (FNLA); A.V. Perreira (Democratic Liberal Party-DLP); M.L. Victor (Democratic Progress Party of the Angolan National Aliance-PDP-ANA); A. Kilandamoko (Angolan Social Democratic Party-PSDA); D. Chipenda (independent supported by the Angolan National Democratic Party-PNDA); R.V. Pereira (Angolan Reformers Party-PRA); S. Cacete (Democratic Front); A. Neto (Angolan Democratic Party-PDA); J.E. dos Santos (MPLA); H.Lando (Democratic Liberal Party of Angola-PDLA).

| 27 Aug. 1992 | The National People's Assembly approve a number of constitutional changes including the abolition of the death penalty. The country's official name is changed from the People's Republic of Angola to the Republic of Angola. |

1 Sept. 1992   The Angolan and Zairean government sign a security agreement aimed at improving relations at their common border and to remove obstacles to the repatriation of Angolans from Zambia.

5 Sept. 1992   FLEC supporters kill two government soldiers. In response the government sends in 300 anti-riot police. Government soldiers mutiny, attack the provincial governors palace and take control of Cabinda city. FLEC vow that elections will not be held in Cabinda. Chevron Oil pulls out all but a skeleton staff. Airlines are warned not to fly over Cabinda.

9 Sept. 1992   President dos Santos promises that if the MPLA win the election it will form a government of national unity.

10 Sept. 1992   UNITA spokesman, Jorge Valentin, says in Luanda that should UNITA win the election, personalities from the MPLA could participate in a government of national unity.

12 Sept. 1992   Chief of General Staff, Gen. A. Carreira announces that the situation in Cabinda Province is now calm.

20 Sept. 1992   UNITA forces burn government vehicles and capture a number of Presidential Guards in Bie Province, allegedly to frustrate an attempt on Savimbi's life.

21 Sept. 1992   UNITA occupy Cuito airport, and close it down.

22 Sept. 1992   UNITA forces release the captured Presidential Guards and re-open Cuito airport. However, several FALA battalions place Ganda and Chongoroc districts in Benguela Province under seige.

22 Sept. 1992   President dos Santos, at a news conference in Huambo, condemns UNITA's attempts to create instability before the elections.

27 Sept. 1992   The government's People's Armed Forces for the Liberation of Angola (FAPLA) and UNITA's military wing, the Armed Forces for the Liberation of Angola (FALA) are formally disbanded.

28 Sept. 1992   A new national army, the Angolan Armed Forces (FAA) is established, under the joint command of General A. dos S. França Ndalu and General A.C. Pena Ben-Ben, who are sworn in as Chiefs of General Staff.

29-30 Sept.1992   Angola's first multiparty elections take place. Eleven candidates contest the Presidency and eighteen parties seek representation in the 223 seat National Assembly. The United Nations provide extensive logistical and technical support. 800 foreign observers monitor the voting at nearly 6,000 polling stations and note that the elections have been free and fair.

5 Oct. 1992   UNITA withdraws from the Angolan Armed Forces (FAA).

11 Oct. 1992   Heavy fighting breaks out in Luanda. Tension mounts between UNITA soldiers and anti-riot police.

13 Oct. 1992	South African Foreign Minister, `Pik' Botha, flies to Huambo, meets Dr. Savimbi, urges him to pursue discussion and dialogue rather than reactivate the civil war and puts forward a possible political compromise on genuine power sharing in a government of national unity.
13 Oct. 1992	Dr. Savimbi alleges that the elections have been rigged. Western observers admit the process has been flawed, but more by inexperience than design and look to a brokered political deal.
17 Oct. 1992	Election results are published. The incumbent J.E. dos Santos wins 49.57 percent of the Presidential vote, just short of the 50 percent required to avoid a second round of elections, and J. Savimbi 40.07 percent of the vote. In the Legislative elections the MPLA-PT receive 53.74 percent of the vote (70 seats), UNITA 34.10 percent (44 seats). Ten other parties share the remaining sixteen seats.
30 Oct-1 Nov. 1992	Heavy fighting in the capital city concentrates in the area around UNITA headquarters and two hotels housing UNITA members active during the election campaign. Among key UNITA leaders killed are UNITA's deputy leader Jeremias Chitunda and Elias Salupeto Pena, senior official and nephew of Jonas Savimbi.
1 Nov. 1992	A United Nations brokered ceasefire agreement comes into force.
1-5 Nov. 1992	Serious fighting in Luanda and in the central and southern town of Benguela, Huambo, Lobito and Lubango.
2 Nov. 1992	The Portuguese government sends service vessels and 200 marines to assist with the evacuation of 40,000 Portuguese nationals and its fleet of C130 transport planes is put on standby.
3 Nov. 1992	Plans to evacuate European Community nationals are suspended, because the airport is closed.
4 Nov. 1992	Luanda airport is re-opened for special flights for evacuation purposes.
6 Nov. 1992	The United Nations Under-Secretary-General for Peace-Keeping Operations is despatched to Angola to attempt to resolve the crisis and restore peace. The UN is prepared to extend the UNAVEM mandate beyond 30 November and suggests the deployment of UN peace-keeping troops.
7 Nov. 1992	Angola declares South Africa's Foreign Minister `Pik' Botha persona non grata, for allegedly supplying UNITA with logistical aid, in a recent `flare up' of the conflict. Pretoria deny supporting armed conflict in any way.
10 Nov. 1992	United Nations officials Marrack Goulding and Margaret Anstee meet Savimbi in Huambo for discussions on the consolidation of the ceasefire and United Nations mediation.
15 Nov. 1992	President dos Santos announces that a government will be formed, with or without UNITA.
17 Nov. 1992	Following discussions with Goulding and the United Nations Special Representative in Angola, Margaret Anstee, Savimbi accepts the election results, declares his willingness to participate in the second round of

Presidential elections and to attend the forthcoming multiparty talks convened by the MPLA-PT.

21 Nov. 1992   The MPLA government convenes a national unity congress to discuss the formation of a government. UNITA fails to attend, claiming the required safety guarantees for its delegates have not been given.

26 Nov. 1992   Parliament is convened. F.J.F. Van-Dúnem is elected chair of the Assembly. The seventy elected UNITA representatives do not take their seats.

27 Nov. 1992   Dos Santos and Savimbi issue the Namibie Declaration committing themselves to accepting the Bicesse Peace Accord, to implementing a ceasefire and to a continuing United Nations presence in the country.

27 Nov. 1992   Marcolino Moco, Secretary-General of the MPLA-PT is appointed as Prime Minister to head the transitional government to be sworn in on 1 December 1992.

29 Nov. 1992   UNITA launch a military offensive in northern Angola, capturing Uige and the strategic air base at Negage.

1 Dec. 1992   Fierce fighting rages at Uige, 250 km north of Luanda. A.B. Costa, a United Nations observer from Brazil is killed when he and four other UN observers are caught in crossfire. UNITA forces also attack Negage, 20 km south of Uige and fighting spreads to other northern towns and then to central Angola.

1 Dec. 1992   Angolan authorities hold the crew of a South African plane that had made an emergency landing in Luena, Moxico Province.

2 Dec. 1992   President dos Santos announces the appointment of a new government headed by Marcelino Moco, with six posts allocated to UNITA.

3 Dec. 1992   The South African government announces that it is withdrawing its diplomatic representatives from Angola.

3 Dec. 1992   The Front for the Liberation of Cabinda - Cabinda armed forces (FLEC-FAC) warns the government of Sao Tomé and Príncipe that it must evacuate all its nationals from Cabinda as soon as possible. All government soldiers should also abandon the territory.

22 Dec. 1992   UNITA announces a six stage plan of action, beginning with its withdrawal from the northern provincial capital Uige and from the airbase Negage opening the way for the restablishment of state administration.

22 Dec. 1992   UNITA forces are said to be leaving the northern towns after intervention by the United States diplomat Jeffrey Davidow.

23 Dec. 1992   A United Nations report says that the situation has undergone a catastrophic deterioration. The UN mandate has been extended but success is not assured.

3 Jan. 1993   Government troops attack UNITA forces in the southern city of Lubango, Huita provincial capital and recapture the north western towns, Taxito and Ndalatando.

5 Jan. 1993	The Prime Minister, Marceline Moco declares 'Angola is at war'.
6 Jan. 1993	State radio says UNITA has been expelled from most of Cunene Province.
6 Jan. 1993	UNITA Information Secretary Jorge Valentine declares 'This is really war. We are obliged to respond if we are not all to die'.
7 Jan. 1993	Savimbi calls for the United States to broker a ceasefire as government troops besiege UNITA headquarters. Fighting rages round Benguela and breaks out in Cuito, capital of Bie province.
8 Jan. 1993	A delegation from the Zimbabwe and Cape Verde governments flies to Huambo to discuss and prepare for a meeting between Savimbi and the Ad Hoc Peace Committee of the OAU.
11 Jan. 1993	Government troops take Luena, Moxico Province capital.
12 Jan. 1993	Fighting is reported in fifteen of Angola's eighteen provinces, following a government offensive, and UNITA response.
13 Jan. 1993	The outgoing United States Secretary of State, Lawrence Eagleburger, states that UNITA is 'largely to blame' for the fighting in Angola.
14 Jan. 1993	From mid-January UNITA hits back and scores a number of military successes.
15 Jan. 1993	Interior Minister A. Pitva Petroff announces in Madrid that Spain and Portugal will continue cooperating in the training of the National Police.
18 Jan. 1993	United Nations representative, Margaret Anstee, describes the situation as a 'full-scale civil war'.
19 Jan. 1993	UNITA captures the strategic oil town of Soyo. Gulf Oil begins evacuating foreign workers from Cabinda.
19 Jan. 1993	Angolan officials express concern over sightings of white mercenaries, the involvement of South Africans and protests to Zaire over Zairean support for UNITA.
20 Jan. 1993	Angola's Ambassador to Congo, J.A. Prata, accuses Congolese politicians of interference in Angola's domestic affairs, notably in the Cabinda enclave and of involvement in arms smuggling for the separatist movement FLEC, led by H. N'Zita.
21 Jan. 1993	United Nations representative, Margaret Anstee, describes the UN mandate in Angola as 'increasingly irrelevant'.
23 Jan. 1993	Clashes in Cuando Cubango Province.
26 Jan. 1993	The United Nations Secretary-General Boutros Boutros-Ghali delivers an ultimatum urging the Security Council to withdraw all but thirty of the 600 military observers unless a ceasefire is reached at the peace talks to which Savimbi finally has agreed to send representatives.
27 Jan. 1993	The new United States administration of President Clinton announces that

it is 'actively reviewing' US policy towards Angola.

27 Jan. 1993   Talks between UNITA and the government, chaired by Margaret Anstee, begin in Addis Ababa, Ethiopia, with the ambassadors of Portugal, Russia and the USA attending as observers.

28 Jan. 1993   Intense fighting in Menongue, Cuando Cubango provincial capital.

30 Jan. 1993   Peace talks are adjourned.

1 Feb. 1993   Currency is devalued.

2 Feb. 1993   President dos Santos carries out a minor Ministerial reshuffle which includes the appointment of J.M. Peixoto as Minister in the President's Office in charge of Civic Affairs.

7 Feb. 1993   A second round of peace talks between the government and UNITA, scheduled to begin in Addis Ababa, Ethiopia, is repeatedly delayed because of the absence of the main UNITA delegation.

18 Feb. 1993   Ten of the seventy UNITA members of the National Assembly take their seats, 'choosing peace and dialogue over war'.

23 Feb. 1993   Food aid is being airlifted by the World Food Programme (WFP) to Lobito, Benguela, Uige, Luena, Lubango, Cazombo, Saurimo, Mbanza Congo, Makela de Zombo Toto. A weekly convoy travels from Luanda to Sumbe: otherwise overland transport is impossible. WFP's Director in Angola reports that refugees in Malange are dependent on the Catholic charity Caritas' airlifted food relief.

23 Feb. 1993   In a statement issued in Lisbon, the three international observer delegations to the peace talks from Portugal, Russia and the United States, insist that the fulfilment of the May 1991 Bicesse peace accord is the only political solution to the conflict.   An OAU meeting, also held in Lisbon unequivocally and unanimously condemns UNITA's resumption of war.

24 Feb. 1993   The Governor of the National Bank and the Finance Minister are dismissed for exceeding their authority when they devalued the currency on 1 February 1993, without previously contacting government departments.

1 Mar. 1993   The peace talks are cancelled because of the failure of UNITA to attend.

7 Mar. 1993   The fifty six-day siege of Huambo ends with government forces withdrawing in the face of intense UNITA bombardment. General Joao de Matos, FAA Chief of Staff calls on Angolans to prepare for a 'difficult conflict' which could continue for one to two years, with casualties higher than those sustained in the previous sixteen years of civil war.

9 Mar. 1993   Savimbi declares that UNITA will only resume negotiations if United Nations representative, Margaret Anstee, is withdrawn and replaced, that the UN mediation committee is restructured and that a provisional government of national unity is established that will last for at least two years.

12 Mar. 1993   The United Nations Security Council adopts resolution 811(1993) accusing

UNITA of being solely responsible for the resumption of conflict, demands that UNITA accept unreservedly the results of the 1992 elections, condemns UNITA violations of the Bicesse peace accord, its withdrawal from the newly established Angolan Armed Forces and its seizure of towns and cities.

25 Mar. 1993	A joint resolution of the United States Senate and House of Representatives condemning UNITA and calling for the recognition of the Angolan government is passed unanimously.
12 Apr. 1993	Peace talks, chaired by Margaret Anstee, resume in Abidjan, Côte d'Ivoire. By the end of April a forty seven point 'memorandum of understanding' is reportedly close to signature.
27 Apr. 1993	Savimbi agreed to a ceasefire 'in principle'.
28 Apr. 1993	Government delegate General H. Carreiro condemns UNITA's occupation of large areas of the country as illegal. UNITA however will not surrender territory seized since the renewal of hostilities in September 1992 until a United Nations peacekeeping force arrives.
8 May 1993	The Abidjan peace talks are adjourned, following disagreement over the withdrawal of UNITA forces.
12 May 1993	United Nations representative, Margaret Anstee, requests to be released from her responsibilities despite government requests for her to continue.
17 May 1993	Peace talks resume.
19 May 1993	The United States State Department announces America's decision to recognize the Angolan government 'which was democratically elected in September 1992', signalling an end to support for UNITA.
21 May 1993	The United Nations representative formally announces the indefinite suspension of the Abidjan talks, with consensus reached on forty six and forty seven points (all but point eleven) of the 'memorandum of understanding'.
24 May 1993	South Africa says it will not follow Washington's lead and recognize the Angolan government until a 'fully representative' administration is in power.
26 May 1993	UNITA intensifies military operations and, after a four-day battle takes control of the key northern oil town, Soyo.
31 May 1993	Fighting spreads. Zairean troops are gathering with UNITA forces at the border at Cabinda. Zambian forces are being amasssed in the north-east border zone to guard against UNITA attacks, and similar preventative action is taken by Namibia in the south.
2 June 1993	The United Nations Council extends until 15 July the mandate of the United Nations Angola Verification Mission (UNAVEM II) but halves its operation to around fifty military observers.
3 June 1993	At a United Nations-sponsored conference in Geneva, departing United Nations special envoy, Margaret Anstee, issues an urgent appeal for humanitarian aid to Angola. Donor countries will need to raise at least

US$227 million to help 2,000,000 Angolans suffering from hunger, drought and disease.

4 June 1993	Bilateral talks take place in Windhoek between Foreign Minister Venacio de Moura and South Africa's 'Pik' Botha, said to focus on the issue of alleged South African mercenaries fighting in Angola and Angolans serving in the South African security forces. Trilateral talks are also held, including the Foreign Minister of Namibia, T.B. Gurirab, reviewing security in the region.
8 June 1993	Heavy shelling, by UNITA, in Cuito is reported.
17-20 June 1993	Reports include renewed fighting in Cuito, with heavy civilian casualties, the siege of Menongue, 250 km south of Cuito and the seizure by UNITA of the northern cities of Ucua and Quibaxi.
21 June 1993	Full diplomatic relations with the United States are formally established, and marked by talks between President dos Santos and visiting United States Assistant Secretary of State for African Affairs, George Moose.
5 July 1993	The new United Nations representative in Angola, Alioune Blondin Beye cites UN figures to emphasize that more than 1,000 people are dying daily from the direct and indirect consequences of the 'world's worst war'.
9 July 1993	Savimbi meets United Nations envoy, A. Blondin Beye, and expresses UNITA's readiness to resume peace talks and to facilitate humanitarian relief operations.
10 July 1993	The international observers to the peace process, representatives of Portugal, Russia and the USA meet in Moscow, call on UNITA to comply with the peace agreement and Security Council resolutions.
15 July 1993	The United Nations Security Council adopts Resolution 851, (1993) extending UNAVEM II's mandate until 15 September 1993 and demanding UNITA end all military action and accept the results of the 1992 elections.
16 July 1993	An aircraft operated by the United Nations World Food Programme is shot down by UNITA as it attempts to land at the northern city of M'Banza Congo. All relief flights are suspended until 19 July 1993, when operations to non-war zones only are resumed.
28 July 1993	Huito is reported to be falling to UNITA after a six-month siege and heavy casualties.
2 Aug. 1993	The Zairean government unilaterally closes two border posts on the Angolan border.
5 Aug. 1993	Angolan Armed Forces (FAA) claim its bombing campaign against Huambo has destroyed UNITA headquarters there.
9 Aug. 1993	The British government lifts its arms embargo, in force since independence in 1975. It accepts the assessment of the international observers that the Angolan government has a 'legitimate right of self-defence'.
11 Aug. 1993	Government troops rally and repel UNITA forces in Cuito despite heavy

daily shelling.

20 Aug. 1993	President dos Santos signs an agreement with the United Nations World Food Programme (WFP) to provide emergency food aid to war victims.

22 Aug. 1993   The FAA retakes Camenongue in Moxico Province and makes gains in Huila.

2 Sept. 1993   Sao Tomé and Príncipe emerges as brokers in the efforts to restart peace talks when United Nations envoy A.B. Beye flies there for talks with President Trovoada, a personal friend of Savimbi. The government however boycotts the talks.

15 Sept. 1993   The United Nations Security Council adopts Resolution 864, (1993) extending the mandate of UNAVEM II until 15 December 1993, gives UNITA a further ten days to comply with its demands, but provides for further sanctions including trade and travel restrictions.

19 Sept. 1993   Savimbi declares a unilateral ceasefire, and a suspension of the eight-month seige of Cuito. Ceasefire to take effect from 'zero hour' on 20 September 1993.

21 Sept. 1993   State radio reports continued and widespread fighting.

24 Sept. 1993   UNITA puts forward plans for negotiations, in talks with the UNAVEM II's military commander Chris Garuba, calling for both sides to disavow the Bicesse Peace Accord and the UN-monitored elections, and to establish a power-sharing government based on military occupation.

24 Sept. 1993   The government announces a five-point peace plan calling for UNITA's withdrawal from all areas occupied since the 1992 elections, a ceasefire, humanitarian aid and evacuation of wounded and foreigners, recognition of the 1991 Bicesse peace agreement and of validity currently in force in Angola.

25-26 Sept.1993   Deputy Foreign Minister J. Chiesti claims that UNITA have started new hostilities in Benguela Province.

26 Sept. 1993   The mandatory oil and arms embargo against UNITA, imposed by the United Nations, comes into effect.

29 Sept. 1993   At the end of a three-day visit to Angola President M. Trovoada of Sao Tome and Príncipe announces that President dos Santos has agreed to meet Savimbi and that he has received assurances from UNITA that it would recognize the election results.

6 Oct. 1993   UNITA announces it is prepared to recognize the results of the 1992 elections, although it maintains they were 'fraudulent', and further accepts the validity of the May 1991 Bicesse Accord, although it needs updating. It asserts its willingness to cooperate with the UN representative, A.B. Beye, and takes note of United Nations resolutions.

9 Oct. 1993   President dos Santos calls for a preliminary meeting between representatives of UNAVEM II, the troika of observers and UNITA to clarify UNITA's position.

21 Oct. 1993	Food aid from the United Nations World Food Programme (WFP) arrives in Cuito, besieged by UNITA for nine months in desperate need, with 99% building damaged by shelling and an estimated 25,000 people killed. Phillipe Borel, director of the WFP describes the situation as catastrophic.
25-27 Oct.1993	In response to the government's request, a series of meetings are held between UNITA, UNAVEM II and the international observers in Lusaka, Zambia.
1 Nov. 1993	The United Nations representative in Angola, A.B. Beye informs the UN Security Council that UNITA agrees to withdraw its forces to the UN-monitored confinement areas where they are being held awaiting demobilization. The Security Council accordingly agrees to postpone the implementation of further sanctions until 15 December 1993.
8 Nov. 1993	The United Nations Under-Secretary for Humanitarian Affairs makes an urgent appeal to all UN member states for contributions to the relief programme in Angola.
9 Nov. 1993	The Deputy Foreign Minister, J.B. Miranda, estimates the death toll from war related causes at 2,000 a day - a figure twice as high as the United Nations estimate.
9 Nov. 1993	Malawi and Angola establish diplomatic relations.
16 Nov. 1993	Direct talks between the government and UNITA resume in Lusaka. A five point agenda is agreed upon: a ceasefire, the mandate of UNAVEM II, the police, the armed forces, and national reconciliation.
23 Nov. 1993	The Angolan Armed Forces (FAA) General Staff report that UNITA have carried out attacks of various kinds in the areas of Menongue, Gabela, Caxito, Ucuma, Balombo, Mupa, Waku Kungo and Zenza do Itombe in the period 15-21 November.
24 Nov. 1993	Fresh fighting in Cuito forces the evacuation of Western aid workers.
10 Dec. 1993	Agreement on three fundamental issues on the cease fire are reached: the demobilization and confinement of UNITA troops, the handing over of UNITA weapons to the United Nations, and the integration of UNITA generals into the Angolan Armed Forces.
10 Dec. 1993	FNLA leader Holden Roberto calls for a national conference to enable other political parties and civil society organizations and churches to be represented in the peace process.
11 Dec. 1993	United States President Bill Clinton receives the credentials of Jose Patricio, the first Ambassador of Angola to the United States.
13 Dec. 1993	UNITA withdraws from the peace talks, but subsequently agrees to resume negotiations. Although no final settlement is concluded, significant progress is made in Lusaka on key issues.
15 Dec. 1993	In recognition of the success of the peace talks the United Nations Security Council extends UNAVEM II's mandate until 16 March 1994 and agrees to postpone the implementation of additional sanctions against UNITA.

22 Dec. 1993	The peace talks are adjourned until 5 January 1994.
6 Jan. 1994	Second round of peace talks in Lusaka begin. These focus on the formation and operation of a new national police force.
30 Jan. 1994	After protracted negotiations an agreement is reached providing for a police force to be formed under United Nations supervision, of 26,700 members, with UNITA providing 5,500 members. The Rapid Intervention Force is to remain in existence but with UNITA participation.
30 Jan. 1994	Government commanders are preparing for a new UNITA offensive in Bie province.
12 Feb. 1994	The government halts aid flights to UNITA-controlled areas of the country, in retaliation for an intense UNITA bombardment of the encircled town of Cuito, that halted aid to the devastated city.
17 Feb. 1994	Negotiations in the continuing second round of talks in Lusaka concentrate on the issue of national reconciliation. A document is signed agreeing to five fundamental principles, which are defined as the 'expression of the will of the people translated into the political wills of both the government and UNITA. Both sides reaffirm their acceptance of the 1992 election results.
28 Feb. 1994	The United Nations launch a revised appeal for US$179 million in emergency humanitarian aid for Angola. The UN agencies now identify 3,000,000 Angolans in need of assistance, compared with the 2,000,000 identified in June 1993.
14 Mar. 1994	President dos Santos reshuffles his Cabinet. Appointments: A. Craveiro - Finance Minister; J.A.L. Rocha - Territorial Administration; A. Malungo - Assistance and Social Reintegration; J. da R.S. de Castro - Youth and Sports; A. dos S. Franca - Special Adviser to the President.
16 Mar. 1994	The United Nations Security Council unanimously adopts Resolution 903 (1994) extending the mandate of UNAVEM II to 31 May 1994. The Council decides not to impose additional sanctions against UNITA, but warns the position will be reviewed in the context of progress in the negotiation process.
24-31 Mar.1994	Fourteen political parties, four of which are represented in Parliament, form a new political grouping, the Democratic Civilian Opposition, and meet to discuss peace and national reconstruction. A comprehensive declaration of its goals is issued.
28 Mar. 1994	Negotiations continue in Lusaka, mediated by United Nations Secretary-General's Special Representative A.B. Beye, with the main focus on national reconciliation and the role of UNITA in central and provincial government structures. The division of ministerial portfolios is in dispute and Beye decides to move to the last point on the agenda: the conclusion of the electoral process.
8 Apr. 1994	The fourteen Angolan opposition parties demand an end to media censorship and call for a free independent, pluralist and responsible press.

20 Apr. 1994	Agreement is reached in Lusaka on four general principles for the concluson of the second round of Presidential elections and to ensure that these will be free and fair. The United Nations will be responsible for monitoring, verifying and declaring whether conditions have been created to hold the elections.
29 Apr. 1994	Agreement is reached on eight specific points, including the decision that the date of the second round of elections will be set by the National Assembly, after a declaration by the United Nations that the stipulated conditions have been created.
3 May 1994	Talks resume in Lusaka between the government and UNITA.
3 May 1994	UNITA is reported to have informed the United Nations Representative, A.B. Beye, that it is calling off the talks in protest against continued government attacks on UNITA strongholds.
5 May 1994	Agreement on the second round of the Presidential elections is officially confirmed.
25 May 1994	A further round of talks resumes in Lusaka, focusing on the distribution of government posts for UNITA.
26 May 1994	Fighting erupts in the central city of Cuito, spreading to Cuanzo, Norte, Cuanza Sul and Benguela provinces.
26 May 1994	The government authorizes the resumption of UN relief flights to Huambo and Uige.
30 May 1994	A Presidential spokesman confirms the government has offered UNITA four Ministerial portfolios, covering health, tourism, geology and mines, and commerce. Seven Deputy Ministers for UNITA are also proposed.
31 May 1994	Humanitarian flights by the World Food Programme (WFP) to Malange and Huambo come under attack from both UNITA and government forces, despite assurances guaranteeing relief supplies.
8 June 1994	UNITA announces it will accept the government's power-sharing proposal submitted in May, now expanded to provide UNITA with 140 local government posts, seven Provincial Deputy Governorships, three Provincial Governorships, and six Ambassadorial positions.
11 June 1994	It is agreed that UNITA will occupy the seventy parliamentary seats it won in the 1992 elections. However, UNITA insists it be given the governorship of Huambo Province.
12 June 1994	The government states that its existing offer to UNITA is final and non-negotiable.
14 June 1994	The civilian death toll in Cuito, after intense fighting and shelling in early June, is said to have risen to 500.
14 June 1994	The escalation in fighting forces the UN World Food Programme (WFP) to order the cancellation of all humanitarian supplies to Angola.

14 June 1994	The OAU at its summit meeting in Tunis urges UNITA to adopt a positive attitude to the government's proposal.
18-19 June 1994	The United Nations Representative, A.B. Beye, holds a series of meetings with government officials and UNITA leaders in Luanda and Huambo.
28 June 1994	A document of national reconciliation is signed in the Zambian capital, Lusaka.
7 July 1994	South African President Nelson Mandela, responding to a request from the United Nations Secretary-General's Special Representative in Angola, A.B. Beye, hosts a meeting between the Presidents of Angola, Mozambique and Zaire. A Joint Defence and Security Commission is established, bringing together the Foreign and Defence Ministers of Angola and Zaire.
10 July 1994	The government rejects Zambia's proposals relating to Huambo, maintaining it has recently made sufficient concessions. Negotiations remain deadlocked.
18 July 1994	UNITA representatives meet South African Foreign Minister, Alfred Nzo, in Pretoria for 'open agenda' talks. The UNITA delegation includes Jardeo Muekalia, UNITA representative in Washington and Jorge Valentim, UNITA's chief negotiator at the Lusaka peace talks.
25 July 1994	UNITA President Jonas Savimbi formally accepts the proposition relating to Huambo that includes the appointment of a neutral governor assisted by a deputy from each side.
28 July 1994	Aid agencies warn of catastrophe unless aid routes are re-opened within two weeks.
3 Aug. 1994	The government insists that UNITA officials should join government institutions only after the movement's total demilitarization, a process expected to take nine months.
9 Aug. 1994	A procedural accord is signed covering eleven points and paving the way for talks on full reconciliation.
11 Aug. 1994	An agreement is concluded on security issues and on the mandate and composition of a new UN Angola Verification Mission, to be known as UNAVEM III.
18 Aug. 1994	The United States renews its oil and arms embargo on UNITA.
18 Aug. 1994	UNITA officially acknowledges it has lost control of the north-eastern diamond-mining town, Cafunfo.
30 Aug. 1994	The government and UNITA agree to accept a 7,000-man United Nations peacekeeping force. Details of the agreement are released at the summit meeting of the SADC in Gaborone.
5 Sept. 1994	At peace talks in Lusaka, UNITA agrees to approve a new mandate for UNAVEM III. The agreement is formally conveyed in a letter to the United Nations Security Council.
9 Sept. 1994	The United Nations Security-Council says it will not

strengthen the existing oil and arms embargo against UNITA by additional measures because UNITA has met the requirements set out in Resolution 932 (1994).

14 Oct. 1994   Government forces bomb UNITA positions in Luanda South province. UNITA forces capture the town of Chinibuande.

19 Oct. 1994   Reports that Savimbi has been injured in an assassination attempt, and flown to Sao Tomé for emergency medical treatment are denied by UNITA.

20 Oct. 1994   The government apologizes for an air attack on an Zairean army base on the Zaire River, citing pilot error.

22 Oct. 1994   United Nations Special Representative, A.B. Beye, confirms that Savimbi is 'alive and well'.

27 Oct. 1994   The United Nations Security Council unanimously adopts Resolution 952 (1994) renewing the mandate of UNAVEM II until 8 December 1994 and restoring its strength to the previous level of 350 military observers and 126 police observers.

31 Oct. 1994   The government and UNITA representatives initial a peace agreement in Lusaka. The protocol envisages a ceasefire within forty eight hours and UNITA's thorough integration into the national army and civil services.

1 Nov. 1994   Government forces seize the UNITA held town of Soyo, the north-west on-shore oil centre.

6 Nov. 1994   Government forces claim to have surrounded Huambo. United Nations envoy A.B. Beye flies to Luanda for an emergency meeting with dos Santos.

8 Nov. 1994   Government longrange artillary pound Huambo, UNITA's main stronghold, causing 'mass slaughter' of civilians.

10 Nov. 1994   Huambo falls, forcing Jonas Savimbi to leave, and the army consolidates its position around the city.

13 Nov. 1994   The government claims to have captured Mbanza Congo, capital of Zaire Province, from UNITA.

14 Nov. 1994   The signing of the peace agreement by Presidents dos Santos and Savimbi is postponed to 20 November. The United States Assistant Secretary of State for African Affairs, George Moose, urges both sides 'to exercise maximum restraint'.

15 Nov. 1994   A truce agreement is signed in Lusaka by General P. Neto, for the government, and General E. Manuvakola, Secretary-General of UNITA, to come into effect twenty four hours later.

16 Nov. 1994   The government orders a ceasefire. UNITA calls on the United Nations to send observers to monitor it.

17 Nov. 1994   Government forces recapture Uige, the last provincial capital still held by UNITA.

20 Nov. 1994	Despite the absence of Savimbi, the peace agreement is signed in Lusaka by dos Santos and Manuvakola and comes into effect on 22 November 1994.
23 Nov. 1994	Savimbi announces his support for the Lusaka Protocol and declares his willingness to meet dos Santos.
27 Nov. 1994	UNAVEM monitors are sent to Huambo where continued fighting is reported with each side continuing to accuse the other of violations of the ceasefire.
2 Dec. 1994	United Nations Special Envoy to Angola reports that the ceasefire is holding despite sporadic fighting.
5 Dec. 1994	A UNITA delegation is reported to have arrived in Luanda for a first meeting of the Joint Political and Military Commission to oversee the implementation of the Lusaka peace agreement.
8 Dec. 1994	The United Nations Security-Council unanimously adopts Resolution 966 (1994) extending UNAVEM II's mandate until 8 February 1995. Thereafter it is expected that an extended mission UNAVEM III will be deployed, dependent on the strict observance of the ceasefire.
14 Dec. 1994	UNITA claims government forces attacked Chivala, east of UNITA's base at Jamba, in a serious violation of the 22 November 1994 ceasefire.
28 Dec. 1994	United Nations envoy A.B. Beye arrives in Lusaka to try to set up a meeting between dos Santos and Savimbi and to explore the possibility of a summit of Southern African leaders in Luanda.
10 Jan. 1995	At a meeting in Chipipa, Huambo Province, between General A.C. Pena `Ben-Ben', UNITA Chief of General Staff and his government military counterpart Joao de Matos, both sides agreed to an immediate ceasefire, separation of troops in sensitive areas, release of prisoners and the creation of stable conditions.
11 Jan. 1995	Angolan Chief-of-Staff General J.B. de Matos acknowledges that `hundreds' of South African mercenaries are fighting both with and against government forces.
12 Jan. 1995	Deputy Defence Minister R. Sebastiao leaves for Portugal for a week's visit. Discussions with the Portuguese Defence Ministry will focus on training and the creation of better conditions for the Angolan Armed Forces (FAA).
18 Jan. 1995	United Nations special envoy A.B. Beye meets Jonas Savimbi in the central highlands. Agenda for discussion includes implementation of the Lusaka Peace Accord, the political and military situation and humanitarian aid for UNITA controlled areas.
23 Jan. 1995	President dos Santos appoints A. da S. Tomas as the new Minister of Finance.
7-12 Feb.1995	UNITA holds its eighth Congress in Bailundo, 330 miles south-east of Luanda. Gives its support to a meeting between Savimbi and dos Santos,

conditions are favourable, and agrees to adhere to the Lusaka Peace Accord.

8 Feb. 1995   The United Nations Security Council approves the composition of UNAVEM III, to consist of 8,000 personnel, 7,000 peacekeepers, 350 military observers, 260 police observers, together with international and local civil servants. The cost, $383m. for twelve months, is to be charged to member states. Foreign Minister V. da S. Mours pledges $64.7m on behalf of the Angolan government.

9 Feb. 1995   The Angolan Ambassador to Pretoria A. Rodrigues meets President Mandela and receives an offer of help in clearing an estimated 26m. land mines in the country.

13 Feb. 1995   The following UNITA appointments are announced:
General L. Gato - UNITA Secretary-General; A. Sakala - Secretary for Foreign Affairs; M. Dachala - Information Secretary; J. Valentim - Director of the Office Monitoring the Implementation of the Lusaka Accords; J. Jamba - Secretary for Culture; C. Celo - Justice and Human Rights.

17 Feb. 1995   Namibian President Sam Nujoma warns business people in the northeast Kavango region to stop illegal trade with Angola.

3 Mar. 1995   Responsibility for an attack in Zaire Province is claimed by the Armed Forces for the Liberation of Kongo (FALKO). Its Chief of Staff, S. Malando, describes its aim as securing the freedom of the region of Kongo, which includes Angola's Zaire, Uige and Bengo provinces.

5 Mar. 1995   In a report to the Security Council, United Nations Secretary-General Boutros Boutros-Ghali, criticizes both sides for their lack of goodwill in the implementation of the peace process and warns that unless commitment to this was demonstrated by 25 March, the arrival of the 7,000 UNAVEM III infantry personnel will be postponed.

22 Mar. 1995   In a minor government reshuffle President dos Santos appoints F.F. Muteka as Minister without Portfolio. He will head the government delegation to the Joint Commission.

24 Mar. 1995   The next United States Ambassador to Angola is to be Donald Steinberg, special assistant to President Clinton and senior Director for African Affairs at the United States National Security-Council.

28 Mar. 1995   At the close of a Joint Commission meeting, the United Nations Special Envoy to Angola, A.B. Beye announces that the first stage of troop disengagement has been completed. Preparations for the deployment of the peacekeepers are proceeding.

4 May 1995   Russia agrees to a Russian military contingent being placed at the disposal of the United Nations Control Commission in Angola.

6 May 1995   President dos Santos and Jonas Savimbi meet in Lusaka. Dos Santos claims that all conditions have been created for the `unhesitating' implementation of the Lusaka Protocol.

17 May 1995   During talks with President Nelson Mandela in Cape Town, Dr. Savimbi commits himself to cooperate to consolidate peace in whatever way is deemed necessary.

31 May 1995	UNAVEM III operation commander, Colonel Bento Soares, reports that the deployment of the logistical units has been postponed to allow for the re-opening of Angola's fifteen main roads. The Uruguayan units will spearhead the operation of disarming and escorting guerrillas to internment camps in early June.
15-24 June 1995	Dr. Savimbi tours Côte d'Ivoire, Benin, Gabon, Congo and Zaire and is widely quoted as saying he will be willing to accept the post of Vice-President.
17 June 1995	It is officially confirmed that the MPLA has recommended that the Constitution be revised to include two Vice-Presidents and that UNITA leader Jonas Savimbi be invited to occupy one of the posts.
18 June 1995	Franco van Dunem, currently speaker of the National Assembly, is named as the MPLA Vice-President.
20 June 1995	UNITA receives the official proposal to appoint Savimbi as Vice-President.
11 July 1995	A. dos S. Franca `Ndalu', hitherto Special Adviser to the President, is appointed Ambassador to the United States.
14-15 July 1995	United Nations Secretary-General Boutros Boutros-Ghali visits Angola to assess the prospects for peace. He declares there is political will on both sides to reinforce the national reconciliation and peace processsss. The remaining contingents of peace-keepers should be in position by the end of August.
16 July 1995	Savimbi claims he has not received an official offer of the post of Vice-President.
22 July 1995	Colonel General Pedro Maria Tonha `Pedalo', Minister of Defence since 1980, dies in London. No replacement is named.
4 Aug. 1995	United Nations Special Representative A.B. Beye reports that conditions are being created for the confinement of UNITA troops with the construction of 500 barracks.
7 Aug. 1995	The United Nations Security Council unanimously adopts Resolution 1008 (1995) extending UNAVEM III's mandate until 8 February 1996 while expressing concern at the slow pace of implementation of the Lusaka Protocol.
10 Aug. 1995	Presidents dos Santos and Savimbi meet in Franceville, Gabon. Savimbi agrees to serve as one of the two Vice-Presidents but insists that a formal offer be extended to UNITA, rather than to him personally. The government insists Savimbi will only be able to take up his post after his troops have been disarmed.
15 Aug. 1995	The Front for the Liberation of Cabinda-Armed Forces of Cabinda (FLEC-FAC) wants Cabinda to become a Portuguese protectorate, after which discussions on transition to independence could take place.
18 Aug. 1995	Rebellion in the Cabinda enclave escalates. The FLEC-Renovada faction, headed by José Tiburcio, infiltrates Cabinda city and attacks the airport.

31 Aug. 1995	Five political parties combine to form the Patriotic Front, standing for political realism, democracy and territorial integrity. Member parties are: the Social Democratic Party of Angola, the Angolan Liberal Party, the Angolan Liberal Democratic Party, the National Salvation Patriotic Renewal Party, and the Democratic Progressive Party of Angola.
31 Aug. 1995	UNAVEM III report that ceasefire violations have been reduced by half.
1 Sept. 1995	The government and UNITA issue a joint declaration on the free movement of people and goods, an expansion of the 1994 Lusaka Protocol. Unauthorized checkpoints are to be removed.
21 Sept. 1995	The Joint Commission voices concern over increasing ceasefire violation.
22 Sept. 1995	Savimbi tells Zairean Radio that he has accepted the position of Vice-President but will only take it up when the demobilization of the government's Armed Forces for the Liberation of Angola (FALA) is complete, probably in February 1996.
24 Sept. 1995	Dos Santos and Savimbi meet again in Brussels, their third meeting in three months.
25-26 Sept. 1995	At a donors' conference in Brussels, hosted by the European Commission, dos Santos and Savimbi together plead for international financial support to rebuild the shattered Angolan economy. Pledges totalling US$1 billion in aid and reconstruction are made.
26 Sept. 1995	A ceasefire between the government and the Front for the Liberation of the Cabinda Enclave - Renewal (FLEC-Renewal) comes into effect.
3 Oct. 1995	President dos Santos expresses concern at the slow pace of the peace process highlighting delays in troop confinement, in the deployment of UNAVEM III and in mine clearing.
11 Oct. 1995	General A.C. Pena 'Ben-Ben', UNITA Chief of General Staff, callsfor a more dynamic approach to troop confinement and offers the use of his troops for camp construction.
12 Oct. 1995	The UN Security Council expresses concern over delays in the formation of the new national army, the 'repatriation' of mercenaries and the quartering of UNITA.
13 Oct. 1995	While on a tour through Southern Africa capitals, Jonas Savimbi meets President Nelson Mandela and holds substantial discussions with Thabo Mbeki. A principal topic of concern is the presence and role in Angola of South African mercenaries from the Pretoria based Executive Outcomes (EO) company.
18 Nov. 1995	The government and the Cabinda Democratic Front (CDF) hold talks in Congo on establishing a military truce.
20 Nov. 1995	The confinement of UNITA troops begins in Vita Nova, Huambo Province.
29 Nov.- 4 Dec. 1995	Government troops attack and capture towns in northern Zaire Province.

27 Dec. 1995	UNITA leaders assure observers in Bailundo that the Lusaka Protocol will be implemented.
17-18 Jan.1996	The fifteenth annual UNITA conference, attended by 700 delegates, is held in Ballundo. Discusses the issue of troop confinement, the implementation of the Lusaka Accords and UNITA's participation in the Government of National Unity.
mid Feb. 1996	A technical group to coordinate mine sweeping operations is established. The group includes the National Institute for the Removal of Obstacles and Explosive Devices, as well as some NGOs.
16 Feb. 1996	It is reported that 14,000 UNITA soldiers are confined in various centres under the control of UNAVEM III. UNITA had promised to demobilize 16,500 soldiers before 8 February, but delayed the operation. The UN Security Council expressed its impatience with the delay by renewing the mandate of UNAVEM for only three instead of six months.
28 Feb. 1996	Daniel Chipenda, a key player in the liberation struggle and founder member of the MPLA dies.
Mar. 1996	Discussions are held between Savimbi and various opposition groups in order to establish alliances in the future GNU.
1 Mar. 1996	A summit meeting between President Dos Santos and Jonas Savimbi takes place in Gabon. The two men agree to form a Government of National Unity within four months, and discuss military demobilization.
1 Mar. 1996	Political leaders agree at a summit meeting to form a Government of National Unity in June. Jonas Savimbi is offered the post of Vice-President. They also discuss the formation of the unified armed forces.
4 Mar. 1996	Jonas Savimbi, UNITA leader, holds talks with President Mandela in Togo.
7 Mar. 1996	At the invitation of President dos Santos, Namibian President Nujoma visits Angola to discuss bilateral cooperation and security along the Angolan-Namibian border.
7 Mar. 1996	The Angolan Republican Conservative Party, led by Martinho Mateus is established.
Apr. 1996	Russia expresses concern about the pace of the peace process as it has not progressed as predicted.
9 Apr. 1996	A new political party is registered by the Supreme Court - the United Front for the Salvation of Angola, led by Jose Augusto da Silva Coelho.
10 Apr. 1996	Army Chief Joao de Matos states that an operation is to be staged to round up armed rebels after an attack in Benguela on a UN vehicle in which two UN soldiers and an Oxfam worker were killed. Tension remains high in the diamond-rich province of Lunda where diamond traffickers servicing UNITA's internal economy are on the increase.
10 Apr. 1996	The government and the Cabinda-based Front for the Liberation of the Cabinda Enclave (FLEC) Renewal agree to end hostilities and work out

mechanisms towards a peace plan. The meeting in Windhoek is facilitated by the Namibian government.

15 May 1996
The government and the Front for the Liberation of the Cabinda Enclave - Cabinda Armed Forces (FLEC-FAC) sign a cease-fire agreement.

22 May 1996
Cabindan separatists state that forty-one people, mostly civilians, have been killed in clashes with government troops. This occured shortly after a ceasefire agreement had been negotiated between the government and FLEC-FAC.

24 May 1996
The Joint Ceasefire Commission approves a plan to integrate government and UNITA armies into a single force. The process is to commence on 25 May at four of the twelve UN-supervised camps where UNITA troops have been reporting for demobilization. However, the government is disappointed at the slow pace of disarming and integrating UNITA guerrillas; The United Nations has also accused UNITA of dragging its feet. Since November, fewer than 23,000 of the 63,000 UNITA troops have moved to the camps.

28 May 1996
UNITA radio reports that the Angolan Armed Forces are violating the Lusaka Protocol by not returning to barracks.

early June 1996
The Social Renewal Party, at its second ordinary meeting, relieves A.J. Muachicungo from his post as party leader. The party states that its ideological foundation should be centre-left.

3 June 1996
President Dos Santos dismisses his cabinet and replaces Prime Minister Moco by Fernando Jose da Franca van Dunem. He also bans foreign exchange dealings in an effort to solve the economic crisis.

6 June 1996
President Mandela's state visit to Angola is postponed for the second time. The reason given is that it would be inconsiderate to impose a state visit on his Angolan counterpart, who is grappling with a transition in government.

7 June 1996
A new cabinet is appointed. Only seven former ministers have lost their portfolios. A new Speaker is also elected - Roberto de Almeida, on 13 June.

18 June 1996
Both the government and UNITA have reached the targets set for reducing their armed forces - a quarter of the forces have been demobilized. However, there have been consistent reports that elite forces from both sides have been kept out of the process, together with heavy arms.

19 June 1996
According to the government, the renewed attacks on FAA troops by FLEC-FAC took place in Cabinda.

20 June 1996
UNITA radio reports that government troops are continually violating the ceasefire agreement. Two days later it claims that South African mercenaries were spotted at the Cabindan Gulf Oil Company's Malongo Base.

2 July 1996
UNITA and the government agree to preserve the post of Prime Minister in the future Government of National Unity, without prejudice to the creation of two vice-presidencies.

11 July 1996
The UN Security Council extends its peace-keeping operations in Angola for three months, but states that the implementation of the Peace Accords is

behind schedule. The Council especially criticized UNITA's lack of progress in reducing its armed forces.

25 July 1996   Hundreds of human bodies are discovered in Soyo, Zaire Province during a mine-clearing excercise. Soyo was occupied by UNITA in 1993 and recaptured by government forces in 1994. The National Assembly institutes an inquiry into the matter. Many women and children seem to have been among the victims. UNITA declines to comment.

26 July 1996   The government issues a communique in which it re-affirms its commitment to national reconciliation and peace. It states that the Soyo discovery should not be seen as an isolated incident - thousands of citizens lost their lives in the strife. The government will establish a working commission to identify the victims.

30 July 1996   Talks between the government and FLEC-FAC on a ceasefire break down in Libreville, Gabon. The government states that it is prepared to resume discussions once the Cabinda faction shows some goodwill.

early Aug.1996 Angola and Portugal sign two protocols: the first provides for the abolition of bilateral diplomatic service and special entry visas; the second commits some $1m for the construction of schools in Angola.

12 Aug. 1996   A programme to repatriate illegal immigrants commences. The action will continue for about three months, as an estimated 6,000 people will be rounded up and returned to their countries of origin. Nationals from Mauritius, Senegal, Mali, Gambia and other African countries are involved.

16 Aug. 1996   UNITA fails to meet the deadline to have all its 62,500 troops demobilized. It blames insufficient funding for the delay. On the same day, the government approved a $65m. financial aid package to facilitate the return of 100,000 soldiers from both sides to civilian life.

25 Aug. 1996   It is reported that UNITA has decided at its congress that it will join the coalition government, but will not nominate Jonas Savimbi for the Vice-President's post, as this will be mainly ceremonial.

end Aug. 1996   Talks between the government and UNITA on a revision of the constitution collapse, as the two sides fail to agree on a juridical framework to accommodate UNITA in a Government of National Unity.

Sept. 1996   The demobilization of UNITA troops ends. Hereafter youths under the age of eighteen are to be demobilized. However, concerns are expressed over desertions, the small amounts of heavy artillery which have been handed over and the small number of senior officers sent by UNITA to join the general staff of the new defence force.

Oct. 1996   The government calls on Southern African countries to exert pressure on UNITA to implement the Lusaka Peace Protocol. Angolans continue to flee into neighbouring states, and the government claims that UNITA troops are hiding in Cabinda. Savimbi refuses to go to Luanda, as he claims that his safety cannot be guaranteed.

Oct. 1996   US Secretary of State Warren Christopher fails to make progress in the peace process when he visits Angola. He states that the US will not tolerate any resumption of conflict by UNITA. He places the onus firmly on Savimbi, but also criticizes the government for not confining to quarters a feared paramilitary force known as the Rapid Intervention Police.

5 Oct. 1996   Angola and Portugal sign a defence agreement on the establishment of joint military industries. UNITA radio criticizes this pact, as Portugal, a peace process observer, should not unbalance the implementation of the Lusaka Accord by signing this treaty.

9 Nov. 1996   UNITA releases a list of names of officials who are to participate in the Government of National Unity and Reconciliation.

18 Nov. 1996   Spain states that it will send a technical team to Angola to train elite units of the security forces.

Dec. 1996   It is reported that UNITA deputies will join the National Assembly on 17 January 1997 and the new Government of National Unity will be established on 23 January, which will focus on the reconstruction of infrastructure in the war-ravaged country.

11 Dec. 1996   The UN Security Council agrees a final extention of UNAVEM III until 28 February 1997 and the resumption in the same month of its progressive withdrawal. Obstacles to a unified government, apart from problems regarding demobilization, are UNITA's claims of government efforts to exert control over areas formerly held by UNITA, such as Kwanza Norte Province. Its main concern is to maintain control over the northern provinces bordering Zaire, which constitute the mainstay of UNITA's economy.

Jan. 1997   Jonas Savimbi meets South African President Mandela and Deputy President Mbeki in Umtata (Eastern Cape). They discuss Savimbi's future role in the Angolan government. Savimbi seems to have accepted President Mandela's advice to enter the government not as Vice-President, but rather as an adviser. This is followed by a visit to Luanda of Deputy President Mbeki and Foreign Minister Alfred Nzo who attempt to pressurize for the installation of the new unity government.

11 Jan. 1997   It is reported that thirteen political parties have left the Civilian Opposition Parties group, to establish a coalition under the name of CUFA (Congregation of the Union of Angola's Leading Forces). CUFA intends to support President Dos Santos in the second round of presidential elections provided for in the Lusaka Protocol. Joao Domingos Francisco is the chairman of CUFA.

23 Jan. 1997   The government and UNITA decide to postpone the formation of the Government of National Unity until after 12 February, when the UNITA members of the National Assembly, elected in 1992, are due to arrive in Luanda.

25 Jan. 1997   The date accepted for the installation of the new unity government passed without any developments. Behind the scenes, meetings take place but without any visible results.

Feb. 1997   Guerrillas fighting for the oil-rich enclave of Cabinda warn that they will target Western companies such as Chevron, Elf, Agip and Ranger Oil if the latter refuse to withdraw.

Feb. 1997   The swearing in of the new unity government is delayed, probably until March, due to UNITA's demand to discuss the programme of action of the Government of National Unity and Reconciliation (GURN) before the inauguration. Savimbi has dropped his demand to be appointed as the President's Chief Adviser, but he wants to be recognized as the head of the main opposition party.

11 Feb. 1997   The UN Secretary-General Kofi Annan announces that the UN Angola Verification Mission (UNAVEM III) will be extended for two months after February if a Government of National Unity has been established by the end of February; should this not be the case, UNAVEM III will be withdrawn by the end of March 1997.

Mar. 1997   Russian field engineers will clear landmines in Angola, according to an agreement concluded on humanitarian assistance between Russia and Norway.

1 Mar. 1997   Rebels of the Renewed Cabinda Enclave Liberation Front claim that they have killed forty-two Angolan soldiers in combat. It is believed that UNITA troops are involved in supporting the beleaguered Zairean President Mobutu Sese Seko.

14 Mar. 1997   The Council of Ministers meet in Luanda, chaired by President dos Santos. New ministries are created and old ones abolished. UNITA's parliamentary deputees arrive but insist that they will not join the government until its draft programme has been discussed. UN Secretary General urges UNITA to commit themselves to the implementation of the Lusaka Protocol.

11 Apr. 1997   The Government of National Unity and Reconciliation is sworn in at a ceremony attended by thirteen foreign heads of state. However, Jonas Savimbi boycotts the occasion, as he fears for his safety in Luanda. Savimbi is given a special role as leader of the opposition, entitling him to question the President on political matters, and several perks, such as a salary, a house in Luanda and bodyguards. UNITA has four ministers and seven deputy ministers in the Cabinet.

mid Apr. 1997   The demobilization of an estimated 100,000 troops from both the MPLA and UNITA armies commences. About 28,000 of UNITA's 63,000 strong army are to be absorbed into the unified armed forces.

24 May 1997   The first national conference of the National Democratic Party of Angola (PNDA) ends with the election of a new Central Committee and Political Bureau. Some members are expelled for violation of the party statute.

June 1997   Fighting breaks out in the diamond rich province of Lunda Norte between UNITA and government forces. Both the United Nations and the ruling MPLA are playing down the intensity of the conflict. President dos Santos accepts an offer of talks by Jonas Savimbi to discuss the matter.

BOTSWANA

30 Sept. 1966   Independence is declared. A republican government, with a president elected by the legislature, is instituted.

30 Sept. 1966	Signs agreement with the United Nations Development Programme for the application of the special fund's projects in Botswana.
30 Sept. 1966	Signs public officers agreement with Great Britain.
30 Sept. 1966	Signs multilateral agreement with the United Nations, the International Labour Organisation, the Food and Agriculture Organisation, UNESCO, International Civil Aviation Organisation, International Atomic Energy Agency and the Universal Postal Union.
30 Sept. 1966	Signs agreement with Great Britain on the status of the armed forces of the United Kingdom in Botswana.
30 Sept. 1966	Signs multilateral declaration of acceptance of the obligations found in the Charter of the United Nations.
Oct. 1966	About fifty United States Peace Corps voluntary workers arrive to assist mainly in the fields of teaching and agriculture.
17 Oct. 1966	Botswana is admitted as the 120th member of the United Nations.
25 Oct. 1966	Eleven South African and Rhodesian refugees deported by Botswana arrive in Zambia.
28 Nov. 1966	The first High Commissioner to Zambia, Richard Mannathoko presents his credentials.
15 Dec. 1966	Z.K. Matthews presents his ambassadorial credentials to President Johnson of the United States.
18 Dec. 1966	The South African government lodges a protest with Botswana over the broadcasting of anti-South African programmes.
3 Jan. 1967	Signs multilateral convention on road traffic.
1 Feb. 1967	A strike by 956 meat workers in Lobatsi over salaries costs the Meat Commission approximately 20,000 pounds sterling per day.
7 Feb. 1967	Signs an agreement with Great Britain whereby British military personnel have the right to freely enter or leave Botswana.
31 Mar. 1967	A government spokesman says the activities of some 200 South African political refugees in Botswana will be curbed.
1 Apr. 1967	British government agrees to provide up to 13 million pounds stirling of budgetary and development aid.
15 Apr. 1967	Botswana and Zambia Cabinet ministers issue a joint statement refusing rights to use their countries as springboards for hostilities against neighbouring states.
July 1967	The United People's Party is formed.
5-6 July 1967	Sir Seretse Khama pays a state visit to Malawi during its independence

celebrations. Makes the keynote speech at the banquet outlining Botswana's foreign policy towards Africa.

25 July 1967	Chiefs warned by Minister of Home Affairs, A. Dambe, that they would be liable for prosecution should they sign false papers enabling aliens to obtain passports.
26 July 1967	House of Chiefs introduces a motion to repeal African Court Proclamation no. 19 of 1961 stating that no African Court shall have jurisdiction to try any case wherein the witness is a non-African.
26 July 1967	Opposition is voiced against the Bushmen Protection Bill as dissenters claim that Bushmen will never be assimilated should the Bill be passed.
3-8 Aug. 1967	Sir Seretse Khama pays an official visit to Zambia.
30 Aug. 1967	British soldiers are withdrawn and Botswana police assume responsibility for guarding the Francistown relay-station.
18 Sept. 1967	At the OAU meeting in Kinshasa, Minister of State M. Nuvako persuasively argues that his country's sovereignty shall not be violated by `freedom fighters'.
12 Oct. 1967	Signs agreement with the United Nations and its specialized agencies.
12 Oct. 1967	Revises standard agreement with the United Nations Development Programme (Special Fund).
19 Oct. 1967	R.N. Mannthoko presents his ambassadorial credentials to Emperor Haile Selassie of Ethiopia.
30 Oct. 1967	The High Commissioner to Kenya, R.N. Mannathoko presents his credentials to President Kenyatta.
22 Nov. 1967	An attempt is discovered to sabotage the President's aeroplane.
1 Dec. 1967	The repatriation of Zambian citizens from Botswana is arranged.
1 Dec. 1967	Amends Public Officer's Agreement with Great Britain.
5 Jan. 1968	Signs multilateral treaty banning nuclear weapon tests in the atmosphere.
12 Jan. 1968	Signs multilateral agreement concerning Universal Postal Convention.
20 Mar. 1968	Tells the United Nations Secretary, U Thant, that the use of force to bring down the Rhodesian government would not be supported.
29 Mar. 1968	Signs multilateral agreement on the treatment of prisoners of war.
29 Mar. 1968	Signs multilateral agreement on the amelioration of the condition of the wounded, sick, shipwrecked members of armed forces at sea.
29 Mar. 1968	Signs multilateral agreement on the amelioration of the conditions of the wounded, sick in armed forces in the field.

21 May 1968	President Kenneth Kaunda arrives on a four-day visit. He promises aid in the form of 5000 bags of maize and to allocate places in Zambian institutions for trainees and students.
12 June 1968	Signs a multilateral agreement on the amendment to Article 109 of the Charter of the United Nations.
27 June 1968	A joint report on the Botswana-South Africa border is signed, based on the London Convention of 1884. Unmarked sections are to be fenced.
2 July 1968	Signs multilateral agreement on the permanent control of outbreak areas of red locust.
24 July 1968	Signs agreement with the International Development Association.
24 July 1968	Signs multilateral agreement with the International Monetary Fund.
24 July 1968	Signs multilateral agreement with the International Bank for Reconstruction and Development.
16 Sept. 1968	Signs multilateral convention abolishing requirement of legalization of foreign public documents.
9 Oct. 1968	Signs an agreement with Great Britain for the provision of personnel to assist in the training of the police force.
18 Nov. 1968	Signs agreement on the conflicts of laws relating to the form of testamentary dispositions.
Jan. 1969	United Nations Development Programme experts complete a report on the Shashi complex.
6 Jan. 1969	Signs multilateral agreement on the status of refugees.
7-15 Jan.1969	The Commonwealth Prime Ministers' Conference in London recognizes the particular problems encountered by Botswana as a result of the Rhodesian crisis.
7-15 Jan.1969	Sir Seretse Khama, President, calls at the London Conference of Commonwealth Prime Ministers for direct rule by Britain and the withdrawal of the 'Fearless' proposal for Rhodesian independence.
10 Feb. 1969	Signs multilateral agreement on the service of judicial and extrajudicial documents in civil/commercial matters.
25 Feb. 1969	Signs multilateral convention relating to the status of stateless persons.
27 Feb. 1969	Signs an extradition agreement with South Africa.
Apr. 1969	Legislation is passed aimed at bringing trade unions under tighter control.
1 Apr. 1969	Signs multilateral agreement on Commonwealth telegraphs.
11 Apr. 1969	Signs multilateral agreement on diplomatic relations.

18 Apr. 1969	Signs multilateral agreement on the rescue of astronauts, the return of astronauts.
28 Apr. 1969	Signs multilateral treaty on non-proliferation of nuclear weapons.
23 May 1969	Sir Seretse Khama reacts to the Rhodesian constitutional proposals.
24 May 1969	Signs basic agreement with the United Nations Children's Fund.
June 1969	Bathoen Gaseitsiwe resigns as chief of the Ngwaketse and becomes leader of a new opposition grouping, the Botswana National Front.
8 July 1969	Signs an agreement with Great Britain.
15 July 1969	Signs multilateral agreement with the World Food Programme.
25 July 1969	Signs a multilateral agreement on the international regulations of the the World Health Organisation.
Aug. 1969	Discrimination penalties are announced for anyone transgressing on grounds of race, colour, nationality or creed.
Aug. 1969	President Khama denies that Botswana has been used by South Africa to ferry arms to Biafra. South Africa's Defence Minister, P.W. Botha also denies the allegation.
22 Aug. 1969	The President announces that parliament will be dissolved the following day. This signifies that elections will be held within five months according to the Constitution's stipulations.
1 Sept. 1969	Signs agreement concerning the guarantee by Great Britain and the maintenance of reserves in sterling by Botswana.
10 Sept. 1969	Signs OAU convention governing specific aspects of refugee problems.
24 Sept. 1969	Sir Seretse Khama addresses the United Nations General Assembly and defines his Southern Africa policy.
29 Sept. 1969	Certain amendments are made to the constitution relating to citizenship.
18 Oct. 1969	General election, announced by Sir Seretse Khama on 29 August, takes place with a victory for the Botswana Democratic party.
22 Oct. 1969	Sir Seretse Khama is sworn in for a second term of presidency and announces his new Cabinet. Creates a new ministry, Home Affairs, Health and Labour.
17 Nov. 1969	President Khama opens Parliament and in his speech refers to instability of the Southern Africa region engendered by policies of the Smith regime.
11 Dec. 1969	Signs Customs Union Agreement with South Africa, Lesotho and Swaziland.
14 Jan. 1970	Signs multilateral declaration recognising as compulsory the jurisdiction of International Court of Justice in conformity with article 26.

Mar. 1970   Theneas Makepe presents his ambassadorial credentials to Emperor Haile Selassie of Ethiopia.

Mar. 1970   The United States Agency for International Development announces support for a project to link Livingstone in Zambia to Francistown in Botswana.

2 Mar. 1970   Czechoslovakia's first ambassador to Botswana, Malos Vojta, presents his credentials.

28 Mar. 1970   President Khama addresses the Botswana Democratic Party annual conference at Molepolole particularly on the issue of instability in the region.

9 Apr. 1970   Signs agreement with Great Britain for the avoidance of double taxation and the prevention of fiscal evasion with respect to taxes and income.

9 Apr. 1970   Signs multilateral memorandum of understanding to amend Customs Union agreement dated 11 December 1969.

18 Apr. 1970   The Botswana government declares that it has no reason to change the existing view that Botswana and Zambia have a common border, despite the South African denial.

16 June 1970   On the death of the Minister of Agriculture, T. Tsheko, President Seretse Khama appoints J.G. Haskins to the portfolio whilst retaining the Ministry of Finance.

July 1970   Kenyan Vice-President pays an official visit to Botswana and opens the Agricultural Show and Trade Fair.

Aug. 1970   B.K.T. Chiepe presents her ambassadorial credentials to the Federal Republic of Germany.

Aug. 1970   The South African government rejects Botswana's claim that it has a common border with Zambia.

Aug. 1970   The United States Secretary of State announces that his government is willing to offer financial aid for the construction of a road from Botswana to Zambia.

24-30 Aug. 1970   The Botswana People's Party holds its national convention and is critical of government policies pertaining to the citizenship laws, teacher recruitment, racial discrimination, Tribal Land Act and the like.

Sept. 1970   Yugoslavia and Botswana decide to establish ambassadorial relations.

18 Sept. 1970   Gaoitwe Chiepe presents her ambassadorial credentials to President Pompidou of France.

30 Sept. 1970   Botswana reiterates its opposition to the proposed British arms sales to South Africa.

13 Nov. 1970	Sir Seretse Khama addresses the Foreign Policy Society in Copenhagen and says South African investment will be accepted provided it does not compromise any development projects.
14 Nov. 1970	Signs agreement with Denmark on technical cooperation.
Dec. 1970	Soviet (non-resident) ambassador, D.Z. Belokolos presents his credentials to President Khama.
Dec. 1970	Swedish ambassador to South Africa, Baron Carl Rappe becomes ambassador to Botswana and presents his credentials to President Khama.
30 Dec. 1970	Signs agreement with Great Britain concerning officers designated by Great Britain for service in Botswana.
10 Feb. 1971	Signs development credit agreement with the International Development Association on the Lobatsi Water Supply Project.
13-20 Feb. 1971	At the Commonwealth Conference of Heads of State in Singapore, Sir Seretse Khama talks about the general position of Southern Africa and condemns Britain's sales of arms to 'apartheid' South Africa.
Mar. 1971	First Botswana High Commissioner to Nigeria, Miss G.K.T. Chiepe presents her credentials to General Gowon.
8 Mar. 1971	Botswana High Commissioner to Malawi, Phineas Makepe, presents his credentials to President Banda.
14 May 1971	Signs an agreement relating to the Peace Corps with the United States.
June 1971	Japanese Ambassador to Zambia, Mr. Matsuo, also becomes Ambassador to Botswana.
July 1971	Swazi Prime Minister, Prince Makihosini, concludes a state visit to Botswana.
1 July 1971	De Beers begins its diamond mining operations at Orapa.
1 Sept. 1971	Simon Hirschfield, Botswana's first African Commissioner of Police, takes office.
14 Sept. 1971	Signs agreement with Great Britain on the maintenance of reserves of sterling by Botswana.
Oct. 1971	P.L. Udo arrives in Botswana to establish the Nigerian High Commission.
20 Dec. 1971	Signs multilateral agreement on the recognition and enforcement of foreign arbitral awards.
17 Jan. 1972	Tanzania's High Commissioner in Zambia is accredited to Botswana.
4 Feb. 1972	The first Nigerian to be seconded to Botswana after the 1971 technical agreement between the two countries, T. Aguda assumes position of Chief Justice.

17 Feb. 1972	High Commissioner, Emmanuel Onlumetse, presents his credentials to President Kenyatta of Kenya.
31 Mar. 1972	Signs agreement with the African Development Bank.
10 Apr. 1972	Signs multilateral convention on the prohibition of development, production and stockpiling of bacteriological and toxic weapons.
11-12 Apr. 1972	Presidents Kaunda and Khama meet in Livingstone and issue a communiqué after their wide-ranging talks.
17 Apr. 1972	High Commissioner to Malawi, Mr. Ontumetse presents his credentials to President Banda of Malawi.
27 Apr. 1972	Signs a multilateral financing agreement with the International Development Association and Sweden on the Second Road Project.
May 1972	E.M. Ontammentse presents his ambassadorial credentials to Emperor Haile Selaisse.
30 June 1972	Signs multilateral agreement with the International Development Association and Sweden on the Livestock Project.
July 1972	Amos Dambe presents his ambassadorial credentials to President Nixon.
24 Aug. 1972	Signs boundary treaty with South Africa.
12 Oct. 1972	Signs Convention for the Suppression of Unlawful Acts against the Safety of Civil Aviation.
12 Nov. 1972	Signs multilateral agreement prohibiting the use of nuclear weapons and other weapons of mass destruction and their emplacement on the sea bed, ocean floor and in subsoil thereof.
4 Dec. 1972	The Embassy established by Israel in Swaziland is also responsible for Botswana.
8 Dec. 1972	Signs agreement with Denmark on a government loan.
24 Dec. 1972	Signs agreement with South Africa on the establishment of a Botswana Government Labour Representative Office in South Africa.
1973	Minor Cabinet changes occurred during the year under review: D.K. Kwelagobe becomes Minister of Commerce and Industry; K.P. Morake becomes Minister of Local Government and Lands; Water Affairs is added to Mineral Resources and creates a new ministry under the responsibility of M.K. Segoko; E.M.K. Kgabo takes over the new Ministry of Information and Broadcasting.
12 Feb. 1973	Signs agreement with the United Nations on the amendments to the United Nations Charter.
3 Mar 1973	Signs multilateral treaty on international trade in endangered species of wild fauna and flora.

30 Mar 1973	Signs a financial agreement with the Commonwealth Telecommunications Organisation.
Apr. 1973	British High Commissioner, Eleanor Emery is appointed.
23 May 1973	Application by Botswana of the International Health regulations adopted by the twenty-second World Health Assembly.
28 Aug. 1973	Sir Seretse Khama visits Tanzania.
3 Sept. 1973	President's Khama and Nyerere issue a joint communiqué at the end of Khama's visit and express their support for the Southern African liberation struggle.
11 Sept. 1973	Two of the eleven mine workers shot dead on the Carletonville mine are from Botswana.
9 Oct. 1973	Botswana and Lesotho issue a joint communiqué at the end of Sir Seretse Khama's visit and affirm their support for non-racialism and democracy.
Nov. 1973	Botswana reserves its stance at the OAU Council of Ministers emergency meeting on the call to extend their oil embargo to South Africa.
12 Nov. 1973	The heads of government of Botswana, Lesotho and Swaziland meet at their first summit meeting.
13 Nov. 1973	Botswana breaks relations with Israel.
Feb.- Apr.1974	Faction fighting at the Western Deep Levels gold mine in South Africa cause 400 Botswana mine workers to return home.
1 Feb. 1974	Abraham Tiro, one of the student founders of the South African Students' Organization is killed by a letter bomb whilst taking refuge in Botswana.
13 Feb. 1974	The South African government rejects allegations of their involvement in the death of Abraham Tiro and protests to both the United Nations and Botswana.
Mar. 1974	Botswana requests the closure of the Republic of China's embassy as the government decides to recognize the People's Republic of China.
Mar. 1974	Thirty two political refugees cross into Rhodesia from Botswana and are arrested for illegal entry. They are not impelled to leave Botswana.
5 Mar. 1974	Signs multilateral agreement on the service abroad of judicial and extra judicial documents in civil or commercial matters.
10 Mar. 1974	Four refugees from Rhodesia are allegedly kidnapped in Francistown.
11 Mar. 1974	Signs multilateral convention on international liability for damage caused by space objects.
15 Mar. 1974	Signs loan agreement with the International Bank for Reconstruction and Development.

Apr. 1974	A South African political exile, Godfrey Beck and his family are deported back to South Africa for security reasons.
22 Apr. 1974	Signs agreement with Benelux countries on the abolition of visas.
9 May 1974	Signs a development credit agreement with the International Development Association.
27 June 1974	Signs guarantee agreement with the International Bank for Reconstruction and Development.
8 July 1974	Border incident occurs involving eight white South Africans held for five hours.
17 July 1974	Signs loan agreement with the International Bank for Reconstruction and Development.
Aug. 1974	Botswana government withdraws from the two-year old negotiations with South Africa, Lesotho and Swaziland over a joint monetary agreement. This occured shortly before the final agreement was reached.
6 Sept. 1974	Sir Seretse announced that within two years, Botswana would have its own national currency and Central Bank.
16 Sept. 1974	Sir Seretse Khama intimates that the Rhodesia Railways operation in Botswana would be taken over as soon as possible.
21 Sept. 1974	Nominations for presidential candidates to be handed in.
27 Sept. 1974	Deadline for nominations to the thirty two parliamentary constituencies.
3 Oct. 1974	Signs agreement with Germany on technical cooperation.
3 Oct. 1974	Signs agreement with Germany concerning the financial and technical assistance for development of the Francistown-Serule Road.
13 Oct. 1974	Ethan Dube, a full time worker at ZAPU's Lusaka headquarters is abducted.
26 Oct. 1974	Holds second post-independence general election resulting in a win for Sir Seretse Khama's Botswana Democratic Party.
30 Oct. 1974	Sir Seretse Khama is sworn in as the President of Botswana for the third time.
30 Oct. 1974	New cabinet is announced.
Nov. 1974	Parliament agrees to request R5 million loan from the Arab oil-exporting states to enable the construction of two large oil storage depots.
18 Nov. 1974	Sir Seretse opens a new session of Parliament and confirms he will play an active role in bringing about peaceful change in Southern Africa post the transfer of power to Mozambique from Portugal.
25 Nov. 1974	The Botswana police station on the Kazungula border is fired upon by South

African security forces in an engagement with Zambian patrols. The Botswana Cabinet issues a statement placing responsibility on South Africa.

Dec. 1974   Botswana joins the United Nations Commission on Namibia.

Dec. 1974   President Sir Seretse Khama plays a leading role with President Kaunda of Zambia in promoting a settlement in Namibia and Rhodesia leading to the Lusaka Agreement.

3 Jan. 1975   Mr. Callaghan visits Sir Seretse Khama, as part of a visit to Africa to ascertain views on the Rhodesian settlement issue.

6 Jan. 1975   Diplomatic relations formally established with the People's Republic of China at ambassadorial level.

Feb. 1975   The Sua Pan Soda Ash Project is shelved.

26 Feb. 1975   Botswana becomes a member of the World Health Organization.

28 Feb. 1975   Botswana signs the Lomé Convention.

Mar. 1975   Demonstrations on the Gaborone campus of the University occur in support of their fellow students in Swaziland.

Mar. 1975   The Russian embassy is established in Gaborone.

24 Apr. 1975   Signs agreement with Denmark on volunteers from Denmark.

25 May 1975   Signs agreement concerning the Francistown-Nata Road Project.

June 1975   A boundary fence is constructed in consultation with South Africa.

June 1975   Potential collapse of the beef industry upon which 80% of the population depend. This is averted by a reduction in the European Community levy to June 1976.

June 1975   World Bank announces that it expects to lend Botswana approximately R30 million during the following five years.

26 June 1975   Botswana categorically refuses to attend the OAU summit conference in Kampala due to President Amin's human rights record.

July 1975   Government establishes its own Central Bank under the governorship of H.C.L. Hermans.

July 1975   Government White Paper proposes a revolutionary policy on tribal grazing land.

July 1975   Two Rhodesians are killed in an explosion near Francistown.

July 1975   A wildcat strike on the Selebi-Pikwe copper mine marks the onset of militant trade unionism.

19 Sept. 1975   Signs loan agreement with the United States for the construction and equipping of the Northern Abattoir.

Oct. 1975	Sir Seretse Khama spends the month in hospital and is recuperating from an illness.
Oct. 1975	A country-wide aerial survey for minerals is conducted.
Oct. 1975	The University of Botswana, Lesotho and Swaziland is in jeopardy after the Lesotho government nationalizes the main campus in Roma.
19 Oct. 1975	Rhodesian soldiers open fire on Matsiloje village close to the border.
27 Oct. 1985	Signs amendment on Customs Union Agreement dated 11 December 1969.
21 Nov. 1975	Signs loan agreement with the International Bank for Reconstruction and Development on a Third Road Project.
Dec. 1975	The Botswana government recognizes SWAPO.
Dec. 1975	Diplomatic relations are established with Mexico.
Jan. 1976	The new University of Botswana and Swaziland devises a plan to accommodate students who had to suspend their studies due to the nationalization of the Lesotho campus.
1 Jan. 1976	Accepts the constitution of the Universal Postal Union.
14 Jan. 1976	The Presidents of Tanzania, Botswana, Zambia and Mozambique hold a private meeting on Angola in Dar-es-Salaam following the deadlocked OAU Conference.
Feb. 1976	Presidents of Tanzania, Zambia, Botswana and Mozambique meet in Quelimane, Mozambique and endorse the need for the armed struggle to achieve majority rule in Rhodesia.
Feb. 1976	Sir Seretse Khama plays a prominent role in the OAU emergency summit. He refuses to accept the MPLA as the legitimate government and insists on support for a Government of National Unity.
24 Feb. 1976	Signs agreement with Great Britain concerning the public officer's pensions.
14 May 1976	Signs agreement with the United Development Programme concerning assistance.
28 May 1976	Signs loan agreement with the International Bank for Reconstruction and Development on an Education Project.
4 June 1976	Signs exchange of notes with Great Britain concerning officers designated by Great Britain in the service of specific organizations and institutions.
July 1976	Botswana is to erect a fence along its border with Rhodesia.
July 1976	Sir Seretse Khama visits China and in a speech claims that South Africa and Rhodesia have violated Botswana's borders and air space.

19 July 1976	High Commissioner to Tanzania, Aloysius Kgarebe presents his credentials to President Nyerere.
23 Aug. 1976	The Bank of Botswana issues its new currency with Pula and Thebe replacing South African Rands and Cents. Withdraws from the Rand Monetary Area.
Sept. 1976	Botswana celebrates the tenth anniversary of its independence.
Sept. 1976	Sir Seretse Khama receives the country's two highest awards: Nalediya Botswana and the Presidential Order of Botswana.
6 Sept. 1976	The Presidents of the five Front Line States (Tanzania, Botswana, Zambia, Mozambique, Angola) end a summit conference in Dar-es-Salaam. They agree to intensify the armed struggle in Zimbabwe.
26 Sept. 1976	The five Front Line States including Botswana, put forward their own programme for settling the Rhodesian problem. They are unhappy about some aspects of the Anglo-American plan.
17 Oct. 1976	The Front Line States including Botswana, appeal to Britain to assume full responsibility for residual powers during the two-year transition to majority rule in Rhodesia.
Nov. 1976	Botswana reports a new influx of Angolan refugees.
Nov. 1976	Ten women are abducted by Rhodesian security forces; the residence of ANC refugees in Francistown is bombed; and a man was murdered near Matsiloje.
2 Nov. 1976	Sir Seretse Khama is fitted with a pacemaker and flown to South Africa for cardiac treatment.
22 Nov. 1976	More than 500 students assemble at the Ministry of Education to protest at the reduction of student stipends.
23 Nov. 1976	Government closes Gaborone University until further notice due to demonstrations.
23 Nov. 1976	High Commissioner to Kenya, Aloysius Kgarebe presents his credentials to President Kenyatta.
Dec. 1976	Three people are kidnapped; the village of Moroka is burned; barracks in Francistown are machine-gunned.
1 Dec. 1976	The Minister of Mineral and Water Affairs, K. Segokgo commits suicide.
1 Dec. 1976	The obligation of the Bank of Botswana to value the Pula equal to the Rand ceases.
17 Dec. 1976	South African Minister of Justice, Jimmy Kruger alleges that guerrillàs are being trained in Botswana bases for operations in South Africa.
18 Dec. 1976	A brief clash occurs between Rhodesian and Botswana forces at the border near Francistown.

20 Dec. 1976	Botswana to raise the question of clashes on the Rhodesian border at the United Nations Security Council.
20 Dec. 1976	Botswana considers an offer of military aid from the Soviet Union.
31 Dec. 1976	The target of one million Pula is reached in the Botswana University Campus appeal.
Jan. 1977	Chief Besele Montshiwa of the Baralong is deposed as Tribal Authority by the government.
Jan. 1977	Ivor Richard, chairman of the adjourned Geneva Conference on the Rhodesian settlement issue consults with Southern African leaders, including Botswana.
Jan. 1977	A student demonstration occurs at the United States Embassy due to Washington's decision to abstain in the United Nations Security Council resolution condemning Rhodesian violations of Botswana.
Jan. 1977	A woman is shot in the north-east by Rhodesian forces.
12 Jan. 1977	The Foreign Minister addresses the United Nations Security Council on Rhodesian violations of Botswana territory.
12 Jan. 1977	Rhodesian troops exchange fire with 'armed men' inside Botswana states official communiqué.
14 Jan. 1977	An immediate and total cessation of all hostile acts against Botswana by Rhodesia is demanded by the United Nations Security Council after a three-day debate on the subject.
21 Jan. 1977	A shooting incident near the Botswana border is reported. The man was crossing into Rhodesia and refused to halt.
29 Jan. 1977	Two plane-loads of arms arrive in Gaborone from Lusaka for the expansion of the paramilitary Botswana Police Mobile Unit. This has been increased from 500 to 700 men.
30 Jan. 1977	About 500 pupils are kidnapped from the Manama Secondary School together with five teachers, two priests and a school clerk. They were taken from Rhodesia across the Botswana border.
Feb. 1977	Botswana seeks material assistance from the United Nations who is sending a fact-finding team under the chairmanship of A.A. Farah.
16 Feb. 1977	First military restricted area on the southern border of Rhodesia with Botswana is created.
19 Feb. 1977	Cross-border operations from Rhodesia in Botswana confirmed by a defence communiqué announces the death of a Rhodesian police inspector. He has been killed by nationalists north of Francistown.
24 Feb. 1977	Tension rises on the Rhodesia-Botswana border with an announcement that Rhodesia was planning an attack, which the Office of the Botswana

President said would be tantamount to a declaration of war.

25 Feb. 1977	Refugees now total 861 South Africans, 575 Namibians, 2638 Rhodesians and 404 others.
Mar. 1977	Botswana sends delegation to the first Afro-Arab summit in Cairo.
Mar. 1977	The Minister of External Affairs visits Libya.
31 Mar. 1977	The Botswana Defence Bill is passed providing both for a Defence Force and a Defence Council.
31 Mar. 1977	The findings of the United Nations mission to Botswana are published and provide evidence of destruction on Botswana's side and that the refugees are causing economic difficulties.
Apr. 1977	Border security assistance is promoted by a United Nations mission recommendation to raise international capital amounting to $25 million.
Apr. 1977	Botswana sends a delegation to the meeting of the Co-ordinating Bureau of Non-aligned Countries in New Delhi.
Apr. 1977	Sends delegation to the joint meeting of the European Community and the ACP countries in Fiji.
Apr. 1977	Botswana tightens its security legislation and a bill providing for a Botswana army is tabled.
Apr. 1977	The ruling Botswana Democratic Party has its annual conference and announces that a youth wing is to be established.
2 Apr. 1977	Signs agreement with South Africa for the avoidance of double taxation and prevention of fiscal evasion with respect to taxes on income.
19 Apr. 1977	Deputy Police Chief Mompati Merathe is appointed as the first commander of the Botswana Army.
May 1977	Diplomatic relations are established with the German Democratic Republic.
May 1977	Libyan representatives pay a reciprocal visit to Botswana.
16 May 1977	A company-size Rhodesian force goes on an invasion into Botswana.
16 May 1977	The death of the Minister of Home Affairs, Bakwena Kgari, is announced.
20 May 1977	Signs loan agreement with the International Bank for Reconstruction and Development for the Fourth Road Project.
June 1977	The European Community announces that the 90% reduction on the levy normally applied to Botswana beef entering the Common Market will be extended to the end of 1978.
June 1977	Sends delegation to the Commonwealth Meeting in London.
June 1977	Sends delegation to the Security Council and the United Nations condemns

	Rhodesian border incursions.
8 June 1977	Signs additional protocol to the Geneva Conventions of 12 August 1949 relating to the protection of victims of non-international armed conflict.
July 1977	By this date, the border has been violated over 100 times.
7 July 1977	Signs grant agreement with the United Nations Capital Development Fund.
30 Sept. 1977	Botswana announces the imminent establishment of an air force.
5 Oct. 1977	Signs agreement with Great Britain on the avoidance of double taxation and the prevention of fiscal evasion with respect to taxes and income.
9 Oct. 1977	The South African government demands an explanation from Botswana as to why four men were removed from the Johannesburg to Bulawayo train.
Nov. 1977	Preliminary zoning plans for the Tribal Grazing Land Policy are announced.
Nov. 1977	Japanese interests are attempting to establish a consortium of potential investors in the Sua Pan soda ash and brine deposits.
6 Nov. 1977	Lord Carver, British President Commissioner-designate visits Botswana.
Dec. 1977	Botswana establishes diplomatic relations with Cuba.
Dec. 1977	World Bank announces a $6.5 million loan for long-term livestock development.
23 Dec. 1977	Signs additional protocol to the Geneva Convention relating to the victims of armed conflict.
Jan. 1978	Arrival of the Soviet Union's first resident Ambassador to Botswana, Michail Petrov.
7 Jan. 1978	Signs convention on international trade in endangered species of wild fauna and flora with reservations.
12 Feb. 1978	Accession by Botswana to Convention on International Trade in Endangered Species of Wild Fauna and Flora.
17 Feb. 1978	Botswana serves a fifteen year sentence on a South African, Rene Beyleveld, on charges of trying to undermine Botswana's security by joining the Rhodesian Selous Scouts. He was arrested in Botswana.
27 Feb. 1978	Rhodesian forces capture a Botswana army patrol near Kazungula.
15 Mar. 1978	Signs loan agreement with the International Bank for Reconstruction and Development.
29 Mar. 1978	Signs agreement with West Germany concerning financial assistance.
29 Mar. 1978	The Botswana Defence Force kills two South Africans and a Briton as mercenary suspects in the Tuli Block.

29 Mar. 1978	420 children are abducted from a Methodist mission school at Tegwani in Rhodesia and marched across the border to Botswana.
May 1978	Sir Seretse Khama pays an official visit to Britain.
1 May 1978	Signs grant agreement project with the United Nations Capital Development Fund upgrading fund distribution facilities.
22 May 1978	Sir Seretse Khama states in Geneva that there has been an increasing influx of refugees in Botswana since the signing of the Rhodesian internal settlement plan on 3 March.
June 1978	The estimated number of refugees in Botswana is 12,000.
1 June 1978	Sir Seretse Khama appoints E.S. Masisi as Minister of Health and L.S.M. Seretse as Minister of Agriculture.
21 June 1978	The government withdraws the passports of seventeen Botwana National Front members who are due to attend the World Festival of Democratic Youth in Havana.
July 1978	Botswana is given one of the vice-chairmanships of the OAU at the Khartoum meeting.
July 1978	President of the Botswana Appeal Court, I. Maisels, sets aside the fifteen year prison sentence delivered on Bernard Beyleveld for allegedly threatening Botswana's security.
14 July 1978	Cuba's former Ambassador to Tanzania, A. Zorrilla, confers in Gaborone with Botswana's acting Foreign Minister, Daniel Kwelagobe and delivers a message from the Cuban Foreign Minister.
Aug. 1978	The government announces that the Defence Force patrol commander involved in the March shooting is charged with murder.
Sept. 1978	Announces the formation of a Presidential Commission to review all local government institutions.
11 Sept. 1978	Signs loan agreement with the International Bank for Reconstruction and Development.
11 Sept. 1978	Students demonstrate at the murder charge levelled against the patrol commander and the University is closed down.
14 Sept. 1978	Eight University students and two heads of departments are ordered out of Botswana.
14 Sept. 1978	More than 100 students of the National Vocational Training School clash with the police.
18 Sept. 1978	The Botswana Trade Union stages a demonstration in solidarity with student protests.
18 Sept. 1978	Signs a grant agreement with the UN concerning the control of communicable diseases.

Oct. 1978	Minister of External Affairs, A. Megwe addresses the United Nations General Assembly.
26 Oct. 1978	Signs agreement with Denmark on a Danish government loan to Botswana.
13 Nov. 1978	The patrol commander accused of murder is acquitted.
21 Nov. 1978	Sir Seretse Khama accuses the official opposition of left-wing policies and for causing disruption in the pre-election period.
Dec. 1978	Approximately 100 Patriotic Front guerrillas are rounded up by the Defence Force and sent back to Zambia.
11 Dec. 1978	Signs agreement with West Germany concerning financial co-operation, continued promotion of the National Fuel Reserve Project.
Jan. 1979	About sixty armed guerrillas believed to be ZAPU members are arrested in Botswana.
Jan. 1979	South African police force and alleged ANC members clash. Botswana denies that the latter have fled into their country.
8 Jan. 1979	The government states that a force of 100 Rhodesian soldiers attacked a Botswana Defence Force camp but withdrew after a brief battle.
13 Jan. 1979	A clash occurs between the South African police and suspected ANC members, fifty miles from the Botswana border. The South African claim that they had fled accross the Botswana border is to be investigated.
Feb. 1979	The air lift of Rhodesian refugees in Botswana halts and poses problems for the Botswana government.
12 Mar. 1979	Botswana and the Soviet Union hold talks aimed at developing cultural and scientific co-operation.
15 Mar. 1979	Four men are arrested in Gaborone for having guns and explosives. They are believed to be members of the ANC.
19 Mar. 1979	A South African exile, Mr. Thmoedi is sentenced to three and a half years in jail for illegal possession of firearms.
22 Mar. 1979	Signs agreement with West Germany concerning financial co-operation.
Apr. 1979	The Botswana government builds a refugee camp for South African students at Molepolole.
Apr. 1979	Diplomatic relations are established with Cuba.
12 Apr. 1979	Botswana recognizes the new government of Uganda under President Lule.
13 Apr. 1979	Rhodesian troops capture fourteen persons in a house in Francistown occupied by ZAPU members.
23 May 1979	Ratifies additional protocol to the 1949 Geneva Conventions relating to the

protection of victims of armed conflict.

June 1979	Government declares a state of drought.
12 June 1979	David Sibeko, a member of the Pan-Africanist Congress presidential council, dies after being assassinated and his body is flown home to Botswana for burial.
July 1979	Botswana plays a prominent role in the Commonwealth Conference in Lusaka.
July 1979	SADCC holds its first meeting in Arusha and Botswana plays an important role.
25 July 1979	Queen Elizabeth II, as head of the Commonwealth, pays a two-day state visit to Botswana and other African states.
Aug. 1979	A brief air engagement occurs when a Botswana reconnaisance plane is attacked by Rhodesian helicopters.
24 Aug. 1979	Sir Seretse Khama dissolves Parliament.
Oct. 1979	The chief ZAPU representative in Botswana and five other officials are expelled after a shooting and stoning confrontation with the police at Dukwe.
20 Oct. 1979	Third national election since independence takes place.
23 Oct. 1979	Sir Seretse Khama is sworn in as President for his fourth term of office.
Nov. 1979	Sir Seretse Khama goes to London for a physical check-up and hospital rest; thereafter convalesces in Botswana.
21 Jan. 1980	Repatriation of Rhodesian refugees begins.
Feb. 1980	Free education is introduced.
18 Feb. 1980	Sir Seretse Khama resumes his full schedule of official duties.
Mar. 1980	The Legislature is divided along ethnic lines on a motion urging the condemnation of discriminatory practices. This is interpreted as aiming at the Kalanga-speaking people.
25 Apr. 1980	This is declared National Defence Day.
23 June 1980	The President goes to England for a regular medical check-up. The foreign press report that he has terminal cancer.
13 July 1980	The President of Botswana, Sir Seretse Khama dies at the age of 59 after a long illness.
18 July 1980	Dr Quett K.J. Masire is formally elected as President by the National Assembly.
22 July 1980	President Masire appoints his Cabinet which contains a number of minor

changes.

20 Sept. 1980	A by-election is held to fill Masire's place in the Ngwaketse-Kgalagadi constituency. It is won by Patrick Tshane.
Oct/Nov. 1980	President Masire, as chairman of SADCC makes a sixteen day tour to Luxembourg, Brussels, the Netherlands, Norway and Britain.
Jan. 1981	Botswana hands four refugees over to the South African authorities after they ignored warnings not to leave the Dukwe Camp.
10 Jan. 1981	Government claims that South African troops have opened fire on Botswana forces at Mohembo.
11 Jan. 1981	The Botswana Defence Force returns fire on the South African troops.
Feb. 1981	President Masire attends a one-day Summit of Front Line States in Lusaka.
19 Mar. 1981	Botswana lodges an official protest with the South African government. They claim that the South African troops had warned the Botswana Defence Force that an attack was immenent due to a shooting of a South African soldier.
Apr. 1981	The head of the Botswana Defence Force feels it necessary to assure the public that the military should not be involved in partisan politics.
Apr. 1981	President Masire attends a meeting of the Front Line States in Luanda to discuss the Crocker initiative on Namibia and a summit of Southern African states in Mbabane.
6 Apr. 1981	President Masire attends a meeting in Mbabane with the leaders of Mozambique, Lesotho and Swaziland.
16 Apr. 1981	United States Assistant Secretary of State for Africa, Chester Crocker, visits Botswana as part of his initial tour of Southern Africa.
May 1981	First signs appear, with Zaire's withdrawal from the de Beers diamond marketing system, (CSO) that the market was declining with gravely detrimental results for Botswana, both economically and politically.
June 1981	President Masire pays a state visit to Nigeria, followed by the OAU Summit in Nairobi and a SADCC Heads of State meeting in Zimbabwe.
29 June 1981	Botswana forces allegedly exchange fire with South African troops along the Namibian border.
July 1981	Botswana adopts a new constitution.
July 1981	President Samora Machel of Mozambique visits Botswana.
Aug. 1981	The first meeting of the Botswana-Zambia Permanent Commission of is held in Livingstone. They discuss the completion of the Bot-Zam road and the possibility of a Kazungula Bridge over the Zambezi.

Sept. 1981	President Masire appoints a Presidential Commission on Economic Opportunities.
Sept. 1981	President Masire attends a meeting of the Front Line States in Nigeria to discuss South Africa's incursions into Angola.
Sept./Oct. 1981	President Masire visits India and Australia, where he attends the Commonwealth Prime Ministers' Conference.
Nov. 1981	The President announces a new Industrial Policy Plan to attract investors.
21 Dec. 1981	Botswana does not sign the Preferential Trade Area in Eastern and Southern Africa Agreement (PTA) because of requirement provisions stipulated by the Southern African Customs Union. Ultimately however, Botswana expects to become a member.
Jan. 1982	A new opposition party, the Social Democratic Party (SDP) applies for registration.
23 Jan. 1982	Botswana, together with the other Front Line States, meet in Lusaka to discuss the Namibian proposals, together with Kenya, Nigeria and SWAPO.
Feb. 1982	The Chieftainship of the Barolong is settled, and Kgosi Besele Montshiwa is reinstated after his deposal in 1976.
Feb.- July 1982	Botswana chairs the OAU Council of Ministers.
6 Feb. 1982	Peter Lengene, a political refugee is kidnapped by South African agents.
Mar. 1982	Botswana claims that it had shot down a South African army helicopter over the Caprivi Strip.
Mar. 1982	Daniel Kwele resigns from the ruling party and from the National Assembly after he is dropped from the Cabinet.
Mar. 1982	The English and Setswana versions of the government-owned Daily News are combined.
Mar. 1982	Cabinet reshuffle as a result of Daniel Kwele being dropped and charges are made at the Assistant Minister level.
Mar. 1982	Work begins on the new Gaborone International Airport.
7 Mar. 1982	Botswana attends a two-day meeting in Maputo with the other member of the Front Line States on South Africa's aggressive policies.
Late Apr. 1982	Botswana shoots down a civilian plane for violating its airspace.
30 Apr. 1982	President Masire hosts a meeting between President Kaunda of Zambia and Prime Minister Botha of South Africa at the Tlokweng border gate near Gaborone.
May 1982	Angry protests in the Mahalapye area follow the announcement that President Masire's face would replace that of Sir Seretse Khama on the currency and that only his picture be displayed in public places.

4 May 1982	Botswana, together with the Front Line State's members reject the current Western attempt to secure a Namibian settlement.
June 1982	The Botswana Progressive Union, a new opposition party, is founded.
June 1982	Masire attends a meeting of the Front Line States with Namibia as its focus.
July 1982	A Conference on Culture and Resistance is held at the University of Botswana.
July 1982	France opens a consular and trade commission office in Gaborone.
July 1982	Botswana hosts the fourth SADCC Heads of Government meeting in Gaborone. The SADCC Secretariat, based in Gaborone is officially opened.
Aug. 1982	A bomb blast occurs in a SWAPO safe house in Gaborone.
Aug. 1982	Rumours circulate that six kidnapped tourists in Zimbabwe have been driven across the Botswana border.
Sept. 1982	The Universities of Swaziland and Botswana sever ties.
Oct. 1982	Botswana and Zimbabwe in a joint communiqué, reject United States attempts to link Cuban troop withdrawal in Angola with the Namibian negotiations.
Oct. 1982	An incident centres on the role of the non-Setswana speaking Kalanga minority which is interpreted as tribalization.
Oct. 1982	Masire is scheduled to make a state visit to Zimbabwe but border tensions dampen the visit.
Nov. 1982	President Masire makes a state visit to France and Algeria.
17 Nov. 1982	Signs cultural, scientific and technical co-operation agreement with France.
Dec. 1982	Increase in violence necessitate s the creation of a special police branch which is named the Special Services Group.
11 Dec. 1982	A privately owned South African aircraft is shot down over north-western Botswana.
4 Jan. 1983	Vice-President Lenyeletse Seretse dies after a long illness.
Feb. 1983	More than fifty refugees per day are crossing the Zimbabwe-Botswana border as troubles intensify in Matabeleland.
Feb. 1983	The Palapye-Serowe road is opened with the result that all major villages are served by tarred roads with the exception of Maun.
Feb. 1983	The number of refugees at Dukwe increase from 833 to 3,000. South African Airways announces its withdrawal from Gaborone until the airport is upgraded.

9 Mar. 1983	Joshua Nkomo crosses into Botswana over the ill-guarded border leading to a deterioration in Botswana/Zimbabwe relations.
Apr. 1983	An attempt is made to register another political party, the Liberal Party.
5 Apr. 1983	Claims are made that ZAPU have established a five-member High Command in the Dukwe camp. At about the same time, twenty-one Batswana are abducted by the Zimbabwe army.
19 Apr. 1983	A high-level Zimbabwe delegation led by the Minister of Home Affairs visits Gaborone to discuss their deteriorating relationship.
31 May 1983	Botswana and Zimbabwe establish diplomatic relations at ambassadorial level.
5-11 Sept.1983	President Masire pays an official visit to Romania.
11-15 Sept.1983	President Masire visits Yugoslavia.
May 1984	President Masire visits the United States.
8 Sept. 1984	First general election under President Masire and the fourth since independence takes place. Botswana Democratic Party wins although the Botswana National Front slightly improves its position.
10 Sept. 1984	President Masire is re-elected for a further five-year term.
13 Sept. 1984	A communiqué issued by the ANC condemns South Africa's attempt to compel Botswana to sign a security pact.
14 Sept. 1984	A slightly re-arranged Cabinet is announced.
8 Oct. 1984	President Masire announces that 60% of the population are receiving food aid due to the drought.
25 Oct. 1984	Three members of the South African Defence Force are slightly injured in a shooting incident whilst on a patrol boat in the Chobe River.
11 Jan. 1985	Botswana's currency is devalued by approximately 15% against a basket of currencies.
28 Jan. 1985	President Masire dismisses two ministers and demotes a third in a cabinet reshuffle. The Minister of Agriculture and his assistant are replaced by Daniel Kwelagobe and Geoffrey Oteng. Health Minister is replaced by Patrick Balopi.
5 Feb. 1985	Border tensions with South Africa mount and Foreign Minister 'Pik' Botha issues a statement voicing South Africa's concern that Botswana is harbouring ANC members.
13 Feb. 1985	Two refugees are injured in an explosion in a house in Gaborone.
22 Feb. 1985	It is announced that South Africa will not insist on Botswana signing a security pact.

Mar. 1985	A South African farming couple is killed near the Botswana border.
22 Apr. 1985	A large cache of arms is discovered in Gaborone.
14 May 1985	A black South African political refugee, Vernon Nkadimeng, is killed by a car bomb.
14 June 1985	South African commando raids ten houses in different parts of Gaborone and at least fifteen people are killed.
20 June 1985	South African police reveal details of documents seized during the Gaborone raid.
21 June 1985	The Security Council unanimously adopts UN Resolution 568 (1985) condemning the South African raid.
15 July 1985	Peter Mmusi is re-elected Chairman of the Botswana Democratic Party for a third successive two-year term.
25 Sept. 1985	South Africa and Botswana cannot reach agreement on compensation for damage caused during the June raid.
26 Sept. 1985	Brazil and Botswana establish diplomatic relations at ambassadorial level.
Oct. 1985	A communiqué is issued after a meeting of the Zimbabwe/Botswana permanent commission on defence and security after their meeting in Gaborone. Botswana agrees to hand over criminals fleeing across the border.
16 Nov. 1985	A car bomb explodes in Gaborone and kills two adults and two children.
20 Nov. 1985	Two members of Parliament from the ruling Botswana Democratic Party defect to the Botswana National Front.
4 Jan. 1986	Two white South Africans are killed in a land-mine explosion just south of the border with Botswana.
7 Jan. 1986	'Pik' Botha increases South African pressure on Botswana to take action against the ANC.
13 Mar. 1986	France decides to open an embassy in Gaborone.
Apr. 1986	The government passes the National Security Act.
19 May 1986	The South African Defence Force carries out raids on alleged ANC offices and camps in the Gaborone suburb of Mogoditshane.
5 June 1986	Signs multilateral agreement with South Africa, Mozambique and Zimbabwe on the establishment of the Limpopo Basin Permanent Technical Committee.
14 June 1986	South African commandos strike Gaborone on the first anniversary of the June 1985 raid.
27 July - 4 Aug. 1986	A United Nations mission visits Botswana after their appeal for international aid.

25 Sept. 1986	Approximately 2,000 workers go on strike over salaries.
30 Sept. 1986	Botswana celebrates twenty years of independence.
Dec. 1986	Plans are suspended concerning the transfer to Botswana Railways by the National Railways of Zimbabwe of certain sections of railway line. This is due to a disagreement with Bophuthatswana.
Jan. 1987	The southern border village of Ramotswa is raided.
Feb. 1987	Botswana hosts a summit with business people from overseas and from the region invited to participate for the first time.
1 Feb. 1987	It is announced that Botswana citizens will be required to have Bophuthatswana visas to enter the 'homeland', to be applied for thirty days in advance. Botswana circumvented this by building a turn-around facility at Rakhuna.
9 Feb. 1987	The South African Transport Service tries to resolve the railway crisis by suggesting that they take over for an interim period. This does not prove acceptable.
9 Feb. 1987	Bophuthatswana argues that Botswana is still in charge of railway operations within its borders and Zimbabwean passport holders, too, would need visas.
9 Feb. 1987	Zimbabwe and Botswana announce that no personnel or locomotives would pass the border.
Apr. 1987	British Caledonian Airways becomes the first European airline to initiate a service between Gaborone and London.
Apr. 1987	Bophuthatswana offers to withdraw all its demands if Botswana will resume handing over trains at Mafikeng. Botswana remains firm.
9 Apr. 1987	A vehicle bearing South African number plates explodes in Gaborone. It kills three Botswana citizens and demolishes a house.
May 1987	Elizabeth Bathobakae, deputy mayoress of Jwaneng and a member of the Botswana Democratic Party claims that the Botswana National Front plan to overthrow the government.
May 1987	The Morupule Power Station opens in central Botswana. Previously Botswana was dependent on South Africa for 75% of its electricity.
10 June 1987	Botswana police detain the editor of the Botswana Guardian, Charles Mogale, for security reasons.
2 July 1987	The South African company, de Beers Consolidated Mines Limited, and Botswana reach agreement on the purchase of Botswana's stockpile of diamonds.
10 Aug. 1987	Steven Burnett, latterly of the British Special Air Service Regiment is convicted in the Botswana High Court of attempting to murder Ronnie Watson, an anti-apartheid activist.

10-13 Aug. 1987	President Chissano of Mozambique visits Botswana and holds talks with President Masire.
26 Sept. 1987	A referendum is held to endorse a proposed change to the constitution. This pertains to the post of supervisor of elections, whose office hitherto formed part of the Office of the President.
Mid-Oct. 1987	'Pik' Botha leads a delegation to Botswana for talks with Pontashego Kedikilwe, Minister of Presidential Affairs and Public Affairs, on the Sua Pan Project.
Nov. 1987	The constitution is further amended, restricting the holding of the presidency and vice-presidency to Botswana citizens by birth or descent.
Mid-Dec. 1987	A series of explosions occur in Gaborone.
Mar. 1988	A white South African businessman is detained for a day by the Botswana Defence Force in a game reserve, apparently for being dressed in camouflage.
28 Mar. 1988	South African commandos attack a house in Gaborone, killing three Batswana and one South African refugee.
Apr. 1988	Air Botswana becomes the first SADCC airline to establish air links with Namibia.
28 Apr. 1988	Chapson Butale is appointed as Minister of Works and Communications following the resignation for health reasons of Colin Blackbeard.
13 May 1988	Minister of External Affairs, Gaositwe Chiepe goes to South Africa and holds discussions with Deputy Minister of Foreign Affairs, Kobus Meiring.
17 May 1988	Zimbabwean Vice-President visits Botswana and attempts to persuade Zimbabwean refugees to return home.
20 June 1988	Two white South African soldiers are captured south of Gaborone after a shooting incident with the police.
July 1988	Botswana pays Zimbabwe 83,000,000 Pula in compensation for the takeover of the Botswana section of the railway previously run by Zimbabwe.
7 Aug. 1988	The Botswana presidential plane is shot down over southern Angola. President Masire sustains moderate injuries.
Sept. 1988	Botswana-Zimbabwe agreement is signed pertaining to imports and exports.
Sept. 1988	Pope John Paul II visits Botswana.
16 Sept. 1988	Minister of External Affairs has discussions with Pik Botha in Pretoria.
20 Sept. 1988	Rescue attempt of the two commandos fails.
12 Oct. 1988	It is reported that Barry Vivier, one of the three South Africans involved in the June raid, has been released.

Nov. 1988	An agreement is concluded between African Explosives and Chemicals Industry of SA and Soda Ash Botswana for the development of a plant north-west of Francistown.
Dec. 1988	The two commandos involved in the Gaborone raid are sentenced to ten years each under the National Security Act.
11 Dec. 1988	A bomb blast kills a fourteen year old boy.
12 Dec. 1988	It is alleged that the South African Defence Force has raided the village of Ditlharapeng near the border, in which two people were killed. This is refuted by the South Africans.
23 Jan. 1989	The University of Botswana is indefinitely closed and all 2000 students expelled following unrest.
Feb. 1989	The United States Defence Department announces a $7,900,000 military support programme for the Botswana Defence Force.
1 Apr. 1989	Botswana takes over and no longer relies on the National Railways of Zimbabwe.
July 1989	Five members of the ANC are sentenced in Gaborone for the possession of AK-47 rifles and ammunition.
31 July 1989	The refugee status of the camp at Dukwe is terminated.
3 Aug. 1989	President Masire is named co-winner of the Africa Prize for Leadership for the Sustainable End of Hunger for his management of the 1981-1987 drought.
25 Sept. 1989	Some 12000 primary school teachers call off their pay strike.
Oct. 1989	Colonel Garang of the Sudanese People's Liberation Movement is assured of diplomatic support from Botswana during his visit to that country.
7 Oct. 1989	The Botswana Democratic Party is returned to office with an increased majority in the legislative elections.
10 Oct. 1989	President Masire is sworn in for his third term of office.
13 Oct. 1989	President Masire announces his reshuffled cabinet.
May 1990	A campaign is launched to attract the Asian manufacturing industry.
July 1990	It is reported that China will provide financial and technical assistance in relaying the railway line between Francistown and Serula.
July 1990	President Masire goes to Libya and holds talks with Colonel Gadhafi.
July 1990	President Masire visits Namibia and agrees to establish a joint commission to promote trade and communications, and to create a protocol on defence and security.
26 July 1990	Signs agreement with Namibia on creation of a joint commission of

co-operation.

26 July 1990	Signs agreement with Namibia on culture and education co-operation.
26 July 1990	Signs treaty of understanding with Namibia on defence and security.
Aug. 1990	King Mswati of Swaziland visits Botswana and holds talks with President Masire.
4 Sept. 1990	Signs multilateral memorandum of understanding on road transportation in the common customs area pursuant to the Customs Union Agreement of Botswana, Lesotho, South Africa and Swaziland.
26 Sept. 1990	Signs air service agreement with Namibia.
23-26 Oct.1990	President Masire visits Mozambique.
26 Nov. 1990	Diplomatic relations are established with Malaysia.
5 Dec. 1990	A long-term agreement is signed with the United States company, Lazare Kaplan International, for the established of a diamond cutting and polishing factory.
10 Dec. 1990	An agreement on development assistance is signed with Sweden.
Feb. 1991	The Finance Minister announces a P36,000,000 budget deficit, the first since 1982.
Aug. 1991	Botswana plans to expand its veterinary cordon fences into the north-west in conformity with European Community regulations.
10 Oct. 1991	Unification of three opposition parties takes place - the Botswana People's Party, the Botswana Progressive Union, and the Botswana National Front. It is known as the Botswana People's Progressive Front.
Nov. 1991	An estimated 12000 strikers are dismissed by the Directorate of Public Service Management.
9 Nov. 1991	University students protest against the firing of striking workers.
30 Dec. 1991	Botswana and South Africa establish reciprocal diplomatic missions.
14 Jan. 1992	250 United States troops arrive in Gaborone for a fortnight to carry out training exercises with the Botswana Defence Force.
9 Mar. 1992	President Masire is forced to make cabinet changes after the resignation of Vice-President, Peter Mmusi who is also Minister of Local Government and Lands, and Daniel Kwelagobe, Minister of Agriculture. Improper land transfers are given as the reason.
9 Mar. 1992	Vice-President and Minister of Local Government and Lands Festus Mogae is appointed whilst also retaining the portfolio of Finance and Development Planning. Keatlemang Morake is appointed as Minister of Agriculture.

17 Mar. 1992	The Botswana National Front and the Botswana People's Party call on the government to resign and call an election within six months.

17 Aug. 1992   Signs multilateral treaty with the Southern African Development Community (SADC).

Feb. 1993   The forecast budget deficit for 1992-3 is estimated at P567,000,000 due to the diamond recession and severe drought.

4 May 1993   The Bank of Botswana issues its annual report and focusses on the gloomy prospects for the diamond industry.

12 May 1993   Botswana's six political parties meet in Francistown to discuss reforming the electoral system prior to the 1994 elections.

July 1993   Peter Mmusi and Daniel Kwelagobe make a come back after the land scandal and are elected party chairman and secretary-general respectively of the Botswana Democratic Party.

Sept. 1993   Reports that the controversial military airbase near Francistown is nearing completion. Due to United States and French agreements, Botswana is financially covered.

9 Sept. 1993   The seventh National Development Plan for 1991-7 reveals that economic planners are considering tax cuts and deregulation in order to promote economic growth and reduce the country's dependence on diamonds.

Oct. 1993   Although a final decision is still to be made, the Botswana National Front threatens to boycott the 1994 elections unless electoral reform is instituted.

Nov. 1993   Namibia has laid a claim to the Sedudu/Kasikili Island in the Chobe River which was generally thought to belong to Botswana. Botswana retaliates by hoisting the flag and several shooting incidents have been reported.

Jan. 1994   Botswana makes recommendations, together with South Africa and Zimbabwe, for ending the crisis within the Royal Lesotho Defence Force.

17 Feb. 1994   The military air base, nearing completion, continues to cause tension locally and regionally. Namibia expresses concern. It is now reported that it will cost the Botswana government several million United States dollars.

10 Mar. 1994   President Mugabe of Zimbabwe leaves Botswana after a four-day visit. Border problems were discussed.

30 Apr./7 May 1994   Primary elections for the ruling Botswana Democratic Party are to be held.

29 June 1994   Botswana becomes the first Southern African country to lend money to the International Monetary Fund.

26 Aug. 1994   President Masire dissolves Parliament.

14 Sept. 1994   President Masire reports that the country's annual growth rate of 3,5% threatens to outstrip the country's resources.

27 Sept. 1994   Sir Ketimule Masire (Botswana Democratic Party), Dr Koma (Botswana

National Front) and Dr. Maripe (Botswana People's Party) are declared validly nominated presidential candidates.

27 Sept. 1994   Government signs a memorandum pertaining to British technical assistance, which concerns training and consultants in Botswana.

Oct. 1994   Peter Mmusi dies.

15 Oct. 1994   Elections are held and although it was won by the Botswana Democratic Party, surprise gains are made by the opposition Botswana National Front.

26 Oct. 1994   Newly elected members of parliament meet to elect four more MPs from a selection of names to which they had contributed.

17-19 Feb. 1995   A teenage girl is the victim of a ritual murder and protesters demonstrate in Gaborone. At least one youth dies and two policemen are seriously wounded.

6 Apr. 1995   President Masire announced a reduction in the voting age from 21 to 18.

9 June 1995   Botswana Soda Ash faces liquidation but will not cease operating.

12 June 1995   President Masire arrives in Harare for a four-day state visit to Zimbabwe, his second since independence.

18 July 1995   Pontashego Kedikilwe is elected as the new Chairman of the Botswana Democratic Party after the death of Peter Mmusi.

1 Aug. 1995   Angola, Botswana and Namibia sign an agreement establishing a joint commission to ensure the development of an environmentally suitable management plan for the Okavango River Basin.

26 Aug. 1995   The execution of five convicted murderers was the first in five years.

28 Aug. 1995   Details of the deal between Soda Ash Botswana's shareholders and the company's creditors - specially the lending banks - reveal the extent to which the lenders have been penalized.

6 Nov. 1995   South Africa and Botswana set up a water commission to promote joint water supply projects.

8 Nov. 1995   Chairman Kedikilwe insists that the decision by the ruling party to put forward a constitutional amendment limiting a president to serving a maximum of two five year terms, would not be retrospective. In this case President Masire would be able to contest the 1999 elections.

Feb. 1996   Botswana and Namibia sign an agreement on the dispute surrounding Sedudu/Kasikili river island, to be submtted to the International Court of Justice. Both countries have committed themselves in advance to the outcome of the court's ruling.

Mar. 1996   Joint committees between Botswana and Namibia are established to control illegal crossing and cross-border smuggling.

May 1996	An envisaged alliance by the opposition parties to oust the ruling Botswana Democratic Party fails because the Independent Freedom Party and the Botswana People's Party join the ruling party in criticizing another opposition party, the Botswana National Front.
June 1996	The ruling Botswana Democratic Party agrees to long-demanded electoral reforms, which took the opposition parties by surprise. The opposition hopes that this will enable them to oust the government in the 1999 elections. The introduction of an Independent Electoral Commission, with a High Court judge acting as head, has been generally welcomed. The lowering of the voting age from twenty-one to eighteen is also no longer opposed by the ruling party.
21 June 1996	The Botswana Defence Force confirms the purchase of thirteen F-5 fighter bombers from Canada, fifty German-build Leopard tanks from the Netherlands and the intended sale of thirty-six Scorpion tanks from the United Kingdom. The army is to be extended by 3,000 and the purchase of armaments, worth 66 million pounds sterling is planned. Defence Chief Ian Khama defends this build-up, as he sees potential for conflict in Southern Africa.
Aug. 1996	The Department of Immigration states that in 1995, more than 40,300 illegal immigrants have been repatriated to their countries of origin. 14,000 were Zimbabwean nationals, while the rest came from fourteen other African countries. In the first six months of 1996, 5,400 illegal immigrants were caught. A detention centre for illegal immigrants is planned to be built in Francistown.
Nov. 1996	The Minister of Labour and Home Affairs states that the prisons are overcrowded due to the escalating crime rate and the growing number of illegal immigrants.
Dec. 1996	The Botswana Defence Force receives the first of a number of Canadian F-5 fighter-bomber aircraft, ordered earlier.
June 1997	Conflicting reports state that Botswana has purchased thirty-two tanks from Austria, whilst others deny that the sale has been made. The Botswana High Commission to Namibia denies that there is an arms build-up in Botswana, but that the creation of a credible army is a long-term plan. He assures that the country is on friendly terms with all its neighbours.

LESOTHO

3 Oct. 1966	Basutoland achieves independence as the Kingdom of Lesotho at midnight 3 October and becomes a member of the British Commonwealth.
4 Oct. 1966	Paramount Chief Moshoeshoe II is sworn in as King of the newly independent Kingdom of Lesotho.
4 Oct. 1966	Signs with United States an agreement for the continued application to Lesotho of certain treaties concluded between the United States and the United Kingdom.
4 Oct. 1966	Signs the Charter of the United Nations.

4 Oct. 1966	Signs multilateral supplementary convention on abolition of slavery, slavery traffic, institutions and practices similar to slavery.
4 Oct. 1966	Signs multilateral agreement on the nationality of married women.
4 Oct. 1966	A revised standard agreement on the provision of technical assistance by the United Nations Special Fund Project for Lesotho is agreed upon with the UNDP.
4 Oct. 1966	Signs termination treaty with UN for the application of agreement of 27 June 1963 between UN and Great Britain and Northern Ireland for the provision of operational, executive and administration personnel to the Trust, non-self governing and other territories.
17 Oct. 1966	The United Nations admits Lesotho as its 121st member.
31 Oct. 1966	Signs the International Labour Organisation's Convention (no. 64) on contracts of employment of indigenous workers.
31 Oct. 1966	Signs the International Labour Organisation's Convention (no. 5) on minimum age for industrial employment.
31 Oct. 1966	Signs the International Labour Organisation's Convention (no. 11) on rights of agricultural workers.
31 Oct. 1966	Signs the International Labour Organisation's Convention (no. 14) on industrial undertakings.
31 Oct. 1966	Signs the International Labour Organisation's Convention (no. 19) on equality of treatment for national foreign workers.
31 Oct. 1966	Signs the International Labour Organisation's Convention (no. 26) on minimum wage.
31 Oct. 1966	Signs the International Labour Organisation's Convention (no. 29) on forced or compulsory labour.
31 Oct. 1966	Signs the International Labour Organisation's Convention (no. 45) on employment of women in mines.
31 Oct. 1966	Signs with the International Labour Organisation Convention (no. 65) on penal sanctions for breach of contract - employment.
31 Oct. 1966	Signs with the International Labour Organisation Convention (no. 87) on freedom of association and protection of right to organise.
31 Oct. 1966	Signs the OAU's Charter.
31 Oct. 1966	Signs the OAU's protocol on mediation, conciliation and abitration.
Nov. 1966	Ghana designates an ambassador to Lesotho.
5 Nov. 1966	At the summit meeting of the Organization of African Unity held at Addis Ababa, Lesotho is admitted as a new member.

7 Nov. 1966	Adheres to the Food and Agriculture Organisation's (FAO) Constitution.
7 Nov. 1966	Signs agreement with the World Health Organisation for the provision of technical advisory assistance.
17 Nov. 1966	Signs agreement with the UNDP for special projects in Lesotho.
24 Nov. 1966	King Moshoeshoe II leaves Accra after a six-day state visit to Ghana.
Dec. 1966	I.A. Maisels Q.C., one of South Africa's leading advocates and a former judge to the High Court of Rhodesia is appointed Judge of the Court of Appeal of Lesotho.
Dec. 1966	Work starts on a transmitting station, five miles out of Maseru.
7 Dec. 1966	The Prime Minister, Chief Leabua Jonathan, meets the South African Prime Minister.
13 Dec. 1966	The Prime Minister, Chief Leabua Jonathan, announces on his return from the Far East that he found an interest in Lesotho. Diplomatic relations are feasible with Nationalist China, Japan and South Korea.
15 Dec. 1966	The Ambassador of Lesotho presents his credentials to the President of the United States.
27 Dec. 1966	King Moshoeshoe II is placed under house arrest by Chief Jonathan under the terms of the Emergency Powers Act.
28 Dec. 1966	Chief Jonathan makes a statement regarding a plot between the king and the opposition leaders to take over the government.
29 Dec. 1966	The College of Chiefs meets the king to discuss the role of the king in the traditional law and his demand for more political power.
Jan. 1967	Archbishop Fortescue Makheta is nominated as Suffragan Bishop of Lesotho.
5 Jan. 1967	The leaders of both opposition parties are put under arrest. They are charged with incitement to commit public violence and of taking part in illegal meetings.
5 Jan. 1967	King Moshoeshoe II signs a tripartite agreement to adhere to the role assigned to him by the Constitution.
18 Jan. 1967	The Lesotho Government invites all South African political refugees, who wish to leave the country, to make formal application.
4 Feb. 1967	Signs treaty on diplomatic relations with Malawi.
17 Feb. 1967	Signs agreement with Great Britain concerning public officers.
24 Feb. 1967	Signs investment guarantee agreement with United States.
26 Feb. 1967	Chief Jonathan sends a formal note to the UN Secretary-General protesting against the training of youth to commit acts of sabotage by certain countries.

13-20 Mar.1967	Signs an amendment with South Africa concerning insured parcels.
26 Mar. 1967	Signs International Telecommunications Convention.
13 Apr. 1967	Signs nursing examination agreement with Botswana and Swaziland.
12 May 1967	Chief Jonathan commences a goodwill visit to Malawi.
23 May 1967	Signs amendment to Articles 24 and 25 of the World Health Organization's Constitution.
7 July 1967	Signs World Health Organization's nomenclature regulations.
6 Sept. 1967	Signs continuation of the Universal Postal Union Final Protocol and detailed general regulations.
22 Sept. 1967	Exchange of notes with United States on the Peace Corps.
27 Sept. 1967	Signs air service agreement with South Africa.
29 Sept. 1967	Signs the UNESCO constitution.
5 Oct. 1967	Agreement with the United States for the continued application to Lesotho of certain treaties concluded between the United States and Great Britain.
6 Oct. 1967	Chief Maserbane introduces a bill providing for the extradition of fugitives from South Africa.
15 Oct. 1967	Agreement with the United States for the continued application to Lesotho of certain treaties concluded between the United States and Great Britain.
23 Oct. 1967	Chief Jonathan announces in the Assembly that South Africa made a grant of R25,000 to pay for the expansion of Lesotho Mounted Police.
7 Nov. 1967	Basic agreement for technical advisory assistance from the World Health Organization.
11 Nov. 1967	Signs multilateral basic agreement with FAO.
13 Nov. 1967	Signs basic agreement with Taiwan on technical cooperation.
26 Dec. 1967	The 50th annual conference of the official Lesotho Opposition Party, condemns the foreign policy of Chief Jonathan who allows unchecked interference of foreign countries, particularly of South Africa, in domestic affairs.
Feb. 1968	Chief Jonathan announces that he is prepared to co-operate with South Africa in eradicating communism, terrorism and stock theft, but all South African political refugees will have to leave the country.
Feb. 1968	The former British Governor-General of Malawi accepts an invitation by Chief Jonathan to act as adviser on government matters.
Mar. 1968	Chief Jonathan warns the king, Moshoeshoe II, that 'ruthless action' will be

taken against him, unless he refrains from political activity.

15 Mar. 1968	The Senate votes to unseat the Vice-President, because of unbecoming conduct by involving himself too deeply with political issues.
15 Mar. 1968	Lesotho and South Africa fail to reach agreement on a common extradition treaty, because South Africa insists on the inclusion of Namibia.
20 Mar. 1968	Lesotho informs the United Nations Secretary-General that it will not use force to bring down the Rhodesian government.
23 Mar. 1968	The first Ambassador from Lesotho presents his credentials to France's President.
16 May 1968	Agreement respecting development assistance signed with C.A.R.E.
1-30 June 1968	Lesotho establishes diplomatic relations with Kenya.
18 June 1968	Signs multilateral agreement for the amelioration of conditions of wounded and sick of armed forces in the field.
18 June 1968	Signs multilateral agreement for the amelioration of conditions of the wounded, sick and shipwrecked members of the armed forces at sea.
18 June 1968	Multilateral agreement on treatment of prisoners of war.
3 July 1968	Agreement amending the arrangement between Great Britain and Lesotho for the avoidance of double taxation and the prevention of fiscal evasion with respect to taxes on income.
9 July 1968	Signs multilateral agreement on treaty on non-proliferation of nuclear weapons.
24 July 1968	Chief Jonathan reshuffles his cabinet, abolishing the Ministry of Justice. All matters relating to the administration of justice except those dealing with the constitution will be referred to the newly created post of minister to the Prime Minister.
25 July 1968	Signs articles of agreement with the International Bank for Reconstruction and Development.
25 July 1968	Signs articles of agreement with the International Monetary Fund.
Aug. 1968	Chief Jonathan warns the Basuto Congress Party to refrain from destructive criticism of his 'good neighbour' policy towards South Africa.
31 Aug. 1968	The Prime Minister announces that he will ask South Africa to remove one of Lesotho's political refugees. This is necessary as they collaborated with the opposition party whose leaders obtained money from East Germany to overthrow the government.
15 Sept. 1968	Signs African Convention on the Conservation of Nature and Natural Resources.
19 Sept. 1968	Signs multilateral agreement on settlement of investment disputes between

states and nationals of other states.

Oct. 1968	Lesotho's envoy presents his credentials as Ambassador in Cameroon, as High Commissioner in Ghana, Sierra Leone and Uganda.
24 Oct. 1968	Signs a treaty against discrimination in education with UNESCO.
Nov. 1968	Lesotho's new Ambassador presents his credentials to the President of the Ivory Coast.
11 Nov. 1968	Signs treaty obtaining assistance from the World Food Programme.
13 Nov. 1968	Signs technical cooperation agreement with Taiwan.
Dec. 1968	An agreement is reached between Lesotho and South Africa to implement the Oxbow hydro-electric scheme to be financed by the UN Development Programme.
14 Feb. 1969	Signs treaty with Canada on the provision of telecommunications equipment to the University of Botswana, Lesotho and Swaziland.
Mar. 1969	Relations between Chief Jonathan and King Moshoeshoe remain tense, but the king denies rumours of his abdication.
27 Mar. 1969	Signs loan agreement with South Africa.
28 May 1969	Signs multilateral agreement on transit trade of landlocked states.
15 Aug. 1969	Chief Jonathan, arrives in Zambia. He assures President Kaunda of Lesotho's support of African unity.
22 Aug. 1969	Signs trade agreement with Zambia.
10 Sept. 1969	Signs OAU agreement on refugee problems in Africa.
12 Sept. 1969	Signs diplomatic treaty with Malawi.
26 Sept. 1969	The new ambassador to Kenya presents his credentials to President Kenyatta.
Oct. 1969	Chief Jonathan announces that the first post-independence election will be held on 27 January 1970.
22 Oct. 1969	Signs diplomatic agreement with Malta.
7 Nov. 1969	To prepare for the election, parliament and registration of voters is suspended.
13 Nov. 1969	Chief Jonathan's BNP promises to negotiate with South Africa for the release of the 'conquered' territory of the Orange Free State.
16 Nov. 1969	Signs Convention on the Privileges and Immunities of the United Nations.
26 Nov. 1969	Signs multilateral agreements on privileges and immunities of the United Nations' specialized agencies.

26 Nov. 1969	Signs Vienna Convention on diplomatic relations.
27 Nov. 1969	The leader of the Opposition Basutoland Congress Party and a number of supporters appear at the Magistrate Court due to an incident during the previous week when he addressed a political meeting.
1 Dec. 1969	Signs agreement with Denmark on the mutual waiver of visas.
11 Dec. 1969	Signs multilateral agreement on the Southern African Customs Union.
15 Dec. 1969	Chief Jonathan addresses a news conference and says that at the forthcoming elections his party will continue to pursue friendly relations with South Africa. He predicts that all seats will be won by his party, but that would not be a declaration of a one-party state.
15 Dec. 1969	Signs agreement with Sweden on the mutual waiver of visas.
21 Dec. 1969	Signs friendship treaty with Taiwan.
22 Dec. 1969	Signs agreement with Norway on the mutual waiver of visas.
Jan. 1970	The Congress Party appeals to the UN, OAU and the Commonwealth against the actions of Chief Jonathan.
1 Jan. 1970	Signs an extradition treaty with Sweden.
6 Jan. 1970	Signs agreement with Great Britain on the maintenance of sterling reserves.
9 Jan. 1970	Signs agreement with United States respecting the sale and distribution of United Nations stamps in Lesotho.
12 Jan. 1970	Signs multilateral convention on simplification of customs and protocol formalities.
21 Jan. 1970	Signs an agreement with Israel relating to visas.
27 Jan. 1970	The result of the first general election since independence ends with the defeat of Chief Leabua Jonathan's ruling party.
29 Jan. 1970	Signs an agreement with Iceland respecting mutual waiver of visas.
30 Jan. 1970	Following his defeat at the general election Leabua Jonathan declares a state of emergency and a curfew from 6 p.m. to 6 a.m. for a fortnight, suspends the constitution and orders the arrest of opposition leaders. Serious disturbances follow.
31 Jan. 1970	King Moshoeshoe II is placed under house arrest. The King's position is to be clarified.
Feb. 1970	The French Ambassador to Zambia is also appointed Ambassador to Lesotho.
2 Feb. 1970	Police headquarters in Maseru announces that a dusk-to-dawn curfew, previously only applicable to Maseru, is extended to all major centres. The leaders of the Congress Party are arrested.

3 Feb. 1970	Chief Jonathan declares that he agrees with most African leaders that the Western concept of democracy is not compatible with African problems.
8 Feb. 1970	Chief Jonathan bans the Communist Party.
11 Feb. 1970	The brother of King Moshoeshoe, Chief Seeiso, who is third in the line of succession is arrested.
12 Feb. 1970	Chief Jonathan issues a warning to interfering foreigners, and asks them to leave the country before the government takes action against them.
24 Feb. 1970	Signs agreement with San Marino respecting a mutual waiver of visas.
25 Feb. 1970	Chief Jonathan meets the detained opposition leader. They agree that the restoration of peace and order was the only basis to return to constitutional government.
26 Feb. 1970	The acting President of the Revolutionary Command of the Pan-African Congress says that the revolutionary forces will act against Chief Jonathan if he hands over PAC freedom fighters in Lesotho to South Africa.
27 Feb. 1970	The leader of the royalist Marematlou Freedom Party is placed under indefinite house arrest. Restrictions are also imposed on the General Secretary of the Party.
3 Mar. 1970	The former Police Commissioner, Clement Loepa, who marched on the capital to reinstate the deposed king, is killed by the Lesotho police.
10 Mar. 1970	Lesotho's new Ambassador to France presents his credentials to President Pompidou.
13 Mar. 1970	Chief Jonathan announces that the new constitution being drawn up will emphasise the unity of the Basuto nation.
10-30 Mar.1970	During this period a great number of people are killed, or injured and 88 houses are destroyed in the home village of King Moshoeshoe II. Demonsrations by the Basutoland Congress Party also result in killings.
22 Mar. 1970	The government issues a warning to the opposition Congress Party that its continued existence will depend on the behavior of its leaders.
31 Mar. 1970	Chief Jonathan announces that King Moshoeshoe II has technically abdicated and is leaving the country with his family for an indefinite period.
Apr. 1970	Violent clashes occur during the month between the police and opposition groups with an estimated 400 persons killed.
3 Apr. 1970	King Moshoeshoe II leaves Lesotho for the Netherlands where he intends staying no longer than six months. In his absence his wife, Queen Mamohato, will assume the duties of regent with the full approval of the government.
4 Apr. 1970	Serious rioting breaks out, at diamond diggings in the Letseng-la-terai area, where police intervention results in a number of persons killed.

5 Apr. 1970	A joint communiqué of the four leaders and distributed under the authority of Chief Jonathan, deplores the violence that sweeps the country.
6 Apr. 1970	The Prime Minister's office announces that a large quantity of explosives were found in the stores of a wealthy businessman. A master plan, describing in detail the destruction of Chief Jonathan's government, was also found.
9 Apr. 1970	A meeting between Prime Minister Jonathan and three opposition leaders, dealing with the country's political crisis breaks up without an agreement.
14 Apr. 1970	At the preparatory conference of non-aligned countries, the Lesotho delegate says that the release of the members of the BCP depends on their recognition and acceptance of the present regime.
1 May 1970	The leaders of Lesotho's four main political parties resolve to ignore the results of the January general election as a first step towards solving the country's constitutional crisis.
1 May 1970	Signs agreement with Finland, respecting the mutual waiver of visas.
7 May 1970	The leader of the Opposition, Mr. Mokhele, is released from detention and declares his willingness to serve with his Party in a coalition government under the leadership of Chief Jonathan.
11 May 1970	With the resumption of the High Court sessions, normality seems to return to Lesotho's political scene.
25 May 1970	Chief Jonathan criticizes in a broadcast the OAU and the Commonwealth for violating their promises not to interfere in each other's domestic affairs.
2 June 1970	Lesotho police announces the release of sixty-eight people detained under the emergency regulations. They included the head of the Marematlou Freedom Party.
30 June 1970	Speaking at a ceremony in honour of the British High Commissioner, Chief Jonathan warns the U.K. against using its aid to Lesotho as a political lever.
24 July 1970	Regarding the refugee problem Lesotho says that the OAU and the United Nations member states must be positive in their handling of the refugee problem, namely the asylum question.
12 Aug. 1970	Chief Jonathan expresses regret that the party leaders are unwilling to attend a round table talk to end the constitutional crisis.
30 Aug. 1970	At the 15th session of the OAU Ministerial Council, Lesotho abstains from voting for the resolution condemning France, Britain and Germany for supplying arms to South Africa. Lesotho's reservation on the resolution of the Namibian question is registered.
1 Sept. 1970	Chief Jonathan, attends the seventh Summit Conference of the OAU.
8-10 Sept.1970	A Lesotho delegation attends the Third Non-Aligned Summit Conference at Lusaka.

Oct. 1970	Chief Jonathan announces that the country will take a five year holiday from politics to recover from the years of party feuding.
14 Oct. 1970	It is reported that King Mosheshoe II has discussed the amendments to the constitution and his possible return to Lesotho with a delegation of senior chiefs.
19 Nov. 1970	Speaking at the opening of the United States Embassy in Maseru, Chief Jonathan says that quiet diplomacy even though slow, is the best way of assisting Africans in countries still under minority rule.
30 Nov. 1970	The Dutch Foreign Ministry announces that King Moshoeshoe II will return to Lesotho on 3 December. Chief Jonathan comments that the monarchy must be maintained as a symbol of peace and unity.
Dec. 1970	The High Court sentences to imprisonment thirty-one dissidents who organised a private gang against the Lesotho police.
4 Dec. 1970	King Moshoeshoe returns to Lesotho from 'his voluntary exile' in the Netherlands after the suspension of the constitution and undertakes not to involve the monarchy in politics.
11 Dec. 1970	Lesotho signs a customs agreement with South Africa, Botswana and Swaziland.
Jan. 1971	Chief Jonathan announces the country's first development plan for the period 1970 to 1975.
1 Jan. 1971	Signs multilateral agreement on international health regulations.
7 Jan. 1971	Signs agreement with Great Britain concerning officers designated by the British government in the service of Lesotho.
7 Jan. 1971	Signs agreement with Great Britain respecting Overseas Service Aid Scheme (OSAS).
10 Jan. 1971	Chief Jonathan declares Lesotho a hunger-stricken area and appeals for international aid.
13 Jan. 1971	Signs an agreement with Malawi respecting air services.
14-21 Jan.1971	At the Conference of the Heads of Government of the Commonwealth, Chief Jonathan gives his views on South Africa, on the permanence of the Commonwealth, the Russian naval presence in the Indian Ocean and on Rhodesia.
20 Jan. 1971	Signs additional regulations with the World Health Organisation amending international sanitary regulations.
30 Jan. 1971	The constitution is suspended.
Feb. 1971	The Common Market meeting in Brussels announces that Lesotho, Botswana and Swaziland will be given three forms of agreement with the EEC.

Feb. 1971	The Lesotho government declares that it has no quarrel with the British decision to supply helicopters to South Africa.
6 Feb. 1971	Radio Johannesburg reports that the Lesotho Government considers the situation in Uganda an internal affair.
19 Feb. 1971	The curfew imposed in 1970 following the General Elections is lifted in Lesotho as announced by the police in Maseru, except on the main roads from midnight to 5 a.m.
3 Mar. 1971	Lesotho's Ambassador presents his credentials to President Kenyatta of Kenya.
30 Mar. 1971	Signs a treaty with Great Britain on the African Auxiliary Pioneer Corps pensions.
26 Apr. 1971	Signs an agreement with West Germany confirming continued application of extradition treaties of 1872 and 1960.
8 May 1971	Lesotho does not contribute to the OAU for the support of freedom-fighters in Southern Africa.
11 May 1971	The Cabinet decides to restore the two courts suspended at the same time as the constitution.
23 May 1971	Chief Jonathan says in an interview with the Johannesburg Sunday Times that the dialogue with South Africa has already begun.
8 June 1971	India establishes diplomatic relations with Lesotho. The Indian High Commissioner presents his credentials to the President of Malawi as he will be based in Blantyre.
11 June 1971	The United Kingdom announces the resumption of normal relations with Lesotho, which were interrupted at the suspension of the constitution.
23 June 1971	At the 16th session of the OAU Ministerial Council, Lesotho votes against the anti-dialogue with South Africa motion.
29 June 1971	Seven men are imprisoned for conspiring to overthrow the government.
30 June 1971	Signs an agreement with Republic of Korea respecting mutual waiver of visas.
17 July 1971	Signs an agreement with Benelux Countries on the abolition of visas.
19 July 1971	A goodwill mission arrives in the Ivory Coast with a message from Chief Jonathan to President Hophouet-Boigny that Lesotho supports the question of peace in Africa.
20 July 1971	Signs an agreement with United Nations Development Programme on residential housing for the Oxbow Project.
Aug. 1971	The Lesotho High Commissioner to Kenya relinquishes his post.
31 Aug. 1971	A cabinet reshuffle is gazetted.

14 Sept. 1971	Signs an agreement with Great Britain prolonging the Sterling Area Agreement.
31 Sept. 1971	The Cabinet is reshuffled for the first time since the 1970 aborted general elections.
5 Oct. 1971	Signs agreement with San Marino on treaty of extradition.
7 Oct. 1971	Signs an agreement with Greece on the mutual waiver of visas.
12 Oct. 1971	Signs multilateral agreement on suppression of unlawful seizure of aircraft.
12 Oct. 1971	Signs multilateral agreement establishing International Red Locust Control Organisation.
25 Oct. 1971	Lesotho votes against the admission of the Republic of China to the United Nations.
Nov. 1971	The Nigerian High Commissioner presents his credentials to King Moshoeshoe.
4 Nov. 1971	Signs multilateral agreement on elimination of all forms of racial discrimination.
9 Nov. 1971	Signs the Final Protocol with the Universal Postal Union constitutary parcel agreements, general and detailed regulations.
Dec. 1971	On an official visit to Madagascar, Chief Jonathan and President Tseranana sign a joint communiqué reasserting their faith in dialogue in the UN and the OAU. The two countries intend to strengthen their good relations and to establish diplomatic relations.
4 Dec. 1972	The Embassy established by Israel in Swaziland is also responsible for Lesotho.
7 Dec. 1971	Signs agreement with Madagascar respecting mutual waiver of visas.
2 Jan. 1972	Restrictions imposed on Ntsu Mokhehle, leader of the main opposition Congress Party are lifted and 50 political detainees are released. These moves are aimed at a probable establishment of a national coalition government.
7 Jan. 1972	Signs a treaty with Kenya respecting reciprocal performance of consular functions.
7 Jan. 1972	Signs treaty with Greece on legal proceedings in civil/commercial matters.
7 Jan. 1972	Signs supplementary convention with Turkey on legal proceedings in civil and commercial matters.

7 Jan. 1972	Signs treaty with Norway on legal proceedings in civil/commercial matters.
10 Jan. 1972	The Lesotho High Commissioner presents his credentials to President Amin of Uganda.
13 Jan. 1972	Signs air services agreement with Malawi.
18 Jan. 1972	Signs treaty with Belgium respecting legal proceedings in civil and commercial matters plus supplementary convention on 1922.
18 Jan. 1972	Signs agreement with Netherlands on the application of the convention between Great Britain and Northern Ireland and Netherlands on legal proceedings in civil/commercial matters.
18 Jan. 1972	Signs treaty with Sweden on legal proceedings in civil/commercial matters.
20 Jan. 1972	The African-American Conference of Lusaka ends with a call by African delegates, Lesotho among them, for America's involvement in the liberation of African countries still under colonial rule.
10 Feb. 1972	Signs multilateral agreement for prohibition of the use of asphyxiating gases in war.
29 Feb. 1972	Signs treaty with Spain on legal proceedings in civil/commercial matters.
3 Mar. 1972	Signs multilateral agreement on the law of treaties.
7 Mar. 1972	The Office of the Prime Minister announces that the government of Lesotho asked nearly all black African States to with-hold further favourable moves toward South Africa until a joint approach is approved by the OAU.
29 Mar. 1972	Signs multilateral convention on internatonal liability for damage caused by space objects.
Apr. 1972	The Secretary of SWAPO accuses the Lesotho and Malawi governments of sabotaging the liberation war inside Namibia.
4 Apr. 1972	The Commissioner of Police is dismissed and is replaced by the Director of Intelligence and an Assistant Commissioner of Police.
7 Apr. 1972	Signs an agreement with UNICEF on its activities in Lesotho.
10 Apr. 1972	Signs multilateral agreement on the prohibition of development, production and stockpiling of bacteriological and toxic weapons.
24 Apr. 1972	Signs multilateral agreement on abolishing requirements of legalization of foreign public documents.
4 May 1972	South Africa and Lesotho decide to establish reciprocal consular representation at consul-general level.
8 May 1972	Signs a memorandum of understanding with Great Britain on the provision of British technical assistance.

19 May 1972	Exchange of notes with Denmark respecting the treaties of commerce of 1660, 1670 and 1814.
12 June 1972	The Ninth Assembly of the OAU's Summit approves a recommendation of twelve countries, Lesotho among them, to work out a new draft convention on inter-African technical co-operation.
6 July 1972	Signs treaty with Austria on legal proceedings in civil/commercial matters.
24 July 1972	One of the longest serving cabinet ministers, who served as Minister of Works, Health and Social Welfare and recently Minister of Works and Telecommunications, resigns.
27 July 1972	Signs multilateral agreement on offences and other acts committed on board aircraft.
30 July 1972	The High Commissioner of Lesotho presents his credentials to President Amin of Uganda.
Aug. 1972	Lesotho's delegation attends the fourth conference of the Non-Aligned countries in Guyana.
25 Aug. 1972	Signs multilateral agreement in Vienna on Consular Relations.
6 Sept. 1972	Signs multilteral convention on prohibition on development, production and stockpiling of bacteriological and toxic weapons.
4 Oct. 1972	At a ceremony marking Lesotho's sixth anniversary of independence, Chief Jonathan says that racial discrimination is the root cause of failure to a solution through dialogue in Southern Africa.
6 Nov. 1972	Signs assistance treaty with UNICEF.
9 Nov. 1972	The Ambassador of Lesotho presents his credentials to President Nyerere of Tanzania.
28 Nov. 1972	Lesotho and South Africa conduct enquiries in connection with the alleged abduction of a South African fugitive charged under the Terrorism Act.
Dec. 1972	The former Interior Minister of South Africa, who had resigned from the National Party, warns that there are 'dangerous gaps' in South Africa's relations with Botswana and Lesotho.
Dec. 1972	Israel decides to upgrade its relations with Rwanda, Swaziland, Botswana and Lesotho. A permanent Chargé d'Affairs, residing in Swaziland, will deal with Botswana and Lesotho.
4 Dec. 1972	The Embassy established by Israel in Swaziland is also responsible for Lesotho.
16 Jan. 1973	Signs agreement with the Organisation of African Unity on privileges and immunities.
16 Jan. 1973	Signs multilateral treaty on the privileges and immunities of the Organisation

of African Unity (OAU).

Feb. 1973	The opposition urges Chief Jonathan, to convene fresh inter-party talks to prepare for reinstating the constitution which was suspended in 1970 and re-open parliament.
1 Feb. 1973	Signs treaty with Commonwealth Fund for technical cooperation.
4 Feb. 1973	Signs memorandum of understanding with Canada on financial assistance.
19 Feb. 1973	Signs treaty with Yugoslavia regarding legal proceedings in civil/commercial matters.
19 Feb. 1973	Signs agreement with Hungary on legal proceedings in civil and commercial matters.
19 Feb. 1973	Signs a treaty with Yugoslavia on legal proceedings in civil and commercial matters.
20 Feb. 1973	Signs convention with Poland on tonnage measurement of merchant ships.
26 Feb. 1973	Signs project agreement with the Agency for International Development.
3 Mar. 1973	Signs multilateral agreement on international trade in endangered species.
12 Mar. 1973	Speaking at a ceremony, Chief Jonathan announces that Lesotho will return to Parliamentary rule after a suspension of three years. The new Assembly will consist of newly elected nominees of the various parties. He also announces that the main task of the Assembly will be to work out a new constitution.
23 Mar. 1973	Signs credit agreement with International Development Association on the Thaba/Bosiu rural development project.
24 Mar. 1973	Chief Jonathan announces that the first session of the newly constitued Parliament will be held in April.
Apr. 1973	Lesotho is studying the feasibility of introducing television.
27 Apr. 1973	King Moshoeshoe II delivers the speech from the throne at the first session of the Interim Assembly. He identifies the government programme for education, agriculture, communications, health and economy. Legislation will be introduced to establish a Boundaries Commission with South Africa.
27 Apr. 1973	The Interim Assembly is formed. The Basotho National Party, the Maramatlou Freedom Party, the United Democratic Party are represented but the Basuto Congress Party refuses to be represented unless its demands are first discussed with the Prime Minister.
30 Apr. 1973	Chief Jonathan addresses the Assembly and reaffirms Lesotho's commitment to 'dialogue', both in domestic and foreign policy. He condemns the Western world's contravention of UN policy against Rhodesia and declares that the problems of Southern Africa are an international issue.
May 1973	At the Tenth Assembly of the OAU Heads of State, Lesotho becomes part

of study groups which proposes to move the OAU headquarters from the Ethiopian capital.

10 May 1973   Signs treaty with International Atomic Energy Agency for application of safeguards.

24 May 1973   King Moshoeshoe II represents Lesotho at the Tenth Assembly of Heads of State and government of the OAU.

29 May 1973   At the 10th Assembly of the Heads of State of the OAU Lesotho becomes part of the 'good offices' committee to find a solution to Ethiopia and Somali frontier dispute.

8 June 1973   Signs agreement with Federal Republic of Germany on assistance to Lesotho's health service.

12 June 1973   Signs agreement with Catholic Church for provision of relief services.

12 June 1973   Signs agreement with the International Atomic Energy Agency for the application of safeguards in connection with the treaty on the non-proliferation of nuclear weapons.

July 1973   The Kenyan High Commissioner presents his credentials to King Moshoeshoe.

3 July 1973   Signs an agreement with African Development Bank.

24 July 1973   Chief Jonathan lifts the emergency imposed in 1970 and a former leader of the opposition is released from detention.

25 July 1973   Signs treaty with International Development Association on development credit.

25 July 1973   Lesotho's three year old state of emergency ends as Chief Jonathan declares in a broadcast. However he warns people to abstain from acts of 'hooliganism and subversion'.

27 July 1973   Lesotho's first High Commissioner to Nigeria presents his credentials.

24 Aug. 1973   Signs agreement with South Africa on establishment of labour representatives in South Africa.

24 Aug. 1973   Chief Jonathan says in a broadcast that relations with South Africa and the establishment of diplomatic relations is hampered by South Africa's policy of colour discrimination against Basotho citizens.

27 Aug. 1973   Signs constitution of the African Civil Aviation Commission.

28 Aug. 1973   Signs agreement with Norway on extradition.

30 Aug. 1973   Signs treaty with Great Britain concerning the British International Voluntary Service.

5-9 Sept. 1973 Lesotho participates at the Fourth Non-Aligned Summit Conference in

Algeria.

19 Sept. 1973	The Zambian High Commissioner to Botswana is accredited to Lesotho and presents his credentials to King Moshoshoe.
21 Sept. 1973	The interim National Assembly declines an opposition motion, proposing diplomatic relations with South Africa.
27 Sept. 1973	Signs multilateral agreement on road traffic.
2 Oct. 1973	Signs agreement with Federal Republic of Germany on the exchange of notes regarding services of football coach.
3 Oct. 1973	Signs agreement with Belgium concerning supply of wheat.
9 Oct. 1973	President Sir Seretse Khama visits Lesotho and reaffirms his country's commitment to the promotion of non-racism.
15 Oct. 1973	The leader of the Opposition and several followers decide to participate in the Assembly, being expelled from the party in consequence.
23 Oct. 1973	Signs multilateral optional protocol on compulsory settlement of disputes arising out of the Law of Sea Convention of 29 April 1958.
23 Oct. 1973	Signs multilateral agreement on territorial sea and contiguous zone.
23 Oct. 1973	Signs multilateral convention on freedom of transit.
23 Oct. 1973	Signs multilateral declaration recognizing the right to a flag of states with no sea-coast.
23 Oct. 1973	Signs multilateral agreement on the high seas.
Nov. 1973	Mr. Makroane, an opposition member in the Interim Assembly, announces the formation of a United Front, consisting of opposition members. The aim of the Front is national reconciliation.
12 Nov. 1973	The President of Botswana, Sir Seretse Khama, the Prime Ministers of Swaziland and Lesotho hold their first summit meeting in Gaborone, in a cordial atmosphere. They decide to establish a Consultative Commission which would meet at regular intervals to discuss topics of mutual interest.
19 Nov. 1973	At the eighth Extraordinary Session of the OAU, Lesotho, with Swaziland and Botswana, makes reservations about the paragraph in the proceedings calling for an oil embargo against South Africa.
16 Dec. 1973	Chief Jonathan threatens to arrest four men for treason after receiving a document calling for representative government, favourable to the Basotho people, which was signed by the leader of the Opposition.
7 Jan. 1974	The country's British-trained Mobile Police Unit foils an attempt by the oposition Basotho Congress Party to overthrow the government of Chief Jonathan.
Feb. 1974	Lesotho refuses an offer to exchange political refugees wanted by South

Africa. South Africa denies that the men wanted by Lesotho for the 7th January coup were in South Africa.

1 Feb. 1974	Signs memorandum of understanding with the Commonwealth Fund for Technical Cooperation.
4 Feb. 1974	Signs memorandum of understanding with Canada on financial assistance.
21 Feb. 1974	Signs multilateral agreement on rescue of astronauts, return of astronauts and return of space objects.
25 Feb. 1974	A bill to fight terrorism is tabled at the Interim National Assembly by Chief Majara.
27 Feb. 1974	Signs agreement with Great Britain on public officers' pensions.
Mar. 1974	The government introduces a Security Bill into the interim assembly aimed at prohibiting the flow of foreign funds from abroad to political organisations in the country.
7 Mar. 1974	The Star (Johannesburg) reports from Maseru that forty-nine supporters of the opposition BCP party had been executed following the January coup. The Lesotho Government states in a broadcast on Radio Lesotho The Star report is speculation.
11 Mar. 1974	Signs memorandum of understanding regarding Canadian assistance.
25 Mar. 1974	Signs economic, financial and technical assistance and cooperation agreement with Libya.
25 Mar. 1974	Signs financial assistance agreement with Libya.
8 Apr. 1974	Foreign Ministers of Lesotho and South Africa hold discussions and resolve certain misunderstandings on the principle of good neighbourliness.
28 Apr. 1974	Some South African parlamentarians maintain that the policy of their Premier, John Vorster, rests on forming a 'powerbloc' of independent Southern African states which could comprise South Africa, Rhodesia, Lesotho, Botswana, and Swaziland.
8 May 1974	Signs treaty with Agency for International Development on the establishment of a regional testing resource and training centre.
June 1974	The parliamentary leader of the opposition BCP party is willing to accept the extension of Lesotho's 'five year political holiday' provided all political parties are appointed. He adds that a national government is necessary to unite the people.
25 June 1974	The Lesotho Government's spokesman objects to the reported release of nine Opposition Party supporters who had fled to South Africa. He claims that

this results from Lesotho government's refusal to extradite South African political refugees.

July 1974   Lesotho and Liberia decide to establish diplomatic relations at ambassadorial level.

1-4 July 1974   President Tolbert of Liberia pays a state visit. Speaking at a banquet in Maseru he attacks the white domination in Southern Africa. In his answer Chief Jonathan states that Lesotho will never break its pledge of solidarity with the cause of African liberation.

4 July 1974   President Tolbert signs an agreement in which both governments give their full support to the Organization of African Unity.

5 July 1974   A comprehensive Cabinet change is organized by the Prime Minister. This is strongly criticized by the opposition parties.

25 July 1974   Signs development credit agreement with the International Development Association on an Education Project.

26 July 1974   The Ambassador of Lesotho presents his credentials to President Giscard d'Estaing of France.

31 July 1974   Signs agreement with German Federal Republic on the development of metal working/motor mechanics.

7 Aug. 1974   Signs treaty with Taiwan concerning mutual waiver of visa fees.

26 Aug. 1974   Signs treaty with Israel concerning assistance to Lesotho Health Service.

Sept. 1974   The World Bank mission arrives to plan employment for 10,000 Basotho miners repatriated from South Africa.

30 Sept. 1974   Signs specific agreement with Sweden on development cooperation.

9 Oct. 1974   Thirty-two men are remanded in custody in Maseru on charges of high treason arising out of the disturbances in January.

28 Oct. 1974   The High Commissioner of Lesotho presents his credentials to President Nyerere of Tanzania.

4 Nov. 1974   Multilateral agreement on the control of drugs outside the scope of the Convention of 1931.

4 Nov. 1974   Signs International Opium Convention.

4 Nov. 1974   Signs multilateral agreement on suppression of white slave traffic.

4 Nov. 1974   Signs multilateral protocol amending the 1961 Single Convention on Narcotic Drugs.

4 Nov. 1974   Signs multilateral agreement on political rights of women.

4 Nov. 1974	Signs multilateral Convention on Conflict of Nationality Law.
4 Nov. 1974	Signs multilateral protocol amending 1926 Convention on Slavery.
4 Nov. 1974	Signs multilateral agreement on the status of stateless persons.
4 Nov. 1974	Signs multilateral Convention on Abolition of Slavery.
4 Nov. 1974	Signs protocol on military obligation of double nationality.
11 Nov. 1974	King Moshoeshoe II arrives in Tanzania on a five-day state visit. Speaking at a banquet in his honour, he condemns South Africa and Rhodesia for their racist policies, and surrounded as Lesotho is by South Africa, it would never become another Bantustan.
20 Nov. 1974	The Interim National Assembly decides that a commision should be established to propose a new system of government to Lesotho, as the British system was opposed to Lesotho's interests. This Commission will investigate the constitutional wishes of the people.
21 Nov. 1974	Radio Kampala reports that following a meeting at Entebbe Airport, King Moshoeshoe II and President Amin agreed that Lesotho and Uganda would establish diplomatic relations.
25 Nov. 1974	The trial of thirty-two alleged supporters of the BCP, on charges of high treason for overthrowing the government is adjourned to allow the defence to prepare its case.
3 Dec. 1974	Signs telecommunications development treaty with Sweden.
5 Dec. 1974	Signs multilateral monetary agreement with South Africa and Swaziland.
19-22 Dec. 1974	Observers from Lesotho attend the meeting of the OAU Liberation Committee in Dar-es-Salaam. The meeting recommends further increase in military aid to the Patriotic Front guerrillas.
31 Dec. 1974	Signs agreement with the UN Development Programme.
23 Jan. 1975	Signs agreement on scientific and technical cooperation with Yugoslavia.
27 Feb. 1975	Signs agreement with Great Britain concerning public officers' pensions.
28 Feb. 1975	Lesotho becomes a signatory to the Lomé Convention.
10 Mar. 1975	Signs agreement with West Germany regarding technical co-operation.
10 Mar. 1975	Twenty-two members of the Basotho Congress Party are found guilty of treason and are condemned to nine years in prison.
23 Apr. 1975	Signs multilateral agreement on psychotropic substances.
19-29 May 1975	The Minister of Foreign Affairs visits China. Chinese authorities described it as a `friendly visit by invitation'.

26 June 1975	Signs loan agreement with Iran.
24 July 1975	Signs loan agreement with Denmark.
3 Sept. 1975	Signs agreement with United Nations Capital Development Fund on a grant providing for sanitation in rural schools.
3 Sept. 1975	Signs agreement with United Nations Capital Development Fund on co-operative low-cost housing.
3 Sept. 1975	Signs agreement with United Nations Capital Development Fund concerning Lesotho Credit Union League.
3 Sept. 1975	Signs agreement with United Nations Capital Development Fund on a pilot asparagus plant.
11 Sept. 1975	Signs Protocol amending the Convention on International Civil Aviation.
27 Oct. 1975	Signs amendment to Customs Union Agreement of 11 December 1969.
7 Nov. 1975	Signs agreement with Federal Republic of Germany for financing pre-investment studies for water-supplies in various townships.
28 Nov. 1975	Signs multilateral Convention for Suppression of Circulation and Traffic in Obscene Publications.
5 Dec. 1975	Lesotho, Swaziland and South Africa sign a monetary agreement.
Jan. 1976	Signs financial agreement with European Economic Community.
5 Jan. 1976	Signs financial agreement with European Economic Community.
23 Jan. 1976	Signs agreement with Yugoslavia on scientific and technical co-operation.
23 Jan. 1976	Signs trade agreement with Yugoslavia.
12 Feb. 1976	Swaziland and Lesotho establish diplomatic relations.
4 Mar. 1976	Signs technical assistance agreement with Swaziland on village water supply and rural access roads construction.
10 Mar. 1976	Signs treaty with International Development Association on development credit for Second Highway Project.
31 Mar. 1976	Signs agreement with Great Britain concerning officers designated by Great Britain to serve in Lesotho: extension of 1971 agreement.
18 June 1976	Signs agreement with Co-operative for American Relief Everywhere (CARE) on rural development and self-help programme.
13 July 1976	Signs International Telecommunications Convention, Final Protocol and Four Additional Protocols.
2 Aug. 1976	Signs treaty with Great Britain concerning officers designated by Great

Britain in the service of specified organizations or institutions in Lesotho.

27 Aug. 1976	Signs amendments with World Health Organization on Articles 34 and 55 of its Constitution.
Oct. 1976	A dispute prevails between Lesotho and South Africa regarding Transkei citizens rights to travel without passports from the one country to the other.
Oct. 1976	Chief Jonathan, takes a unilateral action and breaks up the existing Lesotho, Botswana and Swaziland University and establishes the National University of Lesotho and calls for the replacement of an African for vice-chancellor.
5 Oct. 1976	Signs cultural co-operation treaty with India.
14 Oct. 1976	Signs multilateral agreement with International Civil Defence Organisation.
1 Nov. 1976	Chief Jonathan lodges a complaint with the UN Security Council on Transkei.
12 Nov. 1976	Signs agreement with the European Coal and Steel Community.
12 Nov. 1976	Chief Jonathan appoints, for the first time, two members of the Opposition to his Cabinet.
22 Dec. 1976	The United Nations Security Council approves by consensus a resolution appealing to all states to provide immediate aid to Lesotho counteracting its economic difficulties arising from the closure of its border posts with the newly declared `independent' Transkei.
23 Dec. 1976	The Commission of the European Communities announces that it has agreed to grant Lesotho help from the European Development Fund towards the cost of improving roads, providing international links between the north-west and the south-east of the country.
28 Dec. 1976	Signs agreement with Denmark on volunteers.
30 Dec. 1976	UN Secretary-General, Dr. Kurt Waldheim, is sending a mission to Lesotho to study the border situation and to advise on an assistance programme.
Jan. 1977	President Nyerere invites Lesotho to become the sixth member of the five Front Line States. Lesotho's government is still considering the invitation.
5 Jan. 1977	Signs financial agreement with European Economic Community.
11 Jan. 1977	Signs loan agreement with OPEC Special Fund concerning balance of payments support.
Feb. 1977	Chief Jonathan renews his land claims against South Africa. He also complains that South Africa has withdrawn its maize and wheat subsidies causing great hardship.
Feb. 1977	Signs agreement with Montreal Engineers Company on Phuthiatsana Irrigation Project.

10 Feb. 1977	Lesotho attends the first conference of the Union of African Parliaments held in Mauritania.
24 Feb. 1977	Lesotho attends a closed door session of the Human Rights Commission, where the Ugandan situation is discussed.
Mar. 1977	Lesotho applies to the UN General Assembly for help to maintain its South African refugee programme.
4 Mar. 1977	Signs technical assistance agreement with Switzerland.
12 Mar. 1977	Signs agreement with Binnie and Partners on Phuthiatsana Irrigation Project.
29 Mar. 1977	Signs agreement with Yugoslavia on trade.
2 Apr. 1977	Signs agreement with West Germany on financial assistance.
21 Apr. 1977	Signs agreement with the Federal Republic of Germany concerning financial assistance.
30 Apr. 1977	Signs agreement with India on cultural co-operation.
20 May 1977	Signs development credit agreement with the International Development Association.
31 May 1977	Signs visa abolition agreement with Japan.
3 June 1977	Signs agreement on basic agricultural service programme with the European Economic Community.
24 June 1977	Signs agreement with Sweden on the financing of Lesotho's internal telecommunications for S.Kr.6,000,000.
29 June 1977	Signs agreement with Sweden on the financing of the Lesotho international telecommunication link with Nairobi.
July 1977	The African-American Institute of New York grants Lesotho $70,000 to help the Lesotho Government accommodates South African student refugees.
1 July 1977	Signs memorandum with Ireland on a hand-flat knitting factory.
1 July 1977	Signs a memorandum with Ireland on the Basotho Pony Project.
1 July 1977	Signs memorandum with Ireland on Hololo Valley Project.
12 July 1977	President Amin of Uganda appoints a new envoy to Lesotho.
Aug. 1977	Lesotho receives a donation of $29,000 from Denmark.
2 Aug. 1977	Signs a technical co-operation agreement with Taiwan.
11 Aug. 1977	Signs agreement with West Germany on construction of a hall of residence at NUL.
11 Aug. 1977	Signs agreement with West Germany on lighting equipment for Maseru

airport.

11 Aug. 1977 Signs agreement with West Germany on lighting equipment for the Maseru district.

Sept. 1977 The United Nations High Commissioner for Refugees announces a Scandinavian contribution to help refugees in Southern Africa. He names Lesotho among seven other countries as first asylum.

Sept. 1977 The Prime Minister of South Africa, Mr. Botha, warns Britain that any move to impose sanctions on South Africa regarding the Rhodesian independence question would affect neighbouring states, Lesotho amongst them.

Sept. 1977 Lesotho is represented at a Conference on Women and Development, sponsored by various UN agencies, held in Mauritania.

21 Sept. 1977 Signs agreement with Irish Leprosy Association on provision of a doctor.

28 Sept. 1977 Signs an agreement with Opportunities Industrial Centre International (OICC) on vocational training.

4 Nov. 1977 Signs development agreement with Fund for Research and Investment for the Development of Africa Ltd.

13 Nov. 1977 The Anglican Bishop of Lesotho, the Rev. Desmond Tutu announces his resignation to become secretary-general of the South African Council of Churches.

30 Nov. 1977 Signs agreement with International Development Association for the development of the Second Education Project.

1 Dec. 1977 Signs financing agreement with European Economic Community.

2 Dec. 1977 Signs agreement with Canada on assistance to small-scale diamond mining sector.

2 Dec. 1977 Signs memorandum of understanding with Canada on Canadian assistance for BEDCO.

2 Dec. 1977 Signs memorandum of understanding with Canada on project to expand facilities at the National University of Lesotho.

2 Dec. 1977 Signs agreement with Canada on the grant of $2,460,000.

18 Dec. 1977 Signs agreement with United States on land and water resource development.

30 Dec. 1977 Signs agreement with United States on Southern Africa development and personnel training.

30 Dec. 1977 Signs agreement with United States on Thaba-Bosiu rural development.

14 Feb. 1978 The United Nations High Commissioner for Refugees reports after a Southern African tour that it was impossible to give an accurate figure of

South African refugees in Lesotho.

17 Feb. 1978	Lesotho notifies the European Economic Community and the United Nations on neighbouring Transkei's stringent non-entry regulations.
Mar. 1978	Signs memorandum of understanding with West Germany on assignment of a radiologist.
16 Mar. 1978	Signs agreement with West Germany on Lesotho's telecommunication system.
16 Mar. 1978	Signs memorandum of understanding with West Germany on secondment of economic advisor.
Apr. 1978	A minor Cabinet reshuffle is announced.
6 Apr. 1978	Signs multilateral treaty on customs co-operation.
14 Apr. 1978	Signs multilateral agreement for the suppression of unlawful acts against civil aviation.
26 Apr. 1978	Signs agreement with West Germany on financial assistance.
27 Apr. 1978	Amends grant agreement with Great Britain.
18 May 1978	Signs agreement with West Germany on establishment of a fund for feasibility and pre-feasibility studies. (Semonkong Road)
25 May 1978	Signs development credit agreement with International Development Association on basic agricultural services programme.
June 1978	Diplomatic links are established between Cuba and Lesotho but so far no official confirmation is given by Lesotho.
9 June 1978	Signs agreement with Great Britain on the establishment and function of the British Council in Lesotho.
19 June 1978	Religious groups from Lesotho take part at the Meeting of the Evangelical Community for Apostolic Action.
20 June 1978	Signs agreement with USAID on the Lesotho Southern Perimeter Road.
26 June 1978	Signs treaty with West Germany concerning project promotion of a commercial training institute.
27 June 1978	Signs agreement with UN High Commissioner for Refugees on supplementary aid.
28 June 1978	Signs grant agreement with the United States relating to Southern Africa Academic Project.
6 July 1978	Signs agreement with Romania on education, science and culture.
25 July 1978	Signs agreement with World University Service of Canada on technical assistance programme.

15 Aug. 1978	Signs treaty with West Germany on the extension of laundry and catering services at National University of Lesotho.
15 Aug. 1978	Signs supplementary agreement with UNICEF on extension of laundry and catering services at National University of Lesotho.
21 Aug. 1978	Signs agreement with Canada on Lesotho community development sites.
26 Aug. 1978	Signs agreement with Mozambique on scientific and cultural co-operation.
26 Aug. 1978	Signs trade agreement with Mozambique
26 Aug. 1978	Signs air service agreement with Mozambique.
1 Sept. 1978	An agreement is concluded between the United States and the UN High Commissioner for Refugees in an assistance programme for Southern African refugees in Lesotho, Botswana and Zambia.
6 Sept. 1978	Signs agreement with UNICEF on construction of classrooms.
11 Sept. 1978	Signs agreement with Sweden on labour development.
14 Sept. 1978	Signs grant agreement with United Nations Capital Development Fund on the expansion of the Pilot Asparagus Plant.
18 Sept. 1978	Signs grant agreement with United Nations Capital Development Fund on the control of communicable diseases.
27 Sept. 1978	Signs agreement with West Germany on supply of rolled oats to Lesotho.
Oct. 1978	Lesotho takes part at an unprecedented meeting of South African black trade unionists and those affiliated to the Organisation of African Trade Union Unity.
Oct. 1978	West Germany gives ninety-two Southern African refugees in Lesotho scholarships for vocational and university education in West Germany.
1 Nov. 1978	Signs agreement with Denmark on technical co-operation.
7 Nov. 1978	Signs agreement with West Germany on financial cooperation.
7 Nov. 1978	Signs agreement with West Germany on village water supply.
14 Nov. 1978	Signs treaty with West Germany on development credit regarding Basic Agricultural Services Programme.
13 Dec. 1978	Amends grant agreement with Great Britain.
18 Dec. 1978	Signs agreement with West Germany on financial cooperation.
18 Dec. 1978	Signs agreement with West Germany on Roma Ramabanta road.
20 Dec. 1978	Signs agreement with West Germany on financial cooperation.

21 Dec. 1978	Signs memorandum with Great Britain on provisions of certain technical aid.
19-22 Dec.1978	Observers from Lesotho attend the OAU Standing Liberation Committee Meeting in Dar-es-Salaam.
8 Jan. 1979	Signs agreement with South Africa on the issuing of notes and coin.
Feb. 1979	Lesotho strongly protests to South Africa over two death incidents at the frontier and asks the United Nations to take action.
23 Feb. 1979	Lesotho is one of the fifteen countries who join the motion to decolonize the Western Sahara at the OAU Ministerial Council's 32nd session held in Nairobi.
23 Mar. 1979	Signs financing agreement with European Economic Community on annual micro-projects programme.
23 Mar. 1979	Signs financial agreement with European Economic Community on the financing of Mafetong-Tsoloane Road.
28 Mar. 1979	Signs treaty with Economic Commission for Africa, granting Lesotho $7,000.
19 Apr. 1979	Signs an amendment on Lerotholi Technical Project agreement with West Germany.
24 Apr. 1979	Signs agreement with West Germany on financial cooperation.
30 Apr. 1979	At a rally in Maseru to celebrate the 20th anniversary of the ruling party, Chief Jonathan reiterates his demand for the return of part of the Orange Free State by South Africa.
May 1979	Lesotho recognizes the new Ugandan government.
May 1979	Two separate incidents at opposite ends of the country involving a number of people killed gives rise to the speculation that the Basuto Congress Party is seeking to infiltrate the country to carry out subversive activities.
9 May 1979	Signs agreement with Israel on recruitment of international experts.
11 May 1979	Signs treaty with West Germany for the support of the Lesotho national transport system.
17 May 1979	Signs loan agreement with the African Development Fund.
22 May 1979	Signs admendment to the agreement with the United Nations High Commissioner for Refugees on the extension of laundry and catering services.
30 May 1979	Signs financial co-operation agreement with West Germany.
June 1979	Maseru and Havana announce that Lesotho and Cuba have established formal diplomatic relations.
June 1979	Lesotho takes part at a workshop organised by the Commonwealth Regional

Health Secretariat of the Malaria Control Conference.

7 June 1979	Signs treaty with Great Britain on retrospective terms arrangement.
19 June 1979	Signs treaty with Great Britain on the Lesotho/United Kingdom Second Triennium.
26 June 1979	A statement released in Maseru indicates that the Lesotho government intends to clamp down on political refugees. The order is connected with the recent bomb explosion.
July 1979	Chief Jonathan announces that the paramilitary police mobile unit of Lesotho is to be developed into a full army.
July 1979	The Lesotho Minister of Health and Social Welfare visits Mozambique accompanied by nine officials, to study problems of primary health care and concludes an agreement over exchange of health personnel.
4 July 1979	Signs treaty with West Germany for the promotion of the Lerotholi Technical Institute.
11 July 1979	Signs memorandum of understanding with Australia on the recruitment of Australian citizens for selected positions in its public service and statutory authorities.
14 July 1979	The OAU's Ministerial Summit Conference at Monrovia forms a committee to study recent developments in Zimbabwe and Namibia. The committee of eleven countries includes Lesotho.
18 July 1979	Signs agreement with West Germany on assignment of German volunteers.
31 July 1979	Signs agreement with the United Nations High Commissioner for Refugees on supplementary aid for South African refugees.
Aug. 1979	A new wave of violence is reported from Maseru. The National Basotho Party is thought to be behind the upheaval. Chief Jonathan may be considering new elections.
Aug. 1979	The anti-apartheid editor of a newspaper in Transkei has fled to Lesotho and asks for political asylum.
3 Aug. 1979	Accedes to the World Meteorological Organisation.
13 Aug. 1979	Signs agreement with the United Nations High Commission for Refugees on supplementary aid.
30 Aug. 1979	Signs agreement with West Germany amending loan project agreement of 31 May 1978.
30 Aug. 1979	Signs agreement with West Germany on project fund for feasibility studies.
30 Aug. 1979	Signs agreement with the United States on renewable energy technology projects.

30 Aug. 1979	Signs agreement with the United States on Instructional Material Resource Centre Project.
30 Aug. 1979	Signs agreement with the United States on farming systems research.
14 Sept. 1979	Signs agreement with Leprosy Mission on the development of national leprosy control programme.
27 Sept. 1979	Signs air services agreement with Botswana.
30 Sept. 1979	Signs grant agreement with the United States for rural water and sanitation.
17 Oct. 1979	Signs agreement with West Germany on financial cooperation.
27 Nov. 1979	The Lesotho Commissioner of Police denies that the Lesotho police has killed fifty members of the opposition Basotho Congress Party. Neighbouring Orange Free State farmers in South Africa say that they are harbouring Lesotho refugees who claim torture for sympathising with Basotho Congress Party.
27 Nov. 1979	Signs consultancy contract on oil supplies with Zinder-Companies Inc.
29 Nov. 1979	Signs supplementary aid agreement with the United Nations High Commissioner for Refugees for assistance to South African refugees.
Dec. 1979	Increasing sabotage is directed against the government of Chief Jonathan. Lesotho Radio calls upon Lesotho refugees to return to their country and blames South Africa for armed attacks on Lesotho.
Dec. 1979	Work commences on a modern brick plant with financial assistance provided by West Germany.
4 Dec. 1979	Signs co-operation agreement with France concerning the National University of Lesotho.
7 Dec. 1979	A new national currency known as the Maloti is introduced.
12 Dec. 1979	Signs agreement with South Africa on the use of a road camp site at Cobham Forest.
21 Dec. 1979	Signs loan agreement with the African Development Bank on the financing of projects: BEDCO and LNDC.
21 Dec. 1979	Signs co-operation agreement with France on hydraulic resources.
Jan. 1980	Refugees from Lesotho still trickle into South Africa.
Jan. 1980	South Africa is accused of backing the outlawed Basotho Congress Party leader and his Lesotho Liberation Army.
8 Jan. 1980	Signs debt release agreement with West Germany.
24 Jan. 1980	Signs supplementary agreement with the United Nations High Commissioner for Refugees for the construction of additional classrooms.

1 Feb. 1980	The Soviet Union and Lesotho decide to establish diplomatic relations. The Lesotho Government reassures South Africa that Lesotho will not allow its territory to be used as a springboard for attacks on South Africa.
26 Feb. 1980	A huge arms cache is discovered in the North East of Lesotho. The find is made in an area where the Lesotho police and members of the Basotho Congress Party have recently clashed.
17 Mar. 1980	Signs agreement with West Germany on project support on water and sewerage.
19 Mar. 1980	Lesotho becomes the eleventh member of the UPA (Union of African Parliaments) Committee at the fourth conference held in Kinshasha.
22 Mar. 1980	Twenty-eight people, who were housed at the refugee camp in the Orange Free State, return to Lesotho.
24 Mar. 1980	Lesotho Security Police detains under the country's 60-day detention law the Chairman of the Financial Fund of the World Council of Churches. No reasons are given.
1 Apr. 1980	A delegation from Lesotho attends the inaugural meeting of the Southern African Development Co-ordination Conference in Lusaka. The main areas of co-operation on which agreement was reached is issued in a communiqué.
2 Apr. 1980	Signs multilateral agreement on technical co-operation between the European Economic Community, Botswana, Lesotho and Swaziland.
8 Apr. 1980	Signs agreement with West Germany concerning support of the transport system Lesotho Freight Service Corporation.
17 Apr. 1980	Signs multilateral convention against the taking of hostages.
24 May 1980	Lesotho accepts the invitation to attend the Moscow Olympic Games.
27 May 1980	Signs multilateral financial agreement between the European Economic Community, Botswana, Lesotho and Swaziland.
10 June 1980	The National Assembly of Lesotho passes a bill granting amnesty to political exiles responsible for subversive activities.
20 June 1980	The paramilitary police announces the imposition of strict security measures at the South African border to curb the infiltration of guerrillas.
21 June 1980	Lesotho shows to Soviet and Cuban diplomats arms and ammunition of South African origin as evidence of its involvement in an alleged plot to overthrow the government.
27 June 1980	Signs agreement with Switzerland on technical co-operation: BEDCO.
14 July 1980	Signs agreement with the Arab Fund for technical assistance.
24 July 1980	King Moshoeshoe II attends the funeral of Sir Seretse Khama of Botswana. King Moshoeshoe is one of three African leaders who attends the funeral

service in the royal cemetery.

20 Aug. 1980	Lesotho takes part in the work of an OAU committee which deals with the recognition of Ogaden as an integral part of Ethiopia.
20 Aug. 1980	The South African Prime Minister P.W. Botha and Chief Jonathan, meet in an attempt to improve relations between the two countries.
3 Sept. 1980	Signs multilateral agreement on nomenclature of classification of goods in customs tariffs.
22 Sept. 1980	Chief Jonathan's brother is seriously wounded in an attack on two houses. The attack was perpetrated by a group of unknown men.
10 Oct. 1980	Signs agreement with United Nations High Commissioner for Refugees on the construction of additional classroooms and accommodation.
22 Oct. 1980	Signs agreement with Sweden on financial co-operation.
23 Oct. 1980	Signs agreement with West Germany on financial co-operation.
24 Oct. 1980	Signs financial agreement with West Germany on a rural airfield development programme.
29 Oct. 1980	Signs supplementary agreement with United Nations High Commissioner for Refugees on aid for South African refugees.
1981	A motion is introduced to the Lesotho National Assembly by Chief Jonathan to hold a referendum as the Basuto people are ready for a general election.
28 Jan. 1981	Signs loan agreement with South Africa on an agricultural development project.
Feb. 1981	The Minister of Information and Broadcasting informs a mass rally of students that in mid-February the police foiled a South African attempt to attack the capital.
6 Apr. 1981	The Heads of State of Lesotho, Botswana, Mozambique and Swaziland meet in Mbabane to discuss South Africa's incursions and subversive activities against these Southern African states.
May 1981	Under an amnesty declared for all Basuto Congress Party members allegedly implicated in `subversive activity', many return to Maseru.
8 June 1981	Signs agreement with the Centre for Integrated Rural Development for Africa on the establishment of a centre.
11 June 1981	Lesotho and South Africa decide to set up a consultative committee to resolve the misunderstandings arising out of the movement of people across the common border.
17 July 1981	Chief Jonathan reshuffles his cabinet, a move which is considered as preparatory for a referendum on a general election, the first in eleven years.

31 July 1981	The Lesotho government protests strongly to South Africa against a mortar barrage which hit petrol installations near Maseru. It accuses South Africa of harbouring criminal elements as 'a springboard of aggression'.
Sept. 1981	The internal wing of the main opposition party, the former exiled Basutoland Congress Party, calls on its members to avoid all methods of violence as a means of achieving liberation.
2 Sept. 1981	An explosive charge is detonated and damages the Maseru airport buildings. Other bombs damaged the U.S. Cultural Centre, the Hilton Hotel and a bar owned by the Agriculture Minister.
9 Sept. 1981	A bomb explosion in Maseru destroys the West German Ambassador's car. This is one of a series of attacks which pose a threat to government of Chief Jonathan.
27-28 Nov.1981	A Lesotho delegation attends the second Southern African Development Co-ordination Conference in Maputo. Development projects are discussed with potential aid and donor countries.
Feb. 1982	A report on the progress of the economic evolution since independence in 1966. A Ten-Year Plan (1980-1990) is mooted which aims at agricultural and food self- sufficiency but also to establish small industries and emphasizes road construction and tourism.
18 Feb. 1982	The nine-nation Southern African Development Co-ordination Conference agree on establishing an energy committee. The next meeting to be held in November in Lesotho. Ministers call for member countries, Lesotho amongst them, to pay their subscriptions.
Apr. 1982	Lesotho is one of nine member states of the Organisation of African Unity Executive Bureau. The Bureau deals with details and issues omitted at the Heads of States' Summits.
7 Apr. 1982	Lesotho security forces shoot an insurgent of the Lesotho Liberation Army, which is the exiled wing of the Basutoland Congress Party. The man was intercepted as he crossed into Lesotho from South Africa.
May 1982	A plot concerning members of the Lesotho Liberation Army is uncovered. These men trained in South Africa, intended to overthrow the Lesotho government. The men are found guilty of high treason.
June 1982	Lesotho's claim to certain portions of the land incorporated in South Africa is discussed in the South African Parliament.
June 1982	The Lesotho National Assembly gives the police emergency powers. This Security Bill gives the police the right to stop and search vehicles and their occupants without a search warrant.
7 June 1982	At the 39th Session of the OAU Liberation Committee in Arusha, the Tanzanian Foreign Minister reports on South Africa's aggressiveness and its acts of destabilization against Lesotho.
16 July 1982	A man is killed in a bomb explosion on the South African Lesotho border.

This is the third violent death. The two countries blame each other.

8 Aug. 1982	Changes in the cabinet are announced following the assassination of the Works Minister.
9 Aug. 1982	At the nineteenth Annual Summit Conference of the OAU only twenty-seven out of the forty-seven members attended. Lesotho attends and the head of the delegation notes the racist military aggression of South Africa and its large scale economic embargo against Lesotho.
25 Aug. 1982	Signs grant assistance treaty with Denmark.
Nov. 1982	A second attempt to hold the nineteenth OAU Summit Conference also fails. A new contact committee is therefore set up, consisting of twelve members, Lesotho amongst them.
23 Nov. 1982	Lesotho and Swaziland attempt to prove themselves innocent of allowing insurgents of the banned ANC to use their territory as springboards for attacks on South Africa.
Dec. 1982	South African troops raid houses and kill thirty-seven people in Maseru, in retaliation for sabotage incidents in South Africa commited by the banned ANC.
Dec. 1982	The raid by the South African Defence Force into Lesotho is strongly condemned by the Lesotho government and by Britain, the United States and the United Nations Secretary-General.
Jan. 1983	The third annual meeting of SADCC's Council of Ministers takes place in Maseru. Emphasis is on securing the funds already pledged by donors to be used in transport and communications sector.
May 1983	Lesotho establishes diplomatic relations with China.
21 May 1983	Signs agreement with Bulgaria on cultural and scientific cooperation.
19 Oct. 1983	At an emergency meeting of the FAO held in Rome, the Director-General states that the food supply situation is worsening. He names the twenty-two worst affected countries, Lesotho amongst them.
19 Dec. 1983	The government announces that a mercenary attack launched from South Africa is imminent. It intends to remove Chief Jonathan from power. South Africa denies the allegation
6 Jan. 1984	A meeting is held in Pretoria between the South African Foreign Minister and six opponents of Chief Jonathan who protest against the invitations issued to China, North Korea, Romania, the Soviet Union and Yugoslavia to establish embassies in Lesotho.
4 Apr. 1984	The Prime Minister declares a state of emergency as a result of the effects of the drought.
18 Apr. 1984	Signs agreement with the Federal Republic of Germany concerning financial cooperation.

May 1984	Lesotho government refuses to sign security agreement with South Africa.
16 Aug. 1984	The cabinet is re-shuffled.
Dec. 1984	King Moshoeshoe announces the dissolution of the interim National Assembly from 5 January 1985 in preparation for the forthcoming elections.
Jan. 1985	A draft treaty is drawn up between South Africa and Lesotho concerning the second phase of the feasibility study for the Highlands Hydroelectric Water Scheme.
10 Mar. 1985	A Lesotho government official discloses that six people, allegedly members of the Pan-African Congress, which engaged a Lesotho security patrol at a sensitive border area, have been killed. The Minister of Information denies that the six were members of PAC, but belonged to the underground movement of the LLA seeking to overthrow Chief Jonathan's government.
29 Mar. 1985	PAC members are threatened with mass expulsion from Lesotho. They are accused of attacking a platoon Lesotho Paramilitary Force and of training members of the Lesotho Liberation Army in Libya.
Apr. 1985	The President of the Basotho Democratic Alliance, Charles Molopo, is expelled from the party. He was originally the Minister of Information in Prime Minister Jonathan's government but resigned and formed the Alliance as an opposition party.
19 Apr. 1985	Sweden announces the forthcoming opening of a diplomatic mission in Maseru.
24 June 1985	Lesotho's first daily newspaper, The Nation, begins publication in Maseru. The sale of the paper is country-wide.
30 June 1985	A Chinese government delegation pays a goodwill visit to 3 July 1985 Lesotho.
2 July 1985	Lesotho establishes diplomatic relations at ambassadorial level with Mongolia.
24 July 1985	Signs development credit agreement with the International Development Association.
31 July 1985	The Prime Minister, Chief Jonathan, announces that the first general elections in fifteen years will be held on 17 and 18 September.
9 Aug. 1985	The country's security police raids the offices of the Communist Party of Lesotho and confiscates literature.
14 Aug. 1985	It is announced that none of the opposition parties had nominated candidates for any of the sixty elected National Assembly seats.
14 Aug. 1985	The first general election in fifteen years is cancelled as opposition parties refuse to take part, because Chief Jonathan denies them access to the voters' roll.

29 Aug.- 4 Sept.1985	King Moshoeshoe visits China.
18 Sept. 1985	Prime Minister Jonathan and the new Lesotho Cabinet are sworn in.
1 Oct. 1985	Improvements are noted in South African-Lesotho relations. South Africa no longer insists that Lesotho signs a non-aggression pact and conversely Lesotho refuses to be used for attacks on South Africa.
11 Oct. 1985	Chief Jonathan renews his declaration of a state of emergency throughout the country as a result of the drought.
11 Oct. 1985	A Lesotho representative holds talks in Pretoria with South African Foreign Minister Pik Botha on Lesotho's territorial integrity and security.
20 Dec. 1985	South Africa warns its neighbours, Lesotho amongst them, to expect retaliation should they assist the ANC. The warning follows a pre-dawn raid in Maseru in which nine people were killed. Lesotho blames South Africa for the attack, contrary to their denial.
15 Jan. 1986	Signs agreement with the Federal Republic of Germany concerning financial cooperation.
20 Jan. 1986	A bloodless military coup ends the rule of Chief Jonathan with the seizure of power by General Lekanya. South African pressure, in the form of an economic blockade comes to an end.
27 Jan. 1986	The post-coup government consists of fifteen members of the Council of Ministers. A further five are also sworn in.
6 Feb. 1986	Radio Maseru reports a general amnesty both in an out of the country, to those citizens who had been convicted of offences of a political nature.
20 Feb. 1986	Lesotho informs South Korea of its decision to resume diplomatic relations.
Mar. 1986	Despite the general amnesty three former ministers of Chief Jonathan's government are detained for arming Chief Jonathan's youthful followers.
Mar. 1986	Lesotho deports nineteen North Korean construction and agricultural technicians. They were accused of arming Chief Jonathan's Basutoland National Party.
Mar. 1986	Two former officers of the Lesotho paramilitary force, who opposed the coup of 20th January, die while in detention.
26 Mar. 1986	After talks in Cape Town between President Botha of South Africa and a Lesotho delegation led by Major-General Lekhanya, a joint statement is issued in which the two countries agree that lasting peace and stability are of primary importance for economic development. It is also agreed not to allow their respective territories to be used for purposes of terrorism.
18 Apr. 1986	Signs bilateral monetary agreement with South Africa.
18 Apr. 1986	Signs trilateral agreement amending the monetary agreement between South Africa, Lesotho and Swaziland.

22 Apr. 1986	Signs agreement with the Federal Republic of Germany concerning financial cooperation.
5 July 1986	FAO states that the drought crisis is now over in Lesotho.
21 Aug. 1986	Lesotho's ruling Military Council announces house arrest for Chief Jonathan and six of his supporters. They are accused of disruptive activities.
22 Aug. 1986	Three North Korean diplomats are expelled due to interference in Lesotho's internal affairs.
15 Sept. 1986	Lesotho's High Court upholds an application by Premier Jonathan and sets him free challenging the validity of the government order which put him under house arrest.
Oct. 1986	Changes in the designation of ministerial portfolios and assignments of ministerial responsibilities are announced.
Oct. 1986	The Secretary-General of the Christian Council of Lesotho is expelled. This causes a rift between King Moshoeshoe and General Lekhanya.
24 Oct. 1986	An exchange of notes with South Africa regarding the priveleges and immunities accorded to the members of The Joint Permanent Technical Commission.
24 Oct. 1986	Signs treaty with South Africa on Lesotho Highlands Water Project.
3 Nov. 1986	Lesotho's first Prime Minister, Chief Maserebane dies. He was briefly in office after independence and held various offices during Chief Jonathan's premiership.
15 Nov. 1986	Two former ministers in the government of Chief Jonathan, are abducted and shot dead. The two men were among those who were placed under house arrest together with Chief Jonathan, and released when it was declared unlawful.
April 1987	The World Bank grants a R15m. loan to cover the initial costs of the Lesotho Highlands Water Scheme.
5 Apr. 1987	Chief Jonathan dies of natural causes in a Pretoria hospital in South Africa.
30 Apr. 1987	Lesotho and South Africa sign an agreement for the mutual establishment of a trade mission.
12 June 1987	The security police arrests Charles Motele, the leader of the opposition United Democratic Party (UDP) for attacking the country's military government for abuse of power. He called for the restoration of parliamentary government and asked for British, US and French help to solve unsolved murders.
15 Aug. 1987	Two gunmen attack two houses belonging to the Pan Africanist Congress, a movement banned in South Africa. The houses were unoccupied at the time.

20 Jan. 1988	The first anniversary of the coup which overthrew Chief Jonathan is marked by an amnesty for over 200 prisoners.
Mar. 1988	The Military Council intends to continue the ban on all political activities pending agreement on a new constitution.
19 Mar. 1988	The first government re-shuffle takes place since the military came to power.
29 Mar. 1988	Signs Protocol I, II and III with South Africa on the Lesotho Highlands Water Project.
31 Mar. 1988	There are 4000 spontaneously settled South Africans in Lesotho.
15 Apr. 1988	The High Court declares null and void the state of emergency declared by General Lekhanya proclaimed in February as part of a campaign against crime.
20 May 1988	A prominent exiled politician, Ntsu Mokhehle, returns after fourteen years for peace talks with a member of the ruling Military Council. He has been reassured of the personal safety of all exiled members of the Basutoland Congress Party if they come back in a spirit of peace.
5 July 1988	The International Monetary Fund approves a loan to support a three-year economic and financial reform programme.
Sept. 1988	The South African Defence Force Chief of Staff visits Maseru to hand over a hospital built with South African finance.
Sept. 1988	The state of emergency declared in February 1988 and rescinded on 15 April, is nevertheless extended.
Sept. 1988	The Minister of Law, Constitutional and Parliamentary Affairs is dismissed by the ruling Military Council without a reason given.
Sept. 1988	The Pope's arrival in Lesotho is delayed by a storm which made the Zimbabwe plane make a diversion to Johannesburg's Jan Smuts Airport. The delay lasted nine hours. His message is that strife and racial tension must be solved by peaceful dialogue.
14 Sept. 1988	A bloody gun battle mars the arrival of the Pope in Maseru. South African commandos storm a hijacked pilgrim bus to free seventy one hostages held captive by four armed guerrillas.
16-19 Oct.1988	The King visits Nigeria and agrees to explore areas of co-operation.
25 Oct. 1988	King Moshoeshoe II visits South Africa and discusses bilateral relations with the South African President.
Nov. 1988	Leading figures from the three suspended political parties, BCP, BDA and BNP apply to the High Court for the restoration of the 1966 constitution.
Jan. 1989	The 'Mirror' newspaper in Maseru appoints a news editor to carry on the crusade against corruption in government. The dismissed editor, Johnny Wa Ka Maseko, is deported to Kenya protesting that he was a Lesotho citizen. But he is in in fact a South African who fled the country in 1980.

1 Apr. 1989	Signs bilateral monetary agreement with South Africa.

1 Apr. 1989   Signs trilateral agreement amending the trilateral monetary agreement between Lesotho, Swaziland and South Africa.

Oct. 1989   Head of State, Major-General Lekhanya, denies killing a student. He admits to firing a shot to apprehend the student George Ramone when he visited Lesotho Agricultural College and heard a woman scream. He refused to name the people he was visiting at the college. He is under pressure to resign over Ramone's death.

16 Oct. 1989   Signs multilateral memorandum of understanding to amend the Customs Union agreement of 11 December 1969.

12 Dec. 1989   Signs agreement with South Africa on the establishment of a common works area at Caledon River for the purpose of the implementation of the Lesotho Highlands Water Project.

2 Feb. 1990   Signs agreement with South Africa on the establishment of trade missions.

20 Feb. 1990   The Military Council chairman, Major-General Lekhanya finds it imperative to remove three members of the council and the Minister of Transport, because of their subordination and behaviour against army unity.

21 Feb. 1990   Major-General Lekhanya announces his disagreement with King Moshoeshoe II over the dismissal of three Military Council members and his hindrance of democratization. He therefore, for the time being, assumes power while confirming that the King remains Head of State.

22 Feb. 1990   A ministerial reshuffle is announced.

13 Mar. 1990   Two colonels recently expelled from the Military Council and the Army are released from detention.

2 Apr. 1990   Signs multilateral agreement amending customs union agreement between South Africa, Botswana, Lesotho, Swaziland of 11 December 1969.

8 Apr. 1990   China severs diplomatic relations with Lesotho, after Lesotho resumed official ties with Taiwan.

9 Apr. 1990   Signs memorandum of understanding with South Africa on road transportation agreement between Botswana, Lesotho, South Africa and Swaziland.

30 Apr. 1990   Major-General Lekhanya reiterates his commitment to civilian rule by 1992. He is determined that the introduction of democracy will have to take place against a backdrop of national stability.

July 1990   The Lesotho government is launching a countrywide campaign to explain to its citizens the details of the forthcoming national constitutional assembly aimed at paving the way to democratization. He also appoints a commission to represent the country's rural population in the Constituent Assembly.

17 July 1990   The Minister of Interior, Chieftainship Affairs and Rural

Development is replaced.

4 Sept. 1990	Signs multilateral memoradum of understanding on road transportation in the Common Customs Area.
2 Nov. 1990	Signs air transport agreement with South Africa.
2 Nov. 1990	Signs memorandum of agreement with South Africa on the design, construction and maintenance of the international border bridge over the Caledon river at Ficksburg/Maputsoe.
Jan. 1991	King Moshoeshoe II is deposed in favour of his son, by General Lekhanya. General Lekhanya returns Lesotho to military rule, which might pose danger to political parties and the government of the day. King Moshoeshoe instructs his son to accept the crown for fear that if it was refused a republic would be introduced.
30 Apr. 1991	The military leader Major-General Lekhanya is ousted in a bloodless military coup and is forced to announce his own resignation on the radio. He is then driven to a maximum security prison to await trial on charges of corruption.
May 1991	Following the bloodless coup of 30 April, South African troops are placed on the Lesotho border, concerned with the safety of the joint Lesotho Highlands Water Scheme. The new military ruler, Colonel Elias Ramaema, reassures the South African Foreign Minister that there are no major policy changes and the country will return to civilian rule after the 1992 elections.
1 May 1991	Lekhanya is released and retires to his small holding near Maseru.
2 May 1991	Colonel Elias Ramaema is sworn in as the new Chairman of the Lesotho Military Council. Several new members are also sworn in.
10 June 1991	Twenty officers of the Royal Lesotho Defence Force are relieved of their duties.
17 June 1991	Eighteen high-ranking military officers are arrested following an unsuccessful coup which intended to arrest officers supporting Major-General Lekhanya.
4 July 1991	The Constituent National Assembly ends its session by adapting the draft constitution to re-establish democracy. The parties are asked to prepare for the general election of 1992. An American delegation and a United States mission will be called to supervise the elections.
2 Aug. 1991	Major-General Lekhanya is placed under house arrest following allegations that he is plotting to return to power.
Sept. 1991	A new Information and Broadcasting Minister is appointed by the Military Council. This new arrangement separates the administration of the Ministry of Foreign Affairs and the Ministry of Information and Broadcasting.
3 Sept. 1991	The deposed King of Lesotho, Moshoeshoe II arrives in Swaziland where he is expected to seek political asylum.

18 Oct. 1991	Signs memorandum of understanding on road transportation in the Common Customs Area Agreement between Botswana, Lesotho, South Africa and Swaziland.
19 Nov. 1991	Signs protocol on the Lesotho Highlands Water Project regarding Phase IA.
21 May 1992	Lesotho announces its decision to establish diplomatic relations with South Africa, as soon as possible.
22 June 1992	The present High Commissioner to Kenya, Tokonye Katcho is named the new Foreign Minister, following the resignation of Captain Pius Molapo.
20 July 1992	King Moshoeshoe II returns to a joyous reception after two years of exile. He commits himself to promote democracy and install a multiparty government.
17 Aug. 1992	Signs establishment of Southern Africa Development Community (SADC) treaty.
14 Jan. 1993	The election date is announced. It will take place on 27 March.
12 Feb. 1993	In line with the military government's decision to dissolve its Council of Ministers, nine Lesotho ministers lose their position. The present King Letsie III announces that he will step down in favour of his father Moshoeshoe II.
27 Mar. 1993	Elections are held resulting in the landslide victory of the Basotho Congress Party taking all but one of the parliamentary seats, thereby overthrowing General Lekhanya. The Commonwealth Observer Group declares the elections free and fair. Ntsu Mokhele the BCP Leader, shifts his position from the South African Pan African Congress to the African National Congress. The issue of the monarchy is not yet resolved.
2 Apr. 1993	The new Prime Minister, Ntsu Mokhele of the Basuto Congress Party, is sworn in.
8 Apr. 1993	Ten new ministers are sworn in.
3 June 1993	A new Minister of Justice and Human Rights is appointed.
17 June 1993	Construction and Allied Workers are on strike, demanding wage increments. The strike does not effect work on the Lesotho Highlands Water Project.
July 1993	Clashes occur between the police and trade unionists which casts doubt on the newly elected government's commitment to improve labour-government relations.
July 1993	The use of the Internal Security Act to charge the striking unionists and the heavy-handed policing of the incident casts doubt on the government commitment to human rights.
July 1993	The government re-declares a state of food emergency due to the persistent drought.

21-23 July 1993	A United Nations sponsored forum meeting to discuss the transition process.
30 July 1993	Dalton Katopola, Minister of Trade and Industry resigns on grounds of ill health.
6 Aug. 1993	The IMF announces the approval of $10.5 million loan to promote economic and financial reform. It will be drawing from the Fund's Enhanced Structural Adjustment Facility which exists to implement structural reform in the world's poorest economies. This is the third annual loan to Lesotho. Real growth in Lesotho's G.D.P. amounted to 2.4% in 1992-3, despite the drought.
17 Aug. 1993	Five political parties have registered with the Registrar General to date.
Sept. 1993	The ruling Basutoland Congress Party is pressurized to reclaim part of the South African Orange Free State province as this was land secured after the British-Boer conflict at the end of the 19th century.
7 Sept. 1993	Public sector strikes involving 6000 civil servants ends with the acceptance of a 35% pay rise, backdated to 1 July.
Dec.1993	Lesotho receives a loan of $1 million from the OPEC fund to assist in the financing of the Oxbow-Mokhotlong Road Project. However, the total cost is estimated at $62.3 million.
3 Dec. 1993	Junior officers of the Lesotho Defence Force mutiny against senior officers rejecting the move to merge the defence force with the Lesotho Liberation Army.
Jan. 1994	The formation of a peace-keeping force in Southern Africa is triggered by the Lesotho crisis of 1993.
1 Jan. 1994	In order to match the anticipated inflation rate, the Lesotho Electricity Corporation announces an increase of 10% on tariffs.
12 Jan. 1994	Taiwan breaks diplomatic ties with Lesotho after the Maseru Government switched diplomatic recognition to Beijing.
1 Feb. 1994	After three weeks of sporadic fighting, Lesotho's feuding army factions return to their barracks under a Commonwealth brokered arrangement.
4 Mar. 1994	Signs treaty on Lesotho Highlands Water Project with South Africa.
23 Mar. 1994	The Prime Minister adds a new minister and three deputies to his Cabinet, separating the portfolios of Labour and Employment from Trade, Industries and Tourism.
14 Apr. 1994	Dissident soldiers shoot the Deputy-Prime Minister and seize four cabinet ministers apparently over a planned probe into the army. Dissatisfaction over army pay causes the incident.

23 May 1994   After the kidnapping of ministers, the situation deteriorates due to the undisciplined police force.

31 May 1994   The police end their strike after reaching agreement on pay rise.

June 1994   Unrest in the military, police and prison services continues. To avert a civil war representatives from all communal organizations call for a national conference. The government, however, fears that such a conference might pass a vote of no confidence.

June 1994   A civilian adviser from the British Ministry of Defence is seconded to the Lesotho Government to assist with the establishment of a Ministry of Defence.

8 June 1994   The Front Line States meet in Harare, where President Mandela declares that South Africa will play a crucial role in solving Southern Africa's problems. The member countries decide to send a special force to Lesotho.

15 June 1994   The new Minister of National Resources responsible for the Lesotho Highlands Water Project takes the oath of office.

19 July 1994   Reports are denied that Zimbabwe and Botswana are sending troops to Lesotho. However, members of the defence forces of South Africa, Botswana and Zimbabwe have begun work in Maseru as a commission of inquiry into the recent military unrest.

17 Aug. 1994   The struggle to restore King Moshoeshoe II to his throne erupts in violence.

14 Sept. 1994   King Letsie III restores Prime Minister Mokhehle and his government to power much to popular acclaim.   Foreign Ministers of Zimbabwe, Botswana and South Africa act as mediators in the process. However the Basutoland Congress Party is unhappy with the provisions of the agreement exonerating Letsie and his father King Moshoeshoe II.

22 Oct. 1994   After talks on border disputes three border passes between South Africa and Lesotho are re-opened.

17 Nov. 1994   A bill to reinstate King Moshoeshoe II as the country's monarch is presented for first reading in parliament.

23 Dec. 1994   Signs treaty with South Africa on Lesotho Highlands Water Project.

25 Jan. 1995   King Moshoeshoe regains his throne.

9 Feb. 1995   The office of the Prime Minister announces the creation of a new Cabinet portfolio, by the appointment of a Deputy Prime Minister.

23 Feb. 1995   The first major cabinet reshuffle is announced by the Prime Minister.

6-7 Apr. 1995   A two-day meeting is held between government officials and army officers from Lesotho, Botswana, South Africa and Zimbabwe. The focus is on constitutional order following tension between the government and the security forces.

18 May 1995	Lesotho and Namibia sign an agreement abolishing visa requirements for travel between the two countries.
22 May 1995	Rioting breaks out in Maseru when a crowd go on the rampage and urge the government to take steps over the deteriorating security situation, following the indefinite go-slow strike by the police force.
24 May 1995	Two members of parliament are abducted by the National Security Service and questionned about arms caches. The arms are connected to the Azanian People's Liberation Army and used to attack South African farmers living and working near the border.
18 July 1995	A cabinet reshuffle is announced.
Sept. 1995	Amnesty International urges the government to discipline the security forces which it accuses of serious human rights violations.
Oct. 1995	A new party, the Progressive National Party is founded. Its leader is the former deputy leader of the Basotholand National Party.
15 Jan. 1996	King Moshoeshoe II is killed in a car accident less than two years after regaining the throne.
18 Jan. 1996	The Traditional College of Chiefs name the King's eldest son, Crown Prince David Mohato Bereng Seeiso as his successor.
3 Feb. 1996	Eleven suspected stock thieves from Lesotho are killed by Eastern Cape security forces.
7 Feb. 1996	Crown Prince Mohato Bereng Seeiso is sworn in and installed as new monarch and Head of State.
23 Feb. 1996	Government ministers from both South Africa and Lesotho meet to discuss cross-border raids and livestock rustling, after the killing of eleven suspected stock thieves. The meeting decides on measures to eliminate this problem.
Mar. 1996	A commission of inquiry into the death of King Moshoeshoe has been appointed by the Prime Minister. It comprises detectives from Scotland Yard.
19 Mar. 1996	Opposition United Party President Makara Sekautu and former defence force member Lepoqo Molapo are charged with high treason for allegedly attempting to overthrow the government, through a broadcast on state radio on the 29 February.
Apr. 1996	A military police unit is established as part of the Lesotho Defence Force to provide security to military and government facilities.
23 Apr. 1996	Prime Minister Mokhehle announces an amnesty for dissident army members.
May 1996	An investigation into King Moshoeshoe II's death on 15 January concludes that the driver had been drinking and fell asleep at the wheel.

6 May 1996

A cabinet reshuffle is announced. Four ministers are dismissed from the Cabinet: Molapo Qhobelo, Tseliso Makhakhe, Ntsukunyane Mphanya and Sekoala Toloane. It is believed that these ministers are linked to a pressure group associated with a court case applying for nullification of BCP elections.

15 May 1996

A week after his appointment as Minister of Trade and Industry, Dr. K. Raditapole resigns. Finance and Planning Minister Dr. Moeketsi Senaoana also resigns from the Cabinet.

20 June 1996

Dr. Victor Ketle is appointed Minister of Finance and Development Planning.

15 Sept. 1996

Five dismissed workers of the Lesotho Highlands Water Project are killed and several injured after clashes with the police. The government announces a full independent inquiry into this incident at Buthabutha.

6 Nov. 1996

Pakane Khala, Minister of Information, dies.

Dec. 1996

The High Court annuls the National Executive Committee election of the Basotholand Congress Party which took place in March 1996. The Court rules that the old NEC should organize a new poll. An earlier court order stated that the factions within the BCP should reach a settlement, but that they had failed to comply.

Jan. 1997

An Independent Electoral Commission is promised by Prime Minister Ntsu Mokhehle. The Commission is to prepare for the 1998 general elections and will start their activities in April. This move is designed to silence claims of rigging.

Jan. 1997

A rift within the ruling Basotholand Congress Party has deteriorated into public denigration. Information and Broadcasting Minister Monyane Moleleki, an ardent supporter of Prime Minister Mokhehle, declares that deposed cabinet minister Molapo Qhobela has been vilifying the Prime Minister and takes advantage of a protracted legal battle to destabilize the government.

24 Jan. 1997

A new National Executive Committee is elected for the Basotholand Congress Party.

5 Feb. 1997

A police mutiny under the leadership of Pakiso Molise takes place. Molise and seven officers demand amnesty for the murder of which three fellow officers are accused.

14 Feb. 1997

The Lesotho High Court nullifies the election of a new National Executive Committee of the Basotholand Congress Party, which was held on 24 January 1997. Prime Minister Mokhehle is treated in South Africa in a hospital, and the gulf between factions in his ruling party deepens.

16 Feb. 1997

The Lesotho Army ends an eleven-day old police mutiny, resulting in the surrender of thirty-three officers.

21 Feb. 1997

Ten rebel police officers appear in court and are remanded in custody until 7 March.

28 Feb. 1997	Dr. Ntsu Mokhehle is removed as party leader of the ruling Basotho Congress Party at the annual conference of the BCP in Maseru.
14 Mar. 1997	South Africa grants asylum to two Lesotho policemen who fled to South Africa after the police mutiny was put down by the army. A delegation from Lesotho is sent to South Africa to request the return of the policemen who are to face charges in Lesotho.
16 Mar. 1997	Mass demonstrations in support of Prime Minister Mokhehle takes place. But members of a faction within the BCP call for his resignation.
11 Apr. 1997	During a visit of Foreign Minister Maope to Beijing, Chinese Foreign Minister expresses his appreciation that Lesotho has pursued the one China policy, and not sought official links with Taiwan. He wishes to develop its relations with Lesotho based on mutual benefit, respect and equality.
18 Apr. 1997	The removal of Dr. Ntsu Mokhehle as leader of the BCP is declared invalid by Justice Winston Churchill Maqutu in the Lesotho High Court. The judge rules that as Mokhehle's term of office expired in January, he will remain as interim leader until the next annual conference, when a new leader will be elected. The BCP is ordered to hold a party conference within three and a half months to elect a new leader.
22 Apr. 1997	Parliament approves the first Independent Electoral Commission which will oversee the general elections in 1998.
June 1997	Nstu Mokhehle leaves the Basotho Congress Party, founded by him forty-five years previously and forms the Lesotho Congress for Democracy, taking with him the majority of MPs from the BCP. He intends to carry on as premier until the general election in 1998. However, Leader of the BCP insists that this is still the ruling party and accuses Mokhehle of staging a political coup.
16 June 1997	A demonstration attended by several thousand, is launched against the 'usurped' government of Ntsu Mokhehle.

MALAWI

6 July 1964	Malawi, formerly known as Nyasaland, becomes an independent sovereign state.
6 July 1964	New government and ministerial appointments announced.
6 July 1964	Accession to GATT negotiations for establishment of a new Schedule III. Brazil, Parts I and II; and other GATT rectifications to the French text and texts of the following 5-9th Schedules.
6 July 1964	Succeeds to the following GATT treaties; accession of Israel; Spain; Procès-verbal of rectifications concerning the Protocol amending Part I and Art XXIX and XXX; Protocol amending the Preamble and Parts II and III; Protocol of rectification to the French text and extension of time for signature; and provision accession of Argentina; Tunisia; United Arab Republic; Yugoslavia; successsion to relations between Contracting Parties and Poland.

8 July 1964	The Ghanian High Commissioner to Malawi, Timothy Owusu presents his credentials to the Governor-General.
8 July 1964	Sam P. Gilstrap, American Ambassador to Malawi presents his credentials to the Governor-General.
17-21 July	President Banda clarifies his country's position on the impossibility of severing all ties with South Africa. This speech was made at the OAU's First Session of the Assembly of Heads of State and Government, Cairo, 17-21 July 1964.
4 Aug. 1964	Colin Cameron, Minister of Works, resigns.
6 Aug. 1964	Malawi applies for United Nations membership.
7 Aug. 1964	Signs supplementary agreement with Great Britain concerning public officers.
24 Aug. 1964	Signs Agreement with South Africa on Double Taxation.
1 Sept. 1964	Signs treaty with Great Britain on cereals production and trade policies.
7 Sept. 1964	Malawi refuses a request from Ghana to extradite Khow Daniel Amehya, leader of the African Democratic Congress in London. He was allegedly involved in a conspiracy to murder President Nkrumah.
8 Sept. 1964	Dr Banda dismisses Foreign Affairs Minister, Kanyama Chiume; Orton Chirwa, Minister of Justice and Attorney-General; Augustine Bwanausi, Minister of Development and Housing and Works. The following Ministers tendered their resignation, Yatuta Chisiza (Home Affairs); William Chokani (Labour) and H.B.N. Chipembere.
8 Sept. 1964	Prime Minister Banda tells Parliament that the Chinese Embassy in Dar es Salaam is behind a conspiracy involving some of his dissident ministers. This involves a R18 million loan offer should Malawi recognize the Chinese government.
11 Sept. 1964	Adheres to the International Civil Aviation Treaty
15 Sept. 1964	South Africa and Malawi exchange notes on postal services including insured parcels on 15 September and 26 September.
24 Sept. 1964	Minister of Transport and Communications, J. Msonthi is given the additional portfolio of Minister of Education.
28 Sept. 1964	During riots in Zomba, G. Shakuamba, the Minister of Social Development is injured. The Malawi Congress Party District Headquarters are gutted.
1 Oct. 1964	Regulations passed giving the Malawi Prime Minister power to restrict anyone in the interest of public order without recourse to the courts. Henry Chipembere, post his 8 September resignation from the Cabinet, is restricted under these regulations.
9 Oct. 1964	Malawi unanimously recommended to the General Assembly by the Security Council for United Nations membership, thus making it the 113th member.

13 Oct. 1964	The United States gives the Malawi Broadcasting Corporation a new 10-Kilowatt radio transmitter.
16 Oct. 1964	Dr. Banda claims the 'full support' of the northern provinces. However considerable resistance is noted in the Fort Johnston, Zomba, Blantyre and Limbe areas.
23 Oct. 1964	Exchange of notes dated 23 October and 27 October continuing the trade agreement between South Africa, Zambia and Malawi.
24 Oct. 1964	Signs the Charter of the United Nations and becomes a member of the ILO, FAO, UNESCO, ICAO, WHO, International Telecommunications Union, IAEA, UPU, and WMO.
24 Oct. 1964	Assistance from the United Nations Special Fund treaty is signed.
24 Oct. 1964	Signs multipartite treaty for technical assistance.
27 Oct. 1964	Signs and accepts the UNESCO Constitution.
28 Oct. 1964	Malawi Young Pioneers are trained by Israeli and Malawi instructors. The main objective of the youth movement is 'Kamuzuism'.
7 Nov. 1964	The Prime Minister's Office releases a statement saying that the programme of Africanization of the Civil Service 'will be carried out with ever increasing speed, efficiency and effectiveness'.
17 Nov. 1964	Frontier problems with Tanzania are addressed by Dr. Banda.
17 Nov. 1964	The Minister of Education, John Masonthi asks France to provide teaching personnel for secondary schools and the university.
25 Nov. 1964	A.F. Ahlal appointed as the United Arab Republic's Ambassador to Malawi.
26 Nov. 1964	Succeeds to 1963 multipartite treaty concerning banning of nuclear weapon tests.
26 Nov. 1964	Succession to the treaty banning nuclear weapon tests in the atmosphere.
30 Nov. 1964	Ratifies amendments to the International Civil Aviation Protocol.
7 Dec. 1964	Dr. Banda recongizes the People's Republic of China.
20 Dec. 1964	Some 300 Malawi Chiefs reaffirm their support to Dr. Banda at an 'indaba'.
28 Dec. 1964	Tanzania accused, in an editorial of the Malawi News, of planning an incursion into Malawi and training forces as well as the detention of Malawi citizens and the censorship of mail.
8 Jan. 1965	The Secretary-General of the Malawi Congress Party issues a statement barring Whites and Asians from becoming members.
19 Jan. 1965	President Banda confirms arrest of armed infiltrators from Tanzania.

9 Feb. 1965	Strained relations exist between Malawi and Zambia after the latter gave refuge to erstwhile cabinet ministers after the revolt of 1964.
12 Feb. 1965	Raid on Fort Johnston believed to be an attempt to overthrow the government.
17 Feb. 1965	Assumes obligations of the 1949 Road Traffic Treaty and notification concerning distinguishing signs in international traffic.
22 Feb. 1965	Signs multipartite treaty concerning the activities of UNICEF.
4 Mar. 1965	Accepts GATT treaty on trade and development.
4 Mar. 1965	Signs treaty with the United States concerning the Peace Corps.
12 Mar. 1965	Accepts GATT treaty concerning provisional accession of Iceland; Switzerland; United Arab Republic.
22 Mar. 1965	Assumes the obligations of the following International Labour Organisation conventions: employment of women on underground work in mines (no. 45); maximum length of contracts of employment for indigenous workers (no. 86); penal sanctions for breaches of contracts of employment for indigenous workers (no. 65); minimum wage-fixing machinery (no. 26) and in agriculture (no. 99); right to bargain collectively (no. 98); rights of association of agricultural workers (no. 11); workmen's compensation in agriculture (no. 12).
22 Mar. 1965	Ratifies the following International Labour Organisation conventions: discrimination in employment occupation (no. 111); equal remuneration for men and women workers (no. 100); labour inspection in industry and commerce (no. 81); migration for employment (no. 97); night work of women employed in industry (no. 89); protection and integration of indigenous populations in independent countries (no. 107); workmen's compensation for equality of treatment for national and foreign workers (no. 19); abolition of penal sanctions for breaches of contracts of employment for indigenous workers (no. 104).
25 Mar. 1965	Signs rectification to the World Health Organization treaty on technical advisory assistance.
25 Mar. 1965	Malawi becomes a member of the International Labour Organisation.
4 Apr. 1965	Austrian good-will mission arrives to select students for training.
9 Apr. 1965	Accepts the Constitution of the World Health Organization.
9 Apr. 1965	Signs facilitation of international maritime traffic treaty.
13 Apr. 1965	Penal Code Amendment Bill presented to Parliament, retrospective to 1 January 1965. Clarifies the Law of Treason.
4 May 1965	Signs air transport agreement with Ghana.
8 May 1965	Rebels surprised by government forces in the Fort Johnston area.

14 May 1965	Vincent Gondwe appointed as Malawi's Ambassador to the United States.
19 May 1965	Accedes to the Vienna Convention on Diplomatic Relations.
24 May 1965	Signs treaty with Israel abolishing visas for diplomatic and service passports.
2 June 1965	Ratifies entry into force of amendments to Articles 23, 27 and 61 of the United Nations Charter.
8 June 1965	Accedes to Single Convention on Narcotic Drugs, 1961.
8 June 1965	Cultural cooperation discussed with French Secretary of State for Foreign Affairs.
10 June 1965	With respect to the suppression of white slave traffic, Malawi accedes to the agreement of 4 May 1949 and the convention of 4 May 1949.
July 1965	Attempted assassination of the Deputy-Speaker H.T. Kaunda.
2 July 1965	Dr. Banda alleges that Malawian rebels are being trained in Tanzania.
6 July 1965	East African governments boycott Malawi's independence celebrations.
7 July 1965	President Banda announces that 2,000 Mozambican refugees have arrived on Likoma Island, a missionary centre on Lake Malawi.
8 July 1965	Signs Final Act of the United Nations Conference.
15 July 1965	Dr. Banda, whilst speaking on the Constitution Amendment Bill, recalls that those non-Malawi citizens resident in the country were eligible for citizenship application during the period of twelve months from July 1964. Due to the problems in registration, this period is now extended for a further twelve months.
19 July 1965	Accepts Articles of Agreement of the International Development Agency.
19 July 1965	Signs and accepts the Articles of Agreement of the International Finance Corporation.
19 July 1965	Signs and accepts Articles of Agreement of the International Monetary Fund.
19 July 1965	Signs and accepts Articles of Agreement of The Bank for Reconstruction and Development.
20 July 1965	Multilateral operational assistance treaty is signed.
20 July 1965	Banda announces that Malawi is to become a republic within the Commonwealth on 6 July 1966.
22 July 1965	Succession to International Opium Conventions of 1912 and 1946.
22 July 1965	With respect to the suppression of obscene publications, Malawi accepts the agreement of 4 May 1949 and accedes to the convention of 12 November 1947.

22 July 1965	Succession to Protocol bringing under international control drugs outside the scope of the Convention of 13 July 1931 for limiting the manufacture and regulating the distribution of narcotic drugs.
26 July 1965	Accedes to the 1952 Universal Copyright Convention.
29 July 1965	R.P. Chisala appointed as Malawian Ambassador to Ghana, and presents credentials.
2 Aug. 1965	Accedes to the treaty pertaining to the privileges and immunities of the specialized agencies - IBRD, FAO, ICAO, IDA, IFC, ILO, IMLO, ITU, UNESCO, UPU, WHO, WMO.
2 Aug. 1965	Accedes to treaty on the abolition of slavery, the slave trade and institutions and practices similar to slavery.
4 Aug. 1965	Accepts obligations contained in the United Nations Charter.
4 Aug. 1965	Emperor Haile Selasie of Ethiopia visits Malawi, and together with Dr. Banda supports the OAU decision on Southern Rhodesia. They agree to support all efforts toward the liberation of that country.
5 Aug. 1965	Accedes to the multilateral treaty on the permanent control of outbreak areas of the red locust.
17 Aug. 1965	Accepts treaty on the inportation of educational, scientific and cultural materials.
22 Aug. 1965	Banda accuses ex Foreign Affairs Minister, Chiume of preparing Malawians in Tanzania for an invasion.
31 Aug. 1965	Entry into force of amendments to Articles 23, 27 and 61 of the United Nations Charter.
13-17 Sept.1965	Dr. Banda pays an official visit to Madagascar.
28 Sept. 1965	Malawi establishes diplomatic relations with Kenya at High Commission level. B. Katenga presents credentials.
7 Oct. 1965	Signs multilateral treaty on the privileges and immunities of the Organisation of African Unity (OAU).
11 Oct. 1965	Dr. Banda warns of new subversion attempts by former cabinet ministers.
13 Oct. 1965	Accedes to the treaty on the suppression of traffic in persons and of exploitation of prostitution of others.
17 Oct. 1965	The Malawi Peoples Congress, meeting in Lilongwe, unanimously vote Dr. Banda as the President-Designate. Approves the Republican Constitution thus making Malawi a one-party state.
19 Oct. 1965	Leading rebel associate of former Minister of Education Chipembere, Medson Silombela arrested near Fort Johnston.

25 Oct. 1965	Accedes to the Universal Postal Union.
29 Oct. 1965	M. MacDonald, the High Commissioner for Kenya takes up post as the Special Representative of Great Britain in a number of Eastern and Central African states, including Malawi.
3 Nov. 1965	Accedes to the treaty pertaining to the continental shelf.
3 Nov. 1965	Accession to fishing and conservation of living resources of the high seas treaty.
3 Nov. 1965	Accession to treaty on the high seas.
3 Nov. 1965	Accedes to the treaty on a uniform law for cheques.
3 Nov. 1965	Accedes to the treaty on territorial seas and contiguous zone.
10 Nov. 1965	Banda introduces the Public Hanging Bill. Clarifies that it is intended for those involved in the 'rebellion' near Fort Johnston.
15 Nov. 1965	'Rebel' leader, Medson Silombela sentenced to death for the murder of a Malawi Congress Party official.
18 Nov. 1965	Accedes to 1929 convention pertaining to the suppression of counterfeit currency and its optional protocol.
6 Dec. 1965	Malawi and Austria agree to establish diplomatic relations at ambassadorial level, with the Austrian Ambassador to Kenya, Dr. Kudernatsh also accredited to Malawi.
6 Dec. 1965	Malawi and the Netherlands agree in principle to establish diplomatic relations.
7 Dec. 1965	New United States Ambassador, M.P. Jones, sworn in.
17 Dec. 1965	Signs treaty on the compulsory settlement of disputes.
22 Dec. 1965	Medson Silombela's appeal against the death penalty dismissed in the Malawi Supreme Court.
1 Jan. 1966	International Sanitary Regulations concerning disinfecting of ships and aircraft against yellow fever and smallpox comes into force.
11 Jan. 1966	President Banda introduces the Forfeiture Bill in Parliament. It provides for the disposal of property belonging to persons declared subject to forfeiture and deprives them of redress in Malawi Courts.
19 Jan. 1966	Dr. Banda announces several senior Assistant Secretary posts but reiterates he would not Africanize for the sake of Africanization.
19 Jan. 1966	President Banda, speaking in Parliament, rebukes President Nyerere of Tanzania for abetting Malawian 'rebels'.
7 Feb. 1966	A Cabinet reshuffle entails Aleke Banda to assume responsibility for the Minister of Works which becomes a department of the Ministry of

Development and Planning; Chibambo becomes the Minister of Health.

15 Feb. 1966	The Malawian government orders the United Arab Republic to close its embassy in Blantyre.
25 Feb. 1966	Accedes to the multilateral treaty on the suppression of traffic in women and children.
8 Mar. 1966	Dr. Banda recognizes the military regimes in Nigeria and Ghana.
19 Mar. 1966	Madagascar and Malawi sign an agreement on culture, tourism and trade in Tananarive.
21 Mar. 1966	Signs GATT treaty concerning acceptance of Tunisia: third extension of provisional accession.
21 Mar. 1966	Signs GATT treaty of acceptance of Iceland's provisional accession.
1 Apr. 1966	Signs GATT treaty recognising the accession of Switzerland.
11 Apr. 1966	Ratifies amendments to United Nations Charter.
18 Apr. 1966	Dr. Banda states that the 1964 Malawi government would continue in office until 1971. The necessary legislation to be effected at Parliament's next session.
19 Apr. 1966	Banda advises four members of the Rhodesian official opposition party, the United People's Party to pursue a policy of non-violence.
21 Apr. 1966	Banda calls for the expulsion of Malawian rebels from Tanzania prior to any talks between the two governments.
26 Apr. 1966	Queen Elizabeth II agrees to remain as Colonel-in-Chief of the Malawi Army after Malawi becomes a republic within the Commonwealth.
16 May 1966	The Japanese Ambassador to Kenya is appointed non-resident ambassador to Malawi.
17 May 1966	Accedes to the multilateral treaty on the privileges and immunities of the United Nations.
20 May 1966	Dr. Banda accepts, unopposed, nomination as the country's first President. He will be known as the President designate until 6 July.
21 May 1966	Parliament approves a new constitution making Malawi a one-party state and giving the President the right to prorogue or dissolve Parliament.
4 June 1966	Announces that new army barracks are to be built at Mzuzu costing 400,000 Pounds Sterling.
7 June 1966	Signs International Labour Organisation convention on systems of recruiting workers (no. 50).
7 June 1966	Signs International Labour Organisation convention on written contracts of employment of indigenous workers (no. 64).

15 June 1966	Ministerial responsibilities re-allocated as the Ministry of Community and Social Development ceases to exist. Ministry of Local Government assumes responsibility for community development.
17 June 1966	First Japanese Ambassador to Malawi Urabe, presents credentials to the Governor-General.
27 June 1966	Former Minister of Local Government, Chipembere announces his intentions of returning to Africa and to public life despite President Banda's threats.
29 June 1966	Accedes to the multilateral treaty on the political rights of women.
4 July 1966	Amnesty granted to 800 people as an act of clemency due to the forthcoming Republic. Detention orders also revoked on 229 people held under the Preservation of the Public Security Regulations.
6 July 1966	Dr. Banda is sworn in as the first Republican president. He is also Commander-in-Chief of the Malawi Army.
6 July 1966	President Banda warns population that Henry Chipembere, leader of the Cabinet revolt was not being groomed by Western powers to take over the government.
7 July 1966	President Banda outlives his foreign policy of selective non-alignment during the opening of Parliament.
12 July 1966	Malawi and Norway agree that visas are no longer necessary for visits not exceeding three months.
12 July 1966	President Banda affords de jure recognition to Nationalist China.
18 July 1966	Inter-government talks take place between Malawi and Tanzania.
18 July 1966	Exchange of notes on extra contributions by Great Britain toward increases in emoluments of officers in public service of Malawi.
20 July 1966	Signs GATT treaty recognizing the accession of Yugoslavia.
25 July 1966	Accession to African Development Bank treaty.
29 July 1966	Visits of two peace envoys from Tanzania cancelled due to the political refugee issue.
1 Aug. 1966	Danish loan treaty is signed.
11 Aug. 1966	Apostolic Nuncio in Lusaka, Archbishop Poledrini presents his credentials to President Banda. He is accredited to Malawi on a non-residential basis.
23 Aug. 1966	Ratifies multilateral treaty on the settlement of investment disputes between states and nationals of other states.
8 Sept. 1966	Signs multilateral treaty on the nationality of married women.
16 Sept. 1966	Acceptance of multilateral treaty on the privileges and immunities of the specialized agencies - FAO: Annex II, second revised text.

21 Sept. 1966	The Malawi High Commissioner, R.P. Chisala, presents his credentials to President Kenyatta of Kenya.
29 Sept. 1966	The opening of Nationalist China's first embassy in Central Africa is announced. The opening, in Blantyre, will be effected by Chen Yei Yuan who will become Ambassador to Malawi.
4 Oct. 1966	Israeli Ambassador, Haru, presents his credentials to President Banda.
4 Oct. 1966	Signs development credit agreement with the International Development Agency on the Highway Engineering Project.
10 Oct. 1966	Zambian Minister for Home Affairs Chona assures Malawi that his country did not encourage subversive elements against them.
13 Oct. 1966	Accession to multilateral treaty in military obligations in cases of double nationality.
25 Oct. 1965	Accedes to the Universal Postal Union.
25 Oct. 1966	Accession to agreement on insured letters and boxes.
25 Oct. 1966	Notification of the postal parcels agreement.
31 Oct. 1966	Dr. Banda forbids the mention of Henry Chipembere's name. Anyone mentioning the name will be reported to the Malawi Youth Pioneers.
12 Nov. 1966	Border incident with Mozambique occurs. Fifty Malawians, captured by a Portuguese army patrol, are interrogated in Mozambique and later released. Four people are killed when the patrol penetrated three miles into Malawian territory.
17 Nov. 1966	Signs GATT treaty recognizing the provisional accession of Argentina: third extension.
17 Nov. 1966	Signs GATT treaty of provisional acceptance of the United Arab Republic: second extension of provisional accession.
17 Nov. 1966	Exchange of notes with Great Britain on conditions of service in respect to British officers in the public service of Malawi.
22 Nov. 1966	Signs multilateral treaty recognizing the compulsory jurisdiction of the International Commission of Jurists.
29 Nov. 1966	Postal service agreement with South Africa concerning money and postal orders.
12 Dec. 1966	Accedes to the convention on the transit trade of land-locked countries.
17 Dec. 1966	Application of treaties between the United States and Great Britain to Malawi.
1 Jan. 1967	Malawi News Agency starts operations.
18 Jan. 1967	Dr. Banda states that the Tanzania government was no longer lending active

support to Malawian rebels.

3 Feb. 1967	Dr. Banda forbids the import of publications from the People's Republic of China.
8 Feb. 1967	Dr. Banda comments on the relationship between Malawi and Tanzania, especially concerning the training of rebels. These, he states were given land to cultivate for food because the Tanzanian government was no longer giving them money.
16 Feb. 1967	Signs the multilateral treaty on the simplification of customs procedures.
24 Feb. 1967	Accedes to the convention abolishing requirements for foreign public documents.
2 Mar. 1967	Signs GATT treaty recognizing the accession of the Republic of Korea.
13 Mar. 1967	Signs trade agreement with South Africa.
24 Apr. 1967	Cabinet changes are announced: Chakuwamba is to become Minister for Local Government from Chidzanja who has resigned. Chakuwamba is to relinguish the Ministry of Works and Supply. This will be taken over by Msonthi who will remain Minister for Transport and Communications.
May 1967	An organization IMEX (Malawi) is formed to encourage South African capital investment in Malawi.
1 May 1967	Investment guarantees treaty with the United States.
4 May 1967	Enters into development credit agreement with the International Development Agency for an Education Project.
12 May 1967	Chief Leabua Jonathan of Lesotho arrives in Blantyre at the start of a goodwill visit.
15 May 1967	President Banda announces the release of more than 1600 prisoners as an act of presidential clemency to mark Malawi's National Day.
31 May 1967	President Nyerere declares that Tanzania does not recognize the artificial boundary around the Lake's shore but rather the original boundary which passes through the middle of the Lake.
14 June 1967	President Banda has discussions with British Prime Minister Harold Wilson on the Rhodesian problem during his visit to both the United States and Great Britain.
28 June 1967	A Bill introduced in Parliament whereby those insulting, ridiculing or showing disrespect to President Banda, the Malawi flag, or the national symbols will be liable to two years in prison and a fine of 1000 Pounds Sterling.
4 July 1967	Tanzanian Minister of Information and Tourism, Makame, reiterates his country's stance on the boundary dispute between his country and Malawi.
5 July 1967	Accession to multilateral treaty on the international circulation of visual and

auditory material of an educational, scientific and cultural character.

5-6 July 1967	President Seretse Khama of Botswana visits Malawi, as guest of honour at the Republican anniversary celebrations.
11 July 1967	Accession to the case of statelessness treaty.
1 Aug. 1967	Signs agreement with Republic of South Africa regarding the employment and documentation of Malawi nationals in RSA.
3 Aug. 1967	A junior Minister, Rev. Tobias Banda, Parliamentary Secretary to the Ministry of Health, is suspended for nepotism and for interfering with local authorities.
5-13 Aug.1967	President Banda pays an official visit to Nationalist China and supports the position of Nationalist China in the United Nations.
23 Aug. 1967	President Banda deposes the Paramount Chief of the Angoni, W.P. Gomani, for political activities.
28 Aug. 1967	Malawi announces it would not send a representative to the OAU Summit meeting in Kinshasha as it coincided with the Malawi Congress Party Convention.
10 Sept. 1967	President Banda announces at the annual convention of the Congress Party, the opening of formal diplomatic relations with South Africa at legation level.
26 Sept. 1967	Malawi Ambassador to the United States, Nyemba Mbekeani presents his credentials to President Johnson.
26 Sept. 1967	The High Commission for Malawi in the United Kingdom, T.S. Mangwazu, arrives in London.
3 Oct. 1967	President Banda announces strengthening of ties with Portugal and Malawi's High Commissioner will also become Ambassador to Portugal.
4 Oct. 1967	President Banda reveals to Parliament that a group of heavily armed rebels had shipped into the country with the intention of assassinating both him and his Ministers. These are later captured.
23 Oct. 1967	The Jehovah's Witness sect is outlawed as a subversive organisation by a Presidential Decree.
24 Oct. 1967	Ministers of Health and of Trade and Industry are dropped in a Cabinet reshuffle, which takes effect on 1 November. The Ministries of Natural Resources, Trade and Industry, and Development and Planning are merged into a single Ministry of Economic Affairs.
Nov. 1967	The Chairman of the Resources and Planning Council of the South African government visits Malawi and endorses President Banda's plan to build a new capital at Lilongwe.
3 Nov. 1967	President Banda is quoted as saying that relations with Tanzania and Zambia have been hostile since the 1964 Cabinet crisis.

24 Nov. 1967	Accepts accession of Argentina, Iceland, Poland, Republic of Korea, Switzerland and the United Arab Republic to GATT and Ireland for signature.
12 Dec. 1967	Philip Richardson, Malawi Chargé d'Affaires, presents his credentials to the South African Minister of Foreign Affairs. His counterpart in Malawi, Jan F. Wentzel, also presents his credentials to President Banda.
1-8 Jan.1968	Eight Europeans and Asians are ordered to leave the country without reasons being given.
3 Jan. 1968	Bill to be submitted at the next Parliamentary session is designed to lift the restrictions on the number of non-members of Parliament who may be appointed as Cabinet Ministers. It will also amend the constitution regarding the Presidential Electoral College, and will give Parliament more legislative powers regarding criminal and civil appeals.
5 Jan. 1968	Succession to the Geneva Conventions: prisoners of war; protection of civilian persons in time of war; wounded and sick in armed forces in the field, and at sea.
23 Jan. 1968	Accepts by signature provisional accession of Tunisia to the fourth extension of GATT.
Feb. 1968	Signs development credit agreements with the International Development Agency for the following projects: Highway; Lilongwe Agricultural Development; Shire Valley Agricultural Project.
7-10 Feb.1968	An official Zambian delegation visits Malawi. It is headed by Foreign Minister Kamanga.
10 Feb. 1968	Malawi states intention to open a High Commission in Lusaka, Zambia as soon as practicable.
5 Mar. 1968	Mini-skirts banned. Any foreign girl wearing these will be asked to leave the country under ban, and the shop selling them will be closed.
13 Mar. 1968	Portugal denies that it is ceding Portuguese territory to Malawi, and states that a recent visit of four Malawian parliamentarians to Portugal was one of courtesy.
20 Mar. 1968	Die Welt in Hamburg publishes President Banda's attack on certain European countries for the condemnation of white minority regimes in Southern Africa.
21 Mar. 1968	Air transport agreement signed with South Africa.
2 Apr. 1968	Signs treaty on double taxation on income with Great Britain.
8 Apr. 1968	Signs multilateral treaty concerning assistance from the World Food Programme (United Nations and FAO on behalf of WFP)
8 Apr. 1968	Vincent Gondwe is appointed Malawi Ambassador to Ethiopia.
22 Apr. 1968	Amendment to Danish government loan.

24 Apr. 1968	Malawi sends a goodwill mission to Zambia. It is led by Minister of Transport, Communications and Power, Msonthi.
May 1968	The South African government appoints a Military Attaché to its Legation in Malawi.
8 May 1968	President Banda announces that South Africa would finance the construction of a railway line from Southern Malawi to Mozambique. The building of the line will be carried out by a South African consortium.
10 May 1968	Five men are sentenced to death for the murder of a former member of the Malawi Congress Party.
13 May 1968	Malawian Ministers attend the three day Fourth East and Central African Summit Conference held in Dar-es-Salaam.
15 May 1968	President Banda assumes responsibility for the Ministry of Works and Supplies. Aleke Banda retains the Ministry of Economic Affairs but for reasons of continuity also becomes Deputy Minister of Works and Supplies.
17 May 1968	President Banda goes to Kenya for talks on technical exchanges.
20 May 1968	President Banda begins a tour to the United Kingdom, Israel and West Germany.
11-16 June 1968	President Banda pays a state visit to Kenya.
12 June 1968	Entry into force of amendments to Article 109 of the United Nations Charter.
14 June 1968	Death sentences are passed on eight of the rebel band of 1967. All plead not guilty and have thirty days in which to appeal.
4 July 1968	1427 prisoners released to mark Malawi's second Republican anniversary. This also marks President Banda's tenth anniversary of returning to Malawi from abroad.
7 Aug. 1968	An official statement reflects the attitude of Malawi towards Boy Scouts and Girl Guides due to their colonial links.
15 Aug. 1968	The Algiers venue for the September OAU Summit is deemed unacceptable to Malawi due to its relationship with Israel.
29 Aug. 1968	South Africa's Foreign Minister, Dr. Muller visits Malawi.
6 Sept. 1968	Signs a loan treaty with Denmark to establish a Technical Training Centre in Malawi.
9 Sept. 1968	President Banda resuscitates and extends territorial dispute with Tanzania.
15 Sept. 1968	Signs the Africa Convention on Nature and Natural Resources Conservation.
21 Sept. 1968	President Banda lays claim to the supposed boundaries of the seventeenth century Maravi Empire. This elicits sharp reactions from Tanzania and Zambia. The latter postponed indefinitely its plans for a diplomatic mission

in Malawi.

22 Sept. 1968	The President announces that the national languages move to English and Chichewa (formerly Chinyanja)
22 Sept. 1968	Delegates to the Malawi Congress Party Convention thank the South African government for making available four million Pounds Sterling towards the construction of a new capital city, Lilongwe.
24 Sept. 1968	Signs treaty with Great Britain on minimum sterling proportion.
27 Sept. 1968	Signs air services agreement with Great Britain.
Oct. 1968	Minister of Trade and Industry, Aleke Banda emphasizes that Malawi welcomes capital investment from the West.
31 Oct. 1968	Alfred Chiwanda, Minister of Labour resigns his portfolio but retains his Mwanza parliamentary seat. His vacancy is filled by Minister of Transport and Communications, John Msonthi.
13 Nov. 1968	Commissioner to Kenya, J. Mseku presents his credentials to President Kenyatta.
18 Nov. 1968	Alex Nyasulu is appointed Minister of State in the President's Office, with especial responsibility for National and Regional Development. This entails relinquishing his post as Minister of State in the Ministry of External Affairs.
21 Nov. 1968	Application of the extradition treaty between the Netherlands and Great Britain to Malawi.
16 Dec. 1968	Rectification on Danish loan.
30 Dec. 1968	Ministry of Information and Tourism established, headed by Aleke Banda, who also becomes Minister of Finance. Future changes to the Ministry of Natural Resources are indicated.
7 Jan. 1969	Succession to the agreement on the international regime of railways.
7-15 Jan.	At the London Conference of Commonwealth Prime Ministers, President Banda strongly opposes the use of force, asking who would raise an army to invade Rhodesia.
27 Jan. 1969	President Banda introduces two new Ministers to replace the Ministry of Natural Resources. These are the Ministry of Agriculture (G. Chakuamba) and the Ministry of Natural Resources (Richard Chidzanja)
27 Jan. 1969	Signs financial agreement with the Commonwealth Telecommunications Organisation.
27 Jan. 1969	Terminates Commonwealth Telegraphs Agreement.
4 Feb. 1969	Malawi represented at a 3-day meeting in Dar-es-Salaam of foreign ministers from East and Central Africa. This is in preparation for the Lusaka East and Central African Heads of State meeting to be held in Lusaka in April.

5 Feb. 1969	Accedes to GATT's provisional extension to Tunisia.
21 Feb. 1969	Vice-President, Kapwepe tells the National Assembly that it was up to Malawi to follow up a 1968 Zambian visit to establish diplomatic relations.
4 Mar. 1969	Ryuichi Ando, Japanese Ambassador to Kenya, and also accredited to Malawi, presents his credentials to Dr. Banda.
26 Mar. 1969	Denunciates agreement on a uniform law for cheques.
2 Apr. 1969	Diplomatic relations established with Portugal, and the first Portuguese Ambassador presents his credentials. He is Dr. Vasco Futscher Pereira.
8 Apr. 1969	President Tsiranana of Madagascar arrives in Malawi for an eight-day official visit.
14-16 Apr.1969	Malawi attends the Fifth East and Central African Summit Conference in Lusaka. Expresses reservations on the final communiqué on Rhodesia, South Africa and Mozambique. It would also not commit itself to the Manifesto on Southern Africa.
21 Apr. 1969	Eight men hanged in Blantyre for their role in the 1967 rebel movement.
29 Apr. 1969	The reconstituted Ministry of Health is to be known as the Ministry of Health and Community Development. It will be the portfolio of Alec Nyasulu.
17 May 1969	Discussions are held with Tanzania at Mbeya. Further talks to be held in Blantyre.
23 May 1969	Accession by Malawi to the Vienna Convention on the Law of Treaties.
24 May 1969	Accession to Customs Convention on Containers.
7 June 1969	Watchtower Bible and Tract Society is banned and anyone furthering their aims will be liable to seven years imprisonment.
7 June 1969	Convention on double taxation between Netherlands and Great Britain applies to Malawi.
9 June 1969	Accepts authentic trilingual text of the Convention on International Civil Aviation.
11 June 1969	Succession to a right to a flag of states having no sea coast.
1 July 1969	First Italian Ambassador to Malawi, Dr. G. Grotta presents his credentials to President Banda.
6 July 1969	President Banda defends his relations with South Africa and Portugal on the third Republican anniversary.
8-11 July 1969	Malawi takes part at the consultative meeting of the non-aligned countries in Belgrade.
9 July 1969	Accedes to the International Sugar Agreement.

25 July 1969	Signs International Health Regulations.
28 July 1969	Norwegian Ambassador to Malawi, S. Gjellum presents his credentials to President Banda. He is based in Kenya.
6 Aug. 1969	Malawi and Turkey are to establish diplomatic relations.
14 Aug. 1969	French Ambassador, Jacques Nouvel, presents his credentials to President Banda.
10 Sept. 1969	Signs specific aspects of the OAU Convention on Refugee Problems in Africa.
20 Sept. 1969	President Banda intervenes to secure the release of two Portuguese servicemen who had been detained in Zambia. This is in exchange for three Zambians held in Mozambique.
1 Oct. 1969	President Banda warns against infiltrations of hostile 'agents' from Zambia or Tanzania.
13 Oct. 1969	Cabinet reshuffle: Gomile Kumtumanja relinquishes the post of Minister for the Southern Region (now Gwanda Chakvanba) but retains Ministry of Local Government and Ministry of Education; Richard Chidzanja becomes Minister of Agriculture and Natural Resources. Regional ministers will no longer have individual Cabinet portfolios.
28 Oct. 1969	Accedes to the treaty on the international exchange of publications.
9 Nov. 1969	Governor-General of Mozambique, Dr Baltazar Rebello de Souza pays a six-day goodwill visit to Malawi.
14 Nov. 1969	Signs Universal Postal Union Additional Protocol to Constitution and General Regulations; insured letters and boxes; postal parcels; the Universal Postal Convention.
21 Nov. 1969	Parliament to be increased from fifty to sixty members as the present constituencies are too large.
22 Nov. 1969	All four expatriate judges of the High Court resign in protest against the new legislation allowing President Banda to empower local courts to try all types of cases, including capital ones and to impose the death penalty. Courts to be renamed Traditional Courts.
24 Nov. 1969	President Banda announces four new portfolios. Ministry of Education and Local Government has been split (Education: M.M. Lungu). Local Government: G. Ndaema). The Ministry of Transport, Communications and Labour has been divided (Labour: R.J. Sembeieka, and Transport and Communications: J. Msonthi). Ministry of State in the President's Office portfolio is created (A.B. Chiwanda)
29 Nov. 1969	Malawi and Nigeria establish diplomatic relations. The Nigerian High Commisioner to Uganda has also been appointed as envoy to Malawi.
Dec. 1969	President Banda remarks that of the rebel ex-ministers, two were dead, two were in exile in Britain and the United States and only two remained in

Africa.

3 Dec. 1969	Treaty abolishes visas with Belgium, Luxembourg and Netherlands.
26-28 Jan. 1970	Malawian delegates attend the sixth East and Central African Summit held in Khartoum. Malawi dissents on certain resolutions including that on the intensification of the liberation struggle in Southern Africa.
27 Jan. 1970	The American Peace Corps is asked to withdraw from Malawi by August.
11 Feb. 1970	Development credit agreement with the International Development Agency concerning the Malawi Power Project.
11 Mar. 1970	Accedes to the World Intellectual Property Organisation.
25 Mar. 1970	Accedes to the Paris Convention Concerning the Protection of Industrial Property.
24 Apr. 1970	Due to the alleged arrest of Local Government Minister, Gladstone Ndema, the Labour Minister Richard Sembereka is appointed to head the Ministry of Local Government.
30 Apr. 1970	Ndema is found guilty of abusing his position as Member of Parliament and Minister of Local Government and is expelled from membership of the Malawi Congress Party.
11 May 1970	Malawi reaffirms its support for Israel. Aleke Banda speaks at a reception marking Israel's National Day.
14 May 1970	The new United States Ambassador to Malawi, William C. Burdett presents his credentials to President Banda.
19 May 1970	South Africa's Prime Minister, John Vorster arrives for a visit. He is accompanied by Foreign Minister Muller.
20 May 1970	Acceptance of amendment to Articles 24 and 25 of the World Health Organization Constitution.
2 July 1970	President Banda receives the credentials of M. Etuk as High Commissioner for the Federal Nigerian Republic, on a non-residential basis.
11 July 1970	The first Malawi Ambassador to the Vatican, R.W. Katenga-Kaunda presents his credentials to Pope Paul.
29 July 1970	Proposed Constitutional amendments would add ten nominated members to the House who would all be Malawians.
4 Aug. 1970	John Gwengwe is appointed as Minister of Trade and Industry in place of John Tembo who assumes governorship of the Reserve Bank of Malawi.
20 Aug. 1970	The new Danish Ambassador, Kai Johansen presents his credentials to President Banda.
24 Aug. 1970	Dr. Chin-Youn Chao, Ambassador of Nationalist China to Malawi presents his credentials.

6-12 Sept.1970	A convention of the Malawi Congress Party is held at Mzuzu, at which Dr. Banda is nominated life President of the Party.
14 Sept. 1970	Accession to treaty on the prohibition of the use in war of asphyxiating, poisonous or other gases and bacteriological methods of warfare.
11 Nov. 1970	Madagascar and Malawi dispense with the need for a visa for nationals entering the other country for periods of less than three months.
13 Nov. 1970	The newly-appointed Belgian Ambassador presents his credentials to President Banda.
20 Nov. 1970	Zambia's first Acting High Commissioner R.K. Ching'ambo leaves for Blantyre.
1 Dec. 1970	A Bill seeking to make President Banda Life President, passes through its second Parliamentary reading.
12 Dec. 1970	The Speaker of Parliament, I.K. Surtee is expelled from membership of the Malawi Congress Party and the MP for Thyolo North, A.M. Namalima is suspended. Both are accused of abusing their positions.
17 Dec. 1970	The Zambian Ministry of Foreign Affairs establishes diplomatic relations with Malawi at full High Commission level. Reuben K. Chinambu presents his credentials.
21 Dec. 1970	Michael Botha, South Africa's Minister of Bantu Administration and Development visits Malawi for four days.
1 Jan. 1971	International Health Regulations enter into force.
21 Jan. 1971	President Banda criticizes the eight-nation Commonwealth group formed to study the South African arms issue.
1 Feb. 1971	Amends the trade agreement signed with South Africa on 13 March 1967.
2 Mar. 1971	Danish government loan to Malawi.
2 Mar. 1971	Signs technical co-operation treaty with Denmark.
5 Mar. 1971	Signs treaty with Great Britain regarding the production and trade policies of cereals.
8 Mar. 1971	Botswana High Commissioner, Phineas Makepe, presents his credentials to President Banda.
12 Mar. 1971	M. Lungu appointed as Minister of Health and Community Development, in addition to Minister of Education.
27 Mar. 1971	Treaty with Great Britain concerning officers designated by the United Kingdom in the service of specified organizations or institutions in Malawi.
11 Apr. 1971	President Banda personally selects the Malawi Congress Party candidates from constituency lists.

17 Apr. 1971	General election takes place in which all Malawi Congress Party candidates are returned unopposed. Irregularities are reported in seven constituencies when results announced on 19 April.
21 Apr. 1971	President Banda appoints a new Cabinet.
21 Apr. 1971	British High Commissioner, W. Haydom presents his credentials to President Banda.
29 Apr. 1971	Ratifies the Convention on International Civil Aviation.
3 May 1971	Signs agreement with South Africa for avoidance of double taxation and prevention of fiscal evasion of taxes on income.
18 May 1971	First Malawi High Commissioner to Nigeria, V. Gondwe, presents his credentials to Major-General Gowon.
16 June 1971	First Iranian Ambassador presents his credentials to President Banda.
17 June 1971	Turkish Ambassador, Sardum Terem presents his credentials to President Banda.
24 June 1971	The seven candidates from the constituencies demonstrating irregularities are returned unopposed.
25 June 1971	Ratifies the agricultural labour section of the International Labour Organisation Convention.
30 June 1971	New Austrian Ambassador, Dr. George Reisch, presents his credentials to President Banda.
1 July 1971	Britain agrees to lend Malawi eleven million Pounds Sterling over three years, interest free, for development projects.
2 July 1971	At the State Opening of Parliament President Banda announces that both the Malawi legation in Pretoria and the South African mission in Blantyre would be upgraded to embassies.
6 July 1971	Dr. Banda is sworn in as Life President. Also receives the Kamuzu Foundation Fund with contributions by commerce, agriculture and industry.
14 July 1971	Government appoints first black Police Commissioner, M. Kawawa.
5 Aug. 1971	South African Ambassador to Malawi, J.F. Wentzel, presents his credentials to President Banda.
16-20 Aug. 1971	President Banda on state visit to South Africa.
26 Aug. 1971	High Commissioner to Kenya presents his credentials to President Kenyatta.
1 Sept. 1971	Malawi Ambassador to Ethiopia presents his credentials to Emperor Haile Selassie.
5 Sept. 1971	President Banda opens the Ninth Convention of the Malawi Congress Party in Lilongwe.

14 Sept. 1971	Signs a treaty with Great Britain concerning minimum sterling proportion: guarantee by Great Britain and maintenance by Malawi.
14 Sept. 1971	Signs treaty with the United States regarding the Peace Corps and Peace Corps programme.
20 Sept. 1971	Ratifies protocol relating to an amendment to Article 56 of the International Civil Aviation treaty.
21 Sept. 1971	Malawi High Commissioner to the United Kingdom, B. Katenga, presents credentials to Queen Juliana of the Netherlands.
24 Sept. 1971	President Banda arrives in Tete, Mozambique, for a 2-day official visit.
18 Nov. 1971	Minister of State in the President's office resigns due to pressure of Party work and private business.
8 Dec. 1971	It is reported that Malawi bought nine armoured scout cars from South Africa.
30 Dec. 1971	Signs commercial scheduled air transport agreement with Cyprus.
2 Jan. 1972	Signed development credit agreement with the International Development Agency concerning the Karonga Development Project.
11 Jan. 1972	Signs treaty with Great Britain pertaining to officers designated by the United Kingdom in the service of the Government of Malawi.
25 Feb. 1972	Extradition treaty is signed with South Africa.
Mar. 1972	Ambassador to Israel, C.M. Mkona, presents his credentials.
10 Mar. 1972	President Kaunda appoints Reuben Chinambu as Ambassador to Malawi.
17-24 Mar. 1972	President Fouché of South Africa visits Malawi. He is accompanied by Foreign Minister Hilgard Muller.
4 Apr. 1972	President Banda makes a number of new ministerial appointments and changes to the ministerial organization affecting trade and industry, and information and tourism. The latter would cease to exist in its present form and will become joined to Trade and Industry, while the Department of Information will be known as the Department of Information and Broadcasting.
10 Apr. 1972	Signs the multilateral bacteriogical (biological) and toxic weapons treaty: development, production and stockpiling: prohibition and destruction.
11 Apr. 1972	D. Pestalozzi, Swiss Ambassador to Malawi presents his credentials. He is based in Kenya.
17 Apr. 1972	Botswana High Commissioner to Malawi, Ontumetse, presents his credentials.
24 Apr. 1972	Accession to the treaty on judicial and extrajudicial documents in civil or commercial matters: service abroad.

1 May 1972	Colonel Matemere takes over command of the Army from a British Army officer, Brigadier Clements.
8 May 1972	West German Ambassador, von Wartenburg, presents his credentials to President Banda.
13 May 1972	Signs agreement with the International Development Agency concerning the Lilongwe Agricultural Development Project.
18 May 1972	Malawi High Commissioner to Kenya, E. Phakamea, presents his credentials to President Kenyatta.
24 May 1972	A South African Airways Boeing 727 is hijacked on a flight from Johannesburg to Salisbury and lands in Malawi. The two highjackers surrendered to the Malawi police on 26 May.
12 June 1972	Malawi is not represented at the Ninth Assembly of the OAU Heads of State and Government in Rabat. No explanation is given.
15 June 1972	In an attempt to promote tourism, Malawi relaxes its ban on the mini skirt, shorts and slacks for women. These are now permissable at hotels, holiday resorts, airports and railway stations.
26 June 1972	President Banda announces a cabinet reshuffle for the third time in four months. The President assumes responsibility for Agriculture and Natural Resources; John Gwengwe returns to the Ministry of Transport and Communications; Wadson Deleza retains the Ministry of Labour only.
30 June 1972	Rhodesia Herald is banned in Malawi after Rhodesian press allegations regarding Malawi assistance to FRELIMO.
July 1972	Danish Ambassador, Hans Kuhne, presents his credentials to President Banda.
6 July 1972	A banquet is held to mark the sixth anniversary of Malawi's independence. Chiefs Buthelezi and Mangope from South Africa attend.
8 July 1972	Amends air services agreement with Great Britain.
14 July 1972	Aaron Gadama ceases to be Minister of Community Development and Social Welfare and becomes Minister without Portfolio; the Minister of Local Government, Pearson Nkhoma also assumes responsibility for the Ministry of Community Development and Social Welfare, which, however retains its separate identity.
31 July 1972	The United Kingdom agrees to grant one million Pounds Sterling towards the construction of an army barracks in Lilongwe. This results in doubling the strength of the second battalion.
Aug. 1972	Ambassador to Ethiopia presents his credentials to Emperor Haile Selassie.
4 Aug. 1972	President Banda orders the suspension from the Malawi Congress Party of the Minister of Transport and Communications, John Gwengwe for breaching party discipline.

4 Sept. 1972	Ministerial changes take place: Malani Lungu assumes responsibility for the Ministries of Local Government and Community Development and Social Welfare, whilst relinguishing the Ministry of Health. This portfolio is assumed by Makhumula Nkhoma, who relinguishes the Ministries of Local Government and Community Development and Social Welfare.
10-16 Sept.1972	At the annual convention of the Malawi Congress Party, President Banda comments on his relationship with other Southern African states, and also on the nine resolutions passed at the Convention and the importance of good manners and tradition.
15 Sept. 1972	Ratifies Amendment to Article 61 of the United Nations Charter.
18 Sept. 1972	Hijackers Foud Kamil and Ajaj Yaghi each sentenced to eleven years imprisonment with hard labour in the Malawi High Court.
19 Sept. 1972	President Banda announces that Malawi is to receive some of the Asians expelled from Uganda.
21 Sept. 1972	Signs, with some reservations, the multilateral civil aviation treaty concerning the suppression of unlawful acts.
Oct. 1972	Israeli Ambassador, Jacob Monbaz, presents his credentials to President Banda.
10 Oct. 1972	Times of Zambia reports that several hundred members of the Watchtower sect have fled from Malawi to the Eastern Province of Zambia.
25 Oct. 1972	One of the two Malawi ministers attending the Zambia independence celebrations denies the persecution of the Watchtower sect.
30 Oct. 1972	Radio Lourenco Marques announces that about 7000 members of the Watchtower have fled to the Mozambican border area of Tete.
2 Nov. 1972	Zambian Minister of Home Affairs, Lewis Changufu is convinced, after discussions with Malawian officials, that the fears of the Watchtower refugees are unfounded and that they are to return home.
10 Nov. 1972	Acceptance of instrument for amendment to the International Labour Organisation.
Dec. 1972	The number of Watchtower refugees in Zambia reportedly total approximately 20,000.
7 Dec. 1972	Malawi denies the presence of FRELIMO bases from which Mozambique could be attacked.
15 Dec. 1972	The first Greek Ambassador to Malawi, Marcus Economides, presents his credentials. He is South African based.
21 Dec. 1972	Signs multilateral treaty for the suppression of unlawful acts against the safety of civil aviation.
1 Jan. 1973	The Daily News begins circulation following the merger of the Malawi Press Ltd. and the Blantyre Printing and Publishing Company.

Feb. 1973	Belgian Ambassador, Edgar Vehille arrives to present his credentials to President Banda.
6 Mar. 1973	Ratifies the Africa convention on nature and national resources conservation.
13 Mar. 1973	Minister of Trade, Industry and Tourism, Aleke Banda, is dismissed from the Cabinet, after being deprived of his membership and office in the ruling Malawi Congress Party.
14 Mar. 1973	Signs treaty regarding crimes against internationally protected persons, including diplomatic agents.
29 Mar. 1973	Danish government loan to Malawi.
31 Mar. 1973	Signs Commonwealth Telecommunications Organisation financial agreement.
8 May 1973	Ministry of Information and Broadcasting refutes a Reuter report of 4 May alleging border clashes between Malawi and Mozambique.
8 May 1973	Swedish Ambassador F. Dolling presents his credentials to President Banda.
9 May 1973	John Borrell, a British free-lance journalist, arrives in London after his expulsion from Malawi.
23 May 1973	Signs additional regulations of amendment to Articles 1, 21, 63-71 and 92 of the International Health Regulations.
11 June 1973	Director of the news programmes on Malawi Broadcasting Corporation, Joseph Wadda arrives in Cyprus after being given seventy-two hours in which to leave Malawi.
12 June 1973	Malawi High Commissioner to Zambia, Callisto Mkona, presents his credentials to President Kaunda.
10 July 1973	Whilst addressing Parliament, the President comments on the introduction of legislation against 'lying journalists'. He refers in particular to the report on fighting between Malawi and Mozambican troops, legislation on the illegality of mini-skirts and 'other obscenities' also relevant.
26 July 1973	Signs air services agreement with Swaziland.
18 Aug. 1973	Ministry of Information and Broadcasting dissolved. It is later announced that its functions have been divided between the President's Office and Cabinet and the Ministry of Trade, Industry and Tourism. The incumbent Minister, Rodwell Munyenyembe is appointed Minister of Community Development and Social Welfare, a portfolio previously held by the Minister of Local Government.
2 Sept. 1973	President opens the Malawi Congress Party Convention in Mzuzu.
7 Sept. 1973	Signs development credit agreement with the International Development Agency concerning the second Power Project.
4 Oct. 1973	Accession to the Single Convention on Narcotic Drugs, 1961; entry into force is dated 8 August 1975.

6 Oct. 1973	British High Commissioner to Malawi, K. Ritchie, presents his credentials to President Banda.
20 Oct. 1973	The first Spanish Ambassador to Malawi, Eduardo Gasset, presents his credentials to President Banda.
29 Oct. 1973	Minister of Youth and Culture, Chaknamba Phiri tells Parliament that the decision to end European representation in Parliament does not mean that they are being ousted from the country.
1 Nov. 1973	President Banda explains the background to the ending of sectional representation in Parliament.
19 Nov. 1973	South African Ambassador, Louis Vorster, presents his credentials to President Banda.
Dec. 1973	The Malawi Ambassador to South Africa, A. Funsani, presents his credentials to President Fouché.
3 Dec. 1973	Signs International Sugar Agreement.
14 Dec. 1973	Accession by Malawi to the Convention on the Prevention and Punishment of Crimes Against Internationally Protected Persons Including Diplomatic Agents.
2 Feb. 1974	British Foreign Secretary, Sir Alec Douglas-Home, arrives in Malawi.
12 Feb. 1974	The first Canadian High Commissioner Brondbidge, accredited to Malawi on a non-residential basis, presents his credentials to President Banda.
14 Feb. 1974	Minister of Education, John Msonthi, is dismissed from the Malawi Congress Party.
19 Feb. 1974	Rodwell Munyenyembe, Minister of Community Development and Social Welfare, assumes responsibility for the Ministry of Education. The two Ministries remain separate but under one Minister.
5 Mar. 1974	Ambassador B.W. Katenga presents his credentials to Emperor Haile Selassie of Ethiopia.
6 Mar. 1974	Mayor of Lilongwe, Dominic Kainja Nthara, is appointed Minister of Community Development and Social Welfare.
20 Mar. 1974	President Banda appoints three people to serve as National Executive Members of the Malawi Congress Party. They are Effie Mtika, Chidzanja Nkhoma, and Dominic Kainja Nthara.
4 Apr. 1974	Seventy-four Malawi miners returning from South Africa die in an air disaster at Francistown, Botswana. President Banda suspends recruitment of Malawian mine workers to South Africa.
30 Apr. 1974	The fourteen-month suspension from the Malawi Congress Party of Aleke Banda, formerly its Secretary-General, comes to an end.
May 1974	Two Lebanese hijackers are secretly released after serving only twelve

months of eleven years hard labour, reports the Sunday Times, on 23 June.

1 May 1974	Richard Banda, Rodwell Munyenyembe and Watson Deleza become members of the National Executive Committee of the Malawi Congress Party.
6 May 1974	President Kaunda of Zambia returns home after a day-long visit to Malawi.
18 May 1974	Signs loan agreement of $10m. with the Agricultural Development and Marketing Corporation and the Chase Manhattan Bank.
21 May 1974	Adheres to the International Plant Protection Convention.
30 May 1974	President Banda announces the establishment of a Ministry for Organisation of African Unity Affairs. This will be named at a later date and will operate from the Office of the President and the Cabinet.
3 June 1974	A $3m. contract is awarded to the French Kier Group for the hydro-electric scheme at Tedzane Falls.
13 June 1974	Signs development credit agreement with the International Development Association concerning the Transport, Engineering and Services Project.
5 July 1974	Signs second additional protocol to the Universal Postal Union; the General Regulations; insured letters; postal parcels, as well as the Universal Postal Convention.
6 July 1974	President Tolbert of Liberia attends the tenth independent anniversary celebration.
17 July 1974	Signs financial assistance treaty with the Federal Republic of Germany.
23 July 1974	Portuguese government announces that it would withdraw its diplomatic representation from Zomba.
Aug. 1974	Italian Ambassador, Dr. Alberto Rossi, and United States Ambassador R. Stevenson present their credentials to President Banda.
6 Aug. 1974	Signs multilateral treaty on the Status of the World Tourism Organisation (WTO).
Sept. 1974	The governments of Cameroon and Malawi decide to establish diplomatic relations at ambassadorial level.
1-7 Sept.1974	The annual convention of the Malawi Congress Party is held in Lilongwe with its theme 'Building the Nation'.
15 Sept. 1974	The IMF announces certain changes in the par or central rates of Malawi's currency.
17 Sept. 1974	Delegates from South Africa's Chamber of Commerce fly to Malawi for discussions with both the President and the Minister of Labour aimed at ending the ban on recruiting Malawians for work on the South African gold

mines.

24 Sept. 1974	Malawi's Ambassador to South Africa, A.D. Funsani is recalled and leaves the Republic after only ten months.
Oct. 1974	Ambassador Nelson Mizere takes up his appointment in South Africa.
21 Oct. 1974	Signs amendments of Articles 34 and 55 of the World Health Organization constitution.
Dec. 1974	Several thousand Malawi miners leave South Africa.
19 Dec. 1974	Signs development credit with the International Development Agency concerning the second Highway Project.
31 Dec. 1974	Signs a financial assistance treaty with the Federal Republic of Germany.
1 Jan. 1975	Lilongwe is officially declared the country's capital, and is granted a charter by President Banda on 7 April.
5 Jan. 1975	James Callaghan, the U.K. Foreign and Commonwealth Secretary, flies to Malawi for talks with President Banda, as part of his visit to African countries.
8 Jan. 1975	Dr. Banda's first state visit to Zambia since it gained independence in 1964.
11 Jan. 1975	Preliminary survey is announced which will chart Zambia's railway connections with Angola and Malawi.
1 Feb. 1975	Malawi signs the Lomé Convention between the European Economic Community and forty-six African, Caribbean and Pacific countries.
7 Feb. 1975	Belgian Ambassador, J.R. Blancquaert, presents his credentials to President Banda.
9 Apr. 1975	President Kenyatta receives the credentials of Malawi's High Commissioner, Edson Phakamea.
27 May 1975	Grant agreement is signed with the UN Capital Development Fund.
27 May 1975	Signs a development credit agreement with the International Development Association concerning Phase III of the Lilongwe Agricultural Development Project.
27 May 1975	Signs development credit agreement with the International Development Association for the second Sedhiou Project.
25 June 1975	Signs the multilateral African Civil Aviation Commission constitution.
Sept. 1975	Henry Chipembere dies in the United States.
Sept. 1975	Jehovah's Witnesses flee to Zambia after their refusal to become members of the Malawi Congress Party.
20 Sept. 1975	Signs treaty with France on cultural and technical co-operation.

3 Nov. 1975   Approximately 3000 Jehovah's Witnesses have been repatriated from Zambia back to Malawi.

18 Nov. 1975   President Banda accuses exiled Malawians in Tanzania and Zambia of plotting to overthrow him.

24 Nov. 1975   Signs a development credit agreement with the International Development Agency regarding the second Education Project.

Late Nov.1975   Malawi seals her borders with Tanzania and Zambia for at least one month.

3 Dec. 1975   Accepts International Coffee Agreement.

13 Dec. 1975   Exchange of notes with South Africa amending the trade agreement of 13 March 1967.

31 Dec. 1975   Acceptance of Resolution no. 1 extending the International Sugar Agreement of 1973.

1 Jan. 1976   Accepts the constitution of the Universal Postal Union.

Feb. 1976   Richard Allen Banda, Minister of Justice, is expelled from the Malawi Congress Party and all official posts.

1 Apr. 1976   Signs financial assistance treaty with West Germany.

17 Apr. 1976   Parliament is dissolved.

22 Apr. 1976   President Banda dissolves the Cabinet and assumes all ministerial powers.

May 1976   Malawi gives 250 Asian British passport-holders until the end of June to leave the country. This includes seventy-one families of Goan origin.

1 May 1976   President Banda announces the arrest of a `group of agents' sent from Tanzania to assassinate him.

24 May 1976   Eighty-five candidates nominated to the National Assembly are returned unopposed while two others fail to have their nomination paper accepted in time.

1 June 1976   Banda appoints a new Cabinet, and reduces the number of Ministers by four.

15 June 1976   Acceds to the International Coffee Agreement.

18 June 1976   Signs Resolution no. 2 extending the International Sugar Agreement.

24 June 1976   Signs a loan agreement with the World Bank for the Karonga Rural Development Project.

July 1976   Malawi doubles the size of her army and plans further expansion of the fighting forces.

19 July 1976   Danish loan to Malawi by treaty signature.

9 Aug. 1976   Amnesty International (London) states that over 1,000 people are detained

without trial in Malawi.

26 Aug. 1976	Watson Deleza is appointed Minister of Labour.
Sept. 1976	Minister for Local Government, Community Development and Social Welfare, D. Kainja Nthara is expelled from the Malawi Congress Party and four Members of Parliament are suspended from the Malawi Congress Party.
Sept. 1976	Lesotho and Malawi establish diplomatic relations on a non-residential basis and Rasekaai is accredited as High Commissioner.
8 Oct. 1976	Commander of the Army, Major-General Matewere becomes the first army general.
28 Oct. 1976	The Malawi Congress Party's Secretary-General, Albert Nqumayo, is expelled. He is also Minister without Portfolio.
Nov. 1976	President Banda makes new ministerial appointments. Minister of Local Government, B.L.R. Kapi Chila Banda; Minister at Large, R.B. Chidzanja Nkhoma; Minister without Portfolio, R.T.C. Munyen Yembe; Minister of Education, E.B. Muluzi; Minister of Health, A.A. Chatsika.
19 Nov. 1976	Signs financial assistance treaty with West Germany.
31 Dec. 1976	International Sugar Agreement definition accepted.
25 Jan. 1977	Nqumayo and Gwede are found guilty of conspiring to overthrow the lawfully constituted government in the Southern Regional Traditional Court. They are sentenced to death on 14 February but lose their appeal.
28 Apr. 1977	Signs development credit agreement with the International Development Association pertaining to the third Power Project.
28 Apr. 1977	Signs guarantee agreement with IBRD for the third Power Project.
30 May 1977	Ministers exchange posts and Bakil Muluzi becomes Secretary-General of the Malawi Congress Party and Rodwell Munyenyembe assumes responsibility for the Ministry of Education.
7 July 1977	President Banda dismisses the entire Cabinet and all deputy ministers and parliamentary secretaries. He also dissolves the Executive Committee of the Malawi Congress Party.
8 July 1977	Banda forms a new government with most of the appointments remaining the same, with several exceptions, Minister without Portfolio, Elson Muluzi; Health, Sebastian Muwangalira; Education, Winford Lweya; Local Government, Tadeus Phaiya.
15 July 1977	Signs multilateral operational assistance treaty.
15 July 1977	Signs treaty on assistance from United Nations Development Programme.
15 July 1977	Signs multilateral treaty for technical assistance.

9 Aug. 1977	Amnesty International (London) reports that over 1000 people are detained without trial in Malawi.
7 Nov. 1977	President Banda claims that Chiume, dismissed former Minister of Foreign Affairs and now in exile, is planning to overthrow the government.
22 Nov. 1977	The Guardian (London) reports that the Socialist League of Malawi is recruiting Malawi exiles for training in Cuba.
13 Dec. 1977	Accedes to the International Fund for Agricultural Development establishment agreement.
29 Dec. 1977	Signs the International Sugar Agreement of 1977.
18 Jan. 1978	Signs development credit agreement with the International Development Association for a third Highway Project.
14 Feb. 1978	Winford Lweya is dismissed as Minister of Education and expelled from the Malawi Congress Party.
16 Feb. 1978	Mr. Mwangonga Mkandawire is appointed Minister of Education.
22 Feb. 1978	Signs multilateral agreement establishing the International Tea Promotion Association.
29 June 1978	Elections are held in which voting is allowed for the first time since 1964, and only members of the Malawi Congress Party are allowed to stand. In the previous elections candidates were returned unopposed.
3 July 1978	Election results announced.
5 July 1978	President Banda announces his new Cabinet.
7 July 1978	Signs guarantee agreement with the International Bank for Reconstruction and Development.
Aug. 1978	Western journalists banned once more after being allowed into the country briefly for the first time since 1973.
Aug. 1978	President Banda dismisses Minister of Health, Gerald Kalimapapadzala and he, himself takes over the portfolio.
3 Oct. 1978	Lewis Chimango and Katola Phiri become Minister of Health and Minister of Local Government respectively.
2 Jan. 1979	Elia Phiri becomes Minister of Transport and Communications, David Kaunda assumes Local Government portfolio, and Edward Muruwezi ceases to be Minister Without Portfolio. There will be no parliamentary secretaries at present.
Feb. 1979	Fingers blown off the hands of Dr. Attai Mpakati who is in exile in Maputo. He, allegedly, is planning on overthrowing the government.
7 Mar. 1979	President Banda admits in Parliament that his agents were responsible for the letter bomb sent to Dr. Mpakati.

12 June 1979	Malawi closes its representative office in Rhodesia.
4 July 1979	President Daniel Moi arrives on an official visit which coincides with the fifteenth independence celebrations.
23 July 1979	Queen Elizabeth II makes a state visit.
30 July 1979	Cabinet reshuffle announced as Henry Harawa becomes Minister of Transport and Communications and Zondwayo Jere becomes Minister of Commerce, Industry and Tourism.
15 Sept. 1979	Signs treaty with Canada concerning Canadian investments in Malawi.
18 Oct. 1979	Southern African Regional Tourism Council treaty recommends the continued operation with Malawi, South Africa, and Swaziland as members, with suitable amendment to the original treaty.
2 Nov. 1979	Main alteration in the Cabinet makes John Sangala Local Authorities Minister and David Kaunda becomes Minister Without Portfolio. The President now has four portfolios for himself - Justice, Foreign Affairs, Agriculture, Natural Resources and Public Works and Supplies.
17 Dec. 1979	Accession of Malawi to the International Convention Against the Taking of Hostages, as adopted by the General Assembly of the UN.
31 Dec. 1979	A minor cabinet reshuffle occurs. Wadson Deleza retains Labour Ministry also takes on Ministry of Social Welfare, John Sangala (Minister of Local Government) also assumes the portfolio of Community Development. All eight parliamentary secretaries cease to hold their posts from 1 January 1980.
6 Jan. 1980	Loan agreement signed with South Africa.
13 Feb. 1980	David Kaunda is expelled from the Malawi Congress Party.
14 Feb. 1980	Aleke Banda is expelled from the Malawi Congress Party.
27 Feb. 1980	President Banda directs that there would only be acting Ministers of Youth and Culture (Dick Matenje) or Minister of the South (Alfred Chiwandagame). The regional Chairman of the Malawi Congress Party in the South will not be replaced for the present.
Aug. 1980	The International Development Association is to spend K22 million on its third five year Educational Development Programme in Malawi.
Nov. 1980	Asylum in Tanzania is sought by two Malawian air force officers.
Dec. 1980	The Netherlands provide Medical equipment valued at K3.1 million to be utilized in district hospitals.
7 Jan. 1981	Chaziya Phiri becomes Minister of Finance, Louis Chimang becomes Minister of Local Government and of Community Development, and Twaibu Sangala becomes Minister of Health.
20 Feb. 1981	Size of the Cabinet is increased by splitting the Ministry of Agriculture

(President Banda) and Natural Resources (John Liwewe) in two and Ministry for Housing and Community Development (David Chiwanga) is established.

20 Mar. 1981	Gwanda Chakuamba is sentenced to twenty-two-years imprisonment for sedition. He was formerly the Minister of Youth and Culture.
1 May 1981	Two new hospitals opened, financed by the European Community and Great Britain respectively.
19 June 1981	Algeria's first Ambassador to Malawi, Mohamed Khouri, presents his credentials.
1 July 1981	Cultural functions of the Ministry of Youth and Culture are transferred to the Ministry of Education which is now known as the Ministry of Youth and Sport while the latter becomes the Ministry of Education and Culture. The Department of Tourism is detached from the Ministry of Trade, Industry and Tourism and is renamed the Ministry of Trade and Industry. It now forms part of the Department of Information and Tourism under the Office of the President and Cabinet.
1 July 1981	Mozambique and Malawi upgrade their diplomatic relations to ambassadorial level.
12 Aug. 1981	Border dispute between Zambia and Malawi is declared over land in Zambia's Eastern Province.
3 Oct. 1981	Tentative agreement reached on Tanzania-Malawi border issues. It replaces the Songwe River which is always changing course.
12 Oct. 1981	Follow-up talks held on Malawi-Tanzania border issue end on an amicable note with further talks envisaged.
16 Dec. 1981	Youth and Sport Minister, Dunn Chihphwanya, is dismissed.
24 Dec. 1981	The leader of the Malawi Freedom Front, Orton Chirwa, and his family are arrested.
5 Jan. 1982	Ministerial reorganization results in Dick Matenje becoming Minister of Education and Culture (and also Secretary-General of the Malawi Congress Party); Stephen C. Hara becomes responsible for Education and Culture, Stanford Demba for Forestry and Natural Resources and Harrison Y. Kayira for Trade and Industry. Muluzi, a succession favourite, is dropped.
11 Jan. 1982	Ten Zambian nationals are held for straying into Malawi.
Feb. 1982	President Kaunda of Zambia makes his first official visit to Malawi since independence.
22 Feb. 1982	It is announced that the leader of the opposition Socialist League of Malawi is deported from Zambia.
24 Apr. 1982	The Malawian Kwacha is devalued by 15% against the special drawing right of the International Monetary Fund.
19 May 1982	President Banda assumes responsibility for the Transport and

Communication portfolio due to Muluzi's resignation.

23 July 1982	D.S. Katopola becomes Minister of Local Government and Louis Chimango becomes Minister of Transport and Communication.
28 July 1982	Opposition leader, Orton Chirwa and his wife are further accused, in the treason trial, of plotting to assassinate President Banda.
12 Oct. 1982	Malawi denies any links with the RENAMO movement in Mozambique.
23 Oct. 1982	Exchange of notes with South Africa dated 23 October and 4 November amending the loan agreement of 4 January 1980.
27 Oct. 1982	President Banda and Major-General Joaquim Chissano, Mozambique's Minister of Foreign Affairs, meet and shortly thereafter RENAMO facilities in Malawi are closed.
12 Feb. 1983	Loan agreement is signed with South Africa concerning financial and technical assistance for the purchase and transport of fertilizer.
28 Mar. 1983	Dr. Attai Mpakati, the National Chairman of LESOMA is found shot dead in Harare.
5 May 1983	Orton Chirwa and his wife are sentenced to death, but leave is granted for an appeal.
19 May 1983	Four senior politicians killed. The government claims they were in a car accident whilst Malawian exiles claim it was part of a succession power struggle.
12 June 1983	The same Malawi Committee comprised of representatives of the Socialist League of Malawi, the Malawi Freedom Movement, and the Congress for the Second Republic hold a unity meeting.
27-28 June 1983	Parliamentary elections held for the 101 elective seats, recently enlarged by Presidential Decree from 87.
4 July 1983	New cabinet is sworn in. President Banda retains four key portfolios.
25 July 1983	A new Ministry of Community Services is created with George Kandawire as Minister.
28 July 1983	Two new members, B. Banda and Titus C. Kaleya, are appointed to the national executive committee of the ruling Malawi Congress Party.
20 Sept. 1983	The International Monetary Fund authorizes a three-year extended arrangement whereby purchases up to 100,000,000 special drawing rights may be made.
26 Nov. 1983	Signs a loan agreement with South Africa for financial and technical assistance for storage of reserve seed stocks.
21 Dec. 1983	Information is received in London that the Chirwas have lost their appeal against their death sentence.

16 Jan. 1984	The Kwacha is henceforth pegged to a basket of currencies of seven of Malawi's major trading partners.
Mar. 1984	Members of the Zimbabwe branch of the Congress for the Second Republic join the Socialist League of Malawi.
2 Apr. 1984	President Banda announces the dissolution of the Cabinet and temporarily assumes all ministerial posts himself.
4 Apr. 1984	President Banda reconstitutes the Cabinet. Changes included Edward Bwanali (Finance), Stephen Hara (Transport and Communications), Stanford Demba (Youth) and Poltone Mtenje (Forestry and Natural Resources).
18 May 1984	Signs agreement with the Federal Republic of Germany concerning financial co-operation.
28 June 1984	Death sentences for Orton and Vera Chirwa are commuted to life imprisonment.
11 July 1984	Malawi pledges 5000 Kwacha towards the plight of refugees in Africa at the second International Conference for Assistance to Refugees in Africa held in Geneva.
2-9 Sept.1984	The Malawi Congress Party Convention is held in Zomba.
27 Sept. 1984	Exchange of notes with Israel concerning the abolition of visitors' visas and visa fees.
23 Oct. 1984	Signs a general co-operation agreement with Mozambique to set up a joint commission concerning their bilateral relations.
12 Jan. 1985	A minor cabinet reshuffle occurs.
5 Mar. 1985	Signs loan agreement with the International Fund for Agricultural Development for the Kasungu Agricultural Development Project.
2 Apr. 1985	The Kwacha is devalued by 15%.
16-19 Apr.1985	President Banda makes a four-day state visit to Great Britain. Meets with Margaret Thatcher on 17 April.
May 1985	A link road is opened through northern Malawi to the Tazara railway.
15 May 1985	Sally Mugabe, wife of the Zimbabwean Prime Minister meets with President Banda at the end of a four day visit.
16 May 1985	Diplomatic relations are established with Tanzania.
21 June 1985	President Banda reshuffles the Cabinet as George Mkandawire assumes the Forestry and Natural Resources portfolio. Pulton Mtenje becomes Minister of Youth.
28 June 1985	Another minor Cabinet change is effected as George Mkandawire is dismissed as a Minister and a Member of Parliament.

30 Sept. 1985	The Ministry of Youth is abolished and all its business reverts to the Office of the President and Cabinet.
2 Jan. 1986	President Banda dissolves the Cabinet and personally takes charge of the Government.
17 Jan. 1986	President Banda reappoints all ministers to the Cabinet, mostly with changes of portfolio. The exceptions are the Minister Without Portfolio, Robson Chirwa and Minister at Large, Sydney Somanje.
25 Apr. 1986	Malawi and Tanzania sign an agreement giving Malawi greater access to Dar-es-Salaam.
1 May 1986	The governments of Malawi and Finland establish diplomatic relations.
9 May 1986	At the end of President Mugabe's three-day visit to Malawi, a Joint Commission of Cooperation and Friendship is established.
11 July 1986	Albania and Malawi establish diplomatic relations.
Sept. 1986	President Banda faces the most serious external crisis during his tenure of office. His support for RENAMO and their use of bases inside Malawi provokes censure from Presidents Machel, Kaunda and Mugabe.
17 Dec. 1986	The Malawi government hands over Mozambican prisoners released into Malawi by RENAMO.
18 Dec. 1986	Agreement signed in Lilongwe between Malawi and Mozambique on the principles agreed upon at the Nampula Meeting. Principles include good-neighbourliness, friendship and co-operation.
Mar. 1987	Malawi despatches a contingent of soldiers to assist President Chissano in the civil war against RENAMO.
15 Apr. 1987	President Banda dissolves Parliament and the Cabinet in preparation for the general elections.
27-28 May 1987	General election is held for the 112 elective seats in the National Assembly.
1 June 1987	The Bangkok Home Service reports that Thailand and Malawi have established diplomatic relations.
3 June 1987	The new Cabinet is announced.
13 Sept. 1987	The Malawi Congress Party Convention opens and Banda declares 'I will appoint no successor to me'.
6 Nov. 1987	A Malawian charter plane is believed to have been shot down over Mozambique. There were three British and one South African among the passengers.
2 Jan. 1988	President Banda dissolves the Cabinet.
14 Jan. 1988	The reshuffled cabinet is appointed in which Maxwell Pashane replaces Robson Chirwa as Minister Without Portfolio and as administrative secretary

of the Malawi Congress Party. Chirwa becomes Minister of Trade, Industry and Tourism; Michael Mlamba becomes Minister of Education and Culture.

Feb. 1988   External Affairs Secretary, Ron Nkomba denies that Malawi supports RENAMO and that it is impossible to prevent them from crossing Malawi's unprotected borders.

Feb. 1988   Phase I of the import liberalization plan comes into effect whereby exchange controls comprising 25% of the import bill are lifted.

2 Mar. 1988   The International Monetary Fund provides a new standby arrangement of 13,020,000 special drawing rights.

July 1988   The office of the United Nations High Commissioner for Refugees estimates that 570,000 Mozambicans had taken refuge in Malawi.

8 Aug. 1988   Phase II of the import liberalization plan, which extends to 30% of the imports is implemented.

13 Sept. 1988   President P.W. Botha visits Malawi, the sole African state to have diplomatic relations with South Africa. It is thereafter announced that Malawi's debt to South Africa would be rescheduled and the 3000 tonnes of maize will be given by the Republic to the Mozambican refugees in Malawi.

Jan. 1989   Four students are expelled from the University of Malawi for writing an article critical of government education policy.

19 Jan. 1989   Malawi becomes the 133rd member of the International Maritime Organization.

13 Feb. 1989   President Banda accuses northern civil servants of regionalism and a secessionist plot. Education Minister Mlambala is ordered to prevent teachers from working outside their home areas.

Mar. 1989   Malawi appeals for major international assistance following a cyclone, an earthquake on 11 March and floods on 13 March. Over 200,000 people are left homeless.

30 Mar. 1989   Margaret Thatcher of Great Britain visits President Banda.

31 Mar. 1989   Margaret Thatcher visits a Malawian refugee camp.

4 May 1989   Pope John Paul II visits Malawi and praises the country for having received 650,000 Mozambican refugees.

2 July 1989   President Mwinji of Tanzania pays a five-day state visit to Malawi, on the occasion of its twenty-fifth independence anniversary.

24 Sept. 1989   The Malawi Congress Party Convention opens in Lilongwe.

13 Oct. 1989   Opposition (Mafremo) leader, M. Mhongo, killed in fire bomb attack in Zambia.

20 Oct. 1989   The Ncala Railway which links Malawi to the Indian Ocean is re-opened for commercial traffic.

Dec. 1989	The United States cancels debts valued at US $40,400,000.
30 Jan. 1990	President Banda dissolves the Cabinet.
23 Feb. 1990	President Banda appoints a new cabinet.
3 May 1990	Further cabinet reshuffle takes place as Veteran Minister of Local Government Edward Bwanali is dropped, and also dismissed from the Malawi Congress Party. He has been mooted as a possible successor to President Banda. Mfunjo Mwakikunga becomes Minister of Community Services as Local Government also becomes the portfolio of Forestry and Natural Resources Minister, Stanford Demba.
27 Apr. 1990	President Banda dismisses the new Cabinet.
11 Jan. 1991	Violence breaks out in the Tete Corridor, Malawi's trade lifeline. This is followed by negotiations between the Government and RENAMO.
Feb. 1991	Forty-five people are killed by rebels and the Tete Corridor, Malawi's key transport route is closed.
Apr. 1991	Floods and mudslides affect the south-eastern region leaving 516 dead or missing and between 40-50,000 people homeless.
May 1991	Jack Mapanje, Malawi's foremost poet is released after four years in detention without trial.
June 1991	New trade agreement signed with South Africa, which supersedes the 1967 agreement.
7 Jan. 1992	President Banda appoints a new government. John Tembo becomes Minister of State in the President's Office.
6 Apr. 1992	Chakufwa Chihana, leader of the Southern African Trade Union Co-ordination Council is arrested on his arrival at Lilongwe Airport.
16 Apr. 1992	Dr. Banda dissolves the National Assembly.
17 Apr. 1992	Mgr John Roche, Roman Catholic bishop-elect of Mzimba is served with an expulsion order and given twenty four hours in which to leave the country.
21 Apr. 1992	The Zambian-based United Front for Multi-Party Democracy declares its intention of participating in the forthcoming elections.
5 May 1992	Strike action brings Lilongwe and Malawi to a halt. At least forty people are killed and several hundred injured.
12-14 May 1992	World Bank donors decide in Paris to suspend all non-humanitarian aid to Malawi for 1992-3 due to its human rights record.
26-27 June 1992	Single-party elections held and the government's claim of an 80% turnout is disputed by the exiled opposition alliance.
11 July 1992	Opposition trade union leader Chihana is released on bail, together with ten other political prisoners. The former however is re-arrested three days later.

| 22 Aug. 1992 | Norway rejects a request to support a telecommunications project due to Malawi's human rights abuses. |

22 Aug. 1992   Norway rejects a request to support a telecommunications project due to Malawi's human rights abuses.

29 Aug. 1992   Government bans a pro-democracy rally.

31 Aug. 1992   Father Tom Leahy, one of the clerics involved in the pro-democracy movement, is deported.

21 Sept. 1992   The Alliance for Democracy is formed. It is the first organized opposition for thirty years.

Oct. 1992   A group of former civil servants and former senior members of the Malawi Congress Party announce the formation in mid-October of a United Democratic Front.

2 Oct. 1992   Delegates to the Annual Convention of the Malawi Congress Party reject unanimously proposals for the introduction of a multiparty system.

12 Oct. 1992   President Banda announces that a referendum will be held to determine whether the population favours a multiparty system.

14 Oct. 1992   Two of the five sedition charges against Chakufwa Chihana are dropped in the High Court.

20 Oct. 1992   Orton Chirwa, one of the country's most prominent political prisoners, dies in prison.

Nov. 1992   Two people are beaten to death outside the Chihana trial court.

17 Nov. 1992   The Alliance for Democracy is banned.

1 Jan. 1993   The editor of a new dissident newspaper, New Express, is arrested and 20,000 copies of the paper are confiscated.

10 Jan. 1993   Malawi's first officially approved opposition rally takes place.

11 Jan. 1993   A Referendum Commission is formed to oversee the 15 March poll to ascertain feeling towards multipartyism.

18 Jan. 1993   The Malawi Congress Party's campaign rally is aborted. It attracted four party officials whilst an opposition rally attracted approximately 30,000 people.

20 Jan. 1993   Cabinet changes are as follows: Minister of Energy and Mines - Michael Mlambala; Minister of Education and Culture - Kate Kainja; Minister at Large - Sonet Kitonga.

24 Jan. 1993   Vera Chirwa is released from prison after twelve years.

Feb. 1993   President Banda postpones the forthcoming multi-party elections from 14 March to 14 June to allow international organizations to prepare for their participation. The voter registration is also extended, from two weeks to one month.

Mar. 1993	The Malawi Freedom Movement is dissolved and merges with the Alliance for Democracy.
8-15 Mar. 1993	Chakufwa Chihana appeals against his two-year prison service in order to campaign for the referendum. At the end of the hearing the judge states that due to the excess of new material, judgment would not be before the end of March.
24 Mar. 1993	Legal and opposition sources claim that the Minister of Justice, Friday Makuta, has resigned.
29 Mar. 1993	Sentence on Chakufwa Chihana is reduced from two years to nine months.
Apr. 1993	President Banda passes legislation granting immunity to the Malawi Congress Party, its officials and members as well as government ministers. This pertains to prosecution for violence and intimidation during the referendum campaign.
May 1993	Machipisa Munthali is awarded substantial compensation for false imprisonment after spending twenty seven years in prison.
May 1993	President Banda agrees to a single ballot box system. The government have previously insisted on dual ballot boxes.
14 June 1993	A referendum on multipartyism is held. Opposition leaders claim a substantial victory.
16 June 1993	There is widespread jubilation after the referendum but President Banda refuses to resign.
21 June 1993	A compromise agreement is reached after the government initially refused opposition demands for interim power-sharing.
29 June 1993	Parliament amends Section 4 of the Constitution thus paving the way for multipartyism. Political parties are legalized.
30 June 1993	The first group of political exiles return home.
21-23 July 1993	A United Nations sponsored forum meets to discuss the transition process.
30 July 1993	Dalton Katopola, Minister of Trade and Industry resigns on grounds of ill health.
17 Aug. 1993	Five political parties have registered with the Registrar General to date.
7 Sept. 1993	Public sector strikes involving 6000 civil servants ends with the acceptance of a 35% pay rise, backdated to 1 July.
11 Sept. 1993	President Banda reshuffles the Cabinet with the most significant appointment being that of Hetherwick Ntaba as Minister of External Affairs, a post which the President held since 1964. Other important changes are that of Nyemba Mbekeani to the Trade and Industry Ministry and Lovemore Munro to the portfolio of Justice.

17 Sept. 1993	Great Britain and the European Community resume their aid programmes to Malawi.
Oct. 1993	An interim Presidential Council replaces President Banda. It is drawn from the ranks of the Malawi Congress Party.
2 Oct. 1993	President Banda undergoes brain surgery at the Garden City Clinic, Johannesburg.
2 Nov. 1993	The Presidential Council makes the following appointments leaving Dr. Banda without ministerial responsibility for the first time since 1964: Home Affairs - Gwanda Chakuamba; Agriculture - Elia Phiri; Forestry - Mfunjo Mwakikunga; Information and Tourism - Johnson Mkandawire; Local Government - Alfred Kienda; Youth, Sports and Culture - Ndusu Junio.
5 Nov. 1993	Malawi signs the treaty establishing the Common Market for Eastern and Southern Africa.
9 Nov. 1993	Malawi and Angola establish diplomatic relations.
16 Nov. 1993	National Assembly approves legislation which formally establishes two bodies to oversee the transition to democracy - the National Consultative Council and the National Executive Council.
16 Nov. 1993	All provisions relating to detention without trial are repealed, as is the Decency in Dress Act.
17 Nov. 1993	The Constitutional Amendment Bill repeals the institution of life presidency, among others.
3 Dec. 1993	The army becomes involved by attempting to disarm the Malawi Youth Pioneers.
7 Dec. 1993	Dr. Banda resumes full presidential powers.
10 Dec. 1993	Major-General Wilfred Mponera is named as Minister of Defence with a specific brief to oversee the disarmament of the Malawi Youth Pioneers and army grievances.
7 Jan. 1994	Minister of Defence announces that the exercise to disarm the Malawi Young Pioneers is now complete.
18 Jan. 1994	Kanyama Chiume, leader of the Congress for the Second Republic returns after thirty years in exile.
4 Feb. 1994	The Reserve Bank of Malawi lifts exchange controls.
8 Feb. 1994	The Malawi Youth Pioneers are disbanded and the pertinent legislation is repealed.
13 Feb. 1994	Dr. Banda is elected as the candidate for the Malawi Congress Party in the presidential poll, with Gwanda Chakuamba as his running mate.
17 Apr. 1994	National Assembly is dissolved. The Electoral Commission finds evidence of violence, bribery and theft or seizure of voter registration certificates.

Findings are validated by the Joint International Observer Group.

16 May 1994	The new constitution is formally approved by the outgoing National Assembly.
17 May 1994	The country's first multiparty elections end thirty years of one-party rule. Bakili Muluzi and his United Democratic Front oust President Banda and the Malawi Congress Party.
19 May 1994	Dr. Banda concedes defeat.
21 May 1994	Muluzi is inaugurated as President. All political prisoners released and three prisons are closed and all death sentences are converted to life sentences.
25 May 1994	President Muluzi announces a new Cabinet.
1 June 1994	Possible alliance talks between the United Democratic Front and the Alliance for Democracy break down.
10 June 1994	President Muluzi announces the establishment of an independent commission of inquiry to investigate the deaths in 1983 of three Ministers and a Member of Parliament.
20 June 1994	The Alliance for Democracy and the Malawi Congress Party sign a memorandum of understanding.
25 Aug. 1994	Dr. Banda retires from active politics. The leadership of the Malawi Congress Party has effectively been transferred to Gwanda Chakuamba, the Secretary-General.
28 Sept. 1994	A new Cabinet is sworn in with Chakufura Chihana as second Vice-President and Minister if Irrigation.
8 Nov. 1994	Minister of Finance, Aleke Banda adds the Ministry of Economic Planning and Development to his responsibilities.
16 Nov. 1994	The International Monetary Fund approves a credit of fifteen million SDR.
4 Jan. 1995	The Commission of Inquiry, established to investigate the circumstances surrounding the death of four prominent politicians in 1983, publishes its proceedings.
Apr. 1995	The army commander, General Manken Chigaawa is shot dead by thieves.
Apr. 1995	Five soldiers are arrested for anti-government plotting.
May 1995	Dr. Banda is placed under house arrest. He is examined by three foreign doctors and declared too ill and frail to appear in court. The trial nevertheless goes ahead.
July 1995	A charge is laid against John Tembo and four members of the Malawi Congress Party of attempting to murder the country's Roman Catholic bishops in 1992.
Nov. 1995	Prison conditions have not changed since multiparty elections in 1994.

24 Nov. 1995	Malawi makes first of 30,000 public service retrenchments in line with an independent inquiry into civil service conditions.
Dec. 1995	Kamuzu Banda is acquitted by the High Court from blame in the 1983 deaths of four politicians that he and his aides were accused of ordering.
Dec. 1995	Chakufwa Chihana, leader of the Alliance for Democracy and coalition partner in the government accuses the UDF of lacking transparency, good governance and involvement in high-level corruption.
Jan. 1996	Former President Kamuzu Banda apologizes to Malawians for any hardship suffered during his time in office. He calls for reconciliation.
2 May 1996	President Muluzi reshuffles his cabinet after his coalition partner Chakufwa Chihana of the Alliance for Democracy (AFORD) resigns. No AFORD ministers are dropped from the cabinet. Instead, Health Minister Sam Mpasu is dismissed. He was involved in a corruption scandal when he was Minister of Education.
June 1996	A terrorist group known as the Movement for the Restoration of Democracy in Malawi, surfaces in Mozambique. It seems to be linked with Banda's Young Pioneers who were disarmed in 1993 by the army.
3 June 1996	The Alliance for Democracy announces that it has severed its alliance with the UDF after a resolution adopted at a special national conference of the party. AFORD government ministers shall resign. Five AFORD NEC members are removed and one is suspended. In reaction to AFORD's decision, the government assures the nation that its business will continue as usual. President Muluzi welcomes the collapse of the coalition. It leaves his party four seats short of a parliamentary majority, but he promises to cooperate with opposition parties.
16 June 1996	The Alliance for Democracy announces its shadow Cabinet.
25 June 1996	Five members of AFORD refuse to vacate their cabinet posts after the coalition government breaks up. Banda's Malawi Congress Party are demanding that the five deemed to have joined the ruling UDF. The Speaker rejects this and members of AFORD and the MCP walk out, threatening to take the matter to court.
July 1996	A miner reshuffle of cabinet and the additional appointment of Joseph Kubalo as Minister of State in the Office of the President and Cabinet is regarded by donors, who are pressurising President Muluzi to trim his cabinet, as unnecessary. He is reportedly a close friend of the President.
25 July 1996	The Ministry of Defence announces that members of the Malawi Parachute Battalion will hold a joint six-week training exercise with their United States' counterparts.
Sept. 1996	Conflict within the ruling UDF party is exposed when Rolf Patel, MP for Thyolo North, resigns from the UDF. Frustrated MPs, angered by the unilateral appointment of Luke Jumbe as UDF Regional Governor for the South, threaten to design.
2 Sept. 1996	Two associates of former President Banda are arrested on charges of

attempted murder and conspiracy - top aide John Tembo and long-time companion Cecilia Kadzamira. The charges are for plotting to kill three cabinet ministers in 1995.

9 Dec. 1996   The ruling UDF fails to obtain a quorum in Parliament in the absence of the opposition parties AFORD and MCP, who have been boycotting parliament since July in protest at President Muluzi's appointment of five opposition members into his Cabinet without consulting their own parties. These ministers announced that they are standing as independents, and have not crossed the floor.

5 Mar. 1997   President Bakili Muluzi accuses opposition parties of 'blackmail' over an eight month boycott of Parliament. The boycott results from the fact that six members of the opposition, Alliance for Democracy (Aford) remain in the Cabinet despite a split in the coalition. Aford wants the six to lose their parliamentary seats to fight by-elections. The boycott is also supported by the Malawi Congress Party.

9 Mar 1997   Seventeen criminal suspects suffocate in an overcrowded police cell. Subsequently, six policemen are suspended.

Apr. 1997   A public service strike is continuing despite arrests of trade union leaders.

3 Apr. 1997   Opposition Party, the Malawi Congress Party, announces that it will end the ten-month boycott of parliament after an agreement with President Muluzi has been brokered by the Catholic Church. The President promised that there will be stability in parliament.

May 1997   Local elections are set for August 1997, after postponements from November 1995 to June 1996, to October 1996. The former local authorities under Banda were dissolved in 1995. Fear of loss of control over local authorities and their resources, as well as substantial wins by the opposition are reasons why decentralization is so slow.

16 May 1997   Minor cabinet changes are announced.

MAURITIUS

12 Mar 1968   Mauritius becomes independent after 158 years of British rule, with Seewoosagur Ramgoolam as Prime Minister.

12 Mar. 1968   A Defence Agreement between Britain and Mauritius is signed.

12 Mar. 1968   Signs treaty with Great Britain on facilities for a detection station.

12 Mar. 1968   Signs Public Officers Agreement with Great Britain.

12 Mar. 1968   Signs mutual assistance treaty with Great Britain.

12 Mar. 1968   Signs treaty with Great Britain on assistance or advice in staffing, administration and training of the police forces of Mauritius.

12 Mar. 1968   Acceptance of obligations of the UN Charter.

12 Mar. 1968	Signs Convention on the Exploration and Use of Outer Space, including the Moon and Other Celestial Bodies.
12 Mar. 1968	Mauritius enters into diplomatic relations with the Soviet Union and the People's Republic of China.
18 Apr. 1968	A.L. Williams, general secretary of the Labour party is appointed Governor-General of Mauritius in succession to Sir John Dennie.
23 Aug. 1968	The Algerian Foreign Ministry announces that Mauritius is admitted to the Organization of African Unity.
3 Sept. 1968	Signs treaty with the United States on facilities for the US Air Force aircraft at Plaisance Airfield, necessary to the Apollo Project.
4 Sept. 1968	Recognizes the compulsory jurisdiction of the International Court of Justice.
4 Sept. 1968	Application of the 1948 Berne Convention for the Protection of Literary and Artistic Works.
15 Sept. 1968	Signs African Convention on the Conservation of Nature and Natural Resources.
16 Sept. 1968	Signs treaty with Great Britain on minimum sterling proportion.
23 Sept. 1968	Acceptance of the IBRD's Articles of Agreement.
23 Sept. 1968	Accepts the International Development Association's Articles of Agreement.
23 Sept. 1968	Accepts the International Finance Corporation's Articles of Agreement.
25 Oct.1968	Accedes to the UNESCO Constitution.
9 Dec. 1968	Accession to the WHO Constitution.
20 Dec. 1968	Succession to the Convention Abolishing the Requirements of Legalization for Foreign Public Documents: designations of [competent] authorities.
23 Dec. 1968	Accession to the International Sugar Agreement of 1968.
17 Jan. 1969	Signs Constitution of the African Civil Aviation Commission.
8 Apr. 1969	Accepts amendment to Articles 24 and 25 of the WHO Constitution.
8 Apr. 1969	Ratifies the Convention on the Non-Proliferation of Nuclear Weapons.
16 Apr. 1969	Accedes to Convention on Astronauts and Objects Launched into Outer Space.
30 Apr. 1969	Succession to the 1963 Convention on Nuclear Weapon Tests in the Atmosphere, in Outer Space and Under Water.
15 May 1969	Signs treaty on visas with Israel.
2 June 1969	Ratifies 1965 agreement on the settlement of investment disputes between

states and nationals of other states.

18 July 1969	Succession to both the International Agreement and International Convention on the Suppression of White Slave Traffic.
18 July 1969	Succession to the 1949 agreement on the suppression of obscene publications and the 1947 Convention.
18 July 1969	Succession to the Single Convention on Narcotic Drugs.
18 July 1969	Succession to the 1953 Slavery Convention.
18 July 1969	Signs multilateral agreement on the right to a flag of states having no sea coast.
18 July 1969	Succedes to the Protocol bringing under international control drugs outside the scope of the Convention of 13 July 1931 for Limiting the Manufacture and Regulating the Distribution of Narcotic Drugs.
18 July 1969	Succedes to the 1947 privileges and immunities with respect to FAO, (Annex II, 2nd revision); IMCO (Annex XII, revised); ICAO, ILO, ITU, UNESCO, UPU, WHO, WMO and the UN.
18 July 1969	Succession to 1929 Agreement on the Suppression of Counterfeiting Currency.
18 July 1969	Succession to the 1953 Convention on the Political Rights of Women.
18 July 1969	Succession to the 1957 agreement on the nationality of married women.
18 July 1969	Succession to the 1946 agreement uniting the manufacture and regulating the distribution of narcotic drugs.
18 July 1969	Succession to the 1930 agreement on military obligations in cases of double nationality.
18 July 1969	Succession to the 1923 agreement on the international regime of maritime ports.
18 July 1969	Succession to the 1912 International Opium Convention and its 1946 amendment by Protocol.
18 July 1969	Succession to the 1952 agreement on the importation of commercial samples and advertising material and the 1950 agreement on the importation of educational, scientific and cultural materials.
18 July 1969	Succession to the 1921 agreement on the freedom of transit.
18 July 1969	Succession to the 1927 agreement on the execution of foreign arbitral awards.
18 July 1969	Succession to 1954 agreement on customs facilities for Touring and Protocol 4.

18 July 1969	Succedes to various aspects of the Customs Convention: containers; temporary importation of aircraft and pleasure boats and private road vehicles.
18 July 1969	Succedes to the multilateral agreement on the conflict of nationality laws.
18 July 1969	Signs agreement on the compulsory settlement of disputes.
18 July 1969	Succession to multipartite agreement on the case of statelessness.
18 July 1969	Succession to 1936 multilateral agreement on broadcasting in the cause of peace.
18 July 1969	Succession to arbitration clauses.
18 July 1969	Succession to the Convention on the Abolition of Slavery, the Slave Trade and Institutions and Practices Similar to Slavery.
18 July 1969	Succession to the 1921 agreement on traffic in women and children.
18 July 1969	Succession to the Vienna Convention on Diplomatic Relations.
23 July 1969	Mauritius hosts a ten-day conference to regulate tea exports.
28-31 July 1969	During a visit to Paris the Prime Minister discusses the proposed cooperation with Madagascar, Comoro Islands and Reunion in the field of tourism and emigration of Mauritians to France and New Caledonia.
15 Aug. 1969	Obtains assistance from the World Food Programme through multilateral treaty signed with United Nations and FAO on behalf of the WFP.
20 Aug. 1969	Accedes to the Constitution and General Regulations of the Universal Postal Union.
29 Aug. 1969	Accession to the 1964 agreement on insured letters and boxes; and to postal parcels agreement.
29 Aug. 1969	Accedes, with reservations, to the 1964 Universal Postal Convention.
29 Aug. 1969	Application of the Agreement of 7 January 1960 between Great Britain and the UN Special Fund concerning assistance from the Special Fund.
29 Aug. 1969	Application of 1960 agreement between the United Nations and Great Britain for the provision of technical assistance and the application of 1963 agreement for the provision of operational, executive and administrative personnel to the Trust, Non-Self Governing and other Territories for whose international relations, Great Britain is responsible.
10 Sept. 1969	Signs specific aspects of the OAU Convention on Refugee Problems in Africa.
4 Nov. 1969	Signs agreement with the United States concerning the distance measuring equipment at Plaisance Airfield, Mauritius.
1 Dec. 1969	A Government of National Unity is formed in order to overcome the latent

antagonism between the predominantly Hindu community and the Muslim, Chinese, Creole and European minorities. The life of the Legislative Assembly is extended until 18 November 1976.

2 Dec. 1969   Ratifies, with declarations, the following ILO Conventions: right of association and combination of agricultural workers (no. 11); minimum wage-fixing machinery in agriculture (no. 99); workmen's compensation in agriculture (no. 12); compulsory medical examination of children and young persons employed at sea (no. 16); minimum age for admission of children employed at sea (nos. 7 and 58); abolition of forced labour (no. 105); forced or compulsory labour (no. 29); For indigenous workers, the following apply: maximum length of contracts of employment (no. 86); regulation of written contracts of employment (no. 64); minimum age for admission of children in industrial employment (nos. 5 and 59); weekly rest in industrial undertakings (no. 14); labour inspection in industry and commerce (no. 81); migration for employment (no. 97); minimum wage-fixing machinery; labour clauses in public contracts (no. 94); right to bargain collectively (no. 98); national identity documents for seafarers (no. 108); certification of able seamen (no. 74); unemployment indemnity as a result of ship loss or floundering (no. 8); protection against accidents in the loading and unloading of ships (no. 32); regulations of special systems of recruiting workers (no. 50); statistics of wages and hours of work in the principal mining and manufacturing industries (no. 63); minimum age of young persons as trimmers or stokers (no. 15); unemployment (no. 2); protection of wages (no. 95); accidents necessitating workmen's compensation (no. 19); workmen's compensation (no. 17); workmen's compensation for occupational diseases (no. 42); equality of treatment for national and foreign workers concerning workmen's compensation (no. 19).

30 Jan. 1970   Adheres to the Convention on International Civil Aviation.

11 Feb. 1970   The first official contact of independent Mauritius with South Africa is made by a trade delegation to discuss ways of strengthening the links between the two countries.

18 Feb. 1970   Signs visa agreement with Belgium, Luxembourg and the Netherlands.

1 Mar. 1970   Adheres to the authentic trilingual text of the Convention on International Civil Aviation.

20 Mar. 1970   Signs multilateral agreement pertaining to the Agency for Cultural and Technical Co-operation.

7 Apr. 1970   Signs treaty with WHO on technical advisory assistance.

11 May 1970   Investment guarantees treaty with the United States.

13 May 1970   Accedes to the Vienna Convention on Consular Relations, and Option of Protocol Regarding the Compulsory Settlement of Disputes.

22 June 1970   A cultural and technical co-operation agreement is signed with France.

14 July 1970   The government grants harbour facilities to Soviet trawlers.

17 Aug. 1970	Succession to various aspects of GATT: Procés-verbal of rectification concerning the Protocol amending Part I and Article XXIX and XXX, the Protocol amending the Preamble and Parts II and III and the Protocol of Organizational Amendment; Protocol amending the Preamble and Parts II and III; Protocol modifying Article XXVI; Protocol modifying certain provisions; Protocol modifying Part I and Article XXIX; Protocol modifying Part II and Article XXVI; Protocol of amendment to introduce a Part IV on trade and development; Protocol of provisional application; Protocol of rectification to the French text; Protocol of rectifications, 3rd, 4th and 5th; Protocol of rectifications and modification to the annexes and to the texts of the schedules (4th); Special Protocol modifying Article XIV; Special Protocol relating to Article XXIV.
18 Aug. 1970	Suceeds to the Geneva Conventions of 1949: civilian persons in times of war; prisoners of war; wounded and sick in armed forces in the field; wounded, sick and ship-wrecked members of armed forces at sea.
20 Aug. 1970	Succession to the Universal Copyright Conventions and Protocols 1, 2, 3.
20 Aug. 1970	Succession to 1960 Convention on Discrimination in Education.
24 Aug. 1970	Succession to the multipartite agreement on refugee seamen.
1 Sept. 1970	Signs multilateral treaty relating to an amendment to the Convention on International Civil Aviation.
24 Sept. 1970	Accedes to the Wheat Trade Convention of the International Grains Arrangement.
5 Oct.1970	Succession to the Convention on the High Seas.
5 Oct.1970	Succession to the Convention on the Continental Shelf.
5 Oct.1970	Succession to the multilateral agreement on the living resources of the high seas; fishing and conservation.
5 Oct.1970	Succession to the Convention on Territorial Sea and Contiguous Zone.
2 Nov. 1970	The Foreign Minister of Mauritius explains to Lord Lothian, Minister of State and Commonwealth Office, that his conclusion of a technical agreement with the Soviet Union does not mean a change in his country's foreign policy.
21 Dec. 1970	Signs treaty with Great Britain on officers designated by Great Britain in the service of the government of Mauritius.
1971	General strike results in a State of Emergency and the postponement of elections schedules for 1972.
1 Jan. 1971	Entry into force of the International Health Regulations adopted by the 22nd World Health Assembly.
8 Jan. 1971	Succession to the Convention on the Prohibition of the Use in War of Asphyxiating, Poisonous or Other Gases and Bacteriological Methods of Warfare.

11 Feb. 1971	Signs the Convention on the Prohibition of the Emplacement on the Sea-Bed and the Ocean Floor and in the Subsoil thereof of Nuclear Weapons and other Weapons of Mass Destruction. This was ratified in Washington, London and Moscow on 23 April 1971, 3 May 1971 and 18 May 1971 respectively.
18 Mar. 1971	Signs treaty with the United States over the Peace Corps.
9 Apr. 1971	Signs credit agreement with the International Development Association on the Mauritius Tea Development Authority Project.
19 Apr. 1971	Treaty is signed with UNICEF on its activities in Mauritius.
9 June 1971	Ratifies amendment to the Convention on International Civil Aviation.
11 June 1971	Adheres to the International Plant Protection Convention.
16 June 1971	Accedes to the 1971 Wheat Trade Convention.
24 July 1971	Signs the Universal Copyright Convention and Protocol 2 which is applicable to works of certain international organizations.
5 Aug. 1971	Signs multilateral treaty with the Agency for Cultural and Technical Co-operation.
13 Sept. 1971	Acceptance of 1944 International Air Services Transit Agreement.
15 Nov. 1971	Ratifies Protocol relating to the amendment of Article 56 of the Convention on International Civil Aviation.
23 Dec. 1971	The government issues a Public Order Bill which provides inter alia for people's restriction of movement, preventive detention, and a ban on public meetings during sessions of parliament.
28 Jan. 1972	Signs air services agreement with India.
10 Apr. 1972	Signs Convention on Bacteriological (Biological) and Toxic weapons. This was ratified in London, Moscow and Washington on 11 January 1973, 15 January 1973 and 7 August 1972 respectively.
8 May 1972	Accepts the provisional accession of Tunisia to GATT, eighth extension.
30 May 1972	Accedes to the Convention on the Elimination of Racial Discrimination.
23 June 1972	Signs development credit agreement with the International Development Association on the DBM Project.
10 Nov. 1972	Amends the first annex 1972 to the treaty signed with Great Britain on officers designated by Great Britain in the service of specified organizations or institutions in Mauritius.
12 Nov. 1972	Accepts instrument for amendment to the ILO Constitution.
20 Dec. 1972	Signs IAEA agreement on the application of safeguards in connection with the Treaty on the Non-Proliferation of Nuclear Weapons.

3 Mar. 1973	Signs Convention on International Trade of Endangered Species of Wild Fauna and Flora. This was ratified on 28 April 1975.
8 May 1973	Accedes to the multilateral agreement on psychotropic substances.
22 May 1973	Signs treaty with France on the protection of investments.
25 May 1973	Accepts accession of the People's Republic of Bangladesh to GATT.
29 June 1973	Ratifies amendment to Article 61 of the UN Charter.
29 June 1973	Signs treaty with the International Development Association on the Coromande/Industrial Estate Project.
9 July 1973	Signs credit agreement with the International Development Association on the Rural Development Project.
12 July 1973	Signs air services agreement with Great Britain.
26 July 1973	Approves the World Tourism Organisation (WTO) Statutes.
10 Sept. 1973	Accedes to various aspects of the Universal Postal Union agreement: Additional Protocol to the Constitution, insured letters and boxes; postal parcels; Universal Postal Convention.
17 Sept. 1973	Designation of authorities under Article 6 of the multipartite agreement on the abolition of legalization of foreign public documents.
23 Oct.1973	Signs guarantee agreement with the IBRD on third DBM Project.
15 Nov. 1973	Signs air services treaty with the Netherlands.
24 Nov. 1973	The Soviet Airline Aeroflot and Air Mauritius establish an airlink between Moscow and Mauritius.
Dec. 1973	Coalition MLP and PMSD is dissolved following disagreement over foreign policy and increase in taxation.
12 Dec. 1973	Accedes to the Convention on Civil and Political Rights and its Optional Protocol.
12 Dec. 1973	Accedes to the Convention on Economic, Social and Cultural Rights.
17 Dec. 1973	It is announced that on the advice of the Prime Minister, three ministers are dismissed. They were members of the Parti Mauricien social-démocrate and as such represent French-speaking Creoles.
19 Dec. 1973	Acceptance of the International Sugar Agreement.
1 Jan. 1974	Entry into force of amendments to the International Health Regulations, especially to Articles 1, 21, 63-7 and 92.
1 Jan. 1974	Accedes to the treaty establishing the African Development Bank.
30 Jan. 1974	Further amends the treaty signed with Great Britain concerning officers

designated by Great Britain in the service of specified organizations or institutions on Mauritius.

2 Feb. 1974	The Minister of Foreign Affairs announces the reorganization of the Cabinet.
12 Apr. 1974	Signs loan agreement with IBRD for the Port Project.
12 Apr. 1974	Signs credit agreement with the International Development Association over the Education Project.
24 Apr. 1974	Signs guarantee agreement with the IBRD on the second DBM Project.
5 July 1974	Signs various aspects of the Universal Postal Union viz: second additional Protocol to the Constitution; General Regulations; Insured Letters; Postal Parcels; Universal Postal Convention.
29 July 1974	Signs loan agreement with the IBRD for the Education Project.
29 Aug. 1974	Signs treaty with the UNDP for assistance.
29 Aug. 1974	Termination of the applicability (28 May 1968 and 29 August 1969) over the Agreement of 27 June 1963 between the United Nations and Great Britain on the provision to the Trust, Non-Self Governing and other territories whose international relations Great Britain is responsible: operational, executive and administrative personnel; technical assistance; assistance from the Special Fund.
7 Apr. 1975	Accepts agreement on privileges and immunities of the IAEA.
3 July 1975	Signs agreement with Great Britain on public officers' pensions.
27 July 1975	Signs treaty on international trade in endangered species of wild fauna and flora.
23 Oct.1975	Signs guarantee agreement with the International Bank for Reconstruction and Development for the third DBM project.
5 Dec. 1975	Definitive acceptance of Resolution no. 1 extending the International Sugar Agreement of 1975.
1 Jan. 1976	Signs Multilateral agreement to the constitution of the Universal Postal Union.
26 Jan. 1976	Accepts amendments to Articles 34 and 55 of the WHO Constitution.
31 Mar. 1976	Terminates mutual defence and assistance treaty with Great Britain.
1 July 1976	Suspends treaty of 18 February 1970 on the abolition of visas with Belgium, Luxembourg and the Netherlands.
7 Sept. 1976	Definitive signature of the 1973 International Sugar Agreement.
Dec. 1976	General elections result in the MMM becoming the single largest in the Legislative Assembly, but Ramgoolam forms a new coalition with the

Independence Party.

8 Dec. 1976	Signs amendment to treaties with Great Britain on both the officers designated by Great Britain in the service of specified organizations or institutions in Mauritius, and those designated in the service of the Mauritian government.
9 Dec. 1976	Signs loan agreement with the International Bank for Reconstruction and Development concerning the Port Project.
1 June 1977	Acceptance of the establishment of the African Training and Research Centre in Administration for Development.
29 Aug. 1977	Signs guarantee agreement with the IBRD concerning the fourth Development Bank of Mauritius Project.
25 Nov. 1977	Signs multilateral agreement establishing the International Tea Promotion Association.
20 Dec. 1977	Acceptance of International Sugar Agreement of 1977, which Mauritius signed on 1 December 1977.
23 Dec. 1977	Signs multilateral treaty on protocol additional to Geneva Convention Relating to Victims of Armed Conflict.
27 Feb. 1978	Accepts multilateral agreement on the prohibition and prevention of illicit import, export and transfer of ownership of cultural property.
26 Apr. 1978	Signs loan agreement with the IBRD for the second education project.
26 Apr. 1978	Signs guarantee agreement with the IBRD relating to the power transmission project.
18 May 1978	Acceptance of Inter-Governmental Maritime Consultative Organization and acceptance of amendment to Article 10.
27 May 1978	Acceptance of multilateral convention on the means of prohibiting and preventing illicit import, export and transfer of ownership of cultural property.
30 May 1979	Signs treaty with Spain establishing diplomatic relations.
14 Nov. 1979	Signs agreement with Switzerland relating to regular air transport.
18 Dec. 1979	Accession by Mauritius to the Convention against All Forms of Discrimination against Women.
17 Jan. 1980	A minor reshuffle of the cabinet takes place. Among the four new ministers a former opposition parliamentarian is sworn in.
19 Mar. 1980	At the fourth conference of the Union of African Parliaments in Kinshasa (Zaire) an executive committee is formed by eleven countries. Mauritius is one of the members.
May 1980	Mauritius is represented at the summit conference of African Unity held at

Nice (France).

24 May 1980   Mauritius is one of the African countries which accepts the invitation to
                   join the Moscow Olympic Games.

4 June 1980   The French cabinet approves an agreement for military cooperation
                   between France and Mauritius. French military personnel will train
                   Mauritians for a unit similar to the French Gendarmerie.

26 June 1980   Forty-eight members of the seventy-member Mauritius Parliament call for
                   the return of the Indian Ocean island Diego Garcia, which was ceded to
                   Britain in 1965.

1-4 July 1980   At the seventeenth annual summit conference of the OAU held in
                   Freetown (Sierra Leone), Mauritius reiterates its demand for the return to
                   Mauritius of the Indian Ocean Island of Diego Garcia, at present a
                   British-owned American naval base.

17 July 1980   The dispute over the return of Diego Garcia to Mauritius continues. The
                   Mauritian Prime Minister's argument is that Britain misled Mauritius
                   when it did not inform it that the island would be leased to the US for
                   military purposes.

20 Aug. 1980   The Chinese Vice-Premier, Mr. Ji, arrives on a 10-nation tour of Africa
                   and the Middle East. Mr. Ji, who is also head of the Communist Party
                   International Relations Department, will also visit Mauritius.

Sept. 1980   The proposed Pan-African News Agency (PANA) will supply
                   telecommunication equipment and teletype operators to Mauritius, one of
                   the eleven member countries.

28 Feb. 1981   The Peoples Progressive Party of Mauritius is given the under-secretariat
                   responsibility at the founding of the Inter-African Socialist Organization
                   (IAS) in Tunis.

Apr. 1981   A left-wing alliance is formed between the PSM (Parti Socialiste
                   Mauricien) and the official opposition movement, Mouvement Militant
                   Mauricien (MMM).

May 1981   The election of François Mitterand as President of France is regarded by
                   Mauritius as by other African nations, a socialist victory which will be
                   one more step towards detente and for the struggle against colonialism.

May 1981   Father Trevor Huddleston, Archbishop of the Indian Ocean and President
                   of the Anti-Apartheid Movement, is based on the island of Mauritius.

2 July 1981   The negotiations between the UK and Mauritius, regarding the payment of
                   cost of resettling the evicted Diego Garcia population back to Mauritius,
                   end in a stalemate.

Feb. 1982   The Mauritian government restricts the activities of the Libyan
                   government representatives, such as financial aid to private organizations
                   and individuals, or to help political parties. The government will also not
                   allow publication of pro-Libyan propaganda and establish influence on the
                   country's Muslim community.

Feb. 1982	The Mauritian Minister of Agriculture expresses his pessimistic opinion about the EEC joining the International Sugar Agreement (ISA).
Mar. 1982	The governments of Britain and Mauritius agree on the terms of compensation for the 900 families dislodged from the island of Diego Garcia, to make way for Anglo-US military base.
31 Mar. 1982	Mauritius joins seven African states and boycotts the opening session of the Labour Commission of the OAU in Salisbury, Zimbabwe. The boycott is due to the admission of the Saharan Arab Democratic Republic into the Organisation.
11 June 1982	The general election resulted in a leftist alliance victory between the MMM and the PSM. A. Jugnauth becomes Prime Minister and Paul Berenger, Minister of Finance. Its political programme consists among others of the establishment of a 'Mauritian-style' socialism; an 'Indian type' republic; a member of the Commonwealth; a president without executive powers; the return of the Diego Garcia archipelago; the reduction of commercial links with South Africa.
15 June 1982	A new Mauritian cabinet is sworn in following general elections.
29 June 1982	The Supreme Court decides that following the total left-wing victory of the recent elections four extra seats will be allocated to the opposition.
17 July 1982	An Indian Ocean Commission is set up grouping, initially, Mauritius, the Seychelles and Madagascar.
21 July 1982	Mauritius says that it may appeal to the World Court on a claim to the sovereignty of the Diego Garcia.
5 Aug. 1982	The head of the Mauritian government is one of the representatives in Tripoli for the nineteenth Annual Conference of the OAU. For the first time since the organisation was founded, the annual meeting could not take place because of the lack of the required quorum.
25 Aug. 1982	The Indian Prime Minister, Indira Ghandi, arrives for a three-day visit. The topics discussed are the UN declaration making the Indian Ocean a zone of peace, the disapproval of turning Diego Garcia into a US military base and agreement on industry, oil refining, scientific research and expansion of marine resources and shipping.
Oct.1982	Mauritius receives from the British High Commission a cheque for 4 million Pounds Sterling in settlement of compensation for the displaced islanders from the Chagos Archipelago, including Diego Garcia.
8-9 Oct 1982	At the ninth Franco-African summit held in Kinshasa, Mauritius is represented at ministerial level.
22 Oct.1982	The left-wing alliance which swept to victory in the June general elections faces a government crisis. The Prime Minister announces the formation of a new government from which the Mauritian Socialist Party will be excluded.
25 Nov. 1982	The Foreign Minister leads a delegation to the second attempt of the OAU's

Summit Conference to be held in Tripoli. However the conference failed to materialize.

1 Dec. 1982   The first number of a daily 'Le Socialist' appears. It is the mouthpiece of the Mauritian Socialist Party.

12 Dec. 1982   The Mauritian Militant Movement (MMM) which shares power with its ally the Mauritian Socialist Party (PSM) takes 116 seats of the 126 municipal seats at the elections which take place in five towns.

Jan. 1983   Mauritius, Madagascar and Seychelles agree to constitute an Indian Ocean Commission (IOC). The presidency will rotate annually between foreign ministers in alphabetical order of member states and a permanent liaison office to be set up in each country. The possibility exists that Comoros, Reunion, India and Australia will add to the eventual expansion.

Feb. 1983   Archbishop Trevor Huddleston, Bishop of Mauritius and Primate of the Indian Ocean will relinquish his post in April.

12 Mar. 1983   Mauritius is represented by its Prime Minister at the seventh summit conference of the ninety-seven non-aligned nations in New Delhi.

23 Mar. 1983   MMM/PSM alliance collapses, splits and eleven ministers resign from the cabinet. A new government is formed which includes ten MMM and five PSM members.

Apr. 1983   Jugnauth forms a new political party, the Mouvement Socialiste Militant (MSM) party.

1 May 1983   PSM led by the deputy Prime Minister, announces the dissolution of the party and its incorporation into the Mauritian Socialiste Mouvement (MSM). The creation of a new government majority is thus reached by the fusion of PSM and the MSM, in a party called the Mouvement Socialiste Mauricien (MSM).

8-12 June   Mauritius is represented by its Foreign Minister at the nineteenth OAU Summit Conference in Addis Ababa.

12 June 1983   The Prime Minister announces the dissolution of the National Assembly before 21 June in preparation for the elections on 21 August. The electoral crisis is provoked by the dissolution of the MMM-PSM coalition.

22 Aug. 1983   The three-party alliance wins forty-one out of the sixty- two elective seats in the general elections. Jugnauth forms a new Council of Ministers with Duval as his deputy. According to foreign diplomats the results show that the registered electors voted on ethnic lines. The status of Mauritius will be changed to that of a republic within the Commonwealth.

27 Aug. 1983   The Prime Minister announces the formation of the new government, which is considered an oddly assorted coalition by the Western powers.

6 Sept. 1983   The Governor General says debt and unemployment are the two main problems. It is intended to nationalize sugar factories, to reduce the retirement age and introduce a forty hour week in the sugar industry, encourage health, trade unionism and to preserve the freedom of the media.

6 Sept. 1983   The new government is continuing in its diplomatic and political efforts to regain the Chagos Archipelago and the island of Tromelin. The government is in favour of strict neutrality and non-alignment and works towards making the Indian Ocean a peace zone.

30 Sept. 1983   It is reported that the Mauritian cabinet adopts a draft law declaring the island a republic. If the move is accepted by 75% of the parliament, Mauritius, as a republic, will remain in the Commonwealth.

3 Oct.1983   The Prime Minister represents Mauritius at the tenth annual summit of the African Unity and Political Alignment, held in France.

Dec. 1983   A bill to make Mauritius a republic fails to obtain the necessary three-quarters majority. The bill receives 47 voters, six short of the required majority.

20 Dec. 1983   Signs loan agreement with the IBRD for technical assistance.

14 Jan. 1984   The government closes down the Libyan embassy and all the five diplomats are told to leave the country immediately. These were ordered because of Libyan interference in the internal affairs of the country.

Feb. 1984   A partial reshuffle of the cabinet takes place. Sir S. Boolell is dismissed. A faction within the ruling party forms the Rassemblement des Traviallaistes Mauricenes (RTM)

4 Apr. 1984   More than forty journalists are charged with unlawful assembly and obstruction after a demonstration against a proposed press bill. This bill would prohibit `unbecoming' press reports of parliamentary affairs.

7 May 1984   Signs agreement with France on co-operation in the fields of education, arts and culture.

June 1984   The government and the press form a committee to study their relationship. A former high court judge will preside over the committee.

16 June 1984   The head of the Mauritian opposition is suspended from parliament due to an incident which took place during the budget debate when the opposition protests about the fact that they were not given the right of reply on television.

July 1984   The Mauritian Director of Public Prosecution drops the proceedings against the forty-four journalists who demonstrated against a controversial press law.

Aug. 1984   Mauritius and Gabon agree in principle to establish diplomatic relations. Agreements covering cultural, scientific and technical co-operation are signed.

Oct.1984   A MMM congress emphasizes four fundamental points: the quest for national unity and cultural diversity; the consolidation of democracy; a policy of non-alignment and a solution to the economic crisis.

10 Nov. 1984   The sixth Legislative Assembly reaffirms the government programme to press for the return of the Chagos Archipelago, which includes Diego Garcia and the Tromelin Island; to continue its commitment to the UN Charter and

to give its support to the UN's efforts to liberate countries under colonial yoke and racial domination.

11-12 Dec. 1984	Mauritius is represented at ministerial level at the 11th annual Francophone Summit in Bujumbura, Burundi.
Dec. 1985	Four members of the Legislative Assembly are arrested in the Netherlands, accused of drug dealing. Four ministers resign through failure of Jugnauth to name other deputies implicated.
Dec. 1985	Ramgoolam dies.
Jan. 1986	Extensive reshuffle of the Council of Ministers occurs.
Jan. 1986	Sir V. Ringadoo, former Minister of Finance, appointed as Governor-General.
Mid 1986	Inquiry of drug trafficking incident.
July 1986	Eleven dissidents are expelled from the MSM.
July 1986	Three ministers resign citing lack of confidence in the leadership and the party.
Aug. 1986	A further reshuffle of the Council of Ministers; and Boolell becomes Deputy Prime Minister.
Nov. 1986	Three members of the Legislative Assembly resign after their implication in a drug scandal, thus reducing the ruling coalition to thirty seats.
Jan. 1987	Jugnauth announces that elections will take place within the year.
Mar. 1987	Six further coalition deputies involved in drug trafficking, are named by the Commission of Inquiry.
Mar. 1987	New allegations implicate Duval in the drug trafficking. He offers to resign. Jugnauth rejects this offer.
July 1987	Jugnauth dissolves the Legislature.
30 Aug. 1987	Prime Minister Jugnauth, Head of the Mauritian Socialist Movement, is returned to office as the result of the general election in August. An alliance between the MSM, PMSD and MLP is formed.
Sept. 1987	A new Council of Ministers takes office.
July 1988	Harish Boodhoo, leader of the demised PSM, announces the revival of the party.
15 Aug. 1988	Sir Gastan Duval, the Deputy Prime Minister and leader of the PMSD, resigns over differences with the Prime Minister. The PMSD withdraws from the coalition. Wins thirty-nine of the sixty-two elective seats.
23 Oct. 1988	Municipal elections are held for 126 seats. The MLP does not participate and calls for a boycott.

6 Nov. 1988	A Hindu priest attempts to assassinate Prime Minister Jugnauth.
3 Mar. 1989	A second attempt to assassinate the Prime Minister takes place.
11 June 1989	At a by-election for a legislative seat, the MSM-MLPP candidate wins, thereby giving the governing coalition a 47-23 seat edge in the Assembly.
23 June 1989	Sir Gastan Duval, leader of the opposition PMSD is arrested in connection with the assassination of a political activist in 1971. He is released later pending trial.
July 1990	Prime Minister Jugnauth agrees to form an alliance with the MMM, in order to secure an election in 1992 for MMM leader Paul Berenger as President. The MLP refuses to accept the proposal.
21 Aug. 1990	The Prime Minister fails to get the necessary 75% of the Legislative Assembly to amend the constitution which would allow a republican form of government within the Commonwealth.
End Aug. 1990	Jugnauth dismisses Boolell from the government together with two MSM ministers.
24 Sept. 1990	Prime Minister Jugnauth forms a new cabinet replacing six MLP ministers with six MMM ministers.
12 Mar. 1991	Prime Minister Jugnauth announces that Mauritius will become a Republic on 12 March.
Aug. 1991	Jugnauth dissolves the Legislative Assembly.
15 Sept. 1991	A general election is held. The Legislative Assembly, the MSM and the MMM combine to win fifty-seven of the sixty-two seats.
24 Sept. 1991	At the first meeting of the Legislative Assembly seven opposition members refuse to take their seats claiming electoral fraud.
Oct. 1991	Jugnauth announces that Mauritius will become a Republic on 12 March 1992.
10 Dec. 1991	The Legislative Assembly passes the Act amending the constitution thereby providing a republican form of government.
Jan. 1992	The Mauritian Foreign Minister delivers an ultimatum to the British government, calling for it to recognise Mauritian sovereignty over the Chagos Archipelago. If the UK refuses to comply with the demand, Mauritius will refer the matter to the UN or the International Court of Justice.
12 Mar. 1992	Mauritius becomes a Republic within the Commonwealth, with Ringadoo as Interim President.
Apr. 1992	Opposition demands Jugnauth's resignation following the controversy provoked by his wife's picture on a bank note.
June 1992	Ringadoo resigns as President due to ill health.

30 June 1992	Cassam Uteem, the Minister for Industry and Technology, becomes President of the Republic. Sir R. Ghurburrun is nominated as Vice-President.
Oct.1992	Ramgoolam announces his return to the UK to complete his legal studies. However, he is to retain MLP leadership and attend a requisite number of legislature sessions.
Dec. 1992	Jugnauth curtails a session of the National Assembly.
Jan. 1993	Jugnauth convenes a National Assembly session without prior notice.
Aug. 1993	A municipal by-election is won by the PSMD in a traditional MMM constituency.
18 Aug. 1993	Once again a crisis arises in the government alliance of the MSM and the MMM parties. The Prime Minister dismisses Paul Berenger, who is also the Secretary General of the MMM, for criticizing the government.
Late 1993	Legal proceedings, initiated by the MSM to exclude Ramgoolam from the National Assembly, are disallowed.
Oct.1993	Berenger is suspended as Secretary-General of the MMM.
18 Oct. 1993	A split occurs in the MMM party. The breakaway group accuses the party chairman of having broken up the coalition in order to negotiate with the Labour Party leader. A central committee meeting is called for 23 October. Two ministers resign from the MMM executive body.
11 Nov. 1993	Two new ministers are appointed following the resignation of the previous office holders.
16 Nov. 1993	The National Assembly returns after three month's holiday and the Prime Minister retains power with a majority of forty-nine MPs against seventeen of the opposition.
17 Jan. 1994	The new Japanese Ambassador arrives and presents his Letters of Credence.
21 Feb. 1994	The Prime Minister dismisses the Agriculture, Natural Resources and Justice Minister over his defiance of a Council of Ministers' decision to close a sugar factory.
31 Mar. 1994	The young brother of the Prime Minister is sworn in as Employment and Public Works Minister.
Apr. 1994	The government and opposition agree to a joint crusade against drug trafficking. Mauritius seems to have become the drug centre of the Indian Ocean region because the Mauritian Anti-Drug and Smuggling Unit has not performed well.
9 Apr. 1994	An electoral agreement is signed between the MLP and the MMM. Both parties make several concessions, amongst them the right of the Labour Party to name the members of a MLP/MMM coalition. The number of ministerial portfolios are reduced from twenty-four to twenty-one, with twelve for the MLP and nine for the MMM.

20 Apr. 1994	Three MPs of the MSM resign from the party and join members of the opposition. The Prime Minister has discussions with various MPs to prevent the defections.
May 1994	The former MMM members are expected to announce the formation of a new political party on 26 June. The name of the new body is still being considered.
22 May 1994	The nomination of a new PMSD leader is announced.
June 1994	Nababsing forms a new party - the Renouveau Militant Mauricien. (RMM)
9 June 1994	The Prime Minister says that his government will continue until the end of its term of office in 1996, when new elections will take place.
26 Aug. 1994	The Prime Minister reshuffles his cabinet which affects seven portfolios including Foreign Affairs.
29 Oct 1994	The Energy Minister is dismissed from his post because he awarded a contract to the Central Electricity Board.
Nov. 1994	Berenger and de L'Estrac resign from the National Assembly to contest a by-election.
29 Nov. 1994	The Minister of Industry and the leader of the Opposition resign from the National Assembly.
Dec. 1994	MSM indicates that it will not oppose the by-election.
29 Jan. 1995	Two opposition candidates of the alliance of the MLP and the MMM succeed in the parliamentary elections.
Feb. 1995	By-election is won by the MLP/MMM candidates.
Aug. 1995	A disagreement arises over the death penalty. Parliament abolishes it but the President refuses to endorse it.
Sept. 1995	The Prime Minister refuses to accept the resignation of both Energy and Environmental Protection Ministers. The reason for these resignations is involvement in drug trafficking.
Sept. 1995	The government acquires a Chilean-built vessel to monitor its exclusive coconut zone. This cannot be detected by radar.
5 Sept. 1995	Zimbabwe and Mauritius discuss proposals for a preferential trade agreement. An exhibition from forty-five Mauritian companies is organized to promote trade with Zimbabwe.
16 Nov. 1995	The crisis and the eventual dissolution of Parliament is pre-empted by a rejected oriental language policy amendment. Parliament is dissolved and elections announced.
22 Dec. 1995	The coalition alliance is defeated when the opposition alliance wins all sixty elected seats in the elections. Sir A. Jugnauth is removed from office.

| 27 Dec. 1995 | The new Prime Minister, Dr Navinchandra Ramgoolam, is sworn in, with Berenger as deputy. Dr Ramgoolam is the son of Sir Seewoosagur Ramgoolam. Four parliamentarians are selected as 'best losers' and will become the token opposition in the sixty-six seat assembly. |

| end Dec. 1995 | Newly elected Prime Minister Navin Ramgoolam forms a new 21-member government after winning all sixty seats through an alliance between the Labour Party and the Mauritian Militant Movement. |

| 5 May 1996 | The leader of the opposition Mauritius Social Democratic Party is Sir Gaëtan Duval. |

| 14 May 1996 | The brother of the late Sir Gaetan Duval, Herve Duval is chosen by the Electoral Commission to take the parliamentary seat left vacant by the former's death. |

| 6 Aug. 1996 | Finance Minister Randheersing Bheenick resigns under pressure from the Militant Mauritian Movement. Prime Minister Navin Ramgoolam decides to take his portfolio. The resignation is the culmination of a long controversy in the government relating to measures taken in the 1996-97 budget. |

| 27 Oct. 1996 | The government alliance Labour Party Mauritian Militant Movement wins 100 seats out of 111 vacant seats during the municipal elections. |

| 18 Nov. 1996 | In local elections in Port Louis, which had to be postponed from 26 October after an attack in which three people died, two candidates from the Islamic Hisbollah Party are elected. The other thirteen other elected councillors belong to the government alliance Labour Party/Mauritian Militant Movement. |

| 27 Nov. 1996 | Labour MP Vasant Bunwares is appointed as Finance Minister. |

MOZAMBIQUE

| 23 June 1975 | Samora Machel makes a triumphant entry into Lourenço Marques. |

| 24-25 June 1975 | Mozambique becomes an independent People's Republic at midnight. An independence ceremony is held on 25 June 1975. Samora Machel assumes the Presidency, he is invested as Head of State and is in future to be known as 'Comrade President'. |

| 25 June 1975 | A constitution is published which lays down that 'the People's Republic of Mozambique is a popular democratic state in which all patriotic strata participate in the construction of a new society free from exploitation of the people by the people'. The legislative organ will be the People's Assembly of 210 members, to include FRELIMO leadership, representatives of the armed forces and of democratic mass organizations. Social aims and foreign policy objectives are set out. |

| 25 June 1975 | At independence diplomatic relations are established with Albania, Cambodia, China, Congo, Denmark, Egypt, the German Democratic Republic, Guinea, India, Iraq, the Democratic People's Republic of Korea, Nigeria, Norway, Romania, Somalia, the Soviet Union and Sweden. |

| 26 June 1975 | The British Foreign and Commonwealth Secretary, James Callaghan, informs the House of Commons that the British Navy's Beira patrol to prevent oil reaching Rhodesia through Beira, has been withdrawn, following Mozambique's independence. |

29 June 1975 — A communiqué from the office of the President states 'it is FRELIMO which will direct the activity of the government, the decision taken by the party organs on such activity... being final'.

29 June 1975 — The composition of the first Council of Ministers is announced. All are members of FRELIMO.

1 July 1975 — The first Council of Ministers is sworn in.

9-25 July 1975 — The Mozambique Council of Ministers holds its first meeting.

18 July 1975 — Mozambique takes its seat at the Organisation of African Unity (OAU) for the first time at its 25th ordinary session in Kampala, Uganda.

24 July 1975 — A series of nationalization measures commence. All private schools and colleges, including missionary schools, hospitals, clinics and all private doctors and lawyers practices are taken over.

25 July 1975 — Radio Salisbury reports the imposition of a dusk-to-dawn curfew along the border with Mozambique.

26 July 1975 — The Ministry of Information publishes some major policy decisions. Radical change is necessary and 'the Government's fundamental task is to revolutionize the state machine'. Priority is accorded to rural collective farms and the promotion of communal villages. Information services will be 'reorientated' to serve national unity.

31 July 1975 — Accepts obligations of the United Nations Charter.

9 Aug. 1975 — A communiqué of the Malagasy Ministry of Foreign Affairs announces that Madagascar and Mozambique have decided to establish diplomatic relations and to exchange Ambassadors.

17 Aug. 1976 — The government announces an extended forty-four hour-week for all people working in the Mozambique Health Service, representing a political task to the service of the people.

19 Aug. 1975 — Legislation denies residence to any foreigner who has stayed, or proposes to stay, outside the country for more than ninety days without valid reason. Thousands of Portuguese thereby effectively lose their right to return.

29 Aug. 1975 — Diplomatic relations are established with Cuba.

30 Aug.-
7 Sept.1975 — President Nyerere of Tanzania visits Mozambique. An agreement between Tanzania and Mozambique is signed establishing a broad basis of cooperation in economic and ideological fields. A permanent commission of cooperation is to be established. Both countries pledge total moral, material and political support for South African national liberation movements.

1 Sept. 1975 — Great Britain establishes diplomatic relations with Mozambique.

| 11 Sept. 1975 | Mozambique is admitted to membership of the World Health Organization (WHO). |

| 11 Sept. 1975 | Diplomatic relations are to be established at ambassadorial level with Swaziland. |

| 13 Sept. 1975 | The government orders the University of Lourenço Marques closed for two years. The students are required to do urgent work in various other parts of the country. |

| 23 Sept. 1975 | By this date various categories of foreigners eligible for Mozambique citizenship, including persons holding, or eligible for, dual nationality are obliged to decide whether to take out Mozambican citizenship or to stay on as 'foreigners'. |

| 24 Sept. 1975 | The United States establishes diplomatic relations with Mozambique. |

| 7 Oct. 1975 | Repatriation begins for some 60,000 refugees who had fled to Tanzania during the war of independence. The first 21,000 will return overland over a three month period. The United Nations estimate the cost of the entire repatriation programme as about $7m. and appeal to member countries for donations. |

| 8 Oct. 1975 | Obtains assistance from the WFP through an agreement signed with FAO and the UN on behalf of the WFP. |

| 9 Oct. 1975 | President Machel denounces Jehovah's Witnesses as 'enemies of the people'. |

| 13 Oct. 1975 | The National Service of Popular Security (SNASP) is created by decree, responsible solely to the President, with the aim of 'detecting, neutralizing and combatting all forms of subversion, sabotage and acts directed against the people's power and its representatives, the national economy or the objectives of the People's Republic of Mozambique'. SNASP's powers are made retroactive to September 1974. No provision is made in the decree for appeal or recourse to Habeas Corpus. |

| 15 Oct. 1975 | Portugal and Mozambique conclude a Treaty of General Co-operation. |

| 17 Oct. 1975 | A communiqué from FRELIMO's political leadership denounces foreign-supported religious sects, including Jehovah's Witnesses, the Nazarene Church, the Church of the Apostle and the Assemblies of God, for allegedly plotting against the government. |

| 7 Nov. 1975 | The Portuguese government recalls its ambassador Dr. Albertino de Almeida, as well as three diplomats declared personae non grata by the Mozambique government. |

| 14 Nov. 1975 | Brazil establishes diplomatic relations with Mozambique. |

| 17 Nov. 1975 | Five Roman Catholic missionaries are expelled as 'counter-revolutionaries' and their homes and belongings taken over as a result of the nationalization measures. |

| 22 Nov. 1975 | All export of the country's most important crop - cashew nuts - is placed under full government control. |

11 Dec. 1975	Application of the Internatonal Health Regulations as amended by the Additional Regulations of 23 May 1973.

13 Dec. 1975   At the conclusion of a three-day meeting of the Joint General Staff of the Popular Forces for the Liberation of Mozambique (FPLM) President Machel violently attacks certain sectors of the armed forces and of FRELIMO. He claims the time is right for a purge of dissident elements.

16 Dec. 1975   The World Council of Churches (WCC) claims to have given $1.2m. in aid to African liberation movements in Angola, Mozambique and Guinea-Bissau over the past three years.

17-18 Dec.1975   An attempt is made by about 400 African troops and police to take control of key points in Lourenço Marques and overthrow Machel's government. Loyal FRELIMO troops suppress it.

19 Dec. 1975   The situation returns to normal, telecommunications links are resumed and the airport is re-opened.

19 Dec. 1975   A FRELIMO policy document is quoted, laying down government guidelines regarding religion - against which the masses will be protected. 'The Catholic Church is a reactionary organization... it is necessary once and for all to put an end to the influence of this Church and the activities it pursues'.

20 Dec. 1975   A government communiqué reports that the rebellion has finally been put down.

13 Jan. 1976   Zambia and Mozambique sign an agreement on the construction of a road between Katete (Zambia) and Bene (Northern Mozambique) to facilitate Zambia's access to the coast and strengthen economic links between the two countries.

14 Jan. 1976   Portugal suspends all flights to Mozambique after accusing the government of persecuting the Portuguese settlers who have remained in Mozambique. Negotiations on an air transport agreement are broken off.

19 Jan. 1976   The 26th Session of the Organisation of African Unity (OAU) Liberation Committee opens in Lourenço Marques. The Committee decides by acclamation to propose to the Council of Ministers that Mozambique be admitted as a member and that the Mozambican Foreign Minister be elected chairman of the next session to be held in Dar-es-Salaam, Tanzania.

22 Jan. 1976   Foreign Minister, J.A. Chissano, announces that all Portuguese citizens arrested prior to independence for 'crimes against decolonization' will shortly be released.

3 Feb. 1976   The capital city, Lourenço Marques, is renamed Maputo.

3 Feb. 1976   During a speech in honour of Dr. Eduardo Mondlane, on the anniversary of his death, President Machel announces that all privately-owned buildings and land are to be taken over and that the government will, in future, collect all rents, even if the owners are in Mozambique.

3 Feb. 1976   On the 'day of the heroes of the national liberation' it is announced that everyone will have to pay one day's salary each month into a 'solidarity

bank'. The proceeds will be used to help the oppressed people of the world, particularly those of Namibia, Rhodesia and South Africa.

5 Feb. 1976   The Portuguese government views the nationalization of property as a further transgression of guarantees given regarding white settlers at pre-independence talks in Lusaka.

12 Feb. 1976   Signs agreement with the Soviet Union concerning cooperation in the fisheries sector.

12 Feb. 1976   Signs trade agreement with the Soviet Union.

23-24 Feb.1976 President Machel claims that Pafuri village, at the junction of the borders between Rhodesia, South Africa and Mozambique, has sustained an aerial and artillery bombardment by Rhodesian forces.

24 Feb. 1976   A Rhodesian security force's communiqué reports fighting along the Rhodesian-Mozambique border and large quantities of arms destroyed or seized in 'follow-up hot pursuit operations'.

3 Mar. 1976   The closure of the Mozambique border with Rhodesia is announced by President Samora Machel in a speech to FRELIMO's Central Committee. All communications with Rhodesia are banned, all Rhodesian property and assets are confiscated, sanctions are imposed, Mozambique is placed in 'a state of war'.

4 Mar. 1976   South Africa's Prime Minister Vorster, in a special statement in Parliament, claims that Mozambique's action in closing its border with Rhodesia, and placing itself on a war footing, could ignite a conflagration in Southern Africa.

4 Mar. 1976   A Portuguese government delegation leaves for Mozambique to investigate allegations of arbitrary arrest and ill-treatment of Portuguese citizens including detention in 'political re-education centres'. The delegation is headed by the Secretary of State for Co-operation, Dr. Gomes Mota and includes Portuguese government law officers and the head of the National Prison Service.

6 Mar. 1976   OAU congratulates Mozambique on the closure of its frontier, routes, railways and ports to Rhodesia. The General Secretariat appeals to all OAU member states to give every assistance to Mozambique 'in this hour of great sacrifice which the young Republic is making for Africa'.

11 Mar. 1976   Rhodesia notes an increase in guerrilla activity and incursions in the north-eastern war zone as well as along the length of the 700-mile border with Mozambique.

17 Mar. 1976   Mozambique's first United Nations representative, Ambassador J.C. Lobo, presents his credentials to the Secretary-General Dr. Kurt Waldheim.

23 Mar. 1976   South Africa's Minister of Police, J.T. Kruger, confirms that seventeen FRELIMO soldiers are being held by South Africa after crossing the border in pursuit of refugees.

4 Apr. 1976   The first session of the Joint Commission for Co-operation between

Tanzania and Mozambique begins in Dar-es-Salaam. The thirty-two member Mozambican delegation is led by the Minister for Economic and Development Planning, M. dos Santos, and includes five ministers. Four sub-commissions are set up to cover Trade, Industry and Finance; Diplomatic and Consular Affairs; Education and Culture; Communications, Transport and Public Works.

7 Apr. 1976	FRELIMO troops are reported to have opened fire on a Rhodesian police post at Vila Salazar.
8 Apr. 1976	South Africa frees seventeen FRELIMO troops arrested in March after pursuing a party of Portuguese refugees fleeing from Mozambique.
11 Apr. 1976	Tanzania, Zambia and Mozambique agree to set up a joint institute for training their defence and police forces.
13 Apr. 1976	The government announces it has released a group of twenty Rhodesian citizens into the custody of the British Embassy in Maputo. The group include consular officials and their families detained when the border with Rhodesia was closed.
25 Apr. 1976	Signs basic agreement with the World Health Organisation for its provision of technical and advisory assistance.
19 May 1976	Signs treaty with Soviet Union on cultural and scientific co-operation.
22 May 1976	An estimated 1,500 Tanzanian troops are helping President Machel crush anti-government dissidents in the Macua and Makonde ethnic areas and are guarding the Cabora Bassa dam.
23 May 1976	President Samora Machel ends a six-day official visit to the Soviet Union. An official communiqué pledges solidarity, urges the abolition of all military bases in the Indian Ocean and attributes the success of the anti-colonial struggle to the alliance with socialist countries.
29 May 1976	According to government decree, students at the Eduardo Mondlane University will now have to give as many years of public service as they spent at university.
4 June 1976	Accession to the agreement establishing the African Development Bank.
10 June 1976	Following a three-hour rocket and mortar barrage of the Zona tea estate from Espungabera in Mozambique and other attacks on farms and border posts, Rhodesian Air Force Hunter jets destroy guerrilla mortar positions on the Mozambican side of the border.
13 June 1976	Accession by Mozambique to the agreement establishing the International Fund for Agricultural Development.
14 June 1976	Further rocket and mortar attacks on Rhodesian targets are reported.
17 June 1976	Rhodesian Prime Minister Ian Smith declares that if Mozambique and Zambia allow 'terrorists' to operate from within their borders they will have to accept that Rhodesia will use the right of hot pursuit.

26 June 1976   President Machel, in a two-hour speech marking the first independence
                    anniversary, attacks lawlessness, corruption, indiscipline, calls on the masses
                    to organize themselves in vigilante groups and says People's Tribunals will
                    be established throughout the country.

26 June 1976   The government reports an attack on the village of Mapai by Rhodesian
                    security forces, and a second assault on the railway town of Malvernia, with
                    casualties on both sides.

29 June 1976   Foreign Minister Chissano, addresses the OAU Council in Port Louis,
                    Mauritius and indicates Mozambique will need nearly 240 million pounds
                    sterling over a two-year period to compensate it for applying economic
                    sanctions against Rhodesia.

2 July 1976   The United Nations Secretary-General, Dr. Kurt Waldheim, reports that a
                    special UN mission has visited Mozambique and estimates the direct cost of
                    sanctions over the next two years at $275m.

5 July 1976   FRELIMO installations set up in Tanzania during the Mozambique war of
                    liberation are handed over to TANU and the government of Tanzania.

24 July 1976   A South African coaster, the Limpopo, comes under attack off Mozambique,
                    about ten miles north of Cabo de Ouro, which marks the limit of
                    Mozambique's territorial waters. The attack is later dismissed as a 'mistake'.

5 Aug. 1976   Salisbury reports a mortar attack on the Rhodesian Army post at Rudna,
                    north of Umtali.

6 Aug. 1976   Accepts UNESCO constitution.

8 Aug. 1976   Rhodesian forces carry out a retaliatory raid on a camp near Nhagomia
                    village where refugees are concentrated, as part of a hot-pursuit operation.

11 Aug. 1976   FRELIMO's sustained mortar barrage on Umtali, Rhodesia, on Forbes
                    border post and on Vila Salazar make open warfare between Mozambique
                    and Rhodesia appear imminent.

16 Aug. 1976   The second phase of repatriation of over 10,000 Mozambique refugees living
                    in Southern Tanzania is launched. The programme is being undertaken by
                    the Tanzanian government in co-operation with the UNCHR and the
                    Tanganyika Christian Refugee Service (TCRS).

17 Aug. 1976   Obtains interest free loan from Great Britain.

20 Aug. 1976   UNHCR representative in Mozambique states that Nhagomia camp had
                    formerly housed 8,000 refugees and that it had not been a guerrilla camp,
                    as claimed by Rhodesia.

29 Aug. 1976   The Rhodesian government produces documentary evidence that the camp
                    which Rhodesian forces raided thirty miles inside Mozambique, on 8
                    August, was indeed a base camp for several thousand Rhodesian African
                    nationalist guerrillas, under the control of the Zimbabwe People's Army.

6 Sept. 1976   The Presidents of five Front Line States - Nyerere of Tanzania, Kaunda of
                    Zambia, Machel of Mozambique, Neto of Angola and Seretse Khama of

Botswana - end a summit conference in Dar-es-Salaam, declairing that they have agreed to further intensify the armed struggle in Rhodesia.

14 Sept. 1976	Signs treaty with United States on the transfer of agricultural commodities.
15 Sept. 1976	Signs agreement obtaining assistance from UNDP.
26 Sept. 1976	The five Front Line Presidents put forward their programme for Rhodesia's political future.
28 Sept. 1976	In Lusaka the Rhodesian guerrilla leader, Robert Mugabe, demands that military control in Rhodesia, during the proposed transitional government period, be taken over by his 15,000 troops now in Mozambique.
14 Oct. 1976	TASS publishes a categorical denial that Mozambique has authorised the Soviet Union to establish an air and naval support base on Bazaruto Island which would threaten the West's oil route through the Mozambique Channel.
16 Oct. 1976	Kenya orders 300 Mozambicans to leave the country immediately as it does not recognize them as refugees. They are not granted the option, as outlined in the UN Human Rights Charter, of leaving for a third country.
21 Oct. 1976	Signs agreement with WHO on the provision of technical advisory assistance.
24 Oct. 1976	More than 3,000 Mozambican refugees have been repatriated from Tanzania. They are to join Ujamaa (communal) villages.
21 Nov. 1976	The Cuban Premier, Fidel Castro, assures Mozambique of unconditional support in the continuing fighting with Rhodesia.
26 Nov. 1976	Rhodesian security forces call on air support in a fresh border flare up with FRELIMO.
28 Nov. 1976	An agreement is signed in Maputo in which the Cuban Communist Party pledges itself 'entirely' to the defence of Mozambique in the event of Rhodesian aggression.
6 Jan. 1977	President Machel pledges all support and co-operation necessary to achieve a negotiated settlement of the Zimbabwe problem. This assurance is given to the chairman of the Geneva Conference, Ivor Richard, during his visit to Maputo.
10 Jan. 1977	Insurance companies are nationalized retroactively from 1 January 1977.
12 Jan. 1977	A Rhodesian Canberra bomber is shot down close to the Mozambique border possibly by FRELIMO using a SAM-7 missile.
20 Jan. 1977	Mozambique launches its first diplomatic mission accredited to a foreign state when chargé d'affaires F.C. Lukanga presents his credentials in Dar-es-Salaam.
3-7 Feb. 1977	The third FRELIMO Party Congress is held in Maputo. It is announced that FRELIMO has been restructured from a guerrilla movement into a

Marxist-Leninist 'vanguard party' dedicated to the development of scientific socialism. Samora Machel is unanimously elected President of FRELIMO for another five years.

21-25 Feb.1977	The first African Conference on Cinema is held in Maputo.
8 Mar. 1977	The government claims the right to decide the future careers of school leavers. The two final years of high school are to be done away with. Students will move immediately to replace the estimated 20,000 Portuguese men and women who are to leave Mozambique by June.
10 Mar. 1977	The Council of Ministers announces a limited amnesty for certain categories of offenders.
16 Mar. 1977	President Machel sets a two month deadline for all Portuguese passport-holders to leave the country. They will not be permitted to return.
23 Mar. 1977	A military communiqué announces the arrest of several high-ranking army officers and political commissars on charges of 'causing a separation between the population and the armed forces'.
23 Mar. 1977	A joint communiqué is issued by Cuba and Mozambique after a visit by Fidel Castro. 'Relations of friendship' are to be strengthened and consolidated.
28 Mar. 1977	An agreement with North Korea is signed in Maputo on bilateral cooperation in education and culture.
29 Mar. 1977	Soviet head of state President Podgorny arrives in Maputo.
31 Mar. 1977	A twenty-year Treaty of Friendship and Cooperation is signed between the USSR and Mozambique. Cooperation will continue to develop in the military sphere on the basis of relevant military agreements.
1 Apr. 1977	The Council of Ministers impose a ban on residents leaving Mozambique temporarily, even for holidays, visits or medical treatment, in an apparent move to prevent foreign exchange from leaving the country.
11 Apr. 1977	The British Foreign Secretary, Dr. David Owen, visits Maputo during a week long tour of Africa. A day is spent in discussing the Rhodesian question with Mozambique's leaders.
1 May 1977	The petroleum industry is nationalized.
15 May 1977	President Machel extends the deadline for Portuguese passport-holders to leave the country. Airports are crammed with 'refugees' leaving to avoid detention in re-education camps. More than 100 a day are arriving in Lisbon.
16-21 May 1977	An International Conference in Support of the Peoples of Zimbabwe (Rhodesia) and Namibia held in Maputo is attended by eighty-seven member states of the United Nations, several observers and non-governmental organizations. President Machel delivers the Keynote address to the opening session.

23 May 1977	Portugal's Foreign Minister, Dr. J.M. Ferreira, declares Portugal is not prepared to ratify its co-operation agreements with Mozambique so long as the security of Portuguese citizens and property there is not assured.
29 May 1977	Rhodesian security forces carry out a pre-emptive strike against a Zimbabwe African National Liberation Army (ZANLA) base at Chicualacula (formerly Malvernia) and attack two FRELIMO camps, according to Mozambique's Minister of Defence.
30 May 1977	Rhodesia announces a further raid into Mozambique against a terrorist headquarters and main supply base in the area of Mapai, which is the controlling centre for all incursions in the south-east of Rhodesia. Rhodesian authorities deny that Rhodesian forces have attacked any units of Mozambique's army.
31 May 1977	Lieutenant-General Peter Walls, Rhodesian Commander of Combined Operations says in Salisbury that Rhodesian troops have occupied the town of Mapai, and will stay in Mozambique as long as it is necessary to destroy ZANLA terrorists in the area.
1 June 1977	Dr. Kurt Waldheim, the United Nations Secretary-General, strongly condemns the Rhodesian actions.
1 June 1977	Rhodesian forces begin to withdraw from Mapai.
2 June 1977	The Rhodesian Prime Minister, Ian Smith, defends his five-day military drive into Mozambique to eliminate guerrillas in their bases. He maintains that there is no question of aggressive intentions against Mozambique itself.
2 June 1977	The Soviet Union officially condemns the Rhodesian raid into Mozambique.
4 June 1977	Mozambique and Cuba sign an agreement providing for cooperation in the spheres of health, public works, transport, agriculture and fisheries.
6 June 1977	Ratifies the following ILO Convention: rights of association and combination of agricultural workers (no. 11); regulation of hours of work in commerce and offices (no. 30); discrimination in employment and occupation (no. 111); organization of employment service (no. 88); abolition of forced labour (no. 105). With regard to industrial undertakings, ratifies application of weekly rest (no. 14); limiting of hours of work (no. 1). Ratifies labour inspection in industry and commerce (no. 81); equal remuneration for work of equal value for men and women workers. In the field of workmen's compensation, ratifies accidents (no. 17) and occupational diseases (no. 18).
9 June 1977	Signs treaty with UNICEF on their activities in Mozambique.
10 June 1977	It is officially announced in Salisbury that security forces have raided a ZANLA base and captured large quantities of weapons and equipment.
15 June 1977	The twenty-year Treaty of Friendship and Cooperation signed on 31 March is ratified by the Supreme Soviet of the USSR.
16 June 1977	In Rhodesia, Lieutenant-Colonel Roland Lever, army commander in the Chipinga area claims, in a published interview, that FRELIMO troops have been involved in about thirty out of forty seven serious border incidents.

18 June 1977	President Samora Machel accuses Rhodesia of waging 'open warfare' against Mozambique.
18 June 1977	Ian Smith categorically denies that there are any Rhodesian troops in Mozambique.
20 June 1977	The United Nations Security Council meets to discuss the Rhodesian incursions into Mozambique.
28-30 June 1977	The United Nations Security Council meets again. The Mozambican Minister of Development and Economic Planning, M. dos Santos claims Rhodesian attacks have caused property losses amounting to $13,000,000 and that it is imperative the international community should contribute to Mozambique's defensive military capability.
29 June 1977	President Machel reshuffles his government. A. Guebuza becomes Defence Vice-Minister and Armed and Security Forces Political Commissar. S. Viera becomes Head of Defence and Security of the FRELIMO party.
29 June 1977	Rhodesia claims Mozambican soldiers have been responsible for 102 incidents in 1977, including robbery, looting and theft of vehicles and cattle.
30 June 1977	A United Nations Security Council resolution, approved by consensus, condemns Rhodesian acts of aggression against Mozambique and calls on all countries to give material assistance, to strengthen its defence capability and to provide financial, technical and material aid to help Mozambique offset the economic loss resulting from its imposition of sanctions.
4 July 1977	During an official visit to Mozambique by Cape Verde's President A. Pereira, it is agreed to establish a Joint Commission to review the implementation of the cooperation and friendship agreement between the two countries, originally signed in June 1976.
5 July 1977	Signs agreement with the United Kingdom of Great Britain concerning cereals to be supplied to Britain.
15 July 1977	Signs treaty with Great Britain and Northern Ireland concerning an interest-free loan.
16 July 1977	Agreements of cooperation are concluded between the Congolese and Mozambican governments and between the Congolese Labour Party (PCT) and FRELIMO.
17 July 1977	The government publishes a document analyzing Mozambique's social and economic problems. Party cells should be established in all state agencies.
31 Aug. 1977	A provisional National People's Assembly holds its opening session.
12 Sept. 1977	President Machel announces that a national association of journalists will be established to control the activities of the organs of the national press.
21 Sept. 1977	Air pooling agreement between SAA and DTA.
22-23 Sept.1977	A two-day meeting of the Presidents of the Front Line States to consider Anglo-US proposals for a constitutional settlement in Rhodesia, concludes

that these form a sufficient basis for further negotiations.

25 Sept. 1977	General elections begin, with voting for deputies to People's Assemblies at local, district and provincial level. Lists of candidates are presented exclusively by FRELIMO.

7 Oct. 1977   The Tanzanian government tightens restrictions on Tanzanians crossing the border into Mozambique, in a bid to discourage illegal trading and fishing.

11 Oct. 1977   In Jamaica, a joint communiqué, issued by Prime Minister Manley and President Machel, states that bilateral relations are to be strengthened through trade, economic and cultural cooperation and expresses their solidarity with the liberation movements in Southern Africa.

16 Oct. 1977   Cuba and Mozambique declare their support for the Patriotic Front in Rhodesia.

17 Oct. 1977   A twenty-year Friendship and Co-operation Treaty providing for joint military and economic assistance is published in Havana.

18 Oct. 1977   Signs treaty with Great Britain concerning an interest free loan.

Nov. 1977   Mozambique is admitted to membership of the United Nations Food and Agriculture Organization (FAO) at its 19th biennial conference in Rome.

28 Nov. 1977   Combined Operations Headquarters in Salisbury announces two ground-air attacks by security forces on the main ZANLA base north of Chimoio and on Tembue camp, north of the Zambesi River.

29 Nov. 1977   The raids are officially condemned in Great Britain and the United States.

1-4 Dec. 1977   General elections culminate in elections to a National People's Assembly. The 226 candidates are nominated by FRELIMO's Central Committee, and presented to the ten provncial asemblies and are adopted almost unanimously.

2 Dec. 1977   Signs agreement with the United States of America relating to the transfer of agricultural commodities.

18 Dec. 1977   The Presidents of the Front Line States meet in Beira and reaffirm conditional support for the Anglo-American Rhodesian settlement proposals.

18 Dec. 1977   The Rhodesian air base and military camp near Umtali, Grand Reef, is attacked by guerrillas; is repulsed, and follow-up operations continue.

23 Dec. 1977   The first post-electoral session of the People's Assembly begins and designates a Permanent Commission led by the Head of State, Samora Machel. It unanimously adopts a resolution stating that the People's Assembly is the supreme organ of power. All its activities are to be based on the will of the Mozambican people to continue the people's democratic revolution under the guidance of FRELIMO.

6 Jan. 1978   Field Marshall Lord Carver, Britain's commissioner-designate to Rhodesia, and the United Nations representative General Prem Chand, fly to Maputo for three days of talks with President Machel in a move to revive the

Anglo-American settlement plan for Rhodesia.

13 Jan. 1978   President Machel opposes an internal settlement for Rhodesia and supports the Anglo-American peace proposals as a basis for negotiations.

14 Jan. 1978   Tanzania and Mozambique sign an agreement to establish a centre to train diplomats in Dar-es-Salaam.

19 Jan. 1978   Cubans are reported to be training guerrillas of Robert Mugabe's ZANU (Zimbabwe African National Union) wing of the Patriotic Front in Mozambique.

24 Jan. 1978   Provisionally applies the 1977 International Sugar Agreement.

23 Mar. 1978   Mozambique introduces compulsory military service for all men and women over the age of eighteen. The law, approved by the Permanent Commission of the People's Assembly takes effect immediately.

25-26 Mar.1978   President Machel attends a Front Line Summit Meeting in Dar-es-Salaam concerning the Rhodesian settlement situation.

11-13 Apr.1978   The first national conference of journalists is held, the National Journalists' Organisation (ONJ) is formally constituted, its statutes and programme approved and an executive committee elected.

22 Apr. 1978   Reorganization of the Council of Ministers.

23 Apr. -   An internationally coordinated exchange of prisoners takes place between
1 May 1978   Mozambique, East Germany and the United States.

Late Apr.1978   The Permanent Commission of the People's Assembly approves a number of bills to improve the efficiency of the Council of Ministers and of provisional governments and decides to set up district and city executive councils.

21 May 1978   A Treaty of Friendship and Co-operation is signed with North Korea, effective from 1 July 1978 and valid for twenty years. Bilateral co-operation in increasing defence capabilities is provided for.

27 June 1978   Signs treaty with Great Britain and Northern Ireland concerning an interest free loan.

31 July 1978   Rhodesian security forces raid the nationalist guerrilla bases of ZANU forces, owing allegiance to Robert Mugabe deep inside Mozambique.

7-16 Aug.1978   FRELIMO examines the conduct of certain members, notes serious cases of deviation, indiscipline and corruption directly violating FRELIMO's revolutionary ideology. J. Ribeiro de Carvalho is expelled from the Central Committee, together with three others.

10 Aug. 1978   The World Council of Churches gives a grant of 40,000 Pounds Sterling to the Zimbabwe Patriotic Front for use in humanitarian programmes in Botswana, Zambia and in Mozambique.

14 Aug. 1978   The third ordinary session of the People's Assembly ends after unanimously

approving the text of the new constitution. This new constitution includes a further objective for the PRM, that of 'the building of a people's democracy and the construction of the material and ideological bases for a socialist society'. Eleven deputies are elected to represent Mozambique in the International Parliamentary Union (IPU) in Geneva.

18 Aug. 1978	J. Ribeiro de Carvalho is dismissed as Minister of Agriculture.
16-20 Sept.1978	President Agostinho Neto of Angola pays a state visit, at the head of a seventy-two member delegation. A joint communiqué reaffirms the importance of the Non-Aligned Movement as a force for peace, and the intentions of both Angola and Mozambique to build societies based on Marxist-Leninist principles.
19 Sept. 1978	A Treaty of Friendship and Co-operation between Mozambique and Angola is signed in Maputo by Presidents Machel and Neto. Co-operation between FRELIMO and the MPLA-PT at state level is assured.
19-24 Sept.1978	Raids into Mozambique are carried out by Rhodesian forces, twenty-five 'terrorist' bases are attacked in a wide area around Chimoio. Arms, ammunition and documents are captured.
27 Sept. 1978	Rhodesia's Lieutenant-General Wells says there is 'no single day of the year when we are not operating beyond our border' and that in many instances his forces have the cooperation of local people in Mozambique and Zambia.
22 Oct. 1978	The Bulgarian Head of State, Todor Zhivkov, arrives in Maputo for an official visit during which a Treaty of Friendship, Co-operation and Mutual Help is signed. Additional agreements cover the fields of science, culture, agriculture, industry and economic cooperation.
23 Oct. 1978	President Machel appoints M.F. da Graca Machungo as Minister of Agriculture, J.Z. Carrilho as Minister of Industry and Energy and J.B. Cosme as Minister of Public Works and Housing. J. Chambal becomes Director of the National Commission of Village Communes.
6 Nov. 1978	Signs loan agreement with Denmark.
18 Nov. 1978	In terms of an agreement signed by the Ministers of Defence of Mozambique and Hungary, Hungary is to provide military equipment, including tanks and aircraft, as well as military advisers and instructors to Mozambique.
11 Dec. 1978	The Mozambican Ministry of Defence announces that on 10 December Rhodesian aircraft have bombed military barracks near Beira port, and that other targets inside Mozambique have been bombed between 29 November and 8 December 1978.
6 Jan. 1979	President Machel states that the mounting bombing attacks by Rhodesian aircraft are seriously disrupting the country's transportation and distribution system.
22 Jan. 1979	The Anglican cathedral at Maciene and a number of other churches in the vicinity have been closed and all religious services banned. Fifteen Roman Catholic churches have been closed, the majority in Gaza province

includes Maputo. Fear of alien influence is blamed.

30 Jan. 1979	A special non-aligned ministerial conference on Southern Africa opens in Maputo. Mozambique puts forward a draft final document aimed at establishing a common stand on the problems of Namibia, Rhodesia and South Africa. In his opening speech President Machel accuses the imperialist West of trying to topple the governments of Angola and Mozambique.
2 Feb. 1979	The Co-ordinating Bureau of the Non-Aligned Movement adopts a 5,000 page document analyzing the Southern African situation. The `Maputo Statement' is to be distributed as an official document of the United Nations.
11 Feb. 1979	A massive public health campaign ends. More than eleven million people have been innoculated.
15 Feb. 1979	A new category of state officials is created by Presidential Decree to improve liaison between central and local government. The state inspectors will have a rank equivalent to that of provincial governor and will be directly responsible to the President.
22-24 Feb. 1979	Erich Honecker, Chairman of the East German Council of State and General Secretary of the Socialist Unity Party (SED) Central Committee, visits Mozambique. A twenty-year Treaty of Friendship and Cooperation is signed on 24 February providing for consultation in times of crisis and for `co-operation in the military sector through bilateral agreements'.
24 Feb. 1979	In a joint communiqué President Machel and Erich Honecker pledge their continued support for black liberation movements in Southern Africa, condemn the recent Chinese invasion of Vietnam and welcome the revolution in Iran.
25 Feb. 1979	Portuguese President A.R. Eanes says at a news conference in Guinea Bissau that there are great outstanding difficulties between Portugal and Mozambique and that he has no plans for meeting President Machel.
26 Feb. 1979	Mozambique and South Africa sign a railway cooperation agreement, under the terms of which the railway administrations will assist each other by rendering professional services. The importance of the ports of Maputo and Matola is recognized.
28 Feb. 1979	The People's Assembly passes a law providing for the imposition of the death penalty for certain crimes against the security of people and state and for those whose reintegration into society appears impossible.
9 Mar. 1979	President Banda of Malawi denies responsibility of his secret agents in dispatching the letter bomb to Dr. Attati Mpakati, leader of the Socialist League of Malawi (LESOMA) in Mozambique. Dr. Mpakali is recovering from his wounds in Maputo.
12 Mar. 1979	Rhodesian aircraft attack an arms depot at Chokwe and a ZANLA headquarters and barracks at Barragem, Gaza Province.
16 Mar. 1979	An air strike is carried out against a ZANLA arms, ammunition and explosives dump at Dondo, twenty-five miles from Beira.

17 Mar. 1979	Further Rhodesian air strikes are carried out on guerrilla bases in the Chimoio area.
23 Mar. 1979	It is announced in Maputo that an attack on fuel depots near Beira has caused extensive damage, estimated at 10,000,000 Pounds Sterling.
28 Mar. 1979	RENAMO claims to have sabotaged the railway line between Tete and Mutarara carrying coal from the Moatize mine. Two bridges are blown up. These, and other attacks are later confirmed by FRELIMO.
29 Mar. 1979	A law is passed allowing the establishment of revolutionary military courts to try crimes falling under the country's security laws.
31 Mar. 1979	A military revolutionary court in Maputo passes death sentences on two alleged Rhodesian spies and eight others accused of treason and sabotage. All ten men are executed by firing squad on the same day.
1 Apr. 1979	The Portuguese government condemns the execution of the Portuguese citizen, R.M.N. da Silva, on 31 March 1979, which has grave implications for relations between Portugal and Mozambique. Concern is expressed at the circumstances surrounding his sentencing and also regarding all Portuguese citizens still detained in Mozambican prisons.
3 Apr. 1979	In Maputo the Portuguese delegation, led by Industry Minister Alvaro Barreto, walks out of talks in protest over the execution of R. da Silva. No concessions over nationalized Portuguese assets are granted. President Machel cancels a meeting with Mr. Barreto.
8 Apr. 1979	Accepts the Constitution of the UN Industrial Development Organisation.
12 Apr. 1979	Mozambique recognizes the new government of Uganda under its new President Professor Y. Lule, following the fall of Kampala on 11 April 1979.
18 Apr. 1979	Four Portuguese nationals released from detention by the Mozambican authorities arrive in Lisbon and give an account of their interrogation and torture. An estimated forty Portuguese are still detained in Mozambican prisons, while twenty-one Portuguese nationals have been executed.
18-21 Apr.1979	President Ceausecu of Romania visits Mozambique. A Treaty of Friendship and Co-operation is signed on 20 April, as well as a programme of economic cooperation and an agreement between their respective political parties.
20 Apr. 1979	Rhodesian fighter aircraft attack guerrilla camps in southern Mozambique.
1 May 1979	President Machel orders the dissolution of all trade unions founded under Portuguese colonial rule and decrees their assets be transferred to local workers' committees. These production councils are to implement FRELIMO's policies. A Hero of Work Medal is being created.
17 May 1979	The EEC grants nearly $60,000 emergency aid to help fight a cholera epidemic, at the request of the World Health Organization (WHO).
22-27 May 1979	An East German military delegation, led by the Defence Minister, General Heinz Hoffmann, visits Mozambique. A military cooperation protocol is signed on 26 May 1979.

1 June 1979	The People's Assembly dissolves the Colonial Police Corps (CPM) and creates a People's Police Force (PPM) in terms of a law enacted by the Permanent Commission on 31 May 1979. Its Commander-in-Chief is President Machel; it will support the Mozambique People's Liberation Forces (FPLM) in the defence of sovereignty and national integrity and the People's National Security Service (SNASP) in preventing and fighting counter-revolutionary activities.
4 June 1979	Rhodesian troops and aircraft attack `terrorist' bases at Chivinga, Tete Province.
9-11 June 1979	The first summit of the five former Portuguese African colonies is held in Luanda, Angola. President Machel attends. Mutual cooperation between Angola, Mozambique, Guinea Bissau, Cape Verde and Sao Tomé and Principe is to be strengthened, liberation struggles are to be supported and joint lines of action are to be followed.
12 June 1979	Rhodesian security forces report that up to 1,000 regular soldiers of Mozambique's army are fighting alongside ZANLA guerrillas.
Early July 1979	RENAMO commander A.M. Matsangai meets Western reporters in a bush camp in central Mozambique and explains the movement's aims and outlines its strength and recent activities. Its goal is the liberation of the people from FRELIMO's Marxist oppression and the creation of conditions for the choice of a free political future.
4 July 1979	An official delegation from Lesotho is visiting Mozambique to study problems in primary health care. An agreement will be concluded for an exchange of health personnel.
9 July 1979	Two networks of enemy agents and counter-revolutionaries are broken up. Six are arrested in Manica Province following a bomb attack on a hydro-electric plant. In Tete province a `spy' operating via Malawi is arrested and accused of supplying military information to assist Zimbabwe/Rhodesia raids on Mozambique.
8 Aug. 1979	Mozambique releases twenty-four detained Portuguese citizens, of whom twenty three return to Portugal.
23 Aug. 1979	Instuments of ratification of the Treaty of Friendship and Cooperation with East Germany are exchanged in East Berlin.
25 Aug. 1979	Eight Mozambicans are sentenced to death in Beira by the Revolutionary Military Tribunal and executed. They were found guilty of crimes against the state - high treason, spying, terrorism and armed attacks.
31 Aug. 1979	South African sources report five senior Soviet officers killed in a clash with RENAMO guerrillas near Metuchira, Nampula district in Northern Mozambique.
5 Sept. 1979	Rhodesian forces launch a four-day major ground and air strike into Southern Mozambique described as a measure to pre-empt a joint ZANLA-Mozambican campaign. The principal forms of the attack is the town of Aldeia da Barragem and the road and rail links there through Gaza province.

6 Sept. 1979	Rhodesian government spokesman claims President Machel is supporting ZANLA insurgents integrating his soldiers with the guerrilla units and is planning large-scale joint operations.
7 Sept. 1979	Robert Mugabe, ZANU leader, announces from his London headquarters that twelve Rhodesian civilians held in Mozambique have been handed over to the Apostolic Delegate in Maputo. Eleven of these are members of the Marymount Mission captured by Mugabe's forces.
8 Sept. 1979	Salisbury communiqué claims sixteen targets destroyed including brigade headquarters at Mapai, bases at Maxaila and Mabalane and five bridges in Gaza province.
11 Sept. 1979	Rhodesian invading forces meet unexpectedly stiff resistance as they move against a base at Mapai on the banks of the Limpopo.
15 Sept. 1979	J.L. Cabaço of Transport and Communications claims in London that the principal targets had been economic installations and estimates the cost of the damage at some 17,000,000 pounds sterling.
27 Sept. 1979	A second major Rhodesian raid targets a ZANLA camp near Chimoio. The five day attack meets strong resistance, led by ZANLA senior commander R. Nhongo, as well as Soviet and East German advisers, anti-aircraft fire as well as intervention by Mozambican tanks.
11-13 Oct.1979	Further bombing raids by Rhodesia take place.
13 Oct. 1979	Mozambique forces capture a RENAMO base near Gorongoso town, which has been under attack by the guerrillas.
14 Oct. 1979	Mozambican authorities claim Rhodesian troops have been driven slowly back across the border.
20 Oct. 1979	RENAMO claim the capture of the town of Macossa in Sofala province. This is confirmed by government sources on 22 October 1979. It also claims successes in Manica province, disruption of non-civilian traffic and the capture of large caches of arms.
22 Oct. 1979	Mozambique forces finally succeed in shelling the RENAMO fortified base on a 5,500 ft high plateau in the Gorongoza mountains.
22 Oct. 1979	President Machel announces the release of 1,153 prisoners from 're-education' camps, together with the release of 600 people who deserted from FRELIMO during the war of independence. Both categories will be resettled in the northern province of Niassa.
2 Nov. 1979	RENAMO guerrillas report the capture of Maringue, Mazamba, and an attack on the town of Inhaminga.
16 Nov. 1979	RENAMO communiqué claims its forces have cut all telephone lines between the western province of Tete and the rest of the country. Tete is now totally isolated. RENAMO is opening two new fronts against the FRELIMO government.
6 Dec. 1979	Five people, including a Rhodesian, Sinai Finai, said to be an agent of

Rhodesia's secret service, are condemned to death for high treason, espionage and terrorism and executed.

8 Dec. 1979   Forty-five ex-RENAMO guerrillas are pardoned at a public rally in Beira, in a move calculated to encourage other guerrillas to surrender.

20 Dec. 1979   President Machel gives Mozambican casuality figures in the conflict with Rhodesia as 1,338 dead, 1,538 wounded and 751 kidnapped. He estimates direct war damage at $50,000,000 and indirect damage due to lost trade, tourism and transit income, at $550,000,000.

23 Dec. 1979   Mozambique lifts sanctions against Rhodesia.

27 Dec. 1979   A government statement confirms the death of Gen. Josiah Tongogara, commander of Robert Mugabe's military wing of the Patriotic Front, ZANLA, in a car crash near Massinga, Inhambane, forty-four miles north of Maputo.

9 Jan. 1980   Zambia and Mozambique have sent military missions to Rhodesia to observe the implementation of the ceasefire by Patriotic Front troops, according to the British High Commission in Lusaka.

10 Jan. 1980   Tanzania is withdrawing its troops from Mozambique since Mozambique is no longer threatened by Rhodesia.

22 Jan. 1980   South Africa officially warns Mozambique that it will not hestiate to strike back if Mozambique continues to shelter guerrillas conducting murderous operations against South Africa. The government rejects the accusations as propaganda.

25 Jan. 1980   President Machel promises that seventy-one members of the Karanga tribe, detained in Mozambique jails for up to two years at Robert Mugabe's request, will be released. British officials are pressing for the matter to be resolved.

28 Jan. 1980   The ZANU 'dissidents' are flown to Salisbury from Beira. Included are prominent military and political leaders formerly opposed to Robert Mugabe's leadership on strategic and ideological grounds. Logistics are handled by the Commonwealth Monitoring Force.

19 Feb. 1980   South Africa warns Mozambique against harbouring 'terrorists', who are conducting acts of sabotage against South Africa from bases in Mozambique.

18 Mar. 1980   President Machel criticizes state enterprises, denounces excessive state involvement, announces that many small businesses will be returned to private hands and invites expatriates to return to Mozambique. To relieve the food crisis he announces the creation of 'green zones', agricultural areas outside the urban centre of Maputo.

20 Mar. 1980   President Machel dismisses M.A. dos Santos as Minister of Internal Trade, and J.B. Cosme as Minister of Public Works and Housing. Dr. H.F.B. Martins resigns as Minister of Health.

24 Mar. 1980   Lord Soames, Governor of Southern Rhodesia, visits Mozambique, and discusses the possibility of Mozambique becoming an adherent to the Lomé Convention and of aid to Mozambique from the European Development Fund.

3 Apr. 1980	President Machel dismisses M. dos Santos as Minister of Planning and Chairman of the National Planning Commission and J. Rebelo as Minister of Information. Both, leading FRELIMO ideologues, retain senior posts in the party hierarchy.
10 Apr. 1980	Mozambique and Bulgaria sign a defence cooperation agreement in Maputo, at the end of a week-long visit by the Bulgarian Defence Minister Mr. Dobrijurov.
13 Apr. 1980	Tanzania and Mozambique agree on a seven point programme to forge closer bilateral links.
May 1980	Mozambique accuses South Africa of supplying its armed opposition, RENAMO or Andrea Group - named after its late leader Andrea Matsangai.
May 1980	The national airline company Deta is dissolved and a new company Linhas Aéreas de Moçambique (LAM) created in its place.
May 1980	Three leading FRELIMO officials in Sofala Province are suspended for corruption.
13 May 1980	The RENAMO attack a dam near Mavuze and cut off power to Beira. An extensive Mozambique Army operation follows.
20 May 1980	F. Langa, a member of FRELIMO's Central Committee, commits suicide after being investigated for embezzlement.
23 May 1980	President Machel and Prime Minister Robert Mugabe of Zimbabwe, meet in Beira. An agreement is reached on joint operations between the two countries to halt RENAMO rebel activity.
24 May 1980	Mozambique is one of the African countries to have accepted invitations to attend the Moscow Olympics.
27 May 1980	A Mozambique delegation flies to Salisbury to work out detailed plans for joint operations with government officials and Zimbabwean army and intelligence heads, designed to combat anti-FRELIMO guerrillas operating on their borders.
27 May 1980	RENAMO denies in Lisbon that the movement is receiving assistance or supplies from South Africa.
30 May 1980	The national universities of Tanzania and Mozambique sign a two-year agreement covering the exchange of students, teachers, teaching materials and information.
16-18 June 1980	Over three days a new currency unit, the metical, named after the 'mithgal', an Arabian unit used in pre-colonial days, is introduced to replace the escudo.
10 July 1980	Mozambique states its forces have attacked the RENAMO main camp on Sitonga Mountain in West Manica Province.
4-9 Aug. 1980	President Machel pays a state visit to Zimbabwe. Six agreements, are signed covering information, trade, energy, banking and air and land transport.

29 Aug. 1980	The government makes an international appeal for food aid.

31 Aug. -
2 Sept. 1980   J. Chissano visits France for talks with President Giscard d'Estaing and French ministers on co-operation and the situation in Southern Africa. Plans are elaborated for financing by France's Central Economic Co-operation Fund and for food aid.

Mid-Sept. 1980   Richard Luce, British Under-Secretary of State for Foreign and Commonwealth Affairs, visits Mozambique and recommends adherence to the Lomé Convention as a means of facilitating British aid.

10-13 Sept.1980   President Machel pays an official visit to Bulgaria.

13-17 Sept.1980   President Machel visits Romania.

17-20 Sept.1980   President Machel visits East Germany.

21 Sept. -
3 Oct.1980   Railway line between Beira and Umtali closed following RENAMO attacks.

25 Sept. 1980   President Machel announces that for the first time the Mozambican Army is to have a formal officer corps identified by marks of rank. All officers will have to be full party members. FRELIMO will issue military medals.

25 Sept. 1980   Following a decision by FRELIMO's Permanent Political Committee President Machel is appointed to the rank of Field Marshal; A. Chipande, A. Guebuza and S.M. Mabote are appointed to the rank of Lieutenant-General and M. dos Santos, M. Matsinhe, J. Chissano and J. Veloso to the rank of Major-General.

18 Oct. 1980   President Machel meets the Zimbabwean Prime Minister at Quelimane to discuss security concerns.

20 Oct. 1980   Mozambique and Zimbabwe agree to conclude a security pact and to co-operate closely to prevent guerrilla activities in both countries.

23 Oct. 1980   M.F. da G. Machungo, Minister of Planning and Agriculture, announces that the creation of trade unions is to be postponed, because the workers organizations are too weak and disorganized.

17-23 Nov.1980   President Machel visits the Soviet Union. Discussion centres on the possibility of Mozambique joining the Council for Mutual Economic Assistance (CMEA or COMECON). Agreements aimed at promoting trade between the two countries are signed.

27-28 Nov.1980   The second Conference on Regional Economic Co-operation in Southern Africa is held in Maputo. Mozambique signs a three-year economic co-operation agreement with five Nordic countries (Sweden, Denmark, Norway, Finland and Iceland) reported to involve Nordic aid amounting to $66,000,000.

29 Nov. 1980   A guerrilla attack on the Cahora Bassa hydroelectric complex disrupts power supply to South Africa. RENAMO claims responsibility.

1 Dec. 1980   RENAMO attacks Espungabera village in the north of Gaza.

6 Dec. 1980	RENAMO claims responsibility for dynamiting power pylons and disrupting Cahora Bassa electricity supplies.

31 Dec. 1980	Under an amnesty, announced on this date, more than 600 soldiers implicated in the 'counter-revolutionary act' of 17-19 December 1975 are released.

10 Jan. 1981	Mozambique and Zimbabwe sign a defence and security agreement under which an attack by South Africa on either country will be taken as an assault on both. The agreement is 'all embracing' and allows both countries to deal with internal dissident activity.

16 Jan. 1981	AIM reports that eleven basic commodities are soon to be rationed.

16 Jan. 1981	The World Food Programme (WFP) renews its emergency food assistance to alleviate continuing food shortages, and FAO approves an emergency food aid grant.

30 Jan. 1981	General Constand Viljoen, Chief of the South African Defence Force announces an attack by a South African commando on the planning and control headquarters of the ANC in the Maputo suburb of Matola. Documents, weapons and 'sabotage equipment' are seized.

1 Feb. 1981	South Africa warns that, if necessary, further strikes against ANC bases in neighbouring countries will follow.

6 Feb. 1981	Lieutenant-General A. Guebuza, Armed Forces Political Commissar, tells a FRELIMO party meeting in Maputo that FRELIMO must increase its vigilance and claims South Africa has been building up large concentrations of troops and military equipment on the border with Mozambique.

8 Feb. 1981	The funeral of the twelve ANC members killed in South Africa's raid is addressed by M. Machungo, Minister of Planning and Agriculture, who pledges solidarity with the South African people and the ANC and by the ANC's President Oliver Tambo who calls the raid a good example of 'international terrorism' intended to impress President Reagan. Mozambique will continue to support the ANC.

14 Feb. 1981	The Times reports growing indicators that RENAMO is receiving backing from South Africa, arms and ammunition, food and military instruction.

14 Feb. 1981	President Machel declares that Mozambique remains 'solidly with the ANC, the legitimate representative of the South African people', and adds that FRELIMO and the ANC will fight shoulder to shoulder until apartheid falls.

14 Feb. 1981	Eight Army officers are paraded by President Machel at a mass rally in Maputo and are accused of treason and complicity with South Africa in the raid on the military base at Matola, where two of them were in command.

17 Feb. 1981	The Front Line States' summit meeting at Lusaka warns South Africa to stop training dissidents hostile to Mozambique's government.

19 Feb. 1981	Radio Lisbon states that the presence of Soviet warships in Mozambican waters on working visits is closely linked with the South African commando raid.

20 Feb. 1981	Members of FAM (Free Africa Movement) based in Malawi are brought to trial for crimes commited in Mozambique. Four are sentenced to death and twenty-seven other rebels receive long prison sentences for undergoing military training and recruiting new members.
23 Feb. 1981	The South African Prime Minister, P.W. Botha says Soviet threats will not prevent South Africa from attacking ANC bases in Mozambique.
4 Mar. 1981	Six Americans are ordered to leave Mozambique within forty-eight hours, for allegedly engaging in `espionage, subversion and interference in Mozambique's internal affairs'.
5 Mar. 1981	The Mozambican Security Ministry alleges a Central Intelligence Agency (CIA) spy network has been gathering information and has close links with the South African security services. Many arrests are made and four United States diplomats are expelled.
12 Mar. 1981	AIM reports that the Ministry of Security is holding two Americans in custody. The arrests are confirmed of businessmen A. Zimmerman and C. Mohrer, lecturer at Eduardo Mondlane University.
17 Mar. 1981	A South African corporal is killed in a border ambush incident at Ponta do Ouro.
20 Mar. 1981	The United States government announces the suspension of its entire food assistance to Mozambique in retaliation for the expulsion pending a complete review of bilateral relations.
23 Mar. 1981	J. Chissano begins a four-day visit to Lisbon, thereby resuming high-level contacts with Portugal.
2 Apr. 1981	Two RENAMO attacks on the garrison town of Espungabera are reported, with refugees fleeing into Zimbabwe.
5 Apr. 1981	Petrol and diesel fuel rationing is introduced.
10 Apr. 1981	Further sabotage on the Cahora Bassa supply line cuts the power supply to South Africa again.
13 Apr. 1981	The United States Chargé d'Affaires in Maputo announces that the two American nationals arrested on charges of spying have been released.
24 May 1981	The FRELIMO Central Committee has decided to create a national organization of teachers (ONP) with the principal objective of organizing, leading and uniting teachers in all subjects, by ensuring the correct application of the party programme in the field of education.
25 May 1981	Official talks in Maputo, with Portugal, result in the signature of three agreements and a protocol concerning economic, social and health co-operation between the two countries.
June 1981	RENAMO attacks communal villages.
12 June 1981	Violent fighting is reported in the Espungabera area with up to 3,000 RENAMO guerrillas said to be involved. More than 1,200 Mozambicans flee

into Zimbabwe.

25 June 1981	Lieutenant General Guebuza, during a visit to Great Britain, asserts that Mozambique has moved to the brink of a very serious and dangerous war with South Africa.
1 July 1981	Mozambique and Malawi raise their diplomatic relations to ambassador level following an agreement aimed at strengthening peace and co-operation in the region.
2 July 1981	The agreement for the supply of electricity to South Africa from the Cahora Bassa dam is suspended, following prolonged disruption of supplies.
5 July 1981	A communiqué announces that of the two men sentenced to death by the Military Revolutionary Tribunal, one, Enoque Cam is found guilty of being a South African agent and of supplying South African security forces with information on the location of ANC cadres in Mozambique.
8 July 1981	Mozambican Air Force pilot, Lieutenant A.F. Bomba, defects to South Africa in a MiG-17 and is granted political asylum. Arrangements are completed in late October for the return of the Soviet built plane to Mozambique.
13 July 1981	President Machel meets Zimbabwean Prime Minister, Robert Mugabe, at Umtali. It is reported that Zimbabwe is willing to commit several battalions to a border operation against RENAMO.
16 July 1981	M. Antonio, Governor of Manica Province, states that FRELIMO's newly created rural centres are becoming the focus of the struggle, with FRELIMO attempting to organize the local population into collectivized villages, while RENAMO tries to prevent this.
23 July 1981	A FRELIMO Central Committee member and former Lieutenant-Colonel in the Army General Staff in Maputo, F. Baptista, arrested as part of a CIA spy ring escapes from prison, together with Lieutenant-Colonel J. Dlakhama formerly head of the armoured cars division at the time of the South African raid on Matola.
13 Aug. 1981	500 former members of the Portuguese secret police are released from a re-education centre in Niassa Province.
20 Aug. 1981	Mozambique signs trade and two-year co-operation agreements with Sweden. The latter agreement includes a donation of 420,000,000 Kroner ($79m) for energy, agriculture, forestry, education and telecommunications.
25 Aug. 1981	The collectivization programme acquires a military dimension with the FRELIMO party often being assisted by the army and with force being used to move people into the new villages, contrary to official government policy.
29 Aug. 1981	RENAMO broadcasts its political programme on the 'Voice of Free Africa' radio station. Principal aims include the extinction of the communist system in Mozambique and the formation of a government of national reconciliation.
30 Aug. 1981	Power and water supplies to Beira are disrupted by guerrilla activity.
12 Sept. 1981	The Mozambican Defence Ministry accuses South Africa of violating

Mozambican air space more than forty times in the previous eighteen months.

27 Sept. 1981	Zimbabwe and Mozambique sign an extradition treaty, needed to counter destabilizing forces operating in the border area.
29 Sept. 1981	President Machel announces that seventy-six inmates from the Ruarua re-education camp in Cabo Delgado Province have been released bringing to over 1,200 the number of those recently released from re-education centres in Northern Mozambique. Those released are ordered to remain in Northern Mozambique and to become 'pioneers'.
21 Oct. 1981	A friendship agreement signed between Mozambique and Czechoslovakia establishes a framework for closer economic and political co-operation.
22 Oct. 1981	A new petroleum law provides for state control over oil production and exploration.
Late Oct.1981	Road and rail links between Beira and Umtali, Zimbabwe are broken and the oil pipeline between the two countries is damaged.
Early Nov.1981	Cahora Bassa power lines are repaired and electricity supplies recommence.
5 Nov. 1981	President Machel extends his two-year campaign against incompetence and corruption in all government departments by ordering a purge of the armed forces, police and militia.
20 Nov. 1981	Lieutenant-General Mabote meets a Zimbabwean delegation at Chimoio to study and co-ordinate the defence of the common border area and the suppression of RENAMO, who raid into Zimbabwe and disrupt Zimbabwean transport routes.
24 Nov. 1981	President Eanes of Portugal pays a five-day state visit to Mozambique.
Early Dec.1981	Traffic links to Zimbabwe are restored.
5 Dec. 1981	A joint communiqué issued by Presidents Machel and Eanes refers to an agreement on military co-operation, but gives no specific details.
7 Dec. 1981	The Times reports that the Deputy Chief of Staff of the Portuguese Armed Forces, General Lopes Alves has remained in Mozambique to make detailed arrangements for Portuguese aid in protecting the country from South African attacks. These include officer training and counter-insurgency training courses.
7 Dec. 1981	AIM reports that Mozambican forces capture a major RENAMO base in Manica Province, some twelve miles from the Zimbabwean border. Documentary evidence is said to reveal South African involvement in supplies and in tactical planning.
17 Dec. 1981	RENAMO guerrillas abduct a British ecologist, a Chilean citizen together with a number of workers and students in the Gorongosa wildlife reserve.
19 Dec. 1981	Signs cooperation agreement with France.
21 Dec. 1981	A RENAMO spokesman claims that guerrillas have sabotaged the Maputo to

Zimbabwe railway line, blown up four electricity pylons and seized three villages in Tete, Manica and Sofala provinces.

23 Dec. 1981   President Machel and Prime Minister Robert Mugabe of Zimbabwe sign a friendship agreement. During Robert Mugabe's first state visit to Mozambique discussions centred on growing military threats from South Africa and the need for a common counter-strategy.

14 Feb. 1982   RENAMO guerrillas attack and capture the garrison town of Mabalane, partly occupied by Tanzanian soldiers. The action is in response to talks on military co-operation between Tanzania and Mozambique.

15 Feb. 1982   Following an agreement to strengthen military and economic co-operation between Mozambique and Tanzania a detachment of Tanzanian troops will help train government troops and replace a detachment of Soviet instructors.

Early Mar.1982   The Western press reports that RENAMO activities affect six of Mozambique's ten provinces and that larger bands of guerrillas are attacking towns instead of villages, with alleged increase in brutality against FRELIMO supporters.

4 Mar. 1982   President Machel appoints military commanders for all Mozambique's provinces, to strengthen the role of the army in territorial defence, to reinforce the presence of the FRELIMO party, to promote collective agriculture and maintain security. All are veterans of the independence war.

7 Mar. 1982   A joint communiqué is issued by the Front Line States, following a two day meeting in Maputo outlining joint action to counter the undeclared war situation provoked by South Africa. They pledge to step up their support for the ANC in an intensification of the armed struggle.

12 Mar. 1982   The government releases new evidence indicating South African support for RENAMO. Four meetings have been held between RENAMO and South African officials at Zoabostad, northern Transvaal. The role of linkman has been taken over by Orlando Christina, former Portuguese secret police agent.

1-5 Apr. 1982   President Machel visits Gaza Province. J. Pelembe is suspended from both his posts as provincial governor and first party secretary in the province. Dr. J.O. Monteiro takes over from him.

18-19 Mar.1982   A national FRELIMO conference is held in Maputo.

17-19 Apr.1982   President Rene of Seychelles and President Machel issue a joint communiqué calling for African countries to sign a convention against mercenaries. Links between Mozambique and the Seychelles are to be strengthened.

27 Apr. 1982   A protocol is signed in Lisbon covering technical and military cooperation, providing for training of Mozambican military personnel in Portuguese military colleges and allows for the possibility of Portuguese military instructors working in Mozambique.

5 May 1982   The FRELIMO party and Tanzania's Chama Cha Mapinduzi sign a cooperation agreement. Closer ties are reaffirmed at all levels in relations of friendship and solidarity.

21 May 1982	Zimbabwe reports that the Beira oil pipeline has been sabotaged for the second time in seven months.
24 May 1982	The British Foreign Office announce the release of a British national captured by RENAMO on 17 December 1981 at Chitengo, Gorongosa. The prisoner, John Barlison, a zoologist gives a full account of his observations of the nature and strength of RENAMO.
28 May 1982	At the end of a four day visit to Cuba by President Machel a joint communiqué issued emphasizes `close and unshakeable friendship' and increased cooperation between FRELIMO and the Cuban Communist Party.
31 May 1982	The government launches a counter-offensive against RENAMO bases in Manica Province, intended to clear Mozambique's main transport links to Zimbabwe. RENAMO claim that it is aided by Zimbabwean and Tanzanian troops.
2 June 1982	General Alexes Yepishev, head of the main political directorate of the Soviet Army and Navy, and leader of a senior Soviet military delegation visiting Mozambique, declares that the Soviet Union will increase its military cooperation with and support to Mozambique.
7 June 1982	Jorge M. da Costa, a senior official in the Mozambique Security Ministry defects to South Africa. He claims Soviet influence in Mozambique is increasing. Finance Director in the President's Office Zulficar has also defected. His whereabouts are not disclosed.
8 June 1982	Mozambique's Ambassador to Portugal, Joao Ataide, defects.
14 June 1982	The government announces it will issue identity cards to all Maputo's residents.
Mid June 1982	Because of security problems some Malawi-Zimbabwe road traffic is being re-routed through Zambia, adding nearly 700 miles to the journey.
23 June 1982	President Machel announces that a late-night curfew is to be imposed, thousands of guns are to be distributed to residents of Maputo and increased protection will be provided for areas with large numbers of diplomatic and foreign workers.
27-30 June	The Portuguese Prime Minister, Sr Pinto Balsemiao visits Mozambique. Several cooperation agreements are signed.
12 July 1982	Following da Costa's defection a number of senior officials in the Security Ministry are placed in preventive detention.
26 July 1982	An Italian embassy spokesman in Maputo reports that Maimaalane Mission in northern Inhambane province has been raided and an Italian priest kidnapped.
29 July 1982	AIM alleges that South Africa has carried out thirty-three violations of Mozambique air space, mainly over Gaza Province, during the first seven months of 1982.
5 Aug. 1982	Mozambique is reported to have received a dollar loan from the EEC of

nearly $10,000,000, valued at 298,000,000 meticals.

7-9 Aug. 1982   During President Machel's visit to Tripoli for a meeting of the OAU, agreements are signed with Libya on friendship and cooperation, economic and technical cooperation and military co-operation.

10 Aug. 1982   RENAMO attacks a train in north-western Mozambique, on the line linking Beira with Malawi.

14 Aug. 1982   The Cahora Bassa power line is cut, and the power supply to South African grid disrupted. ESCOM (The South African Electricity Supply Commission) confirm this.

18 Aug. 1982   Ruth First is killed by a parcel bomb, opened in her office at Eduardo Mondlane University, Maputo.

19 Aug. 1982   The government claims it has destroyed seven RENAMO guerrilla bases.

20 Aug. 1982   South African Defence Minister, General Magnus Malan, warns that South Africa may act to destroy SAM-3 and SAM-6 missiles he claims are deployed along the border with South Africa.

23 Aug. 1982   RENAMO member of executive council, M.G. Mahluza, claims that RENAMO controls Gaza, Imhambane, Manica and Sofala provinces and asserts that RENAMO's fighting strength is some 12,000 well armed men.

25-27 Aug.1982   The Indian Prime Minister Mrs. Indira Gandhi pays an official visit to Mozambique. Several accords on technical co-operation are signed. President Machel and Mrs. Gandhi call for the demilitarization of the Indian Ocean.

Sept. 1982   Senior government officials claim that a 300-strong RENAMO force, operating from at least four bases in southern Malawi have launched a major offensive into Zambezia Province. Western press reports also refer to a RENAMO offensive moving eastwards from Malawi from August onwards.

15 Sept. 1982   The People's Assembly has decided that a general election will be held between July and September 1983.

17 Sept. 1982   Five foreign missionaries are captured by RENAMO from their mission in Southern Mozambique.

25 Sept. 1982   The government claims that forty-two RENAMO bases have been captured since the beginning of the year.

30 Sept. 1982   The Mozambican Military Tribunal announces sentences of from six to eight years for twenty 'rebels' returned by Zimbabwe. Two other RENAMO men captured taking wounded RENAMO fighters back to base near Mabote are sentenced to death by firing squad.

4 Oct. 1982   Lisbon radio reports a government decision to order an inquiry into RENAMO activities in Portugal.

7 Oct. 1982   FRELIMO instructs the party secretariat to revitalize party cells.

11 Oct. 1982   The Malawi High Commissioner in Zimbabwe, M.A. Banda, states that his

government does not support the use of its territory by RENAMO and is working closely with Mozambique to eliminate sources of conflict between the two countries.

11 Oct. 1982   A pumping station on the Beira-Zimbabwe fuel pipeline is destroyed in a RENAMO attack. Landlocked Zimbabwe and Malawi are again reliant on South African ports for their foreign trade.

18 Oct. 1982   Zimbabwean Security and Transport Ministers meet their Mozambican counterparts in Beira to discuss economic, security and defence matters.

20 Oct. 1982   President Machel and President Kaunda of Zambia, accompanied by senior foreign policy, security and transport officials, discuss the regional dimension of rebel attacks and South Africa's destabilization strategy, in Quelimane. They decide to intensify political and economic co-operation, 'which implies also military co-operation'.

27 Oct. 1982   President Banda meets Major-General J. Chissano. Shortly afterwards RENAMO facilities in Malawi are apparently closed.

Nov. 1982   RENAMO is active in seven of Mozambique's eleven provinces. Three provinces, Manica, Sofala and Inhambane are considered unsafe outside the major towns.

2 Nov. 1982   Government forces capture a major guerrilla base about thirty miles from the Malawi border.

26 Nov. 1982   South African intelligence sources report 600 Zimbabwean soldiers deployed to protect the Beira to Mutare (Umtali) oil pipeline.

Dec. 1982   Western press report that several hundred guerrillas have crossed into Mozambique from the Kruger National Park, South Africa, but have suffered serious reverses.

3 Dec. 1982   'Pik' Botha warns that South Africa will not tolerate the introduction of Cuban troops and will not hesitate to launch counter-measures against Mozambique, if it allows nationalist guerrillas to operate against South Africa from its territory.

8-9 Dec. 1982   In an attack on Beira RENAMO guerrillas destroy quantities of oil and damage installations. It is confirmed that over twenty-five tanks are destroyed, the feeder system of pipes extensively damaged and fuel worth up to $12,000,000 (much of which was destined for Zimbabwe) is lost.

9 Dec. 1982   RENAMO spokesman in Lisbon claims the Beira oil attack is a warning to Zimbabwe not to assist Mozambique in its anti-RENAMO campaign. Further attacks on economic targets important to Zimbabwe may follow, as may military attacks against Zimbabwe itself.

11 Dec. 1982   The raid is followed by the arrest of D. Hamilton, British businessman and managing director of Manica Freight Services, together with several of his staff. He is accused of complicity in the raid.

14-17 Dec.1982 President Machel meets religious leaders - Catholic, Protestant, Muslim and Hindu, held to clarify points of dispute between church and state. The Roman

Catholics request compensation for their nationalized schools and hospitals. This is refused and a bitter attack is launched by Machel on the Catholic hierarchy.

17 Dec. 1982   The South African Foreign Minister, `Pik' Botha, and the South African Director-General of Foreign Affairs, Hans van Dalsen, meet the Mozambique Minister of Agriculture, Sergio Vieria and Major-General Veloso at the border town of Komatipoort. Talks are directed towards lessening tensions and removing the threat of generalized war.

12 Jan. 1983   The government launches an international appeal for emergency food aid for the victims of drought.

17 Jan. 1983   Four men accused of being RENAMO insurgents are summarily executed at a public meeting in Macia, seventy-five miles north of Maputo, in the presence of Foreign Minister, J. Chissano and Gen. S. Mabote who ordered the execution.

28 Jan. 1983   A thirty percent shortfall in sugar production deals a new blow to Mozambique's hard-pressed economy.

2 Feb. 1983   RENAMO carries out ambushes in central Mozambique on this date and on 7 February.

13 Feb. 1983   Iran and Mozambique agree to establish diplomatic relations and to exchange ambassadors.

17 Feb. 1983   North Korean Deputy Foreign Minister, K.C. Pong affirms his country's committment to increased political, military and economic support for Mozambique in the face of growing tension in southern Africa.

18 Feb. 1983   Representatives of Mozambique, South Africa and Swaziland sign an agreement in Pretoria establishing a tripartite permanent technical committee to ensure the most beneficial utilization of their common rivers.

22 Feb. 1983   D. Hamilton is sentenced to twenty years' imprisonment and five Mozambicans are sentenced to death for involvement in acts of sabotage and terrorism organized by RENAMO.

3-8 Mar. 1983   The first assembly of military and political cadres of RENAMO is held in Geneva. A six-man Cabinet and government in exile is formed. Afonso Dlakama is reaffirmed as Commander-in-Chief and leader of the movement.

16-18 Mar.1983 The eleventh session of FRELIMO's Central Committee notes with pleasure the improvement of relations with a number of Western countries.

17 Mar. 1983   The permanent commission of the People's Assembly issues a new law on crimes against the security of the people and of the people's state. It introduces more severe penalties, including the death penalty, for crimes seriously affecting the economic and political situation in the country.

31 Mar. 1983   The permanent commission of the People's Assembly passes a law reintroducing public flogging.

9 Apr. 1983   The FRELIMO government reject international appeals for clemency and

executes six men in public in Maputo.

17 Apr. 1983   Orlando Christina is killed in a `shooting incident' near Pretoria.

26-30 Apr.1983 The fourth Congress of FRELIMO is held in Maputo, its agenda as outlined by the FRELIMO National Conference in March 1982. Notable topics are the level of agricultural production, the decentralizatin of decision making, the expansion in size of the Central Committee and a considerable degree of self-criticism.

5 May 1983   South Africa and Mozambique hold talks at ministerial level at which the activities of RENAMO and of the ANC are discussed.

21 May 1983   Government portfolios are reallocated.

22 May 1983   In a seven hour speech to a rally in Independence Square, Maputo, President Machel describes the vital roles of the four key Ministries, Defence, Interior, Security and Justice, in maintaining discipline, and in the functioning of government.

23 May 1983   The South African Air Force attacks six alleged ANC targets in Maputo suburbs, in retaliation for an ANC car bomb attack on the air force headquarters in Pretoria.

28 May 1983   Appointments announced in the second stage of a government reshuffle reflects both increasing security problems and recent criticims of the government's handling of the economy. Key moves include President Machel's own assumption of overall control of defence, the appointment of three new ministers, four reassignments, five newly created deputy ministers and a new ministry. Noticeable trends are towards decentralization and the appointment of people with relevant professional qualifications.

15 June 1983   Internal Trade Minister, da Silva, makes an international appeal for emergency food aid, to offset the effects of drought which has cut production in six of Mozambique's ten provinces by as much as 80 percent.

18-19 June 1983 A joint statement by the Ministries of Defence, Interior, Justice and Security orders the unemployed to leave the cities by the end of the month, after which stringent measures will be taken and a rigid pass system enforced.

19 June 1983   President Machel admits, in a speech at Quelimane, that much of Zambezia Province is affected by RENAMO guerrilla offensives.

1 Aug. 1983   In a statement after a two-day meeting in Kadoma, Zimbabwe the Information Ministers of the six Front Line States, including Mozambique, decrees that foreign journalists based in South Africa will be barred from working in any of these countries. The new information strategy will be applied immediately to counter South African propaganda and a distorted view of Southern Africa.

8 Aug. 1983   President Machel announces the appointment of eight new army commanders, to intensify operations against RENAMO in Zambezia Province.

21 Aug. 1983   RENAMO kills two Soviet mining technicians and kidnaps twenty-four others, in a dawn raid on Morrua mine, Zambezia Province. The operation appears designed to highlight the Russian presence in Mozambique.

31 Aug. 1983	Amnesty International's report alleges the government is contravening fundamental human rights in its arbitrary use of the death penalty.
2-3 Sept.1983	Cape Verde's President A.M. Pereira visits Mozambique for discussions with President Machel on Southern Africa and on cooperation between the five Portuguese-speaking African countries.
28 Sept. 1983	The army claims to have destroyed RENAMO's largest Inhambane provincial base at Tomé.
3 Oct. 1983	President Machel begins a European tour which will include visits to Belgium, the Netherlands, Portugal, Yugoslavia, France and Great Britain. The reported intentions are to persuade West European countries to invest in Mozambique and to provide more political support.
6 Oct. 1983	Formal negotiations are opened at a ministerial level conference in Luxembourg on the renewal of the Lomé Convention. Mozambique sends government representatives.
9 Oct. 1983	President Machel states that Mozambique's relations with the Soviet bloc remain excellent and are based upon mutual respect and common objectives.
17 Oct. 1983	South African forces destroy an ANC office in a residential block in Maputo, one week after a series of explosions in Warmbaths, Transvaal attributed to the ANC.
18 Oct. 1983	South Africa's attack on the ANC in Maputo is widely condemned by the United Nations Secretary General, by the United Nations Special Committee against Apartheid, by the ANC and the OAU, by the Front Line States and Ethiopia, Egypt and Algeria.
28 Oct. 1983	RENAMO sabotage the Cahora Bassa power lines.
31 Oct. - 3 Nov.1983	The Founding Conference of the Organisation of Mozambican Workers (OTM) is held in Maputo. The trade union is headed by A. Macamo, director of Production Councils since its inception. The Organization will be closely controlled by FRELIMO.
9 Nov. 1983	It is reported that the United States Ambassador to Mozambique, P.J. de Vos, has presented his credentials to President Machel, and, in a rare American tribute to Mozambique's leader, praised his outstanding role as a statesman.
7-9 Dec. 1983	Directors of national news agencies from the six Front Line States, including Mozambique, meet in Luanda. The media heads call for reporting to be covered by journalists based in their own states, rather than in South Africa and for it to stress opposition to the 'Pretoria regime'. Facilities should be offered to the ANC.
18-19 Dec.1983	Mozambique attends the fourth summit of the Heads of State of the five Portuguese-speaking African countries, in Bissau. Discussion focusses on conflicts in Southern Africa and South Africa is condemned for its aggression against countries in the region, notably Angola and Mozambique.
20 Dec. 1983	South Africa's 'Pik' Botha accompanied by L. Le Grange, Minister of Law and Order and General Magnus Malan, Defence Minister, meet a

Mozambican delegation led by Major-General Veloso in Mbabane, Swaziland. No details are released, but topics discussed are said to include security and the ending of hostilities.

27 Dec. 1983　Lieutenant-General S.M. Mabote, Chief of General Staff claims that some 3,000 guerrillas have been captured in military offensives since March 1983.

15 Jan. 1984　President Machel announces a reorganization of FRELIMO's defence and military responsibilities. He appoints Colonel S. Viera as Deputy Defence Minister, Major-General A. Panguene as Deputy Defence Minister and Armed Forces Political Commissar, Major-General A.H. Thoi as Commander of the Air Force. New military commanders are appointed for Maputo and Sofala provinces.

16 Jan. 1984　A meeting is held in Pretoria between delegations from Mozambique and South Africa to consider measures necessary to ensure that neither state should serve as 'a springboard for aggression and violent actions against the other'. Another three working groups, concentrating on economic matters, meet in Maputo.

25 Jan. 1984　RENAMO releases twelve Soviet technicians captured on 21 August 1983. Eight are said to have been previously rescued by government troops, and two to have died.

14 Feb. 1984　Mozambican and South African delegates meet Portuguese officials in Lisbon to discuss the Cahora Bassa complex and financial and security problems relating to it.

20 Feb. 1984　After a meeting between Major-General Veloso and R.F. 'Pik' Botha a joint statement announces that Mozambique and South Africa have agreed on the central principles concerning security arrangements and that they intend to enter into a formal agreement.

2 Mar. 1984　At a further meeting in Cape Town Mozambique and South Africa reach agreement on the principal features of a military security pact to prevent cross-border aggression, declare that neither country will serve as a base for acts of violence or aggression against the other, and agree to establish a joint security commission to monitor the pact.

16 Mar. 1984　President Samora Machel of Mozambique and the South African Prime Minister, P.W. Botha, sign on the border between the two countries, a non-aggression and good-neighbourliness pact, to be known as the Nkomati Accord. Both countries agree not to service as a base for acts of violence or aggression against the other. Provision is made for enforcement.

18 Mar. 1984　FRELIMO soldiers are reported to have been killed by guerrillas while escorting a convoy in Tete province. Zimbabwe may send troops to defend the main road through Tete.

21 Mar. 1984　The ANC's President, Oliver Tambo, says in London that the clause in the Nkomati Accord denying the ANC transit facilities through Mozambique was a temporary problem which would be overcome.

24 Mar. 1984　The government's pledge to regulate the ANC in Mozambique is realized when dozens of ANC houses are searched in Maputo.

24 Mar. 1984	Maputo radio claims that about seventy guerrillas have surrendered to government forces.
26 Mar. 1984	The Mozambican-South African Joint Security Commission holds its first meeting in Maputo. Heads of neighbourhood councils are instructed to compile lists of ANC members living in their areas.
30-31 Mar.1984	Clashes take place in Inhambane province between government forces and RENAMO guerrillas.
4 Apr. 1984	A FAO report indicates that death due to starvation has reached an extraordinary magnitude in Mozambique. Between 40,000 and 100,000 people are believed to have died as a result of prolonged drought.
5 Apr. 1984	ANC headquarters in Lusaka confirm that all resident ANC personnel are to leave Mozambique, with the exception of a ten-member diplomatic mission, fifteen teachers or technicians employed by the government, and Mr. Joe Slovo.
9 Apr. 1984	A passenger train forty-five miles north of Maputo is attacked by RENAMO.
10 Apr. 1984	Successful RENAMO attacks on Maputo electricity and water supplies are reported.
14 Apr. 1984	Twenty-five ANC members leave Maputo by air.
27 Apr. 1984	A convoy of lorries transporting food to Zimbabwe is attacked by RENAMO on the main Tete road.
27-28 Apr.1984	Mozambique hosts a Summit Meeting of the Heads of State of the five Lusophone African countries in Maputo. President Machel is praised for his political courage in concluding the Nkomati Accord.
29 Apr. 1984	Six leaders of the Front Line States end a one-day Summit in Arusha, Tanzania, by declaring support and understanding for the recent peace accord between Mozambique and South Africa.
2 May 1984	Mozambique, Portugal and South Africa sign a new agreement in Cape Town on the supply of electric power to South Africa from the Cahora Bassa hydroelectric dam. New tariffs are negotiated, and a specific provision for safeguarding the power lines is drawn up.
25 May 1984	The Joint Commission set up to monitor the Nkomati Accord meets in Pretoria. South Africa reaffirms its committment to the non-aggression pact. Mozambique, for its part, has expelled 800 members of the ANC.
Early June 1984	The government announces an amnesty for all surrendering 'bandits' - RENAMO guerrillas - and pledges assistance towards reintegration into civilian life.
12 June 1984	The United States announces that a Congressional ban on direct economic assistance to Mozambique has been lifted. Financial assistance will become available for development projects. For emergency relief aid up to $500,000 will be available in 1984 and up to $30,000,000 in 1985.

16 June 1984	Changes in the Interior and Security Ministries are the main focus of the government reshuffle completed by President Machel.
1 July 1984	South African Foreign Minister, 'Pik' Botha meets President Machel in Maputo for talks concentrated on continuing RENAMO activities which have virtually isolated Maputo from the rest of the country.
3 July 1984	Mozambican authorities announce the destruction of ninety-three RENAMO bases, the deaths of 1,200 guerrillas and the capture of 340 others.
12 July 1984	Signs agreement with the Netherlands on technical co-operation.
17 July 1984	President Machel begins a five-day visit to China. Arrangements are made for a Chinese soft loan to the value of $13,000,000 repayable over ten years, and a donation of consumer goods worth $2,000,000.
Aug. 1984	President Machel announces a major military offensive in Zambezia Province, led by eight veteran military commanders.
Aug. 1984	The main RENAMO base at Tomé, northern Inhambane, is overrun by government forces.
5-7 Aug. 1984	At the meeting of Foreign Affairs Ministers of the five Lusophone African countries in Bissau the ministers decide to combine their efforts to neutralize the actions of the 'armed forces' destabilizing Angola and Mozambique.
6 Aug. 1984	An Italian missionary priest and Mozambican workers are killed by RENAMO near their mission at Quelimane, Zambezia Province.
10 Aug. 1984	Swaziland announces that a security agreement has been signed with Mozambique with the intention of preventing border clashes.
17 Aug. 1984	At a meeting with the South African Foreign Minister, R.F. 'Pik' Botha in Maputo, the government presents detailed evidence of violations of the Nkomati Accord by South Africa, including continuing support for RENAMO.
20 Aug. 1984	RENAMO states it will enter Maputo if no agreement is reached by October. Its demands include a constitutional change ending one party rule, dissolution of the People's Assembly, a government of national reconciliation and RENAMO leadership of the government and of the armed forces.
31 Aug. 1984	The Portuguese Prime Minister, Dr. Mario Soares, begins a four-day official visit to Mozambique.
3 Sept. 1984	Twelve Portuguese nationals, detained in Mozambique without charges being brought, are released, seven from Beira, four from Maputo, and one from Quelimane.
6 Sept. 1984	A new investment code, designed to encourage foreign investment, comes into force.
8 Sept. 1984	In a RENAMO attack on a sugar refinery in Zambezia Province a member of FRELIMO's Central Committee, Z. Tomas, is killed.

9-14 Sept.1984   Major-General Veloso pays an official visit to Great Britain to discuss aid
                        and debt rescheduling.

12 Sept. 1984   Two Italian workers on a hydroelectric scheme near Moamba are kidnapped
                        and killed, allegedly because they were repairing power lines.

24 Sept. 1984   Membership of the IMF and World Bank is ratified in Washington, with a
                        quota of 61,000,000 special drawing rights.

28 Sept. 1984   Talks are held in Pretoria between Mozambique and South Africa as the
                        Nkomati Accord seems threatened by increased RENAMO activity.

29 Sept. 1984   Two Portuguese technicians are kidnapped about thirty miles north of
                        Maputo and are later killed.

3 Oct. 1984   South African Minister of Foreign Affairs, R.F. `Pik' Botha, announces in
                       the Pretoria Declaration that RENAMO and the Mozambique government
                       have agreed in principle to end their conflict and to work for peace, that an
                       eventual ceasefire will be monitored by South African troops and that peace
                       negotiations will continue. Reactions to the announcement are conflicting.

5 Oct. 1984   The South African based hotel group, Sun International, explores
                       Mozambique's tourist prospects. This follows meetings between Sol
                       Kerzner and Mozambique's Tourism Secretary, A. Materrula.

19-23 Oct.1984   President Machel makes his first official visit to Malawi accompanied by
                       General Mabote and the governors of Niassa, Zambezia and Tete provinces
                       bordering Malawi, in an attempt to cut off Malawi support for RENAMO.
                       The defence and security forces of both countries agree to work together to
                       ensure peace along the 1,400 km border.

30 Oct. 1984   South African Foreign Minister `Pik' Botha concludes talks in Pretoria
                       with delegations from the Mozambique government and from RENAMO,
                       designed to bring about a ceasefire.

Nov. 1984   Mauritius establishes diplomatic relations with Mozambique.

2 Nov 1984   RENAMO announces it is withdrawing from the tripartite talks. Its
                       spokesman, Jorge Correia accuses the government of not negotiating in
                       good faith, and South Africa of being an `unconditional ally' of the
                       Mozambique government. It has instead promised a major guerrilla
                       offensive deploying 21,000 fighters in all ten provinces.

6-11 Nov. 1984   The Extra-ordinary Conference of the Mozambican Women's Organization
                       is held in Maputo. Its role in the building of socialism is defined and
                       resolutions on gender issues are taken. President Machel plays a dominant
                       role.

6 Dec. 1984   In a RENAMO attack on an agricultural complex in Niassa Province, seven
                       East German technicians, one Yugoslav and five Mozambicans, are killed.

Late Dec. 1984   Beira is reportedly without electricity for one week.

20-21 Dec. 1984   Angola's President dos Santos visits Mozambique where discussions with
                       President   Machel   covering   the   activities   of   South   African

supported guerrillas and other security concerns are held. Mutual support and solidarity is declared.

25 Dec. 1984   President Machel accuses South Africa of continuing to support RENAMO and of equipping and supplying them in violation of Article 3 of the Nkomati Accord. South Africa claims to have complied with the letter and spirit of the Accord.

5 Jan. 1985   In RENAMO attacks on two buses in an area north of Maputo, twenty-seven people are killed.

13 Jan. 1985   Mr. Kafe, Foreign Minister of the Comoros, denies reports that his country has formed a link in an arms supply chain from the Middle East to RENAMO.

13 Jan. 1985   Two British citizens travelling by road to Maputo are murdered by RENAMO guerrillas, thought to have been operating from South African soil. The South African President, P.W. Botha, condemns this in the strongest of terms.

18 Jan. 1985   Agreement is reached on military aid from the United States. America will initially spend about $100,000 a year training Mozambican officers in the United States. In the second phase, to cost possibly $1m a year, non-lethal military equipment will be supplied.

Late Jan. 1985 All foreign aid workers are advised to return to five regional centres and to cease working in remote areas. The government has declared it can no longer guarantee the safety of foreigners.

22 Jan. 1985   A member of FRELIMO's Central Committee, A. Ntaula, is murdered by RENAMO in Niassa Province.

31 Jan. 1985   South Africa remains committed to helping to bring the civil war in Mozambique to an end but is frustrated by the `unreasonable' demands from RENAMO. The Movement believes it is on the point of winning the war, according to South African Foreign Minister `Pik' Botha.

6 Feb. 1985   President Kaunda flies to Maputo for one-day talks with President Machel. The discussion focusses on South Africa's non-fulfilment of Nkomati.

15 Feb. 1985   At the end of the fifth Summit Meeting of the five Lusophone countries, the Sao Tomé Declaration is issued. The communiqué charges South Africa with violations of the Nkomati Accord and calls on all African countries to aid Mozambique.

5 Mar. 1985   President Machel flies to Dar es Salaam for a day of talks with President Nyerere.

14 Mar. 1985   The Joint Security Commission meets in Maputo. Both South Africa and Mozambique express concern over the increase in violence in Mozambique.

16 Mar. 1985   South African Foreign Minister, `Pik' Botha, presents details of investigations into South African Defence Force (SADF) connections with RENAMO and details of sources of financial support for RENAMO from various European and Latin American countries.

20 Mar. 1985   In an attempt to salvage the Nkomati Accord, talks take place between President Machel and `Pik' Botha. Both sides reaffirm their commitment to the Accord.

28 Mar. 1985   South Africa declares that it is now seeking ways of cooperating with the FRELIMO government to eliminate the RENAMO threat, including working with the international community to block RENAMO supplies.

14 Apr. 1985   A South African delegation led by Foreign Minister `Pik' Botha, and Defence Minister, General Magnus Malan hold talks in Maputo with representatives of the Mozambique government, on the eve of the first anniversary of the Nkomati Accord. They discuss ways to end the increased violence in Mozambique.

22-24 Apr. 1985   President Pinto da Costa of Sao Tomé and Príncipe pays an official visit to Mozambique and holds discussions on the Southern African situation.

Late Apr. 1985   RENAMO claims to possess a number of Soviet-built Sam-7 ground-to-air missiles and to have shot down three government planes.

28 Apr. 1985   As part of a `final offensive' against the capital, RENAMO damages a railway bridge linking Maputo with South Africa and obstructs coal delivery to its power station.

28 Apr. -   The President of Portugal, General A.R. Eanes, pays a private visit to
1 May 1985   Mozambique. Military cooperation is discussed. Portugal agrees to train Mozambican troops.

May 1985   RENAMO incursions into Maputo begin, and continue sporadically for about ten months. Factories are attacked, shops looted and people kidnapped.

1 May 1985   A joint operational centre on the Lebombo-Ressano Garcia border post, permanently staffed by government officials of both countries is to begin functioning. To be named the Nkomati Operational Centre it will straddle the border a short distance from the site of the signing of the Nkomati Accord.

2 May 1985   The International Institute of Strategic Studies, in a report issued in London, states that RENAMO attacks have increased in number and intensity since the signing of the Accord in March 1984 and attributes this to South Africa's decision to provide RENAMO with a massive supply drop around the time of the signing and to the entry of more than 1,500 armed and trained personnel into Mozambique.

30 May 1985   RENAMO demands direct talks with Portugal over the release of four recently captured Portuguese citizens.

12 June 1985   President Machel, accompanied by Defence Minister Lieutenant-General A.J. Chipande and Chief of General Staff Lieutenant-General S.M. Mabote, meets Robert Mugabe in Harare, Zimbabwe. As a consequence, Zimbabwean troops, estimated at 7,000-10,000 are deployed in joint operations with the Mozambique Army against RENAMO from early July.

24 June 1985   RENAMO ambushes a passenger bus near Maluane, c. fifty km. north of Maputo, kill twenty-four people, abduct twenty, leaving eight wounded.

29 June 1985	RENAMO repeats their bus ambush. Sixty-four people are killed in the two incidents.
2 July 1985	In response to a request from President Machel, Great Britain is to provide training for up to 500 Mozambican troops under a 500,000 Pound sterling military aid programme. The training, to take place in Zimbabwe, is to begin in January 1986.
2 Aug. 1985	The British Embassy in Maputo reports that the two foreign workers abducted by RENAMO at Luabo, Zambezia Province have been identified and the Embassy is requesting the help of Mozambique in securing their release. RENAMO however will only negotiate directly with the governments of Britain and of Ireland.
8 Aug. 1985	A further fifteen people die in another RENAMO ambush.
13 Aug. 1985	The Beira-Mutare oil pipe-line is damaged by rebel action. Zimbabwean troops are to carry out repairs.
28 Aug. 1985	A major Zimbabwean-Mozambican joint offensive succeeds in capturing RENAMO's base, Casa Banana at Gorongosa, Sofala Province.
Sept. 1985	A second front is opened up against RENAMO in Maputo Province.
15 Sept. 1985	A five-hour meeting of the Heads of State of the Front Line States takes place in Maputo hosted by President Machel. The final communiqué includes a tribute to the cooperation between Zimbabwe and Mozambique in countering the activities of RENAMO.
16 Sept. 1985	Documentary evidence of continued South African support for RENAMO, obtained from the captured `Casa Banana' base, is presented by President Machel to `Pik' Botha in Maputo.
17-24 Sept. 1985	President Machel pays his first visit to the United States, holding talks with President Reagan on 19 September 1985. Discussions focus on matters relating to Mozambique's economic development.
19 Sept. 1985	South Africa concedes that there have been `technical' violations of the Nkomati Accord, but counter-claims that Mozambique is continuing to support the ANC.
25 Sept. 1985	A military arsenal explodes in Maputo, possibly by accident.
27 Sept. 1985	President Machel holds talks in London with the British Prime Minister, Margaret Thatcher.
30 Sept. 1985	The contents of the Gorongosa documents are made public at a press conference held by Security Minister Sergio Vieira in Maputo.
9 Oct. 1985	Chief of South Africa's Armed Forces, General Constand Viljoen, admits that the South African military has on occasions violated the Nkomati Accord and has acted without the authority of the Pretoria government.
17 Oct. 1985	It is reported that the Joint Security Commission has been suspended at President Machel's request. However, high-level contacts between South

Africa and Mozambique covering security matters and bilateral relations continue.

22 Oct. 1985   South Africa's Foreign Minister and his Deputy meet Mozambique's Minister of Security and President Machel's Security Adviser at Komatipoort in an effort to restore co-operation.

Nov. 1985   Foreign Minister J. Chissano, Economics Minister J. Veloso and two deputy Defence Ministers visit Moscow and hold discussions with Gorbachev, Foreign Minister E. Shevardnadze and Defence Minister S. Sokolov and receive a cordial reception.

14 Dec. 1985   The Mozambican Parliament has decided that general elections will be held in 1986, despite RENAMO activities. The decision is announced to the Deputies by Foreign Minister J. Chissano.

Jan. 1986   An upsurge in RENAMO activity includes: the destruction on 9 January of a sugar refinery at Marromeu, Sofala Province; the cutting of the Maputo Swaziland railway on 10 January; an attack on an international passenger train on 15 January; sabotage of power lines to Maputo, cutting electricity supply for three days in mid-January.

27 Jan. 1986   Zimbabwean troops announce the recapture of the town of Marromeu from RENAMO, indicating an extension of their area of operations within Mozambique. Their commanding officer Colonel Flint Magama is killed in a helicopter crash.

Feb. 1986   RENAMO presence and effectiveness is increasing in Tete, Zambezia and Niassa Provinces bordering on Malawi, and in the region of Maputo.

14-15 Feb.1986   RENAMO recaptures their former headquarters, Casa Banana, Gorongosa, from government troops, who fled. This setback deepens growing disillusion in Zimbabwe with its decision to help Mozambique militarily.

18 Feb. -
3 Mar.1986   The Political Bureau meets. The Party apparatus and Party leadership are to be strengthened. Party publications are to be revived. The Bureau is committed to elections in 1986.

21 Feb. 1986   Four RENAMO rebels are sentenced to death after being found guilty of attacking civilian vehicles.

21 Mar. 1986   RENAMO raiders attacking the Vidreira glass factory in the Matola suburb of Maputo fall into a government forces ambush.

27 Mar. 1986   South Africa claims that clandestine visits by senior officials to RENAMO in the field are part of its continuing effort to revive peace negotiations.

28 Mar. 1986   In a restructuring, the Council of Ministers is divided into three sections, each under the authority of a senior FRELIMO Political Bureau member. A concerted effort is planned to revitalize the economy and to bring the military situation under control. The most significant change is the recall of Lieutenant-General J.A. Chipande from Delgado Province to resume full responsibility for defence issues, and release President Machel of these.

29 Mar. 1986   It is reported that RENAMO's military wing has approached Zimbabwean

Prime Minister, Robert Mugabe, to act as broker in setting up a peace conference without informing RENAMO's political wing in Lisbon and its Secretary-General Evo Fernandes.

29 Mar. 1986   Relations with the ANC become warmer. Moses Mabhida, general secretary of the S.A. Communist Party (SACP) and member of the ANC's National Executive Committee is buried in Maputo with full military honours in a state funeral led by President Machel.

Late Mar. 1986   The Mozambican Youth Organization (OJM) holds its second national conference in Maputo. Machel attends almost every session. Disorganization in the armed forces is criticized.

30 Mar. 1986   Mozambican air force Antonov-6 transport plane crashes at Pemba, Cabo Delgado Province. Forty-four people are killed including Maria Chipande, wife of Defence Minister General A. Chipande, founder member of FRELIMO in 1962 and former women's guerrilla army leader in her own right. Seven other leading provincial leaders die in Mozambique's worst air crash to date.

30 Mar. -
1 Apr 1986   President Machel and senior Defence Ministers pay a `working and friendly' visit to the Soviet Union, holding talks with the Soviet leader, Mikhail Gorbachev, and other senior officials. A new agreement on defence is signed.

Apr. 1996   Mozambique receives $20 million from Norway for a cooperation programme and 600 million yen from Japan.

21 Apr. 1986   A car bomb explodes in a residential area of Maputo causing severe damage and injuring fifty people. RENAMO claim responsibility and its Lisbon spokesman, Jorge Corveira, declares that RENAMO cells are now operating in the capital.

24 Apr. 1986   A Cabinet reshuffle, affecting principally the economic portfolios, is announced and the Governor of the Central Bank (Banco de Moçambique) is replaced.

25 Apr. 1986   President Machel attends the coronation of King Mswati III of Swaziland and invites the monarch to visit Mozambique.

9-14 May 1986   Trials are held of six Mozambicans charged with terrorist activities, and of a Kenyan charged with espionage. The Mozambicans are sentenced to death by the court in Maputo, and the Kenyan, P. Nguilache (alias J.O. Odawa), said to have been recruited by the CIA in Nairobi in 1980, trained in South Africa and to have spied for the SA military, to a thirty-year jail term.

17-19 June 1986   President Machel pays a three-day working visit to Zimbabwe, accompanied by Deputy Defence Minister, Lieutenant-General A. Panguene and Air Force Commander, Major-General A.H. Thai. Closer economic, political and military cooperation is discussed.

5 July 1986   Colonel-General S. Mabote, Armed Forces Chief of Staff openly accused the Malawian government of aiding RENAMO materially and logistically. RENAMO is active in all ten provinces and poses a major threat to travellers outside the principal towns. Malawi later denies the allegations.

17 July 1986	Mario Machungo is appointed to the newly created post of Prime Minister. Members of the Council of Ministers and provincial governors will now report to him.
22-23 July 1986	The People's Assembly discuss the report from the National Elections Commission recommending that the second general election goes ahead. Despite RENAMO activities, the great majority of local assemblies elected in rural areas in 1980 are still functioning.
26 July 1986	The Prime Minister is sworn into office.
1 Aug. 1986	An electrified fence along part of South Africa's border with Mozambique is put into operation. Designed ostensibly to prevent illegal crossings and stock theft, it is also an obstacle to the entry of ANC guerrillas and refugees from the civil war.
15 Aug. - 15 Nov.1986	A general election is scheduled to take place. All candidates are proposed by FRELIMO. Local and provincial deputies are to be chosen by secret ballot.
11 Sept. 1986	President Machel, together with Presidents Kaunda and Robert Mugabe visits President Banda of Malawi and threaten to close the border with Malawi unless support for RENAMO is stopped, to install missiles along the border, and to disrupt Malawi's trade.
17 Sept. 1986	John Tembo, Malawi Congress Party representative, leads a delegation to Maputo. He announces Malawi will no longer allow RENAMO bases in its territory and proposes a joint security commission to monitor bilateral issues.
22 Sept. 1986	The Minister of Cooperation, J.C. Veloso, appeals to the international community for help in averting famine.
25 Sept. 1986	RENAMO begins a major offensive, captures and retains several small towns, Mutarara, Caia, Milange, Gité, Nametil, and claims to have seized the military camp at Mueda, some sixty km from the Tanzanian border. The Beira transport corridor is further threatened.
27 Sept. 1986	Albania establishes diplomatic relations at ambassadorial level with Mozambique.
30 Sept. 1986	The establishment of diplomatic relations between Mozambique and Nepal is agreed upon in New York.
6 Oct. 1986	Six South African soldiers are injured in a land-mine explosion close to the point where the borders of South Africa, Swaziland and Mozambique meet. South Africa immediately blames Mozambique of breaking the Nkomati Accord by allowing the ANC to operate from Mozambican territory.
8 Oct. 1986	The South African government bans further recruitment of Mozambican workers with immediate effect and announces that the work permits of those already in South Africa will not be renewed.
12 Oct. 1986	A joint communiqué issued after an emergency meeting of leaders of the Front Line States accuses South Africa of engaging in 'a race to generalized war'.

Mid Oct. 1986	It is announced that military supplies are to be sent to Mozambique from Great Britain and training is to be given to a special battalion to guard the Nacala battalion.
Mid Oct. - Nov. 1986	Some 200,000 Mozambican refugees enter Malawi fleeing from war and guerrilla attacks, mainly in Tete and Zambezia provinces.
19 Oct. 1986	President Machel flies to Zambia for a meeting with Presidents Kaunda of Zambia, Mobutu of Zaire and dos Santos of Angola.
19-20 Oct. 1986	President Machel is killed in an aircraft crash, on the night of 19-20 October, along with several senior aides, party officials and members of the diplomatic corps. The President's plane, a Soviet-built Tupolev 134A jet, flying back from Zambia, crashes some 200 yards inside South African territory, about five km north-west of the border town of Namaacha. Pilot error is blamed but there is speculation as to other possible causes.
20 Oct. 1986	In the morning, President P.W. Botha of South Africa expresses deep regret and profound shock as he makes the first public announcement of Machel's death. In the evening, the death of the President is formally announced on Mozambique radio by Marcelino dos Santos.
22 Oct. 1986	A fourteen-member commission of inquiry into the cause of the air crash is announced by the FRELIMO Political Bureau.
22 Oct. 1986	The electoral process is temporarily suspended; and resumed, 10 November 1986, with a revised timetable - district assemblies to be elected by 25 November 1986 and provincial assemblies and the People's Assembly by 15 December 1986.
24 Oct. 1986	The government controlled newspaper Noticias, implies that sabotage by the South African government caused the air crash. On the same day a team of Soviet and Mozambican officials arrive in South Africa to begin a joint investigation with South Africa, into the causes of the crash. The six-man Soviet delegation is led by Ivan Dontsov, Head of the Soviet State Committee for Civil Aviation and Mozambique's by the Deputy Health Minister Dr. Fernando Vaz. Both delegations are met at Komatipoort by General Lothar Neethling, head of the South African police forensic unit.
28 Oct. 1986	Samora Machel is buried in Maputo. Major-General Marcelino dos Santos delivers the funeral oration and many tributes are paid to Mozambique's revolutionary hero. A period of sixty days of mourning is declared.
29 Oct. 1986	Leaders of the six Front Line States meet in Maputo. They dismiss RENAMO's declaration of war on Zimbabwe as South African inspired, but see it as signalling increased attacks on the Beira Corridor.
3 Nov. 1986	FRELIMO's Central Committee elects Joaquim A. Chissano to succeed President Machel as President of the Party, Head of State and Commander-in-Chief of the Armed Forces.
3 Nov. 1986	South Africa's President Botha in congratulating J. Chissano on his election as Head of State, declares that states with differing socio-economic and political systems can live together in harmony... provided they adhere to the principles enunciated in the (Nkomati) Accord.

4 Nov. 1986   Thousands of Mozambicans storm the Malawian embassy building in Maputo, ransack it and stone the South African Trade Mission, in protest at the death of Samora Machel. Intervention by Security Minister Colonel S. Vieira eventually disperses the crowd.

6 Nov. 1986   President Chissano is sworn into office. In his inaugural speech he assesses the problems facing the country, including South Africa's destabilization policy, pledges adherence to the Nkomati Accord and announces the rehabilitation of the economy as the central objective in the economic sphere.

6 Nov. 1986   South African Foreign Minister 'Pik' Botha claims that Mozambique and Zimbabwe are plotting the military and political overthrow of the Malawian government. Details of the plot are contained in a document, purporting to be minutes of a meeting in Maputo, on 16 October, between President Machel and a senior Zimbabwe military delegation, found at the site of the air crash in which Machel was killed.

8 Nov. 1986   RENAMO captures five foreigners, including a British citizen, when they overrun Ulongue, Angonia district, Tete Province, twenty-five miles from the Malawi border.

10 Nov. 1986   Mozambique's second general elections resume.

14 Nov. 1986   The Red Cross and Red Crescent Societies launch an emergency appeal for assistance to Mozambique refugees in Malawi.

24-26 Nov.1986   The contents of three of the four flight recorders from the Tupolev 134A crash are examined in Zurich, Switzerland, by experts from South Africa, the Soviet Union, and Mozambique, with assistance from Swiss technicians and representatives of the International Civil Aviation Organization (ICAO).

26 Nov. 1986   President Chissano demands that Malawi 'go beyond simple declarations to the effect that it does not support RENAMO' and creates conditions of security. Malawi, reluctantly, activates the Joint Security Commission.

Dec. 1986   A counter-offensive against RENAMO in Zambezia Province is launched. Several areas in southern Zambezia are cleared and the road from the provincial capital Quelimane to the north is re-opened.

2 Dec. 1986   RENAMO leader A. Dhlakama names F.N. Moises as Secretary of Information and B. Lemane as spokesman in the United States. The appointments are interpreted as an attempt to 'africanize' the movement.

4 Dec. 1986   President Chissano reaffirms his government's adherence to the Nkomati Accord during his first press conference as Head of State.

11-13 Dec.1986   In the course of his first state visit to Tanzania, President Chissano obtains an offer of renewed military support against RENAMO. A contingent of 1,000 Tanzanian troops are subsequently despatched to Quelimane, Zambesia Province.

14-15 Dec.1986   The second general election comes to an end with Parliament, the People's Assembly elected by the eleven Provincial Assemblies. All government and senior party leaders are elected for membership of the Assembly by comfortable margins. The elections, repeatedly postponed since 1982 are finally completed.

| 16 Dec. 1986 | Mozambique alleges that members of the Malawian armed forces are participating in RENAMO raids into Zambezia Province. |

16 Dec. 1986   Swaziland reports that Mozambican government forces have planted landmines in an area on the Swazi side of the border.

17 Dec. 1986   RENAMO leader, A. Dhlakama, confirms that RENAMO's aim is now to close the Beira Corridor. He is reported to have moved into the captured town of Milanje to take command of operations.

17 Dec. 1986   RENAMO releases fifty-seven foreign hostages on the border with Malawi.

18 Dec. 1986   An accord on mutual cooperation and a protocol covering defence, state security and public order between Malawi and Mozambique are signed.

19 Dec. 1986   The Malawi government flies the released RENAMO prisoners to Maputo, allegedly against their will, apparently to provide the Mozambique government with information about RENAMO. This is described as a Christmas `gesture of goodwill'.

22 Dec. 1986   A further eight foreign hostages are released as a gesture of Christmas goodwill. These include three Portuguese Jesuit missionaries.

2 Jan. 1987   RENAMO attack the town of Monapo, Nampula Province, wrecking industrial installations.

Early Jan.1987   J. da S. Ataide, a former Mozambican ambassador to Portugal, is made spokesman and propaganda official for RENAMO in Europe, based in Lisbon.

8 Jan. 1987   Six ANC officials claimed by `Pik' Botha to be responsible for supplying arms and explosives to the ANC in South Africa via Swaziland, are to leave Mozambique shortly following pressure from Pretoria. These include the ANC's Maputo office chief representative Jacob Zuma, who is also a member of the ANC's National Executive Committee.

10 Jan. 1987   Appointments to the Central Committee Secretariat are announced.

11 Jan. 1987   Cabinet changes are announced. Lieutenant-General A.E. Guebuza is appointed Minister of Transport and Communications, P.M. Mucumbi Minister of Foreign Affairs, F. Vaz Minister of Health and M. de A. Matsinhe Minister of Security. Two new ministries are created, Culture headed by Luis Bernardo-Honwana and Labour, headed by A.R. Mazula.

15 Jan. 1987   President Chissano and the Prime Minister of Zimbabwe, Robert Mugabe meet at Victoria Falls. Increased military assistance from Zimbabwe is pledged.

19 Jan. 1987   RENAMO claims to have shot down an army helicopter near Vita Raiva de Andrada, Sofala Province, to have attacked military bases in Gorongosa, manned by Zimbabwean and Tanzanian troops and captured garrison personnel and equipment, to have attacked five military bases and mounted a series of ambushes in Maputo Province.

Feb. 1987	The Office of the United Nations High Commissioner for Refugees in Swaziland reports the Mozambique refugees situation in Swaziland has reached crisis proportions.
4 Feb. 1987	A RENAMO unit attacks a tea processing plant at Socone and destroys two factories.
11 Feb. 1987	Five more tea factories are sabotaged by RENAMO and stock piles destroyed at Gurue, Zambezia Province.
13 Feb. 1987	Zimbabwean and Mozambican troops have retaken five towns in Northern Mozambique, Sena, Mutara, Vitanova, Baue and Vilacaia. Zimbabwe army commander General Mujuru visits the recaptured towns and 'is satisfied the operation is going well'.
19 Feb. 1987	President Chissano arrives in Lusaka to begin a three-day official visit to Zambia. Political economic and cultural issues are analyzed and it is agreed to intensify co-operation through the permanent joint commission of both countries and their bilateral co-operation programme.
Early Mar.1987	Malawi decides to deploy troops against RENAMO. A contingent of 300 soldiers is to be despatched during the first week of April to guard the Nacala railway line from Nacala port to Malawi.
1 Mar. 1987	The United Nations General Secretary appeals for more than $200 million in humanitarian aid for Mozambique. An estimated 3,500,000 people are urgently in need of international assistance.
2 Mar. 1987	RENAMO spokesman in Lisbon, Paulo Oliveira, reports the demotion of founder member Evo Fernandes, who has been removed from RENAMO's National Council and the expulsion from the movement of Jorge Correira, a former Lisbon spokesman.
2-5 Mar. 1987	In the course of a state visit to Zimbabwe President Chissano rules out the possibility of negotiating a power-sharing agreement with RENAMO.
5 Mar. 1987	President Chissano confirms that Tanzanian troops have arrived at the coastal town of Quelimane to aid Mozambique in the war against RENAMO.
5 Mar. 1987	President Chissano leaves Zimbabwe for an official and friendly visit to Angola. A joint communique declares South Africa as the main cause of tension in Southern Africa and underlines SADCC's role in the development of their economies.
9 Mar. 1987	Government troops claim to have retaken the town of Luabo, Zambezia Province, as part of a continuing counter offensive.
12 Mar. 1987	The Minister of Construction and Water, M.J. Carrilho is dismissed and replaced by J.M. Salomao.
25 Mar. 1987	RENAMO's Lisbon-based spokesman, Paulo Oliveira, releases a RENAMO statement warning Malawi it will 'pay a high price' if it enters the regional war in Mozambique and that foreign technicians rehabilitating the Nacala railway line will be at risk if Malawi continues to provide 'military escorts' for the trains.

Apr. 1987	Government troops register a series of successes in the north, recapturing towns and regaining control of the coastline. RENAMO increases its operations in the south of the country.
6 Apr. 1987	President Chissano visits Quelimane, Zambezia Province to restore confidence to the armed forces and help improve their position in the field.
8 Apr. 1987	President Chissano publicly opposes talks with RENAMO and expresses regret that 'certain countries' are trying to push Mozambique to the negotiating table.
14 Apr. 1987	RENAMO appeals for international recognition as a legitimate nationalist movement and urges Western governments to support its war against Mozambique's Marxist government.
7 May 1987	President Chissano claims his forces are on the offensive and have destroyed two RENAMO bases at Michadvine, Gaza Province following their success in capturing Morrumbara base, Zambezia Province. RENAMO denies these claims, describing them as propaganda only, timed to coincide with his visit to Britain.
7 May 1987	President Chissano holds talks in London with British Prime Minister Margaret Thatcher. In the course of his visit Mozambique obtains a pledge of an additional 15,000,000 Pounds Sterling. Britain's military training programme, based in Zimbabwe, is to be expanded and a British military attaché is to be posted to Maputo in an advisory capacity.
11 May 1987	FRELIMO's Politburo rejects the findings of the Margo Commission of Inquiry into the death of Samora Machel and declares the investigation is still open.
15 May 1987	RENAMO abducts seven hostages from a rural mission near the town of Gondola in central Mozambique run by the International Missionary Organisation, 'Youth with a Mission'.
25 May 1987	In a battle at Malema, Nampula Province RENAMO kills four Malawian and seven Mozambican soldiers and five Malawian railway workers. Malawi protests to the South African military attaché at the South African embassy in Lilongwe.
29 May 1987	Four groups of four commandos raid four houses in Maputo, simultaneously. One contained offices of the African National Congress. The commander escapes by boat. The attack was thought to be in retaliation for car bomb explosions in Johannesburg for which the ANC claimed responsibility.
June 1987	The Assistant Secretary of State for African Affairs, Chester Crocker, defends the United States Administration's Mozambique policy at hearings before the Senate Africa Subcommittee, claiming Mozambique is pursuing 'a more independent, non-aligned foreign policy course that has distanced it from Moscow'.
June 1987	Heavy fighting throughout the month in Gaza Province, Southern Mozambique, causes heavy casualty on both sides.
16 June 1987	Chissano, speaking in Mueda, describes the death of Samora Machel as 'an

act of murder' by `our enemies'.

17 June 1987	A South African businessman, Mr. Tippet (alias David Horne), is shot on the Mozambique border and dies on 19 June 1987. Mozambique authorities maintain the shooting by a Mozambican soldier took place in the neutral zone between Mozambique and Swaziland, and that groups of smugglers are involved in the 'business transactions' with Mozambican authorities.
20 June 1987	Wide-ranging changes to senior military positions are announced and the Defence Ministry is restructured.
20 June 1987	RENAMO attacks the settlement of Makowa in the Rushinga district of Zimbabwe, killing ten civilians and leaving behind pamphlets in English and Shona and identifying themselves as RENAMO.
20 June 1987	The national security service detains G.O.N. Alerson whom they claim is a member of a South African commando unit targeting ANC members based in Mozambique. He is charged with responsibility for a bomb explosion in Matola, Maputo on 13 March 1987. The South African Defence Force (SADF) denies that he is a SADF member.
21 June 1987	In Lisbon, RENAMO claims to have attacked a Zimbabwean army base, near Dukosa, twenty miles east of the Mozambican border. RENAMO spokesman Paulo Oliveira says the guerrillas have set up fixed bases within Zimbabwe and `the war in Zimbabwe has begun'.
21 June 1987	Government forces claim victories in four provinces of Mozambique.
22 June 1987	Several hundred troops are sent to the Rushinga area. Zimbabwe's government in Harare, however, refuses to confirm the RENAMO attack of which a first hand account is given by a Roman Catholic nun.
25 June 1987	The speech delivered by Chissano at a mass rally in Maputo's Independence Square during the celebrations of the twenty-fifth anniversary of the foundation of FRELIMO is the high point of his campaign against negotiations with RENAMO.
27 June 1987	An official of the United States State Department meets Louis Serapiao, RENAMO representative in Washington, for `humanitarian purposes', following the kidnapping of an American nurse and missionary, Kindra Bryant in Manica Province, in May 1987.
9 July 1987	The international Commission of Inquiry, convened by South Africa, and chaired by Mr. Justice Cecil Margo into the October 1986 aircrash in which President Machel was killed, issues its report. Human error is blamed. No evidence is found to suggest the aircraft was improperly lured off course.
9-10 July 1987	Donor countries attending a meeting of the World Bank Consultative Group for Mozambique, in Paris, agree to provide aid to the value of $700 m. during 1987.
18 July 1987	The government accuses RENAMO of being responsible for a raid at Homoine in Inhambane Province in which some 380 villagers were killed.
24 July 1987	FRELIMO's Political Bureau blames South Africa, as the mentor of

RENAMO, for the Homoine massacre. South Africa denies involvement, and demands an apology. RENAMO states that the massacre was the work of a group of army mutineers, local militiamen, who fired on the army barracks.

30 July - 3 Aug.1987	President Chissano visits Bulgaria.
Aug. 1987	The head of the Vatican's Justice and Peace Commission and of the Papal Commission 'Cor Unum' co-ordinating the work of all Roman Catholic humanitarian and charitable bodies, Cardinal Roger Etchegaray, tours parts of Mozambique devastated by RENAMO.
4-7 Aug. 1987	President Chissano visits the Soviet Union, and receives considerable media attention. Talks are held with Mr. Gorbachev and other Politburo members.
6 Aug. 1987	A joint Mozambique-South Africa investigation into the Homoine massacre is to be undertaken. This decision is announced in Cape Town after the first senior ministerial talks between the two governments since the death of Machel in October 1986.
10 Aug. 1987	RENAMO is reported to have attacked and largely destroyed the town of Manjacaze, Gaza Province.
12 Aug. 1987	The provincial governor of Inhambane, J.P. Zandamela, reports that the death toll in the Homoine massacre has risen to 408 people.
13 Aug. 1987	At the end of a four-day visit to Botswana, President Chissano reiterates the government's belief that RENAMO is supported by South Africa, declaring it trained, armed and led by the South African regime.
14 Aug. 1987	The International Committee of the Red Cross issues an appeal for no repetition of the massacres of civilians at Homoine and Manjacaze.
18 Aug. 1987	Seven missionaries, an Australian, an American and five Zimbabweans, captured from a mission farm near Gondola are released by RENAMO in Malawi. Australia, the United States, Zimbabwe and Malawi all helped to arrange their release.
26 Aug. 1987	RENAMO claims to have killed three British 'experts' whom it later describes as special military troops assigned to guard the Nacala railway line.
28 Aug. 1987	Defence Minister General A.J. Chipande, flies to East Berlin, following a four-day visit to the Soviet Union, for a meeting with his East German counterpart, General Heinz Kessler. The priority needs of the Mozambican armed forces are discussed.
Sept. 1987	The Defence Minister, General A. Chipande, returns from a tour of five Warsaw Pact countries (USSR, German Democratic Republic, Poland, Hungary and Bulgaria) and reports that all these countries accord Mozambique moral, political and material support.
29 Sept. 1987	President Chissano meets French President François Mitterand in Paris. Mozambique's defence capacity is discussed. Requests for military assistance are to be examined by a French fact-finding mission to be sent on a strictly exploratory visit to Mozambique.

1 Oct. 1987	President Chissano addresses the United Nations General Assembly.
5 Oct. 1987	President Reagan is asked by President Chissano to assist Mozambique with increased ecnomic aid. The U.S. Administration declines to assist militarily against RENAMO. Chissano reaffirms his non-aligned stance.
10 Oct. 1987	The government launches a three-week offensive against RENAMO in the south, and captures several bases, including Morrumane.
28 Oct. 1987	RENAMO saboteurs cut the railway line from Maputo to Swaziland.
29 Oct. 1987	RENAMO attacks a convoy of ninety civilian vehicles, escorted by 100 government troops, travelling about eighty km north of Maputo, at Taninga. The provisional death toll is given as 278. An outraged FRELIMO Political Bureau places the blame for RENAMO's tactics on South Africa.
1 Nov. 1987	Defence Minister pledges that the Army will defend the Taninga road - which it was already supposed to be doing - in the face of anger and criticism over military incompetence.
4 Nov. 1987	RENAMO supporters meet for one hour with President Reagan's National Security Adviser in Washington.
6 Nov. 1987	Mozambican armed forces shoot down an Air Malawi aircraft causing the death of the crew and ten passengers most of whom were executives on an internal flight. Mozambican military sources claim the aircraft had violated Mozambican air space.
20 Nov. 1987	Mozambique signs an agreement with Portugal and South Africa to rehabilitate the Cahora Bassa project. In the discussions held in Pretoria, Portugal indicates it is not prepared to finance any further restoration project since the dam's debt to the Portuguese government is already $1.200m, but once guaranteed power is flowing it will again lend finance.
25 Nov. 1987	Mozambican security forces capture the RENAMO base at Matsequentra, three km from the South African border after two days of heavy fighting. The government offensive to clear the area of guerrillas believed responsible for the Taninga massacre, began on 20 November 1987 and is still continuing.
28 Nov. 1987	Vehicles travelling near the town of Maluane are attacked by RENAMO. It is feared the government is losing control of transport arteries.
30 Nov. 1987	Two senior RENAMO leaders Mateus Lopes and Joao da Silva Ataide are killed in a car crash in Malawi in mysterious circumstances.
30 Nov. 1987	RENAMO guerrillas launch an attack on Jersey tea estate on Zimbabwe's eastern border, twenty miles south of Mount Selinda village.
End Nov. 1987	South African and Mozambican generals meet to set up a joint security system that could involve deploying South African troops inside Mozambican territory to protect the Cahora Bassa power lines.
1 Dec. 1987	At the end of a four-day visit, Minister of State at the Great Britain Foreign and Commonwealth Office, Lynda Chalker, pledges continued military assistance to Mozambique in the form of training and supplies of non-lethal

equipment.

6 Dec. 1987	RENAMO raid the village of Mucodza, Sofala Province.

15-22 Dec. 1987   Elections to various levels of assemblies throughout Mozambique are completed with the indirect election of the 250-member People's Assembly. All candidates were nominated by FRELIMO.

17 Dec. 1987   President Chissano, in an address at the opening of a session of the People's Assembly, announces that FRELIMO is to submit draft legislation on issuing an amnesty for rebels who lay down their arms.

24 Dec. 1987   The International Committee of the Red Cross ends its relief flights and recalls its planes to Harare for security reasons.

28 Dec. 1987   RENAMO kills civilians and sets fire to thirty-two vehicles travelling in convoy near Maluane, some thirty miles north of Maputo.

31 Dec. 1987   RENAMO derails a train, loots it, and takes prisoners.

Jan. 1988   RENAMO continues to attack district capitals in the south - 19 January, Namaacha on the Swaziland border. 23 January, Guija on the north bank of the Limpopo.

Jan. 1988   RENAMO continues to mount ambushes on roads leading to Maputo.

Jan. 1988   Joint missions consisting of government personnel and representatives of United Nations agencies and other donors visit six of the ten provinces to evaluate emergency aid requirements for themselves.

12 Jan. 1988   RENAMO is reported to have destroyed a refugee village at Namacata, ten km east of Quelimane.

20 Jan. 1988   At a meeting of government representatives from Mozambique, South Africa and Portugal, agreement is reached in principle on security and the maintenance of power supplies from the Cahora Bassa hydroelectric dam.

Early Feb. 1988   The coordinator for relief efforts in Mozambique, Prakas Ratilal uges that aid be used for long term rehabilitation rather than the continual provision of food aid.

Feb. 1988   The French Foreign Minister, J.B. Raimond, visits Maputo, signs agreements for medical assistance and discusses security on the northern rail line from Nacala to Malawi in the rehabilitation of which the Caisse Centrale de Cooperation Economique (CCCE) is involved.

Feb. 1988   Malawi's External Affairs Secretary, Ron Nkomba, claims it is impossible to prevent RENAMO using Malawi's unprotected frontiers to launch attacks on Mozambique because of the large numbers of displaced Mozambicans living in border areas.

6 Feb. 1988   RENAMO attacks Moamba, fifty km north-west of Maputo.

16 Feb. 1988   RENAMO attacks Bela Vista, the most southerly district capital, between Maputo and the Natal border, but is driven back by the Mozambique army.

18 Feb. 1988	In a communiqué issued at the end of a five-day official visit to Mozambique by the Tanzanian Prime Minister and First Vice-President, Joseph Warioba, the two countries reiterate their countries' solidarity, reaffirm their ever increasing level of friendship and co-operation and totally condemn the South African apartheid regime.
25-26 Feb.1988	Tripartite talks are held between Mozambique, Portuguese and South African officials. The three countries reaffirm their commitment to the rehabilitation of the Cahora Bassa hydroelectric dam.
27-28 Feb.1988	RENAMO captures the town of Marrapula, in north-east Mozambique.
13 Mar. 1988	Nine Zimbabweans are ambushed and killed by RENAMO attacks on the Limpopo railway line inside Zimbabwe. A British grant of 14m. Pounds Sterling has funded rehabilitation work, but the line is in poor condition and Zimbabwean troops may be needed to safeguard repair operations.
17-20 Mar.1988	RENAMO claims to have killed fifty-nine government soldiers only five kilometres from Maputo.
21 Mar. 1988	RENAMO official and sometime Head of Information in Europe, Paulo Oliveira, surrenders to the government authorities in Maputo. He provides them with information concerning RENAMO training and sources of support with specific references to links with South Africa.
21 Mar. 1988	It is reported that on a recent visit to Praia, Cape Verde by Mozambican Prime Minister, Mario Machungo, Mozambique and Cape Verde pledge solidarity with each other and the consolidation of their friendship.
Late Mar.1988	Mozambican and Zimbabwean forces reportedly kill 260 RENAMO guerrillas and capture three RENAMO bases at Chiconjo, Maginge and Nhahombe in Gaza Province.
31 Mar. 1988	The IMF approves a loan of 18,300,000 special drawing rights in support of the second year of the three-year programme under the Structural Adjustment Facility (SAF).
End Mar. 1988	By the end of March 1988, Chissano has toured the provinces of Inhambane, Maputo and Gaza in the South, Sofala, Manica and Zambezia in the centre and Tete and Cabo Delgado in the north. Rallies are held, and problems raised with the people. No negotiations are to be held with RENAMO.
20 Apr. 1988	An investigation, sponsored by the US, reveals a pattern of RENAMO's systematic brutality that could have taken as many as 100,000 lives.
21 Apr. 1988	Evo Fernandes, former RENAMO Secretary-General, is found dead near Malveira da Serra, about thirty kilometres from Lisbon. The Mozambican authorities deny any involvement in his death, or in his abduction four days earlier on the evening of 17 April. Internal feuding within RENAMO is blamed.
26 Apr. 1988	A Zambian spokesman states that thirty-seven RENAMO guerrillas have been captured in eastern Zambia.
26-27 Apr.1988	An international conference on emergency aid is held in Maputo. Emergency

support worth $270 million is pledged by twenty-two donor governments, eight UN agencies and forty non-governmental organizations.

28 Apr. 1988   Foreign Minister, Pascoal Mocumbi, speaking to journalists in Lisbon denies that FRELIMO or its security service, SNASP, are in any way involved in the murder of Evo Fernandes.

28 Apr. 1988   United States Deputy Assistant Secretary of State for Africa, Roy Stacey says at a Maputo press conference that the United States Administration is well aware of South African supplies and support for RENAMO.

29 Apr. 1988   The military commander of Inhambane Province, Lieutenant-Colonel E. Lambo claims that eighteen RENAMO camps have been destroyed and 196 cadres killed in the province in the first four months of 1988.

3 May 1988   Lisbon police announce that Moroccan and French police have detained three Portuguese men in connection with the abduction and murder of Evo Fernandes, two in Casablanca on 29 April 1988 and one in Paris on 30 April 1988.

7 May 1988   President Chissano calls for stronger unity between Mozambique and Malawi, following a meeting between the two countries at Cuamba, Niassa Province. Malawi has committed 600 soldiers to defend the Cuambo-border railway line.

7 May 1988   A car-bomb explosion in Maputo seriously injures exiled South African civil rights lawyer Albie Sachs.

10 May 1988   President Chissano announces a limited Cabinet reshuffle. A. Zandamela becomes Minister of Agriculture and L. Simao Minister of Health.

21 May 1988   The Zambian Secretary of State for Defence and Security, A. Shapai, states that Zambian forces have pursued RENAMO into Mozambique, destroying two bases, following a RENAMO raid on a Zambian village in Chadiza district.

26-27 May 1988   Aid donors at a conference in Maputo assemble a plan mostly of food aid and transport assistance worth $270,000,000. Responsibility for the country's crisis is attributed to South African backed RENAMO insurgency.

26-28 May 1988   Mozambican Minister of Co-operation, Major-General J. Veloso, and South African Foreign Minister `Pik' Botha hold talks in Cape Town and agree to reactivate the joint security commission established under the 1984 Nkomati non-aggression pact.

2 June 1988   Government forces recapture the border town of Milange in Zambezia Province.

9 June 1988   Zimbabwe and Mozambique sign a military co-operation agreement in Maputo, after two days of security consultative talks. The Zimbabwean delegation, led by Defence Minister, Enos Nkala, includes Home Affairs Minister, M. Mahachi, and senior police, government and army officials.

21-22 June 1988   Tripartite talks are held between Mozambique, Portugal and South Africa concerning the Cahora Bassa hydroelectric scheme. Agreement is reached in principle on an increase in the electricity tariff paid by South Africa. Security will be provided by the Mozambican army, with logistical support from South Africa.

24 June 1988	Chairman of the Maputo City Executive Council, J.B. Cosme, announces that churches, places of worship and residences are to be returned to their respective religious groups.
28 June 1988	President Mugabe of Zimbabwe maintains Zimbabwe will continue to keep its estimated 10,000 troops in Mozambique until its routes to the sea are completely free from attack, and until 'the enemy' is neutralised'.
July 1988	The office of the United Nations High Commissioner for Refugees (UNHCR) estimates that 570,000 Mozambican refugees are now in Malawi, with more arriving at a rate of 20,000 - 40,000 a month.
7 July 1988	President Chissano, at the end of a four-day visit to Malawi, says in Blantyre that he is convinced Malawi is not supporting RENAMO. Appreciation is expressed of Malawi's humanitarian aid to Mozambican refugees, now said to number 600,000.
7 July 1988	The re-established Joint Security Commission meets for the first time in three years in Pretoria. The Mozambican side is led by the Commander of the Army, Lieutenant General T. Dai, the South African side by Neil van Heerden, Director-General of the Department of Foreign Affairs.
10 July 1988	Government forces retake Gile, Zambezia Province.
19-23 July 1988	The second National Conference of FRELIMO is held in Maputo as part of the preparations for the fifth Party Congress to be held in 1989. The 391 conference delegates debate, among other matters, the nature of the Party itself, the state of the country's mass democratic organizations, the war against RENAMO, major social problems and international relations.
26-29 July 1988	A session of FRELIMO's Central Committee is held. Major topics include resurgent racism, tribalism, regionalism and military service. Decisions taken form part of the basis on which FRELIMO's Political Bureau draws up a set of seven theses for FRELIMO's fifth Congress due in July 1989.
End July 1988	Justice Minister O.A. Danto, gives as 1,600 the number of RENAMO who have surrendered under the seven-month old amnesty. The majority have surrendered in the central provinces of Manica and Zambezia, the scene of heavy fighting in recent years.
3 Aug. 1988	President Mugabe arrived in Maputo for his first official visit as Head of State. He agrees to a force of 10,000 Zimbabwean troops to protect the Limpopo railway corridor from RENAMO attacks. The British government has agreed to provide 14,000,000 Pounds Sterling to rehabilitate the route.
3 Aug. 1988	Mozambique's first ambassador to Great Britain, Major-General A. Panguere, presents his credentials in London.
16 Aug. 1988	The United Nations Special Co-ordinator for Emergency operations in Mozambique reports that Mozambique still faces a food shortfall of 400,000

tonnes in 1988-89.

20 Aug. 1988	A dispute with West Germany arises when the German ship, the Edda, makes an unscheduled stop off in Inhambane province and contact is made between the Captain and three crew members and a RENAMO unit. In September, when the Edda reappears in Mozambican waters it is detained at Quelimane and kept there until March 1989 when it is released as 'a gesture of goodwill' but also under threat of cancellation of all West German aid to Mozambique.
21 Aug. 1988	United States Democrat Senator, Chairman of the Africa Subcommittee of the Senate Foreign Relations Committee, informs newsmen in Maputo that South African aid to RENAMO is an area of concern for the US Congress.
2 Sept. 1988	RENAMO guerrillas who surrendered to Malawi police are handed over to the Mozambican ambassador in Lilongwe.
12 Sept. 1988	President P.W. Botha meets with President Chissano at Songo, northern Tete Province, near the Cahora Bassa Hydro-electric Scheme for talks concerning electricity supply to South Africa, upgrading Maputo harbour, employment of Mozambican workers in South Africa and the reactivation and reinforcement of the Nkomati Accord.
17-19 Sept. 1988	British Foreign and Commonwealth Secretary, Sir Geoffrey Howe, during a three-day visit announces a new 30,000,000 Pounds Sterling aid package, and continuation of the military training programme until March 1995.
Oct. 1988	A delegation of Amnesty International visits Mozambique for the first time.
Oct. 1988	RENAMO retakes Inhaminga, Sofala Province despite the government's perimeter defence.
20 Oct. 1988	It is agreed to establish a joint commission for co-operation and development to be concerned mainly with the functioning of the Cahora Bassa hydroelectric dam, the rehabilitation of ports and railways, support for agricultural projects and the training of Mozambican technicians.
25 Oct. 1988	South African Foreign Minister 'Pik' Botha formally inaugurates the SA Trade Mission in Maputo and claims South Africa is committed to co-operation with Mozambique.
30 Oct. 1988	Chissano flies to Cuba for medical treatment.
1 Nov. 1988	RENAMO attacks a passenger train about fifty km northwest of Maputo.
9 Nov. 1988	Zambian security forces raid RENAMO guerrillas, in a hot pursuit operation ten km inside Mozambique in retaliation for their attacks on villagers in the Petauke district of Zambia.
15 Nov. 1988	At the end of a joint security meeting in Maputo between the Mozambican Army commander, Lieutenant-General T. Dai and the South African Army chief Lieutenant-General K. Liebenberg, a communiqué is released noting the continuing acts of terrorism and undertake to 'make efforts to eliminate such acts'.
15 Nov. 1988	An agreement is signed lifting the suspension of the recruitment of

	Mozambican workers for the South African mining and agricultural centres, originally imposed October 1986.
16 Nov. 1988	The withdrawal of Tanzanian troops is under way.
22 Nov. 1988	RENAMO attacks a Franco-Portuguese railway construction site at Namyalo in northern Mozambique.
23 Nov. 1988	Chissano returns from Cuba.
23 Nov. 1988	South African Transport Minister, E. Louw, visit Maputo to discuss South Africa's use of the Maputo port.
24 Nov. 1988	The Secretary-general of the Mozambique Christian Council, the Rev. F.S. Banze, reveals in Harare that President Chissano has sanctioned efforts by church authorities to talk directly to RENAMO. A Peace and Reconciliation Commission, headed by the Anglican Bishop of Maputo, D. Sengulane, will attempt to convince them they should accept the government's amnesty, and work for peace and will then report back to President Chissano.
28 Nov. 1988	The SAS Drakensberg docks in Beira to unload non-lethal military equipment, worth 10m. rand to be used by Mozambican forces protecting reconstruction work on the Cahora Bassa power lines. The supplies are handed over by South Africa's Deputy Minister of Defence, W. Breytenbach, to Mozambique's Minister of Industry, A. Branco.
29 Nov. 1988	Police in Harare report that eight Zimbabweans have been killed in Chiredzi district bordering on south-western Mozambique.
30 Nov. 1988	RENAMO attacks the Chibabara district headquarters.
1 Dec. 1988	Tanzanian troops, believed to number several thousand, are withdrawn from Mozambique.
Early Dec.1988	Four RENAMO bases are reportedly destroyed by Zimbabwean troops operating fifteen kilometres inside Mozambique.
5 Dec. 1988	A second shipment of 'non-lethal' military equipment to the Mozambican army is delivered by South Africa, supposedly for the protection force guarding reconstruction work on the Cahora Bassa power lines.
7 Dec. 1988	Portuguese, Mozambican and South African delegations meet in Maputo to discuss the Cahora Bassa situation. Recent aerial surveys undertaken both north and south of the Save River, report the shock total of 891 pylons destroyed or knocked down by RENAMO's sabotage.
12 Dec. 1988	RENAMO attacks Chibuto in the Limpopo valley, Chissano's home district and its barracks housing the Gaza Provincial Military Command.
14 Dec. 1988	A Joint Commission on Economic Affairs established between Mozambique and South Africa meets for the first time in Maputo. It has as its brief, relations in the field of labour, transport, agriculture, tourism, health and building operations.
21 Dec. 1988	A tripartite agreement on the repatriation of refugees from Malawi is signed

by Mozambique, Malawi and the United Nations Commissioner for Refugees. Repatriation is to be voluntary and to be carried out in stages.

22 Dec. 1988   Defence Minister, General A. Chipande, presents the report of the Co-ordinating Commission for the Implementation of the Amnesty Law to the People's Assembly. The highest number of 'bandits' accepting amnesty come from the central and southern provinces, and includes twenty three who formerly had held leading positions in RENAMO.

31 Dec. 1988   President Chissano announces that the Amnesty Law will be extended for another year. During 1988 some 3,000 RENAMO guerrillas had surrendered.

6 Jan. 1989   In a minor cabinet reshuffle President Chissano relieves Graca Machel of her Education portfolio and replaces her by A. dos Muchangos. She remains a member of FRELIMO's Central Committee and of the People's Assembly Standing Committee. D.G. Tembe becomes Trade Minister.

25 Jan. 1989   A further meeting of the Joint Security Commission is held at which South Africa is accused of continuing to cooperate with RENAMO.

Early Feb.1989 RENAMO attacks the sugar complex at Maragra, seventy km north of Maputo.

4-5 Feb. 1989   RENAMO attacks a train leaving Maputo for South Africa and a sugar plantation west of Maputo.

7 Feb. 1989   'Pik' Botha states that his government is trying to encourage a United States brokered settlement of the civil war in Mozambique.

10 Feb. 1989   President Chissano and 'Pik' Botha meet in Maputo and agree that if the United States, or other countries, wish to participate in a peace process, they are invited to discuss this with Mozambique and South Africa.

13 Feb. 1989   In a statement, distributed in Lisbon, RENAMO rejects South Africa's peace plan and states peace is only possible through direct negotiations between RENAMO and the Mozambique government.

16 Feb. 1989   President Chissano confirms South Africa has contacted Mozambique proposing joint US-Soviet intervention to settle the conflict. The issue is to be studied and more information sought.

Mar. 1989   A UNICEF and Mozambique government report estimates 600,000 people killed as a result of the war and that 494,000 children have died from malnutrition associated with war.

Mar. 1989   Terms of the government's proposal for peace, set out in a 12-point plan for a negotiated settlement are submitted to permanent members of the United Nations Security Council.

7 Mar. 1989   Widespread starvation and deaths are reported from Memba district, Nampula Province and from Gité and Ile districts, Zambezia Province.

10 Mar. 1989   A United States senior official states that Washington knows of RENAMO bases within ten miles of the South African border, supplied from South Africa. No effort is made to block the supply route.

16 Mar. 1989	Justice Minister A. Dauto formally announces the abolition of the Military Tribunal. Security offences will now be tried by the provincial courts, appeals will be heard by the Supreme Court and death sentences must be ratified by the Supreme Court.
17 Mar. 1989	Portugal orders the Third Secretary at the Mozambican Embassy in Lisbon, R.C. Marques, to leave Portugal, under suspicion of being involved in the murder of Evo Fernandes. Mozambique refuses to waive Marques' diplomatic immunity and relations between the two countries remain strained.
23 Mar. 1989	South African Foreign Minister 'Pik' Botha visits Maputo and meets with President Chissano and the Soviet Deputy Foreign Minister, Anatoly Adamishin, the highest level contact to date between the Soviet and South African governments.
29 Mar. 1989	British Prime Minister Margaret Thatcher meets President Chissano at Nyanga, Zimbabwe, where British military instructors help train Mozambican troops and discusses the possibility of increasing this training programme. The possibility of a negotiated settlement is also raised.
Apr. 1989	Mass starvation is reported from Nampula and Zambezia provinces.
Apr. 1989	At a donors conference in New York, backed by the United Nations, the government requests $362m. for emergency needs, but donor response is disappointing.
17 May 1989	A high-powered Soviet military delegation arrives to finalize a military agreement concerning training of forces and supplies of equipment.
1 June 1989	An estimated 700-800 Soviet military experts are to be withdrawn from Mozambique over the next two years. Defence Minister, General A. Chipande announces that 'more than half of the advisers are leaving and they will be replaced by Mozambicans'.
5-9 June 1989	RENAMO holds its first Congress within Mozambique. Afonso Dhlakama retains the overall leadership position. R.M. Domingas becomes Head of External Relations. The leadership structure now consists of a four-member Cabinet and a ten-member National Council comprising one representative from each province.
24 June 1989	President Chissano dedicates most of his Independence Day speech to an appeal to RENAMO to end the war, and achieve peace.
24-25 June 1989	Afonso Dhlakama meets church officials representing the Mozambican Christian Council, in Nairobi, Kenya.
25 June 1989	Mozambique has circulated a plan to end the war with RENAMO, to selected embassies in Maputo, which envisages dialogue with RENAMO members who accept the government's terms.
28 June 1989	Reports in Lisbon say RENAMO has accepted a 12-point peace plan put forward by the Mozambican Christian Council.
7 July 1989	A preferential trade agreement between Mozambique and South Africa comes into force.

9 July 1989	Presidents Chissano and Mugabe meet in Beira reportedly to discuss the future of the Zimbabwe military presence in Mozambique.

12 July 1989 — United States Assistant Secretary of State for African Affairs, Herman Cohen, discusses peace proposals with President Chissano.

12 July 1989 — Security forces attack RENAMO headquarters at Gorongosa, Sofala Province.

17 July 1989 — President Chissano publicly admits the government's intention of opening talks with RENAMO, without in any way recognizing RENAMO 'as a real political movement or party'.

19 July 1989 — South African acting President F.W. de Klerk, visits Mozambique accompanied by 'Pik' Botha and holds talks with President Chissano. RENAMO no longer receives official South African assistance.

19 July 1989 — RENAMO attacks villages in Gaza.

21-22 July 1989 — President Moi of Kenya holds two days of discussion with President Chissano regarding his role as mediator in the peace process.

23 July 1989 — President Chissano formally announces that President Moi is to mediate between the government and RENAMO, and that other African leaders will be invited to assist in the peace process.

24-30 July 1989 — FRELIMO holds its fifth Congress in Maputo. Pragmatic changes to party policy include endorsement of the President's proposals for a negotiated peace agreement and a decision to broaden the basis of party membership. Chissano is unanimously re-elected President of the Party and Head of State. All reference to Marxism-Leninism is dropped.

30 July 1989 — Elections were held for the Central Committee, enlarged from 130 to 160, and for a 12-member Political Bureau (enlarged from 10).

8-14 Aug. 1989 — Talks are held between RENAMO and Mozambique church leaders under the auspices of the Kenya government, at an undisclosed location in Nairobi. Kenyan President Daniel arap Moi acts as mediator. The government's principles are delivered to RENAMO leader Afonso Dhlakama.

15 Aug. 1989 — RENAMO issues its sixteen-point statement putting forward its stance on peace negotiations, elections, respect for secular traditions, its status and future. The statement, together with a covering letter in English, is hand-delivered to journalists' offices in Nairobi.

17 Aug. 1989 — The government pardons all those convicted under the 1979 State Security Act. Of the 1,600 criminals released, at least 100 cases are linked to security matters. This decision is part of an effort to reform the justice system.

25 Aug. 1989 — President Chissano dismisses RENAMO's conciliatory sixteen-point statement on the peace process as 'meaningless'.

Late Aug.1989 — A major offensive by Mozambican and Zimbabwean forces has recaptured from RENAMO every sizeable town they held in Sofala and Manica provinces.

Sept. 1989	Portugal's Prime Minister, A.C. Silva, pays a highly successful visit to Mozambique which culminates in the signing of fourteen protocols and agreements covering economic, financial, and social matters. Portugal pledges 'unfailing solidarity' with the Mozambican people.
18 Sept. 1989	The People's Assembly unanimously ratifies an agreement on the reaffirmation of land borders and the demarcation of maritime borders between Mozambique and Tanzania.
20 Sept. 1989	Presidents Robert Mugabe of Zimbabwe and Daniel arap Moi of Kenya meet in Nairobi to review the previous month's discussions between church leaders and RENAMO.
Oct. 1989	RENAMO launches raids in the southern three provinces, notably in Chissano's home province of Gaza. A string of atrocities take place on 7 October, 10 October and 11 October in villages and on the roads.
12 Oct. 1989	During a trip to the provinces President Chissano addresses a rally in Gilé, Zambezia, a town occupied by RENAMO from 1986 to 1988, and receives overwhelming support for FRELIMO.
15 Oct. 1989	Chissano announces that RENAMO will be allowed to stand in the 1991 elections if it renounces violence and lays down arms.
17 Oct. 1989	Symbolically Chissano addresses a rally at Gorongosa on the tenth anniversary of the deaths of the first RENAMO commander Andre Matsangaissa, killed in a raid against Gorongosa Town. The same fate is predicted for Dhlakama.
6 Nov. 1989	The Seventh National Meeting on the Emergency Situation opens in Maputo, bringing together representatives of the United Nations organizations, donor countries, agencies and officials concerned with relief efforts in all ten provinces. International Co-operation Minister, Major-General J.S. Veloso says 5,600,000 people are now displaced or affected by the emergency, critical shortages are imminent.
16 Nov. 1989	At the third consultative group meeting co-ordinated by the World Bank for Mozambique in Paris, attended by representatives of twenty two countries and eleven international organizations, the Prime Minister M. da G. Machungo calls for international assistance. Mozambique's needs for external aid are put at a total of $1,400 million.
25 Nov. 1989	A Zambian UNIP delegation visits Maputo to sign an agreement establishing a joint security commission to contain RENAMO incursions into Zambia. Zambian security forces may cross into Mozambique in pursuit of RENAMO.
Dec. 1989	The United States distributes a seven-point plan to the government, to RENAMO and to the mediators. It strongly resembles the government's principles for dialogue circulated in July 1989.
8 Dec. 1989	Presidents Mugabe and Moi meet again in Nairobi and approve a report recommending direct talks between the two sides, without pre-conditions. The government insists, on the contrary, that RENAMO must first recognise the Mozambican constitution and the existing order.

15 Dec. 1989   President F.W. de Klerk of South Africa visits Mozambique. Chissano indicates that the South African government will have to increase its efforts to stop supplies reaching RENAMO.

20 Dec. 1989   President Chissano agrees to a proposal that his government meets with RENAMO and 'unblock the impasses' in the peace process. This information is conveyed to the Heads of State of the Lusophone African countries at their ninth summit held in Praia, Cape Verde, 18-20 December 1989.

31 Dec. 1989   According to the commission implementing the Amnesty Law only 1,063 'rebels' surrendered in 1989. The amnesty is not renewed for a third year.

2 Jan. 1990   Foreign Affairs Minister Pascoal Mocumbi says, in Maputo, that the time is becoming ripe for direct talks between the two conflicting sides.

5 Jan. 1990   The government dismisses the director of the national daily 'Noticias' and the editor of the television station TVE resigns. Press freedom is not one of the rights listed in the new draft constitution.

9 Jan. 1990   President Chissano unveils the draft of a new constitution at a public rally in Maputo. It will be circulated for public debate. The draft includes an initial separation between state and FRELIMO, direct universal suffrage, the right to strike and the independence of the judiciary.

23 Jan. 1990   On his return from a summit of Front Line African leaders in Lusaka, Zambia, Chissano denies that a date for direct talks with RENAMO has been set.

24 Jan. 1990   The United States removes Mozambique from the list of Marxist nations denied preferential loan and trade agreements.

Feb. 1990   Combined Mozambican and Zimbabwean forces launch major offensives, concentrating on RENAMO strongholds in Manica and Sofala provinces.

11 Feb. 1990   President Chissano praises the release of Nelson Mandela but does not consider it sufficient grounds for ending sanctions against South Africa.

14 Feb. 1990   RENAMO attacks a train near the town of Ressano Garcia, seventy five km north-west of Maputo, killing sixty six passengers and destroying 400 yards of rail and concrete sleepers. The victims are mainly Mozambican workers returning from the South African gold mines.

16 Feb. 1990   RENAMO abducts a British scientist and a Zimbabwean businessman, near the village of Inchope, halfway between Beira and Mutare. The situation in the Beira Corridor is seen to have altered for the worse.

23 Feb. 1990   At a press conference in Maputo, Soviet ambassador Nikolai Dybenko insists that there is no significant change in the main direction of Soviet cooperation with Mozambique.

25 Feb. 1990   Speaking in Bloemfontein, Nelson Mandela calls on South African President de Klerk to make any assistance to RENAMO a criminal offence, to treat Mozambican refugees more sympathetically and to dismantle the electrified fence along the border.

Mar. 1990	A delegation from the Parliament of the USSR, the Supreme Soviet, led by Praesidium member Yuri Borodin visits Mozambique. He recommends continued support for the Samora Machel Military Academy in Nampula and confirms that the Supreme Soviet is committed to mutually advantageous relations.
9 Mar. 1990	The Central Office for Organizing and Discussing the Draft Project for Revising the Constitution set up to co-ordinate the national debate, holds its first meeting in Maputo. The office has central and regional commissions drawn from all social groups.
9 Mar. 1990	Three senior Defence Ministry officials are dismissed: Lieutenant-General J. Munhepe, Director-General for Training and Cadres, Colonel I. Mangueira, Director-General of Logistics and Major L. Mathe, Director-General of Weaponry. No reasons are given.
13 Mar. 1990	President Joaquim Chissano making his first official visit to the United States meets President George Bush for two hours of talks. Chissano declares he is now prepared to enter into direct talks with RENAMO and the American Administration agrees to provide aid for development and reconstruction.
22 Mar. 1990	Soviet Foreign Minister Eduard Shevardnadze holds talks with President Chissano in Maputo. He pledges continued Soviet support for the government's attempts to seek a political solution to the conflicts.
Apr. 1990	The government appeals for emergency aid of $136.1m. focussing on the needs of 1.4m. internally displaced Mozambicans and 154,000 returnees. $106m. was raised, $30m. short of the target.
3 Apr. 1990	East German officials announce that there will be no fresh intake of Mozambicans in 1990. Existing contracts will be honoured. Mozambique's most important link with the German Democratic Republic is under threat.
4 Apr. 1990	The establishment of a permanent co-operation commission between Ghana and Mozambique is announced at the end of a three-day visit by President Chissano. Issues of mutual concern are discussed, including the peace initiatives in Mozambique and Angola.
9-12 Apr. 1990	President Chissano pays an official visit to Portugal and is awarded the Order of the Infante Dom Enrique. He indicates the government is ready to begin direct talks with RENAMO, but that dialogue on peace cannot be limited to them only, as many interested parties as possible are being contacted.
22 Apr. 1990	Government forces recapture Chigubo in the Gaza interior. For the first time in seven years RENAMO does not hold a single district capital.
26 Apr. 1990	The Mozambique government requests $136,000,000 in emergency aid in its 1990 appeal launched at the United Nations headquarters in New York. Donors are reported to have responded with pledges of $120,000,000.
12 May 1990	RENAMO attacks a passenger train near the border town of Ressano Garcia. At least forty people, mostly miners returning from South Africa, are killed.
18 May 1990	Mozambique's Army claims to have destroyed a RENAMO logistics centre near the border with South Africa.

| 4 June 1990 | The International Monetary Fund announces approval of a three-year arrangement in an amount equivalent to SDR 85,400,000 ($112,800,000) under the Enhanced Structural Adjustment Facility (ESAF). |

11 June 1990 — A new pro-FRELIMO military force, NAPRAMA, led by the mystic M. Antonio, emerges in Zambezia Province and has some success.

11 June 1990 — A senior Mozambican delegation arrives in Blantyre, Malawi. RENAMO leader Afonso Dhlakama is reported to be in Blantyre but the two sides do not meet.

13 June 1990 — The Malawian government says the planned direct talks were postponed because of 'apparent difficulties' including a lack of security. Mediator B.A. Kiplagat, Kenya's Permanent Secretary for Foreign Affairs says 'There was no RENAMO delegation, there was no Kenyan delegation, and there was no meeting'. Confusion reigns.

8-10 July 1990 — The first direct talks between the FRELIMO government and RENAMO take place in Rome, arranged by the Italian government and the Vatican. Their representatives observe the talks, together with the Roman Catholic Archbishop of Beira, Mgr Jaime Gonçalves. The encounter is reportedly successful in its commitment to a search for a working platform to end the war.

31 July 1990 — President Chissano announces that the FRELIMO Politbureau is unanimously in favour of introducing a multi-party system in time for the next elections, scheduled for 1991.

11 Aug. 1990 — A RENAMO battalion trained in Kenya is reported to have entered Mozambique near the village of Tsangano in Tete Province.

14 Aug. 1990 — Peace talks between the government and RENAMO resume for a second round in Rome. RENAMO's 'delaying tactics' are criticized by Chissano.

16 Aug. 1990 — FRELIMO's Central Committee endorses the holding of multiparty elections in 1991 and effectively assures the abandonment of the one-party system.

16 Sept. 1990 — RENAMO sabotages the power lines supplying Maputo, in order to improve its bargaining power.

18 Sept. 1990 — The third round of peace talks is postponed. RENAMO states in Lisbon, that it will boycott the talks as long as the government's military offensive on its bases in the Gorongosa area continues.

19 Sept. 1990 — Opening the eighth session of the People's Assembly, Chissano reports that official visits have been made to Algeria, Ghana, Libya, Portugal, Rwanda, Spain, Switzerland, Uganda, the United Kingdom and the United States.

4 Oct. 1990 — The Mozambique Workers' Organisation (OTM) is legally recognized. The OTM must observe its established statutes; the state will abstain from any form of administrative intervention that might limit OTM's trade union freedom rights.

23-26 Oct. 1990 — President Quett Masire visits Mozambique.

2 Nov. 1990   The National Assembly unanimously adopts the new Constitution and its 206 articles covering basic principles, fundamental rights, duties and freedoms, and organs of state.

3 Nov. 1990   RENAMO immediately announces their rejection of the new Constitution on the grounds that it has been adopted by a National Assembly that RENAMO considers invalid.

3 Nov. 1990   The new political party UNAMO, the Mozambique National Union announces that it intends backing President Chissano's candidacy in the Presidential elections. Its Secretary-General, Carlos Reis, describes the ideology of UNAMO as 'social democratic'.

10 Nov. 1990   The third round of talks on ending the civil war begin in Rome. RENAMO demand the complete withdrawal of Zimbabwean troops as a precondition for a ceasefire.

30 Nov. 1990   The new Constitution providing for multi-party democracy and a free-market economy, comes into effect. The country's name is changed from the People's Republic of Mozambique to the Republic of Mozambique. Sovereignty, previously vested in 'the workers and peasants united and led by FRELIMO', now resides in the people. The President is to be elected by direct, universal, secret suffrage for a five-year term, for a maximum of only two consecutive terms.

1 Dec. 1990   A significant step toward a ceasefire is taken when delegations from the government and RENAMO reach an agreement confining Zimbabwean troops to two strategic transport routes along the Beira and Limpopo Corridors.

10 Dec. 1990   A joint Mozambique government and World Bank report, released at a donors meeting in Paris, warns that half of the country's 16,000,000 people face starvation. Donors pledge $1,200 million in aid for 1991.

20 Dec. 1990   Further talks take place in Rome under the auspices of the Verification Commission.

24 Dec. 1990   Three RENAMO commanders arrive on schedule in Maputo, following the legalization of opposition parties. This is interpreted as a move to transform the war from a military conflict into an electoral battle.

28 Dec. 1990   The Zimbabwean army completes its withdrawal from Mozambique, and hands over its positions to Mozambican units loyal to the government.

3 Jan. 1991   President Chissano makes four changes to the Council of Ministers. A. Mazula is appointed Minister of State Administration, T. Hunguana Minister of Labour, R. Maguni Minister of Information, and O. Mutemba Minister of Industry and Energy.

Early Jan. 1991   Following the withdrawal of Zimbabwean troops, RENAMO attacks the key Tete highway three times preventing United Nations food aid from Harare to Malawi reaching the refugees. Their activities violate the partial ceasefire.

8 Jan. 1991   700 Mozambican students involved in disturbances on 23 December, in Cuba, in which several people were injured and one died, are to be repatriated. The decision is made by Mozambique's Minister of Health, Leonardo Simao, who

led a delegation to Cuba to investigate the clashes between Cuban and Mozambican students.

26-27 Jan.1991   The government and RENAMO resume talks in Rome. No official statement concerning the agends is released.

30 Jan. 1991   The Law on Political Parties, providing the legal foundation for the establishment of a multi-party state, is promulgated by Chissano.

1 Feb. 1991   Talks in Rome are reported to have been broken off by RENAMO at the end of January following its complaints of violations of the ceasefire agreement. Zimbabwean troops are said to be still operating in seven provinces, and well outside the rail corridor areas. The Joint Verification Commission (JVC) is said to lack impartiality.

6 Feb. 1991   The Law on Political Parties comes into force.

9 Feb. 1991   RENAMO attacks a crowded restaurant at Chinonanquila, ten miles south-west of Maputo city, causing death and destruction.

11 Feb. 1991   RENAMO attacks a protected convoy on the Tete highway, killing forty-five people. The route from Tete to the Malawian border is now closed again affecting Malawi's imports of emergency food aid and her tobacco exports. The Joint Security Commission of Malawi and Mozambique are considering the problem of the Tete Corridor's security.

19 Feb. 1991   Radio Mozambique reports that Mozambique armed forces' officers will, with effect from this year, receive military training at French military academies. France will increase its military assistance to Mozambique, and, that as a result of the presence of French military specialists, the rehabilitation of the Nacala railway lines has already begun.

21 Feb. 1991   A RENAMO spokesman in Nairobi, J. Vaz says RENAMO intends restarting attacks on Beira and Limpopo corridors. RENAMO claims the Zimbabwean troops have not been redeployed to the corridors as prescribed under the Rome agreement, but the international Joint Verification Commission finds no evidence to corroborate this claim.

23 Feb. 1991   Minister A. Guebuza says RENAMO's reading of the Rome Agreement differs from the governments as it relates to the definition of a corridor.

27 Feb. 1991   The Cuban government makes new scholarships available for 300 Mozambican students, despite the December 1990 riots, and the repatriation of the students concerned.

11-18 Mar.1991   Mediators of the peace process meet in Rome. It is decided to resume peace talks in April 1991.

5 Apr. 1991   Three opposition political parties have emerged all having strong racial, regional or ethnic constituencies. These are CORMO, Independent Congress of Mozambique, PALMO, the Mozambique Liberal Democratic Party and UNAMO, the Mozambique National Union.

26 Apr. 1991   A sixth round of peace talks in Rome, previously set for 8 April was postponed until 15 April, then until 26 April, each time at RENAMO's

request. President Chissano, announcing a further deferment until 2 May 1991, is sceptical about RENAMO's intentions.

6 May 1991   A sixth round of peace talks finally open in Rome. Main topics are the new pluralist political system, a draft electoral law and a timetable and monitoring arrangements for multiparty elections. RENAMO refuses to discuss a ceasefire until these matters are resolved.

6-11 May 1991   The Liberal and Democratic Party of Mozambique (PALMO) holds its first party congress in Beira. Its draft programme places the key sectors of the economy in the hands of 'genuine and original' i.e. black Mozambicans, specifically excluding citizens of Asian, European or mixed descent. A bitter leadership contest sees M. Bilal elected President.

11-12 May 1991   RENAMO increases its attacks to coincide with the Rome meetings. Power lines to Maputo are sabotaged, vehicles are attacked on the main road north and the main rail link with South Africa cut.

18 May 1991   The United States sends its Assistant Secretary of State for African Affairs, Herman Cohen, to Rome to help move the discussions onwards.

22 June 1991   An attempted coup, planned for 25 June 1991, the 16th anniversary of Mozambique's independence, is uncovered. Radio South Africa says many of the plotters are retired army officers, with support from the president officer corps, alarmed by government plans to demobilize the armed forces at the end of hostilities.

24 June 1991   The government's initial communiqué indicates the arrest of several army officers and civilians (unnamed) suspected of plotting the overthrow of the government. Their aim is said to be reversing the trends towards political pluralism and a negotiated settlement.

27 June 1991   The government names eighteen people involved in the coup including Colonel-General S. Mabote, Armed Forces Chief of Staff until 1986 and two brothers of the late President Samora Machel.

29 June 1991   RENAMO captures the town of Lalaua in Nampula Province. Attrocities are reported.

July 1991   The People's Assembly approves new laws guaranteeing press freedom and reorganizing the state security services.

19 July 1991   RENAMO leader Afonso Dhlakama cancels a meeting with United States Deputy Assistant Secretary of State for African Affairs, Jeffrey Davidow, claiming plans to assassinate him as the reason.

20 July 1991   The Mozambique Democratic Party (PADEMO) is launched in Maputo. PADEMO co-ordinator Uchia Recua indicates the party supports federalism and national unity and opposes tribalism, regionalism and racism.

24 July 1991   President Chissano appoints E. da C. Comiche as Finance Minister.

1-9 Aug. 1991   The seventh round of peace talks are held in Rome. RENAMO is reported to be demanding that the forthcoming elections be supervised by the United Nations. The movement formally rejects the document of principles proposed by the mediators and favourably viewed by the government.

11 Aug. 1991	Interior Minister Colonel M.J. Antonio is detained for questioning in connection with the attempted coup of 24 June 1991.
12-23 Aug.1991	FRELIMO holds its sixth Congress in Maputo, re-electing President Chissano as party chairman, and electing a new Central Committee, chosen by secret ballot for the first time.
16 Aug. 1991	Indonesia announces that Mozambique has agreed to establish diplomatic relations with Jakarta. FRETLIN (the Revolutionary Front for an Independent East Timor) detect no change in Mozambique's stand in regard to the East Timorese, or to FRETIN's office in Maputo.
4 Sept. 1991	At the end of a two-day visit to Teheran, by Foreign Minister P. Mocumbi, it is announced that Mozambique will open an embassy in Teheran and that Iran will open one in Maputo in the near future.
6 Sept. 1991	The Attorney-General's office is pressing charges against fifteen people on crimes against state security following the attempted coup d'etat which was detected and investigated by SNASP, the now disbanded security service. Eleven of these are senior armed forces officials.
6 Sept. 1991	The Security Minister and his Deputy are relieved of their posts. By decree A. Niquidade is appointed Director-General of the State Information and Security Service.
7 Sept. 1991	F. Gundana, formerly Minister to the Presidency, is elected by FRELIMO's Central Committee, by secret ballot, to be the new Secretary-General of FRELIMO.
7 Sept. 1991	RENAMO attacks and destroys a village near Xai-Xai, Gaza Province.
2 Oct. 1991	The government appoints veteran journalist and writer Albino Magaia as Director of the newspaper 'Noticias'. The appointment follows the ratification of the Press Law establishing rules of ownership and new legal structures for the newspaper.
7-19 Oct.1991	The eighth round of peace talks is held in Rome with Italian mediators present. On 19 October 'Protocol Number 1 on Fundamental Principles' is signed. A Control Commission is to be created and a ceasefire is in operation.
Nov. 1991	RENAMO leader Afonso Dhlakama undertakes a European tour, including visits to Lisbon, to meet Portuguese leaders, and to Geneva, for talks with the United States Secretary of State for African Affairs, Jeffrey Davidow. This apparently is in a bid to involve Portugal and the United States in the peace talks.
9 Nov. 1991	The peace process temporarily breaks down when RENAMO presents a document denying the legitimacy of the government and says the talks are suspended 'indefinitely'.
13 Nov. 1991	The government and RENAMO sign a second protocol, on party law, under which it is agreed that RENAMO will start functioning as a political party immediately after the signing of a general peace accord. A new round of

talks is to start in December 1991.

18-20 Dec. 1991	The ninth round of peace talks is held in Rome. A joint communiqué indicates that agreement has been reached on the holding of Presidential and Parliamentary elections supervised by the United Nations and the Organization of African Unity, a year after the signing of a peace agreement.
23 Dec. 1991	In an attempt to delay a peace agreement, RENAMO seizes the village of Namarroi threatening the destruction of the British Christian Aid development project, into which 500,000 Pound Sterling has been poured over three years. It has been regarded as the model for regeneration after thirteen years of civil war.
7 Jan. 1992	The Malawi-Mozambique Joint Defence and Security Commission holds its fourth meeting in Maputo, reviews progress, resolves to work jointly to implement the co-operation agreement in the spheres of defence and security. Border problems are discussed, focussing on the need for the reopening of the Milange-Muloza border.
8 Jan. 1992	More than a thousand tonnes of food destined for 17,000 war victims in Milange district are held up by Malawi's closure of a key border post.
10 Jan. 1992	Presidents Banda and Mugabe meet RENAMO leader Afonso Dhlakama in Blantyre and discuss steps to be taken towards achieving lasting peace.
21 Jan. 1992	The tenth round of peace talks resumes in Rome.
18 Feb. 1992	Peace talks deadlock over new RENAMO proposals which breach its 1991 agreement. The chief government negotiator accuses RENAMO of undermining all decisions taken to date. RENAMO insists that the constitution be reviewed.
19 Feb. 1992	Mozambique's Chief of Staff accuses RENAMO of using chemical weapons in the Ngungwe area near the South African border.
23 Feb. 1992	The chairman of the Joint Verification Commission reports a RENAMO attack on the town of Macia, Gaza Province.
4 Mar. 1992	Zimbabwe security forces increase controls on the eastern border with Mozambique. Up to 400 refugees are crossing daily, fleeing drought and an upsurge of RENAMO activity, and increasing the possibility of RENAMO infiltration into Zimbabwe.
12 Mar. 1992	The government and RENAMO sign Protocol Number 3, drawn up with Italian mediation in Rome. The agreement establishes the principles of the future electoral system, enshrines the freedom of the press and of association and addresses the issue of the return and re-integration of refugees and displaced people.
17 Mar. 1992	Mozambique's Ambassador to Zambia, Shafurdin Khan, is murdered in his home in Kabulongo, apparently by people searching for documents.
10 Apr. 1992	Colonel M.J. Antonio resumes his duties as Minister of the Interior after charges against him relating to the attempted coup d'état of August 1991 are dropped on 4 February 1992 by the prosecutors.

3 May 1992	Lieutenant-Colonel Bugalo, acting commander of the Mozambican air force, is detained in connection with the disappearance of military equipment. A number of other officers and civilians are being interviewed concerning possible illicit sales and smuggling.
3 May 1992	Foreign Affairs Minister P. Mocumbi says the next round of peace talks will centre on military issues. Meantime they are postponed until June.
7 May 1992	The death in combat of RENAMO commander General Gomes is reported. RENAMO kills and mutilates eight people in revenge.
10 May 1992	MONAMO (Mozambique Nationalist Movement) ends its first congress with the re-election of Maximo Dias as Secretary-General. It will register with the Ministry of Justice by September at the latest. MONAMO is also declared to be the Mozambique Social Democratic Party (PMSD).
16 May 1992	Presiding Judge of the Maputo Judicial Court, A.S. Cutumula and his wife Dr. A.L. Maite, are killed in an ambush on the Namaacha road. The fate of other members of the family in the vehicle is not known.
19 May 1992	United States officials say America will become formally involved in the next round of negotiations.
10 June 1992	Peace talks between mediators and political and military delegations resume in Rome, focussing on three issues: the formation of a single non-partisan army; the ceasefire; and guarantees for a full transition between the ceasefire and general elections. Countries invited as observers are France, Portugal, Great Britain and the United States.
11 June 1992	The government delegation is led by the Minister of Transport and Communications, A. Guebuza and RENAMO's by the Head of its Organization Department, Raul Domingos. RENAMO has again introduced issues not on the agenda.
18 June 1992	Agreement is reached on the agenda for the revision of the constitution and the deadlock in the talks is overcome.
3 July 1992	President Mugabe of Zimbabwe meets Afonso Dhlakama in Gaborone. Also present is LONRHO chairman Tiny Rowland.
6 July 1992	Talks begin on military issues. RENAMO wants joint armed forces of only 15,000 during a transitional phase before elections, the government proposes 50,000.
16 July 1992	RENAMO and the government sign a joint humanitarian declaration designed to allow unrestricted passage for food convoys.
18 July 1992	President F.W. de Klerk of South Africa makes his second visit to Maputo for a `summit' with President Chissano. South Africa is pressured to halt aid to RENAMO from within South Africa and Mozambique to deal with the problem of illegal arms entering South Africa from Mozambique.
18-19 July 1992	The Mozambique People's Progress Party (PPPM) holds its first constituent Congress, attended by 150 delegates from all the country's provinces as well as delegates from Portugal, Swaziland, South Africa and Brazil. Elected is a

110-strong national body, a fourteen member executive, a President, P. Kamati and a Vice-President M. Mabote.

19 July 1992   President Chissano announces that he will meet RENAMO leader Afonso Dhlakama for a first face-to-face meeting in Rome on 4 August. The statement follows a four-hour discussion with President Mugabe.

21 July 1902   Dhlakama demands that RENAMO members be given immunity from prosecution or official harassment.

29 July 1992   In a broadcast, President Chissano says he sees strong possibilities of success in his planned meeting with Dhlakama, in Rome on 4 August 1992.

End July 1992   Mutiny over pay arrears spreads to several sections of the armed forces.

7 Aug. 1992   Meeting for the first time in Rome, President Chissano and RENAMO leaders sign a peace accord to end the civil war by 1 October 1992. The agreement pledges complete political freedom, guarantees personal security, accepts the role of the international community and the United Nations, and respects the principles of Protocol No. 1 and political rights.

16 Aug. 1992   President Chissano appeals to RENAMO to end the war immediately, instead of waiting for the formal signing of the ceasefire on 1 October 1992.

21 Aug. 1992   The President of the Mozambique National Union (UNAMO) is arrested in his home province of Zambezia, accused of speculation and sentenced to a prison term.

24 Aug. 1992   The Minister of Defence accuses RENAMO of preparing a military offensive in the Zambezi River valley.

19 Sept. 1992   A communiqué, issued by the government, indicates that during talks in Gaborone, on 18 September, President Chissano and A. Dhlakama have agreed that the armed forces will total 30,000 men, that the State Information and Security Service will continue to operate, but that a commission will be established to guarantee the service's impartiality.

4 Oct. 1992   President Chissano and RENAMO leader Dhlakama sign a General Peace Accord in Rome - the climax of more than two years of negotiations in the presence of more than thirty African Heads of State or other dignatories. A United Nations chaired ceasefire accord verification will be established and will be responsible for guaranteeing the implementation of truce regulations.

9 Oct. 1992   The Mozambique legislature approves a number of amendments to the Constitution, effectively incorporating the terms of Protocol Number 3, signed on 12 March 1992 and covering arrangements for the future electoral system.

13 Oct. 1992   The United Nations Security Council endorses a proposal from Secretary-General Boutros Boutros-Ghali to appoint an interim Special Representative for Mozambique, and to dispatch twenty-five military observers.

14 Oct. 1992   Following Parliamentary ratification on 13 October, President Chissano promulgates legislation approving the actual peace treaty, as well as a general

political amnesty.

15 Oct. 1992	The first United Nations observers arrive in Maputo.
21 Oct. 1992	The withdrawal of Zimbabwean troops begins.
21 Oct. 1992	It is reported that RENAMO has taken control of four towns, Angoche, Maganja da Costa, Memba and Lugela. Dhlakama claims that these raids are 'defensive actions'.
23 Oct. 1992	RENAMO units occupy Lugela, Zambezia Province. The government protests against violations of the peace accord to the interim Head of the United Nations peacekeeping meeting, Aldo Ajello.
4 Nov. 1992	The first of the joint working commissions, the Supervision and Control Commission (CSC) holds its first meeting. Membership of the other three commissions, to implement the General Peace Agreement under United Nations auspices, is announced.
9 Nov. 1992	United Nations peace monitors are redrafting a ceasefire timetable that will be more realistic and more viable, according to the United Nations special representative, Aldo Ajello.
14 Nov. 1992	A new political party, the National Democratic Party (PANADE) appears, based on 'Christian values and human dignity'. PANADE's political positions appear to mirror the desire of ecclesiastics, led by Jaime Gonçalves, Archbishop of Beira, to play a political role.
15 Nov. 1992	The 3,500 Zimbabwean troops, guarding strategic trade routes, remain in position to protect corridors essential for the transport of drought relief aid to Zimbabwe, Zambia and Malawi.
24 Nov. 1992	Government forces recapture Lugela, central Zambezia.
25 Nov. 1992	The road linking Maputo with Beira is opened for the first time in twelve years.
10 Dec. 1992	RENAMO leader A. Dhlakama talks with President Mugabe of Zimbabwe and withdraws his objection to Zimbabwean troops remaining until they can be replaced by United Nations forces.
12 Dec. 1992	The opposition party, the Democratic Party of Mozambique (PADEMO), calls for the elections to be postponed, and for a transitional government to be formed for a two-year duration. This proposal is approved by the Mozambique Nationalist Movement (MONAMO) and the Patriotic Action Front (FAP). The National Convention Party (PCN) would prefer elections held at the end of 1993.
15 Dec. 1992	Donors meeting in Rome pledge most of the cost of UNOMOZ, estimated at more than $330,000,000.
16 Dec. 1992	The United Nations Security Council approves a plan for supervision of the peace process. The United Nations Operation for Mozambique (UNOMOZ) calls for 7,500 UN troops to disarm both armies, to integrate portions of the two forces into a national army and to organize multiparty elections. The cost

of the operation is estimated at $331m.

16 Jan. 1993 The Portuguese Ministry of Defence provides details of ten military projects that will receive assistance from the Portuguese government within Mozambique.

16-17 Jan. 1993 The first congress of the Mozambique United Front (FUMO) is held in Maputo. Headed by Dr. Domingos Arouca it expects to be the third largest opposition party.

4 Feb. 1993 The United Nations Secretary-General's Special Representative, Aldo Ajello, indicates that delays in the arrival of UN forces are partly the result of difficulty in finding governments prepared to provide troops.

15 Feb. 1993 Fewer than 100 of the 7,500 United Nations peacekeeping troops have arrived.

17 Feb. 1993 Zimbabwe Ministry of Defence confirms that its troops, guarding the strategic Beira and Limpopo corridors, scheduled to have left by November 1992, will be withdrawn as soon as United Nations forces are in place.

18 Feb. 1993 Official mediators express increasing concern at the slow pace in the implementation of the October 1992 General Peace Agreement. RENAMO leader A. Dhlakama is said to be equally concerned.

9 Mar. 1993 RENAMO representatives withdraw from the Ceasefire and Control Commissions, thereby halting preparations of assembly points for demobilizing troops. RENAMO claims the government has not provided its Maputo-based officials with sufficient accommodation, transport or food.

11 Mar. 1993 The Zimbabwean government is investigating accusations that about 1,000 Zimbabwean 'dissidents' are being trained at RENAMO's military base in Gorongosa.

13 Mar. 1993 FRELIMO's first secretary for Beira city reports preparations by RENAMO to resume hostilities should they lose the election.

14 Mar. 1993 RENAMO delegate for Sofala Province, M. Pereira, addressing a RENAMO rally in Buzi accuses the State Information and Security Service (SISE) of promoting a campaign for the assassination of RENAMO members.

18 Mar. 1993 President Chissano travels to Nigeria for talks with President Babangida who has agreed to send troops to Mozambique as part of the UNOMOZ Force.

24 Mar. 1993 RENAMO is reputed to be creating its own police force in the areas it controls.

7 Apr. 1993 Dhlakama says his forces will only be instructed to report to assembly points when RENAMO has received $15m. to support its political activities.

14 Apr. 1993 The United Nations Security Council unanimously adopts Resolution 818 calling for the timetable for the implementation of the October 1992 peace treaty to be finalized, and for both sides to guarantee the freedom of movement and verification capabilities of UNOMOZ.

14 Apr. 1993	Zimbabwean troops guarding the Beira and Limpopo corridors finally withdraw.
20 Apr. 1993	RENAMO confirms it will not rejoin the Commissions until its logistical problems are solved.
25 Apr. 1993	The United Nations Secretary-General Special Representative confirms that elections will probably not take place before mid-1994. Problems of finance are noted with the UN having raised only $140m. of the $332m. budgeted for the peace process.
28 Apr. 1993	According to local reports $125m. have been pledged by Italy, Portugal and South Africa for the reconstruction of the Cahora Bassa-South African power line. Work on the line is expected to begin in September and the supply of power is scheduled to resume in 1996.
30 Apr. 1993	United Nations Special Representative, A. Ajello, reveals that two trust funds totalling $30m. have been created, one of which would be used to support RENAMO, the other for other political parties. The World Bank has allocated $770m. for the Mozambican peace process and UNOMOZ operation costs are estimated at $260m.
May 1993	Dhlakama makes his own fund-raising tour of Europe with special pleas to Germany and the Netherlands for financial assistance to RENAMO in its transformation into a political party.
7 May 1993	According to a United Nations operation in Mozambique (UNOMOZ) communiqué, 4,721 UNOMOZ soldiers have arrived. Armed contingents are being supplied by Bangladesh, Botswana, Italy, Uruguay and Zambia, unarmed units by Argentina, India, Japan and Portugal.
11 May 1993	A six-member advance party of Japan's Self-Defence Forces (SDF) leaves for Mozambique to be followed by a further forty-five SDF troops on 15 May 1993. The Japanese force is to be involved in transport operations and will remain in Mozambique until the end of November 1993.
Early June 1993	Representatives of about thirty donor governments and humanitarian organizations meet in Maputo to monitor financial payments and expenditure. Collective disappointment is expressed at the slow pace of negotiations.
3 June 1993	The work of the peace accord commissions, disrupted in March 1993 by the withdrawal of RENAMO representatives, resumes.
12 June 1993	The repatriation of an estimated 1,300,000 Mozambican refugees is formally inaugurated with the return of refugees from Zimbabwe under the supervision of the Office of the UN High Commissioner for Refugees.
13 June 1993	According to government figures more than 10,000 refugees in South Africa, Swaziland and Zimbabwe have returned voluntarily to Mozambique between October 1992 and May 1993. Most have settled in Gaza Province.
14 June 1993	It is reported that UNOMOZ has proposed postponing the first multi-party elections until October 1994, a full year after the date originally agreed upon.
15 June 1993	United Nations Secretary-General's Special Representative, A. Ajello, says

that the disarming of government troops and RENAMO forces will begin in Zambezia and Nampula provinces on 21 June 1993.

24 June 1993   According to a note from the Ministry of Justice, the Mozambique Democratic Party (PADEMO) is now officially registered as a political organization.

8 July 1993   United Nations Secretary-General, Boutros Boutros-Ghali, complains that the peace process is far behind schedule because both sides fail to adhere to the timetables provided.

13 July 1993   The UN World Food Programme (WFP) will provide Mozambicans with food aid worth $8.3m over the next nine months.

17 July 1993   The meeting arranged between Chissano and Dhlakama in Maputo is cancelled by RENAMO.

21 July 1993   RENAMO accuses the government of 'gross violations' of the General Peace Agreement of October 1992, alleging that government forces have attacked RENAMO buses in Tete Province between 6 and 17 July 1993.

23 July 1993   Ajello appeals to the conflicting forces to allow the United Nations time to investigate their complaints before taking military action.

14 Aug. 1993   The Joint Commission for the Formation of the Mozambique Defence Armed Forces (CCFADM) reaches agreement on the formation of the future Mozambique Defence Armed Forces (FADM). Guidelines cover the timetable, structure of supreme command, and selection of personnel for training.

19 Aug. 1993   An agreement is signed between Mozambique, Swaziland and the UN High Commissioner for Refugees (UNHCR) providing for the return of 24,000 Mozambicans from Swaziland.

23 Aug. 1993   Talks between President Chissano and RENAMO leader, A. Dhlakama, begin in Maputo. Discussions are expected to last two weeks.

26 Aug. 1993   A commission is appointed to consider the demands of the Presidential Guard and to investigate the causes of their mutiny in March 1993, suppressed by Commando units with undue violence.

3 Sept. 1993   Talks between Chissano and Dhlakama end with consensus on two of the three main points under discussion - territorial administration before national elections and control of the police. The outstanding issue is that of press freedom.

10 Sept. 1993   Dhlakama appears to renege on part of the agreement when he says that reintegation of RENAMO-controlled areas into the state administration system will only occur 'with restrictions', and that political parties will only be able to work in these areas with permission from RENAMO leadership.

13 Sept. 1993   The United Nations Security Council unanimously adopts Resolution 863 urging both sides to ensure that the momentum of implementing the General Peace Agreement is maintained, and to agree on an electoral law as soon as possible so that multiparty elections can be held no later than October 1994.

15 Sept. 1993	The Multiparty Conference on the Country's Electoral Law resumes its discussions, focussing on the composition of the National Electoral Commission.
17 Sept. 1993	The group of eight 'unarmed opposition' parties withdraws from the Multiparty Conference.
20 Sept. 1993	The United Nations proposes a postponing the elections until October 1994. This is cautiously welcomed by both the government and RENAMO.
23 Sept. 1993	Representatives of the government and RENAMO meet Ajello to discuss a revised timetable for the implementation of the General Peace Agreement. No agreement is reached, and a further meeting scheduled for 28 September does not take place.
26 Sept. 1993	Senior RENAMO leaders state RENAMO is prepared to contest elections in October 1994, even if the demobilization programme remains incomplete. The government rejects this.
15 Oct. 1993	An agreement is signed in Maputo to repatriate 350,000 Mozambican refugees from South Africa.
20 Oct. 1993	The United Nations Secretary-General, Boutros Boutros-Ghali, announces that after four days of talks with Chissano and Dhlakama in Maputo an agreement has been reached on the creation of an Electoral Commission. A draft electoral law will be ready for submission to the Assembly of the Republic by the end of November. A new timetable for demobilization will be ready shortly.
22 Oct. 1993	The Supervision and Control Commission approves a new election timetable stipulating the holding of a general election in October 1994, the demobilization of troops between January and May 1994 and the establishment of a fully operational army by September 1994.
5 Nov. 1993	The United Nations Security Council adopts Resolution 882 renewing the mandate of UNOMOZ for a period of six months. The Council requests Boutros-Ghali to report by 31 January 1994 and every three months thereafter on the progress of implementation of the General Peace Agreement and on the timetable for electoral and military developments.
6 Nov. 1993	Italy's Foreign Minister informs Ajello that his country intends to leave the Italian contingent in UNOMOZ until the completion of the UN operation.
11 Nov. 1993	An agreement on demobilization is signed. Under its terms all troops from both sides will be confined to forty-nine designated areas, in a process beginning on 30 November and scheduled to take six months. An estimated 82,000 troops and their 40,000 dependents will be supplied with food by the UN World Food Programme.
14 Nov. 1993	Portuguese instructors will, from December, be training government and RENAMO soldiers in administrative issues affecting the Mozambique Defence Armed Forces.
18 Nov. 1993	Outstanding difficulties over the electoral law are overcome when Chissano and Dhlakama agree that Mozambicans abroad will be allowed to vote, where

Elections Commission feels it is possible.

24 Nov. 1993   Troops are called in to restore order in Maputo after riots erupt over the doubling of mini-bus taxi fares. Opposition parties call for government action to cancel the recent fuel price increases.

3 Dec. 1993   A Malawian army operation against the Malawi Young Pioneers (MYP) sends several thousand Pioneers into hiding or fleeing across the Mozambique border where they reportedly find shelter with RENAMO.

21 Dec. 1993   A. Ajello travels to Nampula to investigate a claim by Dhlakama that an assassination attempt has been made against him there. The incident is dismissed as a `misunderstanding'.

24 Dec. 1993   Swazi soldiers are on the alert at the Swazi-Mozambique border after clashes between soldiers of the two countries.

29 Dec. 1993   A report issued by the United Nations Operations Technical Demobilization Unit reveals that by the end of December only about 12,000 of the 90,000 soldiers to be confined had presented themselves at assembly points. The government has confined 13 percent of its troops, RENAMO 19 percent.

3 Jan. 1994   Justice Minister, A. Danto, says an estimated $76m. will be required to finance the October elections, of which the government will be able to contribute $4m. Donors have promised about 50 percent of the estimated costs, but the electoral budget is currently facing a massive deficit.

4 Jan. 1994   It is announced that Great Britain has agreed to reschedule 12,500,000 Pounds Sterling of Mozambique's debt, 11,000,000 Pounds Sterling of which will be rescheduled under priority terms.

9 Jan. 1994   Radio Maputo announces that Portugal, Great Britain and France have received the mission of training the future Mozambique army.

14 Jan. 1994   The United Nations Secretary-General's Special Representative, A. Ajello, says the government has effectively stopped confining its troops. Less than 20 percent of the total force has arrived in specific areas.

18 Jan. 1994   Deputy Planning Minister, T. Salomao, admits the government is facing logistical difficulties, but complains the confinement centres lack sufficient capacity.

18 Jan. 1994   Mozambique condemns the violation of its national territory by the Swaziland Defence Force along the Mozambique-Swaziland border. A meeting is held to discuss patrolling and protection of common borders.

31 Jan. 1994   The Democratic Renewal Party (PRD) is now officially registered, bringing the number of officially registered political parties in Mozambique to thirteen.

2 Feb. 1994   The British Defence Attaché, Lieutenant-Colonel J. Wyatt, announces that the training of the new army's first six infantry battalions is set to begin on 21 February 1994.

11 Feb. 1994   The twenty members of the National Elections Commission (CNE) are sworn in.

12 Feb. 1994	The Roman Catholic Church expresses the hope that a government of national reconciliation will be established after the October elections. The Archbishop of Beira, Monsignor Jaime Goncalves, stresses that a political party victorious at provincial level must be called on to participate in the provincial government.
14 Feb. 1994	Director of the African Affairs Department in the German Foreign Ministry, A. Guntz, assures RENAMO that Germany will soon be delivering a radio transmitter to the movement.
18 Feb. 1994	Ajello reveals that the movements of an Italian UNOMOZ battalion have been restricted following allegations of child abuse.
19 Feb. 1994	South Africa warns people in the Ressano Garcia area that the electrified border fence may soon be re-activated to stem the hole of illegal immigrants and to counter cattle rustling and gun running.
23 Feb. 1994	Mozambique's representative P.C. Afonso tells the United Nations Security Council that the two sides are assembling their forces at a slow and uneven pace. As of 21 February the United Nations has received 26,768 government troops into its assembly areas but only 10,268 members of the RENAMO forces.
23 Feb. 1994	The United Nations Security Council unanimously adopts Resolution 898 (1994) authorizing the establishment of UN police component of UNOMOZ - a move towards preparation for elections.
4 Mar. 1994	The Foreign Minister, P. Mocumbi, warns that the government will ask the UN Supervisory and Control Commission CSC to become involved in the removal of the 1,000 armed members of the Malawian Young Pioneers from Mozambique.
4 Mar. 1994	RENAMO leader, A. Dhlakama, reveals his shadow cabinet on Radio Lisbon: Ministers: Internal Administration: A. Faife; Information: A. Murrial; Agriculture: P.R. Baza.
5 Apr. 1994	A RENAMO communiqué claims Rombezia is under the command of Ghimo Phire, and is backed by ethnic groups in the north of Mozambique who believe they are under-represented in government.
5 Apr. 1994	The government confirms reports of the existence in Zambezia Province of the armed separatist group, Rombezia, demanding an independent state between the Rovuma and Zambezi rivers.
7 Apr. 1994	The two joint commanders of the new army, Lieutenant-General L. Lidimo selected by the government and Lieutenant-General M. Ngonhamo selected by RENAMO, begin their first day in office.
8 Apr. 1994	Dhlakama meets President Chissano and expresses concern over the increasing movement of armed groups in Zambezia Province.
11 Apr. 1994	In a decree, President Chissano announces that the country will hold its first multiparty elections on 27-28 October 1994. The registration of voters will take place from 1 June to 15 August 1994.

15 Apr. 1994   At a special RENAMO Congress in Maringue, 400 delegates adopt an electoral strategy, adapt RENAMO's structures to the ongoing political situation and choose Afonso Dhlakama as Presidential candidate.

16 Apr. 1994   Four accords authorizing the creation of the new Mozambique Defence Armed Forces (FADM) are signed in Maputo by senior military officials representing the government and RENAMO. The agreements deal with general organization, hierarchical structure and the organization and training of special forces and air force personnel.

5 May 1994   The United Nations Security Council adopts Resolution 916 (1994) renewing the mandate of UNOMOZ for a final period ending on 15 November 1994.

5 May 1994   President Chissano temporarily suspends the troop demobilization process, saying it 'has not been balanced'.

12 May 1994   The last group of refugees in Nkhata Bay, Lake Malawi is dispatched to Mozambique under the United Nations High Commissioner for Refugees' voluntary repatriation exercise.

13 May 1994   United Nations Special Representative Aldo Ajello reports no progress in the confinement and demobilization of troops or in the formation of the Mozambique Defence Armed Forces.

16 May 1994   Ajello confirms a UNICEF report alleging RENAMO's use of an estimated 2,300 child soldiers. They create an organizational dilemma since, because of their age, they do not technically have the right to go to the military assembly areas.

18 May 1994   United Nations Special Representative, A. Ajello, confirms that government troops will complete their confinement by 1 July and demobilization by 15 August 1994 and RENAMO forces one month earlier.

23 May 1994   The United Nations High Commisioner for Refugees says thousands of Mozambican refugees are opting to stay in South Africa rather than return under the mass-repatriation scheme that began in April 1994.

27 May 1994   The thirteen 'unarmed opposition' parties end a national conference in Xai-Xai, Gaza Province and indicate they intend establishing a coalition and choosing a single opposition candidate for the Presidential election. A Commission is established to deal with the release of funds for the election campaign.

31 May 1994   Malawian President Bakili Muluzi visits Mozambique on a 'solidarity' visit. Prospects for bilateral cooperation are said by Chissano to be good.

1 June 1994   Voter registration for the October elections begins.

3 June 1994   The United Nations repatriation of 24,000 registered refugees from Swaziland is completed.

10 June 1994   The government is reported to be withdrawing from the UN Supervision and Control Commission, following the denunciation of FRELIMO by the United Nations concerning an enormous discrepancy in the figures for the numbers of soldiers it is demobilizing.

16 June 1994	The IMF announces approval of an additional loan under the Enhanced Structural Facility (ESAF) in an amount equivalent to SDR 29,400,000 (about US$42m.) in support of the government's fourth annual reform programme.
21 June 1994	A third President candidate emerges - Carlos Jack, former Vice-Chairman of the Mozambique United Front (FUMO) - said to be receiving support from Portugal and the United States.
25 June 1994	A new political party, the Mozambique Democratic Alliance (ADM) emerges. It aims to build a state on the rule of law, based on the principles of the Human Rights Charter, and defends equal opportunities in all fields of social life.
10 July 1994	At a rally in Maputo, President Chissano confirms that he is under pressure from foreign governments to agree to a power-sharing agreement in advance of the elections, but he rejects the idea of a coalition.
11 July 1994	Ajello reports that the troop confinement is virtually complete.
12 July 1994	The chairman of the National Elections Commission, Dr. B. Mazula, announces that to date, over 3,2m. people have been registered as voters.
15 July 1994	A visit by a South African delegation, headed by Defence Minister Joe Modise, results in an agreement to establish a joint defence and security commission. The commission will give urgent attention to cross-border arms and drug smuggling, stock theft and abductions.
18 July 1994	South African Police announce the arrest of a Mozambique army officer, and two accomplices for arms smuggling and the uncovering of a cache of AK47 assault rifles, rocket launchers and SAM7 missiles.
19 July 1994	The United Nations Security Council insists that the demobilization of all forces is completed by 15 August 1994, and suggests the new national army should comprise, initially, a force of only 15,000 men.
20-22 July 1994	South African President Nelson Mandela pays his first state visit to Mozambique. Discussions focus on the peace process and Mandela promises to provide logistical support for the October elections.
23 July 1994	Another independent candidate in the Presidential elections comes forward - Mario Carlos Machel, a nephew of the late President Samora Machel.
25 July 1994	The first meeting of the Mozambique-South Africa Joint Commission on Defence and Security is scheduled to take place to coordinate border operations.
Late July 1994	The protracted peace process deteriorates into crisis by a series of troop mutinies across the country, involving both government and RENAMO forces.
4 Aug. 1994	Four Mozambican parties - the Liberal and Democratic Party of Mozambique (PALMO), the National Democratic Party (PANADE), the Democratic Renewal Party (PRD) and the Mozambican National Party (PANAMO) - form a coalition called the Democratic Union (UD) to contest the elections.

4 Aug. 1994   South African Security Minister Sidney Mufamadi, says that Mozambique, South Africa and Swaziland have signed an initial police cooperation accord to control arms smuggling.

12 Aug. 1994   President Joaquim Chissano is himself demobilized as a General in the People's Forces for the Liberation of Mozambique (FPLM).

12 Aug. 1994   The RENAMO movement registers as a political party.

14 Aug. 1994   The requirements to run for office in the Presidential and Parliamentary elections, based on the country's Constitution and Electoral Law, are published.

16 Aug. 1994   The United Nations Observer Mission in Mozambique is confident that all troops who have opted for demobilization will be processed by 22 August 1994. FPLM have demobilized 49,000 of the 64,000 troops, RENAMO 16,000 of its 23,000.

16 Aug. 1994   The new Mozambique Defence Armed Forces (FADM), with a joint government - RENAMO command, is formally inaugurated.

18 Aug. 1994   RENAMO leader, Afonso Dhlakama, is formally demobilized during a ceremony held at RENAMO headquarters in Maringue.

24 Aug. 1994   Chissano reports that the new national army FADM will have only 11,000 of its intended 30,000 members operational by the time of the elections in October 1994.

10-13 Sept. 1994 A peace workshop in Assissi, Italy, discusses the lack of willingness to abandon the use of available military forces.

13 Sept. 1994   The United Nations Special Representative, Aldo Ajello, confirms that the trust fund, worth $11,600,000 established to transform RENAMO from a resistance movement to a political party, has been completely depleted. Monthly payments of $300,000 to Dhlakama were not intended for his personal use.

13 Sept. 1994   At a meeting of the Council of Ministers in Maputo the Information Minister, R. Maguni, is suspended from his post. He is replaced by M.T. Mobisse.

15 Sept. 1994   The United States says it will allocate $1,000,000 towards RENAMO's election campaign finances. RENAMO has threatened to withdraw from the election process unless it has sufficient funds allocated to it.

16 Sept. 1994   The National Election Commission announces the distribution of the 250 parliamentary seats across the country's eleven electoral areas, with Nampula and Zambezia provinces allocated the two largest numbers, fifty and fifty-three, respectively.

22 Sept. 1994   The election campaign begins.

26 Sept. 1994   One month before the elections the Electoral Commission has registered 81% of eligible voters, some 6,309,000 people, and 250 seats will be contested. Twelve political parties are participating. The international community has already pledged $56m. to the electoral process.

27 Oct. 1994	RENAMO announces its withdrawal from the elections, claiming conditions are not in place for the election results to be accepted as free and fair.
27 Oct. 1994	RENAMO's claims are rejected by the National Elections Commission (CNE) and RENAMO's action declared invalid since parties can only withdraw upto seventy two hours before voting begins.
27-29 Oct. 1994	Elections take place.
28 Oct. 1994	Dhlakama abandons the boycott of elections after talks with United Nations officials, Western diplomatics, representatives of the Roman Catholic Church and Zimbabwean President Robert Mugabe. Voting is extended by one day.
29 Oct. 1994	The National Elections Commission (CNE) estimates that over ninety per cent of the electorate have voted. International observers indicate that voting was peaceful and without major incident.
31 Oct. 1994	Dhlakama states that if the elections are fair we will not contest them. We will accept and recognize the results.
15 Nov. 1994	Dhlakama accepts the election results, although complaining of a number of irregularities in the electoral process. RENAMO deputies will take their seats in Parliament. RENAMO is not planning to resume the conflict.
15 Nov. 1994	Adopting Resolution 957 (1994) the United Nations Security Council extends the mandate of UNOMOZ until the inauguration of the new government, expected by 15 December 1994.
19 Nov. 1994	In a report to the United Nations Security Council its Special Representative A. Ajello, discounts RENAMO's allegations of irregularities and declares the elections free and fair. This view is endorsed by the 2,500 international monitors.
19 Nov. 1994	Final results of the elections are released. In the Presidential elections Chissano polled 53.30% of valid votes, Dhlakama 33.73%. In the legislative elections FRELIMO won an eight seat overall majority in the National Assembly over RENAMO and the Democratic Union (UD).
22 Nov. 1994	Chissano has already begun consultations with a view to carrying out a 'significant' Cabinet reshuffle. He will form his government on the basis of competence and experience.
24 Nov. 1994	Chissano and Dhlakama meet for discussions, but no announcement of Cabinet changes is made.
8 Dec. 1994	At the first session of the Assembly of the Republic RENAMO delegates withdraw from proceedings after a dispute over voting procedures.
9 Dec. 1994	President Joaquim Alberto Chissano of FRELIMO is sworn in to serve a new five-year term. He appeals for reconciliation and promises to work for the reconstruction and rehabilitation of Mozambique.
10 Dec. 1994	Mozambique becomes a full member of the Organization of the Islamic Conference (OIC).

16 Dec. 1994	Chissano announces his first Cabinet appointments.

18 Dec. 1994	RENAMO agrees to resume parliamentary activity, and subsequently nominates its representatives on parliamentary committees.

20 Dec. 1994	Seven opposition political parties decide to form an extra parliamentary political force called the United Salvation Front (FUS) to exert influence on the Assembly of the Republic on social, political and economic issues.

23 Dec. 1994	The new government is sworn in.

23 Dec. 1994	Chissano rejects RENAMO's demands for the governorships of the five provinces in which it won a majority of votes in the legislative elections. Instead he finds it necessary to appoint governors 'faithful to the government'.

5 Jan. 1995	Dhlakama reports that a commission has been established to discuss the return of RENAMO to Parliament. It will draft regulations for Parliament and for Members of Parliament.

16 Jan. 1995	RENAMO leader Dhlakama is planning to move RENAMO headquarters to Quelimane, Zambezia Province, for logistical and financial reasons.

24 Jan. 1995	President Chissano appoints governors of Nampula, Sofala and Zambezia, three of the five provinces in which RENAMO has a majority of the votes. All three appointees are FRELIMO members - R. Mualeia, Nampula, O. Candua, Sofala and F.P. Tomas, Zambezia - despite RENAMO's demand for control of these provinces.

2 Feb. 1995	A split in the opposition party, the Independent Party of Mozambique (PIMO) results in dissidents forming their own Patriotic Independent Party, led by M.A. Mussagy, former head of PIMO's Control Commission. PIMO is accused of fomenting Islamic fundamentalism.

5 Feb. 1995	President Chissano reports that the Mozambique Defence Armed Forces (FADM) remains 18,000 men short of its intended 30,000 member strength and that he is considering the reintroduction of compulsory military service to make up the shortfall.

8 Feb. 1995	Mozambique Defence Armed Forces (FADM) Supreme Command is investigating the alleged existence of bases used by Zimbabwean guerrillas under the command of Zimbabwe Unity Movement (ZUM) leader Edgar Tekere, in Manica Province, along the border with Zimbabwe.

9 Feb. 1995	Britain's Minister of State for Overseas Development, Baroness Lynda Chalker visits Mozambique, meets Chissano, Dhlakama, Foreign Minister L. Simao and diplomats from donor countries. Great Britain has made 20m. Pounds Sterling available to Mozambique in 1995.

14-16 Feb. 1995	RENAMO holds its national conference in Quelimane. It accepts that it will not be awarded the governorships of those provinces in which it has won the majority of the votes, but demands a portion of the state earnings of these provinces. This is refused by Prime Minister P. Mocumbi. All RENAMO departmental Heads who have been elected to Parliament are being relieved of their RENAMO party posts. No replacements are named.

19 Feb. 1995	Finance Minister, T. Salomao, confirms the government has decided to institute substantial cuts in its military expenditure, under pressure from the international community and the International Monetary Fund (IMF).
3 Mar. 1995	Dhlakama announces the appointments of F.X. Marcelino (also known as J. de Castro) as RENAMO's Secretary-General, and of C. Pensado as Head of the Department of Political Affairs.
15 Mar. 1995	The Paris Club of creditor countries and international financial institutions pledge some $780m. in loans and grants to Mozambique. In addition, Mozambique expects to be allowed some $350 in debt relief in 1995.
24 Mar. 1995	On an official visit to Malawi, President Chissano pressures Malawi to encourage the return of their Young Pioneers from Mozambique, and the return of Mozambican refugees to Mozambique. Some 80,000 are overdue for repatriation.
3 Apr. 1995	The following new Cabinet appointments are made:- I. Murargy, Secretary-General in the President's office; A. da C.M. Manhanze, Minister in the President's Office for Defence and Security Affairs; C. Taju, Secretary-General of the Council of Ministers.
12 Apr. 1995	The formation of the Mozambique Communist Party (PACOMO) is announced. It intends to build on the positive aspects of the Communist system established by FRELIMO after independence.
21 Apr. 1995	President Chissano appoints A. da C.M. Manhaze, Minister in the Presidency for Defence and Security Affairs and L. Lidimo as Chief of General Staff of the Armed Forces.
May 1995	Demobilized soldiers in central Sofala Province are setting up a political party, the Party of Demobilized Mozambicans (PDM) to represent the interests of both RENAMO and government ex-soldiers.
3 May 1995	President Chissano confirms that the government will not be awarding Dhlakama special status as leader of the opposition since he is not an elected member of Parliament. However he will be treated with 'dignified status'.
Mid May 1995	Opposition political parties hold their second National Conference, funded by the German Friedrich Ebert Foundation, in southern Inhambane Province. They decide to set up an Extra-Parliamentary Forum to convey their concerns to the President and to Parliament, and a Permanent Technical Secretariat to address main political issues.
17 May 1995	President Chissano appoints J.C. de Zumbive as Director-General of the State Information and Security Service (SISE).
17 May 1995	The European Union Commissioner with responsibility for relations with Africa, J. de D. Pinheiro, signs a $65m. aid package during a visit to Mozambique.
24 May 1995	The British ambassador in Maputo, Richard Edis, is reported to have offered British military assistance and balance-of-payments support during a meeting with President Chissano, as well as project aid and assistance with the 1996 local elections.

31 May 1995	The United Nations High Commissioner for Refugees (UNHCR) reports that the programme for the voluntary repatriation of Mozambican refugees from Zimbabwe, launched in June 1993, has been completed. 1,700,000 refugees from six Southern African countries have been repatriated.
31 May 1995	The government of the drought-devastated southern province of Inhambane warns that 100,000 people are at risk of starvation.
June 1995	Mozambique and Malawi set up a Joint Commission to co-ordinate the fight against crime along their common borders and to examine ways to liberalize movement between the two countries.
15 July 1995	The Malawi-Mozambique Joint Security and Defence Commission agree to increase border patrols and to draw up an extradition treaty to facilitate the legal repatriation of criminals. Major problems remain armed robbery, theft of vehicles and cattle as well as drug trafficking.
24 July 1995	At the end of a week-long meeting FRELIMO's Central Committee announces changes to its Secretariat. Five of the six members are replaced, the appointments reflecting a break with the old guard and the promotion of younger members who had not fought in the war of independence. M. Tome becomes FRELIMO's Secretary-General.
25 July 1995	Defence Minister A. Mazula confirms Portugal is to cooperate in the organization of Mozambique's military intelligence.
4 Aug. 1995	Interior Minister, M. Antonio, confirms that armed Zimbabwean dissidents, 'Chimwenjes' are active in Manica Province. The government is preparing a force to act against them.
7 Aug. 1995	The Planning and Finance Ministry's Technical Unit for the Reorganization of Enterprises (UTRE) announces plans to privatize more than twenty state companies.
2 Sept. 1995	State Administration Minister, A. Gamito, speaking on Radio Mozambique, indicates that the country's first local elections will take place in eleven towns only - in Maputo and provincial capitals.
6 Sept. 1995	The Department for the Prevention and Control of Natural Disasters reports that 1,500,000 people in central and southern Mozambique are affected by famine.
8 Sept. 1995	Reports of 'Chimwenje' activity continue to filter out of Manica Province, focusing on their alleged bases at Zomba and Macoca, Sussendenga district, and their preparations for a military incursion into Zimbabwe. Civilian collaborators in the RENAMO stronghold of Dombe are reported.
12 Sept. 1995	An agreement is signed with Portugal in Maputo under which Portugal will provide training to Mozambican police instructors, equipment and technical advice.
20 Sept. 1995	Zimbabwean Defence Minister, M. Matiachi, denies all unconfirmed reports concerning the 'Chimwenje'.
30 Sept. 1995	The Minister of State Administration, A. Gamito, reveals that local elections

scheduled for 1996 are unlikely to be held throughout the whole country. The World Bank has provided loans totalling $24m. but remaining funds will only cover the costs of elections in five cities.

4 Oct. 1995   The government warns that Maputo Province faces a food crisis related to the poor harvest, and to spiralling inflation.

6 Oct. 1995   Widespread rioting occurs in Maputo, in protest against rising food prices.

16 Oct. 1995   The Malawian ambassador to Mozambique, C. Phiri, announces that the two countries have established a joint commission to investigate the presence in Mozambique of members of the disbanded Malawi Young Pioneers (MYP).

27 Oct. 1995   South Africa's Deputy President, Thabo Mbeki and Deputy Foreign Minister, Aziz Pahad visit Mozambique and meet the Prime Minister, P. Mocumbi, and RENAMO leader, A. Dhlakama, in Nacala. Issues discussed include national reconciliation and peace in Southern Africa.

31 Oct. 1995   The General Staff of the Mozambique Armed Forces (FADM) issues a statement distancing itself from reports of a coup plot by officers drawn from RENAMO and guided by right-wing elements.

1 Nov. 1995   Dhlakama is disillusioned by the alleged marginalization of RENAMO by FRELIMO, but pledges he will not return to war. The role of the police seen `as still FRELIMO's police' gives cause for concern.

6 Nov. 1995   President Chissano says he is unconcerned about coup allegations, and there is no cause for alarm.

12 Nov. 1995   United States Assistant Secretary of State for African Affairs, George Moose, arrives in Maputo. Deputy Defence Minister, A.H. Thai, urges the US to assist in the consolidation of the new army, the FADM.

13 Nov. 1995   Mozambique is admitted as the fifty-third member of the Commonwealth at the Heads of Government Meeting in Auckland, New Zealand, as a `unique and special case'.

13 Nov. 1995   The national press reports that RENAMO is maintaining active military bases, at Catema and Masala, in the central district of Maringue, garrisoning more than 1,000 armed men. They are said to be awaiting orders to distribute their weaponry and restart the war.

14 Nov. 1995   A. Dhlakama says there is no national reconciliation in the country, and RENAMO members are being discriminated against and murdered. He claims rumours of coup plots are a deliberate attempt to discredit him by the State Information and Security Service (SISE).

15 Nov. 1995   The European Union representative in Maputo, Francisco Viqueira, warns of a worsening political climate, a hardening of attitudes and a threat of renewed violence. Its concern is presented in a memorandum to Chissano and Dhlakama, warning of the discouragement this will be to aid and investment.

21 Nov. 1995   The Tripartite Commission, comprising representatives of Mozambique, Malawi and the United Nations High Commissioner for Refugees (UNHCR), announces that the programme for repatriating Mozambican refugees from

Malawi has been officially completed. More than 1,000,000 refugees have returned home.

Jan. 1996   Western donors, such as the European Union, Spain and Portugal as well as the UN Development Programme are making their support for Mozambique's first municipal elections conditional on consensus between the parties represented in the Assembly. Deep divergencies between FRELIMO and RENAMO exist over the municipal elections.

mid Jan. 1996   It is decided to crack down on alleged dissidents from Zimbabwe organized in the Chimwenje group, after a number of violent incidents in Sofala Province. Later, a considerable number of troops are placed along the border, reducing attacks.

6 Feb. 1996   South African Defence Minister Joe Modise announces that South Africa will assist Mozambique to clear approximately three million landmines laid during twenty-five years of guerrilla warfare.

May 1996   Conflict between the Catholic Church and the government is apparent after two Muslim holy days are declared as public holidays - Id el Fitr and the Id al Adha. The Catholics Bishops interpreted this as a move to marginalize the church, as the government does not recognize any Catholic feast days. RENAMO expresses support for the Catholic bishops, although the Muslims gave significant support to RENAMO during the 1994 elections.

May 1996   The governor of the Province of Manica confirms the movements of armed men on the border with Zimbabwe. The latter's police force has stepped up patrols on the border against alleged Chimwenje guerrillas.

6 May 1996   Presidents Chissano and Mandela sign an agreement which allows South African farmers to settle in Niassa Province. Mozambique's RENAMO opposes the deal and is concerned about the land conflicts which could arise in ten to twenty years.

20 May 1996   Kuwait and Mozambique establish diplomatic links.

12 June 1996   Zimbabwe and Mozambique announce their cooperation in the fight against the armed Zimbabwean Chimwenje dissidents, who operate from Manica Province against both countries.

18 June 1996   A cooperation agreement is signed with Cuba in the sector of executive training and the exchange of Information.

July 1996   RENAMO leader Afonso Dhlakama meets South African General Constand Viljoen at the latter's request. Not aimed at creating `Boer colonies' the arrival of South African farmers in Mozambique is within the framework of development in the Southern African region.

10 July 1996   The problem of Chimwenje rebels is discussed at a tripartite meeting between security chiefs from Mozambique, Zimbabwe and Malawi in Blantyre, Malawi. The rebels are under the command of a former RENAMO general, Armando Mabache. Although former incidents involved small numbers and small arms, a landmine planted recently in Manica Province was hit by a bulldozer of the Italian consortium Italia-2000, repairing damaged power lines from Cahora Bassa. The second landmine was detected and removed.

Aug. 1996	RENAMO leader Dhlakama refutes allegations that the former rebel movement used chemical weapons during the civil war.
early Aug. 1996	Seven alleged members of the Chimwenje dissident group are sentenced to between two and sixteen years in prison for `mercenarism and armed rebellion'. The group comprises two Zimbabweans and five Mozambicans.
16 Sept. 1996	Iranian Defence Minister Forouzandeh holds talks with the government in Mozambique. Interest is expressed by Iran to assist with mine clearing and military training.
Oct. 1996	A new political party, the Party of All Mozambique Natives (PARTONAMO), is established.
Oct. 1996	The business sector threatens to strike if steps are not taken to curb violence and crime. The Mozambique Human Rights League condemns the government's hidden plans, accusing it, with the police, of involvement in organized crime.
17 Oct. 1996	It is reported that China has presented `non-lethal' military equipment to the Defence Force, valued at $5m.
Nov. 1996	Parliament amends the constitution to allow for the creation of autonomous local government, a requisite for local elections.
Nov. 1996	The police, meeting administrators of five urban districts, decide to establish groups of armed community vigilantes to curb the crime wave.
2 Nov. 1996	Radio Maputo announces that political parties represented in the Extra Parliamentary Forum have established a coalition, which plans to contest the 1997 local elections.
8 Nov. 1996	President Chissano dismisses Interior Minister Manuel Antonio, who came under pressure for the soaring crime rate. The Minister controlling the police, Edmundo Carlos Alberto, is also dismissed. The number of armed robberies show an increase of 71% in the past year.
Jan. 1997	Former rebel movement RENAMO threatens to boycott local elections, unless the law of local authorities is amended to comprise not only cities, towns and administrative post headquarters...... Nation-wide municipal elections should be held.
Feb. 1997	The Council of Ministers bans landmines with immediate effect. The production, sale, use and unauthorized transportation of landmines are prohibited.
25 Feb. 1997	An international conference on landmines is held in Mozambique. The aim is to persuade countries to follow South Africa's example and ban anti-personnel mines.
26 Feb. 1997	The Council of Ministers bans land mines with immediate effect. This includes the production, sale, use and unauthorized transportation of antipersonnel landmines.
19 Mar. 1997	Social Action Minister Alavida Abren is dismissed and his Deputy, Filipe

Mandlane appointed as Acting Minister.

17 Apr. 1997   A former British soldier and his wife, living in Malawi, have been found murdered in Mozambique near the Malawian border.

19 May 1997   The ruling FRELIMO party holds its seventh congress in Maputo. The party has increased its membership by over 150 percent since its last congress in 1991.

22 May 1997   RENAMO leads country-wide demonstrations against alleged poor governing by the ruling FRELIMO party, and protests against the high cost of living. RENAMO leader Dhlakama vows to continue the protests nationwide, but insists that this does not mean another war.

NAMIBIA

21 Mar. 1990   Namibia becomes independent at midnight and SWAPO leader, Sam Nujoma, is sworn in as President by United Nations Secretary-General Perez de Cuellar.

21 Mar. 1990   The new Cabinet is sworn in and the Constituent Assembly, elected in November 1989, assumes the functions of Parliament.

21 Mar. 1990   Namibia becomes a full member of the OAU, SADCC, Non-Aligned Movement and the Commonwealth.

21 Mar. 1990   Signs treaty establishing diplomatic relations with Algeria.

21 Mar. 1990   Signs agreement with Angola on general cooperation and the creation of the Angolan-Namibian Joint Commission on Cooperation.

21 Mar. 1990   Signs treaty establishing diplomatic relations with Finland.

21 Mar. 1990   Signs treaty establishing diplomatic relations with Germany.

21 Mar. 1990   Signs treaty establishing diplomatic relations with Ghana.

21 Mar. 1990   Signs treaty establishing diplomatic relations with Japan.

21 Mar. 1990   Signs treaty establishing diplomatic relations with Korea, Democratic People's Republic.

21 Mar. 1990   Signs treaty establishing diplomatic relations with Korea, Republic (South).

21 Mar. 1990   Signs treaty establishing diplomatic relations with Malawi.

21 Mar. 1990   Signs treaty establishing diplomatic relations with Nigeria.

21 Mar. 1990   Signs treaty establishing diplomatic relations with Rumania.

21 Mar. 1990   Signs treaty establishing diplomatic relations with the Union of Soviet Socialist Republics.

21 Mar. 1990   Signs treaty establishing diplomatic relations with the United States.

21 Mar. 1990	Signs treaty establishing diplomatic relations with Yugoslavia.
21 Mar. 1990	South Africa publishes a bill declaring that no child born in Namibia after independence day will be entitled to South African citizenship.
22 Mar. 1990	Signs treaty establishing diplomatic relations with China.
22 Mar. 1990	Finland donates material and equipment of the Finnish Battalion with UNTAG to Namibia.
22 Mar. 1990	Signs treaty establishing diplomatic relations with Germany (Democratic Republic)
22 Mar. 1990	Signs agreement with World Food Program pertaining to assistance.
23 Mar. 1990	Signs treaty establishing diplomatic relations with Congo.
23 Mar. 1990	Signs treaty establishing diplomatic relations with Iran.
24 Mar. 1990	Signs treaty establishing diplomatic relations with Switzerland.
Apr. 1990	Foreign Minister Gurirab visits Great Britain.
Apr. 1990	Staff of UNTAG leave Namibia.
3 Apr. 1990	Signs treaty establishing diplomatic relations with Cuba.
4 Apr. 1990	Signs bilateral monetary agreement with South Africa.
9 Apr. 1990	The United Nations Council for Namibia votes to dissolve itself and hands over its assets to the Government.
12 Apr. 1990	Signs treaty establishing diplomatic relations with Italy.
12 Apr. 1990	Signs basic agreement with World Health Organization.
Mid Apr.	Finance Minister Herrigel confirms that Namibia will continue to use the South African rand as its currency until 1992.
23 Apr. 1990	Namibia is admitted as the 160th member of the United Nations.
25 Apr. 1990	Signs agreement with World Food Program concerning emergency food assistance.
30 Apr. 1990	Namibia is admitted as a full member of the World Health Organisation.
30 Apr. 1990	Foreign Affairs Minister Theo Ben Gurirab addresses the United Nations General Assembly special session on economic cooperation. He intimates that Namibia is drawing up foreign investment legislation to provide relevant guarantees.
7 May 1990	The charge against Donald Acheson, accused of the murder of Namibian nationalist Lubowski, is dropped.

| 11 May 1990 | Signs agreement with the United Nations Transition Assistance Group (UNTAG) on the donation of certain property. |

11 May 1990   Signs agreement with South Africa concerning the appointment of representatives, privileges and immunities for the representatives and their staff.

19-20 May 1990   Namibia and Angola agree to a joint border security commission during Angolan Defence Minister Pedale's visit to Namibia.

20 May 1990   Signs agreement establishing a permanent joint commission with Egypt.

21 May 1990   Signs agreement on economic cooperation with Germany.

31 May 1990   Signs treaty establishing diplomatic relations with the Sahrawi Arab Democratic Republic.

June 1990   On a visit to the United States, President Nujoma meets President Bush. The two presidents sign four economic and technical aid agreements.

June 1990   President Nujoma signs a bilateral agreement with the Overseas Private Investment Corporation in an attempt to woo United States private investment.

June 1990   Namibia applies to become a member of the IMF.

7 June 1990   Signs treaty establishing diplomatic relations with Bulgaria.

20 June 1990   Signs cultural and educational agreement with Nigeria.

20 June 1990   Signs investment incentive agreement with the United States.

22 June 1990   Signs memorandum of understanding with the Commonwealth Secretariat with respect to the Commonwealth Fund for Technical Cooperation.

29 June 1990   Signs agreement with Zambia regarding the issue of visas.

July 1990   British Defence Minister, Tom King, visits Windhoek.

July 1990   At President Nujoma's invitation, the African National Congress opens an office in Windhoek.

July 1990   Namibia becomes the fifth member of the Southern African Customs Union.

6 July 1990   The first post-election budget is presented revealing a deficit of R210 million.

11 July 1990   Signs treaty establishing diplomatic relations with Peru.

18 July 1990   Signs agreement on economic and technical cooperation with China.

25 July 1990   Signs treaty establishing diplomatic relations with Maldives.

26 July 1990   Signs agreement with Botswana on the creation of the Namibia-Botswana Joint Commission of Cooperation.

26 July 1990	Signs agreement on cultural, educational cooperation with Botswana.
26 July 1990	Signs air services agreement with Botswana.
26 July 1990	Signs a protocol of understanding with Botswana on defence and security.
30 July 1990	Signs general agreement on economic, scientific, technical and cultural co-operation with Mozambique.
1 Aug. 1990	The Central Bank begins operation.
1 Aug. 1990	Government announces the discovery of a coup plot.
2 Aug. 1990	Signs treaty establishing diplomatic relations with Albania.
2-5 Aug. 1990	State visit by President Nujoma to Zambia.
5 Aug. 1990	Signs agreement establishing diplomatic relations with Zambia.
5 Aug. 1990	Signs treaty regarding the supply of electric power with Zambia.
6 Aug. 1990	UNITA of Angola denies involvement in an alleged coup attempt against Namibia.
7 Aug. 1990	The Namibia Newspaper offices are damaged in a grenade attack and President Nujoma issues a warning to those seeking to destabilize Namibia.
9 Aug. 1990	Signs treaty establishing diplomatic relations with Greece.
13 Aug. 1990	Signs treaty establishing diplomatic relations with Benin.
17 Aug. 1990	Agrees on the annual consultation minutes on development cooperation with Finland.
17 Aug. 1990	Signs agreement with the United Nations High Commissioner for Refugees on vehicles, transfer, repatriation, reconstruction and resettlement.
27-30 Aug. 1990	Prime Minister Hage Geingob visits Mozambique.
28 Aug. 1990	Signs treaty establishing diplomatic relations with Jamaica.
Sept. 1990	Prime Minister Geingob withdraws border guards and special constables and replaces them with trained members of the Namibian Defence Force.
12 Sept. 1990	Signs treaty on basic cooperation with the United Nations Children's Fund.
18 Sept. 1990	Signs agreement with Angola on the development of the water potential of Kunene River with Angola.
18 Sept. 1990	Signs agreement on health and social services cooperation with Cuba.
19 Sept. 1990	Signs agreement on Peace Corps with the United States.
21 Sept. 1990	Signs treaty establishing diplomatic relations with Belgium.

24 Sept. 1990	Signs treaty on certain projects with the United Nations Development Program.
25 Sept. 1990	Agrees on minutes between NORAD and the National Planning Commission.
25 Sept. 1990	Signs agreement regarding financial support from Norway in areas of health.
25 Sept. 1990	Namibia is admitted as a member of the IMF and the World Bank.
26 Sept. 1990	Signs air services agreement with Botswana.
28 Sept. 1990	Signs economic, technical and related assistance agreement with United States.
28 Sept. 1990	Signs general agreement with the United States for special development assistance.
28 Sept. 1990	Signs treaty establishing technical assistance with the World Health Organisation.
Oct. 1990	Major-General Soloman Hawala is appointed army commander of the Namibian Defence Force.
Oct. 1990	Amnesty International calls on SWAPO to account for 350 prisoners.
1 Oct. 1990	Verifies project document with the United Nations Development Programme in preparation of the Namibia Donor Conference.
3 Oct. 1990	Signs treaty establishing diplomatic relations with Afghanistan.
5 Oct. 1990	Signs treaty establishing diplomatic relations with Austria.
11 Oct. 1990	Signs agreement with the European Community on budgetary support.
15 Oct. 1990	Signs agreement with Norway on financial support in the areas of health and education.
16 Oct. 1990	Signs treaty establishing diplomatic relations with Chile.
18 Oct. 1990	Signs treaty with Japan regarding economic cooperation to be extended in connection with the Food Aid Convention.
19 Oct. 1990	Signs treaty on bilateral development cooperation with Sweden.
19 Oct. 1990	Signs treaty with Sweden on budgetary support.
19 Oct. 1990	Signs agreement with Sweden on the Bank of Namibia.
19 Oct. 1990	Signs agreement with Sweden on the Personnel and Consultancy Fund.
19 Oct. 1990	Signs treaty with the United Nations Development Program on financial systems development.

30 Oct. 1990	Signs treaty establishing diplomatic relations with Mongolia.
Nov. 1990	An aid agreement is signed with Germany to the value of R170 million.
2 Nov. 1990	Signs revision treaty with the United Nations Development Program on the preparation of the Donor Conference.
9 Nov. 1990	Parliament approves a motion to request the International Committee of the Red Cross to help locate missing persons. The Red Cross is not expected to comply but will continue to search for missing people at the behest of families.
13 Nov. 1990	Signs agreement establishing a Joint Permanent Water Commission with Botswana.
13 Nov. 1990	Signs memorandum of agreement with South Africa on the supply of water.
16 Nov. 1990	Signs contract with European Community on targeted budgetary support.
16 Nov. 1990	Signs contract with the European Community on primary health workers.
16 Nov. 1990	Signs contract on legal training project with the European Community.
16 Nov. 1990	Signs contract with European Community on ground water investigations.
19 Nov. 1990	Signs agreement on development cooperation with Finland.
22 Nov. 1990	Signs agreement on air services with Zambia.
24 Nov. 1990	The British government announces that it will provide a second year of training for the Namibian Defence Force.
25-26 Nov.1990	Ministers of Energy from Angola and Namibia meet in Luanda.
29 Nov. 1990	Signs treaty on economic cooperation with Germany.
4 Dec. 1990	The National Assembly adopts a foreign investment bill which introduces a liberal regime.
14 Dec. 1990	Prime Minister Geingob announces that his government will donate R1 million to South Africa's ANC in a show of solidarity.
14 Dec. 1990	Signs treaty with India regarding contributions to the Africa Fund.
14 Dec. 1990	Signs treaty with Egypt on their Technical Cooperation Fund for Africa.
1991	Signs treaty with Norway concerning energy sector cooperation.
Jan. 1991	The use of passports between the South African enclave of Walvis Bay and Namibia is no longer necessary.
5 Jan. 1991	Six bombs are dropped by fighter aircraft in northern Namibia.
22 Jan. 1991	Signs agreement on development and cooperation with Denmark.

23 Jan. 1991	Holds sectoral talks with Angola.
24-26 Jan.1991	President Nujoma visits the People's Republic of the Congo.
25 Jan. 1991	Signs agreement on budgetary support from Finland.
25 Jan. 1991	Signs cultural agreement with India.
26 Jan. 1991	Signs general cooperation agreement with Congo.
28 Jan. 1991	Signs general agreement on development and cooperation with Iceland.
30 Jan. 1991	Signs agreement on plan of operation for a fisheries research project with Iceland.
1 Feb. 1991	Signs agreement with the Commonwealth Development Corporation relating to operation conditions.
1 Feb. 1991	Signs financial agreement with France.
1 Feb. 1991	Exchange of letters with Sweden abolishing visas.
1 Feb. 1991	Reviews development cooperation with Finland.
5-7 Feb. 1991	President Nujoma visits Gabon.
8 Feb. 1991	Signs agreement with Finland on the geological mapping project in Namibia.
13 Feb. 1991	Angolan fighter aircraft allegedly bomb Bagani in northern Namibia.
18 Feb. 1991	President Nujoma restructures his Cabinet and creates two new ministries which comprise Fishing and Marine Resources (Helmut Angula) and Youth and Sports (Pendukini Hhana).
20 Feb. 1991	Namibia-Norway country programme consultations.
20 Feb. 1991	Signs agreement on development and planning with Norway.
22 Feb. 1991	Signs agreement with European Community on the establishment and the privileges and immunities of the delegation.
22 Feb. 1991	Signs agreement on cultural and scientific cooperation with the Soviet Union.
6 Mar. 1991	Signs agreement on cultural cooperation with Cuba.
6 Mar. 1991	Signs agreement with Cuba establishing a Joint Scientific, Technical and Trade Cooperation.
14 Mar. 1991	Negotiations over Walvis Bay held with South Africa are deadlocked at Groote Schuur in the Cape.
22 Mar. 1991	Signs agreement with Denmark on abolition of visas.

22 Mar. 1991	Signs agreement with Norway on abolition of visas.
22 Mar. 1991	Signs agreement with South Africa to curb and prevent illegal fishing.
22 Mar. 1991	Signs project grant agreement with the United States for basic education reform.
27 Mar. 1991	Signs cultural agreement with China.
27 Mar. 1991	Signs another project grant agreement with the United States for basic education reform.
28 Mar. 1991	Signs agreement with Denmark concerning four development projects.
4 Apr. 1991	Financial protocol with France is established for the purchase of premises for the Franco-Namibia Cultural Centre in Windhoek.
18 Apr. 1991	Signs technical cooperation agreement with Germany.
18 Apr. 1991	Signs treaty with Japan on economic cooperation for the purpose of food production. Another exchange of notes concerns a low income housing project.
19 Apr. 1991	Signs treaty with Sweden concerning support towards development of the Namibian Central Statistics Office.
22 Apr. 1991	Signs treaty on abolition of visas with Finland.
22 Apr. 1991	Signs agreement with the United Nations Development Programme.
22-25 Apr.	State visit by President Nujoma to Tanzania.
23 Apr. 1991	Specifies British assistance in the fields of education and culture.
24 Apr. 1991	Signs specific agreement on Personnel and Consultancy Fund with Sweden.
24 Apr. 1991	Signs treaty with Sweden on development cooperation.
24 Apr. 1991	Signs agreement with Sweden on continued cooperation with the Bank of Namibia.
24 Apr. 1991	Signs agreement on budgetary support with Sweden.
24 Apr. 1991	Signs agreement on education with Sweden
24 Apr. 1991	Signs treaty with Sweden on transport and communications support.
25 Apr. 1991	Signs agreement of cooperation with Tanzania.
25 Apr. 1991	Signs joint communiqué with Tanzania on visit of President of Namibia to Tanzania.
25 Apr. 1991	Signs agreement with Tanzania on the establishment of a joint commission of cooperation.

8 May 1991	Signs agreement with North Korea on cultural cooperation.
13 May 1991	Signs joint communiqué with Indonesia establishing diplomatic relations.
14 May 1991	Signs trade agreement with Romania.
14 May 1991	Signs treaty with Botswana concerning education.
5 June 1991	Signs agreement on cultural cooperation with Germany.
14 June 1991	Signs agreement with Norway on cooperation.
14 June 1991	Signs agreement with Norway on general terms and procedures of development cooperation.
19 June 1991	Signs agreement with Finland on development cooperation.
21 June 1991	Signs treaty with UNICEF on cooperation.
21 June 1991	Signs treaty with the UN Development Programme on Public Service Restructuring.
28 June 1991	Signs agreement with the International Committee of the Red Cross.
28 June 1991	Signs memorandum of understanding with Great Britain concerning the provision of personnel.
8 July 1991	Signs cultural treaty with India.
12 July 1991	Signs treaty with Angola establishing air transport cooperation.
12 July 1991	Signs treaty with Ecuador establishing diplomatic relations.
12 July 1991	Signs agreement on development cooperation with Finland.
12 July 1991	Signs agreement with Germany on financial cooperation.
25 July 1991	Two Spanish vessels are reported to have been fishing illegally in Namibian waters.
25 July 1991	The South African government admits it spent one million rand in attempting to prevent a SWAPO victory in the pre-independence elections.
31 July 1991	Signs financial agreement with France.
31 July 1991	Signs agreement with France, incorporating articles of association of the Franco-Namibian Cultural Centre.
31 July 1991	An agreement is signed with France whereby they will provide a helicopter for four months and an aeroplane for two months to assist in the surveillance of Namibian waters.
1 Aug. 1991	Signs agreement with Japan on economic cooperation for the purpose of the increase of food production in Namibia.

16 Aug. 1991	Signs contract no. 91.750.72.01 with the European Community on the curriculum development program.
21 Aug. 1991	Signs agreement with the United Nations concerning the United Nations Information Centre in Namibia.
Sept. 1991	Signs agreement with North Korea on economic and technical cooperation.
2 Sept. 1991	Signs agreement on cultural and scientific cooperation with the USSR.
5 Sept. 1991	Signs agreement with China on economic and technical cooperation.
Sept. 1991	The Namibian National Party dissolves itself. It is reconstituted as the Monitor Action Group and will serve as a pressure group.
13 Sept. 1991	Signs joint communiqué with Brazil on the occasion of the visit of Fernando Collor, President of Brazil.
13 Sept. 1991	Signs agreement with Finland on development cooperation.
19 Sept. 1991	Signs agreement with Canada on training of personnel.
20 Sept. 1991	A joint technical committee is established by South Africa and Namibia to serve in an advisory capacity facilitating the administration of Walvis Bay. In addition, a similar Committee will investigate the demarcation of the Orange River boundary.
24 Sept. 1991	Signs agreement with Norway on cooperation for promotion of economic and social development.
27 Sept. 1991	Signs agreement with Germany concerning cooperation.
Oct. 1991	An arms and ammunition factory is due to commence production. It is situated near Keetmanshoop.
11 Oct. 1991	Signs agreement with Austria on the visit of an Austrian delegation in Namibia.
21-30 Oct.	Namibian nationwide census is undertaken.
24 Oct. 1991	Signs agreement with Angola on the development of a hydro-electric generating scheme.
28 Oct. 1991	Construction of a border fence between Angola and Namibia will commence.
29 Oct. 1991	President Nujoma announces that Namibia is to open a Namibian interests office in South Africa.
Nov. 1991	Namibia establishes a border post in the Caprivi Strip to act as a deterrent to Zambian smugglers. As there was no consultation with the Zambian government, it causes a diplomatic incident.
6 Nov. 1991	Signs agreement on development cooperation with Finland.

6 Nov. 1991	Signs agreement on budgetary support with Finland.
7 Nov. 1991	Signs financial agreement with France.
20 Nov. 1991	Signs development agreement with the Netherlands.
22 Nov. 1991	Signs agreement with Zambia on scientific and cultural cooperation.
22 Nov. 1991	Members of a Joint Commission, of which Namibia is one, created by the 13 December 1988 Brazzaville Protocol to facilitate conflict resolution, is dissolved.
30 Nov. 1991	The Democratic Turnhalle Alliance becomes a single political party.
30 Nov. - 4 Dec.1991	SWAPO wins a landslide victory in regional and local elections.
2 Dec. 1991	Signs contract no. 91.75072.04 with the European Community.
2 Dec. 1991	Signs contract no. 91.75072.05 regarding targeted budgetary support from the European Community.
2 Dec. 1991	Signs contract no. 91.75072.06 with the European Community regarding studies and action for the preparation of likely projects.
2 Dec. 1991	Signs contract no. 91.75072.06.01 with the European Community regarding the feasibility study for the establishment of an agricultural information system.
7-11 Dec. 1991	The SWAPO party congress is held. President Nujoma is unanimously re-elected as president and Moses Garoeb becomes secretary-general.
9 Dec. 1991	Signs treaty with the Seychelles establishing diplomatic relations.
31 Dec. 1991	Signs specific agreement with Sweden on direct employment by Namibia of foreign personnel.
1992	Obtains letters of credence from the Rwandan ambassador, which assumes that diplomatic relations have been established with Rwanda.
1992	Signs agreement with Finland on a cross-curriculum culture project.
1992	Signs agreement with Finland on the fact finding study on a small scale mining project in Namibia.
21 Jan. 1992	Signs a treaty with Germany on advisory assistance to the Department of Water Affairs.
21 Jan. 1992	Signs treaty with Germany on advisory assistance to the Ministry of Fisheries and Marine Resources.
21 Jan. 1992	Signs treaty with Germany on technical cooperation.
28 Jan. 1992	Provisional population figures as revealed by the 1991 census total the population at 1,401,711.

31 Jan. 1992	President Nujoma arrives in Nigeria at the commencement of a tour of West Africa which also includes Ghana and Gabon.
Feb. 1992	Namibia predicts that it will have to spend R19 million on maize imports due to the drought.
3 Feb. 1992	Signs agreement with Nigeria on cultural, educational and health cooperation.
3 Feb. 1992	Signs joint communiqué with Nigeria on the visit of the President of Namibia to Nigeria.
3 Feb. 1992	Signs agreement with Nigeria on economic, scientific and technical cooperation.
5 Feb. 1992	Signs agreement with Ghana on economic and technical cooperation.
6 Feb. 1992	Signs treaty with Venezuela on technical cooperation in matters of energy and mining.
14 Feb. 1992	Signs agreement with Finland on development cooperation.
16 Feb. 1992	The composition of SWAPO's new twenty-one-member politburo is announced.
26 Feb. 1992	Signs treaty with Norway regarding the fisheries sector.
2 Mar. 1992	Signs joint communiqué with Iran during President Nujoma's visit to the Islamic Republic of Iran.
12 Mar. 1992	Ministry of Information reports that fisheries patrol boats have been instructed to confiscate illegal vessels inside Namibia's 200 mile exclusive economic zone.
16 Mar. 1992	Signs a treaty for cooperation with the European Community.
27 Mar. 1992	Signs cooperation agreement with Sweden.
Apr. 1992	World Bank report concludes that the civil service wage bill will have to be cut by 20 percent over the next four years. Expenditure will have to be diverted into capital expenditure in order to underpin economic growth.
Apr. 1992	Minister of Lands, Resettlement and Rehabilitation reports on a successful mission to Botswana whereby repatriation of Botswanans of Namibian origin would commence. The immediate count is some 2500.
10 Apr. 1992	Signs agreement with Finland on the improvement and strengthening of forestry colleges in the SADCC region.
10 Apr. 1992	Finance Minister Herrigel resigns and is replaced by Gert Hanekom, whose portfolio of Agriculture, Water and Rural Development is assumed by Anton von Wietersheim. This is the second cabinet reshuffle since independence.
10 Apr. 1992	Signs agreement with Japan on the preliminary study of projects for building

of a fisheries research vessel.

16 Apr. 1992	Signs treaty with Japan on economic cooperation.
27 Apr. 1992	Signs agreement with Finland on development cooperation.
30 Apr. 1992	Signs joint communiqué with Papua New Guinea on the establishment of diplomatic relations.
May 1992	President Nujoma launches an appeal for an emergency relief programme due to the critical situation of subsistence farmers.
6 May 1992	Signs basic agreement with Germany on the secondment of development workers of the German development service.
8 May 1992	Signs treaty with Nigeria on the Namibia-Nigeria Joint Commission.
13 May 1992	Signs agreed minutes with Sweden on the mid-term review of development cooperation between the two countries.
21 May 1992	Signs agreement with Germany on financial cooperation. Includes an economic cooperation programme.
24 May 1992	President Mugabe mediates in talks held in Kasane to resolve the boundary dispute between Botswana and Namibia over the Sidudu/Kasikili Island.
27 May 1992	Signs agreement with Sweden on cooperation in the field of development of the Namibian Central Statistics Office.
2 June 1992	Signs agreement with Kenya on the abolition of visas.
2 June 1992	Signs agreement with Kenya on general cooperation.
2 June 1992	Signs joint communiqué with Kenya on the occasion of the visit of President Nujoma to Kenya.
4 June 1992	Signs agreement of cooperation with Uganda.
12 June 1992	Hassam Habibi, first Vice-President of Iran visits Namibia.
20 June 1992	Signs another agreement with Germany on financial cooperation.
12 July 1992	Signs agreement with Germany on financial cooperation.
13 July 1992	Prime Minister Geingob requests the United States Secretary of State, James Baker, to use influence to pressurize South Africa to hasten the Walvis Bay negotiations.
24 July 1992	Signs agreement with France on assistance of air surveillance.
Aug. 1992	The middle of the Orange River is demarcated as the boundary with South Africa but is subject to further discussion.
Aug. 1992	Norway and Sweden cancel emergency drought aid in protest against the purchase of a R75 million jet aircraft for President Nujoma.

17 Aug. 1992	Signs agreement with Zimbabwe on economic, technical and cultural cooperation.
17 Aug. 1992	Signs multilateral treaty establishing the Southern African Development Community (SADC).
20 Aug. 1992	Namibia accedes to the 1970 Nuclear Non-Proliferation Treaty.
21 Aug. 1992	Agreement is reached after months of negotiation with South Africa over the administration of the Walvis Bay enclave. Both countries will be represented on the Walvis Bay Joint Administration Body but neither country is prepared to relinquish its territorial claim.
2 Sept. 1992	Signs treaty with the African Development Foundation on the funding of development projects.
3 Sept. 1992	Signs agreement with the United States on the Living in a Finite Environment (UFE) Project.
8 Sept. 1992	Signs an agreement with Germany on the secondment of a group of advisers of the Federal Armed Forces to Namibia.
8 Sept. 1992	Signs agreement on economic and technical cooperation with China.
8 Sept. 1992	Signs agreement with Germany on equipment aid.
14 Sept. 1992	Signs agreement with South Africa on the Viooldrift and Noordoewer Joint Irrigation Scheme.
14 Sept. 1992	Signs agreement with South Africa on the establishment of a permanent water commission.
14 Sept. 1992	Signs a trade agreement with the Korean Democratic People's Republic.
15 Sept. 1992	Accedes as the 105th contracting party of GATT.
17 Sept. 1992	Signs an agreement with the United States on the project grant amendment no. 1.
17 Sept. 1992	Signs project grant agreement with the United States on the Reaching out with Education to Adults in Development Project (READ).
25 Sept. 1992	Signs agreement with UNESCO on the establishment of a UNESCO office in Namibia.
30 Sept. 1992	Signs loan agreement with the African Development Fund.
30 Sept. 1992	Signs agreement with the African Development Fund on the investigation study for Western Ovambo and Kaokoland.
6 Oct. 1992	Signs agreement with Belgium on development cooperation and technical assistance.
20 Oct. 1992	Signs agreement with South Africa regarding trade tests for apprentices and other prospective artisans.

29 Oct. 1992	Signs agreement with Brazil on the creation of the Namibian-Brazil Joint Commission of Cooperation.
29 Oct. 1992	Signs agreement with Brazil on the abolition of official and tourist visas between both countries.
30 Oct. 1992	Signs agreement with Japan on the supply of equipment for the production of educational programmes.
4 Nov. 1992	Signs a memorandum of understanding with Sweden.
6 Nov. 1992	Justice Minister Tjiriange signs an agreement with South Africa providing for the secondment of South African judges to serve on the Namibian bench.
30 Nov. - 4 Dec. 1992	SWAPO wins resoundingly in regional and local elections in the first polls since independence. This will result in its domination of the new National Council.
24 Dec. 1992	A memorandum of understanding with Botswana is signed, establishing a joint panel of experts to determine the boundary at the Chobe River, especially at the Kasikili/Sedudu Island.
3 Jan. 1993	The National Society for Human Rights accuses the government of torturing refugees and refusing to help them resettle in new countries.
11 Jan. 1993	Thirty World Teach volunteers from the United States arrive in Namibia to begin a one-year programme at schools around the country.
12 Jan. 1993	Namibia introduces a language policy for schools providing for the gradual introduction of English as the medium of instruction from Grade 4.
15 Jan. 1993	Nangolo Mbumba of Namibia and Carl von Hirschberg of South Africa meet to begin work on a joint administrative authority for Walvis Bay. They meet on the day bulldozers drive the military border point between Walvis Bay and Swakopmund into the sand.
15 Jan. 1993	The Namibian government denies that its soldiers were fighting alongside the Angolan army in the renewed civil war against UNITA.
21 Jan. 1993	Namibia joins the Preferential Trade Area of Eastern and Southern Africa (PTA).
27 Jan. 1993	UNITA complains that Namibia is involved in supporting the Angolan army and they claim to have captured a Namibian soldier.
Feb. 1993	Namibia creates a New York-based Fund for the University of Namibia and aims to raise $20 million.
5 Feb. 1993	Namcor, the National Petroleum Corporation of Namibia, reaches agreement with the Norwegian company Nopec, to conduct a multi-client off-shore seismic survey.
9 Feb. 1993	The middle of the Orange River as the common border between South Africa and Namibia is announced by a joint tehnical committee meeting in Pretoria. This delimitation is subject to the approval of both governments.

Mar. 1993	The Minister of Agriculture reports that more than 80 percent of the commercial maize crop has been lost to the drought.
4 Apr. 1993	Dirk Mudge, Chairman of the opposition Democratic Turnhalle Alliance announces his resignation from the National Assembly.
15 Apr. 1993	Changes are made to the Cabinet, aimed at promoting the manufacturing industry. Hidipo Hamutenya becomes Minister of Trade and Industry, exchanging portfolios with Ben Amatila who becomes Minister of Information and Broadcasting.
May 1993	President Nujoma launches an appeal for an emergency relief programme due to the critical situation of the subsistence farmers.
11 May 1993	The National Council, whose twenty-six members were inaugurated in January, begins its first session.
1 June 1993	General Sales Tax is cut by 3 percent and both company and income tax are reduced.
4 June 1993	The foreign ministers of Angola (Venancio de Moura), Namibia (Theo-Ben Gurirab) and South Africa (`Pik' Botha) meet for trilateral talks in Windhoek.
16 June 1993	President Nujoma holds talks in Washington with United States President Bill Clinton.
8 July 1993	Delegations from South Africa and Namibia agree to the joint management of the Rooikop Airport in Walvis Bay.
30 July 1993	The Namibian government approves of a seal culling exercise which will double the 1992 quota.
Aug. 1993	The Rehoboth Community applies to the United Nations for recognition as an indigenous group in the hope that their request for self-government will be strengthened.
16 Aug. 1993	The South African multiparty negotiation council passes a resolution calling for the incorporation of Walvis Bay and a number of off-shore islands into Namibia.
17 Aug. 1993	Permanent Secretary to the Ministry of Works, Transport and Communications states that plans to build a new deep water harbour at Möwe Bay on the skeleton coast will not be affected by Walvis Bay's integration into Namibia.
18 Aug. 1993	President F.W. de Klerk formally announces that South Africa will relinquish its claim to sovereignty over Walvis Bay.
8 Sept. 1993	Namibia's Foreign Minister meets with South Africa's `Pik' Botha to discuss a date for the incorporation/reintegration of Walvis Bay into Namibia.
13 Sept. 1993	The Namibian dollar is launched and a simultaneous bilateral monetary agreement is signed with South Africa to link the new currency to the Rand.

Nov. 1993	The enthronement of the King of the Damara and the SWAPO project to restore the Kwanyama Kingdom raise fears that national unity could be undermined.
Nov. 1993	The Sedudu/Kasikili Island in the middle of the Chobe River proves to be a contentious factor in the relationship between Botswana and Namibia.
5 Nov. 1993	Namibia becomes a signatory to the Common Market for Eastern and Southern Africa (COMESA).
17 Nov. 1993	Government intervenes in the strike at De Beers Centenary AG Group's Consolidated Diamond Mines. They send in riot police to bolster local police and to halt violence on the picket line.
3 Dec. 1993	Namibia welcomes the unanimous adoption of the Transfer of Walvis Bay to Namibia Bill by the Multiparty Negotiating Council.
Feb. 1994	Tension over the construction of a militiary air base rises.
11 Feb. 1994	Israel and Namibia establish diplomatic relations.
17 Feb. 1994	South Africa's Minister of Defence, Kobie Coetsee and his Namibian counterpart, Peter Mushihange sign an agreement handing over the military facilities of Walvis Bay to Namibia. This will become operative at the end of February.
17 Feb. 1994	Sam Nujoma will be SWAPO's sole presidential contender in the elections.
21 Feb. 1994	About 1000 looters ransack a township near Walvis Bay.
28 Feb. 1994	Walvis Bay and the Penguin Islands are transferred to Namibian sovereignty. President Sam Nujoma visits the port for the first time since 1959.
1 Mar. 1994	Namibia is to establish its own navy following the integration of Walvis Bay.
Apr. 1994	An agreement pertaining to naval cooperation is signed with Brazil. This is seen as the first step in establishing a maritime wing of the Defence Force.
20 Apr. 1994	The first private commercial radio station commences broadcasting from Windhoek.
3 June 1994	Worst seal disaster occurs with unusual sea conditions affecting fish shoals upon which the seals feed.
23 June 1994	A two month inquest into the murder of Anton Lubowski, a leading member of SWAPO, ends. Judge Harold Levy concludes that the crime was committed by an Irish contract killer, Donald Acheson, working for South Africa's Civil Co-operation Bureau.
Late June 1994	The United States donates five Cessna aircraft to Namibia under a N$11.9 million biodiversity aid programme. This is considered the first phase in creating an airwing for the Defence Force.

18 July 1994	Auditor-General Fanuel Tjingaete complains at the lack of government accountability and accuses the ministeries of Foreign Affairs, Health and Social Services, Education and Culture of fraud.
21 July 1994	Opposition Democratic Turnhalle Alliance demands the exposure and disciplining of those responsible for corruption.
Aug. 1994	Launch of the new Democratic Coalition of Namibia comprising the National Patriotic Front, German Union and the South West African Union.
9-10 Aug.1994	President Nelson Mandela of South Africa visits Namibia.
15-16 Aug.1994	Local elections are held in Walvis Bay for the first time since it came under Namibian control. They result in a victory for SWAPO.
18 Aug. 1994	A High Court ruling paves the way for the legal return of the disbanded Koevoet members.
28 Oct. 1994	The controversial Land Reform Bill is passed by Parliament. It allows for the expropriation of disused land, and now requires the approval of the National Council.
5 Nov. 1994	United Democratic Front President Justus Garoeb confirms his candidacy in the Namibian presidential elections.
7 Nov. 1994	Only two presidential candidates register by the deadline despite Garoeb's protestations. Hileni Latvios of the Federal Convention of Namibia is refused an extension.
18 Nov. 1994	Namibia joins the International Maritime Organization as its 150th member.
6 Dec. 1994	South Africa writes off the debt owed by Namibia estimated at R800 million.
7-8 Dec. 1994	First post-independence elections are held. A landslide victory for SWAPO and President Nujoma results in a sufficient majority to amend the Constitution.
25 Jan. 1995	Signs cultural agreement with India.
Feb. 1995	The Namibian government is poised to award a contract to a Norwegian-Swedish firm to conduct a two year feasibility study on constructing a new dam on the Kunene River at the Epupa Falls.
9 Feb. 1995	Namibia cuts company and personal tax rates.
15 Feb. 1995	Namibia and Botswana fail to reach agreement over the ownership and boundary of an island in the Chobe River. The International Court of Justice will arbitrate.
17 Feb. 1995	President Nujoma tries to prevent illegal trade with Angola. He repeats orders to troops and police to shoot at vehicles crossing the Okavango River should drivers refuse to stop.

Mar. 1995	Reports on developing links between the right-wing Freiheitliche Movement leaders in Austria with Namibian leadership. The Movement is Austria's largest opposition party.
2 Mar. 1995	Namibia offers tax concessions in the form of an export processing zone or EPZ, at Walvis Bay. The creation of employment is an important aspect of the scheme.
15 Mar. 1995	Amendments to the Pension Funds Act and Long Term Insurance Act require 35% of Namibian investments to be locally placed by June 1995.
20 Mar. 1995	The day before his inauguration for a second term of office, President Nujoma announces a new Cabinet and creates a new post of Prisons and Correctional Services, and Basic Education and Culture. He himself takes responsibility for the Home Affairs portfolio in an effort to combat escalating crime. He is also Commander in Chief of the army, the police and immigration amongst other services.
21 Mar. 1995	Sam Nujoma is sworn in for his second presidential term of office.
6 Apr. 1995	President Nujoma, in his capacity as Minister of Home Affairs, is given as the first defendent in a defamation suit brought by former members of the Security Forces who had been named in the 1994 Lubowski inquest.
May 1995	The co-founder of the Democratic Turnhalle Alliance, Dirk Mudge, resigns as the party's chairman and retires from politics.
18 May 1995	Lesotho and Namibia sign an agreement abolishing mutual visa requirements.
22 June 1995	Namibia announces it would seek foreign drought aid. It was revealed that drought aid had been used, in some cases, to dig deep boreholes on land occupied by government ministers.
Aug. 1995	The annual seal cull on the Atlantic Coast begins.
1 Aug. 1995	Angola, Botswana and Namibia sign an agreement establishing a joint commission to ensure the development of the Okavango River Basin. This is to be done through an environmentally suitable management plan.
15-16 Aug.1995	SWAPO wins eight of the ten seats in Walvis Bay's first non-racial local elections.
28 Aug. 1995	All government ministeries are ordered to cut back on expenditure by 4% to pay for emergency drought relief after the failure of appeals for foreign aid.
28 Aug. 1995	Namibian military personnel to be trained by Zimbabwe.
6 Sept. 1995	A Home Affairs Minister is appointed ending months of criticism since Nujoma occupied the portfolio.
15 Sept. 1995	About 300 Herero protest outside the German Embassy in Windhoek to coincide with the visit of Chancellor Helmut Kohl. They are demanding compensation for the Herero massacres of 1896 and 1907.

15 Sept. 1995	President Sam Nujoma appoints Jerry Edandjo as Minister of Home Affairs.
15 Sept. 1995	Germany provides $20 million to assist long-term housing projects.
15 Sept. 1995	German Chancellor Helmut Kohl, on a two-day visit to Namibia, promises assistance in return for the promotion of the German language and culture.
22 Sept. 1995	Namibia to form a border guard to supplement the defence force troops and police guarding Namibia's northerly border with Angola.
11 Oct. 1995	Prime Minister Geingob reacts to unemployed former members of PLAN who took a deputy minister hostage in Windhoek's Katutura township. The former PLAN members demand employment and cash pay-outs.
19 Dec. 1995	The Cabinet agrees to spend N$45 million in incorporating 2000 former guerrillas of the demobilized People's Liberation Army of Namibia into the police and defence force.
Feb. 1996	Namibia and Botswana sign an agreement on the dispute surrounding the Sidudu/Kasikili river island, to be submitted to the International Court of Justice in The Hague. Both countries have committed themselves in advance to the outcome of the Court's ruling.
Mar. 1996	Joint committee between Namibia and Botswana are established to control illegal crossing and cross-border smuggling.
7 Mar. 1996	President Sam Nujoma pays a working visit to Angola where bilateral cooperation and security along the Namibian-Angolan border is discussed.
9 Apr. 1996	The Cabinet is reshuffled.
22 Apr. 1996	Minister Ben Amathila announces that the country's northeastern border will remain closed until the UN peacekeeping forces have consolidated their position. The border along the Kavango River was closed after three Namibians were killed and a woman assaulted.
late Apr. 1996	SWAPO Secretary-General, Moses Caroeb, is replaced by Deputy Foreign Affairs Minister Netumbo Nduitwah.
30 May 1996	A military co-operation agreement is concluded with Russia covering both training of the Namibian Defence Force and the supply of military equipment.
21 June 1996	President Sam Nujoma pays a five-day state visit to Bonn and discusses cooperation and the improvement of relations with Chancellor Kohl, who regards Namibia as one of Germany's main focusses in Africa. Germany is Namibia's prime aid donor.
24 June 1996	Bilateral issues are the focus of discussions with French President Jacques Chirac during President Nujoma's state visit to France. Namibia's drought and water crisis as well as French investment in the country are discussed. The French President praises Namibia for its democratic government and policy of reconciliation.
22 July 1996	Namibia and the United Arab Emirates establish diplomatic relations at

                          ambassadorial level.

13 Sept. 1996   President Nujoma announces a cabinet reshuffle in order to give new
                          ministers the opportunity to extend their experience. The National Planning
                          Commission is placed within the office of the President.

14 Nov. 1996   A breakaway faction of SWAPO transforms into a political party under the
                          name of the National Democratic Party for Justice, with Nghiwele Ndjoba
                          as its president.

end Jan. 1997   Russian Defence Minister Rodionov meets his Namibian counterpart
                          Phillemon Malima in Moscow, where they discuss Russian-Namibian
                          military cooperation.

11 Mar. 1997   Namibia is to establish extradition agreements with twenty-six countries, the
                          Ministry of Information declares.

21 Mar. 1997   President Nujoma pardons 1,212 prisoners to mark Namibia's seventh
                          anniversary of independence.

30 Mar. 1997   Nineteen senior Nigerian military officers leave Windhoek after a week-long
                          visit. The Nigerian War College might offer assistance to the Namibian
                          Defence Force. The South African call for isolation of Nigeria after the
                          execution of opposition activists was only reluctantly followed by President
                          Nujoma; and Nigeria is keen to keep contact with Southern Africa.

early Apr. 1997   President Nujoma tells Parliament that he would be prepared to stand for a
                          third term of office, despite the fact that the constitution limits the
                          incumbent to a maximum of two terms. This causes concern among the
                          opposition, human rights groups and Western diplomats.

31 May 1997   SWAPO adopts a resolution to amend the constitution in order to allow a
                          third term of office for President Nujoma. The change will apply only in
                          Nujoma's case - all future presidents will service only two terms.

SOUTH AFRICA

30 May 1961   The Union of South Africa officially ceases to exist, at midnight.

31 May 1961   South Africa is declared a Republic, independent and outside the
                          Commonwealth. C.R. Swart, the former Governor-General, is sworn in as
                          the first President of the Republic of South Africa.

4 June 1961   The Iraqi Foreign Minister, Hashim Jawad, announces that Iraq will not
                          recognize the government of South Africa because of its apartheid policies.

14 June 1961   Signs agreement with Great Britain in regard to guaranteed preferences on
                          the British market.

21 June 1961   Signs multilateral protocol on international civil aviation.

26 June 1961   Signs ILO Convention, no. 116, concerning the partial revision of
                          conventions adopted.

| 27 June 1961 | The government of Ghana imposes a total ban on the export of all Ghanian produce to South Africa and South West Africa, as a protest against apartheid. |

29 June 1961   During its plenary conference in Geneva, the International Labour Organisation adopts a Nigerian resolution condemning the racial policies of the South African government and calling for South Africa's withdrawal from the ILO, by 163 votes to nil, with 89 abstentions. The South African government has no intention of acceding to this request.

30 June 1961   The 'Treason Trial' ends. The total cost of the four year trial is estimated at R1 million.

4 July 1961   A United Nations eight-man committee with instructions to investigate conditions in the Mandated Territory of South West Africa, is refused permission to enter the Territory. The Minister for External Affairs, Eric Louw announces that if members of the committee try to enter they will be detained and sent back and that this will involve the United Nations in an act of aggression.

4 July 1961   The Sierra Leone government imposes a ban on all trade and commerce with South Africa, as a protest against its apartheid policies. Ports and airports will be closed to all South African ships and aircraft; no white South Africans will be allowed to enter Sierra Leone; those already in the country will not be granted re-entry visas.

5 July 1961   The International Monetary Fund (IMF) announces it has entered into a stand-by agreement with South Africa under which South Africa may draw up to the requivalent of $75,000,000 in various currencies, during the next twelve months.

15 July 1961   H.A. Fagan, former Chief Justice and Minister of Native Affairs, agrees to become leader of the National Union. Its founder, J. du P. (Japie) Basson will remain party chairman.

24 July 1961   Signs multilateral agreement under Article 18 of the Antarctic Treaty.

1 Aug. 1961   The Prime Minister announces that there will be a general election on 18 October 1961. The necessary proclamation will be issued on 28 August 1961, nomination day 15 September 1961, and the House of Assembly will be dissolved.

2 Aug. 1961   A re-organisation of the Cabinet is announced by Dr. Verwoerd.

4 Aug. 1961   Signs treaty with France amending the air agreement of 17 September 1954.

15 Aug. 1961   An electoral alliance is announced between the United Party (UP) and the National Union (NU) in Bloemfontein, in the form of a nine-point pact determining basic objectives.

26 Aug. 1961   A.K. Ganyile, a Pondo leader and refugee in Basutoland, is kidnapped with two companions by six South African policemen, taken across the border into South Africa, and imprisoned in the Transkei.

18 Sept. 1961   Signs multilateral agreement on aviation.

4 Oct. 1961	Separate elections for the four Cape Coloured representative seats are held. They are won by Independents with United Party support.
11 Oct. 1961	Signs multilateral treaty amending the Phyto Sanitary Convention of 1954.
11 Oct. 1961	The Foreign Minister, E. Louw, defends South Africa's apartheid policy in the United Nations, against African criticism. On the same day the Assembly adopts a Liberian censure motion on South Africa, with sixty-seven in favour, one against, twenty abstaining, nine not participating in the vote (including Britain and the United States) and three absent.
18 Oct. 1961	The government increases its strength in the elections. The final results are: Nationalists 105, United Party 49, Progressives 1, National Union 1.
23-26 Oct.1961	South Africa's racial policies are debated by the Special Political Committee in the United Nations, with South Africa participating.
25 Oct. 1961	Signs treaty with Italy regarding air services.
26 Oct. 1961	Signs multilateral treaty for the protection of performers, producers of phonograms and broadcasting organizations.
14 Nov. 1961	The British Prime Minister, Harold Macmillan, informs the House of Commons that responsibility for the conduct of Britain's relations with South Africa, will be transferred from the Commonwealth Relations Secretary to the Foreign Secretary, from 1 December 1961. Sir John Maud will continue to hold the posts of Ambassador to South Africa and of High Commissioner for Basutoland, Bechuanaland and Swaziland.
28 Nov. 1961	The United Nations General Assembly adopts an eight nation resolution, by seventy-two votes to two, with twenty-seven abstentions, calling on all member states to take such separate and collective action, as is open to them to bring about the abandonment of South Africa's racial policies. It did not specifically call for sanctions.
Dec. 1961	Handbills are distributed by the organization Umkonto we Siswe (the Spear of the Nation) announcing new methods to be adopted in the struggle for freedom and democracy.
1 Dec. 1961	Signs agreement with the International Bank for Reconstruction and Development.
9 Dec. 1961	Signs multilateral treaty extending the declaration on the provisional accession of Tunisia to the General Agreement on Tarrifs and Trade.
11 Dec. 1961	Albert Luthuli is awarded the Nobel Peace Prize in Oslo. The government issues a special ten-day passport, with restrictions on his movements and public appearances.
12 Dec. 1961	Dr. Verwoerd tells the Union Council of Coloured Affairs that the Council will be transformed into a coloured 'Parliament' with a 'Cabinet', initially of four members, within the framework of a ten-year plan for the development towards self-determination of the Cape Coloured population.
16 Dec. 1961	Five bomb explosions occur in the Johannesburg area and five others at Port

Elizabeth.

18 Dec. 1961	Three further attempts to sabotage buildings in and near Johannesburg are discovered.
18 Dec. 1961	Signs treaty with Sweden to further extend the period of validity of traffic rights.
18 Dec. 1961	Signs treaty with Denmark extending the period of validity of traffic rights granted to Scandinavian Airlines System.
18 Dec. 1961	Signs treaty with Norway to further extend the period of validity of traffic rights.
21 Dec. 1961	As a result of investigations into the Port Elizabeth explosions, Security Police arrest and charge Robert H. Strachan with causing malicious damage to property.
17 Jan. 1962	The Department of Justice announces that charges against A.K. Ganyile have been dropped, the government regrets the incident, Ganyile is released, returns to Basutoland and later claims damages against the Minister of Justice and the policemen concerned.
17 Jan. 1962	Leaders of the South African National Convention Movement, a Coloured opposition organisation, completely reject Dr. Verwoerd's plan as offering them only a status of permanent inferiority, giving them 'sovereignty in no area but subservient in all'.
21 Jan. 1962	The President of the Newspaper Press Union of South Africa, M.V. Jooste, issues the draft of a voluntary Press Code, including proposals for the setting up of a three-man Board of Reference.
23 Jan. 1962	Dr. Verwoerd, announces his plan for the granting of 'self-rule' to the Transkei. It is to have its own Parliament and Cabinet, separate citizenship and control over agriculture, education, health, social services and roads with defence, foreign affairs and justice remaining in the hands of the central government in the meantime.
31 Jan. 1962	The government's proposals for self-government for the Transkei are submitted to the committee of twenty-seven chiefs and headmen appointed by the Transkeian Territorial Authority to press its claims.
31 Jan. 1962	Signs treaty with Luxembourg relating to air services.
19 Feb. 1962	The first part of the South African Press Commission's first report is tabled in Parliament by the Minister of the Interior, de Klerk. The report, which has taken eleven years to draw up consists of two volumes totalling 700 pages, with nineteen annexures running to 1,566 pages. It strongly recommends that the South African Press Association (SAPA) gives more say in its affairs to the Afrikaans-language press.
20 Feb. 1962	Signs treaty amending the statute of the International Atomic Energy Agency.
22 Feb. 1962	Signs a parcel post agreement with Canada.

12 Mar. 1962	The Defence Minister, J.J. Fouché, outlines the basic principles of South Africa's defence policy and gives details of measures being taken to build up the Defence Forces and to make South Africa self-supporting in military equipment.
21 Mar. 1962	The Minister of Finance, Dr. Eben Dönges, introduces a budget of national security with increased expenditure on defence.
23 Mar. 1962	The Minister of Water Affairs announces an ambitious scheme to harness the Orange River for power and irrigation at a cost of R450 million, spread over about thirty years.
29 Mar. 1962	The Defence Minister, J.J. Fouché, discloses that South Africa is buying supersonic Mirage III jet fighters from France, and that South African forces are being equipped with French Alouette helicopters.
6 Apr. 1962	Signs a multilateral agreement for the accession of Israel to the General Agreement on Tarrifs and Trade.
30 Apr. 1962	Signs treaty with Germany extending the economic agreement of 28 August 1951.
May 1962	Under a government sponsored Bill, which received its third reading in the House of Assembly on 8 February 1962, a Coloured Development Corporation with a share capital of R500,000 (250,000 Pounds Sterling) is established to aid coloured businessmen in developing and enlarging their own industries in the townships reserved for them.
3 May 1962	Signs a multilateral procès-verbal extending the declaration on the provisional accession of the Swiss Confederation to the General Agreement on Tarrifs and Trade.
4 May 1962	The Transkeian Territorial Authority approves the draft Constitution as a whole, after considerable controversy, mainly concerning the composition of the Legislative Assembly.
6 May 1962	United Nations representatives of the committee to investigate conditions in South West Africa, Victorio Carpio (Philippines) and Dr. Martinez de Alva (Mexico), begin informal talks with Dr. Verwoerd and South African officials in Pretoria. They subsequently visit South West Africa and return to Pretoria.
8 May 1962	R.H. Strachan is found guilty of conspiring to cause bomb explosions and is sentenced to three years' imprisonment.
17 May 1962	Dr. Jan Steytler, leader of the Progressive Party, launches a nationwide protest campaign against the General Laws Amendment Bill, published by the government on 12 May 1962 defining the crime of sabotage in the widest terms.
23 May 1962	Signs an amendment to agreement with Great Britain on sugar for Swaziland.
24 May 1962	A Bill replacing the Republic of South Africa (Temporary Provisions) Act, due to expire on 31 May 1962, is enacted and receives the Royal Assent.

It is designed to regulate finally the operation of British law in relation to South Africa.

26 May 1962	A joint statement is issued, agreed to by Dr. Verwoerd, Victorio Carpio, Dr. de Alva and the Foreign Minister, Eric Louw, indicating that no evidence has been found in SWA of genocide by South Africa, or of any excessive military occupation. The conditions there do not constitute a threat to world peace.
28 May 1962	Signs convention with Great Britain on the avoidance of double taxation and the prevention of fiscal evasion with respect to taxes on income.
End May 1962	Victorio Carpio repudiates the Pretoria statement.
4 June 1962	Signs agreement with Great Britain for the temporary suspension of the margin of preference on tin plate.
11 June 1962	Signs cultural agreement with the Federal Republic of Germany.
12 June 1962	Signs amendment to the co-operation agreement with the United States.
20 June 1962	Signs agreement with Japan on the safe-guards of materials transfered to Japan of the International Atomic Energy Agency.
20 June 1962	The International Commission of Jurists in Geneva, issues a 2,000-word statement asserting that the `Sabotage Bill' reduces the liberty of the subject to a degree `not surpassed by the most extreme dictatorship of the Left or the Right'.
27 June 1962	Parliament passes the General Law Amendment Act - the `Sabotage Bill' - sponsored by the Minister of Justice, B.J. Vorster, defining sabotage in the widest terms and prescribing a minimum sentence of five years and a maximum of death. Its purpose is to combat communism.
July-Mid Sept.1962	Seventy-five serious fires attributed to widespread arson are reported in Natal.
10 July 1962	Signs the International Wheat Agreement.
23 July 1962	Ben Turok is sentenced to three years imprisonment for attempting to cause an explosion in the centre of Johannesburg in February.
26 July 1962	Signs multilateral recommendations under Article IX of the Antarctic Treaty.
30 July 1962	Under the provisions of the General Law Amendment Act of 1962 a list of 102 persons prohibited from attending gatherings is published in the Government Gazette. It includes Patrick Duncan, Albert Luthuli, Duma Nokwe, Ronald Segal, Walter Sisulu, Oliver Tambo and Benjamin Turok.
1 Aug. 1962	Signs multilateral agreement for the accession of Portugal to the General Agreement on Tarrifs and Trade.
3 Aug. 1962	The United Nations Special Committee on South West Africa disowns the Pretoria statement.

8 Aug. 1962	Signs treaty with Great Britain, extending to South West Africa the Convention of 28 May 1962 on the avoidance of double taxation and the avoidance of fiscal evasion with respect to taxes on income.
15 Aug. 1962	The Liquor Laws Amendment Bill, under which Africans are for the first time allowed to buy liquor freely, comes into effect. Introduced on 9 June 1961, given a second reading on 19 June 1961, its third on 24 June 1961 and subsequently approved by the Senate, its long delay in implementation is attributed to the large number of applications for liquor licences received.
16 Aug. 1962	Signs amendment with Great Britain on the Ottawa Trade Agreement of 20 August 1932.
17 Aug. 1962	The Defence Minister, J.J. Fouché, announces that the striking power of the Defence Force has been increased twenty-fold as compared with two years earlier, while that of the Navy is to be increased ten-fold in the next few years.
31 Aug. 1962	Signs a visa agreement with Austria.
7 Sept. 1962	The South African Congress of Democrats is banned by the Minister of Justice under the Suppression of Communism Act.
14 Sept. 1962	Signs a visa agreement with Belgium.
15 Sept. 1962	Signs multilateral treaty, amending the ICAO Aviation agreement of 7 December 1944.
28 Sept. 1962	Signs International Coffee Agreement.
13 Oct. 1962	The first restriction to house arrest under the Sabotage Act is imposed in Johannesburg on Helen Joseph.
19 Oct. 1962	The office of the Minister of Agricultural Economics and Marketing is wrecked by an explosion in Pretoria.
End-Oct. 1962	The Minister of Justice continues issuing a series of house arrest orders confining people to their homes for a period of five years.
6 Nov. 1962	At its 17th session, the United Nations General Assembly adopts a resolution on South Africa's racial policies, deploring the failure of the South African government to abandon its racial policies, and establishing a Special Committee to keep these under review. The resolution favours diplomatic and economic sanctions against South Africa and asks that the UN Security Council consider expelling South Africa from the Council.
9 Nov. 1962	The Minister of Justice states that there have been twenty-three attempts of sabotage from late September to date. Nearly sixty African suspects are reported to have been arrested.
15 Nov. 1962	Thirty-eight African and Asian delegations table a draft resolution in the Trusteeship Committee asking for an effective United Nations 'presence' in South West Africa, and asking the General Assembly to reaffirm 'the inalienable right of the people of South West Africa to independence and national sovereignty'.

15 Nov. 1962	Ugandan Prime Minister Milton Obote announces a boycott of South African goods.
16 Nov. 1962	A list of 437 persons said to have been office-bearers, officers, members or active supporters of the banned Communist Party of South Africa, is published. Listed persons are banned from belonging to thirty-six specified organizations and are ordered to cease membership of such organizations by 1 February 1963.
21 Nov. 1962	In an outbreak of violence at Paarl, Cape Province, two whites are beaten to death and seven blacks are shot during a march on a police station by about 100 blacks.
29 Nov. 1962	President Swart appoints a one-man commission to inquire into the riots at Paarl.
Dec. 1962 - June 1964	In this period over 300 sentences are passed for such crimes as political murder, arson, acts of sabotage and bomb throwing, as well as for membership of banned organizations such as Poqo and the African National Congress. Forty death sentences are imposed in addition to numerous sentences of life imprisonment and lesser terms, at trials throughout the country.
1 Dec. 1962	Signs loan agreement with the International Bank for Reconstruction and Development concerning the seventh Transport Project.
7 Dec. 1962 - 13 Mar. 1963	The Paarl Riots Commissioner, Justice J.H. Snyman hears evidence at Paarl and elsewhere. Detailed information on the nature and activities of the Poqo organization is obtained. It is equated with the Pan Africanist Congress.
21 Dec. 1962	The International Court of Justice at the Hague rules, by the narrow majority of eight votes to seven, that it has jurisdiction in the case brought by Ethiopia and Liberia alleging that South Africa has violated its mandate over South West Africa.
21 Dec. 1962	Dr. Verwoerd intimates that the government proposes to introduce legislation providing for the extension of the territorial sea limit for South Africa and South West Africa from three to six nautical miles and the establishment of a contiguous fishing zone extending to twelve miles from the base line.
1 Jan. 1963	Thousands of Commonwealth citizens resident in South Africa, mostly Britons, become technically aliens through failing to apply for permanent residence by 31 December 1962 under the Commonwealth Relations Act enacted on 15 June 1962.
18 Jan. 1963	Parliament opens with the debate of 'no confidence' moved by the Leader of the Opposition Sir de Villiers Graaff. The Prime Minister defends the government's Bantustan policy by attempting to establish the fact that it had been implicit in the National Party programme since it came to power in 1948.
5 Feb. 1963	A white family is savagely killed in their caravan whilst camping on the Bashee River in the Engcobo area of the Transkei. Forty Africans are later arrested and twenty-two sentenced to death for the murders.

8 Feb. 1963	Signs a Most-favoured-Nation trade agreement with Spain.
8 Feb. 1963	The government publishes the draft of the Bantu Laws Amendment Bill intended to remove most of the remaining rights of Africans in white areas, including security of employment or residence.
11 Feb. 1963	The Defence Minister, J.J. Fouché, announces in the House of Assembly that he intends to increase the strength of the permanent army by fifty per cent.
19 Feb. 1963	The Minister of Defence announces the re-establishment, as of 1 April 1963 of the 'Cape Corps' of Coloured men to be employed in non-combatant roles.
22 Feb. 1963	Signs agreement with Australia on air pooling.
23 Feb. 1963	At the annual conference of the United Nations Economic Commission for Africa in Leopoldville, fifteen African states table a draft resolution requesting the United Nations Economic and Social Council to deprive South Africa of membership of the ECA until it has 'set a term to its policy of racial discrimination'. The resolution is adopted by thirty votes, with Britain, France and Spain opposing it.
27 Feb. 1963	Signs a treaty with the Federation of Rhodesia and Nyasaland amending the trade agreement of 16 May 1960.
4 Mar. 1963	Walter Sisulu, former Secretary-General of the African National Congress is convicted of having incited African workers to strike in protest against the Republic of South Africa Constitution Act of 1961, and of having furthered the aims of the ANC. He is sentenced to six years' imprisonment.
14 Mar. 1963	The Publications and Entertainments Bill, which has been before a Select Committee for nearly two years, passes its third reading in the House of Assembly by sixty votes to forty. The Minister of the Interior is to appoint a Publications Control Board to control the importation, distribution, exhibition, sale or possession of publications deemed 'undesirable'.
15 Mar. 1963	The Defence Minister, J.J. Fouché, gives the Senate details of South Africa's defence programme and replies to statements made by Harold Wilson on the British Labour Party's attitude to arms supplies to South Africa.
20 Mar. 1963	The Budget, introduced by the Minister of Finance, Dr. T.E. Dönges, provides the record sum of R202 million for defence and internal security.
21 Mar. 1963	Justice Snyman, judge in the Cape Division of the Supreme Court, produces an Interim Report of his inquiry into the Paarl riots. This developed into an investigation into the Poqo organization, operating from Basutoland in collusion with subversive groups in the Transkei and its involvement in the murders and terror in the Eastern Province and the Transkei. The report is immediately tabled in the House of Assembly by the Minister of Justice, B.J. Vorster, who announces that he accepts the Judge's findings and will act on them.
25 Mar. 1963	Potlako Leballo, claiming to be the leader of the PAC, confirms in Maseru,

Basutoland, that Poqo and the PAC are one and the same organization and that its revolutionary council is discussing the timing and manner of an uprising to be launched in South Africa during 1963.

1 Apr. 1963	The Foreign Office of the Philippines announces that it has instructed its Commerce Department, the National Marketing Corporation and the Bureau of Customs, to implement a boycott of all South African goods as well as to halt exports to South Africa.
3 Apr. 1963	Signs a treaty with Great Britain on the temporary suspension of the tariff preference on crude sperm oil.
6 Apr. 1963	Signs a parcel post agreement with Japan.
8 Apr. 1963	Signs an amendment to the constitution of the International Labour Organisation.
14 Apr. 1963	Signs a treaty with Bechuanaland protectorate on aeradio-tele-communications and metereological services at Maun.
18 Apr. 1963	The Foreign Minister states that the South African government is unable to assist the United Nations Special Committee on Apartheid since its establishment is contrary to the provisions of the United Nations.
20 Apr. 1963	Signs the Olive Oil Agreement.
23 Apr. 1963	Dr. Verwoerd, states in Parliament that if political refugees in the British Protectorates are allowed to organize revolution against South Africa then these Territories must expect retaliation.
24 Apr. 1963	Signs the Vienna Convention on Consular Relations.
24 Apr. 1963	The Minister of Justice introduces a General Laws Amendment Bill implementing Justice Snyman's recommendations establishing emergency courts to deal with cases arising from Poqo activities, and gives the Minister power to detain anyone without trial in solitary confinement for ninety days, and thereafter for further periods of ninety days, at the Minister's discretion. The Minister is also given powers to detain without trial anyone who has been convicted of an offence endangering the security of the state. Only Helen Suzman, representing the Progressive Party, opposes the Bill in toto.
26 Apr. 1963	At a meeting in Oslo, the Foreign Ministers of Denmark, Finland, Norway and Sweden and the Icelandic Ambassador call upon South Africa to change its racial policies and to cooperate with the United Nations.
30 Apr. 1963	Algeria announces a total boycott of South Africa.
30 Apr. 1963	Three listed white communists serving sentences of house arrest, escape to Bechuanaland.
May 1963	The Security Police begin 90-day arrests. A widespread purge of 'subversive elements' is undertaken.
1 May 1963	Prime Minister Vorster announces that Robert Sobukwe has been taken to

Robben Island, where he will be detained indefinitely in terms of the General Laws Amendment Bill of 29 April 1963.

7 May 1963	Signs air agreement with Portugal.

8 May 1963	Exchanges notes with Scandinavia amending the Air Agreements of December 1961.

8 May 1963	The United Nations Special Committee on Apartheid publishes its first Interim Report, recording with satisfaction the number of countries that have broken off diplomatic and commercial relations with South Africa, but noting with regret that nearly twenty member states still maintained these.

8 May 1963	The British Ambassador in Pretoria and High Commissioner for the Protectorates, Sir John Maud, confirms that a distinction is made between ordinary political refugees and people who flee to the Protectorates to organize revolution. It is Britain's policy 'to prevent action in any territory designed to foment violence in the Republic'.

16 May 1963	Signs the Ocean Mail Contract with the Union Castle Company.

23 May 1963	Signs additional regulation, amending the international sanitary regulations of the World Health Regulations on No. 2.

24 May 1963	The Transkei Self-Government Bill is enacted, giving, for the first time, limited self-government to Africans in a defined area. It incorporates the draft Constitution for the Transkei, as finally approved by the Transkei Territorial Authority in December 1962.

5 June 1963	Signs treaty with Great Britain on the release from the bound margin of preferences of ten percent ad valorem on certain preserved fruit granted to South Africa.

25 June 1963	Signs provisional air agreement with the Federal Republic of Germany.

25 June 1963	The final report by Justice Snyman on the Paarl Riots, is submitted to Parliament. It analyzes the main causes of the riots.

27 June 1963	Signs treaty with Bechuanaland Protectorate on postal services and insured parcels.

28-30 June 1963	The governing body of the International Labour Organisation meeting in Geneva, discusses emergency measures against South Africa and the problems its membership poses. It is resolved that South Africa should be excluded from ILO meetings.

2 July 1963	Cameroon closes its sea and air ports to both Portugal and South Africa.

4 July 1963	Signs treaty with Swaziland on postal services including parcel post.

12 July 1963	Hungary announces the breaking-off of trade relations with South Africa.

12 July 1963	The Security Police surround a house in Rivonia and arrest eighteen people, including Walter Sisulu, former Secretary-General of the banned ANC and Ahmed Kathrada, who had also gone 'underground' from house arrests.

13 July 1963	The government of India announces that it is cutting India's last remaining links with South Africa by refusing landing and passage facilities to South African aircraft.
13 July 1963	The Security Police discose the existence of an underground group the Yu Chi Chan, said to include people trained in Peking and Algeria for sabotage in South Africa.
15 July 1963	Dr. Verwoerd announces that the government has decided to withdraw from the Economic Commission for Africa (ECA) owing to the hostility shown by African states.
16 July 1963	Ivory Coast closes sea and airports to South Africa and Portugal.
18 July 1963	The United Nations Special Committee on Apartheid releases its second Interim Report recommending an effective embargo on the supply of arms and ammunition, and of petroleum.
18 July 1963	Harold Wolpe, a Johannesburg solicitor, and listed Communist, is arrested on the Bechuanaland border.
22 July 1963	Ethiopia closes her airspace to South African aircraft.
26 July 1963	The British High Commissioner for Basutoland, Bechuanaland and Swaziland issues the Prevention of Violence Abroad Proclamation, which makes it an offence for persons to conspire against, or incite or instigate violence in South Africa or other neighbouring territories. It comes into immediate effect.
30 July 1963	In the Geneva session of the United Nations Economic and Social Council, an Argentinian resolution states that South Africa shall not take part in the work of the ECA until conditions for constructive co-operation have been restored by a change of its racial policy. The resolution is adopted by six votes to two, with ten abstentions.
30 July 1963	Yugoslavia closes its consular office in Johannesburg.
31 July - 6 Aug.1963	The United Nations Security Council debates the South African situation. The government reaffirms its decision not to participate in the debate since discussion would concern matters falling solely within its domestic jurisdiction.
Aug. 1963	The Christian Institute of Southern Africa, a non-racial interdenominational organization, is founded under the directorship of the Rev. C.F. Beyers Naudé.
1 Aug. - 30 Sept.1963	Signs multilateral treaty for the prolongation of the International Sugar Agreement.
6 Aug. 1963	Guinea announces that she has broken off diplomatic, commercial and cultural relations with South Africa and Portugal, and banned the entry of their nationals into Guinea.
7 Aug. 1963	The United Nations Security Council adopts a resolution calling upon all states to cease forthwith the sale and shipment of arms, ammunition and

military vehicles to South Africa.

7 Aug. 1963	South Africa is denied landing and overflying rights by the United Arab Republic as from this date.

8 Aug. 1963   Signs amendment to the sugar agreement of 3 June 1957 with Great Britain.

10 Aug. 1963   Dr. K.G. Abrahams is arrested in the Gobabis area of South West Africa, and subsequently charged with being the chairman of the Yu Chi Chan Club (YCCC) aimed at overthrowing the government by revolution. A previous attempt to arrest him on 19 July 1963 was obstructed by the local community at Rehoboth, SWA. Conflicting accounts surround the circumstances of his arrest. He himself claims to have been abducted from Bechuanaland, where he had been travelling between Ghanzi and Lobatsi.

11 Aug. 1963   Harold Wolpe, a listed Communist arrested on the Bechuanaland border, and Arthur Goldreich, caught in the Rivonia raid escape from the Johannesburg Central police station, 'go to ground' and on 28 August emerge in Bechuanaland.

19 Aug. 1963   Dr. Abrahams makes a habeas corpus application to the Cape Supreme Court and demands his return to Bechuanaland where he claims to have been already granted political asylum.

19 Aug. 1963   Indonesia announces the severance of diplomatic and commercial relations with South Africa, and the closure of Indonesian ports to South African vessels.

19 Aug. 1963   Sudan closes her sea and airports to South Africa and Portugal.

19 Aug. 1963   The Abrahams case is discussed by Sir Hugh Stephenson, the new British Ambassador in Pretoria and High Commissioner for Bechuanaland and the Permanent Secretary of the South African Foreign Ministry, in the light of the request by the British Colonial Office for a full report.

20 Aug. 1963   The Israeli government informs the United Nations Special Committee on Apartheid that it has taken all necessary steps to ensure that no arms, ammunition, or strategic materials may be exported from Israel to South Africa in any form, directly or indirectly.

20 Aug. 1963   Mauritius closes her sea and airports to South Africa and Portugal.

22 Aug. 1963   South African Airways (SAA) announces the re-routing of its services to Europe via Luanda (Angola), Brazzaville, the Cape Verde Islands, and Las Palmas.

28 Aug. 1963   Goldreich and Wolpe are found to be in Francistown, Bechunaland, having flown there from Swaziland.

30 Aug. 1963   The Prime Minister announces, in a statement before the Supreme Court in Cape Town, that Dr. Abrahams will be returned to Bechuanaland. Dr. Abrahams, and his three companions, are returned to Ghanzi on 31 August 1963, and the charge of sabotage is withdrawn on 11 September 1963.

31 Aug. 1963   Libya closes her sea and airports to South Africa and Portugal and denies

them overflying rights.

Sept. 1963	South African Airways is excluded from flying over the African continent, except for Portuguese territory.
3 Sept. 1963	Dr. Verwoerd suggests that the three Protectorates might develop to independence under South Africa's guidance rather than under Britain's and offers to administer them as self-governing Bantustans.
9 Sept. 1963	At a meeting in Stockholm the Foreign Ministers of Denmark, Finland, Iceland, Norway, and Sweden confirm that their countries neither permit, nor intend to permit any exports of arms to South Africa. Their ultimate aim is the guaranteeing of equal rights to all citizens.
12 Sept. 1963	Chad closes its air space to South Africa and Portuguese aircraft, as well as to all other planes carrying goods or passengers to or from the two countries.
14 Sept. 1963	Signs multilateral Convention on Offences Committed on Board Aircraft.
16 Sept. 1963	The final report of the United Nations Special Committee on Apartheid gives a detailed review of developments in South Africa's racial policies since 6 November 1962. It is unanimously approved and published on 18 September 1963.
17 Sept. 1963	Regulations incorporating new measures to prevent aircraft transporting 'criminals or refugees' in or out of the three British High Commission Territories are published in the Government Gazette. Thirty-seven air ports are designated as compulsory landing points (twelve for Basutoland, seventeen for Bechuanaland and eight for Swaziland).
23 Sept. 1963	The United Arab Republic Ministry of Economy announces that all economic ties with South Africa will be severed.
23 Sept. 1963	At the World Health Organization's Regional Conference for Africa, in Geneva, twenty-six African delegates leave the opening session in protest against the presence of South African and Portuguese delegates. The Conference is left without a quorum and adjourned on 24 September 1963.
27 Sept. 1963	The Danish Foreign Minister states in the United Nations General Assembly that the Scandinavian Foreign Ministers have refused an invitation by Dr. Verwoerd to visit South Africa to see for themselves what the racial situation really was. Such a journey is not seen as furthering a solution to the South African problem in accordance with the principles of the United Nations Charter.
30 Sept. 1963	Tanganyika formally ends all imports and exports, direct and indirect, from and to South Africa.
2 Oct. 1963	Kuwait breaks off diplomatic relations with South Africa and all Kuwaiti air and seaports are closed to South African aircraft and vessels.
9 Oct. 1963	The United Arab Republic government informs the United Nations that it has banned South African ships from entering UAR ports, and that, while they will still be allowed to use the Suez Canal they will be denied all

facilities there.

9 Oct. 1963	The Rivonia Trial opens in a special court at Pretoria. Eleven men are charged with complicity in more than 200 acts of sabotage aimed at facilitating revolution and armed invasion of South Africa. The indictment is quashed on the grounds that the State has not provided sufficient details of the alleged offences, but a new indictment is prepared and the trial proceeds.
10 Oct. 1963	An urgent resolution is considered by the United Nations Political Committee condemning the government of South Africa for its repression, and requesting it to abandon the trial now in progress and to grant unconditional release to all political prisoners and to all persons subjected to other restrictions for having opposed the policy of apartheid. It is approved, and the following day, 11 October 1963, passed by the General Assembly by 106 votes to one.
11 Oct. 1963	Signs multilateral sugar agreement.
15 Oct. 1963	The Netherlands Permanent Representative at the United Nations announces that his government has banned the export and transit to South Africa of weapons and munitions which could be used for the oppression of the non-white population.
17 Oct. 1963	The Rev. Dr. Arthur William Blaxall, an Anglican clergyman is convicted on charges of aiding the activities of the Pan-Africanist Congress (PAC) and the ANC. He had pleaded guilty and does not appeal against the sentence. However, on instructions from Mr. Vorster he is released on parole the following day.
21 Oct. 1963	The Canadian Minister for External Affairs announces that the government has imposed an embargo on further sales or shipments of Canadian military equipment to South Africa.
28 Oct. 1963	The United Nations General Assembly Social, Humanitarian and Cultural Committee approves a Declaration on the Elimination of All Forms of Racial Discrimination in which South Africa's policy of apartheid is specifically condemned.
Nov. 1963	The Minister of Security announces that 543 people have been detained under the 90-day clause. Of these 151 have been released, 275 have been charged in court, sixty-one are due to be charged shortly, five have escaped and fifty-one are still being questioned.
7 Nov. 1963	Signs treaty with Great Britain on the suspension of the margin of preference on crude sperm oil.
8 Nov. 1963	Signs multilateral agreement on radio regulations.
13 Nov. 1963	Signs multilateral treaty on the provisional accession of Yugoslavia to the General Agreement on Tarrifs and Trade.
16 Nov. 1963	Signs treaty extending the declaration on the provisional accession of Argentina to the General Agreement on Tarrifs and Trade.

18 Nov. 1963	Eric H. Louw, Foreign Minister since January 1955, announces his intention to retire.
20 Nov. 1963	The first elections to the forty-five seats for elected members of the Transkei Legislative Assembly take place. There are no political parties, the choice being between candidates supporting Chief Kaiser Matanzima and those supporting Paramount Chief Victor Poto Ndamase of the West Pondos, believed to favour multi-racialism. All adults are entitled to vote; voters comprise all Xhosa, not only in the Transkei, but throughout South Africa.
21 Nov. 1963	It is officially announced on Eric Louw's seventy-third birthday that the South African Ambassador in London, Dr. Hilgard Muller, will be sworn in as Foreign Minister on 9 January 1964.
22 Nov. 1963	Signs multilateral treaty banning nuclear weapon testing in the atmosphere.
28 Nov. 1963	Signs treaty with Great Britain on the temporary suspension of the tariff preference on crude sperm oil enjoyed by South Africa.
2 Dec. 1963	It is officially conceded that the majority of the members elected to the first Transkei Legislative Assembly support Chief Poto. The voting percentage in most areas is reported to be over 70% and the total number of voters to have exceeded 800,000.
3 Dec. 1963	The Rivonia Trial, concerning two charges of sabotage, one under the Suppression of Communism Act, and one under the General Law Amendment Act, begins before Justice de Wet. The Prosecutor, Dr. Percy Yutar gives details of explosives to be used to commit acts of destruction, to be followed by guerrilla activity and military invasion.
4 Dec. 1963	The United Nations Security Council unanimously adopts a resolution calling on the South African government to cease its repressive measures and calls on all states to embargo materials for arms manufacture. A small group of recognized experts is to be established to examine methods of resolving the South African situation.
6 Dec. 1963	The Transkei Legislative Assembly meets for the first time in Umtata and elects Chief Kaiser Matanzima as Chief Minister by fifty-four votes to forty-nine for Chief Victor Poto, with two papers spoilt. Chief Matanzima forms a political party with the backing of the non-elective chiefs and their supporters; Chief Poto goes into opposition as the leader of the democratically elected members.
10 Dec. 1963	Signs multilateral treaty on consent to marriage, minimum age for marriage and registration of marriages.
11 Dec. 1963	The first of the 'Bantustans' comes into existence when the Minister for Bantu Administration and Development, de Wet Nel, opens the Transkei Legislative Assembly at Umtata. Chief Kaiser Matanzima is installed as Chief Minister.
12 Dec. 1963	Accepts Procès-verbal extending the provisional accession of Tunisa to the General Agreement on Tarrifs and Trade.

23 Dec. 1963	Signs treaty with Southern Rhodesia on the removal of the operation of the trade agreement of 16 May 1960.
23 Dec. 1963	Signs treaty with Southern Rhodesia on the continuation of the extradition agreement of 19 November 1962.
23 Dec. 1963	Signs treaty on extradition (Northern Rhodesia) with Great Britain.
23 Dec. 1963	It is announced in Pretoria that Dr. Carel de Wet, M.P. for Vanderbijlpark, Transvaal and grandson of General J.C. de Wet, a leading Boer commander in the South African War of 1899-1902, has been appointed Ambassador to the United Kingdom.
4 Jan. 1964	In a New Year message, the South African Prime Minister says it is justifiable for the whites to refuse to commit national suicide and to fight for self preservation.
6 Jan. 1964	Signs treaty with France on the installation of a scientific space tracking station in South Africa.
13 Jan. 1964	The United Nations Secretary-General names four experts to examine the problem of apartheid in South Africa in accordance with the UN Security Council Resolution of 4 December 1963. They are: Sir Edward Asafu-Adjaye (Ghana); Josip Djerdja (Yugoslavia); Sir Hugh Foot (United Kingdom); and Alva Myrdal (Sweden).
17 Jan. 1964	Leader of the Opposition, Sir de Villiers Graaff, demands a judicial inquiry into the activities of the Broederbond, and demands the resignation of the Prime Minister from this society. Dr. Verwoerd refuses to resign.
24 Jan. 1964	It is announced that efforts by Britain's Foreign Secretary, Mr. Butler and Glasgow University to obtain permission from the South African government for Albert Luthuli to leave Natal and be installed as Rector of Glasgow University have failed.
27 Jan. 1964	The appointment of the group of experts to examine the problem of apartheid, in terms of the United Nations Security Council resolution of 4 December 1963, is completed.
30 Jan. 1964	Signs treaty with Great Britain on the suspension of the margin of preference on butter.
4 Feb. 1964	The International Court of Justice announces that in the South West Africa cases (Ethiopia v. South Africa; Liberia v. South Africa) the counter-memorial of South Africa has been filed. 20 June 1964 is fixed as the time limit for the filing of replies by Ethiopia and Liberia and 20 November 1964 for the filing of South Africa's rejoinder.
4 Feb. 1964	The number of men required for military training in 1964 is to increase by 60%, i.e. from 10,368 to 16,537.
5 Feb. 1964	The South African government informs the United Nations Secretary-General that it is unable to agree to a visit by the group of experts as it would be an interference in the internal affairs of the Republic.

6 Feb. 1964	The Rt. Rev. Robert Selby Taylor, Bishop of Grahamstown, is elected Archbishop of Cape Town and Metropolitan of the Province of South Africa, in succession to Dr. Joost de Blank who recently returned to Britain on medical advice.
7 Feb. 1964	The Transkei opposition leader Paramount Chief Victor Poto forms South Africa's first African political party - the Democratic Party. Its aims include the retention of the Transkei as an integral part of South Africa.
8 Feb. 1964	The leader of the South African opposition, Sir de Villiers Graaf, agrees with the government that the composition of the proposed United Nations Committee to Study Apartheid is such as to preclude any possibility of an objective or impartial inquiry and that the group should not be received in South Africa.
15 Feb. 1964	The governing body of the International Labour Organisation (ILO) meeting in Geneva, votes in favour of suspending South Africa from participation in its Annual General Conferences. The resolution is passed by thirty-two votes to fourteen with two abstentions.
23 Feb. 1964	A new weekly air service between Johannesburg and New York, with an intermediate stop at Rio de Janeiro is inaugurated in spite of the opposition of the UN Special Committee on Apartheid.
28 Feb. 1964	A Bill, presently before Parliament, provides for the establishment of a Coloured Representative Council comprising thirty elected and sixteen nominated members. The State President will be able to confer power on the Council to make laws for coloureds in respect of finance, local government, education, community welfare and pensions.
Mar. 1964	The South African delegation walks out of the World Health Organization (WHO) having been deprived of its voting rights.
5 Mar. 1964	Signs multilateral declaration on the provisional accession of Iceland to the General Agreement on Tarrifs and Trade.
7 Mar. 1964	The Minister of Posts and Telegraphs, Dr. Hertzog, confirms that the government's policy regarding television is unchanged. There is no question of television being introduced.
9 Mar. 1964	The United Nations Special Committee on the Policies of Apartheid resumes its meetings and decides to draft an appeal to the Security Council and the General Assembly to ensure implementation of resolutions on South Africa adopted by them. They recommend that South Africa halt current trials of anti-apartheid leaders and refrain from executing persons already sentenced to death.
11 Mar. 1964	About two hundred delegates from all parts of the world attend the Accra Conference for Solidarity with the Workers and People of South Africa.
20 Mar. 1964	Signs treaty with Great Britain on the elimination of the margin of preference of ten percent ad valorem on boxwood.
21 Mar. 1964	The 1964-65 Budget provides for R210m. on defence, an increase of R52m. over the previous year. The Minister of Defence, Dr. Dönges, admits it is

a large increase but is confident the House will furnish 'the wherewithal to discourage foreign aggression'.

23 Mar. 1964	Signs multilateral treaty embodying results of the 1960-61 Tariff Conference pertaining to the General Agreement on Tarrifs and Trade.
31 Mar. 1964	Signs treaty with Denmark, Norway and Sweden on the temporary amendment of 1958 air agreements.
31 Mar. 1964	The United Nations Special Committee on Apartheid publishes a report recommending that the Security Council call on South Africa to refrain from executing people sentenced to death for political offences, to end political trials in process and grant amnesty to all political prisoners.
17 Apr. 1964	The Conference on Sanctions against South Africa ends in London by issuing the declaration that total economic sanctions are feasible and practicable, and calls for world action to end apartheid.
18 Apr. 1964	Dr. N.E. Alexander and four others are found guilty of sabotage and are sentenced to ten years imprisonment. The judge finds that the accused participated in the activities of the National Liberation Front (NLF), a continuation of the Yu Chi Chan Club, whose aims was to further violence and revolution.
18 Apr. 1964	Signs agreement with France and a third party.
20 Apr. 1964	At the Rivonia Trial, Nelson Mandela, former leader of the banned ANC, blames the actions of the government for adoption of policies of violence by African leaders. He surveys the history and aims of the ANC and gives reasons why Umkonto we Sizwe (the Spear of the Nation) was formed.
20 Apr. 1964	The United Nations Group of Experts on Apartheid submits its report to the Secretary-General. It proposes a National Convention to set a new course for South Africa's future and envisages the removal of a mass of restrictive and discriminatory legislation.
24 Apr. 1964	The Prime Minister maintains that the country is economically so strong that it can withstand economic sanctions. The only vulnerable spot is oil supply.
1 May 1964	Signs treaty with Great Britain on the elimination of the margin of preference of ten percent ad valorem on prepared or preserved groundnuts.
1 May 1964	President Kayibanda of Rwanda says the people and government condemn apartheid but think a realistic view should be taken of the probable effects of economic sanctions.
6 May 1964	Signs treaty with Great Britain on the temporary suspension of the margin of preference guaranteed to the UK on tin plate.
6 May 1964	The Bantu Laws Amendment Bill passes its third reading, giving the Minister of Bantu Administration the powers to declare prescribed areas in which the number of Africans to be employed could be determined, to override local authorities in African affairs and to redirect redundant labour to African Reserves. This comprehensive piece of apartheid legislation is an essential component of the overall plan for separate development.

9 May 1964	Opening the first Legislative session of the Transkei-Legislative Assembly, President Swart says that the Transkei now has an all-Westernized system of government. The Republic of South Africa will continue to assist the Transkei and will train its successors in office.
16 May 1964	The Commission of Inquiry into the South African Press tables the second part of its report, severely criticizing the reporting on South African affairs by foreign correspondents, or local correspondents working for foreign news agencies, an antagonism towards Afrikaners and the government. The Commission recommends the setting up of a press council to control newspapers and correspondents.
23 May 1964	Albert Luthuli's first five year ban expires but he is immediately served with a new and stricter order.
30 May 1964	The leader of the Basutoland National Party, Chief Leabua Jonathan, indicates that Basutoland is so economically dependent on South Africa that the imposition of economic sanctions is not feasible.
3 June 1964	Signs treaty with Southern Rhodesia on the continuation of the workman's compensation agreement of 11 October 1958.
5 June 1964	Dr. Verwoerd says that the government has no intention of trying to incorporate Bechuanaland, Basutoland or Swaziland into South Africa.
5 June 1964	A resolution to expel South Africa from the Universal Postal Union is approved by the Union's congress in Vienna, by fifty-eight votes to thirty, with twenty-six abstentions.
9 June 1964	The Prime Minister announces the appointment of a one-man commission of enquiry, consisting of a Judge of Appeal, to investigate all secret organizations likely to influence unlawfully the State, the people, or the administration of justice. The inquiry is to be held in secret.
12 June 1964	At the conclusion of the Rivonia Trial eight of the accused are sentenced to life imprisonment. The central figure in the trial is Nelson Mandela who argues that he was driven to acts of sabotage by the frustration of all legitimate means of political protest. His argument is rejected by the Judge. The State has not charged the accused with High Treason, and Mr. Justice de Wet accordingly decides not to impose the supreme penalty.
13 June 1964	In terms of a new General Laws Amendment Bill, the death penalty is extended to people who have undergone sabotage training within South Africa; the Minister of Justice is again empowered to detain people for indefinite periods after they have served prison sentences; and the twelve-day 'jail without bail' law of 1962 is renewed.
13 June 1964	At the Rand Criminal Sessions three Africans are imprisoned for twelve years and one for eight years on a charge of sabotage.
18 June 1964	The United Nations Security Council, taking into account the recommendations and conclusions of its Group of Experts, condemns the apartheid policies of the government of South Africa and the legislation supporting those policies.

19 June 1964	Sabotage groups blast three pylons, one in the Transvaal and two on the Cape Flats.
19 June 1964	Parliament ends its session after 103 days and the passing of 100 bills.
22 June 1964	Signs treaty with Great Britain on the introduction of a system of levies for certain cereals and related products.
July 1964	The police make many arrests throughout the country under the provisions of the General Laws Amendment Act.
21 July 1964	The United Nations Committee on the Policies of Apartheid of the Government of South Africa expresses very serious concern at the reported arrest of Abraham Fischer, defence attorney in the Rivonia Trial.
24 July 1964	A time bomb placed in the main concourse of the Johannesburg railway station explodes during the evening rush hour, causing extensive injuries. Frederick John Harris is later tried and sentenced to death for this offence.
29 July 1964	The Prime Minister issues a statement making it clear that the government will not yield to outside pressure to reduce the sentences in the Rivonia Trial.
31 July 1964	The Minister of Justice, B.J. Vorster, states at a Nationalist Party meeting that he is not prepared to lift the ninety-day detention clause, because of activity in five places in Africa where saboteurs are being trained for sabotage in South Africa and because of the regrouping of Communists since the Rivonia Trial.
4 Aug. 1964	Cabinet changes follow the retirement of Paul Sauer, Minister of Lands, Forestry and Public Works. Jan F.W. Haak becomes Minister of Planning and of Mines: the three portfolios previously held by Paul Sauer are allocated to the following Ministers in addition to their existing portfolios:- Lands, D.C.M. Uys, Forestry, W.A. Maree and Public Works, P.W. Botha.
13 Aug. 1964	Signs Sugar Agreement with Great Britain (South Africa, Great Britain, Swaziland).
15 Aug. 1964	Minister of Defence Fouché, announces that private enterprise will be responsible for the manufacture of aircraft for the South African Air Force. Jet trainers, to replace the SAAF's Harvards will be the first aircraft to be made locally.
18 Aug. 1964	Signs second declaration on the extension of the standstill provisions of Article XVI:4 of the General Agreement on Tarrifs and Trade.
22 Aug. 1964	A spokesman at the Police Headquarters in Pretoria states that the strength of the South African Police Reserve has reached 17,554 and that reservists are attached to almost every police station in South Africa.
24 Aug. 1964	Signs treaty with Malawi on double taxation.
15 Sept. 1964	Signs agreement with Portugal on postal services (for Mozambique).

15 Sept. 1964	Signs treaty with Northern Rhodesia on postal services.
15 Sept. 1964	Signs treaty with Malawi on postal services.
19 Sept. 1964	The Minister of Bantu Administration and Development de Wet Nel says that 'Tswanaland', a number of African reserves skirting the border with Bechuanaland, will be the next Bantustan to be granted self-government.
24 Sept. 1964	South African ordinance workshops have produced the first Belgian F.N. rifle, which is now ready to go into production.
7 Oct. 1964	It is announced in Rawalpindi that the government of Pakistan has decided to ban all exports from Pakistan to South Africa and has issued instructions to Pakistani shipping companies not to enter South African ports. Landing and passage facilities have already been refused to South African aircraft.
7 Oct. 1964	Signs multilateral treaty on univeral postal regulations.
7 Oct. 1964	Signs multilateral agreement accepting the constitution of the Universal Postal Union.
9 Oct. 1964	The demand to the United Nations by four Caprivi chiefs and officials of the newly-formed Caprivi African National Union, for the withdrawal of South Africa and the right to self-determination is reported.
9 Oct. 1964	The United Nations Special Committee on the Policies of Apartheid, at the special meeting, urgently demands that South Africa refrain from executing three leaders of the ANC, sentenced to death in March 1964. The appeals of the three - V. Mini, W. Khayinga and Z. Mraba - against their sentences had been rejected by the Supreme Court.
10 Oct. 1964	The United Party leader, Sir de Villiers Graaff, tells its Free State Congress that the Party rejects the idea of one man, one vote and will retain white leadership over all South Africa.
13 Oct. 1964	Signs agreement with Portugal (for Angola) with regard to rivers of mutual interest and the Kunene River Scheme.
13 Oct. 1964	Signs agreement with Portugal (for Mozambique) providing for the extension of cooling facilities for citrus fruit.
13 Oct. 1964	Signs treaty with Portugal (for Mozambique) on railway matters.
13 Oct. 1964	Signs an economic agreement with Portugal.
16 Oct. 1964	Signs treaty with Southern Rhodesia on air transport.
23 Oct. 1964	Signs treaty with Great Britain for the continuation of the trade agreement of 16 May 1960.
26 Oct. 1964	The United Nations Special Committee on the Policies of Apartheid decides to issue an appeal to member states and organizations to assist families of persons persecuted by the government for their opposition to the policies of apartheid.

30 Oct. 1964	Accepts multilateral procès-verbal extending the declaration of 13 November 1962 on the provisional accession of the United Arab Republic to the General Agreement on Tarrifs and Trade.
6 Nov. 1964	Shock and profound indignation is expressed by the Special Committee on the Policies of Apartheid, at its emergency meeting over the execution of the three ANC leaders in Port Elizabeth.
11 Nov. 1964	Signs agreement with Greece on the reciprocal exemption from taxes on income derived from the operation of ships or aircraft.
17 Nov. 1964	Harold Wilson, the British Prime Minister, announced in the House of Commons that the British government has decided to impose an embargo on the export of arms to South Africa. Outstanding commitments by the Ministry of Defence will be fulfilled, but no new contracts will be accepted. The contract to supply sixteen Buccaneer aircraft is under review.
20 Nov. 1964	The trial of Abram Fischer, Q.C., and thirteen others, charged with being members of the banned Communist Party, begins.
25 Nov. 1964	In a by-election at Edenvale, near Johannesburg in which the Broederbond is the main issue, the National Party's candidate Dr. Piet Koornhof, general secretary of the Broederbond since 1962, retains the seat for the Nationalists with an increased majority of nearly 1,000.
26 Nov. 1964	The Prime Minister, Dr. Verwoerd, welcomes the British Labour government's announcement that the supply of the sixteen Buccaneer aircraft is being sanctioned. Immediate action concerning the Simonstown Agreement has been avoided.
28 Nov. 1964	Dr. Verwoerd enters into a dispute with the British Prime Minister, Harold Wilson over a contract to supply Buccaneer aircraft, and threatens to abrogate the Simonstown Agreement if the planes are not supplied.
30 Nov. 1964	Signs trade agreement with Southern Rhodesia.
1 Dec. 1964	Signs multilateral customs agreement on the welfare material for seafarers.
5 Dec. 1964	The Minister of Justice, B.J. Vorster, announces the suspension, from 11 January 1965, of the clause in the General Law Amendment Act providing for detention for ninety days. All detainees will have to be released or charged in Court by that date.
10 Dec. 1964	It is announced that the Prime Minister's Economic Advisory Council has accepted a five-year plan designed to give South Africa an annual economic growth rate of five and a half per cent.
21 Dec. 1964	Signs treaty with Great Britain on the supply of military equipment to South Africa.
30 Dec. 1964	Signs multilateral treaty [1955(xix)] establishing the United Nations Conference on Trade and Development.
20 Jan. 1965	It is reported in London that the British government will not issue a permit for the export of the ground-to-air missiles South Africa requires.

22 Jan. 1965	Parliament opens with debate on a motion of 'no confidence' in the government in which the opposition attacks the separate development, Bantustan policy on the grounds that the creation of independent states could offer an entreé for communism inside the Republic.
25 Jan. 1965	Abram Fischer, Q.C., standing trial under the Suppression of Communism Act, fails to arrive in court, forfeits his bail and disappears. Letters are read in court enumerating the reasons for his action and making a bitter attack on government policy. A warrant of arrest is issued.
30 Jan. 1965	Minister of Justice B.J. Vorster, tells Parliament that 1,095 people have been detained under the ninety-day clause during the eighteen months the imprisonment-without-trial law has been in operation.
5 Feb. 1965	The Prime Minister, speaking to the House of Assembly, states that territorial separation is not the essential part of the apartheid policy - political separation is. He will not hesitate to use force to ensure white domination in the white man's own area.
12 Feb. 1965	A proclamation applies a section of the Group Areas Act to all public places of recreation, including sporting events, theatres and concerts so that such places in white areas could not be frequented by non-whites and vice versa.
13 Feb. 1965	The unofficial Dutch mission, under Professor W.G. de Gaay Fortman, coming to South Africa to discuss apartheid, is cancelled. The tour will no longer be undertaken because the government has refused permission for the mission to meet Dr. Albert Luthuli.
25 Feb. 1965	Archbishop Owen McCann of Cape Town becomes South Africa's first Cardinal when he is invested by Pope Paul in St Peter's Basilica.
26 Feb. 1965	Signs multilateral agreement between the International Atomic Energy Agency, South Africa and the United States for the application of safeguards.
4 Mar. 1965	Prime Minister H.F. Verwoerd, discloses that the restriction on Seretse Khama, now Prime Minister of Bechuanaland, visiting South Africa has been lifted and friendly relations with Bechuanaland are now desired.
6 Mar. 1965	Justice D.H. Botha, the Commissioner appointed to inquire into the activities of secret societies - the Broederbond, the Freemasons and the Sons of England - is unable to make any finding against any organizations.
15 Mar. 1965	The prolonged hearing of the dispute over the constitutional position of South West Africa is resumed by the International Court of Justice at The Hague. Extensive evidence is led on behalf of South Africa.
18 Mar. 1965	The Director-General of the South African Atomic Energy Board, announces in Pretoria that South Africa's first nuclear reactor has 'gone critical'.
24 Mar. 1965	Provincial Council elections show a sharp swing to the government side and shock the opposition UP. Although provincial, the campaigns are conducted on national, particularly racial, issues.

| 30 Mar. 1965 | The proposal is made that members of the International Court of Justice should make a personal visit to South West Africa, South Africa, Liberia, Ethiopia, and elsewhere in Africa as the Court might wish. The invitation is rejected. |

2 Apr. 1965   Twelve people are found guilty of charges brought under the Suppression of Communism Act, by being members of the Communist Party, taking part in its activities and furthering its aims. On 13 April they are sentenced to terms of imprisonment ranging from one to five years.

6 Apr. 1965   The International Court of Justice at The Hague hears the arguments of Ethiopia and Liberia in the South West Africa cases presented by E.A. Gross of the New York Bar. It is alleged that South Africa has infringed its League of Nations Mandate by applying its racial policies in the territory.

7 Apr. 1965   The United Nations Special Committee on the Policies of Apartheid, meets and is informed of the executions in South Africa of W. Bongco and F.J. Harris for acts arising from their opposition to apartheid.

9 Apr. 1965   Signs multilateral agreement on the facilitation of international maritime traffic.

13 Apr. 1965   Signs treaty with Great Britain on the temporary waiver from 1 July 1964 to 5 May 1965 of the margin of preference on flat white maize.

22 Apr. 1965   Signs agreement with Swaziland on air services.

24 Apr. 1965   The Minister of Bantu Administration and Development, formally opens the Transkei Assembly Session, giving a preview of the more important legislation to be introduced. Bills include one to establish a separate Transkei flag and one to reorganize the Regional, Tribal and Community Authorities and consolidate existing legislation.

29 Apr. 1965   Signs treaty with Denmark, Norway and Sweden on the temporary amendment of the air agreements of 1958.

30 Apr. 1965   The Indians Education Bill is passed, providing for the transfer of the control of education of Indians from the Provincial Councils to the Indian Affairs Department of the central government, despite opposition from the UP.

4 May 1965   Units of the SADF are now being equipped with a rifle made completely in South Africa. It is the R1-7.62 mm rifle, developed from the Belgian FN rifle, with improvements.

7 May 1965   The Deputy Minister of Bantu Administration and Development, M.C. Botha, announces in Parliament that Local Authorities must issue permits to householders who wish to have more than one servant sleeping on their premises. This is construed as a move to keep the suburbs white at night.

8 May 1965   The opposition leader Sir de Villiers Graaff, speaking in the Legislative Assembly, claims that the number of Africans in white areas will continue to increase indefinitely if the country's rate of economic development is maintained.

8 May 1965	Chief Leabua Jonathan, leader of the Basutoland National Party which is to form the Protectorate's first government, tells political refugees that they are welcome to stay provided they do not use Basutoland as a base for operations against South Africa.
12 May 1965	Signs multilateral agreement amending the international sanitary regulations - WHO regulation no. 4.
13 May 1965	The Official Secrets Act Amendment Bill is passed. It is designed to prevent the publication of information which would hamper or nullify the operations of the security police.
15 May 1965	Signs treaty with Portugal concerning SAA and TAP on air pooling.
18 May 1965	The Separate Representation of Voters Amendment Bill lays down that the four white Members of Parliament elected to represent Coloureds will sit for fixed five-year terms and will no longer be elected eight days before the White Parliamentary elections. The effect is to prolong the terms of the present M.P.s for Coloureds and postpone a new election for Coloured voters who might elect Progressive Party members.
19 May 1965	A Commission is appointed to inquire into an experiment involving twelve gold mines in which African miners have been employed.
21 May 1965	The Minister of Defence states that South Africa has already made progress in building up her own military power and is almost independent in the provision of small arms.
22 May 1965	Minister of Defence Fouché announces that R12m. had been spent on the defence radar screen in the Transvaal.
25 May 1965	Signs agreement with Belgium on reciprocity regarding admission to medical practice.
3 June 1965	President Kaunda of Zambia says that an eight million Pound Sterling air base is being built by South Africa in the Caprivi Strip and accuses South Africa of warmongering. The Minister of Transport, B.J. Schoeman, replies that the air strip being constructed at Katimo Mulilo, is intended only for administrative purposes when roads in the Caprivi Strip are impassable.
5 June 1965	The Constitution Amendment Bill of South Africa provides for an increase in the number of members of Parliament from 160 to 170.
7 June 1965	The Police Amendment Bill, passed unopposed, empowers the police to search without warrant any person or premises within one mile of South Africa's borders and to seize anything found. It is designed to combat the infiltration of saboteurs from other parts of Africa.
10 June 1965	Signs agreement with Southern Rhodesia for the avoidance of double taxation and the prevention of fiscal evasion with respect to taxes on income.
15 June 1965	Signs multilateral agreement on arbitration for a global commercial communications system.

15 June 1965	The Constitution Amendment Bill, published on 5 March 1965, but amended by a Select Committee provides that the number of Parliamentary seats will be increased by ten, and that the 'loading' and 'unloading' of constituencies should be applied on a country-wide instead of a provincial basis.
19 June 1965	The government has instructed its Ambassador to The Hague to inform the Dutch government of its displeasure over a grant of 100,000 guilders being made to the Defence and Aid Fund for assistance to the victims of apartheid. This is seen as interference in the domestic affairs of South Africa.
22 June 1965	The Suppression of Communism Amendment Bill authorizing the Minister of Justice to prohibit the publication of statements or writings of those furthering or defending the aims of Communism.
25 June 1965	The Criminal Procedure Amendment Bill is enacted. Among its provisions this Bill empowers the Attorney General to order the Court not to give bail to defendants and to arrest and detain, for up to six months before a trial, any state witness who might be open to intimidation, or be considered likely to abscond. The General Bar Council of South Africa criticizes the Bill as a grave interference with the rule of law and the administration of justice.
1 July 1965	Signs multilateral treaty for the extension of the International Wheat Agreement 1962.
1 July 1965	The police raid the editorial offices of the Rand Daily Mail in Johannesburg and confiscate documents relating to a series of articles on prison conditions written by Harold Strachan.
3 July 1965	A restriction order is served on Harold Strachan of Durban in terms of the Suppression of Communism Act. He has already been imprisoned for three years for conspiring to cause explosions.
3 July 1965	South Africa appoints ambassadors, R.H. Coaton to Argentina, J.C.H. Maree to Australia, A.A.M. Hamilton to Spain.
8 July 1965	Signs multilateral agreement on transit trade of land-locked states.
10 July 1965	The Netherlands Foreign Minister Dr. Luns says at The Hague that the Dutch government's gift of 20,000 Pounds Sterling to the Defence and Aid Fund is pledged to an organization legally active in South Africa for many years, and is part of their international care and responsibility role.
5 Aug. 1965	South Africa's first atomic reactor, Safari I, is opened by the Prime Minister at Pelindaba near Johannesburg. Nuclear power will be used for peaceful purposes only.
8 Aug. 1965	Following the findings of the Viljoen Commission into the employment of African labour in twelve gold mines, the experiment is terminated. The Minister of Mines, J.W. Haak, says the government has decided that the colour-bar in the mining industry should be withdrawn.
20 Aug. 1965	The Transkei Chief Minister, Chief Kaiser Matanzima, tells an election rally in the Umzimkulu District that the Transkei has been given self-government

so that people can rule themselves according to their customs. He promises that European-owned farms will soon be bought by the South African government and distributed to the people.

24 Aug. 1965	Signs a treaty with Great Britain on the temporary waiver from 5 May 1965 to 7 January 1966 of the margin of preference on flat white maize.
4 Sept. 1965	Dr. Verwoerd clearly indicates that no Maoris will be acceptable in any New Zealand rugby team visiting South Africa in future. There is a strong reaction in New Zealand to this declaration of policy.
10 Sept. 1965	Regulations covering the detention of 180-days detainees held as witnesses, are published in the Government Gazette.
21 Sept. 1965	The leader of the opposition United Party presents the party's Race Federation Programme to delegates to the Natal Congress.
13 Oct. 1965	William Rowntree is nominated as the new American ambassador to South Africa to replace J.C. Salterwaite, due to leave South Africa on 18 November 1965.
14 Oct. 1965	Signs treaty with France on air pooling, concerning SAA and UTA.
19 Oct. 1965	New electoral divisions are defined and plans are open for inspection. 160 electoral divisions are provided for the House of Assembly - an increase of ten - and in addition there will be six for South West Africa and four for Cape Coloured voters.
27 Oct. 1965	The Prime Minister opens a new international radio service, 'The Voice of South Africa', intended to counter the hostile propaganda beamed to the Republic from foreign sources.
1 Nov. 1965	Signs multilateral agreement on the prolongation of the International Sugar Agreement.
2 Nov. 1965	Members of the Basutoland Congress Party demand the incorporation into Basutoland of 'Congo Territory', a large area of the Orange Free State, Natal and Eastern Cape Province.
3 Nov. 1965	Following a decision of the Johannesburg Bar Council the name of Abram Fischer is struck off the roll of advocates.
6 Nov. 1965	A R500,000 grant offered to the proposed new Afrikaans University in Johannesburg by the Johannesburg City Council, is accepted by the University Committee.
11 Nov. 1965	On the eve of the Rhodesian Declaration of Independence, South Africa's Prime Minister announces that South Africa will continue to maintain normal friendly relations with both Britain and Rhodesia, adopting an official neutral position.
11 Nov. 1965	Abram Fischer, Q.C. is re-arrested in Johannesburg.
13 Nov. 1965	The Archbishop of Cape Town, the Most Reverend Robert Selby Taylor, says in his charge to the Synod of the Church of the Province of South

Africa, constituted in Cape Town, that barriers erected to keep races apart are creating in the minds of many a serious conflict between loyalty to their conscience and obedience to the law.

17 Nov. 1965	Signs multilateral agreement further extending the international wheat agreement of 1962.
14 Dec. 1965	Accepts Procès-verbal extending the declaration of 13 November 1962 on he provisional accession of Yugoslavia to the General Agreement of Tarrifs and Trade
14 Dec. 1965	Accepts Procès-verbal extending the declaration of 5 March 1966 on the provisional accession of Iceland to the General Agreement on Tarrifs and Trade.
15 Dec. 1965	The United Nations General Assembly, in its twentieth session, passes a resolution strongly condemning the apartheid policies and calling for economic and diplomatic sanctions against South Africa.
20 Dec. 1965	A re-organisation of the South African Defence Force replaces the General Staff with a body to be known as the 'Supreme Command' with the Commandant-General as Chairman and the Executive Commanders as members.
31 Dec. 1965	The government's attitude to Rhodesia's unilateral declaration of independence is defined by the Prime Minister, Dr. Verwoerd, when he says that South Africa will not be coerced into any form of boycott.
1 Jan. 1966	In a New Year message, Prime Minister Verwoerd emphasizes that South African policy is one of non-interference in the issues between Rhodesia and the United Kingdom. Regular relations will be maintained with both parties.
28 Jan. 1966	The Prime Minister states that detention under the 180-day clause of the Criminal Procedure Amendment Act has been applied in the case of twenty-three people, all of whom were required as witnesses in criminal cases, including those against Abram Fischer and Fred Carneson.
1 Feb. 1966	All South African refugees are to report to the Basutoland police for documentation or face deportation to South Africa. A closer check is to be kept on political asylum figures.
4 Feb. 1966	Abram Fischer is committed for trial by a Pretoria magistrate. He pleads not guilty to all allegations.
7 Feb. 1966	The Suppression of Communism Amendment Bill provides for the extension by a further year the power of the Minister of Justice to detain prisoners convicted under the Suppression of Communism Act for further periods after the expiry of their sentences. This power had been applied to Robert Sobukwe and his detention will be extended.
25 Feb. 1966	Seven Africans are detained in the Transkei on an allegation of conspiracy to commit murder. Five are opposition members of the Legislative Council and the plot concerns the possible assassination of the Prime Minister, Chief Kaiser Matanzima.

18 Mar. 1966	The Defence and Aid Fund is banned as an unlawful organization under the Suppression of Communism Act. It is an autonomous South African body providing legal aid for persons accused of political offences and support for the families of political prisoners. The fund's office in Cape Town, East London, Johannesburg and Port Elizabeth are searched by police, as well as the homes of its office bearers, including that of the author, Alan Paton.
23 Mar. 1966	Abram Fischer goes on trial in the Pretoria Supreme Court facing various charges of illegal activity, including membership of the Communist Party, conspiring to commit sabotage and to provide training for guerrilla warfare.
28 Mar. 1966	The trial of Fred Carneson, a listed communist and former editor of 'New Age' opens before the Supreme Court in Cape Town, the charges being sabotage and contravention of the Suppression of Communism Act on three counts. On 25 May he is sentenced to a total of five years and nine months' imprisonment.
29 Mar. 1966	Signs treaty with Zambia on postal services.
30 Mar. 1966	Six political parties participate in the General Elections, with 356 candidates contesting 166 seats. The result is a sweeping victory for the National Party, who have a majority of eighty-two seats over the combined opposition. United Party members declined from forty-nine to thirty-nine, and the Progressive Party duly obtained one seat.
1 Apr. 1966	An official list is published of forty-four people who have left South Africa and whose writings will not be allowed under the Suppression of Communism Act.
6 Apr. 1966	The Chairman of the opposition Democratic Party in the Transkei, K.M. Gunzana, is elected leader to succeed Paramount Chief Victor Poto who is to retire.
6 Apr. 1966	Signs agreement with Italy on the postal administration between South Africa and Italy on the exchange of money orders.
9 Apr. 1966	Following the victory of the National Party in the General Election, Dr. Verwoerd forms a new government.
20 Apr. 1966	Signs multilateral agreement on the further extension of the International Wheat Agreement, 1962.
29 Apr. 1966	Signs multilateral treaty on the partial revision of radio regulations.
29 Apr. 1966	Signs treaty with Denmark, Norway and Sweden on the extension of the period of validity of traffic rights at Zurich in respect of South African territory granted to SAS by the 1958 agreement.
4 May 1966	The court finds Abram Fischer guilty on all fifteen counts of the indictment, including alleged sabotage, Communist Party membership and being a contact between the South African Communist Party and its overseas committee in London.
5 May 1966	Signs treaty with the Federal Republic of Germany on postal services.

5 May 1966   Signs treaty with the Federal Republic of Germany on postal services.

9 May 1966   Abram Fischer is sentenced to life imprisonment on the charge of conspiracy with the ANC and Unkonto we Sizwe to commit sabotage and to twenty-four years' imprisonment on six counts concerning Communist Party membership.

10 May 1966   Signs treaty with Great Britain for the release from the bound margin of preference on raw coffee.

11 May 1966   The President of the National Union of South Africa (NUSAS), Ian Robertson, receives a banning order under the Suppression of Communism Act.

14 May 1966   The government grants an amnesty in celebration of the fifth anniversary of the Republic. Over 30,000 prisoners stand to benefit.

20 May 1966   After the State President assents to the Transkei Flag Bill, the new ochre-red, white and green tricolour of the Transkei is hoisted in the capital Umtata for the first time.

31 May 1966   The Republic celebrates its fifth anniversary with a massive military demonstration in Pretoria. A crowd of more than 500,000 sees nearly 20,000 troops and 200 aircraft take part in the proceedings.

4 June 1966   Senator Robert Kennedy arrives in South Africa as the guest of NUSAS. He speaks at several universities, meets ex-Chief Albert Luthuli, banned leader of the ANC, but at no time does any member of the government meet him and official hostility is evident.

8 June 1966   South Africa officially refuses an invitation to send representatives to an international seminar on apartheid, to be held in Brazil, in August and September 1966. The seminar is considered to be simply part of the political campaign waged against South Africa at the United Nations.

22 June 1966   A spokesman for the World Council of Churches says in Geneva that the government has refused permission for Bishop Zulu to attend the world conference on 'Church and Society' in July. The Anglican Prelate was to have been one of the eight conference presidents.

7 July 1966   Signs treaty with Great Britain on the temporary waiver of the margin of preference on flat white maize.

16 July 1966   The latest list of banned people totals 936 in three categories: 467 listed communists, 515 banned under the Suppression of Communism and Riotous Assembly Acts and three banned only under the Riotous Assemblies Acts. Forty-nine names are both listed as communists and banned.

18 July 1966   The International Court of Justice at The Hague rejects the complaints by Ethiopia and Liberia against South Africa, in which they alleged breaches of duties as the mandatory power to South West Africa, with the President of the Court, Sir Percy Spender of Australia, deciding the issue with his casting vote. The government welcomes this decision: the South West African National Union and SWAPO reject the decision absolutely.

20 July 1966	Accepts the accession of Yugoslavia to the General Agreement on Tarrifs and Trade.
20 July 1966	Signs a parcel post agreement with the Netherlands.
29 July 1966	Addressing the Senate, President Swart announces that legislation is to be introduced by the government to prohibit interference by one population group in the political affairs or institutions of another population group. It is aimed at thwarting Progressive Party plans to counter the four October elections of the four Coloured People's representatives in the Assembly. On a different topic, he makes it clear that no proposal to leave the United Nations is at present being contemplated by the government.
6 Aug. 1966	The Universities Amendment Act and the Extension of University Education Amendment Act give the Minister of Education Arts and Science, complete control over student life in South African universities.
12 Aug. 1966	Under the Suppression of Communism Amendment Bill tabled in Parliament, any attorney or advocate who has committed an offence under the Act at any time is liable to be struck off the roll. Other clauses give the Minister of Justice powers to cut listed people off from contact with any organization he chooses to specify. The Bill is rejected outright by the Progressive Party member Helen Suzman.
17 Aug. 1966	Accepts the accession of Switzerland to the General Agreement on Tarrifs and Trade.
22 Aug. 1966	Signs agreement with the Union Castle Co. on ocean-freight.
23 Aug. 1966	The South African Minister of Posts and Telegraphs complains that Radio Tanzania's broadcasts from Dar-es-Salaam are interfering with broadcasts in South Africa.
6 Sept. 1966	The Prime Minister, Dr. H.F. Verwoerd, is fatally stabbed in the House of Assembly by Demitrio Tsafendas, a messenger who had been serving the Press Gallery. Dr. T.E. Dönges, the Minister of Finance, temporarily takes over the duties of Prime Minister.
6 Sept. 1966	Signs treaty with Botswana on air transport between Bechuanaland National Airways (BNA) and South African Railways and Harbours.
8 Sept. 1966	Signs guarantee agreement with the International Bank for Reconstruction and Development.
10 Sept. 1966	Dr. Verwoerd is buried in Hero's Acre, Pretoria. A mile-long cortège is watched on its three-mile journey by a crowd of some 250,000 people.
13 Sept. 1966	The Parliamentary caucus of the National Party unanimously elects B.J. Vorster, Minister of Justice, as its new leader. He automatically becomes Prime Minister, promises to uphold Dr. Verwoerd's policies and will retain the Cabinet Portfolio of Police, temporarily.
14 Sept. 1966	Justice van Wyk of the Appellate Division of the Supreme Court is appointed as a one-man Commission to inquire into all aspects of the assassination.

27 Sept. 1966

The United Nations General Assembly votes by 114 votes to two (South Africa and Portugal), with three abstentions (Britain, France and Malawi) to terminate the mandate and to declare the administration of South West Africa to be the responsibility of the United Nations. The government views the Resolution as illegal and unconstitutional, and proposes to ignore it.

5 Oct. 1966

A new Afrikaans-medium university is established in Johannesburg, the Rand Afrikaans University.

12 Oct. 1966

Minister of Defence Botha announces in Cape Town that the posts of Secretary for Defence and Commandant-General of the Defence Force are to be combined under one head.

13 Oct. 1966

The General Laws Amendment Bill of 1966 is published. The bill entitles police officers to detain up to fourteen days anyone suspected of offences against security.

17-20 Oct. 1966

Tsafendas is brought to trial before the Judge-President of the Cape Provincial Division of the Supreme Court and two Assessors. He is found mentally unfit to stand trial.

21 Oct. 1966

D. Tsafendas, accused of assassinating Dr. Verwoerd in the House of Assembly, is committed to detention in prison at the State President's pleasure.

1 Nov. 1966

The United Nations General Assembly adopts a fifty-four nation resolution by 114 to 2 against (South Africa and Portugal) with three abstentions (Malawi, France and Great Britain) calling for the establishment of a fourteen-member ad hoc Committee to recommend practical means for the administration of South West Africa. The Assembly also decides that South Africa's Mandate over SWA is terminated.

3 Nov. 1966

Signs multilateral recommendations under Article IX of the Antarctic Treaty.

7 Nov. 1966

The government announces that President Swart will retire on 31 May 1967.

11 Nov. 1966

Signs multilateral agreement on telecommunications and treaties of 21 October 1965.

14 Nov. 1966

Signs treaty with Portugal (for Angola) on air transport.

17 Nov. 1966

Accepts Procès-verbal extending the declaration on the provisional accession of the United Arab Republic to the General Agreement on Tarrifs and Trade.

25 Nov. 1966

The new British Ambassador to South Africa, Sir John Nicholls, presents his credentials to the State President.

28 Nov. 1966

The Bantu Administration Minister M.C. Botha, announces measures leading to the creation of South Africa's second 'homeland' in the Northern Transvaal.

29 Nov. 1966	Signs treaty with Malawi on postal services.
30 Nov. 1966	Signs multilateral treaty on the safety of life at sea.
14 Dec. 1966	Signs multilateral treaty on load lines.
20 Dec. 1966	The United Nations General Assembly passes a draft Resolution, by eighty-seven votes to one (Portugal) and twelve abstentions, indicating that the situation in South Africa constitutes a threat to international peace and that universally applied mandatory economic sanctions are the only means of achieving a peaceful solution.
14 Dec. 1966	The Minister of Agricultural Technical Services, J.J. Fouché, claims that South Africa is strong enough to withstand sanctions for at least three years.
28 Dec. 1966	The Lesotho government announces it will deport eight South Africans, whom it describes as a danger to peace.
1 Jan. 1967	Signs multilateral Sugar Agreement of 1958.
10-11 Jan.	B.J. Vorster and Chief Jonathan of Lesotho meet in Cape Town. A joint statement emphasizes their belief in peaceful co-existence. Economic aid and technical assistance are also proposed.
11 Jan. 1967	The projected North Sotho 'nation' in the Northern Transvaal province is to run its own affairs of state. Matters passing to its control include education, finance, justice, public works, agriculture, forestry and community development.
18 Jan. 1967	A report prepared by UNESCO, published in Paris, states that the policy of apartheid 'is not only an inadmissable answer to the racial and group conflict, but is itself the major cause of racial and group conflict there'. The report is based essentially on official government publications and reports from scientific and research institutions within and outside South Africa relating to discriminatory practices.
18 Jan. 1967	The Lesotho government invites all South African political refugees to make formal application to leave the country, to indicate proposed dates of departure and countries of choice. Transit rights through South Africa will be arranged.
19 Jan. 1967	The National Party Parliamentary caucus nominates Dr. T.E. Dönges, Minister of Finance since 1958 as candidate for the Presidency, on a second ballot. The United Party opposition nominates Major Piet van der Byl.
24 Jan. 1967	Prime Minister B.J. Vorster announces in Cape Town that Dr. Dönges, nominated as the government's candidate for the Presidency, has tendered his resignation as Minister of Finance. His portfolio is to be taken over by Dr. Diederichs. Mr. J.W. Haak becomes Minister of Economic Affairs and Dr. Carel de Wet, South African Ambassador in London will take over the portfolio of Mines and Planning.

27 Jan. 1967	The head of the South African Defence Force, Commandant General Hiemstra, announces the successful conclusion of Anglo-South African talks on aspects of the Simonstown naval agreement for the defence of sea routes around Southern Africa.
7 Feb. 1967	A bill is published, which requires every Coloured male between the ages 18-24 to register for selective service in training camps. It is passed in Committee on 8 March and approved 9 March 1967.
8 Feb. 1967	A spokesman for the Royal Navy that the British Command at Simonstown Naval Base will close on 12 April 1967. South Africa will in future assume greater responsibility for the defence of the sea route around the Cape.
15 Feb. 1967	Suppression of Communism Further Amendment Bill is approved by 106 votes to forty at its third reading. It is made retrospective to 27 June 1962.
18 Feb. 1967	The government drops two Bills which were designed to enforce racial segregation on university campuses.
22 Feb. 1967	The Minister of Defence, P.W. Botha, discloses that South Africa's northern borders are protected by a radar complex constituting an early warning system and that her coasts will be covered by the Decca navigational system costing R6m.
28 Feb. 1967	The electoral college elects T.E. Dönges as the next State President by 163 votes to fifty-two, cast for Major van der Byl.
2 Mar. 1967	The Population Registration Amendment Bill, with reference to racial legislation concerning the Coloured population, is published. The President is empowered to define, by proclamation, the ethnic and other groups into which Coloured persons and Blacks may be classified.
4 Mar. 1967	Dr. Theophilus Ebenhaezer Dönges, is elected South Africa's second State President and will assume office on Republic Day, 31 May 1967.
13 Mar. 1967	Discussions are conducted with Malawi on the occasion of a visit to South Africa by three Malawian Cabinet ministers.
13 Mar. 1967	Signs treaties with Denmark, Sweden and Norway regarding the extension of the period of validity of the traffic rights at Zurich in respect of South African territory granted to SAS.
13 Mar. 1967	Signs trade agreement with Malawi.
13 Mar. 1967	Signs treaty with Lesotho on the amendment of the insured parcel agreement of 27 June 1963 and 1 July 1963.
27-31 Mar.1967	The project of a dam across the Zambezi River at Cahora Bassa in Mozambique, involving the building of a hydro-electric power station, is discussed at talks with the South African government in Lisbon.

31 Mar. 1967	A government spokesman in Gaborone, indicates that Botswana intends to curb the activities of 200 South African political refugees.
8 Apr. 1967	The government publishes a Bill entitled the Prohibition of Mixed Marriages (Amendment) Bill. In effect, marriage between a white South African man and a 'non-white' woman, even if they were married abroad, will not be recognized in South Africa.
19 Apr. 1967	The Minister of Defence announces in Paris that he has signed an agreement for the purchase of French submarines of the Daphne class, their cost being the equivalent of twelve million Pounds Sterling.
19 Apr. 1967	Prime Minister B.J. Vorster declares at the opening of the Sixth Session of the Transkei Legislative Assembly that the government will assist blacks in their development and will transfer more functions and responsibilities to the government of the Transkei as the latter becomes able to handle them efficiently.
26 Apr. 1967	A draft resolution on South West Africa is submitted to a special session of the United Nations General Assembly by fifty-six countries. It declares that obstruction to its proposals by South Africa will constitute a flagrant defiance of the authority of the United Nations and requests the Security Council to take enforcement action.
3 May 1967	An official announcement by the government of Lesotho indicates that preparations for anti-South African political refugees to be flown from Lesotho across South Africa to other African states to the north have reached an advanced stage.
3 May 1967	Signs multilateral Convention on the International Hydrographic Organisation.
15 May 1967	Signs multilateral treaty on the extension of the International Wheat Agreement.
19 May 1967	The United Nations General Assembly adopts a resolution establishing an eleven member United Nations Council for South West Africa to administer the Territory and to enter immediately into contact with South Africa to lay down procedures for its transfer. The resolution is supported by eighty-five votes, two against (Portugal and South Africa) and thirty abstentions, including the USSR, the United States, Great Britain and France.
31 May 1967	Senator J.F. Naudé becomes Acting State President, following the incapacitation of Dr. T.E. Dönges. He is sworn in on 1 June 1967.
6 June 1967	The Physical Planning and Utilization of Resources Bill is enacted.
9 June 1967	The Defence Amendment Bill, designed to make military service compulsory for practically all white young men, is passed with the support of the opposition.
14 June 1967	Signs treaty with Great Britain on the avoidance of double taxation and the prevention of fiscal evasion with respect to taxes on income.
21 June 1967	The General Laws Amendment Bill or 'Terrorism Bill' which makes

terrorism a separate offence to be equated with treason is gazetted. Under its terms terrorism is defined as including acts committed with intent to endanger the maintenance of law and order and conspiracy or incitement to this end. It is made retrospectove to 27 June 1962.

22 June 1967	Signs treaty with Norway on a scientific project.

July 1967 — Thirty-seven Africans are charged in Pretoria under the Terrorism Act. The State alleges that the accused have engaged in terrorist activity in South West Africa between June 1962 and May 1967. Defence contends that the Terrorist Act cannot apply to South West Africa which is mandated territory but this argument is rejected by the court.

July 1967 — The Portuguese Foreign Minister, Dr. A.F. Nogueira visits South Africa for talks with B.J. Vorster concerning regional co-operation.

4 July 1967 — Signs multilateral agreement for the accession of the Republic of Korea to the General Agreement on Tarrifs and Trade.

17 July 1967 — Extends treaty with the United States on the civil uses of atomic energy of 8 July 1957.

21 July 1967 — Albert Luthuli, Nobel Peace Prize winner and former President of the banned ANC, dies.

26 July 1967 — Signs treaty with Italy on the amendment of the air agreement of the 21 May 1956.

30 July 1967 — Dr. Raymond Hoffenberg of Groote Schuur Hospital, Cape Town and senior lecturer at the University of Cape Town Medical School, is banned under the Suppression of Communism Act. No explanation is given and the order leads to immediate protests by University staff and students.

1 Aug. 1967 — Signs treaty with Malawi relating to the employment and documentation of Malawi nationals in South Africa.

4 Aug. 1967 — The Defence Amendment Act comes into force, under which every young white male will be liable for military service. The amendments are based on making all medically fit citizens, except for those who join the permanent force, the South African police, the railways or prison services, liable for military training. Expenditure on citizen forces and commando training will increase by almost R1m. in 1968 to an estimated figure of about R30m.

11 Aug. 1967 — B.J. Vorster says in Koffiefontein, Orange Free State, that the restrictions imposed on Dr. Hoffenberg are attributable to his promotion of the aims and objects of communism.

8 Sept. 1967 — It is officially disclosed that South African police are in Rhodesia actively helping in the fight against Nationalist guerrillas. This follows an attempt by several hundred guerrillas to invade South and South West Africa, from Zambia, at the urging of the Liberation Committee of the OAU in Kampala in July 1967.

8 Sept. 1967 — Prime Minister B.J. Vorster announces the arrest of a fully trained KGB agent, Yuri N. Loginov, in Johannesburg, while on a special mission to

South Africa. His arrest arouses widespread interest among Western intelligence services.

10 Sept. 1967   At the opening of the Malawi Congress Party's (MCP) annual congress at Mzuzu, President Banda announces that formal diplomatic relations will be established between Malawi and South Africa at legation level by 1 January 1968.

10 Sept. 1967   Speaking at a special news conference the Rhodesian Prime Minister, Ian Smith, welcomes the participation of the South African Police in Rhodesian anti-terrorist operations.

23 Sept. 1967   Addressing a National Party rally at Volksrust, the Prime Minister, B.J. Vorster says that South Africa's fight against foreign-trained terrorists will continue in any area where South Africa is allowed to fight. He defends South Africa's decision to send police to Rhodesia.

27 Sept. 1967   Signs treaty with Lesotho on air services.

Oct. 1967   Helen Joseph, placed under house arrest for five years in 1962, is similarly restricted for a further five years.

6 Oct. 1967   A Bill is introduced into the Lesotho parliament providing for the extradition of fugitives from the Republic of South Africa.

8 Oct. 1967   Signs multilateral treaty on the principles governing the activities of states in the exploration and use of outer space.

17 Oct. 1967   Signs multilateral treaty on the conservation of Atlantic tunas (with final act and resolution adopted by the conference of plenipotentiaries).

21 Oct. 1967   Rhodesian Prime Minister, Ian Smith, arrives in Pretoria by military aircraft, accompanied by his Minister of Law and Order, D. Lardner-Burke, for talks with B.J. Vorster. Rhodesian constitutional questions and Rhodesia's relationship with Britain are discussed.

25 Oct. 1967   Signs amendment to multilateral treaty on the safety of life at sea.

Nov. 1967   The Chairman of the Resources and Planning Council visits Malawi and endorses President Banda's plan to build a new capital in Lilongwe. To this end South Africa agrees to provide finance for the first building phase.

8 Nov. 1967   Signs treaty with Austria on the state of the Commonwealth war cemetery at Klagenfurt.

13 Nov. 1967   Signs treaty with Belgium on air services.

15 Nov. 1967   Signs treaty with Great Britain on consular privileges.

17 Nov. 1967   The Malawi Ministry of External Affairs announces that the first Malawi Chargé d'Affaires in South Africa will be P. Richardson. He will take up his post on 11 December 1967 and present his credentials the following day.

21 Nov. 1967	Signs treaty with Great Britain on the temporary suspension of the margin of preference on tin plate.
Dec. 1967	Dr. Christiaan Barnard makes medical history by transplanting the first heart to a man dying of terminal heart ailments.
3 Dec. 1967	The Minister of Defence, P.W. Botha, announces a reshuffle of senior defence force posts to increase the efficiency of the country's Defence Department, the Defence Production Board and the Defence Organisation. Consequently Lieutenant-General C.A. Fraser, at present Chief of the Army, becomes Joint Commander, Combat Forces, in which capacity he will take command in times of war or emergency, of the fighting formations of Army and Air Force elements.
11 Dec. 1967	J.F. Wenzel presents his credentials to President Banda as South Africa's first Chargé d'Affaires and head of legation in Malawi.
13 Dec. 1967	At the twenty-first session of the United Nations, South Africa's apartheid policies are condemned as 'a crime against humanity'.
14 Dec. 1967	Britain continues its ban on arms supplies to South Africa.
30 Dec. 1967	The Foreign Minister Dr. Muller apologizes to Zambia for the actions of the five members of the South African police detained on the Victoria Falls Bridge by the Zambian authorities on 29 December 1967. They are released on 12 January 1968.
31 Dec. 1967	Prime Minister B.J. Vorster warns that the government would re-assess the Simonstown agreement during 1968. This reaction follows the British government's decision to maintain the South African arms embargo.
3 Jan. 1968	The State President-elect, Dr. Theophilus Ebenaeser Dönges, dies after a long illness.
30 Jan. 1968	Signs a modification to the annexure of the air agreement of 19 October 1959 with Switzerland.
1 Feb. 1968	J.J. Fouché is nominated and unanimously elected President following the death of Dr. T.E. Dönges.
2 Feb. 1968	Accepts the accession of Poland to the General Agreement on Tariffs and Trade.
2 Feb. 1968	Accepts the accession of Argentina to the General Agreement on Tariffs and Trade.
4 Feb. 1968	The Prime Minister of Lesotho, Chief Jonathan, is reported to be prepared to co-operate with the South African government.
7-8 Feb. 1968	Mr. Fouché, the newly elected President, resigns from the cabinet and institutes changes in the government. D.C.H. Uys becomes the newly designated Minister of Agriculture and of Water Affairs and M.C.G.J. van Rensburg takes over the Posts and Telegraphs portfolio.
9 Feb. 1968	Mr. Justice Ludorf, presiding judge in the Pretoria terrorist trial, imposes

sentences on the thirty accused of conspiring to overthrow the South West Africa administration. All are sentenced to imprisonment, nineteen to life, nine to twenty years, and two to five years.

15 Feb. 1968   The International Olympics Committee (IOC) decides to re-admit South Africa to the Olympic Games. The government has made five relevant concessions and the country is expected to participate in the Mexico City Olympics late in 1968.

16 Feb. 1968   The Commission, headed by S.L. Muller, appointed to study political interference and representation of population groups publishes its report. Its recommendations, which feature in subsequent legislation, are debated in the House of Assembly in late February and early March 1968.

22 Feb. 1968   The Prohibition of Mixed Marriages Amendment Bill is adopted against the opposition of the United and Progressive Parties.

26 Feb. 1968   The South African Indian Council Bill, dealing with the affairs of the Indian Population, is passed with the support of the Opposition. It establishes the Council as a statutory body with twenty-five nominated members. No Indian 'homeland' is to be established.

28 Feb. 1968   Prime Minister Vorster announces that the new Coloured Persons Representative Council will be comprise forty elected and twenty nominated members. It will take over from the existing Council of Coloured Affairs and will have extended legislative and administrative powers.

28 Feb. 1968   The Ivory Coast Foreign Minister urges African nations to seek a dialogue with South Africa.

12 Mar. 1968   P.W. Botha, the Minister of Defence, reports to the Senate on the progress of the Arms Industry and defines the main aims of South Africa's defence policy.

14 Mar. 1968   The United Nations Security Council censures South Africa for its flagrant defiance of Council Resolution 245 (1968) calling for the freeing of the dependents in the South West Africa 'Terrorism' trial and demands that South Africa release and repatriate them.

21 Mar. 1968   Signs treaty with Malawi on air transport.

26 Mar. 1968   Three Bills dealing with the future of the Coloured population are introduced: the Prohibition of Improper Interference Bill; the Separate Representation of Voters Amendment Bill, and the Representative Council Amendment Bill. All are adopted during 1968.

27 Mar. 1968   Signs agreement with France with regard to the launching of the eole balloons.

28 Mar. 1968   Raymond Hoffenberg leaves South Africa on an exit permit, without possibility of return, to take up a research and consultant's post in London founded for him by the British Medical Council. Later, on 23 April 1968, Prime Minister Vorster reiterates that he fully agrees with the restrictions placed upon him in South Africa.

3 Apr. 1968	The Prime Minister announces that the five 'non-White' University Colleges - those of Fort Hare, Zululand and the North, of the Western Cape and of Durban-Westville - will be released from their association with the University of South Africa, will be called universities and will, subject to certain conditions, be free to provide for their own teaching and conduct of examinations.
5 Apr. 1968	The Minister of Defence, P.W. Botha, tells the House of Assembly that countries aiding and inciting terrorism and guerrilla warfare against South Africa could provoke retaliation against them. This is interpreted as a warning to Zambia that 'terrorist' bases there could be attacked by South Africa.
5 Apr. 1968	The United Nations Council for South West Africa leaves New York for London on its way to SWA, in an attempt to discharge the functions and responsibilities entrusted to it by the Assembly.
8 Apr. 1968	The Minister of Finance states that South Africa is not bound to any particular market and will therefore sell its gold wherever it was to its best long-term interest.
10 Apr. 1968	J.J. Fouché is inducted as President in Cape Town.
18 Apr. 1968	The United Nations Council for South West Africa decides to return to New York from Dar-es-Salaam following problems over the chartering of aircraft and the denial of landing clearance in South West Africa.
22 Apr. - 13 May 1968	The International Conference on Human Rights is held in Teheran. A resolution is adopted condemning the South African government for its apartheid policy.
30 Apr. 1968	The bill establishing five universities for blacks, releasing their association with the University of South Africa, comes into force.
May 1968	South Africa appoints a military attaché to the South African Legation in Malawi.
4 May 1968	In terms of the Armaments Development and Production Bill, the Armaments Development and Production Corporation of South Africa (ARMSCOR) will take over and expand the undertakings of the Armaments Board, establish new undertakings, and assist other companies in the production of armaments. The Bill provides for a share capital of R100 m., or more.
8 May 1968	The South African government decides to finance the first phase of the construction of a new railway line between Southern Malawi and Mozambique. The contract for the construction is awarded to a South African consortium.
20 May 1968	Signs agreement with France relating to the certificates of airworthiness for imported aircraft.
21 May 1968	The Coloured Persons-Representative Council Amendment Bill is adopted after is final reading in the Senate, with the support of the Opposition. It provides for the enlargement of the existing Council, to one of forty elected

and twenty nominated members, for giving it a limited measure of jurisdiction over Coloured affairs (education, pensions and local government) and for a Budget of about R50,000,000 per annum.

21 May 1968	The Prohibition of Improper Interference Bill passes it final stages in Parliament, against the votes of the Opposition. It prohibits multiracial membership of political parties, participation in the affairs of political parties belonging to one racial group by members of another group or acceptance by political parties of funds from abroad.
21 May 1968	The Separate Representation of Voters Amendment Bill is passed, which extends the term of office of white representatives of Coloureds until 1971 and provides that such representation will then end.
1 June 1968	The government announces, in a White Paper, plans to reorganize the administration of South West Africa which will give Pretoria considerably more authority over the affairs of the Territory. The White Paper stresses the complete legality of the proposed new arrangement.
5 June 1968	Signs multilateral treaty on wheat trade.
17 June 1968	The United Nations General Assembly proclaims that South West Africa shall henceforth be known as 'Namibia' and condemns South Africa for its refusal to withdraw from the territory.
26 June 1968	Following official meetings held in Sweden (15-19 June) and later in Britain, the United Nations Special Committee on the Policies of Apartheid appeals for factual and statistical information to be given about countries still supplying arms to South Africa, and proposes that freedom fighters in South Africa be recognized as prisoners-of-war under the Geneva Convention.
28 June 1968	Signs an amendment to the air transport agreement of 23 May 1947 with the United States.
1 July 1968	Signs multilateral treaty on the non-proliferation of nuclear weapons.
4-19 July 1968	At a meeting of the World Council of Churches in Sweden, the Rt Rev A.H. Zulu, Bishop of Zululand and Swaziland, Church of the Province of South Africa (Anglican) is elected as one of the presidents.
11 July 1968	Ratifies a treaty with Switzerland on the avoidance of double taxation with respect to taxes on income.
17 July 1968	The Minister of Health, Dr. A. Hertzog, says there can be no exception to the government's policy of differential salaries for the various race groups.
18 July 1968	The Minister of Finance attacks the United States and other former 'gold pool' countries for attempting to reduce the monetary role of gold.
23 July 1968	The new French ambassador to South Africa, Baron Philippe de Luze, presents his credentials to President Fouché.
9 Aug 1968	Prime Minister Vorster reorganizes his cabinet in order to strengthen the 'verligte' enlightened elements in the government. Four new cabinet

ministers are appointed: Community Development and Public Works, Blaar Coetzee; Interior and Police, S.L. Muller; Water Affairs and Forestry, S.P. Botha; Information, Social Welfare, Pensions and Immigration, C.P. Mulder.

12 Aug. 1968   Over 5,000 soldiers supported by tanks, armoured cars and air force units begin manoeuvres in an exercise code named Operation Subasa designed to test the ability of South African defence forces to deal with terrorist activities.

14 Aug. 1968   Widespread student protests are held against the banning by the government of the appointment of an African lecturer, A. Mafeje, to a post in the Department of Social Anthroplogy at the University of Cape Town. Prime Minister Vorster subsequently threatens to take action against student protests if the University authorities do not do so in reasonable time.

16 Aug. 1968   Prime Minister Vorster says that the number of diplomats from African and Asian countries can be expected to increase as South Africa's policies become better understood. His task is to ensure that Southern Africa remains free from the threat of communism.

20 Aug. 1968   A special conference of National Party office-bearers in Pretoria endorses Prime Minister Vorster's policies concerning the admission of black diplomats, cooperation between English and Afrikaans speaking South Africans and sport, in which racial segregation will be maintained.

Sept. 1968   The Minister of National Education, Senator Jan de Klerk, announces the appointment of a Commission of Inquiry into Universities in the Republic, under the chairmanship of Justice J. van Wyk de Vries, with the mission of investigating all aspects of university life.

4 Sept. 1968   Signs an extradition agreement with Swaziland.

9 Sept. 1968   A new nationalist party in Dar-es-Salaam, the National Liberation Front of South Africa (NALFSA), formed to direct the freedom struggle inside South Africa, applies for recognition of the OAU's African Liberation Committee.

17 Sept. 1968   Prime Minister Vorster criticizes the decision to include a coloured cricketer, Basil d'Oliveira, in the British MCC team to tour South Africa in 1968. South African sports policy does not permit this, and the MCC is asked to cancel the tour.

22 Sept. 1968   A Commission of the South African Council of Churches publishes a report condemning apartheid as a false faith hostile to Christian belief.

24 Sept. 1968   Signs multilateral treaty on the authentic trilingual text of the Convention on International Civil Aviation.

25 Sept. 1968   The appeal of the thirty-one members of SWAPO against their conviction for acts of terrorism is to be heard by the full bench of the eleven judges of the Appellate Division of the Supreme Court in Bloemfontein. International concern is based on the argument that South Africa lacks jurisdiction over Namibia following the United Nations decision in 1966 to revoke its mandate over the territory.

8 Oct. 1968	Signs multilateral treaty on the principles governing the activities of states in the exploration and use of outer space.
9 Oct. 1968	Defence Minister Botha announces that a missile base for experimental tests and launchings is to be established on the Zululand coast about 150 miles north of Durban. This site will be of great strategic importance for the defence of the sub-continent.
12 Oct. 1968	The Secretary-General of the Supreme African Sports Council, J.-G. Ganga, says he will admit white South Africans to the African Games provided that competitions in South Africa are held without racial discrimination.
21 Oct. 1968	An open letter is released by twelve leading clergymen from the Church of the Province of South Africa and other Protestant churches indicating that it is impossible for all political utterances from the pulpit to cease.
21 Oct. 1968	Signs an agreement with Japan on the double taxation on income derived from the exploitation of ships or aircraft in international traffic.
22 Oct. 1968	Signs treaty with Greece concerning the graves of members of the armed forces of the Commonwealth in Greek territory.
23 Oct. 1968	Following his victory at the general elections in which his party, the Transkei National Independent Party (TNIP) won twenty-eight of the forty-five seats, Chief Kaiser Matanzima reorganizes the Transkei cabinet.
27 Oct. 1968	The Minister of Police, S.L. Muller, speaking at a National Party meeting, warns that several hundred South African born black `terrorists' will try to infiltrate the country, and that at least 2,000 have been trained by liberation movements. Guerrilla activity is still taking place in the Caprivi Strip and forty-six Africans in the area have been detained.
14 Nov. 1968	The Ciskei `homeland' is established.
21 Nov. 1968	Signs treaty with Canada on the Canadian Pension Plan.
26 Nov. 1968	Signs amendments to the multilateral treaty on safety of life at sea, 1960.
2 Dec. 1968	The twenty-third Assembly of the United Nations passes a resolution condemning the apartheid policies of the South African government on virtually identical terms to that adopted at the twenty-second session.
12 Dec. 1968	The Tswana Territorial Authority is established.
12 Dec. 1968	Signs the International Sugar Agreement.
14 Dec. 1968	A move to expel South Africa from UNCTAD (The United Nations Conference on Trade and Development) is defeated in the United Nations General Assembly.
17 Dec. 1968	The first rocket to be wholly developed and manufactured in South Africa is successfully launched from the new rocket launching range at St. Lucia Bay on the east coast. The Minister of Defence asserts that the rockets are defensive not offensive weapons.

21 Dec. 1968	A three-month campaign to register coloured voters ends with only approximately half of the total of 700,000 qualified voters registering.
3 Jan. 1969	The Conservative Party agrees with the Republican and National parties to accept the principle of coalition at this stage, with the ultimate aim of amalgamation.
21 Jan. 1969	Signs treaty with Portugal (for Angola) on the first phase development of the water resources of the Cunene River Basin.
1 Feb. - 21 June 1969	During the Parliamentary session the government introduced 129 Bills. The Bills passed include measures intended to safeguard internal security arousing widespread objections from the Opposition and the legal profession.
3 Feb. 1969	The Leader of the Opposition introduces a no-confidence motion, that the government policy of separate development has failed and he proposes the establishment of separate nation-states in a federal system, in which the white population group would retain its leadership role.
7 Feb. 1969	The Prime Minister announces that white entrepreneurs will be given long-standing contracts in the `homelands' to speed up economic development.
11 Feb. 1969	Four former National Party members join the newly formed Herstigte Nasionale Party.
12 Feb. 1969	The South Africa Act Amendment Bill, repealing the provisions of the South Africa Act of 1909 for the possible incorporation into South Africa of Rhodesia and the former High Commission Territories (Botswana, Lesotho and Swaziland), is passed with the approval of the Opposition at its second reading.
18 Feb. 1969	John Vorster formally opens a new submarine cable between Cape Town and Lisbon.
22 Feb. 1969	The fifteenth Annual Conference of the Trade Union Council of South Africa (TUCSA) alters its constitution in such a way as to debar Africans from membership.
23 Feb. 1969	A new weekly air service between Johannesburg and New York, with an intermediate stop at Rio de Janeiro, is inaugurated in spite of the opposition of the UN Special Committee on Apartheid.
28 Feb. 1969	Minister of Justice Pelser says forty-two persons are under house arrest in terms of the Suppression of Communism Act, eight of the orders being renewed for a further five years.
Mar. 1969	Helen Suzman introduces a private members' motion on the subject of capital punishment asking for a commission of inquiry to examine the efficacy of the death penalty. No other Members of Parliament supported the motion.
4 Mar. 1969	The Prime Minister declares in the Senate that the National Party will exercise its power to put into practice, as far as possible, the separation of

the races.

10 Mar. 1969	The Rhodesian Prime Minister, Ian Smith, meets John Vorster for talks of a confidential nature.
18 Mar. 1969	Minister of Defence, P.W. Botha, attends the launching in France of the first of three Daphne class submarines being built for the South African Navy.
26 Mar. 1969	Ten African men and one woman receive prison sentences of from five to twenty years in the Pietermaritzburg Supreme Court on charges of having contravened sections of the Terrorism Act and the Suppression of Communism Act and of having plotted violent revolution and open warfare in South Africa in collusion with foreign Communist-led groups in Ethiopia, Algeria, the Soviet Union, Tanzania and Zambia.
26 Mar. 1969	Signs air transport agreement with Austria.
31 Mar. 1969	Rectifies exchange of notes with France to air services treaty dated 31 January 1966.
Apr. 1969	John Vorster says members of the South African Police Force will remain on Rhodesia's borders while this is necessary in South Africa's own security interests.
Apr. 1969	A petition, bearing over 10,000 signatures, to restore academic freedom to these universities is sent to the government.
8 Apr. 1969	Ratifies extradition treaty with Botswana.
9 Apr. 1969	The Abolition of Juries Bill, providing for the ending of trial by jury comes into force.
10-16 Apr.1969	A nation-wide student campaign is conducted to commemorate the tenth anniversary of the Extension of University Education Act which enforced racial segregation on the universities.
23 Apr. 1969	The Prime Minister announces to the House of Assembly that the government carried on discussions with other nations to fill the power vacuum in the Indian Ocean after Britain's proposed withdrawal in 1970.
24 Apr. 1969	Minister of Defence, P.W. Botha, submits a White Paper to Parliament providing for a 5 year defence plan, with an estimated expenditure of R1,647,000,000 (about 1,000,000,000 Pounds Sterling).
30 Apr. 1969	Separate acts give five University Colleges for blacks full university status although the Central government retains tight control.
May 1969	Twenty-four Africans appear in the Grahamstown Supreme Court on charges relating to sabotage. Twelve of the alleged Poqo members are acquitted, and twelve receive prison sentences.
5 May 1969	P.W. Botha, the Minister of Defence, announces that an air-to-air projectile has been perfected by South Africa.

| 13 May 1969 | The Minister of Justice announces that the former Pan-Africanist Congress leader, Robert M. Sobukwe, has been released from detention. He is permitted to live in Kimberley, subject to restrictions. Being banned under the Suppression of Communism Act, he may not be quoted. |

16 May 1969   For purposes of intense security legislation the South African Bureau of State Security is established (later referred to as BOSS).

16 May 1969   The Publications and Entertainments Amendment Bill gives the Publications Control Board powers to prohibit subsequent editions of any South African periodical whose contents have been declared undesirable.

30 May 1969   Statistics of police action during the year 1 July 1967 - 30 June 1968 include 47,370 cases involving the safety of the state and good order and that 45,230 persons have been prosecuted for such crimes or offences.

4-10 June 1969   The Minister of Defence, P.W. Botha, accompanied by General Hiemstra, Lieutenant-General J.P. Verster, Chief of the Air Force and Lieutenant-General W.P. Louw, Chief of the Army, visits France. He denies that the visit involves the purchase of arms.

5 June 1969   A Bill is tabled in Parliament banning henceforth any merger between newspapers published in South Africa, unless authorized by the relevant ministry. The government can veto the acquisition of a newspaper, or the majority interests in a newspaper, by anyone not possessing South African nationality, or by a group controlled by non-South Africans.

12 June 1969   The leader of the Labour Party appeals to the voters to reject apartheid regulations.

15-17 June 1969   The Minister of Foreign Affairs, Dr. Hilgard Muller visits Portugal, and says that Portuguese and South African forces stand as a bulwark against the domination of the African continent by foreign powers.

23 June 1969   Twenty-four Africans from the Graaff-Reinet district appear in the Grahamstown Supreme Court on charges under the Sabotage Act. They are alleged to have conspired or incited others to kill whites or police in the Graaff-Reinet district of the Cape Province between January 1966 and January 1967.

27 June 1969   A Bill on Separation of Races is passed, which includes the provision that no person could be classified white if one of his parents was classified coloured. It prohibits the hearing of third-party objections to race classification and empowers the Secretary for the Interior to change a person's race classification.

30 June 1969   A Bill affecting state security called the General Laws Amendment Bill is passed, despite rejection by the Opposition and severe criticism by the Bar and a number of judges. It contains far-reaching provisions and restrictions affecting the administration of justice and the disclosure of evidence. Security matters are now defined as including any matter relating to the Bureau of State Security (BOSS), and its relationship with any person. The government denies it is creating a dictatorial and despotic institution but this radical measure is seen as having far-reaching implications for the independence of the judiciary.

July 1969 - Feb. 1970	A number of groups of Africans are tried for subversive activities. The group includes Winnie Mandela.
1 July 1969	In preparation for the Council's taking-over the responsibilities, the Department of Coloured Affairs is replaced by the Department of Coloured Relations.
3 July 1969	Twelve Africans on trial at the Supreme Court in Grahamstown, accused of having conspired to take over a town and kill whites are acquitted on the charge, but are given prison sentences ranging from seven to one year's imprisonment for being members of the illegal organization, Poqo. Twelve others are acquitted.
10 July 1969	The lengthy and expensive trial of Laurence Gandar and Benjamin Pogrund, of the Rand Daily Mail, on charges under the Prisons Act ends with both being found guilty but receiving light sentences. The press wins a moral victory, but the trial discourages editors from publishing reports on prison conditions.
End July 1969	Representatives of the International Commission of Jurists (ICJ) and the American Lawyers' Committee for Civil Rights under Law arrive in South Africa to investigate recent legislation that seems to contravene basic principles of law and to create a trend of increasing state power over the individual without giving access to courts to seek redress. Meetings are held with senior officials of the Ministries of Justice, of the Police and of the Interior.
1 Aug. 1969	The Minister of Bantu Administration and Development, M.C. Botha, outlines the government's homelands policy, in Pretoria. He declares that whites are trustees of the blacks, but this trusteeship is not permanent, and he forsees the establishment of autonomous nations, coexisting peacefully on the basis of a practical interdependence.
6 Aug. 1969	South Africa signs the Agreement on Rescue and Return of Astronauts and Space Objects.
9 Aug. 1969	The French Minister of State for National Defence confirms the continued supply of French arms to South Africa, except for anti-guerrilla equipment.
12 Aug. 1969	The United Nations Security Council's resolution calls on South Africa to withdraw its administration from Namibia immediately, and, in any case, before 4 October 1969. South Africa is condemned for refusing to comply with previous United Nations resolutions.
23 Aug. 1969	An alleged Soviet spy, Y.N. Loginov, who was arrested in 1967, is handed over to a non-communist country, West Germany.
23 Aug. 1969	The Republican Party issues its election manifesto which does not oppose separate development but demands increased services to combat crime.
2 Sept. 1969	P.W. Botha, the Minister of Defence, announces the establishment of a third naval base at Saldanha Bay, about eighty miles north of Cape Town.
5 Sept. 1969	John Vorster appoints a Commission of Inquiry under Justice H.J. Potgieter, of The Appellate Division of the Supreme Court to investigate

South Africa's security network, and to hear objections to its security legislation. Terms of reference include threats of conventional war, guerrilla war, terrorism and internal subversion; recommendations are to be submitted concerning the effectiveness of security and amendment to legislation.

10 Sept. 1969	Nine Africans are charged before the Pretoria Supreme Court with taking part in terrorist activities between 1966 and 1968 in the Elandsfontein, Transvaal.
16 Sept. 1969	The Prime Minister announces that a general election will be held in April 1970.
19 Sept. 1969	Four agreements are signed in Lisbon connected with the construction of the Cahora Bassa Dam in Mozambique, the main one being between the governments of South Africa and Portugal.
24 Sept. 1969	At the first election of Coloured Persons' Representative Council, the anti-Apartheid Labour Party gains a majority of forty elective seats.
24 Sept. 1969	Ratifies multilateral treaty on the rescue and return of astronauts and the return of objects launched into outer space.
30 Sept. 1969	The final results of the Coloured Persons' Representative Council election are announced at which the Labour Party obtained a large majority of seats: Labour Party 26, Federal Party 11, Republican Party 1, National People's Party 1, Conservative Party 0, Independendents 1. Percentage poll 48.75%.
Oct. 1969	All known 'verkramptes' are expelled from the National Party, including Dr. A. Hertzog, Jaap Marais, W.T. Marais and Louis Stofberg.
Oct. 1969	Over 2,000 'verkrampte' delegates gather in Pretoria to form a new party under the leadership of Dr. Hertzog. Launched as Die Herstigte Nasionale Party (HNP) its programme emphasizes exclusive Afrikaner nationalism and 'true Christian principles'.
2 Oct. 1969	South Africa formally rejects a United Nations Security Council resolution calling on it to give independence to Namibia and to withdraw its administration from that territory before October.
7 Oct. 1969	The government announces the twenty nominated members of the Coloured Persons' Representative Council for the four provinces. These include thirteen defeated candidates; all are supporters of separate development; thus the government ensures that the defeated Federal Party will command a majority in the new Council. All other contesting parties condemn the government's action.
9 Oct. 1969	P.W. Botha announces the location of the first missile base for experimental tests.
16 Oct. 1969	The United Party declares that it will oppose the National Party's policy and will moot a certain measure of self-government for the urban black.
19 Oct. 1969	The Progressive Party decides to fight the election in opposition to the government's policy of separate development.

21 Oct. 1969	Signs amendments to a multilateral treaty for the safety of life at sea, 1960.
26 Oct. 1969	The United Nations Committee on Non-Self-Governing Territories adopts a resolution drawing the attention of the Security Council to the deteriorating situation in Namibia following Pretoria's refusal to relinquish its hold over the mandated territory. The resolution is passed by ninety-six votes to two, with six abstentions (Britain, France, Australia, Botswana, Malawi and Ivory Coast).
31 Oct. 1969	The twenty-fourth General Assembly meeting of the United Nations condemns South Africa for its persistent refusal to withdraw from Namibia.
Nov. 1969	The Attorney-General of the Transvaal prosecutes Dr. Hertzog and Jaap Marais under the Commissions Act of 1947 for allegations made concerning the finance allocated to BOSS.
20 Nov. 1969	The first session of the Coloured Persons' Representative Council is officially in Bellville and immediately takes up the question of equal pay for coloureds for equal work.
21 Nov. 1969	South Africa votes against the lengthy resolutions regarding Southern Rhodesia's independence, passed by the twenty-fourth General Assembly of the United Nations.
21 Nov. 1969	The twenty-fourth General Assembly of the United Nations condemns South Africa for its collaboration with Portugal and Southern Rhodesia and for the intervention of its forces against the peoples of Angola and Mozambique; and for its apartheid policies.
29 Nov. 1969	Signs multilateral treaty on the intervention on the high seas in cases of oil pollution casualties.
1 Dec. 1969	The trial begins at the Supreme Court in Pretoria of twenty-two Africans, including Winnie Mandela, accused of pro-Communist and subversive activities, of instigating guerrilla warfare and of organizing Africans in Communist countries. Winnie Mandela refuses to enter a plea. A British subject, Philip Gording, held incommunicado in prison since May 1969 appears as a state witness, is given immunity from prosecution and is released on 8 December 1969.
11 Dec. 1969	South Africa, Botswana, Lesotho and Swaziland sign a new customs agreement in Pretoria, to come into operation on 1 March 1970.
30 Dec. 1969	The International Monetary Fund announces that it will agree to purchase gold from South Africa, subject to certain conditions. The price of $35 per oz. is agreed upon.
1969-1970	The establishment of the additional five members functioning as Cabinets is announced. Basutho ba Bozwa (Southern Sotho); Lebowa Territorial Authority (North Sotho); Venda Territorial Authority; Machangana Territorial Authority (Shangana, Tsonga); Zulu Territorial Authority.
1 Jan. 1970	The Weights and Measures Bill providing for the metrification of weights and measures, thereby introducing the metric system, comes into effect.

9 Jan. 1970	The first week after the announcement of the agreement with the International Monetary Fund the price of gold falls below $35 per oz.
30 Jan. 1970	The Prime Minister announces that the government is watching the situation in Lesotho following the elections and that necessary measures have been taken to ensure the safety of South Africans there.
6 Feb. 1970	The Prime Minister announces that all Coloured people will be removed from the common voters' roll.
11 Feb. 1970	A delegation from Mauritius arrives in Cape Town to discuss ways of strengthening links between Mauritius and South Africa.
16 Feb. 1970	Twenty-two Africans are acquitted of unlawful activities. Three are subsequently released, but the nineteen others are charged again under the Terrorism Act, and immediately taken into custody. They include Winnie Mandela.
18 Feb. 1970	Minister of Defence Botha, appeals in the House of Assembly to the British government to uphold its honour in respect of the Simonstown Agreement, otherwise South Africa will have to explore other avenues to strengthen its maritime forces.
23 Feb. 1970	The Bantu Laws Amendment Bill is passed.
26 Feb. 1970	The Bantu Homelands Citizenship Bill is passed, whereby every African is issued with a certificate of citizenship of his respective 'homeland'.
6 Mar. 1970	The National Party manifesto reaffirms its belief in separate development programmes for the white, black, Coloured and Indian population.
10 Mar. 1970	South Africa's consular representation will not be withdrawn from Rhodesia and South Africa's relations with the Republic of Rhodesia will remain unchanged.
13 Mar. 1970	A total of 407 candidates are nominated for the 166 seats in the House of Assembly. Eight parties and five independents will contest 155 of the constituencies.
18 Mar. 1970	The Deputy Leader of the Herstigte Nasionale Party (HNP), Jaap Marais, is committed for trial in the Pretoria Supreme Court on three charges under the Official Secrets Act.
23 Mar. 1970	South Africa is banned from competing in the Davis Cup, as a result of South Africa's apartheid stand in sport.
26 Mar. 1970	On this date all Africans become citizens of their ethnic 'homelands'. However, they will not become foreigners in the Republic of South Africa.
26 Mar. 1970	Signs treaty with Portugal (for Mozambique), amending Article XXXII of the Mozambique Convention.
Apr. 1970	The Leader of the United Party reiterates his party's proposal for a Federal Constitution.

Apr. 1970	The Herstigte Nasionale Party publishes its manifesto describing its aim of a society dominated by Christian national concepts and Afrikaans as the only official language.
2 Apr. 1970	Signs agreement with Australia relating to air services.
13 Apr. 1970	B.J. Vorster states that he is prepared to meet demands that mixed sports should be allowed.
14 Apr. 1970	The United Nations Special Committee on Apartheid urges a boycott of all South African racist sporting organizations and supports an African proposal to exclude the Republic from both the Munich Olympics and the Olympic Movement itself.
22 Apr. 1970	The general election results in the return to power of the National Party for the sixth time since 1948, but with a reduced majority. There is an overall swing of two and a half percent to the United Party, and of five and a half percent away from the National Party with three percent going to the Herstigte Nasionale Party. The NP wins 117 seats with 820,968 votes cast. The UP wins forty-seven seats with 561,647 votes cast. The Progressive Party wins one seat with 51,760 votes cast.
24 Apr. 1970	It is confirmed in London that thirteen African countries have threatened to withdraw from the Commonwealth Games in Edinburgh, if the South African cricket tour of Britain goes on.
27 Apr. 1970	The Prime Minister announces that his newly re-elected government is to continue its outward looking foreign policy as well as its policy of separate development.
11 May 1970	The Prime Minister announces a Cabinet reshuffle.
13 May 1970	Signs multilateral treaty on certain dairy products.
15 May 1970	The International Olympic Committee expels South Africa from the International Olympic Movement as a result of South Africa's apartheid stand in sport.
18 May 1970	Following the results obtained in the general election held in April, a new cabinet is sworn in.
19-21 May 1970	John Vorster visits Malawi and stresses the desire for continued contact and co-operation between South Africa and Malawi, despite existing differences in outlook.
21-22 May 1970	Private talks are held between John Vorster and Rhodesian Prime Minister Ian Smith.
22 May 1970	The English Cricket Council bows to British government pressure and calls off the all-white South African cricket tour.
29 May 1970	Minister of Justice, P.C. Pelser, announces that the Attorney-General of the Transvaal is to prosecute thirty of the 357 people arrested in Johannesburg after an illegal march in protest against the continued detention of the twenty-two Africans held under the Terrorism Act.

3-7 June 1970	The Prime Minister, accompanied by Dr. Muller, visits Portugal, and holds several meetings with the Portuguese Prime Minister and senior ministers. The friendly talks cover a wide field and include the Cahora Bassa scheme.
9-10 June 1970	The Prime Minister visits Spain and holds discussions with senior officials. A meeting is held with General Franco.
10 June 1970	John Vorster holds talks in Paris with the French Prime Minister covering French investments in South Africa.
12 June 1970	The seventh 'homeland' is inaugurated with the installation of Chief Gatsha Buthelezi as Chief Executive Officer of the Zululand Territorial Authority (ZTA).
13 June 1970	P.W. Botha announces that South Africa is establishing a new submarine base at Simonstown at a cost of $7.7m.
14-17 June 1970	Prime Minister Vorster and Dr. Muller arrive in Geneva. A meeting is held with twelve South African ambassadors to European countries, and with the head of the South African mission to the United Nations in Geneva, concerned with means of improving South Africa's image in Europe.
24 June 1970	Exchange of notes with Portugal on the issue of copyright in maps.
1 July 1970	The question of the resumption of arms supplies by Britain to South Africa is discussed by the Foreign Minister, Dr. H. Muller and the new British Foreign Secretary, Sir Alec Douglas-Home, in London, in the context of the Simonstown Agreement.
6 July 1970	The British Conservative government's intention to resume arms supplies is announced in the House of Commons. Other Commonwealth governments are formally informed of this intention on 10-11 July 1970. Hostile reactions follow.
11 July 1970	The United States Secretary of State reiterates America's adherence to the policy of not supplying arms and military equipment to South Africa.
20 July 1970	The Prime Minister announces in the House of Assembly that South African scientists have succeeded in developing a new process for uranium enrichment, and are building a pilot plant for this process.
20 July 1970	The British Foreign Secretary, Sir Alec Douglas-Home, makes a statement in the House of Commons on the question of arms for South Africa, emphasizing the vital importance of the sea routes around South Africa.
23 July 1970	The United Nations Security Council condemns all violations of its embargo against South Africa. After five meetings on this question Resolution 281 (1970) is subsequently passed calling on all states to strengthen the arms embargo. It is adopted by twelve votes to none against, France, Great Britain and the United States abstaining.
23 July 1970	The Minister of Defence tells Parliament that South Africa in fact spends less than 3percent of her national income on defence.
27 July 1970	An Uranium Enrichment Bill is announced, establishing the

Uranium Enrichment Corporation of South Africa.

29 July 1970	The International Court of Justice in the Hague unanimously condemns the continuing presence of South Africa in Namibia and defines the legal consequences.
3 Aug. 1970	Signs amendments with Portugal (for Mozambique) on the Mozambique Convention.
15 Aug. 1970	Several pamphlet bombs, scattering ANC pamphlets, explode in a number of cities.
19 Aug. 1970	The Chinese community is granted official 'white' status for the first time, but only for sport and leisure. Subsequently the leader of the HNP, Dr. Hertzog, accuses the government of betraying South Africa's traditional principles of racial segregation.
24 Aug. 1970	A second trial of the nineteen Africans, acquitted in February begins after they have been in detention for seventeen months. They are all acquitted and released on 14 September 1970 only to be served subsequently with orders by the Minister of Justice placing them under restriction.
15 Sept. 1970	The Prime Minister announces that his government is willing to enter into a non-aggression pact with any other African country. The Opposition fully supports this.
24 Sept. 1970	Signs visa agreement with Spain.
28 Sept. 1970	The Minister of Justice announces in the House of Assembly that as of 1 January 1970 there were 809 persons serving prison sentences imposed under security laws.
30 Sept. 1970	B.S. Ramotse is sentenced to fifteen years imprisonment by Justice G. Viljoen in the Pretoria Supreme Court. He is found guilty of taking part in terrorist activities and plotting the violent overthrow of the state.
5 Oct. 1970	Signs multilateral Convention on the Conflict of Laws Relating to the Form of Testamentary Dispositions.
28 Oct. 1970	The provincial elections continue to demonstrate the slight swing away from the National Party, with the United Party making a net gain of six seats. The result: National Party 118 seats, the United Party fifty-nine seats, others nil.
4 Nov. 1970	President Houphouét-Boigny of the Ivory Coast announces he is planning an African Summit Conference to urge a dialogue with South Africa. This initiative meets with very various reactions throughout the continent, but is welcomed in South Africa.
9 Nov. 1970	Signs agreement with Netherlands modifying existing agreement on air services.
13 Nov. - 1 Dec.1970	The Archbishop of Canterbury, Dr. Michael Ramsey, visits South Africa on the occasion of the 100th anniversary of the establishment of the Anglican Church in South Africa. He repeatedly expresses his views on political and

social problems arising from the government's apartheid policy.

19 Nov. 1970   John Vorster appoints Theo Gerdener as Minister of the Interior in succession to Marais Viljoen. The latter retains the Labour portfolio and takes over Posts and Telegraphs in addition. The South African Broadcasting Corporation will come under the direct control of the Ministry of National Education.

20 Nov. 1970   The South African Foreign Minister signs an economic agreement with the Malagasy Republic, which provides for a financial loan from South Africa to help the Malagasy tourist industry.

21 Nov. 1970   Six prominent members of the HNP resign, having lost all confidence in the leadership of the party. Resignations include that of Dr. Willie Lubbe, editor of the party's newspaper 'Die Afrikaner'.

5 Dec. 1970   The government's policy for the coloured people is restated by a Cabinet Minister. Any policy, or lack thereof, which can lead to integration on whatever basis between whites and coloureds is rejected; the idea of a specific homeland for the coloured people is impracticable; extended and consistent liaison between the coloureds and the white authorities is promised. The government remains firmly committed to the principle of parallel development.

11 Dec. 1970   South Africa signs a customs agreement with Botswana, Lesotho and Swaziland.

15 Dec. 1970   At the twenty-fourth General Assembly of the United Nations, South Africa joined all the leading maritime powers in opposing a section of the Resolutions on Peaceful Uses of the Sea-Bed.

16 Dec. 1970   Signs multilateral treaty on the suppression of unlawful seizure of aircraft.

24 Dec. 1970   The Minister of Bantu Administration and Development leaves Malawi after a four-day visit during which cooperation between nations of Southern Africa is endorsed.

14-21 Jan. 1971   A conference of Heads of Government from the Commonwealth is held in Singapore at which Britain's proposed sale of arms to South Africa is extensively debated. A study group is set up to consider the question in the context of the security of maritime trade routes in the South Atlantic and Indian Oceans.

20 Jan. 1971   The Anglican Dean of Johannesburg, the Very Rev. Gonville Aubie ffrench-Beytagh, is detained by the police, accused of subversive activities.

1 Feb. 1971   Signs an amendment with Malawi on the provisions of the trade agreement of 13 March 1967.

2 Feb. 1971   Signs the Convention of Wetlands and Water Fowl.

2 Feb. 1971   The Minister of Justice says, in Parliament, that for as long as the present government is in power the Immorality Act will not be repealed.

8 Feb. 1971   The text of a letter from South Africa to the International Court of Justice

at The Hague, officially requesting it to cooperate in supervising a plebiscite in Namibia, is released. The Court is considering a request by the United Nations Security Council for an opinion on the legal consequences of South Africa's continued presence in the territory in defiance of United Nations resolutions.

8 Feb. 1971	Minister of Labour Marais Viljoen announces total exemption for Coloureds from job reservation in the building industry on the Reef and in Pretoria.
11 Feb. 1971	Signs treaty with Israel on the reciprocal recognition of air worthiness certificates between South Africa and Israel.
11 Feb. 1971	Signs multilateral treaty pertaining to nuclear weapons on the seabed.
16-22 Feb.1971	A number of religious ministers and lay workers from Europe and America are told to leave the country.
19 Feb. 1971	It is reported that the Security Police have detained about twenty Africans, Coloureds and Asians. The detainees are said to be members of the Unity Movement of South Africa, founded in 1943 by Coloured schoolteachers.
19 Feb. 1971	The South African arms question is discussed in a closed session of the Singapore Commonwealth Conference.
20 Feb. 1971	The British Prime Minister reiterates his government's attitude to the sale of arms in South Africa, at the Commonwealth Conference in Singapore. Accordingly the South African government has assured Britain that it had no aggressive intentions and that maritime arms would be used only to secure the sea routes.
22 Feb. 1971	The South African Defence Ministry announces that the British government, following its obligations as per the Simonstown Agreement, is willing to give an export licence for Wasp helicopters as requested by South Africa.
25 Feb. 1971	The Chief of the Security Police announces that raids undertaken on this date at offices of Christian and student organizations in the country's main cities have revealed quantities of documents concerning ffrench-Beytagh's activities. The Dean is consequently remanded until 28 May 1971 and again until 30 June 1971. The original charges are withdrawn: a new indictment is drawn up under the Terrorism Act.
25 Feb. 1971	The OAU publishes a statement condemning Britain's proposed sale of helicopters to South Africa.
Mar. 1971	The Bantu Homelands Constitution Bill is enacted in the last week of March.
3 Mar. 1971	A Constitution Amendment Bill, empowering the government to proclaim any African language an official language in any self-governing territory, when considered fit passes its second reading at a joint sitting of both Houses of Parliament. Seven different African languages will thus be given official recognition.
15 Mar. 1971	Signs treaty with Netherlands for the avoidance of double taxation and the prevention of fiscal evasion with respect to taxes on income.

19 Mar. 1971	Prime Minister Vorster says that his government is prepared to engage in dialogue, without preconditions, with other African countries prepared to talk. His offer meets with mixed reactions throughout the continent.
22 Mar. 1971	A statement by Ghana's Minister of Foreign Affairs in the Ghanaian National Assembly indicates a readiness to visit South Africa.
26 Mar. 1971	The Prime Minister of Swaziland visits Cape Town for talks with John Vorster and confirms that a policy of friendship and cooperation towards the Republic is being maintained.
29 Mar. 1971	Signs Wheat Trade Convention.
30 Mar. 1971	Prime Minister Vorster holds his first-ever international press conference and asserts that discussion of separate development with Africa's black leaders will be welcomed. A policy of external dialogue is to be pursued.
30 Mar. 1971	Referring to allegations that a vendetta is being conducted against churches and religious workers in South Africa, Prime Minister Vorster says that of 1,440 religious workers only six have been deported in the last ten years, seventeen were refused extensions of permits and two were refused visas.
End Mar. 1971	The Bantu Homelands Constitution Bill is enacted. It empowers the government to grant self-government, on an equal footing with that of the Transkei, to any area with a Territorial Authority, upon the latter's request, at any time, by simple proclamation, after consultation with the Territorial Authority concerned, but without parliamentary enactment.
1 Apr. 1971	Accepts the accession of Ireland to the General Agreement on Tariffs and Trade.
13 Apr. 1971	The Chief Minister of Transkei demands full control of all departments of state.
16 Apr. 1971	The Minister of Bantu Administration and Development, M.C. Botha, replies to Paramount Chief Kaiser Matanzima's demands for increased control and for the transference to the Transkei of certain lands technically within its boundaries, from the Republic. Certain police stations will be transferred to Transkeian jurisdiction.
21 Apr. 1971	The Prime Minister refers to the Chief Minister of Transkei's demands of 13 April and points out that Defence could not be transferred as it would mean changing the Constitution of the Transkei Act of 1963.
21 Apr. 1971	Prime Minister Vorster makes a lengthy statement on South Africa's relations with Zambia.
22 Apr. 1971	The Ciskei Territorial Authority elects a twenty-member select committee to draft a Constitution for an independent Ciskei.
22 Apr. 1971	Speaking in the House of Assembly the Prime Minister lays down guidelines for international sports meetings in South Africa. He makes it clear, however, that there has been no change in sports policy on the club, provincial and national levels.

23-26 Apr.1971	Prime Minister Vorster denies that he has broken any confidence in disclosing exchanges with Zambia and he added that it was fallacious that he indicated that he was willing to discuss Rhodesia's future with President Kaunda.
28 Apr. 1971	The President of the Ivory Coast reiterates his initiative for opening a dialogue with South Africa. While Swaziland approves the dialogue, Tanzania and Mauritius refuse to participate and many member states of the OAU strongly oppose it.
1 May 1971	The Tswana Legislative Assembly comes into being.
3 May 1971	Chief Kaiser Matanzima denies in the Transkei Legislative Assembly that he is agitating for independence at this state, but he will continue to make certain legitimate land claims.
3 May 1971	Signs treaty with Malawi on the avoidance of double taxation and the prevention of fiscal evasion with respect to taxes on income.
5 May 1971	A wide-ranging bill providing severe penalties for dealing in or using dangerous drugs is published.
6 May 1971	Minister of Defence P.W. Botha announces in the House of Assembly that South Africa has reached such a degree of self-sufficiency that it does not need any arms from the outside world for internal security.
14 May 1971	The International Court of Justice at The Hague rejects the government's application that a plebiscite be organized in Namibia and rejects the offer of additional documentation about the situation there.
16 May 1971	Prime Minister Vorster declares that if the positive signs of cooperation with the rest of Africa are interpreted correctly, South Africa could become the leading state of Southern Africa.
21 May 1971	Joins the International Telecommunications Satellite Organisation (Intelsat).
26 May 1971	Signs multilateral articles of agreement on the Southern African Regional Tourism Council.
1 June 1971	The Venda and Ciskei territorial authorities are replaced by legislative assemblies.
9 June 1971	The Minister of Coloured Affairs pledges himself to strive for equal pay for equal work for Coloureds.
11 June 1971	Minister of the Interior Theo Gerdener, indicates that the Public Service Commission will make a comprehensive study to create a more satisfactory ratio between white and non-white salaries in government service.
14 June 1971	The World Council of Churches cancels a special consultation in South Africa because of unacceptable conditions imposed on it by Prime Minister Vorster.
15 June 1971	Signs amendment of Article 50(A) of the Convention on International Civil Aviation.

20 June 1971   At the meetings of Council of Ministers of the OAU, dialogue with South Africa is firmly rejected.

21 June 1971   The International Court of Justice at The Hague declares that South Africa is under obligation to withdraw its administration from Namibia immediately and thus put an end to its occupation of the territory. John Vorster reacts by indicating that as the judgment is only advisory, it can not be considered binding, and South Africa will act as it sees fit.

22 June 1971   A Pretoria court rules that the former leader of the banned PAC, Robert Sobukwe, will not be allowed to use his exit permit (granted by the Minister of the Interior) to leave South Africa permanently because the Minister of Justice refuses to lift his banning order confining him to the magisterial district of Kimberley.

27 June 1971   The Chairman of Armscor announces that under an agreement with a French aviation company, Mirage III and F jet fighters will be built in South Africa with the help of French personnel.

28 June 1971   Father Cosmos Desmond, British born Roman Catholic priest, is placed under house arrest in Johannesburg by an order signed by the Minister of Justice.

30 June 1971   Membership of the Bank for International Settlement is extended to the South African Reserve Bank.

5 July 1971   The Minister of Information outlines his government's plan for the nine `homelands' of South Africa in London. They are to become sovereign states in their own right, independent, entitled to maintain their own languages cultures and identities in their own way, according to their own wishes in their own geographical territories.

17 July 1971   Signs multilateral treaty on the partial revision of the 1959 radio regulations.

25 July 1971   Joe Kachingwe is appointed Malawi's first Ambassador to South Africa and assumes office in Pretoria on 29 July 1971.

27 July 1971   Prime Minister Vorster completes a tour of African `homelands' in the Northern Transvaal during which he holds talks with leaders of the North Sotho, Tswana and Venda homelands. The importance of working together is emphasized. Regular consultation is promised.

29 July 1971   The International Court of Justice in The Hague unanimously condemns the continuing presence of South Africa in South West Africa and defines the legal consequences.

2 Aug. 1971   The trial of the Very Rev. Gonville Aubie ffrench-Beytagh begins in the Pretoria Supreme Court. Sidney Kentridge appears as Council for the Defence. The Dean himself explains his attitudes and beliefs in evidence given by him on 14-20 September 1971.

4 Aug. 1971   The government gives limited powers of internal self-government to `homeland', Damaraland, in Namibia.

5 Aug. 1971   The Minister of Defence says that South Africa has become so self-sufficient

in the manufacture of arms that she is considering exporting weapons. European countries have accepted that military equipment of a high quality is being produced.

7 Aug. 1971	A Malagasy government delegation arrives for a five-day visit aimed at consolidating relations between the two countries. It is agreed to establish a permanent joint commission to explore further fields of co-operation.
10 Aug. 1971	Eleven bombs explode, scattering ANC propaganda leaflets in the four major cities. The blasts occur twelve months after similar actions in the same cities.
16-20 Aug.1971	President Hastings Banda, President of Malawi, pays a state visit to South Africa, meeting the State President and the Prime Minister. On his return, he declares that 99% of the Africans whom he met supported his policy of contact with Pretoria.
25 Aug. 1971	The leader of the Zulu Territorial Authority, Chief Buthelezi, calls for a National Convention of all races in South Africa to decide the country's future political direction. John Vorster rejects this completely, but it is supported as a constructive proposal by both the opposition United Party and the Progressive Party.
30 Aug. 1971	The government announces programmes for expanded development and augmented political powers for the Ovambo and Kavango homelands in Namibia.
11 Sept. 1971	The Australian Cricket Board decides to withdraw its invitation to the South African Cricket Team to tour Australia. Minister of Sport F.W. Waring blames acts of anarchy and threats of a misguided minority for this decision.
15 Sept. - 17 Dec. 1971	At the twenty-fifth session of the General Assembly of the United Nations, six resolutions denounce the South African government's apartheid policy.
18 Sept. 1971	During a meeting with representatives of the nine member churches of the World Council of Churches in South Africa, Prime Minister Vorster reaffirms that he will not consider allowing a WCC delegation to come to South Africa under any conditions. Nor will he allow any funds to be sent from South Africa to the World Council.
23 Sept. 1971	Signs multilateral treaty for the suppression of unlawful acts against the safety of civil aviation.
26 Sept. 1971	Minister of Coloured Affairs, J.J. Loots announces that larger Coloured group areas will gradually be transformed into fully fledged municipalities, under the Coloured Persons Representative Council.
27 Sept. 1971	South Africa invites the United Nations Security-General to pay Namibia a fact-finding visit.
28 Sept. 1971	President Idi Amin of Uganda offers to dispatch a ten-man investigatory mission to South Africa. South Africa replies by inviting Amin himself, or one or more members of his government instead - an alternative which proves unacceptable.

28 Sept. 1971	Signs Customs Convention on the Temporary Importation of Professional and Scientific Equipment.
30 Sept. 1971	It is officially announced that the British and South African naval units will engage in a month of joint manoeuvres in South African waters from 4 October to 3 November 1971.
30 Sept. 1971	Signs amendment to the trade agreement of 20 August 1932 with Great Britain.
Oct. 1971	The new leader of the Progressive Party, Colin Eglin, together with Helen Suzman, undertake a visit to seven black African states.
4 Oct. 1971	Chief Leabua Jonathan, Prime Minister of Lesotho, warns that violent confrontation between blacks and whites will be an inevitable consequence of apartheid. Mr Vorster responds with restraint, in the interest of friendship.
4-28 Oct.1971	Three leaders of 'homelands' governments - Paramount Chief Kaiser Matanzima (Transkei), Chief Gatsha Buthelezi (Zulu Territorial Authority) and Chief Lucas Mangope (Councillor of the Tswanas) - visit Great Britain at the invitation of the British government to study British institutions and the independence processes undergone by the former High Commission Territories.
5 Oct. 1971	The Prime Minister announces at the National Party Congress the incidences on the border of Zambia and the Caprivi Strip. He reminds the Congress of his previous warnings that South Africa will not tolerate the incursion of communist trained terrorists into South African territory and they will be pursued to the land from where they came.
6 Oct. 1971	The Minister of State of the Ivory Coast, Koffia Ndia, visits South Africa, reraffirming the country's commitment to dialogue.
7 Oct. 1971	SWAPO claims it was not responsible for placing landmines in the Caprivi Strip and that the guerrillas were not operating from Zambia, but from inside Namibia.
8 Oct. 1971	The United Nations Security Council meets in emergency session to hear a complaint by Zambia against numerous violations by South African forces against the sovereignty, airspace and territorial integrity of Zambia. South Africa categorically rejects the Zambian allegations.
11 Oct. 1971	Signs visa agreement with Iran.
12 Oct. 1971	The Security Council unanimously adopts an amended resolution, sponsored by four African states, which declares that army violation of the border of a member-state is contrary to the UN Charter. It calls on South Africa to respect Zambia's sovereignty.
12 Oct. 1971	Signs amendments to the multilateral treaty on the safety of life at sea.
13 Oct. 1971	Signs treaty with Australia on postal parcels.
15 Oct. 1971	Accepts the accession of Romania to the General Agreement on Tarrifs and

Trade.

18-19 Oct.1971   The seventh Summit Conference of the East and Central African states, held in Mogadishu, adopts a Declaration urging armed struggle to liberate Southern Africa, to which they grant total support. This rejection of South Africa's dialogue policy is welcomed by the leaders of both the ANC, Alfred Nzo and the PAC.

24 Oct. 1971   The Security Police raid more than 100 homes throughout the country in a search for illegal political literature.

28 Oct. 1971   It is officially confirmed that one of nineteen Indians detained, Ahmed Timol, a Moslem teacher, has jumped to his death from the tenth floor of the main police building in Johannesburg - the seventeenth death in detention under security laws. Following calls from the opposition and others for a judicial inquiry into deaths of police detainees, the Prime Minister states on the following day, 29 October 1971, that he finds no need for this.

28 Oct. 1971   Winnie Mandela is given a six-month suspended sentence for defying a banning order. She is to appear in court on 16 November 1971 on a second similar charge.

29 Oct. 1971   The Prime Minister emphasizes that following the church's subversive activities, that a comprehensive and serious investigation in connection with terrorism and sabotage can be expected.

Early Nov. 1971   Chiefs Buthelezi and Mangope visit West Germany in early November and hold discussions with ministers and officials.

1 Nov. 1971   After a protracted trial the Anglican Dean of Johannesburg, the Very Rev. Gonville Aubie ffrench-Beytagh is found guilty on ten points of subversive activities against the state and is sentenced to five years' imprisonment with a grant of leave to appeal. The sentence is followed by wide-spread criticism and protests, both within and without the country.

3 Nov. 1971   The Cape Provincial Council approves the Local Authorities Voters' Amendment Ordinance, removing the names of Coloured persons from the common voters' rolls of municipal and divisional councils in the Cape Province, depriving them of rights enjoyed for over 100 years.

3 Nov. 1971   The Transkei Territorial Government is to gain authority over the Xhosa nation living outside its territory. National Boards of Transkeian officials are to be set up in all South African urban areas with populations of more than 100 Xhosas.

12 Nov. 1971   The biennial Congress of the United Party requests the government to hold a referendum before sovereign independence is granted to 'homelands'. The party remains opposed to the separate development policy.

12 Nov. 1971   Signs amendments to the General Agreement on Tariffs and Trade.

12 Nov. 1971   Accepts the accession of the Congo to the General Agreement on Tariffs and Trade.

13-14 Nov.1971	The World Council of Churches meeting in Geneva states that the sentence against Rev. ffrench-Beytagh will stir up the world's indignation against South Africa.
16 Nov. 1971	Signs amendments to the Convention on Narcotic Drugs, 1961.
24 Nov. 1971	Signs agreement with Portugal (for Mozambique) pertaining to rivers of mutual interest.
29 Nov. 1971	The United Nations General Assembly asks all world governments to apply a full-scale embargo on arms supplies to South Africa, condemns the establishment of Bantustans and asks national and international sports organizations to refuse any recognition to any sporting activity involving racial, religious or political discrimination.
2 Dec. 1971	Robert Sobukwe, former PAC leader, is finally refused permission to leave the country, the Appellate Division of the Supreme Court dismisses his appeal against a lower court decision.
4 Dec. 1971	The Defence Minister denies that South Africa has sent troops to Malawi to quell the security threat on Malawi's southern border, but military equipment is being supplied.
4 Dec. 1971	Speaking at the installation of Prince Goodwill Zwelithini as Paramount Chief of the Zulu nation in Nongoma, the Minister of Bantu Administration and Development supports the traditional system of Chieftainship. His speech is resented by the Chief Executive Officer of the Zulu Territorial Authority, Chief Gatsha Buthelezi, who construes it as directed against himself.
13 Dec. 1971	Signs treaty with Australia concerning an international observer scheme for landbased whaling stations.
12 Jan. 1972	The Paramount Chief of the Zulus, Prince Goodwill Zwelithini, is officially removed as a member of the Zulu Legislative Assembly by an amendment to the Constitution. His position henceforth will be similar to that of the State President.
27 Jan. 1972	Signs Convention on Psychotropic Substances.
28 Jan. 1972	The Ministry of Foreign Affairs says that South Africa will not attend the African session of the United Nations Security Council in Addis Ababa. It is not a member and the circumstances are not exceptional enough to request permission to do so.
2 Feb. 1972	An abridged version of the security report by Justice H.J. Potgieter's Commission of Inquiry on State Security is submitted to the House of Assembly. The report finds that South Africa's security is being threatened by numerous enemies in almost every sphere of society.
4 Feb. 1972	At the United Nations Security Council's Special Session on Colonialism and Racial Injustice in Southern Africa in Addis Ababa, a resolution is adopted condemning the government for its racial policies and calling for strict adherence by all states to the arms embargo.

4 Feb. 1972	The Prime Minister states in the House of Assembly in Cape Town that the United Nations General-Secretary, Dr. Waldheim, will be welcome and the government is willing to discuss with him, inter alia, black self-determination.
10 Feb. 1972	The United Nations Secretary-General, Dr. Waldheim, announces in New York that he has received a formal invitiation to visit South Africa for discussions without pre-conditions.
11 Feb. 1972	The House of Assembly approves, by eighty-six votes to forty-three, a motion to appoint a Select Committee to inquire into and report upon the objects, organization, activities, financing and related matters of the National Union of South African Students (NUSAS), the South African Institute of Race Relations, the University Christian Movement (UCM), the Christian Institute of Southern Africa and their subordinate organizations.
15 Feb. 1972	The Department of Bantu Development is planning for the consolidation of the 'homelands' by buying land in terms of the 1936 legislation.
21 Feb. 1972	The Chairman of the South African Coloured Peoples Representative Council reports that the Prime Minister favours Coloureds gradually taking over all posts in the administration of coloured affairs.
25 Feb. 1972	Signs extradition agreement with Malawi.
29 Feb. 1972	Certificates of citizenship in the 'homelands' are to be issued by seven homeland authorities in their respective capitals in terms of the Bantu Homelands Citizenship Act of 1970.
Mar. 1972	The United Nations Secretary-General, Dr. Kurt Waldheim, initiates discussions on the future of Namibia during a five-day visit to South Africa.
4 Mar. 1972	Dr. Basil Moore, Johannesburg Methodist Minister, staff member of the Christian Institute and acting Secretary of the University Christian Movement, is restricted for five years under the Suppression of Communism Act.
4 Mar. 1972	The largest single construction work undertaken in South Africa, the Hendrik Verwoerd Dam on the Orange River, is officially opened by State President Fouché.
4 Mar. 1972	The United Party scores significant victories in municipal elections in Johannesburg and Randburg, continuing a noticeable swing against the National Party.
6 Mar. 1972	The Democratic Party, formed by a splinter group from the National Party, indicates that it represents a coalition of the policies of the National, United and Progressive parties, and outlines its proposed reforms. These include granting the African population representation on municipal councils on the same basis as the white population.
16 Mar. 1972	The Head of the Security Police, General Venter, reports that nobody is still being held incommunicado under the Terrorism Act, and that all those people detained by the Security Police have now been released. However investigations continue.

17-24 Mar. 1972   President Fouché pays a state visit to Malawi and appeals for peaceful co-existence and cooperation between African states. An extradition agreement between the two countries is published in Pretoria on 24 March 1972.

29 Mar. 1972   Signs treaty with Brazil on the issue of avoiding double taxation on profits derived from shipping and aviation.

Apr. 1972   A Legislative Assembly for Vendaland opens for the first time.

Apr.- June 1972   Serious student unrest occurs at both black and white English-language universities leading to forceful police action against demonstrators in Cape Town, Johannesburg and elsewhere. Of the total 618 persons arrested in connection with student protests all those tried in court, for various alleged offences, are acquitted - except one student fined R50 for addressing a meeting.

1 Apr. 1972   The names of the four 'homelands' are changed: from Basotho ba Borwa (Southern Sotho) to Basotho-Qwaqwa; from Tswanaland to Bophuthatswana; from Machangana to Gazankulu; from Zululand to Kwazulu.

1 Apr. 1972   Under its new constitution Kwazulu Territorial Authority becomes Kwazulu Legislative Assembly. Its members undertake to honour and respect the State President and the Paramount Chief, but do not swear allegiance to the South African government and the Zulu royal family is denied executive powers.

5 Apr. 1972   Signs additional articles relevant to the constitution of the Universal Postal Union.

6 Apr. 1972   In the Natal Supreme Court in Pietermaritzburg, at the end of the longest trial of its kind in South Africa, thirteen defendants (nine Africans, two Indians and two Coloureds) are sentenced to imprisonment from five to eight years for contravening the Terrorism Act. They are found guilty of conspiring to overthrow the government by force.

10 Apr. 1972   Signs multilateral treaty on the prohibition of the development, production and stockpiling of bacteriological and toxic weapons and their destruction.

14 Apr. 1972   The appeal by the Anglican Dean, the Very Rev. Gonville Aubie ffrench-Beytagh, against his conviction and sentence under the Terrorism Act is upheld in the Appellate Division of the South African Supreme Court in Bloemfontein. The Dean thereupon leaves South Africa for Britain on the same day.

19 Apr. 1972   The National Party increases its majority in the Oudtshoorn by-election. In the campaign heavy emphasis is placed on the dangers of the United Party race policies.

4 May 1972   The Foreign Minister announces that South Africa and Lesotho have decided to establish reciprocal consular representation.

4 May 1972   The Transkei Legislative Assembly requests independence for the Transkei, subject to the inclusion of additional white areas.

24 May 1972	The Security Intelligence and State Security Council Bill is adopted defining the functions and duties of the Bureau of State Security (BOSS), and setting up a State Security Council, with the Prime Minister as Chairman, to advise government on national policy and strategy on security. It has the support of both opposition parties.
24 May 1972	The first hijacking of a South African Airways plane takes place on a flight to Malawi. The two men responsible are subsequently apprehended and tried.
June 1972	A sixteen day inquest at the Regional Court in Johannesburg concludes that A.E. Timol, a political detainee who fell to his death from the tenth floor of a building while in police custody, committed suicide, and nobody is held accountable.
1 June 1972	Bophuthatswana is granted self government.
1 June 1972	Signs multilateral treaty on the conservation of Antarctic seals.
2 June 1972	Student protest erupts into violence outside St. George's Cathedral in Cape Town. Force is used to dispel demonstrators.
6 June 1972	A proclamation is issued under the Riotous Assemblies Act banning political gatherings, processions, and protests for five weeks in the Cape, Johannesburg, Pretoria, and thirteen other places.
7 June 1972	The Chief Executive Councillor of Kwazulu, Chief Buthelezi, condemns plans to consolidate Zululand in terms of the 1936 Trust and Land Act.
12 June 1972	The Post Office Amendment Bill provides for the interception of mail and telephone and other communications where necessary in the interests of state security. Only the Progressive Party member, Helen Suzman, votes against it.
16 June 1972	The resignation of the Minister of the Interior, Theo Gerdener, is announced and will take effect from 31 July 1972.
16 June 1972	The government gives its details of its proposals to consolidate 157 'black spots' and sixty eight Zulu areas into a homeland. Kwazulu will be consolidated as rapidly as possible. However, Chief Gatsha Buthelezi rejects these plans.
23 June 1972	The Malagasy Foreign Minister declares that his country is going to reconsider its policy of dialogue with South Africa.
27 June 1972	South Africa suspends any further dealing with the Malagasy government.
1 July 1972	Gazankulu holds its first General Assembly.
12 July 1972	A new black political party, the Black People's Convention is formed after a three-day conference in Pietermaritzburg. The objective of the Convention is to unite South African blacks into a political organization seeking to realize their liberation and emancipation from both psychological and physical oppression. It is open only to black members.

14 July 1972   The Minister of Defence, P.W. Botha, announces that Coloureds are to have their own defence force units undergoing twelve months voluntary national service, to be called the South African State Corps Special Service Battalion.

31 July 1972   The Prime Minister announces that, following the resignation of five members of the Cabinet, he has reorganized his government.

31 July 1972   Signs amendment to the trade agreement of 20 August 1932 with Great Britain.

1 Aug. 1972   The Ciskei is given self-government. Chief Justice Mabandla becomes Chief Minister, and the heads of the territory's six departments become Ministers. The following day Mabandla makes a huge land claim asking for all the white-owned land between the Kei and the Fish Rivers in the Eastern Cape and between the coast and the Orange River.

5 Aug. 1972   The state-owned Atlas Aircraft Corporation is to build an advanced subsonic fighter to be airborne in 1974. Also during the next eighteen months the first Mirage F-1 supersonic interceptors being built under licence from France will be in service with the South African Air Force.

7 Aug. 1972   Chief Matanzima (Transkei) outlines proposals for the creation of Xhosaland - a new black super-state to include the Transkei, Ciskei and white-owned land between the Fish and Kei Rivers, and East Griqualand.

10 Aug. 1972   Naval Headquarters at Simonstown announce that the second series of joint British South African exercises off the Cape Coast will begin on 14 August 1972 and will continue for seven days.

11 Aug. 1972   The Minister of Bantu Administration and Development declares that no more land will be allocated to the `homelands' other than that stipulated in the 1936 Land Act.

18 Aug. 1972   The first four Bantu Affairs Administration Boards are gazetted. They are intended to facilitate centralized administrative control and improved mobility of labour.

25 Aug. 1972   Harry Schwarz wins the Transvaal party leadership of the United Party (UP) from Marais Steyn.

12 Sept. 1972   Dr. H. Muller is elected as the National Party's leader in the Transvaal, following the resignation of B. Schoeman. His election is considered to make him the successor-designate to John Vorster as Prime Minister.

28 Sept. 1972   Proposals for the consolidation of `homelands' in the Transvaal which will have the effect of reducing twenty six or twenty-seven specified areas to nine are announced. The purchase of white-owned land, involving a total of 310,000 hectares, for addition to black areas is a long and difficult task.

Oct. 1972 -   A wave of strikes by black workers begins in the autumn of 1972 and esca-
Feb. 1973   lates dramatically in the first months of 1973, the main centre of unrest being Durban.

2 Oct. 1972   Lebowa, the Northern Sotho `homeland', becomes the fourth self-governing

'homeland', with Bheshego as its temporary capital. Under its new constitution there will be a cabinet consisting of a Chief Minister and five other Ministers. External affairs, defence and communications will continue to be controlled by the South African government.

25 Oct. 1972   The International Monetary Fund announces it has concurred in a proposal by the government for a change in the par value of the Rand representing a 4.202 percent devaluation in relation to gold but an effective appreciation of about 4 percent in comparison with the current market exchange of the Rand.

1 Nov. 1972   At the end of a lengthy trial in the Supreme Court in Pretoria, four Indians are convicted of conspiracy under the Terrorism Act and sentenced to a minimum of five years imprisonment. Their intention was the violent overthrow of the system of government.

2 Nov. 1972   The first session of the newly elected Bophuthatswana Legislative Assembly is opened in Mafeking by President Fouché.

15 Nov. 1972   The United Nations General Assembly passes six resolutions in plenary denouncing the government's apartheid policy and various aspects of that policy. Each resolution is sponsored by some fifty African, Asian and Communist countries, the various resolutions receiving in every case over 100 votes in favour, being opposed by South Africa and Portugal and abstentions varying from one to twenty-one votes.

23 Nov. 1972   Passports have been withdrawn from three white staff members of the Institute of Race Relations.

1 Dec. 1972   Signs treaty with Great Britain on air services (Hong Kong) via Seychelles.

1 Dec. 1972   Signs amendment to an agreement regarding the establishment of civil air services with Great Britain.

2 Dec. 1972   Signs International Convention for Containers.

3 Dec. 1972   Theo Gerdener resigns from the National Party on account of his involvement with Action South and Southern Africa (ACASA), an independent organization dedicated to better communication, which he founded.

5 Dec. 1972   It is announced that White, Coloured and Asian workers affiliated to the Trade Union Council of South Africa (TUCSA) have voted overwhelmingly in favour of extending full trade union rights to Africans. Minister of Labour Viljoen opposes it.

8 Dec. 1972   Signs treaty with Swaziland on the avoidance of double taxation and the prevention of fiscal evasion with respect to taxes on income.

16 Dec. 1972   The Black People's Convention (BPC) holds its first National Congress. Its Constitution declares it intends to preach and popularize the philosophy of Black Consciousness and black solidarity.

1973   Under a delimitation carried out to take effect at the next elections the number of seats in the House of Assembly is increased from 166 to 171

generally of benefit to the ruling National Party.

12 Jan. 1973	A notice providing for compulsory education for Indians is gazetted.

18 Jan. 1973   The Kwazulu government issues a document signed by all six Executive Councillors inviting the South African government to test its consolidation plan for the homeland by holding a referendum among all race groups in Natal and Kwazulu.

19 Jan. 1973   Prime Minister Vorster, confirms that the government has not been consulted over Rhodesia's closure of its border with Zambia, but that the government will assist in opposing terrorism.

23 Jan. 1973   The Prime Minister announces that a first-ever multi-racial commission will investigate the political and socio-economic future of the Coloured community.

24 Jan. 1973   Premier Vorster, decrees that in the future the 'homelands' will be allowed to accept direct foreign financial aid.

25 Jan. 1973   Signs a treaty with the Federal Republic of Germany on double taxation.

27 Jan. 1973   Chief Matanzima of the Transkei suggests that a federation between blacks and whites would save South Africa from destruction.

Feb.- Apr.1973   The government's reaction to the strikes is a revision of wage levels for unskilled workers; training facilities for blacks; an improvement of communication between black labour and employers.

Feb.- Apr.1973   Widespread industrial unrest among black workers is experienced. The underlying cause is identified as the fact that black workers have assumed increasing importance in the country's economy, yet they are denied the right to strike or bargain collectively and their trade union is not officially recognized.

1 Feb. 1973   The government grants internal self-government to two further 'homelands', namely to Venda and Gazankulu territories.

12 Feb. 1973   Signs multilateral treaty and operating agreement relating to the Intelsat.

19 Feb. 1973   Unrest among black workers over wage improvement continues. Police arrest 244 African workers, of whom 169 are subsequently charged.

20 Feb. 1973   The Minister of Labour announces instructions to the Wage Board to revise certain determinations applying to unskilled labourers in major centres. Minimum wages rise by over thirty per cent.

21 Feb. 1973   The first general elections to the Ciskei's Legislative Assembly are held in the territory's nine districts. There are no political parties; the candidates are elected to the twenty elective seats in their individual capacity, the remaining thirty seats are filled by Chiefs appointed ex officio.

27 Feb. 1973   The Commission of Inquiry, appointed by the Prime Minister, to investigate the activities of four organizations, among them the National Union of South African Students (NUSAS) submits a detailed interim report on NUSAS to

the Assembly, recommending action against eight NUSAS leaders. The Commission, under the chairmanship of A.L. Schlebush, comprises five other National Party MPs and four opposition United Party MPs. The approval of the report by its four UP members is widely criticized.

27 Feb. 1973   On the same day banning orders under the Suppression of Communism Act of 1950 are served on eight NUSAS leaders. On the following day violent student clashes take place in Johannesburg.

Early Mar. 1973   The Portuguese Foreign Minister, Dr. Rul Patricio, pays a five-day official visit to South Africa. He declares, on 6 March 1973, that there are no plans for a military alliance between Portugal, South Africa and Rhodesia.

2 Mar. 1973   It is announced in Johannesburg that restriction orders have been issued against six leaders of the South African Students Organization (SASO) and against two men closely associated with the Black People's Convention (BPC).

3 Mar. 1973   Signs multilateral treaty on international trade in endangered species of wild flora and fauna.

8 Mar. 1973   The Minister of Justice defends the banning orders on eight black leaders on the grounds that he is preventing acts of terrorism worse than any previously experienced. The opposition queries why, in such a case, the leaders are not taken to court.

8 Mar. 1973   The Prime Minister, B.J. Vorster, officially opens the South African Navy's R15m. Maritime Operational and Communications Headquarters at Silvermine, near Simonstown.

12 Mar. 1973   In the wake of strikes in Natal in February, The Guardian publishes a documented report on the low wages paid to black workers in South Africa by companies with British connections.

14 Mar. 1973   The Supreme Council for Sports in Africa (SCSA) asks the national Olympic committees of Belgium, Great Britain, Japan, the Netherlands and West Germany, to do everything in their power to prevent members of their respective countries from participating in the Pretoria Games from 23 March to 7 April 1973.

20 Mar. 1973   Sports Minister, Dr. P. Koornhof, says the government will not allow organizations inside or outside the country to disrupt the South African games.

20 Mar. 1973   Evidence of guerrilla training in the Soviet Union and Tanzania is given in the trial of six people, on nineteen charges under the Terrorism Act, appearing before Justice Boshoff in Pretoria.

21 Mar. 1973   The banning orders on NUSAS leaders are discussed by the Principals of four English language universities with the Prime Minister, who is unsympathetic. Extra-Parliamentary action to bring about change in the form of government in South Africa will not be tolerated.

27 Mar. 1973   A major detailed Administration statement is made by the United States Assistant Secretary of State for African Affairs, David Newsom, to the

African Sub-Committee of the House of Representatives, chaired by Congressman Charles Diggs concerning American business involvement in South Africa. It stresses that peaceful change in South Africa can be fostered if American firms promote better conditions for blacks.

28 Mar. 1973	At a meeting of its general council the British Trade Union Congress decides to accept an invitation from TUCSA to send a delegation to South Africa to investigate trade union conditions.
29 Mar. 1973	The British government publishes in Trade and Industry, guidelines for British companies operating in South Africa.
3 Apr. 1973	Chief Kaiser Matanzima (Transkei) calls for a federation of white and black states in South Africa. His party stands for a policy of separation of races on an equal and parallel basis, rejecting racial discrimination and white dominance.
4 Apr. 1973	In the British House of Commons the Trade and Industry Sub-Committee of the Select Committee on Expenditure proposes an inquiry 'To investigate how far wages and conditions of employment of African workers employed by British companies in South Africa represent a factor affecting investment prospects, export performance, and the reputation abroad of British industry'. The proposal is accepted.
9 Apr. 1973	The International Commission of Jurists condemns the bannings of black leaders.
9 Apr. 1973	The New Zealand Prime Minister announces that the invitation to an all-white South African rugby team had to be withdrawn because of its racial selection.
10 Apr. 1973	Minister of Defence, P.W. Botha, defines South Africa's defence policy in a White Paper tabled in the House of Assembly. While primarily defensive, the policy must also include a significant retaliatory capability.
11 Apr. 1973	Forty members are elected to Lebowa's Legislative Assembly, the remaining sixty seats being allocated to nominated chiefs. Cedric Phatudi becomes Chief Minister.
14 Apr. 1973	The Bophuthatswana government rejects the South African government's consolidation proposals and, in return, claims large portions of North Western and Western Transvaal and sizeable areas of the Northern Cape and the Free State.
14 Apr. 1973	Signs multilateral treaty on the issue of telegraph and telephone regulations.
20 Apr. 1973	The South African Police Force stationed in the Caprivi Strip, bordering Zambia, suffer casualties in clashes with 'terrorists'.
24 Apr. 1973	The ambush and killing of policemen by Zambian based terrorists is reported from the Caprivi Strip. Zambia denies that it harbours 'freedom fighters'.
25 Apr. 1973	Prime Minister Vorster, confirms in the House of Assembly that the blacks would receive all the land provided for in the 1936 Native Trust and Land

Act.

25 Apr. 1973	The Schlebush Commission of Inquiry issues its third interim report, focussing on the Wilgespruit Fellowship Centre, an institution stated to be working towards radical social and political change and employing procedures counter to accepted religion and religious practice. The Prime Minister gives its controlling body, the South African Council of Churches (SACC) three weeks to clear it up.
27 Apr. 1973	Details of the government's final consolidation proposals for the 'homelands' involving land in the provinces of Natal and Transvaal are given at a press conference by the Minister of Bantu Administration and Development, M.C. Botha. They are tabled in Parliament and approved on 6 June 1973. Resettlement of 363,000 Africans is expected to result. Gatsha Buthelezi protests over the limited concessions and threatens non-cooperation.
29 Apr. 1973	The Prime Minister indicates that the 'homelands' will be perfectly free to form a federation among themselves, once they have achieved full independence. However he is not prepared to share the sovereignty of the white people with any other national group.
4 May 1973	The Minister for Bantu Administration and Development hands over the symbols of authority to the Kwazulu Legislative Authority.
12 May 1973	A Bill prohibiting demonstrations near the Houses of Parliament in Cape Town is passed with the support of the opposition United Party.
15 May - 11 July 1973	The British Trade and Industry Sub-Committe holds eighteen public sittings; twenty eight companies give oral evidence, 100 others written evidence. Most state they have given unscheduled wage increases to black workers in the period before and during the House of Commons inquiry.
16 May 1973	The Minister of Justice banns all protest meetings in the centre of Cape Town, following student protests. Several arrests are made.
18 May 1973	Signs multilateral treaty on the issue of the simplification and harmonization of customs procedures.
21 May 1973	The Bantu Labour Relations Regulation Amendment Bill is read for the first time in the House of Assembly. It creates more effective machinery for communication between employers and African workers and gives the Minister of Labour wide powers to stimulate improvements in working conditions. Africans are given a more direct role in wage negotiations.
24 May 1973	In connection with the uranium enrichment programme, disclosed by the Prime Minister in July 1970, it is announced in the House of Assembly that the government has decided to make funds available for preparatory work for establishing a full-scale prototype plant for the economic enrichment of uranium.
25 May 1973	Final land consolidation proposals for Bophuthatswana are announced. They involve moving more than 120,000 Tswana people from their present lands.
26 May 1973	A comprehensive policy statement on South Africa's new multi-national

sports concessions is made by Sports Minister Dr. P. Koornhof in the House of Assembly. Separate participation will be maintained at club, provincial and national levels. Mixed competition will be only at international level.

20 June 1973   Prison sentences ranging from five to fifteen years are imposed by Justice W.G. Boshoff in Pretoria on six defendants convicted under the Terrorism Act. They are found guilty of various charges including conspiring in South Africa, the Soviet Union, Somalia and Britian with the ANC, to overthrow the South African government by force and preparing for violent revolution.

20 June 1973   The Minister of Defence denies that South African troops are supporting Portuguese armed forces in Mozambique, as alleged by FRELIMO.

29 June 1973   A racially-open movement, Verligte Action, concerned with improving the political situation emerges.

July-Sept. 1973   'Homeland' leaders Chief Buthelezi, Professor Ntsanwisi, and T.M. Molahlawa warn the South African government of worsening race relations.

4 July 1973   The Bantu Labour Regulations Amendment Bill becomes operative. The conditions under which Africans - for the first time - have the legal right to strike, the procedures to be followed, and the exclusion from it of certain essential services categories of workers are laid down.

20 July 1973   The Minister of Coloured Affairs announces that the government has decided to appoint a judicial commission to investigate student grievances and conduct at the University of the Western Cape, closed between 11 June and 15 July 1973, following various demands and protests.

28 July 1973   The Deputy Minister of Bantu Administration and Education, Punt Janson, invites guidance in humanizing the pass laws and influx control measures by which African mobility is regulated, in the interests of the communities.

30 July 1973   The former Minister of the Interior, Theo Gerdener, announces details of his scheme for a new political organization whose aim will be to work for two separate states in South Africa, one for Africans and the other for White, Indian and Coloured peoples with equality for all.

Aug. 1973   Banning orders continue. Passports are refused, or withdrawn.

1 Aug. 1973   A High Court is established in Umtata, capital of the Transkei. The first Chief Justice sworn in is a white South African.

7 Aug. 1973   Students strike at the University of Fort Hare. The Students Organization (SASO) is held responsible for the agitation. Further violence erupts on the campus on 28 August 1973.

15-16 Aug. 1973   Elections are held in Venda. Traditionalist Chief Patrick R. Mphephu is returned to power despite electoral victory for the opposition Vendaland Independent People's Party, additional seats being filled by nominated headmen.

24 Aug. 1973   Signs treaty with Lesotho relating to the establishment of an office for a Lesotho government labour representative in South Africa.

24 Aug. 1973	Signs boundary treaty with Botswana.
25 Aug. 1973	The Prime Minister warns the opposition parties, the United Party and Progressive Party, that his government may have to end interference by whites in the political affairs of Africans and vice-versa. He is particularly opposed to representatives of black and Coloured communities being invited to speak at their congresses which can only heighten friction between racial groups.
29 Aug. 1973	Signs treaty with Brazil regarding the exemption from customs duties to consuls and consulates of both states.
Sept. 1973	The Premier of West German Schleswig-Holstein says during a visit to South Africa that more German entrepreneurs should be attracted to the 'homelands'.
11 Sept. 1973	Eleven rioting miners are shot by police and twenty-seven injured at the Western Deep Levels mine, Carltonville in a confrontation arising from a pay dispute. The incident arouses international concern.
13 Sept. 1973	Chief Gatsha Buthelezi, the Chief Councillor, announces that the South African government has agreed that members of the Kwazulu Executive Council should be allowed to possess firearms.
20 Sept. 1973	The United States House of Representatives Judiciary Sub-Committee opens an inquiry into the South African operations of 320 American firms, with a view to determining whether they follow fair employment practices.
25 Sept. 1973	The New Zealand government announces that it terminates all tariff preferences previous granted to South Africa, as from 1 January 1974.
Oct. 1973	A plan is launched by the government and leading blacks, for the formation of twenty-two councils to represent the country's 6,000,000 urban Africans.
3 Oct. 1973	Prime Minister Vorster indicates that there is nothing to prevent employers taking the necessary steps to bring about improvements in the productive use of black labour. The government will not obstruct changes in the country's traditional work patterns.
5 Oct. 1973	The Minister of Labour exercises his power under the Bantu Labour Relations Regulation Bill to order minimum wage increases of between fifty and ninety per cent for a large proportion of the more than 100,000 Africans employed in the civil engineering and road-making industries in main urban areas.
5 Oct. 1973	The United Nations General Assembly rejects South Africa's credentials. The Assembly President rules, however, that the measure does not affect the delegations right to participate, and the Prime Minister affirms South Africa's intention to remain in the United Nations despite mounting opposition.
5 Oct. 1973	A State Presidential Proclamation, widening powers of the Group Areas Act, is published in a bid to prevent multi-racial matches at Pietermaritzburg's Aurora Cricket Club.

7-20 Oct. 1973	A delegation of British Trade Union leaders carry out an intensive programme of visits and talks, investigating trade union conditions and meeting the Prime Minister and several other government ministers. Their leader, Victor Feather, President of the European Trade Union Confederation, outlines a six point plan for industrial prosperity and black workers advancement. The government rejects it.
12 Oct. 1973	The Minister of Labour says that the government will neither abolish job reservation nor recognize black trade unions.
16 Oct. 1973	Signs treaty with Spain for the prevention of double taxation on income derived from the operation of ships or aircraft in international traffic.
16-17 Oct. 1973	Elections are held in Gazankulu. Professor Hudson Ntsanwisi is unanimously re-elected leader of the Gazankulu Legislative Assembly.
21 Oct. 1973	It is reported that the government has banned twenty black leaders of black organizations, including the South African Students' Organization (SASO), the Black People's Convention (BPC) the Black Community Programme (BCP), the Black Allied Workers' Union and the Black Workers' Project. Members of the South African Black Scholars' Association (SABSA) are interrogated by security police.
24 Oct. 1973	In the elections the Transkei National Independence Party wins twenty-five seats, the Democratic Party ten, Independents eight. Another sixty-four Assembly seats are filled by chiefs appointed ex officio by the government.
27 Oct. 1973	The Carltonville inquests exonerates the police from any blame for the shootings at the Western Deep Levels on 11 September 1973, in which eleven black miners were killed and which caused an international outcry.
8 Nov. 1973	A meeting convened by Chief Lucas Mangope, Chief Minister of Bophuthatswana, held in Umtata in camera and attended by eight 'homeland' leaders to work out a common approach to the government, lays emphasis on the concept of one black nation. Resolutions are passed for the estblishment of a black bank, abolition of influx control and consolidation of 'homelands' into single units.
9 Nov. 1973	At its Biennial Congress in Bloemfontein the United Party adopts a new six-point declaration of principles, and ratifies a new federal plan committed to a federal constitution.
9-11 Nov.1973	The Progressive Party supports the idea of a federation of autonomous states in Southern Africa.
16 Nov. 1973	Dr. Beyers Naudé, Director of the Christian Institute is found guilty by a Pretoria regional court of refusing to testify before the Schlebusch Commission, because its hearings were held in secret.
17 Nov. 1973	The Democratic Party officially comes into being at a one-day conference in Johannesburg attended by some 200 delegates from the four provinces. Theo Gerdener is unanimously elected leader of the party.
28 Nov. 1973	An Arab oil embargo against South Africa, brings the prospects of rationing and the extension of conservation measures.

30 Nov. 1973	The United Nations General Assembly adopts, by ninety one votes to four, the Convention on the Suppression and Punishment of the Crime of Apartheid. To become international law its ratification by twenty countries is still required.
4 Dec. 1973	Following the placing of an embargo on the supply of oil to South Africa from Arab countries, the Prime Minister announces restricted trading hours, but states that petrol rationing is not as yet being introduced.
7 Dec. 1973	Further bannings are gazetted, including that of the former leader of the South African Indian Congress, Yusuf Cachalia who has already spent twenty years under restriction.
11 Dec. 1973	Land consolidation proposals for the Transkei and Ciskei are announced, involving black acquisition of Port St Johns and Indwe.
14 Dec. 1973	The United Nations adopts a resolution declaring that the South African government has no right to represent the people of that country and that representation should instead be vested in the African national liberation movements.
15 Dec. 1973	The British Trade Union Congress (TUC) publishes a report on black labour conditions. Among the major recommendations it advocates is the organization of black workers into trade unions.
19 Dec. 1973	Signs International Sugar Agreement.
24 Dec. 1973	Signs agreement with Botswana relating to the establishment of a Botswana government labour representative in South Africa.
1 Jan. 1974	With effect from this date the New Zealand government terminates all tariff preferences previously granted to South Africa.
4 Jan. 1974	The leader of the United Party in the Transvaal, Harry Swartz, signs a five-point 'declaration of faith' with Chief Gatsha Buthelezi of Kwazulu. Its purpose is to provide a blueprint for government by consent and racial peace in a multi-racial society, stressing opportunity for all, consultation, the federal concept, and a Bill of Rights.
30 Jan. 1974	The United Party controlled Johannesburg City Council announces the dismantling of petty apartheid practices.
Feb. 1974	The report of the one-man Commission of Inquiry into the University of the Western Cape by Justice J.T. van Wyk urges that disruption and incitement at all South African universities be made a legally punishable offence.
1 Feb. 1974	Abraham Tiro, a leader of the South African Students' Organization, who after his expulsion from Turfloop University in 1972 had fled the country in September 1973, is killed by a parcel bomb near Gaborone, Botswana.
4 Feb. 1974	The Prime Minister announces the holding of early elections. The National Party bases its election campaign on its record in office over the previous twenty-six years and on the need for a strong government.
8 Feb. 1974	The Prime Minister warns that the government will not hesitate to intervene,

should campaigns by City Councils - led by Johannesburg - to eliminate petty apartheid measures cause friction, or disturb the peace.

8 Feb. 1974   The Minister of Justice, P.C. Pelser discloses in Parliament that during 1973 a total of sixty-seven people were banned by the government for political reasons. Of these sixteen were prosecuted and eleven convicted for not complying with their restriction orders.

9 Feb. 1974   The Publications and Entertainments Bill placed by the government before the House of Assembly incorporated the recommendations of the Commission of Inquiry chaired by Jimmy Kruger, Deputy Minister of the Interior. The most controversial section abolishes the existing right of appeal from the Publications Control Board decisions to the Supreme Court - regarded by the opposition United Party as a damaging blow to the rule of law.

18 Feb. 1974   The Lebanese government decides to break off diplomatic relations with South Africa.

23 Feb. 1974   The Prime Minister condemns, in the strongest terms, a gift of $450,000 announced by the World Council of Churches (WCC) to Southern African liberation movements.

6 Mar. 1974   The British Parliamentary Report on Black Labour Conditions indicate that sixty-three of 141 British companies investigated have been paying African workers below the relevant poverty line. Three main recommendations are made the British government should initiate a new code of practice for British firms operating in South Africa; British companies should pay African workers not less than the minimum effective level and should encourage the lawful development of collective bargaining.

6 Mar. 1974   What is officially described as the first meeting of its kind, the Prime Minister holds a one-day conference with the black 'homeland' leaders to discuss mainly economic and urbanization questions.

14 Mar. 1974   Chief Matanzima calls upon the South African government to grant full independence to the Transkei within five years. The Prime Minister states that he is prepared to negotiate.

15 Mar. 1974   The creation of a community of separate and sovereign states is laid down as the official policy of the National Party in its election manifesto. Simultaneously it rejects absolutely a federal system.

15 Mar. 1974   Two Bills conferring wide new security powers on the government are passed by Parliament. The Affected Organizations Act is intended to prevent such organizations from receiving financial support from overseas sources to achieve political objectives in South Africa. The Riotous Assemblies Amendment Act empowers the authorities to prohibit any public or private gathering of more than one person, whether lawful or unlawful, if it is thought to pose a threat to law and order. Both Acts are strongly opposed by the United Party and the Progressive Party.

18 Mar. 1974   At the close of nominations for the 1974 elections a total of 334 candidates have been nominated for 171 seats: National Party 137, United Party 110, Herstigte Nasionale Party 46, Progressive Party 23, Democratic Party 7 and

others 11.

18 Mar. 1974	The Minister of the Interior, Connie Mulder, announces that senior officials of the World Council of Churches (WCC) have been banned from South Africa. Entry will be refused to any member of the Council's Executive or Central Committee.
20 Mar. 1974	Responding to the British Labour government's reimposition of an embargo on arms sales to South Africa, John Vorster tells Britain that South Africa does not depend on British arms.
20 Mar. 1974	Signs agreement with Swaziland on the issue of notes and coin.
25 Mar. 1974	Signs amendment with Great Britain to the agreement on civil air services signed on 26 October 1945.
29 Mar. 1974	Chief Minister Cedric Phatudi of Lebowa signs the 'Seshego Declaration' with the United Party Transvaal leader, Harry Schwarz and the United Party M.P. for Durban North aiming at peaceful change, a federal system - and a stake in society for blacks.
Early-Apr. 1974	The President of Paraguay, A. Stroessner, pays a five-day State visit to South Africa. Paraguay is given a $20m. loan for agricultural development. Agreements are signed on economic cooperation.
2 Apr. 1974	Signs multilateral treaty on the extension of the Wheat Trade Convention, 1971.
3 April 1974	Signs treaty with Paraguay on cultural exchanges and cooperation in science and technology.
4 April 1974	Following the aircrash death of over seventy miners, President Banda unilaterally suspends labour recruitment to South Africa. The move leads to protracted, but inconclusive negotiations for better conditions for migrant workers.
8 April 1974	The Prime Ministers of Lesotho and South Africa meet to clear up certain misunderstandings and reaffirm their belief and determination that both countries base their relations on the principle of good neighbourliness.
24 April 1974	The general elections result in the return of the National Party for the seventh consecutive time since 1948. While the United Party suffers a setback the Progressive Party increases its representation from one seat to six. The newly created Democratic Party has no success and the Herstigte Nasionale Party meets with resounding defeat.
25 April 1974	The World Council of Churches (WCC) calls for an end to multi-million pound investment in South Africa by international banks, to help bring about the collapse of the economy and the end of apartheid. The report, commissioned by the council, is released simultaneously in London, Geneva, Frankfurt and New York.
26 April 1974	The Minister of Defence, P.W. Botha, announces an expansion programme for the naval base at Simonstown.

29 April 1974   A number of Cabinet changes are announced by the Prime Minister.

30 April 1974   The claims of the government of Lebowa to more than one third of the total area of the Transvaal are set out in a report of the Select Committee of Inquiry into the Consolidation of Lebowa, tabled in the Lebowa Legislative Assembly by the Minister of the Interior, C. Ramusi.

30 April 1974   The new government decides that the Senate will be dissolved by the State President and replaced by an enlarged Upper House at the end of May.

6 May 1974   The British Lions rugby team leave London to begin a controversial twenty-two match tour of South Africa and Rhodesia, ignoring threats by the Supreme Council for Sport in Africa (SCSA). Kenya, Zambia, Tanzania and Uganda sever all sporting links with Britain.

17 May 1974   After a two-hour discussion, the Transkei and South African governments agree to appoint a committee of experts to prepare the way for Transkei independence. An assurance is given by Chief Kaiser Matanzima that the Transkei will continue as a democratic multi-party system after its independence.

21 May 1974   The British Prime Minister, Harold Wilson, states in the House of Commons that the export license for a Westland Wasp helicopter to South Africa will be revoked.

22 May 1974   The South African Olympic and National Games Association (SAONGA) reports that all South Africa's attempts to secure re-admission to the Olympic Games have failed, despite the tremendous strides made to comply with the demands of the IOC.

22 May 1974   Signs an amendment to the agreement on civil uses of atomic energy with the United States.

29 May 1974   After joint talks with Ian Smith of Rhodesia, the Prime Minister B.J. Vorster commits South Africa to co-operative coexistence with, and non-interference in the internal affairs of a black-ruled Mozambique. A reciprocal pledge is forthcoming from FRELIMO's Joachim Chissano on 17 September 1974.

30 May 1974   Following the elections, ten new senators are chosen and appointed by the Prime Minister, on the same day that the electoral colleges elect their forty-four Provincial Senators.

30 May 1974   South Africa tells Britain that unless the Wasp helicopter is delivered the Simonstown Agreement on naval cooperation will have to be reviewed.

5 June 1974   The Japanese government announces that South Africans will no longer be granted visas to enter Japan, to take part in sporting, cultural or educational activities. The ban comes into effect on 15 June 1974.

15 June 1974   Minister of Defence P.W. Botha, announces during a press visit to the Caprivi Strip that the Defence Force has taken over protection of the country's northern borders as a full military operation, replacing the police in the area. Zambia protests over this change. It becomes clear that South Africa is recruiting, arming and training blacks for its army anti-terrorists

units to repel a possible guerrilla onslaught on its northern border.

20 June 1974	Signs amendment to multilateral agreement of 26 July 1967 for the application of safeguards (IAEA/SA/USA).
21 June 1974	The Minister of Finance announces a change in the South African exchange rate practice. Henceforward the Rand is tied strictly to the U.S. dollar.
30 June 1974	Cooperation with Iran in the fields of nuclear energy, petroleum, mining and trade is announced.
July 1974	The leader of the opposition party, Colin Eglin, together with F. van Zyl Slabbert, undertakes a fact-finding tour of several African countries, including Botswana, Kenya, Nigeria and Zambia.
July 1974	Removals of thousands of Africans are taking place near Middleburg in the Eastern Transvaal, and more are planned for the Eastern Cape Albany district.
7 July 1974	New Zealand imposes a blanket ban on virtually all visits by sports teams from South Africa.
22 July 1974	The Deputy Chairman of the Coloured Representative Council, J.A. Rabie, calls for full citizenship for Coloured people, and urges a separate voters roll to elect sixty Coloured representatives to Parliament and the Provincial Councils.
11 July 1974	Strikes in Durban, common since January 1973, continue as white mechanics and engineers join the ranks of some 400 black and coloured workers.
23 July 1974	Following criticism of the press, particularly the English press, by the Prime Minister, a code of conduct is adopted by the National Press Union which is criticised by newspaper editors and certain academics.
24 July 1974	Dissatisfaction with the Coloured Persons Representative Council (CPRC) climaxes with a motion of no confidence in separate development. This is followed, on 29 July, by a walkout of the Federal Party after its third defeat in three days by the Labour Party, led by Sonny Leon.
30 July 1974	The Cabinet meets to discuss the crisis in the government policy towards the coloured community, following the capture of the Coloured Representative Council (CRC) by the anti-Apartheid Labour Party. The government has prorogued the Council until further notice.
31 July 1974	In a by-election held in Natal the United Party candidate wins a seat against the Democratic Party candidate. The ruling National Party did not contest the seat.
31 July - 1 Aug. 1974	The South African Council of Churches adopts a resolution, at its national conference, that a just war cannot be fought in defence of a basically unjust society.
1 Aug. 1974	Signs treaty with the Federal Republic of Germany relating to the visit of the German nuclear-powered vessel `Otto Hahn'.

1 Aug. 1974	It is officially announced that the police's counter-insurgency potential will be increased by the establishment of a long-service volunteer unit to fight 'terrorists' in Rhodesia.

1 Aug. 1974   The government expands its defence potential by enrolling blacks for defence services. This policy has the support of 'homeland' leaders.

12 Aug. 1974   The Commission of Inquiry into Certain Organizations submits its final report on NUSAS to Parliament. It finds that its leaders are traitors, guilty of providing terrorist groups and the like. The Commission recommends that the application of students to NUSAS should end and that NUSAS should not be allowed to accept funds from overseas.

14 Aug. 1974   A sharp increase in defence expenditure is announced. This follows the White Paper tabled on 10 April 1973, by the Minister of Defence. This demand was necessary for the strengthening of the defence force on the borders of the Caprivi Strip with Angola and Zambia.

19 Aug. 1974   The Prime Minister meets for four hours in Cape Town with a delegation of politicians from the Coloured Representative Council (CRC), led by Sonny Leon. He informs them that the government cannot meet their demands.

26 Aug. 1974   A Defence Bill is passed laying down penalties for any person or organization inciting anyone to avoid military service.

3 Sept. 1974   Joint routine exercises are held between the British Royal Navy and the South African Navy, under the Simonstown Agreement, and again from 14 October 1974.

5 Sept. 1974   The Prime Minister again meets Coloured leaders in Cape Town in a attempt to resolve the crisis in the government's Coloured policy.

9 Sept. 1974   The U.K. Department of Trade confirms that all arms sales to South Africa are halted.

10 Sept. 1974   The Minister of Defence states that South Africa will provide bases and communication facilities to the maritime forces of Western nations interested in the defence of the Cape route.

11 Sept. 1974   The government is empowered to set up a Publications Board which would endeavour to present and uphold the Christian view of life.

13 Sept. 1974   The Minister of Justice officially announces that NUSAS has been declared an 'affected organization' under the Affected Organizations Act and will not be allowed to retain any funds obtained from overseas.

16 Sept. 1974   The United States decides to sell helicopters and reconnaissance aircraft to South Africa.

16 Sept. 1974   The Minister of Defence announces that South Africa will soon build its own tanks.

19 Sept. 1974   The Prime Minister wishes the new Mozambique government well, but warns that South Africa will have to act in self-defence if Mozambique

makes its territory available to guerrilla forces as a base for direct attacks against South Africa.

22-23 Sept. 1974   The Prime Minister pays a secret visit to the Ivory Coast in pursuit of his policy of seeking dialogue with black African states.

23 Sept. 1974   The United States government officially advises American companies operating in South Africa to negogiate with (unregistered) African trade unions.

25 Sept. 1974   The New Zealand government announces that it terminates all tariff preferences previously granted to South Africa, as from 1 January 1974.

26 Sept. 1974   The United Nations General Assembly's Political Committee decides to grant observer status to the ANC and the PAC. The South African delegation is subsequently withdrawn from the Political Committee.

30 Sept. 1974   The United Nations General Assembly asks the Security Council to review the relationship between the United Nations and South Africa in the light of the constant violation by South Africa of the principles of the Charter and the Universal Declaration of Human Rights.

7 Oct. 1974   Signs regional agreement on low frequency and medium frequency broadcasting in ITU regions 1 and 3.

8 Oct. 1974   The Minister of Bantu Administration and Development states that, in 1973, 475,387 foreign Africans were working in South Africa. Of these 36,480 were from Botswana, 148,856 from Lesotho, 139,714 from Malawi, 129,198 from Mozambique, 3,249 from Rhodesia, 10,032 from Swaziland and the remainder from other African territories.

9 Oct. 1974   The Publications Act replaces the Publications Control Board with an entirely new censorship machine operative at three different levels. A fundamental change is the specific exclusion of appeal to the courts.

12 Oct. 1974   Fourteen people, including leading members of the South African Students Organization (SASO) and the Black People's Convention (BPC) are arrested and held under the Terrorism Act, following the pro-FRELIMO rally in Durban on 25 September 1974. Their arrest is the signal for widespread unrest at the University of the North, Turfloop.

14 Oct. 1974   The Minister of Sport, Piet Koornhof, announces a relaxation of apartheid rules for sport and declares the government is working towards eliminating racial discrimination in the selection of contestants for international events.

15 Oct. 1974   A Second General Law Amendment Bill is introduced by the Minister of Justice, J.T. Kruger, involving the repeal of the `Masters and Servants' laws governing the employment of labourers on farms, in mines, and of domestic workers. The Bill is passed late in October with the support of the opposition.

15 Oct. 1974   The United Nations Secretary-General accepts the credentials of the South African delegation led by `Pik' Botha and including, for the first time, three black delegates, Chief Kaiser Matanzima (Transkei), Dr. M.B. Naidoo (South African Indian Council), and Dan Ulster (Coloured People's

Representative Council.

23 Oct. 1974	The Prime Minister makes a major policy speech in the Senate, promising that South Africa will contribute its share to order, development and technical and monetary aid to African countries, particularly to close neighbours.
24 Oct. 1974	In the United Nations Security Council 'Pik' Botha says that South Africa will do everything in its power to move away from discrimination based on race or colour.
25 Oct. 1974	Cameroon, Kenya, Mauritania and Iraq call for the expulsion of South Africa from the United Nations. The proposition is vetoed by Britain, France and the United States. The vote on South Africa's expulsion constitutes the first on the specific question of expelling a member country and also the first in which there is a triple veto.
30 Oct. 1974	The main report of the Van Wyk de Vries Commission of Inquiry into Universities is tabled. It advances some positive recommendations, while in a minority report, G.R. Bozzoli, Principal of the University of the Witwatersrand, warns tht certain chapters represent an attack on the English-language universities.
1 Nov. 1974	A seventh black 'homeland', Qwa-Qwa, becomes self-governing.
1 Nov. 1974	Signs multilateral treaty on safety of life at sea.
4 Nov. 1974	The Chamber of Mines secures the Rhodesian government's approval for the recruitment of black labour from Rhodesia.
5 Nov. 1974	In a major policy speech, the Prime Minister talks of peace with black Africa, and of close economic ties in Southern Africa. He asks for six months' grace for South Africa, and requests political commentators to 'give South Africa a chance'.
6 Nov. 1974	At the National Party's Cape Province Congress, four Cabinet Ministers call for changes and the removal of unnecessary irritating legislation.
6 Nov. 1974	The South African Indian Council ceases to be totally government-appointed when half of its thirty seats are filled by election.
8 Nov. 1974	The Prime Minister's major proposal for the Coloured people is the creation of a consultative cabinet with equal numbers of white ministers and Council representatives meeting under his chairmanship. This 'new deal' is rejected by leaders of the Coloured community, by the leader of the Labour Party and by the Opposition parties.
12 Nov. 1974	At a request made by the Permanent Representative of Tanzania, representing the African Group of the United Nations, the South African Delegation is refused participation in the Session of the UN General Assembly.
16 Nov. 1974	Six of the eight 'homeland' leaders meet United Party leaders and issue a statement supporting federation as the solution for South Africa's race problem. All eight leaders question the Prime Minister's offer of

independence.

16 Nov. 1974	The Prime Minister tells black 'homeland' leaders that one-man-one-vote in a Parliament for whites and blacks will never come about. Black majority rule in the 'homelands' will prevail and the whites will govern South Africa. The six months grace period was not intended 'to turn South Africa upside-down'.
20 Nov. 1974	The Masters and Servants Act and sections of the Bantu Labour Act are repealed. The repealing Act, the Second General Laws Amendment Act, makes it an offence to cause hostility between sections of the population and prohibits the furnishing of information, without ministerial permission, about business matters in response to any order, direction or request emanating outside the Republic.
21 Nov. 1974	An agreement is signed in Blantyre by which South Africa undertakes to lend Malawi R19m. to build a railway line between Lilongwe, the capital, and the Zambian border.
27 Nov. 1974	In a by-election at Wonderboom (Pretoria) the National Party candidate retains the seat by 5,745 votes against 1,077 cast for the Herstigte Nasionale Party.
5 Dec. 1974	A comprehensive monetary agreement is signed between South Africa, Lesotho and Swaziland.
7 Dec. 1974	International Monetary Fund announces the termination of South Africa's request of the 1969 arrangements for the sale of South African gold.
13 Dec. 1974	Signs an amendment to the trade agreement of 13 March 1967 with Malawi.
22 Dec. 1974	The Minister of Foreign Affairs, H. Muller, defines the government's policy of ending discrimination inside South Africa and of detente in external relations.
Jan.- Feb.1975	A number of measures are taken at government, provincial and municipal level to liberalize the applications of apartheid rules. Attempts to organize sports on a multi-racial basis are, however, blocked by cabinet ministers.
5 Jan. 1975	The British Foreign Minister, James Callaghan, arrives in Port Elizabeth for a three-hour meeting with Prime Minister Vorster. Talks focus on the Rhodesian situation and the possibilities for political settlement.
22 Jan. 1975	At a meeting between John Vorster and eight 'homelands' leaders, strong representations are made to the Prime Minister on the disabilities of Africans in urban areas. The meeting produces some concessions but falls short of African demands.
23 Jan. 1975	At a meeting between the Prime Minister and a liaison committee of the Coloured Representative Council (CRC), important decisions include reaffirmation in principle of parity in salaries for Coloureds and Coloured representation on statutory bodies.
30 Jan. 1975	Dr. Nicolaas Diederichs, Minister of Finance, is elected as the National Party's candidate to succeed J.J. Fouché as State President at the end of his

term of office on 9 April 1975.

31 Jan. 1975   New Cabinet appointments are announced: Senator Owen P.F. Horwood - Finance; J. Chris Heunis - Economic Affairs; S.J. Marais Steyn - Indian Affairs and Tourism. P.W. Botha, the Minister of Defence, becomes Leader of the Assembly.

Feb. 1975   Differences over the role to be played by the Parliamentary Opposition lead to a spate of expulsions and defections from the United Party.

10 Feb. 1975   It is confirmed by the Department of Foreign Affairs that the Foreign Minister, Dr. H. Muller, visited Lusaka for talks with the foreign ministers of Tanzania, Zambia and Botswana and with leaders of the Rhodesian ANC.

11 Feb. 1975   A Rhodesian government spokesman announces that elements of the South African police were withdrawing from certain forward positions on the Zambezi River, a move made after undertakings from the Zambian government about guerrilla infiltrations there.

11 Feb. 1975   A new Reform Party is founded.

11 Feb. 1975   A second report by the Commission of Inquiry, under the chairmanship of Justice Van Wyk de Vries, appointed in 1968 to investigate the activities of South Africa's white universities and the University of South Africa (UNISA) is submitted to Parliament. The report, completed in 1972, recommends that the Minister of Education be empowered to declare any inter-university or student organization undesirable, if it is engaged in political activities. NUSAS is particularly targeted.

11-12 Feb. 1975   Prime Minister Vorster visits Liberia for talks with President Tolbert. It is confirmed that the government's 'homelands' policy is explained and discussed.

17 Feb. 1975   The Prime Minister confirms his visit to Liberia and describes the talks as long and fruitful.

18 Feb. 1975   All activities of the South African Students' Organization (SASO) are suspended until further notice. The announcement is made at the University of the North at Turfloop, Transvaal.

21 Feb. 1975   Dr Diederichs receives the unanimous vote of the Electoral College, consisting of members of both Houses of Parliament, to become State President.

26 Feb. 1975   Signs trade agreement with Taiwan.

5 Mar. 1975   A sharp indictment of apartheid is published by the World Health Organization (WHO).

8 Mar. 1975   The Commission for the Programme against Racism of the World Council of Churches (WCC) calls for actions to discourage tourism and visits by churchmen, political figures and sportsmen to South Africa and condemns Prime Minister Vorster's détente policy.

10 Mar. 1975   All South African policemen in Rhodesia are being confined to camps.

South Africa is slowly disengaging from the settlement situation in Rhodesia.

11 Mar. 1975	The Liberian legislature expresses support for President Tolbert's policy of contact with South Africa.
16 Mar. 1975	Bram Fischer is released from prison, following widespread appeals on his behalf, on health grounds, by the United Nations Secretary-General, Dr Kurt Waldheim, by the British Labour Party and by liberal Members of Parliament, as well as by many prominent South Africans.
17-18 Mar. 1975	Meetings are held in Cape Town between Prime Ministers Vorster and Ian Smith, with discussions focussing on the détente policy and the future of Rhodesia.
19 Mar. 1975	The second elections to the Coloured Persons' Representative Council result in thirty-one of the Council's forty elective seats being won by the anti-apartheid Labour Party, which now has an absolute majority in the Council. Its leader, Sonny Leon, states that his party's minimum demand is full equality with whites - complete economic and political freedom.
19 Mar. 1975	On the day of the elections the Minister of Coloured Relations gives notice of a Bill enabling him to exercise the powers and functions of the Council in certain circumstances.
19-21 Mar. 1975	The first elections of twenty members of the Legislative Assembly take place in Qwaqwa.
25 Mar. 1975	Signs multilateral treaty for the modification and further extension of the Wheat Trade Convention.
26 Mar. 1975	Presenting his Budget for 1975/76, the Minister of Finance, Senator Owen Horwood announces a 36% rise in proposed defence expenditure, the defence budget being raised to R948,122,000. The White Paper following the Budget announces plans for an expansion and reorganization of the Defence Forces.
27 Mar. 1975	The government's final proposals for the consolidation of the 'homelands' are announced. The total number of separate homeland areas will be reduced from 113 to thirty-six.
27 Mar. 1975	Minister of Defence P.W. Botha, presents a White Paper outlining defence policy and justifying the increased expenditure which now accounts for one-fifth of the country's revenue budget.
7 Apr. 1975	The Prime Minister announces that a pilot plant for the manufacture of enriched uranium has gone into production. The overall production cost is expected to be between 25% and 35% lower than that of enrichment methods in other countries.
8 Apr. 1975	The government registers a strong protest after a South African Airways plane is hit by bullets as it lands in Luanda, Angola. Until an investigation is completed, SAA will not use Luanda as a stopover.
9 Apr. 1975	President Fouché ends his seven-year term of office.

10 Apr. 1975	Chief Kaiser Matanzima announces that the government has agreed to assist the Transkei in setting up its own army. Training of recruits will begin within a few months.
12 Apr. 1975	Atlas Corporation completes deliveries to the South African Air Force (SAAF) of a first series of Impala MK-2 jet fighters.
14 Apr. 1975	Despite opposition, the Coloured Persons' Representative Council Amendment Bill is approved.
19 Apr. 1975	Dr. Nicholaas Diederichs, former Finance Minister, is inaugurated as South Africa's third State President.
20 Apr. 1975	The names of the nominated members of the Coloured Persons Representative Council are announced. They include four Labour Party members, giving that party a total of thirty-five of the Council's sixty seats. It is accepted that Sonny Leon will be Chairman of the Council's Executive Committee.
24 Apr. 1975	Under an amendment to the Defence Act the definition of superior officer is changed with the effect that white and black members of the Defence Force will have equal status.
25 Apr. 1975	The Foreign Minister announces that South Africa will begin recruiting blacks for its diplomatic service in the near future.
30 Apr. 1975	The World Meteorological Organization (WMO) decides at its seventh Congress in Geneva to suspend South Africa from membership until it renounces racial discrimination.
1 May 1975	The Minister of Bantu Administration and Development announces that the government has decided on far-reaching concessions for urban Africans involving home ownership and trading rights.
6 May 1975	The government announces that its aim is to provide all black children with free and compulsory education as soon as possible.
7 May 1975	Prime Minister Vorster emphasizes the need for continuing his policy of increasing détente in Southern Africa.
8 May 1975	Former advocate Bram Fischer, sentenced to life imprisonment for communist activities, dies in Bloemfontein.
14 May 1975	Prime Minister Vorster gives the first official confirmation of his two-day meeting with President Houphouet-Boigny in the Ivory Coast on 22-23 September 1974. Discussions focussed on the improvement of relations between African states.
18 May 1975	It is disclosed that John Vorster has invited the Presidents of the Ivory Coast and Liberia to visit South Africa.
20 May 1975	The Foreign Minister, Dr. Muller, confirms that the government will continue to co-operate with Rhodesia, whatever solution is found to the political problems there and that South Africa will not apply economic sanctions.

28 May 1975	In its report submitted to Parliament, the Le Grange (formerly Schlebusch) Commission, declares that certain activities of the Christian Institute of Southern Africa are a danger to the State. The Commission's findings are rejected by the Institute, by other South African churchmen and by the South African Council of Churches (SACC).
30 May 1975	The Minister of Justice announces that the Christian Institute has been declared an affected organization under the Affected Organization's Act of 1974.
June-Sept. 1975	People arrested include lecturers at the Universities of Cape Town and Natal, leaders of NUSAS, an assistant to Dr. Beyers Naudé and the Afrikaans author Breyten Breytenbach. Most are detained under the Terrorism Act.
2 June 1975	Under an amendment to the Suppression of Communism Act, approved without objection, it ceases to be automatically an offence to quote banned persons after their restriction order has been withdrawn, or has lapsed.
5 June 1975	The Cape Supreme Court, sitting in Port Elizabeth, sets aside the 1973 election of Lennox Sebe and three other members of the Ciskei Legislative Assembly on the grounds of irregularities at the capital, Zwelitsha. Lennox Sebe is accordingly ineligible for the office of Chief Minister.
6 June 1975	A proclamation is published in the Government Gazette providing for the detention of offenders for up to three years in rehabilitation centres to be set up in the `homelands'. The regulations are strongly attacked in the English press and controversy continues into July 1975.
9 June 1975	The final report of the Le Grange Commission, dealing with the University Christian Movement (UCM), defunct since 1972, is submitted to Parliament. The Commission finds that the UCM, as a multi-racial body, has engaged in dangerous activities aimed at propagating violent resolution.
12 June 1975	The Minister of Indian Affairs announces that South African Indians will be free to move from one province to another without prior permission, with the exception of the Orange Free State.
13 June 1975	Robert Sobukwe, former leader of the banned Pan-Africanist Congress (PAC), although still under a banning order, is admitted to practice as an attorney in Kimberley.
16 June 1975	The British Foreign and Commonwealth Secretary, James Callaghan, announces in the House of Commons that the Simonstown Agreement with South Africa has been terminated. There will be no further joint excercises between the Royal and South African navies. The facilities will remain available to countries of the free world wishing to co-operate in the defence of the Cape Sea Route.
16 June 1975	The Minister of Economic Affairs, J.C. Heunis, announces that the government has agreed to increase the education and industrial training of Africans in white areas.
17 June 1975	The British Minister of State for Defence says that the ending of the Simonstown Agreements means an end to all the military co-operation between Britain and South Africa associated with them. In South Africa

	P.W. Botha sees the ending of the agreements as a challenge and the government will continue to improve and develop Simonstown's facilities.
19 June 1975	Lennox Sebe is appointed general and economic adviser to the Ciskei Cabinet.
19 June 1975	Signs multilateral treaty on the civil liability for oil pollution damage.
6 July 1975	It is reported that Israel and South Africa are increasing their cooperation and contacts in the military sphere, and negotiating joint economic ventures, including the construction of a major new railway in Israel, and the building of a desalination plant in South Africa.
23 July 1975	The South African Council of Churches (SACC) warns the government that unless the country's racial policies are reversed it will not be possible to achieve peace.
23 July 1975	Signs multilateral treaty with GATT on the extension of the provisional accession of Colombia.
25 July 1975	Congresses of both the Progressive and the Reform parties, held simultaneously in Johannesburg, unanimously approve the merger of the two parties under the name of South African Progressive Reform Party (PRP). The new party's leader is Colin Eglin. It has eleven seats in the 171-member House of Assembly.
1 Aug. 1975	An order has been issued withdrawing the remaining South African Police from Rhodesia.
6 Aug. 1975	In a by-election in Caledon, Cape Province, the National Party makes substantial gains at the expense of the United Party.
8 Aug. 1975	Signs single treaty on narcotic drugs, 1961, as amended by the Protocol of 25 March 1972.
9 Aug. 1975	France's President Giscard d'Estaing, announces that the French government has decided to supply no further continental (ground or air) armaments to South Africa. This political decision does not affect naval armaments or existing contracts.
11 Aug. 1975	Decisions on the future constitution of the Transkei are agreed upon at a meeting of a Cabinet committee of the South African and Transkei governments, presided over by John Vorster in Pretoria.
12 Aug. 1975	A statement issued simultaneously is Lusaka and Salisbury, gives details of proposals agreed to after two days of talks between John Vorster and Ian Smith, which could lead to a settlement of the Rhodesian constitutional problem.
13-18 Aug. 1975	During a visit to Paraguay by the Prime Minister, and the Minister of Foreign Affairs, four agreements on South African aid to Paraguay are signed in Asuncion.
19-29 Aug. 1975	A number of new arrests are made under the Terrorism Act.

22 Aug. 1975	Prime Minister Vorster officially opens the Orange-Fish River Tunnel, believed to be the world's longest continuous tunnel (c.50 miles), constructed at a cost of 76,400,000 Pounds Sterling.
22 Aug. 1975	Signs treaty with Swaziland on the establishment of an office for the Swaziland government labour representative in South Africa.
11-20 Sept. 1975	At the invitation of Dr. Connie Mulder, the Ivory Coast's Minister of Information, M.L. Dona-Fologo, visits South Africa on a fact finding tour. It is described as the first visit to South Africa by a West African minister.
12 Sept. 1975	The Coloured Persons Representative Council (CRC) adjourns without passing its budget and urges the government to meet its demands for Parliamentary representation and full rights as citizens.
12 Sept. 1975	Signs commercial agreement with Greece on air services.
16 Sept. 1975	South Africa fails to return for the 30th Session of the United Nations General Assembly in New York. Its relations with the United Nations are said to be under review.
19 Sept. 1975	While officially opening the Biennial Congress of the Coordinating Council of South African Trade Unions in Pretoria, the Minister of Labour announces government plans to establish black industrial committees which will have direct bargaining powers with employers.
26 Sept. 1975	The Organization of African Trade Union Unity (OATUU) condemns the South African government's plan for black works councils.
30 Sept. 1975	Winnie Mandela is released from her banning order and house arrest.
2 Oct. 1975	Chief Kaiser Matanzima announces in Umtata that the Transkei will become fully independent on 26 October 1976.
5 Oct. 1975	Winnie Mandela ends thirteen years of enforced silence with a strong attack on the country's Terrorism Act.
20 Oct. 1975	The Prime Minister holds discussions on constitutional developments with the chairman and other members of the Coloured Persons' Representative Council, and makes various proposals. These are rejected and an immediate referendum among white voters on the issue of full citizen rights for Coloured people is called for.
27 Oct. 1975	Signs an amendment to a customs union agreement of 11 September 1969 with Botswana, Lesotho and Swaziland.
4 Nov. 1975	Lennox Sebe again becomes Chief Minister of the Ciskei, having won a by-election on 24 October 1975.
11 Nov. 1975	State President, Dr. N. Diederichs, summarily dismisses Sonny Leon as Executive Chairman of the Coloured people's Representative Council (CPRC), following his refusal to sign a government-approved budget for the Coloured community and his total rejection of apartheid and its laws.
12 Nov. 1975	Four other members of the Coloured Persons' Representative Council resign.

This is seen as the first step in the destruction of the CPRC.

18 Nov. 1975   Signs multilateral treaty on the extension of the International Sugar Agreement, 1973.

19 Nov. 1975   Chief Lucas Mangope of the Bophuthatswana homeland, receives a mandate from his Democratic Party to begin negotiations for the independence of that territory.

20 Nov. 1975   The Bophuthatswana Legislative Assembly concludes a two-day Special Session during which it formally votes to open negotiations with South Africa for independence.

23 Nov. 1975   A newly formed extreme right-wing organization, the Afrikaner Resistance Movement, is being investigated by the authorities.

26 Nov. 1975   The Afrikaans writer Breyten Breytenbach is sentenced in the Pretoria Supreme Court to nine years imprisonment for offences under the Terrorism Act. He has pleaded guilty to entering South Africa to start an organization, Atlas or Okhela, intended to be the white wing of the ANC.

27 Nov. 1975   At a meeting in Durban, between S. Leon and several Indian and African leaders, a call is made for the formation of an alliance of black and brown people. It receives some support but is opposed by the Federal Party.

12 Dec. 1975   The Christian Institute appeals to the Prime Minister, John Vorster, asking him to reconsider the withdrawal or confiscation of the passport of six of their leaders, including that of Dr. Beyers Naude.

15 Dec. 1975   Signs a visa agreement with Uruguay.

16 Dec. 1975   The United Nations General Assembly approves a series of resolutions demanding sanctions against South Africa.

18 Dec. 1975   Signs multilateral customs agreement on the temporary importation of pedagogic material.

18 Dec. 1975   Signs multilateral treaty on customs - the ATA Carnet for the temporary admission of goods with annex.

5 Jan. 1976   A full-scale television service is officially opened by the Prime Minister. He issues a warning against slanted news and unbalanced presentations.

22 Jan. 1976   A government reshuffle, including the appointment of three new ministers and two new deputy ministers is announced on the eve of the opening of the 1976 Parliamentary session. The most significant change is the appointment of Dr. Andries Treurnicht, the conservative former chairman of the Afrikaner Broederbond, as Deputy Minister of Bantu Administration and Bantu Education.

27 Jan. 1976   Signs treaty with Uruguay on the exchange of postal parcels.

30 Jan. 1976   A Parliamentary Internal Security Bill provides for the establishment of a Commission of ten members of Parliament, to investigate internal security matters, in secret, referred to it by the State President and drastic penalties

will be imposed on those refusing to testify before it. Its reports will have to be submitted to Parliament, although all or part of them can be kept secret, if it is 'not in the public interest' to disclose their contents. It is strongly opposed by the Progressive Reform Party and the Herstigte Nasionale Party. The United Party refuses to sit on the Commission.

2 Feb. 1976	Signs second additional treaty to the constitution of the Universal Postal Union of 10 July 1964.

5 Feb. 1976 — The Defence Amendment Bill, making provision for the employment of South African conscripted troops anywhere outside South Africa, is approved. The Defence Force may now, at all times, be deployed to prevent or suppress any armed conflict outside the Republic which is, or may be, a threat to the Republic.

7 Feb. 1976 — The Minister of Justice announces that apartheid laws will be done away with in sixteen hotels, allowing them to cater for all races. International status will be granted as from 16 February 1976.

12 Feb. 1976 — The report of the Snyman Commission into the disturbances on the campus of the University of the North at Turfloop, finds that the South African Students Organization (SASO) was responsible for the unrest at Turfloop and other black campuses, and was aimed at overthrowing the political system in South Africa.

4 Mar. 1976 — In the House of Assembly, the Prime Minister criticizes Mozambique's action of closing its border with Rhodesia. He warns of the dangers inherent in the situation and of the aggravting factor presented by the Russian and Cuban involvements in Southern Africa.

12 Mar. 1976 — It is announced that all South African troops have been withdrawn from Angola except those guarding the Cunene River hydro-electric projects.

14 Mar. 1976 — Chief Gatsha Buthelezi makes a major policy statement in Soweto, before an audience of 10,000 people, denouncing the government's homelands policy and indicating that the country must move towards majority rule. He calls for a series of black national conventions to discuss foreign investments, homelands independence and foreign policy, particularly détente with black Africa.

20 Mar. 1976 — The Roman Catholic Church decides in principle to open its 192 all-white schools to black pupils. Legal questions relating to this will be discussed with the government.

22-24 Mar.1976 — The Minister of Information and the Interior, Dr. Connie Mulder, pays a three-day official visit to the Ivory Coast. Talks are held on Communist penetration in Africa.

27 Mar. 1976 — Remaining troops are withdrawn from the Angolan border after the MPLA government has undertaken through Soviet and British good offices, and the mediation of the United Nations Secretary-General to respect the border, and assure the safety of the project and their personnel.

29 Mar. 1976 — Opposition amendments to the Parliamentary Internal Security Commission Bill are defeated in the House of Assembly, where it is given its third

reading. The Prime Minister declares that the government believes Parliament, and not the courts, should combat subversion.

31 Mar. 1976   In the 1976-77 budget, defence expenditure is raised to R1,350 m, or 17.2 percent of the total expenditure.

5 Apr. 1976   Signs multilateral treaty modifying and further extending the Wheat Trade Convention, 1971.

9-12 Apr. 1976   Prime Minister Vorster, accompanied by his Foreign Minister Dr. Muller, visits Israel. A joint Ministerial Committee will meet at least once a year to review economic relations and to discuss, inter alia, scientific and industrial cooperation.

23 Apr. 1976   A draft constitution for the Transkei is published in Umtata.

27 Apr. 1976   South Africa's diplomatic representation in Taiwan has been raised from Consultate-General to full ambassadorial level.

2 May 1976   Signs treaty with Israel amending the extradition treaty.

3 May 1976   The Parliamentary Internal Security Commission Bill, providing for the establishment of a commission of members of the House of Assembly to investigate internal security matters, is approved in the Senate, and enacted shortly afterwards.

5 May 1976   In the Parliamentary by-election in Durban North, the Progresive Reform Party's candidate gains the party's first seat in Natal, bringing the PRP's representation in the House of Assembly to twelve. The United Party suffers a serious defeat.

29 May 1976   The South African Electricity Supply Commission (ESCOM) announces in Pretoria that it has decided to order two nuclear power stations from France.

10 June 1976   The Internal Security Bill is enacted. Originally published on 4 May 1976, as the Promotion of State Security Bill, it is designed to amend and widen the scope of the 1950 Suppression of Communism Act. It is strongly condemned by the opposition and by the legal profession.

16 June 1976   Demonstrations by secondary school pupils, protesting against the compulsory use of the Afrikaans language as a medium of instruction, escalate into an outbreak of violence in Soweto, during which police open fire on the protesters. Casualties occur, the first being Hector Petersen. Rioting, arson, looting and lawlessness spread.

16-24 June 1976   During these days, rioting, arson, destruction and protest spread to other localities and townships, mainly in the Transvaal, but reaching Natal as well as several black `homelands'.

17 June 1976   Parliament meets in an Extraordinary Session at the request of the leader of the Opposition, Colin Eglin. The resignation of the Minister of Bantu Affairs is called for, and that of his conservative Deputy, Andries Treurnicht.

17 June 1976   The Minister of Justice and Police, J.T. Kruger, announces his decision to

appoint a one-man judicial commission in the person of Justice P.M. Cillié, Judge-President of the Transvaal, to investigate the disturbances in Soweto.

17 June 1976   The Status of the Transkei Bill passes its second reading in the Senate, despite opposition from the United Party and the Progressive Reform Party.

18 June 1976   The report of the Commission, under the chairmanship of Professor Erika Theron, to investigate matters relating to the Coloured community in South Africa, is submitted to the House of Assembly. The Commission makes 178 recommendations, approved by majority vote, the most important of which the government subsequently rejects, i.e. that political rights be restored to Coloured people in Parliament.

18 June 1976   The United Nations Security Council is called into session at the urgent request of the African states. It issues a unanimous condemnation of South Africa for resorting to massive violence against demonstrators opposing racial discrimination.

23-24 June 1976   Prime Minister Vorster holds talks with the United States Secretary of State, Dr. Kissinger, in West Germany.

25 June 1976   Acting Prime Minister P.W. Botha, says in the House of Assembly that the government has no objection to 158 of the 178 recommendations in the Theron Report, but that there is no prospect of a qualified franchise, a return to the common voters' roll or direct representation of Coloureds in Parliament. Nor will the Prohibition of Mixed Marriages Act be repealed.

25 June 1976   The death toll in the riots is officially given as 174 blacks and two whites, the number of wounded 1,222 blacks and six whites, the number of persons arrested 1,298. Property damaged or destroyed is officially listed as sixty-seven state owned beer halls and bottle stores, fifty-three administration buildings, thirteen schools, eight state hostels, 154 vehicles, as well as banks, clinics, bus sheds, hostels and factories - public buildings and amenities built up over the previous twenty-five years.

27 June 1976   The National President of the Black People's Convention declares that riots have ushered in a new era of political consciousness.

6 July 1976   The government announces that teaching in Afrikaans in black schools will no longer be compulsory.

15 July 1976   The Minister of Justice, J.T. Kruger, announces that the provisions of the Internal Security Act, allowing for the unlimited detention without trial of persons deemed to be threatening public order, will apply in the Transvaal Province with immediate effect for one year. All public gatherings are banned and schools in Soweto and other riot areas will remain closed.

20 July-19   In more than seventy townships, a further series of disturbances occur,
Aug. 1976   leading to considerable destruction of property and loss of life. These riots are apparently now organized by militant youths, demanding change and liberation.

21 July 1976   The closure of schools in black townships is rescinded by the Minister for Police, Justice and Prisons.

30 July 1976	The Opposition press strongly attacks the detention of four journalists under the Terrorism Act.
Aug. 1976	The police begin arresting black leaders, not only members of the Black People's Convention (BPC) and the South African Students' Organization (SASO), but also members of the Soweto Black Parents' Organization.
Aug.-Sept. 1976	The government's policies are repeatedly and strongly criticized by prominent churchmen.
2 Aug. 1976	French officials disclose that France is to supply South Africa with two destroyer escorts.
4 Aug. 1976	Riots erupt again in Soweto and spread to other townships in South Africa. The Minister of Justice again bans public meetings under the Riotous Assemblies Act, until the end of August.
7-8 Aug. 1976	A new deal for urban blacks is announced in Pretoria by the Minister of Bantu Administration and by the Minister of Justice and Police.
9 Aug. 1976	The Theron Commission Report is discussed at a meeting between the Prime Minister and the sixteen-member Liaison Committee of the Coloured Persons' Representative Council (CPRC).
9 Aug. 1976	Violence again erupts in the black townships. The Prime Minister says he does not regard the present combination of external and internal pressures on South Africa as critical.
10 Aug. 1976	The government extends its powers under the Internal Security Act from the Transvaal only to the whole of South Africa.
11-12 Aug. 1976	Violence spreads to Cape Town,to the black townships of Langa, Nyanga and Guguletu and then, for the first time, to Coloured townships.
13 Aug. 1976	The government fully supports the United States initiative for a peaceful settlement of the Rhodesian crisis.
Mid Aug. 1976	Widespread arrests of black leaders and dissidents, office-bearers, priests, teachers and doctors follow a speech to the National Party Congress in Durban by Justice Minister Kruger, in which he claims that black power will have to be destroyed if race riots are not to become endemic. All the main black opposition groups are affected.
16-20 Aug. 1976	At the 5th Conference of Non-Aligned Nations in Colombo, Sri Lanka, a resolution is adopted calling for an oil embargo on France and Israel because of their arms sales to South Africa.
20 Aug. 1976	At a Nordic Council meeting in Copenhagen, the Foreign Ministers of Denmark, Finland, Iceland, Norway and Sweden recommend an international weapons embargo against South Africa.
20 Aug. 1976	Sends notification of approval of recommendations relating to the objectives of the Antarctic treaty of 1 December 1959.
21 Aug. 1976	The leaders of seven of the country's nine black homelands i.e. all except

Chiefs Matanzima (Transkei) and Mangope (Bophuthatswana) meet in Johannesburg to review the political situation and issue a joint statement of appeals, demands and recommendations.

23-25 Aug. 1976

A three-day strike is observed in Soweto by between 150,000 and 200,000 workers.

24-27 Aug. 1976

Violent ethnic clashes between Zulus and others, involving circa 10,000 blacks in running fights cause chaos in Soweto which the police appear unable to control. Police collusion is alleged.

29 Aug. 1976

Speaking at a ceremony to mark his tenth anniversary as Prime Minister, John Vorster admits that the country has problems, internationally and economically, but claims that these do not constitute a crisis. His remarks are strongly criticized by the opposition.

Sept. 1976

Government ministers repeatedly declare that there is no crisis, and that whatever concessions may be made to meet the demands of the blacks, the policy of separate development will be continued.

Sept. 1976

Unrest, disturbances and riots spread to Cape Town itself, with interaction with the police on 1, 2 and 7-8, 10-13 September. Sporadic outbreaks of violence continue to occur in Soweto and in central Johannesburg.

2 Sept. 1976

The ban on public gatherings throughout the country is reimposed until 31 October 1976.

3-6 Sept. 1976

Prime Minister Vorster flies to Zurich for talks with the United States Secretary of State, Dr. Henry Kissinger. The focus is on the conditions necessary for negotiations on independence for Namibia and for majority rule in Rhodesia.

10 Sept. 1976

The President of the Senate, Marais Viljoen, opening the 1976 Session of the Coloured Persons' Representative Council announces a number of government decisions aimed at removing obsolete practices and usages causing dissatisfaction among Coloured people.

13 Sept. 1976

The Cillié Commission of Inquiry into the riots in Soweto on 16 June 1976 holds its first public hearing in Johannesburg. Evidence is taken on the extent of the damage and of casualties.

13 Sept. 1976

Speaking to the Transvaal Congress of the ruling National Party in Pretoria, the Prime Minister again rejects major changes in the country's race policies.

13-15 Sept. 1976

A second strike call in Soweto leads to absenteeism estimated at 75-80 per cent in Johannesburg.

14 Sept. 1976

Security Police continue to arrest prominent members of the Coloured community. Several black journalists who covered the Soweto riots are also detained.

15-16 Sept. 1976

Some 200,000 Coloured workers stay away from work in the Cape Town area. The extent of the strike is unexpected and unprecedented.

17 Sept. 1976

A total of sixty-five documents concerning the establishment of an independent Transkei are signed in Pretoria by the Prime Minister and Chief Kaiser Matanzima. Among them is a non-aggression pact, designed to come into force at independence on 26 October 1976.

17 Sept. 1976   The United States Secretary of State, Dr. Kissinger, visits South Africa and holds discussions with political leaders, both white and black. Demonstrations against his visit are held in Soweto.

20 Sept. 1976   A seven-man delegation of Coloured leaders flies from Cape Town to Pretoria to meet the Prime Minister for discussions on the future of the Coloured community. They appeal to John Vorster for the immediate release of the Chairman of the Coloured Labour Party, the Rev. Allan Hendrickse, unsuccessfully.

23 Sept. 1976   Renewed rioting breaks out in Johannesburg. The Minister of Information, Dr. Connie Mulder, warns of tougher measures, including the use of the army, to deal with the unrest. Four more black journalists are detained, bringing the total number of journalists held to thirteen, eleven of whom are black.

24 Sept. 1976   A crucial meeting of the Coloured Cabinet Council is boycotted by the Labour Party.

29 Sept. 1976   In the Cape Town Supreme Court a British journalist, David Rabkin, his wife and a university lecturer, Jeremy Cronin, are sentenced to ten, one, and seven years' imprisonment respectively for offences under the Terrorism and Internal Security Acts to which they have pleaded guilty. They have advocated violence leading to insurrection. Since Mrs. Rabkin was expecting a baby, the court suspended eleven months of her twelve-month sentence and she returns to Britain with her new born daughter in October.

29 Sept. 1976   General elections are held in the Transkei.

29 Sept. 1976   Voters go to the polls in the Transkei's pre-independence elections. The results are a foregone conclusion following the Transkei government's detention of eight leading opposition Democratic Party officers in July and August.

1 Oct. 1976   France confirms that it is selling two new combat submarines to South Africa, to help it protect the oil route round the Cape in the face of the Soviet naval escalation in the Indian Ocean.

5 Oct. 1976   The elected leaders in the Coloured Persons' Representative Council reject the government's emergency mini-budget and demand the summoning of an all-race National Convention to consider the country's future.

8 Oct. 1976   At a seven-hour meeting with eight of the black `homeland' leaders (i.e. all except Chief Matanzima, Transkei) Prime Minister Vorster declares there is no merit at all in the idea of holding a round table conference to plan a new constitution.

8 Oct. 1976   A meeting is held between John Vorster and eight `homeland' leaders to discuss the unrest which has left at least three-hundred-and-forty dead, around two-thousand injured and hundreds under arrest. He rejects their demands for a multi-racial   constitution and the release   of black leaders   in   detention. This failure   precipitates a   move towards a common   political   front between traditional   leaders   and   radical   black   students   to   fight for

freedom.

| 15 Oct. 1976 | The results of the Transkei general elections are announced. The ruling Transkei National Independence Party (TNIP) win sixty-nine of the seventy-five election seats in the new National Assembly. |

17 Oct. 1976   The township of Soweto flares into violence again. An estimated 75,000 Pounds Sterling damage is caused. Incidents are also reported from Cape Town, Pretoria and Krugersdorp.

21 Oct. 1976   The Minister of Justice J. Kruger says that 697 people are being held for security reasons: 123 under the Internal Security Act; 217 under the Terrorism Act; thirty-four are jailed for their protection as witnesses; 323 are held for cases pending in relation to public security.

22 Oct. 1976   Teachers and pupils are arrested at the Morris Isaacson High School in Soweto.

24 Oct. 1976   Further trouble erupts at a funeral in Soweto when a crowd of 4,000 attacks police. Retaliatory fire causes deaths and injuries.

24 Oct. 1976   The authorities release the leader of the Coloured Labour Party, the Rev. Allan Hendrickse after holding him in prison for two months.

25-26 Oct. 1976   Transkei is declared an independent state at midnight. South Africa formally divests itself of all sovereignty over Transkei. The new flag is raised and a 101 gun salute ushers in the new `state'.

26 October 1976   At its opening session the Transkei National Assembly elects Paramount Chief B.J. Sigcau as the Transkei's first President.

Nov. 1976   Splits appear within the National Party between the `verligte' (enlightened) academics, businessmen and MPs and the `verkrampte' (conservatives) led by Dr. Andries Treurnicht.

1 Nov. 1976   A five-day strike called by militant students in the Soweto Students' Representative Council (SSRC) meets with only limited response.

8 Nov. 1976   Signs multilateral treaty, extending the International Sugar Agreement, 1973.

11 Nov. 1976   The United Nations General Assembly adopts nine resolutions against apartheid at the end of a two-and-a-half week debate on the South African question.

16 Nov. 1976   President Pérez of Venezuela announces in New York that he has ordered the severance of commercial relations with South Africa.

17 Nov. 1976   Leaders of the three opposition parties meet in an attempt to form a united opposition front. Fundamental principles are laid down by Colin Eglin, leader of the Progressive Reform Party (PRP). Chairman of the Steering Committee, former Transvaal Judge, K. Marais, presents a detailed draft constitution based on a federal structure.

18 Nov. 1976   The Cillié Commission into recent riots is given a detailed account of the

loss of life and damage to property in the Greater Cape Town area.

19 Nov. 1976	Fourteen officials representing non-registered multiracial trade unions are reported to have been served with banning orders. Two main bodies are targeted: the Johannesburg based Urban Training Programme (UTP) and the unions and service organizations affiliated to the Trade Union Advisory and Co-ordinating Council (TUACC) with a membership of more than 60,000.
23 Nov. 1976	Eight more banning orders are served, mostly on white students connected with black labour organizations.
24 Nov. 1976	School pupils and students from Soweto who have fled to Botswana, Swaziland and Lesotho to escape continuous Security Police searches for ringleaders of unrest, have rejected the government's amnesty offer which expired on 22 November 1976. An estimated 700 have fled since June, more than 500 of them to Botswana, whose government has requested international assistance in the matter.
27 Nov. 1976	The arrest of five people, detained under the Terrorism Act, coincides with the Security Police search of the Johannesburg headquarters of the Christian Institute and the South African Council of Churches.
End Nov. 1976	The inaugural conference of the Black Unity Front is held in Johannesburg. Formed after the abortive meeting between John Vorster and 'homeland' leaders on 8 October 1976, its aim is to group middle-class blacks into a moderate anti-apartheid system guided by a steering committee of urban blacks.
Dec. 1976	Both the United Party and the Progressive Reform Party formally approve the Marais Committee's proposals as a basis for a constitution.
Dec. 1976	Serious fighting and rioting break out in the Cape Town townships of Guguletu, Nyanga and Langa, peak periods being the first week and Christmas weekend. Youths and migrant workers clash; deaths, destruction and arrests follow.
2 Dec. 1976	At the end of an eight-month trial a University lecturer, Eddie Webster and four white students are acquitted of all charges against them under the Suppression of Communism and Unlawful Organizations Act.
15 Dec. 1976	The South African Institute of Race Relations reports that 433 people are known to be still in custody. According to their sources, these comprise fifty-six school children, seventy-two university students, twenty-six student leaders and office-bearers of the South African Students' Organization and related organizations, twenty-five members of other Black Consciousness organizations, sixteen churchmen, thirty-five teachers and lecturers, fifteen journalists, sixty state witnesses, six trade unionists, thirteen former political prisoners, one member of the Coloured Labour Party and eighty-one who have no known connection with political organizations. Of this total, 102 were in preventative detention, with no charges pending. In addition, according to the SAIRR, 144 people are under banning orders, restricting their movements and prohibiting them from attending gatherings.
16 Dec. 1976	Calls for judicial inquiries into the death of detainees in police custody are made by the South African Institute of Race Relations, backed by Colin

Eglin, leader of the Progressive Reform Party (PRP) and by Sonny Leon, leader of the Coloured community, who addresses his request to the International Commission of Jurists in Geneva.

17 Dec. 1976   The government confirms that guerrillas are being trained for operations in South Africa from bases in Botswana and Mozambique. Minister of Justice Kruger names three South African exiles in London as the men behind the campaign: Joe Slovo, Moses Kotane and Ronnie Kasrils.

20 Dec. 1976   Signs multilateral treaty on the international regulations for the prevention of collisions at sea, 1972.

21 Dec. 1976   The lengthy trial ends of nine black nationalist student leaders, first detained by Security Police in October 1974, following a pro-FRELIMO Durban rally. They are found guilty under the Terrorism Act and sentenced to periods of imprisonment, three for six years and six for five years.

29 Dec. 1976   The Minister of Bantu Education announces moves towards the introduction of free and compulsory education for blacks. This is the fifth concession to black demands since the Soweto riots of 16 June 1976. It has also reversed the Afrikaans ruling in schools, suspended the `homeland citizenship' requirement for blacks leasing houses in townships, introduced a home ownership scheme and agrees in principle to give increased powers to Bantu Councils in black areas.

29 Dec. 1976   Police announce the release of the last of the 113 detainees held under Section 10 (preventive detention) of the Internal Security Act. Restriction orders are placed on six of those released, including Winnie Mandela.

31 Dec. 1976   In his New Year's Eve address the Prime Minister warns the country that South Africa will have to face the Communist onslaught in Southern Africa alone.

31 Dec. 1976   An official of the Department of Justice claims that all detainees held in preventive detention under the Internal Security Act have been released.

31 Dec. 1976   The prohibition of public gatherings (under the Riotous Assemblies Act) is extended to 31 March 1977, and thereafter to 30 September 1977.

1 Jan. 1977   Four senior members of the Soweto Students' Representative Council (SSRC) are arrested.

10-12 Jan. 1977   Prime Minister Vorster pays a three-day goodwill visit to Transkei. Tributes are paid to him for his assistance in helping Transkei gain independence in a peaceful manner.

19 Jan. 1977   Six members of the thirty-six member United Party Parliamentary caucus are expelled from the Party for refusing to abide by the Party's decision to accept the Marais programme for the formation of a new united opposition party. They decide to establish themselves as a `centrist' Independent United Party.

21 Jan. 1977   At the opening of Parliament the State President states that it has become necessary for South Africa to maintain an increased military capability on the northern border of Namibia to prevent terrorist incursions and to protect the

local inhabitants. This is being done at the explicit request of the governments of Ovamboland, Kavango and Caprivi.

24 Jan. 1977

Introducing a motion of no-confidence in the government, the leader of the United Party (UP) Sir de Villiers Graaff delineates the multiple dimensions of the crisis facing South Africa - in economics, race relations and international affairs. He argues that it is time to destroy apartheid before it destroys South Africa.

25 Jan. 1977

A group of clergymen of seven Christian churches - including the Roman Catholic, Anglican and Methodist churches - calling themselves 'Ministers Fraternal' publish a report blaming the riot police for their role in the violence in the Cape Town townships at Christmas 1976. Their report is banned.

25 Jan. 1977

The Minister of Justice and Police, J. Kruger claims the internal unrest and riots are not the result of the government's apartheid policies but are instigated by Communists and the ANC.

25 Jan. 1977

Under an Indemnity Bill, retroactive to 16 June 1976, police and other members of security forces acting in good faith to prevent disorder, maintain public safety or preserve life and property, will be immune from civil or criminal prosecution. It is passed with the support of the opposition, on 1 February 1977.

25 Jan. 1977

Under the Civil Protection Bill, introduced on this date, the Minister of Defence is given power to declare a State of Emergency for three months in the event of natural disasters, or internal disorders and civil disruption.

27 Jan. 1977

Police in Cape Town arrest thirty two members of the Comrades Movement, a student organization arising from the unrest in the townships in 1976. They face several charges of arson.

28 Jan. 1977

Prime Minister Vorster denies the possibility of South Africa pressuring the Rhodesian government into accepting a dictated solution. Demands to shut South Africa's borders and impose boycotts will not be acceded to.

5 Feb. 1977

The government, for the first time, releases the official list of all detained under the Preventive Detention clause of the Internal Security Act since its introduction on 11 August 1976. The total number of detainees is given as 135.

9 Feb. 1977

The Prime Ministers of South Africa and Rhodesia meet in Cape Town for talks on the Rhodesian problem and the possibilities for settlement.

9 Feb. 1977

Signs a multilateral trade procés verbal extending the declaration on the provisional accession of Colombia to GATT.

10 Feb. 1977

The Southern African Catholic Bishops' Conference decides to uphold the rights of conscientious objectors, expresses its perturbation over reports of police brutality and deaths in detention, calls for an investigation and protests against the provision of legal indemnity for the police. At the close of their conference, a twenty-one point action programme is issued for guidance in future stances to be taken.

11 Feb. 1977   In a 'Declaration of Commitment' the Bishops' Conference states it will promote black consciousness in solidarity with all those who work for the legitimate aspirations of oppressed people.

11 Feb. 1977   The appointment of South Africa's Ambassador to the United States, R.F. 'Pik' Botha, as the country's next Foreign Minister, is announced by the Prime Minister and welcomed by black delegates at the United Nations.

12 Feb. 1977   The Prime Minister of Lesotho, Leabua Jonathan, claims the whole of the Orange Free State, Matatiele in Natal, the Herschel district in the Transkei and the Southern Sotho homeland of Qwa Qwa for Lesotho - areas, he says, fraudulently taken from it during the Basotho wars.

13 Feb. 1977   'Kowie' Marais announces that it has not been possible for the opposition parties to arrive at an agreed interpretation of the 'fourteen principles' contained in his programme.

15 Feb. 1977   Between March 1976 and 15 February 1977, a total of eighteen black people have died while in police custody, the causes of death being officially described as suicide, accident or natural causes.

17 Feb. 1977   The Anglican church joins the growing confrontation between church and state, when the Archbishop of Cape Town, the Most Rev. William Barnett issues a statement condemning South African society as morally indefensible. He expresses particular concern over deaths in detention and the imprisonment and interrogation of people 'until they die'.

23 Feb. 1977   The Minister of Justice and the Police, Jimmy Kruger states that a full-scale judicial commission of inquiry into deaths in detention is not necessary since there is a full judicial enquiry into each separate death.

24-26 Feb. 1977   Justice spokesman for the opposition parties, Radclyffe Cadman for the United Party, and Helen Suzman for the Progressive Reform Party, reject Kruger's explanations and call for a full-scale judicial commission of enquiry.

2 Mar. 1977   The United Party suffers reverses in municipal elections in the Transvaal and fails to contest the Randburg seats because of internal dissension. It loses control of Johannesburg for the first time in thirty-one years. Of the forty-six seats in this key election, the National Party wins fifteen (a gain of five), the Progressive Reform Party nineteen (a gain of two) and the United Party eleven.

7 Mar. 1977   The Defence Amendment Bill, first published on 31 January 1977, becomes law. Under it the State President is empowered to invoke powers of censorship and of commandeering premises. Service in defence of the Republic now includes anti-terrorist operations as well as the prevention and suppression of internal disorder and there can be greater flexibility and speed in mobilization.

8 Mar. 1977   Chief Matanzima names various areas of South Africa that should be added to Transkei. The Ministry of Bantu Administration denies that any historical claim to the land exists. Any land still to be acquired by Transkei has already been scheduled in the 1976 agreement.

| 9 Mar. 1977 | Paramount Chief Sigcau of Transkei tells the Assembly that legislation is to be introduced making it a capital offence to criticize Transkeian sovereignty or office bearers of the state. It will be made retrospective to October 1975. |

10 Mar. 1977   In the Senate the United Party calls for the convening by the Prime Minister of a conference of all race groups to discuss a constitutional structure which would satisfy the legitimate political aspirations of all groups. John Vorster rejects this call, reiterating that the National Party did not, and never would support power-sharing between whites and blacks.

10 Mar. 1977   The Minister of Bantu Administration and Development, M.C. Botha, reports that following Transkei's land claims a thorough inquiry was made by the South African Archives into the documents and charts involving the land concerned. No claim to the land can be substantiated. The report has been made available to Chief Matanzima.

10 Mar. 1977   Under the Criminal Procedure Bill, opposed by both the United Party and the Progressive Reform Party, the judicial system is altered by the introduction of pre-trial interrogation by judicial officers.

19 Mar. 1977   In a joint declaration the leaders of the United Party, Sir de Villiers Graaff and the Democratic Party, Theo Gerdener, express their agreement to form a new party on the basis of equal rights for all racial groups in South Africa. No actual unification is immediately announced.

21 Mar. 1977   Steven Biko, former SASO leader, released on 30 November 1976 after temporary detention under security laws, is re-arrested.

30 Mar. 1977   During an emergency debate in Transkei's Parliament in Umtata, Chief Matanzima threatens to cut diplomatic links with South Africa and to launch an 'armed struggle' unless the land claim to East Griqualand is settled. The opposition leader, Cromwell Diko, hints at possible military assistance from the Soviet Union.

30 Mar. 1977   In the 1977-78 Budget introduced by the Minister of Finance, Senator Owen Horwood, the amount to be spent on defence is given as R1,654 m., twenty-two per cent more than in 1976-77 and constituting more than 18 per cent of the national budget. To raise money the Defence Force will launch a Defence Bond scheme.

31 Mar. 1977   A Defence White Paper analyzes South Africa's defence requirements in the context of the Soviet and Cuban intervention in Angola. South Africa is to be placed on a war footing.

1 Apr. 1977   'Pik' Botha becomes Minister of Foreign Affairs, in succession to Dr. Hilgard Muller who retires.

2 Apr. 1977   The South African Newspapers' Union issues its own press code for the daily handling of news.

2 Apr. 1977   Signs treaty with Botswana on the avoidance of double taxation and the prevention of fiscal evasion with respect to taxes on income.

15 Apr. 1977   Signs multilateral agreement on the total catch quota of hake in 1977.

25 April 1977	The Chief of Staff (Operations) says that the development of South Africa's defence has made the country completely self-sufficient from an arms point of view.
25 Apr. 1977	The government for the first time allows twenty local journalists, five correspondents of international news agencies and two official photographers to visit the prison on Robben Island, where 370 men convicted under security legislation are held. The material conditions are considered in general to be satisfactory, but the lack of contact with the outside world is very severe.
27 Apr. 1977	Police confront some 10,000 students demonstrating against rent increases in Soweto and violence ensues. The offices of the Urban Bantu Council in Soweto are attacked. The government later suspends rent increases for one month, pending investigation of alternative financing.
9 May 1977	A Second Defence Amendment Bill passes its final stages in the House of Assembly, with the support of the entire opposition. The existing twelve months' maximum national service will be increased to twenty-four months and the subsequent period of service increased to a maximum of 240 days.
11 May 1977	According to a report by the South African Institute of Race Relations, a total of 617 black persons, of whom it names 558, are known to have died by violence since June 1976 in the townships, including at least eighty five children and youths, of whom fifty three have been shot.
11 May 1977	In a by-election at Westdene, Johannesburg, 'Pik' Botha as National Party candidate defeats the Herstigte Nasionale Party by 9,126 votes to 652 - the biggest majority ever obtained in a Parliamentary election. The opposition United Party did not contest the seat.
12 May 1977	'Pik' Botha sees his election victory as a mandate to bring about internal change and to move away from discrimination.
16 May 1977	Winnie Mandela, placed under restriction in Soweto on 28 December 1976 is now banished to a black township outside Brandfort, Orange Free State. She is free to live in Swaziland, or Transkei, but elects to remain in South Africa.
17 May 1977	A committee of inquiry appointed by the Administrators of Natal and the Cape Province, declares that East Griqualand (claimed by Transkei) has never been a black tribal territory, but has for 115 years been an area of Griqua, coloured and white settlement. The area is subsequently transferred from the Cape Province to Natal with effect from 1 January 1978.
19-20 May 1977	The United States Vice President, Walter Mondale and the Prime Minister, John Vorster, meet in Vienna for two days of high level talks. Some measure of agreement is reached on the Namibia and Rhodesia situations, but on the central issue of the government's apartheid policies, vital differences in outlook remain.
21-22 May 1977	The United States Ambassador to the United Nations, Andrew Young, pays a two-day visit to South Africa at the invitation of Harry Oppenheimer. He meets Soweto student leaders, black and white community leaders, newspaper editors and addresses a business dinner. He maintains economic

pressure can bring about radical changes.

24 May 1977	Minister of National Education, Dr. Piet Koornhof, tells a conference in Cape Town that South Africa is moving in the direction of a confederal or 'canton' political system, and cultural pluralism. He is publicly supported by the Minister of Defence, P.W. Botha, chairman of the special committee on adaptations to the present Westminster-style of government.
24 May 1977	The leadership of the Herstigte Nasionale Party is relinquished by its veteran founder, Dr. Albert Hertzog. He is succeeded by the deputy leader, Jaap Marais.
27 May 1977	The Independent United Party decides to adopt the name of the South African Party (SAP).
27 May 1977	The Prime Minister rejects the idea of a 'canton' system saying it is certainly not practical politics at this stage.
28 May 1977	At its inaugural Congress in Pretoria, the South African Party commits itself to a federal or confederal solution to the country's political future, the maintenance of separate group identities under white leadership, and the rejection of power-sharing at every level.
28 May 1977	Differences about citizen and land become a major issue between the government and the Bophuthatswana 'homeland', due to become independent in December 1977.
June-Oct. 1977	Political unrest results in destruction of property by rioting demonstrators, in clashes with police and in hundreds of arrests. The authorities nevertheless reaffirm their ability to maintain law and order.
3 June 1977	The Explosives Amendment Bill is supported by all parties. It provides for a minimum sentence of three years' imprisonment without the option of a fine for threatening to explode any explosive device or knowingly to render false information in respect of a threatened explosion. During 1976 the police had had to investigate 149 bomb threats.
4 June 1977	A five year restriction order is served on Father S. Mkhatshwa, Secretary of the South African Catholic Bishops' Conference (SACBC), signed by the Minister of Justice.
11 June 1977	It is announced that Security Police have arrested the leader of the Soweto Students' Representative Council (SSRC), Dan S. Montsitsi in connection with plans to commemorate the Soweto uprisings. Four white students are also arrested in the same connection.
11 June 1977	Stellenbosch University announces that it is to open its doors to black, coloured and Asian students for all post-graduate degree courses and will also accept non-white undergraduates for courses not offered at their own universities.
15-16 June 1977	Sporadic outbreaks of violence occur on the anniversary of the Soweto, Sharpeville riots, but there are fewer incidents than were anticipated and the called for work stayaway is only partially successful.

16-19 June 1977	A four-day conference to examine racism, colonialism and apartheid in South Africa is held in Lisbon, Portugal, organized by an Afro-Arab solidarity group, the United Nations and the Helsinki-based World Peace Council. It is timed to coincide with the Sharpeville anniversary.
20 June 1977	Twelve Africans (eleven men and one woman) appear in court in Pretoria accused of setting up a transport route to smuggle recruits out of South Africa through Swaziland into Mozambique for military training and of using the same route to bring arms, ammunition and explosives back into the country. The charges also include creating secret cells for banned organizations and sabotage of a railway line in October 1976.
23 June 1977	The Chief Executive Officer of the Kangwane Territorial Authority, Chief M. Dhlamini, is removed from office following a vote of no-confidence after he refuses to sign a land consolidation proposal by Pretoria. In a Supreme Court action against the Minister of Bantu Administration and Development, it is found that Dhlamini has been wrongfully deposed and that the subsequent election of Enos J. Mabusa, and six others, is null and void.
23 June 1977	Violence erupts in Soweto again and at least 146 arrests are made by the police.
24 June 1977	The programme for a new white 'centrist' party is published by Sir de Villiers Graaff, leader of the United Party, Vause Raw, Chairman of the UP's steering committee and Theo Gerdener, leader of the Democratic Party. A confederal basis is recommended.
28 June 1977	The United Party, the official opposition since 1948, disbands itself. The decision to disband is opposed by a group of Parliamentarians, a senator and six members of the House of Assembly led by J.D. du P. (Japie) Basson, who intends to cooperate with the Progressive Reform Party to form a new opposition.
29 June 1977	A new opposition party, the New Republic Party (NRP) is formed at a special congress in Johannesburg, by a merger between the United Party and the Democratic Party.
30 June 1977	The Security Police detain J. Tugwana of the Rand Daily Mail, the fifth journalist to be held without trial since February 1977.
6 July 1977	The Coloured Labour Party strengthened its position by forging an alliance with six members of the Coloured Representative Council (CRC) founded on the rejection of apartheid. Unity talks are held and it is decided unequivocally to tell the government that the present political dispensation is unacceptable.
14 July 1977	The New Zealand government announces steps to discourage sporting contacts with South Africa.
23 July 1977	The co-founder of the recently formed New Republic Party, Theo Gerdener, announces that he is withdrawing his support from it.
25 July 1977	The trial ends in the Natal Supreme Court in Pietermaritzburg of five Africans - all of whom have previous convictions for subversive activities or sabotage - with sentences of life imprisonment. Four others are sentenced to

prison terms of from seven to eighteen years for various terrorist activities. Among the defendants, described by the Judge as dedicated revolutionaries, is Themba Harry Gwala.

26 July 1977 The 'Committee of 10' formed by prominent Soweto residents, issue a programme for the election of a new community board to have total autonomy in Soweto including powers to levy taxes and to control education, the police and local elections. The Minister of Justice rejects this and the government remains committed to community councils with limited powers, control being retained by the Bantu Administration Board.

27-31 July 1977 There is further unrest in the townships throughout the country including those of Alexandra (Northern Johannesburg), Atteridgeville and Saulsville (Pretoria) and in Soweto.

End July 1977 Two contentious pieces of legislation come into operation. The first, the Criminal Procedure Act, replacing an earlier Act of the same name, effectively replaces the British-style 'innocent until proved guilty' system with the continental inquisitorial system, but without the checks and balances European countries have developed. The second, the Lower Courts Amendment Act, vests considerable new powers in the country's regional courts, providing magistraters with the jurisdiction to hear terrorism and sabotage cases, greatly increasing the scope of the Terrorism Act.

Aug.-Sept. 1977 Long prison sentences are imposed in a number of trials for subversive activities.

3 Aug. 1977 Dr. Motlana, on behalf of the 'Committee of 10' repeats the call for non-ethnic elections for an autonomous Soweto city council.

10 Aug. 1977 About 100 white sympathisers join evicted black squatters in a passive protest against the demolition of shanty dwellings outside Cape Town. This was the third day of an operation to remove an estimated 26,000 squatters from three camps.

10 Aug. 1977 Signs multilateral treaty relating to the meeting of the whaling nations to allocate quotas for 1976/77 and 1977 whaling seasons.

16 Aug. 1977 The Minister of Justice asks for an extension of emergency powers granted to one area troubled by faction fighting to the entire KwaZulu 'homeland'. His request is turned down.

20 Aug. 1977 The constitutional proposals are approved by a special session of the National Party Parliamentary caucus. They are subsequently approved unanimously by National Party congresses in the Cape Province, Natal and the Orange Free State.

23 Aug. 1977 American President Carter announces at a press conference that South Africa has promised that no nuclear explosive test will be made now or in the future.

24 Aug. 1977 Government proposals for a new constitutional dispensation are disclosed by the Prime Minister John Vorster. They involve the creation of three separate Parliaments, for whites, coloureds and Asians, of the office of an executive State Presidents, of a Cabinet Council drawn from the three Parliaments, and

of an advisory President Council.

26 Aug. 1977

The Prime Minister attacks the double standards of foreign countries in the nuclear field, but announces, conditionally, his willingness to discuss South Africa's accession to the nuclear non-proliferation treaty.

Late Aug - Sept. 1977

The government's constitutional proposals are widely rejected by black and coloured leaders and severely criticized by white opposition leaders and academics.

31 Aug. 1977

The Prime Minister gives further details of the constitutional plan at a meeting in Durban. While Indian and coloured people are entitled to political rights no separate Parliament is to be created to accommodate urban blacks. Legislation already exists for them to elect their own town councils with powers greater than other local authorities. Also they exercise their political rights in their own homelands.

2 Sept. 1977

The Bophuthatswana electoral office publishes the results of the general election giving Chief Lucas Mangope's Democratic Party a landslide victory over the opposition Seoposengwe Party.

2-3 Sept. 1977

Foreign Minister 'Pik' Botha pays a two-day visit to Israel when Southern African issues are discussed with Prime Minister Begin and Foreign Minister Dayan.

4 Sept. 1977

Foreign Minister 'Pik' Botha meets the President of the Ivory Coast at Lake Geneva for talks covering the dangers threatening Africa internally and externally, and including the Rhodesian situation.

5 Sept. 1977

The Progressive Reform Party and the Basson group merge as the Progressive Federal Party (PFP) with Colin Eglin as party leader, Ray Swart as party chairman and 'Japie' Basson as deputy chairman. Its seven key principles include full citizenship rights for all South Africans and the negotiation of a new constitution at a national convention.

9 Sept. 1977

Full details of the proposed constitutional dispensation are given in a memorandum delivered to the Coloured Persons' Representative Council (CPRC) by the Minister of Coloured Relations, and released on 11 September 1977 by sources close to their Executive. The details are also revealed officially by the Transvaal leader of the National Party, Dr. Connie Mulder, who claims it to be an honest well-intentioned offer.

12 Sept. 1977

The death in detention of Steven Biko, founder and first President of the South African Students' Organization (SASO), and later honorary President of the Black People's Convention (BPC) arouses serious internal and international reactions. The circumstances of his death are the subject of statements by the Minister of Justice, J. Kruger, on 12, 14 and 16 September. Messages of concern continue including those from Cyrus Vance US Secretary of State and Dr. Kurt Waldheim, the United Nations Secretary-General.

13 Sept. 1977

At the Transvaal National Party Congress the constitutional proposals are accepted by 1,236 votes out of 1,243.

19 Sept. 1977

The Coloured Persons' Representative Council (CPRC) decide to reject the government's constitutional proposals and call for a National Convention to negotiate a new constitutional dispensation.

19 Sept. 1977	The Trade Union Council of South Africa (TUCSA) elects its first black chairman, Ronnie Webb, at the Council's annual congress in Durban.
20 Sept. 1977	The Prime Minister announces in Pretoria that he has decided that the House of Assembly and the four Provincial Councils should be dissolved and fresh elections be held on 30 November 1977. Nominations must be declared on 20 October 1977.
20 Sept. 1977	Signs trade agreement with the Federal Republic of Germany.
21 Sept. 1977	Signs agreement with Mozambique on air pooling between SAA and DETA.
22 Sept. 1977	It is reported that the President, Vice-President and Secretary-General of the Hervormde (Reformed Church of the Netherlands) have been refused visas to visit South Africa.
23 Sept. 1977	The Netherlands government suspends its cultural agreement with South Africa and proposed visits by several other Dutch groups are cancelled.
25 Sept. 1977	Steven Biko's funeral in King William's Town is attended by some 15,000 people. Twelve Western diplomats are present, including the American Ambassador.
30 Sept. 1977	The World Intellectual Property Organization (WIPO), Geneva, bans South Africa from further meetings of the organization and to seek its expulsion from its membership.
30 Sept. 1977	The ban on open-air gatherings is further extended until 31 March 1978.
30 Sept. 1977	The Ciskei 'homeland' government proclaims the introduction of emergency powers, after violent incidents and rioting. The powers allow for ninety days detention without trial, banishment without decree, prohibition of unauthorized meetings and heavy fines or prison sentences for showing disrespect or disobedience to chiefs and headmen, who remain the instruments of official policy.
30 Sept. 1977	Radclyffe M. Cadman is elected national leader of the New Republic Party (NRP). He expects opposition parties to cooperate, but is confident the NRP will become the government of South Africa.
3 Oct. 1977	M.C. Botha, Minister of Bantu Administration and Development announces that he will not stand for re-election and will resign as Minister in November 1977.
5 Oct. 1977	Sir de Villiers Graaff announces his retirement from politics, having been leader of the opposition from 1956 until the dissolution of the United Party on 28 June 1977.
7 Oct. 1977	A government notice gazetted on this date provides for the establishment of an Ndebele Tribal Authority.
12 Oct. 1977	Signs multilateral agreement on the additional act of 1972, amending the

International Convention for the Protection of New Varieties of Plants.

16 Oct. 1977   A total of 128 members of the United States Congress, from both the Democratic and Republican parties send a written request to the South African Ambassador in Washington urging the government to invite an appropriate international body to examine South Africa's laws and practices relating to detention and to make recommendations, with special reference to the death of Mr. Biko.

19 Oct. 1977   Following a Cabinet decision on 18 October 1977, the government, by proclamation under the Internal Security Act, declared eighteen organizations unlawful, arrested some seventy leading Africans, placed a number of people in restriction (including Donald Woods) and closed down the daily newspaper 'The World' and its associated 'Weekend World'. The actions provoke worldwide shock and protest. The Minister of Justice issues a statement justifying these draconian measures, and declares the organizations concerned a threat to law and order. The principal associations affected include the Black People's Convention (BPC), the South African Students' Organization (SASO), the Black Parents' Association, the Black Women's Federation and the Union of Black Journalists. Persons arrested included eight members of the Soweto 'Committee of 10'.

19 Oct. 1977   Emergency powers are proclaimed by the government of Venda.

19 Oct. 1977   The Foreign Minister hands over a seventy-six room presidential palace, which cost an estimated R1.8 m. to build to Transkei Head of State, Chief Botha Sigcau as a gift from the Pretoria government. Transkei will celebrate its first anniversary of independence on 26 October 1977.

19 Oct. 1977   The United States declares that the Carter Administration will be re-examining its relations with the South African government.

21-25 Oct. 1977   The United States, the Netherlands, Great Britain, West Germany and Belgium all recall their Ambassadors for consultations.

24 Oct. 1977   As the United Nations Security Council debate on South Africa opens in New York, a major diplomatic effort begins to deal with South Africa's severe treatment of its critics and with African demands for mandatory United Nations sanctions.

24 Oct. 1977   The Minister of Justice, Police and Prisons receives a report of a police investigation into Mr. Biko's death and a post-mortem report submitted to the Attorney General of the Transvaal and signed by Professor Johan Loubser, Chief State Pathologist, by Professor I.W. Simpson (University of Pretoria) and by Jonathan Gluckman (pathologist appointed by the Biko family) whose findings are unanimous. Death has been caused by extensive brain damage. Mr. Biko has sustained at least a dozen injuries between eight days and twelve hours of his death.

26 Oct. 1997   The Attorney General of the Transvaal, Jacobus E. Nothling, announces that an inquest into Biko's death will be held, but that he would not institute criminal proceedings. On 28 October the Attorney General of the Eastern Cape, Carel van der Walt, also declines to institute criminal proceedings.

27 Oct. 1997   President Carter announces that the United States government will support

the decision against the sale of arms to South Africa.

1 Nov. 1977	Signs Convention on Road Traffic.

2 Nov. 1977   Benin, Libya and Mauritius insist that the United Nations Security Council bypass the Western powers arms embargo resolution and instead take up a series of hardline African resolutions paving the way for a total economic and diplomatic blockade of South Africa. They force their resolutions to a vote and America, Britain and France exercise their vetoes.

2 Nov. 1977   The South African Indian Council (SAIC) unanimously rejects the government's proposed new constitution, after two days of lengthy debate and widespread opposition by other Indian leaders.

2 Nov. 1977   The United States Secretary of State, Cyrus Vance, announces that two further diplomats have been withdrawn from South Africa, and that the United States will prohibit all exports of military and police equipment to South Africa.

3 Nov. 1977   After a meeting between the Prime Minister John Vorster, with his Ministers of Bantu Administration and seven of the eight 'homeland' leaders, a statement is issued in Pretoria that influx control regulations are to be amended to provide greater freedom of movement for urban blacks. 'Pass books' are to be abolished and replaced by documents issued by the 'homeland' governments.

4 Nov. 1977   The United Nations Security Council unanimously adopts a seven-point resolution imposing a mandatory arms embargo against South Africa.

8 Nov. 1977   The French Ministry of Defence will no longer permit delivery of two escort vessels (corvettes) and two submarines under construction in French naval yards.

8 Nov. 1977   The Prime Minister, reacting to the arms embargo, says that the measure, even if supplemented by an oil embargo, will not seriously harm the Republic.

9 Nov. 1977   It is announced that Transkei and South Africa have signed an extradition agreement. Transkei authorities refuse to say whether it covers political offences. Transkei Interior Minister, Stella Sigcau, daughter of the country's President Botha Sigcau, resigns. No reason is given.

9 Nov. 1977   The Prime Minister of Swaziland says that his government will not allow the country to be used as a base for guerrilla attacks against South Africa. He denies that there are training camps within Swaziland.

10 Nov. 1977   The Minister of Finance, Senator Owen Horwood, announces the government is to spend an additional R250 m. on low-cost housing for Blacks, Coloureds and Asians during the next three years. Changes in property rights will give security of tenure to Blacks living in urban areas.

10 Nov. 1977   Signs agreement of co-operation with France regarding the Koeberg Nuclear Power Units 1 & 2.

11 Nov. 1977   The government adopts powers enabling the Minister of Economic Affairs

to compel companies to produce strategic and military goods should the need arise. The main consideration is preventing parent companies from controlling the operations of South African subsidiaries should they attempt to forbid local production of strategic equipment.

13 Nov. 1977	The Anglican Bishop of Lesotho, the Rev. Desmond Tutu announces that he is giving up his current post to become Secretary-General of the South African Council of Churches (SACC) which is taking an increasingly radical position against apartheid.
14 Nov. 1977	The Chairman of the Olympic Games organizing committee announces that Rhodesia and South Africa will be excluded from the 1980 Moscow Olympics.
14 Nov. 1977	The inquest into the death of Black Consciousness leader, Steve Biko, opens in Pretoria. Evidence given concerning the autopsy report is widely reported both locally and overseas.
15 Nov. 1977	A non-aggression pact between Bophuthatswana and South Africa is the first of sixty-six treaties signed by the two governments at a special pre-independence ceremony in Pretoria. The agreements will take effect on 6 December 1977.
17 Nov. 1977	A black high school student, Sipho Malaza dies while in Security Police custody. His death is the twenty-first in detention since March 1976.
17 Nov. 1977	The P.K. le Roux Dam, an integral part of the Orange River development project to provide electric power, irrigation and flood control - is officially inaugurated by John Vorster the Prime Minister. It was constructed at a cost of R94m.
18 Nov. 1977	The United Nation's Special Committee against Apartheid approves a draft international declaration against apartheid in sports.
21 Nov. 1977	A Soweto Action Committee is formed to back the plan for the future of Soweto proposed by the 'Committee of 10' most of whose members are in detention.
23 Nov. 1977	A National Party candidate and leading economist, Dr. Robert Smit and his wife, Jeanne-Cora, are found murdered in their home in Springs in curious circumstances. Police decline to offer any interpretation.
24 Nov. 1977	A bomb explodes in the Carlton Centre, Johannesburg, injuring sixteen people.
30 Nov. 1977	John Vorster achieves an overwhelming victory in the General Election, taking 136 of the 165 parliamentary seats. The National Party gains eighteen seats from the combined opposition parties. The only opposition party to hold its own is the Progressive Federal Party, which now becomes the official opposition with seventeen seats. The New Republic Party retain ten, the South African Party win three, the Herstigte Nasionale Party none.
1 Dec. 1977	Counsel for Steve Biko's family, Sydney Kentridge, makes his final submission calling for a verdict that Steve Biko died as the result of a criminal assault on him by one or more of the eight members of the Security

Police in whose custody he was on 6 and 7 September. During his four hour address Sydney Kentridge reserves his most serious criticism for two Security Police officers, Colonel Piet Goosen and Major Harold Snyman and two doctors who examined Steve Biko, Dr. Ivor Lang and Dr. Benjamin Tucker.

2 Dec. 1977   The fifteen-day inquest into the death of Steve Biko ends with a three-minute finding by the presiding magistrate, Martinus Prins, who rules that no one can be found criminally responsible for his death in detention. The verdict causes deep concern within South Africa and a storm of protest overseas. Shock is expressed by the United States Secretary of State and consternation by the United Nations Secretary-General.

2 Dec. 1977   Two members of Steve Biko's family, as well as eight other blacks, some of them friends of the Biko family, are detained by police in a pre-dawn raid in Soweto.

3 Dec. 1977   The record of the Biko inquest will now go to the Attorney General of Transvaal who can decide whether there should be any further investigation or any other action taken.

6 Dec. 1977   Bophuthatswana becomes independent at midnight. Its Parliament sits for the first time and elects Chief Lucas Mangope as the country's first President. He immediately raises the issues of land consolidation and citizenship. A twelve-man Cabinet, including two whites, is appointed.

8 Dec. 1977   Sir David Napley, President of the Law Society of England (who attended the Biko inquest as an independent observer at the invitation of the Association of Law Societies of South Africa) issues a twenty-five page report on the inquest in which he severely criticizes police procedure, evidence and investigation (`perfunctory in the extreme'). Regarding the magistrate's findings he is in accord, but adds `I do not, however, apprehend that it would have been irregular for the Magistrate to have found that the death was caused by one or more of a group of persons without specifying such persons with particularity'.

9 Dec. 1977   The United Nations Security Council unanimously adopts an African-sponsored resolution setting up a United Nations committee to monitor enforcement of the mandatory arms embargo decreed against South Africa on 4 November 1977.

14 Dec. 1977   The United Nations General Assembly in its thirty-second regular session passes fourteen resolutions on the policy of apartheid and a further resolution on 16 December 1977.

16 Dec. 1977   Signs an agreement for the application of safeguards and privileges with the International Atomic Energy Agency.

20 Dec. 1977   Canada announces it is to withdraw all government support for trade with South Africa. Trade commissioners will be recalled and the Consulate-General in Johannesburg will close. Diplomatic relations will be maintained to give Canada the opportunity to impress on the South African government the necessity for change.

6 Jan. 1978   Donald Woods, banned editor of the Daily Dispatch (East London) reaches

Britain with his family, having fled South Africa via Lesotho and Botswana. The pro-government Afrikaans press launches a virulent campaign against him: the British and American press in contrast give wide and sympathetic coverage to the story of his escape.

8 Jan. 1978   The murder of political scientist and author Dr. Richard Turner, in Durban, by an untraced assassin, is thought to have political implications. As one of eight leaders of NUSAS (the National Union of South African Students) Dr. Turner was served with a banning order in 1973.

11 Jan. 1978   A meeting is held in Ulundi between Chief Gatsha Buthelezi (Inkatha), Sonny Leon (Coloured Labour Party) and Y.S. Chinsamy (Indian Reform Party) who agree to formulate a common strategy against the government's race policies.

12 Jan. 1978   The Transkei government is to ban the South African Methodist Church, and replace it with a Transkei Methodist Church, which will acquire all the previous church's assets. The South African Council of Churches calls on Transkei to reconsider its decision.

22 Jan. 1978   At a meeting of the newly organized Soweto Students' League it is decided to continue the students' boycott of State schools, to call for a national conference to launch a new education system and to take no part in elections to the Soweto Community Council.

25 Jan. 1978   Government assurances are given that reform will be introduced, appeals for return to schools are made and between fifty and seventy per cent of pupils respond.

25 Jan. 1978   In a government reorganization following the elections of 30 November 1977, John Vorster reappoints most his Ministers, but mades a limited number of changes.

26 Jan. 1978   Signs agreement with Taiwan on mutual fishing relations.

26 Jan. 1978   Amnesty International's detailed report on human rights violations in South Africa is banned. It presents comprehensive documentation on deaths in detention, detention without trial, treatment of convicted political prisoners, bannings and banishment.

26 Jan. 1978   At the request of the African delegates, Donald Woods addresses the United Nations Security Council and urges member states to pursue a policy of disengagement from all ties with South Africa.

31 Jan. 1978   Jimmy Kruger announces in the House of Assembly that new measures for the protection of political detainees and prisoners are being considered and that all police instructions on their treatment will be reviewed.

1 Feb. 1978   When nominations for the Soweto Community Council close, only twenty-nine candidates have been nominated. Sixteen are later disqualified on technical grounds, nine are returned unopposed and the other four will stand for election in two wards.

2 Feb. 1978   Chief Matanzima announces that all South Africans seconded to the Transkei Army will leave Transkei by 31 March 1978.

2 Feb. 1978	The Attorney-General of the Eastern Cape states that he will not prosecute any police involved in the arrest and detention of Black Consciousness leader Steve Biko.
3 Feb. 1978	The Minister of Foreign Affairs, `Pik' Botha, says in the House of Assembly that the Biko affair has done unending harm to South Africa.
9 Feb. 1978	Winnie Mandela, restricted to a black township at Brandfort (Orange Free State), is sentenced to six months' imprisonment (suspended for four years) for breaking her banning and house arrest order by receiving unauthorized visits by friends and relatives. Earlier four white women had been sentenced to prison terms for refusing to give evidence as to whether they had visited Winnie Mandela.
9 Feb. 1978	South Africa is to make its own missiles. Kentron (Pty) Ltd, a newly formed subsidiary of ARMSCOR (the South African Armaments Corporation) will produce these.
15 Feb. 1978	The Prime Minister states that South Africa is still committed to granting independence to Namibia before the end of 1978.
16 Feb. 1978	The Minister of Bantu Administration and Development, Dr. Connie Mulder, announces that he will in future be known as the Minister of Plural Relations and Development, reflecting the plural nature of the population.
18 Feb. 1978	The election of the first government sponsored Soweto Community Council is poorly supported. Nine candidates are returned unopposed, nineteen wards attract no candidates at all. In the two wards contested the percentage poll is less than 6 per cent. The elections fill only eleven of the thirty seats.
27 Feb. 1978	Robert M. Sobukwe, founder of the Pan Africanist Congress, dies of cancer at the age of fifty-three and is buried in his home town, Graaff Reniet.
28 Feb. 1978	The Minister of Justice announces that detainees held under security laws will soon be allowed to have monthly visits from doctors and legal representatives.
10 Mar. 1978	Percy Qoboza, editor of the banned newspaper, The World, is released from detention, together with nine other black leaders seized in security raids in October 1976.
11 Mar. 1978	The government agrees to eliminate racial segregation in theatres but not in cinemas.
13 Mar. 1978	The first public rally of the new South African Black Alliance (SABA) is held under the leadership of Chief Gatsha Buthelezi in Cape Town. Its main objective is to convene a National Convention of representatives of all population groups to seek a peaceful, negotiated solution to the country's problems. The Dikwankwetla Party from the Qwa Qwa `homeland' is joining the alliance. The organizations represented will not merge, however, since to do so would infringe the Political and Interference Act of 1968 which bans inter-racial mixing in political parties.
15 Mar. 1978	A Durban magistrate rules that no one is to blame for the death of a young Indian dentist, Dr. Hoosen Haffejee, who died in police custody in August

1977. It is found that he committed suicide.

21 Mar. 1978

South Africa is informed by the International Olympic Committee (IOC) that it may not re-apply to join the world sporting body. Consequently South Africa will not be able to send any teams to the Olympic Games in Moscow.

21 Mar. 1978

It is reported that about 15,000 students have returned to secondary schools in Soweto and that thirty-two of the forty state-run schools in the townships will re-open by the beginning of April.

23 Mar. 1978

Three more detainees are released: the Chairman of the `Committee of 10', Dr. N. Motlana, a member of the Committee, L. Mosala, and Soweto journalist, Aggrey Klaaste.

29 Mar. 1978

Chief Minister of Venda, Chief Patrick Mphephu is to hold talks with John Vorster on the issue of homeland independence.

1 Apr. 1978

The Office of the Canadian Consul-General in Johannesburg closes.

4 Apr. 1978

Dr. Andries Treurnicht is re-appointed as a Deputy Minister of Plural Relations. Opposition spokesperson Helen Suzman calls this an insensitive move.

10 Apr. 1978

Chief Kaiser Matanzima, Prime Minister of Transkei, announces that his government has decided to sever its diplomatic relations with the Republic of South Africa. The announcement follows the adoption of a Bill transfering the control of East Griqualand from Cape Province to Natal, with effect from 1 April 1978.

11 Apr 1978

Fifty Pan Africanist Congress (PAC) members arrested by Swaziland government orders, are to be expelled from Swaziland. They are accused of being involved in faction fighting and of providing arms and training people in the use of arms. South Africa has not requested their detention or deportation.

11 Apr. 1978

The South African Prime Minister expresses regret at Chief Matanzima's declaration, which is to his own disadvantage, but states that South Africa will continue to honour its obligations to Transkei, including financial assistance.

13 Apr. 1978

Chief Matanzima says he will demand majority rule in South Africa.

Mid-Apr. 1978

Brigadier C.F. Zietsman, the head of the Security Police, confirms that African National Congress (ANC) guerrillas have been involved in skirmishes with counter-insurgency forces in the Eastern Transvaal.

17 Apr. 1978

Minister of Defence, P.W. Botha, announces that a new army base is to be built at Phalaborwa, and that a new airbase has been constructed at Hoedspruit in the Eastern Transvaal.

25 Apr. 1978

Sixteen of the independent members of the Transkei Assembly announce that they have formed the Transkei National Progressive Party (TNPP) under the leadership of C. Mda, a former chief whip of the TNIP and earlier a member of the Democratic Party.

28 Apr. 1978	The South African Defence Headquarters state that Transkei soldiers will not be admitted for training courses in South Africa until diplomatic relations are normalized.
28 Apr. 1978	Venda's request for 'independence' has been granted and the second half of 1979 set as the target date.
End-Apr. 1978	A new black political movement, the Azanian People's Organization (AZAPO), is formed at an inaugural conference at Roodepoort, near Johannesburg. It is open to Blacks, Coloureds and Indians, but closed to Whites. It adopts the slogan of the banned Black People's Convention - 'One Azania, one People' and will oppose all institutions created by the government, from homelands to Community Councils.
2 May 1978	PAC Central Committee announce in Dar es Salaam that its chairman, Potlako Leballo, is to retire for health reasons.
4 May 1978	AZAPO's two principal leaders, I. Mkhabela and L. Mabasa are arrested in Soweto. Anglican Bishop Desmond Tutu protests and queries why the authorities are so unwilling to listen to the voices of authentic black leaders.
6 May 1978	Eschel Rhoodie, the Secretary for Information, reveals that he has been operating a secret fund for which he was accountable only to a three-member Cabinet Committee and which has never been approved by Parliament.
8 May 1978	The newly-formed Transkei National Progressive Party (TNPP) is recognized as the official opposition in the National Assembly.
8 May 1978	John Vorster declares that he has personally authorized the Department of Information to use secret funds without Parliamentary approval for purposes in the highest national interest. There will be a full investigation into alleged irregularities.
10 May 1978	Transkei abrogates its non-aggression pact with South Africa. From this date, Chief Matanzima says no South African military aircraft will be allowed overflying rights, neither will ships of the South African Navy be allowed into Transkeian waters.
12 May 1978	The Minister of Justice, Police and Prisons, Jimmy Kruger, tells Parliament that nearly 700 terrorists were arrested in 1977 and of these ninety-one had had terrorist training. At present sixty-six terrorist trials are in progress.
24 May 1978	Legislation for three major components of the governments plans to defuse black grievances is introduced. Bills provide for ninety-nine year leases to be granted to qualified urban blacks; for black identity documents to be replaced by travel documents issued by 'homeland' governments; and for the word 'Bantu' to be replaced by the word 'Black' in all government legislation.
26 May 1978	The Transkei Minister of Justice orders the Methodist Church of South Africa to cease all activities, and cede its property within six months. The property is insured for R3.6m.
2 June 1978	A new independent Methodist Church of Transkei is proclaimed at a conference in Umtata.

| 3 June 1978 | Security Police chief, Brigadier C.F. Zietsman, announces that about 4,000 South African exiles are undergoing guerrilla training in Mozambique, Angola, Tanzania and Libya; of these about three quarters have been recruited by the ANC. |

15 June 1978   The Department of Information is to be disbanded and replaced by a Bureau for National and International Communications, for which Dr. Connie Mulder will be responsible. Dr. E. Rhoodie will resign. An evaluation of secret projects will be made by General H.J. van den Bergh, head of the Bureau of State Security.

15 June 1978   The new Soweto Council is inaugurated. The Council, under the Chairmanship of David Thebahadi, is given considerable powers, but its decisions have to be ratified by the Minister of Plural Relations, and are not subject to approval by either the Johannesburg City Council or the West Rand Administration Board.

15 June 1978   Signs treaty with the Perishable Products Export Control Board for the ocean conveyance of goods between South Africa and Europe.

16 June 1978   The anniversary of Sharpeville passes off without serious incidents. The main service in Soweto is held by Bishop Desmond Tutu and addressed by Dr. N. Motlana who is later warned by Soweto's Police Chief, Brigadier Jan Visser, against making any more inflamatory speeches.

18 July 1978   The ANC's President-General, Nelson Mandela, celebrates his sixtieth birthday on Robben Island.

20-21 July 1978   In reaction to further deaths of people in police detention, ten policemen have been suspended from duty and six have been charged with murder.

21 Aug. 1978   The State President Dr. Nicolaas J. Diederichs dies of a heart attack. Following an earlier heart attack on 12 August he had been temporarily succeeded as State President by Senator Marais Viljoen.

24 Aug. 1978   John Vorster announces that while Dr. Connie Mulder will remain Minister of Plural Relations and Development, the Bureau for National and International Communications will be placed under the Ministry of Foreign Affairs as from 1 September 1978.

6 Sept. 1978   Sonny Leon, leader of the Labour Party in the Coloured Representative Council (CRC), resigns, ostensibly for health reasons. His resignation raises the possibility of a split between the Left and Right wings of his party.

12 Sept. 1978   On the eve of the first anniversary of the death of Steve Biko, police arrest sixteen people including his brother, his sister and her husband and close friends of the family. No reason is given to them but police say the arrests are preventive measures covered by the 1977 Internal Security Act.

13 Sept. 1978   The Venda Independence Party (VIP) boycotts the opening of the Venda Parliament despite having won thirty-one of the forty-two elected seats. The boycott is prompted by the arrest, after the election of twelve of the new VIP Parliamentarians. They were detained together with nearly forty other opposition supporters.

15 Sept. 1978   France returns the deposit paid by South Africa for two corvettes and two submarines. Their order was cancelled by France in November 1977 in accordance with an international arms embargo against South Africa.

20 Sept. 1978   Prime Minister Vorster announces that he will resign shortly, for health reasons, but that he will be available for election as the next State President.

21 Sept. 1978   Seven more people are detained in Venda, bringing the total number of detentions since the opposition Venda Independence Party won a majority of elected seats in the Legislative Assembly. The Pretoria government's inaction in persuading Venda to charge or release the detainees is widely criticized, since South Africa is still technically responsible for the administration of Venda.

25 Sept. 1978   The trial begins of eleven Soweto students charged under the Terrorism Act. The fifty-six page indictment alleges that as officers, members or supporters of the now banned Soweto Students' Representative Council (SSRC) they conspired to commit sedition and terrorism between May 1976 and October 1977.

27 Sept. 1978   A Parliamentary Commission of Inquiry has found no irregularities in the accounts of the Department of Information. However a wider inquiry is still in progress to examine the purposes for which the money was spent and to establish whether the officials involved have received any financial gain from their actions.

28 Sept. 1978   The caucus of the National Party elects as party leader, and thereby as Prime Minister, Pieter Willem Botha, the Minister of Defence and leader of the National Party in the Cape Province. He declares that there will be no immediate changes in the composition of the Cabinet and that he himself will retain the Defence portfolio.

29 Sept. 1978   The Electoral College elects B.J. Vorster as State President by 173 votes to the nineteen cast for Sir de Villiers Graaff, former Leader of the opposition, nominated by the New Republic Party and the twelve cast for Professor G. Bozzoli, Vice-Chancellor of the University of the Witwatersrand, proposed by the Progressive Federal Party.

30 Sept. 1978   Signs treaty with Japan on certain portions of land granted to the Commonwealth War Graves Commission at Yokohama.

End Sept. 1978   An Ivory Coast delegation arrives in Transkei on an official visit. The mission is the first from a black African country.

2 Oct. 1978   The Transkei will resist the government's plan for a mass removal of nearly 20,000 blacks from the Crossroads settlement near Cape Town, to a settlement centre on land due to be incorporated into Transkei.

3 Oct. 1978   At the end of a ten-day inquest, J.A. Coetzee, Deputy Chief Magistrate of Port Elizabeth, rules that no one is to blame for the death of L. Tabalaza who died after falling from the fifth floor of the Port Elizabeth Security Police headquarters on 10 July 1978. Mr. Tabalaza was not a detainee under the Terrorism Act, nevertheless a high level police inquiry had been ordered into his death.

10 Oct. 1978	B.J. Vorster is sworn in as State President in Pretoria, the occasion being marked by a display of the country's military forces, including a fly-past of Mirage fighter bombers and Impala jet trainers.
10 Oct. 1978	P.W. Botha makes a number of changes in the allocation of portfolios, but retains the post of Minister of Defence himself. Louis le Grange becomes Minister of Public Works and Tourism. A new post of Deputy Minister for Defence and National Security is created, and the MP for Bloemfontein West and Chairman of the National Party defence group in Parliament, H.J. 'Kobie' Coetzee is appointed to it.
26 Oct. 1978	A report drawn up by the Progressive Federal Party calls for power-sharing among all the races in the country, under a federal constitution, providing for political rights without the danger of majority domination. Elections would be on the basis of proportional representation.
26 Oct. 1978	The Nederduitse Gereformeerde Kerk (NGK) unanimously rejects proposals for a merger with its three sister churches in the African, Coloured and Indian communities. The policy of different churches for the different peoples is reaffirmed.
31 Oct. 1978	A full scale police search, headed by a specially trained anti-terrorist unit is launched following a shoot-out between police and suspected nationalist guerrillas some forty miles west of Louis Trichardt, Northern Transvaal.
2 Nov. 1978	Justice Anton Mostert, Chairman of a one-man Commission of Inquiry into exchange control contraventions (set up in December 1977) discloses evidence of corruption and the misappropriation of public funds, taken during his investigations into the Information scandal. This improper application of taxpayers money involves, among other things, the financing of the newspaper 'The Citizen'. Judge Mostert publishes some of the evidence despite a request from P.W. Botha not to do so.
3 Nov. 1978	The Prime Minister appoints a judicial commission to investigate the allegations of corruption. Its three members, Justice R.P. Erasmus of the Orange Free State Division of the Supreme Court, A.J. Lategan, the Cape Attorney-General and G.F. Smallberger the Chief State Law Adviser will present findings to a Special Session of Parliament.
6 Nov. 1978	The Commission begins its investigation into any misappropriation of funds by the former Information Department and into any irregularities of private benefit to individuals that may have occurred. Judge Erasmus decides to hear all evidence in camera.
7 Nov. 1978	Dr. Connie Mulder resigns from the Cabinet, but retains his seat as a Member of Parliament.
7 Nov. 1978	The Prime Minister announces that Judge Mostert's Commission of Inquiry into exchange control contraventions has been terminated and replaced by a twelve-man Parliamentary Commission with the same instructions as that of the Judge. This termination arouses widespread anger.
8 Nov. 1978	Britain announces a probe into allegations that the West Indian island of Antigua has been used in illegal arms traffic to South Africa.

11 Nov. 1978	Dr. Connie Mulder resigns from his post as leader of the National Party in the Transvaal.
14 Nov. 1978	Prime Minister Botha announces an important Cabinet reshuffle, involving the promotion of moderate ('verligte') members, the most dramatic of which is the appointment of Dr. Piet Koornhof as Minister of Plural Relations.
15 Nov. 1978	John Vorster, State President and former Prime Minister, appears before the Erasmus Commission.
17 Nov. 1978	Prime Minister Botha gives evidence before the Erasmus Commission, at his own request.
18 Nov. 1978	Minister of Justice, J.T. Kruger, says the PAC has launched two insurgency campaigns Homecoming and Curtain Raiser against South Africa. The South African police have arrested twenty-three of the insurgents already.
20 Nov. 1978	From this date the Bureau of State Security (BOSS) becomes a full portfolio of National Security under the Prime Minister who is now Prime Minister and Minister of Defence and of National Security.
21 Nov. 1978	The Transvaal National Party leadership election produces a decisive win for Dr. Andries Treurnicht, Deputy Minister of Plural Relations. This is interpreted as a right-wing backlash against recent moves to 'humanize' apartheid.
21 Nov. 1978	It is announced that all Cabinet Ministers on the boards of newspaper groups are to resign their directorships.
21 Nov. 1978	The government decides to disband the Foreign Affairs Association, a front organization founded by the former Department of Information to project a favourable image of South Africa, and to promote dialogue on both internal and external levels.
24 Nov. 1978	The Southern African Freedom Foundation (SAFF) is exposed as a government front financed out of public funds.
28 Nov. 1978	In his first major speech since his election as Transvaal leader, Dr. Treurnicht revives the concept of a 'Colouredstan' to accommodate South Africa's one million Coloured people - an idea in direct contravention of the National Party's current policy of power-sharing.
1 Dec. 1978	Transkei's first President, Paramount Chief Botha Sigcau, dies from a heart attack. Prime Minister K. Matanzima announces his retirement from active politics, but his preparedness to accept nomination as President.
1 Dec. 1978	The government extends the Erasmus Commission's terms of reference to 30 May 1979.
5 Dec. 1978	The Erasmus Commission presents its report on its investigations into allegations of corruption and misappropriation of funds by the former Department of Information to Parliament. It alleges ineptitude, moral turpitude, malpractice and misappropriation in dealing with funds. It discredits Dr. Connie Mulder, General Hendrik van den Bergh and Dr. Eschel Rhoodie and his brother Dr. Deneys Rhoodie, who served as his

deputy at the Information Ministry, but exonerates State President Vorster and Prime Minister P.W. Botha. For reasons of state security no details are given of the 160 to 180 secret projects controlled by Dr. Rhoodie.

6 Dec. 1978   Signs agreement with Japan on fisheries.

7 Dec. 1978   State President Vorster opens the first emergency session of Parliament to be held in peace-time and promises action against anyone found guilty of the maladministration and misappropriation of public funds. His Ministry does not accept collective responsibility for the scandal and will not resign.

19 Dec. 1978   Signs International Sugar Agreement, 1977.

29 Dec. 1978   Rev. H.J. Hendrickse is elected leader of the Coloured Labour Party of South Africa at its thirteenth Congress in Bloemfontein. The party declares its support for the banned ANC, and urges universal suffrage in a South African unitary state.

8 Jan. 1979   Signs agreement with Lesotho on issuing of notes and coin.

13 Jan. 1979   A clash between police and suspected guerrillas is reported near the Botswana border. Botswana denies that it is being used as a springboard for attacks on his neighbours despite this being the third shooting incident in the Northern Transvaal with the guerrillas apparently coming from Botswana.

13 Jan. 1979   The government is reported to have frozen the South African assets of the former Information Secretary, Dr. Eschel Roodie, and to have seized secret funds deposited in private accounts outside the country.

24 Jan. 1979   The former Minister of Information, Dr. Connie Mulder, resigns his seat in parliament at the insistence of the Prime Minister, P.W. Botha. Announcing his decision, Dr. Mulder claims that his conscience is clear and decisions made were in the interests of the country.

24 Jan. 1979   The Transvaal Attorney-General, Jan Nothling, states that General Hendrick van den Bergh, former head of BOSS, will not be prosecuted for disparaging remarks made about the Erasmus Commission, since this would involve the publication of evidence, not in the national interest. This decision is strongly criticized by the opposition parties.

2 Feb. 1979   Opening Parliament, State President Vorster promises South Africa a new deal, new economic and financial measures and a new constitutional dispensation.

5 Feb. 1979   The official opposition Progressive Federal Party refuses to congratulate John Vorster on his appointment as State President on the grounds that not all the evidence of the Erasmus Commission has been made public. PFP leader Colin Eglin describes the real tragedy of the information scandal as the immobilization of government and the diversion of attention away from the real problems facing the country.

6 Feb. 1979   In reply to the opposition's motion Prime Minister P.W. Botha offers to resign if opposition politicians can show that either he or his cabinet were aware of the information scandal.

| 7 Feb. 1979 | Figures released by the South African Institute of Race Relations indicate a fall of twenty per cent in political trials in 1978, compared with 1977. Authorities are showing increasing recourse to preventive detention rather than administrative banning of opponents. |

19 Feb. 1979   The former Transkei Prime Minister, Chief Kaiser Matanzima, is elected President of Transkei. His brother, Chief George Matanzima, is elected leader of the ruling Transkei Congress Party (TCP).

21 Feb. 1979   George Matanzima becomes Premier.

26 Feb. 1979   Mozambique and South Africa sign a railway cooperation agreement.

4 Mar. 1979   In reaction to newspaper reports, Prime Minister P.W. Botha states through the media, that he will not be `blackmailed into a deal with anybody' and challenges Dr. Rhoodie to return to South Africa.

4 Mar. 1979   Iran breaks off diplomatic, political, economic and military ties with South Africa, and will no longer supply oil to this country.

6 Mar. 1979   The trial of eighteen suspected PAC members which began in December 1977 and has already taken over 100 court sessions, resumes in Bethal. The defendants face two main charges under the Terrorism Act, and a number of alternative counts under other legislation.

6-7 Mar. 1979   General Hendrik van den Bergh has a lengthy meeting with Dr. E. Rhoodie in Paris and indicates afterwards that it has been agreed that Dr. Rhoodie will not divulge details of his tapes to the media.

8 Mar. 1979   Foreign Minister `Pik' Botha, says in Switzerland that South Africa will consider adopting a more neutral position in world affairs and become pro-African rather than pro-Western.

9 Mar. 1979   The government gives official notice that it has refused to allow the Herstigte Nasionale Party to be registered as a political party, in terms of an amendment to the Electoral Act made in 1978. The party's leader, Jaap Marais, indicates that the party will continue to put up candidates for election, but as independents.

14 Mar. 1979   On his return from Paris, General Hendrik van den Bergh has his own passport impounded on orders from the Minister of the Interior, and the Prime Minister makes it clear that the General had no government authority to negotiate with Dr. Rhoodie.

15 Mar. 1979   Four people, believed to be members of the ANC, are arrested in Gaborone, Botswana, and charged with the illegal possession of explosives and firearms. They receive sentences of from two to four-and-a-half years imprisonment.

16 Mar. 1979   A warrant is issued for Dr. Rhoodie's arrest on a charge of fraud, with an alternative charge of theft.

16 Mar. 1979   The terms of reference of the Erasmus Commission are extended to investigate and evaluate, by 31 March 1979, the government's political culpability. The Prime Minister also authorizes that appointment, from 1

June 1979, of an Advocate-General who will investigate and report to Parliament on any allegation, suppported by a sworn affidavit, of corruption on malpractices by the government.

17 Mar. 1979   It is reported that during February 1979, Dr. Eschel Rhoodie has claimed in interviews in Quito, Ecador, that he was the initiator of the South African government's policy of detente conducted in 1974-76. He subsequently threatens to release forty-one tape recordings containing details of secret South African propaganda and security operations.

18 Mar. 1979   Dr. Rhoodie reiterates that he possesses documentary evidence of secret projects involving the transfer of funds to major political figures in several Western countries. He denies being guilty of any criminal offence.

18 Mar. 1979   The government admits responsibility for the death of the black leader, Joseph Mdluli on 19 March 1976 and agree to pay damages to his family. A claim for loss of support, against the Minister of Justice and Police, will be settled out of court.

20 Mar. 1979   Former South African Supreme Court judge, Judge J.F. Ludorf, claims he has evidence that two hired German killers were paid to murder the former South African representative to the International Monetary Fund, Dr. Robert Smit and his wife. The Prime Minister's office states that there is no connection between the Smit murders and irregularities in the former Information Department, but speculation continues.

22 Mar. 1979   President Vorster, in a lengthy statement, challenges Dr. Rhoodie to release any document which may implicate him in the Information affair; emphasizes that the question is not whether state money has been available for secret projects, but whether that money has been misused; denies he was informed of the secret funding of 'The Citizen' and rejects as contemptible Dr. Rhoodie's attempt to drag Minister Horwood into the affair.

22 Mar. 1979   The Prime Minister, in a cautiously worded statement issued by his office, says the Cabinet knew of secret projects, but not about the state funding of 'The Citizen', or of irregularities that have taken place. He says he has undertaken to resign only if it can be proved that members of his Cabinet were aware of one specific project - the funding of The Citizen - before he came into power in September 1978.

22 Mar. 1979   President Vorster's statement is immediately followed by calls for his resignation by the opposition parties on the grounds that he has violated the fundamental constitutional principle that the State President acts in political matters only on the advice of his Cabinet, and that he has pronounced on evidence material to the Erasmus Commission.

23 Mar. 1979   The Prime Minister defends John Vorster's statement, denying that a constitutional crisis has been created.

23 Mar. 1979   The two major opposition parties demand the immediate resignation of President Vorster because of his intervention in the Information scandal, which is said to have created a major constitutional crisis.

25 Mar. 1979   Dr. Connie Mulder, in effect, accuses President Vorster of lying and states that the decision to found and finance 'The Citizen' was known to him from

the start. He provides precise dates and times of meetings concerning the Information Department's secret projects, from 23 October 1974 onwards, held in the Prime Minister's office.

26 Mar. 1979   The opposition moves to impeach President Vorster for his controversial intervention. However it requires the signature of thirty Members of Parliament to convene a special debate and the opposition parties can only convene twenty-seven votes.

28 Mar. 1979   It is disclosed that summaries of Dr. Rhoodie's tape recordings have already been made available to a syndicate including the British Broadcasting Corporation and the United States National Broadcasting Corporation.

30 Mar. 1979   The draft Constitution is published. It is widely criticized and the government decides not to introduce it in the current Parliamentary session. Instead it is now submitted to a Parliamentary Select Committee.

30 Mar. 1979   The Foreign Minister 'Pik' Botha, whose portfolio now includes the South African Information Services, promises to give opposition leaders full access to all current secret projects. He has decided to terminate, with effect from 1 April 1979, all confidential and sensitive projects that do not serve the national interests in the most effective manner.

2 Apr. 1979   In an interim report, the Erasmus Commission exonerates P.W. Botha and all members of his government from having had any prior knowledge of irregularities in the former Department of Information. The Commission's findings are the result of a special two-week inquiry, focussing on whether members of the Cabinet knew of the funding of 'The Citizen' before 26 September 1978.

4 Apr. 1979   Dr. Andries Treurnicht, the leader of the National Party in the Transvaal, gives Dr. Connie Mulder an ultimatum to accept the findings of the Erasmus Commission by noon on 5 April 1979, failing which he will be expelled from the party. Dr. Mulder states he cannot accept the report.

5 Apr. 1979   The White Paper on Defence warns that the military threat against South Africa is intensifying at an alarming rate. A total national security strategy is being developed to counter the 'total onslaught'. This involves a major increase in naval defence spending, the overhaul of the air defence system and the creation of a parachute brigade.

6 Apr. 1979   Dr. Connie Mulder is expelled from the National Party over his role in the Information Department scandal.

9 Apr. 1979   The Botswana government is building a camp to house over 5,000 student refugees from South Africa at Molepolole, thirty-five km. west of Gaborone. This will be a country settlement and not a training camp.

9 Apr. 1979   Signs agreement with Portugal on mutual fishery relations.

11 Apr. 1979   The home of the leader of the opposition Progressive Federal Party, Colin Eglin, is attacked. The attack follows a pattern characteristic of the secret society known as 'Scorpio'.

12 Apr. 1979   Prime Minister, P.W. Botha, announces that three members of the staff of

the United States Embassy in South Africa, have been given a week to leave the country. They have photographed sensitive military installations by a secret camera installed in a diplomatic aircraft.

19 Apr. 1979   In a major policy statement, the Prime Minister declares that in future, South Africa will be guided solely by its own interests, and those of the Southern African region.

19 Apr. 1979   The American government has supplied no reasonable explanation or apology for the photographing of the uranium enrichment Pelindaba plant. Instead they have acted against two South African attachés in the United States.

19 Apr. 1979   The International Press Institute (IPI) appoints an official observer in South Africa, Joel Mervis, to report on matters affecting the conduct and freedom of the press. He will observe court actions and Press Council complaints brought against editors, journalists and publishers, and their outcome.

20 Apr. 1979   The Federation of South African Trade Unions (FOSATU) is founded. It aims to be a national, non-racial, umbrella body co-ordinating South Africa's black trade union movements.

26 Apr. 1979   Dr. Connie Mulder refused to give evidence before the Erasmus Commission, alleging it has declined to grant him a fair hearing.

1 May 1979   The first interim report of the Wiehahn Commission is tabled in Parliament. Its recommendations include registration of black trade unions, including migrant workers, abolition of the principle of statutory job reservation; retention of the closed shop; the creation of a National Manpower Commission and an Industrial Court to resolve industrial litigation. The report is welcomed in trade union and business circles.

2 May 1979   The Minister for Cooperation and Development, Dr. Piet Koornhof, announces that relevant urban black leaders will be consulted about the position of blacks outside the 'homelands'. His deputy, Dr. Willie Vosloo, announces the reversal of the government's policy on Alexandra Township: it will be renewed with the emphasis on high-density family housing rather than hostels.

2 May 1979   The Minister of Labour, S.P. Botha, says that the government accepts the Wiehahn Report in principle, but some of its recommendations will have to be implemented with caution and care.

8 May 1979   The recommendations of the Riekert Commission are tabled. These include more black involvement in government administration boards; active promotion of home ownership; wider opportunities for black traders in white areas; dismantling of the Department of Plural Relations; streamlining of recruitment procedures in 'homelands'; curfew on blacks in white areas to be lifted; scrapping of random pass arrests.

11 May 1979   Eleven Soweto school pupil leaders are convicted of sedition and sentenced in Johannesburg to terms of imprisonment, most of which are suspended, since the accused have already been held for long periods. The charges arise from the June 1976 demonstrations.

11 May 1979   The executive of the South African Confederation of Labour (SACL)

approves the government's White Paper accepting the Wiehahn Report by thirteen voters to eleven.

17 May 1979   The Advocate General Bill is introduced by L. Muller, Minister of Transport, against strong opposition from the Progressive Federal Party and the New Republic Party. The Bill, resulting from the Information Department scandal, will prevent anyone publishing or broadcasting material relating to the alleged misappropriation of state funds without the written permission of an Advocate General who will be specially appointed. The holding of inquiries by the Advocate General will be secret. This `totalitarian measure' and `press gag' is widely condemned.

21 May 1979   Signs multilateral treaty pertaining to the South East Atlantic fisheries agreement on the total catch quota of hake in 1979.

30 May 1979   Following fierce opposition to the Advocate General's Bill, the government refers it to a Parliamentary Select Committee - on which it will have an overwhelming majority. The official opposition series of amendments have little chance of success.

4 June 1979   In its final report the Erasmus Commission amends its interim report and states that President Vorster has to bear joint responsibility for continued irregularities in the former Department of Information while he was in office as Prime Minister. It exonerates P.W. Botha and the Minister of Finance, Senator Owen Horwood.

4 June 1979   B.J. Vorster resigns from his position as State President. Marais Viljoen, the President of the Senate, is sworn in as acting State President.

6 June 1979   In the by-election at Randfontein (formerly Dr. C. Mulder's seat) the National Party candidate wins, but with a very much reduced majority over the Herstigte Nasionale Party.

7 June 1979   S.P. Botha introduces the second reading of the Industrial Conciliation Amendment Bill, under which a national manpower commission is to be set up, the registration of trade unions and employers' organizations is to be regulated and safeguards against inter-racial competition are to be repealed, except in certain industries. The Bill is opposed by the PFP and by various trade unions, including the multiracial Trade Union Council of South Africa.

12 June 1979   A member of the three-man Presidential Council of the PAC, David M. Sibeko, dies in Dar es Salaam, Tanzania, after being shot the previous night. Mr. Sibeko was Director of the PAC's Foreign Affairs and formerly PAC representative at the United Nations in New York. His assassination shocks political exiles.

13 June 1979   Marais Viljoen, former President of the Senate and acting State President, is elected State President by members of both Houses of Parliament and is sworn in on 19 June 1979.

14 June 1979   An amendment to the Inquest Act prevents any reporting on a suspicious death before an inquest. Its intention is to discourage publicity surrounding deaths in detention. In the same week amendments are gazetted to the Police Act curbing the reporting of allegations of brutality and maladministration in the Police Force.

14 June 1979	Cabinet changes are announced by Prime Minister, P.W. Botha.
14 June 1979	Botswana authorities announce the arrests in Gaborone of nine black dissidents in connection with the assassination of Mr. Sibeko.
14 June 1979	In the face of widespread protest the Prime Minister announces that provisions in the Advocate General Bill preventing the press from publishing details of the misuse of government funds, without the permission of a government official, have been dropped for the present.
16 June 1979	Six PAC members, all from Itumbi Camp, Southern Tanzania, appear before a magistrate's court in Dar es Salaam, charged with the murder of PAC leader, David Sibeko.
17 June 1979	The government's White Paper on the Riekert Commission rejects two crucial recommendations - that employers of illegal labour, and not workers, be prosecuted, and that the 72-hour time limit for 'illegal' blacks in prescribed areas be abolished.
19 June 1979	J.T. Kruger, formerly Minister of Justice, Police and Prisons, is elected President of the Senate on the nomination of P.W. Botha.
20 June 1979	The government's White Paper on the Riekert Report accepts that existing laws enforcing racial separation may have to be reviewed and that greater mobility of urban blacks between different urban areas is desirable. However, certain restrictions will remain in force.
21 June 1979	The Information Service of South Africa Special Account Bill is passed against the votes of the opposition parties. Under it, the unauthorized expenditure by the former Department of Information is accepted as a statutory accomplished fact.
22 June 1979	The Advocate-General Bill is passed in amended form against PFP opposition.
22 June 1979	Signs amendment to multilateral treaty on endangered species of flora and fauna.
26 June 1979	South Africa's longest political trial ends in Bethal, Transvaal with seventeen defendants sharing a total of 147 years' imprisonment. They were charged under the Terrorism Act with reviving the banned PAC, sending people out of South Africa for insurgency training and inciting riots in Kagiso township in June 1976.
28 June 1979	Dr. C. Mulder, together with two other former National Party members, Cas Greyling and Sarel Reinecke, and four other men announce the formation of an Action Front for National Priorities with the aim of forming a new right-wing party whose ideological position would lie between those of the National Party and the Herstigte Nasionale Party.
16 July 1979	The Secretary of Health announces that all senior doctors in the Public Service, irrespective of race, will in future receive equal salaries.
19 July 1979	Dr. E. Rhoodie is arrested at the French Riviera resort Juan les Pins. He will appear in Aix-en-Provence for extradition proceedings on 31 July 1979,

following the receipt of extradition documents from South Africa.

26 July 1979	The annual conference of the South African Council of Churches decides that some restrictions on interracial contact in South Africa are so objectionable that they cannot be obeyed with a clear conscience.

26 July 1979   The Schlebush Commission investigating a future constitution for South Africa, meets for the first time. The Chairman, A.L. Schlebusch, Minister of Justice and of the Interior, says that the Commission views the government's previous constitutional proposals as merely one of the sets of proposals under consideration, that he is happy to hear evidence from blacks, and that the commission will hold most of its hearings in public.

29 July 1979   The government is reported to have paid the family of the Black Consciousness leader, Steve Biko, R65,000 in settlement of claims for his death in custody in 1977. The Minister of Police, Louis le Grange, says the state is not admitting liability and the file on the Biko affair has now been closed.

7 Aug. 1979   The Prime Minister, P.W. Botha, draws up a comprehensive national strategy, reappraising the apartheid policy and reiterating his aim of establishing a constellation of independent African states.

13 Aug. 1979   The leader of two independent 'homelands'. Chief K. Matanzima and President Mangope of Bophuthatswana, support Mr. Botha's call for a constellation of states.

15 Aug. 1979   Addressing the National Party's Natal Provincial Congress in Durban, the Prime Minister puts forward a twelve-point plan for achieving a permanent solution to the country's multi-racial problems.

22 Aug. 1979   Dr. Eschel Rhoodie is extradited from France and handed over to the South African authorities. He appears briefly in Pretoria's Supreme Court charged with fraud and theft.

29 Aug. 1979   The National Party wins two uncertain victories in by-elections, with sharply reduced majorities in both seats.

30 Aug. 1979   Dr. Connie Mulder is acquitted and discharged on charges of contempt by the Pretoria Supreme Court. Justice W.G. Boshoff rules that there is no evidence that the questions Dr. Mulder has been called to answer before the Erasmus Commission, had any relevance to the Commission's mandate at that time.

31 Aug. 1979   P.W. Botha becomes the first South African Prime Minister to visit Soweto. His visit includes talks with the Soweto Community Council during which he promises that Soweto debts, totalling some R9m. will be written off.

3 Sept. 1979   Dr. Frederick van Zyl Slabbert is chosen as the Leader of the Opposition Progressive Federal Party (PFP) in succession to Colin Eglin, who is elected the party's National Chairman.

6 Sept. 1979   The Minister of Cooperation and Development, 'Piet' Koornhof, says that blacks in urban areas will not have political rights in the white political system but only in the 'homelands'.

12 Sept. 1979	South Africa's new Ambassador to the United Nations, Adrian Eksteen, presents his credentials to the Secretary-General, Dr. Kurt Waldheim.
12-13 Sept. 1979	At midnight the Republic of Venda becomes independent. Chief Mphephu will become Venda's first President.
19 Sept. 1979	The Chairman of the Commission of Inquiry into Consolidation of the 'Homelands', Hennie van der Walt, speaking at the National Party's Transvaal Congress, states that the proposals for redistribution of land will go beyond the provisions of the 1936 Land Act, hitherto regarded by the government as immutable.
21 Sept. 1979	The United Nations Security Council condemns the establishment of Venda as totally invalid.
25 Sept. 1979	The Minister of Manpower Utilisation, Fanie Botha, tells the Conference of the Federated Chamber of Industries that migrant workers from the 'homelands' are to be allowed to join registered black trade unions. An announcement is gazetted on 28 September 1979.
26 Sept. 1979	The Prime Minister tells the Cape Congress of the National Party that he is prepared to consider constructive suggestions for revision of the section of the Immorality Act which forbids miscegenation and of the Prohibition of Mixed Marriages Act.
27 Sept. 1979	The Minister of Community Development, Marais Steyn, announces that restaurants may open to all races without having to apply for special permits.
30 Sept. 1979	AZAPO elects new leaders at its first Congress, near Johannesburg. The 200 delegates choose as leader, Curtis Nkondo, a former Soweto teacher who resigned in protest against the separate school system for blacks. AZAPO declares itself opposed to all institutions created by the government and to the principle of ethnically-based institutions and advocates the creation of a single Parliamentary state.
2 Oct. 1979	The South African Barbarians rugby team completes its controversial tour of Britain with minimal disruption but against a background of condemnation from African and Commonwealth countries.
3 Oct. 1979	The results of four Parliamentary by-elections show a decided swing to the Herstigte Nasionale Party and low percentage polls. The National Party retains its seats, but by very reduced majorities.
8 Oct. 1979	Dr. Eschel Rhoodie is found guilty on five of seven charges of fraud or theft involving R63,000 of secret government funds and sentenced to six years imprisonment. He is granted bail the following day.
10 Oct. 1979	The PAC appoints V. Make as its new chairman and H. Isaacs to replace the assassinated Mr. Sibeko as its Director of Foreign Affairs.
Nov.-Dec. 1979	Black workers in the motor industry are involved in strike action in connection with demands for recognition by independent black trade unions.
1 Nov. 1979	Accepts Article VII of General Agreement on Tariffs and Trade.

2 Nov. 1979	The government announces a plan to allow white and black businessmen to form partnerships as part of a strategy to draw blacks into free enterprise.
7 Nov. 1979	Signs amendment to a multilateral treaty on plant protection.
7 Nov. 1979	The former Information Minister, Dr. Connie Mulder is elected leader of the newly-formed National Conservative Party.
7 Nov. 1979	The National Party loses its Edenvale, Johannesburg seat to the PFP, its first by-election defeat since it came to power in 1948. In three other disputed constituencies - Durbanville, Worcester and Eshowe - the National Party retains its seats but with reduced majorities.
9 Nov. 1979	A meeting between the Prime Minister, P.W. Botha and Coloured leaders for preliminary discussion on the constitutional future of the Coloured people ends in deadlock. The Labour Party leaders refuse to give evidence before the all-white Schlebusch Constitutional Commission.
12 Nov. 1979	The Minister for Coloured Relations, S.J.M. Steyn, states that no elections are planned after the current five-year term of the elected Coloured Representative Council (CRC) expires on 31 March 1980. He indicates that the CRC may be replaced by a nominated interim council, pending new constitutional arrangements.
15 Nov. 1979	The trial of twelve members of the banned ANC in Pietermaritzburg ends with the death sentence for one defendant and a total of 173 years' imprisonment for the others. Following an international campaign for clemency, the death sentence on James Mange is overruled by the Bloemfontein Appeal Court, on 11 September 1980, and he is sentenced to twenty years' imprisonment.
22 Nov. 1979	The Prime Minister, P.W. Botha, outlines a project for a constellation of states to some 250 leading businessmen. Its objective would be to improve the lives of all peoples in the Southern African region.
22 Nov. 1979	Signs multilateral GATT protocol supplementary to Geneva 1979 protocol.
5 Dec. 1979	The Prime Minister announces the appointment of a Commission of Inquiry into the reporting of defence matters, to be headed by Justice M.T. Steyn. The Commission is to inquire into and make recommendations on the dividing line between the rights of the media to inform and the right of the public to be informed on the one hand, and the interests of the security of the state on the other.
6 Dec. 1979	The Prime Minister announces a reorganization of the governmental administrative structure, under which the number of central executive institutions is to be reduced from thirty-nine to twenty-two, with responsibilities being distributed between eighteen ministries.
10 Dec. 1979	The government relaxes the Group Areas Act permit system on a wide range of shared facilities.
10 Dec. 1979	The Minister of Community Development announces that blacks will in future be admitted to certain amenities previously reserved for whites, including libraries, private hospitals, restaurants, theatres, concerts,

exhibitions, and drive-in cinemas.

11 Dec. 1979	Alexandre Moumbaris, who was serving a twelve-year sentence, convicted under the Terrorism Act, escapes from Pretoria Central, and succeeds in reaching Zambia. Two white academics from the University of Cape Town, escape with him.
12 Dec. 1979	Signs agreement with Lesotho on the issue and use of a road camp site on Cobham State Forest.
18 Dec. 1979	Signs multilateral treaty on import and licensing procedure (GATT).
18 Dec. 1979	Signs multilateral treaty relating to bovine meat (GATT).
24 Dec. 1979	The Security Police detains the President and six Executive Members of the recently formed Congress of South African Students (COSAS).
29 Dec. 1979	Signs multilateral treaty on dairy arrangements (GATT).
Jan. 1980	The Schlebush Commission holds hearings in Cape Town on the country's constitutional future. Among the organizations submitting memoranda, or alternative proposals, are the PFP, the NRP, the South African Indian Council and Inkatha.
3 Jan. 1980	A police station at Soekmekaar, Northern Transvaal, is attacked.
6 Jan. 1980	Signs loan agreement with Malawi.
10 Jan. 1980	Security Police in Port Elizabeth, detain three black civil rights leaders after the Port Elizabeth Black Civic Organisation (PEBCO) decide to implement a city-wide strike and demonstrations against the planned removal of residents from Walmer. Banning orders are placed on all three on their release from detention on 27 February 1980.
12 Jan. 1980	A British Sports Council team begins a three-week fact-finding tour of South Africa to investigate racial discrimination in sport and to report on its findings.
21 Jan. 1980	It is revealed in Switzerland that the International University Exchange Fund's Deputy Director, Craig Williamson, has been working as an agent for the South African Security Police. This is confirmed by the Minister of Police, Louis le Grange, on 24 January 1980.
25 Jan. 1980	A bank and twenty-five hostages are seized at Silverton, Pretoria. Two of the hostages die; several are injured; all three ANC guerrillas are killed.
31 Jan. 1980	The Swiss government send an official protest to the South African government over the illegal activities of South African agents operating in Switzerland and liaising with Anti-Apartheid organizations. The International University Exchange Fund (IUEF) Director, Lieutenant-General Erikssen, resigns with effect from July 1980, his health having deteriorated after the exposure of Craig Williamson. Financial irregularities are also alleged.
6 Feb. 1980	The Prime Minister explains that the administrative rationalization is to be implemented in four states, and announces that the Department of National

Security (DONS) is to become the Directorate of National Intelligence (DNI). Mr. Botha further rejects calls made by Helen Suzman, (PFP) for a Parliamentary investigation into allegations that DONS has intercepted mail and tapped telephones to build up dossiers on NP opponents.

6 Feb. 1980

The Minister of Cooperation and Development, Dr. Piet Koornhof, announces that the '72-hour curfew' will be lifted on a trial basis in Pretoria and Bloemfontein, as part of a movement to remove restrictions.

7 Feb. 1980

Transkei announces it is re-establishing diplomatic relations with South Africa because South Africa is now willing to negotiate over disputed land.

12 Feb. 1980

The Quail Commission, examining, at the request of the government of the Ciskei, the question of the feasibility of independence of the Ciskei releases its report. It finds that ninety per cent of all Ciskeians favour a one-man one-vote system within South Africa and advises against independence as a first option.

15 Feb. 1980

Prime Minister P.W. Botha decides to invite leaders of the black 'homelands' to join in a discussion on a 'statement of intent', by all South Africans.

18 Feb. 1980

In a joint statement the leaders of seven black 'homelands' set out the basis of a possible consensus solution for South Africa's constitutional future.

19 Feb. 1980

The South African Defence Force has taken over from the police the security of Northern Natal since the area is becoming a third front in Security Force action against guerrilla infiltration.

21 Feb. 1980

South Africa warns Mozambique it will not hesitate to strike back if Mozambique continues to shelter guerrillas conducting murderous operations and acts of sabotage against South Africa.

22 Feb. 1980

The South African Coloured Persons' Council Bill is introduced into Parliament. A government memorandum released on the same day gives obstruction by the Labour Party as the reason for the abolition of the previous Coloured Persons' Representative Council. The Bill is opposed by the PFP and the NRP.

28 Feb. 1980

An Angolan priest, the Reverend David Russell, is sentenced to a year's imprisonment for defying his banning order and attending a church synod meeting. He is released on 18 December 1980 after the Supreme Court has, on 5 December 1980, ruled an appeal that his sentence should be suspended except for fourteen days.

29 Feb. 1980

Justice Petrus Cillié submits to Parliament his report on the violent racial disturbances beginning in Soweto in June 1976, and covering the period to February 1977. The report concludes that the immediate cause of the riots was the government's decision to introduce the use of Afrikaans on an equal basis with English as the official teaching medium in black schools. Underlying dissatisfaction had been exploited by activists.

Mar. 1980

A campaign is launched for the release of Nelson Mandela. Organizations supporting the campaign include the Soweto 'Committee of 10', Inkatha, AZAPO, the Labour Party, the Natal Indian Congress and the South African

Council of Churches (SACC).

3 Mar. 1980
A large cache of arms is discovered in a township near Springs, East of Johannesburg. Together with the buried arms are bundles of ANC leaflets.

9 Mar. 1980
Prime Minister P.W. Botha announces that all South Africa's races will take part in a constitutional conference, but he emphasizes that he rejects one-man, one-vote and systems based on consensus and federalism.

11 Mar. 1980
After a Cabinet meeting, both P.W. Botha and Dr. Treurnicht issue statements calling for party unity.

11 Mar. 1980
Signs agreement with Taiwan for the reciprocal exemption from taxes on income.

11 Mar. 1980
Signs agreement with Taiwan for the reciprocal treatment of navigation.

11 Mar. 1980
Signs air service agreement with Taiwan.

11 Mar. 1980
Signs agreement with Taiwan for scientific and technological cooperation.

12 Mar. 1980
The Nederduitse Gereformerde Kerk (NGK) together with its sister church for blacks (the NGK in Afrika), Coloureds (the NG Sendingkerk) and Indians (the Reformed Church in Africa) issue a statement stating that the Churches bring no objection in principle if the authorities judge that circumstances justify reconsideration of the Immorality Act and the Mixed Marriages Act.

12 Mar. 1980
A court in Pretoria sentences nine blacks to terms of imprisonment from five to seven years on charges of training as guerrillas outside South Africa or recruiting others to undergo training.

13 Mar. 1980
The former Prime Minister and President, John Vorster, re-emerges into public life with a speech in Bloemfontein in which he questions P.W. Botha's policy initiatives and backs the hard-line taken by Dr. Treurnicht. Separate development, he says, is the salvation of South Africa.

15 Mar. 1980
The Prime Minister states that those who disagree with the government's 12-point strategy, accepted by all four National Party Provincial Congresses in 1979, and unanimously endorsed by the Cabinet, do not belong within the National Party.

16 Mar. 1980
Dr. Connie Mulder, leader of the recently-formed Nasionale Konservatiewe Party (NKP), foresees a new political alliance bringing to power a conservative government.

21 Mar. 1980
The Prime Minister dismisses allegations that the Cabinet is divided, and denies that there are differences in principle between Dr. Treurnicht and himself.

21-23 Mar. 1980
A weekend of events commemorate the twentieth anniversary of the Sharpeville shootings on 21 March 1960. Speakers attack the policy of apartheid.

26 Mar. 1980
The 1980 Defence Budget amounts to R2,074 million or fifteen percent of

the total Budget.

Apr.-July 1980	Serious unrest among the Coloured population leads to a school boycott, joined by students and teachers and accompanied by widespread demonstrations ending in violence. Over thirty people are killed in rioting, while several hundred are detained by police.
1 Apr. 1980	The South African Coloured Persons' Council Bill comes into force. It abolishes the Coloured Persons' Representative Council (CRC) and provides for the creation of a Coloured Persons' Council (CPC) to consist of not more than thirty members nominated by the State President, with an Executive comprising an Administrator of Coloured Affairs and four other members, also appointed by the State President.
2 Apr. 1980	Among those giving the 'Constellation' plan warm, but qualified support, is Harry Oppenheimer. Opening the 'Constellation of Southern African States' exhibit he says that this excellent idea can only succeed if racial discrimination is eliminated and a settlement is reached over Namibia.
4 Apr. 1980	ANC insurgents launch a rifle, rocket and grenade attack on Booysens Police Station, Johannesburg. Pamphlets are scattered demanding the release from Robben Island of Walter Sisulu.
11 Apr. 1980	The Minister of Manpower Utilization announces the removal of the ban on the employment of skilled black construction workers in white areas.
11 Apr. 1980	The Prime Minister states that the government has no intention of releasing Nelson Mandela.
11 Apr. 1980	The United Nations Security Council unanimously adopts a resolution condemning South Africa for continued, intensified and unprovoked acts against Zambia. South Africa blames terrorist attacks launched from Zambia for border instability.
12-13 Apr. 1980	Chief Buthelezi urges his supporters to use the official community councils in black urban areas as part of the democratic struggle against the apartheid system.
14 Apr. 1980	The Steyn Commission of Inquiry appointed to investigate relations between the Security Forces - both Military and Police - and the press proposes that new restrictions should be introduced on the publication of details of acts of political violence and the manufacture of arms. The system of accreditation of journalists should be more strictly applied and foreign correspondents should be subject to a more vigorous registration procedure.
15 Apr. 1980	The (Coloured) Labour Party National Executive Committee resolves to expel from the party anyone accepting nomination from the government to the Coloured Persons' Council (CPC).
15 Apr. 1980	The leader of the PFP states that the PFP as a party has not taken a decision regarding the campaign to have Nelson Mandela released, but he, personally, has urged his release providing he renounces violence.
20 Apr. 1980	Mounting protests by Coloured students against the educational and political system escalate further. Representatives of more than sixty Coloured high

schools, teacher training colleges and the University of the Western Cape resolve to continue their boycott of classes. The boycott begins on 21 April 1980 and is widely observed by approximately 100,000 students from seventy schools for three weeks.

21 Apr. 1980   The Coloured schools boycott is joined by pupils at a number of Indian schools in Pretoria and Natal. Support is also pledged by Black Consciousness groups.

29 Apr. 1980   Hundreds of Coloured school children are arrested in Johannesburg during a student-police confrontation during the school boycott in terms of the Riotous Assemblies Act. The Prime Minister warns in Parliament that such actions would meet with the full might of the state.

6 May 1980   The Advocate-General's report confirms that the Herstigte Nasionale Party's office telephones have been illegally tapped and calls intercepted. He recommends stricter controls over the State Security Services' monitoring of mail and telephone conversations.

6 May 1980   Black PEBCO activist Thozamile Botha breaks his banning order and escapes to Lesotho.

7 May 1980   The interim majority report of the Schlebusch Commission is tabled. A minority report by the PFP members of the Commission opposes the proposal to create a President's Council which would not include black representatives.

8 May 1980   Prime Minister P.W. Botha announces that his government accepts the recommendations of the Schlebusch Commission including the replacement of the Senate by a President's Council comprised of sixty Whites, Coloureds, Indians and Chinese. Also proposed is the nomination of twenty additional Members of Parliament to be appointed on a proportional basis by the leaders of the political parties.

8 May 1980   In the Fauresmith by-election the National Party retains its seat against a double right-wing challenge from the Herstigte Nasionale Party and the recently formed National Conservative Party.

12 May 1980   The British Sports Council urges the International Olympic Committee (IOC) and all other international sporting governing bodies to bring South Africa back into international competition.

20 May 1980   Signs multilateral Convention on the Conservation of Antarctic Marine Living Resources.

22 May 1980   In a joint sitting of both Houses of Parliament it is unanimously agreed to re-entrench the language rights in the constitution in anticipation of the abolition of the Senate.

26 May 1980   Fifty-three churchmen are arrested at a demonstration in central Johannesburg against the detention of a fellow clergyman who had supported the schools boycott by Coloured students. They are released on bail the following day, after being charged under the Riotous Assemblies Act, and warned to appear in court on 1 July 1980.

27 May 1980   The schools boycott spreads to universities and to rural areas and the 'homelands' following warnings against political protests, widespread detentions are reported.

28 May 1980   The schools boycott spreads to the black townships and riot police are in action in Durban and Port Elizabeth. At Elsies River, near Cape Town, police fire on Coloured children, killing two and wounding three.

29 May 1980   The Republic of South Africa Constitution Fifth Amendment Bill, establishing a framework for deliberations on the country's future constitutional, economic and social development is introduced into Parliament. The Bill is based closely on the majority recommendations of the Schlebusch Commission.

June-July 1980   A further series of strikes in the motor industry, affecting especially the Volkswagen works at Uitenhage, ends on 14 July with an agreement including a twenty-five percent increase in minimum wages for blacks in the industry.

1 June 1980   The SASOL I fuel plant complex at Sasolburg, fifty miles south of Johannesburg, is attacked. On the same night SASOL II at Secunda suffers an unsuccessful limpet mine explosion which fails to set off fires. Oliver Tambo, President of the ANC, claims that both attacks were made by ANC guerrilla units.

6 June 1980   Dr. Renfrew Christie, an academic and former student leader from the University of Cape Town, is sentenced to ten years imprisonment, with four other sentences of five years each to run concurrently, after being found guilty on five charges under the Terrorism Act. He is said to have supplied information to the ANC concerning South Africa's nuclear programme, and to have exposed vital installations to the danger of sabotage.

7-8 June 1980   The South African Black Alliance (SABA) condemns the proposed composition of the President's Council and the nomination of its members.

11 June 1980   The Wiehahn Commission publishes its recommendations on the training of black workers, including government- supported training in industrial relations.

12 June 1980   The government publishes details of proposed legislation under which the Minister of Defence could designate any place, area or installation as a national key point for which adequate security measures would have to be taken.

12 June 1980   The Republic of South Africa Constitution Bill receives its third reading. Among its provisions are the abolition of the Senate and the creation of a sixty-member President's Council comprising Whites, Coloured, Indian and Chinese representatives nominated by the State President for a five-year term. A new office, that of Vice State President, will be created: he will act as chairman of the President's Council. It is opposed by the PFP principally on the grounds of the exclusion of blacks.

13 June 1980   Following a meeting 4-13 June 1980, held at the request of the African group, the United Nations Security Council unanimously adopts a resolution strongly condemning South Africa for its massive repression and for its

defiance of General Assembly and Security Council resolutions. Inter alia it calls for the release of all political prisoners, including Nelson Mandela.

13 June 1980   John Wiley, the leader of the South African Party (SAP), announces that his party is to disband. SAP representatives will retain their seats and join the National Party, thus increasing the NP strength in the House to 136.

16 June 1980   The ANC issues a call for the intensification of the liberation struggle on all fronts, but demonstrations on the anniversary of Sharpeville are generally low key.

18-19 June 1980   Renewed rioting occurs in the Cape. Criminal elements in the Coloured community are blamed. Official figures give twenty-nine dead and 141 injured. Damage to shops and businesses runs into millions of rands.

23 June 1980   The Prime Minister warns the country that confrontation awaits it if his proposed President's Council fails. Pretoria is prepared to create consultative bodies for Coloured, Indian and Black leaders, but not to accept majority rule as the ultimate end.

25 June 1980   Helen Joseph, the seventy-five year old political campaigner, is served with a two-year banning order. She is already a `listed person', has had several restrictions previously imposed upon her, as well as being detained and sentenced to imprisonment. She regards her banning order - her fourth - as a `certificate of merit'.

26 June 1980   Zimbabwe's Prime Minister, Robert Mugabe, announces that he will cut diplomatic ties with South Africa.

July 1980   Boycotts continue at a number of black high schools and higher primary schools, particularly in the Eastern Cape, with violent disturbances recurring.

1 July 1980   The Chamber of Mines of South Africa announces wage increases of fifteen percent and twenty-eight percent respectively, for black face and surface workers in the gold and coal mining industries.

8 July 1980   Foreign Minister `Pik' Botha announces that all senior members of the South African diplomatic mission in Salisbury have been withdrawn.

16 July 1980   The `Committee of 81', representing all Coloured schools and colleges in the Western Cape, decide to end class boycotts.

17 July 1980   The United States expresses deep concern to the South African Ambassador, Donald Sole, over government and police response to strikes and demonstrations. Mentioned particularly are the pervasive ban on peaceful assembly, widespread detentions without charge or trial, and bannings of moderate leaders of all racial groups.

18 July 1980   The Nigerian President of the Supreme Council for Sport in Africa (SCSA) states that Britain and other countries maintaining sporting ties with South Africa are toying with the unity of the Commonwealth, African and Caribbean countries, particularly object to the British Lions Rugby Union tour of South Africa that ended on 14 July 1980.

19-20 July 1980	'Homeland' leaders do not necessarily reject the concept of the President's Council, provided it is revised to include black representation. A similar stance is taken by the Urban Council's Association of South Africa, speaking for leaders of the officially-recognized community councils in black urban areas.
23 July 1980	The Prime Minister announces that the government is establishing formal machinery to promote its concept of a 'constellation of Southern African states'. Dr. Gerhard de Kock, the Finance Ministers Chief Economic Adviser, is appointed co-ordinator of Constellation Affairs to chair a Constellation Committee to examine, inter alia, proposals for a multilateral development bank, industrial decentralization and financial arrangements between participants.
30 July 1980	Following decisions by the 'Committee of 81' on 16 July and 30 July 1980 Coloured students suspend their boycott of schools in the Western Cape.
1 Aug. 1980	A strike by black municipal workers in Johannesburg, ends when police supervise the removal of over 1,000 dismissed men. The Chairman of the unofficial Black Municipal Workers' Union (BMWU), Joseph Mavi, is arrested and subsequently charged under the Sabotage Act, together with the BMWU Secretary.
5 Aug. 1980	It is reported that the Netherlands government, co-sponsors of the International University Exchange Fund (IUEF) along with the governments of Canada, Denmark, Norway and Sweden, has withdrawn its financial support for the Fund and that Denmark and Norway have also ended their contributions.
5 Aug. 1980	The trial begins in Pretoria of nine men accused of having planned the siege of a suburban bank in Pretoria in January, in which five people died, of belonging to the banned ANC and of having undergone military training in Angola.
7 Aug. 1980	A delegation of the South African Council of Churches meets the Prime Minister and other government leaders, following calls by churchmen for urgent discussions on the causes of unrest in the country. The government undertakes to end all compulsory mass removals.
8 Aug. 1980	The government abandons the proposal to create a separate black advisory council.
11 Aug. 1980	After a meeting between P.W. Botha and the leader of the (Coloured) Labour Party and the Freedom Party, the government reportedly abandons its proposals to create a nominated Coloured Persons' Council (CPC).
15 Aug. 1980	The offices of a member of the Prime Ministers' team, responsible for drawing up plans for a Southern African 'constellation of states', Professor Jan Lombard, are destroyed at the University of Pretoria. A rightwing group, the Wit Commando later claims responsibility for the bomb attack.
20 Aug. 1980	The Prime Minister meets Lesotho's Chief Leabua Jonathan in an attempt to improve relations between the two countries.
22 Aug. 1980	Leaders of Port Elizabeth's black secondary school children, decide to end

a four-month boycott of classes. Negotiations have taken place between the local parents' committee and the Port Elizabeth Students Council (PESCO).

26 Aug. 1980	Prime Minister P.W. Botha, announces a reorganization of his government, with effect from 7 October, including the appointment of seven new ministers.
27 Aug. 1980	The government decides to lift the ban on political meetings affecting the main metropolitan areas. Announcing this, Minister of Justice Alwyn Schlebusch, says he will not hesitate to reintroduce the ban if it is necessary to maintain public peace.
1 Sept. 1980	Dr. Andries P. Treurnicht, Minister of Public Works, Statistics and Tourism, is unanimously re-elected as the National Party's leader in the Transvaal. As the chief spokesman for the conservative wing he re-affirms that the party will continue to work for independent national groups on a geographical basis.
2 Sept. 1980	Zimbabwe announces it has severed diplomatic relations with South Africa, but will maintain a trade mission in Johannesburg.
3 Sept. 1980	General Constand Viljoen is appointed as Chief of the South African Defence Force (SADF) and Lieutenant-General Jan Geldenhuys as Chief of the Army, with effect from 7 October 1980.
3 Sept. 1980	John Wiley, former leader of the South African Party, is elected as National Party member for Simonstown, defeating the PFP candidate by 1,182 votes in an eighty-two per cent poll.
4 Sept. 1980	At a congress in Bloemfontein, the Prime Minister says that the National Party has to draw together as many people as possible, allowing them to maintain their separate identities, but uniting them in a common front against Marxism.
19 Sept. 1980	The town of Mafeking is officially surrendered by the Republic of South Africa to the Republic of Bophuthatswana, and upon its transfer changes its name to the African form 'Mafikeng'.
22 Sept. 1980	Signs treaty with Zimbabwe for the reciprocal appointment of trade representatives.
24 Sept. 1980	Closure of more than seventy black schools, mainly in the Cape Province, is ordered by the government following five months of boycotts by pupils. Talks with community leaders have failed and incidents of violence continue.
29 Sept. 1980	The former Secretary for Information, Dr. Eschel Rhoodie, is acquitted by the Bloemfontein Appeal Court of five charges of fraud. His conviction and sentence are set aside.
2 Oct. 1980	The Prime Minister appoints fifty-six members to the President's Council, comprising forty-one Whites, seven Coloureds, seven Indians, and one Chinese.
3 Oct. 1980	The leader of the New Republic Party, Vause Raw, states that his party is prepared to give the President's Council a chance as a start on the road to

a negotiated future.

5 Oct. 1980   Chief Lennox Sebe, Chief Minister of the Ciskei, accepts independence in principle, and wins endorsement for his stand at a rally in Zwelitsha, near East London. He pledges to hold a referendum on the issue.

6 Oct. 1980   Parliament meets in special session to elect the National Party candidate, Alwyn Schlebusch, as the nation's first Vice-President. In this role, he will be Chairman of the President's Council, from 1 January 1981.

17 Oct. 1980   The Prime Minister, P.W. Botha, concludes a five-day state visit to Taiwan, during which he and his twenty-member delegation meet Taiwan's Premier and other officials and discuss substantial cooperation in economic and technical projects.

23 Oct. 1980   In the by-elections at East London North, the seat is won by the conservative NRP, defeating the PFP's candidate D. John Malcomess who had previously held the seat.

23 Oct. 1980   Amendments to loan agreement with Malawi.

31 Oct. 1980   The draft laws are gazetted providing some benefits for black people. These include greatly increased mobility and security of tenure for blacks qualified to be in white areas. Piet Koornhof claims the proposed Bills are the beginning of a process of normalizing race relations.

3 Nov. 1980   A nationwide strike is launched by black journalists for increased pay and for recognition of their union, the Media Workers' Association of South Africa (MWASA).

5 Nov. 1980   Disturbances break out in the black townships of Port Elizabeth and police open fire on rioting crowds. Tensions rise in the areas.

10 Nov. 1980   Signs multilateral treaty extending the declaration on the provisional accession of Colombia to GATT.

12 Nov. 1980   The Minister of (black) Education and Training announces that compulsory education for black children will be introduced in stages, with a first programme beginnning near Pretoria.

13 Nov. 1980   South Africa's Medical Association agrees to ask its ethical committee to conduct a public investigation into issues raised by the death of Steve Biko in police custody in November 1977.

26 Nov. 1980   At the end of the Soekmekaar and Silverton trial in Pretoria, three young black men are found guilty of high treason, as well as of attempted murder and robbery with aggravating circumstances and are sentenced to death. Six others are given prison sentences. The ANC calls on the world community to intervene to save the men.

29 Nov. 1980   At a National Party rally in Ladysmith (Natal), the Prime Minister restates his policies. The government is not thinking in terms of a union or a federal form of government for all population groups, nor of one man, one vote, but proposes to establish a constellation of states.

10 Dec. 1980	A new Coloured political movement, the Congress of the People (COPE) is launched in Cape Town's Bellville district.
12 Dec. 1980	A white extremist group, the `Wit Kommando' claims responsibility for the bombing of the offices of Professor F.A. Maritz at the University of South Africa.
12 Dec. 1980	During the thirty-fifth Regular Session, the United Nations General Assembly adopts two resolutions concerning South Africa's nuclear capacity, requesting the Security Council to prohibit all forms of co-operation with South Africa in the nuclear field and demanding that South Africa submit all its nuclear installations to inspection by the International Atomic Energy Agency.
16 Dec. 1980	The United Nations General Assembly adopts a total of eighteen resolutions on the situation in South Africa and problems created by the application of the government's apartheid policy.
17 Dec. 1980	The results of the referendum on the issue of independence for Ciskei, held on 4 December 1981, are announced. They show a decided majority in favour of independence.
23 Dec. 1980	Four black newspapers, Post Transvaal, Saturday Post, Sunday Post and the Sowetan, are banned on a technicality on the same day that the eight week strike of black journalists ends.
29 Dec. 1980	Justice Coetzee in the Rand Supreme Court refuses to lift an order barring resumption of publication of four black newspapers. Security police serve three-year banning orders on the President and Vice-President of the black journalists' trade union, Media Workers of South Africa. A storm of protest erupts, even from the strongly pro-government Afrikaans press.
9 Jan. 1981	Draft legislation is published giving owners and managers of hotels and restaurants the right to admit blacks.
14 Jan. 1981	Under a proposed amendment to the Population Registration Act South Africans of all races will have their fingerprints taken and recorded on a central fingerprint register. A uniform identity document will be issued to all races.
19 Jan. 1981	In a referendum organized by King William's Town municipality, the voting is overwhelmingly against incorporation into the Ciskei, despite a recommendation from the van der Walt Commission on consolidation of the homelands that this be done.
20 Jan. 1981	The Minister of the Interior informs the Argus Printing and Publishing Company that if it applied for re-registration of the Post newspapers these would be banned because they had aimed at creating a revolutionary climate in South Africa. This decision is widely condemned.
22 Jan. 1981	Percy Qoboza, who had resigned as editor of the Post papers on 13 January 1981 and left immediately for the United States, says in Washington that in the light of the Minister's remarks it is difficult to see how a credible newspaper for blacks can ever be created in South Africa.

22 Jan. 1981	Student committees decide to end the boycott of black schools, the Congress of South African Students (COSAS) having declared itself in favour of suspending the action in order to 'regroup forces and formulate a new strategy'.
23 Jan. 1981	In the House of Assembly, twelve new nominated members are sworn in. They include Professsor Owen Horwood, former Leader of the Senate.
27 Jan. 1981	A Marine Traffic Bill empowers the Minister of Transport Affairs to order ships to be stopped or searched if they are believed to be carrying drugs or cargo in persons constituting a threat to the sovereignty, integrity or political independence of South Africa. The Bill is passed on 2 February 1981 with the support of all parties.
27 Jan. 1981	Former President John Vorster says he has decided to withdraw from politics for family reasons.
27 Jan. 1981	The government decides to close The Post and The Sunday Post because they have become media for communist viewpoints.
28 Jan. 1981	Prime Minister Botha announces that general elections to the House of Assembly and the Provincial Councils will be held on 29 April 1981, on the grounds that seventeen parliamentary and thirteen provincial by-elections are due in the near future. They are to be held eighteen months earlier than is necessary under the Constitution.
28 Jan. 1981	The Security Police arrest Major A.M. Kozlov, a senior officer in the Soviet KGB, during his third visit to South Africa in 1980, on charges of spying in South Africa.
28 Jan. 1981	Signs loan agreement with Lesotho.
30 Jan. 1981	General Constand Viljoen, Chief of the South African Defence Force, announces that earlier in the day a South African commando has attacked and destroyed the planning and control headquarters of the ANC at Matola, Maputo, Mozambique.
2 Feb. 1981	A new black daily paper, promising to expose political ills, appears in Johannesburg. The Sowetan has the same format as the banned Post and Sunday Post and is apparently following the same editorial policies.
3 Feb. 1981	The President's Council is formally inaugurated as a policy-advisory, problem-directed, reform-orientated and future-looking body. The new tri-racial Council, consisting of sixty-one nominated White, Coloured and Indian members is the first multi-racial institution of its kind to be established in South Africa.
5 Feb 1981	Police announce the arrest of a number of whites in connection with sabotage acts for which the Wit Kommando has claimed responsibility on 15 August 1980 and on 12 December 1980.
6 Feb. 1981	The government withdraws three controversial Parliamentary Bills relating to freedom of movement of the black population for penetrating revision by a ten-member technical committee headed by Justice Rossouw.

8 Feb. 1981	Mozambique stresses its continued support for the ANC, in a statement made at the funeral of twelve ANC members killed in the South African raid on Matola, Maputo, on 30 January 1981.
14 Feb. 1981	A new right-wing group `Aksie Eie Toekoms (Action for our Own Future) (AET)' is founded in Pretoria, mainly by Afrikaner academics. It stands for strict racial segregation at all levels.
20 Feb. 1981	Prime Minister P.W. Botha announces that the Ciskei will become fully independent on 4 December 1981.
21 Feb. 1981	The Republic of South Africa Constitution Amendment Bill, providing for the extension of the terms of office of nominated and indirectly elected members of the Assembly, after the dissolution of Parliament and empowering the State President to alter the names of electoral divisions by proclamation, is condemned by the opposition as gerrymandering.
22 Feb. 1981	The Minister of Manpower Utilisation warns that the government is planning to take a tougher line with the rapidly expanding and increasingly militant black trade unions. The newly established industrial court may be used to discipline certain unions.
22 Feb. 1981	The Soviet Union supports Mozambique after the South African raid on Matola by sending two warships to Maputo. More are expected soon.
23 Feb. 1981	The Prime Minister declares that Soviet threats will not prevent South Africa from attacking ANC bases in Mozambique.
27 Feb. 1981	The Minister of Police announces the arrest of five further alleged Wit Kommando members.
2 Mar. 1981	The United Nations General Assembly Credentials Committee rejects the credentials of the South African delegation, by six votes to one.
6 Mar. 1981	The United Nations General Assembly resolution calls on the Security Council to impose comprehensive sanctions against South Africa to compel it to end its illegal occupation of Namibia.
18 Mar. 1981	The PAC announces in Dar es Salaam that it has reinstated seventy-two members expelled from the movement in July 1978.
23 Mar. 1981	Nominations for the elections close with candidates for the 165 seats in the House of Assembly being nominated as follows: National Party, 155; Progressive Federal Party seventy-seven, Herstigte Nasionale Party, eighty-nine; New Republic Party, thirty-eight; National Conservative Party, nine and Aksie Eie Toekoms, two.
23 Mar. 1981	The HNP's policies are defined by its leader, Jaap Marais: no concessions to the black man; withdrawal of South Africa from the United Nations; no mixing of races in sport, parks, hotels or theatres; a homeland for Coloureds and no political mixing with them and an inflation rate of only two percent.
24 Mar. 1981	The government announces that it is terminating its preferential trade agreement concluded with Rhodesia in 1964.

25 Mar. 1981	Dr. C.P. Mulder, speaking for the National Conservative Party (NCP) discloses that his party has reached an understanding with the HNP not to nominate candidates against one another.
25 Mar. 1981	The leader of the NRP, Vause Raw, states that the country's major parties are divided and in disarray and that the NRP could lay the base for a regrouping of moderates.
30 Mar. 1981	From 1 June 1981, holders of Zimbabwean passports will require visas to enter South Africa. The Zimbabwean government reciprocates amid deteriorating relations in both political and economic spheres.
30 Mar. 1981	The Irish government's efforts to persuade the Irish Rugby Football Union to call off its tour of South Africa fail.
3 Apr. 1981	The PFP issues its election manifesto, laying emphasis on the party's aim of caring for the voter, linking the future security and welfare of the whites with the security and welfare of blacks.
6 Apr. 1981	The Heads of State of Botswana, Lesotho, Mozambique and Swaziland meet in Mbabane, to discuss South African military incursions and subversive activities against black Southern African states.
13 Apr. 1981	The Transkei Legislative Assembly approves a Criminal Law Amendment Bill making it illegal for anyone to publish anything about the Transkei government without ministerial approval.
16 Apr. 1981	The government seizes the passport of Bishop Desmond Tutu, the Anglican General Secretary of the South African Council of Churches, apparently because of his speeches made in the United States in March 1981.
17 Apr. 1981	The government announces that King William's Town will not be handed over to the Ciskei at independence.
20-21 Apr. 1981	A bomb explosion during the night at a power station near Durban, causes an extensive blackout and temporarily paralyzes industry in the area. It is attributed to members of the ANC.
29 Apr. 1981	The elections result in the return to power, with a slightly reduced majority, of the National Party and notable gains for the opposition Progressive Federal Party. Right-wing opposition groups, led by the HNP, more than quintuple their votes, but gain no seats.
30 Apr. 1980	The Prime Minister warns neighbouring states against supporting 'terrorist' movement operations from their territories, but re-iterates that he is ready to conclude non-aggression pacts with them.
May 1981	Police make more than seventy arrests at student and trade union demonstrations, protesting against official celebrations marking the twentieth anniversary of the founding of the Republic of South Africa.
8 May 1981	Relations between Zimbabwe and South Africa deteriorate further when the Minister of Police, L. le Grange, threatens retaliatory action if Robert Mugabe persists in supporting the ANC.

| 12 May 1981 | P.W. Botha is re-elected as National Party leader. |

14 May 1981 | The United Nations General Assembly publishes a roster of sixty-five multi-national companies supposedly in 'criminal collaboration' with South Africa and a blacklist of some 270 sportsmen and women who have furthered sports contacts with South Africa. This publication was subsequently updated.

22 May 1981 | The Minister of National Education has approved amendments to certain Acts, to encourage the normalization of sports relations.

25-27 May 1981 | There are several sabotage attacks - in Soweto, on the Natal coast, East London and in Durban - for which the ANC claim responsibility.

30 May 1981 | State President M. Viljoen describes the twenty years since South Africa became a Republic as a 'golden era' during which the country has experienced phenomenal growth and development in the economic, industrial, scientific and technological fields.

1 June 1981 | Festivities to mark the twentieth anniversary of the South African Republic reach a climax with a massive military display in Durban, attended by P.W. Botha, the Prime Minister.

1 June 1981 | Three offices of the PFP are petrol-bombed in Johannesburg. Responsibility is claimed by the South African Liberation Support Cadre (SALSC).

3 June 1981 | Rioting breaks out in the Coloured townships south-west of Johannesburg. A class boycott and arrests follow.

11 June 1981 | Lesotho and South Africa decide to establish a consultative committee to resolve misunderstandings arising from the movement of people across their common border.

15 June 1981 | In two separate statements, the ANC and the UN Committee Against Apartheid call for a more concerted and intensified effort from the international community to bring about change in South Africa.

15 June 1981 | Six South African members of the PAC are sentenced to fifteen years' imprisonment, by the Tanzanian High Court, for the killing in Dar es Salaam of David Sibeko, PAC representative at the United Nations.

16 June 1981 | On the anniversary of the Soweto uprising, police and troops cordon off Soweto and other black townships in the Johannesburg and Pretoria areas, stopping and searching all vehicles. Sporadic clashes occur near the Regina Mundi Roman Catholic Church in Soweto.

21 June 1981 | Police confirm the capture of eight leaders of the Nigeria-based South African Youth Revolutionary Council (SAYRCO).

30 June 1981 | Zwelakhe Sisulu, President of the Black Media Workers Association of South Africa, and son of Walter Sisulu, is arrested under security laws that provide for unlimited detention without trial.

30 June 1981 | The campaign against dissident South African students continues with the banning of three more students immediately after the serving of restriction

orders on Andrew Boraine, President of the National Union of South African Students (NUSAS) and son of opposition M.P., Dr. Alex Boraine.

17 July 1981   The Government Gazette announces an extension to the provisions of the 1964 Tear Gas Act to widen the range of those empowered to use tear gas.

21 July 1981   Explosions occur at two electrical power stations in the Eastern Transvaal. Responsibility is claimed by the ANC's military wing Umkhonto We Sizwe.

31 July 1981   The first person to be banned under the 1976 Internal Security Act, Fatima Meer, is banned again for a further five years.

1 Aug. 1981   For the sixth time in eight months, a leader of the Media Workers' Association of South Africa (MWASA) is banned. Its Acting President and senior reporter on the East London Daily Dispatch, is served with a two-and-a-half year banning and house arrest under the Internal Security Act.

12 Aug. 1981   A rocket attack is launched on the Voortrekkerhoogte military area near Pretoria, which leads to the larger black townships in the Pretoria-Johannesburg area being temporarily sealed off.

14 Aug. 1981   Co-operation and Development Minister, Piet Koornhof, states that uncontrolled squatting cannot be tolerated, and will not be allowed in the interests of the squatters themselves... No squatting will be allowed on the relevant site in Nyanga.

18 Aug. 1981   Deadlock is reached between the Peninsula Administration Board and the Nyanga squatters.

18 Aug. 1981   Three black men are found guilty of high treason and of having been involved in the sabotage of SASOL fuel installations and the attack on Booysens Police Station. They are sentenced to death, with appeals being lodged on their behalf.

19 Aug. 1981   A mass arrest of 2,000 Nyanaga squatters is carried out, under immigration legislation allowing summary deportation. They are to be charged under the Admission of Persons to the Republic Regulation Act of 1972.

20 Aug. 1981   Mass protests in Cape Town over the enforced removal from Nyanga camp are followed by widespread criticism both within and without South Africa.

20 Aug. 1981   South Africa bans three white Zimbabweans from visiting South Africa and addressing members of the University of Cape Town.

25 Aug. 1981   Confrontation between South Africa and Transkei over the deportation and return to Transkei of squatters from the Cape Town area.

22 Sept. 1981   The Broederbond reverses its 1972 decision to expel HNP members from its ranks. This is interpreted as confirmation of growing Afrikaner discontent over P.W. Botha's 'enlightened approach' to racial matters.

23 Sept. 1981   The Rand Supreme Court rules that blacks from the homelands can establish the right to reside permanently in towns in white South Africa.

24 Sept. 1981   In the first post-independence election in Transkei, the ruling Transkei

National Independence Party (TNIP) is returned to power winning virtually all seventy-five elected seats.

30 Sept. 1981   The sixth and final report of the Wiehahn Commission, inquiring into labour legislation, is tabled in Parliament. Dealing with the mining industry, its main recommendation is that Blacks as well as Whites and Coloured workers should be issued with blasting certificates.

Early Oct. 1981   A separate alliance of right-wing parties is formed, comprising the National Conservative Party (NCP) and the Aksie Eie Toekoms (AET) together with the Afrikaner Weerstandsbeweging (AWB) or Afrikaner Resistance Movement, led by Eugene Terre'blanche, and the Kappie Kommando, an organization of Afrikaner women.

6 Oct. 1981   Dr. D. de Villers wins the Piketberg, Western Cape, seat for the National Party with a slightly reduced majority.

8 Oct. 1981   Equal education for all races, including a provision that will allow white government schools to admit blacks, is proposed in the Human Sciences Research Council, Committee report, chaired by Professor J.P. de Lange. Eleven guiding principles are laid down.

11 Oct. 1981   In a provisional White Paper on the De Lange education report, the government reaffirms its commitment to the policy of separate education departments.

16 Oct. 1981   The Status of Ciskei Bill is signed by the State President, having been opposed at all stages by the opposition parties. It confers Ciskei citizenship on approximately two million Xhosa people, of whom about half live permanently outside Ciskei's borders.

23 Oct. 1981   President Kaiser Matanzima of Transkei announces his intention to retire from the Presidency in February 1982, to devote more time to tribal and family affairs. By April 1982 this has not happened.

26 Oct. 1981   The ANC claims responsibility for an attack on a police station at Sibasa, near the capital of Venda, Thohoyandou. Nevertheless the Venda government charge three ministers of the Lutheran Church with murder.

26 Oct. 1981   The South African Indian Council requests the Prime Minister to reverse the Cabinet's decision not to return Pageview and District Six to their respective Indian and Coloured communities. The Prime Minister refuses this request and a massive boycott of the Indian elections follow.

1 Nov. 1981   A new Labour Relations Amendment Act becomes effective, banning only links between unions and political parties.

3 Nov. 1981   The government appoints a judicial Commision of Inquiry, under the chairmanship of Justice C.F. Eloff, to investigate the inception, development, objects, history and activities of the South African Council of Churches (SACC), as well as organizations and people giving money or assets to the Council.

4 Nov. 1981   The first elections to the South African Indian Council are held. Of the SAIC's forty-five members, forty are up for election, five being nominated,

but only 10.5 per cent of the electorate vote.

20 Nov. 1981   A total of eighty-two agreements between South Africa and Ciskei are signed in Cape Town by Chief Sebe and the Prime Minister and other Cabinet Ministers.

20 Nov. 1981   Signs multilateral agreement on the control of pollution of water resources in the South African region.

3 Dec. 1981   Ciskei becomes the fourth black 'homeland' to be granted independence. Chief Sebe is elected President by the National Assembly, consisting of both elected members and thirty-seven hereditary chiefs.

14 Dec. 1981   Ciskei accepts independence. Chief Lennox Sebe becomes its first president.

26 Dec. 1981   Guerrillas open fire on Wonderboom police station, Pretoria. Subsequently two guerrillas allegedly connected with the attack are arrested, and an arms cache uncovered.

29 Dec. 1981   Winnie Mandela is banned for a further five years and continues to be restricted to the small town of Brandfort.

1982   The Security Police continue to take measures including detentions and banning orders against students, journalists, clerics, black leaders, and a British citizen Steven Kitson. Guerrilla activity by the ANC increases markedly.

5 Jan. 1982   The forty-five mercenaries alleged to have commandeered an Air India Boeing and forced it to fly to Durban, after attempting a coup in the Seychelles in November 1981, appear in magistrates' courts in five South African cities. They are all to go on trial in South Africa.

7 Jan. 1982   The Acting General Secretary of the Lutheran Church in South Africa claims that in addition to four ministers detained in Venda, T. Muofhe, a Lutheran elder, has died in custody. Brigadier T.R. Malandzi, head of Venda's National Force confirms this.

8 Jan. 1982   The ANC President, Oliver Tambo, declares, at a gathering in Dar es Salaam, Tanzania, celebrating the seventieth anniversary of the founding of the ANC, that under the slogan 'Unity in Action' that 1982 will be a year of massive actions against the apartheid system.

11 Jan. 1982   The United Nations Special Committee against Apartheid launches the International Year of Mobilisation for Sanctions against South Africa.

21 Jan. 1982   A spokesman for the Lutheran World Federation, meeting in emergency session in Geneva, says there are now twenty-one people detained in Venda, two of whom are believed to have 'died of torture'. Attempts by the President of the South African Council of Churches, the Reverend Peter Storey and Bishop Tutu, to visit the detained clergymen are frustrated and they are expelled from Venda.

1 Feb. 1982   The official Commission of Inquiry into the media, appointed in June 1980, under the chairmanship of Justice M. Steyn, tables its report. It recommends that a general council of journalists should be established by law to regulate

entry into the profession and sit in judgement on journalists accused of violating a statutory code of conduct. The report's findings and recommendations are widely opposed.

3 Feb. 1982   The six-man Commission of Inquiry into security legislation, under the chairmanship of Justice P.J. Rabie, presents its report and recommendations. It suggests that a Ministry of Law and Order be established with two separate components of Police, and a Directorate of Internal Security.

3 Feb. 1982   The Venda Attorney General announces he has ordered an inquiry into the death of Mr. Mufhe to be held in the Sibasa Magistrate's Court in May.

3 Feb. 1982   Three draft Bills revising and streamlining South Africa's security laws are placed before Parliament, their object being to regroup and consolidate more than thirty existing security laws. The proposed legislation consists of:
(i) an Internal Security Bill, to deal with the four redefined offences of 'terrorism', 'subversion', 'sabotage' and 'communism';
(ii) a Protection of Information Bill to replace the existing Official Secrets Act; and
(iii) a Bill to combat a new offence of intimidation. These embody the recommendations of the Rabie Commission.

5 Feb. 1982   Dr. Neil Aggett, acting Transvaal Regional Secretary of the African Food and Canning Workers' Union (AFCWU) is found dead in his cell at the Security Police Headquarters in John Vorster Square, Johannesburg, having been detained, along with several other Trade Union leaders on 27 November 1981. Widespread concern and condemnation, both external and internal, follow. He is said to be the forty-sixth person to have died in Security Police custody since 1963.

5 Feb. 1982   Signs treaty with Taiwan concerning cooperation in agricultural science and technology.

11 Feb. 1982   A call for a thirty minute work stoppage, in protest against the death of Dr. Aggett, is supported by virtually all independent black unions, and tens of thousands of workers. Outrage at his death cuts across racial lines, with white opposition politicians, lawyers, academics and churchmen leading demands for the end of prolonged detention without trial in solitary detention and the intolerable pressures it creates.

16 Feb. 1982   The Prime Minister confirms that the government accepts the Rabie Commission on security legislation recommendations, although these are criticized by the legal profession and politicians.

17 Feb. 1982   Signs security agreement with Swaziland.

18 Feb. 1982   Botswana accuses South Africa of kidnapping a former Soweto student leader, Peter Lengene, from Gaborone and transporting him to South Africa. The Minister of Police confirms his presence in South Africa.

19 Feb. 1982   The Minister of Justice, Kobie Coetsee, announces that the most comprehensive and intensive investigation is being carried out into the death in detention of Dr. Neil Aggett. A formal inquest will be held soon.

20 Feb. 1982   Prime Minister P.W. Botha describes the National Party policy of inter-racial

consultation and joint responsibility, as 'a form of power-sharing'. He expects that every Cabinet Minister will submit to this statement.

24 Feb. 1982

Twenty-two Members of Parliament refuse to support a motion of confidence in Prime Minister P.W. Botha at a National Party Parliamentary caucus meeting. The Prime Minister gives them eight days to decide whether they wish to remain in the Party: they must recant by 11 a.m. on 3 March 1982.

25 Feb. 1982

Louis le Grange, Minister of Police and Prisons, states in the House of Assembly that twenty-one trade unionists have been detained since the beginning of 1981, of whom ten have been released without charge and ten are still being held.

28 Feb. 1982

More than 200 of the Transvaal National Party vote on either Dr. Treurnicht or Mr. Botha's interpretation of Party policy. The vote is 172 to thirty-six votes in favour of the Prime Minister. Dr. A. Treurnicht is immediately suspended as the Transvaal Party chairman.

2 Mar. 1982

The inquest into Dr. Aggett's death begins, and is immediately adjourned for six weeks, to allow further investigation.

2 Mar. 1982

Dr. Andries Treurnicht resigns as Minister of State Administration and of Statistics and announces the formation of the Conservative Party. It becomes the third largest Parliamentary group with sixteen Members of Parliament.

3 Mar. 1982

In municipal and rural council elections in the Transvaal the National Party is still dominant, but loses ground to both the left and the right. The Herstigte Nasionale Party is elected to public office for the first time, winning six of Pretoria's thirty-six seats.

6 Mar. 1982

F.W. de Klerk, Minister of Mineral and Energy Affairs, is unanimously elected the new leader of the Transvaal National Party.

7 Mar. 1982

Six Front Line States meet in Maputo and decide to coordinate further their military and economic policies to counter South Africa's economic and military aggression.

7 Mar. 1982

The Commission of Inquiry into the constitutional, political, economic and social development of Natal/KwaZulu, set up by Chief Buthelezi in August 1980, publishes its report. Its central recommendation - that Natal should be merged with the KwaZulu 'homeland' to form a new multi-racial regional administration - is rejected by the government.

10 Mar. 1982

Over fifty squatters begin a hunger strike in St. George's Cathedral, Cape Town, protesting against evictions from Nyanga squatter camp. The strike ends on 1 April 1982 after a meeting with Dr. P. Koornhof.

10 Mar. 1982

The trial begins in the Natal Supreme Court of the mercenaries accused of hijacking an airliner to flee from the Seychelles after a failed coup on 25-26 November 1981.

11 Mar. 1982

Chief Gatsha Buthelezi maintains that majority rule, tempered by safeguards for whites and other minorities, offers the only realistic alternative to deepening confrontation.

11 Mar. 1982	Two former Soweto student leaders, K. Seathlolo and Mary Loate, are sentenced to fifteen and ten years' imprisonment under the Terrorism Act.
14 Mar. 1982	A bomb wrecks the ANC offices in Islington, London, shortly before the beginning of a mass rally organized by the Anti-Apartheid Movement.
14 Mar. 1982	In a radio and television interview, Prime Minister P.W. Botha, sets out the principles on which he is leading the government towards a new Constitutional dispensation.
15 Mar. 1982	Evidence of the government's complicity in the abortive coup plot against the Seychelles' Socialist government, is taken in camera.
18 Mar. 1982	The Preferential Trade Agreement with Zimbabwe, due to expire next week, has been extended.
20 Mar. 1982	At a meeting in Pretoria, attended by some 7,000 to 8,000 people, the Conservative Party of South Africa (CPSA) is launched. It brings together, in alliance with Dr. Treurnicht and the National Party rebels, the National Conservative Party (NCP or Nasionale Konservatiewe Party) and the Aksie Eie Toekoms (AET). It outlines fifteen guiding principles, of which the most important is that every group should have its own political structure and authority.
23 Mar. 1982	South Africa is to expand its military call-up to include all white men aged between seventeen and sixty-five, almost doubling the size of its forces. Commando units are to be strengthened.
24 Mar. 1982	The United Nations Security Council Commission of Inquiry, investigating the abortive Seychelles coup, fails to reach a definitive conclusion on the extent or level of South African knowledge or responsibility.
25 Mar. 1982	In announcing the 1982 Defence Budget, Owen Horwood reaffirms that the government's highest priority remains that of giving South Africa an effective defence capability and a self-sufficient arms industry.
25 Mar.- 20 Apr. 1982	The Seychelles coup trial is adjourned to allow the defence and prosecution to go to the Seychelles to hear key witnesses.
26 Mar. 1982	Eight political detainees are released. They will all appear as state witnesses in the 'Barbara Hogan case' on 30 April 1982.
28 Mar. 1982	ARMSCOR's Chairman announces that South Africa has produced a world-beating 155-millimetre artillery system - the G5 gun.
8 Apr. 1982	The Bloemfontein Appeal Court turns down appeals by three ANC members sentenced to death in November 1980.
13 Apr. 1982	The inquest into Dr. Aggett's death reopens, and it is argued that he met his death by 'induced suicide'.
14-16 Apr. 1982	A special Commission, empowered by the Supreme Court, hears evidence in Victoria, Seychelles, relating to happenings at the airport during the attempted Seychelles coup.

15 Apr. 1982   The main provisions of the Constitutional Amendment Bill give rise to speculation that Coloured and Indians are to be appointed to senior government posts.

21 Apr. 1982   A Group Areas Amendment Bill introduced on 7 March 1982 and enacted on 21 April, maintains the existing commitment to the principle of separate residential areas, schools and amenities for different races, but excludes sports from its provisions.

30 Apr. 1982   President Kaunda of Zambia meets the Prime Minister, P.W. Botha on the Botswana border to discuss the political situation in Namibia and South Africa. This is the first meeting between any leader of a Front Line State and a South African premier since the Victoria Falls meeting between B.J. Vorster and President Kaunda on 25-26 August 1976.

6 May 1982   Three leaders of the black South African Allied Workers' Union (SAAWU) are charged under the Terrorism Act. They are remanded in custody until 28 May and their names added to the pending 'Barbara Hogan trial'.

11 May 1982   The leader of the Herstigte Nasionale Party, Jaap Marais, is charged in the Pretoria Regional Court with disclosing secret information on the country's oil supplies.

11 May 1982   The Prime Minister announces that eight very important Western intelligence agents, held by the Soviet Union, and one South African soldier, held in Angola, have been exchanged somewhere in Europe for Major A.M. Kozlov, a senior Soviet intelligence officer arrested in South Africa in July 1980.

12 May 1982   The multiracial President's Council presents its recommendations for a reform of the constitutional and political system. Its principal proposal is that a degree of power-sharing between the White, Coloured and Indian communities should be introduced at central government level. The Black community is specifically excluded, except at local government level. The proposals are rejected by Black leaders and criticized by both wings of the opposition.

21 May 1982   A full bench of eleven judges of the Appeal Court upholds an appeal against a conviction under the Terrorism Act, on the grounds that the Act is inconsistent with Bophuthatswana's Declaration of Fundamental Rights enshrined in it's Constitution and based on the European Convention on Human Rights.

22 May 1982   The Intimidation Act specifies that it is an offence to assault or threaten any person in order to compel or induce that person 'to do or to abstain from doing any act or to assume or to abandon a particular standpoint'.

1 June 1982   The inquest into Dr. Aggett's death is adjourned for the third time when police object to the use, as evidence, of a statement made by Neil Aggett fourteen hours before his death, in which he declares under oath, that he has been assaulted and tortured.

2 June 1982   The State President commutes the death sentences on three black men, for their part in the attack on the Soekmekaar Police Station in 1980, to life imprisonment.

3 June 1982	The Protection of Information Act is given Presidential Assent. Under threat of heavy penalties the Act implicitly places the onus on the press not to publish reports of a detention where this might endanger state security.
3 June 1982	Revised figures for the Defence Budget indicate the funds available to the South African Defence Force have been increased to R3,068 million.
4 June 1982	A senior ANC member, P. Nyaose and his wife, are killed by a car bomb in Swaziland. Their deaths are blamed on the South African government by Alfred Nzo, the ANC Secretary-General.
4 June 1982	The Supreme Court rules that the statement of Neil Aggett is admissable as evidence.
5 June 1982	The Commission of Police reports a wave of bomb attacks on major installations, buildings used by government departments and quasi-government organisations.
5 June 1982	Prime Minister P.W. Botha persuades a combined gathering of the Provincial and Parliamentary caucuses of the National Party to accept the new constitutional proposals.
7 June 1982	The inquest into the death of Dr. Neil Aggett reopens after a seven week break.
10 June 1982	The newspaper proprietors and editors of all the main South African newspapers, both English and Afrikaans, unanimously opposed to the government's planned legislation, decide at an emergency meeting in Johannesburg to establish a media council which will operate independently from the State.
14 June 1982	Albertina Sisulu, wife of ANC leader, Walter Sisulu is placed under a banning order for the fifth time since 1963.
14 June 1982	The Minister of Cooperation and Development, Dr. Piet Koornhof, announces in the KwaZulu Legislative Assembly in Ulundi, that the KaNgwane national state and the Ingwavuma district in the north of KwaZulu are to be incorporated into the Kingdom of Swaziland. This Cabinet decision is strongly opposed. Outrage is expressed not only by the governments of KwaZulu, KaNgwane and 'homeland' leaders but by all four opposition parties.
16 June 1982	An ANC spokesman in Lusaka calls for increased participation by white sympathizers in the black emancipation struggle.
16 June 1982	On the anniversary of the Soweto uprising, police bar forty-seven local and overseas journalists from entering Soweto and tear gas is later fired to disperse crowds at the Regina Mundi Cathedral.
17 June 1982	Dr. Koornhof defends the proposed border adjustment between Natal and Swaziland as 'a step towards the fullfilment of a long-cherished ideal of the Swazi people... to be united under one king in one country'.
18 June 1982	The Government Gazette publishes a Proclamation by which the forty-two member KaNgwane Legislative Assembly is dissolved, and, together with the

Ingwavuma district, placed under the direct control of the Department of Cooperation and Development, despite the opposition of the great majority of the Legislative Assembly.

20 June 1982   The Swaziland government welcomes South Africa's offer to hand over parts of KaNgwane and KwaZulu to Swaziland, since, it claims the territory is historically Swazi.

23 June 1982   A Defence Amendment Bill provides for a re-organization of the defence system intended to give the South African Defence Force (SADF) adequate manpower to deal with almost every conceivable threat, internal or external, but as flexibly as possible so as to ensure the minimum of disruption to normal life.

24 June 1982   The police confirm that three leading members of the black journalist trade union, the Media Workers Association of South Africa have been arrested and detained under the General Laws Amendment Act.

25 June 1982   The Durban Supreme Court cancels the state's announcement of 18 June 1982 that it has repossessed the Ingwavuma region of KwaZulu, on the grounds that the government did not meet its legal obligation to consult fully with the KwaZulu authorities before making its announcement. The State President responds by issuing a new Proclamation, under a different law, once again placing Ingwavuma under government control.

29 June 1982   After the Court is told by the Head of Interrogation at John Vorster Square, Major Arthur Cronwright, that the Security Police have withheld statements by Dr. Aggett because they contain secret information relating to the Communist Party, and that he had given permission for Dr. Aggett to be interrogated for a sixty-two hour period, the inquest is adjourned until 20 September 1982.

29 June 1982   Libya, as chairman of the OAU, supports Swaziland's claims to South African territory. Its Foreign Minister outlines Libya's position during a visit to Mbabane, at the end of June.

30 June 1982   The Provincial Council of Natal passes at a special sitting, a resolution urging the government to hold a referendum in Natal and in the Ingwavuma region of KwaZulu on the proposed land deal. The government has also been challenged to hold a referendum by Enos Mabuza, former Chief Minister of KaNgwane.

1 July 1982   It is announced that some political prisoners have been granted remission of their sentences and released.

1 July 1982   Helen Joseph, who has been under a series of banning orders since she became the first South African to be placed under house arrest in October 1962, is released from such restrictions.

2 July 1982   The Internal Security Act becomes operative. Opposition parties oppose the massive powers given to the authorities to investigate any organization or publication.

6 July 1982   Following an order granted to the KwaZulu government by the Supreme Court in Natal, officials of the Department of Cooperation and Development

begin withdrawing from the disputed Ingavuma area. The Prime Minister denies that he is going to reconvene Parliament to deal with this crisis, but may exercise this option later.

6 July 1982   The Prime Minister announces a government reorganization, including the creation of a new portfolio of Constitutional Development, the rearrangement of six ministries and the appointment of three new Ministers.

16 July 1982   South Africa's first State President, Charles Robberts Swart, dies, aged eighty-seven.

30 July 1982   The Federal Congress of the National Party supports the set of constitutional reforms outlined by Prime Minister P.W. Botha, and explained to the Congress by the Minister of Constitutional Affairs, Chris Heunis. If enacted, Parliamentary rule, based on the Westminster model, will be replaced by a Presidential system, with real power still concentrated in white hands. The tri-cameral structure is specifically designed to maintain National Party control of legislation.

5 Aug. 1982   The twentieth anniversary of the arrest of Nelson Mandela is marked by a call for his release by China, publicized in the Communist Party organ, the People's Daily and an appeal signed by more than 2,000 mayors from fifty-three countries, made public by the United Nations Centre Against Apartheid in New York.

6 Aug. 1982   Three ANC members are sentenced to death for attacks directed against the Moroka and Orlando Police stations in Soweto and the Wonderboom Police station in Pretoria in which four policemen were killed. The attacks took place in May 1979 and December 1981.

8 Aug. 1982   Lieutenant-General Johann Coetzee, Head of the Security Police, announces that Ernest Dipale, arrested under the new Internal Security Act and charged with furthering the aims of a banned organization, has been found hanged in his cell at John Vorster Square. He is the forty-seventh person to die in detention. PFP's justice spokesperson, Helen Suzman, calls for the whole structure of detention laws to be changed.

9 Aug. 1982   The PFP's spokesman on Police Affairs, Ray Swart, calls for a commission of inquiry into all aspects of the conditions of detainees under security legislation. The Minister of Law and Order promises a clear-cut policy statement on the treatment of security detainees, but it will not be a formal code of conduct, nor will it be embodied in a law.

13 Aug. 1982   The Minister of Manpower, S.P. Botha, states there have been 182 strikes in the first six months of 1982, involving 51,000 workers. Disputes in the gold mines have been violent, resulting in riots and some deaths.

17 Aug. 1982   Dr. Ruth First, wife of ANC leader Joe Slovo, and herself a political activist, is killed by a letter bomb in Maputo.

19 Aug. 1982   In a by-election in Germiston the National Party retains its seat, but with a reduced majority, reflecting a considerable swing to the Conservative Party.

25 Aug. 1982   The World Alliance of Reformed (Presbyterian and Congregational) Churches (WARC) suspends the Nederduitse Gereformeerde Kerk (NGK)

and the Nederduitse Hervormde Kerk (NHK) from membership because of their support for apartheid. They may still attend meetings, but no longer have the right to vote.

26 Aug. 1982   The World Alliance of Reformed Churches (WARC) chooses the South African Reverend Alan Boesak, of the Dutch Reformed Mission Church, as its new President.

6 Sept. 1982   Former American Secretary of State Dr. Henry Kissinger, lectures South Africans on the need for racial reform and a new Constitution during a two-week private visit to South Africa.

14 Sept. 1982   The Transvaal Congress of the National Party overwhelmingly supports P.W. Botha's constitutional proposals.

21 Sept -
21 Dec. 1982   During the proceedings of the General Assembly of the United Nations resolutions are adopted appealing for clemency for ANC members sentenced to death for alleged guerrilla activities, asking the IMF to refrain from granting credit or assistance to South Africa, and condemning a South African raid into Lesotho on 9 December 1980.

22 Sept. 1982   The Nederduitse Hervormde Kerk (NHK) severs its ties completely with the World Alliance of Reformed Churches (WARC) rather than accept WARC's ruling that apartheid is contrary to the scriptures.

30 Sept. 1982   The Appeal Court in Bloemfontein rules that the Presidential Proclamation issued in June, purporting to restore Ingwavuma to South African jurisdiction, is null and void since the State President acted ultra vires. It is announced that a Commission under the chairmanship of Frans Rumpff, will be appointed to investigate and report on conflicting claims between KwaZulu and Swaziland.

1 Oct. 1982   A report compiled by the Detainees' Parents Support Committee provides detailed evidence of systematic torture as an integral feature of the detention system.

9 Oct. 1982   Applications for parole by the thirty-four mercenaries involved in the Seychelles attempted coup are refused. Most are due to be released in January 1983.

16 Oct. 1982   The Southern African Black Alliance (SABA) and the PFP declare their total opposition to the pending constitutional changes involving the creation of a tricameral Parliament.

21 Oct. 1982   Barbara Hogan is sentenced in the Rand Supreme Court to an effective ten years in prison for high treason and membership of the ANC. Hogan admitted her membership, but pleaded not guilty to treason.

27 Oct. 1982   An intensified campaign to enforce the pass laws leads to increased prosecutions in the Cape Town area. The government is working towards stricter enforcement of influx control, particularly in the Western Cape.

28 Oct. 1982   The Reverend Beyers Naudé is served with his second banning order, restricting him for a further three years. The order is the first to be served under the comprehensive new security law, the Internal Security Act of

1982, on the sole discretion of the Minister of Law and Order, and the decision cannot be questionned in court.

3 Nov. 1982   Four leading South African journalists are charged under the new Protection of Information Act. The charges relate to reports concerning National Intelligence Service agent Martin Dolinchek, his involvement in the Seychelles attempted coup, and NIS reaction to his capture by Seychelles security forces.

4 Nov. 1982   The results of four Parliamentary and three Provincial Councils by-elections demonstrate a vote of confidence by the electorate in the governments proposals for constitutional reform.

13 Nov. 1982   Security Police have failed to obtain a single conviction against any of the twenty trade unionists detained and interrogated during the last eighteen months.

22 Nov. 1982   The President's Council, mandated to consider South Africa's constitutional future, releases its final report. Central items of its plan include establishment of a strong executive President chosen by a triracial electoral college, a three-chamber Parliament representing the White, Coloured and Indian communities, and a division between national and communal interests. It reaffirms the need for separation of executive and legislative power.

23 Nov. 1982   Swaziland and Lesotho take steps to clear themselves of suspicion of allowing insurgents of the ANC to use their territory as springboards for attacks on South Africa.

25 Nov. 1982   The government concedes another legal defeat in its attempts to transfer the KaNgwane 'homeland' to Swaziland. Dr. Piet Koornhof, Minister of Development and Cooperation, announces the withdrawal of a Proclamation dissolving the Legislative Assembly of KaNgwane issued in June 1981. As a result of the settlement, Enos Mabuza, Chief Executive Councillor of KaNgwane, withdraws his application to the Pretoria Supreme Court for return of the administration of KaNgwane to the tribal authorities. The government is ordered to pay his legal costs.

25 Nov. 1982   Minister of Law and Order, Louis le Grange, announces a new series of directives for the protection of detainees.

26 Nov. 1982   Signs loan agreement with Malawi.

27 Nov. 1982   Prison authorities release thirty-four of the forty-two mercenaries involved in the hijacking of an Air India plane after the abortive Seychelles coup. Released after four months imprisonment are twenty-one South Africans, six Britons, five Zimbabweans, one Australian and one Austrian. The eight still in prison include the commando leader, Colonel Mike Hoare.

2 Dec. 1982   Afrikaans poet, Breyten Breytenbach, is released from prison after serving seven of the nine years to which he was sentenced in 1975.

3 Dec. 1982   Signs amendment to multilateral Convention on Wetlands.

9 Dec. 1982   South African forces raid houses in Maseru, killing thirty members of the ANC and seven women and children caught in the crossfire. A chain of

sabotage incidents within South Africa are blamed on the ANC command structure in Lesotho. The incursion is widely condemned.

13 Dec. 1982   Security Police arrest the leader, Eugene Terreblanche and eight other members of the Afrikaner Weerstandsbeweging (AWB) after uncovering illegal arms caches in different parts of the country.

17 Dec. 1982   Up to 100 ANC members are reported to have been detained in Swaziland. The arrests are confirmed by the Swaziland Police Commissioner and a large cache of arms in the north of the country is found.

18-19 Dec. 1982   Four explosions occur at the Koeberg nuclear power station for which the ANC claims responsibility.

21 Dec. 1982   At the conclusion of a forty-four-day inquest into the death in detention of the white trade union leader, Dr. Neil Aggett, the Johannesburg magistrate, Pieter Kotze, finds that no one is to blame for his death. The verdict, which completely exonerates the Security Police, is greeted with astonishment and anger.

Jan.- Apr. 1983   Three bomb explosions damage the old building housing the Supreme Court in Pietermaritzburg, and the new building nearing completion.

2 Jan. 1983   Several ANC members detained in Swaziland decide to leave the country voluntarily for Mozambique. A further group of seventeen ANC members leave Mawelawela refugee camp, near Mbabane, fearing a South African attack.

4 Jan. 1983   At its annual conference in Eshowe, Natal, the Labour Party overwhelmingly adopts a resolution stating that it seeks to represent the Coloured community in a restructured Parliament, even though it rejects the racial premises on which the constitutional proposals are based. This decision is welcomed by the Prime Minister but criticized by other political organizations. Three leading members resign immediately after the Conference.

7 Jan. 1983   The Government Gazette proclaims that only one-fifth of District Six, will be returned in its entirety to its earlier status and again be designated a Coloured area.

12 Jan. 1983   The South African Indian Council (SAIC) decides to give the government's constitutional proposals 'a reasonable chance', provided the Indian community approves them in a referendum.

19 Jan. 1983   Chief Buthelezi meets President Matanzima of Transkei at Tongaat, north of Durban, where they dedicate their homelands to opposing the constitutional proposals which exclude blacks.

23 Jan. 1983   At the annual congress of the Transvaal Anti-SAIC Committee held in Johannesburg, it is decided to revive the old Transvaal Indian Congress and to establish a united democratic front to mobilize resistance on a national scale to participation by Indians and Coloureds in the new Constitution.

26 Jan. 1983   The Prime Minister calls a special press conference to announce that a senior South African naval officer, commanding Simonstown dockyard, Commodore Dieter Gerhardt and his wife, have been detained for

questioning in connection with alleged espionage.

27-28 Jan. 1983	The third Annual Meeting of the Council of Ministers of the SADCC and representatives of donor countries and organizations, held in Maseru, is marked by further criticism of South Africa's foreign policy and deliberate interference in the region.
29-30 Jan. 1983	The executive of the non-racial Federation of South African Trade Unions (with a substantial Coloured membership) rejects the racially divisive constitutional proposals.
1 Feb. 1983	The government is to establish a special Cabinet committee to look at the problems of urban blacks.
4 Feb. 1983	Signs meteorological treaty with Taiwan.
7 Feb. 1983	Cedric Mayson, former Methodist Minister, banned for five years in 1977 and detained on 27 November 1981, appears before the Pretoria Supreme Court on charges including treason and being a member or an active supporter of the ANC. He is released on bail, flees the country and arrives in Britain the day before his case is due to resume on 18 April 1983.
15 Feb. 1983	Signs multilateral Convention on Agency in International Sale of Goods.
17 Feb. 1983	Signs agreement with Swaziland and Mozambique on the establishment of a tripartite permanent technical committee on water resources.
18 Feb. 1983	A bomb explosion in an administrative building in the Batho township of Bloemfontein, injures seventy-six blacks while seeking registration for employment. The ANC denies responsibility.
21 Feb. 1983	The Minister of Manpower, Fanie Botha, the leader of the Conservative Party, Dr. Andries Treurnicht, and one of his senior lieutenants, Tom Langley, all resign as Members of Parliament and begin a trial of strength between the Conservative Party and the National Party.
4 Mar. 1983	Four senior newspaper editors are found guilty on between one and three counts under the 1982 Protection of Information Act, and sentenced to fines (mainly suspended) of from R300 to R2000. Information published relating to the involvement of NIS self-confessed agent, Martin Dolinchek, in the Seychelles attempted coup, was held to have been prejudicial to the security or the interests of the Republic.
16 Mar. 1983	In elections to the 100-member Lebowa National Assembly, Dr. Phatudi's ruling Lebowa People's Party wins more than three-quarters of the forty elective seats.
21 Mar. 1983	The twenty third anniversary of Sharpeville, the International Day for the Elimination of Apartheid, is marked by messages issued by the United Nations Special Committee against Apartheid and the Pan Africanist Congress.
26-27 Mar. 1983	The Lesotho government accuses South Africa of launching raids into Lesotho. South Africa denies this.

30 Mar. 1983	Prime Minister P.W. Botha announces that, contrary to previous indications, the constitutional proposals will be put to a referendum of the white electorate.
2 Apr. 1983	Saul Mkheze, leader of a black farming community, is shot dead during a protest meeting at Driefontein, 200 miles east of Johannesburg. The United States State Department calls on 5 April for a full investigation into the circumstances of his death, and on 7 April the Foreign Minister, 'Pik' Botha, says the government 'deeply regretted' such incidents.
7 Apr. 1983	The French government decides to request all sporting bodies to end links with South Africa, since the government is against racial discrimination in all its forms.
9-10 Apr. 1983	At a meeting in Cape Town seven predominantly black trade unions decide in principle to form a federation, estimated to have a potential membership of about 180,000.
11 Apr. 1983	Chief Leabua Jonathan, Prime Minister of Lesotho, tells the National Assembly that Lesotho is faced with a war with South Africa.
13 Apr. 1983	A Defence Amendment Bill provides for an alternative form of national service for conscientious objectors, who oppose military service on religious grounds. The offer is not extended to objectors motivated by political values.
25 Apr. 1983	The Labour Party, in anticipation of probable expulsion, announces it has withdrawn from the South African Black Alliance (SABA).
28 Apr. 1983	The Prime Minister, P.W. Botha, orders the Minister of Law and Order, L. le Grange, to investigate the activities of the Afrikaner Weerstandsbeweging (AWB).
30 Apr. 1983	The Prime Minister meets Lesotho's Minister of Foreign Affairs, discusses the revival of the Highland Water Scheme and emphasizes the paramount importance of economic and geographic facts in establishing realistic relations between the two countries.
Late May 1983	The government is planning to build a large new township, Khayalitsha, twenty-five miles outside Cape Town. More than 150,000 black people living in townships near Cape Town, will be expected to move to the new development. This is a policy reversal of the government's virtual freeze on all building for blacks in the Cape.
5 May 1983	The Republic of South Africa Constitution Bill is placed before the House of Assembly. It is opposed by the Conservative Party, while the PFP abstains. It is read a second time on 18 May, the New Republic Party (NRP) supporting the government, the other opposition parties voting against it.
6 May 1983	New regulations, introduced under the 1979 Promotion of the Density of Population and Designated Areas Act, come into effect, designed to curb the exodus of whites from farms in the border areas.
6 May 1983	The KwaNdebele Legislative Assembly passes a unanimous motion instructing the homeland's Cabinet to begin independence negotiations with South Africa.

10 May 1983	Three parliamentary by-elections in the Transvaal represent a major electoral test for the Conservative Party. They result in the technical regaining of one seat by the National Party from the Conservative Party, while Dr. Treurnicht's success in holding his seat represents an effective defeat for the National Party.
19 May 1983	Signs treaty with Taiwan relating to the acceptance of international tonnage certificates.
20 May 1983	Outside the headquarters of the South African Air Force (SAAF), and other government offices, a car bomb explodes in Pretoria killing nineteen and injuring about 200 people.
20 May 1983	The Minister of Defence, General Magnus Malan, announces that a total of six districts, all on or near South Africa's borders with Swaziland and Mozambique, are now activated under the 1982 Amendments to the Defence Act. In three of them, all white men up to the age of fifty-five, will have to register for commando duty.
21 May 1983	A total of thirty-two organizations join to form the United Democratic Front (UDF) to oppose the constitutional proposals.
23 May 1983	In retaliatory action for the Pretoria car bomb, the South African Air Force (SAAF) launch a raid on six ANC targets in the suburbs of Maputo.
26 May 1983	Traffic flow slows at the border posts between South Africa and Lesotho is reported following bomb explosions in Pretoria and Bloemfontein, for which the ANC office in Lesotho first claims, and later denies, responsibility.
27-29 May 1983	Swazi police discover a hidden arms cache in the Mlilwane game park and three men, said to comprise an ANC military training group in the same park, are arrested as part of a renewed crackdown on ANC activities.
30 May 1983	The Appeal Court hands down a landmark decision in the case Rikhoto v. East Rand Administration Board (ERAB) granting him the right to permanent urban status. This ruling may affect about 150,000 black contract workers in urban areas, who can now apply to have their families living with them.
1 June 1983	An inquest into the death of Ernest Dipale, who had died in custody in Johannesburg Security Police headquarters in August 1982, finds no-one criminally liable for his death.
3 June 1983	Foreign Minister, 'Pik' Botha, meets Lesotho's Minister of Foreign Affairs. They agree on the need to curb cross-border guerrilla activity and to place their relations on a more amicable footing.
6-7 June 1983	Black trade unionist, Oscar Mbetha, is one of ten people found guilty by the Cape Supreme Court on charges of terrorism and/or murder. On 28 June he is sentenced to five years' imprisonment and on 1 August 1983 is elected as one of the three Presidents of the United Democratic Front.
7 June 1983	Dr. Piet Koornhof declares that, pending the implementation of the Orderly Movement and Settlement of Black Persons Bill, interim steps will have to be taken to prevent too many migrant workers from qualifying for permanent residence.

9 June 1983   Three black ANC guerrillas are executed in Pretoria, appeals for clemency having been turned down, and an appeal for a stay of execution having failed. International outrage follows.

11-12 June 1983   The National Forum representing 170 black organizations, holds its first Conference at Hammanskraal near Pretoria. Delegates from political, religious, student and trade union movements unanimously adopt a manifesto identifying racial capitalism as the real enemy and pledging to establish a Socialist republic. AZAPO predominates: absent are movements subscribing to the Freedom Charter adopted by the ANC and its allies.

14 June 1983   Two former members of the Afrikaner Weerstandsbeweging (AWB) are sentenced to fifteen years imprisonment after being found guilty of terrorism.

16 June 1983   The seventh anniversary of the Soweto uprisings is again commemorated by absenteeism from work and popular disturbances.

23 June 1983   Laurence Eagleburger, the United States Under-Secretary of State for Political Affairs, defends his government's policy of 'constructive engagement' with South Africa designed to support those who are committed to change away from apartheid.

28 June 1983   Two bomb blasts cause extensive damage to the Department of Internal Affairs office and the police headquarters at Roodepoort, near Johannesburg. The ANC is held to be responsible.

30 June 1983   Signs multilateral agreement establishing the Development Bank of Southern Africa.

1 July 1983   Under the 1982 Internal Security Act all existing banning orders are automatically revoked a year later, and, as a consequence, more than fifty banning orders are lifted. Fresh banning orders are issued in several cases, including that of Winnie Mandela.

4 July 1983   Professor Carel Boshoff resigns as chairman of the Broederbond. He is critical of the government's constitutional proposals which, he says, may stimulate rather than appease racial conflict.

5 July 1983   The South African Bureau of Racial Affairs (SABRA) issues a statement by Professor Boshoff (Dr. Hendrik Verwoerd's son-in-law) arguing that every race group should have its own geographical sphere in which it can exercise authority - and this applies to Coloureds and Indians also.

13 July 1983   The Transvaal Attorney General announces that AWB leader Eugene Terreblanche and three associates, will face terrorism charges, having been accused of attempting or planning to overthrow the South African government by violent means.

23 July 1983   The last six mercenaries from the attempted Seychelles coup are pardoned, freed and arrive in Johannesburg. The Minister of Law and Order indicates that South African authorities have no further interest in the case.

28 July 1983   South Africa and Lesotho exchange prisoners across the Caledon River, heralding a new rapprochement and a lifting of strict border control measures.

6 Aug. 1983	A bomb explodes at a synagogue in central Johannesburg four hours before State President Viljoen is due to attend a ceremony there.
8-31 Aug. 1983	Debates on the Constitution Bill continue and recommendations of the select committee empowered to suggest amendments to the Bill, but not to propose changes to the principle are discussed.
15 Aug. 1983	The Lesotho Foreign Ministry appeals for international help to stop South Africa applying an economic squeeze designed to force Lesotho to expel up to 3,000 political refugees.
20 Aug. 1983	The United Democratic Front (UDF) is formally launched at a meeting in Mitchell's Plain, near Cape Town, attended by delegates from 320 community groups, trade unions, women's groups and student organizations. It is opposed to the government's constitutional proposals and pledges itself to a single non-racial and unfragmented South Africa.
24 Aug. 1983	It is announced that the referendum will be held on 2 November 1983, with the whites being asked whether they are in favour of the Constitution, 1983, as approved by Parliament.
30 Aug. 1983	The government withdraws its plan to place a quota limit on the admission of black students to white universities, but remains committed to universities that retain their community-directed character.
Sept. - Oct. 1983	Opposition to the Constitution and calls to the white electorate to reject the new dispensation are voiced by a variety of groups including the Southern African Catholic Bishops' Conference, the South African Council of Churches and the leader of six black 'homelands'.
1 Sept. 1983	The Southern African Development Bank, financed primarily by South Africa, is formally established with headquarters in Midrand, near Johannesburg.
5 Sept. 1983	The trial begins in the Cape Town Supreme Court of Commodore Dieter Gerhardt on charges of spying for the Soviet Union. The Judge President grants an application by the state that the proceedings be held in camera.
8 Sept. 1983	The Lesotho government announces that an undisclosed number of South African refugees have decided voluntarily to withdraw from Lesotho. On 10 September it airlifts the first batch of twenty-two ANC members to Mozambique and Tanzania. Another 200 will follow later.
9 Sept. 1983	Parliament approves the new Constitution by 119 votes to thirty-five, after a marathon session lasting 127 sitting days.
10 Sept. 1983	Balthazar Johannes Vorster, Prime Minister of South Africa and leader of the National Party from 1966 to 1978 and State President in 1978-79, dies aged sixty-seven.
11-12 Sept. 1983	The Lesotho Foreign Ministry protests to South Africa, following further clashes with guerrillas in the Leribe district, and an eight-hour attack against Maryland Roman Catholic mission near the border.
16 Sept. 1983	Signs agreement with Swaziland regarding financial and technical assistance.

22 Sept. 1983   The Republic of South Africa Constitution Bill is enacted.

29 Sept. 1983   A commission of inquiry into malpractices in South African prisons is ordered by the Minister of Justice, following disturbances and deaths at the Barberton prison farm complex in the Eastern Transvaal.

5 Oct. 1983   The leaders of six black `homelands' reject the new Constitution. Their statement is also signed by a number of black business and church leaders.

17 Oct. 1983   South African forces raid offices of the ANC in Maputo. The raid is internationally condemened.

2 Nov. 1983   The white referendum is held on the constitutional proposals. The results, announced on 3 November 1983 show that 1,360,223 people (65.95%) have voted in favour, 691,577 (33.53%) against, with 10,669 (0.52%) spoilt papers, on a 76.02% turn out.

15 Nov. 1983   Fanie Botha, a senior Member of the Cabinet, announces his resignation as Minister of Manpower, following allegations that he has refused to hand over diamond leases promised in a secret deal with Brigadier Johann Blaauw.

15 Nov. 1983   The United Nations General Assembly adopts a resolution declaring that the constitutional proposals are contrary to the principles of the UN Charter and further entrench apartheid, and that the results of the referendum on 2 November 1983, endorsed by an exclusively white electorate, are of no validity whatsoever.

17 Nov. 1983   Following the resignation of F. Botha, new ministerial appointments are made.

24 Nov. 1983   A former theology student, Carl Niehaus, is sentenced to fifteen years in prison for high treason in the Rand Supreme Court, his fiancée, Johanna Lourens, to four years.

3 Dec. 1983   Elections to the country's twenty-nine new black local authorities, over the previous ten days, are met with demonstrations and calls for a boycott. The last round of voting finishes in Johannesburg, in Soweto, Dobsonville and Deepmeadow. Elections in Soweto, with a turnout of eleven percent give E. Tshabalala's Sofasonke Party control of the new authority.

5 Dec. 1983   During the proceedings of the thirty-eighth regular session of the United Nations General Assembly, eleven resolutions are adopted on the situation in South Africa, the programme of action against apartheid, the effects of apartheid on Southern Africa, sanctions against South Africa, the work of the Special Committee against Apartheid, relations with Israel, military and nuclear collaboration, investments, oil embargo and apartheid in sport.

9 Dec. 1983   Senior South African officials arrive in Maseru, for discussions on mutual security, movement across the common border, the Customs Union and the Highlands Water Scheme.

15 Dec. 1983   A bomb explosion, shattering the Johannesburg office of the Department of Foreign Affairs, is the forty-second attack by ANC saboteurs in 1983.

20 Dec. 1983   South Africa and Mozambican delegations hold talks in Mbabane, concerning

peaceful co-existence.

29 Dec. 1983	Commodore Dieter Gerhardt, the former commanding officer of the Simonstown naval base, and his wife Ruth Gerhardt, are sentenced to life imprisonment and ten years' imprisonment respectively, being found guilty of high treason on charges of spying for the Soviet Union.
4 Jan. 1984	The (Coloured) Labour Party opts for an election for the eighty representatives to the Coloured House of Representatives, without first holding a referendum.
16 Jan. 1984	A second series of meetings is held between South Africa and Mozambique in Pretoria and in Maputo. Four working groups discuss security matters and economic relations.
26 Jan. 1984	The South African Indian Council (SAIC) calls for a referendum in the Indian community on the acceptability of the Constitution.
14 Feb. 1984	Elections for the Coloured and Indian Parliament under the new Constitution are announced by the government. They are to be held on 22 August 1984; with nomination day likely to be 16 July 1984.
15 Feb. 1984	By-elections are held for two seats in the House of Assembly. The Northern Transvaal seat is won by the CP, the Natal seat is retained by the PFP. Both results are disappointments for the National Party.
15 Feb. 1984	The judicial Commission of Inquiry into the Activities of the South African Council of Churches (SACC) accuses it of pursuing strategies of resistance to government policies and of identifying with the liberation struggle. However, it stops short of recommending a total ban on foreign funding, as requested by the Commissioner of Police.
20 Feb. 1984	At the end of the third meeting between Mozambique and South Africa, in Maputo, a joint statement is released announcing that the two countries have agreed on the central principles concerning security arrangements between them; and that they intend to enter into a formal agreement in this regard.
10-11 Mar. 1984	The ANC mounts a sabotage attack on a petrol depot in which five storage tanks are damaged.
14 Mar. 1984	The nuclear power station at Koeberg becomes operational.
16 Mar. 1984	President Samora Machel of Mozambique and Prime Minister Botha, sign the Nkomati Accord, a non-aggression and good-neighbourliness pact, on the border between the two countries.
17 Mar. 1984	A Defence Force spokesman confirms in Cape Town that South Africa is to stop supplying the United States and Britain with intelligence reports on the movements of Soviet warships around the Cape by the end of the year.
24 Mar. 1984	The harbour of Richards Bay is to be extended at a cost of approximately $75 million.
26 Mar. 1984	The Mozambique-South Africa Joint Security Commission meets for the first time in Maputo, as further raids are carried out against ANC houses and

offices by the Mozambican authorities.

31 Mar. 1984   It is disclosed that South Africa and Swaziland signed a non-aggression pact in February 1982. The two countries now also agree to exchange trade representatives and to establish trade missions in their respective countries.

1 Apr. 1984   South Africa recalls its ambassador to Britain for urgent consultations, after four South Africans and a Briton are charged in Coventry with illegally exporting military equipment to South Africa.

5 Apr. 1984   The Hoexter Commission presents its fifth and final report to Parliament recommending major reforms in the judicial system and containing incisive attacks on the administration of the apartheid system.

11 Apr. 1984   General Magnus Malan tables a wide-ranging Defence White Paper focussing on strengthened border defences to counter sabotage attacks by organizations seen as proxies for the Soviet Union.

24 Apr. 1984   Carnegie Report on Poverty in South Africa reveals the doubling of blacks living below the poverty line (1960-1980).

2 May 1984   South Africa, Mozambique and Portugal sign a new agreement in Cape Town on the supply of electric power to South Africa from the Cahora Bassa Hydro-electric Dam in north-west Mozambique.

5 May 1984   Over 7,000 people attend a rally in Pretoria to mark the foundation on 4 May 1984 of the Afrikaner Volkswag (People's Guard), a cultural organization led by Professor Carel Boshoff. The new Conservative group is expected to challenge the influence of the Broederbond.

10 May 1984   Signs amendment to the Convention on Civil Aviation.

10-12 May 1984   Talks take place in Cape Town between Swaziland and South Africa concerning trade and regional security. South Africa is to open a consulate in Swaziland. It is reported that more than sixty ANC members are in detention in Swaziland and four have been handed over to the South African authorities.

11 May 1984   South Africa's longest serving white political prisoner, David Kitson, is released, seven months short of completing his twenty-year sentence for sabotage and barely three weeks before the Prime Minister is due to meet Margaret Thatcher in London.

16 May 1984   South Africa concedes that almost two million black people have been relocated since 1960, but maintains that only 456,860 were moved for ideological reasons. The fact that some forced removals have taken place is admitted by the Minister for Cooperation and Development, Dr. Piet Koornhof.

18 May 1984   Saboteurs blow up two railway lines south of Johannesburg.

23 May 1984   The Minister of Law and Order states that a total of fourteen armed attacks and explosions have occurred between January and May 1984.

23 May 1984   Signs treaty with Italy for the avoidance of double taxation and the

prevention of fiscal evasion with respect to taxes on income.

25 May 1984   Signs multilateral treaty to amend the International Convention on Civil Liability for Oil Pollution Damage.

29 May -   Prime Minister Botha visits eight countries in Europe - Portugal, Great
12 June 1984   Britain, West Germany, Belgium, France, Austria, Italy and Switzerland - and has an audience with Pope John Paul II on 11 June 1984. He is accompanied on his tour by the Minister of Foreign Affairs, 'Pik' Botha. The tour is seen in South Africa as a diplomatic breakthrough signalling the end of South Africa's isolation.

June - Sept 1984   Further ANC sabotage attacks occur in Durban, Roodepoort and Johannesburg, involving bomb explosions, causing deaths and injuries.

16 June 1984   Sporadic clashes with police take place during the annual commemoration of 16 June 1976. The day is marked by pronouncements by the ANC, the PAC and the United Nations Secretary-General, all calling for an end to repression.

18 June 1984   Chief Gatsha Buthelezi is summoned to Cape Town by Dr. Piet Koornhof and informed that the Rumpff Commission of Inquiry into the implications of the possible transfer of KaNgwane and Ingwavuma, KwaZulu to Swaziland has been disbanded.

19 June 1984   The Foreign Minister gives an assurance that the government will not go ahead with plans for the cession of land to Swaziland, unless it has the majority support of the people concerned.

26 June 1984   The nineteenth quintuennial congress of the Universal Postal Union in Hamburg, expels South Africa on account of its apartheid policy.

28 June 1984   Exiled South African Jenny Schoon, and her daughter Katryn, are killed by a parcel bomb in Lubango, Angola, probably intended for her husband Marius Schoon, named in security trials as an agent of the ANC.

28 June 1984   Owen Horwood announces his resignation from the post of Minister of Finance. He is replaced by Barend du Plessis, hitherto Minister of Education and Training.

28 June 1984   The NP loses the provincial by-election in Potgietersrus to a right-wing coalition led by the CP, but retains Rosettenville, Johannesburg, with an increased majority in a three-cornered fight with the CP and NRP.

9 July 1984   Signs Protocol amending the International Convention for the Conservation of Atlantic Tunas.

12 July 1984   A car bomb explosion in Durban kills five and injures twenty-six.

13 July 1984   The last all-white Parliament ends its last session in Cape Town.

30 July 1984   Campaigning for the new tricameral Parliament begins.

8 Aug. 1984   The government is to grant self-government to KaNgwane. This is seen as confirmation that it has finally abandoned its land deal with Swaziland, of

which KaNgwane was to have been a part.

14 Aug. 1984   Lesotho rejects South Africa's proposal for a draft security treaty.

22 Aug. 1984   Elections to the House of Representatives among the Coloured community show overwhelming support for the Labour Party. Official results record only a 30.9 per cent turn out and protests and boycotts are followed by 152 arrests.

28 Aug. 1984   Elections to the House of Delegates among the Indian community are marked by a low poll, protests, boycotts and active opposition by the UDF. Results show eighteen seats for the National Peoples Party (NPP), seventeen for Solidarity, one for the Progressive Independent Party (PIP), four for independents.

30 Aug. 1984   Prime Minister Botha declares that the government does not see the low turnout at the polls as invalidating the revised constitution.

2-3 Sept. 1984   The revised Constitution comes into effect.

5 Sept. 1984   P.W. Botha is unanimously elected to the post of Executive President by an Electoral College composed of the majority parties in each house - fifty NP members of the white House of Assembly, twenty-five Labour Party members of the Coloured House of Representatives, and thirteen National People's Party members of the Indian House of Delegates.

11 Sept. 1984   Following unrest and rioting in the townships, the Minister of Law and Order prohibits all meetings of more than two persons, discussing politics or which is in protest against or in support or in memorium of anything, until 30 September 1984. The ban extends to certain areas in all four provinces, but is most comprehensive in the Transvaal.

13 Sept. 1984   Six political refugees, including the President of the United Democratic Front (UDF) seek refuge in the British consulate in Durban, and ask the British government to intervene on their behalf.

14 Sept. 1984   The inauguration of the new President, P.W. Botha, takes place. Under the revised Constitution, the post of President combines the ceremonial duties of Head of State with the executive functions of Prime Minister. Mr. Botha is also chairman of the Cabinet, Commander-in-Chief of the Armed Forces and controls the National Intelligence Service which includes the Secretariat of the State Security Council.

14 Sept. 1984   Margaret Thatcher, the British Prime Minister, gives an assurance that the six refugees will not be required to leave the consulate against their will, but also states that Britain will not become involved in negotiations between the fugitives and the South African government.

15 Sept. 1984   Members of a new Cabinet responsible for general affairs of government and three Ministers' Councils are appointed and sworn in on 17 September 1984.

15 Sept. 1984   The leader of the Labour Party, the Reverend H.J. (Allan) Hendrikse and A. Rajbansi of the NPP are appointed to the Cabinet as Chairmen of the Ministers' Councils, but neither is given a ministerial portfolio.

24 Sept. 1984	Minister of Foreign Affairs, 'Pik' Botha, announces that in retaliation for the British government's refusal to give up the six men, the government will not return to Britain four South Africans due to face charges of having contravened British customs and excise regulations, and believed to be employed by ARMSCOR.
26 Sept. 1984	Five of the political detainees are released and on the same day the banning order on Dr. Beyers Naudé is lifted.
26 Sept. 1984	Schools re-open, but 93,000 pupils continue to boycott classes.
2 Oct. 1984	The death toll in rioting and clashes with police has risen to over sixty.
5 Oct. 1984	L. le Grange states that the South African Defence Force units will be deployed increasingly in a supportive role to the police in maintaining an effective protective force against radical elements. On 6-9 October they are deployed in Soweto.
6 Oct. 1984	Three of the six protesters leave the British Consulate in protest against South Africa's action in linking their sit-in with the Coventry case. They are immediately arrested and detained by security police.
8 Oct. 1984	Signs treaty relating to certificates of airworthiness for imported aircraft with the United States.
9 Oct. 1984	The three anti-apartheid protesters in the British Consulate in Durban, declare they will not leave the building voluntarily. The British government will have to evict them.
17 Oct. 1984	The United Nations Security Council, by fourteen votes to none, with the United States abstaining, passes a resolution reiterating its condemnation of the South African regime's policy of apartheid and condemning its continued defiance of United Nations resolutions, the continued massacres of the oppressed people and the arbitrary detention and arrest of their leaders.
22 Oct. 1984	The Minister of Law and Order rejects conditions set on 18 October 1984 by the three remaining fugitives in the British Consulate in Durban for their voluntary exit. They ask the government to waive detention-without-trial orders or to provide them with passports to enable them to plead their case before the United Nations Anti-Apartheid Committee.
23 Oct. 1984	A combined force of about 7,000 South African Defence Force troops and police seal off the townships of Sebokeng, Sharpeville and Boipatong and carry out house-to-house searches, arresting 358 people, some of whom are immediately charged in special courts. Its purpose is to eliminate criminal and intimidatory forces from the townships.
23 Oct. 1984	The government forfeits 400,000 Pounds Sterling bail when the 'Coventry four' fail to appear to answer arms smuggling charges, prevented from doing so by the South African government. Warrants are issued for their arrest.
24 Oct. 1984	The United Nations Security Council endorses a lengthy resolution condemning South Africa's apartheid regime, demanding the immediate cessation of massacres and the prompt and unconditional release of all political prisoners and detainees.

2 Nov. 1984	Amends air services agreement with Great Britain.
9 Nov. 1984	Following pressure from township residents, resignations have occurred among black municipal councillors.
14 Nov. 1984	Signs international telecommunications treaty.
14 Nov. 1984	In a continued attempt to forestall further unrest, the authorities arrest several leading trade union activists belonging to organizations affiliated to the UDF.
17-18 Nov. 1984	The opposition PFP opens its membership to all races, despite the Prohibition of Political Interference Act which forbids mixed political parties. The Party leadership also votes to oppose military conscription now that the South African Army is being used regularly to suppress mounting black unrest. The decision draws strong opposition within the Party.
21 Nov. 1984	Demonstrations begin outside the South African Embassy in Washington, D.C. and continue on an almost daily basis as anti-apartheid protesters demand a stronger anti-South Africa policy from the United States government.
23 Nov. 1984	Signs multilateral agreement regulating the appointment of a Southern African tourism coordinator.
29 Nov. 1984	The NP retains three House of Assembly seats in by-elections, with reduced majorities, losing ground to right-wing parties opposed to the new Constitution.
4 Dec. 1984	Bishop Desmond Tutu, addressing a United States House of Representatives subcommittee, describes the policy of constructive engagement as immoral and evil and hostile to the conditions of blacks in South Africa.
10 Dec. 1984	American President Reagan, in a speech made on International Human Rights Day, calls on the Pretoria government to engage in effective dialogue with the black population and to broaden the changes taking place, so as to address the aspirations of all South Africans.
12 Dec. 1984	The three anti-apartheid activists still in the British Consulate in Durban, leave the building. A. Gumede and one other are immediately arrested and charged with treason.
13 Dec. 1984	During the proceedings of the thirty-ninth regular session of the United Nations General Assembly, a series of seven resolutions on the theme of apartheid are adopted.
13 Dec. 1984	The United Nations Security Council reaffirms the mandatory arms embargo, and, for the first time requests that all states refrain from importing arms, ammunition and military vehicles produced in South Africa.
27 Dec. 1984	Swaziland and South Africa agree to exchange trade representatives who will have the same rights and privileges as diplomatic personnel.
28 Dec. 1984	It is announced that Colonel Hoare, the leader of the attempted Seychelles coup, will shortly be eligible for release from prison under a recent amnesty.

5 Jan. 1985	Senator Edward Kennedy pays an eight-day visit to South Africa.
25 Jan. 1985	Opening parliament, President Botha announces that government intends giving blacks more political rights such as those living outside their designated 'homelands' and an informal forum where black leaders can discuss changes. Also giving blacks property rights to those living in urban areas.
30 Jan. 1985	The South African Medical and Postal Council is ordered to hold an inquiry into the conduct of doctors whò treated the Black Consciousness Leader, Steve Biko, who died at the hands of the security police in 1977.
31 Jan. 1985	Foreign Minister 'Pik' Botha denies South African support for RENAMO and that South Africa is committed to the Nkomati Accord of 1984.
31 Jan. 1985	President P.W. Botha offers a release proposal to jailed ANC leader Nelson Mandela.
31 Jan. 1985	In an address to the Foreign Correspondents Association, Minister of Cooperation and Development, Dr. Gerrit Viljoen announces that the forced removal of blacks will be suspended and government is to review this policy.
5 Feb. 1985	Foreign Minister 'Pik' Botha accuses Botswana of harbouring ANC guerrillas.
10 Feb. 1985	Nelson Mandela, jailed ANC leader, turns down offer of release made to him by President Botha on 31 January.
15 Feb. 1985	President Botha announces that his offer of release to Nelson Mandela still stands and that government is prepared to talk to the ANC if it renounces violence. Four Pan-Africanist Congress security prisoners take up an offer of release and three other ANC prisoners reject this offer in a six-page memorandum submitted to President Botha.
18 Feb. 1985	Top leadership officials of the United Democratic Front (UDF) are arrested. Of the thirteen detained, six are to be charged for high treason.
21 Feb. 1985	Government announces ninety-nine year leasehold rights for blacks in three Cape Town townships in order to stop the riots over the policy of forced removal in that region.
20 Mar. 1985	Dr. Allan Boesak who is President of the World Alliance of Reformed Churches, is exonerated by his church for having had an extra-marital affair with a white woman and allowed to resume his official duties.
21 Mar. 1985	At least seventeen people are killed in Langa, a black township near Port Elizabeth, during a commemoration of the twenty-fifth anniversary of the Sharpeville massacre. Government appoints a Commission of Inquiry into this massacre, chaired by Justice D. Kannemeyer.
25 Mar. 1985	In an important policy shift, South Africa's Deputy Minister of Foreign Affairs, Louis Nel, discloses that his government is seeking ways to cooperate with FRELIMO in Mozambique to eliminate the rebel RENAMO.
Apr. 1985	At its third congress, the United Democratic Front agrees to establish closer

links with the trade union movement and to increase its presence in rural areas. Popo Molefe, Patrick Lekota and Moses Chikana, three key UDF officials are arrested under security laws.

4 Apr. 1985   Signs treaty with Taiwan relating to co-operation in mineral and energy affairs.

15 Apr. 1985   South Africa's Foreign Minister announces that South African troop withdrawal from Angola is to be completed within a week.

19 Apr. 1985   President Botha outlines proposals to improve the lot of blacks. Amongst these are property rights and political representation for urban blacks and future dual citizenship rights to 'homeland' blacks.

24 Apr. 1985   Foreign Minister 'Pik' Botha announces in Parliament that South Africa and Mozambique are to establish joint operational centres on their borders to fully implement the Nkomati Accord.

30 Apr. 1985   The Rand Daily Mail, a leading anti-apartheid newspaper, ceases publication.

May 1985   Sipho Mutsi of the Congress of South African Students dies during police custody and Andries Raditsela, an executive member of the Federation of South African Trade Unions dies hours after charges under the Internal Security Act are withdrawn against him.

May 1985   The ruling National Party wins a parliamentary seat in Newton Park and provincial council seats in the Orange Free State and Eastern Cape.

1 May 1985   Signs agreement with the United States relating to the reciprocal granting of authorization to permit licensed amateur radio operators of either country to operate their stations in the other country.

9 May 1985   Regional Services Councils are introduced giving blacks increasing say in second-tier government. It is decided that blacks in fifty-two townships are not to be forcibly removed.

25 May 1985   The Prohibition of Political Interference Act which bans racially mixed political parties, is to be repealed.

June 1985   The Kannemeyer Commission of Inquiry into the Langa shootings of 21 March 1985, blames the police for the events leading to the shooting.

1 June 1985   Signs agreement with Swaziland on the issue of notes and coin.

14 June 1985   ANC bases in Gaborone, Botswana, are attacked by South African commanders. At least fifteen people are killed.

25 June 1985   At its conference held in Lusaka, Zambia, the ANC opens its national executive committee to all race groups by appointing five Indian, White and Coloured people to the committee.

30 June 1985   John Nyati Pokela, PAC chairman dies in Harare.

July 1985   A Dutch subject, Klaas de Jong, is detained under the Internal Security Act for distributing arms and ammunition to the ANC. He seeks refuge in the

Dutch Embassy in Pretoria.

1 July 1985	Minor cabinet changes are made.
5 July 1985	Two white medical doctors are found guilty of misconduct by the Medical Council in the 1977 death of Black Consciousness leader, Steve Biko.
10 July 1985	Four British men are jailed for conspiring to smuggle military components into South Africa.
21 July 1985	State of Emergency is declared affecting the Eastern Cape, Johannesburg and industrial areas east of Johannesburg.
Aug. 1985	A march to Pollsmoor prison, where a message of solidarity is to be delivered to Nelson Mandela, is prevented by the government. The message is eventually read out at a press conference by Dorothy Boesak, wife of Dr. Allan Boesak, who had called the march. He was detained to prevent him from leading it.
15 Aug. 1985	President Botha, leader of the National Party, takes a hardline stance at the party's Natal congress.
16 Aug. 1985	In response to President Botha's hardline speech at the party's Natal congress, the president of the ANC, Oliver Tambo, reaffirms in Lusaka, that the armed struggle will be intensified and whites will lose their lives and property.
Sept. 1985	At the National Party Congress in the Orange Free State, President Botha announces the government's willingness to restore South African citizenship to blacks deprived of it under the policy of separate development.
16 Sept. 1985	South Africa and Namibian Security Forces cross into Angola in pursuit of SWAPO forces.
21 Sept. 1985	A Convention Alliance is launched to promote the idea of a national convention to formulate a democratic and multi-racial constitution.
27 Sept. 1985	In anticipation of a national day of prayer on 9 October, the government outlaws gatherings and meetings.
Oct. 1985	Dr. Benjamin Tucker is struck off the roll for disgraceful conduct over the death in detention of Black Consciousness leader Steve Biko in September 1977.
9 Oct. 1985	General Constand Viljoen, Chief of South Africa's Armed Forces admits on television that the military, without the government authority, has flaunted the Nkomati Accord by supporting RENAMO.
13 Oct. 1985	The PFP meets the ANC in Lusaka and calls for the release of Nelson Mandela.
25 Oct. 1985	State of Emergency is extended to include Cape Town and seven surrounding areas.
31 Oct. 1985	The ruling National Party loses a string of by-elections to the ultra-right

parties with the exception of Port Natal.

1 Nov. 1985
Government bans television coverage of unrest in black townships in the thirty-eight magisterial districts where the State of Emergency is in force, except with permission from the Commissioner of Police. Curbs on newspaper reports are also imposed.

3 Nov. 1985
Signs multilateral treaty on radio regulations.

4 Nov. 1985
In a cabinet reshuffle, Louis le Grange, Minister of Law and Order, is replaced by Adriaan Vlock, Deputy Minister of Defence and Law and Order.

21 Nov. 1985
Signs multilateral agreement on the control of pollution of water resources in the Southern African region.

28 Nov. 1985
Two strategic oil-from-coal plants based in Secunda are attacked by saboteurs.

Dec. 1985
A shopping centre in Amanzimtoti, Natal, is bombed.

9 Dec. 1985
Twelve of the sixteen UDF members, charged with treason, have these withdrawn.

30 Dec. 1985
Winnie Mandela is arrested for contravening a banning order prohibiting her from being in the magisterial district of Johannesburg and Roodepoort.

7 Jan. 1986
South Africa's foreign minister 'Pik' Botha warns Botswana to take action against ANC operations in its country.

7 Jan. 1986
The ANC in exile in Lusaka, calls on its supporters to take the struggle into white areas.

20 Jan. 1986
Twenty-two black South Africans appear in the Delmas Court for allegedly attempting to overthrow the government.

25 Jan. 1986
Sixty ANC refugees are airlifted out of Lesotho to counter South Africa's threat of a blockade against that country.

31 Jan. 1986
In his opening speech to Parliament, President Botha outlines government policy on the restoration of South African citizenship to blacks, their involvement in decision-making, freehold property rights and uniform identity documents for all population groups.

Feb. 1986
President Botha reprimands Foreign Minister 'Pik' Botha for suggesting that a black could become president of South Africa.

7 Feb. 1986
Dr. Frederick van Zyl Slabbert, leader of the opposition PFP, resigns from parliamentary politics.

25 Feb. 1986
South Africa and Botswana agree to take steps preventing ANC operatives from using Botswana as a transit base into South Africa.

7 Mar. 1986
The State of Emergency imposed on 21 July 1985 lifted.

7 March 1986
The South African Congress of Trade Unions (SACTU), the Congress of

South African Trade Unions (COSATU) and the ANC issue a joint statement in Lusaka, reiterating their commitment to overthrow white supremacy in South Africa.

8 Mar. 1986	Moses Mabhida, General Secretary of the South African Communist Party, dies in Maputo.
12 Mar. 1986	The Eminent Persons Group meets imprisoned ANC leader, Nelson Mandela.
13 Mar. 1986	Signs multilateral Wheat Trade Convention.
26 Mar. 1986	South Africa and Lesotho issue a joint statement that their respective territories are not to be used for acts of terrorism against each other.
14 Apr. 1986	Bishop Desmond Tutu is appointed head of the Anglican Church of South Africa.
18 Apr. 1986	Signs bilateral monetary agreement with Lesotho.
18 Apr. 1986	Signs trilateral agreement amending monetary agreement between South Africa, Lesotho, Swaziland, dated 5 December 1974.
18 Apr. 1986	Signs monetary agreement with Swaziland.
19 May 1986	South African commandos air strike alleged guerrilla targets in Zambia, Botswana and Zimbabwe, jeopardizing the Eminent Persons Group (EPG) mission to South Africa.
22 May 1986	The multi-racial National Council, intended to negotiate a constitutional structure for South Africa, is unveiled.
5 June 1986	Signs treaty with Botswana, Mozambique and Zimbabwe relative to the establishment of the Limpopo Basin Permanent Technical Committee.
12 June 1986	The Eminent Persons Group releases its report on South Africa.
12 June 1986	Government declares a new State of Emergency and hundreds of anti-apartheid activists are arrested.
23 June 1986	The State drops the case against the remaining four charged with treason in the Pietermaritzburg Supreme Court.
24 June 1986	In Britain, Foreign Office Minister Lynda Chalker, meets Oliver Tambo, president of the ANC.
July 1986	The Transkei, Kangwane and KwaNdebele 'homelands' are plagued by violence and Piet Ntuli, Home Affairs Minister for KwaNdebele, is killed in a bomb explosion.
July 1986	The European Community Mission under the leadership of British Foreign Secretary, Sir Geoffrey Howe, pays a weeklong visit to South Africa to assess the situation.
1 July 1986	Influx control restrictions lifted and passes to be replaced by a uniform

identity document for all population groups.

7 July 1986	After enduring more than twenty years of government banning, Winnie Mandela is freed of all state-ordered restriction.
31 July 1986	Signs treaty with Zimbabwe regarding the amendment of the trade agreement of 30 November 1964.
Aug. 1986	Zephania Mthopeng is elected President of the PAC.
Aug. 1986	South African intelligence forces raid Swaziland in search of ANC activists.
12 Aug. 1986	At the Federal Congress of the National Party, President Botha outlines six proposals for discussion with the United States, Britain, France, West Germany and neighbouring African states.
12 Aug. 1986	KwaNdebele 'homeland' rejects independence.
13 Aug. 1986	At the National Party Federal Congress, Chris Heunis, Minister of Constitutional Development and Planning, outlines plans for the creation of a black electorate to choose leaders to be represented on a National Statutory Council which will play a role in power sharing. Government also considers establishing independent 'city states'.
9 Sept. 1986	Three ANC members are executed, amongst them Andrew Zondo, who bombed a shopping centre in Amanzimtoti, Natal, in December 1985.
16 Sept. 1986	The European Economic Community (EEC) imposes sanctions against South Africa, coal being the exception.
30 Sept. 1986	President Botha retires as leader of the Cape Division of the National Party.
24 Oct. 1986	Signs treaty on Lesotho Highlands Water Project.
24 Oct. 1986	Exchange of notes with Lesotho regarding the privileges and immunities accorded to the members of the Joint Permanent Technical Commission.
27 Nov. 1986	Three of the twenty-two Delmas trialists are freed.
8 Jan. 1987	At the ANC's seventy-fifth anniversary, its President Oliver Tambo rules out negotiations with the South African government and declares 1987 'the year of advance to people's power'.
9 Jan. 1987	Security police raid English-language newspapers seizing documents related to an advertisement calling for the legalising of the ANC.
9 Jan. 1987	A bomb explodes in a major departmental store in the centre of Johannesburg.
20 Jan. 1987	The Margo Commission of Inquiry into the death of President Samora Machel has its first hearing in Johannesburg.
28 Jan. 1987	United States Secretary of State, George Shultz, meets ANC leader, Oliver Tambo, in Washington, D.C.

19 Feb. 1987	President Lennox Sebe of the Ciskei escapes an assassination attempt.
Mar. 1987	Joe Slovo resigns as Chief of Staff of Umkhonto we Sizwe, the military wing of the ANC.
16 Mar. 1987	The International Commission of Jurists states in its report that children are being tortured by security forces.
18 Mar. 1987	Israel freezes military contracts and imposes cultural and tourism sanctions on South Africa.
22 Mar. 1987	Archbishop Desmond Tutu meets the ANC in Zambia and fails to convince the organization to abandon the armed struggle.
5 Apr. 1987	Transkei deports white Selous Scout mercenaries.
10 Apr. 1987	Ciskei, Transkei and South Africa sign a security pact forbidding cross-border violence.
30 Apr. 1987	Signs an agreement with Lesotho in regard to the establishment of trade missions.
May 1987	South African agents attack ANC offices and safe houses in Maputo and Harare.
May 1987	Major urban areas hit by a wave of pre-election bomb blasts for which the ANC claims responsibility.
6 May 1987	The ruling National Party wins the general election and the rightwing Conservative Party replaces the PFP as the official opposition in the white House of Assembly.
7 May 1987	The COSATU building in Johannesburg is seriously damaged by two bomb blasts.
4 June 1987	President Botha visits Sharpeville.
11 June 1987	The year old State of Emergency renewed.
16 June 1987	Concludes a reciprocal radio agreement with the Republic of Chile.
July 1987	Key African ANC personnel are assassinated in South Africa's neighbouring states. Amongst them is Cassius Make and Paul Dikeledi, both killed in Swaziland.
1 July 1987	Eight multi-racial Regional Services Councils are established to provide basic services, such as water and electricity.
1 July 1987	The Reverend Frank Chikane succeeds the Reverend C.F. Beyers Naudé as head of the South African Council of Churches.
6 July 1987	A new black party, the Federal Independent Democratic Alliance (FIDA) is launched to oppose apartheid and prepares to work with the government.
9 July 1987	The Margo Commission of Inquiry into the death of President Samora

Machel releases its findings. The plane carrying him crashes due to pilot error and negligence and was not lured off course by a decoy beacon as alleged by the Soviets and Mozambicans.

9-12 July 1987   Sixty-one white South Africans, mainly from the Afrikaans community, meet the ANC in Dakar, in search of a democratic alternative for South Africa. Eric Mntonga, an IDASA official, who organized this meeting, is found stabbed to death.

20 July 1987   Signs an agreement with the Federal Islamic Republic of the Comores relating to the basic conditions governing the secondment of officials to, and the recruitment of other personnel by South Africa on behalf of the government of the Republic of the Comores.

26 July 1987   Prominent anti-apartheid activists are arrested. Amongst them is Azhar Cachalia, national treasurer of the United Democratic Front (UDF).

30 July 1987   A bomb explodes outside the headquarters of the South African Defence Force, injuring soldiers and civilians.

10 Aug. 1987   Ratifies the Convention on Assistance in the case of a Nuclear Accident or Radiological Emergency; also ratifies Convention on Early Notification of a Nuclear Accident.

14 Aug. 1987   Reverend Allan Hendricks, a cabinet minister, resigns from government.

7 Sept. 1987   An intricate prisoner exchange takes place in Maputo, involving 133 Angolan soldiers, anti-apartheid activists, Klaas de Jonge, a Dutch anthropologist, Pierre Andre Albertini, a French university lecturer and Major Wynand du Toit, a South African officer captured in Angola two years ago.

11 Sept. 1987   A revised National Statutory Council is released providing a forum for blacks to discuss policy and assist in drawing up a new constitution.

23 Sept. 1987   Signs treaty with Malawi providing for the training of nurses from Malawi in South Africa.

24 Sept. 1987   Congress of Traditional Leaders of South Africa is launched to articulate the interests of tribal chiefs and act as an extra-parliamentary opposition movement.

27 Sept. 1987   Oliver Tambo, President of the ANC denies that it is in contact with the South African government.

Oct. 1987   Chris Hani is appointed new Chief of Staff and Deputy Commander of Unkhonto we Sizwe.

5 Oct. 1987   President P.W. Botha decides against scrapping the Separate Amenities Act, but agrees that some residential areas can be opened to all races.

6 Oct. 1987   ANC command structure in the Western Cape is arrested.

12 Oct. 1987   Wynand Malan a former National Party M.P. leads the newly formed Afrikaans dominated political party, the National Democratic Movement

(NDM) which is to develop contacts with black politicians.

5 Nov. 1987	Govan Mbeki released from Robben Island after twenty-three years in prison.
1 Dec. 1987	Signs an agreement with the USA regarding co-operation in the development, building, installation and operation of an integrated real-time global seismic data acquisition system.
30 Dec. 1987	The Transkei military overthrows the administration of Stella Sigcau of the Transkei.
31 Dec. 1987	Ratifies International Sugar Agreement.
Jan. 1988	Fierce fighting erupts between Angolan and South African forces for control of the strategic town of Cuito Cuanavale in Angola.
6 Jan. 1988	General Bantu Holomisa, who ousted Stella Sigcau in a coup appoints himself as the Transkei's military and government chief.
12 Jan. 1988	Signs a medical co-operation treaty with the government of the Republic of China, providing advanced training for medical and nursing personnel.
17 Jan. 1988	Percy Qoboza, well-known anti-apartheid journalist and editor of The World newspaper, dies.
31 Jan. 1988	Allan Hendrickse, leader of the Labour Party, replaces Carter Ebrahim as Minister of Education and Culture in the House of Representatives.
5 Feb. 1988	President P.W. Botha opens Parliament and ignores the country's domestic crisis in his opening address.
10 Feb. 1988	Bophuthatswana troops, led by Rocky Malebane-Metsing, fail to overthrow President Lucas Mangope.
24 Feb. 1988	Seventeen anti-apartheid organizations are banned, amongst them the Azanian People's Organization and COSATU.
27 Feb. 1988	Members of the Afrikaner Resistance Movement (AWB) march to Pretoria and call for a Volkstaat for the Afrikaner people.
29 Feb. 1988	Reverend Desmond Tutu and others are arrested as they present a petition to Parliament.
11 Mar. 1988	The Cabinet is reshuffled.
13 Mar. 1988	Church services are held countrywide to warn the government to desist from its confrontational road.
17 Mar. 1988	The 'Sharpeville Six' are granted stay of execution until 18 April.
17 Mar. 1988	Dennis Worrall, former Ambassador to Britain, establishes the Independent Party.
28 Mar. 1988	South African commandos raid Gaborone, in search of ANC members.

| 29 Mar. 1988 | Dulcie September, ANC representative in Paris, is assassinated. |

| 29 Mar. 1988 | Signs Protocol I, II and III to the treaty on the Lesotho Highlands Water Project (Royalty Manual). |

| Apr. 1988 | President Patrick Mphephu of Venda dies. |

| Apr. 1988 | Alan Paton, founder member of the Liberal Party, dies. |

| 7 Apr. 1988 | Albie Sachs, an exiled ANC member, is critically injured in a bomb explosion in Maputo. South African agents are blamed. |

| 11 Apr. 1988 | Signs visa agreement with the government of the Republic of Paraguay. |

| 19 Apr. 1988 | General Jannie Geldenhuys, Chief of the South African Defence Force (SADF) reveals details of South African military operations, code named Modular and Hooper, directed against SWAPO forces in Angola. |

| 21 Apr. 1988 | President P.W. Botha outlines reform plans involving a form of race federation and draft legislation providing for new regional assemblies for blacks living outside the existing 'homelands'. Black leaders, such as Dr. Nthato Motlana, state that such reforms will not attract legitimate black leaders. |

| May 1988 | Alleged South African spy, Olivia Forsyth, seeks refuge in the British Embassy in Angola and claims that she was imprisoned for twenty-two months by ANC guerrillas. |

| 4 May 1988 | Representatives of South Africa, United States, Angola and Cuba, meet in London in search of a solution to the Angolan war and independence for Namibia. |

| 10 May 1988 | An International Commission of Jurists report alleges the widespread use of force and torture by security forces on anti-apartheid opponents. |

| 10 May 1988 | New Nation and South newspapers are banned and twenty-six English-language newspaper editors hand petitions to government, protesting against these curbs on the press. |

| 11 May 1988 | Four white guerrillas, known as the Broederstroom Four, are arrested and an arms cache is discovered. |

| 11 May 1988 | Visa agreement signed with Paraguay on 11 April 1988 enters into force. |

| 24 May 1988 | Signs treaty of extradition with the Republic of China. |

| 26 May 1988 | South Africa and Mozambique agree to revive the Nkomati Accord. |

| 27 May 1988 | Anti-apartheid Afrikaners led by Frederik van Zyl Slabbert, IDASA director, meet with the ANC in Frankfurt, to discuss a post-apartheid South Africa. |

| 10 June 1988 | The State of Emergency renewed. |

| 20 June 1988 | The South African government presents a promotion of Constitutional Development Bill which proposes an advisory and consultative council, |

designed to give blacks a voice in government.

25 June 1988	Angolan, Cuban, South African and United States officials meet in Cairo, in search of independence for Namibia in tandem with a withdrawal of Cuban troops from Angola.
30 June 1988	Zimbabwe foils a South African commando attempt to rescue five alleged South African agents awaiting trial for bomb attacks against the ANC in Zimbabwe.
July 1988	The ANC compiles a set of constitutional proposals for post-apartheid South Africa.
1 July 1988	The government tables three bills cracking down on illegal residents, but allowing legal recognition of some racially mixed residential areas. Those are the draft Group Areas Amendment Bill, the Free Settlement Areas Bill and the Local Government Affairs in Free Settlement Areas Bill.
8 July 1988	The government introduces the Extension of Political Participation Bill, empowering the government to divide the country into a number of regions and calls elections to Legislative Council for each region through which Non-Homeland blacks can articulate their political aspirations. The ANC and the Inkatha Freedom Party express their opposition to these reforms.
12 July 1988	The 'Sharpeville Six' sentenced to hang on 19 July for the killing of a black local councillor, receive an indefinite stay of execution to pursue a possible appeal. This announcement was made hours after British Premier, Thatcher, made a plea of clemency on behalf of the six to President P.W. Botha.
18 July 1988	The pro-government Afrikaans newspaper, Die Beeld, in an editorial coinciding with Nelson Mandela's 70th birthday, urges the government to release him.
20 July 1988	A fourteen-point agreement is signed between South Africa, Cuba, Angola and the United States for a peaceful settlement for Namibia and Angola.
Aug. 1988	The Indian and Coloured Houses of Parliament, the Progressive Federal Party and the Independence Movement, refuse to debate the draft Group Areas Amendments Bill, the Free Settlement Areas Bill and the Local Government Areas Bill.
5 Aug. 1988	Colin Eglin of the PFP decides not to stand for re-election at the Congress, but will remain a party and parliamentary member.
5 Aug. 1988	Dr Zach de Beer succeeds Colin Eglin as leader of the PFP.
8 Aug. 1988	A joint declaration released on talks held in Geneva by Angola, Cuba, South Africa and the United States announcing a formal cessation of hostilities in the Namibian border conflict.
14 Aug. 1988	Nelson Mandela is admitted to the Tygerberg hospital, suffering from a lung ailment.
18 Aug. 1988	At the National Party Annual Congress in Durban, President P.W. Botha rules out any possibility of a black majority government in South Africa.

31 Aug. 1988   The South African Council of Churches (SACC) headquarters, Khotso House, is devastated by a bomb blast. Responsibility for the blast is claimed by a right-wing group.

12 Sept. 1988   President P.W. Botha visits Mozambique and in talks with President Joaquim Chissano, pledges not to support RENAMO, to defend and rebuild the Cahora Bassa power lines and to increase economic cooperation between the two countries. He also visits Malawi and Zaire.

13 Sept. 1988   Three leading anti-apartheid activists, Mohammed Valli Moosa, Murphy Moroke, and Vusi Khanyile, escape from detention and seek refuge in the American Consulate in Johannesburg.

26 Sept. 1988   Indian and Coloured members walk out of Parliament in protest against the draft Group Areas Amendment Bill, the Free Settlement of Areas Bill, and the Local Government Affairs in Free Settlement Areas Bill.

Oct. 1988   The government shelves the three Group Areas Amendment Bills that led to the Indian and Coloured Houses walking out of Parliament and refers the Free Settlement Areas Bill to the President's Council.

12 Oct. 1988   Khanya House, the headquarters of the Southern African Catholic Bishops Conference, is set alight.

12 Oct. 1988   Three Zimbabwean intelligence officers are on trial in Harare for attempting to car bomb a house in Bulawayo, occupied by ANC refugees. The bomb exploded prematurely.

15 Oct. 1988   President P.W. Botha meets Ivory Coast's President Felix Houphouet-Boigny.

16 Oct. 1988   ANC members and South African rugby officials meet in Harare to normalize the sport and get South Africa back into international sport.

19 Oct. 1988   Mohammed Valli Moosa, Murphy Morobe and Vusi Khanyile end their 37-day sit-in at the American Consulate-General in Johannesburg.

26 Oct. 1988   All race municipal elections are held to elect segregated local authorities.

Nov. 1988   Justice Michael Corbett appointed South Africa's new Chief Justice.

1 Nov. 1988   The government suspends the anti-apartheid alternative newspaper, The Weekly Mail, until 28 November.

15 Nov. 1988   Barend Hendrik Strydom, a former right-wing member, massacres six blacks in a Pretoria street. He appears in court on six charges of murder and 17 of attempted murder.

18 Nov. 1988   Three UDF officials, Patrick Lekota, Popo Molefe and Moses Chikane, as well as South African Council of Churches member, Tom Manthatha, are convicted of treason in the Delmas Trial.

18 Nov. 1988   The three Zimbabwean intelligence officers standing on trial for a bomb attack on an ANC house in Bulawayo, are sentenced to death.

23 Nov. 1988	The Sharpeville Six are reprieved by State President, P.W. Botha.
26 Nov. 1988	Harry Gwala of the ANC and Zephania Mothopeng of the PAC are released from prison.
Dec. 1988	Delmas trialist Patrick Lekota is sentenced to twelve years imprisonment, and Popo Molefe, to ten years. Six others, amongst the eleven convicted, are given suspended sentences for terrorism.
Dec. 1988	Johnstone Makatini, director of foreign relations for the African National Congress since 1977, dies in Lusaka.
Dec. 1988	Nelson Mandela is transferred to the Victor Verster Prison.
2 Dec. 1988	Zwelakhe Sisulu, editor of the New Nation newspaper, and six other detainees are released.
5 Jan. 1989	The ANC agrees to close its military training base in Angola and in return South Africa must stop aid to the rebel Angolan UNITA movement, the Angolan president, José Eduardo dos Santos says in an interview.
19 Jan. 1989	Chris Heunis, Minister of Constitutional Development and Planning, is appointed Acting State President by President P.W. Botha who is recovering from a stroke suffered on 18 January. But he will continue making key decisions.
25 Jan. 1989	Minister of Manpower and Public Works, Pietie du Plessis, resigns over a financial scandal involving his department and a company in which he holds interest.
2 Feb. 1989	Ailing President P.W. Botha resigns as leader of the ruling white National Party, but remains President. F.W. de Klerk, the Education Minister, is to take over the post of party leader.
2 Feb. 1989	A Free Settlement Board is to come into effect on 1 March to legalize multi-racial free settlement areas in carefully chosen zones in main cities and towns.
4 Feb. 1989	The National Democratic Movement, the Progressive Federal Party and the Independent Party merge to form the Democratic Party.
16 Feb. 1989	The United Democratic Front and COSATU distance themselves from Winnie Mandela and her private militia.
21 Feb. 1989	Fifty political detainees who had gone on hunger strike are released from prison.
10 Mar. 1989	Signs an agreement concerning the status of the United Nations Transition Assistance Group to Namibia.
21 Mar. 1989	The political power struggle continues between President P.W. Botha and F.W. de Klerk and a compromise is reached between the two, according to which P.W. Botha is to announce a date for an October election. He is not expected to stand for re-election for another five-year term.

1 Apr. 1989	Signs monetary agreement with Lesotho.
6 Apr. 1989	In a parliamentary speech, President P.W. Botha announces the dissolving of Parliament by the end of May and indicates that he will not stand for re-election as President.
9 Apr. 1989	The Democratic Party is formally launched.
20 Apr. 1989	Signs an air service agreement with the Republic of Zaire.
30 Apr. 1989	Helen Suzman announces her retirement from Parliament.
1 May 1989	Dr David Webster, a social anthropologist at the University of the Witwatersrand and a leading anti-apartheid activist, is shot dead outside his home.
3 May 1989	President P.W. Botha announces that a general election is to be held on the 6th September.
3 May 1989	Signs memorandum of understanding amending the Customs Union Agreement of 11 December 1969.
11 May 1989	C. Heunis, Minister of Constitutional Development, announces that he will resign his post on 1 July and not stand for re-election in the September general election. Other Ministers also resign.
9 June 1989	The three-year old State of Emergency is renewed for another twelve months.
12 June 1989	Three whites, Damion de Lange, Ian Robertson and Susan Donelly, are convicted for terrorism for being in possession of arms cache in Broederstroom.
15 June 1989	Signs an agreement with the government of the Republic of China relating to cooperation in the field of population development.
19 June 1989	Signs an agreement on cultural matters with the Republic of China.
29 June 1989	F.W. de Klerk, Leader of the National Party, explains to the NP Federal Congress in Pretoria the Party's next five-year plan, giving blacks a say in running the country and at the same time maintaining white superiority.
5 July 1989	Jailed leader of the ANC, Mr Nelson Mandela, meets President P.W. Botha at his official residence.
12 July 1989	Nelson Mandela issues a statement subsequent to his meeting with President Botha on the 5th July, that only dialogue with the outlawed ANC will bring peace to the country.
19 July 1989	F.W. de Klerk meets President Joaquim Chissano of Mozambique.
14 Aug. 1989	President P W Botha resigns as South Africa's President.
21 Aug. 1989	The OAU Committee on Southern Africa issues a political declaration in Harare (The Harare Declaration)

28 Aug. 1989	During a meeting in Livingstone, Zambia, President Kenneth Kaunda supports acting South African President F.W. de Klerk's moves to reform apartheid.
6 Sept. 1989	The National Party wins the general election with an overwhelming majority.
14 Sept. 1989	F.W. de Klerk is elected President of South Africa and is officially installed on 20 September.
16 Sept. 1989	President de Klerk nominates his new cabinet.
15 Oct. 1989	Seven jailed senior ANC leaders and Jafta Masemola of the Pan African Congress who was convicted of sabotage in 1963 are released from prison.
29 Oct. 1989	The ANC holds a huge rally to welcome back the seven released leaders.
28 Nov. 1989	President de Klerk issues a statement that the National Security Management System (NSMS) is to be disbanded.
Dec. 1989	An all-inclusive black political conference is held with the main groups being the Mass Democratic Movement and the Black Consciousness Movement. The Conference adopts the Harare Declaration which sets out pre-conditions for negotiations and outlines a new constitutional future.
Dec. 1989	The Pan-African Movement (PAM) which is to act as a front for the banned Pan-Africanist Congress, is formed.
Dec. 1989	Signs an agreement on the establishment and operation of a common works area at the Caledon River for the purpose of the implementation of the Lesotho Highlands Water Project.
13 Dec. 1989	President de Klerk and Nelson Mandela meet to discuss the country's political future.
16 Dec. 1989	Five anti-apartheid leaders, imprisoned in 1988 for political activities, are freed from Robben Island. Amongst these five is the General Secretary of the United Democratic Front, Popo Molefe and its Publicity Secretary, Patrick Lekota.
Jan. 1990	Eight veteran ANC leaders, together with the leader of the Mass Democratic Movement (MDM) and the Congress of South African Trade Unions (COSATU) meet the external hiearchy of the ANC in Lusaka.
15 Jan. 1990	Accedes to the Montreal Protocol on Substances that Deplete the Ozone Layer.
25 Jan. 1990	Extracts of a document written by Nelson Mandela in anticipation of a meeting with President P.W. Botha in the beginning of 1989, is published by a Cape Town newspaper.
2 Feb. 1990	At the opening of Parliament, President F.W. de Klerk unbans the ANC, the Pan African Congress, the South African Communist Party and thirty three internal political organizations which includes the United Democratic Front.
11 Feb. 1990	Nelson Mandela, leader of the ANC, freed after twenty-seven years in jail.

27 Feb. 1990	Nelson Mandela meets ANC officials in Lusaka.
Mar. 1990	Violence erupts in South Africa's 'homelands'. Ciskei falls in a military coup.
15 Mar. 1990	Major cabinet portfolio changes are made to co-ordinate economic policy and constitutional negotiations.
31 Mar. 1990	The ANC decides not to hold talks with the South African government scheduled for 11 April, due to the killing of defenceless demonstrators in Sebokeng. Meeting between Nelson Mandela and Chief Buthelezi of the Inkatha Freedom Party, is also called off.
2 Apr. 1990	Nelson Mandela is appointed Deputy President of the ANC and the organization is to shift its headquarters from Zambia to Johannesburg.
4 Apr. 1990	Signs bilateral monetary agreement with the government of Namibia.
5 Apr. 1990	The Venda homeland falls in a military coup.
6 Apr. 1990	Signs agreement with Togo regarding wildlife management in the Keran National Park.
9 Apr. 1990	Signs memorandum of understanding amending the Customs Union Agreement of 1969.
18 Apr. 1990	In a parliamentary speech, President de Klerk rules out any possibility of black majority rule.
27 Apr. 1990	Senior ANC leaders such as Joe Slovo, Thabo Mbeki and others, return to South African after a quarter of a century in exile.
May 1990	Government admits to failure of its 'homeland' policy and that those 'homelands' will be reintegrated into South Africa.
2-4 May 1990	The Groote Schuur talks take place between the South African government and the ANC. They reach agreement on conditions for full-scale negotiations on ending political conflict in South Africa.
6 May 1990	P.W. Botha resigns from the National Party in protest against President F.W. de Klerk's reform proposals.
8 May 1990	President F.W. de Klerk tours nine European countries.
9 May 1990	Nelson Mandela begins a six-nation African tour.
18 May 1990	Signs agreement with Namibia concerning the appointment of representatives and privileges and immunities for representatives and their staff.
4 June 1990	Nelson Mandela leaves South Africa for a thirteen-nation international tour.
8 June 1990	National State of Emergency is to be lifted with the exception of Natal.
19 June 1990	Signs trade agreement with the government of the Republic of Malawi.

22 June 1990	Offices of the Minister of National (Black) Education, Stoffel van der Merwe, and that of Deputy Consitutional Development Minister, Rolf Meyer, are bombed by white far-right wing members.
2 July 1990	A week long labour stayaway, organized by the ANC and its allies, begins in protest against factional black violence in Natal.
6 July 1990	The right wing bomb campaign continues when a powerful bomb explodes in Johannesburg, injuring twenty-seven people.
25 July 1990	Senior ANC member, Sathyandranath 'Mac' Maharaj and over forty other members of the ANC and the SACP, are detained for allegedly attempting to overthrow the government (Operation Vula).
6 Aug. 1990	The Pretoria Minute is signed at a meeting between the South African government and the ANC, according to which the latter agreed to suspend the armed struggle.
10 Aug. 1990	Signs trade agreement with Hungary.
24 Aug. 1990	More than five hundred people die in eleven days of fighting between township residents and migrant Zulu workers in the PWV region, and the government declares a State of Emergency in this region.
Sept. 1990	The Goldstone Commission of Inquiry is established to investigate the Sebokeng massacre of 26 March, in which at least eleven people were killed during a protest march by township residents.
Sept. 1990	The government launches Operation Iron Fist to curb township violence.
Sept. 1990	President F.W. de Klerk pays a three-day visit to the United States of America.
4 Sept. 1990	Signs a memorandum of understanding on road transportation in the Common Customs Area.
7 Sept. 1990	Dr. Zach de Beer is elected as leader of the Democratic Party.
9 Sept. 1990	Signs co-operation agreement with Cote d'Ivoire regarding the technical management of the Abokouamekro Game Park.
24 Sept. 1990	Winnie Mandela is formally charged with four counts of kidnapping and of assault, and will stand trial with seven others in the events surrounding the murder of Stompie Moeketsi in December 1988.
8 Oct. 1990	Signs agreement with the government of the Democratic Republic of Madagascar regarding merchant shipping and related maritime matters.
15 Oct. 1990	The Reservation of Separate Amenities Act is repealed.
20 Oct. 1990	The formerly whites only National Party opens its membersip to all race groups.
25 Oct. 1990	Signs a trade agreement with the government of Romania.

30 Oct. 1990	Signs agreement for the establishment of permanent offices of interest with the Republic of Poland.
Nov. 1990	ANC supporters are arrested for allegedly plotting to assassinate President Lucas Mangope of Bophuthatswana.
Nov. 1990	An attempted coup to topple the Transkei government fails.
Nov. 1990	The Cabinet is reshuffled to prepare the way for constitutional negotiations. These are to commence early in 1991, according to government sources.
Nov. 1990	A Conference of black and white churches held. Delegates agree on a common declaration of principles on the country's political future. However, the Dutch Reformed Church disassociates itself from key parts of the Declaration.
Nov. 1990	The government and the ANC reach agreement on guidelines for the release of political prisoners and the return of 40,000 exiles.
2 Nov. 1990	Signs an air transport agreement with Lesotho for services between and beyond their respective territories.
2 Nov. 1990	Signs memorandum of agreement regarding the design, construction and maintenance of the international border bridge over the Caledon River at Ficksburg/Maputsoe.
13 Nov. 1990	The Harms Commission report criticizes the army and police counter-insurgency units, but has no evidence that police operated death squads. The activities of the Civil Co-operation Bureau are severely criticized.
13 Nov. 1990	Signs memorandum of agreement for the supply of water between the governments of Namibia and South Africa.
16 Nov. 1990	Signs treaty with Romania establishing consular and trade relations.
13 Dec. 1990	Oliver Tambo, President of the ANC, returns to South Africa after having fled the country thirty years ago.
14 Dec. 1990	The ANC holds its first Consultative Conference in South Africa, after thirty years.
8 Jan. 1991	At its seventy ninth anniversary, the ANC declares 1991 a year of political emancipation, and demands an interim government and constituent assembly. Calls on the government to implement agreements entered into in terms of the Groote Schuur and Pretoria Minutes.
29 Jan. 1991	Nelson Mandela and Chief Mangosuthu Buthelezi of the Inkatha Freedom Party, meet in Durban and issue a statement on a joint peace strategy.
29 Jan. 1991	Signs the Southern African Convention with Regard to Energy and Energy-Related Matters.
1 Feb. 1991	President F.W. de Klerk announces during the opening of Parliament, that the Land Act, the Group Areas Act and the Registration of Population Act

is to be scrapped. He also unveils a manifesto for a New South Africa.

12 Feb. 1991	According to the D.F. Malan Accord, signed between the South African government and the ANC, the government reaffirms the right to peaceful protest and that ANC guerrillas will not be harassed.
16 Feb. 1991	The Committee of Commonwealth Foreign Ministers, meeting in London, issues a statement to the effect that sanctions against South Africa will remain until the South African government's promise to repeal the Group Areas Act, the Land Acts and Population Registration Act is put into concrete action.
Mar. 1991	The first group of political exiles return to South Africa and the government releases forty (mainly ANC) political prisoners. Amongst these, is Piet 'Skiet' Rudolph, a prominent Right Winger facing charges of planting bombs and theft of arms and ammunition.
2-3 Mar. 1991	It is announced at a Convention that the United Democratic Front is to end its activities and will formally disband on the 20th August.
3 Mar. 1991	The SACP is formally launched in Natal at a rally held at Currie's Fountain Stadium in Durban.
12 Mar. 1991	A White Paper on Land Reform is tabled to repeal the Group Areas and Land Acts.
22 Mar. 1991	Signs an agreement with the Republic of Namibia to curb and prevent illegal fishing.
Apr. 1991	The Inkatha Freedom Party and the ANC adopt a five-year plan to end violence between their supporters.
Apr. 1991	President de Klerk rejects ANC's ultimatum that it will abandon constitutional talks unless it dismisses the Minster of Defence, General Magnus Malan and the Minister of Police, Adriaan Vlok, and that those and other demands be met by 9th May.
Apr. 1991	President F.W. de Klerk and Nelson Mandela visit the United Kingdom in quick succession.
8 Apr. 1991	The government appoints a new Minister of Trade, Industry and Tourism, Dr George Marais, a new Minister of Transport Peter J. Welgemoed, David de Villiers Graaf as Deputy Minister of Trade, Industry and Tourism, and A.T. Meyer as Deputy Minister of Agriculture.
15-16 Apr. 1991	The ANC and the PAC hold a joint conference in Harare, brokered by President Robert Mugabe.
19 Apr. 1991	Signs agreement concerning the exchange of representatives and their privileges and immunities with the Democratic Republic of Madagascar.
May 1991	The ANC boycotts a government-sponsored conference to end violence, accusing the government of fomenting it.
2 May 1991	In response to the ANC ultimatum to suspend negotiations if its demands are

not met by 9th May, President de Klerk during his budget vote in Parliament, offers to include black South African opposition groups in his cabinet and amend tough security laws.

9 May 1991   A broad consensus is reached between the government and the ANC to end black violence in townships a day before the ANC's 9th May ultimatum to suspend negotiations unless its demands are met.

12 May 1991   Inkatha supporters rampage through a squatter camp in the Kagiso Township in the West Rand, killing at least twenty-two people.

14 May 1991   Winnie Mandela sentenced to six years imprisonment on charges of kidnapping and being accessory to assault of four township youths at her her Soweto home in December 1988.

14 May 1991   Signs loan agreement with the Transkei relating to financial and technical assistance for the construction of five police stations.

23 May 1991   The ruling National Party loses the Ladybrand by-election to the Conservative Party.

8 June 1991   President F.W. de Klerk pays a two day visit to Kenya.

17 June 1991   The Population Registration Act is repealed.

21 June 1991   The Internal Security Act is amended to remove certain police powers allowing detention without trial.

23-24 June 1991   A peace summit brokered by the clergy and business and attended by all major political parties, but boycotted by the Conservative Party, is held to end the violence.

28 June 1991   South Africa decides to sign the Nuclear Non-Proliferation Treaty.

2 July 1991   The ANC holds its first National Conference in Durban after a break of more than thirty years. Cyril Ramaphosa is appointed its Secretary General. Nelson Mandela is elected President, and Walter Sisulu, deputy President of the organization.

8 July 1991   Signs memorandum of understanding with Great Britain concerning drug trafficking.

10 July 1991   The United States lifts certain sanctions against South Africa.

21 July 1991   The government admits to providing a slush fund to Inkatha and its associated trade union, the United Workers Union of South Africa (UWUSA).

23 July 1991   The Inkathagate scandal claims its first victim, when M.Z. Khumalo, personal assistant to Chief Buthelezi, resigns after admitting that he acted as a middle man who organized covert funds paid by the Security Police for two Inkatha rallies.

24 July 1991   Protocol on the establishment of diplomatic relations with Hungary.

30 July 1991	In a major cabinet reshuffle, Law and Order Minister, Adriaan Vlok and Defence Minister General Magnus Malan, are demoted to ministries of Correctional Services and Water Affairs & Forestry, respectively.
Aug. 1991	The National Party outlines its constitutional proposals to be tabled at its Federal Congress on 4th September which calls for a scrapping of the current single presidential head of state, to be replaced by a council of three to five members.
Aug. 1991	Umkhonto we Sizwe, the military wing of the ANC, holds its first conference in South Africa after thirty years and calls for a formal ceasefire in the country.
9 Aug. 1991	A bloody confrontation takes place between the right wing Afrikaner Weerstandbeweging (AWB) and government security forces in Ventersdorp.
9 Aug. 1991	Signs a multilateral agreement with Transkei, Venda and Ciskei regarding social welfare services in their respective territories.
26 Aug. 1991	Signs a co-operation agreement with Transkei regarding structural adjustment.
4 Sept. 1991	Key points of the National Party's constitutional proposals are outlined at its special Federal Congress. Various political parties react.
4 Sept. 1991	Signs a memorandum of understanding with the United Nations High Commissioner for Refugees on the voluntary repatriation and reintegration of South African returnees.
12 Sept. 1991	Signs trade agreement with the Czech and Slovak Federal Republic.
14 Sept. 1991	A National Peace Accord is signed by all major political organizations at a Conference held at the Carlton Hotel. The PAC and AZAPO attend proceedings, but refuse to sign the accord, while right wing organizations refuse to participate in the session.
18 Sept. 1991	Signs a trade agreement with the government of Poland.
30 Sept. 1991	Signs multilateral agreement with the governments of Transkei, Bophuthatswana, Venda and Ciskei for the avoidance of double taxation, the prevention of fiscal evasion, the rendering of mutual assistance and co-operation and the establishment of a transfer system with respect to Value Added Tax.
2 Oct. 1991	Signs an agreement with the United Nations High Commissioner for Refugees governing the legal status, privileges and immunities of the UNHCR office and its personnel in South Africa.
23 Oct. 1991	Signs an agreement with the League of The Red Cross and Red Crescent Societies regarding the establishment of a delegation in South Africa.
23 Oct. 1991	Exchange of notes with Lesotho to amend the Trade Mission Agreement of 30 April 1987.
26 Oct. 1991	A Patriotic Front Conference convened by the ANC and the PAC takes

place in Durban.

29 Oct. 1991	Signs agreement with the government of the Czech and Slovak Federal Republic on the abolition of visa requirements for holders of diplomatic and service passports.
29 Oct. 1991	Signs Protocol with the Czech and Slovak Federal Republic on establishing diplomatic relations and the abolishment of visas.
30 Oct. 1991	Signs aviation security agreement with the United States.
31 Oct. 1991	Signs an aviation security agreement with the government of the USA.
Nov. 1991	The South African Law Commission releases a draft Bill of Rights.
11 Nov. 1991	Signs memorandum of understanding on multiple co-operation with Israel.
11 Nov. 1991	Signs agreement with Bophuthatswana regarding social pensions, grants and allowances.
15 Nov. 1991	Signs an agreement on the promotion of investments with the government of the Republic of China.
15 Nov. 1991	Signs co-operation agreement with the Republic of China regarading the promotion of investments.
15 Nov. 1991	Signs amended bilateral air services agreement with the Republic of China.
19 Nov. 1991	Signs Protocol IV to the treaty on the Lesotho Highlands Water Project including supplementary arrangements regarding Phase IA.
22 Nov. 1991	Exchange of notes establishing diplomatic relations with Romania.
Dec. 1991	The SACP held its first legal Congress inside the country and Chris Hani replaces Joe Slovo as Secretary-General of the Party.
4 Dec. 1991	Cabinet is reshuffled, and the head of the mining house, Gencor, Derek Keys, is appointed Minister of Trade and Industry.
9 Dec. 1991	Signs co-operation agreement with Ciskei regarding structural adjustment.
18 Dec. 1991	Signs Protocol with the government of Poland on establishing diplomatic relations.
18 Dec. 1991	Exchange of notes with the People's Republic of China regarding the establishment of informal offices in Pretoria and Beijing.
20-21 Dec. 1991	The Convention for a Democratic South Africa (CODESA), holds its first meeting. Seventeen of the nineteen parties attending the Convention sign a Declaration of Intent, committing themselves to multiparty politics.
20 Dec. 1991	Heated verbal exchanges take place between President F.W. de Klerk and Nelson Mandela at the CODESA talks.
30 Dec. 1991	Signs agreement with Botswana regarding the establishment of a

representative office.

Jan. 1992	Outline of a working model for the Convention for a Democratic South Africa (CODESA) is presented.
Jan. 1992	Details are revealed of Armscor involvement in acquiring top secret American technology for the manufacture of weapons in South Africa.
7 Jan. 1992	Danish Coalition indicates to the European Council that it favours the lifting of remaining EU sanctions.
8 Jan. 1992	At its eightieth anniversary celebration, the ANC presents its post-apartheid policies and launches its electoral campaign.
13 Jan. 1992	Exchange of notes with Japan concerning the re-establishment of diplomatic relations.
22 Jan. 1992	President F.W. de Klerk and Nelson Mandela are awarded the Unesco Peace Prize.
23 Jan. 1992	South Africa and Angola re-establish diplomatic ties after a seventeen-year break.
24 Jan. 1992	President F.W. de Klerk opens parliament and suggests a referendum in which the vote of each race group be counted separately.
27 Jan. 1992	The European Community formally lifts economic sanctions against South Africa.
28 Jan. 1992	Eugene Terreblanche, leader of the Afrikaner Resistance Movement (AWB) and nine other members are arrested for staging a riot on 9 August 1991 when President F.W. de Klerk was addressing a meeting in Ventersdorp.
Feb. 1992	The United States blocks the sale of 200 long-range G16 super-guns to Saudi Arabia.
2 Feb. 1992	Exchange of notes with the government of Bulgaria regarding the establishment of diplomatic relations.
5 Feb. 1992	The Goldstone Commission of Inquiry has its first hearing on the South African Defence Force involvement in promoting black on black violence.
5 Feb. 1992	Signs an agreement with Hungary on the abolition of visa requirements for holders of diplomatic and service passports.
6 Feb. 1992	Signs bilateral air transport agreement with Burundi.
7 Feb. 1992	Signs an agreement with the government of the Republic of Poland on the abolition of visa requirements for holders of diplomatic and service passports.
23 Feb. 1992	Signs agreement with Angola on the establishment of representative offices.
24 Feb. 1992	President F.W. de Klerk announces the holding of a referendum on 17 March requesting a mandate to pursue constitutional reform from the white

electorate.

24 Feb. 1992	The ANC submits its constitutional blue-print to CODESA. It suggests a two phase transitional period of multiparty rule for fifteen months, to be followed by a coalition government for up to five years.
28 Feb. 1992	South Africa and the Russian Federation establish full diplomatic relations.
6 Mar. 1992	Signs economic and industrial co-operation agreement with Italy.
9 Mar. 1992	Exchange of notes establishing diplomatic relations with Thailand.
13 Mar. 1992	Signs treaty with Swaziland on the establishment and functioning of the joint Water Commission.
13 Mar. 1992	Signs treaty with Swaziland on the development and utilization of the water resources of the Komati River Basin.
18 Mar. 1992	In a referendum held on 17 March, nearly 70% of white voters vote in favour of the continuation of negotiations to end white minority rule.
27 Mar. 1992	Multilateral agreement between the governments of Lesotho, South Africa and Swaziland amending the Trilateral Monetary Agreement of 5 December 1974.
Apr. 1992	The 1991 census figures released.
Apr. 1992	CODESA outlines its proposals for an interim constitution.
1 Apr. 1992	Signs bilateral monetary agreement with Namibia.
9 Apr. 1992	President F.W. de Klerk pays a state visit to Nigeria.
13 Apr. 1992	Nelson Mandela announces his separation from his wife, Winnie Mandela.
21 Apr. 1992	Five white Democratic Party MP's defect to the ANC.
23 Apr. 1992	The South African government submits its proposal for an interim constitution for South Africa to CODESA.
25 Apr. 1992	Barend du Plessis, the Minister of Finance, resigns because of ill health.
May 1992	In a major cabinet reshuffle, Chief Executive Officer of the Mining House, Gencor, Derek Keys is appointed Finance Minister to replace Barend du Plessis.
1 May 1992	Signs agreement with Zambia on the establishment of representative offices.
8 May 1992	South Africa and Kenya establish formal diplomatic relations.
16 May 1992	CODESA talks end in deadlock. The ANC threatens mass action if the government does not compromise on constitutional issues.
21 May 1992	South Africa and Lesotho establish full diplomatic relations.

21 May 1992	Signs agreement with Côte d'Ivoire on the establishment of diplomatic relations.
22 May 1992	Signs bilateral air transport agreement with Singapore.
25 May 1992	Signs co-operation agreement with Venda regarding structural adjustment.
25 May 1992	Winnie Mandela and the entire executive of the ANC Women's League are suspended.
26 May 1992	Signs bilateral air transport agreement with Netherlands.
9 June 1992	Signs memorandum of understanding with Zimbabwe on the transportation by road of commodities related to drought relief.
11 June 1992	Signs protocol with Italy on the establishment of a joint working group for trilateral development co-operation in Southern Africa.
17 June 1992	Boipatong massacre takes place.
21 June 1992	Following the Boipatong massacre, the ANC suspends bilateral talks with the government.
July 1992	The South African government and the ANC attempt to break the stalemate, resulting from the Boipatong massacre.
July 1992	In response to the Goldstone Commission findings, the South African government announces the disbanding of battalions 31 and 32 and the former Namibian counter-insurgency unit, Koevoet.
July 1992	Two South African military intelligence agents are arrested in London on a mission to kill a former South African policeman, Dirk Coetzee, who confessed in 1989 to leading hit squads against black activists in the 1980s.
8 July 1992	Signs agreement with the International Committee of the Red Cross regarding visits by the ICRC to persons held in South African prisons.
13 July 1992	The tripartite alliance, consisting of the ANC, the SACP and the COSATU, outline mass action plans from the beginning of August and the occupation of cities on 5 August.
23 July 1992	The Waddington report into the Boipatong killing is released.
30 July 1992	The South African government and ANC leaders held talks, brokered by the United Nations Special Envoy to South Africa, Cyrus Vance, to break the political stalemate.
Aug. 1992	The 31 and 32 battalions that were ordered to dissolve by President F.W. de Klerk, is being integrated into RENAMO, according to Mozambican reports.
Aug. 1992	The South African government accepts the United Nations proposals on breaking the political stalemate in South Africa.
Aug. 1992	Five CP MP's leave the party to form the Afrikaner Volksunie.

3 Aug. 1992	A forty-eight-hour strike and a week of mass action starts to force an early transition to majority rule.
3 Aug. 1992	Signs air services agreement with the Russian Federation.
5 Aug. 1992	Nelson Mandela leads more than 50,000 supporters to the Union Buildings in Pretoria.
11 Aug. 1992	Signs air services agreement with the United Kingdom.
13 Aug. 1992	The ANC issues a statemate explaining why it has suspended talks with the South African government and that its fourteen demands have not been met.
17 Aug. 1992	Signs memorandum of agreement with Lesotho regarding the design, construction and maintenance of the international border bridge over the Caledon River at Maseru.
24 Aug. 1992	Exchange of notes with Italy constituting an agreement regarding the establishment of a community centre for refugees in the Transvaal.
24 Aug. 1992	Signs agreement with Mozambique regarding the establishment of trade mission.
27 Aug. 1992	Sweeping changes are made to the police force and a purging of top police personnel.
31 Aug. 1992	Signs agreement with Mozambique concerning fishing matters.
31 Aug. 1992	Multilateral agreement between the governments of Ciskei, South Africa, Transkei and Venda on the cross-border transportation of goods by road.
31 Aug. 1992	Multilateral agreement between the governments of Ciskei, South Afrca, Transkei and Venda on the cross-border transportation of passengers by road.
2 Sept. 1992	Signs agreement with the United Kingdom concerning mutual assistance in relation to drug trafficking.
7 Sept. 1992	The ANC leads a march against the Ciskei government and the Bisho massacre takes place.
8 Sept. 1992	Signs agreement with Israel on co-operation in the field of agriculture.
10 Sept. 1992	Winnie Mandela resigns from the Executive of both the ANC and the Organization's Women's League.
14 Sept. 1992	Signs agreement with Namibia on the establishment of a permanent Water Commission.
14 Sept. 1992	Signs agreement with Namibia on the Vioolsdrift and Noordoewer joint irrigation scheme.
21 Sept. 1992	President F.W. de Klerk and Nelson Mandela, leader of the ANC agree, at a peace summit, to resume constitutional negotiations that were suspended in June.

27 Sept. 1992	The ANC and the South African government reach a compromise at their summit meeting in Johannesburg.
Oct. 1992	The ANC released a report on inhumane treatment of its opponents in the organization's detention camps in Angola, Tanzania and Uganda.
8 Oct. 1992	Signs agreement with Israel on co-operation in the fields of culture, education and science.
8 Oct. 1992	Signs agreement with Israel on co-operation in the field of environmental management and of nature protection and conservation.
8 Oct. 1992	Signs agreement with Israel in the field of tourism.
8 Oct. 1992	Signs agreement with Israel on trade and industrial co-operation.
16 Oct. 1992	The Goldstone Commission reports the finding of a secret operational centre run by Military Intelligence and seize plans to destabilise the ANC.
20 Oct. 1992	Signs agreement with Namibia regarding trade tests for apprentices and other prospective artisans.
27 Oct. 1992	Reggie Hadebe, a prominent Natal ANC leader, shot dead after contacting the Natal Witness newspaper in Pietermritzburg, with evidence that RENAMO is behind the violence in Natal.
28 Oct. 1992	President F.W. de Klerk reshuffles his cabinet.
30 Oct. 1992	Signs air services agreement with Zambia.
Nov. 1992	The Oelof de Meyer report finds corruption and incompetence on a vast scale in Lebowa.
Nov. 1992	The Parsons report on the KwaNdebele 'homeland' is released.
Nov. 1992	The ANC releases its strategic perspectives documents which opts for indefinite power-sharing coalition with the National Party.
1 Nov. 1992	Exchange of notes with Namibia on the joint administration of Walvis Bay and the off-shore islands.
5 Nov. 1992	Signs agreement with Namibia relating to the basic conditions governing the secondment of judges.
7 Nov. 1992	Foreign Minister 'Pik' Botha is declared persona non grata by Angola for having supported the rebel Angolan UNITA.
9 Nov. 1992	Exchange of notes with Croatia regarding the establishing of diplomatic relations.
9 Nov. 1992	Exchange of notes with Slovenia regarding the establishment of diplomatic relations.
12 Nov. 1992	Signs agreement with Bophuthatswana concerning formal Technikon instructional programmes and the performance by the Certification Council

for Technikon education in the Republic of Bophuthatswana.

| 12 Nov. 1992 | Signs agreement with Venda concerning formal school and Technical College instructional programmes and the performance by the South African Certification Council of functions in the Republic of Venda. |

| 12 Nov. 1992 | President F.W. de Klerk spells out a government timetable for a transition to multiracial democracy and that all-race elections will take place by April 1994. |

| Dec. 1992 | The IFP releases a constitution for the KwaZulu-Natal region, calling for an autonomous KwaZulu-Natal state. |

| Dec. 1992 | Twenty-three military officers are purged following revelations of illegal and unauthorized activities by the South African Defence Force. |

| 1 Dec. 1992 | Cabinet decides to replace the SAF trainer Harvard by the Swiss-made Pilatus PC-7 MK2. The joint venture will include twelve SA companies. |

| 1 Dec. 1992 | Signs Protocol with Korea on the establishment of diplomatic relations. |

| 10 Dec. 1992 | The Concerned South African Group (COSAG) issues a statement that multi-party talks should be resumed. |

| Jan. 1993 | Bilateral meetings are held between the government and both the Inkatha Freedom Party and the ANC. These meetings aim to lay a foundation for negotiation between various interested parties by the end of 1993 and how power is to be shared between black and white. |

| 5 Jan. 1993 | Signs air service agreement with the Republic of Malaysia. |

| 14 Jan. 1993 | Convention on the Prohibition of the Development, Production, Stockpiling and Use of Chemical Weapons and on their Destruction (1993). |

| 29 Jan. 1993 | At the opening of Parliament, President F.W. de Klerk warns that South Africa will be plunged into a Yugoslav style civil war if democratic negotiations fail. Multi-party constitutional talks will resume in March. |

| 29 Jan. 1993 | Convention on the Elimination of All Forms of Discrimination Against Women (1979). |

| 29 Jan. 1993 | Convention on the Rights of the Child (1989). |

| 11 Feb. 1993 | Signs agreement with Namibia regarding the movement of animals, animal products, parasites and infectious and contaminated things between the two countries. |

| 11 Feb. 1993 | Signs agreement with Namibia regarding standards of livestock breeding and the importation of breeding animals, semen, ova or eggs in Southern Africa. |

| 12 Feb. 1993 | Exchange of notes with Namibia concerning formal school and technical college instructional programmes and the performance by the South African Certification Council of functions in the Republic of Namibia. |

19 Feb. 1993	Signs agreement with Hungary on co-operation in the areas of culture, education, science and related fields.
19 Feb. 1993	Joint statement on bilateral relations with Hungary.
19 Feb. 1993	Signs agreement with Hungary concerning visa exemption for private passport holders.
20 Feb. 1993	President F.W. de Klerk reshuffles his cabinet. This comes into effect on 1 April 1993.
Mar. 1993	Corruption scandals rock the country. General Bantu Holomisa, head of Transkei, releases government documents alleging state covert operations against the ANC and other groups during the 1980s.
5-6 Mar 1993	A multi-party planning negotiations conference puts constitutional negotiations firmly on track by deciding to establish a new forum before 5 April.
22 Mar. 1993	Joint communiqué concerning the establishment of diplomatic relations with Congo.
24 Mar. 1993	President F.W. de Klerk, in an address to a special joint session of Parliament, reveals details of South Africa's past nuclear programme.
1 Apr. 1993	A one-day constitutional talk takes place when twenty-six political parties meet.
10 Apr. 1993	South African Communist Party General Secretary and member of the National Executive Committee of the ANC, Chris Hani is shot dead outside his home. J.J. Walluz, a white South African of Polish origin, is arrested.
22 Apr. 1993	Conservative Party leader, Dr. Andries Treurnicht, dies.
22 Apr. 1993	People's Action Front (Volksaksiefront-RAF) formed. Its membership comprises right wing militant organizations.
24 Apr. 1993	ANC Chairman, Oliver R. Tambo, dies.
26 Apr. 1993	Delegates from twenty-six groups meet to resume constitutional negotiations.
May 1993	Nelson Mandela tours various European countries.
May 1993	The Afrikaner Volksfront is officially founded in Pretoria. It is to articulate the interest of right-wing groups and has the support of twenty-one organizations, such as the Conservative Party and Afrikaner Volksunie.
May 1993	Clive Derby-Lewis, a former Conservative Party MP and a member of a presidential advisory council, is formally charged with the murder of Chris Hani. His wife Gaye, has already been charged, together with J. Walluz.
May 1993	Former South African military and police commanders meet to form a `Committee of Generals' to resist Pretoria's handover to majority black rule.
7 May 1993	Twenty-three of the twenty-six parties involved in the Multi-Party Talks at

the World Trade Centre, adopt a Declaration of Intent on the setting of an election date for a transitional government.

25 May 1993   In an interview with the Financial Times (London), President F.W. de Klerk insists that power sharing between the countries' main political parties should be constitutionally entrenched in any constitution adopted after the 1994 elections.

June 1993   The election date for South Africa's first democratic election is set for 27 April 1994, at the Multi-Party Talks held in Kempton Park.

June 1993   Nelson Mandela and Inkatha Freedom Party leader Buthelezi meet and pledge to work together. They intend holding joint rallies in war torn areas of conflict.

June 1993   The Pan African Congress agrees in principle to halt hostilities.

3 June 1993   South Africa and Swaziland sign agreements concerning the secondment of judges, officials and the training of personnel.

4 June 1993   South Africa signs the Convention on Biological Diversity (1992).

15 June 1993   The Concerned South African Group (COSAG) storm out of Multi-Party Talks held at Kempton Park.

17 June 1993   The government and the ANC make concessions, allowing COSAG to return to the talks.

17 June 1993   The President's Council closes after an existence of just over twelve years.

26 June 1993   Afrikaner Weerstandbeweging members attack the World Trade Centre where the Multi-Party Talks are being held.

July 1993   Key points of the interim constitution are outlined.

July 1993   A constitutional compromise is agreed on at Multi-Party Talks. The negotiators will decide on regional administrative structures for the country and on binding constitutional principles, the constitution itself will be drawn up by an elected constitution-making body.

8 July 1993   Exchange of notes with Sudan regarding the establishment of a trade representative office of the Sudan in Pretoria.

20 July 1993   Exchange of notes with India concerning the establishment of a Cultural Centre by the Republic of India in South Africa and a Liaison Office by South Africa in India.

28 July 1993   Exchange of notes with Peru on the establishment of diplomatic relations.

3 Aug. 1993   Signs agreement with Namibia regarding the provision of technical and administrative personnel by the government of South Africa to the government of Namibia.

10 Aug. 1993   The second draft interim constitution is unveiled.

12 Aug. 1993	Signs agreement with Paraguay on the partial waiver of visa requirements for holders of ordinary passports.
16 Aug. 1993	South Africa relinquishes sovereignty over Walvis Bay which now falls under the jurisdiction of Namibia.
16 Aug. 1993	Signs bilateral air transport agreement with the Czech Republic.
27 Aug. 1993	Signs bilateral air services agreement with Bulgaria.
31 Aug. 1993	Signs bilateral air transport agreement with Hungary.
Sept. 1993	An outline of the purpose and function of the Transitional Executive Council is announced.
Sept. 1993	Parliament meets to approve four new laws. Parliament votes 211-36 in favour of the Transitional Executive Council Bill which will oversee the transition to democracy. Independent electoral and media commission bills are also passed. Parliament is to meet in November to approve a new constitution.
3 Sept. 1993	Signs bilateral air transport agreement with Poland.
6 Sept. 1993	Signs basic agreement with the UNHCR concerning the presence, role, legal status, immunities and privileges of the UNHCR and its personnel in the RSA.
9 Sept. 1993	Signs agreement with Namibia regarding co-operation in the fields of culture, education and the sciences.
13 Sept. 1993	Signs agreement with the Russian Federation on scientific and technological cooperation.
13 Sept. 1993	Signs agreement with Bahrain on the establishment of diplomatic relations.
14 Sept. 1993	Signs bilateral monetary agreement with the government of Namibia.
24 Sept. 1993	Addressing the United Nations, Nelson Mandela, calls for a lifting of all existing economic sanctions against South Africa.
24 Sept. 1993	Exchange of notes with Swaziland to amend the extradition agreement of the 4th - 5th September 1968.
1 Oct. 1993	Exchange of notes with Swaziland on the establishment of diplomatic relations.
5 Oct. 1993	Exchange of notes with Pakistan on the establishment of bilateral relations.
7 Oct. 1993	The Freedom Alliance is formed. It seeks to gain concession on federalism from the ANC and to displace the National Party.
8 Oct. 1993	Signs bilateral air transport agreement with France.
15 Oct. 1993	President F.W. de Klerk and Nelson Mandela are jointly awarded the Nobel Peace Prize.

15 Oct. 1993   Chris Hani's assassin, Clive Derby-Lewis and Janusz Walluz are sentenced to death. Clive Derby-Lewis' wife, Gaye, is acquitted.

15 Oct. 1993   Multilateral agreement between the governments of South Africa and Mozambique and the UNHCR for the voluntary repatriation of Mozambican refugees from South Africa.

15 Nov. 1993   Interim constitution is approved by nineteen of the twenty-one parties participating in the Multi-Party Talks.

20 Oct. 1993   Signs agreement on co-operation with Romania.

22 Oct. 1993   Signs agreement with the Russian Federation on trade and economic co-operation.

5 Nov. 1993   Protocol on cooperation between the Department of Foreign Affairs of South Africa and the Ministry of Foreign Affairs of the Republic of Georgia.

8 Nov. 1993   Convention between the governments of South Africa and France for the Avoidance of Double Taxation and the Prevention of Fiscal Evasion with respect to Taxes on Income.

10 Nov. 1993   Signs agreement with Poland on the avoidance of double taxation with respect to taxes on income.

11 Nov. 1993   Signs bilateral air transport agreement with Rwanda.

12 Nov. 1993   Signs agreement with Romania for the avoidance of double taxation and the prevention of fiscal evasion with respect to taxes on income and capital gains.

22 Nov. 1993   Signs protocol with India on the establishment of consular and diplomatic relations.

28 Nov. 1993   The Afrikaner Broederbond adopts a new constitution which will allow women and all race groups as members, as long as they all speak Afrikaans. It will in future be known as the Afrikanerbond.

30 Nov. 1993   Signs investment incentive agreement with the United States.

Dec. 1993   Brigadier Oupa Gqozo, head of the Ciskei government, is found not guilty of murdering Charles Sebe.

2 Dec. 1993   Multi-Party negotiators agree to the reincorporation of the TBVC states (Bophuthatswana, Ciskei, Transkei and Venda).

3 Dec. 1993   Signs joint communiqué with Venezuela on the establishment of full diplomatic relations.

7 Dec. 1993   The Transitional Executive Council has its first meeting in Cape Town.

8 Dec. 1993   Winnie Mandela is elected President of the ANC Women's League.

9 Dec. 1993   Exchange of notes with Thailand on the establishment of diplomatic relations.

10 Dec. 1993	Signs protocol with Cyprus on the establishment of diplomatic relations.
14 Dec. 1993	Signs agreement with the UN concerning the legal status, privileges and immunities of the United Nations Observer Mission and its personnel in South Africa.
14 Dec. 1993	Signs agreement with the Commission of the European Union establishing the privileges and immunities of the Commission in South Africa.
15 Dec. 1993	Signs agreement with Namibia relating to the administration of the judicial system after the incorporation/reintegration of Walvis Bay into Namibia.
22 Dec. 1993	Signs joint communiqué establishing diplomatic relations with Vietnam.
Jan. 1994	Moves are made to deploy the 10,000 strong National Peacekeeping Force.
16 Jan. 1994	The Pan-Africanist Congress suspends its armed struggle and its guerrillas disarm.
28 Jan. 1994	Signs joint communiqué concerning the development of bilateral relations with Jordan.
12 Feb. 1994	Nineteen political parties have registered for the forthcoming April 1994 general election.
14 Feb. 1994	Signs agreement with the Republic of China concerning the avoidance of double taxation and the prevention of fiscal evasion with respect to taxes on income.
16 Feb. 1994	Nelson Mandela announces six constitutional concessions to defuse black and white threats of conflict. Amongst them are a change from a single to a double-ballot system and provision for each province to determine its form of government.
17 Feb. 1994	Signs agreement with Namibia relating to defence and civil aviation in Walvis Bay.
17 Feb. 1994	Signs bilateral air services agreement with the government of Luxembourg.
18 Feb. 1994	Signs bilateral air transport agreement with the government of Morocco.
22 Feb. 1994	Signs agreement with the government of Namibia on co-operation in the policing of Walvis Bay.
25 Feb. 1994	Signs agreement with the government of Namibia relating to the promotion of co-operation in the field of administration of justice.
25 Feb. 1994	South Africa opens an embassy in Mbabane, Swaziland.
27 Feb. 1994	Signs agreement with the government of Namibia with respect to road transport and road traffic matters relating to Walvis Bay.
28 Feb. 1994	Signs treaty with the government of Namibia regarding Walvis Bay and the off-shore islands.

Mar. 1994	Several of South Africa's 'homelands' are on the verge of collapse. These include Venda, Ciskei and Lebowa.
Mar. 1994	Moves are made again to activate the forty mile electrified fence between South Africa and Mozambique to deter the flood of weapons entering South Africa from that country. This was switched off in 1990.
Mar. 1994	An outline of proposed amendments to the constitution is published.
Mar. 1994	National Party and ANC Party manifestos are made available.
Mar. 1994	The Goldstone Commission of Inquiry releases report suggesting that top police officers masterminded 'third force' activities aimed at destabilizing the country ahead of the forthcoming April general election.
1 Mar. 1994	Signs agreement with Namibia concerning the multilateral Motor Vehicle Accidents Fund of South Africa and Namibia relating to Third Party compensation matters in view of the incorporation/reintegration of Walvis Bay into Namibia.
1 Mar. 1994	Signs agreement with the government of Namibia concerning hospital and health services in Walvis Bay.
1 Mar. 1994	Signs agreement with the government of Namibia with respect to prisons matters in Walvis Bay.
1 Mar. 1994	Signs agreement with the government of Namibia in respect to health and welfare services in Walvis Bay.
1 Mar. 1994	Signs agreement with the government of Namibia regarding schools and adult education in Walvis Bay.
1 Mar. 1994	Signs agreement with the government of Namibia concerning sea fisheries functions in Walvis Bay.
1 Mar. 1994	Signs agreement with the government of Namibia with a view to regulating certain taxation matters with regard to South African taxes and duties and Namibian taxes in Walvis Bay.
1 Mar. 1994	Signs agreement with the government of Namibia concerning nature conservation functions in Walvis Bay.
1 Mar. 1994	Three days before the 4 March deadline for registering parties, Chief Buthelezi announces that he is considering registering his Inkatha Freedom Party for the forthcoming April general election.
2 Mar. 1994	Signs agreement with Zimbabwe establishing a Joint Commission for Economic, Technical, Scientific and Cultural Co-operation.
4 Mar. 1994	General Constand Viljoen registers a new party, the Freedom Front, for the forthcoming April election.
4 Mar. 1994	Signs agreement with the government of Namibia with respect to mineral and energy matters relating to Walvis Bay.

4 Mar. 1994	Convention between the Republics of South Africa and Hungary for the Avoidance of Double Taxation with respect to Taxes on Income.
8 Mar. 1994	Signs agreement for air services with Japan.
12 Mar. 1994	Chief Lucas Mangope is deposed as leader of Bophuthatswana by the South African army. Dr. Tjaart van der Walt is appointed as the territory's new administrator.
17 Mar. 1994	Signs agreement with the government of Namibia relating to local government matters in Walvis Bay.
19 Mar. 1994	Signs agreement with the government of Mauritius for the avoidance of double taxation and the prevention of fiscal evasion with respect to taxes on income.
28 Mar. 1994	Violent clashes occur between Zulu IFP supporters protesting against the forthcoming April general election and the ANC's security guards protesting the ANC headquarters Shell House.
12 Apr. 1994	Signs joint communiqué with Colombia on the establishment of diplomatic relations.
19 Apr. 1994	Kenyan Professor Washington J. Okumu persuades Chief Buthelezi to participate in the forthcoming general election.
22 Apr. 1994	Signs agreement with the government of Namibia concerning broadcasting services to Walvis Bay.
23 Apr. 1994	An 'Accord on Afrikaner self-determination' is signed.
26 Apr. 1994	Signs agreement with the government of Namibia regarding payment from 1 March 1994 of benefits in terms of the Unemployment Insurance Act, 1966 (Act 30 of 1966) to Walvis Bay contributors.
26 Apr. 1994	Signs agreement with Namibia concerning the carriage of goods by road.
26-29 Apr. 1994	South Africa holds its first democratic general election. The African National Congress wins 62.65% of the vote. The National Party 20.39%, Inkatha Freedom Party 10.54%, Freedom Front 2.2%, Democratic Party 1.7%, Pan Africanist Congress 1.2%, African Christian Democratic Party 0.5%. Nineteen political parties participated in the election and 22 million voted.
29 Apr. 1994	Signs joint communiqué establishing diplomatic relations with Cameroon.
29 Apr. 1994	Signs agreement upgrading existing diplomatic relations with Zimbabwe.
May 1994	Great Britain offers 530 million Pounds Sterling in aid to South Africa over the next three years, targetted towards the RDP.
May 1994	Signs agreement upgrading existing diplomatic relations with Tunisia.
May 1994	US President Clinton announces an aid package of some R2 billion to develop the South African economy over the next three years.

May 1994	The ANC publishes its Reconstruction and Development Programme.
May 1994	The ANC proposes that Self-Defence Unit members between thirteen and eighteen be given catch-up schooling.
4 May 1994	Basel Convention on the Control of Transboundary Movement of Hazardous Wastes and their Disposal.
6 May 1994	Signs agreement establishing diplomatic relations with Ghana.
6 May 1994	Signs agreement establishing diplomatic relations with Mali.
6 May 1994	Signs agreement establishing diplomatic relations with Senegal.
10 May 1994	Nelson Mandela is sworn in as President of South Africa.
10 May 1994	Signs agreement concerning the establishment of diplomatic relations with Sao Tome & Principe.
10 May 1994	Signs bilateral agreement upgrading existing diplomatic relations with Algeria.
10 May 1994	Signs agreement upgrading diplomatic relations with Iran.
10 May 1994	Signs agreement upgrading diplomatic relations with Morocco.
10 May 1994	Signs agreement establishing diplomatic relations with Libya.
10 May 1994	Signs agreement upgrading diplomatic relations with Namibia.
10 May 1994	Signs agreement establishing diplomatic relations with Qatar.
10 May 1994	Signs agreement establishing diplomatic relations with Sudan.
10 May 1994	Signs agreement upgrading existing diplomatic relations with Zambia.
11 May 1994	Signs agreement concerning the establishment of diplomatic relations with Cuba.
11 May 1994	President Nelson Mandela announces his cabinet.
11 May 1994	Signs agreement establishing diplomatic relations with Burkina Faso.
17 May 1994	Signs protocol with the United Arab Emirates concerning the establishment of diplomatic relations.
19 May 1994	Signs bilateral agreement establishing diplomatic relations with Benin.
20 May 1994	Signs agreement establishing diplomatic relations with Kuwait.
22 May 1994	Dr Zach de Beer of the Democratic Party is replaced as leader of the party by Tony Leon, MP for Houghton.
23 May 1994	South Africa becomes fifty third member of the OAU.

24 May 1994	Cyril Ramaphosa, Secretary-General of the ANC, elected chairman of the Constituent Assembly which is to write a new constitution for the country within two years.
24 May 1994	Opening the first session of the first non-racial parliament, President Nelson Mandela adopts a conservative reform policy.
25 May 1994	Signs agreement establishing diplomatic relations with Mongolia.
26 May 1994	Signs agreement upgrading existing diplomatic relations with Egypt.
27 May 1994	Signs agreement establishing diplomatic relations with Angola.
29 May 1994	Signs agreement establishing diplomatic relations with Saudi Arabia.
31 May 1994	South Africa joins the Non-Aligned Movement.
31 May 1994	Signs agreement establishing diplomatic relations with Iceland.
June 1994	The South African Communist Party (SACP) suspends Natal Midlands leader Harry Gwala for six months for verbally abusing SACP members.
1 June 1994	South Africa rejoins the Commonwealth.
1 June 1994	South Africa and Syria establish diplomatic relations at ambassadorial level.
6 June 1994	Signs protocol with the government of France concerning the use of the Satellite Application Centre at Hartebeeshoek.
14 June 1994	At a meeting between President Nelson Mandela and Chairman of the Palestine Liberation Organization Yasser Arafat, the two leaders agree to the opening of a Palestinian embassy in South Africa with Arafat's advisor on African affairs, Salman al-Hirfi, as ambassador.
22 June 1994	Signs agreement upgrading existing diplomatic relations with Botswana.
23 June 1994	The National Party announces its thirty four member shadow cabinet.
24 June 1994	Signs joint communiqué establishing diplomatic relations with Uganda.
30 June 1994	The Minister of Correctional Services, Dr. Sipho Mzimela, announces in parliament that Dimitrio Tsafendas, assassin of Prime Minister Dr. Hendrik Verwoerd (1966), is to be released from prison to a mental asylum.
July 1994	National Intelligence Service restructures its 'de-bugging team' to include ANC experts after allegations that homes and offices of cabinet ministers and President Mandela were being bugged.
July 1994	South African National Defence Force (SANDF) releases a document outlining how defence spending cuts have adversely affected the military capability of the force. Major restructuring of the force's personnel with Ronnie Kasrils, appointed Deputy Defence Minister and MK chief of staff Siphiwe Nyanda SANDF first black chief of staff. Seven former MK members are appointed generals.

6 July 1994	Finance Minister Derek Keys resigns and former banker, Chris Liebenberg takes his place.
11 July 1994	Signs agreement with the Commonwealth Development Corporation.
14 July 1994	Defence Minister J. Modise issues a statement that South Africa is to end the special relationship with Israel. Modise compares Israel's Palestine policy with the apartheid years in South Africa, collaboration between the two countries on nuclear weapons states that South Africa is to assess every contract with Israel.
16 July 1994	The IFP releases its new constitution at its annual general conference held in Ulundi.
16 July 1994	IFP political director, Ziba Jiyane, appointed secretary-general of the party at its annual general conference in Ulundi.
18 July 1994	Signs agreement with Namibia with a view to regulating certain taxation matters in Walvis Bay.
18 July 1994	Signs agreement upgrading diplomatic relations with Tanzania.
20 July 1994	Signs agreement concerning the establishment of a Joint Permanent Commission for Co-operation with the government of Mozambique.
20 July 1994	President Nelson Mandela pays his first state visit to a foreign country (Mozambique) as President of South Africa.
26 July 1994	The Department of Defence is allocated some R10.5 billion, more than 8.7 per cent of the budget.
27 July 1994	Signs joint communiqué on the establishment of diplomatic relations with the Republic of the Maldives.
28 July 1994	Signs joint communiqué on the establishment of diplomatic relations with the Commonwealth of the Bahamas.
28 July 1994	Signs joint communiqué on the establishment of diplomatic relations with the Kingdom of Nepal.
Aug. 1994	Anglican Archbishop, Desmond Tutu, criticizes government for selling arms to Rwanda and the Sudan and for approving salary increases for parliamentarians.
1 Aug. 1994	Deputy President F.W. de Klerk issues a statement that he does not intend to leave the Government of National Unity.
3 Aug. 1994	Convention Abolishing the Requirement of Legalisation for Foreign Public Documents.
4 Aug. 1994	Radio Maputo reports that according to South Africa's Security Minister, Sidney Mufamadi, Mozambique, Swaziland and South Africa have signed an initial police cooperation accord to bring arms smuggling under control.
12 Aug. 1994	Signs memorandum of understanding with the government of Malaysia

concluding agreements that enhance trade and investment.

12 Aug. 1994	Signs joint commmunique concerning the establishment of diplomatic relations with the government of Indonesia.
16 Aug. 1994	Zimbabwe's President Robert Mugabe addresses the South African Parliament.
18 Aug. 1994	President Nelson Mandela makes a major policy speech in Parliament to mark his first 100 days as president.
18 Aug. 1994	Signs agreement with the government of Zimbabwe relating to the promotion of co-operation in the field of administration of justice.
19 Aug. 1994	Signs memorandum of understanding with the government of Zimbabwe.
22 Aug. 1994	Signs trade agreement with the government of India.
29 Aug. 1994	Signs treaty of the Southern African Development Community.
Sept. 1994	Seventy-eight murderers granted clemency or indemnity for alleged political crimes. Amongst them is A.B. Nofomela, former police officer at the Vlakplaas Unit (granted clemency); Major-General Eddy Webb (indemnity) - former chief of the disbanded Civil Cooperation Bureau.
Sept. 1994	Deputy President F.W. de Klerk is appointed chairman of the cabinet committee which will oversee a revamped security and intelligence service. President Nelson Mandela is to take personal charge of the intelligence service.
7 Sept. 1994	State of Emergency is lifted in KwaZulu-Natal.
7 Sept. 1994	Signs joint communiqué establishing diplomatic relations with the Laos People's Democratic Republic.
9 Sept. 1994	Disgruntled former ANC guerrillas march to Pretoria demanding equal rights and pay in the new South African army. President Mandela persuades them to return to barracks.
9 Sept. 1994	Signs joint communiqué establishing diplomatic relations with the government of Jamaica.
9 Sept. 1994	Signs bilateral agreement establishing diplomatic relations with Afghanistan.
10 Sept. 1994	Signs bilateral agreement establishing diplomatic relations with Bangladesh.
13 Sept. 1994	Signs protocol on consultations between the Department of Foreign Affairs of South Africa and the Ministry of Foreign Affairs of the Russian Federation.
14 Sept. 1994	Signs memorandum of understanding concerning development co-operation with the government of Switzerland.
15 Sept. 1994	Signs joint communiqué on the establishment of diplomatic relations with the Republic of Nicaragua.

16 Sept. 1994	Signs agreement establishing diplomatic relations with Sri Lanka.
17 Sept. 1994	The Labour Party decides to disband after twenty-nine years in existence.
20 Sept. 1994	King Goodwill Zwelethini and the Zulu Royal Family severs all ties with Chief Buthelezi. This followed a stoning by Inkatha Freedom Party youth during a meeting between the King, Buthulezi and President Mandela at the king's Enyokeni Palace.
20 Sept. 1994	Great Britain's Prime Minister John Major pays an official state visit to South Africa and addresses Parliament.
20 Sept. 1994	Signs memorandum on bilateral developoment cooperation with Great Britain.
20 Sept. 1994	Signs memorandum of understanding with Great Britain concerning the provision of personnel of the UK Armed Forces and the UK Ministry of Defence to advise on the integration of the defence and other armed forces of South Africa.
20 Sept. 1994	Signs agreement with Great Britain regarding the promotion and protection of investments.
20 Sept. 1994	Signs letter of intent: science, technology and engineering co-operation with the United Kingdom.
21 Sept. 1994	Government releases its White Paper on the Reconstruction and Development Programme (RDP).
22 Sept. 1994	Signs joint communiqué on the establishment of diplomatic relations with the Republic of Ecuador.
Oct. 1994	President Mandela pays an official state visit to the United States of America. An American aid plan to South Africa is unveiled during their visit.
Oct. 1994	Tony Leon is appointed national leader of the Democratic Party.
Oct. 1994	The Black Consciousness Movement of Azania (BCMA) merges with the Azanian People's Organization (AZAPO). BCMA chairman M. Mangena is elected president of AZAPO at its eleventh national congress.
3 Oct. 1994	Signs agreement with the government of the US on missile-related export/import restrictions.
3 Oct. 1994	Signs agreement with the UN Development Programme on Standard Basic Assistance plus exchange of notes.
4 Oct. 1994	Signs joint communiqué establishing diplomatic relations with the Republic of Costa Rica.
7 Oct. 1994	Signs joint communiqué establishing diplomatic relations with the Independent State of Papua New Guinea.
10 Oct. 1994	Signs cooperation agreement with the European Union.

12 Oct. 1994	Exchange of notes establishing diplomatic relations with Guinea-Bissau.
20 Oct. 1994	President Mandela warns disgruntled former Umkhonto we Sizwe combatants, who took leave without permission while being integrated into the new South African army, that they have to adhere to military discipline or face the consequences.
21 Oct. 1994	Signs agreement on the establishment of diplomatic relations with the Republic of Chad.
26 Oct. 1994	Escom intends spending R250 million over five years electrifying 2500 schools and clinics nationwide.
26 Oct. 1994	The SA Chamber of Business states that it is committed to the RDP, but concerned about its 'authoritarian tone'.
4 Nov. 1994	Signs declaration of intent with Flanders.
4 Nov. 1994	Signs agreement with the government of France on co-operation in the fields of education, sport, culture, science and technology.
4 Nov. 1994	Signs joint communiqué on the establishment of diplomatic relations with the Republic of Guyana.
5 Nov. 1994	Influential Afrikaner churchman, Professor Johan Heyns, is murdered.
7 Nov. 1994	Over 2000 Umkhonto we Sizwe soldiers of the ANC's armed wing are dismissed from the SANDF for failing to report for duty.
7 Nov. 1994	Signs joint communiqué on the establishment of diplomatic relations with the Sovereign Democratic Republic of Fiji.
10 Nov. 1994	Signs air services agreement with the government of Ireland.
17 Nov. 1994	The Restitution of Land Rights Bill is passed by President Mandela and signed into law.
22 Nov. 1994	Signs agreement with the government of Switzerland concerning support to the Reconstruction and Development Programme (RDP).
24 Nov. 1994	Signs agreement with the Nederlandse Financierings Maatschappij voor Ontwikkelingslanden N.V.
28 Nov. 1994	Signs memorandum of understanding on South African - Swedish development cooperation.
Dec. 1994	Minister for General Services, Chris Fismer, is to serve as a Minister Without Portfolio.
Dec. 1994	South Africa re-admitted to UNESCO. It was forced out of the organization in 1956 because of its policy of apartheid.
2 Dec. 1994	Signs Marrakesh Agreement establishing the World Trade Organization.
3 Dec. 1994	The Afrikaner Volksfront transforms itself into an umbrella body for thirty

organizations striving for Afrikaner self-determination in a sovereign state, according to its leader Dr. Ferdi Hartzenberg.

17 Dec. 1994   The ANC holds its forty-ninth National Conference in Bloemfontein. Its strategy and tactics document: From Resistance to Reconstruction and Development, is to guide the organization over the next three years.

25 Dec. 1994   Signs agreement establishing diplomatic relatons with Mauritania.

5 Jan. 1995   Allan Boesak, charged with financial impropriety, agrees to not take up the post of Ambassador to the United Nations.

6 Jan. 1995   Joe Slovo, Chairman of the SACP and Minister of Housing, dies of cancer.

6 Jan. 1995   Signs agreement upgrading existing diplomatic relations with Ethiopia.

9 Jan. 1995   Home Affairs Minister Buthelezi, is appointed chairman of the KwaZulu/Natal House of Traditional Leaders Executive Committee.

10 Jan. 1995   General Johan van der Merwe resigns as Police Commissioner. He is succeeded by General George Fivaz.

10 Jan. 1995   Signs joint communiqué on the establishment of diplomatic relations with the Republic of Panama.

10 Jan. 1995   Signs joint communiqué on the establishment of diplomatic relations with the Republic of Trinidad and Tobago.

12 Jan. 1995   Signs joint communiqué on the establishment of diplomatic relations with the Republic of Guatemala.

18 Jan. 1995   Heated discussion occurs at a cabinet meeting and President Mandela casts doubt on the commitment of second Deputy President F.W. de Klerk over the indemnity issue of 3,500 policemen.

25 Jan. 1995   Signs agreement with the government of India on the inter-governmental Joint Commission for Political Trade, Economic, Cultural, Scientific and Technical cooperation.

25 Jan. 1995   Signs protocol on cooperation between the Department of Foreign Affairs of South Africa and the Ministry of External Affairs of India.

25 Jan. 1995   Signs treaty of the principles of inter-state relations with India.

25 Jan. 1995   Signs cooperation agreement with India concerning the fields of science and technology.

26 Jan. 1995   Signs joint communiqué on the establishment of diplomatic relations with the Kingdom of Cambodia.

Feb. 1995   The far right wing decides to boycott the October 1995 local government elections.

Feb. 1995   Portugal disapproves the appointment of white ultra-right personality, Tom Langley, as the country's ambassador designate.

1 Feb. 1995	Convention between South Africa and Belgium for the Avoidance of Double Taxation and the Prevention of Fiscal Evasion with Respect to Taxes on Income.
2 Feb. 1995	Signs memorandum of understanding with the government of the Federal Republic of Germany concerning direct cooperation in the field of labour and labour related matters.
3 Feb. 1995	Signs joint communiqué on the establishment of diplomatic relations with the Republic of Suriname.
10 Feb. 1995	Signs memorandum of understanding with the government of the United Kingdom concerning British technical cooperation.
14 Feb. 1995	The Constitutional Court is inaugurated.
15 Feb. 1995	South Africa establishes diplomatic relations with Palestine.
15 Feb. 1995	President Nelson Mandela announces he will not be standing for re-election in 1999.
Mid Feb. 1995	IFP members walk out of Parliament during the debate on President Mandela's keynote parliamentary address, in which the issue of international mediation and federal plans for KwaZulu/Natal were discussed.
17 Feb. 1995	South Africa signs agreement with Namibia regarding the transfer of military facilities in the enclave of Walvis Bay to Namibia.
17 Feb. 1995	Following violent student protests in Cape Town on 16 February, President Mandela warns in Parliament that he will not tolerate anarchy developing in the country.
20 Feb. 1995	Signs air services agreement with the Austrian Federal government.
20 Feb. 1995	Signs development cooperation agreement with the government of Sweden.
21 Feb. 1995	The Ministry of Mineral and Energy Affairs signs memorandum of understanding with the Ministry of Industry and Energy of Spain on cooperation in the field of energy.
22 Feb. 1995	Signs agreement with the International Organization for Migration regarding the legal status, privileges and immunities of the IOM.
23 Feb. 1995	Signs agreement with the International Committee of the Red Cross.
27 Feb. 1995	Signs bilateral air transport agreement with the government of Gabon.
27 Feb. 1995	Signs agreement with the government of the United Kingdom on cooperation in science and technology.
28 Feb. 1995	Joint statement of intent by President Mandela of South Africa and President Chissano of the Republic of Mozambique and the presidents of the agricultural unions of the Free State and Transvaal.
28 Feb. 1995	Signs agreement with Mozambique regarding tourism.

28 Feb. 1995	Convention on the International Maritime Organization (1948).
1 Mar. 1995	Statement of intent between the governments of South Africa and the United States to establish the South Africa-US Binational Commission.
1 Mar. 1995	The Coloured Liberation Movement for the Advancement of Brown People, launched to generate the interest of South Africa's Coloured people against racial discrimination, claims a membership of 100,000 people.
1 Mar. 1995	Signs agreement with the government of Mozambique regarding cooperation and mutual assistance in combating crime.
2 Mar. 1995	Signs agreement with the government of Zimbabwe for the establishment of a Joint Commission for Economic, Technical, Scientific and Cultural cooperation.
5 Mar. 1995	IFP decides to end its parliamentary boycott of mid-February.
16 Mar. 1995	Signs memorandum of understanding on development cooperation with Belgium.
20 Mar. 1995	Queen Elizabeth II of Great Britain, addresses the South African Parliament.
22 Mar. 1995	Joint communiqué on the establishment of diplomatic relations with the Independent State of Western Samoa.
23 Mar. 1995	Joint communiqué on the establishment of diplomatic relations with the Republic of Bosnia and Herzegovina.
23 Mar. 1995	Memorandum of understanding between the government of South Africa, through the Department of Transport, and the Federal Transit Highway Administration of the Department of Transportation of the US concerning transportation research and technology transfer.
27 Mar. 1995	Winnie Mandela, Deputy Minister of Arts, Culture, Science and Technology, is dismissed from her post.
29 Mar. 1995	Signs agreement with Egypt for the establishment of a Joint Commission of Cooperation.
Apr. 1995	Cabinet approves the establishment of the Truth Commission.
Apr. 1995	A government inquiry concludes that Allan Boesak did not misappropriate Dan Church aid funds. The fund threatens to sue him for the return of missing funds.
2 Apr. 1995	The ANC announces at its Conference on Constitutional Policy, that there will be no enforced coalition after the 1999 general election.
5 Apr. 1995	Signs agreement with Tunisia on tourism cooperation.
5 Apr. 1995	Signs agreement with Tunisa for the establishment of a Joint Commission of Cooperation.
13 Apr. 1995	In a letter to Chief Buthelezi, Deputy President Mbeki rejects the IFP's

international mediation proposals.

14 Apr. 1995	Winnie Mandela resigns as Deputy Minister of Arts, Culture, Science and Technology, hours before her second official dismissal.
21 Apr. 1995	Signs agreement on maritime transport with the Netherlands.
24 Apr. 1995	Voter registration for the forthcoming November local government election is extended to 5 June.
May 1995	The Volkstaat Council abandons the idea of an Afrikaner homeland and opts for a Cultural Citizens' Council, economic development sub-region and a share in the Pretoria area.
May 1995	Chief Buthelezi, denies that the document entitled 'A Minimal Institutional Strategy to Promote Federalism and Pluralism from the KwaZulu/Natal Base' is official IFP policy.
5 May 1995	Signs amendments to articles 24 and 25 of the Constitution of the World Health Organization (1986).
5 May 1995	Signs letter of intent with Bulgaria regarding arts, culture, science and technology and sport.
8 May 1995	Signs agreement with government of Belgium regarding cooperation between the South African police service and the Belgian Gendarmerie.
8 May 1995	Joint communiqué between the Minister of External Relations of Brazil and the Minister of Foreign Affairs of South Africa.
9 May 1995	Signs declaration of intent with the government of Belgium concerning education.
9 May 1995	Signs agreement on encouragement and reciprocal protection of investments with the Netherlands.
10 May 1995	Signs agreement upgrading existing diplomatic relations with Nigeria.
10 May 1995	Signs agreement establishing diplomatic relations with Niger.
17 May 1995	Unita leader Jonas Savimbi meets President Mandela in Cape Town.
17 May 1995	Parliament approves legislation to set up a Truth Commission.
24 May 1995	Signs specific agreement with the government of Belgium on cooperation in the field of health.
24 May 1995	Convention between South Africa and Sweden for the Avoidance of Double Taxation and the Prevention of Fiscal Evasion with Respect to Taxes on Income.
25 May 1995	Signs memorandum of understanding on development cooperation with the government of Australia.
25 May 1995	The IFP withdraws from the inter-governmental forum which provides for

liaison between the central and provincial governments.

26 May 1995   Signs agreement with Finland for the avoidance of double taxation and the prevention of fiscal evasion with respect to taxes on income.

June 1995   President Mandela admits during a Senate speech that he ordered ANC security guards to shoot to kill in protecting ANC headquarters at Shell House from an armed IFP march on the building which occurred on 28 March 1994.

June 1995   Amendments are made to the Truth Commission legislation that was passed in May. Parliament agrees to establish it.

5 June 1995   Letter of intent concerning arts, culture, science and technology and sport between South Africa and Bulgaria.

5 June 1995   Protocol on consultations between the Department of Foreign Affairs of South Africa and the Ministry of Foreign Affairs of Bulgaria.

5 June 1995   Signs agreement on the waiver of visas for diplomatic and official/service passports with Bulgaria.

6 June 1995   The Constitutional Court abolishes the death penalty.

14 June 1995   Signs declaration of intent on cooperation with the Russian Federation in the field of arts and culture.

20 June 1995   Signs extradition agreement with the government of Lesotho.

20 June 1995   The ANC and SACP stalwart, Harry Gwala, dies.

21 June 1995   Convention between the governments of South Africa and Denmark for the Avoidance of Double Taxation and the Prevention of Fiscal Evasion with respect to Taxes on Income.

21 June 1995   A Draft White Paper on Defence is released.

27 June 1995   Signs agreement with the Swiss Federal Council on the promotion and reciprocal protection of investments.

27 June 1995   Protocol of intent on military cooperation between the Ministry of Defence of South Africa and the Ministry of Defence of the Slovak Republic.

28 June 1995   Name changes to three of South Africa's nine provinces are announced: PWV becomes Gauteng; Orange Free State becomes the Free State and the Northern Transvaal becomes the Northern Province.

July 1995   Judicial Commission of Inquiry into Armscor, chaired by Justice Edwin Cameron, finds that it was involved in clandestine arms shipment to conflict zones, the Lebanese government, Christian militia and also to warring factions in the former Yugoslavia.

5 July 1995   Exchange of notes with Australia to establish an arrangement for the exchange of personnel.

7 July 1995	Signs air services agreement with the government of Korea.
7 July 1995	Convention between South Africa and Korea for the Avoidance of Double Taxation and the Prevention of Fiscal Evasion with respect to Taxes on Income.
7 July 1995	Memorandum of understanding between the Ministry of Trade and Industry of South Africa and the Ministry of Trade, Industry and Energy of Korea.
7 July 1995	Signs agreement with the government of Korea on the promotion and protection of investments.
9 July 1995	Ex-Police Commissioner General Johan van der Merwe, implicates Deputy President F.W. de Klerk in being informed about a 'dirty tricks' campaign waged against the ANC to undermine it between 1990 and the 1994 election.
14 July 1995	South Africa and Russia sign a military cooperation agreement.
14 July 1995	Signs agreement with the Ministry of Defence of the Ukraine on cooperation in the military sphere.
14 July 1995	Signs agreement with the government of the Ukraine on military-technical cooperation.
18 July 1995	Signs air services agreement with the government of Australia.
19 July 1995	Signs agreement with India on cooperation in the fields of science and technology.
Aug. 1995	A cooperation agreement is reached between South Africa and Swaziland over the issue of thwarting arms smuggling.
3 Aug. 1995	Signs protocol on environmental protection to the Antarctic Treaty (1991).
10 Aug. 1995	Signs agreement with Swaziland in respect of cooperation and mutual assistance in the field of combating crime.
15 Aug. 1995	Iranian Foreign Minister, Ali Akbar Velayati, visits South Africa in connection with South Africa's agreement to store and market up to 15 million barrels of Iranian oil. This will assist Tehran in sidestepping sanctions imposed by Washington on Iran. The USA criticizes this arrangement.
15 Aug. 1995	Signs agreement with Iran concerning the establishment of a joint Commission of Cooperation.
22 Aug. 1995	Minister of Safety and Security, Sydney Mufamadi, visits violence-torn KwaZulu/Natal. He states that 1000 extra troops and police will be sent to the province as reinforcements.
25 Aug. 1995	Signs cooperation agreement with the United States concerning peaceful uses of nuclear energy.
25 Aug. 1995	Terms of reference of the Sustainable Development Committee of the United States-South African Binational Commission.

Sept. 1995	Chief Buthelezi indicates that he will resign if divisions within the party are not resolved.
Sept. 1995	Cabinet approves immediate demobilization of over 10,000 MK and APLA soldiers and the rationalization of 50,000 personnel from the SANDF. This reduces the military from a force level of 135,000 to 75,000.
11 Sept. 1995	Signs agreement with Germany regarding technical cooperation.
11 Sept. 1995	Signs treaty with Germany concerning reciprocal encouragement and protection of investments.
11 Sept. 1995	Signs basic agreement with Germany concerning the secondment of development works of the German Development Service.
12 Sept. 1995	Signs framework agreement for financial cooperation with the European Investment Bank.
13 Sept. 1995	Signs agreement with Israel concerning the establishment of a joint Commission of Cooperation.
13 Sept. 1995	Convention on Prohibition or Restriction on the Use of Certain Conventional Weapons which may be deemed to be Excessively Injurous or to have Indiscriminate Effects and Protocols (1980).
15 Sept. 1995	Signs agreement with the Palestine Liberation Organisation, representing the State of Palestine, regarding the establishment of a Joint Commission of Cooperation.
19 Sept. 1995	Signs memorandum of understanding with Iran on cooperation in the fields of mining and minerals.
19 Sept. 1995	Signs protocol on consultation with the Ministry of Foreign Affairs in Poland.
22 Sept. 1995	The Constitutional Court rules that President Nelson Mandela exceeded his power by decreasing electoral boundaries.
2 Oct. 1995	Muziwendoda Mdluli of the National Intelligence Agency, is found shot dead in his car in Silverton, Pretoria. He was investigating the possible involvement of fellow-agents in the failed Comoros Islands coup.
11 Oct. 1995	Signs financial protocol with the government of France.
11 Oct. 1995	Signs agreement with the government of France concerning the reciprocal promotion and protection of investments.
24 Oct. 1995	Signs agreement with Lesotho concerning the avoidance of double taxation and the prevention of fiscal evasion with respect to taxes on income.
Nov. 1995	The Draft constitution is unveiled.
1 Nov. 1995	Local government elections are held.

2 Nov. 1995	Former South African Defence Minister, General Magnus Malan and nineteen others are charged with murder and for having established hit squads to destabilize South Africa before the end of apartheid. They are further charged for the 1987 massacre of thirteen people in Durban's Kwamakutha township.
4 Nov. 1995	Signs agreement with France on co-operation in the fields of education, sport, culture, science and technology.
6 Nov. 1995	Convention between the governments of South Africa and Italy concerning the Avoidance of Double Taxation with respect to Taxes on Income and for the Prevention of Fiscal Evasion.
8 Nov. 1995	It is reported that the SANDF's full-time component comprises 75,479 personnel, including 39,473 Africans, 28,192 Whites, 6,982 Coloureds, and 832 Indians.
10 Nov. 1995	Results of the local government elections are published: 51.37% participated, 5.3 million people in total. The ANC is the overall winner, securing 66.37% of the votes cast. Voting was postponed in the Western Cape and KwaZulu/Natal province.
20 Nov. 1995	Signs coopertion agreement with Bulgaria concerning education, arts, culture, science, technology and sport.
21 Nov. 1995	Signs protocol additional to the Geneva Conventions of 1949 and relating to the Protection of Victims of International Armed Conflicts (Protocol I).
21 Nov. 1995	Signs protocol additional to the Geneva Conventions of 1949, and relating to the Protection of Victims of Non-International Armed Conflicts (Protocol II).
27 Nov. 1995	Convention with the government of Canada for the Avoidance of Double Taxation and the Prevention of Fiscal Evasion with respect to Taxes on Income.
27 Nov. 1995	Signs agreement with Canada concerning the promotion and protection of investments.
27 Nov. 1995	Signs agreement with the Russian Federation for the avoidance of double taxation and the prevention of fiscal evasion with respect to taxes on income.
27 Nov. 1995	Signs protocol with the Russian Federation on Consular procedure.
Dec. 1995	South Africa and Australia sign an extradition treaty with effect from 1996.
Dec. 1995	Archbishop Desmond Tutu is appointed head of the Truth Commission.
Dec. 1995	South Africa signs a business arrangement with Malaysia, allowing for the manufacture, under licence in Malaysia, of the South African designed attack helicopter, the Rooivalk.
Dec. 1995	A Coloured breakaway party from the Coloured Resistance Movement is established. It is called the Coloured Liberation Movement (CLM). Its leader is Michael Roman.

1 Dec. 1995	General Magnus Malan and nineteen co-accused are formally charged with murder for killing thirteen people in Durban's Kwamakutha township in 1987.
5 Dec. 1995	Signs economic, technical and related assistance agreement with the United States.
5 Dec. 1995	Signs agreement with the Unites States concerning the program of the Peace Corps in South Africa.
5 Dec. 1995	Signs framework agreement with the United States concerning cooperation in the scientific, technological and environmental fields.
5 Dec. 1995	Signs agreement with the United States on collaboration in energy policy, science, technology and development.
7 Dec. 1995	Signs agreement with the Republic of China regarding technical assistance for the establishment of a vocational training centre.
8 Dec. 1995	Signs agreement with Cuba for the promotion and reciprocal protection of investments.
13 Dec. 1995	Signs general memorandum of understanding with Canada on development cooperation.
15 Dec. 1995	Signs agreement with Denmark concerning community forestry in the Bushbuchridge area in the province of Mpumalanga.
15 Dec. 1995	Signs agreement with Denmark on the development of a White Paper on Biological Diversity for the Republic of South Africa.
15 Dec. 1995	Signs agreement with Denmark concerning capacity building in the Directorate of Environment, Department of Development Planning, Environment and Works in the Province of Gauteng.
15 Dec. 1995	Signs agreement with Denmark concerning capacity building in the Department of Environmental Affairs in the province of Mpumalanga.
15 Dec. 1995	OAU Convention Governing the Specific Aspects of Refugee Problems in Africa (1969).
1 Jan. 1996	At least twenty-eight people are murdered in KwaZulu-Natal on New Year's Day.
9 Jan. 1996	Crime figures released by the police National Crime Information Management Centre confirm South Africa's designation as the most violent country in the world outside a war zone. It is estimated that on average 15 percent of a South African's disposable income is spent on security measures.
10 Jan. 1996	Chief Buthelezi rejects the President's call to resume participation in the constitution-making process and returns to the Constitutional Assembly (CA).
11 Jan. 1996	First Executive Deputy President Thabo Mbeki announces the establishment of an independent judicial inquiry to investigate allegations that government

ministers and senior police officials are being kept under surveillance by the National Intelligence Agency (NIA). The investigation will be undertaken by the National Intelligence Co-ordinating Committee (NICOC).

15 Jan. 1996	The National Party (NP) admits it is involved in a fundamental reassessment of its role in the country's political life.
19 Jan. 1996	President Nelson Mandela holds meetings with Zulu King Goodwill Zwelithini and later declares he will initiate a round of urgent peace talks in Kwazulu-Natal, leading as soon as possible to an 'imbizo' (a traditional Zulu gathering).
21 Jan. 1996	President Mandela meets Inkatha leader Chief Mangosuthu Buthelezi, who endorses the plan for the traditional gathering to discuss ways of ending the bloodshed in Kwazulu-Natal.
23 Jan. 1996	The independent Human Rights Committee (HRC) reports that 837 people have been killed in political violence in 1995 compared to 1,600 in 1994 and 2,009 in 1993.
28 Jan. 1996	President Mandela meets United States black Muslim leader Louis Farrakhan, head of the Nation of Islam. Both state their opposition to racism and sexism. The media, religious leaders and opposition criticize the reception of Farrakhan.
29 Jan. 1996	Two serving members of the army and a third man are arrested in connection with the attack on St James's Church in Cape Town in July 1993.
29 Jan. 1996	The ANC blame the killing of up to fourteen people and the injuring of twenty-six unemployed people in Alberton on 'third force' activity returning to the main industrial area around Johannesburg.
10 Feb. 1996	President Mandela discloses that he has invited Cuban President Fidel Castro to South Africa. This move elicits expressions of concern from the United States and criticism from the National Party.
2 Feb. 1996	The National Party launches a 'core values' document in Pretoria. On the same day it is reported that the Provincial Affairs and Constitutional Development Minister Roelf Meyer will resign his Cabinet post on 1 March 1996 to become Secretary-General of the 'revamped' National Party. Its leader Mr. F.W. de Klerk confirms that while it is not seeking formal alliances, it has held discussions with various parties opposed to the African National Congress (ANC).
9 Feb. 1996	It is announced that a special party congress has been called for in Bloemfontein at Easter by the Pan Africanist Congress (PAC) at which a new leadership could be elected.
13 Feb. 1996	Finance Minister Chris Liebenberg announces that the 1995-96 Budget deficit will be R30.1 billion or 6 per cent of G.D.P.
14 Feb. 1996	President Mandela issues an invitation to Libyan leader Col. M. al Kadhafi. The National Party considers this could jeopardize South Africa's relations with the United States.

16 Feb. 1996	The Supreme Court orders the Potgietersrus Primary School in Northern Province to admit Black pupils.
17-18 Feb. 1996	Violence claims at least sixty lives in Kwazulu-Natal. A pattern is repeated every weekend during February 1996.
18 Feb. 1996	The Algerian government protests over President Mandela's reception of the head of the opposition Islamic Salvation Front's (FIS) parliamentary delegation abroad, A. Haddam, and decides to recall its ambassador from South Africa. This decision is recinded on 21 February 1996.
21 Feb. 1996	Welfare and Population Development Minister, Abe Williams, resigns in the face of corruption allegations relating to missing pension funds. The National Party thus loses one of its seven members of the Cabinet in the government of National Unity.
22 Feb. 1996	Sixteen Black children arrive at the Potgietersrus Primary School to register, protected by police officers.
26 Feb. 1996	Court officials announce that the Potgietersrus school authorities will not challenge the Supreme Court decision.
26 Feb. 1996	Relations with Algeria are restored after intervention by President Mandela. Deputy Foreign Minister, Mr. A. Pahad, is sent to Algeria and, on return, states that the two countries will strengthen ties by signing a bilateral agreement to develop areas of common interest.
3-4 Mar. 1996	President Mandela visits Mali for two days (and Togo for a few hours on 4 March). He and Togolese President Eyadema review the situation in West Africa. South Africa and Mali agree to establish diplomatic relations.
5 Mar. 1996	President Mandela is reported to have held talks with Mr. Jonas Savimbi, President of the National Union for the Total Independence of Angola (UNITA) in Togo on 4 March 1996. Discussions centred on the Angolan peace process and democracy in South Africa.
5-7 Mar. 1996	President Mandela undergoes three days of intensive medical checks to counter rumours concerning the state of his health.
7 Mar. 1996	A Foreign Ministry statement issued in Pretoria, blames 'developments in Angola' for the indefinite postponement of President Mandela's visit to Angola.
11 Mar. 1996	Former Defence Minister General Magnus Malan and nineteen co-accused, plead not guilty to thirteen charges of murder, and other charges, including conspiracy to commit murder and attempted murder, at the opening of their trial in the Durban Supreme Court. The charges relate to a 1987 massacre of thirteen people in KwaMakhutha township south of Durban.
13 Mar. 1996	Finance Minister Liebenberg presents the 1996-97 Budget, reports continuing economic growth and underlining his aim of building on the government's reputation for fiscal discipline.
15 Mar. 1996	The first provisional constitution is unanimously adopted by the Kwazulu-Natal legislature. The ANC secures a major concession - a clause

nullifying an aspect of the constitution incompatible with the final national constitution and various contentious issues (including the monarchy, rural local government and provincial powers) are rendered 'of no force and effect' for periods ranging from six to eighteen months.

19 Mar. 1996   President Mandela's thirteen-year marriage to Winnie Mandela is formally ended when a Rand Supreme Court judge grants his petition for divorce on the grounds of irretrievable breakdown.

20 Mar. 1996   A hearing to decide the financial settlement between President Mandela and Winnie Mandela is held at which the President testifies. Her claim for half of her husband's estate is dismissed because of her absence from court; she is ordered to pay the costs of the hearing. The President subsequently offers an unspecified out-of-court settlement.

21 Mar. 1996   A massacre takes place at Donnybrook, Kwazulu-Natal only hours after President Mandela visits the province. All those killed are ANC supporters.

22 Mar. 1996   A notice banning the carrying of weapons in public in seventy magisterial districts is published in the Government Gazette.

23 Mar. 1996   At a rally in the Tugela Ferry district of Kwazulu-Natal some 6,000 Inkatha Freedom Party (IFP) supporters come armed with fighting sticks, spears, clubs and battle axes in clear defiance of the government's ban on traditional weapons.

28 Mar. 1996   Ministerial changes in the Cabinet are announced.

28 Mar. 1996   Inkatha Freedom Party supporters march through the streets of Johannesburg to mark the anniversary of the 1994 'Shell House killings'. The demonstrators defy a government ban on the carrying of traditional weapons.

28 Mar. 1996   President Mandela announces important changes to the Government of National Unity. Finance Minister Chris Liebenberg, whose resignation takes effect on 4 April 1996, is replaced by Trevor Manuel hitherto Trade and Industry and Tourism Minister; Pallo Jordan, Minister of Posts and Telecommunications is dismissed and replaced by Jay Naidoo formerly Minister in charge of the Reconstruction and Development Programme.

3 Apr. 1996   Five members of the Afrikaner Resistance Movement (AWB) are sentenced to twenty-six years imprisonment each for their part in a bombing campaign in which twenty people were killed and hundreds injured, aimed at disrupting the 1994 elections.

8 Apr. 1996   Iran's official news agency quotes Foreign Minister Alfred Nzo as saying, during his visit to Tehran, that South Africa's relations with Iran are good and that South Africa does not follow American policy in the region. Growing concern is expressed in the West over the substance and direction of South African foreign policy.

11 Apr. 1996   President Mandela warns that local government elections in Kwazulu-Natal, scheduled for 29 May 1996, may have to be postponed again because of widespread violence and intimidation.

13 Apr. 1996   Cyril Ramaphosa, Secretary-General of the ANC and chairman of the

Constitutional Assembly, announced his intention to resign from Parliament once the final Constitution is agreed upon. He will become deputy Executive Chairman of New Africa Investment Ltd. (NAIL).

15 Apr. 1996   The Truth and Reconciliation Commission holds its opening session in East London. Reservations are expressed about the constitutional right of the Commission to grant amnesty to political killers by the families of anti-apartheid activists. Legal groups also argue that evidence of crimes should be heard in a court of law.

17 Apr. 1996   During a working visit to Libya, Foreign Minister Alfred Nzo stresses South Africa's eagerness to strengthen and develop its relations with Libya. The South African people will never forget the support, assistance and the courageous stance shown by the Libyan Arab people to the people of South Africa. Diplomatic relations have already been established and during his visit a cooperation agreement is signed in the economic, scientific, technical and cultural fields.

19 Apr. 1996   The Pan Africanist Congress conference in Bloemfontein over Easter resolve to hold a congress in August to resolve questions of leadership and the way forward. The Pan Africanist Students' Organization (PASO) and the Azanian National Youth Unity (AZANYU) delegates walk out. The Easter meeting is called a 'consultative conference' rather than a congress and no binding decisions can be taken.

24 Apr. 1996   The Constitution Bill is given its first reading and is referred back to the Constitutional Committee for amendments to be considered. In terms of the interim constitution the final constitution has to be agreed by 9 May 1996, or a referendum could be forced.

25 Apr. 1996   Parties table more than 300 amendments to the constitutional legislation. The National Party (NP) fight for the insertion of a right of lockout - as a counter to labour's right to strike - and provision for single-language education. The Congress of South African Trade Unions (COSATU) calls for a one-day general strike on 30 April 1996 to demonstrate opposition to a lockout clause. The ANC is criticized for supporting this call. Both the ANC and the NP are criticized for negotiating in private.

25 Apr. 1996   Senior members of the Zulu royal family are attacked in a royal residence near Durban.

2 May 1996   South Africa and China exchange letters granting each other most-favoured-nation status.

4 May 1996   Violence in Kwazulu-Natal spills over into the streets of central Durban and running gun battles ensue. The march protesting against the ban on carrying traditional weapons is organized by the National Hostel Residents' Association. Reports of killings continue throughout the month. Police reinforcements are sent to the province in a bid to prevent violence escalating further before the regional elections.

6 May 1966   Presidents Joaquim Chissano and Nelson Mandela sign an agreement to allow South African farmers to settle and farm in Mozambique.

7 May 1996   Only a few hours before the expiry of the deadline for the production of the

final document, and after a period of intense negotiations, the main political parties reach agreement on a new constitution.

8 May 1996

The new Constitution is finally approved by the 490-member Constituent Assembly: 421 votes are cast in favour, two against, the Freedom Front (FF) abstains, the Inkatha Freedom Party does not attend the session, nine votes are not recorded. The heart of the constitution is a Bill of Rights listing fundamental freedom.

9 May 1996

Second Executive President F.W. de Klerk announces that the NP will withdraw from the Government of National Unity at the end of June 1996 and move into formal opposition. This decision is said to be occasioned by disagreements over the constitution itself and the growing financial crisis resulting from the collapse of the rand.

12 May 1996

Cyril Ramaphosa confirms that he is resigning as ANC Secretary-General, as well as from Parliament.

13 May 1996

As a result of the NP's withdrawal President Mandela carries out a Cabinet reshuffle replacing all the NP ministers with ANC appointees. The Ministry of General Services is abolished and the Ministries of Agriculture and Land Affairs are amalgamated. The changes are effective from 1 July 1996.

14 May 1996

The NP confirms it will withdraw from all provincial governments at the end of June, with the exception of the Western Cape where it is the majority party.

14 May 1996

Local elections for KwaZulu-Natal are again postponed until 26 June 1996 as a result of persistent violence and administrative difficulties.

22 May 1996

Former South African Defence Force (SADF) Chief Tienie Groenewald is acquitted of all charges related to the 1987 KwaMakhuthu massacre. The trial of seventeen other accused, including that of former Defence Minister Magnus Malan, is adjourned until 10 June 1996.

29 May 1996

Local elections held in the Western Cape result in the National Party securing control of all three district councils.

11-13 June 1996

President Nelson Mandela's first state visit to Angola, planned for these three days, is postponed for the second time at the President's request. However, he commits South Africa to playing a constructive role in developing Angola's economy through increased investment and to assist in the peace process.

13 June 1996

A regional peace summit is held in Durban on the initiative of church leaders. Zulu King Goodwill Zwelithini urges his subjects to stop killing each other.

14 June 1996

Finance Minister Trevor Manuel unveils the government's macro-economic strategy in a framework document entitled Growth, Employment and Redistribution (GEAR).

19 June 1996

Cuban Foreign Minister Roberto Rubaina says his visit to South Africa will pave the way for an extnded state visit by Cuban President Fidel Castro and that the two countries have signed a joint communique committing themselves to strengthening relations.

22-24 June 1996	Violence continued in Kwazulu-Natal. Thirty-seven murdered are reported on 22-23 June and fourteen on 24 June. The victims include an Inkatha Freedom Party (IFP) Chairman.
23 June 1996	A service in Cape Town's St George's Cathedral marks the retirement of the Most Rev. Desmond Tutu as Archbishop of Cape Town and head of the Anglican Church in South Africa. He will remain chairman of the Truth and Reconciliation Commission.
26 June 1996	Local elections are finally held in Kwazulu Natal. Thousands of additional police and troops are deployed and voting proceeds peacefully.
27 June 1996	The Minister of Local Government in Kwazulu-Natal applies to the Supreme Court to have voting in four rural areas declared null and void and for polling to be repeated in those areas. This follows ANC complaints about administrative chaos and intimidation. However President Mandela says the polls have largely been free and fair.
2 July 1996	The results of the local government elections in Kwazulu-Natal indicate that Inkatha polled 44.50 percent of the votes, the ANC 33.22 percent. Ward results give Inkatha 562 seats, the ANC 512 and the NP 187. The ANC wins control of all thirteen of the province's metropolitan councils, with a combined annual budget of R5 billion. Inkatha takes control of most of the rural councils but the budget allocation is less than R100 million.
7 July 1996	In a television broadcast President Mandela confirms that he will not stand for re-election in 1999 and gives clear support to Deputy President Thabo Mbeki as his successor.
9-13 July 1996	President Nelson Mandela makes a triumphant state visit to London.
14 July 1996	President Mandela attends the Bastille Day celebrations in Paris as a guest of French President Jacques Chirac.
15 July 1996	General Constand Viljoen reassures RENAMO leader Afonso Dhlakama that the agreement between South Africa and Mozambique to settle farmers in northern Niassa Province is not designed to create `Boer colonies' but is part of the development of the southern African region and its agricultural activity.
15 July 1996	A grenade attack is launched on the ANC headquarters in Johannesburg. It is blamed by the ANC on a `third force', and is linked by them to controversy over investigtions into the March 1994 Shell House massacre and civil claims by dependents of Zulus killed in it against the ANC party.
25 July 1996	The Constitutional Court rejects an attempt by the families of murdered political activists to have the Truth and Reconciliation Commission stripped of its power to grant amnesties. The Court rules that reconciliation should be placed above revenge and that the Commission can grant amnesty to those who come forward voluntarily, confess freely and can prove that their crimes have been politically motivated.
26 July 1996	A White House statement, issued at the end of a visit by Deputy President

Thabo Mbeki, states that a tentative agreement has been reached in the dispute over an attempt by the United States government to prosecute ARMSCOR over illegal weapons trafficking. Details of the agreement are not made public, but it is said `to meet the needs of both countries'.

26 July 1996   Bantu Holomisa is dismissed as Deputy Environment and Tourism Minister. His responsibilities are assigned to former ANC Youth League leader Peter Mokaba and it is announced that he will face internal ANC disiplinary charges.

30 July 1996   The Minister of Arts, Culture, Science and Technology, Dr Ben Ngubane, is to resign from the government of National Unity following the Inkatha Freedom Party (IFP) resolution that he should join the Kwazulu-Natal provincial government.

2 Aug. 1996   Bantu Holomisa, former ruler of the Transkei, claims that President Mandela had told him that Sol Kerzner (former head of Sun International) had donated two million rand to the ANC before the 1994 elections. He construes this as an attempt by Kerzner to have bribery charges against him dropped. The ANC initially strongly deny accepting payment.

3 Aug. 1996   Following the National Party (NP)'s first federal congress since its withdrawal from the Government of National Unity, its policy plan is unveiled concentrating on anti-poverty strategies. The possibility of the Party changing its name is again discussed.

4 Aug. 1996   During a march organized by the Cape Town-based Muslim organization People against Gangsterism and Drugs (PAGAD) a suspected drug dealer, Rashaad Staggie, is set alight and shot to death. PAGAD spokesmen later claim the motorcade of some 500 vehicles had been delivering an ultimatim to him and to his twin brother Rashid to end drug sales.

10 Aug. 1996   President Mandela confirms that Sol Kerzner did indeed `make the contribution' to the ANC electoral funds, but states that he has told no-one else in the ANC about the donation.

11 Aug. 1996   PAGAD supporters attend a rally in Cape Town. Similar rallies are held in Durban and Johannesburg's Lenasia area, and national support grows. Tensions rise and police and troops patrol. Leaders of PAGAD deny that there are plans for a `jihad' or holy war and maintain theirs is a broad-based campaign against crime, for which they are receiving a ground swell of support.

13 Aug. 1996   At least one PAGAD member is reported arrested on charges of murder and sedition. On the same day PAGAD says it is seeking aid from external sources including the Lebanese Islamic guerrilla movement Hezbollah. PAGAD is urged to support existing channels of law enforcement.

19 Aug. 1996   The major parties begin their political party submission to the Truth Commission. In a forty-three-page document the Freedom Front (FF) leader, General Constand Viljoen, emphasizes the need for reconciliation and nation-building. The PAC acknowledges that its armed wing, APLA, targeted white civilians, takes responsibility for this, but makes no apoligies.

21 Aug. 1996   Former President F.W. de Klerk tells the Truth and Reconciliation

Commission that he reiterates his apologies for suffering caused during the conflict that ended the apartheid system. However, he says that when in power (1948-1994) his National Party (NP) had not, to his knowledge, authorized the security forces to commit murder, torture, rape, assassination or assault.

22 Aug. 1996   The ANC presents to the Truth and Reconciliation Commission a detailed 300-page self-analysis of the ANC's human rights record and strategy during its campaign to end apartheid. The document names thirty-four ANC members who were executed by an ANC military tribunal at an external base in Angola.

26-27 Aug. 1996   The Supreme Court convicts former Police Colonel Eugene de Kock of six killings during his service as commander of a police unit based outside Pretoria, Vlakplaas.

28 Aug. 1996   An agreement is signed for the sale of Anglo American's almost 48 percent shareholding in Johnnies Industrial Corporation to the National Empowerment Consortium (NEC). The decision to sell is interpreted as a response to political pressure to transfer economic power to the black community.

30 Aug. 1996   Bantu Holomisa is expelled from the ANC after a disciplinary hearing.

30 Aug. 1996   The government announces that units from the army and airforce, as well as extra police, will be stationed in Johannesburg in a drive to bring down crime rates. One of the operation's commanders is to be Colonel Buks Pieterse, who as second-in-command to the SADF's 32 Battalion (now disbanded) led cross-border raids into Angola during the Angolian civil war.

5 Sept. 1996   During the Inkatha Freedom Party (IFP) submission to the Truth and Reconciliation Commission, leader Mangosuthu Buthelezi apologises for whatever hurt he may have caused but reiterates that he never instructed any of his followers to engage in acts of violence. He makes public a top secret detailing a plot by the ANC to assassinate him in 1987.

6 Sept. 1996   The bitter debate over the power of central government in relation to the provinces is reopened when the Constitutional Court rejects the new constitution, giving the Constitutional Assembly ninety days to rectify a number of specific aspects. A key objection concerns powers allocated to provincial governments which are substantially less and inferior to those set out in the thirty-four principles agreed by the political parties before the 1994 general elections.

11 Sept. 1996   The Chamber of Mines and the National Union of Mineworkers (NUM) sign an agreement on wages and working conditions averting the likelihood of damaging strikes in the coal and gold mining industries.

12 Sept. 1996   Iranian President Rafsanjani arrives in South Africa as part of a six-nation tour of Sub-Saharan Africa amid opposition to it within and without South Africa. President Mandela reiterates his stance that South Africa will make its own policy decisions.

16 Sept. 1996   Former Police Colonel Eugene de Kock begins his evidence in Pretoria Supreme Court by revealing his part in the apartheid regime's `dirty tricks'

campaign. Pleading in mitigation, his testimony implicates leading NP figures and senior officers in the security forces over a two-week period. He insists he was part of a systematic campaign which encompassed the police, armed forces and covert security units.

17 Sept. 1996 The South African Foreign Affairs Department denies Iranian media reports that the government has endorsed Iran's human rights record and has called for the withdrawal of foreign forces from the Gulf. Foreign Minister Alfred Nzo says only that South Africa is heartened by Iran's willingness to co-operate more fully with the UN's Special Representative of Human Rights. No joint communique is issued.

20 Sept. 1996 The PAC's finance secretary says it will transform itself from a revolutionary movement to a fully-fledged political party run on democratic and business principles. The aim is to counter-act the party's radical reputation and attract funds in preparation for the 1999 general elections.

22 Sept. 1996 The sale of six state-owned provincial radio stations has realized R520 million, to be spent on reducing state debt, new infrastructure and promoting black economic empowerment. These plans are opposed by the South African Broadcasting Corporation (SABC), which wants the money to fund its transformation into a public service broadcasting in all eleven official languages.

26 Sept. 1996 Approval is given by the National Conventional Arms Control Committee for the sale of arms to Rwanda. Only 'defensive arms' are said to be involved. Nevertheless the decision is widely criticized by human rights groups.

1 Oct. 1996 Inkatha agrees to return to the Constitutional Assembly, after an eighteen-month absence, but withdraws again on 7 October 1996, indicating it is considering reviving its demand for international mediation.

11 Oct. 1996 The Constitutional Assembly approves final amendments to the new Constitution. The changes are approved by 369 votes to one, with eight abstentions.

11 Oct. 1996 The seven-month trial of former Defence Minister, General Magnus Malan, ends. Malan and other former military officials are cleared of all charges relating to the murder of thirteen people in KwaMakutha in 1987.

17 Oct. 1996 President Mandela vows 'to leave no stone unturned' in finding the truth behind the air crash ten years before that killed Mozambican leader Samora Machel. Judge Cecil Margo, who headed the official inquiry at the time, says it would be possible to reopen the investigation but only if new evidence is produced.

21 Oct. 1996 Before the Truth and Reconciliation Commission, General Johan van den Merwe, National Police Commissioner 1990-1995, admits that he gave the order in 1988 for the police to blow up the headquarters of the South African Council of Churches. He claims that Adrian Vlok, then Minister of Law and Order gave the instructions and that these had emanated from President P.W. Botha (1984-1989).

21 Oct. 1996 South African Security agent Craig Williamson, on his return to South

Africa, denies involvement in the assassination of Prime Minister Olof Palme in Stockholm in 1986. Swedish investigators have been in South Africa looking into any possible South African connection. The Swedish Foreign Minister, on a visit to Cape Town, reveals that her government gave about $400m. in humanitarian assistance to opponenets of apartheid, much of it to the ANC.

23 Oct. 1996   President Mandela confirms the appointment of Ismail Mahomed as Chief Justice to succeed Michael Corbett in 1997. The appointment is made on the recommendation of the Judicial Service Commission (JSC) which is reported to have voted 15-1 in favour of Mahomed. Mandela had earlier broken with tradition when he expressed his support for Mahomed before the JSC had made its recommendations.

29 Oct. 1996   The South African Schools Bill is approved by the National Assembly by 232 votes to 71.

30 Oct. 1996   Former Police Colonel Eugene de Kock is sentenced to life imprisonment twice over for murder and conspiracy to murder.

31 Oct. 1996   The National Assembly passes legislation providing for abortion on demand within the first twelve weeks of pregnancy and for terminations to be permitted under specified conditions up to the twentieth week of pregnancy. The changes are opposed by Christian and Muslim groups.

4 Nov. 1996   The Chairman of the Truth and Reconciliation Commission, Desmond Tutu, threatens to resign from the Commission of the ANC ..... refuses to seek amnesty for its past human rights abuses. On 10 November he meets a senior ANC delegation who agrees that anti-apartheid activists will appply for amnesty, although 'reconciliation does not require that we should deny or trample upon the moral legitimacy and validity' of their struggle.

4 Nov. 1996   Free State Provincial Premier Patrick 'Terror' Lekota and the entire provincial Executive Committee agree to resign following allegations of corruption and nepotism. On 20 November 1996 Deputy President Mbeki endorses Ivy Matsepe-Casaburri as Lekota's successor.

12 Nov. 1996   A memorandum of understanding on military cooperation has been signed between Malaysia and South Africa. Malaysian Defence Minister D.S.H. Alban confirms in Pretoria that talks on the purchase and production of helicopters have been held.

14 Nov. 1996   The National Conventional Arms Control Committee discusses a White Paper on arms sales to foreign countries. The proposed legislation is aimed at curbing illegal arms deal trading.

14 Nov. 1996   President Mandela announces that Patrick Lekota will be 'redeployed' to the Senate. It is believed he will be appointed to a ministerial post.

21 Nov. 1996   Former President P.W. Botha declares he will never apologize for apartheid and denounces what he calls the 'fierce unforgiving assault on the Afrikaner' by the new government.

27 Nov. 1996   President Nelson Mandela announces that South Africa is to sever diplomatic relations with Taiwan and establish full diplomatic relations with China, with

effect from the end of December 1997. Taiwan expresses regret at the decision and calls on South Africa to reconsider.

4 Dec. 1996   Taiwanese Foreign Minister John Chang Hsiaoyen visits South Africa and holds talks with President Mandela. The President insists South Africa is keen to maintain relations with Taiwan at the highest level short of diplomatic ties.

5 Dec. 1996   The Taiwanese Foreign Minister announces the recall of the Taiwanese Ambassador and the immediate suspension of most Taiwanese aid projects, as well as most of the thirty six treaties and agreements between the two countries.

9 Dec. 1996   General Holomisa announces that he is abandoning a Supreme Court action aimed at forcing the ANC to reinstate him as a member and will instead organize a national conference to consider the formation of a new party.

10 Dec. 1996   President Mandela signs the new Constitution. It incorporates the broad principles of the existing Interim Constitution adopted in 1993 together with amendments and revisions. Analysts declare it one of the most liberal in the world.

12 Dec. 1996   The ANC confirms it has forwarded 300 applications from its members to the Truth and Reconciliation Commission and expects to submit at least another sixty, including those of three Cabinet ministers. The PAC announced that at least 600 of its members, including the 'high command' of its armed wing APLA, have applied. No high-ranking IFP members are known to have applied.

13 Dec. 1996   President Mandela extends both the cut-off date for amnesty applications and the deadline for applications to the Truth and Reconciliation Commission. Amnesty may now be sought for political crimes carried out up to 10 May 1994, the date of his inauguration as President. Applications to the TRC may now be made up to 10 May 1997.

16-17 Dec.1996   Running battles break out between police and PAGAD protestors in Cape Town.

Jan. 1997   Discussions are held on possible new political alliances. The ANC invite the PAC for talks on joining the government; the NP holds talks with the IFP, the DP and community organizations and the DP holds discussions with the IFP and the PAC. Mr. de Klerk says the NP is seeking to establish a new political movement cooperating with parties that shared its value system, supported free enterprise and were anti-Communist.

6-7 Jan. 1997   Three men are arrested following three bomb blasts in Rustenburg, about 100 miles northwest of Johannesburg. The Minister of Safety and Security visits the town to inspect the damage to the mosque and other Muslim owned buildings. Responsibility for the explosions is claimed by the Boere-Aanvals-troepe (Boer Attack Troops - BAT).

13 Jan. 1997   Togo and South Africa establish diplomatic relations. This decision follows a 'friendly' visit by President Mandela to Togo in March 1996.

14 Jan. 1997   South Africa reacts angrily to American threats to cut off aid if the

government sells arms to Syria.

17 Jan. 1997   In a Truth and Reconciliation Commission (TRC) revelation, General Georg Meiring is implicated with more than sixty officers and soldiers in 'dirty tricks' including state-sponsored murder. It also suggests that the former President F.W. de Klerk refused to investigate charges against General Meiring and two other generals despite the Steyn commission of enquiry.

24 Jan. 1997   Three leaders resign from the IFP, Frank Malalose, national chairman and the Premier of Kwazulu-Natal, Ziba Jiyane, Secretary-General and Musa Myeni, leader in the Gauteng legislature. All three are said to be moderates who favour compromise. Their resignation during a fifteen-hour meeting of the IFP's national council follows reports of tensions with Inkatha President Chief Buthelezi.

28 Jan. 1997   The Truth and Reconciliation Commission confirm newspaper reports that five former security police officers have confessed to the 1977 murder of Black Consciousness leader Steve Biko, and have made a formal amnesty application.

6 Feb. 1997   Violence occurs in Johannesburg's Coloured townships, at least four people are killed and up to two hundred injured when police clash with demonstrators during a stayaway called by the South Western Joint Civics Association (SAWEJOCA) in protest against rent and service charges.

7 Feb. 1997   Freedom Front leader General Constand Viljoen has announced he will seek amnesty before the Truth and Reconciliation Commission. He admits involvement in a pre 1994 election plot to establish a 'volkstaat' by force.

7 Feb. 1997   Opening the new session of Parliament President Mandela reviews the governments achievements since the 1994 elections. He promises action in three principal areas - on projects under the Reconstruction and Development Programme, in the fight against corruption (especially in the civil service) and increased economic growth. The war against crime is identified as one of his government's top priorities.

8 Feb. 1997   South Africa radio reports that C. Barnard and A.K. Myburgh have been sentenced to fifty years' imprisonment each for their part in four bomb blasts, shortly before the 1994 election.

13 Feb. 1997   It is reported that President Mandela, as part of his duties as chairman of the Southern African Development Community (SADC) has held talks with President Robert Mugabe in Harare, Zimbabwe and discussed the situations in Angola, Lesotho, Swaziland and Zambia. Talks have also been held with Botswana's President Masire. The next meeting will be with President Chissano of Mozambique.

14 Feb. 1997   The IFP have issued a new Mission Statement calling for a 'social market economy' following a three-day National Council workshop in Ulundi.

19 Feb. 1997   The Presidents of South Africa, Uganda, Mozambique, Botswana and Zimbabwe meet in Cape Town. The five leaders exchange views on problems affecting the sub-continent as well as the crises in Zaire and the Sudan. President Mandela emphasizes the importance of peace and stability in Africa to ensure harmonious co-existence and development.

26 Feb. 1997	Adrian Vlok, former apartheid era Minister of Law and Order, applies to the Truth and Reconciliation Commission for amnesty - the first member of the former NP government to indicate willingness to admit to political crimes.
6 Mar. 1997	The Commissioner for Correctional Services, Mr. K. Sithole, discusses the possibility of incarcerating the worst criminals in disused mine shafts. This proposal is widely attacked, but there are repeated calls for the reintroduction of the death penalty. Justice Minister Dullah Omar reiterates that the government will not reconsider this issue.
7 Mar. 1997	Both the DP and the PAC decline President Mandela's offer to join the Government of National Unity. The degree of opposition allowed to them outside the Cabinet was held to be too restrictive.
10 Mar. 1997	South African arms manufacturer Denel announces that it will unveil six new products at a United Arab Emirates weapons exhibition to increase its sales, especially in the Middle East.
14 Mar. 1997	Protests by thousands of farmers around the country against land reform legislation and loss of tax rebates, and against the government's failure to solve the high number of farm murders end peacefully with the handing over of memorandums on the subjects. The South African Agricultural Union supports the protests.
17 Mar. 1997	Allan Boesak appears in a Cape Town court to face nine charges of fraud and twenty one charges of theft involving more than $800,000 - most of it donated to his Foundation for Peace and Justice by Danish and Swedish aid organizations. The case is postponed until 4 August 1997.
17 Mar. 1997	Denel say no deal has been reached over the sale of arms to Syria.
18 Mar. 1997	A security force presence of more than 1500 police, military and municipal officials moves to control the violence that erupts in central Johannesburg during a march to commemorate the 1994 Shell House shootings. Three people are killed and several wounded. Twenty-five people are arrested.
19 Mar. 1997	The Denel group and Aerospatiale of France sign an agreement to broaden co-operation in various fields, notably helicopters and tactical missiles.
22 Mar. 1997	South African mercenaries, hired by the Papua New Guinea government to help crush a separatist rebellion, arrive back in South Africa. Executive Outcomes say that the men should not be seen as mercenaries, but as consultants.
1 Apr. 1997	South Africa's second biggest labour federation is officially launched following the merger of the Federation of South African Labour Unions and the Federation of Organizations Representing Civil Employees. The new Federation of Unions of South Africa (FEDUSA) has 25 affiliated unions and claims a membership of 515,000.
2 Apr. 1997	National Police Commissioner George Fivaz announces plans to restructure the South African Police Service (SAPS) and later seeks an audience with President Mandela to ensure that there is no political interference with the SAPS.

3 Apr. 1997   The National Party's Roelf Meyer meets with Bantu Holomisa to discuss the formation of a new political movement. A joint statement by the NP and the National Consultative Forum (NCF) said the meeting's purpose is to compare notes and explore possible points of agreement.

4 Apr. 1997   India and South Africa make a series of important agreements around a 'strategic partnership' pact. The 11-point 'Red Fort' declaration, signed by President Mandela and the Indian Prime Minister HD Deve Gowda in New Delhi, stresses the need for an equitable balance in the composition of the expanded Security Council and pledges to revitalise the Non-Aligned Movement (NAM).

6 Apr. 1997   The PAC announces that Clarence Makwetu has been suspended as chairman of the party pending the outcome of a disciplinary hearing. Makwetu has been charged with violating the PAC's constitution by dividing the party and creating factions.

7 Apr. 1997   The ANC leader in the Kwazulu Natal midlands Sifiso Nkabinde is expelled from the ANC and named as a 'spy for the enemy' by Jacob Zuma. Nkabinde denies the allegations and claims he is being used to deflect attention from agents in the ANC's senior ranks.

9 Apr. 1997   President Mandela declares that Minister of Safety and Security Sydney Mufamadi and National Police Commissioner George Fivaz are the best team to combat crime and that the misunderstanding between the two men has been resolved.

17 Apr. 1997   The ANC holds a special one-day summit with its alliance partners COSATU (the Congress of South African Trade Unions) and the SACP (the South African Communist Party) and pledges to take the concerns of its allies into account and to ensure consultation on key policies.

17 Apr. 1997   The government presents proposals to improve basic working conditions and encourage greater labour flexibility. Labour Minister Tito Mboweni describes the Basic Conditions of Employment Bill as a revolution of labour law. Among its provisions is that for a maximum working week of forty-five hours.

17 Apr. 1997   President Mandela, present in his capacity as chief of the Temba clan, rather than Head of State, inaugurates the Council of Traditional Leaders. 150 tribal leaders are inducted into Parliament in a colourful ceremony. The kings of Lesotho and of Swaziland also attend.

23 Apr. 1997   AWB (Afrikaner Resistance Movement) leader Eugene TerreBlanche, is convicted of attempted murder and assault in the Magistrates Court in Potchefstroom.

26 Apr. 1997   Winnie Mandela, former wife of President Mandela, is overwhelmingly re-elected as president of the ANC's Women's League by 656 votes to 114 for her deputy Tandi Modise. Her victory reflects the level of grassroots support she continues to enjoy.

2 May 1997   ANC spkesman, Ronnie Mamoepa, reports that an internal party committee has recommended that all members of the ANC's National Executive Committee since 1961, together with senior members of the armed wing

Umkhonto we Sizwe (MK) should apply to the Truth and Reconciliation Commission (TRC) for amnesties.

7 May 1997   F.W. de Klerk disbands the NP task team, headed by Roelf Meyer, which had been charged with planning strategies for an opposition realignment.

7 May 1997   Former Defence Minister Magnus Malan takes full responsibility for secret apartheid raids into neighbouring countries but says they were all state-sanctioned and legal. He expresses regret over the operations that led to the killings of innocent people, but 'unfortunately this is the reality of war'.

10 May 1997   By this deadline for the receipt of applications for amnesty to the Truth and Reconciliation Commission, 370 have been delivered by the ANC. Notable among those who have not applied are former President P.W. Botha, his successor and current NP leader F.W. de Klerk and IFP leader Chief Mangosutho Buthelezi. Almost 8,000 applications have been received in all.

11 May 1997   The chairman of a PAC disciplinary committee announces that former party President Clarence Makwetu has been expelled from the party for three years.

12-13 May 1997 An ANC delegation, led by Deputy President Mbeki, makes the party's second major submission to the Truth and Reconciliation Commission in the form of a defence of the way in which it had conducted its 'just war' against apartheid.

13 May 1997   The Western Cape regional executive of the PAC rejects the move to expel Clarence Makwetu, declares it will not recognise his dismissal, and will continue to call him President until a special national congress is convened to resolve the matter.

14 May 1997   Speaking before the Truth and Reconciliation Committee for a second time, F.W. de Klerk repeats his assertion that murder and torture had never been a part of government policy. He apologises 'once and for all' for apartheid and the hurt caused by its policies.

15 May 1997   At a news conference, the chairman of the Truth and Reconciliation Commission, the Most Rev. Desmond Tutu says it is difficult to believe De Klerk's ignorance of the atrocities committed under apartheid, given the 'avalanche of information' sent to the then President of South Africa detailing murders and torture committed by the security services.

15 May 1997   Later, the NP accuses the Truth and Reconciliation Commission of bias and announces it will no longer co-operate with it.

17 May 1997   Roelf Meyer announces his resignation from the NP.

21 May 1997   Roelf Meyer announces the formation of a new political grouping, with which he plans to challenge both the ANC and the NP at the 1999 elections. He calls on other disaffected NP members to join him in his New Movement Process.

2 June 1997   In a letter to the Truth and Reconciliation Commission, lawyers for the NP demand an unconditional apology from chairman Desmond Tutu and the

resignation of vice-chairman Alex Boraine who had also publicly criticized de Klerk. A deadline of 4 June is set for response, but the date is later extended to 20 June 1997.

3 June 1997	Talks are held between NP leader F.W. de Klerk and his Freedom Front colleague General (retd) Constand Viljoen. It is agreed that an alliance or permanent co-operation agreement between the two parties is not possible, but they will co-operate on an ad hoc basis on particular issues.
4 June 1997	South Africa announces the development of a revolutionary canon - an externally powered gun codenamed EMAK35, designed by Denel at the request of ARMSCOR.
10 June 1997	It is reported that South Africa and Namibia have signed an agreement on increased co-operation between their armed forces. The South African National Defence Force (SANDF) is already assisting Namibia train its officers and Namibia has requested help in protecting its marine resources.
12 June 1997	A deal is proposed between the IFP and the ANC in Kwazulu-Natal aimed at stopping the conflict. The initiative has brought a decrease in violence.
19 June 1997	The Truth and Reconciliation Commission refuse to accede to the NP demands and calls instead for urgent talks in order to resolve difficulties.
20 June 1997	The NP serves legal papers on the Commission giving notice of a High Court application to be heard on 26 August 1997. The application calls on the court to order Tutu to refrain from making further public statements which 'compromise the credibility and impartiality of the Commission'. It also calls for Alex Boraine's dismissal arguing that he should never have been appointed as a commissioner and is abusing his position to continue pursuing old political battles.
24 June 1997	Defence Minister Joe Modise warns that the proposed R1,4 bn. cut in the defence budget could seriously disrupt the defence force's ability to function and to contribute to the fight against crime. The departments of Defence and State Expenditure are negotiating to end the impasse.

SWAZILAND

6 Sept. 1968	Swaziland attains formal independence from Great Britain.
17 Jan. 1969	Signs constitution of the African Civil Aviation Commission.
18 Feb. 1969	Signs Annex A to the International Sugar Agreement.
Apr. 1969	At the African Labour Ministers Conference in Algiers, the Swaziland Prime Minister abstained from voting with ten other delegates, in supporting the people of Palestine, as the conference's agenda did not contain an item concerning Arab-Israeli relations.
17 Apr. 1969	The Swaziland Ambassador to France presents his credentials to President de Gaulle.
9 May 1969	Makes a declaration on the Statute of the International Court of Justice.

2-11 June 1969	The Prime Minister of Swaziland, Prince Dlamini, visits Uganda, Kenya and Tanzania.
11 June 1969	Signs treaty with South Africa amending the extradition agreement of 4 and 5 September 1968.
17 June 1969	Signs multilateral treaty on OAU privileges and immunities.
July 1969	Three Swaziland cabinet ministers attend the Malawi Independence Anniversary celebrations.
10 July 1969	Signs the Universal Postal Convention.
4 Aug. 1969	The Prime Minister arrives for a short visit to Zambia. President Kaunda declares that Zambia and Swaziland both take the line of non-racialism.
18 Aug. 1969	Signs agreement with the United Nations Development Program.
18 Aug. 1969	Signs multilateral agreement on operational assistance between the United Nations, the International Food Organization, UNESCO, the International Civil Aviation Organization and the World Health Organization.
11 Dec. 1969	Signs amendments to the Customs Union Agreement.
Mar. 1970	At the OAU Ministerial Council Meeting, Swaziland among several other delegates, registers its reservation regarding the Middle East crisis.
3 Apr. 1970	Signs continuation agreement with the United States on investment guarantees.
13 May 1970	Signs agreement with Israel on the issue of extradition between both countries.
18 Apr. 1970	Signs visa treaty with Israel.
22 Apr. 1970	The new Swaziland High Commissioner to Kenya takes up his duties in Nairobi.
3 June 1970	Signs general agreement with the United States for special development assistance.
22 June 1970	Ratifies convention (131) concerning minimum wage fixing as adopted by the International Labour Organisation.
1 July 1970	Signs multilateral agreement with the United Nations/FAO World Food Programme, concerning assistance.
7 July 1970	Signs an amendment to Article 26 of the Convention on International Civil Aviation.
18-21 Aug. 1970	At the 17th Session of the OAU Liberation Committee at Addis Ababa, Swaziland among seventeen other states registers reservation on resolutions regarding Rhodesia and Namibia.

Sept. 1970	Prince Dlamini attends the Third Non-Aligned Summit Conference at Lusaka, Zambia.
1 Sept. 1970	Signs multilateral treaty with the Netherlands, Belgium and Luxembourg concerning visas.
11 Nov. 1970	Signs treaty with the United States relating to the Peace Corps.
Jan. 1971	The first Swaziland Ambassador to Ethiopia presents his credentials to Emperor Haile Selassie.
Feb. 1971	The High Commissioner of India to Malawi is also concurrently High Commissioner to Swaziland.
24 Feb. 1971	Signs treaty with Great Britain concerning officers designated by Great Britain to serve in Swaziland.
26 Mar. 1971	Prince Dlamini has talks with South African Prime Minister John Vorster. He mentions the countries' social, cultural and economic links, resulting in a policy of friendship and cooperation towards the Republic.
Apr. 1971	The Department of Foreign Affairs criticizes the South African press for suggesting that the meeting between the two heads of state was requested by Swaziland. Swaziland does not intend establishing diplomatic relations with South Africa.
8-10 May 1971	The Conference of the United National Independence Party at Mulungushi, Zambia, is attended by Swaziland delegates.
July 1971	Since this date the two commoners in Cabinet have lost their portfolios.
July 1971	The Prime Minister pays a state visit to Botswana. A joint communiqué is issued together with President Seretse Khama emphasizing the importance of close consultation between the two countries.
1 July 1971	King Sobhuza II announces new cabinet appointments.
25 Oct. 1971	At the United Nations General Assembly, Swaziland among many other countries, votes against Peking's admission.
Nov. 1971	The High Commissioner of India presents his credentials to King Sobhuza II.
16 Jan. 1972	Swaziland is represented at the Afro-American Conference held at Lusaka, Zambia.
17 Jan. 1972	The High Commissioner in Zambia is accredited to Botswana and Swaziland.
Mar. 1972	The Ambassadors of the United Kingdom, Israel and Switzerland, present their credentials to King Sobhuza II.
15 Mar. 1972	The parliament and the Senate is dissolved by the King in preparation for the general election on 16-17 May.
21 Mar. 1972	The new Swaziland Ambassador to Ethiopia presents his credentials to

Emperor Haile Selassie.

24 Mar. 1972	Signs loan agreement with Denmark.

14 Apr. 1972 — Sixty six candidates are nominated for the eight constituencies in the first Swaziland general election since independence.

16-17 May 1972 — A general election is held.

18 May 1972 — The ruling Imbokodro National Movement wins twenty one of the twenty four seats in the National Assembly in the general elections.

End May 1972 — Addressing a meeting, the King comments that the advent of an official opposition in Parliament is a new development in Swaziland and something which is inherited from the British colonial administration.

June 1972 — One of the three Ngwane National Liberatory Congress Party candidates elected at the General Election is declared a prohibited immigrant on the grounds that he is a South African citizen.

2 June 1972 — Following the general election, King Sobhuza II appoints a new cabinet.

July 1972 — A bill providing four amendments to the Constitution is submitted to the House of Assembly: (a) increased members of parliament from 6 to 10; (b) increased number of senators from 6 to 10; (c) to remove limitations on number of cabinet ministers; (d) to create public post of Director of Prosecution; (e) to change the title of Director of Prisons to Commissioner of Prisons.

1 Sept. 1972 — M.T. Mtetwa is appointed Commissioner of the Royal Swaziland Police. The former Commissioner becomes Adviser to the Police.

Nov. 1972 — A member of the Opposition Ngwane National Liberatory Congress, who won a High Court case annulling a government order declaring him a prohibited immigrant, is rearrested, as the government believes the original banning order is still valid until the Appeal Court gives its ruling in December.

21 Nov. 1972 — Signs agreement with UNICEF concerning their activities in Swaziland.

Dec. 1972 — Charles J.M. Nathan is appointed Puisne Judge to the Swaziland High Court.

Dec. 1972 — Israel is upgrading its relations with Swaziland, Botswana, Lesotho and Rwanda. A permanent Charge d'Affaires will reside in Swaziland. He will also be accredited to Botswana and Lesotho.

4 Dec. 1972 — Israeli embassy opens in Swaziland.

7 Dec. 1972 — A Swazi delegation attends the tenth anniversary of Tanzania's independence.

8 Dec. 1972 — Signs treaty with South Africa on the avoidance of double taxation and the prevention of fiscal evasion.

Jan. 1973 — The Portuguese Ambassador to Swaziland presents his credentials to King Sobhuza II.

Jan. 1973	At the second All-African Games held in Lagos, Swaziland gains one bronze medal.
Feb. 1973	At the twentieth session of the OAU Ministerial Council, Swaziland is elected as Rapporteur.
Mar. 1973	The Portuguese Foreign Minister pays an official visit to Swaziland.
Mar. 1973	King Sobhuza II announces that Swaziland will develop its own army.
12 Apr. 1973	King Sobhuza II repeals Swaziland's Independence Constitution and assumes full judicial legislative and executive power. He gives as his reason for this action the existence of political parties which had created a constitutional crisis. Political parties were not part of the Swazi traditional social structure.
20 Apr. 1973	It is announced that the Royal Proclamation of the previous week is only an interim measure. A constitutional commission is appointed to choose a constitution pertinent to Swazi tradition and international trends. Targeted date is for October or November.
May 1973	Prince Dlamini represents Swaziland at the OAU tenth Assembly of Heads of State to mark its first decade.
May 1973	A number of opposition party members are taken in custody for continuing various political activities in defiance of the King's order of 12 April.
5 June 1973	Signs basic agreement with the World Health Organization for the provision of technical advisory assistance.
12 June 1973	Signs agreement with Denmark on technical cooperation.
July 1973	A number of people detained for sixty days without trial on the Constitution's suspension, are freed.
18 July 1973	The new Swaziland High Commissioner to Kenya presents his credentials to President Kenyatta.
26 July 1973	Signs agreement with Malawi on air services.
Sept. 1973	On the fifth anniversary of Swaziland's independence, King Sobhuza II announces the appointment of a Royal Constitutional Commission to draw up a new constitution.
5-9 Sept. 1973	Mr. Khumalo, Deputy Premier, represents Swaziland at the Fourth Non-Aligned Summit Conference in Algiers.
13 Oct. 1973	Signs the International Sugar Convention.
Nov. 1973	At the eighth OAU Extraordinary Session of the Ministerial Council in Addis Ababa, Swaziland in conjunction with Lesotho and Botswana, make reservations about the paragraph calling for an oil embargo against South Africa.
Nov. 1973	Swaziland and Egypt decide to establish diplomatic relations at ambassadorial level.

12 Nov. 1973	The first ever summit between the Presidents/Prime Ministers of Botswana, Lesotho, and of Swaziland, is held in Gaborone, Botswana in a cordial and friendly atmosphere.
1 Jan. 1974	Signs additional WHO regulations.
31 Jan. 1974	Signs multilateral treaty relating amending the Convention on International Aviation.
20 Feb. 1974	The new Swaziland High Commissioner of Swaziland presents his credentials to President Nyerere of Tanzania.
5 Mar. 1974	Mr. Kunene of Swaziland presents his credentials to Emperor Haile Selassie of Ethiopia.
12 Mar. 1974	The leader of the opposition Ngwane National Liberatory Congress Party, is detained for criticising the government.
20 Mar. 1974	Signs agreement with South Africa on issue of notes and coin.
18 Apr. 1974	The Swaziland High Commissioner to Zambia presents his credentials to President Kaunda.
5 July 1974	Signs multilateral agreement on insured letters and postal parcels, as well as the Universal Postal Convention.
Sept. 1974	The High Commissioner of Kenya presents his credentials to King Sobhuza II.
6 Sept. 1974	The government introduces its own bank notes and coins under an agreement with the South African government. The new currency Emalangene will remain in the Rand monetary area.
6 Sept. 1974	At the sixth independence anniversary celebration, King Sobhuza announces the appointment of a constitutional committee to draft the new constitution as the Westminster-style constitution was nullified eighteen months ago.
5 Dec. 1974	Signs multilateral monetary agreement with South Africa and Lesotho.
9 Dec. 1974	Signs development credit agreement with the International Development Association on education projects.
9 Dec. 1974	Signs loan agreement with International Bank for Reconstruction and Development on water supply and sewerage.
24 Jan. 1975	A Royal Commission presents King Sobhuza II with a new constitution which may result in the country's first parliament and senate. Independent judiciary of the Executive and the powers of the king are recommended. The king is requested to provide for a special Constitutional Committee.
12 Feb. 1975	Signs treaty with the Netherlands on the application of the convention between Great Britain, Northern Ireland and Netherlands on legal proceedings in civil and commercial matters.
15 May 1975	Signs loan agreement with the International Bank for Reconstruction and

	Development on the Second Highway Project.
26 May 1975	The Swazi Ambassador presents his credentials to President Sadat of Egypt.
28 May 1975	Signs agreement with Denmark on the Francistown-Nata Road Project.
8 July 1975	Signs agreement with the International Atomic Energy Agency on safeguards in connection with the treaty on the non-proliferation of nuclear weapons.
6 Aug. 1975	Signs agreement with Great Britain on public officers' pensions.
Sept. 1975	Swaziland and Mozambique establish diplomatic relations at ambassadorial level.
Sept. 1975	The leader of the opposition is detained without a formal charge.
Sept. 1975	King Sobhuza announces that the Prime Minister is retiring because of ill health. He will be assigned various other duties at an appropriate time.
27 Oct. 1975	Signs amendments to Customs Union Agreement of 11 December 1969.
Jan. 1976	The new University of Botswana and Swaziland draw up a plan to accommodate all students as Lesotho withdrew from the original university triumvirate.
1 Jan. 1976	Signs the constitution of the Universal Postal Union.
Feb. 1976	Lesotho and Swaziland establish diplomatic relations.
13 Feb. 1976	Signs loan agreement with Danish government.
17 Mar. 1976	King Sobhuza II appoints Colonel Maphevu Dlamini, Defence Force Colonel-in-Chief, as Prime Minister.
7 May 1976	Signs agreement with the Universal Postal Union on insured letters and postal parcels.
June 1976	The Swaziland government demands that South Africa return two members of the African National Congress abducted by South African policemen on Swazi soil.
June 1976	A Basotho lecturer in statistics on the Swaziland campus, is deported 'for security reasons'.
3 June 1976	Signs agreement with Great Britain concerning officers designated by the British government in the service of specified organizations and institutions in Swaziland.
8 June 1976	Signs extension to the 1971 Overseas Service Agreement (Swaziland).
Mar. 1977	The longest reigning monarch, King Sobhuza II, abolishes the country's parliamentary system and replaces it with a structure based on tradition.
Apr. 1977	Swaziland expands its army into a fully fledged defence force incorporating an air force and a navy. All Swazis over eighteen years will be liable for

military training.

28 Apr. 1977	Signs agreement with the Federal Republic of Germany on financial assistance.
12 May 1977	Signs a guarantee agreement with the IBRD concerning the National Industrial Development Corporation of Swaziland project.
June 1977	Prince Dumisa Dlamini, a member of the royal family, is detained under the country's sixty-day detention proclamation.
6 June 1977	The United States contributes $2m towards the seven-year project to expand Swaziland's medical services.
21 June 1977	Ratifies convention (no. 144) concerning tripartite consultations to promote the implementation of international labour standards as adopted by the International Labour Organisation.
26 June 1977	Swaziland radio refuses to replace the Addis-Ababa based radio station Voice of the Gospel with South African programmes of the Council of Churches because of their political overtones.
Aug. 1977	An independent commercial television station is due to start transmission in February 1978. Capital cost is financed by the UK-based Electronic Rentals Group.
Oct. 1977	The recent disturbances created by the students, challenges for the first time the authority of the king. There is general discontent.
14 Oct. 1977	Students demonstrate in Mbabane in support of their teachers, who are in dispute with the government over pay and union representation.
28 Oct. 1977	Signs assistance agreement with UN Development Programme.
9 Nov. 1977	The Swaziland government refuses to allow the country to be used as a base for guerrilla attacks against South Africa.
21 Dec. 1977	Signs International Sugar Agreement.
23 Dec. 1977	Signs multilateral treaty on the protocol additional to the Convention on Victims of Armed Conflict.
Jan. 1978	King Sobhusa announces the preparations for the first elections since the constitution was suspended in 1973. He also announces that the political structure under which members will be elected differ greatly from the Westminster electoral system.
25 Jan. 1978	Acceptance of the constitution of UNESCO.
Feb. 1978	The new constitution is completed and is due for presentation.
Feb. 1978	The Swaziland Television Broadcasting Corporation begins operating. Viewers are estimated currently at 10,000 but are expected to grow by 3,000 or 4,000 monthly.

9 Feb. 1978	The Leader of Swaziland's banned opposition party is arrested and taken to the country's maximum security prison, for refusing to surrender his passport to the authorities.
Apr. 1978	Fifty members of the outlawed South African black nationalist organisation, the Pan African Congress, are expelled from Swaziland for violating international refugee and local laws. They are accused of attempting to establish guerrilla training camps.
26 Apr. 1978	Ratifies convention (98) concerning the application of the principles of the right to organize and bargain collectively, adopted by the International Labour Organisation.
26 Apr. 1978	Ratifies convention (no. 87) concerning freedom of association and protection of the right to organize, adopted by the International Labour Organisation.
26 Apr. 1978	Ratifies convention (no. 14) concerning the appplication of weekly rest in industrial undertakings adopted by the International Labour Organisation.
26 Apr. 1978	Ratifies convention (no. 86) concerning the maximum length of contracts of employment of indigenous workers adopted by the International Labour Organisation.
29 Apr. 1978	Ratifies convention (no. 50) concerning the regulation of certain special systems of recruiting workers, adopted by the International Labour Organisation.
June 1978	The government demands a full explanation from South Africa on the death, after only six days in a prison cell, of an Education Department official.
5 July 1978	Three cabinet ministers are removed from office. Those dismissed are the Foreign Minister, who gave an anti-South African speech at the UN; the Minister for Works, Power and Communications because of a deal with a South African motor company; and the Minister for Local Administration for spending $200,000 on a festival which did not materialize.
17 July 1978	Succession by Swaziland on convention abolishing the requirement of legalization for foreign public documents.
Aug. 1978	A new opposition party, the Swazi Liberation Movement, distributes leaflets in the country's main industrial area calling for the overthrow of the government.
31 Aug. 1978	The police seize an arms cache of Communist origin, in Manzini. The Police Commissioner suspects that the find is connected with the outlawed ANC of South Africa.
27 Sept. 1978	Signs loan agreement with International Bank for Reconstruction and Development on the Third Highway Project.
27 Oct. 1978	The first elections are held since the suspension of the Constitution.
4 Nov. 1978	The Swaziland Football Association announces its withdrawal from the International Football Federation, in order to continue sporting links with

South Africa.

Jan. 1979	King Sobhuza appoints four white Swazis to the Assembly and Senate.
Jan. 1979	The Prime Minister pays a state visit to Israel to strengthen their cooperation in economic projects.
Feb. 1979	King Sobhuza reshuffles the cabinet.
5 Apr. 1979	Signs agreement with Spain on diplomatic relations.
26 July 1979	Signs agreement with Southern African Regional Tourism Council.
Oct. 1979	King Sobhusa appoints Prince Mandabala Dlamini as Prime Minister after the death of Maphevu Dlamini.
1 May 1980	Signs agreement with South Africa in respect of a servitude to be granted for the inundation of 3800 acres of land by the Pongolapoort Dam.
Dec. 1981	Stanley Masabela, an ANC activist, is held in police custody, as he did not fulfill the requirement stipulated by the refugee control order.
17 Feb. 1982	Signs security agreement with South Africa.
Aug. 1982	King Sobhusa dies and Queen Mother Dzeliwe becomes regent.
Jan. 1983	Swaziland succumbs to South African pressure and arrests twenty-five ANC members.
12 Mar. 1983	Swaziland is represented by its Prime Minister at the seventh summit conference of the ninety-seven non-aligned nations in New Delhi.
21 Mar. 1983	The Prime Minister, Prince Dlamini is dismissed but refuses to accept it. This is the result of the power struggle between traditionalists and modernists. In the meantime the Kingdom is ruled by the Queen Regent.
24 Mar. 1983	Prince Bhekimpi Dlamini is appointed successor to the dismissed Prime Minister who takes refuge with his family in South Africa.
8-12 June 1983	Swaziland is represented by its Prime Minister at the OAU nineteenth summit conference in Addis Ababa at which Swaziland's Head of State becomes one of the eight Vice-Chairpersons.
July 1983	The dissolution of Parliament on 18 August is announced in preparation for the general election in October.
26 Aug. 1983	A fifteen-year old, Prince Makhosetive, who is at a public school in England, is named as the new king. The choice is not welcomed by all members of the royal family. A dispute ensues from the deposition of Queen Dzeliwe. A judicial clash is avoided when the court refuses to give judgment on the deposition of the Queen Regent. The Prime Minister announces 28 October as the date of the elections.
Sept. 1983	The feud between the royal princes over the appointment of the Queen Regent, ends with the removal from the Supreme Council of State Prince

Ghubeni.

Sept. 1983	Swaziland deports most ANC members and imposes restrictions on those who remain.
13 Sept. 1983	The future king, wearing traditional attire, is formally presented to the Swazi nation by Prince Sozisa. He also announces that Princess Ntombi will hold the regency until her son is enthroned at the age of twenty-one, in five years time.
16 Sept. 1983	Signs an agreement regarding technical and financial assistance with South Africa for the construction of a railway link.
20 Oct. 1983	The government releases details of a new Sedition and Subversive Activities Bill.
Dec. 1983	An alleged coup to depose the Queen Regent Ntombi involves eleven people, including members of the royal family.
June 1984	Dr. Nxumalo, who is regarded as one of the ablest Swazi politicians, is dismissed from his ministerial post after relevations concerning customs duty frauds, implicating highly-placed Swazis.
25 Oct. 1984	Signs loan agreement with the International Fund for Agricultural Development for smallholder credit and marketing project.
27 Dec. 1984	Signs agreement with South Africa regarding exchange of trade representatives.
17 Mar. 1985	The Prime Minister informs a meeting that four officials plotted to kill him and other high ranking members of Swaziland's ruling supreme council, the Liqoqo. They face high treason charges and are detained.
Apr. 1985	Four high-ranking police and former army officers are charged with sedition and subversion which counts as high treason and carries a possible death penalty.
1 June 1985	Signs agreement with South Africa regarding the amendment of Article two of the Agreement on the Issue of Notes and Coin.
10 Sept. 1985	Signs loan agreement with the International Bank for Reconstruction and Development for a cyclone rehabilitation project.
Oct. 1985	A turning point in the struggle for power is the dismissal of Prince Mfanasibili and Dr Msibi.
Nov. 1985	The police are investigating a plot to overthrow the government. The dissidents want to restore Council members and the Commissioner of Police dismissed by the Queen Regent in October, in a purge of alleged anti-government elements.
Dec. 1985	Dr Nxumalo and four other prisoners are pardoned by Queen Regent Ntombi.
20 Dec. 1985	South Africa warns Swaziland, as a neighbouring country, of the heavy price

it will pay if it does not stop aiding the ANC.

31 Dec. 1985	Five prominent Swazis who had been in prison many months without trial, are pardoned by the Queen Regent.
Feb. 1986	Prince Mfanasibili and Majiji Simelane are arrested on charges of attempting to subvert justice.
18 Apr. 1986	Signs bilateral monetary agreement with South Africa.
18 Apr. 1986	Signs trilateral agreement amending monetary agreement between South Africa, Swaziland and Lesotho.
25 Apr. 1986	Crown Prince Makhosetine is crowned as the new King Mswati III.
27 May 1986	King Mswati dissolves the Liqoqo.
28 May 1986	The High Court passes prison sentences on Prince Mfanasibili Dlamini.
9 July 1986	King Mswati reorganizes the cabinet.
19 Aug. 1986	South African security forces raid various targets in Mbabane, aimed at the banned ANC members in Swaziland.
26 Aug. 1986	The South African Foreign Minister, 'Pik' Botha, on a visit to Swaziland, delivers a message from President Botha that there will be no change in South Africa's friendship with Swaziland.
6 Oct. 1986	King Mswati replaces Prime Minister Bhekimpi and appoints Sotsha Dlamini in his place.
12 Dec. 1986	A major South African raid on ANC targets in Swaziland.
4 Jan. 1987	The Swazi government takes firmer action against the ANC. Four members are arrested in Mbabane and a quantity of arms seized from their premises.
Feb. 1987	The UN High Commissioner for Refugees maintains that the refugee problem in Swaziland, arising from the war in Mozambique, is reaching crisis proportions.
11 Feb. 1987	Swaziland deports to Zambia six ANC members, part of a group of twenty, for possessing arms in Swaziland.
May 1987	Twelve prominent officials are charged with sedition and treason.
9 July 1987	A cabinet reshuffle is announced.
28 Oct. 1987	Parliament is dissolved and elections were called for 5 November, one year before the expiry of the indirectly elected government's mandate.
5 Nov. 1987	Elections to the Libandla take place.
12 Mar. 1988	A special treason court, sitting since November, jails seven, including a prince and a former prime minister, to fifteen years each. The Chief Justice

states that the sentence concerns the removal of the head of state in a coup.

31 Mar. 1988	There are 26,700 refugees in Swaziland comprising 6,900 registered South Africans, 7,800 registered Mozambicans and an estimated 12,000 spontaneously settled Mozambicans.
July 1988	Eight political detainees including six members of the royal family are released from detention. The commission of inquiry which investigated the detention closed the case.
12 July 1988	Ten high treason trial prisoners and former top personalities are set free, with the exception of Prince Mfanasibili, who is to serve another six years imprisonment.
16 Aug. 1988	In a blockade that began at dawn, the police arrest 198 people in a massive security operation, in an attempt to stop the prevailing crime wave.
Sept. 1988	The Pope pays a brief visit to Swaziland where he warns the crowd against the dangers of polygamy, marital infidelity and promiscuity. He also says that strife and racial tension must be solved by peaceful dialogue.
2 Nov. 1988	King Mswati III promises to review the controversial land and property decree issued on 30 September.
28 Mar. 1989	Sources in Mbabane report that six people with trade union links have been arrested for the possession of illegal political pamphlets.
1 Apr. 1989	Trilateral agreement to amend the Monetary Agreement signed with South Africa and Lesotho.
19 Apr. 1989	Swazi security forces are put on full alert until 19 April, King Mswati's 21st birthday, when he assumes full executive power. The alert was ordered in connection with the escape and recapture of a Mozambican prisoner who admitted to a plot to overthrow the government contrived by another prisoner, a member of the Swazi royal family.
12 July 1989	King Mswati removes the Prime Minister as he is dissatisfied with his performance. The new Prime Minister is experienced in labour relations.
Oct. 1989	South Africa and Swaziland agree to adjust the borders between them. This means that the KaNgwane homeland and the district of Ingwavuma are reincorporated into Swaziland.
10 Oct. 1989	South African soldiers cross into Swaziland territory pursuing an illegal emigrant to South Africa. The Swazi Prime Minister expresses strong condemnation on this undue act of aggression.
8 Nov. 1989	Angola and Swaziland establish diplomatic relations.
4 Sept. 1990	Signs multilateral memorandum of understanding on road transportation in the Common Customs Area.
Oct. 1990	The king suffers a serious political setback with the acquittal on treason charges of all the accused dissidents. He responds by ordering a second detention and a crackdown on student opposition.

Nov. 1990	King Mswati III, responding to pressure, dismisses the most liberal member of his government, the Minister of Justice.
3 Sept. 1991	The deposed King of Lesotho, Moshoeshoe II, arrives expecting to receive political asylum.
12 Oct. 1991	It is announced that King Mswati III has approved the creation of five new government ministries which will be effected from 14 October, in conjunction with fifteen new ministerial appointments.
25 Feb. 1992	The opposition party, the People's United Democratic Movement (PUDEMO), ignores the ban on political associations and proclaims itself `legal'.
Mar. 1992	In a surprise move, King Mswati appoints a member of the opposition party PUDEMO, to an important committee to reform the country's electoral system.
17 Aug. 1992	Signs multilateral treaty with the Southern African Development Community (SADC).
9 Oct. 1992	King Mswati III dissolves parliament and will rule by decree until new elections are held. The new government will oversee the continuation of the monarchy, a charter of rights and liberties and the introduction of multipartyism. A new election scheme is envisaged to satisfy the wishes of a vocal urban class and the traditional chiefs. A voters' register will be compiled.
3 June 1993	The Swazi Minister of Justice signed 3 different agreements with South Africa. Areas covered by the agreements are: secondment of South African judges and magistrates and training facilities for government officials.
19 Aug. 1993	Swaziland and Mozambique sign an agreement to repatriate Mozambican refugees under the patronage of the United Nations High Commissioner for Refugees.
25 Sept. 1993	Free elections are held on, which puts an end to twenty years of state of emergency. The voters will choose from 2,094 candidates for the fifty-five districts.
11 Oct. 1993	One of the surprise results of the election is Prime Minister Dlamini's loss of position. Under the new constitution, the king will announce the list of nominees to add to those elected by the voters.
4 Nov. 1993	King Mswati appoints a new Prime Minister, Prince Jameson Dlamini. He is a conservative but his cabinet is dominated by strong modernists.
Dec. 1993	A large number of Swazi soldiers are deployed on the Swaziland-Mozambique border following clashes between soldiers of the two countries.
Jan. 1994	Swaziland Defence Force violates the national territory of Mocambique. Mocambique condemns the action and the two countries discuss patrolling and protecting common borders.
25 Feb. 1994	South Africa opens an embassy in Mbabane.

2 Oct. 1994	After electing their first democratic parliament by secret ballot, Swaziland holds a second round of elections with voters choosing district secretaries for fifty-five districts. The district secretaries are expected to coordinate development in their areas and provide a link between Members of Parliament.
Jan. 1995	Bombs are launched on officials' property, but no-one takes responsibility. The government takes seriously the threats of a small opposition party demanding the unbanning of political parties. Swaziland is the only country in southern Africa where political parties are banned.
18 Jan. 1995	At a meeting of the joint Mozambique-Swaziland Security Sub-Commission, Swaziland admits that its forces have violated the Mozambican border and kidnapped and tortured two Mozambican citizens.
Mar. 1995	A spate of arson attacks on various public buildings culminates in a direct attack on the parliament building adjoining the royal kraal. Due to these events the pressure grows for democratic change.
24 Mar. 1995	King Mswati dismisses the Ministers of Finance, Broadcasting, Information and Tourism as they are accused of possessing stolen cars.
Aug. 1995	The most substantial agreement between King Mswati and President Mandela, is the co-operation in thwarting arms smugglers.
15 Aug. 1995	The Senate passes a motion rallying behind the king's statement that the Swazis do not want multiparty politics. The acting Prime Minister promises that the kingdom will get a new democratic constitution.
Oct. 1995	Former Minister of Education, Senator Arthur Khosa, is the new Minister of Foreign Affairs.
20 Jan. 1996	An industrial relations act is passed which imposes draconian restrictions on trade union activities.
25 Jan. 1996	Trade unions refuse to negotiate an end to their crippling week-long strike until the state of emergency banning political parties, public gatherings and free speech is lifted. The unions want to transform the autocratic monarchy into a modern representative democracy modelled on that of South Africa. They also want to revoke restrictions placed on trade union activities.
29 Jan. 1996	The strike called by trade unions is suspended, pending talks with the government.
16 Feb. 1996	The planned strike, which was to be resumed on 19 February has been averted after a mass meeting of the Swaziland Federation of Trade Unions decided to give negotiations with both government and employers a chance. King Mswati, in his speech at the opening of Parliament stated that labour issues were separate from wider political issues. He promised that attention will be paid to the settling of chiefs' boundaries.
Mar. 1996	PUDEMO, Swaziland's largest opposition party, calls for an interim government, representing all interest groups. However, King Mswati appears increasingly on the defensive after meeting regional Heads of State Mandela, Mugabe and Masire on the country's constitutional crisis.

3 Feb. 1997 A three-week strike commences, crippling the country's transportation sector and its sugar and timber industries. This pro-democracy action is coordinated by the Swaziland Federation of Trade Unions, and includes demands on an amendment to the Constitution, an end to the absolute monarchy and the establishment of a multi-party system.

12 Feb. 1997 Four union leaders are arrested, including the General Secretary of SFTU Jani Sithole. They are charged with intimidation.

mid Feb. 1997 International trade union leaders threaten to blockade the country unless King Mswati releases four jailed Swazi trade union leaders and commences government reforms.

mid Mar. 1997 It is reported that King Mswati is reviewing the ban on political parties and unauthorized political gatherings. This is regarded as reaction to the national strike. Mswati's statement that Swazis should decide through individual submissions to the Review Commission whether the ban should be lifted, is regarded by the nation as a cover for the status quo.

May 1997 The Swaziland Federation of Trade Unions, suspended due to failure of delivering certain documents to the Minister for Enterprise and Employment, have the suspension lifted after delivering the end-of-year report and financial statements.

TANZANIA

9 Dec. 1961 Tanganyika becomes independent at midnight 8-9 December.

9 Dec. 1961 Julius Nyerere appointed Prime Minister.

14 Dec. 1961 Tanganyika becomes 104th member of the United Nations.

18 Dec. 1961 The Foster-Sutton Commission of Inquiry report into Zanzibar election riots released.

29 Dec. 1961 The Colonial Office announces that the Sultan of Zanzibar will visit London in March 1962 for talks on the Kenya Coastal Strip.

1962 Britain promises Zanzibar financial assistance, including repayment of Zanzibari loan to Britain of 200,000 Pounds Sterling under the 1895 Agreement.

1962 Swahili to be used as official language in the National Assembly of Tanganyika.

18 Jan. 1962 Zanzibar curfew restrictions that were imposed due to the June 1961 election riots, lifted.

19 Jan. 1962 The Zanzibar Nationalist Party (ZNP) opposes the integration of the Coastal Strip in to Kenya.

22 Jan. 1962 Prime Minister Nyerere resigns to pay more attention to building the Tanganyika African National Union (TANU) and Mr R Kawawa appointed Prime Minister.

Feb. 1962	Freehold tenure to be ended in Tanganyika.

2-10 Feb.1962   Tanganyika attends the Fourth Conference of the Pan-African Freedom Movement of East and Central Africa (PAFMECSA) in Addis Ababa.

Apr. 1962   Sir George Mooring, the British Resident in Zanzibar, announces that the government will stay in office until 1964 unless agreement is reached between the parties on an early election.

5 Apr. 1962   Conference held in London between the Secretary of State (R. Maudling), the Sultan of Zanzibar and Zanzibari representatives over independence for Zanzibar, ends in failure. Coalition government and the opposition Afro-Shirazi calls for fresh elections before any constitutional advances are made.

May 1962   Sheikh Abdul R.M. Babu, General Secretary of the Zanzibar Nationalist Party (and other people) arrested under the Emergency Regulations for arson, and is sentenced to fifteen months imprisonment.

June 1962   The right to strike in Tanganyika ends with provision made for compulsory arbitration.

July 1962   The United Nations Committee on Colonialism investigating Zanzibar affairs, is told by Sheikh Ali Muhsin, leader of the Zanzibar Nationalist Party, that new elections will lead to fresh disturbances and the Committee adopts a Soviet sponsored appeal to Britain to end the emergency and release political prisoners.

Aug. 1962   Mr. Tumbo resigns as High Commissioner to London to become leader of the People's Democratic Party.

10 Sept. 1962   Tanganyika should remain a Commonwealth member after it becomes a Republic, the Commonwealth Prime Ministers agree.

Sept. 1962   Prime Minister R Kawawa introduces the Preventive Detention Bill, saying that 'democracy must defend itself'.

10-19 Sept.1962   Tanganyika attends the Commonwealth Prime Ministers meeting in London.

Nov. 1962   In the presidential election held in November, J. Nyerere obtains 1,123,553 votes against 21,279 for Mr. Mtemvu, leader of the African National Congress.

28 Nov. 1962   Mr. Nyerere, speaking in the National Assembly, calls for an ethic for the nation which will make oppressive action by the President impossible, as 'not Tanganyikan'.

Dec. 1962   State of Emergency in Zanzibar lifted, but parties reach no common agreement.

9 Dec. 1962   Constitutional proposals to create a republican system of government approved by the Tanganyika National Assembly.

9 Dec. 1962   Julius Nyerere appointed President and Mr. R. Kawawa, Vice-President, and the latter continues to carry out functions of Prime Minister.

1963	Tanganyika African National Union (TANU) opens membership to non-Africans.
Jan. 1963	Political meetings re-allowed in Zanzibar since June 1961.
Jan. 1963	President Nyerere states at a TANU conference that Tanganyika should become a statutory single party state.
Jan. 1963	Relations between the government and trade unions further strained after unofficial strikes by sisal plantation workers lead to the restriction of Victor Mkello, President of the Tanganyika Federation of Labour (TFL), and Mr. Sheshe Amiri, acting secretary of the Plantation Worker's Union, to a settlement on the Northern Rhodesian border.
Mar. 1963	Oscar Kambona appointed Minister of External Affairs and other changes made to Tanganyika's government.
Apr. 1963	Tanganyika's African National Congress loses its registration and becomes an illegal organization.
May 1963	A number of people deported, the most notable being a South African, Frene Ginwala, editor of the monthly Spearhead. In its February issue she criticized the idea of a one-party state.
June 1963	An Arusha Hotel closed down after its guests failed to stand when President Sekou Toure of Guinea passed through its lounge.
ʹJune 1963	Reuters News Agency representative, Arthur Maimane, expelled for reporting that differences existed in the Liberation Committee set up in Dar-es-Salaam by the Addis Ababa Conference.
24 June 1963	Zanzibar attains internal self-government.
July 1963	President Nyerere appeals to politicians and civil servants to fight against pomposity. It is speculated that this action was taken after the Arusha hotel incident.
1 July 1963	The Sultan of Zanzibar dies and is succeeded by Prince Jamshid.
8-11 July 1963	Zanzibar elections held and Afro-Shiraz Party gets majority vote, but loses the election to a coalition between the Zanzibar Nationalist Party and the Zanzibar and Pemba People's Party.
Sept.-Oct. 1963	Country troubled by Muslim restiveness, leading to deporation of a Muslim leader to Kenya in September and the rustication of another two from Dar-es-Salaam in October.
Oct. 1963	Victor Mkello, President of the Tanganyika Federation of Labour (TFL), rejects government proposal that the TFL should become part of the Ministry of Labour.
Nov. 1963	Muslim attempts to register new organization have little success.
10 Dec. 1963	Zanzibar becomes an independent state within the Commonwealth.

22 Apr. 1964	Articles of the Union between Tanganyika and Zanzibar are signed, thus creating one sovereign state. An interim period will be followed by the ratification of the Articles, the formation of a Constituent Assembly and the adoption of a Constitution. The state is known as the United Republic of Tanganyika and Zanzibar. Dr Julius Nyerere is President and Sheik Karume and Mr Kawawa as Vice-Presidents.
26 Apr. 1964	The Articles of Union are ratified.
27 Apr. 1964	President Nyerere announces his Cabinet.
5 May 1964	Diplomatic relations are to be established with Romania at an embassy level.
6 May 1964	The United Republic of Tanganyika and Zanzibar becomes a single member of the United Nations.
7 May 1964	It is announced that diplomatic relations between East Germany and Zanzibar will continue with the United Republic of Tanganyika and Zanzibar.
11 May 1964	Eight Zanzibaris are included as members of the National Assembly.
12 May 1964	Accedes to the multilateral agreement on the status of refugees.
27 May 1964	Diplomatic relations policy is outlined by Foreign Minister Kambona and announces that any government which has established diplomatic missions, both in Tanganyika and Zanzibar, prior to 26 April, be permitted to set up consulates in Zanzibar. A small department of the Foreign Affairs Ministry will be established in Zanzibar.
29 May 1964	The first recruits to the army, members of the Zanzibar Youth League, start military training in Dar-es-Salaam.
29 May 1964	Swedish Ambassador, Oho Rathsman, presents his credentials to President Nyerere.
30 May 1964	Andrew Tibandebage is appointed Ambassador to Congo (Leopoldville).
30 May 1964	Daniel Mfinanga becomes Ambassador to the Federal Republic of Germany.
30 May 1964	Philemon Muro becomes the Republic's Ambassador to Sweden.
30 May 1964	Salim Ahmed Salim is appointed Ambassador to the United Arab Republic.
30 May 1964	Sheik Othman Shariff becomes Ambassador to the United States.
June 1964	Relations between students in Zanzibar and China are the focus of a visit by a Chinese delegation. They visit Zanzibar at the invitation of the Afro-Shirazai Youth League.
June 1964	R.W.D. Fowler is appointed British High Commissioner.
1 June 1964	Ethiopia's ambassador, Ato Mekasha, presents his credentials.

8 June 1964	Vice-President Karume calls on all ex-servicemen to arm themselves in defence of the country.
10 June 1964	The government decides to establish an aviation school as part of the armed forces.
15 June 1964	Thirty students arrive in Djakarta on scholarships resulting from an agreement signed between Zanzibar and Indonesia earlier in the year.
16 June 1964	Leopold van Ufford of the Netherlands presents his ambassadorial credentials.
17 June 1964	Emperor Haile Selassie's state visit to the United Republic takes place. He has wide-ranging discussions with President Nyerere.
22 June 1964	Signs declaration with the ILO assuring obligations of the abolition of forced labour (no. 105); age for admission to employment at sea (no. 7); industrial employment (no. 5); trimmers of stokers (no. 15); compulsory medical examination of young persons employed at sea (no. 16); employment of women in underground mines (no. 45); employment service (no. 88); forced or compulsory labour (no. 29); holidays with pay for those in agriculture (no. 101). With relation to indigenous workers, the following apply: contracts of employment (no. 64); maximum length of contracts of employment (no. 86); penal sanctions for breaches of contracts of employment (no. 65). Other conventions include industrial employment (no. 59); labour inspection in industry and commerce (no. 81); migration for employment (no. 97); minimum age for employment at sea (no. 58); minimum wage-fixing machinery (no. 26); protection against accidents in loading and unloading ships (no. 32); protection of wages (no. 95); right to organize and to bargain collectively (no. 98); right of association of agricultural workers (no. 11); seafarers' national identity documents (no. 108); special systems of recruiting workers (no. 50); statistics of wages and hours of work in the mining industries and in agriculture (no. 63). Workmen's compensation as relating to accidents (no. 17); agriculture (no. 12); equality of treatment for national and foreign workers for accidents (no. 19).
22 June 1964	Accedes to multilateral agreement on customs facilities for Touring and Protocol relating to importation of tourist publicity documents and material.
23 June 1964	Cuban Ambassador, Rivalta Perez, presents his credentials to President Nyerere.
25 June 1964	The army's affiliation with TANU is recognized. Within the army, each company leader becomes a chairman of TANU, and the army is represented in the TANU National Executive.
25 June 1964	The United Republic government notifies all foreign missions in Zanzibar that from 30 June they will have consular status.
28 June 1964	Ethiopia is to provide military assistance, in the form of an air force squadron, in terms of an agreement signed in Addis Ababa.
30 June 1964	Second Vice-President, Kawa, outlines Tanzania's defence policy. This will focus on internal security. The basic qualification for entrance to the army

is membership of either TANU or the Afro-Shirazi Party.

July 1964	Ethiopia provides training assistance for the air force.
July 1964	The Polish government offers scholarships to study in tertiary institutions for those single Tanganyika citizens possessing appropriate High School certificates.
July 1964	President Nyerere addresses the OAU's first session of the Assembly of Heads of State and Government in Cairo. He stresses the need to free the Portuguese colonies from the colonial yoke.
1 July 1964	A bill extending the term of the Tanganyikan Parliament for a further year is passed by the National Assembly. This will enable the promulgation of the Constitution to take place.
2 July 1964	Nyerere Polneau becomes the Ivory Coast's first Ambassador to the Republic.
3 July 1964	Accedes to the multilateral treaty on limiting the manufacture and regulating the distribution of narcotic drugs.
30 July 1964	It is announced that West German experts will train a transport and communications squadron.
Aug. 1964	President Nyerere protests against Western criticism of his reception of the Chinese army instructors.
3 Aug. 1964	Discussions are held with the United Arab Republic to provide experts and teachers in various technical fields.
4 Aug. 1964	Treaty maintaining force in respect of Tanganyika of Convention of 29 November 1932 between Denmark and Great Britain regarding legal proceedings in civil and commercial matters; and the Convention of 27 March 1950 between Denmark and Great Britain for the avoidance of double taxation regarding taxes on income.
6 Aug. 1964	Immigration procedure is clarified and the Department of External Affairs of Zanzibar is confined to processing the formalities for the diplomatic corps.
13 Aug. 1964	The first Vice-President states that the East German embassy in Zanzibar will retain its status as an embassy, as there is no embassy in Dar-es-Salaam.
22 Aug. 1964	Succedes to the IBRD.
24 Aug. 1964	Ministerial changes include the appointment of Ali Sultan Issa as Minister Without Portfolio in the Ministry of Agriculture; the Ministry of Finance nd Development changes its name to Ministry of Finance under A.K. Twala; and a new Ministry of Development, Commerce and Planning is established under Abdulrahman Babu.
31 Aug. 1964	President Nyerere protests against criticism of the Republic's acceptance of Chinese military aid.

2 Sept. 1964	Signs a treaty with Great Britain relating to cereals production and trade policies.
2 Sept. 1964	Weapons presented by China are unloaded from a Chinese ship. They are part of a $10 million aid agreement.
7 Sept. 1964	Bulgarian doctors to work in Tanganiyka once an agreement is signed between the two countries.
8 Sept. 1964	A bill is passed in the National Assembly enabling the President to dispense with certain qualifications relating to High Court Judges, and to increase the number of judges from seven to eight.
16 Sept. 1964	Hasan Moyo becomes Minister of Agriculture and Land Distribution. He changes portfolios with Saleh Akida who takes over the Ministry for Works, Communications and Power.
25 Sept. 1964	Members of the Nigerian army, who took over peace-keeping operations from the British, start leaving the country.
Oct. 1964	The British Council donates 20,000 Pounds Sterling for assistance towards a new central library in Dar-es-Salaam.
1 Oct. 1964	A volunteer reserve force is formed to meet special emergencies. Volunteers are posted along the Congo and Mozambican borders.
6 Oct. 1964	The People's Liberation Army of Zanzibar becomes part of the Republic's military forces.
13 Oct. 1964	Accedes to multilateral agreement on the recognition and enforcement of foreign arbitral awards.
24 Oct. 1964	The Mbweni Technical College, financed by USAID, is handed over.
29 Oct. 1964	President Nyerere announces that henceforth the Republic would be known as the United Republic of Tanzania.
30 Oct. 1964	Accepts provisional accession to GATT of Argentina (2nd extension); Switzerland (2nd extension) and extension to the United Arab Republic.
Nov. 1964	The United Arab Republic opens a consulate in Zanzibar and El Sayed Faruk Shelbaya is nominated for the position.
Nov. 1964	Approximately fifty farms belonging to whites are expropriated.
2 Nov. 1964	Daniel Mfinanga is appointed Ambassador to the Soviet Union.
2 Nov. 1964	The former Minister for Land, Settlement and Water, Mr. Tewa, is appointed Ambassador to China.
4 Nov. 1964	The Ministry of Justice is abolished and falls under Second Vice-President. A. Babu becomes Minister of Commerce and Co-operatives, while Mr. Mang'enya takes over the portfolio for Community Development and National Culture, among other changes.

5 Nov. 1964	George Kahama is appointed Ambassador to the Federal Republic of Germany.
7 Nov. 1964	Osei Amantwo is appointed Ghana's High Commissioner.
10 Nov. 1964	At a press conference, the Minister of External Affairs alludes to the 'Western powers' alleged plans to invade the Republic.
11 Nov. 1964	The Indian High Commissioner to Tanzania, R.D. Sathe, announces the imminent establishment of an office in Zanzibar.
17 Nov. 1964	Five people are executed for corruption. They were sentenced by a military court.
17 Nov. 1964	Frontier problems with Malawi manifest themselves as rebel Malawian and ex-Minister Chiume is allegedly ready to leave his refuge in Tanzania to 'invade' Malawi.
24 Nov. 1964	Boubacar Diallo is appointed as Mali's Ambassador to Tanzania.
Dec. 1964	Sheik Babu and Mr Kambona visit new British Labour Ministers and President Nyerere acknowledges a six and a quarter million Pounds Sterling development loan from Great Britain.
Dec. 1964	Approximately 2000 Rwandan refugees are airlifted from the Kivu Province in the Congo Democratic Republic to western Tanzania by the United Nations.
2 Dec. 1964	A Chinese book exhibition opens in Zanzibar.
8 Dec. 1964	President Nyerere, at a mass rally, reports that the United States had sent a letter to the government, assuring it of the falsity of the documents claiming plans to overthrow the government.
8 Dec. 1964	Continuance in force of treaty relating to the activities of UNICEF in Tanganyika.
8 Dec. 1964	It is announced that the Canadian government will offer military training and advisory experts.
15 Dec. 1964	Arms sent from Dar-es-Salaam and bound for Congolese rebels, are impounded by Burundi.
24 Dec. 1964	Call for the merger of the TANU and Afro-Shirazi (ASP) parties to form one national movement.
28 Dec. 1964	Congolese government of President Mobuto issues a statement that the Tanzanian government is prepared to have trade and economic talks with them and would also stop aid to Congolese insurgents.
28 Dec. 1964	Thirty American Peace Corps volunteers arrive and swell the number of Peace Corps volunteers in Tanzania to some 300.
28 Dec. 1964	Two ambulances are presented to Zanzibar by Czechoslovakia.

29 Dec. 1964	Further Cabinet changes take place.

30 Dec. 1964 Tanzania contributes 3000 Pounds Sterling to Somalia as a contribution to drought victims.

4 Jan. 1965 Sheik Abdalla Suleiman el-Harthy, President of the Arab Association in Zanzibar for forty years, is evicted.

8 Jan. 1965 The official name for the armed forces becomes the Tanzania Military Defence Forces.

15 Jan. 1965 Robert Gordon and Frank Carlucci, two American diplomats, are declared persona non grata as a result of alleged subversive activities. Apparently a tapped telephone call was misinterpreted.

17 Jan. 1965 A common policy on prohibited immigrants was agreed upon by the Foreign Ministers of Uganda, Kenya, Tanzania and Zambia.

25 Jan. 1965 An extradition treaty is signed with Rwanda.

Feb. 1965 Ahmed Hassan is appointed Ambassador to the United Arab Republic.

Feb. 1965 Daniel Mfinanga is appointed Ambassador to the United States.

Feb. 1965 George Kahama is appointed Ambassador to the Federal Republic of Germany.

Feb. 1965 Hassan Nur Elmi is appointed Somali Ambassador to Tanzania.

5 Feb. 1965 Eugene Rittweger de Moor presents his credentials as the Belgian Ambassador.

14 Feb. 1965 Tanzania recalls Ambassador Shariff from the United States.

15 Feb. 1965 East Germany will establish a Consulate-General in Dar-es-Salaam.

16-23 Feb. 1965 President Nyerere visits China.

28 Feb. 1965 President Nyerere urges the withdrawal of all forms of West German technical assistance to Tanzania, following their decision to withdraw all military personnel provided under their programmes. This was due to the establishment of an East German Consulate in Zanzibar.

Late Feb. 1965 West Germany ceases military aid to Tanzania once the name of an East German Consul-General is announced.

1 Mar. 1965 The Constitutional Commission is postponed, pending the outcome of the Commission on the One-Party State.

18 Mar. 1965 Announcement is made that the National Assembly is to be dissolved on 11 October.

18 Mar. 1965 Salah O. Hashim assumes his appointment as Sudanese Ambassador to Tanzania.

Apr. 1965	Great Britain's Overseas Development Minister visits Tanzania. She agrees to send an economic mission identifying obstacles to fulfilling the country's five year plan. She refuses aid for the proposed railway link with Zambia.
Apr. 1965	President Nyerere to visit Senegal.
Apr. 1965	Tanzania imposes restrictions on Japanese goods due to the unfavourable trade balance.
9 Apr. 1965	Signs multilateral agreement of the facilitation of international maritime traffic.
12 Apr. 1965	The Tanzanian trade union, NUTA, and the All China Federation of Trade Unions express solidarity.
14 Apr. 1965	Christopher Ngaiza, Tanzanian Ambassador to the Netherlands, presents his credentials.
17 Apr. 1965	President Nyerere introduces the report of the sixteen-man Presidential Commission on the establishment of one-partyism.
18 Apr. 1965	A joint communiqué is issued following President Nyerere's visit to Mali by the two presidents on the attitude of Rhodesia and Portugal towards blacks in Africa.
20 Apr. 1965	President Nyerere, at a London press conference, describes President Tshombe of the Congo as 'a traitor and enemy of Africa'.
21 Apr. 1965	President Nyerere is decorated by Queen Juliana of the Netherlands during his state visit.
27 Apr. 1965	Signs technical co-operation treaty with the Netherlands.
28 Apr. 1965	Ministry of External Affairs denies that Israel has established a Consulate-General in Zanzibar.
30 Apr. 1965	Continuance in force in respect of Tanzania of multipartite agreement on technical assistance.
30 Apr. 1965	Plans are announced to expand the police force from 7000 to 9000 within the next two years.
May 1965	The Federation of Revolutionary Trade Unions and its affiliates in Zanzibar are dissolved and will now fall under the aegis of the Afro-Shirazi Party.
May 1965	The outlawed Watch Tower and Bible Society are deemed still to be operative in the Kilimanjaro Region, and are warned accordingly as a threat to national security.
May 1965	A technical agreement is concluded with Poland.
May 1965	The Swedish Agency for International Assistance donates over ten thousand Pounds Sterling to the Mozambique Institute in Dar-es-Salaam which prepares Mozambicans in secondary schools for advancement studies abroad.

8 May 1965	Electoral procedure is announced whereby a candidate will have to produce at least twenty five supporters in his constituency prior to being able to contest the election.
14 May 1965	Signs multipartite agreement on operational assistance.
14 May 1965	Terminates United Nations treaty on operational executive and administrative personnel.
4 June 1965	Chou En-Lai, the Chinese premier arrives in Tanzania.
8-15 June 1965	President Nyerere visits Nigeria. At the conclusion of his state visit, he reaffirms his country's commitment to a continental union government of Africa.
13 June 1965	During his state visit to Nigeria, President Nyerere is offered scholarships for twelve students at the University of Ife.
13 June 1965	Minister of Finance Bomani refutes the accusation that Tanzania intends to break up the East African monetary area.
14 June 1965	Tanzania is accused of interfering in Malawian politics but President Nyerere has given President Banda an assurance to the contrary.
17 June 1965	Military expansion is to be undertaken in the form of a Navy, National Service units in four more regions, a reserve force and additional training.
28 June 1965	Tanzania and West Germany resolve their differences and are to normalize their relations.
29 June 1965	Presidents Nyerere and de Gaulle meet in Paris during President Nyerere's visit to France.
30 June 1965	The last of the 3000 Rwanda refugees moved from Kivu Province in the Congo arrive in Tanzania.
July 1965	Frontier control posts will be established following an agreement between Kenya, Uganda, Tanzania and Zambia.
July 1965	It is reported that China is prepared to assist with cost of the railway link with Zambia estimated between 75 and 150 million Pounds Sterling.
July 1965	Tanzania formally becomes a one-party with the adoption of a new constitution. Until the TANU and Afro-Shirazi parties are merged, they will be recognized as the only valid parties in their respective territories.
8 July 1965	Signs Convention on Transit Trade of Land-locked countries; and Final Act of UN Conference.
8 July 1965	A tripartite agreement is signed between Tanzania, the Office of the United Nations High Commissioner of Refugees and the Tanganyikan Christian Refugee Service. This will enable the settlement of 10000 Mozambican refugees in Southern Tanzania.
10 July 1965	The National Assembly is dissolved in preparation for the elections.

15 July 1965	Nominations for the forthcoming elections begins. Candidates are not permitted to compaign individually.
15 July 1965	Tanzania supports the East African Federation. This viewpoint is expressed by President Nyerere in laying the foundation stone of the East African Common Services Regional Headquarters in Dar-es-Salaam.
Aug. 1965	An instruction team from the Dutch Navy is expected in Tanzania to train their coast guard units. This was previously undertaken by West Germany, who withdrew following the establishment of an East German consulate in Zanzibar. They have, however, promised two new patrol boats.
Aug. 1965	North Vietnam intends establishing diplomatic relations with Tanzania.
10 Aug. 1965	President Nyerere opens the eleventh season of the East African Central Legislative Assembly and outlines his attitude towards the East African Federation.
20 Aug. 1965	A twelve-man survey team arrives from China to investigate the feasibility of a rail link with Zambia. Great Britain and Canada agree to share the cost of the survey.
22 Aug. 1965	Accusations are made against Tanzania in harbouring Malawi's ex Foreign Affairs Minister, Chiume, who is allegedly preparing an invasion of Malawi from his house in Tanzania. Tanzania's involvement is refuted by President Nyerere.
22 Aug. 1965	Prince Bernhard of the Netherlands arrives in Tanzania on a private visit.
Sept. 1965	Tanzania accepts help in establishing their military air wing from Canada as part of a five-year programme.
2 Sept. 1965	Acceptance of GATT's trade and development agreement.
8 Sept. 1965	Alan McGill, Canadian High Commissioner to Tanzania, presents his credentials.
8 Sept. 1965	Czechoslovakia's first Ambassador to Tanzania presents his credentials. He is Mikulas Surina.
9 Sept. 1965	Burundi Ambassador, Antonie Natahokaja, presents his credentials to President Nyerere.
21 Sept. 1965	General elections are held. Two Cabinet Ministers and six junior Ministers lose their parliamentary seats.
28 Sept. 1965	John Burns, of the United States, is appointed Ambassador and embassies are to reopen following an improved relationship.
29 Sept. 1965	Signs guarantee agreement with the IBRD on the second East African Railways and Harbours Project.
Oct. 1965	Diplomatic relations, at ambassadorial level, are to be established with Syria.

Oct. 1965	Special Representative of the United Kingdom, M. McDonald, takes up the post in a number of African countries, including Tanzania.
Oct. 1965	Tanzania receives a loan of approximately 47,000 Pounds Sterling from US Aid to assist with the second phase of expanding the Community Training Centre at Tengeru.
Oct. 1965	Toshio Urabe of Japan presents his ambassadorial credentials.
Oct. 1965	Waziri Juma is appointed Ambassador to China.
1 Oct. 1965	President Nyerere is inaugurated as president for a further five years.
1 Oct. 1965	President Nyerere granted an amnesty for 26,395 prisoners and 14 people held under the Preventive Detention Act to mark his inauguration as President for his second term of office.
4 Oct. 1965	An agreement is signed with Canada pertaining to the States and establishment of the Canadian Military Advisory and Training Team in Tanzania.
5 Oct. 1965	The German Democratic Republic signs a cultural agreement providing for fourteen teachers in Zanzibar.
7 Oct. 1965	A delegation from the South Vietnam National Liberation Front arrives at the invitation of President Nyerere.
7 Oct. 1965	Twenty two people are now held under the Preventive Detention Act.
8 Oct. 1965	Boubeker Bouumahdi of Morocco presents his ambassadorial credentials to President Nyerere.
12 Oct. 1965	The new Assembly opens with a membership comprising 107 elected members from the mainland, twenty-three members of the Zanzibar Revolutionary Council, fourteen from Zanzibar, ten nominated members from both the mainland and Zanzibar, and twenty regional commissioners.
29 Oct. 1965	Soji Williams, Nigerian High Commissioner, arrives in Dar-es-Salaam.
Nov. 1965	Britain offers Tanzania an interest-free loan of seven and a half million Pounds Sterling towards the 1964-66 Development Plan.
Nov. 1965	G. Rutanzibwa is appointed Tanzanian High Commissioner to Canada.
Nov. 1965	Israeli Ambassador to Tanzania is named as Yitzhak Pundak.
Nov. 1965	S. Chale is appointed as Tanzanian Ambassador to Ethiopia.
2 Nov. 1965	United States agrees to finance a survey for a road joining Tanzania and Zambia.
4 Nov. 1965	It is announced that the workers' Educational Associations of Sweden, Denmark, Norway and Finland will commence training schemes in Tanzania in 1966.

4 Nov. 1965	Signs treaty with Canada relating to the provision of military training and advisory assistance.
4 Nov. 1965	Yugoslavian Ambassador-designate, Zivoji Lakic, arrives.
9 Nov. 1965	Minister of Regional Administration, Mr Kambona, discusses mutual cooperation with President Sekou Toure, during his visit to Guinea.
12 Nov. 1965	President Nyerere calls for sanctions against South Africa, as well as those imposed by Britain against Rhodesia in order to effectively end UDI.
13 Nov. 1965	Students from the University College of Dar-es-Salaam demonstrate against the ineffectiveness of British policy in Rhodesia.
16 Nov. 1965	Harmonization of labour legislation is promoted by a joint meeting of officials from the Ministries of Labour from Kenya, Uganda and Tanzania.
21 Nov. 1965	W. Juma, Tanzanian Ambassador in Peking, presents his credentials.
30 Nov. 1965	Signs treaty with the United States on the application to Tanzania of the Extradition Treaty of 22 December 1931 and the Consular Convention of 6 June 1951.
Dec. 1965	Six Tanzanian pilots receive their wings in Canada after undergoing training with the Royal Canadian Air Force.
2 Dec. 1965	Continuance in force of assistance from the UN Special Fund.
3 Dec. 1965	John Burns is sworn in as United States Ambassador to Tanzania at a ceremony is Washington, D.C., attended by the Tanzanian Ambassador, Chief Lukumbuzya.
7 Dec. 1965	President Osman of the Somali Republic arrives in Dar-es-Salaam on a four day state visit.
14 Dec. 1965	Accepts third extension to Tunisia's provisional accession to GATT; and the first extension of the provisional accession of Iceland.
15 Dec. 1965	Tanzania severs diplomatic relations with Great Britain for the stance on Rhodesia's UDI and the question of majority rule. Canada agrees to act as protecting power.
16 Dec. 1965	Chief Lukumbuzya becomes Ambassador to the United States and presents his credentials.
19 Dec. 1965	Tanzanian government is amenable in assisting Great Britain and the United States in sending oil and other supplies across Tanzania to Zambia.
30 Dec. 1965	Relations are improved with Congo as Tanzania forbids refugees to plan an invasion from Tanzania.
Jan. 1966	Forty volunteers from the West German Volunteer Service are scheduled to arrive.
Jan. 1966	President Banda of Malawi accuses Tanzania of openly aiding and abetting

rebels from Malawi.

Jan. 1966
President Nyerere issues tribute on the death of Mr. Shastri of India and reports that his last work at the Tashkent Conference will be accepted as a great inheritance for the whole Sub-Continent.

Jan. 1966
President Nyerere sceptical that the United Kingdom policy of economic sanctions against the rebel Smith regime in Rhodesia will induce its citizens to hate the regime and give their votes to liberal elements in the country.

Jan. 1966
Tanzania decides not to attend the Commonwealth Prime Minister's Conference on Rhodesia to be held in Lagos, Nigeria, on 11 January. Statement issued by the conference organizers.

1 Jan. 1966
Entry into force of additional regulations amending the International Sanitary Regulations relevant to the disinfecting of ships and aircraft; and the forms of the international certificates of vaccination or revaccination against yellow fever and smallpox.

13 Jan. 1966
Signs agreement with the International Development Association for the Agricultural Credit Project.

23 Jan. 1966
President Nyerere sends message of condolence on the death of Alhaji Sir Abubakar Tafawa Balewa of Nigeria.

31 Jan. 1966
Oscar Kambona, Chairman of the OAU African Liberation Committee, expresses concern over the division between the MPLA and GRAE in Angola, and recognizes only FRELIMO in the liberation of Mozambique at the 8th ordinary session of the committee in Dar-es-Salaam.

Feb. 1966
President Nyerere announces that severing relations with Britain has cost the country seven and a half million Pounds Sterling in aid and resumption of diplomatic relations with Britain depends on whether Rhodesia goes the South African way.

Feb. 1966
President Nyerere calls for continuation of the socialist revolution against exploitation at the second anniversary of the Zanzibar revolution.

13 Feb. 1966
Second anniversary of the Zanzibar revolution commemorated at a military parade in Zanzibar.

18 Feb. 1966
Signs multipartite treaty on agricultural commodities.

21 Feb. 1966
Decree passed prohibiting the re-entry of persons who left Zanzibar between 12 January and 31 May 1964.

22 Feb. 1966
Bill introduced establishing a Permanent Commission of Inquiry to investigate activities of other commissions such as the Judicial Services Commission and institutions such as the Tea Board.

22 Feb. 1966
National Defence Bill, 1966, submitted to National Assembly.

23 Feb. 1966
R. Kawawa, the second Vice-President, announces that Tanzania has 30,000 refugees from seven different countries.

3 Mar. 1966	Tanzania withdraws from the OAU Sixth Session of the Council of Ministers in protest against the seating of representatives of the new Ghana region, but will continue to support and remain members of the OAU.
11 Mar. 1966	President Nyerere states Tanzania's policy of non-interference in the internal affairs of African states especially with regard to the overthrow of K. Nkrumah of Ghana.
15 Mar. 1966	Arusha rural contituency parliamentary election held on 21 September 1965 declared null and void.
15 Mar. 1966	President Nyerere states his views on non-alignment in the British weekly magazine, Punch.
Apr. 1966	President Nyerere declares amnesty commemorating the second anniversary of the Union of Zanzibar and Tanganyika, with effect from 26 April.
Apr. 1966	Rt Rev Robert N. Russell, the Anglican Bishop of Zanzibar, given forty-eight hour notice to leave the island.
1 Apr. 1966	Accepts accession of Switzerland to GATT.
5 Apr. 1966	September 1965 Geita North election results declared null and void.
26 Apr. 1966	President Nyerere announces National Service for Youth at the opening of the TANU Youth League Centre in Dar-es-Salaam.
27 Apr. 1966	Internal Youth Seminar against Racialism and Racial Discrimination opens at University College, Dar-es-Salaam.
30 Apr. 1966	Signs agreement with Canada concerning the provision of military transport and liaison aircraft to Tanzania.
9 May 1966	Presidential Commission of Inquiry appointed into the affairs of the National Union of Tanganyika Workers (NUTA)
9 June 1966	President Nyerere rejects allegations that Tanzania is anti-West in a memorandum presented at the TANU National Executive.
20 June 1966	Ratifies amendments to UN Charter.
10 July 1966	All Tanzanians residing in Zanzibar and over sixteen will be registered with effect from 11 July, first Vice-President Mr Karume announces.
15 July 1966	Signs scientific and technical co-operation treaty with Bulgaria.
18 July 1966	Announcement made in National Assembly by R. Kawawa on the establishment of a Military Academy at Munduli.
18 July 1966	Exploratory talks between Tanzania and Malawi begin.
20 July 1966	Accepts accession of Yugoslavia to GATT.
Aug. 1966	Motion approved in Central Legislative Assembly of Tanzania calling for a speedier progress towards the establishment of an East African Federation.

5 Aug. 1966	Thirty National Service youths arrested for disorderly conduct.
8 Aug. 1966	Accedes to the Articles of Agreement of the International Cotton Institute.
21 Aug. 1966	President Nyerere pays official State Visit to Somalia and maintains that political independence was meaningless without economic independence and freedom.
23 Aug. 1966	South African Minister of Post & Telegraphs complains that Radio Tanzania broadcasts from Dar-es-Salaam are interfering with broadcasts from South Africa.
4 Oct. 1966	Approval of White Paper proposing national service for school leavers and university graduates.
10 Oct. 1966	President Nyerere states that although it is difficult to federate independent countries, a federation of East African countries of Kenya, Tanzania and Uganda, is still possible.
28 Oct. 1966	Establishment of a special court to try political and other offences connected with destruction or theft of state property according to a Government Notice in Zanzibar.
Nov. 1966	O. Kambona says that OAU critics wishing to shift OAU offices from Dar-es-Salaam, are welcome to do so and disbanding of the OAU Liberation Committee would be scrapping the organization itself.
Nov. 1966	President Nyerere submits a memorandum entitled Rhodesia: the case for action, which sets out in chronological order developments of events since October 1965, to the OAU Summit Conference in Addis Ababa.
Nov. 1966	President Nyerere walks out of OAU Summit Conference in Addis Ababa over budgetory allocation to its Liberation Committee and that it be removed from Tanzania if sufficient money is not allocated for its activities.
10 Nov. 1966	President Madiba Keita of Mali arrives to pay a State Visit to Tanzania.
10 Nov. 1966	President Nyerere expresses his views on the recently held OAU Summit Conference in Addis Ababa and the future of the OAU.
17 Nov. 1966	Accepts second extension to the United Arab Republic's provisional accession to GATT; and the third extension to Argentina's provisional accession.
30 Nov. 1966	National Union of Tanzania Students banned.
30 Nov. 1966	Portuguese soldiers from Mozambique cross into Tanzania in the Mtwara region and murder four Tanzanians, according to The Standard newspaper.
3 Dec. 1966	President Nyerere suspends the secret court established to try political offenders.
7 Dec. 1966	General Mobuto of the Congo postpones his visit to Tanzania.
16 Dec. 1966	Bill introduced in National Assembly making it compulsory for university

	students and six form school leavers to join the National Service for a 2-year period.
21 Dec. 1966	President Nyerere responds to British Premier Wilson's statement that Rhodesia will not be given legal independence until its four million Africans had won majority rule.
22 Dec. 1966	President Nyerere meets President Micombero of Burundi and holds talks centering on strengthening ties between their two countries.
30 Dec. 1966	Lieutenant-General Keevy, Commissioner of Police for South Africa, accuses Tanzania of having training camps for terrorists insurgency into Namibia.
Jan. 1967	Visa abolition agreement with Uganda and Burundi.
4 Jan. 1967	Second Vice-President Rashidi M. Kawawa directs that Kiswahili be used for all government business.
28 Jan. 1967	TANU aproves text of the Arusha Declaration which outlines Tanzania's policy on socialism and self-reliance.
Feb. 1967	Cabinet changes.
5 Feb. 1967	Presentation of the Arusha Declaration: TANU's Policy on Socialism and Self-reliance. This declaration outlines Tanzania's new socialist policies.
7 Feb. 1967	President Nyerere addresses youth rally and states that they should be in the vanguard for socialist reconstruction and implementation of the Arusha Declaration. He names them the 'Green Guards'.
8 Feb. 1967	First Vice-President Karume says that students who completed Standard XII schooling in 1966 will be drafted as teachers.
17 Feb. 1967	Signs guarantee agreement with the IBRD on the East African Telecommunications Project.
22 Feb. 1967	Government reshuffle.
27 Feb. 1967	Opening of special national conference of TANU in Dar-es-Salaam where the Arusha Declaration could be accepted or rejected.
2 Mar. 1967	Accepts accession of the Republic of Korea to GATT.
3 Mar. 1967	Arusha Declaration approved.
9 Mar. 1967	In a White Paper, Arusha Declaration principles spelt out in Education for Self-Reliance document as to how the educational system should encourage socialist values by equipping people for mainly a rural existence.
17 Mar. 1967	Swahili becomes medium of instruction in all primary schools.
26 Mar. 1967	TANU announces the dismissal of E. Anangisye, Secretary General of TANU Youth League (the Green Guards), with retrospective effect from 17 March.

Apr. 1967	Border security arrangements between Tanzania and Mozambique strengthened following death of Tanzanians by explosive mines.
4 Apr. 1967	President Nyerere attends African Heads of State meeting in Cairo. Addresses the United Arab Republic National Assembly on 9th April.
5 Apr. 1967	Signs scientific and technical cooperation treaty with Denmark.
5 Apr. 1967	Signs treaty with Denmark on the provision of volunteers from Denmark.
24 Apr. 1967	'The Standard' reports that President Nyerere lifts the suspension on University of Dar-es-Salaam students who demonstrated against national service in October 1966.
26 Apr. 1967	Celebration of third anniversary of Union between Tanganyika and Zanzibar.
1 May 1967	President Nyerere addresses May Day rally in Dar-es-Salaam, encouraging hard work by all workers.
17 May 1967	Josef Nyerere appointed Secretary-General of TANU Youth League replacing E. Anangiswe who was dismissed on 17 March.
31 May 1967	President Nyerere announces that Tanzania does not recognize the artificial boundary between it and Malawi which is marked along the lake shores.
June 1967	Oscar Kambona moved to Ministry of Local Government.
6 June 1967	Signs a fifteen-year joint agreement with Kenya and Uganda establishing the East African Community, to be implemented on 1 December 1967.
7 June 1967	Cabinet reshuffle. Ministers reduced from fifteen to eleven.
9 June 1967	Oscar Kambona, Minister of Local Government and Rural Development resigns from government forty-eight hours after his appointment.
12 June 1967	At a meeting of the UN Committee of 24 in Dar-es-Salaam, Second President R. Kawawa, attacks Portuguese violation of human rights in Mozambique, and also refers to the Namibian and Rhodesian issues.
16 June 1967	Accedes to multilateral convention on global commercial communications satellite system.
27 June 1967	President Banda of Malawi responds to Tanzania's claim to part of Lake Nyasa.
28 June 1967	Second Vice-President, R. Kawawa announces the establishment of a military academy at Monduli in Arusha.
30 June 1967	Al Noor Kassum appointed secretary of the Economic and Social Council of the United Nations, and to assume duties on 30th June.
July 1967	Oscar Kambona, who was dismissed from his Foreign Affairs Ministry in 1965, leaves Tanzania for Britain.

3 July 1967	Major foreign policy speech covering South Africa and Portuguese territories in Africa.
3 July 1967	Policy statement on Tanzania's attitude to Israel by Minister of Information & Tourism, Mr Hasim Makame.
4 July 1967	Tanzanian Minister of Information & Tourism, Hasim Makame, states his country's view on the Tanzania-Malawi boundary dispute.
8 July 1967	Presidents of Tanzania, Zambia, Uganda and Kenya meet in Nairobi to find a solution to the Nigerian crisis.
21 July 1967	Government issues statement that parliamentary members E.M. Anangisye and Hamisi Salumu were detained on 15 July for subversive activities.
26 July 1967	Pan Africanist Congress of South Africa (PAC) activities suspended and offices closed in Dar-es-Salaam because of political infighting.
3 Aug. 1967	Government legislation to enforce the Arusha Declaration expected to be submitted to the National Assembly in September according to Second Vice-President R. Kawawa in an address to National Service members at Rubu.
13 Aug. 1967	President Nyerere refutes statement made by former Minister Oscar Kambona in London that party and government officials are opposed to the Arusha Declaration and are conspiring to overthrow the government.
15 Aug. 1967	Pan Africanist Congress of South Africa (PAC) allowed to operate again in Dar-es-Salaam after its offices were closed on 26th July.
18 Aug. 1967	K. Hanga dismissed as Vice-President of Zanzibar.
20 Aug. 1967	TANU announces new election procedures for its NEC, such as having to satisfy leadership conditions as set out in the Arusha Declaration.
24 Aug. 1967	President Nyerere calls on Oscar Kambona to return from London and explain why he resigned as both Minister and Secretary-General of TANU.
25 Aug. 1967	Oscar Kambona accepts President Nyerere's challenge to return to Tanzania under certain conditions that he will reveal at a press conference on 30 August (which was subsequently postponed).
29 Aug. 1967	Banning of South West African National Union (SWANU), operating from Tanzania.
Sept. 1967	Release of Second Arusha Declaration document - Socialism & Rural Development, outlining President Nyerere's Ujaama or co-operative village philosophy.
Sept. 1967	Tanzania criticizes the issuing of badges by foreign embassies bearing the heads of their governments (China, the US and West Germany in particular), and forbids children and students to wear them.
Sept. 1967	China agrees to build Tan-Zam railway line.

7 Sept. 1967	Zanzibar cabinet change.
8 Sept. 1967	A five-year work orientated Kiswahili adult literacy pilot project signed in Dar-es-Salaam between the UNDP, UNESCO and the Tanzanian government.
21 Sept. 1967	Bill to amend the Interim Constitution setting out qualifications for members of Parliament to comply with Principles of the Arusha Declaration.
21 Sept. 1967	PAC of South Africa resolves its differences at a meeting under the auspices of the OAU Liberation Committee held at Moshi.
22 Sept. 1967	Publication of the Permanent Labour Tribunal Bill 1967 to replace the Trades Dispute (Settlement) Act of 1962. This new bill will establish a permanent labour tribunal to deal with disputes between employers and employees.
26 Sept. 1967	Ratifies postal parcels agreement; the Constitution and General Regulations of the Universal Postal Union; the Universal Postal Convention; and insured letters and boxes.
27 Sept. 1967	President Nyerere opens the first TANU Youth League meeting since the Arusha Declaration.
Oct. 1967	TANU Youth League adopts various resolutions at the end of its general meeting. Amongst them are the expulsion of American Peace Corps volunteers, the expulsion of Oscar Kambona from the Party, and the binding of all members to the Arusha Declaration.
6 Oct. 1967	Signs a treaty with the United Nations and FAO on behalf of the World Food Programme for assistance.
16-22 Oct.1967	TANU bi-annual conference, held at Mwanza. President Nyerere in his opening speech, reviews Tanzania's non-alignment stance, its relation with the Great Britain and attitude to Israel, African unity and other issues.
24 Oct. 1967	Promulgation of the Permanent Labour Tribunal Act, 1967, that makes strikes or work interruptions illegal.
25 Oct. 1967	Parliament approves Bill to amend the country's Interim Constitution.
1 Nov. 1967	Loan from Denmark.
13 Nov. 1967	Signs guarantee agreement with the IBRD on the Power Project.
14 Nov. 1957	TANU outlines details of a six months revolutionary programme of political education for the population at regional and district levels.
22 Nov. 1967	Kenya denies border dispute with Tanzania, especially along the Netline Inkajiado district.
27 Nov. 1967	Third Conference of judges and magistrates held in Dar-es-Salaam.
Dec. 1967	Chinese engineers arrive in Dar-es-Salaam to survey a railway to Zambia.

15 Dec. 1967	President Nyerere attends the East and Central Africa Heads of States Conference in Kampala.
18 Dec. 1967	Agreement accepted by Tanzania and Burundi establishing a African Training and Research Centre in Administration for Development (CAFRAD).
20 Dec. 1967	President Kayibanda of Rwanda begins a three-day state visit to Tanzania.
30 Dec. 1967	Government announces the detention of former Zanzibar Vice-President, Kasim Hanga and Otini Mattiya Kambona, brother of Oscar Kambona - former Secretary-General of TANU and Cabinet Minister in exile in England.
4 Jan. 1968	Former Tanzania Foreign Minister, Oscar Kambona, accuses President Nyerere of dictatorial tendencies.
11 Jan. 1968	Passing of the National Assembly (Qualifications of Members) (Forms and Procedure) Bill of 1968. It requires members of Parliament to make a sworn statement that they fulfil the leadership conditions of the Arusha Declaration before they can retain their seats.
12 Jan. 1968	Oscar Kambona challenged by President Nyerere to return to Tanzania and testify before a judicial commission that he had not banked large sums of money.
28 Jan. 1968	The number of persons detained under the Preventive Detention Act contain former members of the government of Zanzibar and some Goanese allegedly spying for Portugal.
Feb. 1968	Tanzania accused of harbouring terrorists training camps, by S.A. Muller of South Africa, the Deputy Minister of Police.
Feb. 1968	Vice-President Karume calls for inter-marriages between Asians and Africans to free Tanzania from racial discrimination.
8 Feb. 1968	Signs economic and technical co-operation treaty with the United States.
25 Feb. 1968	President Nyerere maintains at a state banquet in the Ivory Coast that African unity is not easy to achieve.
28 Feb. 1968	President Nyerere and the President of the Ivory Coast reach agreement on world peace and African unity.
4 Mar. 1968	Exile Oscar Kambona files papers testifying his compliance with Tanzania's leadership code and socialist conditions.
11 Mar. 1968	President Nyerere declares that he complies with the leadership code of the Arusha Declaration.
21 Mar. 1968	Signs credit agreement supplement to the Highway Project with the International Development Association.
2 Apr. 1968	Application to Tanzania of the 1898 extradition agreement between the Netherlands and Great Britain.

13 Apr. 1968	Tanzania recognizes Biafra.
25 Apr. 1968	Sheikh Abeid Karum states that Zanzibar does not seek integration with Tanzania.
May 1968	Tanzania confirms that it will remain neutral in the violence clash in the offices of FRELIMO in Dar-es-Salaam.
2 May 1968	Newspaper Ordinance Amendment Bill introduced in Parliament. Bill to stop publication of a newspaper considered to be detrimental to the state.
1 June 1968	Signs treaty with Finland on Finnish volunteers in Tanzania.
4 June 1968	Tanzania's former Foreign Minister Oscar Kambona, maintains that Tanzania's image has been damaged by recognizing Ojukwu's rebel regime in Biafra, Nigeria.
12 June 1968	Entry into force of amendments to Articles 23, 27 and 61 of the United Nations Charter. This was ratified on 7 October 1964.
13 June 1968	A Constitution for the 'elder' section of the Tanganyika African National Union (TANU) adopted. This 'elder' section to be called Baraza la Wazee wa (TANU Elders' Council)
14 June 1968	Oscar Kambona states in Lagos, Nigeria, that arms and ammunition that were intended for the Zimbabwe African People's Union in Rhodesia, have been diverted to Ojukwu's rebel regime in Nigeria by President Nyerere.
17 June 1968	President Nyerere leaves on a three-day visit to Peking, China. States that both Tanzania and China are committed to socialism.
18 June 1968	Tanzania announces that it will no longer pay pensions to British officials who worked for the government of Tanganyika.
July 1968	Parliament overturns government decision to grant gratuities to political appointees.
July 1968	President Nyerere denies that Tanzania is allowing Sudanese rebels to operate from within Tanzania against Sudan.
July 1968	Second Vice-President, R. Kawawa, states that defence policy will be for internal security, safeguarding of the countries sovereignty and support the anti-colonial struggle.
1 July 1968	British aid to Tanzania ceases in consequence of the Tanzanian government decision to stop paying pensions to former British officials.
4 July 1968	United Kingdom and Tanzania resume diplomatic relations which were broken in December 1965.
15 July 1968	Zanzibar cabinet reshuffle.
18 July 1968	Multilateral agreement granting co-operative assistance to Tanzania is signed with Denmark and Sweden.

22 July 1968	The oil pipeline from Dar-es-Salaam is in operation from this day.
13 Aug. 1968	Tanzania warns Eastern Bloc countries not to interfere in its external policies and internal affairs.
16 Aug. 1968	Radio Moscow broadcast response to Tanzania statement of 13 August that they respect Tanzania's sovereignty and policies.
21 Aug. 1968	Tanzanian government expresses shock at Soviet invasion of Czechoslovakia.
28 Aug. 1968	Tanganyika African National Union (TANU) Central Committee prohibits beauty competitions.
4 Sept. 1968	Accedes to multilateral agreement on the status of refugees.
Sept. 1968	Tanganyika African National Union Youth League (TYL) introduces new membership code that all members will adhere to the principle of socialism and that they have to be either workers or students.
12 Sept. 1968	President Nyerere rebutts President Banda of Malawi's claim over Tanzanian territory.
13-18 Sept.1968	At the Algiers meeting of the Liberation Committee of the OAU, Tanzania, as part of the Committee, decides to give increased aid to the ANC of South Africa.
15 Sept. 1968	Tanzania signs the African Convention on the Conservation of Nature and Natural Resources. Ratifies it on 22 November 1974.
19 Sept. 1968	President Nyerere denies accusations by Colonel Benjamin Adekunle of Nigeria's 3rd Division of Marine Commandos that Tanzanians, Chinese and Zambians are fighting alongside Biafran forces.
23 Sept. 1968	Signs treaty with Great Britain over minimum sterling proportion.
1 Oct. 1968	Ratifies International Coffee Agreement.
11 Oct. 1968	L. Nagwanda Sijaoana to succeed Mr Shaba (who resigned) as Minister of Health & Housing.
14 Oct. 1968	Signs multilateral agreement on operational assistance inclusive of UNIDO and the Inter-Governmental Maritime Consultative Organization.
16 Oct. 1968	President Nyerere outlines his views on development and democracy in his booklet 'Freedom and Development'.
19 Oct. 1968	TANU expels nine politicians, including former Foreign Affairs Minister, Oscar Kambona.
20 Oct. 1968	Importation prohibited of four Kenyan newspapers - Daily Nation, Sunday Nation, Taifa Les and Taifa Tanzania.
25 Oct. 1968	Swaziland opposition Ngwane National Liberatory Congress to close its office in Dar-es-Salaam, and is given until 8 November to close their

business.

| 26 Oct. 1968 | Signs technical co-operation treaty with Netherlands in respect of taxation experts from the Netherlands. |

26 Oct. 1968   Signs technical co-operation treaty with Netherlands in respect of taxation experts from the Netherlands.

27 Oct. 1968   At a state banquet in honour of President Moktar O. Daddah of Mauritania, President Nyerere says that one way of achieving African unity is through regional economic and social co-operation such as the establishment of the East African Community.

31 Oct. 1968   Signs credit agreement with the International Development Association concerning the Beef Ranching Development Project.

Nov. 1968   Tanzania's Minister of Commerce & Industry (who comes from the Comoro Islands) resigns when government decrees that all Comorans residing in Tanzania and who have not taken out Tanzanian nationality will have to relinquish official positions.

Nov. 1968   Tanzania denies Nigerian accusation that it is arming rebel movements.

1 Nov. 1968   Stephen Mhando appointed as Minister of State in the President's office and to be responsible for Foreign Affairs.

10 Nov. 1968   North Korean Youth experts arrive to train TANU Youth League (TYL) members and to organize the forthcoming February 1969 Youth Festival.

15 Nov. 1968   Comorians informed by first Vice-President, Mr. Karume, to renounce their French status if they want to retain their Tanzanian citizenship.

19 Nov. 1968   Foreign Minister, S. Mhando, expresses relief at the deadlock broken over the Anglo-Rhodesia talks on Rhodesian independence.

21 Nov. 1968   The Ministry of Home Affairs announces that only Tanzanian citizens over the age of twenty-one will be allowed to vote in the 1970 election,

25 Nov. 1968   American Peace Corps workers told to leave Tanzania by end of August 1969.

Dec. 1968   TANU Youth League (TYL) General Secretary, Joseph Myorere, in a report to the General Council of the League, calls on the League's membership to make 1969 'the year of the youth'.

18 Dec. 1968   Zanzibar government workers who originated from countries which are or were under Portuguese rule are to lose their government positions. They should apply for Tanzanian citizenship.

19 Dec. 1968   A.M. Babu, the Minister of Land Settlement & Water Development, appointed as Minister for Commerce & Industries.

19 Dec. 1968   Tanzanian branch of the East African Muslim Welfare Society and the Tanzania Council of the East African Muslim Welfare Society declared unlawful.

20 Dec. 1968   The Nationalist newspaper accuses the Tanzanian standard of being anti-people, racist and subversive, and trying to discredit 'Operation

Vijana'.

29 Dec. 1968   Launching of 'Operation Vijana' announced. This operation to be launched on 1 January 1969, is to foster a national culture, emancipation from decadent Western practices and play an ideological role.

2 Jan. 1969   Demonstrations occur against The Standard newspaper accusing it of subversive activities against TANU and the Tanganyika African National Union Youth League (TYL)

7-15 Jan.1969   At the Land Conference of Commonwealth Prime Ministers, President Nyerere declares that the pledge of no independence in Rhodesia before majority rule must be maintained.

9-10 Jan.1969   President Nyerere comments on a debate on Rhodesia at the Commonwealth Prime Ministers Conference in London that economic sanctions against the Smith regime should be increased, that the Fearless proposals as a solution are unacceptable and that the pledge of no independence before majority rule (NIBMAR) must be maintained unequivocally.

16 Jan. 1969   President Nyerere visits France and discusses the Biafran issue in Nigeria with President de Gaulle.

17 Jan. 1969   Signs the Constitution of the African Civil Aviation Commission and ratifies it on the 26 September 1969.

22 Jan. 1969   Tanzania (together with Kenya and Uganda) instruct their central banks to prevent British citizens of Asian origin taking money out of the country.

27 Jan. 1969   Signs multilateral financial agreement with the Commonwealth Telecommunications Organisation; terminates 1948 and 1963 Commonwealth Telegraphs Agreement.

30 Jan. 1969   Youth Festival celebrations begin with a Biafra Day rally in Dar-es-Salaam.

Feb. 1969   Newly elected chairman of the OAU Liberation Committee's fourteenth Session meeting in Dar-es-Salaam, S. Mhando, Tanzania's Minister of Foreign Affairs, appeals to Africans to increase the struggle for freedom in South Africa, Rhodesia and the Portuguese colonies.

3 Feb. 1969   Dr Eduardo Mondlane, President of FRELIMO, assassinated in Dar-es-Salaam.

19 Feb. 1969   Sheik Mohamed Ahmadi, Zanzibar's former Prime Minister, and former Minister without Portfolio, Ibuni Saleh, released from detention.

24 Feb. 1969   The second Highway Project benefits from the signature of a loan agreement with the IBRD.

24 Feb. 1969   Signs multilateral treaty with the IBRD, International Development Association and Sweden over the second Highway Project.

25 Feb. 1969   The Swedish government, the World Bank and the International Development Association announce that in a joint operation they are lending $30,000,000 to Tanzania for rebuilding the Tanzanian Highway linking the

Zambian Copperbelt with Dar-es-Salaam.

14 Mar. 1969   Ministerial reorganization announced. Affected are those of Water Development & Irrigation Department; Lands, Housing & Urban Development; Health & Housing; Communications; Labour & Works; Information & Tourism.

26 Mar. 1969   Accedes to the provisional accession of Tunisia (5th extension) and the United Arab Republic (4th extension) to GATT.

26 Mar. 1969   Parliamentary elections' voting age lowered to eighteen years of age.

26 Apr. 1969   Fifth anniversary of Union of Tanganyika and Zanzibar celebrated.

5 May 1969   TANU Youth League resolves at its bi-annual Congress that all responsibilities in parastatals, religious organizations and government be held by Tanzanians.

27 May 1969   Signs technical co-operation treaty with Denmark pertaining to the Teachers' College at Iringa.

28 May 1969   TANU opens its fourteenth National Conference in Dar-es-Salaam. President Nyerere announces Tanzania's second five-year Development Plan at the Conference.

29 May 1969   Signs credit agreement with the International Development Association on the second Education Project.

7 June 1969   President Nyerere announces at the closing of the TANU National Conference that Tanzania's historical task is to carry out the African revolution. Nyerere and Kawawa were returned to their posts of President and Vice-President respectively.

July 1969   President Nyerere approves military promotions. Amongst these are Brigadier Marisho Sam Hagai Sarakikya, Chief of Defence Forces, promoted to Major-General of the Tanzania People's Defence Forces.

July 1969   TANU Central Committee meeting calls on government to enact a law to wipe out all feudalistic legacies in Tanzania that allows existence of Chiefs and Sultans in the state of workers and peasants.

8-11 July 1969 Tanzania takes part at the consultative meeting of the Non-Aligned countries, in Belgrade.

25 Aug. 1969   Signs guarantee agreement with the IBRD on the East African Harbours Corporation Project.

26 Aug. 1969   Provides definitive signature to the authentic trilingual text of the Convention on International Civil Aviation.

1 Sept. 1969   Former Vice-President, Kassim Hanga, and other Zanzibaris arrested, the Tanzania Standard announces.

10 Sept. 1969   Tanzania signs specific aspects of the OAU Convention on Refugee Problems in Africa.

24 Sept. 1969	New association agreement signed between the EEC and the East African Community.
28 Sept. 1969	President Nyerere begins a twenty-eight day state visit to North America and Europe.
Oct. 1969	The Electoral Commission alters constitutional boundaries of thirteen districts of mainland Tanzania, raising the number of Parliamentary constituencies from 107 to 120.
Oct. 1969	President Nyerere pays an official state visits to Canada, Sweden, USSR, Hungary and Yugoslavia and is granted an audience with Pope Paul.
13 Oct. 1969	Michael Kamaliza, former Trade Union leader and five others, arrested for activities endangering law and order, according to The Nationalist newspaper.
17 Oct. 1969	Amends 1968 Beef Ranching Development Project agreement with the International Development Association.
Nov. 1969	Zanzibari teachers to undergo military training. Teachers responsible for the training of school children to begin from 13 November.
5 Nov. 1969	President Nyerere attempts to reconcile dissension between FRELIMO's Presidential Council leaders in Dar-es-Salaam.
14 Nov. 1969	Communist China, Tanzania and Zambia sign agreement confirming construction of railway line from the Copperbelt to Dar-es-Salaam.
14 Nov. 1969	Signs Additional Protocol of the Universal Postal Union's Constitution and General Regulations; insured letters and boxes; postal parcels; and the Universal Postal Convention.
24 Nov. 1969	Amends the development credit agreement signed with the International Development Association on 24 February 1969, concerning the second Highway Project.
2 Dec. 1969	Military barracks constructed by the Chinese government for the Maji Maji Battalion handed over to the Tanzanian government.
4 Feb. 1970	The Standard and Sunday News newspapers nationalized. Frene Ginwala appointed Managing Editor of both papers and the Standard will be the government's official paper.
4 Feb. 1970	Two-year ban on Kenyan newspapers, Daily Nation, Sunday Nation, Taifa Tanzania and Taifa Leo lifted.
13 Feb. 1970	National Security Bill published to repeal the Official Secrets Ordinance. Covers issues such as espionage, sabotage and unauthorized dealings with classified information.
25 Mar. 1970	Zanzibari government abolishes all ministerial posts as from 1 June 1970. All ministers and junior ministers will become Chairmen and Vice-Chairmen respectively.

14 Apr. 1970	Signs treaty with the Netherlands on economic and technical co-operation.
7 May 1970	Inquiry opens in Dar-es-Salaam concerning eight people charged with treason. Between July 1968 and 6th September 1969 they conspired to overthrow Tanzania's government by unlawful means.
25 May 1970	Signs multilateral credit agreement pertaining to the second East African Telecommunications Project with Sweden, Kenya and Uganda.
25 May 1970	Signs guarantee agreement with the IBRD concerning the East African Railways Project and the second East African Telecommunications Project.
24 June 1970	Seven people accused of attempting to eliminate President Nyerere and overthrow the Tanzanian government, appear in the High Court in Dar-es-Salaam, charged with treason.
12 July 1970	The Tanzanian Minister of Finance and the Zambia Minister of Development and Finance discuss with their Chinese counterpart the construction of the projected railway between Dar-es-Salaam and the Zambian Copperbelt with Chinese technical and financial aid.
12 July 1970	The Chinese Ministry for Economic Relations with Foreign Countries grants an interest-free loan of approximately 169 million Pounds Sterling to Tanzania for the building of the railway line between Dar-es-Salaam and the Zambian Copperbelt.
15 July 1970	Plans to establish a Tanzanian Air Force completed. Second Vice-President R. Kawawa tells Parliament.
22 July 1970	President Nyerere accompanied by the Presidents of Uganda and Zambia, express their joint view to Britain's High Commissioner to Tanzania, Horace Phillips, on Britain's possible resumption of arms supplies to South Africa.
24 July 1970	Parliament dissolved. National Assembly dissolved.
1 Aug. 1970	President Nyerere announces the reappointment of parliamentary members for Zanzibar and Pemba for the next five years, according to Radio Zanzibar.
24 Aug. 1970	Announcement made by the Chairman of the Electoral Commission, Chief Adam Sapi, that Presidential, Parliamentary and local government elections will be held on 30 October.
11 Sept. 1970	TANU amd the Afro-Shirazi Party at their electoral conference in Dar-es-Salaam unanimously elect Nyerere as sole candidate for Presidential election on 30 October.
16 Sept. 1970	Foreign Minister, S. Mhando, responds to South African Prime Minister J. Vorster's threat that South Africa will pursue guerrillas crossing its borders back into the countries from which they came.
17 Sept. 1970	Vice President Karume of Zanzibar calls on Zanzibaris to foster mixed marriages.

21 Sept. 1970	Hamza Aziz appointed Inspector-General of Tanzania Police.
7 Oct. 1970	TANU Youth League responds to burning of Tanzanian flag in India over the Zanzibari policy of encouraging marriages between Asians and Africans.
9 Oct. 1970	Signs credit agreement with the International Development Association on the Flue-Cured Tobacco Project.
23 Oct. 1970	Swahili magazine 'Film Tanzania' banned by Zanzibari government.
24 Oct. 1970	Zanzibar launches its first national newspaper called 'Truth Prevails where Lies must Vanish'.
26 Oct. 1970	Vice-President Karume announces that of the fourteen people detained for attempting to overthrow the Zanzibari government, four were sentenced to death, nine sentenced to ten years, and one for three years imprisonment. Those executed were former Ministers K. Hanga, O. Shariff and A.M. Tambwe.
30 Oct. 1970	General elections.
Nov. 1970	All Cabinet Ministers returned in Parliamentary elections with the exception of J W. Kilhampa (Minister of Lands, Housing & Urban Development) and B. Munanka (Minister of State in the Vice-President's Office). Also defeated was F. Mbonai, a junior Minister in the same office.
4 Nov. 1970	President Nyerere re-elected as President. Only 72% of the five million registered voters cast their vote.
5 Nov. 1970	New government elected. Cabinet is increased to nineteen and six new Ministers named. One new Ministry of Water Development & Power created.
5 Nov. 1970	To mark his inauguration for another 5 year term of office, President Nyerere grants amnesty to 3484 prisoners and eighteen detainees.
9 Nov. 1970	President Houphouet-Boigny of the Ivory Coast proposal that independent Africa should open dialogue with Pretoria viewed as a betrayal of African rights and aspirations by the Standard newspaper.
27 Nov. 1970	Signs treaty with Denmark on the establishment of an Audio-Visual Institute in Dar-es-Salaam.
14 Dec. 1970	Signs guarantee agreement with IBRD concerning the Kidatu Hydroelectric Project.
17 Dec. 1970	Danish grant for the Miombo Research Centre.
1 Jan. 1971	Entry into force of the International Health Regulations adopted by the twenty-second World Health Assembly.
1 Jan. 1971	President Nyerere awarded the Lenin Centenary Jubilee medal by Soviet Ambassador to Tanzania.
12 Jan. 1971	Zanzibar celebrates its seventh anniversary and Vice-President Karume

speaking on this occasion, states that only the workers and peasants have power over the Tanzanian government.

14-21 Jan. 1971 | President Nyerere circulates a document at the Commonwealth Heads of Government Conference held in Singapore, arguing against British arms sales to South Africa.

28 Jan. 1971 | President Nyerere condemns seizure of power by Idi Amin in Uganda.

5 Feb. 1971 | Signs credit agreement with the International Development Association on the Third Education Project.

9 Feb. 1971 | Bibi Titi Mohamed, former President of the Union of Tanzania Women, and four others sentenced to life imprisonment for plotting to overthrow the Tanzanian government and assasinate Julius Nyerere. Two others given ten-year prison sentences for treason.

11 Feb. 1971 | Tanzania signs prohibition of the emplacement on the seabed and ocean floor and in the subsoil thereof of nuclear weapons and other weapons of mass destruction.

13-20 Feb. 1971 | At the Singapore Commonwealth of Heads of State, President Nyerere declares that he would accept South Africa's assurances that arms received from Britain would not be used for aggressive purposes.

21 Feb. 1971 | President Nyerere announces the formation of a people's militia in the interests of defence and security.

Mar. 1971 | By March 1971, 1600 Ujamaa (socialist) villages are established in Tanzania. Government admits in its Guidelines to the Annual Development Plan, 1971-72, that 'the degree of socialist living and working in these villages is still very uneven'.

5 Mar. 1971 | Terminates agreement of 2 September 1964 with Great Britain on the production and trade production of cereals.

Apr. 1971 | The Standard newspaper criticizes Ivory Coast's proposal of opening dialogue with South Africa.

Apr. 1971 | Government defeated for the first time since independence when MPs rejected the proposed Interim Constitution Amendment Bill.

Apr. 1971 | Tanzanian government issues statement on death of K. Nkrumah of Ghana.

28 Apr. 1971 | Amends 1966 agreement with the International Development Association for the Agricultural Credit Project and the 1970 Flue-Cured Tobacco Project.

2 May 1971 | The Revolutionary Council of Zanzibar sentences to death 19 alleged conspirators of Arab descent who have been preparing a coup d'etat.

9 May 1971 | President Nyerere re-affirms Zambian-Tanzania unity at the United National Independence Party (UNIP) Conference, held at Mulungushi from 8-10 May. States that both countries will stand united against the illegal South African regime.

9 May 1971	Zanzibar's Vice-President Karume announces that nineteen men have been sentenced to death for plotting to overthrow the government.
13 May 1971	A decree deprives a large number believed to be more than 30,000 Zanzibarians, of their nationality due to various immigration irregularities.
June 1971	The Tanzanian government discloses the presence of thirteen thousand Communist Chinese 'Technicians' as part of the labour force working on the railway line from Tanzania to the Copperbelt in Zambia.
7 June 1971	Nigeria and Tanzania agree to exchange diplomatic envoys. Diplomatic relations were suspended in 1968 when Tanzania recognized Biafra.
25 June 1971	Ratifies Convention on International Civil Aviation.
July 1971	Frene Ginwala, editor of the offical Standard and Sunday News newspapers since 1970, dismissed from her post for publishing comments in conflict with President Nyerere's views.
July 1971	Three of the six, sentenced on the 9th February for attempting to overthrow the Tanzania government and assasinate President Nyerere, acquitted by the East African Court of Appeal. Amongst them, former Minister of Labour, M. Kamaliza.
8 July 1971	Danish loan to Tanzania.
14 July 1971	During a visit to London, President Idi Amin of Uganda discloses that he is sending notes to President Nyerere and the Chinese Communist government requesting them not to interfere in Uganda's internal affairs.
15 July 1971	Tanzania refutes claims by Uganda's Idi Amin that it is involved in the killing of Ugandan soldiers and officers.
19 July 1971	President Nyerere denies Ugandan claims that Tanzanian trained guerrillas are fighting in Uganda and that border clashes have occured on the Tanzania-Uganda border. Issues statement on non-recognition of Amin regime and that the East African Community is not threatened.
July - Aug. 1971	Border clashes continue between Tanzania and Uganda right throughout the month of August until President Amin of Uganda accepts an offer of mediation on 2 September.
23 July 1971	The East African Appeal Court repudiates three of the six sentences imposed by the Chief Justice on 19 February. President Nyerere orders the immediate release of two of the trialists, but orders the continued detention of the third, a journalist.
Aug. 1971	The workings of the East African Community are in peril as a consequence of Tanzanian non-recognition of President Idi Amin's regime in Uganda.
6 Aug. 1971	Signs development credit agreement with the International Development Association concerning the third Highway Project.
25 Aug. 1971	According to the Institute of Strategic Studies in the United Kingdom, Tanzania has about 10,000 troops equipped with Chinese and Soviet

artillery.

Sept. 1971	Government publishes bill denying the East African Court of Appeal jurisdiction over appeal against treason charges and that these appeals should instead be heard by a full bench of Tanzania's High Court Judges.
Sept. 1971	TANU holds its fifteenth biennial conference in Dar-es-Salaam. Discusses issues such as the Party Guidelines, the President's Ten Years Post-Independence Report, the implementation of the Second Five-Year Development Plan, the development of Ujamaa co-operatives villages and the adult education programme.
1 Sept. 1971	Tanzanian diplomatic mission officially opened in Lagos, Nigeria.
14 Sept. 1971	TANU Central Committee recommends that Civil Servants be allowed to contest Parliamentary and local government elections without having to relinquish their posts, endorsed by the parties' National Executive Committee.
20 Sept. 1971	Extends 1968 treaty with Great Britain on its guarantee and maintenance pledge by Tanzania on the minimum sterling production.
Oct. 1971	Tanzania applauds the admission of the People's Republic of China into the United Nations Organization.
Nov. 1971	President Nyerere states that the agreement reached between Britain and the Ian Smith regime was a sell-out and whether Tanzania will leave the Commonwealth will be discussed at the OAU.
Nov. 1971	President Kenyatta of Kenya mediates between President Nyerere of Tanzania and President Amin of Uganda with the object of securing continued co-operation of their countries in the East African Community.
13 Nov. 1971	Modifies Netherlands air services agreement of 1969.
19 Nov. 1971	Technical assistance is provided for the expansion of the Faculty of Agriculture in Morogoro by Denmark.
21 Nov. 1971	President Amin of Uganda opens the border with Tanzania that have been closed since the end of April.
23 Nov. 1971	Tanzania signs treaty with the Netherlands pertaining to the employment of volunteers.
30 Nov. 1971	Every Zanzibari citizen leaving school is to serve in a youth camp for two years where he/she will be taught to serve the nation and be employed in various types of agricultural activities. Will not be employed in any department or public enterprise if he/she has not completed this service.
Dec. 1971	Seventy-seven persons sentenced to death have this commuted to life imprisonment on the occasion of Tanzania's Tenth Anniversary Independence Day.
Dec. 1971	Tanzania celebrates its tenth Independence Anniversary.

13 Dec. 1971	Multilateral agreement is signed with Denmark, Finland, Norway and Sweden granting co-operative assistance to Tanzania.
20 Dec. 1971	Abeid Karume, President of Zanzibar, announces that as from 20 December, this presidency will be abolished and that he will assume the title of President of the Revolutionary Council of Zanzibar.
25 Dec. 1971	Dr. W. Kleruu assassinated. He was TANU regional secretary for Iringa.
16 Jan. 1972	The Standard and The Nationalist newspapers should merge and the Party newspaper, Uhuru, should be strengthened, TANU's Central Committee decides at a meeting in Dar-es-Salaam.
23 Jan. 1972	Nineteen of the counter revolutionaries sentenced to death in Zanzibar in May 1971, reprieved and ordered to serve as cattle herdsmen for a period ranging from three, five and ten years.
27 Jan. 1972	President Nyerere announces a series of measures to decentralize the organization of government. Amongst these are that all regional activities be run by the regions themselves, and the abolition of local authorities.
Feb. 1972	Bibi and Titi Mohamed, the two brothers of former Minister Oscar Kambona and ex-MP E. Anansisiye, released from prison.
2 Feb. 1972	Approves the statutes of the World Tourism Organization.
17 Feb. 1972	President Nyerere announces major government changes and a cabinet reshuffle. Amongst this, is the appointment of a Prime Minister, R.M. Kawawa.
3 Mar. 1972	Signs credit agreement with the International Development Association relevant to the Smallholder Tea Development Project.
28 Mar. 1972	Signs treaty with Romania abolishing necessity for visas.
7 Apr. 1972	Sheikh Abeid Karume assasinated. He was Tanzania's First Vice-President and Chairman of the Zanzibar Revolutionary Council. Succeeded on 12 April by Aboud Jumbe, a Minister of State in Karume's office since 1964.
14 Apr. 1972	Abdulrahman Babu detained in connection with the assassination of Sheikh Karume. He is a former government minister and belonged to Sheikh Karume's Afro-Shirazi Party.
14 Apr. 1972	Radio Tanzania announces that Tanzanian forces shot down a Portuguese aircraft crossing the border into Tanzanian air space, after Portuguese aircraft had attacked a Tanzanian village.
23 Apr. 1972	Tanzanian High Commission Office in London set on fire by unknown persons allegedly as protest against Tanzania's socialist policy according to Foreign Minister Malecela.
26 Apr. 1972	The Standard (the government paper) and the Party Nationalist paper merge and the new paper is called 'Daily News'.
28 Apr. 1972	The Public Officers (Eligibility for Election as Constituency Members) Bill

approved, allowing civil servants to stand for election, and if elected, to serve as MPs without resigning their posts.

16 May 1972	Government decentralization policy document that was announced on 27 January is distributed to TANU National Executive Committee meeting at Iringa.
16 May 1972	Portuguese military aircraft shot down in April violating Tanzanian air space recovered.
June 1972	Two Israelis shot dead at the Ubongo Security Centre for breaching security.
1 June 1972	Government announces that leaflets bearing the picture of former Foreign Minister Oscar Kambona and his signature dropped in various parts of Tanzaniza criticizing the party government leaders and Nyerere's socialist policies are banned.
12 June 1972	Series of bomb explosions occur in Dar-es-Salaam and surrounding areas.
12 June 1972	Otini and Mattiya Kambona, brothers of former Foreign Minister, Oscar Kambona, detained following a series of bombings in Dar-es-Salaam.
28 June 1972	Signs guarantee agreement with the IBRD on the East African Development Bank Project.
July 1972	John Mhaville appointed National Executive Secretary of TANU, succeeds Major Hashim Mbita who is appointed Executive Secretary of the OAU Liberation Committee.
1 July 1972	Government decentralization programme becomes effective.
7 July 1972	In an official communiqué after President Numeiry of the Sudan visited Tanzania, both governments reiterate their support for the non-aligned movement, that economic action be taken against Rhodesia and the promotion of mutual cooperation between the two countries.
14 July 1972	Abdulrahman Babu still held in detention over the killing of First Vice-President Sheikh Karume in April. More than fifty people held for questioning are freed.
18 July 1972	Eight Asians detained for engaging in anti-socialist economic crimes against Tanzania. Eight more were detained the following day for similar activities.
Aug. 1972	President Nyerere decries the expulsion of Uganda Asians by Idi Amin.
1 Aug. 1972	Zanzibar government reshuffle of the new government. Comprises ten men and the thirteen members of the Party Central Committee.
13 Aug. 1972	Zanzibar lifts ban on Daily Nation, Sunday Nation, Taifa Leo and Taifa-Tanzania from entering the island.
15 Sept. 1972	Hi-jacking of DC-9 plane from Dar-es-Salaam. Found damaged at Kilimanjaro airport in northern Tanzania.

17 Sept. 1972	Ugandan government announces that Tanzanian troops invade Uganda.
23 Sept. 1972	Amends 1970 treaty establishing an Audio-Visual Institute in Dar-es-Salaam by Denmark.
1 Oct. 1972	India's President Giri calls on Tanzania's Asians to identify with the country's problems and aspirations.
2 Oct. 1972	S.A. Mwamwindi sentenced to death for murdering Dr W. Kleruu, former Regional Commissioner of Iringa, on 25 December 1971.
5 Oct. 1972	Amends technical assistance treaty with Denmark pertaining to the Faculty of Agriculture in Morogoro.
5 Oct. 1972	War between Tanzania and Uganda averted through the mediation of Somalia resulting in the signing of a five-point peace agreement between the two countries in Mogadishu.
25 Oct. 1972	President Amin of Uganda issues decree that Tanzanian (Kenyan and other) Asians are to leave Uganda by 8 November.
27 Oct. 1972	Accedes to the Convention on the Elimination of Racial Discrimination.
3 Nov. 1972	Former Foreign Minister Oscar Kambona announces that he has established a secret base in northern Mozambique from which he intends to launch an attack on Tanzania.
27 Nov. 1972	Obtains assistance from Sweden, Denmark, Finland and Norway for the expansion of milk production and poultry units at the Kibaha Education Centre.
1-7 Dec. 1972	Afro-Shirazi Party holds its fifth Congress in Pemba.
2 Dec. 1972	Signs the final act of the United Nations/Inter-Governmental Maritime Consultative Organization Conference on International Container Traffic.
18 Dec. 1972	Signs guarantee agreement with the IBRD concerning the third Harbours Project.
19 Dec. 1972	Tanzania recognizes East Germany.
22 Jan. 1973	Radio Dar-es-Salaam announces that three Portuguese aircraft from Mozambique invade and bomb Tanzanian territory. Portuguese spokesperson denies this.
6 Feb. 1973	Heads of State of Tanzania, Zaire and Zambia meet in Arusha.
6 Feb. 1973	Tanzanian Foreign Minister denies that Tanzania is training guerrillas to attack Uganda.
Mar. 1973	Border conflicts take place between Tanzania and Burundi, resulting in casualties.
9 Mar. 1973	Signs treaty with France regarding cultural and technical co-operation.

21 Mar. 1973	Burundi military plane invades Tanzanian air space and bombs Tanzanian villages of Kagunga, Kibuti and Mubarazi.
27 Mar. 1973	Tanzania Rural Development Bank obtains financial assistance through treaty signature.
31 Mar. 1973	Denmark contributes to the Regional Development Fund.
3 Apr. 1973	Burundi Ambassador to Tanzania apologizes to Tanzanian Foreign Minister for the bombing of the Kigoma district causing the death of seventy-four people and destruction of property.
4 Apr. 1973	Ratifies amendment to Article 61 of the UN Charter.
13 Apr. 1973	Signs development credit agreement with the International Development Association on the fourth Education Project.
27 Apr. 1973	National Assembly approves bill which enforces the Arusha Declaration Leadership Code.
19 May 1973	Nine people sentenced to death for the assasination on 7 April 1972 of Zanzibari ruler, Sheikh Abeid Karume.
23 May 1973	Additional regulations amending the International Health Regulations multilateral agreement is signed, with particular reference to Article I. Enters into force on 1 January 1974.
23 May 1973	Signs credit agreement with the International Development Association on the second Livestock Development Project.
28 May 1973	President Amin of Uganda and J. Nyerere sign agreement in Addis Ababa with Ethiopia's Haile Selassie acting as mediator, that cordial relations between the two countries be maintained.
10 June 1973	Radio Nairobi announces that Hutu refugees from Southern Burundi have fled into Tanzania during the past month.
22 June 1973	Signs guarantee agreement with the IBRD concerning the third Telecommunications Project.
July 1973	Tanzania-Burundi border conflicts that occurred in March re-occur and result in a number of deaths.
July 1973	Uganda government pays compensation for twenty four Tanzanians who disappeared in Uganda in 1972.
2-3 July 1973	Multilateral agreement signed at the UN Seminar on the Study of New Ways and Means for Promoting Human Rights - the Problems and Needs of Africa.
9 July 1973	Liberia and Tanzania issue joint communiqué that they will cooperate in education, commerce and trade
13 July 1973	Tanzania-Burundi border conflict continues.

10 Aug. 1973	Percy Cleaver, a British freelance cameraman convicted of spying, and is sentenced to three years' imprisonment.
16 Aug. 1973	Definitive signature of the Commonwealth Telecomunications Organization Financial Agreement.
28 Aug. 1973	President Nyerere states at a state banquet in honour of Sir Seretse Khama of Botswana that Tanzania will assist Botswana to build links with Africa. Both leaders pledge their support for the liberation struggle in Southern Africa.
24 Sept. 1973	President Nyerere opens TANU's sixteenth Biennial Conference in Dar-es-Salaam. Discusses population, agriculture and educational issues in his address.
24 Sept. 1973	President Nyerere presents statistics which show that since 1967 2,000,000 people, 15% of the population, have been moved to Ujamaa villages.
28 Sept. 1973	Accepts, subject to constitutional procedures, the extension to the 1968 International Coffee Agreement.
30 Sept. 1973	Capital be moved from Dar-es-Salaam to Dodoma by stages over the next ten years.
Oct. 1973	TANU National Executive Committee imposes ban on wigs, mini-skirts and tight trousers.
4 Oct. 1973	Denmark provides financial assistance, via treaty signature, for district hospitals in Bagamoyo and Maswa; the construction of health auxiliary schools in Kondoa and Rufiji; and the construction of a medical assistance school.
7 Oct. 1973	Aboud Juma, Tanzania's First Vice-President, visits Uganda to attend the eleventh Independence Anniversary. Joint communique issued concerning trade, closer cooperation and African liberation.
18 Oct. 1973	Tanzania breaks off diplomatic relations with Israel.
Nov. 1973	Government nationalizes fifty farms held on ninety-nine year leases in the Kilimanjaro region by individuals.
6 Nov. 1973	Tanzania and Burundi sign agreement whereby Burundi agrees to pay compensation for border incidents that occured in March and June.
14 Nov. 1973	Signs treaty with Denmark regarding the construction of a Danish Volunteer Training Centre in Tanzania.
23 Nov. 1973	Denmark provides financial assistance, via treaty signature, for public libraries.
30 Nov. 1973	Signs financial assistance treaty with West Germany.
8 Dec. 1973	President Nyerere's book entitled 'Freedom and Development' covering speech and articles between January 1968 and January 1973 launched.

10 Dec. 1973	Sudan and Tanzania sign a joint statement of co-operation in various fields.
8 Jan. 1974	Acceptance of the Inter-Governmental Maritime Consultative Organization multilateral agreement.
8 Jan. 1974	Denmark provides financial assistance, via treaty signature, for the establishment of an Adult Education Book Publishing Programme for Tanzania.
8 Jan. 1974	Signs treaty with Denmark providing for financial assistance assigned to the Tanzania Primary Education Programme.
16 Jan. 1974	Tenth Anniversary of the 1964 Zanzibari revolution celebrated with the release of 545 prisoners.
17 Jan. 1974	Signs credit agreement with the International Development Association over the Geita Cotton Project.
21 Jan. 1974	Signs treaty with West Germany concerning financial assistance for the Tabora Water Supply Project.
28 Jan. 1974	Burundi pays compensation to Tanzania for attacks on its territory in March and June 1973.
5 Feb. 1974	President Nyerere holds talks with Britain's Sir Alec Douglas Home that the British government should secure the release of Zimbabwe leader, J. Nkomo and Rev. N. Sithole to secure a peaceful path to Rhodesian independence.
12 Feb. 1974	A new Ministry of National Culture and Youth created. Commander of Tanzania People's Defence Force, Major-General Sarakikya appointed its head.
13 Feb. 1974	Signs credit agreement with the International Development Association concerning the TIB Project.
5 Mar. 1974	Amends treaty with Denmark concerning contributions to the Regional Development Fund.
11 Mar. 1974	President Nyerere arrives in Mauritius on the first leg of a three week overseas tour to Australia, New Zealand and China.
12 Mar. 1974	Zanzibar cabinet reshuffle.
12 Mar. 1974	David Martin, correspondent of the Financial Times and the British Broadcasting Company expelled from Tanzania.
14 Mar. 1974	Amends treaty with Denmark over financial assistance for the Tanzania Rural Development Bank.
26 Mar. 1974	Receives government loan from Denmark after treaty signature.
May 1974	Three former ministers who were in the Zanzibari government that was overthrown in 1964, are amongst the twenty-nine political prisoners released.

May 1974	Burundi completes payment to Tanzania for attacks made on its citizens in March-June 1973.
15 May 1974	Forty-four people convicted of treason for their involvement in the assasination of Zanzibar leader Sheikh Karume. Amongst them is a former Tanzanian cabinet minister, A. Babu, said to have master minded the coup.
18 May 1974	A. Babu and thirty-three others sentenced to death and ten others given jail sentences ranging from ten to fifteen years with hard labour for their involvement in the assasination of Sheikh Karumu of Zanzibar.
June 1974	British government expresses concern that four of its citizens are detained in Tanzania.
4 June 1974	Definite acceptance, as an extension with modifications until 30 September 1975 of the 1968 International Coffee Agreement.
7 June 1974	President Nyerere and Vice-President R. Kawawa unanimously re-elected President and Vice-President of TANU.
19 June 1974	President Nyerere calls for an end to racial discrimination at the opening of the sixth Pan-African Congress (PAC) held in Dar-es-Salaam.
22 June 1974	Danish government loan to Tanzania.
24 June 1974	Loan agreement from the IBRD on the Cashew Nut Development Project.
July 1974	Two days after Tanzanian First Vice-President, Sheikh Aboud Tumbe had talks with President Amin of Uganda, to normalize relations, Amin accuses Tanzania of planning to invade Uganda.
July 1974	TANU celebrates its twentieth anniversary.
5 July 1974	Signs an Additional Protocol to the Universal Postal Union, General Regulations, insured letters, postal parcels and the Universal Postal Convention.
9 July 1974	Signs an Additional Protocol on 5 July to the Universal Postal Union, General Regulations, unused letters, postal parcels and the Universal Postal Convention.
12 July 1974	Signs development credit agreement with the International Development Association on the Sites and Services Project.
2 Aug. 1974	Disinvokes Article XXXV of GATT in respect of Japan.
2 Aug. 1974	President Idi Amin of Uganda calls off threatened invasion of Tanzania.
7 Aug. 1974	Uganda threatens to extend its border into Tanzania to the Kagura River.
21 Aug. 1974	Signs development credit agreement with the International Development Association on the Highway Maintenance Project and the Kigoma Rural Development Project.
23 Aug. 1974	Signs grant agreement with the United Nations Capital Development Fund.

27 Aug. 1974	President Nyerere starts four day state visit to the Congo People's Republic.
6 Sept. 1974	Financial assistance treaty with West Germany covering the Handeni Water Supply Project.
6 Sept. 1974	Signs financial assistance treaty with West Germany concerning the Tanzania Investment Bank.
15 Sept. 1974	The International Monetary Fund announces certain changes in the par or central rates of Tanzania's currency.
26 Sept. 1974	Signs protocol for the continuation in force of the International Coffee Agreement.
27 Sept. 1974	Signs development credit agreement with the International Development Association on the Kilombero Sugar Project.
30 Sept. 1974	President of Tanzania, Zambia and Zaire meet with FRELIMO President Samora Machel in Dar-es-Salaam to discuss the Mozambique issue.
Oct. 1974	Tanzania, Zambia and Zaire ruling party members meet in Dar-es-Salaam to formulate a policy of co-operation.
Oct. 1974	Tanzanian foreign minister, J. Malecela, condemns British naval manoeuvres in South Africa.
Nov. 1974	President Nyerere begins a five day state visit to Sudan. Both countries pledge bilateral political, economic and cultural co-operation. Agree on non-alignment, support for liberation movements.
Nov. 1974	First Vice-President Sheikh Aboud Jumbe admits on British Television that former Prime Minister, Kassim Hanga and others were secretly executed a few years ago.
4-5 Nov. 1974	Uganda warns Tanzania that it will take strong action against her for having violated its air space on 4 and 5 November.
13 Nov. 1974	President Nyerere reshuffles his cabinet.
27 Nov. 1974	TANU party members are to obey its leadership code. They have to commit themselves to socialism and are banned from participating in capitalism enterprises.
20 Dec. 1974	Signs programme loan agreement with IBRD.
28 Jan. 1975	Signs financial assistance treaty with Denmark for the construction of the College of National Education at Monduli.
28 Jan. 1975	TANU central committee issues directives at a meeting in Dodoma that the countries constitution be amended to reflect the party's supremacy and that the constitution should state that Tanzania is a socialist state.
Feb. 1975	Tanzania resumes sporting ties with Britain.
20 Feb. 1975	Signs treaty on financial assistance from West Germany.

11 Mar. 1975	TANU National Executive Committee meeting in Shinyanga constitutional changes proposed calling for the election of only one member of Parliament for each of its districts. This was later approved by Parliament.
24 Mar. 1975	Danish loan to Tanzania.
24 Mar. 1975	Denmark provides assistance for a Primary education programme. Treaty signed.
24 Mar. 1975	Tanzania and Denmark amend financial assistance treaty regarding the Tanzania Rural Development Bank.
28 Mar. 1975	Definitive signature of the International Coffee Agreement.
10 Apr. 1975	Tanzania denounces the movement of the Ugandan Malire Mechanised Socialist Reconnaisance Unit to the Tanzanian border on 7 April.
15 Apr. 1975	Tanzania and Libya agree to establish diplomatic relations.
26 Apr. 1975	One hundred and fifty seven detainees released to mark the eleventh anniversary of the Union of Tanganyika and Zanzibar to form the Republic of Tanzania.
May 1975	Two Kenyan officials returning from an East African Community meeting held in Arusha, Tanzania, stripped naked and harassed by Tanzanian police.
1 May 1975	Ugandan Ministry of Information denies that Ugandan air planes violated Tanzanian air space.
19 May 1975	Zairean rebels calling themselves the People's Revolution Party (PRP) kidnap students and the United States holds Tanzania responsible for their release.
20 May 1975	Tanzania announces the banning of the Zimbabwe African People's Union (ZAPU) and the Zimbabwe African National Union (ZANU) operating from Tanzanian soil. Recognizes the African National Council as the sole party for the liberation of Rhodesia.
23 May 1975	Tanzania signs a treaty with the United States relating to agricultural commodities.
June 1975	With the passing of the Interim Constitution (Amendment) Bill of 1975, TANU attains legal status as the supreme party and that all political activity in Tanzania be conducted by or under its auspices.
June 1975	Tanzania criticizes Kenyan call for the dissolution of the East African Community.
2 June 1975	Signs grant agreement with the United Nations Capital Development Fund.
5 June 1975	Accepts multilateral treaty on the African Training and Research Centre in Administration for Development.
19 June 1975	Accedes to the Convention of the Political Rights of Women.

19 June 1975	Signs loan agreement with IBRD on the Mwanza Textile Project.
1 July 1975	Signs international treaty on the suppression and punishment of the crime of apartheid.
14 July 1975	President Nyerere pays two day state visit to Somalia.
18 July 1975	Signs treaty with Denmark pertaining to technical assistance for the establishment of a hospital equipment maintenance unit.
18 July 1975	Parliament dissolves to prepare for the forthcoming 26 October election.
24 July 1975	Addressing students in Dar-es-Salaam, Tanzania's foreign minister, John Malecela, explains why his country is boycotting the twenty-fifth ordinary session of the OAU, held in Kampala, Uganda.
28 July 1975	Tanzania boycotts the twelfth OAU Heads of State Conference held in Kampala because of the killing of people by the Amin regime in Uganda.
July 1975	President Nyerere announces changes to its military.
15 Aug. 1975	Signs a development credit agreement with the International Development Association on the Dairy Development Project.
19 Aug. 1975	Briton Percy Cleaver, who was sentenced in 1973 for espionage is released.
30 Aug. 1975	President Nyerere pays official visit to Mozambique.
Aug. 1975	Tanzania makes changes to its police force.
Sept. 1975	5,577,569 Tanzanians register to vote for the forthcoming 26 October election. This is 526,629 more than the 1950 general election.
Sept. 1975	TANU and the Afro-Shirazi Party nominate President Nyerere as sole presidential candidate for the October general election at a joint electoral conference.
6 Sept. 1975	Signs agreement with Canada relating to the training of personnel of Tanzania People's Defence Forces in Canada.
7 Sept. 1975	Uganda puts its troops on alert along the Tanzanian border following the killing of a Ugandan citizen by Tanzanian troops in the border area of Mutukula on 31 August.
7 Sept. 1975	During a state visit to Mozambique, Presidents Nyere and Samora Machel sign two agreements sealing ideological ties, economic and diplomatic relations. Agree to establish a commission of co-operation to strengthen their economies and enhance bilateral economic relations.
23 Sept. 1975	TANU seventeenth Biennial National Conference opens. Announces rural reforms and formation of villages, assemblies and councils to run the affair of all villages on a co-operative and socialist basis.
24 Sept. 1975	At a special meeting on border incidents held in Tarime, Kenya calls on Tanzania to stop harrassing its nationals along the Tanzanian border.

Oct. 1975	The repatriation of 21,000 Mozambican refugees who fled to Tanzania during the liberation war in Mozambiqueeee begins.
Oct. 1975	Appointment of two new members of the Zanzibar Revolutionary Council (Ali M. Ali and Kassim Ali - who will be Chairman of the Ports and Shipping Department, and Works and Housing respectively) and the creation of seven new departments.
4 Oct. 1975	At the 'Good Neighbours' Conference held in Arusha, Kenya and Tanzania resolve to cooperate in solving border problems between the two countries.
15 Oct. 1975	East African Authority approves terms of references for reviews of the Treaty of East African cooperation.
19 Oct. 1975	Government owned Sunday News opposed call by President Houphouet-Boigny of the Ivory Coast for Africa to open diplomatic links with South Africa.
31 Oct. 1975	At the October general election, President Nyerere returned to office by a 93.2% vote.
Nov. 1975	Zanzibar High Court upholds the death sentences of 24 people convicted of treason in connection with the assasination of Zanzibari leader, Sheikh Karume, in 1972.
1 Nov. 1975	President Nyerere commemorates his third term of office with the release of 7,380 prisoners and reduced the jail term of 3,685 other prisoners.
7 Nov. 1975	New cabinet appointed.
12 Nov. 1975	Signs guarantee agreement with the IBRD on the second Tanzanian Investment Bank Project.
18 Nov. 1975	President Nyerere starts a four day state visit to Britain. States that the armed struggle for the liberation of Rhodesia and Namibia is inevitable.
18 Nov. 1975	Afro-Shirazi Party (ASP) opens its 6th congress in Mbweni. Zanzibar Party constitution amended 95 resolutions passed covering issues such as farming methods, adult literacy and a new leadership code similar to chat of TAMU.
30 Nov. 1975	Tanzanian government condemns South African invasion of Angola, Radio Dar es Salaam reports.
8 Dec. 1975	Accedes to the Customs Convention on Welfare of Seafarers.
11 Dec. 1975	Danish government loan to Tanzania.
17 Dec. 1975	Signs treaty with Kenya on the territorial sea boundary.
Jan. 1976	First Vice-President Jumbe accuses ex-Sultan Jamshid and Ali Muhsin - former leader of the Zanzibar Nationalist Party - of planning to invade the country.
Jan. 1976	President Nyerere pays five-day state visit to India. In a joint communiqué with Mrs. Gandhi concern over the strife in Angola and South African

aggression is expressed.

1 Jan. 1976	Signs multilateral agreement to the Constitution of the Universal Postal Union.
6 Jan. 1976	Accepts amendment to Articles 34 and 35 of the World Health Organization's Constitution.
9 Jan. 1976	Signs development credit agreement with the International Development Association on the Technical Assistance Project.
11 Jan. 1976	Accedes to the multilateral convention on civil and commercial rights.
18 Jan. 1976	During a state visit to India, President Nyerere defends African support for Soviet and Cuban involvement in Angola and denies African support for communism.
29 Jan. 1976	Development agreement signed with the International Development Association concerning the National Maize Project.
29 Jan. 1976	Signs a development credit agreement with the International Development Association on the fifth Education Project.
Mar. 1976	Armed forces statistics: Tanzania has a 13,000 army, 600 navy, 1000 air forces, 35,000 citizens militia, one police marine unit. Arms: one tank battalion, 1 artillary battallion, 6 motor gunboats, 20 combat aircraft, backing - mainly China.
1 Mar. 1976	Signs a guarantee agreement with the IBRD on the second East African Development Bank Project.
24 Mar. 1976	Signs a treaty with Great Britain concerning public officers' pensions.
Apr. 1976	Zambia, Tanzania and Mozambique agree to establish a Joint Institute for training their Police and Defence Force.
4 Apr. 1976	The Joint Commission for co-operation, established to create closer relations between Tanzania and Mozambique, holds its first meeting in Dar-es-Salaam.
13 Apr. 1976	Signs agreement with the Federal Republic of Germany concerning financial assistance.
6 May 1976	Signs a double taxation treaty with Denmark regarding fiscal evasion on income and capital.
6 May 1976	Zanzibar government changes.
12 May 1976	Signs treaty with Finland relating to the avoidance of double taxation and the prevention of fiscal evasion with respect to taxes on income and capital.
June 1976	Government owned press accuses Kenya of trying to break up the East African Community.
June 1976	TANU and the Afro-Shirazi Party (ASP) agree to merge.

9 June 1976	Signs International Coffee Agreement of 1976.
11 June 1976	Accedes to the Convention on Economic, Social and Cultural Rights.
11 June 1976	Accedes to the Convention of the Suppression and Punishment of the Crime of Apartheid.
15 June 1976	Signs treaty with United States on agricultural commodities.
5 July 1976	Installations established by Mozambique in Tanzania during the Mozambique liberation struggle, handed over to TANU by FRELIMO. Amongst these are a hospital and educational institution.
12 July 1976	Signs a development credit agreement with the International Development Association on the Fisheries Development Project.
12 July 1976	Signs loan agreement with the International Bank for Reconstruction and Development on the Sao Hill Forestry Project.
14 July 1976	TANZAM railway line officially handed over to the Tanzanian and Zambian Presidents by Chinese Vice-Premier, Sun Chien.
18 July 1976	Eleven SWAPO dissidents who were held in protective custody in Zambia, flown to Dar-es-Salaam and held in protective custody.
5 Aug. 1976	Signs the British Expatriates Supplementary (Tanzania) Agreement.
16 Aug. 1976	Over 10,000 Mozambican refugees who fled from Portuguese colonial war are to be repatriated back to Mozambique according to D. Chefeke, the representative in Tanzania of the UN High Commissioner for Refugees.
29 Aug. 1976	Tanzania, Zambia and Mozambique reach common agreement on security issues and on criminals who cross borders.
1 Sept. 1976	Tanzania's Minister for Defence and National Service, Edward Sokoine, states at the opening of the Military Academy that all military personnel will be trained locally, instead of being sent abroad.
14 Sept. 1976	President Nyerere issues statement criticizing United States policy over Southern Africa (shortly before Dr. Kissinger's visit to Dar-es-Salaam and talks with President Nyerere).
16 Sept. 1976	Inter-Governmental Maritime Consultative Organization acceptance.
16 Sept. 1976	Signs a development credit agreement with the International Development Association for the Tobacco Processing Project.
24 Sept. 1976	Signs International Coffee Agreement.
Oct. 1976	President Nyerere issues statement at Lusaka Airport after a Black African pre-Geneva Summit that Britain should play a full role as a colonial power at the Geneva Conference over the Rhodesian issue and also during the black majority transitional government. That a Governor-General also be appointed.

18 Oct. 1976	Trial concerning an appeal made by those convicted of assassinating President Karume of Zanzibar resumes. Accused tell of beatings whilst in detention.
2 Nov. 1976	Signs agreement with the Federal Republic of Germany concerning financial assistance.
5 Nov. 1976	Zanzibar's Afro-Shirazi Party and the TANU merge to form a new party called the Chama Cha Mapinduzi and adopt a new constitution. New party to be proclaimed on 5 February 1977.
12 Nov. 1976	Danish loan to Tanzania.
16 Nov. 1976	President Nyerere commences a five-day state visit to Nigeria.
Dec. 1976	Accusation and counter accusation continues between Kenya and Tanzania over the East African Community.
21 Dec. 1976	Financial assistance from the Federal Republic of Germany for the Arusha Water Supply Project, the Tabora Water Supply Project, the Tanzania Investment Bank Project, Tanzania Rural Development Bank Project, and for the purchase of goods and services.
5 Jan. 1977	Signs loan agreement with the IBRD on the Urban Water Supply Project.
21 Jan. 1977	President Nyerere appointed Chairman of the new Chama cha Mapinduzi political party and Aboud Jumbe elected its Vice-Chairman.
23 Jan. 1977	Two cabinet ministers and two regional commissioners resign after taking responsibility for the death of prisoners at the hands of police and security forces in the Shinyanga and Mwanza regions.
3 Feb. 1977	Tanzania closes its border with Kenya over the collapse of East African Airways, which left Tanzania without an airline.
5 Feb. 1977	Chama Cha Mapinduzi (CCCM) political party formally launched in Zanzibar.
9 Feb. 1977	Death sentences on seven people upheld for plotting a 1972 abortive coup in which Zanzibar leader Sheik Karume was assassinated. Of the thirty-six appallants, some had their death sentences cummuted to prison terms and others had their prison sentences reduced.
13 Feb. 1977	President Nyerere reshuffles his cabinet and appoints Edward Moringe Sokoine as Prime Minister, replacing Rashidi Kawawa, who also lost his post as Vice-President.
25 Feb. 1977	Zanzibar cabinet reshuffle.
16 Mar. 1977	Talks continue between Kenya and Tanzania over the latter's closure of their common border in February.
24 Mar. 1977	Signs agreement with the International Development Association over programme credit.

Apr. 1977	In a document entitled 'The Arusha Declaration Ten Years After', President Nyerere reviews the country's progress since the Arusha Declaration was adopted in January 1967.
6 Apr. 1977	Loan agreement signed with the IBRD concerning the Morogoro Industrial Complex Project.
18 Apr. 1977	Accedes to the Vienna Convention on Consular Relations.
18 Apr. 1977	Tanzania closes its borders permanently with Kenya.
25 Apr. 1977	A new constitution adopted to replace the thirteen year old interim constitution.
24 June 1977	Danish loan to Tanzania.
July 1977	East African Community collapses. Tanzania's Prime Minister, Sokoini, reiterates that his country is still committed to the Community.
18 July 1977	International Fund for Agricultural Development establishment treaty is signed.
2 Aug. 1977	Ratifies Protection of World Cultural and Natural Heritage Convention.
2 Aug. 1977	Signs multilateral Convention Concerning the Prohibition and Prevention of the Illicit Import, Export and Transfer of Ownership of Cultural Property.
24 Aug. 1977	Establishes, together with Rwanda and Burundi, the Organization for the Management and Development of the Kagera River Basin.
Sept. 1977	Tanzania grants over 100 Ugandans formerly employed in the East African Community (EAC) headquarters in Arusha, political asylum.
Oct. 1977	Army increased from 13,000 to 17,000 and battalions from eight to eleven.
5 Oct. 1977	Former Intelligence officer, Juma Thomas Zangira sentenced to a twenty-year imprisonment with hard labour for espionage and sabotage. He released information to John Wilson of Britain between 1971 and 1977, for spying on the OAU Liberation Committee and on the liberation movements based in Dar-es-Salaam.
18 Oct. 1977	Chama Cha Mapinduzi (CCM) holds its first conference in Dar-es-Salaam.
3 Nov. 1977	Signs development credit agreement with the International Development Association for the second national sites and services project.
1 Dec. 1977	A new minister for national culture and youth (Chediel Mgonja) and a junior minister for finance and planning (Venance Ngula) sworn in.
16 Dec. 1977	A nine-point accord released by Kenya to normalize relations with Tanzania.
18 Dec. 1977	Pemba and Zanzibari voters go to the polls to elect ten new members of Parliament.

28 Dec. 1977	Signs guarantee agreement with the IRBD pertaining to the Tanzania Investment Bank.
14 Jan. 1978	Tanzania and Mozambique sign agreement in Maputo that a training centre is to be established in Dar-es-Salaam to train diplomats.
19 Jan. 1978	Obtains rural credit after signing treaty with United Nations Capital Development Fund.
Feb. 1978	Chama Cha Mapinduzi Party's first anniversary celebrated with the release of 7083 prisoners and twenty-six political prisoners. Two of these political prisoners are brothers of former foreign minister Oscar Kambona.
5 Feb. 1978	The following five organizations established and open to all Tanzanians irrespective of whether they are Chama Cha Mapinduzi members or not. These are Youth organizations; Union of Tanzania Women; Union of Tanzania Workers; Union of Co-operative Societies; Tanzania Parents' Association. Only Party members can become leaders.
16 Feb. 1978	Tanzania dismisses the Salisbury Agreement on an internal settlement plan for Rhodesia.
18 Feb. 1978	Signs treaty with United Nations Capital Development Fund on community development.
27 Feb. 1978	Signs treaty with United Nations Capital Development Fund pertaining to rural water supply.
27 Feb. 1978	Cabinet changes made.
Mar. 1978	Juma T. Zangira, who was sentenced to twenty years for spying, has his sentence reduced to twelve years.
2 Mar. 1978	Minor government reshuffle.
2 Mar. 1978	Signs grant agreement with the United Nations Capital Development Fund for Community Development.
5 Mar. 1978	University of Dar-es-Salaam students and students from the Water and Land Institute protest against salary increases and other benefits granted to MPs, ministers and party leaders. About 20% are expelled by President Nyerere.
26 Apr. 1978	Thirteen people are given amnesty to mark the fourteenth anniversary of the union between Tanganyika and Zanzibar. Amongst them is former Tanzanian Minister of Economic Affairs, A. Babu, who was sentenced to death for his involvement in the assassination of Sheikh Karume, the Zanzibar leader.
May 1978	Ten Ugandans suspected of belonging to Uganda military intelligence and masquerading as athletic officials arrested for spying.
May 1978	Tanzania and Burundi issue joint communiqué stating they have decided to establish a permanent joint commission to review cooperation between the two countries.

May 1978	154 Zanzibari prisoners are freed and the sentence of fourteen others is reduced to mark May Day. Amongst those pardoned are eight political prisoners involved in the attempt to overthrow the Zanzibari government in 1972 and the death of Sheikh Karume, Zanzibar's leader.
29 May 1978	327 of the 367 students expelled on 5 March for protesting against salary increases given to MPs and other ministers and party leaders are pardoned.
30 May 1978	Receives operational assistance from United Nations and specialized agencies.
30 May 1978	Signs assistance treaty with United Nations Development Programme.
2 June 1978	Tanzanian government announces takeover of Lonrho assets.
8 June 1978	Statue of assassinated President of the Afro-Shirazi Party, Sheikh Karume, unveiled to commemorate the 10th anniversary of the 1964 revolution in Zanzibar.
22 June 1978	The Tanzania-Kenya border will remain closed unless all the nine points of the Mombasa Agreement signed in December 1977 are fulfilled, Tanzania's Foreign Minister, B. Mkope tells the National Assembly.
30 June 1978	Zanzibar reshuffles its cabinet from nineteen to thirteen members. Thirteen principal secretaries and four junior ministers are appointed.
22-23 July 1978	President Nyerere pays an official state visit to Ethiopia.
28 July 1978	Signs multilateral agreement establishing the International Tea Promotion Association.
22 Aug. 1978	500 Tanzanians, expelled from Zambia, return to Tanzania.
Sept. 1978	Foreign Minister E. Sokoine visits China and an agreement is made on economic and technical cooperation.
27 Oct. 1978	The Ugandan government claims that Tanzanian troops, backed by Cubans, have invaded Uganda and captured the border town of Mutukula.
Nov. 1978	Ugandan troops, who invaded the Kagora forest in Tanzania, are driven out.
Nov. 1978	Uganda-Tanzania border war continues.
9 Nov. 1978	Tanzania recognizes the government of the Saharan Arab Democratic Republic led by the Polisario Liberation Front.
27 Nov. 1978	Tanzanian troops carry out a retaliatory strike against Uganda and capture the border town of Mutukula.
Dec. 1978	Madagascar proposes a joint commission with Tanzania to deal with co-operation in trade, cultural affairs and communication.
8 Dec. 1978	Signs treaty with Denmark concerning a project unit in the Ministry of National Education.

10 Dec. 1978	Uganda drops eleven bombs over Kitengule in the Kagera District.
13 Dec. 1978	158 Tanzanians are expelled from Zambia arrive in Mbeya, southern Tanzania.
4 Jan. 1979	Uganda accuses Libya of supplying arms to Tanzania.
26 Jan. 1979	Border conflict between Tanzania and Uganda continues.
Mar. 1979	Tanzania fails to obtain arms from the Soviet Union.
Apr. 1979	For the 1980 general elections Tanzania will have 111 electoral constituencies (ninety-six in the 1975 election), ten of which will be in Zanzibar.
12 Apr. 1979	Tanzania recognises the new Uganda government of President Lule.
26 Apr. 1979	Tanzania's fifteenth union anniversary is celebrated with the pardoning of 6,413 prisoners by President Nyerere.
May 1979	Tanzania, Seychelles and Malagasy armed forces hold joint military exercises in the Seychelles.
30 May 1979	President Moi of Kenya and President Nyerere meet at Arusha to break the impasse between the two countries. This consequence of Nyerere's closing their common border two and a half years ago after the collapse of the East African Community.
July 1979	Joint Commission established between Algeria and Tanzania at end of President Nyerere's three day visit to Algeria to explore areas of further co-operation.
20 July 1979	President Nyerere welcomes Britain's Queen Elizabeth on her state visit to Tanzania.
12 Oct. 1979	The Zanzibar Revolutionary Council approves a new constitution separate from that of the Tanzanian mainland.
22 Oct. 1979	Tanzania Court of Appeal inaugurated by President Nyerere.
5 Nov. 1979	In a minor cabinet reshuffle, Amir Jamal replaces Edwin Mtei as Minister of Finance and Planning on Mtei's resignation over an attack on Nyerere's socialist policies. This is the fourth time that Jamal has been elected Finance Minister.
21 Nov. 1979	Chama Cha Mapinduzi (CCM) National Executive Committee dismisses seventeen party officials for lack of discipline.
Dec. 1979	Two agreements are signed at the end of President Nyerere's state visit to Iraq. Co-operation in banking, technical, youth and sports affairs is envisaged.
12 Dec. 1979	Tanzania and Uganda sign two agreements according to which Tanzania is to provide defence and police forces to strengthen Uganda's defence-security

over the next two years.

28 Dec. 1979   Chama Cha Mapinduzi (CCM) approves a separate constitution for Zanzibar.

8 Jan. 1980   Zanzibar elects a forty person House of Representatives under a new constitution which came into effect on 12 January.

14 Apr. 1980   East African Summit is held to improve the relations between members of the East African Community - Tanzania, Kenya and Uganda.

15 Apr. 1980   Law Reform Commission of Tanzania established.

11 May 1980   Hussein Shekilango killed in air crash in Uganda. He is a Minister of State in the Prime Minister's Office.

May 1980   Two Chama Cha Mapinduzi members, L. Kintu and Hazi M. Sadik, expelled from the party for criticizing Tanzania's economic policies and co-operating with Ugandan forces when they occupied Tanzanian territory near Bukoba in 1978.

12 July 1980   Zanzibar leader Aboud Jumba says that a coup to topple him has failed.

21 Aug. 1980   Rwandan refugees (36,000) granted Tanzanian citizenship.

Sept. 1980   Tanzania regrets lawless action by its paramilitary unit in Kenyan territory.

26 Oct. 1980   Aboud Jumbe elected President of Zanzibar in the October general election by a 93.65% margin. President Nyerere re-elected for a further five-year term. He receives 93.01% of the vote, his lowest level of support since coming into power.

Nov. 1980   Cabinet reshuffle following the October general election. Amongst them is the appointment of a new Prime Minister, Foreign and Defence ministers.

Nov. 1980   Zanzibar's President Aboud Jumbe elects a fifteen member cabinet.

5 Nov. 1980   In a minor cabinet reshuffle, Professor K. Malima named minister of a new Ministry of Economic and Development Planning.

Jan. 1981   Minister for Communications and Transport, A. Mwingira, also chairman of the Air Tanzania Corporation (ATC) dismissed from his post for mismanagement.

Jan. 1981   President Nyerere admits that Tanzanian troops fought alongside Mozambican government forces and black nationalist guerrilla forces during the liberation war in Zimbabwe.

Jan. 1981   Uganda attempts to influence Tanzania to open the Tanzania-Kenya border and normalize relations between these three countries.

17 Jan. 1981   The Kenyan, Ugandan, Zambian and Tanzanian Presidents meet in Kampala to reaffirm East African co-operation and to symbolize Uganda's reacceptance into the international community.

Feb. 1981	Ministerial portfolio changes made as Trade Minister Ibrahim Kaduma becomes Transport Minister in place of a sacked Augustine Mwingira.
11 Feb. 1981	Kenya and Tanzania agree to normalize border relations between their two countries.
13 Mar. 1981	Six East and Central African leaders meet in the Tanzanian capital to discuss matters of mutual interest.
26 Apr. 1981	Seventeenth anniversary of the Union of Tanganyika and Zanzibar commemorated with the release of ten people detained in 1980 for conspiring to overthrow the government of Zanzibar.
28 Apr. 1981	10,000 Tanzanian troops, remnants of the military forces that overthrew Idi Amin's regime in Uganda two years ago, are to be withdrawn from Uganda, according to Defence Minister Lieutenant-General Abdallah Twalipo.
24 July 1981	Kenya-Tanzania border remains closed. This border was closed in 1977 after the collapse of the East African Community.
22 Aug. 1981	Military co-operation agreement signed between Uganda and Tanzania.
3 Oct. 1981	Tanzania-Malawi border readjusted.
Nov. 1981	Zanzibar cabinet changes.
9 Dec. 1981	Abel Mwanga, Tanzanian Minister of State in the President's Office, has his 1980 parliamentary election victory nullified for soliciting votes.
12 Dec. 1981	Tanzania-Malawi border talks take place in Lilongwe.
21 Jan. 1982	The Chama Cha Mapinduzi Party holds Congress to discuss proposed amendment to the Party's 1980 constitution.
Feb. 1982	Tanzania and Mozambique agree to increase economic and military co-operation between the two countries.
5 Feb. 1982	Tanzania reshuffles its cabinet.
10 Feb. 1982	Uganda, Rwanda, Burundi and Tanzania agree to establish a communication network by mid-1982.
28 Feb. 1982	Twenty-six-hour siege of a Tanzanian airliner, hijacked by a group claiming to represent a 'revolutionary youth movement of Tanzania', comes to an end in Standsted Airport, Essex. Hijackers demand to see Oscar Kambona, former Defence & External Affairs Minister.
5 May 1982	Tanzania's Chama Cha Chapinduzi and Mozambique's FRELIMO Party sign co-operation agreement.
June 1982	About 700 Tanzanian policemen leave Uganda and return home.
1 June 1982	Tanzania signs the Organization of African Unity Convention on Human and People's Rights.

6 July 1982	New Minister for Trade, R.A. Shaaban, appointed in Zanzibar.
Aug. 1982	President Nyerere pays a five-day state visit to Zambia to improve relations between the two countries.
17 Sept. 1982	Five hijackers of the Air Tanzania plane in February found.
Oct. 1982	President Nyerere re-elected chairman of the Chama Cha Mapinduzi Party at its National Congress.
16 Oct. 1982	Two fugitive Kenyan Air Force rebels granted asylum by Tanzania.
25 Oct. 1982	At its National Congress, Chama Cha Mapinduzi (CCM) Party calls for disciplinary measures against party and government leaders who disregard the country's socialist policies.
Jan. 1983	Details of the proposed amendments to the countries' constitution released. Restrictions on the presidential terms are introduced and reintroduction of the dual vice-presidency, one for the mainland and the other for Zanzibar. The National Assembly is given increased powers.
28 Jan. 1983	Twenty seven soldiers and civilians appear in court for attempting to overthrow the government.
10 Feb. 1983	Raschid Kawawa, Chama Cha Mapinduzi Party's Secretary-General, opens the 40th session of the OAU Liberation Committee in Arusha.
21 Feb. 1983	Zanzibar reshuffles its cabinet. A new Ministry of Labour, Manpower and Social Welfare is created and a post of Chief Minister with Ramadhani Haji Faki as its head in a supervisory capacity.
24 Feb. 1983	Edward Sokoine (who resigned in 1980) re-instated as Prime Minister of Tanzania.
Mar. 1983	Department responsible for the civil service and manpower development in the Prime Minister's Office, develops into a fully fledged Ministry. Pius Mwandu is its head.
28 Mar. 1983	Tanzania, Angola and Mozambique's Foreign Ministers attend an international conference in Lisbon in support of Front Line States bordering South Africa.
22 Apr. 1983	An Economic Crime Bill passed to reduce corruption.
27 Apr. 1983	Amnesty granted to 1,183 prisoners to commemorate the 19th anniversary of the Union between Tanganyika and Zanzibar.
17 June 1983	Charges dropped against coup plotters for attempting to assassinate President Nyerere in January 1983.
20 June 1983	Home Affairs Minister & Commissioner of Prisons resigns after the escape from custody of two people accused of plotting to overthrow the government in assasinating President Nyerere.
15 July 1983	Tanzania reiterates its readiness to establish diplomatic relations with Kenya.

19 July 1983	Tanzania and six other Southern and Central African states issue a joint statement at a meeting in Nyanga, Zimbabwe, attended by its Defence and Security Ministers, to strengthen co-operation and counter South African destabilization.
10 Aug. 1983	Tanzanian troops gradually withdraw from the Seychelles because of its improved security situation.
Sept. 1983	Tanzania and Saudi Arabia agree to establish full diplomatic relations, with immediate effect.
20 Sept. 1983	Salim Amour appointed Minister of Home Affairs. He replaces A. Natupe who resigned in June.
Oct. 1983	President Nyerere visits Algeria. Issues joint communique that both countries will strengthen bilateral relations.
17 Nov. 1983	The Tanzania-Kenya border that was closed since 1977, reopened. A few hours earlier the Kenyan, Tanzanian and Ugandan Presidents agreed on a settlement of financial matters arising from the collapse of the East African Community.
3 Dec. 1983	Bashir E. Kwaw-Swanzy sworn in as Attorney-General of Zanzibar.
13 Dec. 1983	Tanzania, Kenya and Uganda agree to exchange High Commissioners.
Jan. 1984	Tanzanian Foreign Minister, Salim Ahmed Salim, reacts to the military coup in Nigeria, stating that his country will not impose its political views on how another country should govern itself.
29 Jan. 1984	Zanzibar President A. Jumbe resigns and Ali Hassan Mwinyi is appointed his interim successor.
31 Jan. 1984	Ali Hassam Mwinyi is sworn in as President of Zanzibar and as Interior Chairman of the Zanzibar Revolutionary Council.
Feb. 1984	Zanzibar cabinet reshuffle.
Mar. 1984	President Nyerere decides to step down as President of Tanzania.
Mar. 1984	Zanzibar President Mwinyi announces that former Attorney General, Woifango Dourado, is the only person in detention. Mr. Dourado calls for changes to the constitution.
1 Mar. 1984	Bills passed to amend the Zanzibar constitution of 1979 and to amend the Act of 1980 which governs the election of the chairman of the Revolutionary Council and the President of Zanzibar.
11 Mar. 1984	Ali Hassan Mwinyi is nominated as sole candidate for Zanzibar's Presidential elections scheduled for 19 April.
Apr. 1984	Ali Hassan Mwinyi replaces Aboud Jumbe as president.
12 Apr. 1984	Prime Minister of Tanzania E.M. Sokoine dies in a road accident near Morogoro town.

24 Apr. 1984	Salim Ahmed Salim is appointed Prime Minister and the cabinet reshuffled. Cabinet is reduced from twenty-one portfolios to fourteen.
May 1984	Zanzibar cabinet is reshuffled. Portfolios reduced from fifteen to ten.
June 1984	A far-reaching draft amendment to the constitution is announced by the Chama Cha Mapinduzi party.
Aug. 1984	President Nyerere indicates that he may not step down from the Presidency in 1985.
24 Aug. 1984	Zanzibar President Ali Hassan Mwinyi is elected as Vice-Chairman of the Chama Cha Mapinduzi Party.
Sept. 1984	Charges are outlined in court against nineteen people who planned to kill President Nyerere and overthrow his government in 1983.
10 Oct. 1984	Bill passed to amend the 1979 Isles Constitution.
14 Nov. 1984	Tanzania and Burundi sign border agreement.
23 Nov. 1984	Nineteen people, who planned to kill President Nyerere and overthrow his government, plead not guilty.
23 Nov. 1984	The Tanzanian government rejects charges of its involvement in the Shaba raid.
9 Dec. 1984	1018 prisoners are given amnesty to mark Tanzania's twenty-third anniversary of independence.
14 Jan. 1985	Zanzibar introduces a new judicial system. Abolishes peoples' courts and adopts the policy that a defendent is innocemt until proved guilty.
7 Mar. 1985	Signs agreement with Ireland on technical cooperation.
8 Mar. 1985	Zanzibar reshuffles its cabinet.
17 Mar. 1985	President Nyerere arrives in London on an official state visit to the United Kingdom, Netherlands and Yugoslavia. Amonst other issues pleads that African countries are given more time to pay their debts. Comments on African achievements and on the Nkomati Accord between Mozambique and South Africa.
16 May 1985	Tanzanian foreign minister issues statement that diplomatic relations will soon be established between Malawi and Tanzania.
July 1985	President Nyerere expresses his thanks to Sweden, Norway, Denmark and Finland on his visit to those countries for aid given to Tanzania.
12 Aug. 1985	Four of the nineteen Tanzanians charged with treason for attempting to kill President Nyerere and overthrow his government freed by the Dar-es-Salaam High Court.
15 Aug. 1985	Ali Hassam Mwinyi to succeed President Nyerere who retires at the end of the year.

18 August 1985	President Nyerere starts ten-day visit to China, North Korea and India.
Oct. 1985	Zanzibaris go to the polls and elect a new government. Idris Abdul Wakil appointed Zanzibar President.
27 Oct. 1985	Tanzanians vote in Ali Hassam Mwinyi as next president to replace J. Nyerere.
4 Nov. 1985	Ali Hassim Mwinyi sworn in as president of Tanzania.
5 Nov. 1985	2300 prisoners granted amnesty to commemorate the retirement of Nyerere and appointment of Mwinyi as President.
6 Nov. 1985	Newly elected President Mwinyi appoints his new cabinet.
4 Apr. 1986	Fourteen people detained without trial since 1983 for plotting to overthrow President Nyerere, have their detention order rescinded by President Mwinyi.
10 June 1986	Former President Nyerere tells Zambian newspaper reporters that he doubts the viability of one-party political systems.
July 1986	Seven Kenyans belonging to the MwaKenya Movement and associated with distributing subversive literature in Kenya, are refused political asylum but allowed to remain in Tanzania until the United Nations High Commissioner for Refugees (UNHCR) finds them an alternative country willing to give them asylum.
23-25 July 1986	President Mwinyi pays state visit to Kenya. Signs trade, cultural, educational and scientific agreements between the two countries. The two Presidents reiterate their commitment to the Arusha Accord of November 1983.
25 Oct. 1986	Parliament passes the national registration bill by a majority of only three votes. This compels all the countries' citizens to carry identification cards.
12 Dec. 1986	President Chissano of Mozambique, on a three-day state visit to Tanzania.
23 Mar. 1987	Tanzania reshuffles its cabinet and creates a new Ministry of Water headed by Pius Ngwandu.
Mar/Apr. 1987	Tanzanian and Malawian troops deployed to Mozambique to fight against RENAMO.
31 July 1987	President Mwinyi pays a four-day state visit to Zambia. Agree to strengthen economic, technical and cultural relations and condemn South Africa for sabotaging the Front Line States' economies.
Aug. 1987	The ruling Chama Cha Mapinduzi Party paper reports that President Nyerere will retire as chairman of the Party.
Oct. 1987	The Chama Cha Mapinduzi Party makes changes to its National Executive Council.
22-31 Oct. 1987	The Chama Cha Mapinduzi Party holds its third Congress in Dodoma.

Agrees to strengthen the party's left wing, and Julius Nyerere agrees to serve another term as Party Chairman. He stated in August 1987 that he intends retiring as Party Chairman.

12 Dec. 1987	Tanzania reshuffles its cabinet.
6 Jan. 1988	President I. Abdul Wakil of Zanzibar reshuffles his cabinet and appoints Omar Ali Juma as Prime Minister to replace Seif Shariff Hamad who was dismissed for plotting to overthrow the President.
12 Jan. 1988	On the anniversary of the Zanzibari revolution, Zanzibar's President Idris Abdul Wakil accuses dissident cabinet ministers of planning to hire mercenaries to overthrow his government.
18 Feb. 1988	At the end of a five-day state visit to Mozambique, Tanzania's Prime Minister and First Vice-President, Joseph Warioba and Mozambique's Prime Minister, Mario da Graca Machungo, issue a joint communique condemning South Africa, and increasing co-operation between the two countries.
28 Apr. 1988	Burundi's President Pierre Buyoya pays a four-day state visit to Tanzania and a joint communiqué is signed with President Mwinyi, stating that cultural, scientific, extradition and judicial agreements made between the two countries.
13 May 1988	Riots take place, protesting against Islamic laws on marriage and inheritance.
14 May 1988	The Chama Cha Mapinduzi Party (CCM) expels seven party officials for disrupting the party and unity of Tanzania. Amongst these is Shariff Hamad, former Chief Minister of Zanzibar who is also dismissed as CCM chairman in Pemba South.
June 1988	A commission appointed to investigate the 13 May riots as a result of remarks attributed to the Chairman of the Tanzanian Women's Organization, Mrs. Sophia Kawawa, that Islamic laws on marriage and inheritance be amended as they suppressed women.
11-13 July 1988	President Daniel Arap Moi of Kenya pays state visit to Tanzania.
1 Sept. 1988	General Ernest Mwita Kiaro replaces retired General David B. Musuguri as Chief of the Defence Force.
21 Sept. 1988	Zanzibar passes law curbing the press.
1 Dec. 1988	Tanzania to withdraw its troops from Mozambique where they were involved in fighting RENAMO.
Feb. 1989	The ANC (South Africa) moves its members out of Angola to Tanzanian camps.
6 Mar. 1989	President Mwinyi reshuffles his cabinet.
2 Apr. 1989	Zanzibar cabinet reshuffled. Four new ministers appointed and three moved to other ministerial posts.

15 May 1989	Tanzania expels Burundi rebels from its territory and commended for this action by Burundi Prime Minister Adrien Sibomama.
4 June 1989	Joint communiqué issued by the Iranian and Tanzanian governments at the end of President Mwinyi's state visit to Iran to establish bilateral economic, technical and scientific links.
13 Aug. 1989	The Bismillah Party formed by followers of detained former Zanzibar Chief Minister Sieff Shariff Hamid. Party seeks to break the union between the Island and Tanganyika according to the Chama Cha Mpinduzi party.
18 Sept. 1989	Border agreement between Mozambique and Tanzania reaffirming the land and maritime border between the two countries.
20 Sept. 1989	President Mwinyi takes over the Defence Portfolio and the Deputy Prime Minister post is abolished. These posts were held by Salim Ahmed Salim who has assumed the post of Secretary-General of the OAU.
16 Oct. 1989	Salim Ahmed Salim's post in the Central Committee of the Chama Cha Mapinduzi is filled by Zanzibar Chief Minister Omar Ali Jumar.
12 Mar. 1990	President Mwinyi dissolves his cabinet. He dismisses seven ministers and exchanges portfolios in an attempt to promote economic reform and fight corruption.
29 May 1990	Julius Nyerere, chairman of the ruling Chama Cha Mapinduzi, informs that he will retire from active politics as from August.
10 July 1990	Tanzanian Defence Force receives communication equipment worth TSh34 million from Britain.
Aug. 1990	At a special CCM congress, presidential and parliamentary elections are announced for October.
Aug. 1990	At its Congress, the CCM amended its constitution, whereby the same person can hold both posts of Party Chairman and President of the Republic.
12 Aug. 1990	President Idris A. Wakil of Zanzibar announces that he will not be standing for Presidency in the forthcoming Zanzibar election in October.
17 Aug. 1990	Ali Hasan Mwinyi receives 99.72% of all votes cast at a special CCM congress and elected its chairman. Rashid M. Kawawa is elected Vice-Chairman with 99.56% of all votes cast.
17 Aug. 1990	Julius Nyerere steps down as CCM Chairman and retires from active politics.
Oct. 1990	Presidential elections are held.
25 Oct. 1990	Zanzibar's new President Dr. Salmin Amour sworn in. He is sole presidential candidate and collected 98% of all votes cast.
30 Oct. 1990	Zanzibar's President Dr. Salmin Amour appoints his new government.

3 Nov. 1990	President Ali Hassan Mwinyi re-elected for a second five-year term of office with a 95.5% majority. He is the only candidate.

9 Nov. 1990   President Mwinyi names his new cabinet.

Mar. 1991   A presidential multipartyism commission is established, headed by Chief Justice Francois Nyalali. Its brief is to collect public opinion on multiparty politics over the next twelve months and report these to the government and to the CCM.

21 Mar. 1991   Opposition political groups banned by President Mwinyi.

7 July 1991   23,108 prisoners pardoned under the presidential pardon issued on Peasants Day.

19 Aug. 1991   13,750 prisoners freed and the rest released, according to the procedure set out in the pardon of 7 July 1991.

25 Oct. 1991   Tanzania cabinet reshuffle.

22 Nov. 1991   The leader of the Union for Multi-Party Democracy, Chief Abdallah Said Fundikira and James Mapalala, leader of the Civic Movement, detained and charged with forming unlawful societies.

22 Nov. 1991   Presidents of Tanzania, Uganda and Kenya meet in Nairobi and declare their commitment to co-operate in the political, economic, social and security sector. Appoint a three-man committee to draft a declaration of intent.

11 Jan. 1992   Zanzibar's revolutionary government launches a newspaper called Nuru.

17-21 Jan. 1992   CCM's National Executive Committee accepts proposals of a commission established earlier to test public opinion on political change. Call for an end of twenty-seven years of one-party rule and recommends that the constitution be amended to allow for the registration of political parties. Recommendation to be ratified at a special congress in February 1992.

30 Jan. 1992   Zanzibar cabinet reshuffle.

Feb. 1992   Former Chief Minister of Zanzibar, Sheik Sharif Hamad argues in favour of the establishment of the Zanzibar United Front (ZUF), now that the CCM Party endorses multiparty politics.

Feb. 1992   The CCM Party endorses multipolicies in Tanzania, and since then five opposition parties have been established. They are the Union for Multiparty Democracy (UMD), the Civic Movement (CM), the Pragmatic Democratic Alliance (PDA), the National Convention for Construction and Reform (NCCR), and the National League for Democracy (NCD)

10 Feb. 1992   Sanctions against South Africa selectively lifted, including amongst them air services.

15 Feb. 1992   Tanzania, Uganda and Kenya sign an agreement to reactivate and strengthen political, economic, social and regional cooperation.

19 Feb. 1992	At an extraordinary CCM national congress, delegates vote unanimously for the introduction of a multiparty system.
7 May 1992	Parliament approves amendments to the constitution to allow multiparty politics. Women will make up 15% of the total number of MPs instead of the proposed fifteen seats.
14 May 1992	Zanzibar House of Representatives votes to amend the 1984 constitution to authorize multiparty politics.
29 May 1992	Tanzania reshuffles its cabinet.
17 June 1992	President Ali Mwinyi endorses a bill legalizing opposition political parties.
4 July 1992	The Daily News of Tanzania reports that over 35 potential political parties have taken application forms for provisional registration from the office of the Registrar of Political Parties.
10-14 July 1992	Minister of Foreign Affairs and International Relations, Ahmed Hassan Diria, chairs a meeting between the transitional Rwandan government and the rebel Rwandan Patriotic Front (in Arusha) to end the civil war which started in October 1990.
28 July 1992	Various political parties provisionally register.
Sept. 1992	Oscar Kambona, who has been in exile for the past twenty-five years, allowed back into Tanzania provided he applies for a visa to enter as soon as he arrives.
14 Sept. 1992	Opposition Democratic Party leader Christopher Mtikila and three of his colleagues have their case withdrawn against them for holding an illegal meeting in Dodoma.
Oct. 1992	Tanzania and Uganda sign a military exchange agreement.
20 Oct. 1992	President Mwinyi reshuffles his cabinet.
20 Dec. 1992	At the 4th CCM Congress, President Hassam Mwinyi re-elected its national chairman for another five-year term and John Malecela its Vice-Chairman.
Jan. 1993	Zanzibar's decision to join the Islamic Conference Organization (ICO) and Tanzania joining the Islam in Africa Organization is criticized by politicians. This is exacerbated by bomb explosions in a Zanzibari supermarket stocking alcoholic drink and is allegedly caused by Islamists.
10 Jan. 1993	Zanzibar confirms that it has joined the Organization of the Islamic Conference and stresses that religious and political issues will be kept separate.
24 Jan. 1993	Minister of Home Affairs, Augustin Mrema, appointed Deputy Prime Minister. He also remains Interior Minister.
28 Jan. 1993	Foreign Minister Ahmed Hassan Diria demoted to Labour and Youth Development in a cabinet reshuffle.

28 Jan. 1993	Zanzibar's membership of the Organization of the Islamic Conference supported by President Mwinyi. Inclusion was on economic rather than religious grounds.
31 Jan. 1993	Police kill and wound another person during opposition demonstrations on Pemba Island.
Feb. 1993	Government bans two privately owned newspapers for flouting African and Tanzanian customs and journalistic ethics.
8 Feb. 1993	Reverend Christopher Mtikila and four of his supporters, held under preventive detention since 27 January for sedition and inciting violence, are released on bail.
Mar. 1993	Religious clashes take place in Arumeru District.
12 Mar. 1993	30,000 government employees will be made redundant by the end of the 1993-94 financial year according to the Information Department.
Apr. 1993	CCM Party wins a landslide victory in a Zanzibar by-election.
13 Apr. 1993	Samuel Sitta appointed head of the newly created Ministry of Legal Constitutional Affairs. Juma H Umar appointed Minister of Tourism, National Resources and Environment, replacing A. Mgumia.
13 Apr. 1993	Thirty nine Muslim fundamentalists appear in a Dar-es-Salaam Court for incitement and holding illegal demonstrations.
25 Apr. 1993	Government expels three Sudanese nationals teaching at an Islamic school in Morogoro, for promoting Islamic fundamentalism. Country is swept by a wave of Islamic disturbances.
29 Apr. 1993	The Council for the Propagation of the Koran banned.
2 June 1993	Charges against thirteen of the twenty-nine Islamic fundamentalists dropped.
13 Aug. 1993	Zanzibar's President Salmin Amour withdraws from the Organization of the Islamic Conference. Membership of the OIC has generated controversy and former President Nyerere asserts that Zanzibar's membership of the OIC violated the constitution and is detrimental to national unity.
23 Aug. 1993	Motion adopted by the Tanzania parliament calling for a constitutional revision to permit the establishment of a separate government for Tanganyika.
5 Sept. 1993	Minister for Education and Culture, Charles Kabeho, resigns for health reasons.
13 Sept. 1993	Pius Msekwa, speaker of the National Assembly, clarifies parliamentary resolution adopted on 23 August which provides for the establishment of a third government, in addition to the Union and the government of Zanzibar.
15 Sept. 1993	Reverend Christopher Mtikila opposition Democratic Party leader (DP) is rearrested and charged after being acquitted of sedition the previous day. Remanded until 24 September when a Magistrate is to rule on his bail

application.

26 Sept. 1993	Stephen Kibona, Minister of Planning in the President's office, dies in hospital in Washington, D.C.
22 Oct. 1993	Reverend C. Mtikila and three oposition leaders arrested for organizing unauthorized demonstrations.
29 Oct.- 19 Nov. 1993	Elections are held.
13-14 Nov.1993	At a special meeting in Dodoma, the CCM Party states that it has agreed on a parliamentary resolution in favour of creating a separate Tanganyika government within the union of Tanzania. Former President Nyerere opposed this motion.
22 Nov. 1993	Election results are announced. Benjamin W. Mkapa appointed president with a 61.8% majority.
1994	Tanzania, Kenya and Uganda sign an agreement that eliminates trade barriers, and a secretariat is established in Arusha to implement this.
Jan. 1994	Baraza newspaper ordered to close down by the office of the Registrar of Newspapers after carrying an article linking Deputy Prime Minister and Ministers of Home Affairs Mrema, with the death of the Iman of Mtoro Mosque, Sheikh Kasim Bin Juma Bin Khamis. Government gives the executive editor an ultimatum to prove the report or face legal action.
15 Feb. 1994	The ruling CCM Party wins the Ileje and Kigoma by-election with a clear majority. Only seven of the twelve opposition parties contest the by-election.
Mar. 1994	Zanzibar government accused of persecuting and harrasing its political opposition, the New African reported.
July 1994	Five major mainland parties stage a demonstration calling for a separate Assembly and government for Tanganyika.
Aug. 1994	Former President Nyerere intervenes to maintain the union between mainland Tanzania and Zanzibar. Criticizes the rule of President Dr Salmin Amour of Zanzibar.
Sept. 1994	The Tanzanian People's Party reshuffles its leadership in preparation for the forthcoming October 1995 election. Mrs Gravel Limo appointed new Secretary-General of the Party.
14 Sept. 1994	Opposition Democratic Party leader, Christopher Mtikila and three of his colleagues, has case withdrawn against them for holding an illegal meeting in Dodoma.
Nov. 1994	SADC members meet in Arusha and agree to establish a non-permanent rapid deployment force to deal with attempted coups and regional conflicts.
Dec. 1994	Jakaya M Kikwette, appointed Minister of Finance and reformist Prime Minister John Malecela replaced by Cleopa, David Msuya.

Dec. 1994	According to a constitutional amendment which is to come into effect only after the next election, Zanzibar's President will not automatically become Vice-President in the union government.
Feb. 1995	National Electoral Commission announces programme for the forthcoming presidential and parliamentary elections.
Feb. 1995	Rioting takes place in the Kariakoz region and a number of people held.
24 Feb. 1995	Tanzania and Israel resume diplomatic relations.
25 Feb. 1995	Minister of Labour and Youth Development, Augustine L. Mrema, dismissed from his position for criticizing government attitude to embezzlement of public funds by administration officials and by Vinu Chavda, a Pakistani businessman. Basil P. Mramba replaces him.
Apr. 1995	Presidential candidates for the forthcoming October election announced.
14 Apr. 1995	Prime Minister Cleopa Msuya states that the Tanzania-Burundi border will remain closed to refugees but ordinary travel and trade will continue.
May 1995	Tanzania and Zanzibari political parties nominate their candidates for the forthcoming October presidential election.
June 1995	Basil P. Mramba replaces Kighoma Malima as Minister of Industry and Trade.
23 July 1995	The CCM Party selects William Mkapa as its presidential candidate for the forthcoming October election.
19 Sept. 1995	The four presidential candidates for the forthcoming election participate in a live television debate outlining their policies.
Oct. 1995	Amnesty granted to prisoners jailed and given life sentences for treason, on 18 December 1985.
Oct. 1995	Health services paralyzed in Dar-es-Salaam due to striking doctors.
5 Oct. 1995	Tanzania expels Burundi's ambassador. Conflict between the two countries because of Burundi refugees fleeing to Tanzania.
22 Oct. 1995	Political party wrangling and electoral chaos prevails.
29 Oct. 1995	The presidential election turns chaotic and is suspended. Voting postponed to 30 October and 31 October in other areas.
1 Nov. 1995	Dr Salmin Amour re-elected President of Zanzibar. He names his new thirteen member cabinet.
22 Nov. 1995	Controversial Tanzanian presidential and parliamentary elections that started on 29 October and ended on 19 November. Results announced. Benjamin W. Mkapa appointed president with a 61.8% majority.
4 Dec. 1995	President Benjamin Mpaka appoints his cabinet with Frederick Sumaye as Prime Minister. The 265 member Parliament is dominated by the CCM

Jan. 1996	The President appoints an Anti-Corruption Commission under Joseph Warioba.
Feb. 1996	Defence ministers from Tanzania and Burundi agree to improve border security and resolve the issue of Burundian refugees in Tanzanian camps. More than 100 Burundian Hutu refugees had been prohibited entry into Tanzania.
4 Feb. 1996	As Zanzibaris of Pemba origin protest against discrimination, police ban all public rallies by the opposition Civic United Front in Pemba's southern region.
Apr. 1996	Former President Nyerere is deeply involved in facilitating the peace process in Burundi - President Mkapa appeals to all sides involved in the conflict in Burundi and Rwanda to realize that only dialogue, not armed force, will solve their problems.
May 1996	The winner of the 1995 election in Zanzibar, Salmin Amour of the Chama Cha Mapinduzi Party, is sworn in as cabinet member of Tanzania. The convention whereby the President of Zanzibar automatically became the Vice-President of Tanzania, was replaced by a provision which gives him a seat in the union cabinet.
May 1996	The government of Zanzibar denies intimidating members of the opposition on the island of Pembu, as those detained have been involved in acts of sabotage.
17 May 1996	Khamis Ahmed is appointed as Minister of Trade and Industry in place of Salim Juma who resigned due to poor health.
21 May 1996	A marine disaster occurs on Lake Victoria when an overloaded vessel, the Bukoba, sinks, causing the death of 615 people. The captain, chief engineer and seven shore-based officials are charged. An international inquiry is ordered by President Mkapa, and a three-day period of national mourning is called.
late June 1996	Changes within the ruling Chama Cha Mapinduzi Party are reported. The National Chairperson is Benjamin Mkapa; the Secretary-General resigns together with four party executives, which allows the new Chairperson to appoint executives of his choice.
5 Aug. 1996	Tanzanian politician in exile, Abdulrahman Mohamed Babu, who was also a prominent Pan-Africanist, dies in London.
8 Oct. 1996	In a parliamentary by-election, the candidate for the National Convention for Reconstruction and Reform, Augustine Mrema is elected as representative for the Temeke constituency in the Dar es Salaam region.
Nov. 1996	Finance Minister Simon Mbilinyi resigns amid bribery allegations. A parliamentary select committee, appointed to investigate allegations implicating three prominent government officials and two top members of the Chama Cha Mapinduzi Party of taking bribes, presents its report to parliament.
10 Dec. 1996	The Anti-Corruption Commission publishes its report. Former President

Mwinyi and both incumbent and past cabinet ministers are accused of corruption and the abuse of public office. Minister of Natural Resources and Tourism Juma Ngasonga, whose name is also mentioned, resigns.

5 Feb. 1997   President Mkapa reshuffles his cabinet.

Mar. 1997   Chama Cha Mapinduzi loses a second by-election.

13 Mar. 1997   CCM Secretary General Horace Kolimba is summoned to the party's control committee to explain his public criticism of the party. As he appears before the committee, he unexpectedly dies.

mid May 1997   The only credible opposition party, the National Convention for Constitution and Reform (NCCR) - Maguezi falls apart when the populist, but erratic chairman is suspended by the intellectual wing of the party.

ZAMBIA

24 Oct. 1964   Zambia becomes independent with Kenneth Kaunda as its first President.

26 Oct. 1964   Acceptance of obligations contained in the UN Charter.

30 Oct. 1964   Adheres to the 1944 Convention on International Civil Aviation.

9 Nov. 1964   Signs and accepts the UNESCO Constitution.

20 Nov. 1964   Signs treaty with Great Britain on the production and trade policies of cereals.

1 Dec. 1964   Civil service posts are africanised. Whites still retain control of key positions in twelve different ministries.

1 Dec. 1964   Zambia becomes a member of the United Nations.

2 Dec. 1964   Zambia becomes the 111th member of the ILO.

2 Dec. 1964   ILO Conventions as follows: age for admission in industrial employment - declaration assuming obligations (no. 5); ratifies the following: equality of treatment of national and foreign workers as regards workmen's compensation for accidents (no. 19); ratifies convention on forced labour (no. 105); forced or compulsory labour (no. 29); maximum length of contracts for employment of indigenous workers (no. 86) and penal sanctions (no. 65) and regulation (no. 64); assumes obligations of migration for employment (no. 97; declaration assuming obligations of agricultural workers' rights of association; declaration assuming obligations of social policy; ratifies special systems of recruiting workers (no. 50); ratifies wage-fixing machinery (no. 26) with regard to women. The following conventions are ratified: night work in industry (no. 89); underground work in mines (no. 45). With reference to workmen's compensation, the following are ratified: accidents (no. 17); agriculture (no. 12).

6 Dec. 1964   ANC leader, Mr Nkumbula, addresses a rally in which he is critical of one-party rule. The rally is disbanded under orders from UNIP.

15 Dec. 1964   A new Bill is introduced which makes racial insults an offence.

Jan. 1965	A transitional development plan is announced, which aims, over the next eighteen months, to spend 35 million Pounds Sterling on projects to produce foodstuffs.
11 Jan. 1965	Succession to the multipartite treaty banning nuclear weapon tests in the atmosphere.
22 Jan. 1965	President Kaunda announces a cabinet reshuffle.
29 Jan. 1965	Restrictions are placed on activities of exiled nationalist movements based in Zambia.
2 Feb. 1965	Assumption of obligations of the 1960 agreement between the UN Special Fund and Great Britain pertaining to projects in Zambia.
2 Feb. 1965	Signs 1946 Constitution of WHO.
8 Feb. 1965	Succession to multipartite agreement banning nuclear weapon tests.
12 Feb. 1965	The government announces that it is due to take control of Zambia Television.
21 Feb. 1965	New labour laws will eliminate outside interference in trade unions and illegal strikes. Office bearers are now required to gain at least three years experience in the trade which their union represents.
22 Feb. 1965	Ratifies ILO Convention of workmen's compensation for occupational diseases (no. 18).
1 Mar. 1965	Accession to the 1952 Universal Copyright Convention.
6 Mar. 1965	Notification of deposit of instrument of accession with declarations to the 1958 Convention of Paris on the Protection of Industrial Property.
11 Mar. 1965	The East Katanga government protests against Zambia supporting the Congolese rebels.
20 Mar. 1965	The movement of foreign diplomats within the country is curtailed: no diplomat is allowed to travel more than twenty-five miles from the capital without notifying the Ministry of Foreign Affairs.
25 Mar. 1965	Signs technical advisory assistance treaty with WHO.
11 Apr. 1965	UNIP resolves to take strong action against political opponents, including the ANC, who are critical of the government.
26 Apr. 1965	Portugal places an embargo on arms shipment consigned to Zambia passing through Mozambique.
26 Apr. 1965	Zambia enters into negotiations with Tanzania to allow for the safe passage of arms shipments bound for Zambia.
28 Apr. 1965	Ratifies entry into force of amendment to Articles 23, 27 and 61 of the UN Charter.

29 Apr. 1965	A limit is set on the number of staff of foreign missions.
End Apr. 1965	All trade unions are now required to affiliate to the state controlled Zambia Trades Union Congress.
11 May 1965	The National Union of Postal and Telecommunications workers suspend their threat to strike over the possibility of Rhodesia declaring independence.
24 May 1965	An extradition treaty between Tanzania, Uganda, Kenya and Zambia comes into effect.
4 June 1965	The Minister of Local Government and Housing, Sikota Wina, objects to a parliamentary opposition, which he regards as a `luxury'.
5 June 1965	South Africa bans the delivery of arms shipments destined for Zambia.
8 June 1965	Differences arise between the Barotse National Council and the central government, centering on the rationalization of customary law into a national code.
14 July 1965	UNIP's activities in Rhodesia are banned.
22 July 1965	The deputy leader of the ANC, Edward Liso, is suspended by Parliament for criticising the President. After the suspension, Harry Nkumbula, leader of the ANC announces that the Party will be boycotting Parliament indefinitely.
29 July - 1 Aug. 1965	Emperor Haile Selassie of Ethiopia pays a state visit to Zambia.
29 July 1965	Kenneth Kaunda makes a call for African unity amidst what he terms 'a new scramble for Africa' by foreign powers.
30 July 1965	Kenneth Kaunda appeals for peace in Vietnam, urging that China be allowed to join the United Nations.
31 July 1965	The government takes over a Lusaka newspaper, The Central African Mail.
1 Aug. 1965	Ethiopia and Zambia issue a joint statement, warning Britain against granting independence to a white minority in Rhodesia. They also call for the release of opposition leaders and a united liberation front.
5 Aug. 1965	Harry Nkumbula, joint opposition leader, resigns from Parliament.
12 Aug. 1965	Accedes to the Single Convention on Narcotic Drugs.
24 Aug. 1965	The Barotse National Council no longer has local government powers. It is to be replaced by five District Councils, bringing it in line with other provinces.
25 Aug. 1965	Zambia boycotts the Commonwealth Law Conference, objecting to the presence of Rhodesian delegates.

26 Aug. 1965	President Kaunda alleges that South Africa intends to disrupt the Zambian economy. He adds that diplomatic relations are impossible at this stage.
26 Aug. 1965	Seretse Khama of Bechuanaland arrives on a state visit.
8 Sept. 1965	The transit of weaponry through Zambia, which is destined to be used by freedom fighters, is banned.
9 Sept. 1965	The embargo against weapons, bound for Zambia being transported through Portuguese territories, is lifted.
17 Sept. 1965	Alice Lenshina, leader of the banned Lumpa Church, is restricted to a remote area.
22 Sept. 1965	Calls are made from within the ANC for Harry Nkumbula's resignation as ANC President, making way for his deputy, Edward Liso. Liso rejects the position.
23 Sept. 1965	Accepts Articles of Agreement of the International Bank for Reconstruction and Development (IBRD).
23 Sept. 1965	Signs 1960 Articles of Agreement with the International Development Association.
23 Sept. 1965	Signs and accepts 1955 Articles of Agreement of the International Finance Corporation.
23 Sept. 1965	Signs and accepts Articles of Agreement of the International Monetary Fund.
6 Oct. 1965	Rhodesia impounds a shipment of weapons bound for the Zambia army.
12 Oct. 1965	Ratifies Protocols dated 14 June 1965; 14 June 1954; 27 May 1947; 21 June 1961 of the Convention on International Civil Aviation.
13 Oct. 1965	Acceptance of the 1944 international air services transit agreement.
23 Oct. 1965	Signs UN Conference on Industrial Development Programmes and Economic Cooperation in East Africa.
25 Oct. 1965	Signs OAU Convention on Privileges and Immunities.
26 Oct - 6 Nov. 1965	A conference, held in Lusaka, discusses the formation of an economic community in East and Central Africa.
2 Nov. 1965	The British High Commissioner in Salisbury is given the responsibility of negotiating for the release of Zambian weapons seized by Rhodesia on 6 October.
5 Nov. 1965	The Minister of Labour and Social Development responds to organizations actively recruiting Zambian labour for work on South African mines, by citing a new employment act which aims to regulate the flow of labour.
12 Nov. 1965	Zambia positions troops along the Zambian-Rhodesian border following Rhodesia's declaration of independence.

14 Nov. 1965	The integration of schools is declared a success by the Minister of Education, J. Mwanakatwe.
17 Nov. 1965	Kenneth Kaunda announces that he has requested military support from Britain to protect power supply at Kariba against being cut off by Rhodesia.
22 Nov. 1965	Affirmative action begins to take effect in the mining industry.
23-26 Nov. 1965	Kenneth Kaunda condemns a racial clash between members of the Zambia Youth Service and whites at the Railway Recreation Club in Livingstone. The club is subsequently closed down by the President. A strike of 300 white railway workers follows the incident on 26 November.
26 Nov. 1965	The power supply from the Kariba Dam to the Copperbelt is cut by unknown sabotteurs.
2 Dec. 1965	Britain and Zambia agree on the stationing of Royal Air Force aircraft in Zambia.
12 Dec. 1965	Signs agreement with Denmark concerning technical co-operation on an agricultural project in Zambia.
14 Dec. 1965	Accession to 1965 agreement on the facilitation of international marine traffic.
14 Dec. 1965	Zambia announces that it will send ministerial delegations to the USSR and USA for talks on military protection of the Kariba power supply.
17 Dec. 1965	The Minister of Transport and Works, H. Band, assures non-Zambians working on Rhodesia Railways of continued employment, as affirmative action programmes are applied.
17 Dec. 1965	Oil sanctions are imposed on Rhodesia. This is followed by a complete supply cut to Zambia by Rhodesia. Britain, USA and Canada with the co-operation of the Congo, Tanzania and Malawi, launch a rescue operation shortly thereafter carrying oil into Zambia by any available means.
17 Dec. 1965	Signs agreement with Netherlands on the employment of Netherlands volunteers.
19 Dec. 1965	Britain announces a three and a half million Pound Sterling aid package to assist Zambia in combatting the effects of sanctions imposed on Rhodesia.
1966	Due to increasingly strained relations with both Rhodesia and Angola, Zambia is forced to alter its trade routes. Copper exports are channelled through Dar-es-Salaam and plans are made to install an oil pipeline by 1968, linking the Copperbelt to Dar-es-Salaam.
1 Jan. 1966	Entry into force of the additional regulations amending the World Health Regulations, no. 2: disinfecting of ships and aircraft and forms of the international certificates of vaccination or re-vaccination against yellow fever and smallpox.
28 Jan. 1966	The Minister of Labour & Social Development, Nalumino Mundia and the

Minister of Commerce and Industry, Mubiana Nalilungwe, are forced to resign after the discovery that both have financial interests in companies benefiting from government aid.

10 Feb. 1966	The Rhodesia Herald is banned in Zambia. President Kaunda cites the bias reflected towards the Smith regime in the Rhodesian press as a major concern.
14 Feb. 1966	Portuguese troops are placed along the Zambia-Mozambique border to prevent further refugees from fleeing into Zambia. Zambia already has 3500 refugees within its borders.
16 Feb. 1966	Signs trade agreement with the United Arab Republic.
Mar. 1966	The Zambian High Commissioner in Ghana is recalled.
4 Mar. 1966	The display of the Rhodesian flag is banned in Zambia.
7 Mar. 1966	Signs multipartite agreement on racial discrimination.
8 Mar. 1966	President Kaunda announces the establishment of a military training school.
29 Mar. 1966	Signs treaty with Zambia which revokes, by Article XXV, the agreement of 12 November 1925.
29 Apr. 1966	Brigadier C.M. Grigg is appointed Major-General of the Zambian army.
30 Apr. 1966	Kenneth Kaunda disapproves of Britain entering into negotiations with Rhodesia over its unilateral declaration of independence.
31 May 1966	The United Front is formed by dissident members of UNIP and the ANC.
July 1966	A 400 million Pounds Sterling four-year National Development Plan is proposed. This plan foresees the development of Zambian hydro-electric schemes.
12 July 1966	Zambia threatens to withdraw from the Commonwealth if the issue over Rhodesia's independence is not resolved.
14 July 1966	Seventeen white police officers are retired, fifteen being declared prohibited immigrants. This comes amidst growing concern over Zambia's security situation.
22 July 1966	Angolan refugees seek refuge in Zambia's North West Province.
28 July 1966	Agreement with Great Britain on the employment in the public service of British officers.
28 July 1966	Signs agreement with Great Britain on British aided conditions of service.
Aug. 1966	Massive strike action in the copper industry affects the economy.
2 Aug. 1966	The NPP, a predominantly white party, disbands.
10 Aug. 1966	President Kaunda advocates the use of force to solve the Rhodesian crisis.

He is critical of Britain's use of sanctions against Rhodesia. He declines to attend the Commonwealth Prime Minister's Conference to be held in September.

11 Aug. 1966	Signs agreement with United States on investment guarantees.

26 Aug. 1966   Zambia tightens immigration regulations, requiring all non-Commonwealth and Rhodesian citizens to obtain visas.

1 Sept. 1966   Accession to the African Development Bank.

4 Sept. 1966   The Minister of Labour adopts a tough attitude towards continued strike action within the copper industry.

9 Sept. 1966   A constitutional amendment comes into effect allowing for a possible increase in size of Zambia's cabinet.

10 Sept. 1966   President Kaunda, although fundamentally opposed to the policies of H.F. Verwoerd, sends a message of condolence to his widow, on his assassination.

18 Sept. 1966   The University of Zambia is officially opened by Kenneth Kaunda, the University's first Chancellor.

4 Oct. 1966   Signs loan agreement with the IBRD on the Highway Project.

13 Oct. 1966   A Commission of Enquiry to the copper industry recommends a 22% wage increase for black miners. The Commission is critical of the prevalence of racialism within the industry.

19 Oct. 1966   Accession to the 1949 Geneva Conventions: prisoners of war; protection of civilian persons in time of war; wounded and sick in armed forces in the field; wounded, sick and ship-wrecked members of armed forces at sea.

24 Oct. 1966   President Kaunda calls for a single, unified trade union operating in the copper industry.

25 Oct. 1966   Zambia accepts eleven South African and Rhodesian political refugees from Botswana.

27 Oct. 1966   Zambia deports twenty five foreigners involved in racial or industrial disputes.

30 Oct. 1966   A riot breaks out in Kitwe after rumours that petrol tanks were sabotaged by Rhodesian agents.

1 Dec. 1966   The police force is to undergo expansion with new recruits receiving paramilitary training.

2 Dec. 1966   Ratifies Convention on Transit Trade of Land-Locked Countries.

16 Dec. 1966   Accession by Zambia to the International Covenant on Economic, Social and Cultural rights.

24 Jan. 1967	Signs agreement with UNICEF on the activities of UNICEF in Zambia.
27 Jan. 1967	Terminates 1948 and 1963 Commonwealth Telegraphs Agreement.
18 Feb. 1967	UNIP wins a by-election at Mazabuka, a former ANC stronghold. During the run up to the election, political meetings were banned, disrupting the ANC's campaign.
20 Feb. 1967	President Kaunda stresses that his wish for a one-party state will not be achieved by legislation, but through elections.
6 Mar. 1967	N. Mundia, the former Minister of Labour and Social Development, is expelled from UNIP.
10 Mar. 1967	Ratifies ILO Convention on employment underground in mines: medical examination for young persons (no. 124).
22 Mar. 1967	Accession to postal parcels agreement; Universal Postal Convention; and the Universal Postal Union.
1 Apr. 1967	The Minister of Education, J. Mwanakatwe, condemns the National Student Association in its bid to establish international ties.
3 Apr. 1967	Ratifies ILO Convention on the minimum age of employment underground in mines (no. 123).
6 Apr. 1967	The government takes control of Zambian television.
13 Apr. 1967	Five foreigners are detained under the preservation of public security regulations. A tribunal subsequently finds that four of the detainees were involved with Rhodesian Intelligence and recommends their deportation.
14 Apr. 1967	A. Simbule, Zambia's High Commissioner-designate in London, in a controversial statement refers to the United Kingdom as a 'humbled toothless bulldog' in its dealings with Rhodesia.
15 Apr. 1967	Zambia and Botswana issue a joint statement in which Zambia respects Botswana's wish not to be used as a base for incursions into neighbouring states.
27 Apr. 1967	President Kaunda presents a manifesto entitled 'Humanism in Zambia' to UNIP. The manifesto is a blueprint for Zambian socialism.
26 May 1967	Signs economic and technical co-operation treaty with the Soviet Union.
21-25 June 1967	President Kaunda's visit to the Chinese People's Republic results in economic and technical co-operation which includes China's offer to build the Zambia-Tanzania rail link.
23 June 1967	Four ANC members of Parliament cross the floor to join UNIP which now holds 60 of the 75 seats in Parliament.
30 June 1967	The Rhodesia Railways which was jointly owned and run by Zambia and Rhodesia is taken over by Zambia Railways.

6 July 1967	Attends UN International Seminar on Apartheid, Racial Discrimination and Colonialism in Southern Africa.
8 July 1967	Presidents of Zambia, Uganda, Tanzania and Kenya meet in Nairobi in an attempt to solve the Nigerian crisis.
3-8 Aug. 1967	Sir Seretse Khama visits Zambia.
15-19 Aug. 1967	UNIP holds its annual conference at Mulungushi. The conference is attended by President Nyerere of Tanzania, President Obote of Uganda and Vice-President Masire of Botswana.
17 Aug. 1967	At UNIP's annual conference, President Kaunda forsees a United States of Africa, with Zambia, Tanzania, Kenya, Uganda and Botswana co-operating economically as a step to unity.
18 Aug. 1967	At UNIP's annual conference President Kaunda is returned unopposed as President of UNIP. Three other outgoing members are also returned: Kalulu, National Chairman; Uina, Director of Publicity and D. Banda, Director of Youth.
19 Aug. 1967	Elections for eleven out of fourteen posts on the UNIP Central Committee are contested on tribal lines: two Lozi cabinet ministers, A. Wina and M. Sipalo, are defeated; the Bemba and their allies now dominate the Central Committee.
21 Aug. 1967	Discrepancies are found in voting procedures for positions on the UNIP National Council.
24 Aug. 1967	A Commission of Inquiry appointed to investigate voting discrepancies at UNIP's Mulunaashi conference finds that errors did occur in counting. However, these findings do not affect overall electoral results.
27 Aug. 1967	Allegations made by Rhodesia that Zambia is harbouring freedom fighters and assisting them in their incursions into Rhodesia, are flatly denied.
30 Aug. 1967	President Kaunda deplores the methods employed in UNIP elections which were based on tribal and provincial lines and appeals for national unity.
7 Sept. 1967	Kenneth Kaunda is forced to reshuffle his Cabinet after the recent changes in UNIP: Simon Kapwepwe - Vice President; Reuben Kamanga - Minister of Foreign Affairs; Elijah Mudenda - Minister of Finance; Sikola Uina - Minister of Education; M. Sipalo - Minister of Agriculture.
25 Sept. 1967	President Kaunda protests to the British government over the repeated violation of Zambian airspace by Rhodesian aircraft.
6 Oct. 1967	Zambia offers political asylum to Kantagese troops who joined Congo mercenaries in a revolt. Zambia reviews its position after renewed fighting leaving the decision-making to the Congolese government.
17 Oct. 1967	Emergency regulations are extended for a further six months.
17 Oct. 1967	Signs treaty with Denmark on training scheme for small independent

building contractors and cooperatives in Zambia.

18 Oct. 1967   Signs loan treaty with Denmark.

28 Oct. 1967   President Kaunda successfully mediates a border dispute between Kenya and Somalia with President Nyerere of Tanzania and President Obote acting as observers.

31 Oct. 1967   Alice Lenshina, leader of the Lumpa sect breaks her restriction orders and is redetained. She receives a six-month prison sentence with hard labour for her actions.

3-5 Nov. 1967   Britain's Commonwealth Secretary, George Thomson, visits Zambia on his way to Rhodesia. Kenneth Kaunda remains sceptical of Britain's stance towards Rhodesia.

5 Nov. 1967   President Kaunda warns that he will not tolerate any attempts to secede in Barotse Province.

16 Nov. 1967   Signs treaty with UN/FAO (on behalf of the World Food Programme) for assistance from the WFP.

Dec. 1967   The replacement of A. Simbule as High Commissioner-designate in London is announced.

15 Dec. 1967   Kenneth Kaunda attends the third East and Central African Summit Conference, held in Kampala.

18 Dec. 1967   Signs general international agreement with the African Training and Research Centre in Administration for Development.

19 Dec. 1967   A Constitution Amendment Bill extends the franchise to persons over eighteen. The new Bill also increases the number of elected members from seventy-five to 105.

20 Dec. 1967   Signs agreement with the ILO on the establishment of an office in Lusaka.

29 Dec. 1967   Five members of the South African Police, deployed in Rhodesia, are held after illegally entering Zambia.

16 Jan. 1968   Changes are made to the decimal currency system when the Kwacha replaces the Zambian pound.

23 Jan. 1968   President Kaunda visits Sudan. His visit is described as an effort to foster pan-African unity between Arab and non-Arab African coutries.

25 Jan. 1968   Accepts amendment to Articles 24 and 25 of the WHO Constitution.

28 Jan. 1968   President Kaunda arrives in Somalia on a state visit. During his visit he commends Somalia and Kenya for resolving a bitter border dispute.

4-6 Feb. 1968   President Kaunda briefly resigns, upset by a provincial and tribal approach to national problems.

5 Feb. 1968   President Kaunda rules that Junior Ministers and Members of Parliament

need to obtain written permission in order to leave Lusaka for the provinces.

21 Feb. 1968	Signs agreement with Great Britain on personnel of the British armed forces to serve as a training team with armed forces of Zambia.
10 Mar. 1968	President Kaunda attacks tribal divisions within UNIP ruling that no UNIP candidate may stand for election in his own tribal area.
15 Mar. 1968	Harry Nkumbula, leader of the ANC is arrested on a charge of insulting the President. His arrest comes shortly after the ANC Deputy-President, Edward Liso, is convicted and sentenced to eighteen months imprisonment.
24 Mar. 1968	The British Government rejects Zambian request for further financial aid to cushion the effects of Rhodesia's sanctions.
3 Apr. 1968	In response to warnings made by South Africa, Zambia stresses that it is bound as a member of the OAU to offer political asylum to refugees and exiled nationals from countries under minority rule. However, it does not allow for the training of freedom fighters within its borders.
6 Apr. 1968	Amends and supplements 1955 double taxation agreement with Great Britain on income which pertains to Great Britain and the Federation of Rhodesia and Nyasaland.
15 May 1968	President Kaunda offers to mediate between Rhodesian nationalists and the white minority.
20 May 1968	The Zambian Foreign Minister announces the recognition of Biafra as an independent state. Nigeria reacts by severing diplomatic ties with Zambia.
21 May 1968	President Kaunda on a four-day State Visit to Botswana, is welcomed by President Seretse Khama as a 'great world figure'.
2 June 1968	Zambia grants amnesty to 19000 members of the Lumpa Sect in exile in the Congo (DR) after a decision by the Congolese to ban the Sect.
27-29 June 1968	The Somali Prime Minister, Mohamed Haji Ibrahim Egal visits Zambia.
July 1968	President Kaunda visits Sweden, Denmark, Finland and the United Kingdom.
11 July 1968	Signs technical co-operation treaty with Denmark.
11 July 1968	Signs treaty with Denmark concerning volunteers from Denmark.
13 July 1968	Vice-President Kapwepwe defends his apparent hate of the British people in particular and the 'White race in general'.
16-20 July 1968	President Kaunda visits London for talks on further economic aid.
21 July 1968	President Kaunda claims that the British government has agreed to give more aid.

22 July 1968	The oil pipeline from Ndola to Dar-es-Salaam is in operation from this day.
25 July 1968	An UNHCR report finds that Zambia has 11000 refugees within its borders.
14 Aug. 1968	President Kaunda bans the UP and restricts its leaders following clashes between UP and UNIP supporters on the Copperbelt.
21 Aug. 1968	An agreement is reached with Tanzania on the construction on the proposed railway line from Zambia to the port of Dar-es-Salaam.
22 Aug. 1968	President Kaunda condemns Soviet aggression against Czechoslovakia.
24 Aug. 1968	Zambia withdraws its recognition of the PAC (South Africa) after the exiled organization contravenes Zambian regulations.
Sept. 1968	Relations with Malawi deteriorate following a claim by President Banda to four districts in Zambia and Tanzania.
2 Sept. 1968	The oil pipeline from Dar-es-Salaam to Ndola is officially opened.
13-18 Sept.1968	At the Algiers meeting of the Liberation Committee of the OAU, Zambia, as part of the Committee decides to give increased aid to the ANC (South Africa).
16 Sept. 1968	During a visit to Paris, President Kaunda discusses Zambia's participation in the building of Kafue Dam.
16 Sept. 1968	President Kaunda rejects the Vice-Presidency of the OAU after Zambia is labelled by some quarters as imperialist over its stance on Biafra.
18 Sept. 1968	President Kaunda on a state visit to France, holds talks with President de Gaulle and M. Couvede Murville.
23 Sept. 1968	Signs treaty with Great Britain on minimum sterling proportion.
5 Oct. 1968	Signs loan agreement with IBRD on the second Highway Project.
5 Oct. 1968	Signs loan agreement with IBRD on the Industrial Forestry Project.
15 Oct. 1968	Zambia expels Rhodesians to Tanzania, charged with press ganging Zambians to join the fight against the Smith regime.
30 Oct. 1968	Signs air services agreement with Great Britain.
2 Nov. 1968	President Kaunda dissolves the National Assembly and announces that general elections will be held on 19 December.
5 Nov. 1968	President Daddah of Mauritania on a state visit to Zambia issues a joint statement with President Kaunda calling for the use of force in Rhodesia.
13-16 Nov. 1968	President Mobuto of the Congo (DR) visits Zambia and at his invitation, President Kaunda accompanies him back to his country.
23 Nov. 1968	Nalumino Mundia, leader of the banned UP, will stand for elections as an ANC candidate.

28 Nov. 1968	Disturbances in the North-Western Province are linked to ANC supporters who allegedly received military training in Angola. The leader of the ANC denies the allegations.
9 Dec. 1968	Portugal accepts responsibility and offers compensation for six separate attacks on Zambian border villages.
18 Dec. 1968	Elias Chipimo is app ointed as High Commissioner in London replacing Ali M. Simbule.
19 Dec. 1968	Kenneth Kaunda is re-elected as President with UNIP winning eighty-one out of 105 seats and the ANC twenty-three with one independent.
19 Dec. 1968	Nalumino Mundia wins the Libonda seat in Barotse Province.
23 Dec. 1968	President Kaunda announces the formation of a new government with a smaller cabinet.
5 Jan. 1969	Nalumino Mundia, banned leader of the UP is elected as Deputy President of the ANC.
8 Jan. 1969	Accession to the Statute of the IAEA.
10 Jan. 1969	The ANC lodges petitions in the High Court against alleged irregularities in various constituencies in the Zambian elections of December 1968.
7-15 Jan. 1969	At the London Conference of Commonwealth Prime Ministers, President Kaunda denounces the terms which would entrench the power of the racial minority at Rhodesia's independence.
15 Jan. 1969	Zambia gives a year's notice in terminating the Joint Services Training Agreement which facilitates the training of Zambian armed forces by British officers in an attempt to realign its defences.
17 Jan. 1969	President Kaunda attending the Commonwealth Prime Minister's Conference in London, reiterates his disappointment with Britain's handling of the Rhodesian issue.
17 Jan. 1969	Signs Constitution of the African Civil Aviation Commission. This is ratified on 10 December 1971.
22 Jan. 1969	The ANC is disqualified from being recognised as the official opposition as it lacks enough members to form a quorum should UNIP resign.
27 Jan. 1969	Signs financial agreement with the Commonwealth Telecommunications Organisation.
3 Feb. 1969	The Chief Whip, Skota Wina, announces penalties for absent MP's.
11 Feb. 1969	President Kaunda calls upon the party officials of the United National Independence Party and the African National Congress not to take the law into their own hands to quell the continuing widespread unrest.
14 Feb. 1969	Zambia enters into negotiations with Italy over the training of Zambian air

force personnel in Italy. Italian made helicopters are purchased.

20 Feb. 1969	President Kaunda arrives in Nairobi to mediate further consultative talks between Kenya and Somali.
9 Mar. 1969	Talks take place between the government and members of the Watchtower Sect in an attempt to halt clashes.
21 Mar. 1969	President Kaunda announces plans which give civil servants a direct say in UNIP and government policy. This will be achieved by making every Permanent Secretary and District Governor a member of UNIP's National Council.
24 Mar. 1969	President Kaunda warns of an impending attack on Zambia by Rhodesia for allegedly harbouring and training freedom fighters.
26 Mar. 1969	The former Minister of Trade, Industry and Mines, Justin Chimba, is to head the newly created Ministry of National Guidance whose brief is to disseminate the concept of Zambian humanism.
11 Apr. 1969	Signs loan agreement with the IBRD on the Education Project.
14-16 Apr. 1969	President Kaunda plays a key role in the adoption of the Lusaka Manifesto at the fifth East and Central African Summit. The manifesto denounces negotiations with the White South and reaffirms a belief in racial equality.
24 Apr. 1969	The State of Emergency is extended for a further six months.
10 May 1969	Former members of the banned UP launch ZANDU with Judan Nkabita as its elected leader. One of the party's first campaigns is to oppose the referendum which seeks to approve constitutional changes.
June 1969	The ANC is banned in the Mumbura district, an ANC stronghold where the Referendum was largely boycotted, following the outbreak of violence.
17 June 1969	A referendum is held which seeks to alter the Constitution and to safeguard human rights. If approved Parliament will be empowered to sanction amendments by means of a two-thirds majority without holding a referendum in each case.
20 June 1969	President Kaunda begins a tour of West African states: Mauritania; Gambia; Guinea; Sierra Leone and Ivory Coast.
30 June 1969	Signs loan agreement with IBRD on the Livestock Development Project.
3 July 1969	Justice Ifor Evans sets aside a sentence imposed on two Portuguese soldiers, who illegally crossed a Zambian border post unarmed, on the grounds that the incident was trivial.
8-11 July 1969	Zambia takes part at the consultative meeting of the Non-Aligned Countries in Belgrade.
14 July 1969	President Kaunda demands an explanation from Chief Justice J.J. Skinner, for Justice Ifor Evans' political judgement.

15 July 1969	Chief Justice Skinner issues a report which rejects President Kaunda's complaint.
16 July 1969	Members of the Zambian Youth Service demonstrating to demand the dismissal of Chief Justice Skinner and Justice Evans, invade the High Court causing damage to property.
17 July 1969	Chief Justice Skinner leaves Lusaka for London, stating that he is not resigning. He subsequently announces his retirement in September.
17 July 1969	President Kaunda announces his intention to amend the Constitution to allow for the Zambianization of the judiciary.
19 July 1969	The Chairman of the Referendum Commission, Judge Thomas Pickett, announces that changes to the Constitution have been approved by a 'Yes' vote of over fifty three percent.
25 July 1969	Justice Ifor Evans resigns.
28 July 1969	The United Nations Security Council condemns Portuguese attacks on a Zambian village near the Mozambique border.
30 July 1969	In three resultant by-elections held after ANC petitions against election irregularities are granted, UNIP members retain their seats with a strong majority.
11 Aug. 1969	In a speech to a National Council meeting of UNIP, President Kaunda announces the nationalization of the mining industry.
12 Aug. 1969	Following his announcement on the nationalization of the mining industry, President Kaunda attempts to deflect anticipated international pressure through Zambian diplomatic missions. Units of the armed forces are also deployed to key installations.
25 Aug. 1969	The Vice-President of Zambia, Simon Kapwepwe resigns to avoid tribal animosity.
25 Aug. 1969	Following the Vice-President's resignation, President Kaunda invokes emergency powers abolishing UNIP's Central Committee and replacing it with an interim Executive Committee. A Commission is established to revise UNIP's Constitution. Government appointments will now be made which will not necessarily reflect the structure of UNIP.
26 Aug. 1969	The President announces the members of the interim Executive Committee. Simon Kapwepwe retains the post of Vice-President but loses his former post of Finance Minister to Elijah Mudenda, the former Foreign Minister. The President will head a new Ministry of State which will oversee the government's takeover of the mining industry. He will also include the Ministry of Foreign Affairs in his portfolio as well as the Defence Ministry which he already holds.
27 Aug. 1969	Simon Kapwepwe withdraws his resignation after talks with President Kaunda.

24 Sept. 1969	Succession to the 1951 Convention on the Status of refugees with declaration and reservations; accession to the 1967 Protocol.
7 Oct. 1969	The following constitutional amendment bills are proposed: An individual may stand as a Parliamentary candidate and simultaneously run for the President's Office; The repeal of the Barotseland agreement of 1964; Aliens who are Commonwealth citizens are put on an equal footing with those who are not; Property may be acquired by the state; The President will have the power to detain or restrict people for up to a year and restrict fundamental rights under an emergency.
17 Oct. 1969	Vice-President Simon Kapwepwe justifies the extension of the emergency by citing the following factors: The presence of refugees in Zambia; The activities of neighbouring hostile minority regimes; The activities of the ANC in Mumbura; The Watchtower and Lumpa sect problems.
Oct. - Nov. 1969	More than 100 political prisoners are released following a presidential amnesty on 25 October, most of them UNIP members. Nalumino Mundia is released on 31 October. Alice Lenshina, leader of the Lumpa Sect, is one of the few not to be freed.
3 Nov. 1969	Godfrey Muwo becomes Zambia's first locally born judge to be sworn in as acting High Court Judge.
3 Nov. 1969	President Kaunda dissolves Zambia's first parliament and fixes the general election for 19 December.
14 Nov. 1969	A further agreement is signed between China, Tanzania and Zambia, confirming the construction of the proposed railway line from the Copperbelt to Dar-es-Salaam.
14 Nov. 1969	Signs multilateral agreement on various aspects of the Universal Postal Union Additional Protocol to Constitution and General Regulations of the same date; postal parcels; and Universal Postal Convention.
20 Nov. 1969	Signs loan agreement with IBRD on the second Education Project.
20 Dec. 1969	President Kaunda is re-elected and his party wins a clear majority in Parliament.
21 Dec. 1969	Talks open between UNIP and ANC in an attempt to resolve their differences and work towards a policy of national unity.
29 Dec. 1969	The Secretary-General of the ANC, Mungoni Liso is charged with assault following clashes between UNIP and the ANC in Mumbwa.
8 Jan. 1970	In a cabinet reshuffle, President Kaunda hands the Defence portfolio to the former Minister of Home Affairs, Alexander Gray Zulu who relinquishes Home Affairs to the former Minister of Transport, Lewis Changufu. Aaron Milner is made the new Minister of Transport and Vice-President Simon Kapwepwe is responsible for a new Ministry of Provincial and Local

Government.

14 Jan. 1970	Zambia recognizes Ghana's new government.

21 Jan. 1970   A Constitutional Amendment Bill is passed which allows for the exclusion of details on defence and security expenditure from public accounts. ANC MP's stage a walkout in protest.

22 Jan. 1970   At the opening of the new National Assembly, measures are announced against ANC members of parliament and supporters.

22 Jan. 1970   President Kaunda announces economic reforms, large-scale Zambianization of existing enterprises and the majority control of major industries.

12 Feb. 1970   The ANC is banned in Livingstone and all party officials are detained, including two MPs.

19 Feb. 1970   Signs double taxation on income treaty with Japan.

19 Mar. 1970   The editor of The Times of Zambia is forced to apologise after his paper's description of Parliament as a 'rubber stamp'.

20 Mar. 1970   Accession to the 1964 agreement on the global commercial communications satellite system; Special Agreement; and Supplementary Agreement on Arbitration.

Apr. 1970   President Kaunda meets Sir Seretse Khama amid reports that South Africa intends to put a halt to the proposed road link between Botswana and Zambia.

Apr./May 1970   President Kaunda undertakes a three week tour of European countries. The main aim of the tour is to persuade Italy, West Germany and France to withdraw their support from the Cabora-Bassa Dam project in Mozambique. His proposals meet with acceptance in Rome. However, neither the West German or French governments will agree.

6 Apr. 1970   Twelve UNIP officials are detained after waging what President Kaunda terms a tribalistic campaign against the appointment of a senior chief.

May 1970   Alice Lenshina is re-detained. 16,000 of her former followers are reported to be still in exile despite a general amnesty.

6 May 1970   Zambia introduces tighter measures to control the entry of refugees (mainly from White-ruled neighbouring states). These measures involve the issuing of identitiy cards and the surrender of weapons at entry point.

14 May 1970   Signs trade agreement with Romania.

14 May 1970   Signs economic and technical co-operation treaty with Romania.

29 May 1970   Signs multilateral treaty on operational assistance.

29 May 1970   Signs multilateral treaty on technical assistance.

5 June 1970	Signs loan agreement with the IBRD on the Commercial Crops Farming Development Project.
6 June 1970	President Mobutu of the Congo arrives in Zambia on a state-visit.
6 June 1970	Zambia introduces tighter measures to control the entry of refugees (mainly from white-ruled neighbouring states). These measures include the issuing of identity cards and the surrender of weapons at entry points.
17 June 1970	Ratifies Convention on Settlement of Investment Disputes between States and Nationals of Other States.
2 July 1970	President Kaunda announces the holding of local government elections. The ANC confirms that it will contest the elections, backing independent candidates in Mumga and Livingstone where the ANC is banned.
5-13 July 1970	Further discussions are held between Zambia, Tanzania and China on the construction of the Tanzanian-Zambian Railway.
10 July 1970	Signs treaty with the UN Council for Namibia on the issuance by the Council of travel and identity documents to Namibians.
12 July 1970	The Zambian Minister of Development and Finance, the Tanzanian Minister of Finance discuss with their Chinese counterpart the construction of the projected railway between the Zambian Copperbelt and Dar-es-Salaam with Chinese technical and financial aid.
21 July 1970	Zambia condemns Britain's decision to resume arms sales to South Africa. This decision follows a Conservative Party victory in Britain in June. In reaction to the news 1000 students attack the British High Commission in Lusaka.
29 July 1970	Signs guarantee agreement with IBRD on the Kariba North Project.
29 July 1970	Signs release agreement with IBRD and Great Britain.
23 Aug. 1970	The Chairman of the Electoral Commission, Justice Pickett, condemns the violence and intimidation which has plagued the election campaign.
28 Aug. 1970	The final election results are announced with UNIP winning 832 out of 968 seats. The ANC wins 124 seats and the independents gain 12 seats.
28 Aug. 1970	President Kaunda arrives in Ethiopia on a four day state visit.
29 Aug. 1970	Signs technical co-operation treaty with Finland.
1 Sept. 1970	During an OAU Summit of Heads of State and Government, Presidents Kaunda and Nyerere meet Nigeria's Major Gowan to forge a reconciliation between Nigeria and the governments of Gabon, Ivory Coast, Tanzania and Zambia who recognized Biafra in 1967.
2 Sept. 1970	Accepts 1960 Convention on Safety of Life at Sea.
2 Sept. 1970	Accedes to the 1966 International Convention on Land Lines.

8 Sept. 1970	Sixteen foreign journalists covering the Non Aligned Summit Conference in Lusaka, are detained. Their arrests come amidst growing suspicion of foreigners.
18 Sept. 1970	President Kaunda endorses Guyana's lead in providing support to freedom fighters. The Prime Minister of Guyana is on a visit to East Africa (which includes Zambia).
19 Sept. 1970	A government proclamation bans lockouts and strikes in essential services.
22 Sept. 1970	The findings of the Chuula Commission, established after the dissolution of UNIP's Central Committee are released. It recommends that the posts of President and Vice-President be scrapped and replaced by a Secretary-General who is nationally elected. It also proposes an enlarged Central Committee consisting of thirty three members. Each province will be represented by two members on this Committee. Provincial Cabinet Ministers will also sit on the Central Committee. The findings are criticized as they will exacerbate racism.
25 Sept. 1970	Approximately forty seven ANC members detained in February are released.
Oct. 1970	President Kaunda outlines Zambia's foreign policy given its hostile regional environment.
14 Oct. 1970	President Kaunda leads an OAU delegation on a mission to dissuade western powers from providing military support to South Africa.
Nov. 1970	During UNIP's National Council meeting, President Kaunda introduces a Code of Leadership which curtails the private business ventures of party leaders and senior civil servants.
9-10 Nov. 1970	President Kaunda suspends two Cabinet ministers, two ministers of state, Lusaka's Police Chief and other high ranking civil servants on allegations of misappropriating public funds.
10 Nov. 1970	President Kaunda announces that following the Zambian Government 51% acquisition of the copper mining industry, further Government participation in industry and trade will follow.
10 Nov. 1970	In his closing speech to UNIP's National Council, the President announces the planned takeover of expatriate banks, building societies and insurance companies.
16 Nov. 1970	Accepts authentic trilingual text of the Convention on International Civil Aviation.
25 Nov. 1970	Two Zambian villagers face charges of treason after allegedly assisting Portugese soldiers to enter Zambia.
6 Dec. 1970	Amidst pressure to Zambianize the defence forces Lieutenant Colonel Kingsley Chinkuli earns promotion as the first Zambian army chief. The Zambian Youth Service becomes a branch of the Ministry of Defence.

10-13 Dec.1970	Three more ANC members cross the floor to join UNIP. This follows President Kaunda's call on all ANC members to join UNIP before the thirty first of December.
Jan. 1971	Entry into force of the International Health Regulations adopted by the 22nd World Health Assembly.
3 Jan. 1971	The Zambianization of the army begins by the dismissal of fifteen British officers who are ordered to leave Zambia by 18 January.
7 Jan. 1971	President Kaunda announces the decentralization of government. The Ministry of State Participation is disbanded and its functions redistributed to six other ministries. Humphrey Mulemba, the former Minister of Trade and Industry will head the new Ministry of Mines and Mining Development. The Vice-President will perform the duties of Justin Chimba's Ministry. The Minister of Legal Affairs, Fitzpatrick Chuula, will take over all judicial subjects previously dealt with by the Vice-President's office.
29 Jan. 1971	President Kaunda appoints a Commission of Inquiry under Chief Justice Brian Doyle. The Doyle Commission will investigate claims made by Justin Chimba, the Minister of Trade and Industry and John Chisata MP that ministers and government officials misappropriated funds from the Central and Southern Province African Farmers Fund.
5 Feb. 1971	President Kaunda, who together with President Nyerere, is a staunch supporter of Obote, condemns the coup in Uganda. He is also critical of Britain's recognition of the Amin regime.
Mar. 1971	A dispute arises between the governments of Portugal and Zambia over the fate of five Portuguese agricultural experts who were abducted by a Mozambican guerrilla group.
13 Mar. 1971	Signs treaty with Great Britain on officers designated by Great Britain in the service of the government of Zambia.
13 Mar. 1971	Terminates treaty with Great Britain on British aided conditions of service.
22 Mar. 1971	President Kaunda calls on the international community to pressurize Portugal to lift its blockade of Zambian imports, including crucial maize shipments, at ports in Angola and Mozambique. Portugal claims that Zambia granted entry to COREMO freedom-fighters who had captured five Portuguese soldiers. Zambia denies the allegations.
29 Mar. 1971	Signs double taxation with respect to fiscal evasion on income treaty with Ireland.
18 Apr. 1971	The President outlaws two tribal groups with a provincial political base within UNIP who were formed after the 1967 National Conference: the Committee of Fourteen comprises non-Bemba groups who fear Bemba domination; the Committee of Twenty-four was established in retaliation.
19 Apr. 1971	President Kaunda makes it clear that there would be no tribal leaders with a provincial political base in his government.
21 Apr. 1971	Correspondence between Vorster and Kaunda refutes Vorster's allegations

that President Kaunda had requested a meeting with South Africa and further its aid against Rhodesia and Portugal.

5 May 1971   Signs treaty with Great Britain on members of the staff of the University of Zambia designated by Great Britain.

7-10 May 1971   UNIP adopts a new constitution at its sixth general conference with far reaching implications: membership on UNIP's Central Committee will henceforth not guarantee a Cabinet post; elections within UNIP will now be held every five years; each Province will send 600, versus the current 100 delegates to general party conferences. The new measures aim to reduce personal or tribal contest. They receive a mixed reaction.

8-10 May 1971   The Conference of the ruling United National Independent Party approves reform proposals additional to those adopted in November 1970.

16 May 1971   More than 100 'essential service' miners are arrested and restricted upon release.

1 June 1971   The Doyle Commission clears all seven ministers and top government officials accused of misappropriating agricultural funds. It also exonerates Reuben Kamanga, Minister of Rural Development, of allegations of rape.

3 June 1971   President Kaunda, acting on the findings of the Doyle Commission, suspends the Minister of Power, Transport and Works, Dingiswayo Banda, the Minister of Trade and Industry, Justin Chimba and Nephas Tembo, Minister of State for Provincial and Local Government and Culture. Mathew Nkdoma is suspended for four months.

28 June 1971   President Kaunda, referring to the South African-French agreement of building jet fighters in South Africa opens that France had after all decided to support the 'racialist government of South Africa'.

7 July 1971   Signs Protocol relating to an amendment of Article 56 of the International Civil Aviation Convention.

8-15 July 1971   University of Zambia students march on the French Embassy, following a decision to permit South Africa to manufacture mirage aircraft under licence. Clashes occur between students and the police. Students later sign a letter accusing President Kaunda of inconsistency in his stance on South Africa. On the fifteenth of July the University is closed. When it reopens ten student leaders who signed the letter are not readmitted.

12 July 1971   The Student Union severely criticises President Kaunda's policies.

6 Aug. 1971   Signs air services agreement with Cyprus.

10 Aug. 1971   ZANDU merges with UPP.

18 Aug. 1971   James Chapoloko, the Minister of Labour and Social Services, is dismissed for alleged subversive ties with the newly formed UPP.

21 Aug. 1971   The Minister of Local Government of Culture resigns and announces the forming of a new Opposition party, the United Progressive Party, who

would press for a general election.

21-22 Aug.1971	The day after Vice-President Simon Kapwepwe's resignation, citing government corruption, he officially announces the formation of the UPP, an opposition party.
23 Aug. 1971	The recently resigned Minister of Local Government and Culture announces that his new party, the United Progressive Party, has reached agreement with the existing opposition, the African National Congress.
24 Aug. 1971	The constitution of the UPP follows a socialist stance. It is anti-capitalist and aims to eliminate tribalism and sectionalism.
27 Aug. 1971	President Kaunda announces that unless the subversive activities of the United Progressive Party and the African National Congress are halted, he would ban them.
10 Sept. 1971	The Minister for Rural Development, Victor Hgundu, resigns, citing corruption, economic chaos and a lack of foresight displayed by both UNIP and the government as his reasons.
13 Sept. 1971	The Ministry of Foreign Affairs announces the expulsion of the East German Trade Mission in Lusaka. It is believed that Simon Kapwepwe, leader of the UPP has close ties with the Mission. Zambians are also barred from visiting East Germany.
17 Sept. 1971	Extends guarantee by Great Britain and maintenance by Zambia of the minimum sterling production.
20 Sept. 1971	The day before the arrival of the Swedish Prime Minister, top UPP officials are detained, except for its leader, Simon Kapwepwe. Kapwepwe appoints new organizers including ten students from the University of Zambia.
28 Sept. 1971	President Kaunda warns government traditional leaders that it will not tolerate opposition on their part. He stresses that traditional leaders have a valuable role to play in the development of Zambia.
29 Sept. 1971	Following talks between Zaire and Zambia, Zaire attempts to move Lumpa refugees further into Zaire. Fighting breaks out after the Lumpas refuse to move and thousands flee back into Zambia, where they are repatriated in the Northern Province. (The Lumpas are a religious sect).
8 Oct. 1971	At the request of Zambia, the Security Council meets in an emergency session to hear Zambia's complaints against 'numerous violations by South African forces against the sovereignty, air space and territorial integrity of Zambia'.
18-19 Oct.1971	The 'Mogadishu Declaration' adopted at the Seventh Summit Conference of East and Central African states in urging armed struggle to liberate South Africa also reiterates its support of Zambia which has been targeted by the white South and consequently prevented from providing its fullest support to the liberation forces of South Africa.
30 Oct. 1971	Following the official registration of the UPP, demonstrations are held against the party by UNIP.

11 Nov. 1971	Home Guard Act allows for the training of Zambian citizens, who will then be empowered to play a role in Zambia's defence. The President will serve as the Commander-in-Chief of the Home Guard.
6 Dec. 1971	Following the proposed Anglo-Rhodesian settlement, President Kaunda takes the unusual step of addressing Parliament. He condemns Britain's policy in Southern Africa and places blame for future violence on its shoulders.
17 Dec. 1971	Signs trade agreement with the Soviet Union.
20 Dec. 1971	By-elections are held for twelve vacant Parliamentary seats. UNIP has one unopposed seat, but in the other wards faces five UPP and six ANC candidates. (The ANC and the UPP have agreed not to split their votes)
12 Jan. 1972	After taking his seat in Parliament, Simon Kapwepwe is severely assaulted by UNIP supporters. President Kaunda condemns the attack.
4 Feb. 1972	Ratifies the Convention on the Elimination of Racial Discrimination.
4 Feb. 1972	The UPP is banned and 123 of its leading members, including Simon Kapwepwe and Peter Chanda (former Ambassador to Ethiopia) are detained. President Kaunda denounces the UPP as a party bent on violence.
25 Feb. 1972	A Commission is established, headed by the Vice-President, to investigate ways of transforming Zambia into a one-party state.
1 Mar. 1972	The DPP is formed, led by Foustino Lembe. It opposes the formation of a one-party state. It is not taken seriously by UNIP as an oppositional force.
6 Mar. 1972	Signs treaty with Romania on visas and the abolition of visa fees.
13 Mar. 1972	President Kaunda announces that internal security measures will be enacted to ensure increased participation by UNIP members. Local UNIP leaders will now be able to make citizen's arrests.
20 Mar. 1972	Ninety-two suspected followers of the Lumpa Church are arrested and charged with attempting to revive the Sect, whose leader Alice Lenshina, is still in detention.
22 Mar. 1972	Signs double taxation treaty with Great Britain on the fiscal evasion of income and capital.
26 Mar. 1972	Accession to the 1953 Convention on the Political Rights of Women.
20 Apr. 1972	Ratifies amendment to the Convention on International Civil Aviation.
1 May 1972	Ratifies the African Convention on the Conservation of Nature and Natural Resources, which was signed on 12 October 1965.
5 May 1972	The Secretary of the unregistered DPP is detained.
5 May 1972	Zambia distances itself from a call made by President Amin for closer ties between the two countries.

26 May 1972	A parcel bomb addressed to President Kaunda explodes when it is opened at State House. It is one of several sabotage attempts directed against UNIP offices.

June 1972	Zambia's foreign exchange reserves have dropped dramatically compared to the previous year. This decline is largely a result of the plummeting price of copper.

15 June 1972	Uganda impounds a Zambian aircraft at Entebbe Airport. The aircraft together with its arms consignment is later released.

20 June 1972	Ratifies ILO Convention on various aspects of minimum wage-fixing machinery - agriculture (No. 99) and developing countries (No. 131); equal remuneration for work of equal value for men and women workers (No. 100).

18 Aug. 1972	The evacuation of all Zambian villages bordering Angola and Mozambique is announced due to an alleged increase in the number of armed incursions into Zambia by Portuguese troops.

31 Aug. 1972	A complete ban in placed on student demonstrations.

14 Sept. 1972	Ratifies amendment to the International Civil Aviation Convention.

25 Sept. 1972	Ratifies instrument for amending ILO Constitution.

26 Sept. 1972	President Kaunda attacks Libya for assisting Uganda in its conflict with Tanzania.

1 Oct. 1972	Alfred Chambeshi, a former detainee of the banned UPP announces the formation of the United People's Party (UPP). He accuses the government of corruption and is fundamentally opposed to the formation of a one-party state.

5 Oct. 1972	During the Indian Head of State's visit to Zambia, President Kaunda announces that Zambia will have a one-party system of particpatory democracy by the end of the year. Whilst in Zambia, President Giri allays fears of 'Asian' expulsions.

9 Oct. 1972	Accession, at London, of the Convention on the Prohibition of Emplacement on the Sea-Bed and the Ocean Floor and in the Subsoil thereof of Nuclear Weapons and Other Weapons of Mass Destruction. Accession at Washington on 1 November 1972, Moscow on 2 November 1972.

13 Oct. 1972	Ratifies amendment to Article 61 of the UN Charter.

15 Nov. 1972	The government acts on the recommendation of the Commission set up to investigate the establishment of a one-party participatory democracy. Under the new Constitution, the President will have full executive powers. The Prime Minister will be appointed by the President, as will the Secretary-General of UNIP. Parliament will consist of 136 members, 125 will be elected and ten nominated by the President. The Speaker will be elected by MPs outside of the National Assembly. The House of Chiefs will be retained. The Prime Minister and Ministers will not vacate their seats during election campaigns, despite the Commission's recommendation that

they do so. The present structure of decentralized government will be maintained to facilitate the process of participatory democracy.   An Ombudsman proposed by the Commission will be appointed to investigate complaints made by the general public. National Councils for the Youth and Women will be established.

7 Dec. 1972	Members of the banned UPP, Justin Chimba, John Chisata, Alfred Chambeshi, Elias Kaenga and Jameson Chapaloka, are awarded damages after being tortured whilst in detention.
13 Dec. 1972	Constitutional Amendment Bill is passed which makes Zambia a one-party state.
14 Dec. 1972	The ANC's case against Zambia's new political dispensation is dismissed with costs. ANC members are invited to join in the process of participatory democracy under a one-party state.
31 Dec. 1972	Simon Kapwepwe and thirty four others are released from detention in what is seen as a gesture of goodwill.
9 Jan. 1973	Rhodesia closes all border posts with Zambia citing security reasons as a cause for the closure: Rhodesia continues to claim that what it terms terrorist attacks are launched from Zambia into Rhodesia.
10 Jan. 1973	Zambia normalizes its relations with the German Democractic Republic after the closure of its Lusaka trade mission in 1971.
11 Jan. 1973	Zambia announces that it will not be sending its copper exports via Rhodesia. All trade links with Rhodesia are subsequently cut off. Copper exports are rerouted to Lobito Bay.
4 Feb. 1973	Ian Smith offers to reopen the border. Zambia responds by sealing border posts.
4 Feb. 1973	The latest in a series of landmine explosions on the Rhodesia-Zambia border since 11 January seriously injures a sergeant. In a letter to the UN Secretary-General Kurt Waldheim two days earlier, President Kaunda highlights the growing tension on its borders, exacerbated by the maiming and deaths of Zambians by landmines planted on Zambian soil by Rhodesian and South African forces.
5 Feb. 1973	At the twentieth session of the OAU Ministerial Council, Emperor Haile Selassie condemns Rhodesia's closure of its borders with Zambia as an 'unprovoked act of aggression...' aimed at paralyzing Zambia's economy.
6 Feb. 1973	Presidents Nyerere, Mobutu and Kaunda meet in a Arusha to exchange views on matters of mutual concern, particularly relating to the struggle for the liberation of Africa.
11 Feb. 1973	A UN Security Council mission arrives in Lusaka to evaluate the Rhodesia-Zambia border issue. After five days of talks in Lusaka, the mission visits Dar-es-Salaam and Nairobi to discuss alternative trade routes for Zambia.

26 Feb. 1973	The mail service between Rhodesia and Zambia is suspended by the Rhodesian Posts and Telecommunications Corporation.
25 Feb. 1973	Rhodesian rail links with Zambia are closed after a Rhodesian train driver is arrested by Zambian troops.
27 Feb. 1973	Signs loan agreement with IBRD on the Integrated Family Farming Project.
10 Mar. 1973	Mines on the Zambian border are also condemned and a call is made for a tightening of the trade embargo against Rhodesia.
10 Mar. 1973	The United Nations Security Council passes a resolution urging all states to aid Zambia in increasing the capacity of alternative trade routes in order to bypass Southern Rhodesia. Southern Rhodesia's actions in planting mines on the Zambian border are also condemned. Calls are made for a tightening of the trade embargo.
26 Mar. 1973	Succession to the International Agreement on the Suppression of White Slave Traffic; and the International Convention on the Suppression of White Slave Traffic.
26 Mar. 1973	Succession to the International Convention on the Suppression of Traffic in Women and Children.
26 Mar. 1973	Succession to the 1953 Slavery Convention; and the Convention on Slavery, Slave Trade and Institutions and Practices Similar to Slavery.
4 Apr. 1973	Accepts amendment to paragraphs A, B, C of Article VI of the IAEA Statute.
9 Apr. 1973	Protocol bringing under international control drugs outside the scope of the 1931 Convention; as amended by the Protocol of 11 December 1946.
9 Apr. 1973	Succession to the Convention of Limiting the Manufacture and Regulating the Distribution of Narcotic Drugs of 1931, as amended by the 1946 Protocol.
9 Apr. 1973	Succession to the International Opium Convention of 1925 as amended by the 1946 Protocol.
9 Apr. 1973	Succession to the 1912 International Opium Convention.
15 May 1973	Four tourists (two Canadians and two Americans) exploring a gorge below Victoria Falls, are shot at from the Zambian side. The Canadian tourists are killed. The incident, one of many during the year, highlights the tension surrounding the border between Rhodesia and Zambia. Calls are made by outraged Canadians to cut off aid to Zambia.
23 May 1973	The UN Secretary-General, Kurt Waldhein, concludes his visit to Zambia. During his visit the deaths of five Zambians are reported killed by landmine explosions.
24 May 1973	Ratifies ILO Convention on the Protection against the Hazards of Benzene Poisoning (No. 136); protection and facilities for workers' representatives (No. 135).

25 May 1973	President Kaunda commissions a new Chinese built transmitting station for Radio Lusaka. He also inaugurates the external service at the Zambia Broadcasting Service. He expands on the revelation that mass communication can play a 'vital role in the defence of a country and can be employed in the counter defence of psychological warfare. Among the languages that will be broadcast to areas in Southern Africa are Afrikaans and Portuguese.
30 May 1973	Signs treaty with West Germany on double taxation concerning income and capital.
30 May 1973	A Summit Meeting again takes place between President Nyerere, Mobutu and Kaunda at Kitwe, Zambia. They are joined by the leaders of the FNLA and MPLA. President Nyerere asserts the need to strengthen the relationship between the Zambian and Tanzanian people and President Mobutu offers military and financial backing.
6 June 1973	Signs loan agreement with IBRD on the third Education Project.
7 June 1973	A call is made at UNIP's National Council Meeting for the process of Zambianization in the management and control of institutions to be accelerated. This call comes after a resolution adopting Kenneth Kaunda's programme to work towards equal opportunities in Zambia.
18 June 1973	Signs loan agreement with IBRD on Program Loan.
27 June 1973	Harry Nkumbula calls on former ANC members to join UNIP at a gathering in Choma, Southern Province, once the stronghold of the ANC. It is at this gathering that he signs the Choma Declaration with President Kaunda.
13 July 1973	Signs Protocol on Space Requirements for Special Trade Passengers Ships.
16 July 1973	Signs guarantee agreement with IBRD on the Kafue Hydro-electric Project (Stage II)
28 July 1973	A summit meeting is concluded between Zaire, Tanzania and Zambia in Lubumbushi, Zaire.
6 Aug. 1973	A bomb explodes in the office of the Minister for Southern Province, killing a secretary and causing extensive damage. It is the first in a spate of such incidents.
10 Aug. 1973	A parcel bomb explodes in the Chinese Embassy in Lusaka killing the wife of a senior Chinese official and injuring another.
15 Aug. 1973	Ratifies specific aspects of the OAU Convention on Refugee Problems in Africa which was signed on 10 September 1969.
20 Aug. 1973	Accedes to multilateral agreement on liability for damage caused by space objects. Accession at Moscow on 21 August 1973, and London 28 August 1973.
25 Aug. 1973	President Kaunda signs the Constitution Amendment Bill at the opening of UNIP's Seventh General Conference at Mulungushi Rock, creating a

one-party state. The implications of the Constitution are as follows: Parliament will consist of 136 members, of these 125 will be elected and then will be nominated by the President. It will also include a Speaker and the Prime Minister. The Party will take precedence over government; primary elections will take place before a general election with the primary electorate composed of Party officials from branch level to constituency level; the Central Committee will take the final decision on Parliamentary candidates. A leadership code will henceforth control a leader's assets and earning capacity. Under UNIP's new Constitution, the Central Committee will consist of not more than twenty five members, twenty of these will be elected by a general conference held every five years and three will be nominated by the President.

27 Aug. 1973	President Kaunda lashes out at western attitudes towards independent African countries. He is particularly upset at big business who needs to adjust its strategies and the media for what he terms their 'callous indifference'.
28 Aug. 1973	Accession to 1967 Convention on the Exploration and Use of Outer Space, including the Moon and other Celestial Bodies.
28 Aug. 1973	Accession to the 1968 Convention on the Rescue of Astronauts and of Objects launched into Outer Space.
28 Aug. 1973	New Cabinet appointments are announced: Mainza Chona (former Vice-President) is made Zambia's first Prime Minister; Grey Zulu (former Minister of Defence) will become UNIP's Secretary-General, with Aaron Milner (former Secretary-General) replacing him.
31 Aug. 1973	Approves WTO Statutes.
31 Aug. 1973	President Kaunda declares that the Zambian government will take immediate control of Nchanga Consolidated Copper Mines and Rian Consolidated Mines (subsidiaries of Anglo-American and American Metal) in which the government has already 51% interest.
8 Sept. 1973	The leader of the banned Lumpa Sect, Alice Lenshina, is released.
11 Sept. 1973	A further parcel bomb incident kills the Asian poet, Chiman Vyass and his wife and injures their son.
13 Sept. 1973	Signs double taxation agreement with Denmark concerning fiscal evasion on income.
26 Oct. 1973	Zambia breaks off diplomatic relations with Israel after the outbreak of the fourth Arab-Israeli war on 6 October.
29 Oct. 1973	A summit meeting is concluded between Zaire, Zambia and Tanzania in Mwanza (Tanzania). During the proceedings the three leaders meet Holden Roberto (FNLA) and Agostinho Neto (MPLA). President Amin also joins the proceedings in a surprise visit.
Nov. 1973	A number of armed incidents on the Zambia Rhodesia border are reported.

30 Nov. 1973	Accession by Zambia to the International Convention on the Suppression and Punishment of the Crime of Apartheid.
4 Dec. 1973	A high Zambian official states that about 100 persons have been sent to Zambia by South Africa in order to interfere with the general elections.
5 Dec. 1973	In the first presidential election under the new constitution, President Kaunda is re-elected.
5 Dec. 1973	The National Assembly, which was dissolved on 1 October, is followed by the elections on 5 December. The result proves that nore than half of the successful candidates were members of the Assembly.
7 Dec. 1973	The number of refugees has almost doubled during the year according to a UN report, from 17000 to 33000. The refugees are mainly fleeing South Africa, Namibia, Angola and Mozambique.
10 Dec. 1973	President Kaunda reorganizes the Cabinet. For the first time in the country's history, it contains leaders of the Army, Air Force, the Police and a woman.
1 Jan. 1974	Entry into force of the Additional Regulations amending the International Health Regulations.
31 Jan. 1974	The British Foreign Secretary, Alec Douglas-Home arrives in Lusaka for talks. One of the key issues under discussion is Britain's present policy towards Rhodesia.
Feb. 1974	Relations with Britain improve after a labour government returns to power.
12 Feb. 1974	A parcel bomb explodes at the Liberation Centre in Lusaka, leaving a representative of the African National Congress (ANC) of South Africa, John Dube, dead and injuring several others.
20 Feb. 1974	President Kaunda heads a large delegation on an eight day visit to China.
8 Mar. 1974	President Kaunda concludes a tour to Pakistan, Saudi Arabia, Egypt and Sudan. On his return, closer cooperation between Zambia and Sudan is announced in the form of a joint commission which will meet annually in both capitals.
29 Mar. 1974	Provides definitive signature to the Commonwealth Telecommunications Organization Financial Agreement.
11 Apr. 1974	Grey Zulu announces that President Kaunda and the Central Committee of UNIP have already declared their assets and liabilities in accordance with the Leadership Code. He adds that the enforcement of the Code will be a continuous process.
21 Apr. 1974	The Lusaka-Livingstone railway line is sabotaged near Nega Nega.
26 Apr. 1974	UNIP National Council adopts a resolution which replaces the 'yes' or 'no' option on ballot boxes with an image of the presidential candidate and the word 'no'. The Council also recommends that there should be only one

Presidential candidate. A proposal is also forwarded to prevent former detainees from claiming compensation for physical and mental abuse. The final Constitutional Amendment Bill which is passed in August, after heated debate, allows ex-detainees to pursue claims.   Calls are made for preventative measures to be taken against rising crime: the death penalty for armed robbery is introduced.

6 May 1974 | President Kaunda visits Malawi and holds private talks with President Banda. Amongst the issues discussed in this 'epoch-making' visit are relations with Mozambique, Rhodesia and South Africa, and transport problems.

7 June 1974 | Leaders now have until the 14 June 1975 to comply with the provisions of the Leadership Code which has been revised. The definition of 'leader' is revised under the new amendments to include people working in a certain income bracket for institutions in which the state has a controlling interest. Concessions are also made to specified leaders to own property. The President has the power to exempt certain leaders from the provisions of the Code. A revised procedure for declaring assets and liabilities is also introduced.

3-6 July 1974 | President Kaunda is the guest of honour at TANU's twentieth anniversary celebrations. This marks his first state visit to Tanzania (apart from his numerous private visits). Addressing a TANU rally on 6 July, President Kaunda states that UNIP has much to learn from TANU's running of a one-party system.

5 July 1974 | Signs various aspects of the Universal Postal Union: the second additional Protocol to the Constitution; General Regulations; postal parcels; Universal Postal Convention.

13 July 1974 | President Amin threatens Zambia and Tanzania over alleged 'invasion plans' headed by Milton Obote.

15 July 1974 | The death sentence is passed on three Zambians found guilty of treason. The men were charged with allegedly recruiting and taking ninety-nine Zambians for military training into Namibia in order to stage a Zambian coup. The defendants appealed against the sentence.

12 Aug. 1974 | The Zambian Prime Minister opens an MPLA Conference in Lusaka. The Conference intending to restore unity within the movement, is unsuccessful.

16 Aug. 1974 | Amends and signs release treaty with IBRD and Great Britain.

16 Aug. 1974 | Amends 1970 loan agreement between IBRD and Kariba North Bank Company and the Kariba North Project.

7 Sept. 1974 | President Kaunda presides over the signing of the independence agreement between the Mozambique Liberation Front and Portugal, in Lusaka.

30 Sept. 1974 | Presidents Kaunda, Nyerere and Mobutu conclude informal summit talks in Dar-es-Salaam. They are joined by Samora Machel and Agostinho Neto and discussions centre around developments in Mozambique and Angola.

3 Oct. 1974 | Confidential proposals on Rhodesia are forwarded to the British government

by Zambia and Tanzania. These include constitutional talks involving political players in Rhodesia.

18 Oct. 1974

Senior government officials from Tanzania, Zambia and Zaire hold a two-day meeting in mid-October to consolidate discussions on co-operation held by their national leaders. Attempts are made to explore a long-term goal of federation.

24 Oct. 1974

Zambia's tenth anniversary independence celebrations are attended by international dignatories from as far afield as Peking.

1 Nov. 1974

Succession to the 1949 multilateral agreement on the suppression of circulation and traffic of obscene publications.

1 Nov. 1974

Succession to 1950 multilateral agreement on importation of educational, scientific and cultural materials.

1 Nov. 1974

Succession with reservations to the Convention on the Status of Stateless Persons.

20 Nov. 1974

President Kaunda arrives in Moscow. He is on a state visit to improve fragile relations between the two countries.

6 Dec. 1974

Signs loan agreement with IBRD on the Lusaka Squatter Upgrading and Site and Services Project.

8 Jan. 1975

President Banda begins a state visit to Zambia, his first since Zambia's independence. His visit affirms the newly established closer ties between the two countries.

15 Jan. 1975

500 University of Zambia (UNZA) students demonstrate in support of MPLA.

20 Jan. 1975

The Minister of Mines and Industry, Andrew Cashita, is removed from office. He is widely regarded as one of the most outstanding members of the young Zambian elite who had worked their way up from civil service to ministerial level. His dismissal comes as changes are made in an attempt to integrate the work of the Central Committee into the running of government.

22 Jan. 1975

Succession to the multilateral agreement on the nationality of married women.

24 Jan. 1975

Ex-detainees are now entitled to join UNIP without being screened by the Central Committee, provided that leaders at branch regional or provincial level are satisfied that they have reformed.

28 Jan. 1975

President Kaunda reinstates the State of Emergency.

30 Jan. 1975

An UNZA lecturer, Lionel Cliffe, is detained.

30 Jan.-1 Feb. 1975

The Lomé Convention is signed betwen EEC and 46 African, Caribbean and Pacific countries. The five-year convention will establish economic co-operation between the signatories.

5-8 Feb. 1975   UNZA students demand the release of Lionel Cliffe. Three days later as the demonstrations intensify, the army cordons off the campus. Four more expatriate lecturers and thirty seven students are detained.

28 Mar. 1975   Leaders of ZANU are detained for questioning after the murder of ZANU's chairman, Herbert Chitepo in Lusaka. Leaders of other nationalist movements are also detained. The offices of ZAPU, ZANU and FROLIZI are closed. ZANU, ZAPU and FROLIZI are subsequently banned.

31 Mar. 1975   President Kaunda orders a special commission of inquiry into the massacre of Zimbabwean freedom fighters on Zambian soil after an apparent power struggle between rival Shona clans. Representatives from various African states as well as the OAU Liberation Committee are included on the commission. President Kaunda states that the cost in supporting the liberation struggle in Rhodesia has taken its toll on Zambia.

3 Apr. 1975   An agreement is signed between Portugal and Zambia, establishing diplomatic relations.

19 Apr. 1975   After a meeting in Washington with President Ford, President Kaunda states that the only solution to the Rhodesian crisis, is a black majority government.

8 May 1975   President Kaunda concludes a two-day visit to Portugal involving high level talks with the Portuguese President and Prime Minister.

27 May 1975   Forty delegates drawn from Botswana, Rhodesia, South Africa and Zambia attend a two-day symposium on detente in Southern Africa, held in Gaborone.

27 May 1975   Mainza Chona resigns at his own request as Prime Minister. He is retained as the Minister of Legal Affairs and Attorney-General. Elijah Mudenda replaces him as the new Prime Minister. Vernon Mwaanga, the former Foreign Minister, is made a member of the Central Committee.

27 May 1975   President Kaunda takes the opportunity to announce a number of changes following the resignation of Mainza Chona. He suspends Ameck Phiri, former Minister for North-Western Province and two MPs for failing to declare their assets, in accordance with the Leadership Code.

16 June 1975   Succession to privileges and immunities of UN specialized agencies: ILO, FAO, ICAO, UNESCO, WHO (revised text of annex VII, 2nd), UPU, ITU, WMO, IMCO (Revised text of annex XII).

24 June 1975   Signs guarantee agreement with IBRD on the Telecommunications Project.

25 June 1975   A Cabinet Minister and five other white Rhodesian Front members hold secret talks with President Kaunda in Zambia, marking the first direct contact between President Kaunda and a Rhodesian government minister since independence.

30 June 1975   In his opening address to UNIP's National Council, President Kaunda challenges the leadership to recognize the importance of the masses and to

modify their lifestyles accordingly. His speech, which takes a strong anti-capitalist line, comes at a point when Zambia faces its most serious economic crisis since independence. The President announces several economic reforms in an attempt to deal with the crisis:
- All privately owned freehold land is abolished and replaced by 100-year leases, with the state acquiring unused properties;
- Estate agents are ordered to close with immediate effect;
- The President also recommends that state subsidies be cut by up to sixty percent;
- Cinemas and the Lonrho-owned Times of Zambia and Sunday Times are nationalized.

18 July 1975   The OAU Ministerial Council meeting and OAU Summit which is held in Kampala, is boycotted for the first time in OAU's history by Zambia, Botswana and Tanzania.

21 July 1975   Uganda accuses the leaders of Zambia, Tanzania and Botswana of spying for the South African and Rhodesian governments.

25 Aug. 1975   A diplomatic initiative begun by President Kaunda in October 1974 and backed by the Presidents of Mozambique, Tanzania and Botswana, reaches its climax when President Kaunda meets the South African Prime Minister, John Vorster, in a railway carriage on the Victoria Falls bridge. In another carriage, white and black Rhodesians face each other for the first time. These talks end in deadlock.

11 Sept. 1975   ANC leaders are relocated from the President State Guest House to a site on the outskirts of Lusaka. The move is seen as a sign of growing Zambian frustration with the ANC faction dispute.

11 Sept. 1975   Zambian troops kill eleven ZANU members with thirteen injured, near Kabwe, in an attempt to halt fighting between ZANU and ZAPU supporters.

13 Sept. 1975   China announces changes to its policy. At a banquet in honour of Grey Zulu, on an official visit to China, it agrees to dialogue between black Africa and white Southern Africa.

18 Sept. 1975   Zambia and SWAPO jointly deny a report which alleges that the Zambian government had ordered SWAPO to cease military operations on its soil. Sam Nujoma confirms that SWAPO does not have military camps in Zambia.

26 Oct. 1975   President Kaunda welcomes a statement made by John Vorster in which peace above violence is chosen. He calls on South Africa to withdraw from the Rhodesian conflict in his response as a prerequisite to peace in the region. Kanuda's statement follows the revival of diplomatic contact with Pretoria in mid-1974 which culminated in the Lusaka Agreement on Rhodesia in December.

27 Oct. 1975   After discussions with President Kaunda, Joshua Nkomo, leader of the anti-Muzorewa faction of the ANC, announces the possibility of resuming constitutional negotiations with the Rhodesian government.

Dec. 1975   The leader of the banned Lumpa Sect is released, after eleven years of detention.

1 Jan. 1976	Signs multilateral agreement on the constitution of the Universal Postal Union.
13 Jan. 1976	An agreement is signed between Zambia and Mozambique on the construction of a road which would facilitate Zambia's access to the coast and strengthen economic ties. Zambia and Mozambique are also investigating the possibility of a rail link.
23 Jan. 1976	President Kaunda announces the dismissal of Skota Uina as a member of UNIP's Central Committee. (Skota Uina was a founding member of UNIP)
27 Jan. 1976	The City of Lusaka and its surrounding areas is constituted as a province, bringing the total number of provinces to nine.
28 Jan. 1976	President Kaunda declares a State of Emergency due to the vulnerability of Zambia's borders.
30 Jan. 1976	In his budget speech, the Minister of Finance, Luke Mwanashiku, cuts public spending and announces sharp increases in the cost of living. Zambia's economic crisis stems from the dramatic drop in the world price of copper in 1974 and 1975.
9 Feb. 1976	Ratifies ILO Convention of Minimum Age for Accession to Employment (No. 138).
15 Feb. 1976	President Kaunda addressing a UNIP meeting speaks of a bloodbath in Rhodesia as inevitable.
18 Feb. 1976	Signs guarantee agreement with IBRD on the Development Bank of Zambia Project.
18 Feb. 1976	Signs treaty with West Germany on financial assistance.
18 Feb. 1976	Zambia goes against a decision adopted by the OAU and other countries to recognize the MPLA government. In doing so, it becomes the first African State to formally withhold recognition of the MPLA government.
3 Mar. 1976	Zambia supports Mozambique's closure of its border with Rhodesia.
16-18 Mar. 1976	Zambia continues to seek a reconciliation between UNITA and the ruling MPLA. Negotiations between an Angolan delegation and Zambia fail to resolve the deadlock. Other issues, such as the future of Angolan refugees in Zambia, are also of concern. Another point of contention is the damage caused to the Benguela Railway during the civil war which links Zambia to the port of Lobito.
17-18 Mar. 1976	An Angolan delegation headed by the Foreign Minister, Jose Eduardo dos Santos, visits Lusaka in an attempt to normalize strained relations between the two countries.
19 Mar. 1976	Talks between Ian Smith and Joshua Nkomo are broken off, leaving Zambia to reverse its strategy of detente in Southern Africa.

31 Mar. 1976	Amends and extends treaty with Great Britain on officers designated by Great Britain in the service of the government of Zambia; and the members of staff designated by Great Britain to the University of Zambia. The latter was further extended by signature on 4 August 1976.
9 Apr. 1976	An International Commission is established by President Kaunda following the murder of Herbert Chitepo, chairman of ZANU. It finds that he was murdered as a result of a power struggle within ZANU, based on tribal lines.
16 Apr. 1976	Zambia formally recognizes the MPLA government in Angola.
21 Apr. 1976	Three former members of ZANU appear before a Lusaka magistrate in connection with the murder of Herbert Chitepo.
27 Apr. 1976	Dr Kissinger launches a joint British-American initiative on Rhodesia in Lusaka. Zambia endorses the move.
3 May 1976	John Mwanakatwe is appointed as Finance Minister in place of Luke Mwanashiku who is made the new Governor of the Bank of Zambia following the arrest of Bitwell Kuuani, who together with his wife, is charged with receiving stolen goods.
5 May 1976	The Central Committee is criticized for suspending, sine die, UNIP elections at section, village, branch and constituency levels.
11 May 1976	Siteke Mwate replaces Rupiah Banda as Minister of Foreign Affairs. Rupiah Banda is alleged to have made appointments in his Ministry based on tribal affiliations.
13 May 1976	Aaron Milner announces the presence of an armed gang in the North-Western Province, led by Adamson Mushala who is reputed to have been trained by the SADF in Namibia. He was a former politician who quit UNIP to join an opposition party. In July, Grey Zulu is forced to cut short a visit to the Province due to the gang's activities. It is difficult to ascertain whether the gang is politically motivated or merely bandits. Their success in eluding the law indicates that they are being sheltered by villagers.
24 May 1976	The Leadership Code is revised to prevent leaders from transferring business interests to relatives. Taking advantage of the loophole, transgressors aim to make Zambia an egalitarian state.
29 May 1976	Zambia sanctions the establishment of a 'third front' by freedom fighters on Zambian soil. The first operation carried out from the base is followed by bomb blasts which rock Lusaka.
June 1976	Four Zambians are sentenced to death for treason following their involvement in the recruitment of 100 Zambians for military training in Namibia with the aim of staging a coup in Zambia. Three others had appealed against their sentence passed in October 1974. Two were successful, but the third was sentenced to death.
13 June 1976	President Kaunda announces the establishment of a United National Defence Force under the command of General Kingsley Chinkuli. The new force

will be directly responsible to UNIP.

13 June 1976	Two bomblasts occur in the Lusaka Post Office, the other in the High Court. The Rhodesian government is blamed by President Kaunda.
13 June 1976	Zambian politicians led by a UNIP Central Committee member, hold a protest march to the residence of the French Ambassador to demand that France cut off its arms sales to South Africa. France has also agreed to build a nuclear power station in South Africa.
20 June 1976	Grey Zulu warns against Rhodesian troops entering Zambia, as threatened.
9 July 1976	The Kwacha is devalued by twenty percent. It is simultaneously linked to the International Monetary Fund's Special Drawing Rights (SDR) and no longer to the US dollar. The Minister of Finance defends the move by citing the closure of Zambia's main trade routes and the decline in the price of copper. Zambia has also borne the cost of sanctions against Rhodesia.
14 July 1976	The railway line connecting Zambia to the port of Dar-es-Salaam is officially handed over to Presidents Kaunda and Nyerere by the Chinese Vice-Premier, Sun Chien.
27 July 1976	At the UN Security Council, Zambia accuses South Africa of violating her borders fourteen times in the first half of 1976.
10 Aug. 1976	The Soviet Union's new Ambassador is received by President Kaunda. Relations with the previous Ambassador had grown increasingly difficult.
13 Aug. 1976	President Kaunda launches an attack on John Vorster, blaming the South African Prime Minister for the escalation of violence in the region and the fact that Rhodesia faces a full-scale war.
17 Aug. 1976	The Zambian and Angolan Presidents meet for the first time at the non-aligned conference in Sri Lanka. This is followed by another meeting in Lusaka when President Neto briefly stops over on his way home.
24 Aug. 1976	Signs treaty with United States on agricultural commodities.
29 Aug. 1976	An agreement is signed between Tanzania, Zambia and Mozambique which will focus on security issues.
11 Sept. 1976	The brother of Aaron Mushala is killed in a clash with security forces. He, together with his brother, is accused of having intended to overthrow the Zambian government.
17 Sept. 1976	Signs second Program Loan agreement with IBRD.
20 Sept. 1976	At UNIP's National Council, President Kaunda presents his ideas for a new society based on 'Communocracy - a people's economy under Humanism' in which power over resources and public affairs is redistributed and employed collectively.
20 Sept. 1976	The Minister of Finance, John Mwanakatwe, highlights Zambia's failure to meet its planned economic target of a 11.5% growth rate set in 1965. Only a 2.5% growth rate was achieved.

22 Sept. 1976	Zambia and Angola agree to establish diplomatic relations at ministerial level. The move follows an assurance given to Zambia that her cargo will be moved up the Benguela route following rail repairs. A joint permanent commission will also be established in order to resolve existing (and possible future) problems.
18 Oct. 1976	Indira Ghandi concludes a four-day visit to Zambia as part of her African tour. She is awarded with Zambia's highest public honour, a Grand Commander of the Order of Grand Companions of Freedom, first division.
Nov. 1976	Ghana is to reopen its mission in Lusaka, closed after the deposition of Kwame Nkrumah ten years ago.
3 Dec. 1976	Signs treaty with United States on agricultural commodities, as well as economic assistance for commodity-related services.
18 Dec. 1976	President Kaunda pays a visit to President Mobutu in Kinshasa.
21 Dec. 1976	Simon Kapwepwe approaches the President in an attempt to rejoin UNIP.
17 Jan. 1977	Signs fourth Education Project loan agreement with IBRD.
22 Jan. 1977	President Kaunda returns to Lusaka from a tour of West Africa which included Nigeria, Ghana, Liberia, Ivory Coast, Guinea and Sierra Leone. The Patriotic Front and its recognition by the Front Line States, receives the support of respective heads of state he visited.
23 Jan. 1977	A parcel bomb kills the ZAPU representative of Joshua Nkomo, Jason Moyo, in Lusaka.
9 Feb. 1977	Signs ILO convention relating to the minimum age for admission to employment.
18 Feb. 1977	A joint team of experts complete their investigations into outstanding border differences between Zambia and Malawi.
16 Mar. 1977	A top level Angolan government delegation visits Zambia, improving relations between the two countries.
26-29 Mar. 1977	On an official state visit to Zambia (amongst other African states), the Soviet Union's President Nikolai Podgorni, issues a joint statement with President Kaunda on areas of common vision that exist between the two countries. A programme involving scientific and cultural co-operation is also ratified by the respective foreign ministers.
24 Apr. 1977	Axon Soko, the Minister of Mines and Industry, is dismissed. He is accused of abuse of powers. (Soko, a prominent Easterner had begun to forge links with Simon Kapwepwe). Another minister, S. Mulenga (Minister of Lands, Natural Resources and Tourism) is accused of anti-UNIP activities. He is also sacked. The President also dismisses Zongani Banda, Minister of State for Power, Transport and Communications, and reshuffles top ranking personnel in the Zambian National Defence Forces. General Kingsley Chipkuli is appointed as Minister to the portfolio of Mines for the reconstituted Ministry of Mines,

while his former deputy, Lieutenant-General Peter Zuze is promoted to Commander.

16 May 1977	Amidst a growing number of border incidents with Rhodesia, Zambia declares itself to be 'in a state of war' with Rhodesia.
25 May 1977	Zambian and South African forces clash openly in two separate border incidents.
8 June 1977	Signs loan agreement with IBRD on Phase II of the Industrial Forestry Project.
8 June 1977	Zambia is accused of a rocket attack on Rhodesia which threatens to cut power at Kariba.
22 June 1977	Police break up a riot of approximately 2000 squatters objecting to a slum clearance project by the Kitwe City Council. The incident is extremely serious and is attributed to the general tension on the Copperbelt.
20 July 1977	The Prime Minister, Elijah Mudenda, is replaced by Mainza Chona. Mudenda however retains his position on the Central Committee of UNIP. His dismissal is never given an official explanation.
21 July 1977	The East African Minister for Finance and Administration, Wilbert Chagula, tells a visiting Zambian delegation to Tanzania to join the East African Community (EAC). An unidentified member of state had previously barred Zambia's entry.
25 July 1977	CCM (Tanzania) proposes a merger with UNIP given previous co-operation that had existed between the two ruling parties. The Zambian delegation on a visit to Tanzania will submit the proposals to UNIP.
2 Aug. 1977	The Minister of Home Affairs, Aaron Milner, is dismissed amidst allegations of currency smuggling. Promises that he will be given an opportunity to defend himself against the charges are never realized.
23 Aug. 1977	Leading oil companies are accused of breaking sanctions by supplying oil to Rhodesia. Zambia is to institute legal proceedings against them.
26 Aug. 1977	The five Front Line Presidents meet in Lusaka to discuss the Anglo-American proposals on the Rhodesian situation. Dr Owen and Andrew Young arrive for talks on the same evening.
Sept. 1977	Zambian security forces kill Samson Mushalla, member of the notorious Mushalla gang, led by his brother, Adamson.
3 Sept. 1977	Following border raids carried out by Rhodesian fighter planes, a night curfew is imposed on Lusaka, Livingstone, Kafue and Chilanga. The curfew lasts for seventeen days and coincides with a visit by Nigerian Head of State.
9 Sept. 1977	Simon Kapwepwe rejoins UNIP after prolonged discussions. he brings with him four of his senior aides, Justin Chimba, John Chisata, Musonda Chamkeshi and Peter Chanda. He makes a call to former members of UPP to join the ruling party.

25 Sept. 1977	President Kaunda receives Ian Smith for talks on the latest Anglo-American proposals in Lusaka. The talks fail to alleviate the deepening tension that exists between the two countries.
6 Dec. 1977	A Parliamentary Select Committee under Finance Minister, John Mwakanatwe, calls for drastic changes to Zambia's political and economic structures. The Committee proposes a reduction in the number of political personnel on the government's payroll. The report also recommends the 'redeployment' of employees. The government is advised to cut costs in the mining industry. Cuts in social services are also envisaged, challenging the concept of Humanism.
16 Dec. 1977	Accession to establishment of IFAO.
23 Dec. 1977	Signs additional protocol relating to the protection of victims of armed conflict.
15 Jan. 1978	Tanzania revokes special tariffs granted to Zambia for the use of the port of Dar-es-Salaam.
21 Feb. 1978	During a debate in the National Assembly, the freedom of the press is raised as an issue.
6 Mar. 1978	Rhodesian forces cross Zambian borders supposedly in 'hot pursuit' of liberation fighters with the main attack in the Luangwa district.
15 Mar. 1978	The UN Security Council acting on a complaint by Zambia against Rhodesian aggression adopts a resolution commending Zambia and other Front Line States for their support of the liberation struggle in Zimbabwe. The resolution also declares that any further acts against Zambia's sovereignty would entail more effective measures.
17 Mar. 1978	Zambia devalues the Kwacha by ten persent. Low world prices for copper and transportation bottlenecks in the export of the metal are causes of Zambia's economic difficulties.
18 May 1978	President Kaunda visits Washington. During his visit he attempts to persuade President Carter to maintain his present policy of not recognizing the internal settlement in Rhodesia. President Kaunda, rather than condemning Soviet and Cuban interventions, insists that the US should look at the underlying causes.
6 June 1978	President Kaunda holds talks with President Mobutu at Lubumbashi, Zaire. The visit appears to heal the diplomatic rift between Zaire and Zambia, following Zairean accusations that Zambia had assisted Shaba rebels. (Zambian territory was used as a transit region but the government refutes that this occurred with the knowledge of the Zambian authorities.)
12 June 1978	President Kaunda offers Zambian assistance to Zaire to solve the problem in Shaba.
28 June - 3 July 1978	Chancellor Helmut Schmidt, on his first official visit to Africa, includes Zambia in his itinerary. Amongst other issues he defends his government's opposition to UN sanctions against South Africa. He also calls for

settlement proposals to be implemented in Rhodesia and promises to increase the copper revenues of developing countries.

22 Aug. 1978	Zambia expels 500 Tanzanians. Their expulsion follows the arrest of several thousand foreigners from neighbouring countries after a house to house search designed to clamp down on crime.
28 Aug. 1978	A joint commission is established between Zambia and Zaire to resolve border issues.
1 Sept. 1978	Amendments to UNIP's constitution affect the rules relating to the presidential election: - A presidential candidate needs to be supported by at least twenty UNIP members in each of Zambia's nine provinces; - Candidates' names need to be approved by the National Council; - Candidates must have been UNIP members for a minimum of five years; - Candidates must not have a criminal record and must be 'disciplined'. These changes disqualify Kapwepwe and Nkumbula from standing. Both will contest the matter in court.
12 Sept. 1978	A new post, to be filled by Grey Zulu, is created: Secretary of State for Defence and Security. Previously such matters were handled by the President but given the increased demands including the worsening situation with Rhodesia, fulltime attention is required.
15 Sept. 1978	President Kaunda confirms that the poor performance due to management and maintenance problems of Tazara (the Chinese built line handed over to Tanzania and Zambia in 1976) has led to the return of Chinese personnel.
19 Sept. 1978	The findings of the Bingham Report confirm the role of British oil companies in breaking UN sanctions imposed on Rhodesia. The revelations boost Zambia's court proceedings against seventeen Western oil companies for damages due to sanctions busting.
21-22 Sept.1978	President Kaunda and the British Prime Minister Callaghan hold talks on Southern African problems in Kano, Nigeria. The talks renew trust between the two countries.
6 Oct. 1978	President Kaunda orders the partial reopening of the border with Rhodesia to gain access to southerly trade links. The government argues that the move is necessitated by a holdup in the delivery of 150000 tons of fertilizer from Mozambique.
7 Oct. 1978	Nyerere and Machel are reported to have met Kaunda in Lusaka in an unsuccessful attempt to persuade him not to reopen the border with Rhodesia.
8 Oct. 1978	A Zambian delegation arrives in Johannesburg for talks with South African officials, following meetings held in Botswana.
19 Oct. 1978	Rhodesia launches air strikes against targets near Lusaka occupying Zambian airspace for thirty minutes and issuing a warning to Lusaka airport control not to allow planes to land or take off.

21 Oct. 1978   Rhodesia strikes again at targets near Lusaka and in the Central Province. Eighteen foreign nationals are arrested after the raids. These arrests, together with targeting incidents of harassment against Zambian whites, increase racial tension.

29 Oct. 1978   A meeting of the Front Line Presidents in Dar-es-Salaam takes place without the presence of President Machel and fails to issue a communiqué afterwards, reflecting the discord over Zambia's decision to reopen the border with Rhodesia.

3 Nov. 1978   Signs agreement with Finland for the avoidance of double taxation and the prevention of fiscal evasion with respect to taxes on income and capital.

Nov. 1978   At a mass rally President Kaunda berates the state of Zambia's defence systems following a failure to detect Rhodesian air raids. Britain responds by donating military equipment at one million Pounds Sterling. Zambians also receive military training in Britain in 1978 and 1979.

4 Nov. 1978   UNIP's Central Committee disqualifies thirty candidates successful in the Zambian primary elections. Arthur Uina, former Foreign Minister, is one of those to be disqualified.

16 Nov. 1978   The Lusaka High Court dismisses a challenge by Harry Nkumbula and Simon Kapwepwe against the validity of President Kaunda's nomination as the sole presidential candidate.

6 Dec. 1978   President Kaunda withdraws from the Anglo-American initiative begun in 1977 to resolve the crisis in Rhodesia.

9 Dec. 1978   The death of the leader of the banned Lumpa Sect, Alice Lenshina, is announced. The Times of Zambia reminds its readers of the threat which she and her followers posed at one point to Zambia's independence.

15 Dec. 1978   President Kaunda is sworn in for a further five-year term as President. Results reveal that he obtained eighty five percent of the votes cast in a sixtyfive percent poll. He does poorly in the Southern Province, a former stronghold of the ANC, but is successful on the Copperbelt.

18 Dec. 1978   President Kaunda, Neto Machel and President Nyerere meet in Beira to draw up a four-point declaration which is supportive of 'posivite aspects' of the Anglo-American proposals. It also stresses its commitment to the Patriotic Front and its war of liberation.

2 Jan. 1979   Grey Zulu is appointed to the newly created Secretariat of State for Defence and Security.

2 Jan. 1979   A new cabinet is announced by the President. Five members of the Central Committee are appointed to Parliament to head ministeries. This gives UNIP greater control than in previous cabinets.

17-23 Feb. 1979   Rhodesian aircraft raid ZIPRA camps. The first attack takes place near Livingstone and the second near Lusaka.

20-21 Feb. 1979   Erich Honecker on a visit to Africa arrives in Zambia. He is received by

President Kaunda. Both leaders emphasize the mutual understanding that exists between the two countries.

12 Mar. 1979	South Africa carries out raids in both Angola and Zambia against what it perceives to be SWAPO bases. Zambia reports that nine villagers died in the raids.
14 Mar. 1979	Dingiswayo Banda, Minister of Labour and Social Services, is suspended pending allegations into illegal hunting. Banda also acted as the National Assembly Chief Whip. He is the tenth national leader to be suspended since January.
10 Apr. 1979	A Rhodesian air raid on a Zambian training area takes place on the eve of the opening of the Afro-Asian Solidarity Conference in Lusaka.
11-14 Apr. 1979	Rhodesian aircraft and troops continue their raids into Zambian territory, targetting ZAPU and ZIPRA bases. On 13 April the bungalow of Joshua Nkomo is destroyed in a raid on Lusaka.
12 Apr. 1979	Zambia formally recognizes the new Uganda government and pledges moral and military support to the new dispensation.
15-17 Apr. 1979	President Ceausescu of Romania visits Zambia on a tour of eight African countries. A treaty os friendship and co-operation is signed. President Kaunda reiterates his commitment to back liberation forces.
16 Apr.-12 May 1979	A dusk to dawn curfew is imposed on all towns situated along Zambia's main railway line from Livingstone to the northern Copperbelt.
4 May 1979	'The Times' of Zambia states that the Conservative Party's victory in Britain could be disastrous for the Southern African region.
10 May 1979	Presidents Kaunda and Neto agree to the establishment of a joint security force to repel Rhodesian and South African attacks. An attack on one of their countries will be seen as an attack on the other.
26 June 1979	Rhodesian troops raid the suspected headquarters of ZIPRA in the Lusaka suburb of Roma.
10 July 1979	Alexander Grey Zulu, Zambia's Secretary of State for Defence and Security, arrives in East Germany at the head of a delegation for talks with the Defence Ministry.
21 July 1979	The Supreme Court dismisses an appeal filed by Harry Nkumbula and Simon Kapwepwe (barred from standing as presidential candidates in the 1978 general elections).
27 July-3 Aug. 1979	Queen Elizabeth arrives in Lusaka on the eve of the Commonwealth Conference amidst controversy given the security risks posed by the Rhodesian raids.
Aug. 1979	The Front Line Presidents meet in Lusaka two days before the Commonwealth Conference commences to formulate a unified policy against the Thatcher government recognizing Zimbabwe-Rhodesia.

1-7 Aug. 1979	The twenty second Commonwealth heads of government meeting takes place in Lusaka with President Kaunda presiding as the Chairman. President Kaunda focuses on the Rhodesian question in his keynote address.
12 Aug. 1979	Diplomatic links are resumed between Zambia and Ugandan delegates in Lusaka for the Commonwealth Conference after ties were suspended eight years ago when Idi Amin came to power.
23 Aug. 1979	Rhodesian forces attack six ZAPU camps within Zambia. This is the tenth raid on Zambian territory since Bishop Muzorewa became Prime Minister.
8 Oct. 1979	In his address to the fourteenth National Council of UNIP, President Kaunda is critical of the OAUs failure to condemn dictators on the African continent, such as Idi Amin (Uganda), Franciso Macias Nguema (Equatorial Guinea) and Emperor Jean-Bede Bokassa (Central African Republic).
12 Oct. 1979	Three bridges including the main bridge on the Tazara railway, are blown up by Rhodesian forces. This effectively cuts off Zambia's main outlet for the export of copper and the import of bulk cargo.
14 Oct. 1979	A mutual non-aggression pact is signed between Zambia, Zaire and Angola, following a meeting of their three Presidents at Ndola (Zambian Copperbelt). The three also agree to intensify economic co-operation.
Nov. 1979	Zambia sues seventeen oil companies for damages caused by their sanctions busting operations.
5 Nov. 1979	Zambian imports are halted by Rhodesia. This is subsequently altered to apply only to maize imports.
20 Nov. 1979	President Kaunda, in response to a spate of bombings from Rhodesia, declares that Zambia is in a state of war. Reservists are to be called up and military leave is cancelled.
22 Nov. 1979	Anglo-Zambian relations deteriorate after Rhodesian raids on road and rail bridges. President Kaunda claims that he finds it unacceptable that Britain, as the administering authority, had no prior knowledge of the wave of attacks. Protests are staged by 2000 demonstrators outside the British High Commission in Lusaka. The British High Commissioner is recalled for consultations.
24 Nov. 1979	Wilson Chakulya, Zambia's Foreign Minister, labels Lord Carrington an 'arch-fascist' for what he sees as his part in the installation of Muzorewa and the side-lining of the Patriotic Front.
27 Nov. 1979	Relations are restored with Britain and President Kaunda orders the cessation of countrywide anti-British demonstrations.
4 Dec. 1979	Ratifies ILO Convention (No. 144) concerning organisations of rural workers and their role in economic and social development as adopted by the International Labour Organisation.
22-23 Dec. 1979	Zambia, together with other Front Line States, lifts sanctions against Rhodesia.

31 Jan. 1980	Zambia reopens border posts at Victoria Falls and Kazungula.

23 Mar. 1980   Zambia redeploys troops stationed along her borders with Rhodesia's Western Province to counter attacks by South African forces.

28 Mar. 1980   President Kaunda arrives in Kenya on a one day state visit, affirming close relations between the two countries.

9 Apr. 1980   President Kaunda on a state visit to the East, visits North Korea where he signs an agreement on economic and technical cooperation.

12 Apr. 1980   During President Kaunda's week long visit to China, agreements are signed on economic, technical and cultural cooperation.

15 Apr. 1980   President Kaunda holds talks with his Indian counterpart, President Reddy. He also meets with Indira Ghandi and discusses the need to defuse tension in South Asia.

21 Apr. 1980   President Kaunda warns the press and individuals against questionning government policies. The Times of Zambia, owned by the multnational Lonrho, is chastised following the publication of a report implicating three Central Committee members in emerald smuggling. Elias Chapimo, a leading banker and former High Commissioner to Britain is also attacked for noting the threat of military coups to African one-party states.

26 Apr. 1980   President Kaunda announces the withdrawal of South African troops who were occuping parts of Zambia's Western Province. This follows a Security Council resolution condemning South Africa for its continued and unjustified aggression against Zambia.

9 June 1980   UNIP advises the United States to slash all rather than part of its aid programme in response to concern over Zambia's arms deal with Soviet bloc countries. The United States does not however, as threatened, cut off its aid programme.

20 June 1980   North Korea offers to train Zambia's army in a pledge to Grey Zulu on a visit to North Korea.

11 July 1980   President Kaunda calls for renewed bilateral relations between Britain and Zambia following the successful resolution of the Rhodesian crisis. President Kaunda is speaking at State House, where he is receiving the credentials of the new British envoy, John Rodney Johnson, who replaces Leonard Alinson.

26 July 1980   The President issues a stern warning on strike action following what has been described as increasing industrial unrest.

11 Aug. 1980   The Times of Zambia reports the hoisting of the Zambian flag over the Kapula district in Zambia's Northern Province on the border with Zaire. The disputed areas of Kaputa and Lake Mweru are claimed by both countries as their own.

30 Aug. 1980   Illegal immigrants living in Zambia's copperbelt towns are deported to Zaire. Their presence is thought to be the major cause of the increase in crime.

| 28 Sept. 1980 | Frederick Chiluba, chairman of ZCTU warns of the prospect of a nationwide strike unless the government responds to workers' demands. |

15 Oct. 1980   A shootout ensues between security forces and an armed gang, believed to be foreigners, on a farm near Chilonga. The incident is followed by a manhunt and the detention of an unspecified number of persons. The gang is later found to have been part of an attempted coup.

23 Oct. 1980   A dusk to dawn curfew is imposed on Zambia's main towns on the eve of the sixteenth anniversary of independence celebrations.

27 Oct. 1980   President Kaunda accuses South Africa of backing an attempted coup planned by disaffected members of Zambia's elite and carried out by Zairean mercenaries. Prominent Zambians are arrested in the crackdown including Elias Chipimo, a former diplomat and banker, Valentine Musakanya, a former governor of the Central Bank, Edward Shamwana, a lawyer, and a top civil servant, Patrick Chisanga, are also detained. Major-General Kabwe together with two other air force officers, is also arrested shortly after being sworn in as head of the air force. South Africa denies the accusations.

7 Nov. 1980   President Kaunda announces that Zambia's security is under control following the revelation of a planned coup in October. The situation remains tense however and the passports of at least five prominent Zambians are seized, including that of Vernon Mwaanga, former Foreign Affairs Minister, and Elias Chipimo. Three trade unionists due to attend an ICFTU conference in London, also have their passports held. Returning to Zambia, Aaron Milner has his Zimbabwean passport temporarily confiscated at the airport.

13 Nov. 1980   The regional director of Agence France Presse, based in Lusaka, is released after spending twenty seven days in detention. Reasons for his arrest remain unclear, although he is accused of financing the defence of the leader of a group of armed dissidents.

20 Nov. 1980   An application for a writ of habeas corpus for Edward Shamvana is dismissed. His arrest is not unconstitutional according to the judgement, as Zambia has been under a continuous state of emergency since independence.

4 Dec. 1980   Wilson Chakulya, former Foreign Minister, moves to Defence as part of a major reorganization of cabinet. W. Phiri replaces Mark Chona as special assistant to the President on political affairs. Frederick Chomba, the former Attorney-General and Minister of Legal Affairs takes over as Minister of Home Affairs from W. Phiri. Justin Chimba moves to the Labour and Social Ministry. The cabinet shake-up which also affects several members of UNIP's Central Committee, will take effect from 8 December and is meant to secure Zambian success.

8 Jan. 1981   The Local Administration Act comes into effect replacing mayors and district chairmen with district governors, while town clerks become executive secretaries. This new system of decentralizatikon creates a power vacuum, as former town clerks and district secretaries vie for the position of district executive secretary.

14 Jan. 1981	Zambia's Asian population is threatened with expulsion by the Secretary of UNIP's Women's League, Chibesa Kankasa if they sympathize with dissident groups.
16 Jan. 1981	Seventeen executive members of ZCTU and MUZ are expelled from UNIP in retaliation for the dismissal of ZCTU officials who had stood in local government elections. The expulsions are followed by industrial action with workers demanding the reinstatement of their leaders. (ZCTU's 380,000 strong membership outstrips that of UNIP)
17 Jan. 1981	The Presidents of Kenya, Tanzania, Zambia and Uganda meet for a one-day summit conference in Kampala. The leaders agree to seek new forms of co-operation to resolve economic problems.
19 Jan. 1981	A five-year co-operation agreement is signed between Zambia and Zimbabwe following talks between Presidents Kaunda and Mugabe in Lusaka. Zambia and Zimbabwe cooperate over vital areas during the course of the year such as the distribution of power from Kariba, negotiations over the assets of the railway system and the repatriation of ZAPU's Zipra guerillas.
29 Jan. 1981	Striking miners return to work after the MUZ leader, David Muila, stresses that the seventeen dismissed officials retain their union jobs. He also highlights the fact that the Prime Minister has pledged that miners would not lose their privileges under UNIP's system of decentralization.
5 Feb. 1981	President Kaunda confirms the arrival of arms consignments from the USSR. The delivery forms part of an arms agreement to be implemented in early 1981.
18 Feb. 1981	Less than three months after a government reshuffle further changes are announced, such as Nalumino Mundia, a former opposition leader, replaces Daniel Lisulu as Prime Minister; Humprey Mulemba takes over from Mainza Chona as UNIP's secretary-general. Other Central Committee changes include the transfer of Elijah Mudenda from the chairmanship of the Social and Cultural Subcommittee to the important Economic and Finance Subcommittee. Lisulu, the former Prime Minister, assumes the chairmanship of UNIP as well as the Social and Cultural Subcommittee of the Central Committee.
19 Feb. 1981	President Kaunda publicly acknowledges a rising tide of public disaffection with his government. However, the cabinet shakeup aims to redress this, moving Zambia forward into a new era.
1 Mar. 1981	President Mobutu of Zaire holds talks with President Kaunda in Lusaka. He requests Zambia to repatriate 15,000 Zairean refugees settled in Zambia. On the issue of the border dispute between the two countries, nothing much is said, apart from the need for closer cooperation in securing borders.
13 Apr. 1981	It is announced that the Presidents of Zambia and Yugoslavia have signed a three-year programme of action on economic cooperation. President Cvijetin Mijatoic is on a four-day visit to Zambia when the agreement is signed.
24 Apr. 1981	Humphrey Mulemba announces the reinstatement of seventeen expelled

union officials to the UNIP fold. It is revealed later that the ban on union leaders travelling abroad has also been lifted.

28 May 1981

Thirteen people - nine Zambians and four Zairean nationals resident in Zambia, are put on trial for high treason in connection with an alleged coup attempt in October 1980. Amongst the trialists are Major-General Kabwe, Valentine Musakanya, Edward Shamwana and Brigadier-General Godfrey Miyanda.

19 June 1981

Ratifies Convention (No. 154) concerning the promotion of collective bargaining, as adopted by the general conference of the International Labour Organisation.

22 June 1981

Two Senior American diplomats are expelled and four other American citizens (three serving as diplomats in Zambia and the fourth a businessman) are declared prohibited immigrants. The moves follow the uncovering of what Zambia's security forces claim to be a CIA plot to undermine Zambia's government. The American Ambassador to Zambia, Frank Wisner, is subsequently recalled.

3 July 1981

Webster Lumbwe, a Political Officer in the Foreign Ministry is charged with spying for the CIA. He is alleged to have been involved with four American citizens who have been declared persona non grata.

7 July 1981

10,000 miners based on the larger of Zambia's two state-run mining companies go on strike, initially to protest against a decision to halt company-supplied emergency food rations. The strike is a sympton of general dissatisfaction with food shortages and severely affects the production of copper. The strike is resolved on 9 July after urgent negotiations with union and government leaders.

7-11 July 1981

President Kaunda leads a sixty three strong delegation on a five-day official visit to Zimbabwe. During his visit Zimbabwean leaders pay tribute to Zambia's role in its struggle towards independence.

17 July 1981

Mine workers at Luanshya and Kabwe stage another walkout. This time the dispute centres around wage disparities between Zambian mine workers and white expatriates. The strike spreads rapidly but most mines have returned to normal by 24 July.

18 July 1981

A further plot is uncovered which involves an attempt to free the October coup detainees. South Africa is again blamed for backing the plot.

23 July 1981

In two of the most violent incidents of the strike, police use teargas to disperse strikers near Kitwe and hundreds of rioting children of mine workers at the nearby township of Minddo.

27 July 1981

Four trade unionists, Frederick Chiluba (Chairman of ZCTU), Newstead Zimba (Secretary-General of ZCTU), Chitalu Sampa (Chiluba's deputy) and Timothy Walamba (Vice-Chairman of MUZ), are detained, accused of inciting illegal strike action with the aim of bringing down the present government.

31 July 1981

ZCTU demands the immediate and unconditional release of its fellow trade union leaders, but avoids a direct confrontation with the state.

1 Aug. 1981	Miners are granted a 10.6% increase in wages.
12 Aug. 1981	A border dispute arises between Zambia and Malawi over land in Zambia's Eastern Province.
15 Aug. 1981	Major-General Kabwe is released and charges against him dropped.
3 Sept. 1981	The Zambia-Zaire joint commission established to resolve border disputes, is boosted by the setting up of district committees to monitor the situation.
29 Oct. 1981	A day after the release of Frederick Chiluba (Chairman of ZCTU) is ordered by a High Court Judge, President Kaunda offers the trade union movement a truce. In the same speech to an economic seminar for government and union officials, he emphasizes that the solution to Zambia;s problems does not lie in outside powers (an allusion to trade unions drawing on Western aid).
11 Dec. 1981	President dos Santos of Angola visits Lusaka. He stresses the joint task of supporting SWAPO and opposing the policies of South Africa.
11 Jan. 1982	A protest is lodged with the Malawi High Commissioner after ten Zambians are detained after straying over the border into Malawi.
18 Jan. 1982	In an attempt to purge his administration of 'inefficiency', President Kaunda makes some major changes including the dismissal of three junior ministers and the suspension of another. Newstead Zimba, the General-Secretary of ZCTU, loses his parliamentary seat on a technicality: only UNIP party members can be MPs. In addition, four District Governors are sacked for allegedly returning to Zambia from a training course in Bulgaria without the consent of UNIP.
22 Feb. 1982	The leader of the opposition Socialist League of Malawi, Attati Mpakati, is deported from Zambia to Zimbabwe. Attati Mpakati had not been granted refugee status since entering Zambia.
25 Feb. - 1 Mar. 1982	President Kaunda pays his first official state visit to Malawi, signalling the warming of relations since Malawi decided to join SADCC.
28 Feb. 1982	Thousands of Zambians flee from villages along the border near Mufilira (in Zambia's Copperbelt Province) when fighting breaks out between marauding Zairean soldiers and Zambian troops.
2 Mar. 1982	Zairean authorities close the border with Zambia in the Sakania area (in southern Shaba Province). The tension in the area is attributed to food shortages in Zaire's Shaba Province and the tightening of customs and immigration regulations in an attempt to halt smuggling on either side of the border.
13-14 Mar. 1982	Presidents Nyerere and Kaunda meet in Lusaka. They enter into an agreement which will establish a joint commission of cooperation. They also aim to improve the running of the jointly owned Tazara railway.
18 Mar. 1982	President Kaunda declares his intention to meet the South African Prime

Minister to discuss potential developments in Southern Africa, in an interview given to a South African journalist.

8 Apr. 1982   Following President Kaunda's state visit to Burundi, a Burundi-Zambia cooperating commission is established.

21 Apr. 1982   The University of Zambia is closed, following a week-long boycott of classes, in protest at the dismissal or suspension of nineteen student leaders. The student body had channelled its frustrations against badly managed and inadequate facilities by protesting at the opening of an Institute of Human Relations whose research activities they felt could be adequately fuflilled by already existing faculties. The student arrests had followed this protest.

26 Apr. 1982   Webster Kayi Lumbwe, a former officer in the Zambian Intelligence and Security Service and the Ministry of Foreign Affairs, arrested in mid-1981 on suspicion of being an agent of the CIA, is found guilty of spying and sentenced to twenty years hard labour.

30 Apr. 1982   President Kaunda meets the South African Prime Minister, P W Botha, in a caravan on the South African/Botswana border. Under the spotlight is the political situation in Southern Africa and in particular, the war in Namibia. The meeting, a first between a leader of any of the Front Line States and a South African leader since the historic meeting at Victoria Falls in August 1975, meets with the disapproval of Tanzania and Zimbabwe, but receives the backing of Angola.

17 May 1982   Zambia and Czechoslovakia sign a cooperation agreement at the end of a three-day visit by Vasil Bilak, a secretary of the Communist Party of Czechoslovakia and a member of the Presidium of its Central Committee.

28-30 Aug. 1982   President Kaunda leads a large delegation to Zaire in an attempt to resolve the border dispute, but the situation continues to simmer.

Sept. 1982   President Kaunda, one of the six Heads of State chosen to try and persuade other African leaders to attend a reconvened OAU Summit in Tripoli, visits Liberia, Cameroon, Sierra Leone and Guinea.

8 Sept. 1982   Kenya and Zambia agree to form a permanent commission for cooperation following a meeting in Nairobi between Presidents Kaunda and Arap Moi.

21 Sept. 1982   Troops are deployed along the border with Zaire following an ambush by Zairean bandits in which two workers are killed. The incident highlights the increase in smuggling and other criminal activities by Zairean nationals.

1 Oct. 1982   UNIP acquires two principal Zambian newspapers: The Times of Zambia and the Sunday Times of Zambia, from Lonrho, the British based multinational company with extensive interests in Southern Africa.

20 Oct. 1982   Presidents Kaunda and Machel meet in the Mozambican town of Quelimane, accompanied by their foreign policy, security and transport officials. The discussions cover South Africa's destabilization strategy and the impact of rebel attacks in Mozambique on the region.

Nov. 1982   George Bush, the United States Vice-President, includes Zambia on his seven-nation African tour. His mission to convince African states to press for the withdrawal of Cuban troops from Angola is unsuccessful.

16 Nov. 1982   South Africa and Angola will exchange prisoners at Lusaka's International Airport.

13-15 Dec. 1982   Colonel Mengistu visits Zambia. During his stay, President Kaunda announces his support for the revolution in Ethiopia. The Ethiopian Head of State pledges his support for Zambia and the battle to free Namibia and South Africa.

7 Jan. 1983   The Kwacha undergoes a further devaluation of twenty percent. This is one of several measures including efforts to conserve foreign exchange. The suspension of payments of principal on Zambia's medium and long-term external debts and price hikes affecting maize meal and fertilizers, to right one of Zambia's most serious economic crises since independence.

13 Jan. 1983   The Prime Minister, Nalumino Mundia, is appointed to the additional post of Minister of Finance, a position he holds until after the October elections. President Kaunda replaces Nalumino Mundia as chairman of ZIMCO.

20 Jan. 1983   Justice Dennis Chirwa finds seven of the accused in the long running treason trial dating back to 1980, guilty of treason and one guilty of failing to report the plot. Three prominent Zambians are amongst the accused. Edward Shamwana, Valentine Musakanya and Yoram Mumba. The remaining four are Zaireans. The plot is believed to have been masterminded by Zambian lawyer, Dierce Annfield, who had fled to South Africa. Annfield, a long-standing friend of Simon Kapwepwe, had persuaded opponents of the ruling party to take control by force after the death of Simon Kapwepwe of a heart attack in early 1980. The seven found guilty of treason are sentenced to death and the eighth defendant to ten years hard labour. All are given leave to appeal.

22-27 Mar. 1983   President Kaunda's first state visit to Britain since independence is seen as marking the formal end of poor relations between the two countries.

29 Mar.-2 Apr. 1983   After his visit to Britain, President Kaunda proceeds to the United States. On 1 April he makes a speech in Washington, D.C. in which he accuses South Africa of attempting to undermine the Zambian government. He also discusses the situation in Namibia with President Reagan and warns of the prospect of a violent racial conflagaration in South Africa.

25 June 1983   Presidents Mobutu, dos Santos and Kaunda gather in Lubumbashi (Zaire) to discuss border security, refugees and improved communication links, including the resuscitation of the Benguela railway line.

8 Oct. 1983   Harry Mwaanga Nkumbula, one of the early leaders of African nationalism in what was then Northern Rhodesia, dies at the age of sixty-seven. He is given a state funeral. This act, together with his former rival, Kaunda, conferring Zambia's highest honour on him in 1982, strengthens loyalty in Mkumbula's former Tonga stronghold in the Southern Province.

26 Oct. 1983   President Kaunda, in a televised discussion focussing on difficulties faced by Zaire, concludes his interview with a pessimistic outlook on the

resolution of his neighbours' manifold problems.

27 Oct. 1983   The general elections take place on the same day as the presidential elections. The elections are peaceful despite allegations of corruption and complaints of too many candidates in certain constituencies. All of President Kaunda's cabinet ministers retain their seats but seven ministers, two District Governors and a Political Secretary are ousted as well as 25% of the sitting MPs. 766 out of 813 aspirant candidates were cleared to stand in 125 constituences as opposed to 369 in 1978.

30 Oct. 1983   President Kaunda is sworn in for a further five-year term having won ninety three per cent of the votes cast in the presidential election in a sixty three per cent poll.

31 Oct. 1983   A new independent newspaper, the Sunday Post, is established, owned and funded by a local media group. It aims to focus on investigative and interpretative journalism.

3 Nov. 1983   President Kaunda announces a new cabinet which will concentrate on economic recovery. Luke Mwanashiku is appointed to the Finance Ministry, taking over from Nalumino Mundia who remains Prime Minister.

16 Jan. 1984   The border dispute between Zambia and Zaire comes under discussion between representatives from both countries at Chilabombwe, Zambia. A decision is taken to step up such meetings.

27 Jan. 1984   Luke Mwananshiku announces the 1984 budget. The government aims to increase exports and to diversify economic activity reducing reliance on the copper industry which is rapidly being exhausted. Zambia's economic structures have not altered since independence.

14 Feb. 1984   Several student leaders are arrested in a dawn raid following a dispute after the introduction of a new meal card system at the University of Zambia.

16 Feb. 1984   Lusaka is the site of talks between Angolan and South African negotiating teams, led respectively by Pik Botha and Lieutenant-Colonel Alexandre Rodriques. The United States delegation, led by Chester Crocker, acts as mediator. Both sides agree on a process of disengagement.

16 Feb. 1984   The University of Zambia is closed indefinitely, following two days of rioting provoked by the arrest of student leaders. Nearly 3000 students are expelled.

21-23 Mar. 1984   Prince Charles, acting in his capacity as a director of the Commonwealth Development Corporation (CDC), undertakes a tour of CDC initiatives in Africa. His itinerary includes Zambia and boosts relations with Britain.

22-24 May 1984   A group of international financiers under the chairmanship of the World Bank Vice-President for Eastern Africa, resolve at a meeting in Paris to provide Zambia with approximately K650m a year between 1984 and 1986 to revitalise its ailing economy. An aid coordination committee is set in place to monitor developments.

25 June 1984   Presidents Kaunda and Mobutu meet in an attempt to resolve tensions along

their shared border.

9 Aug. 1984   Appeals against the death sentence of seven co-accused, convicted of treason, are heard in the Supreme Court. Security is tight during the hearing. Edward Shamwana, one of the accused, argues that there has been a lack of neutrality by the trial court and interference at the highest level. He further alleges that prepared documents concerning torture and poor conditions in detention have been destroyed. The Court reserves judgement on appeal.

16 Aug. 1984   President Kaunda opens the discussions held in Lusaka between Swaziland and the ANC (SA) who are attempting to resolve tensions caused by the signing of a non-aggression pact between South Africa and Swaziland. He appeals to both sides to reach an amicable solution. President Kaunda was initially approached by the ANC to act as a mediator in the conflict.

26 Aug. 1984   Zaire revokes expulsion orders against more than 2000 migrant Zambian workers, most of whom have lived in Zaire all their lives. The round-up in Shaba Province by Zairean authorities is believed to be in retaliation for a Zambian operation 'clean up' on the Copperbelt area where emerald and other form of smuggling is out of control. Among the Zambians held in the swoop, Zaireans predominate.

5 Oct. 1984   Zambia and Lesotho pledge to continue accepting political refugees. They also reiterate that no country in Southern Africa should be used as a base to spring attacks against another country. The pledge is conceived during a three-day visit to the mountain kingdom by Nalumino Mundia.

23 Oct. 1984   In his speech to the nation broadcast on the eve of the twentieth anniversary of independence, President Kaunda reminds Zambians that the restructuring of the economy will imply 'tougher times' in order to achieve desired goals. The President nevertheless does not fail to point out the progress made since independence.

24 Oct. 1984   Zambia celebrates the twentieth anniversary of independence together with the sixtieth birthday of President Kaunda. Foreign heads of state in Lusaka to mark the occasion, include Presidents Nyerere, Machel, Masire, Dos Santos, Moi and Mugabe. A foundation stone is laid at the new party headquarters, wreaths are laid at freedom statue and a colourful march and fly-past add to the celebrations.

3 Nov. 1984   The Tazara Railway authority is forced to temporarily suspend passenger and freight operations due to a lack of funds.

5 Nov. 1984   Wilson Chakulya, at the centre of a diplomatic scandal after his wife Suzanne is arrested on drug trafficking charges earlier in the year (and subsequently jailed), is summarily dismissed from his position on the Central Committee.

18 Dec. 1984   In his address to the Ugandan Parliament, President Kaunda appeals for peace and reconciliation after ten years of disorder and death in Uganda. He is the first foreign head of state to pay an extended visit to Uganda since Milton Obote's return to power.

22 Jan. 1985   President Kaunda reacts to a wave of strikes and stoppages in hospitals by

banning them.

8 Feb. 1985

Mark Tambatamba, the Minister of Health is sent on indefinite leave to enable an investigation to be carried out into his alleged involvement in fake diamond deals.

9-12 Feb. 1985

President Kaunda leads a high profile delegation which includes the Minister of Foreign Affairs, Lameck Goma, to Egypt. He and his Egyptian counterpart, Hosni Mubarak, agree on the need for a joint strategy to deal with South Africa. At the end of his visit he signs an agreement to form a joint economic commission with Egypt.

22 Feb. 1985

President Kaunda returns home after a fifteen day state visit to Egypt, Sweden, Denmark, Norway and Finland. In Denmark on 19 February, President Kaunda warns South Africa of a bloodbath if apartheid is not dismantled.

14 Mar. 1985

Backbenchers, fearful of illegal mineral exploitation, defeat a presidentially endorsed Bill to give a farm to two foreigners to grow cash crops. The defeat jolts Parliament where legislation is normally passed through 'on the nod'.

2 Apr. 1985

Valentine Musakanya, a former governor of the Bank of Zambia and a Zairean citizen, Roger Kambuita, have their convictions overturned. Both had received the death sentence for their role in the alleged coup of October 1980. Anderson Mporokoso, a former officer in the Zambian airforce, also has his ten-year prison term cancelled. The Supreme Court rules that evidence used against the three men was obtained under duress. The appeal court judges uphold the death sentence passed on the remaining five appellants. (Earlier a petition alleging that six of the accused were subjected to inhumane and degrading treatment in prison was dismissed by the High Court).

11-14 Apr. 1985

A donors support conference is held at Arusha, Tanzania, in connection with the ailing Tazara Railway.

24 Apr. 1985

President Kaunda reshuffles top positions in both Cabinet and UNIP. Nalumino Mundia is replaced as Prime Minister by Kebby Musokotwane, previously the Minister of General Education and Culture. The move comes amidst intensive discussions between Zambia and the IMF over the reactivation of Zambia's suspended stand-by borrowing programme. Mundia is subsequently made Ambassador to Washington. UNIP's secretary-general, Humphrey Mulemba, is replaced by Alexander Grey Zulu, the former Secretary of State for Defence and Security. Mulemba is sent as High Commissioner to Canada. In other changes, Basil Kabwe is appointed to the General Education and Culture portfolio and Alex Shapi succeeds Grey Zulu as Secretary of State for Defence and Security. General Malimba Masheke is appointed Minister of Defence and J K M Kalakula is appointed as Minister of Mines.

1 June 1985

A strike at Chambishi mine on the Copperbelt is triggered off by a controversial pension scheme concluded between ZCCM and MUZ (which involves automatic deductions from workers' wages). The unofficial strike spreads to other mines on the Copperbelt. During the strikes, damage to property and looting occurs. Working miners are also attacked. Some 4000 miners are sacked. The losses in production sustained by ZCCM are substantial.

1 July 1985

A bomb blast damages the Lusaka headquarters of the ANC (SA). The attack, as reported in the Western press, is seen as a direct warning by South Africa against Zambia's continued support for the ANC.

3 Sept. 1985

The Zimbabwe Inter-Africa News Agency and the Zambia National News enter into an agreement to cooperate in the dissemination and exchange of information in an effort to decolonize the media.

15 Sept. 1985

President Kaunda succeeds President Nyerere as the next Chairman of the Front Line States.

4 Oct. 1985

President Kaunda announces the immediate introduction of a new foreign exchange auction system. This enables the rate for the Kwacha to be set for the first time and reveals a devaluation from $1.00 = K.2.20 on 4 October to $1.00 = K.5.01.

21 Oct. 1985

The court case of the twenty-four accused charged with alleged involvement in drug trafficking opens in Lusaka. The case causes a political sensation since it includes prominent Zambians, including one of UNIP's founder members and the former Information Minister, Sikota Uina and Vernon Mwaanga, a former Foreign Minister, and prominent businessman, Sikota's wife, is also detained and charged. Diplomats, an assistant controller of customs, prominent businessmen and some South Africans are also involved. During the trial statements are made implicating President Kaunda's eldest son, Panji, and the chairman of the Zambian subsidiary of the Lonrho mining conglomerate, Tom Mtine. Reuben Kamanda, a member of the Central Committee, is also implicated.

4 Apr. 1986

Luke Mwanashiku is replaced as Minister of Finance by veteran politician and trade unionist, Basil Kabwe. Mwanashiku is appointed as Foreign Minister in place of Lameck Goma. The move is seen as an effort by the President to keep his faltering peace initiative and to repair Zambia's flailing economy.

4 Apr. 1986

President Kaunda released twenty-four detainees held on suspicion of drug trafficking since 1985. The detainees could still face criminal charges and are banned from leaving the country.

15 Apr. 1986

Zambian businessmen are accused by President Kaunda of colluding with South Africa in a plot to overthrow the Zambian government.

30 Apr. 1986

Zambia and Zaire sign an agreement after a meeting of a special joint committee to resolve their border dispute. The agreement involves a joint review of the border demarcation in disputed areas in a two-year exercise.

18 May 1986

The University of Zambia's main campus in Lusaka is closed and not reopened until October. The closure follows an escalation of violence, including the use of petrol bombs by students, following a class boycott sparked by the expulsion of a student leader who allegedly attacked the principal.

28 May 1986	A British computer engineer, together with a South African, is accused of spying on Zambia's mining industry for South Africa.
9-11 July 1986	Sir Geoffrey Howe, on an EC mission to Southern Africa to establish a framework for dialogue in South Africa and the ultimate ending of apartheid, visits Zambia, Zimbabwe and Mozambique on the first stage of his tour.
18 July 1986	After a meeting of the Front Line States in Harare, both Zambia and Zimbabwe announce their intention to withdraw from the Commonwealth Games in protest at Britain's refusal to impose economic sanctions against South Africa. A total of thirty two countries decide to withdraw from the Games.
24 July 1986	Sir Geoffrey Howe, on an EC mission to Southern Africa, returns to Lusaka. Upon arrival he is publicly rebuked by President Kaunda for what he sees as a conspiracy between the United States and Britain to support South Africa in their opposition to sanctions.
3-5 Aug. 1986	Six out of seven Commonwealth heads of state attending a mini-summit in London, announce their support for international sanctions to be imposed against South Africa.
5 Aug. 1986	Pik Botha announces the imposition of new regulations affecting the movement of trade traffic between South Africa and some of its neighbours. The measures hold up south-bound traffic from Zimbabwe and Zambia entering South Africa at Beit Bridge, escalating transport costs. South Africa also imposes at 125 per cent deposit on transit traffic. The action is viewed in Lusaka as retaliation for Kaunda and Mugabe's stand on sanctions against South Africa at the Commonwealth mini-summit.
10 Aug. 1986	President Kaunda defends the Zambian security forces against allegations that foreigners had been tortured. Reports in the Western press suggest that some of those (most of them tourists) who have been detained were beaten whilst in prison.
15 Aug. 1986	The UK Foreign Office issues a warning to British travellers in Zambia to avoid the Northern Province and maintain contact with the Lusaka High Commission. The advice follows the arrest and alleged ill treatment of three Britons in July suspected of spying for South Africa. Switzerland also protests to the Zambian Foreign Ministry on 15 August over the alleged assault in detention of Swiss tourists. These visitors are amongst many foreigners who are held on charges of spying for South Africa and maltreated in detention during 1986.
11 Sept. 1986	President Banda holds talks in Blantyre with Presidents Machel, Kaunda and Mugabe. President Banda receives an ultimatum from his neighbours to reduce links with South Africa or face further disruption to export routes. Malawi's position in regard to the South African backed RENAMO is also focussed upon.
Oct. 1986	An unofficial complaint by the IMF over Zambia's arrears (SDR 70 000 000) owed to the Fund and on the government's failure to meet targets for controlling monetary growth and the budget deficit is circulated in the

Western press.

4-5 Oct. 1986   President Kaunda meets with President Mobutu in an attempt to ease strained diplomatic relations.

2 Nov. 1986   President Kaunda complains about the effectiveness of the IMF programme, adding that 'there is a limit to what people will endure'.

3 Dec. 1986   Violent riots break out on the Copperbelt. Defence forces are called in to quell the disturbances. At least fifteen people are killed and scores more are injured. A dawn to dusk curfew is imposed which is lifted on 11 December. The riots are precipitated by the announcement of a 120 percent increase in the price of maize, the staple diet. The price hike is part of an IMF programme which the state is installing, to restore the economy.

11 Dec. 1986   President Kaunda announces his decision to rescind the maize price rise. The country's borders are reopened and the dawn to dusk curfew is lifted. The food shortages are blamed on milling companies which are to be subsequently nationalized.

13 Dec. 1986   Three foreigners are arrested. The three, a Briton, an Australian and a New Zealander, are arrested in connection with the two bomb explosions in Livingstone which coincided with the Copperbelt rioting. The three are accused of being South African agents.

14 Dec. 1986   The detention of approximately 450 people is reported in the Copperbelt Province following food riots (reputedly the worst in the area since independence) in an effort to recover looted goods.

30 Dec. 1986   Presidents Kaunda and Mugabe hold discussions on joint economic ventures designed to reduce their dependence on South Africa.

28 Jan. 1987   Basil Kabwe is reappointed to his former post as Minister of General Education and Culture. The Finance portfolio will now be adopted by the Prime Minister.

19 Feb. 1987   Joaquim Chissano begins a three-day state visit to Zambia. The two leaders pay homage to the late Samora Machel. They also agree to intensify bilateral cooperation although they note with concern the effects of South Africa's policies on their economies. They call for the immediate dismantling of apartheid and for those countries who continue to support the racist regime, to reject it.

8 Mar. 1987   The presence of deposed Ugandan leader on Zambian soil, Milton Obote, causes diplomatic tension between Zambia and Uganda. Uganda charges that Obote is training dissidents to overthrow the Museveni government.

13 Apr. 1987   Zambia and Zaire sign an extradition treaty which will do much to bring crime along the borders under control. The Zambia-Zaire joint permanent commission meeting in Lusaka also agree to the joint funding of oil pipelines in northern Zambia through eastern Zaire. A social security agreement is also concluded which will benefit workers immigrating for or into the other country. A new trade agreement is entered into aimed at the expansion of trade.

25 Apr. 1987	South Africa carries out a raid on the Zambian border town of Livingstone. The raid is the first officially acknowledged incursion by South Africa since May 1986. The raid is internationally condemned as an election ploy by the South African government and raises fears of more cross border raids against Front Line states.
1 May 1987	In his May Day speech, President Kaunda announces his intention to cut ties with the IMF and to find a 'new kind of development strategy' which will resolve the crisis in which Zambia finds itself, beset by rising unemployment and rampant inflation.
5 May 1987	The IMF's resident official is locked out of his office in the Central Bank and President Kaunda accuses the IMF of conducting 'a smear campaign' by attempting to persuade donors to discontinue their aid programmes. The decision to break with the IMF is met with popular support. Zambians march through the streets of Lusaka bearing anti-IMF placards after the announcement. The secretary-general of the OAU pronounces support for Zambia's move.
13 May 1987	Gibson Chigaga, the former Legal Affairs Minister, is named as Zambia's third Finance and National Commission for Development Planning Minister. Chigaga takes over the portfolio from Kebby Musokotwane who remains Prime Minister. The move arouses much comment, particularly in the light of the May Day announcements regarding economic policy.
13 May 1987	The Minister of Home Affairs, Cosmas Chibanda, is dismissed for alleged drunkenness and thirteen Bank of Zambia officials are sacked following a probe into alleged misconduct. Paul Malukutila replaces Chibanda as Home Affairs Minister in what is seen as an effort to strengthen discipline within the leadership.
13 May 1987	Rioting breaks out in the northern copperbelt town of Kitwe with rampaging youths demanding the enforcement of price controls in line with Kaunda's recently introduced economic measures.
Mid-May 1987	The World Bank suspends new loans due to the non-payment of arrears. The Bank undertakes to continue funding existing projects.
20 May 1987	Veteran opposition leader, Alfred Musonda Chambeshi, is arrested. His arrest follows accusations that he planned to conspire with UNITA to overthrow the Zambian government. The government had alleged in court proceedings held the previous month, that he sought to revive the banned UPP as a guerrilla movement, to bring down the government.
29 May 1987	It is reported that more than one hundred businessmen suspected of collusion with South Africa or economic crimes, have had their passports withdrawn.
9 June 1987	President Kaunda calls for the strengthening of UNIP, particularly against a backdrop of economic and political uncertainty. UNIP's popularity and effectiveness has waned over the years.
4 July 1987	Three Zambian Airforce members, together with a Zambian businessman, are held in custody and charged with spying for South Africa.

31 July 1987	Tanzania's President Ali Hassan Mwinyi leaves for Zambia on a four day state visit, accompanied by his Minister of Foreign Affairs. This marks his first state visit to Zambia. The two countries agree to strengthen economic, technical and cultural cooperation. They also condemn South Africa for destroying the Front Line States' economies.
15 Aug. 1987	A New Economic Recovery Interim National Development Plan (NEP) is launched, replacing the IMF programme. The measures include the phasing out of free medical treatment and education.
2 Oct. 1987	The IMF declares Zambia's ineligibility in drawing on the Fund's general resources due to Zambia's failure to meet its obligations over debt repayment.
4 Feb. 1988	The United States suspends its aid programme to Zambia due to the non-payment of arrears.
21 May 1988	Alex Shapi, Minister of State for Defence and Security states that Zambian troops had pursued RENAMO into Mozambique after a raid on a Zambian village in which eight Zambian troops had been killed.
18-22 Aug. 1988	UNIP's tenth general conference is held at Mulungushi Rock. During the proceedings President Kaunda is elected unopposed as party president for the next five years. He is also nominated as the sole candidate for the forthcoming presidential election. The Central Committee is enlarged from twenty five members to sixty eight, ensuring wider representation for diverse interest groups. The development is not without criticism but Kaunda effectively silences his opposition.
7 Oct. 1988	The arrests of six military officers and three civilians are made public, suspected of involvement in an alleged coup plot. Amongst those detained is Lieutenant-General Christon Tembo, a former army commander from April 1985 to January 1987 and at the time of his arrest, Ambassador to West Germany.
8-10 Oct. 1988	A conference organized by SWAPO to discuss proposals for independence takes place in Kabwe, central Zambia.
26 Oct. 1988	President Kaunda, the sole presidential candidate, is re-elected for a sixth five-year term in office. He gains ninety five percent of the vote in a fifty five percent voter turnout. In the parliamentary elections, four Cabinet Ministers fail to gain re-election, four junior ministers also suffer defeat, some ten percent less than in the previous general elections. Among the newly elected deputies are President Kaunda's son, Majwezi Kaunda, who wins convincingly in the eastern Malambo constituency and Humphrey Mulemba, a former secretary-general of UNIP and recent High Commissioner to Canada. He is considered by some observers as a potential challenger to Kaunda which he strongly denies.
8 Nov. 1988	President Kaunda announces a twenty percent devaluation of the Kwacha, one of a number of economic policy initiatives designed to lead to an agreement with the IMF.
22 Nov. 1988	Samuel Ngulube, a member of Zambia's Air Force, is convicted of passing classified information about Zambia's air bases to South Africa.

26 Nov. 1988	An ANC member is killed in a car bomb explosion near Lusaka. South Africa is blamed for the incident.
3 Dec. 1988	Two people are killed and thirteen injured when a car bomb explodes in Livingstone. Alex Shapi, the Secretary of State for Defence and Security blames the South African government for this incident as well as a prior incident which took place on 30 November and killed a Zambian citizen whose car detonated a land mine near a UN transit camp for South African and Namibian refugees.
1 Jan. 1989	President Kaunda announces the fourth National Development Plan to be implemented over five years. The Plan aims to achieve a three percent GDP growth, a reduction in the rate of population growth and a budget deficit cut to two percent of GDP from five percent for 1989. It also aims to reduce inflation to twenty percent. Price controls are to be abolished except on maize meal. The bulk of the total investment is to go to the agricultural sector. The plan also envisages parastatals and the private sector participating more fully in the provision of social services, particularly in health and education. The plan also foresees the development of a local iron and steel industry.
15 Feb. 1989	At the Socialist International Conference held in Harare, President Kaunda appeals to all members to impose comprehensive mandatory sanctions on South Africa, referring to the trade embargoes as 'another form of war against apartheid'.
15 Mar. 1989	The Prime Minister, Kebby Musokotwane, is replaced by former Minister of Home Affairs, General Malimba Masheke, a long standing supporter of Kaunda. Musokotwane, the youngest Cabinet Minister at the age of thirty seven, is given the portfolio of General Education, Youth and Sport in what is regarded as a demotion.
22 Mar. 1989	Speaking at an OAU Summit Conference on Southern Africa held in Harare, President Kaunda lashes out at Washington for hindering the peace process through its continuous support of UNITA.
2-4 May 1989	Pope John Paul II, on his fifth visit to Africa, arrives in Zambia on 2 May. In an open-air mass on 4 May, he extends a message of hope to those suffering in Zambia, particularly AIDS sufferers.
28 May 1989	President Kaunda begins a ten-day tour in which he holds discussions with the heads of state of Guyana, St Vincent and the Grenadines, Jamaica, Cuba, Nicaragua, Canada and the United States. In Nicaragua the President calls on the Bush Administration to revise its policies in Latin America. In Washington, President Kaunda holds talks with George Bush over Southern Africa, focusing on Namibia and the destabilization of the region by South Africa.
3 June 1989	Kebby Musokotwane is replaced by Eli Mwanagonze and appointed as Ambassador to Canada.
4 June 1989	President Kaunda addresses the international AIDS conference in Montreal noting the death of his son from AIDS. Zambia is reported to have one of highest rates of AIDS in Africa. He is on a ten-day tour of the Americas

and the West Indies at the time.

22 June 1989	President Kaunda participates in the effort in Gbadolite, Zaire, to resolve the Angolan situation.

15 Aug. 1989   The World Wildlife Fund (WWF) arranges a debt `swap' with Zambia. The WWF purchases US$2,700,000 of Zambian foreign debt at a discounted rate of eighty percent.   The repayment goes towards the environmental management of the Kafue River Flats.

28 Aug. 1989   President Kaunda meets with the acting South African President, F W de Klerk and Pik Botha in Livingstone, giving credence to his plans to reform apartheid. President Kaunda fails to discuss ANC negotiation proposals with de Klerk.   The main substantive issue on the agenda is the faltering peace process in Angola.

14 Sept. 1989   The Zambian authorities hand over to the UNHCR four South Africans suspected by the ANC of `spying' and of involvement in a spate of bomb attacks on ANC premises in Lusaka in June and July 1989.

18 Sept. 1989   President Kaunda is again present at a meeting arranged by President Mobutu on his yacht on the Congo River just outside Kinshasa, to revive the Angolan peace process.

13 Oct. 1989   The home of exiled Malawian, Mkwapatira Mhongo (chief information office for Mafremo), is attacked in Lusaka. Mhongo is amongst the nine killed in the attack.

31 Oct. 1989   The heads of state of Gabon, Sao Tome and Principe, Zambia and Cote d'Ivoire meet in Yamoussoukto, Cote d'Ivoire, still searching for a solution to the Angolan conflict. The four reaffirm President Mobuto's role as mediator in the peace negotiations.

10 Nov. 1989   Francis Waza Kaunda wins the parliamentary seat in Chinsali (north-west Zambia), President Kaunda's birthplace.   He is the second of the President's sons to enter Parliament.

14 Nov. 1989   Francis Nkhoma, Governor of the Bank of Zambia, appears in court on charges of corruption and misuse of foreign currency. He had earlier been dismissed following an investigation into corrupt practices at the Bank.

25 Nov. 1989   A joint security commission is established between Zambia and Mozambique to ensure the containment of RENAMO incursions into Zambia and to regulate traffic moving along the common border.   Alex Shapi had commented earlier in the month on the destabilizing effects of RENAMO raids into Zambia's Eastern Province.

Jan. 1990   Jacques Bussieres, a Canadian, is appointed as Governor of the Bank of Zambia.   President Kaunda concedes that `Zambinaisation has not succeeded in this particular area'. This comes after the dismissal of Francis Mkhoma.

21 Feb. 1990   Zairean soldiers shoot dead a Zambian fisherman and wound two others who are fishing in the Luapula River on the common border. Zaire claims that the fishermen had strayed into its territory.

27 Feb. 1990   Nelson Mandela visits the headquarters of the ANC in Lusaka where he meets the exiled ANC executive committee, leaders of the Front Line States and Commonwealth representatives. He is accorded treatment normally reserved for heads of state. Nelson Mandela rejects a suggestion by President Kaunda that the ANC should suspend its armed struggle in order to facilitate further reforms by Pretoria.

14-17 Mar. 1990   UNIP's fifth national convention in Lusaka rejects proposals for a multi-party system by voting to retain 'one-party participatory democracy'. President Kaunda tells delegates that Zambia's experience could not be compared to the Soviet Union or other East European countries who had recently chosen a pluralistic approach to politics. He points to other African states where political instability and tribal conflicts have followed the introduction of a multiparty system. Proposals to limit the President's tenure to two five-year terms, to allow for more than one presidential candidate and to require that members of UNIP's central committee and other party officials to be elected by popular vote, are rejected. Despite the outcome of the convention, various members of UNIP voice their criticism of the President and tend to agree that UNIP has assumed too much power.

7 June 1990   Frederick Hapunda is dismissed as Minister of Defence.

19 June 1990   An increase over 100 percent in the price of maize meal, the major food staple, as part of an economic recovery programme, provokes widespread discontent. Panic buying, threats of labour unrest and protest marches, finally explode into riots on 25 June.

25 June 1990   Approximately 2000 students stage a demonstration in Lusaka, demanding the restoration of the price subsidy on maize meal. They also insist on a multiparty system. Calls are also made for the resignation of President Kaunda. Their demonstration culminates in violence as defence forces attempt to contain the crowds led by the students' intent on on marching on State House, President Kaunda's residence. The riots spread to several cities, lasting for almost a week and causing the deaths of over forty-five civilians.

30 June 1990   Disturbances following the increase in the price of maize meal leads to a poorly planned and ultimately unsuccessful coup in which a small group of army officers led by Lieutenant Muamka Luchembe manage to control the national radio for several hours, issuing a message at regular intervals that the army has taken over. They are arrested and imprisoned.

1 July 1990   President Kaunda reshuffles key posts in the army and defence ministry following a failed coup attempt on 30 June: Lieutenant General Gary Kalenge is replaced by his deputy, Major General Francis Sabinda; Hannaniah Lungu, the former Air Force Commander, is sworn in as Minister of Defence, succeeding Frederick Hapunda who advocated a pluralist democracy and was dismissed on 7 June.

16 July 1990   Daphne Parish, a British nurse sentenced to fifteen years imprisonment by an Iraqi military court, is flown to Lusaka following an appeal for clemency

made by President Kaunda. Tiny Rowland (chairman of the Observer and Lonrho), a personal friend, had approached Kaunda in March to seek his help over the Bazoft and Parish cases. (Bazoft, a journalist for the Observer and Parish, were arrested on charges of spying)

25 July 1990	President Kaunda announces the postponement of a referendum on the reintroduction of multi-party democracy, accusing advocates of pluralism of unleashing 'the forces of hate'. The postponement is summarily rejected by pro-democracy activists, including the chairman of the newly established National Interim Committee for Multi-Party Democracy, Arthur Uma.
25 July 1990	President Kaunda, in a speech to the nation in which he postpones the referendum, pardons Lieutenant Mwamba Luchembe and his co-conspirators, for their role in the 30 June attempted coup. He also announces the release of all other political prisoners. These include prisoners serving a life sentence for their role in a 1980 coup attempt, including Edward Shamwana, Goodwin Yoram Mumba, Albert Chilambe Chimballe and Deogratia Symba. Lieutenant General Christon Tembo and three other army officers standing trial for treason in connection with a 1988 coup plot are also pardoned.
17 Sept. 1990	At a mass rally in Kitwe attended by approximately 70 000 people leaders of the MDM threaten mass action if the government does not concede to their demands.
24 Sept. 1990	Amidst growing popular pressure for reform, President Kaunda rescinds an earlier decision for the holding of a referendum planned for August 1991 and recommends the introduction of a multiparty system and the holding of free elections by October 1991.
1 Nov. 1990	General Benjamin Mibenge replaces Luke Mwanashiku as Minister of Foreign Affairs. Mwananshiku is seconded to the IMF in Washington. The Minister of State for Decentralization, Michael Sata, is dismissed for being critical of government policy. He is believed to support the MMD (Movement for Multiparty Democracy)
4 Dec. 1990	The Minister of Defence, Hannaniah Lungu, sworn in after helping to rally loyal troops during an unsuccessful coup attempt, is replaced by the former Deputy Minister of Defence, Dodson Siatalimi.
4 Dec. 1990	President Kaunda dismisses the editors of two of Zambia's leading daily newspapers.
17 Dec. 1990	President Kaunda signs into law a bill approved by the National Assembly on 4 December which allows the formation of political parties other than UNIP. The MMD immediately applies for registration as a political party.
22 Dec. 1990	The National Democratic Alliance (NADA) is formed.
31 Dec. 1990	ZCTU switches its alliance from UNIP to MMD.
20 Feb. 1991	The Zambian and Iranian Ministers of Defence hold the latest round of talks on Iran supplying arms to Zambia.
1 Mar. 1991	Frederick Chiluba is elected president of the MMD. He wins by a two

thirds majority, easily defeating three other potential candidates. Other parties which have sprung into being include NADA, headed by Rev Joshua Mumpanshya, former UNIP diplomat and MP, a DP led by Emmanuel Mwamba, former UNIP diplomat, and MPD headed by Chama Chakomboka, a former ally of Simon Kapwepwe.

25 Mar. 1991   Zambian Finance Minister, Gibson Chigaga, dies of a suspected heart attack as he prepares to address a press conference on arrival at Lusaka airport. He has just negotiated a US$650 million economic restructuring package.

7 Apr. 1991   MMD launches its electoral campaign at a mass rally in Lusaka. Frederick Chiluba addresses the gathering.

18 Apr. 1991   3500 students are ordered off the University campus in Lusaka by heavily armed paramilitary and riot police, following the closure of the University for 'political reasons'. Rumours are circulated that the move may have been prompted by a planned strike on the part of university lecturers to demand the reinstatement of the university press production manager suspended for publishing articles which support political pluralism.

19 Apr. 1991   Dodson Siatalimi is sacked. He becomes the third Defence Minister to be dropped by the President since the unsuccessful coup of July 1990.

12 July 1991   The SPD is created, making it the thirteenth political party since the legalization of multipartyism.

23 July 1991   President Kaunda meets leaders of Zambia's main opposition party, MMD. The meeting is held in Lusaka's Anglican Cathedral and aims to diffuse the constitutional crisis. The MMD has rejected the proposed constitution which will weaken parliamentary powers by transferring them to a strong executive president.

2 Aug. 1991   A new Constitution is adopted by an overwhelming majority which will allow for a multiparty democracy. The landmark decision follows months of wrangling between UNIP and MMD. President Kaunda is finally forced to abandon a constitutional plan conceived in 1990 which would have allowed him to act above the confines of the law.

7 Aug. 1991   Enoch Kavindele, a businessman, withdraws his challenge to Kaunda's leadership of UNIP, after receiving little visible support.

9 Aug. 1991   President Kaunda is unanimously re-elected as party leader at an extraordinary national conference of UNIP.

21 Aug. 1991   Freedom of movement is granted to all diplomats by the President in preparation for the upcoming elections.

21 Aug. 1991   Top ranking officials in the defence and security forces cease to be members of UNIP's central committee. A decision is also made to exclude the use of defence or security facilities for political activities.

4 Sept. 1991   The National Assembly is dissolved by the President, with elections to be held on 31 October. Opposition parties complain that such short notice will give UNIP an added advantage.

24 Sept. 1991   Three UNIP members are arrested in connection with the deaths of four supporters of MMD, their bodies having been found on 21 September. Their deaths lead to further clashes with angry residents attacking the suspects' homes in the Copperbelt town of Luanshya. One of the arrested suspects is the local branch chairman of UNIP.

30 Sept. 1991   President Kaunda is reportedly critical of what he sees as foreign election observers interfering in local politics. This follows an earlier statement by the head of an international team of electoral observers, Jimmy Carter, that the twenty-eight-year-old state of emergency would be lifted on 30 September. A government spokesman confirms that it will not be lifted before the elections.

14 Oct. 1991   President Kaunda's youngest son is sentenced to death for the murder of a woman two years earlier. Kambarage Kaunda who pleaded `not guilty to murder', saying he shot the deceased in self defence when a group threatened to attack him, appeals against the conviction.

18 Oct. 1991   As tension mounts during the run-up to the elections, Chiluba appeals to the Secretary-General of the OAU to send peacekeeping forces to Zambia. Kaunda dismisses such fears on 21 October.

31 Oct. 1991   Frederick Chiluba, leader of the MMD and the former chairman-general of ZCTU, is elected President, forcing Kaunda to step down after twenty-seven years in power. Chiluba gains seventy-five percent of the votes, as opposed to Kaunda's twenty-four percent. The MMD wins 125 of the National Assembly's 150 seats, UNIP wins the remaining twenty-five seats. Official figures indicate that more than half of the electorate did not exercise their right to vote. The MMD focussed on Zambia's economic disarray as part of its election campaign, highlighting UNIP's ineffectiveness in this area. Local and foreign observers declare the runup to the elections to be relatively free from intimidation and violence.

1 Nov. 1991   Namibia unilaterally establishes a border post in the Caprivi Strip to deter Zambian smugglers. The move sparks a diplomatic furore with Zambia declaring that without a post on its side of the border, it will lose customs revenue from undeclared goods.

2 Nov. 1991   Frederick Chiluba is sworn into office announcing that the `era of dictators, of hypocrisy and lies' is over.

5 Nov. 1991   A major reorganization of both the civil service and parastatal bodies is initiated by President Chiluba. The chairmen and managing director of ZCCM are dismissed. They are amongst several senior executives who are axed. Others are questioned about corruption.

7 Nov. 1991   President Chiluba announces his first cabinet and cautions his ministers against putting personal interests above those of national concern. He also appeals to all political parties to pull together as Zambians. Levy Mwanawasa is named as Vice-President and leader of the National Assembly. The post of Minister of Finance goes to Emmanuel Kasonde. Vernon Johnson Mwaanga is given the Foreign Affairs portfolio. Newstead Zimba is chosen as Minister of Home Affairs and a white farmer, Guy Scott, is made Minister of Agriculture and Fisheries.

| 8 Nov. 1991 | The state of emergency is lifted at midnight. It is now illegal to detain people without charge. Security forces are also ordered to remove all road blocks with immediate effect and to cease the random searching of vehicles and homes without warrants. |

18 Nov. 1991   The managing editor of the state controlled Times of Zambia is fired, as is the director-general of the National Broadcasting Service.

24 Dec. 1991   Israel and Zambia resume diplomatic relations, severed after the 1967 Arab-Israeli war. President Chiluba feels that the reasons which led to the rupture are no longer valid.

31 Dec. 1991   The Zambian Foreign Ministry confirms that discussions are under way on the re-establishment of trade and diplomatic links with South Africa.

6 Jan. 1992   UNIP accepts Kenneth Kaunda's resignation as party leader.

31 Jan. 1992   Emmanuel Kasonde, the Minister of Finance announces the new government's first budget. The government's commitment to economic reform is re-emphasized. Exchange controls are liberalized and the Kwacha is devalued by twenty-seven percent. Taxation rates are substantially reduced. Duty-free shops are also abolished, a move which the government foresees as being especially lucrative.

13-14 Feb. 1992   President Frederick Chiluba visits the United Kingdom as part of an effort to seek backing in rescheduling or writing off Zambia's foreign debt of $18,000 million. Chiluba and John Major sign a series of agreements to this effect.

26 Feb. 1992   President Chiluba declares Zambia to be disaster-affected and appeals for international assistance after a devastating drought cuts the maize harvest from over one million to 250,000 tons.

1 May 1992   An agreement is signed between Zambia and South Africa preparatory to the establishment of diplomatic links.

1 June 1992   Grain merchants double the price of maize meal, the second major price increase since the removal of basic food subsidies, drawing criticism from the Minister of Agriculture.

4 July 1992   President Chiluba announces a reduction in Zambia's foreign debt. He also reveals a drop in the annual inflation rate from over 400 percent to seventy-eight per cent.

25 July 1992   Two former Cabinet ministers participate in the launch of a new party, the CNU which had started off as a pressure group within the MMD in February. Baldwin Nkumbula (Minister of Youth, Sports and Child Development) and Akashambacwa Lewanida (Minister of Technical Education and Training) had resigned earlier in the month in protest at what they termed the government's failure to curb corruption.

Early Aug. 1992   The local press reports the dismissal of Ephraim Chibwe, Minister of Works and Supply for alleged 'anomalies' in the acquisition of South African office furniture. The Minister of Information and Continuing Education, Stan

Kristafor, is also reportedly sacked after racist remarks.

1 Oct. 1992	Kebby Musokotwane, former Secretary-General of UNIP, is elected party president at an extraordinary congress.

19 Feb. 1993   Zambia issues an invitation to China to rehabilitate its army. This is followed up by the arrival of an eleven man delegation to do the ground work. This decision flies in the face of an earlier agreement with the World Bank who persuaded Zambia to reduce its expenditure on defence.

4 Mar. 1993   An indefinite state of emergency is declared by President Chiluba over an alleged opposition coup plot. His announcement comes after a document entitled 'The Zero-Option Plan' is leaked to the local press. The document was allegedly prepared by members of UNIP.

5 Mar. 1993   Eleven opposition officials are arrested in connection with the coup attempt, including Kenneth Kaunda's son, Wezi. He is later joined by two of his brothers and more UNIP members bringing the total arrested to at least twenty-five individuals. Kebby Musokotwane, reacting to the initial arrests views the move as an attempt to victimize UNIP.

5 Mar. 1993   President Kaunda is dismissive of reports of an attempted coup stating rather that it is part of a plan by the government and its allies in the US Central Intelligence Agency (CIA) to discredit UNIP.

9 Mar. 1993   Under newly imposed emergency measures, the stipulated period of detention without trial is reduced from twenty-eight days to one week due largely to pressure from international aid donors and the diplomatic community.

11 Mar. 1993   Diplomatic ties are broken with both Iran and Iraq. This comes in the wake of an accusation made by Foreign Minister Mwaanga that Iran and Iraq had funded subversive elements in UNIP. Iran reacts by cancelling previous agreements to supply Zambia with crude oil.

11 Mar. 1993   The state of emergency is ratified by the Zambian parliament. It will remain in force for three months.

18 Mar. 1993   The government blames the outbreak of rioting by street vendors in Lusaka squarely on the shoulders of UNIP agitators.

6 Apr. 1993   The United States writes off an outstanding debt of 59,000m. Kwacha. Other debts are resheduled and a further 28,000 million Kwacha will be revoked in Zambia complying with a rights accumulation programme.

15 Apr. 1993   Four key cabinet ministers are fired by President Chiluba who is under intense public and donor pressure to root out alleged corruption in his cabinet. The President declines to expand on reasons for the dismissals. Instead he hopes that the action will serve as a warning adding that nobody in government is 'indispensable'. Those dismissed are Finance Minister, Ommanuel Kasonde; Education Minister, Arthur Wina; Minister of Agriculture and Fisheries, Guy Scott and Minister of Mines and Mineral Development, Humphrey Mulemba.

27 Apr. 1993   Seven opposition members detained in connection with a planned coup in

	March are released.
21 May 1993	Orders against eight opposition figures detained for their part in the planning of a coup to oust the government are revoked. The eight are then re-arrested on new charges.
25 May 1993	The state of emergency imposed in March is lifted having served its purpose according to President Chiluba.
27 June 1993	Kenneth Kaunda bows out of party politics.
Aug. 1993	Fifteen members of the National Assembly from both the party and the legislature resign. Accusations levelled at the government include protection of corrupt cabinet ministers and failure to act on reports which link party officials with drug trafficking. President Frederick Chiluba describes the furore as 'teething troubles'.
16 Aug. 1993	Fifteen national assembly members who recently resigned launch the National Party (NP).
6 Sept. 1993	Norway withdraws funding aimed at Zambian schools in protest at the government's failure to set up a transparent accounting system. Norway is reviewing its aid programme and is working out specific conditions which must be adhered to or else they will withdraw from other projects.
23 Sept. 1993	Zambia deploys troops and paramilitary policy along its border with Zaire in an effort to combat rising levels of criminal activity in the area.
4 Jan. 1994	Vernon Mwaanga steps down as Minister of Foreign Affairs denouncing cabinet ministers who he claims forced him into resigning. Mwaanga has frequently been accused of drug trafficking and corruption.
9 Jan. 1994	Princess Nakatindi Wina resigns as Minister of Community Development and Social Welfare, together with her husband Sikota Wina as Deputy Speaker of the National Assembly following the Mwaanga resignation. Both protest their innocence amidst drug trafficking allegations. They too claim that they are victims of a growing campaign to purge government of corrupt members.
11 Jan. 1994	President Chiluba reshuffles his cabinet following the resignations of two ministers and the Deputy Speaker implicated in allegations of drug trafficking and corruption. Boniface Kawimbe, the Minister of Health and Dean Mungomba, the Deputy Minister for Economic Co-operation are dismissed in the shake-up. Both are perceived to have formed part of the pressure group to rid government of corrupt members.
11 Feb. 1994	Four members of Parliament who left the MMD to join NP lose their bid to retain their seats after a ruling is upheld by the Supreme Court that any MP who changes party affiliation automatically loses his/her seat.
3 July 1994	The Vice-President Levy Mwanawasa resigns, citing a clash of interests with President Frederick Chiluba who had appointed him 'reluctantly'. He remains the Vice-President of MMD.

4 July 1994	Brigadier-General Godfrey Miyanda previously Minister Without Portfolio, is appointed to succeed Mwanawasa as Vice-President.

17 Aug. 1994
Kenneth Kaunda is placed under surveillance after reports that he has received foreign support in his bid to resume his political career.

15 Oct. 1994
The Deputy Minister of Mines, Mathius Mpande and the Deputy Minister of Agriculture are dismissed. The two had recommended the sale of ZCCM as separate operating units rather than as a single unit. Heated discussion between the two and other senior government officials resulted in their dismissals for indiscipline and impropriety.

25 Jan. 1995
Lands Minister Chuulou Kalima is dismissed by the President due to indiscipline and irresponsibility.

9 Feb. 1995
A Presidential Decree orders all members of cabinet and of parliament to declare within forty-eight hours all their assets and liabilities. The move is linked to the dismissal of Chuulou Kalima.

17 Feb. 1995
Kenneth Kaunda is barred from addressing a rally, part of a by-election campaign.

20 Feb. 1995
Kenneth Kaunda appears in court to deny charges of holding an illegal political meeting. The case is referred to the high court.

23 Feb. 1995
The Governor of the Bank of Zambia, Dominic Mulaisho, is dismissed. He is replaced by Jacob Mwanza, previously a senior adviser to the finance ministry in what is revealed by official sources as a bid to restore confidence in the markets after a sharp drop in the value of the Kwacha.

Feb/Mar. 1995
As members scramble for top positions in MMD the party's unity splits along tribal lines. Chiluba's position as party leader is threatened by the 'hawks' and 'traditionalists' led by Dean Mungomba, former Deputy Development Minister and old guard politicans from Chiluba's own Bemba speaking group.

2 Mar. 1995
Japan reshedules Zambia's debt repayments of 15.6 billion Yen in line with accords reached by the Paris Club of Creditor Countries.

10 Mar. 1995
Zambia and Botswana sign an agreement to establish a Joint Permanent Commission on Defence and Security.

23 May 1995
The managing director of an independent newspaper The Post, Fred Mmembe is arrested when he fails to appear in court on charges of defamation. Two reporters on the Lusaka-based newspaper who also failed to appear in court are being sought. The defamatory charges arise from a report on Chiluba's press aide.

2 June 1995
Constitutional review commissioners reject the final draft of the constitution because of its MMD orientation. They believe that the document, a copy of which was shown to President Chiluba by the Chairman of the Commission, John Mwanakatwe before other commissioners had viewed it does not

reflect the public's interest. They are particularly concerned about clauses governing press freedom and the right to assembly and demonstrations.

4 June 1995

The New Democratic Party, recently launched, intends to ensure equality among all Zambians and to provide a strong opposition. It is led by David Limaka.

c. 10 June 1995

Chama Chakumbuka, leader of NDP will contest the 1996 presidential elections.

16 June 1995

Despite the controversy surrounding the draft constitution formulated by a twenty-two man commission appointed to revise the 1991 constitution, it is released.

24 June 1995

Two MMD MPs, Dean Mungomba and Derrick Chitala are expelled on charges of bringing the party into disrepute.

28 June 1995

Kenneth Kaunda is re-elected president of UNIP, defeating his former protegé, incumbent leader Kebby Musokotwane, by 1916 to 400 votes.

2 July 1995

Following the expulsion of two MMD MPs, Vice-President Levy Mwanawasa announces that he intends to challenge Chiluba's leadership at the next party convention.

10 July 1995

Kenneth Kaunda is threatened with arrest by Home Affairs Minister Chitalu Sampa if he continues to incite civil disobedience in his campaign for an early general election. Kaunda accuses the present government of mismanagement, corruption, abuse of office and tribalism. He plans to regain his former job and introduce policies that include the slowing down of privatization and the possible return of food subsidies.

17 July 1995

Vice-President Brigadier-General Godfrey Miyanda denies that the MMD is in crisis or losing support. On the same day the President reshuffles cabinet, seemingly to consolidate his position. Andrew Kashita, previous Works and Supply Minister, is dismissed and Foreign Affairs Minister, Remmy Mushota is reassigned. The embattled Finance Minister, Ronald Penza is retained. He has been roundly criticized for his handling of the collapsed, privately owned, Meridien BIAO Bank.

30 July 1995

Dean Mungomba, a founder member of the MMD and its party treasurer announces the formation of ZDC. It draws support from disenchanted MMD members including twelve party officials who resigned on 5 July.

11 Aug. 1995

Dingiswayo Banda of UNIP defects to the MMD. This move follows speculation that he faces expulsion from UNIP for his refusal to step down as parliamentary leader in favour of Kaunda's chosen candidate, Patrick Mvunga. His defection is followed by the resignation of two more UNIP MPs.

3 Sept. 1995

Arthur Wina, Chairman of NP and a former minister who served under both Kaunda and Chiluba, dies.

6 Sept. 1995

The Human Rights Commission appointed by President Chiluba two years ago to investigate human rights abuses under Kaunda's twenty-seven year rule and the period since his own party came to power, releases its report. The Commission, chaired by Bruce Munyama finds evidence of the existence of security installations across the country where state torture was committed under Kaunda's rule. These include a network of security tunnels under the presidential residence. Kaunda counters the allegations stating that the torture tunnels were `a gift from a friendly country to the entire sub-region to facilitate the freedom struggle'. The Munyama Commission also targets Zambia's overcrowded prisons and recommends the early release of long term prisoners. The Commission also recommends that security legislation which allows for lengthy detentions and interrogations be amended. It also calls for the incorporation of the UN Declaration of Human Rights into security laws.

19 Sept. 1995   Eight by-elections are held: MMD and UNIP win four seats respectively. The by-elections are viewed as a test of strength between Kaunda and Chiluba before the forthcoming 1996 general elections. Voter turnout is low and there are isolated incidents of violence.

21 Sept. 1995   Two of Kaunda's bodyguards are charged with assaulting Newton Nguni, deputy education minister.

16 Oct. 1995   Home Affairs Minister Chilalu Sampa confirms that Kenneth Kaunda had failed to register as a Zambian citizen at independence in 1964 and had retained citizenship of Malawi (his birth place and that of his parents) until 1970. Chilalu Sampa reveals that the government is investigating the status of Kaunda and until the investigation is finalized Kaunda will be treated `like any alien'.

19 Oct. 1995   The investigation into Kaunda's status as a Zambian citizen is halted as tension mounts over reports of his threatened arrest and deportation. Kaunda's plans to contest the 1996 elections may be further thrown into jeopardy if the new draft constitution is approved. It contains a clause limiting presidential candidates to those who are Zambians by birth.

Late Oct. 1995   Asians who are residents of Livingstone flee after they become the targets of mob violence. The riots are sparked after ritual child murders are linked to two suspects of Indian descent. Property is set alight and goods are looted.

6 Dec. 1995   Zambia's eligibility to borrow from the IMF is restored after its suspension in September 1987.

4 Jan. 1996   An alliance is established between seven opposition parties to agitate for open, free and democratic elections and the founding of a Constituent Assembly to adopt the draft constitution.

Feb. 1996   Dipak Patel, Minister for Commerce and Trade, resigns in protest against the proposed constitutional amendment which will bar second-generation Zambians from contesting presidential elections.

Apr. 1996   Former President Kaunda announces that he would break the law if the government stopped him from contesting the presidential elections. Government reacts by saying that action will be taken by Zambians advocating violence.

May 1996   Simon Zukas Minister of Works and Supply resigns, citing irreconcilable differences with the MMD over proposed constitutional changes.

22 May 1996	Parliament passes a bill which states that candidates in the presidential election have to prove that both their parents were born in Zambia. This amendment is seen as a deliberate attempt to prevent former President Kenneth Kaunda and UNIP leader from standing for re-election. A further amendment stipulates that no ex-President who has served two terms can stand for re-election.
29 May 1996	Ministerial changes are implemented.
June 1996	Aid donors indignant at the government's undemocratic behavior, decide to suspend aid, comprising up to $1,000m. per annum.
June 1996	Eight prominent UNIP members are arrested and charged with membership of an organization known as 'Black Mamba', which is alleged to have been responsible for a number of bomb explosions around Lusaka.
20 June 1996	UNIP party members, demonstrating at the treason trial of their leaders are dispersed by police using tear gas and firing into the air.
July 1996	USAID Director Joseph Stepanek announced that the United States government is to reduce aid to Zambia by 10%, amounting to $3.5m. The constitutional amendments are cited as the reason for the cuts.
July 1996	Four opposition parties form the United Indigenous Opposition Front, which, while not agreeing with President Chiluba, are opposed to 'non-indigenous' Zambians ruling the country. The group is briefing Frontline States about the situation in Zambia.
early July 1996	The ruling MMD party wins local by-elections in a landslide victory. It won sixteen out of twenty-one seats. It is said that council houses were given away to sitting tenants in the run-up to the poll, indicating possible bribery.
Aug. 1996	A new political party, the National Lima Party, is formed by MP Guy Scott, who resigned his parliamentary seat, and Farmers' Union President Ben Kapita. They will contest parliamentary elections and seek representation for farmers in the House.
Sept. 1996	The government refuses a request to hold the 1996 general elections under the 1991 constitution. However, certain concessions are made: a guarantee that the Independent Electoral Commission will remain independent; the fourteen-day notice stipulated for holding public meetings is reduced to seven, counting of votes will be done at polling stations and the assurance that political parties will have equal access to the media.
9 Sept. 1996	Kaunda's UNIP Party refuses to attend a meeting with President Chiluba.
10 Sept. 1996	It is reported that the High Court has discharged two of the eight opposition leaders charged with treason.
12 Sept. 1996	President Chiluba, when receiving Luo Gan, Secretary-General of the State Council of China, expresses feelings of 'genuine friendship' between China and Zambia. Vice-President Godfrey Miyanda reiterates Zambia's one-China policy.

Oct. 1996	President Chiluba sets 18 November as election day, amid deep divisions among political parties.
Nov. 1996	The Commonwealth Press Union honour Zambian editor Fred Momembe by presenting him with the Astor Award for an outstanding contribution to press freedom. This triggered a sharp confrontation with the Zambian government, who had detained and charged the editor after critical comments on Vice-President Miyanda's statement in Parliament of a High Court ruling.
1 Nov. 1996	Six opposition politicians of the UNIP Party charged with treason are cleared, as the state failed to build a case against them.
18 Nov. 1996	President Chiluba's party, the Movement for Multi-Party Democracy, wins the election with a clear majority, despite the boycott by the main opposition party, UNIP and a turn-out of around 40%.
24 Nov. 1996	The President orders the arrest of the heads of two independent Western-funded monitoring groups, who have indicated that the electoral process was not free and fair. At a police raid documents are seized from the offices of the Inter-Africa Network for Human Rights and the Zambia Independent Monitoring Team. After questioning, the heads of the monitoring groups are freed.
2 Dec. 1996	President Chiluba announces his new twenty-three member Cabinet, with very few changes.
mid Feb. 1997	A special projects editor of The Post, the only independent daily newspaper, Masautso Phiri is arrested. Also imprisoned are three journalists from The Chronicle, an independent weekly.
10 Feb. 1997	A hearing by the full bench of seven Supreme Court judges, of a petition filed by five opposition parties which allege that the November 1996 elections were rigged, begins in Lusaka.
24 Feb. 1997	Communication and Transport Minister Paul Kapinga dies.
24 Feb. 1997	Finance Minister Penza is found guilty of contempt of Court, by the Industrial Relations Court, after comments made by him over the ruling of the Court regarding the 45% salary increment awarded to civil servants. The civil servants' trade union took the case to the industrial relations court after the government's reluctance to award the pay rise. Minister Penza has described the court decision as irresponsible.
4 Mar. 1997	The influx of refugees from Zaire outnumbers the country's capacity to contain the situation. Border security in the north will be increased.
11 Mar. 1997	It is reported that the University of Zambia has been closed after student riots over non-payment of allowances.
21 Mar. 1997	A permanent human rights commission is established, which should be regarded as an indication of the government's concern to uphold democracy and the rule of law, Vice-President Miyanda states.
Apr. 1997	The government suspends its proposed Media Council Bill after strong

protests from journalists and diplomats. The Bill would have compelled journalists, newspaper owners and private broadcasters to apply for licences - failure to secure accreditation would have carried a prison sentence.

May 1997   A Chinese delegation holds talks and seeks ways in which to promote military cooperation between the two countries.

May 1997   The editor of The Post, an independent newspaper, is aquitted, together with his two deputees on treason charges for publishing leaked government secrets in 1996.

May 1997   An unresolved dispute involving two islands in the Zambezi River, the common border between Zambia and Zimbabwe, will be submitted for international arbitration if no solution can be found, Zimbabwe's Defence Minister announces. Going to war against a friendly neighbour is ruled out.

19 May 1997   Two factions of UNIP clash at Freedom House in Lusaka, involving cadres supporting UNIP President Kenneth Kaunda and those from expelled UNIP Central Committee member Sam Moyo. The latter are protesting against Moyo's expulsion.

June 1997   The ruling Movement for Multiparty Democracy (MMD) refutes claims that there is a political crisis in Zambia which can lead to civil war, as the MMD was given the mandate to rule in the 1996 elections. His reaction comes after press reports that former President Kaunda and the leader of the Liberal Progressive Front, Rodger Chongwe, are seeking external assistance to solve the political crisis.

ZIMBABWE

17 April 1980   Britain's last colony, Rhodesia, attains recognized and legal independence as the Socialist Republic of Zimbabwe after nearly ninety years of white rule. The new state becomes the 43rd member of the Commonwealth and the 50th member of the Organization of African Unity.

18 April 1980   Diplomatic relations are established with, among others, France, Federal Republic of Germany, United Kingdom and the United States.

14 May 1980   Opening of the first independence parliament by President Canaan Banana with Robert Mugabe as Prime Minister. The President outlines the objectives of the new government: the scrapping of laws based on racial discrimination, and a better future for the country's poor, white farmers are assured that they will not be chased off their land, but a big land resettlement programme will be launched. The country will be non-aligned and seek friendly co-existence with its neighbours.

22 May 1980   Robert Mugabe orders the cancellation of a rugby match between a national team and the British Lions, which is planned for the 10th June, as it could prejudice Zimbabwe's planned participation in the Moscow Olympics. The country plans to join a number of international organizations opposed to sporting ties with South Africa, where the Lions are touring.

27 May 1980	Senior intelligence and military officers from Zimbabwe and Mozambique agree on a detailed plan to combat anti-FRELIMO guerrillas operating on the borders of the two countries. Units of the new Zimbabwe Army have already been diverted to the south east of the country to patrol the border with Mozambique.
June 1980	Deputy Prime Minister, Simon Muzenda, pays an official visit to Peking.
June 1980	Saudi Arabia and Zimbabwe establish diplomatic relations.
26 June 1980	A BBC report, commissioned by Robert Mugabe, criticizes the broadcasting services of Zimbabwe and recommends extensive changes - the main suggestion being that the Zimbabwe Broadcasting Corporation be made independent of government and political interests and serve all Zimbabweans.
27 June 1980	A joint commission of cooperation between Zambia, Mozambique and Zimbabwe is agreed upon in principle.
28 June 1980	Robert Mugabe announces his intention to sever diplomatic ties with South Africa and maintain only economic relations until apartheid has been abolished.
30 June 1980	A combined military unit, consisting of 600 men from both ZANLA and ZIPRA, known as the 21st Batallion, is established.
17 July 1980	The retirement of Lieutenant General Peter Walls, former Rhodesian head of the army and of the combined Rhodesian and guerrilla forces after independence, is announced. After 29 July he will take extended leave until his retirement at the end of 1980.
23 July 1980	Black and white members of Parliament unite to approve a further six months' extension of the State of Emergency which commenced on the eve of UDI in 1965. However, certain provisions of the Emergency Powers Act are being dropped, such as the powers of the police to confiscate or destroy property (except arms), and censorship laws.
4-8 Aug. 1980	President Samora Machel of Mozambique pays an official visit to Zimbabwe. A communiqué is issued on 8 August which focusses on regional cooperation. Support for the UN plan to achieve independence for Namibia and the liberation movement SWAPO is expressed.
6 Aug. 1980	Manpower Minister Edgar Tekere is arrested and charged with murder after the death of a white farm manager, Gerald Adams, at Stamford Farm near Salisbury.
11 Aug. 1980	Lieutenant-General Peter Walls reveals in a BBC television interview that he had appealed to British Prime Minister Margaret Thatcher for annulment of the election immediately after the poll and before the election results were announced. He claims that President Mugabe won the election through intimidation and mentions a pre-independence plot to overrule election results. However, he decided not to proceed with the plan but rather to appeal to Mrs Thatcher. Lieutenant-General Walls maintains that he received no reply from Prime Minister Thatcher.

12 Aug. 1980	United Kingdom officials deny allegations made by Lieutenant General Walls that no response was recieved from Prime Minister Thatcher to his message. It had been decided that all messages would be dealt with by oral reply. Sir Anthony Duff, the Deputy Governor in Salisbury, delivered the message on 3 March 1980. Prime Minister Thatcher could not accept the assessment, due to powerful opinion to the contrary, as stated by the Commonwealth Election Observer Commission.
15 Aug. 1980	Information Minister Nathan Shamuyarira, in a statement to Parliament, declares that Lieutenant-General Walls' remarks were racist and have undermined African confidence in whites holding important positions in the new government. They have also seriously damaged race relations in Zimbabwe.
19 Aug. 1980	Edgard Tekere is released on bail of Z.$50,000 after a personal assurance by Prime Minister Mugabe that Tekere would present himself for trial on murder charges on the appropriate day.
20 Aug. 1980	Heads of the civil service, the permanent and acting secretaries, state that they accept the election result and believe that the outcome indicates that the new government has received their full cooperation. They maintain that they were not party to any message to the British Prime Minister requesting the annulment of the election.
21-28 Aug.1980	President Mugabe pays an official visit to the United States.
25 Aug. 1980	Zimbabwe is formally admitted as the 153rd member country of the United Nations.
29 Aug. 1980	Prime Minister Mugabe launches an attack on Lieutenant-General Walls, by accusing him of disloyalty and stating that he may not be allowed to continue living in Zimbabwe.
31 Aug. 1980	Former Rhodesian Prime Minister, Ian Smith, urges whites to give the new state a chance and not leave Zimbabwe at this stage. About 1000 whites are leaving the country every month.
31 Aug. 1980	Algeria and Zimbabwe establish diplomatic relations.
Sept. 1980	China's Vice-Minister for Economic Relations, Li Ke, pays a thirteen-day visit.
1 Sept. 1980	The Minister of Health announces the introduction of a free health service for patients earning less than $150 per month.
Oct. 1980	Zambia and Zimbabwe sign a health technical cooperation agreement. This comprises exchange of patients requiring specialist treatment and recruitment and cooperation in drugs procurement, training of health personnel, development of traditional medicine and the exchange of consultants.
2 Oct. 1980	Prime Minister Mugabe, speaking in a special broadcast, states that government forces have been deployed to restore law and order by targeting dissidents and taking possession of illegal weapons. This comes as a reaction to widespread violence and killing of civilians.

9 Oct. 1980	Zimbabwe's first High Commissioner in London, Robert Zwinoia, a distinguished academic, takes up office.
13 Oct. 1980	Prime Minister Mugabe visits China for talks with Prime Minister Zhao Ziyang.
19 Oct. 1980	Information Minister Nathan Shamuyarira reintroduces the system of screening foreign journalists by issuing temporary employment permits, valid for one month. Bad press reports in Britain, the West and especially in South Africa have caused this action.
21 Oct. 1980	Zimbabwe and Mozambique sign a security pact. The two countries will cooperate closely on the issue of anti-government dissidents. Prime Minister Mugabe and President Machel, meeting at Quelimane in north-eastern Mozambique focus on rebel activity in Mozambique which has caused a flood of refugees moving into Zimbabwe.
End Oct. 1980	A new national news agency, the Zimbabwe Inter-African News Agency (ZIANA) is established.
1 Nov. 1980	Zimbabwe establishes diplomatic links with the German Democratic Republic, after initial reluctance.
4 Nov. 1980	Trial of Manpower Development Minister, Edgar Tekere, charged with the murder of a white farmer, commences. Pleading not guilty, the Minister and his seven bodyguards refer to the Indemnity Act.
10 Nov. 1980	Street battles take place in Bulawayo between ZIPRA and ZANLA, which leaves eighteen people dead and more than 200 wounded. The tribally-based movements' enmity extends to its leaders, Joshua Nkomo and Robert Mugabe, who blamed each other for the violence.
23 Nov. 1980	Local elections take place, but are marred by political violence between Nkomo's Patriotic Front Party and Mugabe's ZANU-PF Party.
2-7 Dec. 1980	President Julius Nyerere of Tanzania is accorded full state honours during his five-day official visit.
8 Dec. 1980	Cabinet Minister Edgar Tekere and seven bodyguards are acquitted of murder and attempted murder on a majority decision that they had been acting for the purpose of the suppression of terrorism.
17-19 Dec. 1980	President Mugabe pays an official visit to Nigeria. The two countries sign a cooperation agreement, covering trade, agriculture, industries, joint enterprises and exchanges of experts.
19 Dec. 1980	Leaders of the ZANU Party and the Patriotic Front agree to establish a committee to find ways of ending the conflict and creating a climate of unity.
1981	Five Constitutional Amendment Acts are passed relating to a new judicial hierarchy.
Jan. 1981	The government acquires a controlling interest in Zimbabwe's leading newspaper group. The Mass Media Trust, a non-profit organization, buys

the South African Argus Company's 40% shareholding with the aid of a 3.5 million Pound Sterling grant from Nigeria.

10 Jan. 1981   In a Cabinet reshuffle, Manpower Planning Minister, Edgar Tekere, is dropped and Patriotic Front leader Joshua Nkomo demoted from Home Affairs to Public Services Minister. Two additional cabinet posts are created. The Patriotic Front fills five out of twenty-five cabinet seats.

10 Jan. 1981   Zimbabwe and Mozambique sign a defence and security agreement. South Africa is regarded as the aggressor, and an attack on either country would be taken as an assault on both.

15 Jan. 1981   The State of Emergency is renewed.

18 Jan. 1981   The Patriotic Front, in a document to Prime Minister Mugabe, states that it has a right to take part in the administration of security.

19 Jan. 1981   Zambian and Zimbabwean leaders sign a five-year cooperation agreement.

27 Jan. 1981   Joshua Nkomo is appointed Minister Without Portfolio, with special duties in key areas such as security and the formation of the new national army.

31 Jan. 1981   Two white security policemen, Philip Hartlebury and Colin Evans, are detained on charges of espionage for South Africa.

Feb. 1981   South Africa returns a collection of five stone birds removed from the Great Zimbabwe Ruins in the 19th Century by J.T. Bent, an archaeologist-explorer. In exchange, the South Africans receive an outstanding collection of insects.

8-12 Feb. 1981   Fighting between new National Army battalion members near Bulawayo leave approximately 300 soldiers dead.

9 Feb. 1981   Official migration figures are released. Migration for 1980 is 17,240 persons. Immigration stands at 10,833.

12 Feb. 1981   Economic Planning Minister Chidzero announces a three-year plan and calls for foreign investment of 2700 million Pounds Sterling.

13 Feb. 1981   Continuing violence between two former guerrilla armies - ZANLA and ZIPRA - is prevented by troops of the Rhodesian African Rifles, who are called by Prime Minister Mugabe. Their camp near Bulawayo is separated in an effort to reduce tension.

18 Feb. 1981   An agreement to establish diplomatic links with the Soviet Union is signed. It lays down guidelines of non-interference and a ban on partisan support for NGO's.

18 Feb. 1981   Polish/Zimbabwean relations are established.

Mar. 1981   ZANLA and ZIPRA former guerrillas, amounting to nearly 20,000, have been integrated into fifteen new batallions of the Zimbabwean National Army.

23-27 Mar. 1981   A Conference on Reconstruction and Development (ZIMCORD) is held.

Attended by representatives of Western countries, UN and international agencies, pledges for aid exceding 636 million Pounds Sterling are received.

24 Mar. 1981   South Africa terminates its seventeen-year old preferential trade agreement with Zimbabwe.

28-29 Mar. 1981   Local elections are held in the black areas of Salisbury. Landslide victories by the ruling party are scored.

12 Apr. 1981   A new white political group, the Democratic Party, is launched. Its aim is to offer back the hand of genuine friendship in response to the Prime Minister's policy of reconciliation.

14 Apr. 1981   University of Zimbabwe principal is taken hostage by students who demanded the dismissal of white officials for alleged racism.

18 Apr. 1981   On the first anniversary of Zimbabwe's independence, names associated with white rule are changed. Salisbury is to be called Harare.

7 May 1981   Former Prime Minister Ian Smith supports a bill to amend the constitution. A restructuring of the High Court and a reduction of the minimum age for senators from 40 to 30 years has been approved by seventy-one votes.

18 May 1981   Announces a joint radio venture is to be launched by Zambia and Zimbabwe to broadcast anti-apartheid programmes to South Africa.

28 May 1981   Prime Minister Mugabe returns from a tour of China, Japan, India and Pakistan. Pledges of substantial aid were received.

June 1981   The all-white Rhodesian Front Party changes its name to the Republican Front.

7 June 1981   Joshua Nkomo's Patriotic Front Party wins a landslide victory in the local elections held in Bulawayo.

9 June 1981   Prime Minister reiterates support for South African liberation movements.

13 June 1981   More than 1200 Mozambicans flee to Zimbabwe to escape violence between government forces and guerrillas.

14 June 1981   Visit by US Deputy Secretary of State, Clark, and Assistant Secretaries of State, Chester Crocker and Elliot Abrams.

22 June 1981   Mugabe rules out participation in trade sanctions against South Africa.

30 June 1981   The South African-owned Zimbabwe Inter-African News Agency (ZIANA) is taken over by Zimbabwe Mass Media Trust. It will have a national monopoly on news dissemination.

1 July 1981   White farmers give the Republican Front a mandate to represent them.

13 July 1981   A meeting between Robert Mugabe and Samora Machel takes place in Umtali. The Mozambican dissident movement RENAMO's activities are discussed.

17 July 1981	A further extension of the sixteen-year old State of Emergency is approved by Parliament.
28 July 1981	Launching of a new political party, the Zimbabwe Progressive Party, Kingdom Sithole, its President, states that its aim is to stress freedom, peace and democracy.
31 July 1981	ANC representative in Zimbabwe, Joe Gqabi, is assassinated in Harare. Information Minister Nathan Shamuyarira states that South Africa is believed to be responsible.
3 Aug. 1981	The South African government denies responsibility for the assassination of Joe Gqabi, ANC representative.
5 Aug. 1981	As no inter-governmental agreement exists, South Africa prohibits the renewal of labour contracts of 20,000 Zimbabwean nationals.
7 Aug. 1981	Appointment of a white career soldier, General Sandy Maclean as supreme commander of the country's defence forces, ahead of Lieutenant General Rex Nhongo, who commanded the guerrilla forces during the Rhodesian civil war.
9 Aug. 1981	Edgard Tekere is dismissed as ZANU-PF Secretary-General.
13 Aug. 1981	The government announces that it will take control of forty privately-run schools, catering mainly for whites.
20 Aug. 1981	South Africa bars three white Zimbabweans, including a cabinet minister, to address students at the University of Cape Town.
27 Aug. 1981	Government confirms plans to end dual South African/Zimbabwean citizenship.
30 Aug. 1981	Prime Minister Mugabe announces that Zimbabwean children without school places will undergo military training so that they can assist in the defence of the country. Guns and other weapons will only be allowed to be handled during training sessions. He also plans the recruitment of children into his ZANU-PF Party.
Sept. 1981	The design of the first national coat of arms is approved by President Banana.
Sept. 1981	Zimbabwe and Mozambique sign an extradition treaty.
20 Sept. 1981	A demonstration of over 1000 ZANU supporters calls for a one-party state.
9 Oct. 1981	Home Affairs Minister Richard Hove announces new regulations to restrict political rallies and marches, and to allow the police to ban political gatherings.
18-23 Oct. 1981	Teachers and nurses are on strike over pay; 750 arrested in Harare, 200 given suspended sentences.
Nov. 1981	South African-backed RENAMO rebel forces blow up the pipeline and railway bridge over the Pungwe River between Mozambique and Zimbabwe.

1 Nov. 1981	Prime Minister Mugabe, at a commerce and industry conference in Bindura, pledges retention of free enterprise.
17 Nov. 1981	Francis Bertrand, ex-leader of the disbanded United People's Association of Matabeleland, and five other whites are arrested after an arms cache is found in Bulawayo.
17 Nov. 1981	The merger of the three forces - ZANLA, ZIPRA and the Rhodesian security force - is completed.
25 Nov. 1981	Transport Minister Chinamano confirms the loan of twenty-six South African locomotives for use on a joint railway system.
Dec. 1981	Future private health care is in jeopardy, as the government withdraws permission for the construction of the new Kurapa Hospital, on which more than 1 million Pounds Sterling has been spent. Private hospitals are regarded as contrary to its health policy.
10 Dec. 1981	Wally Stuttaford, a Republican Front MP, is detained and held under emergency powers for allegedly conspiring to overthrow the government together with other political elements.
18 Dec. 1981	A bomb explosion in central Harare kills at least six people, injures dozens and destroys the top two floors of the ZANU (PF) headquarters.
23 Dec. 1981	A friendship agreement between Zimbabwe and Mozambique is signed.
23 Dec. 1981	Prime Minister Mugabe states that Zimbabwe should revise its policy of national reconciliation and that economic and political measures will be taken against some supporters and members of previous regimes.
31 Dec. 1981	Two former Zimbabwean Central Intelligence Organization members, Colin Evans and Philip Hartlebury, are imprisoned on charges of spying for South Africa.
Jan. 1982	Embassies in China, Romania and Yugoslavia to be established.
17 Jan. 1982	Robert Mugabe announces that top-level talks are planned between ZANU-PF and ZAPU to discuss the one-party state issue.
20 Jan. 1982	State of Emergency extended for six months.
Feb. 1982	Foreign aid from Canada, the Netherlands and Japan is made available. Canada will extend Z$9.5m credit to assist public sector development; Netherlands will donate $9.5m towards school construction training and infrastructure; Japan signs Z$3.1m over for post-war reconstruction and resettlement of refugees.
9 Feb. 1982	An agreement is signed under which Sweden and Norway will finance construction of Zimbabwe's first telecommunication links independent of South Africa.
17 Feb. 1982	Prime Minister Mugabe's minority coalitian partner, Joshua Nknomo, and tow out of the five Patriotic Front cabinet ministers are dismissed. An anti-government plot is given as the reason.

27 Feb. 1982	Joshua Nkomo's Patriotic Front decide to remain in the government to avoid possible disintegration of the country.
Mar. 1982	Two senior military men, Lieutenant General Lookout Masuku and Dumiso Dabengwa are arrested in connection with the arms caches found on property belonging to the Patriotic Front.
3 Mar. 1982	Former Commander-in-Chief of the Rhodesian Armed Forces, Peter Walls, denies accusations by Prime Minister Mugabe that he had arranged a meeting between Joshua Nkomo, PF leader, and South African officials to seek support for a coup attempt.
4 Mar. 1982	Seven MPs of the Republican Front resign, demonstrating their dissatisfaction with the leadership of Ian Smith and the Party's attitude towards the government of Zimbabwe.
6 Mar. 1982	Agreement reached with Mozambique on the reopening of the 290 km long pipeline carrying petrol to land-locked Zimbabwe from Mozambique's port of Beira.
8 Mar. 1982	Francis Bertrand and three other whites appear in the Bulawayo High Court charged with alleged plots to destroy key installations and force the secession of Matabeleland. They were arrested on 17 November 1981 under the emergency regulations.
23 Mar. 1982	Recognizes the validity of the 1964 trade agreement with South Africa.
Apr. 1982	US Assistant Secretary of State for African Affairs, Chester Crocker, states that Zimbabwe will receive US military aid for the first time - $3 million, to improve communications equipment to buy uniforms, etc. and for ground transport facilities.
3 Apr. 1982	Addressing a political rally, Prime Minister Mugabe warns ZAPU leaders that they will 'land in jail' if they do not stop their dirty tricks.
4 Apr. 1982	ZAPU leader, Joshua Nkomo, recently dismissed from government, tells supporters in an uncompromising speech that he rejects Prime Minister Mugabe's plan for a one-party system. He alleges that the former ZANLA Army has also been responsible for hiding arms.
18 Apr. 1982	Salisbury finally becomes Harare on the second anniversary of independence.
26 Apr. 1982	Prime Minister Mugabe states that the government will not impose a one-party system, but will hold a referendum and use 'persuasion' to achieve this goal.
30 Apr. 1982	The Democratic Party is disbanded. Its aim has been open cooperation with Prime Minister Mugabe but after losing three by-elections in a year, its lack of support is evident.
May 1982	A seven-nation tour of Western Europe is undertaken by Prime Minister Mugabe to discuss the maintenance of maximum pressure on South Africa for a withdrawal from Namibia.

1 May 1982	The main rail link to South Africa is cut near Beit Bridge, electricity installations and a water tank are damaged in five explosions.
2 May 1982	The Defence Ministry announces the retirement of General Sandy Maclean (50), Head of the Defence Force, barely a year after his appointment.
18 May 1982	Four white Zimbabwean are given jail sentences ranging from four to ten years for planning sabotage acts in order to force the secession of Matabeleland.
14 June 1982	President Canaan Banana, at the opening of Parliament, announces plans to form a paramilitary peoples' militia to support the security forces in the maintenance of peace. Dissidents in Matabeleland cause concern as evidenced by this announcement.
24 June 1982	A group of soldiers attack the home of the Prime Minister and exchange fire with guards at the home of the Minister of Supplies, Enos Nkala. Neither of the Ministers has been in danger. Eight soldiers are arrested at a road block and seem to be ex-ZIPRA guerrillas. The attack is seen in the context of violence sweeping the country since Joshua Nokomo's dismissal.
25 June 1982	Joshua Nkomo condemns acts of violence and banditry following the attack on the Prime Minister's residence. He appeals for peace and stability.
July 1982	Three young British tourists are murdered in the Inyanga District, and two white farmers are killed by gangs.
21 July 1982	Former white MP, Wally Stuttaford, appears in the Harare Magistrates Court after being detained on 10 December 1981. He allegedly planned a coup. He is not formally charged, but remains in custody. The Court rules that his detention from the date of arrest to his appearance before court is unlawful.
23 July 1982	Armed dissidents kidnap six tourists, including two Britains, two Australians and two Americans, from an overland tour party at a roadblock approximately fifty miles from Bulawayo.
23 July 1982	The State of Emergency is extended. New regulations, precluding legal detention against civil servants, the police and the military for actions taken for reasons of state security are gazetted. This follows a civil court action in camera by Wally Stuttaford against the security forces for torture.
25 July 1982	Joshua Nkomo appeals to the abductors not to harm the hostages and indicates that he is prepared to assist the government in securing their release. A curfew is imposed in the West of Matabeleland.
25 July 1982	Six Hawker-Hunter fighters and four new Hank aircraft are damaged by an attack on the Thornhill Air Base near Gweru.
29 July 1982	Chief Justice John Fieldsend expresses concern over the arbitrary nature of detention orders.
29 July 1982	Deputy Commander of the National Army, General Lookout Masuku and intelligence expert Dumiso Dabengwa are charged with treason. Two British journalists, Aubrey McDowall and Bill Hipson, are arrested.

29 July 1982   Prime Minister Mugabe accuses the opposition ZAPU Party of direct involvement in the kidnapping of the tourists. The abductors' demands include the release from detention of several senior ZAPU members and the return of party property confiscated after the discovery of arms caches. The dissidents' deadline is 29 July. If not met, hostages will be killed.

Aug. 1982   The Attorney-General tells a High Court judge that two alleged dissident white farmers, Neil and Alan York, who have three times been released by the courts, will not be released from custody by the executive.

Aug. 1982   Zimbabwe's first Ombudsman, Manival Moodley, is appointed to investigate complaints against local authorities, government bodies and organizations. However, complaints against the President, the Prime Minister, cabinet ministers and officers of the Attorney-General are exempted in line with emergency regulations.

17 Aug. 1982   The Republican Front of Ian Smith suffers its first defeat in twenty years when white MPs elect an independent candidate to the Senate.

18 Aug. 1982   Three SADF soldiers are killed by the Zimbabwean army near Sengwe. The South African explanation is that they crossed the border without authority with the aim of freeing political detainees.

24-31 Aug. 1982   Air Vice-Marshal Slatter, Wing Commander Briscoe and Air Commodore Pile are arrested in connection with the attack of an air base in Gweru. Later, they accuse the government of torture.

25 Aug. 1982   The kidnappers of the six tourists held send a note to the police stating that the abducted will not be freed until senior members of the ZAPU Party are relased from detention.

28 Aug. 1982   Two white farmers, Neil and Alan York, who were detained despite High Court orders are set free, apparently on the orders of Prime Minister Mugabe. Two journalists of the Herald Newspaper are also freed.

15 Sept. 1982   A curfew of press coverage on rebel-torn Matabeleland is introduced. A ban on private road traffic in several tribal areas where dissidents are active is also announced.

22 Sept. 1982   Exchange of notes with South Africa for the reciprocal appointment of trade representatives.

15 Oct. 1982   At the end of a state visit by Mozambican President dos Santos, a communiqué is signed by him and Prime Minister Mugabe condemning South Africa's increased utilization of mercenaries and puppets to attack the Front Line States.

Nov. 1982   600 Zimbabwean soldiers establish a camp in Mozambique in order to protect the pipeline which carries Zimbabwe's petrol and diesel fuel.

Dec. 1982   The Ethiopian Head of State, Colonel Mengistu Haile-Mariam, pays an official visit to Zimbabwe.

3 Dec. 1982   A black South African soldier is abducted by a group of Zimbabwean soldiers who crossed the Limpopo. South African authorities claim that

there had been thirty-five other border violations in 1982, and 6000 head of cattle have been rustled.

5 Dec. 1982   Former Rhodesian Prime Minister, Ian Smith, accuses the Zimbabwean government of intimidation after a search of his home and the confiscation of his diary, papers and passport. On a visit to the United States he made unfavourable comments about the government.

9 Dec. 1982   The Mozambique resistance movement, RENAMO attack the oil depot in Beira and destroy a fuel storage depot intended for Zimbabwe, which containes supplies for several months.

24 Dec. 1982   Three people are killed and twenty-one wounded as fifteen armed men, probably supporters of ZAPU, open fire at cars, two buses and a train northeast of Bulawayo on the main road to Gweru.

27 Dec. 1982   The First Paratroop Brigade is placed on alert after the worst outbreak of violence in Western Matabeleland.

1983   Further amendment to the constitution is passed regarding citizenship and land affairs.

10-14 Jan. 1983   Prime Minister Mugabe launches an attack on US policy and the linkage of Cuban troop withdrawal with Namibian independence. He is attending the annual conference of the African-American Institute in Harare.

28 Jan. 1983   Joshua Nkomo accuses the security forces of killing at least ninety-five civilians in Matabeleland. The `Fifth Brigade', a military unit trained by North Koreans, is blamed for the killings who were allegedly given a 'free hand' in Matabeleland.

31 Jan. 1983   British Minister of State for Overseas Development, on a three-day visit to acquaint himself with the country, signs an agreement for a grant of 15 million Pounds Sterling on favourable terms. He deplores acts of sabotage against Zimbabwe's road, rail and oil pipeline links.

Feb. 1983   Two white policemen, Philip Hartlebury and Colin Evans in detention since January 1981, are acquitted on charges of espionage for South Africa, as the judge found that their admissions of guilt had been made under duress.

14 Feb. 1983   Two defence attorneys, Mike Hartmann and Rhett Gardner, are convicted of contempt of court and fined. They represent some of the Air Force officers detained on charges of complicity in the sabotage attack on Air Force planes. The attorneys maintained at a news conference that their clients had been tortured.

19 Feb. 1983   Joshua Nkomo, leader of the opposition ZAPU Party, is prevented from leaving the country to attend a peace conference in Prague. Eight hours after his detention he is released but his passport and travel documents are confiscated. He has to report to the police.

19 Feb. 1983   Prime Minister Mugabe launches a bitter attack against the opposition ZAPU Party at a political rally, accusing its members of dissent.

28 Feb. 1983   Opposition Party leader Joshua Nkomo is placed under virtual house arrest

- he has to inform the police whenever he wants to leave his home.

8 Mar. 1983	Joshua Nkomo flees from his home base in Bulawayo and takes refuge in Botswana, after security forces raided his home, injured his chauffeur and detained some 1000 supporters.
8-12 Mar. 1983	Prime Minister Mugabe attends the seventh summit meeting of the Non-Aligned Movement in New Delhi.
9 Mar. 1983	In Matabeleland, journalists found six decomposed bodies in positions that suggest execution by gunfire. Locals maintain that several were young men killed three weeks previously. The Fifth Brigade is blamed for the killings.
9 Mar. 1983	John and Thandiwe Ndlovu, son-in-law and daughter of Joshua Nkomo, are arrested at Bulawayo Airport, allegedly for questioning.
9 Mar. 1983	President Quett Masire of Botswana meets Joshua Nkomo. The latter declares that he will remain in Botswana for the time while trying to assist in resolving the situation in Zimbabwe.
9-15 Mar. 1983	Ninety-five ZAPU party officials, including two members of the Central Committee, Guduzu and Pallant Mpofu, cross the border into Botswana clandestinely. This leads to the detention of seventeen members of Pallant Mpofu's family.
10 Mar. 1983	Johanna Nkomo, wife of exiled opposition leader, is detained while travelling under her maiden name by train to Harare.
13 Mar. 1983	Joshua Nkomo flies to London, demanding talks with Zimbabwean authorities. However, Nathan Shamuyarira, Zimbabwean Information Minister, also in London, describes Nkomo as a fugitive who has been spreading lies. He promises a safe and free return for Nkomo but no guarantee that he will not face charges. Talks on the issue can only be held in Harare, he states.
16 Mar. 1983	Rebels abduct Robert Dyer-Smith from a farm near Bulawayo.
18 Mar. 1983	Six gunmen, allegedly dissidents loyal to Nkomo, kill two white schoolgirls and their grandparents, Eric and Christine Stratford at their farm in Matabeleland. The killings are condemned by Joshua Nkomo. He denounces the claim that they are ZAPU followers.
22 Mar. 1983	Treason charges are dropped against six of the seven top ZAPU officials, but it is ruled that they will stand trial for allegedly possessing and hiding arms. This arises from an arms cache discovery in 1982.
23 Mar. 1983	Guardian correspondent, Nick Worrall, is banned from working in Zimbabwe, and declared 'an undesirable person and enemy of the State'. This is the official reaction to three critical Guardian articles of which only one has been published and none was written by Worrall.
28 Mar. 1983	Prime Minister Mugabe meets a delegation from the Catholic Commission for Justice and Peace. The Prime Minister assures the members that military excesses will be investigated.

29 Mar. 1983	The Roman Catholic Church Bishops' Conference condemns army brutality in anti-insurgency operations in Matabeleland.
30 Mar. 1983	Information Minister Shamuyarira, rejects the Bishops' claims of army brutality, and states that atrocities have been committed by insurgents. However, he reaffirms the government's intention to investigate.
2 Apr. 1983	Senator Paul Savage, his daughter and a British visitor, are shot in Matabeleland by rebels.
5 Apr. 1983	Robert Mugabe attacks representatives of churches and non-governmental organizations for their allegations of military brutality in Matabeleland and promises stronger action against the rebels of that area. He urges the church to try to understand the government's action against the rebels who have maimed and killed hundreds of innocent people in a campaign to bring down the government.
7 Apr. 1983	A by-election held in the Bulawayo South constituency is won by an independent. He defeats the Republic Front candidate - the first time that a by-election is lost by the Party.
7 Apr. 1983	Tulani Nkomo, son of Joshua Nkomo and MP Sidney Malangu, representing ZAPU, are released from jail. However, John Ndlovu, Nkomo's son-in-law, is still in detention.
14 Apr. 1983	The British Foreign Office declare that the visa granted to Joshua Nkomo has been extended for a month, entitling him to remain in Britain until 12 May 1983.
18 Apr. 1983	At the third anniversary celebrations, President Banana calls on Zimbabweans to brace themselves for a challenging year and to cooperate with the forces of law to combat the 'dissidence menace'.
24 Apr. 1983	ZAPU Deputy Leader Josiah Chinamano and the party's Secetary-General Msika claim that people living in south-eastern Zimbabwe are buying ZANU-PF membership cards in order 'to save their own lives' from army reprisals. Home Affairs Minister Herbert Ushowokunze threatens legal action against such allegations.
27 Apr. 1983	Zimbabwe's High Court acquits two senior aids of opposition leader Nkomo, Dumiso Dabengwa and Lookout Masuku, and four others of charges of treason and arms-caching. However, they are immediately re-detained under the country's emergency by-laws.
2-16 May 1983	A two-man mission of Amnesty International investigates detentions made under the emergency powers regulations, including allegations of torture, kidnapping and murder.
12 May 1983	Britain states in the House of Commons that it has expressed its concern at the highest level on the allegations of torture of the Air Force officers to the Zimbabwean government.
23 May 1983	The trial of six Air Force officers, charged with aiding unnamed South African agents to blow up Zimbabwean war planes, commences. They plead not guilty.

31 May 1983	It is announced that Botswana and Zimbabwe will be establishing diplomatic relations at ambassadorial level, despite strained relations due to Zimbabwean refugees fleeing to Botswana.
July 1983	A West Indian born judge, Telford Georges, is appointed as Chief Justice of Zimbabwe.
14 July 1983	Prime Minister Mugabe dismisses the suggestion of a political solution for the Matabeleland dissident issue and defends the government's detention without trial of Dumiso Dabengwa, aide of Joshua Nkomo, and five others, after acquittal by the Court of treason charges.
15 July 1983	John Ndlovu, son-in-law of Joshua Nkomo, is released after four months in detention without trial.
21 July 1983	The former Prime Minister, Ian Smith, renames the Republican Front (formerly the Rhodesian Front) as the Conservative Alliance, which will be open to persons of any race, creed and colour.
23 July 1983	Air Vice-Marshal Azim Daudpota of Pakistan is appointed Commander of the Zimbabwe Air Force. This is believed to be part of a Pakistani assistance programme to the Air Force.
4 Aug. 1983	Parliament debates whether Joshua Nkomo should lose his parliamentary seat after having missed twenty-one consecutive working days of Parliament. The debate is postponed until 17 August 1983.
9-12 Aug. 1983	Prime Minister Mugabe pays a state visit to Botswana and signs cooperation treaties in the fields of security, trade, transport and the control of animal diseases, especially foot-and-mouth disease.
16 Aug. 1983	ZAPU leader, Joshua Nkomo, returns to Zimbabwe after five months of self-imposed exile in Britain.
17 Aug. 1983	Joshua Nkomo, who had promised a major initiative to solve the dissident problem in Matabeleland, returns to Parliament and merely tries to justify his decision to flee from Zimbabwe. Motion to oust him from Parliament is withdrawn.
23 Aug. 1983	The Minister of Finance, Dr Bernard Chidzero, announces that the IMF has suspended its eighteen month standby credit arrangement, due to a budget deficit.
26 Aug. 1983	Zimbabwe appoints its first woman judge, Ghanian Theresa Eppie Triggner-Scott.
28 Aug. 1983	Six white Air Force officers are acquitted of charges that they plotted to blow up Zimbabwean Air Force planes, but are immediately re-arrested under the emergency regulations.
28 Aug. 1983	The British Foreign Office responds to the re-arrest of the acquitted airmen and expresses its deep concern.
Sept. 1983	The Fifth Brigade is redeployed in Matabeleland - an indication that the security problem has not been solved.

Sept. 1983	New emergency laws are published, extending the State of Emergency. They also include a ban on journalists reporting from designated areas except through official sources and censored despatches. Powers of security forces are enhanced to allow removal of people requisition of land, building or installations, and designate them as protected places. The law authorizes body searches, curfews and the seizure of livestock by security forces and gives carte blanche for the installation of equipment to deter terrorist attacks.
Sept. 1983	A programme to train a 20,000 strong people's militia commences in seven of the nine provinces. The militia force will be used in areas where security is weak and to guard strategic installations.
1 Sept. 1983	Agence France Presse and ZIANA conclude an agreement on the exchange of services. The amount of coverage of African events by Agence France Presse is mentioned as one of the reasons for the agreement.
7 Sept. 1983	Home Affairs Minister Ushewokunze strongly attacks the acquittals of the airmen, and defends the practice that confessions (which were allegedly obtained under torture) are allowed in the trial. However, Zimbabwe law clearly states that illegally-obtained evidence is not permitted in court.
7 Sept. 1983	Prime Minister Mugabe leaves on a state visit to Ireland, the United States and Canada.
9 Sept. 1983	Prime Minister Mugabe reveals in Dublin that he and his Security Minister had decided to redetain the airmen when it became clear that the court would accept their plea of torture by the police. He criticizes the criminal procedure which Zimbabwe inherited from colonial times.
9 Sept. 1983	Vice-Marshal Slatter and Air Commodore Pile are released from detention.
11 Sept. 1983	Zimbabwe's biggest selling newspaper, the Sunday Mail, questions the detention of the airmen and guardedly criticizes Home Affairs Minister Ushewokunze.
14 Sept. 1983	Wing Commander Briscoe is released from prison.
15 Sept. 1983	Home Affairs Minister Ushewokunze says in Parliament that he has no intention of releasing the remaining airmen from detention.
25 Sept. 1983	Prime Minister Mugabe reports that bilateral discussions with Ireland, the United States and Canada were successful, and that aid and cooperation would continue. A technical agreement was signed with Canada.
25 Sept . 1983	Returning from his overseas visit, Prime Minister Mugabe attacks British attitudes to the redetention of airmen. Maintaining that intervention in Zimbabwe's internal affairs will not be accepted, he notes suggestions in Britain that aid to Zimbabwe be stopped, which it is welcome to do, but it should not interfere.
28 Sept. 1983	Army demobilization, cutting the force from 65,000 to 41,500 members, is completed.
30 Sept. 1983	The moderate white independents win their eleventh seat in Parliament,

leaving the conservative Republican Front with fewer than half of the twenty reserved seats for whites.

Oct. 1983	Merger talks between ZANU and ZAPU are held. Claims by a ZANU member that discussions have collapsed, are denied by the Secretary-General of ZAPU, Joseph Msika.
Oct. 1983	Three of the six airmen detained after their acquittal remain in prison because the government believes they were responsible for the crippling of the Air Force.
Oct. 1983	The Zimbabwe High Court orders the release of ZAPU MP Vote Moyo, who was held without trial since 15 June 1982.
21 Oct. 1983	According to reports, former Prime Minister Abel Muzorewa, on a visit to Israel, has urged the establishment of diplomatic relations between Zimbabwe and Israel. He is reported to have said that Zimbabwe is losing out on agriculture and technology due to its political policies. Prime Minister Mugabe denounces these statements.
1 Nov. 1983	Former Prime Minister Abel Muzorewa is arrested because he is suspected of having subversive links with South Africa. Bishop Muzorewa's UANC Party sees the arrest as part of the government's plan to muzzle opposition parties.
3 Nov. 1983	Prime Minister Mugabe gives reasons for Bishop Muzorewa's arrest: his clandestine activities against the state. He warns leaders of minority parties, including Ndabaningi Sithole and Joshua Nkomo, that they risk arrest when conspiring against the government.
8 Nov. 1983	A patrol of the Botswana Army report an incursion by Zimbabwean troops, who fired rifle grenades and mortar shells at the patrol about four kilometres inside Botswana's northern border. Ministry of Defence spokesperson denies the allegations.
8 Nov. 1983	The Zimbabwean High Court rules that ZAPU politician Dumiso Dabengwa is held illegally and orders his immediate release.
10 Nov. 1983	An emergency meeting of the Botswana-Zimbabwe Defence and Security Commission is held in Bulawayo following the alleged incursions. Discussions are frank, but cordial and the issue is amicably resolved. Delegates decide that communications should be improved.
10 Nov. 1983	Ndabaningi Sithole responds to the Prime Minister's accusation of plotting against the government. He states that the government has refused them the right of reply. A spokesperson of ZAPU alleges that non-ZANU-PF members are regarded as dissidents - this smacks of dictatorship and intimidation, he maintains.
11 Nov. 1983	Bishop Muzorewa, detained on 3 November, ends an eight-day hunger strike.
16 Nov. 1983	Air Lieutenant Lewis Walker, who languished alone in prison without being charged for the destruction of thirteen aircraft for almost sixteen months, is released.

25-26 Nov. 1983	Mass arrests of women by police and the army. They are picked up in public hotels, bars and on the streets in a bid to eradicate prostitution. Many innocent women are arrested. Public opposition to the arrest is intense.
21 Dec. 1983	Zimbabwe acknowledges that its troops conduct hot pursuit operations against dissidents taking refuge in Botswana. Zimbabwean Security Minister confirms at a meeting with Botswana officials that a Zimbabwe soldier was shot by Botswana troops outside the border.
22 Dec. 1983	The three remaining Air Force officers who were re-arrested after their acquittal in August, are freed. They are Wing Commander John Cox, Lieutenant Barrington Lloyd and Lieutenant Neville Weir. They are given seven days to leave the country.
29 Dec. 1983	By order of the Prime Minister, women who were arrested in the Government's month-long round-up of prostitutes, are released. About 2,000 women were held at the Musuhumbi Pools detention camp.
1984	An amendment is made to the constitution regarding the composition and qualifications for a Judicial Service Commission. The act to provide for an Ombudsman is also repealed.
3 Jan. 1984	A cabinet reshuffle removes Home Affairs Minister Herbert Ushewokunze from his post where he is regarded as having contributed to the deterioration of Zimbabwe's human rights record by signing hundreds of detention orders. His replacement, Simbi Mubako, is a scholarly moderate. Cabinet is reduced from twenty-eight to twenty-two ministerial posts.
7 Jan. 1984	The Foreign Affairs Ministry protests to the SA Trade Commissioner against police assault on the Zimbabwean Deputy Trade Commissioner, David Buyanga. He was halted at a roadblock on 30 December 1983. Claiming diplomatic immunity, he refused a search of his car; subsequently he was beaten by police and his arm was broken. SA Foreign Minister, Pik Botha, formally apologizes to Zimbabwe.
10 Jan. 1984	A Commission of Inquiry into allegations of atrocities by the security forces against civilians, especially in Matabeleland, begins behind closed doors. It is alleged by church and aid officials that the forces killed more than 2000 members of the minority Ndbele group.
18 Jan. 1984	Zimbabwe and the Soviet Union sign a first bilateral trade agreement.
18 Jan. 1984	The Zimbabwe Parliament extends the state of emergency, to control unrest in Matabeleland. Guerrillas have killed seventy-five people and carried out 284 robberies. There have also been 537 sightings of `dissidents' and 175 incidents of contacts between dissidents and the security forces.
3 Feb. 1984	Home Affairs Minister Mubako announces that additional troops will be sent to Matabeleland to curb increased infiltration by anti-government forces. This follows a marked increase in killings, rape and torture of civilians by rebels. A dawn-to-dusk curfew is also imposed. Private traffic and civilians are banned and food stores closed.
Mar. 1984	Commenting on the Nkomati Accord, Prime Minister Mugabe states that he

will remain an ally in the consolidation of the hardwon peace.

Mar. 1984

Mass graves of about 4,000 guerrillas and their civilian supporters are uncovered at a rifle range near Rusape. The killings took place during the war of independence in the 1970s. Former Rhodesian Prime Minister, Ian Smith, regrets that atrocities which occurred during the war, but regards the announcement as an effort to divert attention from the anti-dissident operation in Matabeleland.

8 Mar. 1984

Home Affairs Minister Mubako eases restrictions on food deliveries to Matabeleland's southern curfew area to prevent starvation. Grocery stores will be permitted to open twice per week and drought relief supplies will be issued.

22 Mar. 1984

The government frees two senior ZAPU members which have been detained since April 1983. They are Isaac Nyathi and Major Masala Sibanda.

Apr. 1984

The United African National Council of Bishop Abel Muzorewa calls for the release of the Bishop, who has been detained without trial since October 1983.

Apr. 1984

ZAPU Minister of Mines, Callistus Ndlovu, deserts the ZAPU Party and joins the ruling ZANU Party.

Apr. 1984

Zimbabwe is elected by the OAU to represent Southern African countries at the ILO Governing Council Congress.

2 Apr. 1984

A report by Roman Catholic leaders, detailing security force brutalities and a policy of starvation against the minority Ndebele group, is handed to Robert Mugabe whilst on a visit to Matabeleland. He denies the allegations.

4 Apr. 1984

ANC leader, Oliver Tambo, visits Zimbabwe to review relations following the signing of a non-aggression pact between South Africa and Mozambique. Mugabe said earlier that Zimbabwe will continue to support the ANC.

9 Apr. 1984

Curfew restrictions in Matabeleland are relaxed. The government claims that the security situation is improving. However, the country's main weekly newspaper challenges this statement.

1 May 1984

Rhodesian Front MP Geoffrey York defects to an independent group, leaving only seven RF seats in Parliament. He argues that the RF has not detached itself from its old associations and attitudes.

23 May 1984

The Supreme Court dismisses an appeal by the government against the acquittal of six white Air Force officers on sabotage charges.

25 May 1984

Zimbabwe joins the Panafrican News Agency (PANA).

June 1984

Pressure is put on the opposition ZAPU Party by threatening that the existing ban on political meetings in the Central Midlands and Mashona and West Provinces will be extended to the provinces if the party will continue to support anti-government dissidents.

11 June 1984

Chief Rekayi Tangwena, the tribal leader most closely associated with the liberation struggle, dies aged 74.

15 June 1984	Violent demonstrations against rebels are held in six cities. More than seven people are killed, 300 injured, ZAPU offices and homes of ZAPU supporters are burned.
18 June 1984	A ban is introduced on all ZAPU meetings in the Midlands Province.
20 June 1984	The ban on all ZAPU meetings in the Midlands Province is extended to Mashonaland West Province.
24 June 1984	Army deserters stage an armed assault on the Prime Minister's official residence in Harare in an attempt to overthrow the government and install Joshua Nkomo as Head of State.
25 June 1984	Minister of Mines, Maurice Nyagumbu, discourages ZANU-PF supporters from taking the law into their own hands, and that it should be left to the army and the police to reinforce the law against rebels.
26 June 1984	Disturbances mark the opening of Parliament when ZAPU and UANC supporters protest with placards against food shortages and the detention without trial of Bishop Muzorewa. ZAPU members turn on these party members and some are beaten.
July 1984	Emmerson Munangaqwa states that Botswana has repatriated more than 1200 Zimbabweans from their Dukwe refugee camp. This includes 300 guerrillas of Joshua Nkomo's ZAPU Party. He also discloses that 400 dissidents were captured, some of whom had been trained in South Africa.
July 1984	Security Minister Munangaqwa, discloses that infiltration of anti-government rebels from South Africa stopped after talks between the two countries.
4 July 1984	A government tribunal recommends that Bishop Muzorewa be kept in detention at least until September. He is accused of conspiring with South Africa and Israel to overthrow the government.
21 July 1984	The Republican Front of Ian Smith renames the party to Conservative Alliance at the Party's congress.
26 July 1984	The State of Emergency is renewed for a further six months. For the first time, opposition party ZAPU votes against the renewal. ZAPU Vice-President's wife, Ruth Chinamano, presents a list of casualties allegedly killed by government troops.
2 Aug. 1984	Six army deserters loyal to ZAPU are sentenced to terms of imprisonment ranging from twelve to twenty-five years. They staged an armed assault and planned to overthrow the government.
8-12 Aug. 1984	Ruling party ZANU-PF holds its first congress in twenty years, and debates a draft constitution which will establish a one-party state 'and the fulfilment of the socialist revolution.'
17 Aug. 1984	Mr Justice Edward Beck declares that the 1975 Indemnity and Compensation Act, which protected the security forces from being sued, is in contravention of the constitution's Declaration of Rights.
4 Sept. 1984	Bishop Muzorewa is freed after ten months detention. He vows to make a

political comeback at the elections scheduled for February 1985.

15 Sept. 1984	Dissidents abducted five people eighty-five miles west of Bulawayo. A pregnant woman, a child and a young boy are killed. The remaining people escape.
17 Sept. 1984	Northwest of Gweru, the chairman of the local ZANU youth wing is shot by guerrillas.
27 Sept. 1984	ZAPU leader, Joshua Nkomo, loses a legal battle against the government and has to vacate an estate confiscated by the government. It was an asset of a banned company with Nkomo, his wife and others as directors. The banning occured after the discovery of arms caches.
29 Sept. 1984	Tunisian and Zimbabwean Ministers of Information sign a cooperation agreement regarding information exchange.
4 Oct. 1984	The ban on ZAPU meetings in both the Midlands and Mashonaland West Provinces is lifted.
6-7 Oct. 1984	Local government elections in Bulawayo are won by ZAPU.
12-14 Oct. 1984	ZAPU holds a two-day congress and re-elects Joshua Nkomo as its leader. The Congress rejects Mugabe's proposed one-party state.
14 Oct. 1984	Violence breaks out in the Midlands Province and at least five opposition ZAPU members are killed.
28 Oct. 1984	Abel Muzorewa, leader of the United African National Council, proposes that black opposition parties should stand together against the ruling party.
10 Nov. 1984	Following the murder of a ruling ZANU committee member, Senator Moven Ndlovu, at least twenty ZAPU members are killed in rioting in the town of Beit Bridge.
Dec. 1984	Handwritten notes, claiming that the six kidnapped tourists which were taken hostage in July 1982 are still alive, are handed to bus conductors in Matabeleland. Western diplomats are sceptical.
Dec. 1984	The High Court in Harare turns down the application for the release of two Zimbabwe intelligence officers who were accused of spying for South Africa. They had been acquitted in 1983 but were immediately redetained. A review tribunal ordered earlier that they be held indefinitely.
Dec. 1984	The ZANU leadership code is adopted. It states that officials may receive only one salary, own no more than 50 acres of land, are prohibited to deal in property or to become a company director.
1985	A further amendment to the constitution provides that the Electoral Supervisory Commission should be fully independent of any person or authority.
1985	President Mugabe on his first official visit to the Soviet Union, signs a bilateral economic and technological accord.

5-8 Jan. 1985	The British Foreign and Commonwealth Secretary, Sir Geoffrey Howe, visits Zimbabwe to discuss the situation in Namibia.
8 Jan. 1985	Joshua Nkomo, starting his election campaign in Masvingo Province, stronghold of Mugabe's ZANU Party, has to take refuge in the police station from angry demonstrators. He is advised to leave. On leaving, his car is stoned and shots are fired.
23 Jan. 1985	Robert Mugabe confirms that the election will be held in March.
1 Feb. 1985	Police Commissioner, Wiridzayi Nguruve, is suspended pending the report of an inquiry into allegations of police involvement in drug trafficking.
15 Feb. 1985	Diplomatic relations at High Commission level are established with New Zealand.
17 Feb. 1985	Violence breaks out among supporters of ZANU-PF and opposition ZAPU members in Kwekwe, Midlands Province. Joshua Nkomo, due to address an election rally, cancels the meeting.
19 Feb. 1985	Justice Minister Zvobgo states that elections will not be held in March or April due to the enormous task of voter registration evaluation and the demarcation of the constituencies.
24 Feb. 1985	Five officials of Bishop Muzorewa's UANC party are dragged from a train in Hwange and shot by supporters of the ruling ZANU-PF party. This follows a weekend of political violence in Bulawayo and factional fighting.
Mar. 1985	The ZAPU party claims that more than fifty key members of its party have disappeared. It blames the ruling ZANU Party. Church and international aid groups active in Matabeleland confirm that community leaders with links to ZAPU have been abducted.
Mar. 1985	Zimbabwe and the Soviet Union sign a cultural and scientific agreement.
1 Mar. 1985	Eight trade unionists and political activists, including ZANU members, are held without charges. They have been campaigning for 'free and democratic' trade unions, and criticized the government for betraying socialist ideals. They focussed especially on the new labour relations act.
2-3 Mar. 1985	Security forces hold the black township around Bulawayo in a state of virtual siege. Traffic flow control and helicopter surveillance are introduced. Arrests are made and arms confiscated.
7 Mar. 1985	Two graves, believed to contain the remains of six foreign tourists captured in 1982, are found. They are identified by a rebel who claims to have belonged to the kidnappers. Forensic tests confirm the finding.
8 Mar. 1985	Six of the eight trade unionists arrested on 1 March are released. Two South African exiles are deported to London for alleged subversive activities on 17 March 1985.
10 Mar. 1985	Joshua Nkomo launches ZAPU's election campaign and addresses a rally of 50,000 people in Bulawayo. He refers to the abduction or murder of 378 ZAPU supporters.

15 Mar. 1985	Diplomatic relations at ambassadorial level are established with Argentina.
27 Mar. 1985	Information Minister Shamuyarira refers to the detention of trade unionists. He accuses them of organizing workers for a general insurrection against the state.
29 Mar. 1985	Roman Catholic Commission for Justice and Peace in Zimbabwe chairman Michael Auret expresses concern over the human rights situation and calls for the withdrawal of the army's Fifth Brigade from Matabeleland. Incidences of violence against people supporting minority parties are listed in a report sent to the Prime Minister.
1 Apr. 1985	Minister of Information, Posts and Telecommunication, Nathan Shamuyarira, announces that Zimbabwe has been elected to chair the Pan-African News Agency for two years.
7 Apr. 1985	A new code of conduct for the ZANU Youth Brigade is drawn up. This follows complaints that Youth Brigade members were forcing people to attend party meetings, and the subsequent death of a schoolboy.
17 Apr. 1985	The government bans the use by ZAPU of an eagle as election symbol arguing that the eagle is part of the Police Support Unit and the Air Force insignia. ZAPU's successful appeal is met by a reinforcement of government powers under the State of Emergency. Twelve other symbols used by opposition parties are also banned.
15 May 1985	Diplomatic relations are established with the People's Democratic Republic of Yemen.
27 June 1985	Elections are held for the twenty seats reserved for whites in the House of Assembly. The Conservative Alliance wins fifteen seats, the Independent Zimbabwe Group four seats and an independent, C. Anderson, one seat. Prime Minister Mugabe reacts by stating that the whites remained by and large the racists of the past.
July 1985	Almost 7000 Zimbabwean troops are stationed in Mozambique (about 125 miles from Mutare to the port of Beira) to protect the oil pipeline from sabotage by the rebel RENAMO forces.
1-2 July 1985	Elections for the majority of Zimbabweans take place. Due to long delays caused by detailed checking of the voter rolls, polling is extended for a further two days.
6 July 1985	The `exclusive white' representation in parliament should be abolished almost immediately, the Prime Minister announces.
7 July 1985	Results of the common roll elections indicate that Robert Mugabe's ZANU Party increased their majority from 57 to 63 out of the 79 seats. This constitutes a 15% increase on the results of the 1980 elections. ZAPU - 19.2%, a drop of 5% from 1980. Smaller opposition parties draw about 2% of the ballots cast.
16 July 1985	Prime Minister Mugabe announces his new Cabinet and dismisses the Minister of Agriculture, Denis Norman, because the country's 100,000 whites backed Ian Smith's party, the Conservative Alliance. Two former

deputy Ministers, John London and Jane Ngwenya, are also dropped.

17 July 1985	The Supreme Court imposes the death sentence on two guerrillas who confessed to the murder of six foreign tourists in 1982.
22 July 1985	Spain's ambassador to Zimbabwe, Jose Luis Blanco-Brianes de Cuellar, is beaten to death. His body is found in a Harare street.
24 July 1985	Joshua Nkomo is stripped of weapons and most of his bodyguards. Responsible Minister is the newly appointed Home Affairs Minister, Enis Nkala.
Aug. 1985	The strategic pipeline between Beira and Zimbabwe is blown up by Mozambican rebels but repairs are carried out by Zimbabwean soldiers, who have guarded the 190-mile pipeline since 1982.
1-2 Aug. 1985	The authorities search ZAPU offices in Bulawayo and Harare, detaining at least ten people.
8 Aug. 1985	Signs loan agreement with the International Bank for Reconstruction and Development for a small-scale enterprise project.
10 Aug. 1985	Opposition ZAPU leader, Joshua Nkomo's passport is confiscated, three ZAPU MPs are arrested and twenty party officials are held after raids on Nkomo's homes in Bulawayo and Harare.
20 Aug. 1985	Five people are executed, two of whom killed three civilians in 1982.
22 Aug. 1985	Prominent ZAPU member announces her resignation from the party and her decision to join the ruling ZANU. She is a former Deputy Manpower Minister.
26-28 Aug. 1985	Prime Minister Mugabe visits Peking on an official state visit. An agreement on economic and technical cooperation is signed.
28 Aug. 1985	A visit to North Korea is paid by Prime Minister Mugabe.
28 Aug. 1985	In a further police crackdown on ZAPU supporters, the new Mayor of Bulawayo, Nick Mabodoko and Alderman Michael Constandinos are detained.
28 Aug. 1985	Zimbabwean army stationed in Mozambique capture the RENAMO headquarters known as Casa Banana, in the Gorangosa National Park, Sofala Province.
29 Aug. 1985	An attack by dissidents on Sweet Water ranch and the town of Makambe in Matabeleland leaves at least eighteen people dead. This later rises to twenty-two.
Sept. 1985	Approximately 17% of Zimbabwe's army and air force are guarding the pipeline which carries all Zimbabwe's petrol and diesel needs from the Mozambican port of Beira. RENAMO guerrillas sabotage this essential commodity.
6 Sept. 1985	Eddison Zvobgo, Minister of Justice and ZANU Chairman for the Masvingo

Provinces announce that the government intends to arm businessmen and school teachers in areas affected by dissidents in Mwenezi.

10-12 Sept. 1985   Four white men, Trevor Hemans, Michael Jacobs, Patrick Higgins and Anthony Hunt, are detained on suspicion of backing dissidents and planning secession in Matabeleland. They are released on 15 September as no charges could be brought against them.

18 Sept. 1985   Two Zimbabwean MPs, Kembo Mdudi and Edward Ndlovu, as well as ZAPU leader Joshua Nkomo are arrested in a crackdown on ZAPU. Nkomo is released after being questioned for an hour on security matters.

23 Sept. 1985   It is reported that Prime Minister Mugabe has appointed a three-man commission to talk to ZAPU on the issue of unity.

24-28 Sept. 1985   Five senior army officers, all former guerrillas of ZIPRA military wing of ZAPU, are arrested for allegedly assisting dissidents.

26 Sept. 1985   After several meetings between ZANU and ZAPU delegations, the parties conclude a seven-point document of general agreement in principle concerning unification of the two parties.

Oct. 1985   At a meeting of the Botswana/Zimbabwe Permanent Commission on Defence and Security in Gaborone, Botswana pledges to apprehend and hand over persons fleeing from Zimbabwe after committing crimes there.

Oct. 1985   In a television interview with the BBC, former Rhodesian Prime Minister Ian Smith says that the concept of one-man - one-vote is a negation of democracy and that most Zimbabwean blacks were illiterate and politically ignorant.

2 Oct. 1985   Prime Minister Mugabe and ZANU leader Joshua Nkomo meet in a first round of talks to discuss the merging of their parties. This follows meetings of a Unity Committee.

10 Oct. 1985   Rebels kill a school headmaster and a villager near Gokwe. They set the body of the schoolmaster alight and also burn down thirteen houses.

14 Oct. 1985   National Assembly Speaker, Didymas Mutasa, discloses that the thirty-member Senate will have no location in the new parliament buildings which are to be constructed at an estimated cost of Z$105 million.

21 Oct. 1985   Seven villagers die in a Matabeleland village store which is set on fire by dissidents.

23 Oct. 1985   A white rancher, his wife and the ranch foreman are killed at their ranch near Bulawayo.

Nov. 1985   New press censorship laws are approved. In terms of this law, any government related body may prohibit all publicity for reasons of public safety, defence interests, economic interests of the state or public morality.

12 Nov. 1985   It is reported that Bishop Abel Muzorewa, leader of the UANC is to withdraw from politics after the party's dismal performance in the election.

13 Nov. 1985	Amnesty International publishes a report accusing the government of torturing opposition party members in Bulawayo. This is denied by the Prime Minister.
30 Nov. 1985	Douglas Lilford, a driving force of the Rhodesian Front and a millionaire, is murdered in his home near Harare.
2 Dec. 1985	The privilege of belonging to more than one nationality is struck from the constitution. The majority of the country's 100,000 whites are therefore either aliens or become Zimbabwean citizens.
2-4 Dec. 1985	Prime Minister Mugabe pays a state visit to the Soviet Union, the first since Zimbabwe became independent.
3 Dec. 1985	A parliamentary committee chaired by Bill Irvine is established. Their brief is to investigate alleged contemptuous statements made by Ian Smith during a BBC television interview. Ian Smith has since unreservedly apologized to Parliament.
31 Dec. 1985	According to the Prime Minister, ZANU and ZAPU agreed to establish a one-party state with socialist principles, based on Marxism-Leninism. The leadership issue is still to be resolved.
1 Jan. 1986	Air Vice-Marshal Josiah Tungamirai becomes the new commander of the Zimbabwean Air Force. He takes over from Air Vice-Marshal Azim Dandrota from Pakistan.
22 Jan. 1986	The twenty-year old State of Emergency is extended - probably for the last time. Bills are tabled to end the State of Emergency yet to wield power contained in emergency legislation including detention without trial.
28 Jan. 1986	Three ZAPU leaders and four senior army officers are charged with plotting a coup.
Feb. 1986	Some 400 RENAMO forces recapture Casa Banana, their headquarters in the Gorongosa National Park which had been taken by Zimbabwean troops in August 1985. The demoralized troops still guard the Beira Corridor but some 5000 of the 12000 have been withdrawn.
7 Feb. 1986	It is reported that Stephen Nkomo, brother of opposition leader Joshua Nkomo and two ZAPU officials, are released from jail.
7 Feb. 1986	A ZANU official, Zimon Ziwore, is sentenced to death for the murder of five opposition supporters of the UANC during the 1985 election campaign.
Mar. 1986	The Cape Verdian president, Aristides Pereira, visits Zimbabwe. Diplomatic relations are to be established between the two countries.
9 Mar. 1986	Joshua Nknomo announces at a political rally that agreement has been reached with ZANU-PF on unification.
11 Mar. 1986	A former ZAPU Secretary-General Moyo, is released from prison after being detained for nearly four years.
12 Mar. 1986	Signs agreement with West Germany concerning financial co-operation.

13 Mar. 1986	Two British citizens, Philip Hartlebury and Colin Evans who have been held for more than four years on charges of spying for South Africa, are refused appeal for freedom.

23 Mar. 1986   In an unprecedented meeting, ZAPU leader Joshua Nkomo and ZANU leader Enos Nkala hold a joint political rally in Matabeleland and call for an end to dissident violence. They plead for political unity.

Apr. 1986   Byron Hove, MP for Gokwe, implicated of misdemeanours, loses both his party post and his parliamentary seat.

7 Apr. 1986   Two dissidents, Gilbert A Gwenya and Austin Mpofu, are hanged for the abduction and murder of six foreign tourists.

12 Apr. 1986   Herbert Ushewokunze, Minister of Transport, is dismissed from the political bureau of the ruling ZANU-PF. He is accused of corruption.

17 Apr. 1986   President Canaan Banana is sworn in for a further six-year term of office.

18 Apr. 1986   Robert Mugabe discloses that the government intends to introduce legislation to abolish the reserved parliamentary seat for whites.

23 Apr. 1986   Ian Smith apologizes to the House of Assembly for derogatory remarks he made about the government and the Zimbabweans at a British television interview in October 1985.

May 1986   ZAPU politician and MP, David Kwidini, defects to the ZANU party.

5 May 1986   ZAPU MP for Gwanda, Edward Ndlovu, is released from detention after being held on charges of plotting a coup.

19 May 1986   The SADF carries out a raid on the alleged ANC office and on an empty house in the suburbs of Harare. No one is hurt.

21 May 1986   The Lawyers Committee for Human Rights releases a report on alleged human rights abuses. It concludes that abuses occured on a significant scale against the Ndebele minority. The continued State of Emergency power is also condemned.

5 June 1986   MP Charles Duke of the Conservative Alliance for the Highlands Constituency in Harare joins the ruling ZANU-PF party.

5 June 1986   Two human rights activists of the Roman Catholic Commission for Justice and Peace, Mike Auret and Nicholas Ndebele, are arrested. Through the personal intervention of the Prime Minister, they are, however, released.

15 June 1986   President Samora Machel visits Zimbabwe and discloses that closer military, political and economic cooperation between Zimbabwe and Mozambique were discussed.

24 June 1986   Two senior customs officials, accused of spying for South Africa, are released by a Supreme Court ruling and granted a High Court order that they could not be re-arrested for the same reasons. However, later on the same night they are re-arrested. The High Court orders the security Minister to justify the re-arrest.

30 June 1986	The abolishment of reserved parliamentary seats for whites as well as parliament's upper house, the Senate, is announced by Justice Minister Eddison Zvobgo. Both moves are permitted in 1987 by the Lancaster House Constitution.
4 July 1986	An anti-American speech is made at an Independence Day reception at the US Embassy in Harare. Youth, Sport and Culture Minister David Karianazira delivers the speech on behalf of Foreign Minister Witness Mangwende. Former President Carter, the Charge d'Affaires and diplomats from several European countries walk out.
4 July 1986	Opposition politician, Kembo Mohadi, is awarded Zim$30,000 in damages for illegal arrest and torture by security agents.
10 July 1986	Robert Mugabe says that the occasion for an attack on US policy at Independence Day was inappropriate but that he stands by its substance. An apology is due to Mr Carter, and the Foreign Minister will be apologizing to him, but not to the Reagan Administration.
11 July 1986	An Air Force Dakota crashes outside a military base in Mozambique and kills seventeen security force personnel, including two of Zimbabwe's most senior officers, Group Captain David Rider and Squadron Leader Charles de Jong.
15 July 1986	The State of Emergency is extended for a further six months.
18 July 1986	Home Affairs Minister Enos Nkala states that he will not tolerate police torturing people under arrest, as this is a violation of human rights.
31 July 1986	The establishment of a new Ministry - the Ministry of Cooperative Development - is announced. The Minister in charge will be Maurice Nyagumbo.
31 July 1986	Exchange of notes to amend the trade agreement with South Africa, dated 1964, the validity of which was extended by exchange of letters on 23 March 1982.
Aug. 1986	A cultural and scientific exchange agreement is signed with the Soviet Union.
Aug. 1986	Diplomatic relations are established with Laos.
Aug. 1986	Indonesia and Zimbabwe establish diplomatic ties.
Aug. 1986	Negotiations on the merger of the ZAPU and ZANU parties reach a breakthrough at a secret meeting between Robert Mugabe and Joshua Nkomo when the latter gives the Prime Minister a written pledge that ZAPU will take on the ZANU name in a merger.
Aug. 1986	Thirty-nine school leavers arrive in Havana to be trained as teachers. This is the result of an agreement with Cuba where 1200 teachers will be trained.
15 Aug. 1986	Five members of the opposition ZAPU are acquitted of the murder of Senator Moven Ndlovu in November 1984.

18 Aug. 1986   In a gesture towards political unity the government releases ten people from detention who were held on suspicion of treason. This includes three army officers.

22 Aug. 1986   Amnesty International is denounced as an enemy of Zimbabwe and anyone supplying it with information will face detention without trial, states Home Affairs Minister Enos Nkala.

Sept. 1986   Deputy Minister of Labour, Manpower Planning and Social Welfare is dismissed following a charge of drunkenness.

Sept. 1986   The Non-Aligned Movement's eighth Summit Meeting is held in Harare and Prime Minister Mugabe accepts the chairmanship of the Movement for the next three years.

Sept. 1986   Pal Losonczi, President of the Hungarian Presidential Council, visits Zimbabwe.

Sept. 1986   The United States announces a freeze on further aid to Zimbabwe after it provided $370 million since 1980.

11 Sept. 1986   Presidents Mugabe, Machel and Kaunda put President Banda of Malawi under pressure to reduce his country's close links with South Africa or face disruption to export routes.

24 Sept. 1986   Minister of Justice, Legal and Parliamentary Affairs outlines proposed changes to the Constitution. These include the establishment of an Executive Presidency, the abolishment of both racial representation and the Senate.

Oct. 1986   An agreement for co-operation in youth training is signed with the German Democratic Republic.

Oct. 1986   Home Affairs Minister Enos Nkala announces that ZAPU political detainees will be released soon. His announcement boosts the merger talks between ZAPU and ZANU.

20 Oct. 1986   After the death of Samora Machel, students display their anger by rioting and stoning buildings belonging to Malawi, South Africa and the United States.

20 Oct. 1986   Prime Minister Mugabe makes a renewed commitment to fight the rebel RENAMO in Mozambique to prevent a takeover in Maputo.

28 Oct. 1986   In retaliation to Zimbabwe's commitment to fight RENAMO, the rebel movement makes a formal declaration of war against Zimbabwe.

Nov. 1986   An agreement for a joint economic commission is signed with the Democratic Peoples' Republic of Korea, to promote trade, as well as technical and economic cooperation.

Nov. 1986   Signs an air traffic agreement with the Soviet Union.

29 Nov. 1986   Dumiso Dabengwa, a prominent leader of the pre-independence guerrilla forces, as well as Norman Fikhali and Dobani Nsigno, are released after

being imprisoned for four years. This is regarded as a key to unity between ZAPU and ZANU.

4 Dec. 1986	Two former members of the Zimbabwe Central Intelligence Organization, Colin Evans and Philip Hartlebury, are released from detention on the understanding that they would leave the country.
20 Dec. 1986	Eddison Zvobgo, Minister of Justice, Legal and Parliamentary Affairs, is dismissed from his provincial party post.
31 Dec. 1986	Prime Minister Mugabe promises trade sanctions against South Africa in the near future, and foresees hard times ahead. However, Zimbabwe must be seeing to play its part in the liberation struggle of Namibia and South Africa
Jan. 1987	An agreement on tourism is signed with Bulgaria.
Jan. 1987	Prime Minister Mugabe undertakes a tour of Asia. He announces an agreement to launch a Non-Aligned Africa Fund of $ 1 bn. to aid the Front Line States, support the liberation movements and create a monitoring group focussing on the South African crisis.
15 Jan. 1987	Robert Mugabe meets Joaquim Chissano, President of Mozambique, at a one-day meeting at Victoria Falls. Zimbabwe pledges to increase military assistance to combat RENAMO.
20 Jan. 1987	Parliament votes in favour of continuation of the twenty-two-year-old State of Emergency.
27 Jan. 1987	Canada's Prime Minister Brian Mulroney is in Zimbabwe on a four-day goodwill tour.
Feb. 1987	Former Prime Minister Ian Smith urges South Africans to unite and thwart global sanctions. Reaction by the government is negative.
Feb. 1987	Zimbabwe intends to establish a trade mission in Moscow.
Mar. 1987	Nicaragua's Foreign Minister visits Zimbabwe.
2-5 Mar. 1987	President Joaquim Chissano visits Zimbabwe. He is accompanied by a twenty-five-member delegation. Robert Mugabe pledges military aid against RENAMO rebels.
2 Apr. 1987	Ian Smith is suspended from Parliament for twelve months after anti-sanctions speeches in South Africa. The government later withdraws the motion.
17 Apr. 1987	ZANU's Central Committee discontinues merger talks with ZAPU, as there had been a deadlock and serves no useful purpose. This announcement comes as a shock to Joshua Nkomo.
May 1987	Edgar Tekere is dismissed from his post as provincial chairman of ZANU in Manicaland. He is found guilty by the Politburo of irresponsibility and tarnishing the party's image.
May 1987	Hungary applies for a $Z25 million barter deal.

May 1987	Three television journalists are held for questioning concerning South African raids into Zambia and Zimbabwe. Two are released after about a week, but Tim Leach, a British TV producer, remains in detention for further questioning.
9 May 1987	Four white Zimbabwean farmers are shot by a gang who attacked a country club in Somabhula.
13 May 1987	Former Prime Minister Ian Smith resigns from the leadership of the Conservative Alliance Party and its legislative commission. The main reason is the reaction to remarks made on sanctions while in South Africa.
15-18 May 1987	Robert Mugabe pays an official visit to Ethiopia where he is awarded the 'Star of Honour'. He discloses on his return that Ethiopia is prepared to train 10,000 ANC guerrillas.
17 May 1987	An unsuccessful rocket attack on a house in a Harare suburb is blamed on South Africa. Earlier in the same week an explosion in a flat killed the wife of an ANC exile, Tsisi Chiliza.
18 May 1987	A fifth farmer is killed by rebels near Gweru.
June 1987	RENAMO rebels murder eleven civilians in the Rushinga area. It is said 'that the MNR has declared war' on Zimbabwe due to the deployment of troops in central Mozambique to guard the Beira Corridor.
3 June 1987	The British TV producer, Tim Leach who was detained for twelve days for alleged links with South African raids on neighbouring countries, is freed.
17 June 1987	RENAMO attacks an army base in Zimbabwe near Dukosa, killing seven soldiers and wounding nineteen.
21 June 1987	ZAPU is banned from holding rallies until violence by anti-government rebels is controlled. More than twelve people have been killed in the past two months including farmers, tourists, ZANU officials and villagers.
23 June 1987	President Banana announces at his opening speech in Parliament that separate representation for the country's white minority will be abolished. The twenty white MPs and the ten senators will be replaced by members elected by the remaining eighty MPs, thereby obviating the need to hold new general elections. President's largely ceremonial position will be replaced by the establishment of an Executive Presidency.
July 1987	A British businessman, Richard Woodcroft and his Zimbabwean partner, Albert Dube, are released from prison fourteen months after their detention for allegedly aiding South African commandos to carry out a bombing raid on ANC offices in Harare.
July 1987	The Katigo Tea Estate near Mumtare is attacked by RENAMO rebels. They destroy property worth 37,500 Pounds Sterling.
Aug. 1987	RENAMO kill three elderly men in the Rushinga area.
19 Aug. 1987	A farmer and his wife are shot by dissidents. The Commercial Farmers' Union calls for a new government approach to security in Southern

Matabeleland area.

19 Aug. 1987	The House of Assembly MPs vote unanimously to abolish the seats in Parliament reserved for whites.
25 Aug. 1987	A tea estate is attacked by RENAMO rebels in the Chipige area. Several Zimbabwean soldiers are killed, and food items stolen. The Zimbabwe army captures four men.
26 Aug. 1987	A British businesman, Derrick Straw, is freed after fifteen months detention without charge. He was held on suspicion of aiding South African commandos.
27 Aug. 1987	A white farmer is killed by dissidents on his farm near Bulawayo.
Sept. 1987	Six whites are detained and accused of espionage for South Africa after one of them, Ivor Harding, is discovered driving into the country from South Africa with sophisticated surveillance equipment in his car.
17 Sept. 1987	Subversive documents are discovered at ZAPU offices in Bulawayo during a police raid, linking ZAPU with anti-government guerrillas in Matabeleland.
21 Sept. 1987	The government orders the closure of all ZAPU offices, accusing the party of conspiracy with anti-government dissidents. ZAPU leader Nkomo considers this action as a 'vendetta'.
Oct. 1987	British Prime Minister Thatcher meets Robert Mugabe in London. She promises an additional 15 million Pounds Sterling aid package.
Oct. 1987	A Zimbabwe-Cuba Friendship Association is launched.
12 Oct. 1987	The ZAPU member for Binga Francis Mukombwe is taken into custody on a charge of supporting dissidents.
13 Oct. 1987	A car bomb at a Harare shopping centre injures eighteen people and destroys five cars. South Africa is blamed for this incident, but South African authorities deny this allegation.
23 Oct. 1987	The twenty successful candidates elected to the House of Assembly to replace the twenty white MPs, are all members of the ruling ZANU. Eleven whites, mostly prominent business people, are among the newly elected MPs.
15 Nov. 1987	Jersey tea estate is attacked by RENAMO rebels. Five school pupils are killed with hatchets, and the ears of seven others are cut off. These are told to leave the estate 'as it belongs to Mozambique'.
26 Nov. 1987	In the Madzi area of north-eastern Zimbabwe, an elderly peasant couple and five young children are massacred by RENAMO guerrillas.
26 Nov. 1987	Sixteen white members of a Christian community are massacred on the Olive Tree and New Adams farms, south of Bulawayo. The group included two Americans and one British citizen.

27 Nov. 1987	Odile Eone Harington is found guilty of espionage for South Africa against the ANC and is sentenced to twenty-five years in jail.
30 Nov. 1987	RENAMO rebels attack a tea estate and burn down thirteen labourers' houses.
22 Dec. 1987	Prime Minister Mugabe and ZAPU leader Joashua Nkomo sign an agreement to merge their rival parties.
30 Dec. 1987	Robert Mugabe is declared Zimbabwe's first executive president.
31 Dec. 1987	The new Executive President, Robert Mugabe, is inaugurated into office for a six-year term. Seven heads of state attend the ceremony - from Uganda, Ethiopia, Angola, Botswana, Mozambique, Tanzania and Zambia.
Jan. 1988	John Austin and Neil Harper, senior customs officers in detention for two years, are freed unconditionally. They allegedly spied for South Africa.
2 Jan. 1988	Unity talks are consolidated by nominating Joshua Nkomo as a senior minister involved in overseeing rural development ministries. Two other ZAPU leaders become ministers: John Nkomo is nominated as the new Minister for Labour, Manpower and Social Welfare and Joseph Msika, the new Minister for Public Construction and Housing.
11 Jan. 1988	Two people are killed and some seriously injured by a car bomb which demolished a house in Bulawayo believed to be used by the ANC.
11 Jan. 1988	Following the car bomb explosion, thirteen whites and one black person are arrested in Bulawayo. South Africa is also accused of involvement by Home Affairs Minister Moven Mahachi.
21 Jan. 1988	The State of Emergency is renewed through a unanimous vote in Parliament. Nkomo's ZAPU party votes along with the governing ZANU Party. Since the unity agreement thirty-five people were killed by dissidents from July to December 1987 and RENAMO rebels carried out 101 attacks near the border with Mozambique.
Feb. 1988	Signs an agreement with China whereby the latter agrees to construct a training college at Chinhoyi. The cost will be borne equally by both countries.
5 Feb. 1988	Legal proceedings against Kevin Woods, Michael Smith and Rory Maguire start in Harare. They are accused of involvement in sabotage and attempted assassination and are said to have confessed to the charges.
Mar. 1988	Romanian Vice-President, Manea Maneseu, visits the country.
Mar. 1988	Soviet Deputy Minister, Vladimir Petrovsky, visits Harare.
Mar. 1988	A Zimbabwe-Nicaragua Friendship Association is launched aiming at promoting trade and cooperation.
13 Mar. 1988	Four Zimbabwe railway workers are killed RENAMO, about twelve miles from Mozambique's border post at Chicualacuala, working at the strategic railway line from Zimbabwe to the Maputo harbour.

Apr. 1988	The German Democratic Republic's Communist Party, signs an agreement with ZANU.
Apr. 1988	The Foreign Minister discloses that the country spent Z$29m. on military and humanitarian assistance to Mozambique.
2 Apr. 1988	At a special congress of Joshua Nkomo's ZAPU Party, the unity agreement with ZANU is ratified.
9 Apr. 1988	ZANU-PF also ratifies the unity agreement. Through the amalgamation with ZAPU, the ruling party controls all but one of the 100 seats in Parliament, making it a de-facto one-party state.
18 Apr. 1988	President Mugabe appoints Joshua Nkomo as one of two vice-presidents of the ruling ZANU Party on the country's eighth anniversary of independence.
27 May 1988	The main square in Harare, Cecil Square, is renamed African Unity Square by President Mugabe at a ceremony.
Apr. 1988	The City Observer newspaper is officially launched in Harare by Information Minister Witness Mangwende, who challenges the newspaper to inform, educate, entertain and provide facts on Council matters.
31 May 1988	A six-week amnesty for rebels ends. 113 men respond to the offer which aims at fortifying the unity agreement and ending dissident activity.
June 1988	A delegation of the Soviet Union's Communist Party visits Zimbabwe and signs a cooperation agreement with ZANU.
9 June 1988	Zimbabwe and Mozambique sign a military cooperation pact, aimed at consolidation of the armed forces.
28 June 1988	President Mugabe pledges that Zimbabwean troops will stay in Mozambique until trade routes to the sea are secure.
30 June 1988	South African commandos allegedly attempt to rescue five South African agents awaiting trial for bombing ANC targets. The rescue mission fails and the commandos escape. One of then, Denis Beahan is caught in Botswana and is returned to Zimbabwe. South Africa denies any involvement.
July 1988	President Robert Mugabe wins the Africa Prize for Leadership for the Sustainable End of Hunger for promoting Zimbabwean agriculture, especially among communal and small farmers.
July 1988	Signs a joint cooperation agreement with Cuba, aimed at enhancing South-South cooperation.
1 Aug. 1988	All espionage charges against five whites accused of operating for South Africa are withdrawn but the five remain in detention under the emergency laws.
Sept. 1988	Pope John Paul visits Zimbabwe and praises the efforts made to restore peace in Matabeleland.
Sept. 1988	The United States resumes its aid programme to Zimbabwe. $17 million will

be provided over two years to assist small farmers.

12 Oct. 1988	Three former members of Zimbabwean intelligence organizations are on trial for murder following a car bomb attack on an ANC refugee shelter which went wrong - the bomb detonated prematurely and killed the driver. The accused are Michael Smith, Phillip Conjwayo and Kevin Woods.
17 Oct. 1988	The three members tried for murder indicate in their statements the involvement of South African covert operations in Zimbabwe.
21 Oct. 1988	Former Secretary-General of ZANU, Edgar Tekere, is expelled from the party, but pledges to continue his crusade against government corruption.
Nov. 1988	The daily newspaper, 'The Chronicle', carries reports of ministers using their power to obtain cars for themselves and their friends from the state-owned motor assembly plant, Willowvale.
15 Nov. 1988	Kevin Woods, Michael Smith and Phillip Conjwayo are sentenced to death for the murder of a Zambian driver, who was killed in a bomb attack on the ANC.
Jan. 1989	President Mugabe establishes a three-member commission to investigate corruption allegations linked to the receipt of scarce cars by ministers and their friends from the Willowvale motor assembly plant, which is state-owned. The Chronicle Newspaper first drew public attention to these activities.
Jan. 1989	The twenty-three-year-old State of Emergency is renewed. Main reason given is the continuing border violence by RENAMO, which caused 420 incidents and led to ninety-three murders of Zimbabweans in the second half of 1988.
13 Jan. 1989	A defence agreeement is concluded with China, who is to supply $104.9 million air defence equipment to Zimbabwe.
Feb. 1989	Geoff Nyarota, editor of the Chronicle newspaper, is promoted to a non-writing post. His outspoken views echo a popular opinion that the socialist government is collaborating with the rich.
6 Feb. 1989	Deputy Sports Minister Charles Ndhlovu is acquitted of seventy-eight out of ninety-nine allegations of fraud and will stand trial on nine charges.
15 Feb. 1989	MP Byron Hove calls for the re-instatement of Geoff Nyarota to his former post as editor. He also expresses alarm at the curtailment of press freedom.
Mar. 1989	The UN High Commissioner for Refugees reports the presence of 166,000 Mozambiquan refugees, 200 South Africans and small numbers from other countries in Africa.
10 Mar. 1989	Defence Minister Enos Nkala announces his resignation after admitting that he has given false evidence to the Commission of Inquiry investigating the Willowvale Motor Industries affair. Junior Minister for Political Affairs, Frederick Shava also resigns.
24 Mar. 1989	President Mugabe condemns the tendency for `getting rich quickly' among

government and party officials and admits that the prestige of government and party leaders has never been so low.

29 Mar. 1989	British Prime Minister Thatcher talks with Robert Mugabe on possible change in South Africa. The latter remains unconvinced that sanctions will not bring change. Margaret Thatcher encourages dialogue with all sides.
12 Apr. 1989	Senior Minister for Political Affairs and administrative secretary of ZANU resigns from his post after a presidential inquiry revealed that he had helped friends to buy cars directly from the Willowvale State assembly plant.
14 Apr. 1989	Three further ministers resign due to the 'Willowgate' corruption scandal: Higher Education Minister Dzingai Mutumbuka, Industry and Technology Minister Callistus Ndlovu and Provincial Governor for Matabeleland-North Jacob Mudenda.
20 Apr. 1989	Former Minister Maurice Nyagumbo dies of poisoning. According to police the death is treated as suicide. This follows the 'Willowgate's' corruption scandal. He is buried in Hero's Acre.
30 Apr. 1989	Edgar Tekere launches a new party, the Zimbabwe Unity Movement (ZUM) in opposition to the President's plans to establish a one-party state. It plans to restore power to the tribal chiefs.
June 1989	President Mugabe announces his intention to abolish the Senate. The forty seats are expected to be added to the 100 House of Assembly seats.
June 1989	The Zimbabwe-USSR Intergovernmental Commission is established. Joint ventures in gold-mining and processing as well are envisaged. The USSR agrees to send ten specialist doctors to Zimbabwe.
8-12 June 1989	The Archbishop of Canterbury Robert Runcie arrives in Harare for a four-day pastoral tour.
9 June 1989	Three white Zimbabweans - Kevin Woods, Barry Bawden and Michael Smith are sentenced to forty years in jail for participating in bombing two ANC buildings in Harare.
28 June 1989	Dennis Beahan, a former British soldier, is found guilty of terrorism and sabotage by the High Court. He is accused of leading a failed attempt to rescue five Zimbabwean saboteurs, amongst them Woods, Bawden and Smith, from a Harare jail.
6 July 1989	ZANU wins a key by-election against Edgar Tekere's new Zimbabwe Unity Movement (ZUM). The latter has been severely restricted in its campaigning. The government prevented it from holding rallies and advertising on the state-controlled media.
6 July 1989	President Mugabe pardons Frederick Shava, who is jailed on perjury charges in the 'Willowgate' affair. This raises an outrage as it negated ZANU's election campaign message that the Party was taking a strong stand against corruption.
18 July 1989	A stormy public meeting addressed by Edgar Tekere, leader of the new ZUM Party takes place at the University of Zimbabwe. The riot squad

moves in and threatens to break up the meeting under Zimbabwe's emergency regulations. Tekere appeals to students to do nothing that can justify government accusations that ZUM is a threat to peace, but rioting and stone-throwing at the police occur. No journalists from Zimbabwe are present, and no reports appear in the local media.

Aug. 1989   An agreement is signed with Cuba who will supply teachers to Zimbabwe. An exchange in expertise in technology is also agreed upon.

End Aug. 1989   A possible partnership between the all-white Conservative Alliance of Zimbabwe (CAZ) and Edgar Tekere's Zimbabwe Unity Movement (ZUM) is discussed when Edgar Tekere, Gerald Smith and Keith Borrows of CAZ meet.

Sept. 1989   Students stage a demonstration against the new investment code, the banning of ZUM campaign rallies and various other grievances.

Oct. 1989   Provincial elections are held. ZANU and ZAPU combine forces.

Oct. 1989   Morgan Tsvangirai the General Secretary of the Zimbabwean Congress of Trade Unions is detained for criticizing the closure of the university. Held under the emergency laws he is acquitted by the High Court, but is immediately rearrested, this time on charges of being a South African agent.

4 Oct. 1989   Students of the University of Zimbabwe riot when two student leaders are arrested for publishing a document critical of the government. This leads to the closure of the campus.

23 Oct. 1989   The University of Zimbabwe reopens for examinations but thirteen students detained during riots are still in custody having been refused bail.

end Oct. 1989   Four by-elections for vacancies in the National Assembly are held. ZUM'S campaign in the constituency of Kariba is curtailed by the detention of eleven activists by the Central Intelligence Organization. Some ZUM party workers are severely beaten, allegedly by ZANU youths. The by-elections are all won by ZANU. All opposition candidates, except one, lose their deposits.

9 Nov. 1989   A confrontation between the government and the judiciary erupts when Chief Justice Mtfasa issues a statement criticizing the speaker, Didimus Mutasa for holding the Supreme Court in contempt and his disregard for the rule of law. This crisis arises from a Supreme Court award of 1,500 Pounds Sterling to Ian Smith for his illegal suspension without pay from the House of Assembly in April 1987. The speaker's reaction is that he will not pay a cent.

14 Nov. 1989   A conscription scheme starting in 1990 is announced. All Zimbabwean males between eighteen and thirty years are to register. A period of six months military training will be followed by six months of non-military training and a further unspecified period.

22 Nov. 1989   Minister of Justice Emmerson Munangagwa informs Parliament that President Mugabe and the cabinet have studied the Supreme Court decision involving the suspension of Ian Smith from the House of Assembly. They are satisfied that the judgement is sound and correct.

22 Nov. 1989	Enos Nkala, former Minister of Defence, is sentenced to a fine of 25,760 Pounds Sterling for vehicle racketeering.
23 Nov. 1989	Parliament adopts a Constitutional Amendment Act which will empower the President to introduce a one-party state and seize private land without compensation. The dissenting vote is that of Edgar Tekere.
26 Nov. 1989	Opposition to the President's aim to transform the democracy into a one-party state is expressed by seven Zimbabwean Roman Catholic bishops.
5 Dec. 1989	Somalia and Zimbabwe establish diplomatic relations at ambassadorial level.
15 Dec. 1989	The Zimbabwe Unity Movement (ZUM) of Edgar Tekere releases its manifesto. It calls for a multi-party state, a free market economy, two legislative chambers and a division of duties between a ceremonial presidency and an executive prime minister.
19 Dec. 1989	A congress is held by the newly united ZANU and ZAPU with a single control committee and politburo. A draft constitution has been approved by the leaders of the two parties. It states that the establishment of a one-party state on Marxist-Leninist principles will be sought.
19 Jan. 1990	The Ministries of Trade and Commerce and of Industry and Technology merge into a single ministry headed by Bernard Chidzero. The Parastatals Commission formed eighteen months ago is disbanded.
15 Feb. 1990	A proclamation is published which announces 28 and 29 March as the dates for simultaneous presidential and parliamentary elections.
23 Feb. 1990	Edgar Tekere, ZUM's leader is to run for president, the party announces. The Conservative Alliance of Zimbabwe (CAZ) will contest the election in alliance with ZUM.
28-30 Mar. 1990	Following a week of violence, voters go to the polls to choose a president and parliamentarians.
2 Apr. 1990	President Mugabe is declared the winner of the presidential election, defeating Edgar Tekere by a ratio of five to one. ZANU wins all but four seats in Parliament. ZUM fails to make a breakthrough but takes about 20% of the national vote.
6 Apr. 1990	ZUM leader, Edgar Tekere, challenges the fairness of the election, after rejecting the findings of the Electoral Commission. He alleges that four of his supporters were killed in Harare and that there have been administrative irregularities.
9 Apr. 1990	President Mugabe announces his new cabinet, which has hardly changed since independence. The former ZAPU party of Joshua Nkomo has only two cabinet posts apart from Nkomo's vice-presidency. Three white ministers are appointed to largely technical ministries - transport, health and mining.
May 1990	Junior nurses strike, nearly forcing health services to close down.
2 May 1990	President Mugabe promises that the government will amend the constitution

to accelerate and simplify the redistribution of land.

18 May 1990	Minister for Justice, Legal and Parliamentary Affairs, Muanngazwe, announces that farmers whose land was compulsorily bought will no longer be paid compensation on foreign currency remittable abroad.
30 May 1990	Students at the University of Zimbabwe call for the formation of a mass democratic movement to campaign against the one-party state establishment.
31 May 1990	Ernest Kadungure, Minister of State for Political Affairs, responsible for youth, dies.
31 May - 5 June 1990	A Chinese educational delegation visits Zimbabwe and commits China to assist the Zimbabwe Technical College in building a laboratory for its Civil Engineering Department, and in despatching Chinese teachers to both the College and the University.
5 June 1990	The government invokes emergency powers in an attempt to stop a strike by teachers who demand pay increases. These are joined by government mechanics, petrol attendants and students. The teachers are ordered back to work and threatened that those who fail to comply will lose their position.
6 June 1990	Striking teachers demonstrating outside parliament are dispersed by riot police using tear gas. The strike is declared illegal under the law which bars strikes in essential services.
20 June 1990	The government dismisses 1000 teachers.
2 July 1990	President Mugabe reaffirms his commitment to socialism and a one-party state.
18 July 1990	Finance Minister Chidzero announces that the government will allow market forces to direct the course of economic activities. Formerly, the government was guided by socialist principles.
25 July 1990	The State of Emergency expires, thereby sweeping powers end such as detention without trial, which was first instituted in 1965, when UDI was declared.
25 July 1990	Zimbabwe's last political prisoner, Leslie Johannes Lesia, is freed. Allegedly a South African spy, he was held without trial since September 1987. He is deported to South Africa.
26 July 1990	President Mugabe announces a general amnesty to mark the country's tenth anniversary of independence. These include 200 former guerrillas who were jailed after an insurgency campaign in Matabeleland.
2 Aug. 1990	The plan by President Mugabe to establish a one-party state meets overwhelming Politburo opposition. Single-party rule is supported by only five of the twenty-six member Politburo.
Nov. 1990	A constitutional amendment bill is published. It proposes to permit flogging and hanging. The bill sends shock waves through both the legal and the white commercial farmers' communities.

2 Nov. 1990	Odile Harington sentenced and jailed in 1987 for twenty-five years for spying against the ANC is released and returned to South Africa.
Dec. 1990	Constitutional changes gives government the right to acquire privately-owned land at a 'fair' price to be paid within a reasonable time. Formerly, it stipulated that the price should be adequate and 'paid promptly'.
Dec. 1990	Zimbabwean troops retreat from Mozambique to positions agreed to in Rome by the Mozambican government and RENAMO.
3 Dec. 1990	Former Chief Justice Enoch Dumbutshena slams government proposals to amend the bill of rights. He describes the proposed changes as retrogressive and calls on the government to reconsider the step.
Jan. 1991	The Economic Structural Adjustment Programme (ESAP) is launched to revive the country's flagging economy, reduce its fiscal debt, and to liberalize imports.
11 Jan. 1991	Agriculture Minister Mangwende, informs the white commercial farmers that the issue of additional land transfers to blacks is not negotiable.
Mid-Jan. 1991	President Mugabe announces in Lagos that he has abandoned his plans for a one-party state. His plan met with stiff opposition, and he is bowing to majority opinion.
16 Jan. 1991	President Mugabe completes a tour of West Africa. He visited Nigeria, Senegal and Ghana. After his visit to Senegal, he announces that the regional integration of Africa should be a matter of urgency. By the year 2000 an economic community at continental level should be established.
28 Feb. 1991	Foreign Ministers from Cameroon and Zimbabwe establish diplomatic relations at ambassadorial level.
22 Apr. 1991	The President meets for the first time since shortly after independence, an official from South Africa - Desmond Krogh of the Reserve Bank.
May 1991	Former Ethiopian Head of State, Mengistu Haile Mariam, is granted asylum by Zimbabwe.
13 June 1991	Assistance by Zimbabwe to Angola after the ceasefire is promised by Zimbabwean Industry and Commerce Minister Kangai. Food and clothing will be donated, as well as logistic assistance for army integration training.
Mid-June 1991	Leader of ZUM is dismissed by his colleagues as president of the main opposition after suspending some members unconstitutionally and rejected a new constitution for the party.
22 June 1991	ZANU-PF decides to abandon the ideologies of Marxism, Leninism and scientific socialism.
Aug. 1991	The Tangwena tribe is evicted from Forestry Commission land that they claim belonged to their ancestors.
25 Jan. 1992	Veteran nationalist leader, Ndabaningi Sithole, returns to Zimbabwe after

spending seven years of self-imposed exile at the Heritage Foundation, Washington, D.C. His return generates excitement and he draws a few thousand supporters to a rally. The government threatens his arrest because of his support for RENAMO rebels, against whom Zimbabwe troops have been deployed, but he moves about freely in Harare.

27 Jan. 1992   Sally Mugabe, wife of the President and member of the ZANU-PF Central Committee and Politburo dies, aged fifty-eight.

Mar. 1992   Security forces increase controls on the country's eastern border with Mozambique as the number of refugees surges to approximately 400 per day. The chances of RENAMO infiltration have increased significantly.

6 Mar. 1992   A national agricultural disaster is declared due to the ongoing drought.

19 Mar. 1992   Parliament passes a bill to nationalize some 5.5m hectares of the country's profitable white farms with little compensation and no right of appeal. The controversial bill is rejected by white farmers who argue that they produce most of the country's food, earn the bulk of export income and are the country's largest private employer.

Apr. 1992   Combat veterans of the former ZANLA and ZIPRA guerrilla armies accuse President Mugabe of having betrayed the aims of ZANU-PF and of the liberation struggle.

21 Apr. 1992   At a meeting in Pretoria, Botswana, Malawi, Mozambique, Zambia and Zimbabwe agree on a joint project to oversee the movement of millions of tons of grain due to arrive at South African ports.

May 1992   Students demonstrating for increased grants clash with riot police on the Harare campus, resulting in the hospitalization of eight injured students. Students in Bulawayo also demonstrate.

1 May 1992   The President fails to attend May Day celebrations for the first time in twelve years. The President of the Zimbabwe Congress of Trade Unions, Gibson Sibanda, describes the depletion of the country's food reserves as 'a national crime' and calls for the removal from office of those responsible.

30 May 1992   The Forum for Democratic Reform is launched, led by lawyers, economists, businessmen and former judges. It plans to broaden political debate and build a credible alternative to the ruling ZANU-PF Party. However, it does not purport to be a political party, but rather a think-tank.

June 1992   The University of Zimbabwe expels its 10,000 students after a month long boycott of classes and demonstrations for higher grants. Students will have to re-apply for admittance.

9 June 1992   Information and Telecommunication Minister, Victoria Chitepo, resigns.

13 June 1992   A Trade Union march in Harare is banned by police who break up the demonstration against the labour relations bill with rifles, tear gas and batons.

July 1992   A number of Zimbabwean opposition parties from the pre-independence era unite in a coalition. This includes the Rev N. Sithole and his

ZANU-Ndonga Party, the UANC, Edgar Tekere's ZUM and the Conservative Alliance of Zimbabwe (CAZ). Their aim is to form a united front dedicated to removing Mugabe's government from office.

3 July 1992	President Mugabe announces a cabinet reshuffle cutting the number of ministries from twenty-one to eighteen.
11 Aug. 1992	A Zimbabwean student at the Patrice Lumumba University in Moscow is shot dead by a Russian police officer. This leads to rioting by African students.
25 Aug. 1992	Zimbabwe cancels the purchase of MIG-29 aircraft from Russia. Reduced tension is Southern Africa is given as the reason.
1 Sept. 1992	Parliament approves a bill granting government funding to political parties with at least fifteen seats in Parliament. This opens the way for the ruling ZANU-PF party to use government funds for its day-to-day operations. The bill is at variance with calls by the World Bank for drastic cuts in state spending.
Oct. 1992	The Forum for Democratic Reform announces its new political status as a political party.
15 Oct. 1992	A high level military and government delegation visits Maputo to discuss the withdrawal of Zimbabwean troops from the eastern border with Mozambique.
15 Feb. 1993	The Zimbabwean and United States troops launch their first joint training manoeuvres. Twenty-six soldiers from Fort Bragg are spending forty-five days with a Zimbabwean commando battalion.
19 Feb. 1993	The Supreme Court overturns a High Court ruling which allowed a Zimbabwean, citizen Terrence O'Hare, to return to the country after emigrating to South Africa. He retained his British citizenship, but will have to apply to immigrate if he wants to return.
28 Mar. 1993	Two main opposition parties, the Forum for Democratic Reform and the Open Forum merge to form the Forum Party of Zimbabwe. The parties' members comprise prominent intellectuals, church leaders, businessmen, and white liberal politicians. The party's leader is Enoch Dumbutshena, who explains that the Forum Party wants to replace dictatorial tendencies with democracy and promote an unfettered market economy.
Apr. 1993	Thousands of Zimbabwean troops withdraw from Mozambique where they initially protected trade routes, but later assisted Mozambique's FRELIMO.
May 1993	The Agriculture Ministry selects seventy farms for resettlement. Forty-nine farmers lodge objections; twenty-two are told that the designation notices have been revoked. Twenty-seven farms will be confiscated against the farmers' will.
May 1993	A conference of African Police Chiefs, organized by Interpol pledges to crack down on drug trafficking and on the dumping of toxic waste in their countries. Closer cooperation between African police forces is proposed.

May 1993	Emmanuel Magoche, leader of the Democratic Party which broke away from ZUM two years previously, resigns.
12 May 1993	Defence Minister Mahachi declares that his country is prepared to launch military attacks into neighbouring countries in pursuit of insurgents. Rumours have it that a Zimbabwe rebel group, Chimwenje trained by RENAMO, are ready to attack Zimbabwe.
24 May 1993	It is announced by Defence Minister Mahachi that the army and airforce are to be merged, resulting in 10,000 job losses.
June 1993	ZUM chairman, Patrick Komayi, resigns from the party and joins the new Forum Party. Edgar Tekere is left as the only founder member.
July 1993	The Peoples' Militia is dissolved, with a loss of 12,000 jobs. This paramilitary unit guarded vital installations. Due to budget constraints as well as improved security and political stability, the unit is no longer needed.
13 Sept. 1993	Egypt and Zimbabwe sign a protocol for military cooperation.
Oct. 1993	Three whites given five years on death row for blowing up an ANC residence, are reprieved. They are Michael Smith, Kevin Woods and Phillip Conjwayo.
28 Oct. 1993	Grassroots conferences by ZANU are announced to calm the discord in the party. The unpopularity originates in the country's economic reform programme, leading to soaring food prices (42.5%).
5 Dec. 1993	The Forum Party claims that Edgar Tekere should have won thirty-three seats, but that the election was rigged. The voters' roll is also not in order, the Party states.
Jan. 1994	Draft legislation is published which will tighten the immigration laws and change the qualifying period for resident status.
17 Jan. 1994	Industry and Commerce Minister, Christopher Ushowokunze, is killed in a road accident.
27 Feb. 1994	The Ethiopian Ambassador to Zimbabwe, Fantahun Haile Mikael, announces that he has formally lodged documents for the repatriation of Mengistu Haile Mariam, who has been granted asylum in Zimbabwe. He is wanted in Addis Ababa for crimes against humanity. Foreign Minister Sharmuyarira reacts sharply against the Ambassador's public announcement.
End Feb. 1994	Peaceful public demonstrations are legal and a ban on them breaches constitutional rights, according to a Supreme Court ruling. This follows a challenge by six trade union leaders, who led a public demonstration after police refused permission.
Mar. 1994	The first beneficiary of the campaign to seize white-owned farms is Witness Mangwende, the Cabinet Minister who promoted the controversial bill. Resettlement authorities planned to settle thirty-three peasant families on the farm.

Mar. 1994	The opposition Democratic Party leader D. Gomo, accuses the ruling ZANU-PF Party of planning to rig the 1995 elections and demands that the election process should be managed by an independent body. The government refuses to accede to the demands, saying that adequate safeguards would ensure that the election will be free and fair.
6-10 Mar. 1994	The President pays a state visit to Botswana. He discusses the problem of illegal border crossings and believes that additional border posts and involving local leaders and villages next to the Botswana-Zimbabwe boundary could curb the problem. This he attributed to unemployment and bureaucracy in the Zimbabwean immigration department.
Mar. - Apr. 1994	The voter registration campaign for the 1995 general election is met with apathy - only a small fraction has registered. The main reason appears to be opposition to the ruling party with no alternative, as the opposition parties seem to have diminished.
Apr. 1994	President Mugabe decides to launch an inquiry into the ninety-eight leases on state farms to black farmers. In a radio interview he announces that all leases of state land to individuals will be cancelled, as it has been acquired to resettle landless peasants.
27 May 1994	President Mugabe maintains that his political opponents are letting themselves be used by whites, turning again to the race issue as elections approach.
28 May 1994	Three hundred Forum Party members meet, representing five provinces and pass a vote of no confidence in its leader, Enoch Dumbutshena. Themba Dlodlo, the party's Secretary-General, is appointed acting president.
June 1994	Malawian President, Bakili Muluzi, visits Zimbabwe. President Mugabe praises the new Malawian government's commitment to national reconciliation.
5 June 1994	Vice-President Nkomo warns undesirable elements in the white community to leave Zimbabwe before it is too late. He reacts to reports that a group of whites in Bulawayo plan to march into the city in ox-drawn wagons in August to mark the defeat of the Ndebeles by white settlers a century ago.
25 June 1994	Edgar Tekere, leader of the opposition party ZUM, proposes the establishment of an army to counter possible attacks of the ZANU-PF party in the run-up to the elections. Opposition leaders attending the Zimrights consultative conference, dissociate themselves from the idea, but urge their members to defend themselves should they be attacked for holding legitimate rallies.
28 June 1994	At the opening of Parliament, the President announces that the country's armed forces will be reduced from 50,000 to 35,000. This is made possible by the improved political situation in South Africa and the return of peace in Mozambique. Demobilization will be undertaken in stages.
July 1994	About 3.4 million Zimbabweans out of a total population of 10 million have registered to vote in the general elections planned for 1995.
16 Aug. 1994	Robert Mugabe addresses the new South African Parliament - the first

African leader to do so. He refers to the rising black expectations which will put pressure on the RDP.

18 Aug. 1994   South Africa and Zimbabwe sign a comprehensive agreement on judicial cooperation.

Late Aug. 1994   Ethiopian Foreign Minister, Seyoum Mesfin, visits Zimbabwe. He states that former leader, Mariam, will be tried in Ethiopia for crimes against humanity. He does not discuss extradition with Zimbabwean officials as the matter is handled by Ethiopian courts.

Sept. 1994   A merger of ZUM, the United Front and several Forum Party of Zimbabwe members, is announced. The new Party which will retain the name ZUM, will have three leaders, ZUM co-leaders, Abel Muzorewa and Edgar Tekere. The third name is to be announced.

1 Sept. 1994   Sudanese Foreign Minister Hussein Suleiman Aba Saleh, visits Zimbabwe. He is satisfied with the Zimbabwean government's denial of allegations that it is supporting rebels in South Sudan.

22 Sept. 1994   President Mugabe states that ZANU-PF will continue redefining its socialist ideology in a manner consistent with its culture and historical experience.

17 Oct. 1994   A break between the factions of the newly formed opposition merger is reported.   The new United Party will have only one leader - Abel Muzorewa. ZUM will continue as a separate party.

21 Oct. 1994   Students create havoc by breaking windows and chasing guests from restaurants as they launch a campaign against alleged white racism. They have earlier been denied access to some clubs and restaurants.

Nov. 1994   South Africa will extend the electrified fence on its border with Zimbabwe by 108 km at a cost of R20 million.

4 Dec. 1994   The United Party declares a merger with the Forum Party for Democracy. The new party will be called United Parties and Bishop Muzorewa is its acting leader.

17 Dec. 1994   A new party, called the Federal Party, is established in Bulawayo. It supports federalism as an answer to ending the tribal domination imposed on Matabeleland by the ruling Shona-oriented ZANU-PF.

Jan. 1995   The Zimbabwe Federal Party states that it wants the country divided into five federal provinces, each led by a prime minister, as follows:- Mashonaland, Manicaland, Masvingo, Midlands and Matabeleland. The party intends to participate in the elections.

16 Jan. 1995   Kumbirai Kangai, ZANU-PF chairman of Manicaland Province, causes an outrage among civil servants when he suggests that all those who did not vote for the ruling party should resign, since they are also working for ZANU-PF if they work for the government.

Feb. 1995   Mines Minister Eddison Zvogbo challenges Mugabe's ruling that the two Vice-Presidents shall be entitled to unopposed party nomination for any seat of their choice. He is backed by Youth Secretary Josiah Tungamiri, who, however, backs down when Mugabe rules that Vice-President Muzende is entitled to an unopposed seat.

Feb. 1995

With elections to be held in March, Mugabe's authority is being challenged as ZANU-PF constituency after constituency rejects candidates proposed by Mugabe and his associates in Harare.

4 Feb. 1995

Bases of Zimbabwean guerrillas are allegedly discovered in Mozambique's Manica Province under the command of ZUM leader Edgar Tekere. The matter is being investigated by the Mozambique Defence Armed Forces Supreme Command. Tekere could launch a civil war against his country from Mozambican territory.

Mar. 1995

A report that Ethiopia's deposed Head of State, Mengistu Haile Mariam, has been granted citizenship by Zimbabwe is denied.

Mar. 1995

The United States proposes the supply of two Hercules C130 transporter aircraft to Zimbabwe as support in the country's peacekeeping operations in Africa.

Mar. 1995

The ZANU-PF Party stands unopposed in fifty-two of 120 constituencies, thereby being almost assured of winning the election.

11 Apr. 1995

In a 54% voter turnout, President Mugabe's ZANU-PF wins the general election for the fourth consecutive time. The party receives more than 82% of the vote and 118 seats. The ZANU (Ndonga) Party, led by N. Sithole, is the sole opposition. The Forum Party does not win any seats. The United Party and ZUM boycott the elections. Opposition parties are handicapped because they did not qualify for financial support from the state.

20 Apr. 1995

President Mugabe announces a new cabinet. A prominent businessman, Ariston Chambati, is appointed as Finance Minster, replacing Bernard Chidzero who is ill. The number of Ndebele ministers is doubled.

May 1995

Three senior staff of the Financial Gazette face criminal defamation charges over their report that President Mugabe allegedly married at a secret ceremony over Easter.

16 May 1995

The United States officially protests to the Zimbabwean government over the arrest of three executives connected to the Financial Gazette on a charge of criminal defamation.

20 May 1995

President Mugabe visits the United States at the invitation of President Clinton. He appeals for increased aid by industrialized countries to Africa.

June 1995

Commander-in-Chief General Charles Boyd, Commander of the US forces in Europe visits Southern African countries including Zimbabwe.

July 1995

The University of Zimbabwe is closed for a week after students protested against alleged discrepancies in subsidy payments.

Aug. 1995

Mozambican Interior Minister Antonio states that armed Zimbabwean dissidents, called Chimwenges, are active in the Mozambican Manica Province. They owe allegiance to opposition leader Edgar Tekere, and operate from former RENAMO bases.

1 Aug. 1995	Violence erupts at the University of Zimbabwe campus when riot police fire tear gas at 1000 demonstrating students who demand that the Council lift the suspension of sixteen student leaders representative of the workers' committee and a law lecturer.

4 Aug. 1995   At a speech delivered at the Harare Book Fair before a distinguished audience, including human rights activists, Robert Mugabe states that homosexuals are sodomists and perverts. Earlier, the government had demanded that the stand of the homosexual rights movement at the Book Fair be closed down.

5 Aug. 1995   Seventy United States Congressmen protest over Robert Mugabe's stance on homosexuals. The President's reaction is that foreigners should not meddle with Zimbabwean affairs.

11 Aug. 1995   President Robert Mugabe urges members of the public to arrest homosexuals, as they reduce themselves `to the status of beasts'.

17 Aug. 1995   The accused three senior staff members of the Financial Gazette - the publisher and two editors - are fined 870 Pounds Sterling over a report that President Mugabe had married his typist.

20 Sept. 1995   Defence Minister Moven Mahachi denies any knowledge of the existence of the group of armed Zimbabwean dissidents known as Chimwenges, who are allegedly preparing a military incursion into Zimbabwe from former RENAMO bases in Manicaland, Mozambique.

8 Oct. 1995   Finance Minister Dr. Ariston Chambati dies. His portfolio is handled by Trade Minister Herbert Murerwa.

9 Oct. 1995   South Korea opens an embassy in Harare.

20 Oct. 1995   Opposition politician Ndabaningi Sithole is granted bail of Z$100,000 when charged of an alleged plot to assassinate President Mugabe.

31 Oct. 1995   Independents and ZANU-PF dissidents win fifteen local government election seats.

11 Nov. 1995   A peaceful march, called to protest against police brutality, is disrupted by ZANU-PF youths, with subsequent rioting. Violence blames the Zim Rights Movement, but the human rights organization denies any involvement in the rioting and condemns the destruction of property.

4 Nov. 1995   An assassination attempt is made on the exiled former dictator Mengistu Haile Mariam. Two Ethiopians are subsequently arrested.

28 Nov. 1995   Outspoken opponent of President Mugabe, Margaret Dango, wins a by-election from ZANU-PF. The election was ordered by the High Court after Ms. Dongo's complaint that she lost the general election through rigging and irregularities.

17 Jan. 1996   Bishop Abel Muzorewa announces that he will challenge President Robert Mugabe in forthcoming elections.

18 Jan. 1996	It is reported that a new political party, the All Zimbabwe Democratic Alliance, has been established. The party is to be launched on the 27 and 28 January 1996.
Feb. 1996	South Africa and Zimbabwe agree in principle to waive visa requirements for civil servants on official duty. Business visitors will be issued with multiple entry visas valid for a year. Ministers also agree that Zimbabwean `border jumpers' should be treated with respect by the police.
5 Apr. 1996	The ZANU-PF party expresses concern at growing voter apathy, as just over 30% of voters cast their ballot in the presidential election in March.
10 Apr. 1996	Rural Development Minister admits that twenty-five farms have been bought for resettlement, but that the necessary infrastructure can not be paid for. This is essential before 271 families can be settled on the farms.
May 1996	Rumours that Vice-President Joshua Nkoma has died in hospital in Cape Town are denied by government officials. It has been re-affirmed that he has been re-admitted to hospital as a private patient.
9 May 1996	President Mugabe appoints a new Finance Minister - Herbert Murerwa, a portfolio which he holds in an acting capacity since the death of former Finance Minister Ariston Chambati. Some other changes in the Cabinet are announced. Press comments note that in defiance to pressure to reduce government spending, two more cabinet posts are created, taking it to fifty.
June 1996	It is reported that Z$83m. are needed to clear an estimated two million anti-personnel mines and 12,000 above surface mines along its borders. The process is being delayed by a shortage of equipment.
12 June 1996	Zimbabwean and Mozambican authorities announce that they will co-operate against the Zimbabwean Chimwenje dissidents who operate against both countries out of bases in central Mozambique.
13 June 1996	It is reported that Vice-President Joshua Nkomo, leader of the minority Ndebele group, will retire as one of the country's two Vice-Presidents because of ill health.
July 1996	Twenty-one armoured personnel carriers are acquired from France at a price of Z$30m.
10 July 1996	The problem of the Chimwenje dissidents is being discussed at a tripartite meeting between Zimbabwe, Malawi and Mozambique. The dissidents have moved their base closer to Zimbabwe and might plan to launch an offensive against Zimbabwe. Land mines, which recently were detonated by a bulldozer belonging to the Italian consortium Italia-2000 might have been planted by the Chimwenjes. Cooperation between the Mozambican and Zimbabwean authorities is reiterated.
19 July 1996	The Defence Minister welcomes the United States Third Special Forces at One Commando barracks. Joint military exercises are planned.
Aug. 1996	The Botswana Immigration Department announces that more than 14,000 illegal Zimbabwean immigrants have been repatriated.

Aug. 1996	Opposition ZANU-Ndonga leader Ndabaningi Sithole, faces allegations of plotting to kill President Mugabe and to destabalize Zimbabwe with the aid of the Chimwenjes. He is remanded to 10 September. The trial will be on 4 November.
early Aug. 1996	Seven alleged members of Chimwenje are sentenced. They comprise two Zimbabwe and five Mozambicans and are charged with 'mercenarism and armed rebellion'. The two Zimbabweans are sentenced to immediate extradition to Zimbabwe.
17 Aug. 1996	President Mugabe married his former secretary Grace Marufu and mother of his two children, during an extravagant ceremony.
27 Aug. 1996	Civil servants strike, demanding salary increases of up to 60%. Workers defy the threats of the government while union leaders urge them to maintain the work stoppage. The strike, in its sixth day, has resulted in the closure of the Zambia-Zimbabwe border at the Victoria Falls, leaving scores of tourists and travellers stranded.
Sept. 1996	Concern is expressed over arbitrary amendments to the constitution by the ruling ZANU-PF party. Since 1980, thirteen amendments have been made, such as reversing Supreme Court rulings, where the government has lost. The latest amendment imposes strict regulations on foreign spouses, who will no longer get automatic citizenship.
Sept. 1996	During a six-nation tour of sub-Saharan Africa Iranian President Rafsanjani visits Zimbabwe. A joint communique calls for a just international economic order and for increased south-south cooperation.
Oct. 1996	Zimbabwe denies that it produces land mines, as alleged by the International Red Cross Society and the UN Humanitarian Land Mine Data Base.
28 Oct. 1996	It is reported that the ruling ZANU-PF party has dropped Marxism-Leninism as a ruling principle. The government adopted IMF market-oriented guidelines in 1990.
Nov. 1996	President Mugabe is to establish a commission that will oversee the end of the state-controlled Zimbabwe Broadcasting Corporation's monopoly. Recommendations for the drafting of a national broadcasting commission are to be made, which will allow private radio and television stations.
Dec. 1996	The strength of the Zimbabwean army has been reduced from 50,000 to 40,000 through a campaign of early retirement.
early Dec. 1996	The fourteenth amendment to the Constitution becomes law. It removes the right of foreigners married to Zimbabwean citizens to have an automatic right to live in the country.
5 Dec. 1996	Education Minister Edmund Garwe resigns after exam papers are leaked at the school where his daughter is enrolled.
9 Dec. 1996	In an interview, President Mugabe dismisses calls from within his ruling party for constitutional change, including a law that will limit his presidency. He has ruled the country since 1960.

22 Dec. 1996	Mrs Sinqobile Mabhena becomes the first woman chief of the Ndebele tribe. This status is bestowed on her at a controversial ceremony.
Jan. 1997	It is reported that Zimbabwe's refugee population has decreased from over 200,000 to about 2400, as most refugees were repatriated to Mozambique and South Africa since the return of peace in the region.
24 Jan. 1997	A North Korean diplomat is caught at the Harare International Airport while attempting to smuggle ivory. There is a long history of incidents in which North Korean officials have smuggled ivory out of the country. This causes embarrassment to President Mugabe, who regards the North Korean government, one of the last Communist regimes, as one of its allies.
31 Jan. 1997	Denmark and Zimbabwe sign a memorandum of understanding on peace-keeping operations, which will allow the trade of skills and technology and will promote the training of officers in Denmark.
11 Feb. 1997	The Supreme Court rules that controversial legislation giving the President sweeping powers to dismiss executives and take control of charity or private associations is unconstitutional. This ruling revokes the 1995 Private Voluntary Organizations Act.
mid Feb. 1997	Christian fundamentalists establish a group called Operation Mobilisation to counter alleged plans to transform the country into an Islamic state. It claims that in exchange for trade and investment the government has allowed Islamic countries to promote their religion.
late Feb. 1997	South Africa and Zimbabwe sign a formal defence cooperation agreement in Pretoria.
25 Feb. 1997	Police are investigating allegations that former President Canaan Banana forced an aide to commit homosexual acts. The case causes embarrassment to President Mugabe, who is vehemently anti-homosexual.
30 Mar. 1997	It is reported that South Africa has deported 14,600 Zimbabweans who were illegally staying in South Africa.
Apr. 1997	Eight Roman Catholic bishops agree to suppress a damning 280-page report documenting over 7,000 atrocities committed by government troops in Matabeleland in the 1980s.
Apr. 1997	Press reports and allegations in parliament claim that the War Veterans Compensation Fund has been 'looted' by cabinet ministers, MPs and ZANU-PF connected persons. More than half of the 22.5 million pounds sterling has been claimed. The government intends to create another fund, to pay political detainees from the Rhodesian era.
May 1997	Agriculture Minister Denis Norman resigns from active politics, leaving the Minister of Health, Timothy Stamp, as the only white member of the Cabinet.
May 1997	A Chinese delegation discusses the possibility of military cooperation with the Minister of Defence and Chief of Staff.
May 1997	5000 soldiers have been retrenched from the Zimbabwean army as part of

a plan to reduce the 40,000 strong defence force by one quarter.

May 1997   A report entitled: Breaking the silence, on atrocities committed in Matabeleland by government forces in the 1980s and compiled by Zimbabwe's Legal Resources Foundation and the Catholic Commission for Justice and Peace, is leaked to Zimbabwe's independent press, despite the Catholic Bishops' agreement to suppress it temporarily. Copies also find their way to South Africa and the United Kingdom. President Mugabe attacks the report, but Amnesty International urges him to accept responsibility for 'crimes against humanity' in Matabeleland.

May 1997   Zimbabwe's Defence Minister Mahachi rules out war with neighbouring Zambia over two islands in the Zambezi River. Should the dispute remain unresolved, it will be submitted for international arbitration.

15 May 1997   The government bans the manufacture, use and transportation of land mines. It will also not allow the use of its territory as a transit point.

late May 1997   Two white South Africans are questioned by Zimbabwean police about a suspected plot to assassinate presidents Mandela and Mugabe during a state visit by President Mandela to Zimbabwe.

Subject Index

Name Index

About the Compilers

JACQUELINE A. KALLEY was International Affairs Librarian at the Jan Smuts House Library, University of Witwatersrand, from 1974 to 1998, and is currently the Information Coordinator at the Electoral Institute of South Africa and Research Associate in the Department of Political Studies at the University of Witwatersrand. She is the author or compiler of several books on South Africa and the Southern African region.

ELNA SCHOEMAN is International Organizations Librarian at the Jan Smuts House Library, University of Witwatersrand. She has compiled several bibliographies on the Southern African region.

L. E. ANDOR previously worked as a librarian at the Institute of Industrial Relations and the National Institute for Personnel Research in Johannesburg.

ISBN 0-313-30247-2